PREFACE

KU-794-164

100752009

The book's title is *Understanding Motivation and Emotion*. This title fit the goals and purposes of the first edition perfectly. For each of the 22 years since that first edition, motivation and emotion researchers have worked in an ever more sophisticated way to understand and to explain motivational and emotional processes. In retrospect, I see the field's recent past as its "golden age," because so many new discoveries were made, so many new insights were gained, and so many new theories were developed and validated. The questions that drove all this activity were those seeking greater understanding and clearer explanation: What do people want?; Why did she do that?; From where do motivation and emotion come?; Why do motivation and emotion change?; and What good are they—what do motivation and emotion predict? In answering these core questions, the field's understanding deepened.

Something important happened in the last several years. All this intellectual effort has borne fruit in terms of practical recommendations about how to go about the task of motivating people. It is great to understand motivation and emotion, but it is even better to take the next step and actually apply that knowledge to improve people's lives. Motivation and emotion study can now do this. As a field, we now understand the nature of motivation and emotion, their causes, the conditions that affect them, and how motivational and emotional processes lead to productive outcomes such as learning, performance, and well-being. The field's understanding is so deep that researchers can now confidently offer practical recommendations. This is the reason the book's final chapter is now titled "Interventions." This new closing chapter functions as a showcase for state-of-the-art intervention programs designed explicitly to enhance people's motivation and emotion so to improve their lives in some important way. But you will not have to wait until the last chapter to learn about the field's practical recommendations, because every chapter now features a series of short-term manipulations and long-term interventions designed to facilitate people's constructive motivation and emotion. Because this is so, it may now be time to retitle the book as, *Understanding and Applying Motivation and Emotion*.

By the time you turn the book's last page, I hope you will gain two important achievements. First, I hope you gain a deep and sophisticated understanding of motivation and emotion. Second, I hope you will gain the practical know-how to apply that knowledge in a concrete and personally meaningful way. Motivational and emotional principles and findings can be applied in many domains, but the most obvious include the home, school, workplace, clinical setting, counseling center, gym, athletic field, all aspects of healthcare, and interpersonal relationships in general.

I assumed some background knowledge on the part of the reader, such as an introductory course in psychology. The intended audience is upper-level undergraduates enrolled in courses in a department of psychology. I also write for students in other disciplines, largely because motivation research itself reaches into so many diverse areas of study and application, including education, health, counseling, clinical, sports, industrial/organizational, and business. The book concentrates on human, rather than on nonhuman, motivation. It includes some experiments in which rats, dogs, and monkeys served as research participants, but the information gleaned from these studies is always framed within an analysis of human motivation and emotion.

WHAT'S NEW IN THE SIXTH EDITION

Following the recent explosion of interest in motivation and emotion, the sixth edition features three new chapters. One new chapter is entitled "Individual Emotions." Adding this chapter creates the new opportunity to look at each of 20 different emotions one by one in an in-depth way. Many emotion researchers specialize in the study of a single emotion, so a comprehensive understanding of contemporary emotion research requires an in-depth analysis of each basic emotion (e.g., anger), each self-conscious emotion (e.g., pride), and each cognitively complex emotion (e.g., gratitude). A second new chapter is entitled "Mindsets." The contemporary study of human motivation continues to embrace cognitive constructs, and "mindset" has emerged as a central cognitive motivational framework that foreshadows a multitude of downstream consequences in terms of that person's thinking, feeling, and acting. The featured three mindsets are the deliberative versus implemental mindset, the promotion versus prevention mindset, and the growth versus fixed mindset. The third new chapter is the aforementioned "Interventions" chapter. In addition to these three new chapters, the sixth edition gives greater prominence to the neuroscience of motivation and emotion, self-control and ego depletion, emotion regulation, the adaptive unconscious, and goal setting and goal disengagement. In addition, the sixth edition makes a deliberate effort to identify practical applications.

Each chapter features a chapter box that addresses a specific concern. For instance, the box in Chapter 3 uses the information on the motivated and emotional brain to understand how antidepressant drugs work. The box in Chapter 8 uses the information on goals to lay out a step-by-step goal-setting and goal-striving program that can be applied to many different objectives. At the end of each chapter, a set of 10 recommended readings appears. These recommended journal articles represent suggestions for further individual study. I selected these particular readings using four criteria: (1) Each reading's focus represents what is central to the chapter, (2) its topic appeals to a wide audience, (3) its length is short, and (4) its methodology and data analysis are reader-friendly.

INSTRUCTOR'S MANUAL/TEST BANK

The sixth edition includes an expanded Instructor's Manual/Test Bank. This supplement includes classroom discussion questions, recommended activities, brief demonstrations of motivational principles, and other tools to help instructors teach their students. Interested instructors should contact their Wiley representative for more information.

ACKNOWLEDGMENTS

Many voices speak within the pages of the book. Much of what I write emerged from conversations with colleagues and through my reading of their work. I have benefited from so many colleagues that I now find it impossible to acknowledge them all. Still, I want to try.

My first expression of gratitude goes to all those colleagues who, formally or casually, intentionally or inadvertently, knowingly or unknowingly, shared their ideas in conversation: Avi Assor, Roy Baumeister, Daniel Berlyne, Virginia Blankenship, Mimi Bong, Jerry Burger, Sung Hyeon Cheon, Steven G. Cole, Mihaly Csikszentmihalyi, Richard deCharms, Ed Deci, Andrew Elliot, Wendy Grolnick, Alice Isen, Carroll Izard, Hyungshim Jang, Sung-il Kim, Richard Koestner, Randy Larsen, Woogul Lee, Wayne Ludvigson, David McClelland, Kou Murayama, Henry Newell, Glen Nix, Brad Olson, Dawn Robinson, Tom Rocklin, Carl Rogers, Richard Ryan, Kennon Sheldon, Paul Silvia, Ellen Skinner, Bart Soenens, Richard Solomon, Silvan Tomkins, Robert Vallerand, Maarten Vansteenkiste, John Wang, and Dan Wegner. I consider each of these contributors to be my colleague and kindred spirit in the fun and struggle to understand human strivings.

My second expression of gratitude goes to those who explicitly donated their time and energy to reviewing the early drafts of the book, including Debora R. Baldwin, Sandor B. Brent, Gustavo Carlo, Herbert L. Colston, Richard Dienstbier, Robert Emmons, Valeri Farmer-Dougan, Todd M. Freeberg, Eddie Harmon-Jones, Wayne Harrison, Carol A. Hayes, Teresa M. Heckert, John Hinson, August Hoffman, Mark S. Hoyert, Wesley J. Kasprow, Norman E. Kinney, John Kounios, Robert Madigan, Randall Martin, Michael McCall, Jim McMartin, James J. Ryan, Kraig L. Schell, Peter Senkowski, Henry V. Soper, Michael Sylvester, Ronald R. Ulm, Wesley White, and A. Bond Woodruff.

I sincerely thank all the students I have had the pleasure to work with over the years. It was back at Ithaca College that I first became convinced that my students wanted and needed such a book. In a very real sense, I wrote the first edition for them. The students who occupy my thoughts today are those with me at Korea University in Seoul, South Korea. For readers familiar with the earlier editions, this sixth edition presents a tone that is decidedly more practical and applied. This balance comes in part from my daily conversations with students.

Ithaca, New York, is doubly important to me, because it was in this beautiful town in upstate New York that I met Deborah Van Patten of Wiley (then Harcourt College Publishers). Deborah was every bit as responsible for getting this book off the ground as I was. Although 22 years have now passed, I still want to express my heartfelt gratitude to you, Deborah. The professionals at Wiley have been wonderful. Everyone at Wiley has been both a valuable resource and a source of pleasure, especially Jay O'Callaghan, Chris Johnson, Carrie Tupa, Danielle Torio, Janet Foxman, Hope Miller, and Sarah Wilkin.

I am especially grateful for the advice, patience, assistance, and direction provided by my psychology editor Eileen McKeever. Thanks.

—Johnmarshall Reeve

To Richard Troelstrup, who introduced me to psychology.

To Edwin Guthrie, who first deeply interested me in psychology.

*To Steven Cole, who mentored and supported me so that
I could participate in this wonderful profession.*

BRIEF CONTENTS

PREFACE   iii

CHAPTER 1   INTRODUCTION   1
CHAPTER 2   MOTIVATION IN HISTORICAL PERSPECTIVE   28
CHAPTER 3   THE MOTIVATED AND EMOTIONAL BRAIN   51

PART I Needs   81

CHAPTER 4   PHYSIOLOGICAL NEEDS   83
CHAPTER 5   EXTRINSIC MOTIVATION   116
CHAPTER 6   PSYCHOLOGICAL NEEDS   152
CHAPTER 7   IMPLICIT MOTIVES   183

PART II Cognitions   211

CHAPTER 8   GOAL SETTING AND GOAL STRIVING   213
CHAPTER 9   MINDSETS   239
CHAPTER 10   PERSONAL CONTROL BELIEFS   268
CHAPTER 11   THE SELF AND ITS STRIVINGS   303

PART III Emotions   335

CHAPTER 12   NATURE OF EMOTION: SIX PERENNIAL QUESTIONS   337
CHAPTER 13   ASPECTS OF EMOTION   369
CHAPTER 14   INDIVIDUAL EMOTIONS   404

PART IV Applied Concerns   429

CHAPTER 15   GROWTH MOTIVATION AND POSITIVE PSYCHOLOGY   431
CHAPTER 16   UNCONSCIOUS MOTIVATION   466
CHAPTER 17   INTERVENTIONS   496

REFERENCES   515

AUTHOR INDEX   603

SUBJECT INDEX   619

DETAILED CONTENTS

PREFACE   iii

CHAPTER 1   INTRODUCTION   1

Motivation and Emotion   2
Motivational Science   4
Two Perennial Questions   6
    What Causes Behavior?   6
    Why Does Behavior Vary in Its Intensity?   7
Subject Matter   9
    Internal Motives   10
    External Events and Social Contexts   11
    Motivation versus Influence   11
Expressions of Motivation   12
    Behavior   12
    Engagement   12
    Psychophysiology   14
    Brain Activations   14
    Self-Report   15
Framework to Understand Motivation and Emotion   15
Ten Unifying Themes   16
    Motivation and Emotion Benefit Adaptation and Functioning   16
    Motivation and Emotion Direct Attention   17
    Motivation and Emotion Are "Intervening Variables"   18
    Motives Vary Over Time and Influence the Ongoing Stream of Behavior   19
    Types of Motivations Exist   20
    We Are Not Always Consciously Aware of the Motivational Basis of Our Behavior   21
    Motivation Study Reveals What People Want   22
    To Flourish, Motivation Needs Supportive Conditions   23
    When Trying to Motivate Others, What Is Easy to Do Is Rarely What Is Effective   24
    There Is Nothing So Practical as a Good Theory   25
Summary   25

CHAPTER 2   MOTIVATION IN HISTORICAL PERSPECTIVE   28

Philosophical Origins of Motivational Concepts   29
Grand Theories   30
    Will   30
    Instinct   31
    Drive   33

Rise of the Mini-Theories   39
    Active Nature of the Person   40
    Cognitive Revolution   40
    Socially Relevant Questions   41
Contemporary Era   43
    The 1990s Reemergence of Motivation Study   45
Brief History of Emotion Study   47
Conclusion   48
Summary   49
Readings for Further Study   50

CHAPTER 3   THE MOTIVATED AND EMOTIONAL BRAIN   51

Motivation, Emotion, and Neuroscience   52
    Day-to-Day Events Activate Specific Brain Structures   53
    Activated Brain Structures Generate Specific Motivations and Emotions   55
Neural Basis of Motivation and Emotion   55
    Cortical Brain   55
    Subcortical Brain   56
    Bidirectional Communication   56
Individual Brain Structures Involved in Motivation and Emotion   58
    Reticular Formation   58
    Amygdala   61
    Basal Ganglia   63
    Ventral Striatum, Nucleus Accumbens, and Ventral Tegmental Area   63
    Hypothalamus   66
    Insula   67
    Prefrontal Cortex   69
    Orbitofrontal Cortex   72
    Ventromedial Prefrontal Cortex   73
    Dorsolateral Prefrontal Cortex   73
    Anterior Cingulate Cortex   74
Hormones   74
Conclusion   76
Summary   76
Readings for Further Study   79

PART I NEEDS   81

CHAPTER 4   PHYSIOLOGICAL NEEDS   83

Need   85
    Three Types of Needs   85
Fundamentals of Regulation   87
    Physiological Need   88

Psychological Drive   88
Homeostasis   89
Negative Feedback   89
Multiple Inputs/Multiple Outputs   90
Intraorganismic Mechanisms   91
Extraorganismic Mechanisms   91
The Homeostatic Mechanism   91
Thirst   92
Physiological Regulation   92
Environmental Influences   94
Hunger   96
Short-Term Appetite   96
Long-Term Energy Balance   97
Environmental Influences   99
Self-Regulatory Influences   101
Weight Gain and Obesity   102
Comprehensive Model of Hunger   102
Sex   103
Physiological Regulation   105
Facial Metrics   107
Sexual Scripts   110
Sexual Orientation   111
Evolutionary Basis of Sexual Motivation   112
Summary   114
Readings for Further Study   115

CHAPTER 5   EXTRINSIC MOTIVATION   116

Quasi-Needs   119
Extrinsic Motivation   120
Incentives, Consequences, and Rewards   120
Incentives   121
Reinforcers   121
Managing Behavior by Offering Reinforcers   122
Consequences   124
Hidden Costs of Reward   130
Intrinsic Motivation   130
What Is So Great about Intrinsic Motivation?   131
Intrinsic Motivation versus Extrinsic Motivation   133
Expected and Tangible Rewards   136
Implications   136
Benefits of Incentives, Consequences, and Rewards   137
Cognitive Evaluation Theory   139
Two Examples of Controlling and Informational Events   140
Types of Extrinsic Motivation   142
External Regulation   144

Introjected Regulation   145
Identified Regulation   145
Integrated Regulation   146
Internalization and Integration   146
Amotivation   146
Motivating Others to do Uninteresting Activities   147
   Providing Explanatory Rationales   148
   Suggesting Interest-Enhancing Strategies   148
Summary   149
Readings for Further Study   151

CHAPTER 6   PSYCHOLOGICAL NEEDS   152

Psychological Needs   153
   Organismic Psychological Needs   154
   Person–Environment Dialectic   155
   Person–Environment Synthesis versus Conflict   156
Autonomy   158
   The Conundrum of Choice   160
   Supporting Autonomy   161
   Benefits from Autonomy Support   165
   Benefits of Giving and Receiving Autonomy Support   165
Competence   167
   The Pleasure of Optimal Challenge   167
   Interdependency between Challenge and Feedback   168
   Optimal Challenge and Flow   168
   Structure   171
   Feedback   173
   Failure Tolerance   174
Relatedness   174
   Involving Relatedness: Interaction with Others   175
   Satisfying Relatedness: Perception of a Social Bond   175
   Communal and Exchange Relationships   176
   Fruits of Relatedness Need Satisfaction   177
Putting It all Together: Relationships and Social Contexts that Support Psychological Need
Satisfaction   178
   Engagement   178
   What Makes for a Good Day?   180
   Vitality   180
Summary   181
Readings for Further Study   182

CHAPTER 7   IMPLICIT MOTIVES   183

Implicit Needs   185
Acquired Needs   186
   Social Needs   187

How Implicit Motives, as Acquired Psychological Needs, Motivate Behavior 188

Achievement 190

Origins of the Need for Achievement 191

Atkinson's Model 192

Achievement for the Future 194

Dynamics-of-Action Model 195

Conditions That Involve and Satisfy the Need for Achievement 197

Affiliation 198

The Duality of Affiliation Motivation 199

Conditions That Involve the Affiliation and Intimacy Duality 200

Conditions That Satisfy the Affiliation Need 201

Power 202

Conditions That Involve and Satisfy the Need for Power 203

Power and Goal Pursuit 205

Is the Implicit Power Motive Bad? 205

Leadership Motive Pattern 205

Four Additional Social Needs 207

Summary 207

Readings for Further Study 209

PART II COGNITIONS 211

CHAPTER 8   GOAL SETTING AND GOAL STRIVING 213

Cognitive Perspective on Motivation 214

Plans of Action 215

Corrective Motivation 217

Discrepancy 218

Affect and Feelings 219

Two Types of Discrepancy 219

Goal Setting 220

Goal–Performance Discrepancy 221

Difficult, Specific, and Congruent Goals Enhance Performance 222

Feedback 225

Criticisms 225

Long-Term Goal Setting 227

Goal Striving 228

Mental Simulations 229

Implementation Intentions 230

Goal Disengagement 235

Epilogue: From where do Goals Come? 236

Summary 237

Readings for Further Study 238

CHAPTER 9   MINDSETS   239

Four Mindsets   240
Mindset 1: Deliberative–Implemental   241
    Deliberative Mindset   242
    Implemental Mindset   243
    Downstream Consequences of the Deliberative versus Implemental Mindsets   243
Mindset 2: Promotion–Prevention   244
    Promotion Mindset   244
    Prevention Mindset   246
    Different Definitions of Success and Failure   246
    Different Goal-Striving Strategies   247
    Ideal Self-Guides and Ought Self-Guides   248
    Regulatory Fit Predicts Strength of Motivation and Well-Being   249
Mindset 3: Growth-Fixed   250
    Fixed Mindset   250
    Growth Mindset   250
    Meaning of Effort   251
    Origins of Fixed-Growth Mindsets   252
    Different Fixed-Growth Mindsets Lead to Different Achievement Goals   254
    Achievement Goals   255
Mindset 4: Cognitive Dissonance   261
    Dissonance-Arousing Situations   262
    Motivational Processes Underlying Cognitive Dissonance   264
    Self-Perception Theory   265
Summary   265
Readings for Further Study   266

CHAPTER 10   PERSONAL CONTROL BELIEFS   268

Motivation to Exercise Personal Control   269
    Two Kinds of Expectancy   270
    Perceived Control: Self, Action, and Control   271
Self-Efficacy   272
    Sources of Self-Efficacy   274
    Self-Efficacy Effects on Behavior   276
    Self-Efficacy or the Psychological Need for Competence?   279
    Empowerment   280
    Empowering People: Mastery Modeling Program   281
Mastery Beliefs   282
    Ways of Coping   282
    Mastery versus Helplessness   282
Learned Helplessness   284
    Learning Helplessness   285
    Application to Humans   286
    Components   288
    Helplessness Effects   289
    Helplessness and Depression   291

Attributions and Explanatory Style 292
Pessimistic Explanatory Style 293
Optimistic Explanatory Style 294
Alternative Explanations 295
Reactance Theory 297
Reactance and Helplessness 297
Hope 298
Expectancy-Value Model 299
Summary 300
Readings for Further Study 302

CHAPTER 11 THE SELF AND ITS STRIVINGS 303

The Self 304
The Problem with Self-Esteem 306
Self-Concept 308
Self-Schemas 308
Motivational Properties of Self-Schemas 309
Consistent Self 310
Self-Verification and Self-Concept Change 311
Why People Self-Verify 312
Possible Selves 313
Agency 315
Self as Action and Development from Within 315
Self-Concordance 317
Personal Strivings 319
Self-Regulation 321
Self-Regulation: Forethought through Reflection 322
Developing More Competent Self-Regulation 323
Self-Control 324
Is the Capacity to Exert Self-Control Beneficial to a Successful Life? 329
Identity 329
Roles 329
Identity-Establishing Behaviors 330
Identity-Confirming Behaviors 330
Identity-Restoring Behaviors 331
What is the Self? 331
Summary 332
Readings for Further Study 333

PART III EMOTIONS 335

CHAPTER 12 NATURE OF EMOTION: SIX PERENNIAL QUESTIONS 337

Six Perennial Questions 339
What is an Emotion? 339

Definition   340
Relation between Emotion and Motivation   343
What Causes an Emotion?   344
Two-Systems View   344
Chicken-and-Egg Problem   345
What Ends an Emotion?   346
How Many Emotions Are There?   347
Biological Perspective   347
Cognitive Perspective   349
Reconciliation of the Numbers Issue   350
What Good Are the Emotions?   352
Coping Functions   353
Social Functions   354
Why We Have Emotions   356
Can We Control Our Emotions?   357
Emotion Regulation Strategies   358
What is the Difference between Emotion and Mood?   361
Everyday Mood   361
Positive Affect   364
Summary   366
Readings for Further Study   368

CHAPTER 13   ASPECTS OF EMOTION   369

Biological Aspects of Emotion   370
James–Lange Theory   371
Contemporary Perspective   372
Brain Activity Activates Individual Emotions   374
Facial Feedback Hypothesis   375
Cognitive Aspects of Emotion   382
Appraisal   382
Complex Appraisal   385
Appraisal as a Process   387
Emotion Differentiation   388
Emotion Knowledge   390
Attributions   391
Emotions Affect Cognition   395
Social Aspects of Emotion   395
Social Interaction   395
Social Sharing of Emotion   396
Cultural Construction of Emotion   398
Summary   401
Readings for Further Study   402

CHAPTER 14   INDIVIDUAL EMOTIONS   404

Basic Emotions   406

Fear   406
Anger   407
Disgust   408
Contempt   410
Sadness   410
Joy   411
Interest   412
Self-Conscious Emotions   414
Shame   414
Guilt   415
Embarrassment   416
Pride   417
Triumph   418
Interrelations among Shame, Guilt, Pride, and Hubris   418
Cognitively Complex Emotions   418
Envy   418
Gratitude   420
Disappointment and Regret   422
Hope   423
Schadenfreude   423
Empathy   423
Compassion   426
Summary   426
Readings for Further Study   427

PART IV APPLIED CONCERNS   429

CHAPTER 15   GROWTH MOTIVATION AND POSITIVE PSYCHOLOGY   431

Holism and Positive Psychology   433
Holism   434
Positive Psychology   434
Self-Actualization   435
Hierarchy of Human Needs   435
Encouraging Growth   437
Actualizing Tendency   439
Organismic Valuing Process   439
Emergence of the Self   440
Conditions of Worth   441
Conditional Regard as a Socialization Strategy   443
Fully Functioning Individual   445
Humanistic Motivational Phenomena   445
Causality Orientations   445
Growth-Seeking versus Validation Seeking   447

Relationships 448
Freedom to Learn 450
Self-Definition and Social Definition 451
Problem of Evil 451
Positive Psychology 453
Happiness and Well-Being 454
Eudaimonic Well-Being 456
Optimism 457
Meaning 458
Positivity 459
Interventions 461
Criticisms 462
Summary 463
Readings for Further Study 464

CHAPTER 16   UNCONSCIOUS MOTIVATION   466

Psychodynamic Perspective 467
Psychoanalytic Becomes Psychodynamic 468
Dual-Instinct Theory 470
Contemporary Psychodynamic Theory 471
The Unconscious 472
Freudian Unconscious 473
Adaptive Unconscious 474
Implicit Motivation 476
Priming 477
Psychodynamics 479
Repression 479
Suppression 480
Do the Id and Ego Actually Exist? 482
Ego Psychology 482
Ego Development 483
Ego Defense 484
Ego Effectance 487
Object Relations Theory 488
Criticisms 492
Summary 493
Readings for Further Study 495

CHAPTER 17   INTERVENTIONS   496

Applying Principles of Motivation and Emotion 497
Explaining Motivation and Emotion 497
Predicting Motivation and Emotion 498
Solving Motivational and Emotional Problems 498
Practice Problems 499

Four State-of-the-Art Interventions   501
    Intervention 1: Supporting Psychological Need Satisfaction   501
    Intervention 2: Increasing a Growth Mindset   504
    Intervention 3: Promoting Emotion Knowledge   507
    Intervention 4: Cultivating Compassion   510
Wisdom Gained from a Scientific Study of Motivation and Emotion   513

REFERENCES   515

AUTHOR INDEX   603

SUBJECT INDEX   619

Chapter 1

Introduction

MOTIVATION AND EMOTION

MOTIVATIONAL SCIENCE

TWO PERENNIAL QUESTIONS

    What Causes Behavior?

    Why Does Behavior Vary in Its Intensity?

SUBJECT MATTER

    Internal Motives

    External Events and Social Contexts

    Motivation versus Influence

EXPRESSIONS OF MOTIVATION

    Behavior

    Engagement

    Psychophysiology

    Brain Activations

    Self-Report

FRAMEWORK TO UNDERSTAND MOTIVATION AND EMOTION

TEN UNIFYING THEMES

    Motivation and Emotion Benefit Adaptation and Functioning

    Motivation and Emotion Direct Attention

    Motivation and Emotion Are "Intervening Variables"

    Motives Vary Over Time and Influence the Ongoing Stream of Behavior

    Types of Motivations Exist

    We Are Not Always Consciously Aware of the Motivational Basis of Our Behavior

    Motivation Study Reveals What People Want

    To Flourish, Motivation Needs Supportive Conditions

    When Trying to Motivate Others, What Is Easy to Do Is Rarely What Is Effective

    There Is Nothing So Practical as a Good Theory

SUMMARY

Every morning on my way to work, I walk by the same beautiful tree. Some of these mornings are bitterly cold. On these winter days, I realize that I can do something that the tree cannot. I can move. I can walk inside a building, put on a coat, or bring along a cup of hot coffee. The tree, however, just stands there day after day. So, I worry about that tree. I worry because the tree cannot take action and do what is necessary to protect itself—from the cold, from a chainsaw, and from bark-eating beetles. My desire to move is an incredible asset, and this asset is the theme of the present book. Indeed, the words *motivation*, *emotion*, and *motive* are all derived from the Latin verb *movere*, which means "to move." This book is about all the forces that generate and sustain *movere*. It is a story about how the motivational and emotional assets we all possess help us move forward toward optimal functioning and greater well-being.

MOTIVATION AND EMOTION

What is motivation? What is emotion? One reason to read this book is, of course, to find answers to these questions. But as a way of beginning the journey, pause for a moment and generate your own answers to these two questions, however preliminary, however tentative, however personal and private. Perhaps scribble your definitions on a notepad or in the margins of this book.

Any effort to define motivation and emotion begins with the choice of a noun inserted into the following two blank spaces: "Motivation is a___." and "Emotion is a___." Figuring out what needs to be inserted into those two blank lines is a fruitful activity.

Are motivation and emotion desires? Are they feelings? or ways of thinking? urges? impulses? strivings? processes, or a set of processes? needs, or a collection of needs? Are they temporary states that rise and fall in a matter of minutes, or are they enduring traits that last a lifetime? On page 9, the text offers a definition with which almost everyone who studies motivation would agree (see "Subject Matter" section). On page 10, the text offers a consensual definition of emotion (see "Internal Motives" section). As you progress through the pages of this book, you will find that your definitions will grow in clarity and sophistication. With ever-growing clarity and with deeper understanding, you will become increasingly able to understand motivational and emotional phenomena and explain how and why they work. You will also become increasingly able to support and enhance motivational strivings in yourself and in others. As the title of the book implies, the journey over the next 600 pages is to *understand* motivation and emotion—and to do so in a way that is clear, sophisticated, and practical.

But the journey can be a long one. So, before taking those first steps, pause for a moment and ask yourself why someone might want to take this journey of understanding in the first place. Why read these pages? Why ask questions in class? Why go online to read motivation- and emotion-related articles? Why stay up until 2:00 in the morning pondering questions of human motivation? Consider two reasons.

First, learning about motivation and emotion is a very interesting thing to do. Few topics spark and entertain the imagination so well. Anything that tells us about who we are, why we want what we want, and how we can improve our lives is going to be interesting. And anything that tells us about what other people want, why they want what they want, and how we can improve their lives is going to be interesting. When trying to explain why people want what they want and why people do what they do, we can turn to theories of motivation to learn about topics such as human nature, strivings for achievement and power, desires for biological sex and for psychological intimacy, and emotions like fear and anger. These theories explain how to cultivate talent and creativity, develop interests and grow competencies, and they help us set goals and make plans.

Second, learning about motivation and emotion is an important and valuable thing to do. Learning about motivation and emotion can be an extremely practical and worthwhile undertaking. It can be quite useful to know where motivation comes from, why it sometimes changes and why other times it does not, under what conditions motivation increases or decreases, what aspects of motivation can and cannot be changed, and whether some types of motivation are more beneficial than are other types. Knowing such things, we can apply our knowledge to situations such as trying to motivate employees, coach athletes, counsel clients, raise children, engage students, or change our own ways of thinking, feeling, and behaving. Understanding motivation and emotion offers a reliable pathway to gain valued outcomes, such as trying to attain expertise, perform better, find meaning, and increase our sense of happiness and personal growth. To the extent that a study of motivation and emotion can tell us how we can improve our lives and the lives of others, the journey will be time well spent.

Studying motivation and emotion is an opportunity to gain both theoretical understanding and practical know-how. As a case in point, consider exercise. Think about it for a moment: Why would anyone *want* to exercise? Can you explain this? Can you explain where the motivation to exercise comes from? Do you understand why people might be more willing to exercise under some conditions yet less willing to do so under other conditions? Can you explain why one person might be more willing to exercise than another? Can you explain why the same person sometimes wants to exercise but other times does not want to exercise? Can you offer any constructive suggestions to increase people's motivation to exercise? If someone hated to exercise, could you intervene in such a way that he or she would truly want to exercise?

And we need to consider not only the motivation to exercise but also the motivation not to exercise. What if exercising makes us feel anxious or stressed? What if exercise makes us feel incompetent and embarrassed? What if we feel tired, or what if we just do not feel like putting forth all that effort? What if time spent exercising takes us away from other things we like to do, such as watching television, reading a book, or logging on to Facebook?

And there are of course many different ways to exercise, assuming that one actually has sufficient motivation to do so. So, we need to ask: Why run laps around a track? Why jump up and down during an aerobics class? Why climb stairs on a machine that does not really go anywhere? Or, why do we sometimes pass by the elevator or escalator to walk up 10 flights of stairs? Or, why do we always take the elevator or escalator, rather than the stairs? Why walk briskly in the park, or swim laps in a pool? Why run when you know your lungs will collapse for want of air? Why jump and stretch when you know your muscles will rip and tear? Why take an hour out of the day when you just do not feel like it or when your schedule simply will not allow it? Why muster together all the energy and effort you will need to overcome the sheer inertia of inactivity? Why exercise when life offers so many other interesting things to do? Why indeed.

These questions ask about exercise, but they could just as easily be about the motivation underlying any activity. If you play the piano, why do you do so? If you are fluent in a second language, why did you go through all the effort to learn that foreign language? If you spent the afternoon working hard to learn something new or to develop a talent, then why?

MOTIVATIONAL SCIENCE

Thirteen different motivation-based reasons to exercise appear in Table 1.1. Who is to say which of these reasons are valid and which other reasons are erroneous? In answering a question such as, Why exercise?, a person can rely on personal experience and intuition to generate an answer. This is a fine starting point, but the study of motivation and emotion is a behavioral science. The term *science* signals that answers to motivational questions require objective, data-based, empirical evidence gained from well-conducted and peer-reviewed

Table 1.1   Thirteen Different Motivational Reasons to Exercise

Why Exercise?	Source of Motivation	Illustration
Fun, enjoyment	**Intrinsic motivation**	Children exercise spontaneously—they run and jump and chase, and they do so simply for the sheer fun of it.
Personal challenge	**Flow**	Athletes get "in the zone" when their sport optimally challenges their skills.
Forced to do so	**External regulation**	Athletes exercise because their coach tells them to do so.
Accomplish a goal	**Goal**	Runners see if they can run a mile in six minutes or less.
Health benefits	**Value**	People exercise to lose weight or to strengthen the heart.
Inspired to do so	**Possible self**	People watch others exercise and become inspired to do the same.
Pursuit of a standard of excellence	**Achievement strivings**	Snow skiers race to the bottom of the mountain trying to beat their previous best time.
Satisfaction from a job well done	**Perceived competence**	As exercisers make progress, they feel more competent, more effective.
An emotional kick	**Opponent process**	Vigorous jogging can produce a runner's high (a euphoric rebound to the pain).
Good mood	**Positive affect**	Beautiful weather can induce a good mood such that people exercise spontaneously, as they skip along without even knowing why.
Alleviate guilt	**Introjection**	People exercise because they think that is what they should, ought to, or have to do to please others or to relieve their own sense of internalized shame or guilt.
Relieve stress, silence, depression	**Personal control**	After a stressful day, people go to the gym, which they see as a structured and controllable environment.
Hang out with friends	**Relatedness**	Exercise is often a social event, a time to enjoy hanging out with friends.

research findings. Motivational science does not accept quotes from famous basketball coaches as definitive answers, however inspirational and attention-getting those quotes may be. Instead, research on motivation and emotion seeks to construct theories about how motivational processes work. It is from these theories of motivation and emotion that hypotheses can be generated to be put to objective empirical test so as to assess their scientific merit. The ongoing processes of putting one's ideas about motivation to empirical test is a crucial process to realizing the title of this book (i.e., *Understanding Motivation and Emotion*), because the motivational concepts one uses need to be chosen carefully, and they need to be continually evaluated against new findings. Inadequate concepts are best tossed aside, useful concepts need to be improved upon, and new explanatory concepts need to be discovered.

A theory is an intellectual framework that organizes a vast amount of knowledge about a phenomenon so that the phenomenon can be better understood and explained (Fiske, 2004). The study of motivation and emotion exists to answer the Why? questions of behavior, thought, and feeling, such as, Why did she do that? and Why does she feel and think that way? Motivational theories therefore exist as answers to these sorts of questions, as in The reason why she did that was because _____. To quote Bernard and Lac (2013, p. 574):

> without an answer to *why*, we are left only with the description of behavior, and description without explanation is ultimately unsatisfying.

To understand the nature of something such as achievement motivation and to explain how it works, a theory of achievement motivation needs to do two things. First, it needs to identify the relations that exist among naturally occurring, observable phenomena. For instance, a theory needs to identify what causes the phenomenon and also what the phenomenon itself causes. A theory of achievement motivation, for instance, will identify variables such as optimal challenge, independent work, and rapid performance feedback as the naturally occurring causes for achievement strivings, and it will identify variables such as effort, persistence, and hope as its naturally occurring consequences. Second, it needs to explain why those relations exist. For instance, why does a challenge (e.g., Here, see if you can do this.) lead some people to experience hope and to exert greater effort while it leads other people to experience only anxiety and to withhold effort? If you can identify the antecedents and consequences to a motivational or an emotional phenomenon, then your understanding will be clearer, more sophisticated, and more helpful. You will be well positioned (well informed) when it comes time to improve your life or the life of a loved one.

Figure 1.1 illustrates the function and utility of a good theory (Trope, 2004). A theory cuts through the complexity and noise of reality to represent how a phenomenon generally works ("Representation" in Figure 1.1). How a theorist conceptualizes the phenomenon may or may not be correct or complete. So, researchers use the theory to generate testable hypotheses. A hypothesis is a prediction about what should happen if the theory is correct. For instance, one hypothesis about achievement motivation might be that people with challenging jobs with rapid performance feedback (e.g., entrepreneurs) should experience greater and more frequent achievement strivings at work than do people who have service-oriented jobs (e.g., nursing; Jenkins, 1987). With a hypothesis in hand, a research study is carried out to collect the data necessary to evaluate the accuracy of the hypothesis. If the findings support the theory's hypothesis, researchers then gain confidence in the validity of the theory; if the findings fail to support the theory, researchers then lose

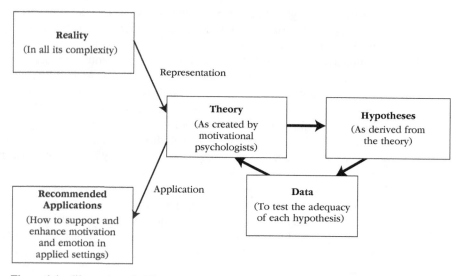

Figure 1.1   Illustration of a Theory

confidence in the theory and either change it or go in search of a better theory (i.e., a better explanation). After a theory has been sufficiently, rigorously, and objectively validated, it becomes useful. A validated theory serves as a practical tool to recommend applications that can improve people's lives ("Application" in Figure 1.1). Overall, by proposing and testing their theories, researchers develop a deep understanding of motivation and emotion (i.e., gain theoretical knowledge), and by refining and applying their theories, researchers develop workable solutions to life's motivational problems (i.e., gain practical know-how).

TWO PERENNIAL QUESTIONS

The study of motivation revolves around providing the best possible answers to two fundamental questions: (1) What causes behavior? and (2) Why does behavior vary in its intensity?

What Causes Behavior?

Motivation's first fundamental question is, What causes behavior? Or, stated differently in terms of *Why?* questions: Why did she do that? Why does he seek out that particular thing at that particular time? We see people behave, but we cannot see the underlying cause or causes that generated their behavior. We watch people show great effort and persistence (or none at all), but the reasons why they seek things out and show great effort remain unobserved. Motivation exists as a scientific field to identify the hidden causes of behavior.

To explain What causes behavior? it is helpful to expand this one general question into five specific questions:

· Why does behavior start?
· Once begun, why is behavior sustained over time?

- Why is behavior directed toward some goals yet away from others?
- Why does behavior change its direction?
- Why does behavior stop?

In the study of motivation, it is not enough to ask why a person practices a sport, why a child reads books, or why an adolescent refuses to sing in the choir. To gain a sophisticated understanding of why people do what they do, we must ask further why athletes begin to practice in the first place. What was the reason (or reasons) why this athlete or this group of athletes first started to participate in this particular sport? What energizes their effort hour after hour, day after day, season after season? Why do these athletes practice one particular sport rather than another? Why are they practicing now rather than, say, hanging out with their friends? When they do practice, why do these athletes quit for the day, or quit during their lifetimes? These same questions can be asked of children as they read books: Why begin? Why continue past the first page? Past the first chapter? Why pick that particular book rather than one of the other books sitting on the shelf? Why stop reading? Will their reading continue in the years to come? For a personal example, let me ask, Why did you begin to read this book today? Will you continue reading to the end of this chapter? Will you continue reading until the end of the book? If you do stop before the end, at what point will you stop? Why will you stop? After reading, what will you do next? Why?

Motivation's first perennial question—What causes behavior?—can, therefore, be elaborated into the study of how motivation affects behavior's initiation, persistence, change, goal directedness, and eventual termination. This question is either one grand question, or it is five interrelated questions. Either way, the first essential problem in a motivational analysis of behavior is to understand how motivation participates in, influences, and helps explain a person's ongoing stream of behavior. Motivation and emotion also influence our thoughts, our feelings, and our aspirations. So, there is some wisdom in expanding the question, What causes behavior?, to a more general question of, What causes activity—not only our behavior, but also our thoughts, our feelings, and our aspirations? The discussion in Box 1 expands on this pursuit for a greater understanding of motivation and emotion.

Why Does Behavior Vary in Its Intensity?

Motivation's second fundamental question is, Why does behavior vary in its intensity? Other ways of asking this same question would be to ask, Why is desire strong and resilient at one time yet weak and fragile at another time? and Why does the same person choose to do different things at different times?

Behavior varies in its intensity, and its intensity varies both within the individual and between different individuals. The idea that motivation can vary within the individual means that a person can be actively engaged at one time, yet that same person can be passive and listless at another time. The idea that motivation can vary between individuals means that, even in the same situation, some people can be actively engaged while others are passive and listless.

Within the individual, motivation varies. When motivation varies, behavior also varies, as people show high or low effort and their persistence is strong or fragile. Some days an employee works rapidly and diligently; other days the work is lethargic. One day a student shows strong enthusiasm, strives for excellence, and shows determined goal-directed

BOX 1   *Why We Do What We Do*

Question: Why is this information important?

Answer: To gain the capacity to explain why people do what they do.

Explaining motivation—why people do what they do—is not easy. People have no shortage of possible motivation theories ("He did that because . . ."), but the problem is that many of these intuitive theories are not really helpful in the effort to explain why people do what they do.

When I talk to people in everyday life, when I ask students about their own motivation theories during the first week of class, and when I read the advice people give online and during television talk shows, the most popular theories people embrace are:

- Self-esteem and praise
- Incentives and rewards

At the top of the list of people's theories of motivation is "increase self-esteem." The view on self-esteem sounds something like, "Find a way to make people feel good about themselves, and then good things will start to happen." "Praise them, compliment them, and give them some affirmation that they are worthy as a person and that brighter days are ahead." The problem with this strategy is that it is wrong. It is wrong because there is practically no empirical evidence to support it (Baumeister, Campbell, Krueger, & Vohs, 2003). Educational psychologists, for instance, routinely find that increases in students' self-esteem do not produce increases in their academic achievement (Marsh & Craven, 2006). A former president of the American Psychological Association (APA) went so far as to conclude that "there are almost no findings that self-esteem causes anything at all" (Seligman, quoted in Azar, 1994, p. 4).

There is great value in a healthy dose of self-esteem. The problem is that self-esteem is not a causal variable. Instead, it is an effect—a reflection of how our lives are going. It is a barometer of well-being. When life is going well, self-esteem rises; when life is going poorly, self-esteem falls. This is very different from saying that self-esteem *causes* life to go well. The logical flaw in thinking about self-esteem as a source of motivation is the act of putting the proverbial cart before the horse. Self-esteem is a cart, not a horse.

Next on people's list of theories of motivation is "provide incentives and offer rewards." This view sounds something like, "When people are unmotivated, dangle a carrot in front of them or slap them with a stick to get them going." The problem with this strategy is twofold. First, incentives and rewards need to be given carefully, because removing them tends to damage the person's preexisting motivation to engage in that same task without the promise of reward (Deci, Koestner, & Ryan, 1999). Second, if you think about it, the person offering the incentive actually ignores or bypasses an understanding of the person's motivation and instead tries to environmentally manufacture the other person's compliance. It is always helpful to stop and ask the difficult—but motivationally crucial—question of why the person is not motivated in the first place. What we will do on each page of this book is look inside the person to identify those internal processes that energize, direct, and sustain behavior.

striving; yet the next day, the same student is listless, does only the minimal amount of work, and avoids being challenged academically. Why the same person shows strong and persistent motivation at one time yet weak and unenthusiastic motivation at another time needs to be explained. Why does the worker perform so well on Monday but not so well on Tuesday? Why do children say they are not hungry in the morning, yet the same children complain of urgent hunger in the afternoon? So the second essential problem in a motivational analysis of behavior is to understand why a person's behavior varies in its intensity from one moment to the next, from one day to the next, and from one year to the next.

Between different people, motivation varies. We all share many of the same basic motivations and emotions (e.g., hunger, anger), but people do clearly differ in what motivates them. Some motives are relatively strong for one person yet relatively weak for another. Why is one person a sensation seeker, who continually seeks out strong sources of stimulation, such as riding a motorcycle, whereas another person is a sensation avoider, who finds such strong stimulation more of an irritant than a source of excitement? In a contest, why do some people strive diligently to win, whereas others care little about winning and strive more to make friends? Some people seem so easy to anger, whereas others rarely get upset. For those motives in which wide individual differences exist, motivation study investigates how such differences arise (antecedents) and what implications they hold (consequences). So another motivational problem to solve is to recognize that individuals differ in what motivates them and to explain why one person shows intense engagement in a given situation while another does not.

SUBJECT MATTER

To explain why people do what they do, we need to explain what gives behavior its energy, direction, and endurance. It is some motive that energizes the athlete, it is some motive that directs the student's behavior toward one goal rather than another, and it is some motive that keeps the artist painting month after month after month. *The study of motivation concerns those internal processes that give behavior its energy, direction, and persistence. Energy* implies that behavior has strength—that it is relatively strong, intense, and hardy or resilient. *Direction* implies that behavior has purpose—that it is aimed or guided toward achieving some particular goal or outcome. *Persistence* implies that behavior has endurance—that it sustains itself over time and across different situations.

As shown in Figure 1.2, motives are internal experiences—needs, cognitions, and emotions. They are the direct and proximal causes of motivated action. External events and social contexts are important too, because they act as antecedents to motives. Antecedents provide the supportive conditions under which motivations and emotions can rise and increase, and antecedents provide the frustrating conditions under which motivations and emotions fall and decrease. Using a movie metaphor, internal motives are the stars while external events are the supporting characters.

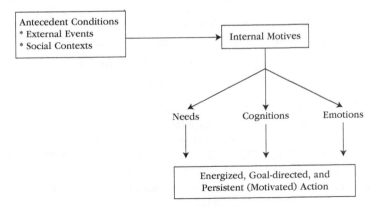

Figure 1.2   Three Categories of Internal Motives

Internal Motives

A motive is an internal process that energizes, directs, and sustains behavior. It is therefore a general term to identify the common ground shared by needs, cognitions, and emotions. The difference between a general motive versus a specific need, cognition, or emotion is simply the level of analysis. Needs, cognitions, and emotions are just three specific types of motives (see Figure 1.2).

Needs are conditions within the individual that are essential and necessary for the maintenance of life and for the nurturance of growth and well-being. Hunger and thirst exemplify two biological needs that arise from the body's requirement for food and water. Food and water are both essential and necessary for biological maintenance, well-being, and growth. Competence and belongingness exemplify two psychological needs that arise from the self's requirement for environmental mastery and warm interpersonal relationships. Competence and belongingness are both essential and necessary for psychological maintenance, well-being, and growth. Needs serve the organism, and they do so by generating wants, desires, and strivings that motivate whatever behaviors are necessary for the maintenance of life and the promotion of well-being and growth. Part I discusses specific types of needs: physiological (Chapter 4), psychological (Chapter 6), and implicit (Chapter 7).

Cognitions refer to mental events, such as thoughts, beliefs, expectations, plans, goals, strategies, appraisals, attributions, and the self-concept. Cognitive sources of motivation revolve around the person's ways of thinking. For instance, as students, athletes, or salespersons engage in a task, they have in mind some plan or goal, they harbor expectations that they will cope well or that they will cope poorly, they have ways of appraising or interpreting what is happening around them, and they have an understanding of who they are and who they are striving to become. Part II discusses specific cognitive sources of motivation: plans and goals (Chapter 8), mindsets (Chapter 9), beliefs and expectations (Chapter 10), and the self (Chapter 11).

Emotions are complex but coordinated feeling–arousal–purposive–expressive reactions to the significant events in our lives (e.g., an opportunity, a threat, a loss; Izard, 1993). Emotions generate brief, attention-getting bursts of emergency-like adaptive behavior. That is, given a significant life event, emotions rapidly and rather automatically generate and synchronize four interrelated aspects of experience into a unified whole:

- *Feelings*: Subjective, verbal descriptions of emotional experience.
- *Arousal*: Bodily mobilization to cope with situational demands.
- *Purpose*: Motivational urge to accomplish something specific at that moment.
- *Expression*: Nonverbal communication of our emotional experience to others.

By generating and synchronizing these four aspects of experience into a coherent whole, emotions allow us to react adaptively to the important events in our lives, such as life's challenges to our survival and well-being. For instance, upon encountering a threatening event, we rapidly and rather automatically feel afraid, our heart rate increases, an urge to escape arises, and the corners of our lips are drawn backward in such a way that others can recognize and respond to our fear experience. Other emotions, such as anger and joy, show a similar coherent pattern that organizes our feelings, arousal, function, and expression in ways that allow us to prepare for and to cope successfully with a different set of circumstances. Part III discusses the nature of emotion (Chapter 12), its different aspects (Chapter 13), and individual emotions (Chapter 14).

External Events and Social Contexts

External events are environmental, social, and cultural offerings that affect a person's internal motives. Environmental events include specific attractive stimuli such as money and events such as being praised. Environmental events can also be unattractive stimuli such as a foul odor or an unattractive event such as being yelled at. Social contexts include general situations, such as a classroom or workplace climate, a parenting style, or the culture at large. It is tempting to think that external events are themselves direct sources of motivation. For instance, if someone says, "I'll give you $20 if you touch your nose," then it seems rather obvious that the $20 bill is directly responsible for your sudden urge to touch your nose. But the motivational power of incentives and rewards ($20) is actually traceable to the dopamine discharge that occurs in your subcortical brain when you expect the delivery of a valued reward (Schultz, Tremblay, & Hollerman, 2000), as will be explained in Chapter 3. So, it is actually the dopamine discharge and the cognitive expectation of a forthcoming benefit (*internal* processes), not the extrinsic reward itself, that energizes, directs, and sustains behavior (nose touching). That is, if the dopamine discharge did not occur, then energetic goal-directed behavior would not occur whenever such a $20 offer came our way. Precisely how environmental events and social or cultural contexts add to and inform a motivational analysis of behavior will be explained in Chapter 5.

Motivation versus Influence

One reason to read a book on motivation might be to learn the techniques necessary to get other people to do what you want them to do. For instance, parents might want to know how to get children to clean their room, and workplace managers might want tips in how to persuade employees to make more sales. In these examples, what people want is not motivation per se but, rather, influence.

Influence is the social process in which one requests that the other change his or her behavior or thought (attitude, opinion) (Hogg, 2010). Influence is an interpersonal process that occurs under various names such as persuasion, compliance, conformity, obedience, and leadership. Motivation, however, is a private, internal process. Instead of leading people to follow a socially engineered way of thinking or behaving, what motivation does is endow the person with the energy and direction needed to engage in and to cope with the environment in an open-ended, adaptive, problem-solving sort of way.

When you motivate someone, you energize and direct their behavior, engagement, and coping. People are motivated when their behavior is strong, purposive, and resilient. When you influence people, you persuade them to respond favorably to your specific request—you get them to do what you want them to do. The study of motivation is, therefore, not about manipulating people; rather, it is about energizing and empowering them toward greater and more able engagement, performance, and well-being.

EXPRESSIONS OF MOTIVATION

In addition to identifying motivation's perennial problems and its subject matter, one more introductory task remains—namely, specifying how motivation expresses itself. In other words, we need to answer questions such as the following: How can you tell when someone is motivated? Or is not motivated? Or is only a little bit motivated? Or is motivated toward one thing rather than another? For instance, as you watch two people—say, two teenagers playing a tennis match—how do you know that one person is more motivated than the other?

Motivation is a private and unobservable (internal) experience. You cannot see another person's motivation. That is, as you walk down the street, you cannot look at passersby and actually see their thirst, the goals they strive for, or extent of their achievement motivation. Instead, we observe what is public and observable to infer such motivations.

Below are five ways that motivation and emotion publically express themselves. But before identifying those five ways, it is important to point out that there are actually two ways to infer motivation in another person. The first way is to observe motivation's publically observable manifestations—behavior, engagement, psychophysiology, brain activations, and self-report. The second way is to pay close attention to the antecedents known to give rise to motivational states. After 72 hours of food deprivation, a person will be hungry. After feeling threatened, a person will feel fear. After winning a competition, a person will feel competent. Food deprivation reliably leads to hunger, a threat appraisal reliably leads to fear, and objective messages of effectance reliably lead to feeling competent. When we know the antecedents to motivation, we can forecast people's motivational states *in advance*, and we can do so rather confidently. But these antecedents are not always knowable. More often than not, motivation must be inferred from its expressions.

Behavior

Seven aspects of behavior express the presence, intensity, and quality of motivation (Atkinson & Birch, 1970, 1978; Bolles, 1975; Ekman & Friesen, 1975): effort, persistence, latency, choice, probability of response, facial expressions, and bodily gestures. These aspects of behavior, listed and defined in Table 1.2, provide the observer with objective information to infer the presence and intensity of another person's motivation. When behavior shows intense effort, long persistence, short latency, high probability of occurrence, facial or gestural expressiveness or when the individual pursues a specific goal-object in lieu of another, such is the evidence to infer the presence of a relatively intense motive. When behavior shows lackadaisical effort, fragile persistence, long latency, low probability of occurrence, minimal facial and gestural expressiveness, or the individual pursues an alternative goal-object, such is the evidence to infer an absence of a motive or at least a relatively weak motive.

Engagement

Engagement refers to how actively involved a person is in a task (Christenson, Reschly, & Wylie, 2012). As shown in Figure 1.3, engagement is a multidimensional construct that consists of the four distinct, yet intercorrelated and mutually supportive, aspects of behavior,

Table 1.2   Seven Behavioral Expressions of Motivation and Emotion

Effort	Exertion put forth during a task. Percentage of total capacity used.
Persistence	Time between when a behavior first starts until it ends.
Latency	Duration of time a person waits to get started on a task upon first being given an opportunity to do so.
Choice	When presented with two or more courses of action, preferring one course of action over the other.
Probability of response	Number (or percentage) of occasions that the person enacts a particular goal-directed response given the total number of opportunities to do so.
Facial expressions	Facial movements, such as wrinkling the nose, raising the upper lip, and lowering the brow (e.g., a disgusted facial expression).
Bodily gestures	Bodily gestures, such as learning forward, changing posture, and intentionally moving the legs, arms, and hands (e.g., a clenched fist).

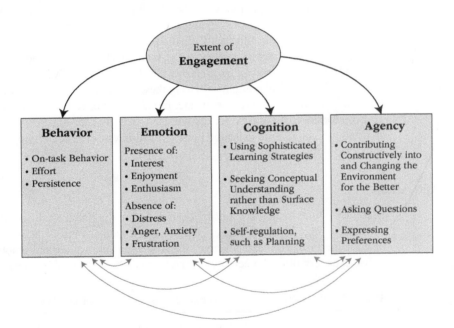

Figure 1.3   Four Interrelated Aspects of Engagement

emotion, cognition, and agency (Christenson et al., 2012; Fredricks, Blumenfeld, & Paris, 2004; Reeve & Tseng, 2011; Skinner, Kindermann, Connell, & Wellborn, 2009). Behavioral engagement refers to how effortfully involved a person is during the activity in terms of effort and persistence, and it is synonymous with the behaviors listed in Table 1.2. Emotional engagement refers to the presence of positive emotions during task involvement, such as interest, and to the absence of negative emotions, such as anxiety. Cognitive engagement refers to how strategically the person attempts to process information and to learn in terms of employing sophisticated rather than superficial learning strategies. Agentic engagement refers to the extent of the person's proactive and constructive contribution into the flow of the activity in terms of asking questions, expressing preferences, and letting others know what one wants and needs. For one example, to infer the underlying motivation of the student who sits next to you during class, observe his or her effort and persistence (behavioral engagement), interest and enjoyment (emotional engagement), deep processing and strategic learning (cognitive engagement), and input and contribution into the flow of the class (agentic engagement).

Psychophysiology

As people engage in various activities, the nervous and endocrine systems manufacture and release various chemical substances (e.g., neurotransmitters, hormones) that provide the biological underpinnings of motivational and emotional states (Andreassi, 2007). The term *psychophysiology* refers to the process by which psychological states (motivation, emotion) produce downstream changes in the body's physiology. Psychophysiology is the study of the interaction between bodily and mental states. In the course of a public speech, for example, speakers manufacture and release into the bloodstream various hormones such as epinephrine (adrenaline) and cortisol, and these hormonal changes produce changes throughout the body (e.g., increased heart rate, blood pressure, respiration rate, and sweating) that can be picked up by blood tests, saliva tests, and various types of psychophysiological equipment. Using these measures, motivation researchers monitor a person's hormonal activity, heart rate, blood pressure, respiratory rate, pupil diameter, skin conductance, skeletal muscle activity, and other indices of physiological functioning, as listed in Table 1.3, to infer the presence and intensity of underlying motivational and emotional states.

Brain Activations

Brain activations underlie every motivational and emotional state, as will be discussed extensively in Chapter 3. When thirsty, the hypothalamus is active. When we feel disgust, the insular cortex is active. Because each motivation and emotion generates a different pattern of neural activity, researchers can use very sophisticated equipment (e.g.,

Table 1.3   Five Psychophysiological Expressions of Motivation and Emotion

Hormonal activity	Chemicals in saliva or blood, such as cortisol (stress) or catecholamines (fight-or-flight reaction).
Cardiovascular activity	Contraction and relaxation of the heart and blood vessels (as in response to an attractive incentive or a difficult/challenging task).
Ocular activity	Eye behavior—pupil size (extent of mental activity), eye blinks (changing cognitive states), and eye movements (reflective thought).
Electrodermal activity	Electrical changes on the surface of the skin (as in response to a significant or threatening event).
Skeletal activity	Activity of the musculature, as with facial expressions (specific emotion), bodily gestures, or shifting one's weight from side to side during a boring hallway conversation (desire to leave).

electroencephalograph) and machinery (e.g., functional magnetic resonance imaging) to detect, monitor, and measure brain-based neural activity. Thus, by observing a rise in hypothalamic or insular activity, researchers can infer that the person is experiencing a rise in thirst or disgust, respectively. In this sense, changes in brain activations are just like changes in behavior, engagement, and psychophysiology.

Self-Report

A fifth and final way to collect the data needed to infer the presence, intensity, and quality of motivation is simply to ask. People can typically self-report their motivation, as in an interview or on a questionnaire. An interviewer might assess anxiety, for instance, by asking how anxious the interviewee feels in particular settings or by asking the interviewee to report anxiety-related symptoms, such as an upset stomach or thoughts of failure. Questionnaires have several advantages. They are easy to administer, can be given to many people simultaneously, and can target very specific information (Carlsmith, Ellsworth, & Aronson, 1976). But questionnaires also have pitfalls that raise a red flag of caution as to their usefulness. Many researchers lament the lack of correspondence between what people say they do and what they actually do (Quattrone, 1985). Furthermore, there is also a lack of correspondence between how people say they feel and what their psychophysiology indicates that they probably feel (e.g., "Oh, I'm not tired, I'm not hungry, I'm not afraid."). Hence, what people say their motives are sometimes are not what people's behavioral, engagement, psychophysiological, and neural expressions suggest their motives are. What conclusion, for instance, can one draw when a person verbally reports low anger but shows a quick latency to aggress, a rapid acceleration in heart rate, and eyebrows that are drawn tightly downward and together?

Because of such discrepancies, motivation and emotion researchers typically trust and rely on behavioral, engagement, psychophysiological, and brain-based measures of motivation and emotion to a greater degree than they trust and rely on self-report measures. Self-reports can be useful and informative, but they also need to be backed up and verified by the person's behavioral, engagement, psychophysiological, and neural activity.

FRAMEWORK TO UNDERSTAND MOTIVATION AND EMOTION

One way to integrate the perennial questions, subject matter, and expressions of motivation is summarized in Figure 1.4. Antecedent conditions affect the person's underlying motive status, and the rise and fall of the person's motive status (needs, cognitions, emotions) expresses itself through a pattern of behavioral, engagement, psychophysiological, neural, and subjective (self-report) activity that can then be expected to contribute positively to important life outcomes.

The summary framework (Figure 1.4) illustrates how motivational psychologists answer their perennial questions. That is, the model explains what causes motivation and emotion (antecedent conditions), illustrates the subject matter of motivation study (needs, cognitions, emotions), articulates how motives express themselves (behavior, engagement, psychophysiology, brain activations, self-report), and explains why the study of motivation and emotion is so important to people's lives (it contributes positively to important life outcomes).

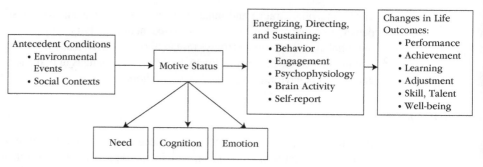

Figure 1.4   Framework to Understand Motivation and Emotion

TEN UNIFYING THEMES

The scientific study of motivation and emotion includes a wide range of assumptions, hypotheses, theories, findings, and domains of application. All of this information can be a bit overwhelming at first. Fortunately, 10 unifying themes can be identified to bring all this information together in a sensible and cohesive way. Those 10 unifying themes are as follows:

- Motivation and emotion benefit adaptation and functioning.
- Motivation and emotion direct attention.
- Motivation and emotion are "intervening variables."
- Motives vary over time and influence the ongoing stream of behavior.
- Types of motivations exist.
- We are not always consciously aware of the motivational basis of our behavior.
- Motivation study reveals what people want.
- To flourish, motivation needs supportive conditions.
- When trying to motivate others, what is easy to do is rarely what is effective.
- There is nothing so practical as a good theory.

Motivation and Emotion Benefit Adaptation and Functioning

Circumstances constantly change, as do the environments we live in (at home, school, work). Demands on our time rise and fall, opportunities come and go, and supportive relationships sometimes turn sour and coercive. When faced with an ongoing and changing stream of opportunities and threats, people need the means to take the corrective action necessary to preserve and enhance their functioning and well-being. Motivations and emotions serve as the means for such corrective action.

When people go for hours without food and when the food supply is scarce, hunger arises. When deadlines become too numerous, stress arises. When a person gains control over a difficult problem, a sense of mastery and competence arises. Changes in hunger, stress, and mastery motivation allow people to become *complex adaptive systems*. Therefore, one theme that runs throughout this book is that motivational and emotional states (e.g., hunger, stress, mastery) provide a key means for individuals to cope successfully with life's inevitable, changing, and somewhat unpredictable demands. Take away the motivational and emotional states, and people would quickly lose a vital resource to adapt, to function productively, and to maintain well-being. Anyone who tries to lose weight, write a creative poem, or learn a foreign language without first recruiting high-quality motivation and emotion will quickly realize that motivation and emotion benefit adaptation and functioning. It is the function of motivational and emotional states to ready and prepare us to adapt and function optimally—to lose weight, to write creatively, and to learn complex skills.

When motivation sours, personal adaptation, functioning, and well-being all suffer. People who feel helpless in exerting control over their fates tend to give up quickly when challenged (Peterson, Maier, & Seligman, 1993). Helplessness sours the person's capacity to cope with life's challenges. Similarly, people who are bossed around and controlled coercively by others tend to become emotionally flat and numb to their own inner psychological needs (Deci, 1995). Being controlled undermines the person's capacity and willingness to generate motivation of his or her own. In contrast, when students are excited about school, when workers are confident in their skills, and when athletes set higher goals today than they pursued yesterday, then their teachers, supervisors, and coaches can rest assured that each of these people is on course to adapt successfully, function optimally, and basically be well. People with high-quality motivation and emotion generally adapt and thrive; people with motivational and emotional deficits generally flounder and suffer.

Motivation and Emotion Direct Attention

Environments demand our attention, and they do so in a multitude of ways. Just driving down the road, for instance, we have many things to do—find our destination, cooperate with other drivers, avoid hitting other cars, listen and respond to our passengers' conversation, avoid spilling our coffee, and so forth. Similarly, a college student must simultaneously make good grades, maintain old friendships, eat healthy, balance budgets of money and time, plan for the future, wash clothes, develop artistic talents, keep abreast of world news, and so on. Who is to say whether our attention is allocated in one direction or the other? Much of that "say" comes from our motivational and emotional states. Motives have a way of gaining, and sometimes demanding, our attention so that we attend to one aspect of the environment rather than to another.

Motives prepare us for action by directing attention to select some behaviors and courses of action over others, as illustrated in Table 1.4. The table's four columns list, from left to right, (1) various aspects of the environment that may be attended to or not, (2) a motive typically activated by that environmental event, (3) a motive-appropriate course of adaptive action, and (4) a hypothetical priority given to each course of action as determined by the intensity of its associated motive. While six courses of action are possible, attention is not allocated equally because the aroused motives vary in strength (as denoted by the number of asterisks in the far-right column). Because interest, thirst, and rest are not urgent at that particular time (one asterisk), their salience is low and they fail to grab attention and prepare motive-congruent action. The motive to avoid a headache's pain is highly salient (five asterisks) and therefore a strong candidate to grab attention and

Table 1.4   How Motives Influence Behavior for a Student Sitting at a Desk

Environmental Event	Aroused Motive	Motive-Relevant Course of Action	Motive's Urgency Attention-Getting Status
Book	Interest	Read chapter	*
Cola	Thirst	Drink beverage	*
Familiar voices	Affiliation	Talk with friends	***
Headache	Pain avoidance	Take aspirin	*****
Lack of sleep	Rest	Lie down, nap	*
Upcoming competition	Achievement	Practice skill	**

Note: The number of asterisks in column four communicates the intensity of the environmentally activated motive. One asterisk denotes the lowest intensity level, while five asterisks denote the highest.

channel behavior toward taking an aspirin. Like many motives, pain has an intrinsic ability to grab, hold, and direct our attention (Eccleston & Crombez, 1999). Motives, therefore, capture attention; interrupt what we are doing; distract us from doing other things; prepare us for motive-congruent action; and impose a motive-congruent priority onto our thinking, feeling, and behaving.

Motivation and Emotion Are "Intervening Variables"

Motivational and emotional processes arise in response to environmental events and, once aroused, cause behavior and outcomes (as illustrated earlier in Figure 1.4). Motivation and emotion are variables that intervene between these causes (antecedents) and effects (outcomes) to explain the *why* that underlies cause–effect relations.

Figure 1.5 graphically illustrates what is meant by the claim that motivation and emotion are intervening variables. The left-hand side of Figure 1.5 shows the direct cause–effect relation between what happens in the environment (X) and how well we adapt and function (Z). For instance, you might receive unfair treatment and then respond with an aggressive act, such as uttering a hurtful comment. In the language of Figure 1.5, the unfair treatment causes your act of aggression (X → Z). What motivation and emotion researchers and practitioners do, however, is to ask why you behaved the way you did. The right-hand side of Figure 1.5 presents a different way of thinking about direct cause–effect relations. Rather than directly effecting outcomes, what antecedent causes do is produce changes in motivation and emotion (line "a"). And what changes in motivation and emotion do is

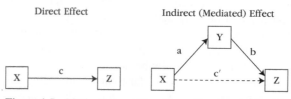

Figure 1.5   Motivation and Emotion as "Intervening Variables"

Note: X represents the antecedent cause, Z represents the life-outcome effect, and Y represents the intervening motivational or emotional state.

produce changes in life outcomes (line "b"). For instance, if the unfair treatment led you to experience anger, then that anger (not the unfair treatment itself) is what led causally to the hurtful utterance. Had the unfair treatment led you to experience a different motivation or emotion—say, compassion for the other—then that compassion would have led to a different way of behaving, such as responding empathically to the other. When the explanatory function of motivational and emotional states are considered, the X → Z direct effect disappears (hence, the line "c" changes from a solid line on the left-hand side of the figure to a dashed line on the right-hand side). Hence, motivational and emotional states "intervene" between environmental causes and life-outcome effects to explain why the antecedent affects the outcome.

The essential point is that theories of motivation and emotion are created to explain the why that underlies the cause–effect line "c" on the left side of Figure 1.5. They do so by showing how the cause changes motivation and emotion (line "a") and how motivation and emotion, once affected, in turn causes the effect (line "b"). Thus, it is more profitable to offer a motivational and an emotional explanation for behavior and life outcomes than it is to offer an environmental explanation.

Motives Vary Over Time and Influence the Ongoing Stream of Behavior

Motivation and emotion are dynamic processes—always changing, always rising and falling. It is helpful to think of motivation as a constantly flowing river of needs, cognitions, and emotions. Not only do motive strengths continually rise and fall, but people also always harbor a multitude of different motives at any one point in time. Typically, one motive is strongest and most situationally appropriate, while other motives are relatively subordinate (i.e., one motive dominates our attention, while others lie relatively dormant, as in Table 1.4). The strongest motive typically has the greatest influence on our behavior, but each subordinate motive can become dominant as circumstances change and time passes and can therefore influence and contribute to the ongoing stream of behavior.

As an illustration, consider a typical study session in which a student sits at a desk with book in hand. Our scholar's goal is to read the book, a relatively strong motive on this occasion because of an upcoming examination. The student reads for an hour, but during this time, curiosity becomes satisfied, fatigue sets in, and various subordinate motives—such as hunger and affiliation—begin to increase in strength. Perhaps the smell of popcorn from a neighbor's room makes its way down the hallway, or perhaps a text message from a friend increases an affiliation motive. If the affiliation motive increases in strength to a dominant level, then our scholar's stream of behavior will shift direction from studying to affiliating.

An ongoing stream of behavior in which a person performs a set of three behaviors, X, Y, and Z (e.g., studying, eating, and affiliating; Atkinson, Bongort, & Price, 1977) appears in Figure 1.6. The figure plots the changes in the strength of each of these three motives that produce the observed stream of behavior. At time one, motive X (studying) is the dominant motive, while motives Y and Z are subordinate. At time two, motive Y (eating) has increased in strength above motive X (perhaps because of the alluring smell of popcorn), while motive Z continues to remain subordinate. At time three, motive Z (affiliating) gains relative dominance (perhaps because of a friend's text message) and exerts its influence on the stream of behavior. Overall, Figure 1.6 illustrates that (a) motive strengths change over time; (b) people forever harbor a multitude of motives of various intensities, any one

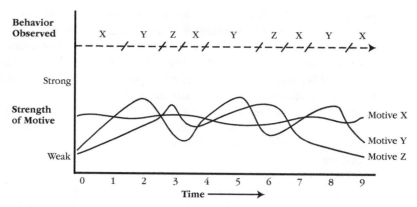

Figure 1.6 Stream of Behavior and the Changes in the Strength of Its Underlying Motives

Source: Adapted from *Cognitive Control of Action*, by D. Birch, J. W. Atkinson, and K. Bongort, in B. Weiner's (Ed.), *Cognitive View of Human Motivation* (pp. 71–84), 1974, New York: Academic Press.

of which might grab attention and participate in the stream of behavior, given appropriate circumstances; and (c) motives are not something a person either does or does not have, but instead, these motives rise and fall as circumstances change.

Types of Motivations Exist

In many people's minds, motivation is a unitary concept. Its key feature is its amount, and what matters about motivation is How much? The thinking is that more motivation is better than is less motivation. Practitioners (teachers, parents, managers, coaches) therefore ask, "How can I foster more motivation in my students, children, workers, or athletes?"

In contrast, motivation theorists emphasize that *types* of motivations exist (Ames & Archer, 1988; Atkinson, 1964; Deci, 1992a) and that human beings are motivationally complex (Vallerand, 1997). For instance, intrinsic motivation is different from extrinsic motivation (Ryan & Deci, 2000a), mastery motivation is different from performance motivation (Ames & Archer, 1988), and the motivation to approach success is different from the motivation to avoid failure (Elliot, 1997). Similarly, emotion is not a unitary concept, because types of emotions exist (Izard, 1991). For instance, a person who is intensely angry behaves quite differently from a person who is intensely afraid. Both are highly motivated and "how much?" matters, but "which type?" (of emotion) is an equally important question to consider, because people who are angry behave very differently than do people who are afraid. So a complete motivational and emotional analysis of behavior answers both questions—How much? and What type?

Watch as an athlete practices, an employee works, and a doctor cares for a patient, and you will see variations in the intensity of their motivation and emotion. But it is equally important to ask why the athlete practices, why the employee works, and why the doctor provides care. Type of motivation and emotion is important because some types yield a higher quality of experience, more favorable performances, and psychologically healthier outcomes than do other types. For instance, students who learn out of an intrinsic motivation (via interest, curiosity) show more creativity and conceptual learning than do students who learn out of an extrinsic motivation (via stickers, deadlines; Deci & Ryan, 1987). In achievement situations, students whose goal is to approach success ("My goal is to make an A.") outperform equally able students whose goal is to avoid failure ("My goal is to avoid making less than an A.") (Elliot, 1999). When people diet, those with autonomous motivation tend to diet successfully because they eat healthier foods, whereas those with controlled motivation tend to diet unsuccessfully because they enact dysfunctional behaviors such as bulimia (Pelletier et al., 2004).

A related theme is that motivation includes both approach and avoidance tendencies. Generally speaking, people presuppose that to be motivated is better than to be unmotivated. The problem is that you sometimes get what you wish for. In actuality and in contrast to common wisdom, several motivational systems are aversive in nature—pain, hunger, distress, fear, dissonance, anxiety, tension, pressure, frustration, perfectionism, helplessness, and so on. While we welcome and embrace many approach-oriented motives (e.g., interest, hope, joy, achievement motivation, and self-actualization), aversive motives (e.g., fear, hunger) are not so welcomed because they essentially poke a proverbial needle in our side until we give the aversive motive its due and adjust our behavior accordingly. Many motivational and emotional states operate under the principle, "the greater the irritation, the greater the change" (Kimble, 1990, p. 36).

The point is that human beings are curious, intrinsically motivated, sensation-seeking animals with goals and plans to master challenges, develop warm interpersonal relationships, and move toward attractive incentives, psychological development, and growth. It is also true, however, that people are stressed, frustrated, plagued by insecurities, pressured, afraid, in pain, depressed, and encounter aversive situations from which they wish to flee. To adapt optimally, human beings have (and need) a motivational repertoire that also features aversive, avoidance-based motives. Hence, a full understanding of the rich fabric of human motivation includes an appreciation for both approach and avoidance tendencies (Carver, 2006; Elliot, 2006).

We Are Not Always Consciously Aware of the Motivational Basis of Our Behavior

Motives vary in how accessible they are to consciousness and to verbal report. Some motives originate in language structures and the cortical brain (e.g., goals) and are thus readily available to our conscious awareness (e.g., "I have a goal to sell three insurance policies today."). For these motives, if you ask a person why he or she selected that particular goal, the person can confidently list the rational and logical reasons for doing so. Other motives, however, have their origins in nonlanguage structures and the subcortical brain and are therefore much less available to conscious awareness. Not many people, for instance, say they feel hungry because of low leptin in the bloodstream; not many people say they acted violently because it was so hot; and not many people say they seek power and social status because their parents imposed very high developmental standards on them during their childhood. These are the motives that originate in the emotional subcortical brain rather than in the language-based cortical brain.

Many experimental findings can be offered to make the point that motives can and do originate in the unconscious. Consider that people who feel good after receiving an unexpected gift are more likely to help a stranger in need than are people in neutral moods (Isen, 1987). People are more sociable on a sunny day than they are on a cloudy day

(Kraut & Johnston, 1979). People commit more acts of violence in the summer months than at other times of the year (Anderson, 1989). Major league baseball pitchers, for instance, are more likely to intentionally hit batters on the opposing team when the temperature is hot rather than when the temperature is cold or moderate (Reifman, Larrick, & Fein, 1991). In each of these examples, the person is not consciously aware of why he or she committed the social or antisocial act. Few people, for instance, would say they helped a stranger because of their mood, and fewer would say they committed murder or hurled baseballs at the heads of opponents because of the hot temperature. Still, these are conditions that cause motivations. The brief lesson is that the motives, cravings, appetites, desires, moods, needs, and emotions that regulate human behavior are not always immediately obvious or consciously accessible. That is, we are not always consciously aware of the motivational basis of our behavior.

Motivation Study Reveals What People Want

The study of motivation and emotion reveals what people want and why they want it. It literally reveals the contents of human nature.

The subject matter of motivation and emotion concerns what we all hope for, desire, want, need, and fear. It examines questions such as whether people are essentially good or evil, naturally active or passive, brotherly or aggressive, altruistic or selfish, free to choose or determined by biological and societal demands, and whether people harbor within themselves natural forces to grow and self-actualize.

Theories of motivation reveal what is common within the strivings of all human beings by identifying the commonalities among people from different cultures, different life experiences, different ages, different historical periods, and different genetic endowments. All of us harbor physiological needs such as hunger, thirst, sex, and pain. All of us inherit biological dispositions such as temperament and neural circuits in the brain for pleasure and aversion. We all share a number of basic emotions, and we all feel these emotions under the same conditions. We all possess the same constellation of psychological needs, including those for autonomy, competence, and relatedness. We are all hedonists (approach pleasure, avoid pain), but we seem to want personal growth and optimal experience even more (Seligman & Csikszentmihalyi, 2000).

Theories of motivation also reveal those motivations and emotions that are learned through experience and are socially engineered through cultural forces (and hence outside the realm of human nature). For example, through our unique experiences, exposures to particular role models, and awareness of cultural expectations, we acquire different goals, values, attitudes, expectations, aspirations, and views of self. These ways of energizing and directing our behavior originate not from inherited human nature but, rather, from environmental, social, and cultural forces. The study of motivation therefore informs us what part of want and desire stem from human nature but also what part of want and desire stem from personal, social, and cultural learning. It reveals what part of motivation and emotion is universal and inherent versus what part is enculturated and acquired.

A careful study of motivation and emotion reveals that we do not so much have a single human nature as we have multiple human natures (Ryan, 2013). Part of our nature is to be inherently malevolent, selfish, passive, and tending toward the antisocial, while another part of our nature is to be benevolent, cooperative, active, and tending toward the prosocial. We have both natures. Whether we tap into and show our malevolent nature or whether we tap into and show our benevolent nature depends significantly on how supportive versus thwarting is the social context that surrounds us and how support versus frustrating are the interpersonal relationships in our lives. When the social environment is nurturing and when our interpersonal relationships are supportive, our benevolent nature arises and regulates our ongoing stream of behavior, but when the social environment is thwarting and when our interpersonal relationships are frustrating, our malevolent nature arises and regulates our ongoing stream of behavior.

To Flourish, Motivation Needs Supportive Conditions

A person's motivation cannot be separated from the social context in which it is embedded. That is, a child's motivation is affected by and somewhat dependent on the social context provided by his or her parents. The same could be said for the motivation of athletes affected by coaches, patients affected by physicians, students affected by teachers, and citizens affected by their culture. These environments can be nurturing and supportive or they can be neglectful, frustrating, and undermining. Those who are surrounded by social contexts that support and nurture their needs and strivings show greater vitality, experience personal growth, and thrive more than those who are surrounded by social neglect, frustration, and abuse (Keyes, 2007; Ryan & Deci, 2000). Recognizing the role that social contexts play in people's motivation and well-being, motivation researchers seek to apply principles of motivation in ways that allow people's motivation to flourish. Four areas of application are stressed in this book:

- Education
- Work
- Sports and exercise
- Therapy

In education, an understanding of motivation can be applied to promote students' classroom engagement, to foster the motivation to learn and develop talent, to support the desire to stay in school rather than drop out, and to inform teachers how to provide a motivationally supportive classroom climate. In work, an understanding of motivation can be applied to improve worker productivity and satisfaction, to help employees set goals, to keep stress at bay, and to structure jobs so that they offer workers optimal levels of challenge, control, variety, and relatedness with their coworkers. In sports, an understanding of motivation can be applied to identify the reasons youths participate in sports, to design exercise programs that promote lifelong physical activity, and to understand how factors such as interpersonal competition, performance feedback, and goal setting effect performance. In therapy, an understanding of motivation can be applied to improve mental and emotional well-being, to cultivate a sense of authenticity and optimism, to foster mature defense mechanisms, to explain the paradox of why mental control efforts so often backfire, and to appreciate the contribution that the quality of the interpersonal relationships we have plays in our own motivation, emotion, and mental health.

As you watch parents, teachers, workplace managers, coaches, and therapists attempt to motivate their children, students, workers, athletes, and clients, you will observe that not all attempts to motivate others are successful. Some of these efforts even backfire and make the motivational problem worse. The same can be said of attempts to motivate the self. For instance, take the time to actually monitor the emotions expressed by children, students, workers, athletes, and clients as they are being motivated by others. When people adapt successfully and their motivational states flourish, people express positive emotions such as joy, hope, interest, and optimism. But when people are frustrated by their environment and their motivational states flounder, people express negative emotions such as sadness, hopelessness, frustration, resentment, and stress. In the chapters to come, much of the text will be devoted to the practical effort to motivate the self and others.

When Trying to Motivate Others, What Is Easy to Do Is Rarely What Is Effective

It is easy to come up with strategies and recommendations about how to motivate self and others. If someone asks you, "How can I motivate my employees to be more creative and to work harder?", I suspect that you can rather quickly offer a seemingly satisfying reply. The problem is that when people's common-sensical answers (e.g., "offer attractive incentives") are put to the objective empirical test, those proposed motivational strategies routinely fall short and prove themselves to be ineffective. They also sometimes create serious harm, such as damaging the very motivation the person sought to promote. If you study motivation and emotion long enough, you will come to the conclusion that what is easy to do in practice is rarely what is most effective. For instance, teachers offer students sticker charts to increase their reading motivation, employers assign goals for their employees to achieve, parents offer their children options to gain their compliance, and we all utter directives and commands to tell others what they should do. In practice, all these things are easy to do (give stickers, assign goals, offer options, and utter directives), but they are also routinely ineffective and even motivationally damaging things to do.

The general finding that "what is easy to do is rarely what is effective" leads motivation and emotion researchers to go back to the drawing board to do the tough work to create effective interventions and motivational supports. For instance, teachers tend to have much better success in motivating their students to read when they do the tough work to transform the lesson plan into a series of activities that children find to be interesting, curiosity-provoking, and personally inspiring. Employers tend to have much better success in motivating their employees' creativity and hard work when they sit down, take the employees' perspective, and invite them to generate their own heartfelt, self-endorsed work goals. Parents tend to have more success encouraging their children to engage in socially constructive behaviors when they offer their children new attractive opportunities for action and explain the otherwise hidden benefits of engaging in such activities. And, everyone tends to have better success in motivating others when they put aside their directives and commands and instead work diligently to understand why the other person currently does not want to do that particular task and instead ask the other for input and suggestions. All of these approaches to motivate and engage others are somewhat difficult to do, but that is what the present book is for. If you will take a moment to glance through the book's final chapter (Chapter 17), you will find several rather sophisticated and highly successful interventions. It may take 16 more chapters to get to that final chapter on effective interventions, but we *will* get there.

There Is Nothing So Practical as a Good Theory

Consider how you might answer a motivational question such as, "What causes Joe to study so hard and for so long?" To generate an answer, you might begin with a commonsense analysis (e.g., "Joe studies so hard because he has such high self-esteem."). Additionally, you might recall a similar instance from your personal experience when you tried very hard, and you might then generalize that experience to this particular situation (e.g., "The last time I studied that hard, it was because I had a big test the next day."). A third strategy might be to find an expert on the topic and ask her (e.g., "My neighbor is a veteran teacher; I'll ask her why she thinks Joe might be studying so hard."). These are all fine and informative resources for helping answer motivational questions, but a truly golden resource is a good theory.

As introduced earlier in Figure 1.1, a theory is a set of variables (e.g., self-efficacy, goals, effort) and the relationships that are assumed to exist among those variables (e.g., strong self-efficacy beliefs encourage people to set goals, and once set, goals encourage high effort). Theories provide a conceptual framework for interpreting behavioral observations, and they function as intellectual bridges to link motivational questions and problems to satisfying answers, solutions, and applications. With a motivation theory in mind, the researcher approaches a question or problem along the lines of, "Well, *according to goal-setting theory*, the reason Joe studies so hard and so long is because . . ." As you read through the pages of each chapter and become familiar with each new theory of motivation and emotion, consider its usefulness in answering the motivational questions you care about most.

Table 1.5 introduces 31 motivation theories that appear in the chapters to come. The theories are listed here for two reasons. First, the list introduces the idea that the heart and soul of a motivational analysis of behavior is its theories. Instead of existing as dry and abstract playthings of scientists, a good theory is a practical, usable tool for solving the problems faced by students, teachers, workers, employers, managers, athletes, coaches, parents, therapists, and clients. To paraphrase Kurt Lewin, there is nothing so practical as a good theory. Theories are as useful as they are because they provide empirically validated (evidence-based) guidance in how to understand and how to solve a problem.

Second, the list of theories can serve as a means for monitoring your growing familiarity with contemporary motivation and emotion study. At the present time, you probably recognize very few of the theories listed in the table, but your familiarity will grow week by week. Months from now, you will feel more comfortable with the 31 different theories listed in Table 1.5. If so, then you can then be confident that you are developing a sophisticated and complete understanding of motivation and emotion. When you know motivation theories, you know motivation.

SUMMARY

The journey to understand motivation and emotion begins by asking the perennial question, What causes behavior? This general question invites the more specific questions that constitute the core problems to be solved in motivation study: What starts behavior? How is behavior sustained over time? Why is behavior directed toward some ends but away from others? Why does behavior change its direction? Why does behavior stop? What are the forces that determine behavior's intensity? Why does a person behave one way in a

Table 1.5 Thirty-one Theories in the Study of Motivation and Emotion (with a Supportive Reference Citation)

Motivation Theory	Supportive Reference Citation for Further Information
Achievement goals	Elliot (1997)
Arousal	Berlyne (1967)
Attribution	Weiner (1986)
Broaden-and-build	Fredrickson (2009)
Cognitive dissonance	Harmon-Jones and Mills (1999)
Cognitive evaluation	Deci and Ryan (1985a)
Differential emotions	Izard (1991)
Drive	Bolles (1975)
Dynamics of action	Atkinson and Birch (1978)
Effectance motivation	Harter (1981)
Ego depletion	Baumeister, Vohs, and Tice (2007)
Ego development	Loevinger (1976)
Expectancy x Value	Eccles and Wigfield (2002)
Facial feedback hypothesis	Laird (1974)
Flow	Csikszentmihalyi (1990)
Goal setting	Locke and Latham (2002)
Implicit motives	Schultheiss and Brunstein (2010)
Interest	Hidi and Renninger (2006)
Learned helplessness	Peterson, Maier, and Seligman (1993)
Mindsets	Dweck (2006)
Motivation intensity	Brehm and Self (1989)
Opponent process	Solomon (1980)
Positive affect	Isen (1987)
Psychodynamics	Westen (1998)
Reactance	Wortman and Brehm (1975)
Self-actualization	Rogers (1959)
Self-concordance	Sheldon and Elliot (1999)
Self-determination	Ryan and Deci (2000)
Self-efficacy	Bandura (1997)
Sensation seeking	Zuckerman (1994)
Stress and coping	Lazarus (1991a)

particular situation at one time yet behave in a different way at another time? What are the motivational differences among individuals, and how do such differences arise? Motivation and emotion exist as scientific disciplines to answer these questions.

The subject matter of motivation concerns those internal processes that give behavior its energy, direction, and persistence. Energy implies that behavior has strength—that it is relatively strong, intense, and hardy or resilient. Direction implies that behavior has purpose—that it is aimed or guided toward achieving some particular goal or outcome. Persistence implies that behavior has endurance—that it continues over time and sustains itself across different situations. The three internal processes that give behavior its strength, purpose, and resilience (i.e., its energy, direction, and persistence) are needs, cognitions, and emotions. Needs are conditions within the individual that are essential and necessary for the maintenance of life and for growth and well-being. Cognitions are mental events, such as beliefs, expectations, and the self-concept, that represent ways of thinking. Emotions are complex but coordinated feeling-arousal–purposive–expressive reactions to significant live events, such as a challenge to our survival or well-being.

Both in its presence and in its intensity, motivation and emotion can be expressed in five ways: behavior, engagement, psychophysiology, brain activations, and self-report. Motivation and emotion express themselves publicly through behaviors such as effort, persistence, latency, choice, probability of response, facial expressions, and bodily gestures. Motivation and emotion also express themselves through acts of engagement, and specifically through behavioral, emotional, cognitive, and agentic aspects of engagement. Motivation and emotion further express themselves publicly through changes in psychophysiology such as changes in heart rate, blood pressure, respiratory rate, and the discharge of hormones such as epinephrine and cortisol. Motivation and emotion also express themselves through brain activations such as increased activity in particular regions of the cortical and subcortical brain. And motivation and emotion express themselves through self-reports, as people complete questionnaires or interviews that ask them specific questions about their subjective experience. In the study of motivation and emotion, self-reports can be useful and informative, but they also need to be backed up and verified by the person's behavioral, engagement, psychophysiological, and neural activity.

Ten themes run throughout motivation and emotion study. These themes are as follows: (1) motivation and emotion benefit adaptation and functioning; (2) motivation and emotion direct attention; (3) motivation and emotion are "intervening variables"; (4) motives vary over time and influence the ongoing stream of behavior; (5) types of motivations exist; (6) we are not always consciously aware of the motivational basis of our behavior; (7) motivation study reveals what people want; (8) to flourish, motivation needs supportive conditions; (9) when trying to motivate others, what is easy to do is rarely what is effective; and (10) there is nothing so practical as a good theory. These 10 themes help organize and unify the otherwise diverse assumptions, hypotheses, perspectives, theories, findings, and applications within contemporary motivation and emotion study. One overall framework to illustrate how motivation is a coherent, interesting, and practical field of study appeared in Figure 1.4.

Chapter 2

Motivation in Historical Perspective

PHILOSOPHICAL ORIGINS OF MOTIVATIONAL CONCEPTS

GRAND THEORIES

    Will

    Instinct

    Drive

        Freud's Drive Theory
        Hull's Drive Theory
        Decline of Drive Theory
        Post-Drive Theory Years

RISE OF THE MINI-THEORIES

    Active Nature of the Person

    Cognitive Revolution

    Socially Relevant Questions

CONTEMPORARY ERA

    The 1990s Reemergence of Motivation Study

BRIEF HISTORY OF EMOTION STUDY

CONCLUSION

SUMMARY

READINGS FOR FURTHER STUDY

In the classic movie *Back to the Future*, Michael J. Fox drives a car that acts as a time machine capable of transporting him back to the 1950s. Imagine being a passenger in such a car and having the chance to stop by the local university to see what the college motivation course looked like.

Besides the students' bobby socks and funny haircuts, one item to notice in this college course would be the lack of a textbook. The first textbook in motivation was not written until 1964 (Cofer & Appley, 1964). Another item would be the syllabus. Featured topics on the mimeographed handout would be drive theory, environmental incentives and reinforcement, acquired drives, conflict, and emotion. You could search the syllabus all you wanted, but none of the really interesting stuff about how to apply motivation would be included—nothing about motivation in the schools, sports psychology, work motivation, obesity and dieting, personal control beliefs, and so on. The course would, however, likely include psychoanalytic and self-actualization concepts—a week on Freud, another week on Maslow. The course would probably feature a weekly laboratory assignment. Each student would be assigned a rat for the semester, and lab time would involve carrying out experiments such as testing the effects of 24 hours of food deprivation on the rat's running speed toward a goal box filled with either appetizing sunflower seeds or unappealing mush. Once the De Lorean time machine returned you to the present, you would probably agree that the study of motivation has changed even more than the haircuts and fashions.

PHILOSOPHICAL ORIGINS OF MOTIVATIONAL CONCEPTS

If technology could send you back 100 years, then you would not be able to find a motivation course at all. Courses in motivation (and the field of motivation itself) have not been around very long—less than 100 years.

The intellectual roots of contemporary motivation and emotion study owe their origin to the ancient Greeks—Socrates, Plato, and Aristotle. Plato (Socrates's student) proposed that motivation flowed from a tripartite, hierarchically arranged soul (or mind, psyche). At the most primitive level, the appetitive aspect contributed bodily appetites and desires, such as hunger and sex. The competitive aspect contributed socially referenced standards, such as social honor and social shame. At the highest level, the calculating aspect contributed decision-making capacities, such as reason and choosing. These three aspects of the psyche motivated and explained different realms of behavior. Also, each higher aspect could regulate the motives of the lower aspects (e.g., reason could keep bodily appetites in check). Interestingly, Plato's portrayal of motivation anticipated Sigmund Freud's psychodynamics rather well (e.g., see Plato's Book IX, pp. 280–281): Roughly speaking, Plato's appetitive aspect corresponds to Freud's id, the competitive aspect to the superego, and the calculating aspect to the ego (Erdelyi, 1985).

Aristotle endorsed Plato's hierarchically organized, tripartite psyche (appetitive, competitive, and calculating), although he preferred different terminology (nutritive, sensitive, and rational). The nutritive aspect was the most impulsive, irrational, and animal-like. It contributed bodily urges necessary for the maintenance of life. The sensitive aspect was also bodily related, but it regulated hedonic pleasure and pain. The rational component was unique to human beings, because it was idea-related, intellectual, and featured the will. The will operated at the psyche's highest level because it utilized intention, choice, and that which is divine and immortal.

Hundreds of years later, the Greek's tripartite psyche was reduced to a dualism—the passions of the body and the reason of the mind. The two-part psyche retained the Greek's hierarchical nature because it made its chief distinction between what was irrational, impulsive, and biological (the body) versus what was rational, intelligent, and spiritual (the mind). The impetus for this reinterpretation rested mostly in the era's intellectual commitment to motivational dichotomies, such as passion versus reason, good versus evil, and animal nature versus human soul. Thomas Aquinas, for example, suggested that the body provided irrational pleasure-based motivational impulses, whereas the mind provided rational will-based motivations.

In the post-Renaissance era, René Descartes, a French philosopher, added to this mind–body dualism by distinguishing between the passive and active aspects of motivation. The body was a mechanical and motivationally passive agent, whereas the will was an immaterial and motivationally active agent. As a physical entity, the body responded to the environment in mechanistic ways through its senses, reflexes, and physiology. The mind, however, was a spiritual, thinking entity that possessed a purposive will. The mind could will the body and govern its desires.

This passive versus active distinction set the agenda for motivation study during the next 300 years. On the one hand, what was needed to understand the passive and reactive motives was a mechanistic analysis of the body. This need gave rise to the biologically based study of physiology. On the other hand, what was needed to understand the active and purposive motives was an intellectual analysis of the will. This need gave rise to the study of philosophy.

For Descartes, the ultimate motivational force was the will. Descartes reasoned that if he could understand the will, then he would understand motivation. The will initiated and directed action, and it chose whether to act and what to do when acting. Bodily needs, passions, pleasures, and pains created impulses to action, but these impulses only excited the will. The will was a faculty (a power) of the mind that controlled the bodily appetites and passions in the interests of virtue and salvation by exercising its power of choice. By assigning exclusive powers of motivation to the will, the study of motivation followed the road of philosophy as Descartes provided the new field of psychology with its first grand theory of motivation.

GRAND THEORIES

The phrase "grand theory" is used here and throughout the chapter to connote an all-encompassing theory that seeks to explain the full range of motivated action—why we eat, drink, work, play, compete, fear certain things, read, fall in love, and everything else. The statement that "the will motivates all action" is a grand theory of motivation in the same way that "the love of money is the root of all evil" is a grand theory of evil. Both identify a single, all-encompassing cause that fully explains a phenomenon (all motivation, all evil). The historical study of motivation—from its philosophical roots to the 1960s—shows that early motivation study embraced a series of three grand theories of motivation—first the will, then the instinct, and finally drive.

Will

Descartes's hope was that once he understood the will, then an understanding of motivation would inevitably unfold. Understanding motivation was reduced to, and became synonymous with, understanding the will. For this reason, a great deal of philosophical energy was invested in the effort. Some progress was made as the acts of willing were identified to be choosing (i.e., deciding whether to act; Rand, 1964), striving (i.e., creating impulses to act; Ruckmick, 1936), and resisting (i.e., resisting temptation; Mischel, 1974). In the end, however, two centuries of philosophical analysis yielded disappointing results. The will turned out to be an ill-understood faculty of the mind that arose, somehow, out of a congeries of innate capacities, environmental sensations, life experiences, and reflections upon itself and its ideas. Furthermore, once the will emerged, it somehow became endowed with purpose. And it turned out that some people showed more willpower than did other people.

To make a long story short, philosophers found the will to be as mysterious and as difficult to explain as was the motivation it supposedly generated. Philosophers discovered neither the will's nature nor the laws by which it operated. Essentially, philosophers painted themselves into the proverbial corner by multiplying, rather than reducing, the problem they were trying to solve. In using the will, philosophers now had to explain not only motivation but also the motivator—the will. As you can see, the problem only doubled. For this reason, those involved with the new science of psychology, which emerged in the 1870s (Schultz & Schultz, 2011), found themselves in search of a less mysterious motivational principle. They found one not within the original intellectual home of philosophy but within the new intellectual home of physiology and biology—the instinct.

Instinct

Charles Darwin's biological determinism had two major effects on scientific thinking. First, it provided biology with its most important idea (evolution). In doing so, biological determinism turned the mood of scientists away from mentalistic motivational concepts (e.g., will) and toward mechanistic and genetic ones. Second, Darwin's biological determinism ended the man–animal dualism that pervaded early motivation study. It introduced questions such as how animals use their resources (i.e., motivation) to adapt to the prevailing demands of an environment. The earlier philosophers had assumed that the will was a uniquely human mental power, one that necessitated that motivation study in humans be separate from motivation study in animals. Darwin reasoned that making this man–animal distinction was a mistake.

For Darwin, much of animal behavior seemed to be unlearned, automated, mechanistic, and inherited (Darwin, 1859, 1872). With or without experience, animals adapted to their prevailing environments: Birds built nests, hens brooded, dogs chased rabbits, and rabbits ran from dogs. To explain this apparently prewired adaptive behavior, Darwin proposed the instinct.

Darwin's motivational concept could explain what the philosopher's will could not—namely, where the motivational force came from in the first place (Beach, 1955). Instincts arose from a physical substance, from the genetic endowment; hence, they were physically real. This inherited and material substance (genes) led the animal to act in a specific way. Thus, the reason why bird build nests and dogs chase rabbits was because they had a genetically endowed, biologically aroused impulse to do so. Essentially, motivation thinkers in the 19th century stripped away the inanimate part of the philosopher's dualism (i.e., the rational soul) and kept the parts that remained, namely the biological and bodily urges, impulses, and appetites.

The first psychologist to pioneer an instinct theory of motivation was William James (1890). James borrowed heavily from the intellectual climate of Darwin and his contemporaries to endow human beings with a generous number of physical (e.g., sucking, locomotion) and mental (e.g., imitation, play, sociability) instincts. All that was needed to translate an instinct into an impulse for action was the presence of an appropriate stimulus. Cats chase mice, run from dogs, and flee fires simply because they biologically must (i.e., because a mouse brings out the cat's instinct to chase, a dog brings out the instinct to flee, and the fire's flames bring out the instinct for self-preservation). The sight of a mouse (or dog or fire) rather mechanically and automatically activated in the cat a complex set of inherited reflexes that generated impulses to purposive action (e.g., chasing, running).

Psychology's affection for, and commitment to, its second grand theory of motivation grew rapidly. A generation after James, William McDougall (1908, 1926) proposed an instinct theory that featured instincts to explore, to fight, to mother offspring, and so on. McDougall regarded instincts as irrational and impulsive motivational forces that oriented the person toward one particular goal. It was the instinct that "determines its possessor to perceive, and to pay attention to, objects of a certain class, to experience an emotional excitement of a particular quality upon perceiving such an object, and to act in regard to it in a particular manner, or, at least, to experience an impulse to such action" (McDougall, 1908, p. 30). Thus, instincts biased perception, generated emotionality, and elicited purposive behavior toward inherently desired goals. In many respects, McDougall's instinct doctrine paralleled James's ideas. The greatest difference between the two was McDougall's rather extreme assertion that without instincts human beings would initiate no action. Without these "prime movers," human beings would be inert lumps, bodies without any impulses to action. In other words, all of human motivation owes its origin to a collection of genetically endowed instincts (i.e., a grand theory of motivation).

Once researchers embraced the instinct as a grand theory of motivation, the next task became identifying how many instincts human beings possessed. Things quickly went out of control. The instinct doctrine became hopelessly speculative as different lists of instincts grew to include over 6,000 (Bernard, 1924; Dunlap, 1919). In the practice of compiling lists of instincts, intellectual promiscuity reigned: "If he goes with his fellows, it is the 'herd instinct' which activates him; if he walks alone, it is the 'antisocial instinct'; if he twiddles his thumbs, it is the 'thumb-twiddling instinct'; if he does not twiddle his thumbs, it is the 'thumb-not-twiddling instinct'" (Holt, 1931, p. 428). The problem here is the tendency to confuse naming with explaining. Notice how the following sentence invokes (names) a motivational entity yet fails to actually explain the "why" underlying the observed behavior: People are aggressive because they have an instinct to fight. This sentence sounds like an explanation when it is in fact vacuous.

In addition, the logic underlying instinct theory was exposed as circular (Kuo, 1921; Tolman, 1923). A circular explanation is one that attempts to explain an observation in terms of itself. Consider the aforementioned explanation of how the instinct to fight motivates acts of aggression. The only evidence that people possess an instinct to fight is that they sometimes behave aggressively. For the theorist, this is the worst kind of circularity: The cause explains the behavior (instinct → behavior), yet the behavior is used as evidence for its cause (behavior → instinct). What is lacking here is some independent way to determine if the instinct really exists. The key to escaping circularity is to make new predictions, such as the following: If two very similar animals (i.e., animals that share the same instincts) were raised with different life experiences, then their instincts should lead them toward similar behaviors (despite their dissimilar personal histories). When researchers performed such experiments on the mothering instinct in rats (Birch, 1956) and the handedness (right- or left-handed) instinct in humans (Watson, 1924), the rats and humans acted in ways that reflected their different life experiences, not their shared instincts.

Psychology's affair with instinct theory began with wholehearted acceptance but ended with sweeping denial.[1] Just as psychology previously abandoned the will, it abandoned the instinct. Once again, psychology found itself in search of a substitute motivational concept to explain behavior's energetic and purposive nature.

Drive

The motivational concept that arose to replace instinct was drive (introduced by Woodworth, 1918). Drive arose from within an intellectual climate of a functional biology, one that understood that the function of behavior was to service bodily needs. As biological imbalances occurred (e.g., lack of food, water), animals psychologically experienced these bodily deficits as "drive." Psychological drive then motivated whatever behavior was instrumental to servicing the body's needs (e.g., eating, drinking). The two most widely embraced drive theories came from Sigmund Freud (1915) and Clark Hull (1943).

Freud's Drive Theory

Freud, a physiologist by training, believed that all behavior was motivated and that the purpose of behavior was to serve the satisfaction of biologically based bodily needs. His view was that biological urges (e.g., hunger) were constantly and inevitably recurring conditions in the body that produced energy buildups within the nervous system (Freud, 1915). While it tried to maintain a constant and low energy level, the nervous system was perpetually being displaced from this objective by the emergence, reemergence, and constant buildup of biological urges. Each energy buildup upset nervous system stability and produced psychological discomfort (i.e., anxiety). If the energy buildup rose unchecked, it could threaten physical and psychological health. Drive therefore arose as a sort of psychologically based emergency warning system that action needed to be taken. Once initiated, the motivated behavior continued until the drive or urge was satisfied. In other words, behavior served bodily needs, and anxiety (drive) acted as a sort of middleman for ensuring that need-servicing behavior occurred as and when needed.[2]

---

[1]Contemporary psychology no longer uses the instinct to explain complex human behavior. Nonetheless, the proposition that nonhuman animals show consistent, unlearned, stereotypical patterns of behavior is an undeniable observation. Bees build hexagonal cells, male stickleback fish attack red coloration, and birds build nests. Contemporary psychologists (but especially ethologists) concede that such stereotypical acts can be attributed to instincts in animals. As James wrote over a century ago, "that instincts … exist on an enormous scale in the animal kingdom needs no proof" (1890, p. 383). In using the term "instinct," ethologists (Eibl-Eibesfeldt, 1989; Lorenz, 1965; Moltz, 1965) now speak of inherited neuronal structures that are unmodified by the environment during development. These inherited neuronal structures give rise not to general patterns of behavior but to particular bits of situationally specific behavior, referred to as "fixed action patterns." Changing instinct's focus from the cause of all complex behavior to only the cause of bits of behavior (fixed action patterns) proved to be a comfortable theoretical compromise. While theoretically expedient, such a compromise clearly shows the decline of a grand theory. Explaining bits of behavior or bits of motivation is just not the same as explaining all of behavior and all of motivation.

[2]One way to understand Freud's view of nervous system energy (i.e., "libido") is through the analogy of a bathtub in which energy (like constantly flowing water) continues to rise and rise. As bodily drives continue to build up energy, the anxious urge to discharge that energy becomes increasingly urgent and expedient (or else the water would overflow). The higher the psychic energy rises, the greater the impulse to act. Adaptive behavior quieted the drive for a time, but the ever-constant buildup of nervous system energy would always return (i.e., the water's inflow never shuts off).

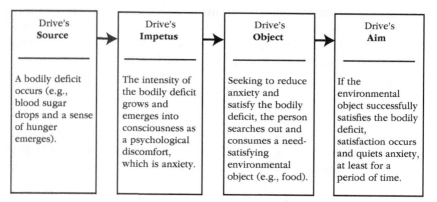

Figure 2.1 Freud's Drive Theory

Freud (1915) summarized his drive theory with four components—source, impetus, aim, and object—as depicted in Figure 2.1. The source of drive was rooted in the body's physiology—in a bodily deficit (e.g., lack of food). Once it reached a threshold level of urgency, bodily deficit became psychological drive. Drive had motivational properties. It had an impetus (force) that possessed the aim of satisfaction, which was the removal of the underlying bodily deficit. To accomplish this aim, the individual experienced anxiety on a psychological level, and it was this anxiety that motivated the behavioral search for an object capable of removing the bodily deficit. Once the need-satisfying object was found, the subsequent satisfaction of the bodily deficit quieted drive/anxiety.

Hull's Drive Theory

Freud was a clinical psychotherapist who built his drive theory from case studies of disturbed individuals. Clark Hull, however, was an experimental psychologist who used modern scientific methods (e.g., random assignment to experimental conditions) to build his drive theory. For Hull (1943, 1952), drive was a pooled energy source composed of all current bodily deficits/disturbances. In other words, particular needs for food, water, sex, sleep, and so forth summed to constitute a total bodily need. For Hull, as for Freud, motivation (i.e., drive) had a purely physiological basis and bodily need was the ultimate source of motivation (i.e., a grand theory of motivation).

Hull's drive theory had one outstanding feature that no motivation theory before it had ever possessed—namely, high versus low motivation could be predicted before it occurred. With both the instinct and the will, it was impossible to predict when and whether a person would be motivated. But if an animal was deprived of food, water, sex, or sleep, however, then drive would inevitably increase in proportion to the duration of that deprivation. Drive was an increasing monotonic function of total bodily need, which itself was an increasing monotonic function of hours of deprivation. The fact that drive could be known from antecedent environmental conditions marked the beginning of a *scientific* study of motivation. This was so because if one knew which environmental conditions created motivation, then one could manipulate (and predict) motivational states in the laboratory. One could also explore the effects of the manipulated motivational state on a host of outcomes (e.g., performance, learning). These years were a very exciting time for motivation psychologists, and many believe that this era represented the "hey day" of motivation study.

Drive arose from a range of bodily disturbances, including food deprivation, water deprivation, mate deprivation, tissue damage (pain), air deprivation, temperature regulation, urination pressures, sleep deprivation, caloric burn from activity, nest building, and care for one's young (Hull, 1943, pp. 59–60). Once it arose, drive energized behavior (Bolles, 1975). Although drive energized behavior, it did not direct it. Habit, not drive, directed behavior. As one contemporary phrased it, "Drive is an energizer, not a guide" (Hebb, 1955, p. 249). Behavior-guiding habits came from learning, and learning occurred as a consequence of reinforcement. Hull's research led him to argue that if a response was followed quickly by a reduction in drive, learning occurred and habit was reinforced. Any response that decreased drive (e.g., eating, drinking, mating) produced reinforcement, and the animal learned which response produced drive reduction in that particular situation. To show how habit and drive (i.e., learning and motivation) produced behavior, Hull (1943) developed the following formula:

$$_sE_r = {_sH_r} \times D$$

The variable $_sE_r$ is the strength of behavior (E stands for "excitatory potential") in the presence of a particular stimulus. $_sH_r$ is habit strength (i.e., the probability that a particular drive-reducing response would occur in the presence of a particular stimulus).[3] D is drive. The observable aspects of behavior—running, persisting, and so on—are denoted by $_sE_r$. The variables $_sH_r$ and D refer to behavior's underlying, unobservable causes. The multiplication sign is important in that behavior occurred only when habit and drive were at nonzero levels. In other words, without drive ($D = 0$) or without habit ($H = 0$), there was no behavioral activity ($E = 0$). One of Hull's contemporaries, Neal Miller, summarized drive theory with his often-quoted phrase, "Drive, cue, response, reward," which meant that drive energized action in the direction of a stimulus (cue) that, when attained (by response), reinforced (reward) that pattern of motivated action (i.e., thirst–water–drink–reinforcement).

Hull (1952) later extended his behavior system beyond $H \times D$ to include a third cause of behavior: incentive motivation, abbreviated as K.[4] In addition to the motivational properties of D, the incentive value of a goal object (its quality, its quantity, or both) also energized the animal. After all, people generally work harder for $50 than they do for $1. Because he recognized that motivation could arise from either internal pushes (D) or from external pulls (K), Hull updated his formula as follows:

$$_sE_r = {_sH_r} \times D \times K$$

Both D and K were motivational terms. The principal difference between the two was that D was rooted in internal stimulation via bodily disturbances, whereas K was rooted in external stimulation via the quality of the incentive. Thus, motivation arose from two sources: internal drive and environmental incentive.

---

[3]The subscripts s and r stand for "stimulus" and "response" to communicate that $_sH_r$ refers to a particular habitual response in the presence of a particular stimulus. Similarly, the subscripts joined with $_sE_r$ refer to the potential "energy" of that particular response in the presence of that particular stimulus.

[4]Incidentally, if you happen to wonder why incentive motivation was abbreviated as K instead of as I, K stood for Kenneth Spence (Weiner, 1972). Spence convinced Hull of the necessity of incorporating incentive motivation into his behavior system. Besides, I was used for another variable, inhibition, which is not discussed here.

Table 2.1   Midcentury Rankings of the 10 Most Important Historical Figures in Psychology

1. Sigmund Freud	**6.** Edward Thorndike
2. Clark Hull	**7.** William James
3. Wilhelm Wundt	**8.** Max Wertheimer
4. Ivan Pavlov	**9.** Edward Tolman
5. John Watson	**10.** Kurt Lewin

In its zenith, Hull's drive theory was as popular as any theory in the history of psychology. That is a strong statement to make, but consider three historical occurrences that validate this claim. First, approximately half of all the articles published in the leading psychology journals in the early 1950s (e.g., *Psychological Review*, *Journal of Experimental Psychology*) included a reference to Hull's 1943 book. Second, books on motivation went from being practically nonexistent at midcentury to commonplace 10 years later (Atkinson, 1964; Bindra, 1959; Brown, 1961; Hall, 1961; Lindzey, 1958; Madsen, 1959; Maslow, 1954; McClelland, 1955; Peters, 1958; Stacey & DeMartino, 1958; Toman, 1960; Young, 1961). Third, in the 1950s the American Psychological Association (APA) invited its members to list the most important figures in the history of psychology (through midcentury). Those survey rankings appear in Table 2.1. Notice the two names at the top of the list.[5]

Decline of Drive Theory

Drive theory—both the Freudian and Hullian versions—rested on three fundamental assumptions: (1) drive emerged from bodily needs, (2) drive energized behavior, and (3) drive reduction was reinforcing and produced learning.

Throughout the 1950s, empirical tests of these three assumptions revealed both support and limitations. First, some motives emerged without any corresponding biological need. For instance, people with anorexia do not eat (and do not want to eat) despite a strong biological need to do so (Klien, 1954). Thus, motivation could emerge from sources other than one's bodily disturbances. Second, research recognized that external (i.e., environmental) sources of motivation could energize behavior. For example, a person who is not necessarily thirsty can feel a rather strong motive to drink upon tasting (or seeing or smelling) a favorite beverage. Hull did add incentive motivation (K) to his formula, but the key point is that motivational energy arose not only from bodily physiology but from many other sources as well. Third, learning often occurred without drive reduction. Hungry rats, for instance, learn even when reinforced only by a nonnutritive saccharin reward (Sheffield & Roby, 1950). Because saccharin has no nutritional benefit, it cannot reduce drive (i.e., cannot serve the needs of the body). Other research showed that learning occurred after drive *induction* (i.e., an increase in drive; Harlow, 1953). Robert White (1959), for instance, explained how behavior was largely motivated by strivings for greater competence (rather than by

---

[5]By the dawn of the 21st century, the list of eminent psychologists had changed quite a bit (Haggbloom et al., 2002). In 2002, Sigmund Freud dropped to third, while Clark Hull dropped to twenty-first. The current top 10, in order from first to tenth, still features numerous motivation researchers: B. F. Skinner, Jean Piaget, Sigmund Freud, Albert Bandura, Leon Festinger, Carl Rogers, Stanley Schachter, Neal Miller, Edward Thorndike, and Abraham Maslow.

drive reduction). Eventually, it became clear that drive reduction was neither necessary nor sufficient for learning to occur (Bolles, 1972). Over time, it became increasingly clear that motivational researchers needed to expand and broaden their intellectual search.

Post-Drive Theory Years

The 1950s and 1960s were transitional decades in the study of motivation. In the early 1950s, the prevalent motivation theories were the well-known, historically entrenched grand theories. Drive theory dominated (Bolles, 1975; Hull, 1952). Additional prominent midcentury motivational theories included optimal level of arousal (Berlyne, 1967; Hebb, 1955), pleasure centers in the brain (Olds, 1969), approach–avoidance conflicts (Miller, 1959), universal needs (Murray, 1938), conditioned motives (Miller, 1948), and self-actualization (Rogers, 1959). As motivation study progressed and new findings emerged, it became clear that if progress was to be made, the field was going to have to step outside the boundaries of its grand theories. The motivation psychologists of the 1970s began to embrace mini-theories of motivation (Dember, 1965). The next section discusses these mini-theories. But it will be helpful to pause a moment to consider the two motivational principles from the 1960s that were offered as possible post-drive theory replacements for a (fourth) grand theory of motivation: incentive and arousal.

Consider incentive. An incentive is an external event (or stimulus) that energizes and directs approach or avoidance behavior. Drive reduction theory asserted that people were motivated by drives, which "pushed" them toward particular goal objects (e.g., hunger pushed the person to go find food). Incentive motivational theories asserted that people were motivated by the incentive value of various objects in their environment that "pulled" them toward these objects (e.g., strawberry cheesecake pulled the person toward the restaurant). The new idea was that just because D needed to be removed from the $D \times K$ equation, then perhaps K could stand on its own as a grand theory of motivation.

The incentive theories that emerged in the 1960s fundamentally sought to explain why people approached positive incentives and why they avoided negative ones (e.g., Bolles, 1972; Pfaffmann, 1960; Young, 1966). These theories adopted the concept of hedonism, which essentially postulates that organisms approach signals of pleasure and avoid signals of pain. Through learning, people formed associations (or expectancies) of which environmental objects were gratifying and thus deserved approach responses and which other objects were pain-inflicting and thus deserved avoidance responses. Incentive theories offered three new features: (1) new motivational concepts, such as incentives and expectancies; (2) the idea that motivational states could be acquired through experience rather than just through inherited biology; and (3) a portrayal of motivation that highlighted moment-to-moment changes (because environmental incentives can change from one moment to the next).

Consider arousal. The rising disaffection with drive theory was countered by a rising affection for arousal theory. The discovery that lay the foundation for this transition came from the neuroscience finding of an arousal system in the brain stem (Lindsley, 1957; Moruzzi & Magoun, 1949). The central ideas in the study of arousal were that:

1. Arousal represents a variety of processes that govern alertness, wakefulness, and activation.

2. A person's arousal level is mostly a function of how stimulating the environment is.

3. A moderate level of arousal coincides with the experience of pleasure and optimal performance.

4. People engage in strategic behavior to increase or decrease their level of arousal.

5. When underaroused, people seek opportunities to increase their arousal: Increases in environmental stimulation are pleasurable and enhance performance, whereas decreases in environmental stimulation are aversive and undermine performance.

6. When overaroused, people seek opportunities to decrease their arousal: Increases in environmental stimulation are aversive and undermine performance, whereas decreases in environmental stimuli are pleasurable and enhance performance.

These six principles can be organized collectively into the "inverted-U" relationship between arousal and performance/well-being shown in Figure 2.2. The inverted-U curve, first introduced more than 100 years ago by Robert Yerkes and John Dodson (1908), helps explain the relationship between level of environmental stimulation and performance and well-being (Berlyne, 1967; Duffy, 1957; Hebb, 1955; Lindsley, 1957; Malmo, 1959). Low environmental stimulation produced boredom and restlessness; high environmental stimulation produced tension and stress. Both boredom and stress are aversive experiences that people strive to escape from. Thus, the inverted-U curve predicts when increases and decreases in stimulation will lead to positive affect and approach behavior and when they will lead to negative affect and avoidance. Eventually, level of arousal (low, optimal, high) came to be understood as something "synonymous with a general drive state" (Hebb, 1955, p. 249): The grand theory was that people prefer an optimal level of arousal and shun too little or too much arousal.

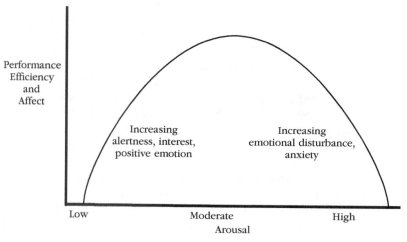

Figure 2.2   The Inverted-U Curve: Relationship between Arousal Level and Performance/Well-Being

Source: From "Drive and the C. N. S.—Conceptual Nervous System," by D. O. Hebb, 1955, *Psychological Review, 62,* pp. 245–254.

RISE OF THE MINI-THEORIES

Unlike a grand theory that seeks to explain all motivation, mini-theories limit their explanatory ambition to specific motivational phenomena. Mini-theories seek to understand or investigate one particular:

- motivational phenomenon (e.g., achievement motivation, the flow experience).
- circumstance that affects motivation (e.g., failure feedback, role models).
- theoretical question (e.g., What is the relationship between cognition and emotion?).

A mini-theory explains some but not all motivated behavior. Thus, achievement motivation theory (a mini-theory) arose to explain how people respond to standards of excellence and hence why some people show enthusiasm and approach, whereas others show anxiety and avoidance, when facing a standard of excellence. Achievement motivation theory leaves a great deal of motivated action unexplained, but it does a very good job of explaining one interesting slice of motivated action.

The following list identifies some of the mini-theories (with a seminal reference) that emerged in the 1960s and 1970s:

- Achievement motivation theory (Atkinson, 1964)
- Attributional theory of achievement motivation (Weiner, 1972)
- Cognitive dissonance theory (Festinger, 1957)
- Cognitive evaluation theory (Deci, 1975)
- Effectance motivation (Harter, 1978a; White, 1959)
- Expectancy × Value theory (Vroom, 1964)
- Flow theory (Csikszentmihalyi, 1975)
- Intrinsic motivation (Deci, 1975)
- Goal-setting theory (Locke, 1968)
- Learned helplessness theory (Seligman, 1975)
- Reactance theory (Brehm, 1966)
- Self-efficacy theory (Bandura, 1977)
- Self-schemas (Markus, 1977)

Each of these 13 mini-theories of motivation will be discussed in the chapters to come. For now, it is important to note the major shift in thinking about the nature of motivation and emotion that underlay the change in emphasis away from instinct, drive, incentive, and arousal toward the mini-theories. It became increasingly evident that any one grand theory was simply unable to carry the whole burden of explaining motivation (Appley, 1991). In addition, three historical trends emerged to explain why motivation study left behind its tradition of the grand theories to embrace the new tradition of mini-theories:

1. Active nature of the person
2. Cognitive revolution
3. Socially relevant questions

In addition, the first journal devoted exclusively to the topic of motivation emerged in 1977, *Motivation and Emotion*. This journal has focused almost all of its attention on the empirical exploration of mini-theories of motivation.

Active Nature of the Person

The purpose of drive theory was to explain how an animal went from inactive to active (Weiner, 1990). The midcentury assumption was that animals (including humans) were naturally inactive, and the role of motivation was to arouse the passive to become the active. So drive, like all early motivational constructs, explained the instigating motor of behavior. As a point of illustration, a common midcentury definition of motivation was, "the process of arousing action, sustaining the activity in progress, and regulating the pattern of activity" (Young, 1961, p. 24). Motivation was the study of energizing the passive.

The psychologists of the second half of the century saw things differently. They emphasized that the person was *always* getting to and doing something. People were inherently active, always motivated. People did not need motivation to start moving, because they were always in motion and always doing something. This understanding paralleled Albert Einstein's 20th-century insight in physics that the natural state of planets was motion (because gravitational forces were always present). Like stars and planets, humans too experienced ever-present pushes and pulls. One midcentury motivational psychologist put it this way: "Sound motivational theory should … assume that motivation is constant, never ending, fluctuating, and complex, and that it is an almost universal characteristic of practically every organismic state of affairs" (Maslow, 1954, p. 69). Perhaps there is no place where this is more evident than in young children: "They pick things up, shake them, smell them, taste them, throw them across the room, and keep asking, 'What's this?' They are unendingly curious" (Deci & Ryan, 1985a, p. 11).

In their mid-1960s review of motivation theories, Charles Cofer and Mortimer Appley (1964) divided the motivation theories of the day into those that assumed a passive, energy-conserving organism versus those that assumed an active, growth-seeking organism. The passive-oriented portrayals outnumbered the active portrayals by 10 to 1. But theories assuming an active organism were beginning to emerge. Today's ideas about motivation and emotion accept the premise of the active organism, and they deal less with deficit motivations (e.g., tension reduction, homeostasis, equilibrium) and more with growth motivations (e.g., competence, possible selves, self-actualization) (Appley, 1991; Benjamin & Jones, 1978; Rapaport, 1960; White, 1960). In the present book, the ratio of passive-to-active portrayals of motivation would be reversed by 1 to 10.

Cognitive Revolution

The early motivational concepts—drive, homeostasis, arousal—were grounded in biology and physiology. Contemporary motivation study continues to maintain this alliance with biology, physiology, and sociobiology, but the tide changed in the early 1970s as psychology's *Zeitgeist* (its "intellectual climate") turned decidedly cognitive (Gardner, 1985; Segal & Lachman, 1972). The historical trend became known as the cognitive revolution. It was a time in which researchers focused on the power of thought, beliefs, expectations, goals, and judgments as the primary causes of behavior. The cognitive revolution spilled into motivation in the same way that it spilled into virtually all areas of psychology (D'Amato, 1974; Dember, 1974).

The importance of the cognitive revolution to motivation study was threefold. First, motivational concepts took a backstage position as a cognitive interpretation of events took psychology's center stage. In some sense, motivation study was not only moved to back-stage but to offstage, because a cognitive perspective on action was initially believed to not need motivational constructs (Hilgard, 1987). The analogy of the day was to the computer and to its motivation-less information-processing operating system.

Second, even motivation researchers themselves began to emphasize internal mental processes and cognitive constructs (e.g., expectancies, goals) and to deemphasize (even banish) biological and environmental constructs. Some of the mentalistic motivational constructs to emerge included plans (Miller, Galanter, & Pribram, 1960), goals (Locke & Latham, 1990), expectations (Seligman, 1975), beliefs (Bandura, 1977), attributions (Weiner, 1972), and the self-concept (Markus, 1977).

Third, psychology's image of human functioning became more "human rather than mechanical" (McKeachie, 1976, p. 831). This ideological shift from mechanical to dynamic and from animal drive to human cognition was captured nicely in the title of one of the popular motivation texts of the day, *Theories of Motivation: From Mechanism to Cognition* (Weiner, 1972). A review of motivation studies from the 1960s and 1970s shows a marked decline in experiments manipulating the deprivation states of rats and a marked increase in experiments manipulating success or failure feedback given after human performance (Weiner, 1990). The experimental design is not much different, but the focus on humans, instead of animals, is unmistakable.

Paralleling the cognitive revolution was the emerging movement of humanism. Humanistic psychologists critiqued the prevailing motivation theories of the 1960s as decidedly dehuman. Humanists resist the machine metaphor that portrays motivation in a deterministic fashion in response to unyielding biological forces, developmental fates (e.g., traumatic childhood experiences), or controls in the environment or society (Bugental, 1967). Ideas from Abraham Maslow and Carl Rogers (Chapter 15) nicely expressed psychology's new understanding of human beings as inherently active, cognitively flexible, and growth motivated (Berlyne, 1975; Maslow, 1987; Rogers, 1961).

Socially Relevant Questions

A third important change helped usher in the mini-theories era: Researchers turned their attention to questions that were relevant to solving the motivational problems people faced in their everyday lives (McClelland, 1978)—at work (Locke & Latham, 1984), in school (Weiner, 1979), in coping with stress (Lazarus, 1966), in solving health problems (Polivy, 1976), in reversing depression (Seligman, 1975), and so on. As researchers studied non-human animals less and humans more, they discovered a wealth of naturally occurring instances of motivation outside the laboratory. Hence, motivation researchers began focusing increasingly on socially relevant, applied questions and problems. Motivation psychologists began to initiate more frequent contact with psychologists in other areas, such as social psychology, industrial/organizational psychology, and clinical and counseling psychology.

Overall, the field became less interested in studying, for instance, hunger as a source of drive and more interested in studying the motivations underlying eating, dieting, obesity, and bulimia (Rodin, 1981; Taubes, 1998).

Emphasizing applied, socially relevant research placed contemporary motivation study in a sort of "Johnny Appleseed" role in which individual motivation researchers left their laboratories to take their questions (What causes behavior?) into psychology's areas of specialization. Motivation's new alliances with other fields in psychology can be illustrated in Figure 2.3. The figure illustrates explicitly how motivation links itself with the reader's other courses in psychology. That is, courses in social psychology, personality, and educational psychology will have some content that is decidedly motivational. Because of this overlap, it is sometimes difficult to say where the study of cognition ends and where the study of motivation begins (Sorrentino & Higgins, 1986) or where the study of perception ends and where the study of motivation begins (Bindra, 1979). As one neuroscientist puts it, "Motivational concepts are needed to understand the brain, just as brain concepts are needed to understand motivation" (Berridge, 2004, p. 205).

The point of Figure 2.3 is to show that the questions in motivation study are highly relevant to practically all other subfields within psychology and, because of this, motivation researchers maintain a constant dialogue with a wide range of allied fields of study. Thus, weak or highly permeable boundaries exist between motivation and other academic fields to the point that today's motivation researcher is as likely to be a social psychologist, a health psychologist, or an educational psychologist as he or she is to be a motivation psychologist per se.

Weak boundaries between motivation and allied fields generally suggest an identity crisis, but in practice, the absence of sharp boundaries facilitated the exchange of ideas

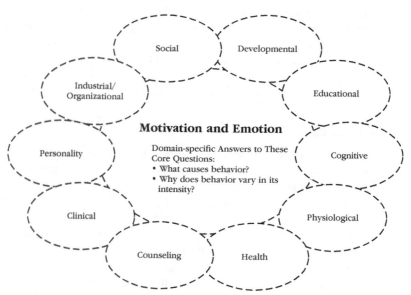

Figure 2.3 Relationship of Motivation Study to Psychology's Areas of Specialization

and fostered an exposure to different perspectives and methodologies (Feshbach, 1984), including those outside of psychology (e.g., sociology; Turner, 1987). As a consequence, contemporary motivation study has gained a special richness and vitality (McNally, 1992). Much of what occurs in contemporary motivation research reflects the search for both a deeper scientific understanding of motivational processes as well as practical and useful applications of motivational principles to improve people's lives (Pintrich, 2003). In fact, it is somewhat unusual to encounter a contemporary scientific investigation about motivation that does not speak at least somewhat to a socially relevant, practical application.

CONTEMPORARY ERA

Thomas Kuhn (1962, 1970) described the history of most sciences, emphasizing that a discipline makes both continuous and discontinuous progress. With continuous progress, participants make slow, incremental, and cumulative progress as new data add to and supplant old data and new ideas add to and supplant outworn ideas. With discontinuous progress, however, radical ideas appear and rival (rather than add to) old ideas. If the radical ideas gain acceptance, researchers' ways of thinking drastically change as old models are torn down to make room for new models to take their place.

Kuhn's developmental view of the history of a scientific field appears in Table 2.2. In its preparadigmatic stage, the primitive beginnings of a discipline take root as participants ask different questions, use different methods, pursue different problems, and basically disagree and argue a lot. The state of the science is chaotic. In its paradigmatic stage, the discipline's participants succeed in reaching a consensus as to what constitutes their common theoretical and methodological framework. This shared framework (a paradigm) allows each contributor to understand the discipline's methods and questions in the same way. Participants are then able to work collaboratively to gain an increasingly detailed and integrated

Table 2.2   Outline of the Typical Development of a Scientific Discipline

1. Preparadigmatic	A budding science emerges. It consists of participants who do not share the same language or the same knowledge base. Debates are frequent about what should be the discipline's methods, core questions, and key problems to address and solve.
2. Paradigmatic	Factionalism gives way to a shared consensus about what constitutes the discipline's methods, questions, and problems to solve. This shared consensus is called a paradigm. Participants who share this paradigm accumulate knowledge and make incremental advances.
3. Crisis and revolution	An anomaly emerges that cannot be explained by the existing consensus/paradigm. A clash erupts between the old way of thinking (that cannot explain the anomaly) and the new way of thinking (that can explain the anomaly).
4. New paradigm	The new way of thinking and explaining brings discipline-changing progress. Embracing the new consensus, participants settle into the new paradigm (the paradigmatic stage). Progress returns to making incremental advances.

understanding of their subject matter. Over time, however, the limitations and inadequacies of the accepted paradigm become apparent as an anomaly surfaces that cannot be explained with the prevailing paradigm. A general discomfort soon runs throughout the field. Participants look for new answers, even if those new answers seem radical. As a result, fresh insights and new discoveries arise, and these insights and discoveries breed a new way of thinking (a paradigm shift). It is not a smooth transition; it involves conflict, rivalry, and in-groups versus out-groups. But if the new way of thinking can succeed in explaining what the old paradigm cannot, then constructive change occurs. Armed with their new way of thinking, researchers eventually settle into the new and improved paradigm, a process that typically takes multiple generations of scientists. Two classic examples of paradigm shifts, for instance, occurred when the Copernican revolution replaced astronomers' ideas of earth centrality and when Einstein's general theory of relativity unseated Euclidean geometry. Astronomy and physics were forever changed by these paradigm shifts.

As a discipline, motivation study has participated in the rise and fall of three major ways of thinking: will, instinct, and drive. Each of these motivational concepts gained wide acceptance, but as new data emerged, each concept proved to be too limiting for further progress. Eventually, each was replaced by the next new-and-improved radical idea. Motivation study is currently in the midst of its mini-theories era. The rejection of drive as a grand theory of motivation produced consequences that were both good and bad. On the bad side, motivation was dethroned as perhaps psychology's most important discipline to a sort of second-class field of study. The dethronement of motivation was so severe that, to some degree, the field collapsed for a decade and a half. Motivational concepts were set aside as the discipline was dominated first by behaviorists who saw motivation as something that took place outside the person (in the form of incentives and reinforcers) and second by cognitivists who saw little need for motivational concepts within their computer-based information processing metaphor.

Motivation study did not, however, disappear. The questions that define motivation, discussed in Chapter 1, endured. Instead of disappearing, motivation specialists dispersed themselves into virtually all areas of psychology. That is, the questions of motivation proved to be significant for and relevant to practically every aspect of psychology (as per Figure 2.3). Motivation researchers therefore branched out in alliances with other fields to form a loose network of researchers who shared a common concern and commitment to motivationally relevant questions and problems. Learning theorists, personality psychologists, social psychologists, clinicians, and others were unable to explain all the behavior they sought to explain without using motivational concepts. For instance, among neuroscientists, motivational concepts (e.g., hunger, pleasure) are vital to understanding why the brain evolved the way it did to such an extent that neuroscience truly needs to ally itself with the study of motivation (Berridge, 2004). What emerged were theories of social motivation (Pittman & Heller, 1988), cognitive motivation (Sorrentino & Higgins, 1986), developmental motivation (Kagan, 1972), motivation in educational settings (Pintrich, 2003), and others. Furthermore, motivation theories specific to particular domains of application emerged: theories to explain the motivation underlying dieting and bingeing (Polivy & Herman, 1985), work (Locke & Latham, 1984, 1990; Vroom, 1964), sports (Roberts, 1992; Straub & Williams, 1984), and education (Weiner, 1979). By the 1980s, motivation psychologists were scattered into literally every area of psychology.

The 1990s Reemergence of Motivation Study

Starting in 1952, the University of Nebraska invited the most prominent motivation theorists of the day to gather annually for a symposium on motivation. In its inaugural year, contributors included Harry Harlow, Judson Brown, and Hobart Mowrer (famous names in motivation study). The next year, John Atkinson and Leon Festinger presented papers. Abraham Maslow, David McClelland, James Olds, and Jullian Rotter presented papers in the third year (again, all famous names in motivation study). The symposium quickly became a success and served a leadership role in defining the field. The symposium continued uninterrupted for 25 years, until a fundamental change occurred in 1978 (Benjamin & Jones, 1978). In 1979, the symposium discontinued its motivational theme and, instead, considered topics that changed from one year to the next, none of which had much to do with motivation. The 1979 symposium focused on attitudes, and later symposiums focused on topics such as gender, addictive behaviors, and aging. Recall that these years correspond to motivation's dethronement as perhaps psychology's most important field to a second-class field. Basically, the Nebraska Symposium, like psychology in general, lost interest in the study of motivation.

The story does not end with motivation in hopeless crisis, however. In recognition of motivation's revival and the advances and accomplishments made during the mini-theories era, the organizers of the 1990 Nebraska Symposium once again invited prominent motivation researchers to gather for a symposium devoted exclusively to the concept of motivation (Dienstbier, 1991). During that conference, the organizers asked the participants—Mortimer Appley, Albert Bandura, Edward L. Deci, Douglas Derryberry, Carol Dweck, Richard Ryan, Don Tucker, and Bernard Weiner (again, all famous names in motivation study)—if they thought motivation was once again strong enough and mature enough as a field to support an exclusive return to motivation topics. Unanimously and enthusiastically, the contributors agreed that motivation was once again a rich and thriving field of study.

In the 1970s, motivation study was on the brink of extinction, "flat on its back," as one pair of researchers put it (Sorrentino & Higgins, 1986, p. 8). The mere fact that the conference organizers had to ask the Nebraska Symposium participants whether motivation was a field that could stand on its own says something about the field's identity crisis. Motivation study survived by allying itself with other fields of study. At the same time, advances in neuroscience, evolutionary psychology, and even statistical methodologies were showing the limits of a purely cognitive analysis of behavior (Ryan, 2007). Cognitions were important to the initiation and regulation of behavior, but cognitions are also inherently intertwined with noncognitive motivations, emotions, and affects that guide, constrain, and even overwhelm cognitive processes. In addition, new journals of motivation and emotion began to emerge, as the first issue of *Cognition and Emotion* appeared in 1987, and the first issue of *Emotion* appeared in 2001. New societies also emerged, such as the Society for the Study of Motivation, in 2008.

Contemporary motivation study once again has its critical mass of interested and prominent participants (see Box 2). To document such an optimistic conclusion, the reader can glance through psychology's major journals (e.g., *Psychological Bulletin*, *Psychological Science*) and expect to find an article related to motivation in practically each issue.

BOX 2   *The Many Voices in Motivation Study*

Question: Why is this information important?

Answer: To become aware of the diversity of voices trying to understand motivation.

Motivational phenomena are complex events that exist at multiple levels (e.g., neurological, cognitive, cultural). In practice, however, most people attempt to explain a motivation by relying on only a single perspective. For instance, when a teenager loses interest in schooling, a parent (or researcher) typically goes in search of "the" one explanation of why interest is low. Another way to think about motivation, however, is to become aware of a full range of possible explanatory forces. Here is a list of nine prominent voices that participate in discussions of contemporary motivation study:

Perspective	Motives emerge from ...
Behavioral	Environmental incentives
Neurological	Brain activations
Biological	Hormones, psychophysiology
Cognitive	Mental events and ways of thinking
Social-cognitive	Socially created beliefs and values
Cultural	Organizations and societies
Evolutionary	Genes and genetic endowment
Humanistic	Encouraging human potential
Psychoanalytical	Unconscious and implicit processes

Most motivational states can (and indeed need to) be understood at multiple levels—from a neurological level, a cognitive level, a social level, and so on. The days are gone when motivation researchers could focus on a single motivational agent and study it in relative isolation, although doing so was once standard practice. Today, practically all motivation researchers emphasize the complex contribution of multiple motivational agents to explain behavior's energy, direction, and persistence. As a point of illustration, consider how to best understand and explain sexual motivation. Behaviorists point to that part of desire that stems from how attractive or reinforcing another person is, as in physical attractiveness. Neuroscientists explain desire as a product of the neurotransmitter dopamine being released into the subcortical brain. Biologists point out the role that the rise and fall of hormones such as testosterone and oxytocin play in the presence or absence of desire and intimacy. Cognitivists add that desire further comes from expectancies, goals, and values. Social-cognitive researchers add that our beliefs and expectations about love and romance arise from interactions with others, such as peers and role models. A cross-cultural perspective shows that people in different cultures experience sexual motivation differently. Evolutionists add that men and women have different mating strategies, and they therefore desire different qualities in a mate. Humanists point to that part of desire that stems from the opportunity to participate in an intimate, growth-promoting relationship. Psychoanalysts add that we desire relationships that are consistent with our childhood attachments and mental model of what an ideal romantic partner should be. What this theoretical eclecticism offers is the opportunity to connect together more pieces of the "Why?" puzzle and therefore to develop a more sophisticated and comprehensive understanding of the nature and function of motivation and emotion.

Motivational questions and problems are just too interesting and too important to ignore, it seems. And the same can be said for journals in a number of specialty areas as well (e.g., *Journal of Educational Psychology, Journal of Personality and Social Psychology, Journal of Exercise and Sport Psychology*). In the 15 chapters still to come, the reader can expect to encounter a growing field—a bit disorganized, but one that is clearly interesting, relevant, and vital. As one motivation researcher phrased it, "If what you have is a way to help people address the significant questions in their lives, then there are 'Help Wanted' signs all over the place."

BRIEF HISTORY OF EMOTION STUDY

The historical and contemporary study of emotion has paralleled and complemented that of motivation, but emotion study has also experienced some of its own unique historical development. Historically speaking, the concept of "emotion" is a relatively recent one. As it is understood today, the concept first emerged with Descartes's *The Passions of the Soul*. For Descartes (1649/1970), *passion* meant emotional "uproar" and implied an unruly, vigorous, and strong bodily reaction. The idea was that a basically passive individual was going along rather well in life until an environmental event produced in him or her an overwhelming bodily reaction that transitioned that state of passivity into one of uproar, one that took control over thought and action. What Descartes called a passion, a contemporary would call an emotion.

What stirred the passions were people, objects, and events. People reacted to such environmental encounters with acceptance or rejection, pleasure or pain, and coping or being overwhelmed. But just why people reacted in such ways to the important events in their lives became an important matter of debate. Evolutionists such as Charles Darwin (1872) argued that emotional reactions were innate and served the purpose of individual adaptation to environmental opportunities and challenges. For instance, an obstacle to one's plans led to an anger reaction, and that aroused passion (emotion) then functionally increased the person's chances of coping successfully with the imposed obstacle. Cultural anthropologists such as Margaret Mead, however, argued that emotional reactions were socially learned and therefore culturally variable. That is, one's culture—not one's biology—taught the person how to react to imposed obstacles. Like so many questions about the nature of emotion, the answer to this question continues to be debated. In fact, questions about the nature, function, and potential self-regulation of emotion essentially define both the historical and the contemporary study of emotion.

One pivotal question throughout the historical study of emotion has been to ask how specific versus how general emotions are. Early emotion theorists such as William James (1884) adopted a non-specificity position. For James, like Descartes, an important life event rather reliably and automatically stirred a general bodily physiological reaction (e.g., changes in heart rate, pupil dilation). An emotion experience was essentially the person's interpretation of what that general pattern of reactivity was (e.g., my heart is racing, my hands are sweating, my breath is shallow and quick; therefore, I must be afraid). Because there were only a handful of physiological patterns, it was assumed that there were only a handful of specific emotions. Some later emotion theorists, such as Stanley Schachter (1964), argued that a person's physiological reaction was a general arousal state, and the person needed environmental cues to interpret any specific emotional reaction. Emotion researchers who studied facial expressions, including Silvan Tomkins (1962, 1963), Carroll Izard (1971), and Paul Ekman (1972), however, argued that people showed many different emotional facial expressions to different life events. Using this logic, there were at least as many individual emotions as there were discrete facial expressions (e.g., an anger expression, a sadness expression). In a similar spirit, cognitive appraisal theories, such as Richard Lazarus (1968), argued that there were as many different emotions as there were cognitive appraisals of the meaning of the events that were happening to the person. For instance, because there are many different types of harm (e.g., being insulted, suffering irrevocable loss, eating spoiled food, failing to live up to an ego ideal), there was a specific emotion for each specific type of harm (e.g., anger, sadness, disgust, shame, respectively).

Overall, emotion study remains a young, incoherent, and largely preparadigmatic field of scientific study. The one shared commonality that gives emotion study its structure and history is that it addresses age-old questions that people care so much about, questions such as the following:

- What is an emotion (i.e., define it)?
- What causes an emotion?
- How many emotions are there?
- What good are the emotions—are they constructive assets or dysfunctional liabilities?
- Can we control our emotions—can emotions be self-regulated and managed?
- What is the difference between emotion and mood?
- What is the relation between emotion and motivation?
- What is the relation between emotion and cognition?

Emotion study will advance as a scientific field as it finds new and more sophisticated ways to answer these core questions. The contemporary answer to all eight of these questions can be found in Chapter 12, entitled "Nature of Emotion: Six Perennial Questions."

CONCLUSION

Much can be gained by wading through 24 centuries of thinking about motivation and emotion. Consider the ancient questions: Why behave? Why do anything—why get out of bed in the morning? Given these questions, the history of motivation began with the search for the instigators of behavior—that is, the search to identify what energizes or initiates behavior. For two millennia (from Plato [ca. 428–348 BC] to Descartes [ca. 1596–1650]), the intellectual effort to understand motivation focused on the will, an immaterial entity that proved to be too difficult an undertaking for the new science of psychology. Biology (physiology) proved to be a more suitable alternative because its subject matter was material and measurable. In answering the Why behave? question, the answer came to be that behavior serviced the needs of the organism. Instinct, drive, arousal, and passion all gained appeal because each clearly energized behavior that served the needs of the organism (e.g., people get out of bed because they are hungry and need to eat something). Incentive added to these motivational constructs because hedonism (approach pleasure, avoid pain) explained how environmental events could also energize behavior by pulling or tempting people out of bed. Century by century, thinkers were improving their answers to the question of what instigates behavior: will, instinct, drive, incentive, arousal.

The whole process was going along rather nicely until a critical mass of motivation researchers realized that—egads!—they were asking and pursuing the wrong question. The question of the instigation of behavior presumes a passive and biologically regulated organism; that is, one who is asleep and upon awaking, needs some motive to get into a behaving mode. At some point, motivation thinkers realized that sleeping was behaving and that the proverbial sleeper was actively engaged in his or her environment. The realization was that to be alive is to be active: Organisms are therefore always active, always behaving. There is no time in which a live organism is not behaving; there is no time in which a live organism is not showing both energy and direction. There is simply no such thing as a live person who is not motivated.

The fundamental questions of motivation study therefore shifted: Why does behavior vary in its intensity? Why does the person do one thing rather than another? These two questions expanded the charge of motivation study. Contemporary motivation study focuses not only on behavior's energy but also on its direction and endurance. This is why the three historical trends of the active organism, cognitive revolution, and socially relevant questions are so important—namely, because the field became less entrenched in the instigators of behavior, in biology, and in animal laboratory experiments and increasingly interested in the directors of behavior, in cognition, and in human problems. This change in perspective opened the intellectual floodgates for the arrival of the field's mini-theories and for the dispersion of motivation study into practically all other fields within psychology.

SUMMARY

A historical view of motivation study allows the reader to consider how the concept of motivation came to prominence, how it changed and developed, how ideas were challenged and replaced, and finally, how the field reemerged and brought together various disciplines within psychology (Bolles, 1975). Motivational concepts have philosophical origins. From the ancient Greeks through the European Renaissance, motivation was understood within the two themes of what is rational, immaterial, and active (i.e., the will) and what is impulsive, biological, and reactive (i.e., bodily desires). The philosophical study of the will turned out to be a dead end that explained very little about motivation, because it actually raised more questions than it answered.

To explain motivation, the new field of psychology pursued a biological–physiological analysis of motivation by focusing on the mechanistic, genetically endowed concept of the instinct. The appeal of the instinct doctrine was its ability to explain unlearned behavior that had energy and purpose (i.e., goal-directed biological impulses) and do so by using a concept whose origins could be identified (i.e., genetic endowment). Instinct proved to be an intellectual dead end as well, at least in terms of its capacity to serve as a grand theory of motivation. Motivation's third grand theory was drive. In drive theory, behavior was motivated to the extent that it served the needs of the organism and restored a biological homeostasis. Like will and instinct, drive appeared to be full of promise, especially because it could do what no motivation theory had ever done before—namely, predict motivation before it occurred from antecedent conditions (e.g., hours of deprivation). Consequently, the theory enjoyed wide acceptance, especially as manifest in the theories of Freud and Hull. In the end, drive theory, too, proved itself to be overly limited in scope, and with its rejection came the field's disillusionment with grand theories in general, although several additional candidate theories emerged with some success, including incentive and arousal.

Eventually, it became clear that if progress was to be made in understanding motivation, the field had to step outside the boundaries of its grand theories and embrace the less ambitious, but more promising, mini-theories. Three historical trends explain this transition. First, motivation study rejected its commitment to a passive view of human nature and adopted a more active portrayal of human beings. Second, motivation turned decidedly cognitive and somewhat humanistic. Third, the field focused on applied, socially relevant problems. The field's changed focus toward mini-theories was part disaster and part good fortune. As disaster, motivation lost its status as psychology's flagship discipline and descended into a second-class status. In reaction, motivation researchers dispersed into virtually all areas of psychology (e.g., social, developmental, clinical, educational) and forged alliances with these other fields to share ideas, constructs, methodologies, and perspectives. This turned out to be motivation's good fortune because the field's scattering proved to be fertile ground to develop a host of enlightening mini-theories. Motivation study in the 21st century is populated by multiple perspectives and multiple voices (see Figure 2.3), all of which contribute a different piece to the puzzle of motivation and emotion study. This change has opened the intellectual floodgates for the arrival of mini-theories of motivation and a new paradigm in which behavior is energized and directed by multilevel influences rather than by a single grand cause.

The historical and contemporary study of emotion has paralleled and complemented that of motivation, but emotion study has also experienced some of its own unique historical development. Emotion study has followed motivation study's emphases on, first, philosophy (Descartes), then biology and evolution (Darwin), to now psychology (James, Tomkins, Izard, Ekman, and Lazarus). Overall, emotion study remains a young, incoherent, and largely preparadigmatic field of scientific study that is held together by its fundamentally important and age-old questions, such as the following: What is an emotion? What causes an emotion? How many emotions are there? What good are the emotions? Can we control and self-regulate our emotions? What is the difference between emotion and mood? Emotion study will develop and progress to the extent that it can find new and ever more sophisticated ways of answering these field-defining questions.

READINGS FOR FURTHER STUDY

Grand Theories Era

BOLLES, R. C. (1975). Historical origins of motivational concepts. In R. C. Bolles, *Theory of motivation* (2nd ed., pp. 21–50). New York: Harper & Row.

COFER, C. N., & APPLEY, M. H. (1964). Motivation in historical perspective. In *Motivation: Theory and research* (Chapter 2, pp. 19–55). New York: Wiley.

HULL, C. L. (1943). Primary motivation and reaction potential. In *Principles of behavior* (pp. 238–253). New York: Appleton-Century-Crofts.

KOCH, S. (1951). The current status of motivational psychology. *Psychological Review, 58,* 147–154.

KUO, Z. Y. (1921). Giving up instincts in psychology. *Journal of Philosophy, 17,* 645–664.

Mini-Theories Era

BENJAMIN, L. T., JR., & JONES, M. R. (1978). From motivational theory to social cognitive development: Twenty-five years of the Nebraska Symposium. In L. T. Benjamin & M. R. Jones (Eds.) *Nebraska symposium on motivation* (Vol. 26, pp. ix–xix). Lincoln: University of Nebraska Press.

DEMBER, W. N. (1974). Motivation and the cognitive revolution. *American Psychologist, 29,* 161–168.

WEINER, B. (1990). History of motivational research in education. *Journal of Educational Psychology, 82,* 616–622.

Contemporary Era

PINTRICH, P. R. (2003). A motivational science perspective on the role of student motivation in learning and teaching contexts. *Journal of Educational Psychology, 95,* 667–686.

RYAN, R. M. (2007). Motivation and emotion: A new look and approach for two reemerging fields. *Motivation and Emotion, 31,* 1–3.

Chapter 3

The Motivated and Emotional Brain

MOTIVATION, EMOTION, AND NEUROSCIENCE
>   Day-to-Day Events Activate Specific Brain Structures
>   Activated Brain Structures Generate Specific Motivations and Emotions

NEURAL BASIS OF MOTIVATION AND EMOTION
>   Cortical Brain
>   Subcortical Brain
>   Bidirectional Communication
>>   Dual-Process Theories
>>   Neurotransmitters

INDIVIDUAL BRAIN STRUCTURES INVOLVED IN MOTIVATION AND EMOTION
>   Reticular Formation
>   Amygdala
>   Basal Ganglia
>   Ventral Striatum, Nucleus Accumbens, and Ventral Tegmental Area
>   Hypothalamus
>   Insula
>   Prefrontal Cortex
>   Orbitofrontal Cortex
>   Ventromedial Prefrontal Cortex
>   Dorsolateral Prefrontal Cortex
>   Anterior Cingulate Cortex

HORMONES

CONCLUSION

SUMMARY

READINGS FOR FURTHER STUDY

As you and a friend walk into the psychology building, you eye a poster recruiting volunteers for a neuroscience experiment. Volunteers will receive $50 for their time, so you look at each other, nod approvingly, and decide to give it a try. Upon arrival, you see an experimental room that looks more like a hospital than a psychology department. A huge machine—an ƒMRI scanner—occupies one room, a second ƒMRI scanner occupies an adjacent room, and lots of computers occupy a third "master control" room to monitor what is happening to the people who lie inside those two huge machines.

The experiment begins. You enter one ƒMRI machine and your friend enters the other. Together, you will play a game and make decisions. The game will have two rounds. In round 1, you will be the "proposer" and your friend the "responder." To start the round, you are given $20 and then asked how you much you want to keep for yourself and how much you wish to give to your friend. The rules are simple: If the responder accepts your offer, you both keep the money agreed upon; if the responder rejects your offer, neither keeps any of the money. This is a game that pits self-interest (keep most of the money for yourself) versus social concern (be fair and share the money).

In round 1, you propose $12 for yourself and offer $8 to your friend. After all, it is your $20 and it is your decision what to do with the money. You send the message, "Keep $12, Give $8," and wait to see if your offer is accepted or rejected. A minute later, you see "Accept Offer."

In round 2, the tables are turned so that your friend is now the proposer and you are the responder. You wait for an offer. The offer arrives: "Keep $18, Give $2." This is not fair. This is not right. It is greed and exploitation. Feeling a bit hot, you press "Refuse Offer." You lose a free $2, but you also stop your greedy so-called friend from taking advantage of you. The experiment ends.

The experimenter invites you and your friend into the master control room so that she can show your in-game brain activity. With a couple of clicks, several brain images appear on the computer screen, as in Figure 3.1. Looking at the brain scans, she explains, "Okay, let me see if I can guess what decisions you made." She points to the brain scan on the upper left side of Figure 3.1—you in the role of the Proposer during round 1. She says, "I can tell from this activity in your nucleus accumbens (a) that you found the $20 to be attractive, and I can tell from this activity in your dorsolateral prefrontal cortex (upper right panel; b) that you exercised self-control over the temptation to keep all the money for yourself. From what I see here on the screen, I'll bet you shared the money." You nod.

Then she points to the brain scans on the lower left side of Figure 3.1—you in the role of the Responder during round 2. She says, "Oh my. I can tell from this activity in your amygdala (c) that you felt rather upset—perhaps even angry—about the offer. And, I can tell from this insular activity (lower right panel; d) that you experienced negative feelings. You refused the offer, didn't you?" Again, you nod.

MOTIVATION, EMOTION, AND NEUROSCIENCE

Neuroscience is the scientific study of the nervous system—and the human brain in particular. The present chapter, however, is not about the nuts-and-bolts biology of the nervous system (e.g., neurons, synapses). Instead, the chapter looks at the human brain in action—how its neural structures and pathways are associated with psychological processes (cognitive neuroscience; Gazzaniga, Ivry, & Mangun, 2008), motivational processes (motivational neuroscience; Reeve & Lee, 2012), and emotional processes (affective neuroscience; Davidson & Sutton, 1995).

Why is the brain important? Most people say that the brain is important because it carries out cognitive and intellectual functions, including thinking, learning, remembering,

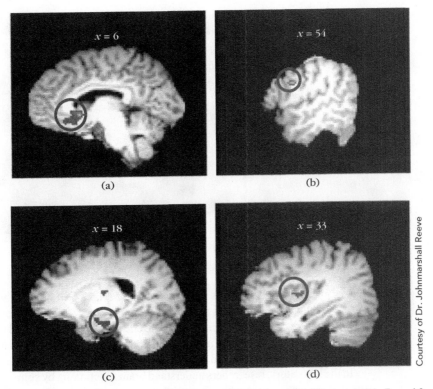

Courtesy of Dr. Johnmarshall Reeve

Figure 3.1   Brain Scans of the "Proposer" in Round 1 and the "Responder" in Round 2

Note: Nucleus accumbens activations appear in the upper left panel (a); dorsolateral prefrontal cortex activations appear in the upper right panel (b); amygdala activations appear in the lower left panel (c); and insula activations appear in the lower right panel (d). All images are taken from *f*MRI imaging.

decision making, and problem solving (Behrens, Fox, Laird, & Smith, 2013). Others, including physicians and those who work in special education, say the brain is important to understand clinical conditions, such as autism, dyslexia, and stuttering. These are important brain processes, but the brain does more. The brain is also the center of motivation and emotion. It generates cravings, needs, desires, preferences, pleasure and pain, liking and wanting and emotions and feelings. This chapter is about the motivated and emotional brain.

Day-to-Day Events Activate Specific Brain Structures

When someone flashes you an angry facial expression, a brain structure called the amygdala actively processes and interprets what is happening. The amygdala actually processes and interprets a wide range of environmental threats and dangers, including encounters with predators, bullies, enemies, loud noises, social criticism, unrealistic deadlines, hostile opponents, disappointments, failures, punishing toothaches, and separations from our loved ones. Other brain structures actively process and interpret environmental benefits and rewards, including a warm smile, a pleasant smell, an unexpected gift, tasty food, a cup of

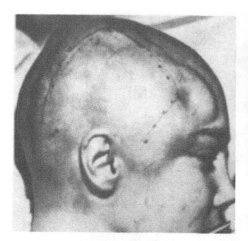 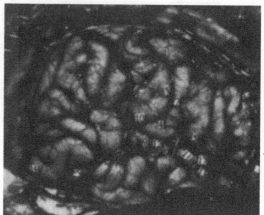

By permission of Liverpool University Press. From "The Excitable Cortex in Conscious Man" by Wilder Penfield; Liverpool University Press, 1958.

Figure 3.2 Photograph of an Exposed Human Cortex

sweet orange juice, a humorous video clip, and finding a $20 bill that we thought we had lost. In the chapter's opening vignette, it was an opportunity to gain money that activated the nucleus accumbens, and it was the social injustice of being exploited and taken advantage of that activated the amygdala and insula. What these examples illustrate is that environmental events in the physical and social world produce brain activations.

In the laboratory, researchers understand brain functioning by stimulating specific brain structures to see what happens. They ask questions such as, "If I apply a mild electrical stimulation to this particular brain area, what will happen?" In doing so, they can isolate the specific functions associated with the various brain structures (e.g., "The amygdala does this, the nucleus accumbens does that ... "). During surgery, for instance, a surgeon may need to saw through the skull to gain access to the brain—to remove a tumor, for instance. With the brain exposed as in Figure 3.2, the surgeon might apply a probe to send a mild electric current to the surface of the brain. Since the brain has no pain receptors, such brain stimulation is actually painless. When the surgeon stimulates one area of the brain, the person may move his or her index finger. When the surgeon repositions the probe to touch another area, a particular sensation or a childhood memory may come to mind.

Unless you are a surgeon, direct stimulation to the brain is a rather impractical idea. The current gold standard to look inside the brain is functional magnetic resonance imaging (fMRI). The fMRI detects changes in brain activity as active brain areas are fueled by glucose and oxygen. Glucose and oxygen are both carried in the blood, and when a brain area becomes active, then blood—and hence the glucose and oxygen within it—flows toward it. So, while a person is lying inside the fMRI scanner, the neuroscientist can expose the person to some environmental stimuli (e.g., an emotional facial expression) and follow the oxygen to observe the brain at work. There are actually several ways to observe brain activity in real time, including measuring electrical brain activity directly with an electroencephalogram (EEG) or measuring metabolic effects of changes in glucose absorption with a positron emissions tomography scanner (PET scan). Whether the researcher uses fMRI, EEG, or PET, this ability to observe and measure the live brain in action has led to an explosion of knowledge about the neural bases of motivation and emotion.

Activated Brain Structures Generate Specific Motivations and Emotions

Half of the equation in a neuroscientific understanding of motivation and emotion is to understand how life events activate specific brain structures (e.g., What class of events activates the insula?). The other half of the equation is to know how specific brain structures, once activated, energize, direct, and sustain motivational and emotional states (e.g., What does the activated insula do? Where in the brain do people experience empathy?). Different brain structures, when stimulated, give rise to specific motivational and emotional states that help us cope with and adjust to what is happening. Stimulating one part of the hypothalamus, for instance, increases hunger, while stimulating a different part of the hypothalamus increases satiety (feeling full). Also, damage to the ventromedial prefrontal cortex (as through an accident or a stroke) dramatically decreases the person's capacity to exert cognitive control over emotions and urges. It is findings like these that led neuroscientists to map out (1) an understanding of which specific brain structures and pathways are the neural basis of specific motivations and emotions and (2) how brain activity in turn creates the motivational and emotional states that energize, direct, and sustain behavior.

NEURAL BASIS OF MOTIVATION AND EMOTION

The brain is astonishingly complex (Bassett & Gazzaniga, 2011). But considered at only a general level, the brain features an outer cortical region and an inner subcortical region, as illustrated in Figure 3.3. The cortical region is sometimes referred to as the cerebral cortex, and it generally includes the bulges and grooves of the frontal, parietal, temporal, and occipital lobes of the brain. The subcortical region is sometimes referred to as the limbic system, and it generally includes the small nuclei that make up the anatomic core or center of the brain.

Cortical Brain

The outer cortical brain—the cerebral cortex (or "cerebrum")—is the bulging, wrinkled surface that most people think of when they think of the brain. It functions at a conscious,

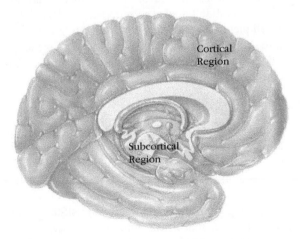

Figure 3.3   Subcortical and Cortical Regions of the Brain

intentional, and purposive level. As such, the cortical brain is associated with cognitively rich motivations such as goals, plans, strategies, values, and beliefs about the self. The cortical brain is active as you set a goal to make an A on your psychology test, formulate a plan of how you will attain that goal, adopt a strategic decision to read the book chapter on Thursday evening, and exercise the self-control needed to resist the temptation to watch television when Thursday evening arrives. In the cortical brain, motivation and emotion are typically deliberate and intentional mental states that the person creates or authors for him- or herself (Szpunar, Watson, & McDermott, 2007).

Subcortical Brain

The subcortical brain is associated with basic urges and impulses and with emotion-rich motivations such as hunger, thirst, anger, fear, anxiety, pleasure, desire, reward, and wanting. For instance, when you are at the airport and pass by one of those shops selling hot fresh cinnamon rolls, the alluring aroma stimulates your subcortical brain to rather automatically generate a desire or an urge to approach the source of the felt pleasure. These urges and emotions occur regardless of whether you want them to—hence, these motivations are largely unconscious, automatic, and impulsive. In the subcortical brain, motivation and emotion are typically reactive events that just happen to the person.

Bidirectional Communication

As will be reviewed in the next section, the brain features many individual structures, but it is important to note that these individual structures are linked together by a network of neural pathways. That is, almost all individual brain structures project out nerve fibers that act as information superhighways to communicate reciprocally with other brain structures. These communication pathways allow the cognitive, motivational, and emotional states that arise in one area of the brain to inform, contribute to, and change the cognitive, motivational, and emotional states that arise in another part of the brain. So, activity in one brain region causes upstream activity in another brain region ("I'm so mad at her, I could yell."), while activity in the second brain region causes downstream activity that in turn modifies the original brain activity ("She probably didn't do that on purpose. It is no big deal. I'm not so angry anymore."). The overall picture of brain function is therefore not one in which individual brain structures are associated with individual functions (e.g., the amygdala does this, the nucleus accumbens does that) but, rather, one of interconnectivity and the brain working in a highly integrated way (O'Doherty, 2004).

Dual-Process Theories

Subcortical brain regions concern basic motivational processes (e.g., "Ice cream—I want it!"), while cortical brain regions concern matters such as self-control, resisting temptation, decision making, assessing risk, and self-regulation. The bidirectional forces between basic motivations and cognitive control over these basic motivations and emotions has been termed the *dual-process model*. Dual-process models of motivation are especially informative in understanding motivation, additions, and risk-taking during childhood and adolescence. During childhood, subcortical brain processes and reward-driven affective processes tend to dominate the cortical brain and its reflective cognitive processes, because childhood is an age in which the cortical brain structures are still developing and maturing (Best, Miller, & Jones, 2009; Cragg & Nation, 2008). During adolescence, children become increasingly able to control strong motivations and emotional processes (e.g., urges, addictions) and to delay immediate gratification for the benefit of long-term goals. Adolescents take more risks than do adults, at least in the use of alcohol, tobacco, legal and illegal drugs, dangerous driving, unprotected sex, and criminal behavior (Arnett, 1991). The basic neurological problem underlying adolescent risk-taking is that mature subcortical brain structures are hot and actively involved in decision making, whereas immature cortical brain structures are cold and less actively involved in decision making (Galvan, 2010; Galvan et al., 2006; Somerville, Hare, & Casey, 2010). This research suggests an overall picture in which the affective subcortical brain and the cognitive cortical brain are two interacting systems (i.e., dual processes) that are often in competition and conflict with one another (Gladwin, Figner, Crone, & Wiers, 2011).

Neurotransmitters

The human brain consists of about 10 billion nerve cells, or neurons. These 10 billion neurons are linked together by about 10 trillion connections. These neurons chemically communicate with one another through the release, transmission, and receipt of neurotransmitters. That is, neural traffic is carried out by neurotransmitters. A "neurotransmitter pathway" refers to a cluster of nerve fibers that project into and communicate with other neurons by using one particular neurotransmitter. The four motivationally relevant neurotransmitter pathways are (1) dopamine, which allows communication among the brain structures involved with reward and pleasure; (2) serotonin, which allows communication among the brain structures involved with mood and emotion; (3) norepinephrine (or adrenaline), which allows communication among the brain structures involved with arousal and alertness; and (4) endorphin, which allows communication among the brain structures involved in the inhibition of pain, anxiety, and fear and in the generation of counteracting good feelings. The serotonin and dopamine pathways appear in Figure 3.4.

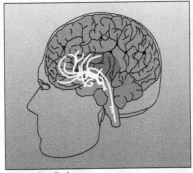
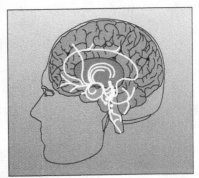

Dopamine Pathways   Serotonin Pathways

Figure 3.4   Two Neurotransmitter Pathways

Source: From *Mapping the Mind*, by R. Carter, 1998, Berkeley: University of California Press. Published by arrangement with Weidenfeld & Nicolson.

INDIVIDUAL BRAIN STRUCTURES INVOLVED IN MOTIVATION AND EMOTION

The 16 brain structures associated with motivational and emotional states are mapped anatomically in Figure 3.5. The figure is the sort of image produced by a MRI or fMRI machine. One structure lies within the brain stem (the final upper portion of the spinal cord)—the reticular formation. Nine structures reside in the subcortical brain—amygdala, ventral striatum, nucleus accumbens, ventral tegmental area, hypothalamus, caudate nucleus, putamen, substantia nigra, and globus pallidus. Six structures reside in the cortical brain—insular cortex, prefrontal cortex, orbitofrontal cortex, ventromedial prefrontal cortex, dorsolateral prefrontal cortex, and anterior cingulate cortex. To complement the anatomical focus of Figure 3.5, Table 3.1 identifies the key motivational and emotional functions associated with each of these 16 brain structures.

Reticular Formation

The reticular formation plays a key role in arousal, alertness, and the process of awakening the brain to process incoming sensory information. The reticular formation is a cluster of neurons within the brain stem about the size of your little finger (see Figure 3.6). It consists

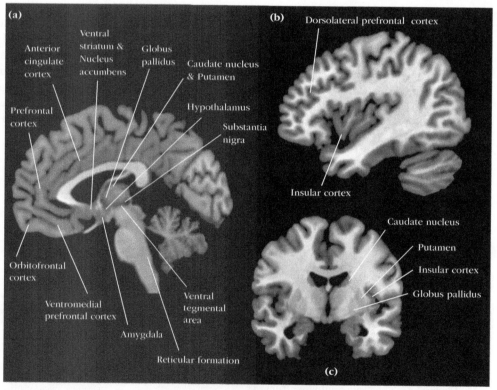

Figure 3.5 Anatomical Locations of the 16 Key Motivation- and Emotion-Related Subcortical and Cortical Brain Structures

Table 3.1   Motivational and Emotional Function of the 16 Specific Brain Structures Featured in Figure 3.5

Brain Structure	Motivational or Emotional Function
Subcortical Brain	
Reticular formation	Arousal, alertness, wakefulness.
Amygdala	Detects, learns about, and responds to the stimulus properties of environmental objects, including both threat-eliciting and reward-eliciting associations.
Basal ganglia[a]	Motivational modulation of movement and action.
Ventral striatum and nucleus accumbens	The brain's reward center. Responds to signals of reward (dopamine release) to produce pleasure and liking.
Ventral tegmental area	Starting point in the brain's dopamine-based reward center. Manufactures and releases dopamine.
Hypothalamus	Responsive to natural rewards in the regulation of eating, drinking, and mating. Regulates both the endocrine system and the autonomic nervous system.
Insular cortex (insula)	Monitors bodily states to produce gut-felt feelings. Processes feelings associated with risk, uncertainty, personal agency, and sense of self.
Cortical Brain	
Prefrontal cortex	Making plans, setting goals, formulating intentions. Right hemispheric activity is associated with negative affect and "no go" avoidance motivation, while left hemispheric activity is associated with positive affect and "go" approach motivation.
Orbitofrontal cortex	Stores and processes reward-related value of environmental objects and events to formulate preferences and make choices between options.
Ventromedial prefrontal cortex	Evaluates the unlearned emotional value of basic sensory rewards and internal bodily states. Responsible for emotional control.
Dorsolateral prefrontal cortex	Evaluates the learned emotional value of environmental events and possible courses of action. Responsible for control over urges and risks during the pursuit of long-term goals.
Anterior cingulate cortex	Monitors motivational conflicts. Resolves conflicts by recruiting other cortical brain structures for executive or cognitive control over basic urges and emotions.

[a]The basal ganglia include the caudate nucleus, putamen, substantial nigra, and globus pallidus.

of two parts: the ascending reticular activating system and the descending reticular formation. The reticular activating system projects its nerves upward to alert and arouse the brain, whereas the descending reticular formation projects its nerves downward to regulate the body (e.g., muscle tonus). Figure 3.6 uses a cat responding to a noise to illustrate that it is the reticular activating system that wakes, alerts, and arouses the brain to ready it to process the incoming information. Once aroused, the alerted brain processes the incoming information (e.g., makes a decision about what to do) and, a second later, responds with appropriate action and coping.

(a)

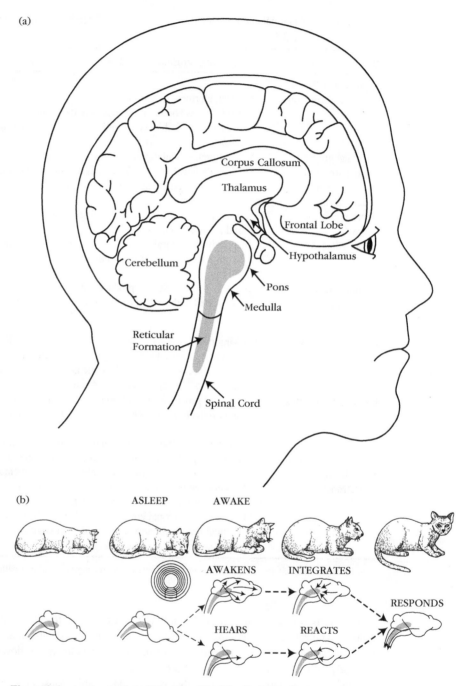

Corpus Callosum

Thalamus

Frontal Lobe

Hypothalamus

Cerebellum

Pons

Medulla

Reticular Formation

Spinal Cord

(b)

ASLEEP   AWAKE

AWAKENS   INTEGRATES

RESPONDS

HEARS   REACTS

Figure 3.6 Anatomy (a) and Function (b) of the Reticular Formation

Source: Adapted from *The Reticular Formation*, by J.D. French, 1957, *Scientific American, 196*, 54–60.

Amygdala

The amygdala (meaning "almond-shaped") is a collection of interconnected nuclei associated with emotion and motivation (Baxter & Murray, 2002; McDonald, 1998). One primary function of the amygdala is to detect, learn about, and respond to emotionally significant and aversive events, although each of its different nuclei serves a different function. Stimulation of one part of the amygdala generates emotional anger, while stimulation of another part generates emotional fear and defensive behavior (Blandler, 1988). Also, impairment of these same amygdala nuclei will produce striking changes, including an overall tameness, affective neutrality, a lack of emotional responsiveness, preference for social isolation over social affiliation, and a willingness to approach previously frightening stimuli (Aggleton, 1992; Kling & Brothers, 1992; Rolls, 1999). These studies make it clear that one key function of the amygdala is to generate and to form stimulus-emotion associations related to self-preservation, such as fear, anger, and anxiety (Hamann, Ely, Hoffman, & Kilts, 2002). If there is an aversive, emotionally charged stimulus in the environment, the amygdala will detect and respond to it.

The amygdala detects environmental threat and generates threat-elicited defensive responses (Cardinal, Parkinson, Hall, & Everitt, 2002; Davis, 1992; Gallagher & Chiba, 1996). Fear is the conscious realization of threat-elicited bodily reactions such as heart rate acceleration, muscular tension, behavioral freezing, and "fear face" facial expressions (LeDoux, 2013). As shown in Figure 3.7, as the person encounters and detects a threatening object, amygdala stimulation occurs and activates neighboring brain structures (e.g., hypothalamus, ventral tegmental area) that release neurotransmitters (dopamine, serotonin, noreadrenaline, acetylcholine) to instigate and regulate a coordinated defensive response, including rapid breathing (Harper, Frysinger, Trelease, & Marks, 1984), heart rate acceleration (Kapp et al., 1982), and high blood pressure (Morgenson & Calaresu, 1973), as well as hormonal discharge and emotional facial expressions (Davis, Hitchcock, & Rosen, 1987). What the amygdala does is (1) detect the aversive characteristics of environmental objects and (b) relay this emotion-laden information to neighboring cortical and subcortical

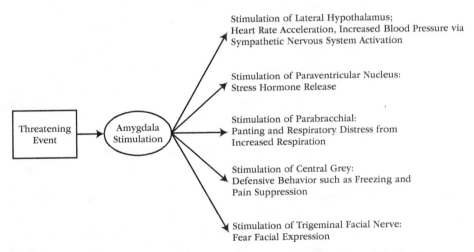

Figure 3.7   Amygdala Connections to Express Fear in Response to a Threat-Eliciting Event

brain regions. As one point of illustration, a rat with a lesioned amygdala will crawl all over a sleeping cat and even nibble playfully on the cat's ear (Blanchard & Blanchard, 1972). What is missing from the fearless rat is its capacity to generate the hard-wired amygdala-coordinated defensive response, as shown in the right-hand side of Figure 3.7. Without an amygdala, the rat lacks the means to respond emotionally to the cat, and it also lacks the capacity to learn to fear the cat when it wakes up and poses a threat. When humans have their amygdala removed (to control epileptic seizures, for instance) they become calm, docile, and emotionally indifferent, even in the face of provocation (Aggleton, 1992; Ramamurthi, 1988).

The amygdala processes the aversive and threatening characteristics of all environmental objects, but it has a special skill in detecting the aversive and threatening characteristics within facial displays of emotion (Adolphs, Tranel, Damasio, & Damasio, 1994; LeDoux, Romanski, & Xagoraris, 1989; Rolls, 1999). If another person lowers her brow and presses her lips tightly together (as when angry), the amygdala automatically, effortlessly, and reliably picks up on this threat-eliciting information.

A second primary function of the amygdala is to detect, respond to, and learn about rewarding and beneficial properties of various environmental objects and events (Baxter & Murray, 2002). What amygdala nuclei detect, learning about, and respond to is the presence versus absence of reward, the value or quality of the available reward, the predictability of the reward, and the costs associated with trying to obtain the potential reward (Berridge & Kringelbach, 2008; Whalen, 1999, 2007). These studies make it clear that a second key function of the amygdala is to generate and to form stimulus-emotion associations related to reward. If there is an attractive, emotionally charged stimulus in the environment, the amygdala will detect it, evaluate it, and respond to it.

The essence of the amygdala in reward is as follows. One area of the brain processes object recognition (I see that this object is a cup of orange juice) and the amygdala processes the reward properties of that object (it is sweet, it is a cool and refreshing temperature) in order to pair the object with its rewarding properties. Thus, a stimulus-reward association is formed, and the person acquires a preference for that object. As new reward-based information about that object becomes available (it tastes sweeter than it did before), the object-reward association is updated. This information is then relayed to other parts of the brain, such as those responsible for storing the learned reward value of objects (orbitofrontal cortex) and for approaching and acting on the valued object (basal ganglia).

An example to communicate the overall threat- and reward-detecting function of the amygdala can be illustrated by a person gambling. In gambling tasks, people need to be able to assess risk, weigh the cost and benefits of choices, and cope with changing outcomes and odds on those outcomes. With each win, the amygdala generates positive emotion and relays that positive emotionality to the ventromedial prefrontal cortex so that the person can make an informed judgment about what to do on the next trial, considering the risks, choices, and changing probabilities. Similarly, with each loss, the amygdala generates and relays negative emotion to the ventromedial prefrontal cortex so that the person can again make an informed judgment about future decisions and behaviors. In this case, the amygdala generates the emotional joy of winning and reward and the emotional pain of losing and danger, while the ventromedial prefrontal cortex uses this emotional information to make a judgment about future predicted winning and losing. However, people with damage to their amygdala behave in a bizarre fashion during such a gambling task, because they have no fear of risk and therefore act recklessly and poorly (Bechara, Damasio, Tranel, & Damasio, 1996). It is good to know when to hold them and when to fold them, and it is the emotionally rich amygdala—not the rational cortical brain—that knows best when to stay and when to quit.

The amygdala has an interesting anatomical relationship with other brain areas. The amygdala sends projections to almost every part of the brain, although only a small number of projections return information to the amygdala. This imbalance helps explain why emotion, especially negative emotion, tends to overpower cognition more than cognition tends to overpower emotion. Hence, a lot of fear and anger messages get blurted out. This is because amygdala nuclei are mostly evolutionarily old structures that produce primitive emotionality. However, the lateral amygdala nuclei have undergone relatively recent development to forge reciprocal projections and pathways with the cortical regions of the brain, especially with the frontal lobes (Cardinal et al., 2002). It is these evolutionary new pathways that allow for some degree of conscious regulation of these biologically basic primitive emotions.

Basal Ganglia

The essence of motivation and emotion is energized and persistent goal-directed behavior. Motivated people move and take action. Movement and action flow out of neural activity in the motor cortex. The motor cortex sends "go" signals to the body's muscles to produce movement. Before such movement occurs, the presupplemental and supplemental motor areas first plan, excite, inhibit, and enact these motor commands. The presupplemental and supplemental motor areas, which are located at the very top of the head (where you might pat a young child on the head), largely send the motor instruction to the premotor and motor cortex and are therefore more related to movement and action than they are to motivation and emotion per se.

Basal ganglia (*basal* meaning at the base of the cortex, *ganglia* meaning a group of nerve cells) are a cluster of many different small nuclei in the subcortical brain that work collectively to provide movement and action with a motivational and an emotional punch. The substantial nigra and globus pallidus motivationally and emotionally prepare action; they make a planned action more or less potent (more or less energized). They are active, for instance, for the game show contestant as she eagerly presses the answer buzzer and for just about anyone in pursuit of rewards and gains. The caudate nucleus and putamen give rise to movement intentions and coordinated (rather than conflicted) action. All basal ganglia—substantial nigra, globus pallidus, caudate nucleus, and putamen—are closely connected to and receive information from the cortical areas of the brain (to receive action plans) and to the motor, premotor, supplemental motor area, and presupplemental motor areas (to execute and carry out those action plans). The collective role of the basal ganglia is to energize (or inhibit) those action plans (Pessiglione et al., 2007).

Ventral Striatum, Nucleus Accumbens, and Ventral Tegmental Area

The basal ganglia also include the ventral striatum. The striatum consists of the nucleus accumbens, caudate nucleus, and putamen (Liljeholm & O'Doherty, 2012). Together, these structures are the brain's reward center, especially the ventral (lower part) of the striatum, which includes the nucleus accumbens. The activation of the ventral striatum (and nucleus accumbens) is practically synonymous with the experience of reward, or what neuroscientists term the hedonic evaluation of stimuli. Through their activation, we learn what to like, what to prefer, and what to want (Smith, Tindell, Aldridge, & Berridge, 2009).

Reward is fundamental to motivation. It is fundamental to survival, to learning, to well-being, and to the generation of goal-directed effort (Schultz, 2000). When a person encounters an environmental object (e.g., a cup of orange juice), its stimulus characteristics are processed in the amygdala and ventral striatum (sweet taste, cool temperature), and the experience of rewarding and pleasurable feelings occurs in the nucleus accumbens (e.g., "I like it.") (Pecina & Berridge, 2005). The nucleus accumbens is active during the experience of a pleasant taste, a pleasant image, social acceptance and inclusion, and several addictive drugs (Berridge & Robinson, 1998; Sabatinelli et al., 2007; Wise, 2002). What specifically stimulates the nucleus accumbens to become active in the first place—what constitutes "reward-related information"—is the release of the neurotransmitter dopamine (Berridge & Kringelbach, 2008). Once activated, the ventral striatum and nucleus accumbens translate the experience of reward into motivational force, approach behavior, and the exertion of physical effort (Pessiglione et al., 2007).

From a neuroscience perspective, reward is dopamine release. As people go about their day, some level of dopamine is always present in the brain. But as people encounter a variety of events, those that signal reward—a pleasant image (looking at a beautiful face), a pleasant taste (sipping sweet juice)—trigger dopamine release (Sabatinelli et al., 2007; Wise, 2002). These triggering events can be natural or learned rewards.

The ventral tegmental area is the manufacturing site for brain dopamine, the nucleus accumbens is the pleasure-generating brain area, and it is the neurotransmitter dopamine that links together the ventral tegmental area and nucleus accumbens to create the biology of reward. As illustrated in Figure 3.8, the nucleus accumbens and the ventral tegmental area are closely connected. The ventral tegmental area is the starting point in the brain's dopamine-based reward center, and it projects fibers into the nucleus accumbens that receive dopamine-release information. Together, these two subcortical brain structures form the neural basis of the dopamine-based reward center. As shown in Figure 3.8, the ventral tegmental area-to-nucleus accumbens pathway extends further upstream into the cortical brain. It is in the prefrontal cortex that the person has a conscious experience of pleasure, and it is the orbitofrontal cortex that stores the learned reward value of environmental objects so that the person will know (will remember) that a particular object has produced rewarding consequences in the past.

Activation of the ventral tegmental area-to-nucleus accumbens dopamine pathway is what allows people to learn the reward value of environmental objects and events. People learn the reward value of any such object or event through stimulus appraisal (amygdala, ventral striatum) and then through extent of dopamine release (ventral tegmental area, nucleus accumbens) (Hampton & O'Doherty, 2007; Hayden, Nair, McCoy, & Platt, 2008; McClure, York, & Montague, 2004; O'Doherty, 2004). The ventral tegmental area also relays reward-related excitatory signals to the basal ganglia, which in turn send

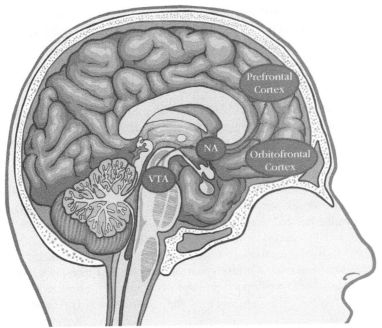

© Oguz Aral/Shutterstock

Figure 3.8   The Dopamine-Based Reward Circuit
The brain's reward system. The dopamine-based reward circuit begins in the ventral tegmental area (VTA) where dopamine is manufactured and then released to the nucleus accumbens (NA). From the NA, the reward center extends into the prefrontal cortex, which is involved in the subjective experience of pleasure, and into the orbitofrontal cortex, which stores the object's learned reward value.

excitatory signals to initiate motivated action (i.e., approach the reward-related event). Overall, the more dopamine that is released, the greater will be the learning, positive emotion, and approach motivation.

When day-to-day events unfold in ways that are better than expected, the ventral tegmental area releases a high level of dopamine, and the increased dopamine serves as information that the event is producing more reward than it was anticipated to deliver. In contrast, when events unfold in ways that are worse than expected, a decreased dopamine release serves as information that a particular course of action is producing less reward than it was anticipated to deliver (Montague, Dayan, & Sejnowski, 1996). Thus, extent of dopamine release from the ventral tegmental area is the essence of reward-related information.

When you anticipate good news or when you anticipate an exciting event, dopamine release occurs. It is not the good news or the event itself that causes the ventral tegmental area to release dopamine but is, instead, the anticipation of rewarding news and the anticipation of a rewarding event that triggers dopamine release. That is, what activates the nucleus accumbens and the experience of pleasure is the *anticipation* of reward. That is, the ventral tegmental area releases dopamine and the nucleus accumbens is activated when we first learn that we are about to receive some money (reward anticipation), not when we actually receive the money (reward receipt). Dopamine release is therefore greatest when rewarding events occur in ways that are unpredicted ("Wow, I'm surprised how nice that flower smells") or underpredicted ("Wow, that flower smells much nicer than I thought it would") (Mirenowicz & Schultz, 1994). For this reason, we typically experience more pleasure in thinking about eating chocolate chip cookies and about engaging in sex than we do when actually munch on the cookies or engage in sex. Of course, if things go better than expected during the eating or mating, then the dopamine release continues and so does its corresponding positive feeling and approach motivation.

The nucleus accumbens can over time become hypersensitive to dopamine stimulation, as occurs with addictive drugs (Di Chiara, 1998). When used repeatedly, many addictive drugs, such as cocaine, heroin, amphetamine, alcohol, and nicotine, cause dopamine-induced neural hypersensitization (a manifold increase in dopamine levels), and once this occurs, it can last for years (Hyman & Malenka, 2001; Robinson & Kolb, 1997). To help smokers quit the habit, some currently marketed pharmaceuticals block the dopamine-related pleasure out of smoking and nicotine stimulation (e.g., the drug Chantix). These prescription drugs prevent much of the nucleus accumbens-based "liking" from nicotine, although much of the nicotine-based (i.e., addiction-based) "wanting" remains.

Wanting is a motivational state that comes from an actual need for something (e.g., when dehydrated, people *want* to drink water). Liking, however, is a motivational state that comes from experiencing pleasure (Berridge & Robinson, 1995). Wanting and liking typically go hand-in-hand, but the two motivational experiences can diverge (Berridge & Robinson, 1998; Dickinson & Balleine, 2002), and this is what typically occurs during addiction. At first, smoking a cigarette, eating a sugary donut, or ingesting cocaine produces liking. But, because pleasure is linked to dopamine-release and because dopamine-release occurs only with unexpected reward, the liking-associated pleasure fades (because the reward becomes expected, rather than unexpected). At this point, wanting can occur without liking—the person can need (i.e., want) the addictive drug because of its addictive properties although that drug no longer produces pleasure (i.e., liking).

Hypothalamus

The hypothalamus is a small subcortical brain structure that comprises less than 1 percent of the total volume of the brain. Despite its small size, it is a motivational giant.

The hypothalamus exists as a collection of 20 neighboring and interconnected nuclei that serve separate and discrete functions. Through the stimulation of its 20 separate nuclei, the hypothalamus regulates a range of important biological functions, including eating, drinking, and mating (via the motivations for hunger, satiety, thirst, and sex). The hypothalamus is responsive to natural rewards (e.g., food, water, mating), and Chapter 4 will detail how hypothalamic stimulation generates wants for, and the pleasures associated with, water, food, and sexual partners. The hypothalamus also regulates both the endocrine system and autonomic nervous system. By regulating these two systems, the hypothalamus is able to regulate the body's internal environment (e.g., heart rate, hormone secretion) in order to adapt optimally to the environment (e.g., cope with a stressor).

The hypothalamus regulates the endocrine system. It does so by exerting control over the pituitary gland—the so-called master gland of the endocrine (or hormonal) system (Agnati, Bjelke, & Fuxe, 1992; Pert, 1986). Anatomically, the hypothalamus is immediately north of the pituitary gland, and it regulates the pituitary gland by secreting hormones into the tiny capillaries that connect the hypothalamus to the pituitary gland. The pituitary gland, in turn, regulates the endocrine system. For instance, to increase arousal, the hypothalamus stimulates the pituitary gland to send hormones through the bloodstream to stimulate the adrenal glands to release its own hormones (epinephrine, norepinephrine) into the blood stream that trigger various bodily organs to initiate the well-known "fight-or-flight" response. A later section in this chapter ("Hormones") will explain how the hypothalamus regulates both the pituitary gland and the stress hormone of cortisol (see Box 3).

The hypothalamus also controls the autonomic nervous system. The autonomic nervous system (ANS) includes all neural innervations into body organs that are under involuntary control (e.g., heart, lungs, liver). It is divided into the excitatory sympathetic system that accelerates bodily functions and alerts the body (as through an increased heart rate) and the inhibitory parasympathetic system that facilitates rest, recovery, and digestion. Therefore, the autonomic nervous system begins at the hypothalamus (the hypothalamus is the autonomic nervous system's head ganglion, or starting point) and extends its nerves throughout the body by innervating its many organs.

Overall, the hypothalamus has two major means to regulate the body's reaction to environmental opportunities and threats, and it therefore has two major means of coping with environmental challenges. It generates both arousal (sympathetic activation) and recovery (parasympathetic activation) via its influence over the autonomic nervous system, and it regulates the endocrine system via its influence over the pituitary gland. The hypothalamus also regulates the motivationally key biological functions of thirst, hunger, and sex. For all these reasons, the small hypothalamus that lies deep within the subcortical brain is a motivational giant.

Insula

The insula is a rather large and highly interconnected structure that lies deep within the brain. Anatomically, it is the fold that lies between the posterior part of the frontal lobe and the anterior part of the temporal lobe and also above the subcortical brain (see Figure 3.4, image C). It is part of the cortical brain, but it is also part of the subcortical brain.

The insular cortex (or insula) consists of two roughly equal halves—an anterior and a posterior part. The posterior insula is the brain structure that receives, monitors, and becomes aware of changes in bodily states such as changes in heart rate; changes in fatigue; changes in pain; changes in autonomic nervous system arousal, tastes, and cravings (Craig, 2003, 2009a). The anterior insula is the brain structure that monitors, evaluates, and consciously represents (becomes aware of) the subjective feelings that arise from these changes in bodily states. Hence, the anterior insula literally monitors and becomes aware of "gut" (bodily based) feelings, such as feeling disgust from the bodily experience of nausea. Notice that the insular cortex operates largely on an unconscious level, but it generates feeling-based information that rises into conscious awareness.

Where do feelings come from? This question will be discussed extensively in Chapter 12, but a study of the insula can answer the questions, Where do "raw" feelings come from? and Where do gut-felt feelings and intuitive hunches come from? The answer is the insular cortex. The insula processes interoceptive information about the state of one's

BOX 3   *How and Why Antidepressant Drugs Alleviate Depression*

Question: Why is this information important?

Answer: To understand how antidepressant drugs alleviate depression.

Each of us wages a lifelong struggle against depression, and about 1 in 10 of us suffers from clinical depression. Aversive, stressful events inevitably come our way because experiences of disappointment, loss, failure, hassle, financial woe, interpersonal neglect, and social rejection represent the all-too-common flow of human experience. When such events affect us in the moment, we feel distress; when such events affect us for days, we feel sad; but when such events affect us chronically, we feel depressed. These life events affect our bodily biochemistry and, when they deplete our biochemical resources, they can leave us vulnerable to depression.

Depression is a complex psychological disorder associated with the stress of coping and a diminished capacity to experience pleasure. Relative to the stress of coping, exposure to uncontrollable stress makes demands on the subcortical brain that gradually deplete brain serotonin. We need serotonin for the motivation to cope, so serotonin deficiency leaves us vulnerable to depression (Kramer, 1993; Weiss & Simson, 1985). The popular antidepressant drugs (e.g., Prozac, Zoloft, Paxil, Cymbalta, Lexapro) are SSRIs, or selective serotonin-reuptake inhibitors. These antidepressants work on the premise that depression is caused by low serotonin turnover in the serotonin pathways. During stressful life events, serotonin is released into the synapse, but it also quickly returns (experiences reuptake) to the sending neuron. To reverse depression, the antidepressant drug prevents serotonin uptake and hence makes serotonin more readily available (rather than allowing

it to be restored via reuptake). The antidepressant acts to restore serotonin levels and usage to normal.

Relative to a diminished capacity to experience pleasure, depression is associated with an inability to experience pleasure and positive feelings for live events. Low dopamine levels can leave the person vulnerable to apathy, boredom, poor concentration, and with little initiative to embrace the day. In contrast, dopamine release generates good feelings, positive affect, and essentially leaves the person primed to a positive mood (Ashby, Isen, & Turken, 1999). Researchers have not been able to produce dopamine-based antidepressive drugs because dopamine decays too rapidly for pharmaceutical usage.

Overall, depression has two faces: serotonin deficiency, which leaves the person less able to cope with life's stress, and dopamine deficiency, which leaves the person less ready to anticipate

and experience pleasure. Drugs targeting serotonin and dopamine both unfortunately produce troubling side effects. Antidepressant drugs not only supply serotonin, but they also "hijack" dopamine pathways to some degree and inadvertently blunt feelings of love, romance, and attachment to others (Zhou et al., 2005). Few people taking antidepressants, for instance, have the experience of falling in love. Some addition-countering drugs (e.g., smoking cessation) blunt dopamine release in general (and not just while taking the addictive substance) and therefore leave the depressed person vulnerable to suicide. Knowing this, pharmacological researchers are now working on a third alternative: namely, drugs that produce neurogenesis, or the growth of new nerve cells. Sprouting new nerve growth is one key biological event that keeps depression at bay.

body (visceral, homeostatic), and it therefore allows the person to mentally construct a consciously aware representation of how he or she feels (Craig, 2009b; Wicker et al., 2003). When people have "a feeling about that thing" (e.g., this person is untrustworthy, my homework is boring, tennis is enjoyable), it is activity in the anterior insular cortex that gives rise to this feeling. Pain is one bodily feeling experience that the insular monitors, but insular activity seems to be involved in practically all subjective feelings (Craig, 2009), including not only negative feelings but positive feelings as well (Lee & Reeve, 2013).

In the anterior insula, people consolidate their internal bodily feeling state information with external social-contextual information about the task they are involved in at the moment to form a basis of the conscious experience of emotion or affect during that task (Craig, 2002, 2009).

The insula also processes and learns about risk and uncertainty (Huettel et al., 2006; Kuhnen & Knutson, 2005). This is important because the role of the insula seems to be to integrate current feelings, a risk prediction forecast (that always has a degree of uncertainty associated with it) that arises from considering the consequences of one's actions, and contextual information to produce a global feeling state that guides decision making (Singer, Critchley, & Preuschoff, 2009). Much of that global feeling state exists as anxiety (Paulus & Stein, 2006). The decision to trust another person, for instance, is one such instance of subjective feelings, risk, uncertainty, considering the consequences of one's actions, and decision making. When a generally cooperative person begins to act in a way that seems exploitive or untrustworthy (recall the chapter's opening vignette), insular activity occurs. The person picks up on social-contextual cues to experience a gut-felt feeling that something is not right. This feeling then enters into the decision-making process whether to continue to trust that person. This same anterior insular activity occurs during financial decision making as well, as in judging the risk and uncertainty of an investment (Kuhnen & Knutson, 2005).

The insula is also responsible for a feeling of "self" and a sense of having a boundary that allows for an intuitive distinction between me (self) and others (not self). Insular activity is also responsible for an intuitive distinction between "action caused by me" and "action not caused by me" (Farrer et al., 2003; Farrer & Frith, 2002). In an experiment, a participant will be asked to perform a simple action (e.g., move a joystick), while the experimenter manipulates what happens when the person performs that simple action. In one case, the participant's action will cause a consequence (moving the joystick makes an image appear on screen), but in another case the consequence will occur at random (when the image appears is controlled by the experimenter, not the participant). In the first case, the person will show insular activation and will experience "self-as-cause." In the second case, the person will not show insular activation and will experience "other-as-cause." Hence, anterior insular activity during action increases an experience of personal agency (Lee & Reeve, 2013). Personal agency (I can change my environment in an intentional way) is fundamentally important to motivation, because people are volitionally motivated to act when they feel "self-as-cause," because they believe their actions produce desired effects, but people are not so volitionally motivated to act when they feel "other-as-cause" (Bandura, 2006). With "self-as-cause" personal agency, people willingly act on their environmental surroundings to change things for the better, but with an "other-as-cause" lack of personal agency, people withhold effort because it seems rather pointless.

Prefrontal Cortex

We have so far discussed only the subcortical brain structures related to motivation and emotion, but we now turn our attention to the cortical brain structures related to motivation and emotion, such as the prefrontal cortex. The prefrontal lobes of the cerebral cortex lie immediately behind the forehead. One lobe is on the right side of the brain—the right prefrontal cortex—while the other is on the left side—the left prefrontal cortex. Together, these two cortical lobes underlie many important motivations, including affect, goals, and personal strivings.

The starting point for many (but not all) negative emotions is the amygdala, while the starting point for many (but not all) positive emotions is the dopamine-network of the ventral tegmental area and nucleus accumbens. The phrase "but not all" is important, because emotions also arise from cortical processes such as thoughts, appraisals, and goals. That is, hearing the dentist's drill from the waiting room is sensory information that is processed by the amygdala to generate threat-elicited coping such as an accelerated heart rate (as summarized in Figure 3.7). When the amygdala is activated, it sends signals not only to the sites summarized in Figure 3.7 but also to the prefrontal cortex where the information creates the conscious awareness of fear or anxiety. Similarly, seeing a pleasant image, such as a very attractive face, is sensory information that is processed by the subcortical brain structures that make up the dopamine circuit. When the dopamine circuit is activated, it sends its reward-related information upstream to the prefrontal cortex where the person has a conscious awareness of pleasure or reward (see Figure 3.8).

The earlier-mentioned right–left hemisphere distinction between the two lobes of the prefrontal cortex is important because right hemispheric brain activity tends to produce negative emotion and "no-go" avoidance motivation, while left hemispheric brain activity tends to produce positive emotion and "go" approach motivation (Davidson, 2004). If you watch a film clip showing puppies and babies (to induce positive emotion), you will show greater left than right prefrontal cortex activity; but if you watch a film clip showing heartache and suffering (to induce negative emotion), you will show greater right than left right prefrontal cortex activity (Fischer et al., 2002). This is important because it leads to an important conclusion about the role of the prefrontal cortex in emotion: Left activations signal positive emotion and approach motivation; right activations signal negative emotion and avoidance emotion (Davidson, 2012). More specifically, left prefrontal cortical activity is associated with parasympathetic nervous system activity, calmness, positive emotionality, approach motivation, and group-oriented desires such as affiliation, while right prefrontal cortical activity is associated with sympathetic nervous system activity, arousal and danger, negative emotionality, and individual-oriented desires such as personal protection.

The prefrontal cortex houses a person's conscious goals (Miller & Cohen, 2001). Thoughts, intentions, goals, and strivings that stimulate the left prefrontal cortex generate positive and approach-oriented feelings, whereas thoughts, intentions, goals, and strivings that stimulate the right prefrontal cortex generate negative and avoidance-oriented feelings (Gable, Reis, & Elliot, 2000). The associated positive versus negative emotion then colors which goals and strivings the person does and does not pursue. The right prefrontal cortex is a cortical bathtub of negative emotion in which thoughts, goals, intentions, memories, and personal strivings bathe as they ready themselves for action—which usually takes the form of anxiety, caution, pessimism, and hence avoidance; while the left prefrontal cortex is a cortical bathtub of positive emotion in which thoughts, goals, intentions, memories, and personal strivings bathe as they ready themselves for action—which usually takes the form of hope, eagerness, optimism, and hence approach.

Different people show different levels of sensitivities to process information in their right versus left prefrontal cortex. That is, biologically basic personality differences exist between people, because some people have sensitive left prefrontal lobes that leave them vulnerable to optimism, positive emotionality, and approach motivation in their day-to-day thinking and planning, while other people have sensitive right prefrontal lobes that leave them vulnerable to pessimism, negative emotionality, and avoidance motivation in their day-to-day thinking and planning (Gable et al., 2000). An active and sensitive left prefrontal cortex provides the person with a behavioral activation system (BAS), which is similar to extraversion, while an active and sensitive right prefrontal cortex provides the person with a behavioral inhibition system (BIS), which is similar to neuroticism (Carver & White, 1994). To get an idea for these two neurologically based dimensions of personality, consider your own reactions to the questionnaire items listed in Table 3.2. The first six items ask how sensitive you are to approach-oriented motivations, emotions, and behaviors, broken down into the three different subscales of reward responsiveness, drive, and fun seeking (i.e., your sensitivity to the "behavior approach system"), while the last four items ask how sensitive you are to avoidance-oriented motivations (i.e., your sensitivity to the "behavior inhibition system").

Some people show greater baseline or everyday activity in their left prefrontal lobe ("left-side asymmetry"), whereas others show greater baseline or everyday activity in the right prefrontal lobe ("right-side asymmetry"), as measured by the electroencephalograph

Table 3.2   Behavioral Activation System (BAS) and Behavioral Inhibition System (BIS) Questionnaire Items

BAS Items

1. When I get something I want, I feel excited and energized.[a]
2. When good things happen to me, it affects me strongly.[a]
3. When I want something, I usually go all-out to get it.[b]
4. I go out of my way to get things I want.[b]
5. I will often do things for no other reason than that they might be fun.[c]
6. I crave excitement and new sensations.[c]

BIS Items

7. If I think of something unpleasant is going to happen I usually get pretty "worked up."
8. Criticism or scolding hurts me quite a bit.
9. I feel pretty worried or upset when I think or know somebody is angry at me.
10. I feel worried when I think I have done poorly at something.

Note: BIS = Behavioral Inhibition System; BAS = Behavioral Activation System. In completing the questionnaire, respondents are asked to agree or disagree with each item using a 1 to 7 response scale (1 = strongly disagree, 7 = strongly agree). The BAS scale consists of three subscales: reward responsiveness (denoted by [a] above), drive (denoted by [b]), and fun seeking (denoted by [c]). The actual BIS/BAS Questionnaire contains 20 items, 7 BIS items and 13 BAS items, so the table shows only a part of the full questionnaire.
Source: Adapted from *Behavioral Inhibition, Behavioral Activation, and Affective Responses to Impending Reward and Punishment: The BIS/BAS Scales*, by C.L. Carver and T.L. White, 1994, *Journal of Personality and Social Psychology, 67*, 319–333. Copyright 1994 by American Psychological Association. Adapted with permission.

(EEG) for instance. People with relatively sensitive right prefrontal lobes—those who show greater right-side asymmetry—score high on the BIS items in Table 3.2, and they show a greater sensitivity to punishment, negative emotion, and avoidance-oriented behaviors. People with relatively sensitive left prefrontal lobes—those who show greater left-side asymmetry—score high on the BAS items in Table 3.2, and they show a greater sensitivity to reward, positive emotion, and approach-oriented behaviors. The correlation between people's scores on the BAS and BIS questionnaires and their prefrontal lobe asymmetry is important because the extent of people's asymmetry corresponds to their typical emotionality (BAS vs. BIS; Sutton & Davidson, 1997). That is, even without exposure to a live event—when people are at "baseline," they show a personality-like disposition to be overly sensitive to negative emotion, anxiety, and avoidance motivation or to be overly sensitive to positive emotion, eagerness, and approach motivation.

Orbitofrontal Cortex

The orbitofrontal cortex lies anatomically beneath the prefrontal cortex, just above the eyes. It is sort of like the floor of the prefrontal cortex. It is the cortical brain structure that stores and processes reward-related information about environmental objects that helps people formulate their preferences and make their choices between options, such as which product to buy or whether to drink orange juice or water (Dickinson & Balleine, 2002; O'Doherty, 2004). As we make our way through the day and compare the incentive (or reward) value of the possible objects and events that might guide our behavior, some objects and some events attract our attention and serve as attractive incentives to our actions. In a demonstration of the orbitofrontal cortex's role in incentive motivation and goal selection, researchers monitored participants' brains while they looked at a menu and selected their order. The orbitofrontal cortex is active when people considered their options, remembered what on the menu was good and what was not, and made their selection among the different environmental objects (menu items) to pursue (Arana et al., 2001).

The orbitofrontal cortex also inhibits inappropriate actions. It is central to the ability to delay gratification, which is essentially quieting the urge for an immediate reward in favor of a delayed reward that is more advantageous. This is a very important capacity, because most long-term plans involve the ability to put aside those things that are immediately attractive (listen to music, get something to eat, turn on the TV) in favor of those things that are part of a longer-term strategy to accomplish goals and complete projects. That is, basic motivations and emotions (e.g., urges, drives, desires) arise from the subcortical brain and are typically automatic and unconscious—you smell fresh coffee brewing and you want it. But the orbitofrontal cortex has dense neural connections into the subcortical brain that allow it to exert self-control (or willpower) over these urges and impulses for immediate action. It is important to note that this orbitofrontal–subcortical brain communication system is reciprocal (two-way or bidirectional), because sometimes urges and emotions need to take precedent over conscious planning, as we do sometimes need to listen to our fears, sense of disgust, and an unexpected opportunity, although we more often need to quiet those urges and desires to focus our attention and behavior away from such distractions and toward our long-term goal pursuits.

Ventromedial Prefrontal Cortex

The ventromedial prefrontal cortex groups together a set of interconnected cortical brain areas that integrate affective-based information from sensory and social cues (Roy, Shohamy, & Wager, 2012). It represents the affective qualities (or value) of basic sensory rewards, such as tastes, and it is constantly updating affective representations of internal bodily states, such as those activated by changes in the autonomic nervous system and the endocrine system. In clinical cases in which the person's ventromedial prefrontal cortex has been damaged (e.g., from a stroke), these individuals show emotional impairments and destructive social judgments (Damasio, 1994, 1996). This is because the ventromedial prefrontal cortex works for cognitive valuing and revaluing of emotional inputs that lead to effective decision making (Davidson & Irwin, 1999; Ochsner & Gross, 2005).

The neural connections between the ventromedial prefrontal cortex and subcortical brain are both dense and bidirectional, just as was the case with the orbitofrontal cortex and the subcortical brain. This two-way communication allows conscious thought to modulate and control emotion, but it also allows emotion to inform beliefs, judgments, and decisions. Hence, via its input from the emotion-laden subcortical brain, the ventromedial prefrontal cortex integrates emotional information with cognitive and social judgments, including what the person believes to be true (social judgment) and whether the person believes something is right or wrong (moral judgment) (Cunningham & Zelazo, 2007). The ventromedial prefrontal cortex also receives input from the insula, which can add emotional disgust to intuitively sway what is believed toward what is not believed. For instance, it is hard to believe that a food is edible or that a person is trustworthy if either creates a gut feeling of disgust within you.

Dorsolateral Prefrontal Cortex

While the ventromedial prefrontal cortex evaluates the emotional value of basic sensory (unlearned or natural) rewards, the dorsolateral prefrontal cortex evaluates the learned emotional value of environmental events and possible courses of action. If someone were to ask you to take a sip of Cola-Cola and evaluate it emotionally in terms of likes and preferences, you would taste the sensory properties of the drink (in the ventromedial prefrontal cortex), but you would also "taste" and evaluate the Coca-Cola brand itself in the dorsolateral prefrontal cortex. The idea is that we have a great deal of learned emotional value and meaning for the objects and events around us, and these emotional memories are largely stored in the dorsolateral prefrontal cortex. When it comes time to make a decision (e.g., What should I buy at the store?), we access this stored environmental information from the dorsolateral prefrontal cortex to help us make an emotionally informed decision.

The dorsolateral prefrontal cortex is also important in the effort to resist temptation during the pursuit of long-term goals (especially the right dorsolateral prefrontal cortex; Knock & Erst, 2007). Sometimes we find ourselves offered a risky opportunity, and neural activity in the dorsolateral prefrontal cortex is important to help us override the temptation to take a risk and to give in to an urge, because the dorsolateral prefrontal cortex contributes important inhibitory forces during decision making. Basically, the opposite of urge-based (subcortical) risk-taking is self- or executive (cortical) self-control. Dorsolateral prefrontal cortex activations occur (to signal that self-control is occurring) when a person pursues a long-term reward in favor of a short-term ventral striatum-based reward (McClure, Laibson, Lowenstein, & Cohen, 2004).

Activity in the dorsolateral prefrontal cortex is also important to keep us from acting selfishly, because it inhibits our urge for self-interest and therefore contributes positively to harmonious social interactions (Knock & Erst, 2007). Because of right dorsolateral prefrontal cortex activity, we can constrain our pursuit of self-interest and make decisions based on our emotional value for social concerns, such as fairness, equality, and equity. Hence, part of our socioemotional competence lies in right dorsolateral prefrontal cortex.

Anterior Cingulate Cortex

There is a lot of conflict in the brain as people wonder "Should I choose this, or should I choose that? Should I take the immediate reward, or keep working for a later but larger reward? Should I approach, or should I avoid?" It therefore makes sense that part of the cortical brain exists to make these sorts of judgment calls. That part of the brain is the anterior cingulate cortex, a mid-frontal cortical brain area that lies above or north of the subcortical brain. It is involved in prioritizing attention, monitoring conflict, making choices, making decisions, predicting the consequences of actions, alerting other brain areas to the need for increased cognitive control to resolve conflict, and regulating the self, such as delaying the gratification of our basic urges and impulses to free us to pursue longer-termed cognitively guided goals, such as delaying the impulsive urge of "I want ice cream!" in the service of "My goal is to lose some weight."

The core function of the anterior cingulate cortex is to monitor conflicts in information processing and, when conflicts arise, to trigger an increased allocation of cognitive resources, such as attention and decision making, to resolve those conflicts in ways that are favorable to one's goals (Botvinick, Cohen, & Carter, 2004; Botvinick et al., 2001; Van Veen et al., 2001). For instance, it is in the anterior (and posterior) cingulate cortex where people consciously and deliberatively undertake a cost-benefit analysis as to whether a goal or a possible course of action has enough reward value associated with it to warrant an investment of effort (Hayden et al., 2008).

In its role as the brain's information-processing conflict detector, the anterior cingulate cortex signals and recruits other cortical brain areas to help it to resolve conflict and to exert greater cognitive control. It uses information gained from these other cortical brain structures to select appropriate action, although it also receives information form the subcortical brain to guide decision making and action selection (Bush et al., 2002; Matsumoto et al., 2003). The anterior cingulate cortex also evaluates the extent of mental effort required on a task, because cognitive conflict is a good indicator of task difficulty (Walton et al., 2003). Overall, the anterior cingulate cortex provides "top-down" executive or cognitive control over decision making, goal pursuit, and action.

HORMONES

While the nervous system relies on neurotransmitters flowing through the nervous system for communication between brain structures, the endocrine system relies on hormones flowing through the bloodstream to communicate between bodily organs, such as the heart, kidney, and pancreas. While many hormones are important to motivation and emotion, we highlight cortisol, testosterone, and oxytocin.

Cortisol is the so-called stress hormone. Cortisol is a hormonal product of the reactivity of the hypothalamic–pituitary–adrenocortical system (Stansbury & Gunnar, 1994; Susman, 2006). In response to stressful events, subcortical brain structures (e.g., the amygdala) stimulate the hypothalamus to stimulate the pituitary gland, which leads the adrenal gland to increase cortical production and release. Cortisol activation occurs during social-evaluative threats (e.g., public speaking), during relationship conflict (Powers, Pietromonaco, Gunlicks, & Sayer, 2006), or while being interpersonally controlled (Reeve & Tseng, 2011b) or devalued/rejected (Stroud, Salovey, & Epel, 2002). Cortisol deactivation (de-stress) occurs during social support (Kirschbaum, Klauer, Filipp, & Hellhammer, 1995; Reeve & Tseng, 2011b; Taylor et al., 2010). Generally speaking, cortisol reactivity serves a short-term adaptive function, as it mobilizes attention and energy in response to a social evaluative threat (Dickerson & Kemeny, 2004). Longer term, however, chronic cortical reactivity (repeated hypothalamic–pituitary–adrenocortical system activation, as from long-term exposure to a conflictual relationship) takes a cumulative toll on the body, a phenomenon termed "allostatic load" (McEwen, 1998). Cortisol-induced allostatic load puts the individual at risk of negative biological outcomes such as diabetes and hypertension, but it has further been linked to maladaptive cognitive outcomes, such as poor memory, impaired problem solving, and poor intellectual functioning (Brown & Suppes, 1998; Kirschbaum et al., 1996). Overall, increased cortical in the bloodstream confirms the activation of the hypothalamic–pituitary–adrenocortical coping system (Dickerson & Kemeny, 2004).

The steroid hormone *testosterone* is associated with high competition, status-seeking behaviors, and sexual motivation (Bancroft, 2002). High testosterone encourages competition. For instance, high testosterone levels help Wall Street stockbrokers make more money (compete better) during the day's trading. More specifically, high testosterone is associated with status-seeking behavior (winning a competition), and it is most strongly associated with status-seeking behaviors after social status has been questioned or threatened (after losing a battle or competition of social dominance) (Josephs et al., 2003, 2006). Testosterone also underlies the mating effort—the investment of time and energy into same-sex competition and mate-seeking behavior (Ellison, 2001). Unmarried men, for instance, have higher testosterone levels than do married men (Gray et al., 2004); men who are not in a committed relationship have higher testosterone levels than do men who are in a committed relationship (Burnham et al., 2003); and men who are not fathers have higher testosterone than do men who are fathers (Gray et al., 2002). High levels of testosterone are associated with having affairs, while low levels are associated with better parenting (e.g., higher nurturance).

Oxytocin, known as the bonding (or even love) hormone, is often referred to as the "tend and befriend stress response" that helps explain why people seek counsel and confide in friends during the stressful events in their lives. Oxytocin increases the salience or attention-getting qualities of social-interpersonal cues, such as emotion recognition and empathy (Bartz, Zaki, Bolger, & Ochsner, 2011), and it is associated with social engagement and the seeking of sociability that can calm and suppress arousal, stress, and depression (Heinrichs, Bumgartner, Kirschbaum, & Ehlert, 2003). Oxytocin also supports the formation and maintenance of attachment bonds between people (Lim & Young, 2006), and it boosts social behaviors such as trusting others, being generous, sharing resources, and being cooperative (Kosfeld et al., 2005; Zak et al., 2007). The tend-and-befriend coping response can be highly effective during times of stress (compared to the well-known "fight-or-flight" coping response) as people seek the counsel, support, and nurturance of others. It is the hormone of oxytocin that underlies this tend-and-befriend coping response during times of stress, and this hormone also supports attachments and bonds with those who are befriended.

Other hormones are integral to basic biological motivations such as hunger and thirst, and these hormones will be featured in the Chapter 4 discussion of the physiological needs.

CONCLUSION

A half century ago, a young neuroscientist, James Olds, was doing his routine laboratory work by implanting an electrode in the brain stem of a rat. One fateful day, the electrode Olds was implanting accidentally bent and ended up in another part of the brain. Not knowing that the electrode had bent, Olds stimulated the rat and watched with amazement as the rat suddenly repeated its behavior and continued enthusiastically to return to the part of the cage where the earlier electrical brain stimulation occurred. The rat liked the stimulation. In fact, the rat *really* liked the stimulation. Follow-up studies showed that animals given the opportunity to stimulate themselves would do so and they would do so repeatedly and with enthusiasm (by pressing a lever that would send an electrical current to their own brain; see Figure 3.9). Olds's research would soon confirm that he had accidentally discovered a pleasure center in the rat's brain (Olds & Milner, 1954).

Researchers soon began bending their electric probes intentionally as they started the field of neuroscience down its path toward understanding the neural basis of reward, pleasure, and aversion (Hoebel, 1976; Olds & Fobes, 1981; Wise & Bozarth, 1984). These efforts to map out the motivational significance of specific brain structures and interconnected neural pathways allowed researchers to understand how the brain creates, maintains, and regulates motivation, emotion, and mood. To summarize the half-century of work since Olds' initial discovery, Figure 3.10 offers a figural representation of the current neuroscientific understanding of reward-based motivated action. As shown on the left side of Figure 3.10, the subcortical and cortical brain structures interact reciprocally with each other, and both feed-forward projections into and receive feedback from the dopamine system; as shown on the right side of Figure 3.10, the dopamine system energizes, directs, and sustains motivated action.

SUMMARY

When thinking about the brain, most people focus their attention on its cognitive and intellectual functions, including thinking, learning, and decision making. But it is more—it is also a motivated and an emotional brain. It generates wants, appetites, urges, needs, reward, cravings, desires, pleasure, feelings, mood, and the full range of the emotions. The neuroscience of motivation and emotion focus on understanding how environmental objects and day-to-day events activate specific brain structures and how these specific brain structures, in turn, are associated with the motivational and emotional states that energize, direct, and sustain behavior.

At a general level, the motivated and emotional brain consists of an outer cortical brain and an inner subcortical brain. The subcortical brain is associated with basic urges and

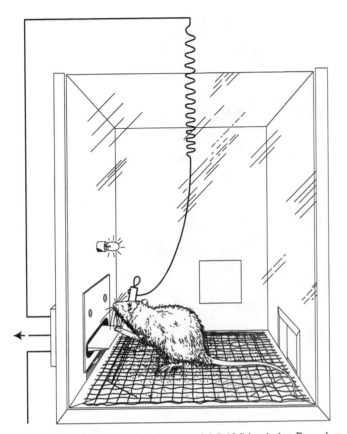

Figure 3.9   Illustration of the Intracranial Self-Stimulation Procedure

Note: When the rat presses down on the lever, the lever press activates a microswitch to send a mild electrical impulse through the wire into the rat's brain via an implanted electrode. With such a procedure, the rat has the means to deliver self-induced stimulation to its brain.

Source: From *Pleasure Centers in the Brain*, by J. Olds, 1956, *Scientific American, 195*, 105–106.

impulses and with emotion-rich motivations such as hunger, thirst, anger, fear, anxiety, pleasure, desire, reward, and wanting. These urges and emotions are largely unconscious, automatic, and impulsive. The cortical brain is associated with cognitively rich motivations such as goals, plans, strategies, values, and beliefs about the self. The mental events are largely conscious, deliberate, and revolve around cognitive or executive control. Both the cortical and subcortical brain features many individual structures, but it is important to note that these individual structures are linked together by a network of neural pathways. That is, almost all individual brain structures project out nerve fibers that act as information superhighways to communicate reciprocally with other brain structures. The overall picture of brain function is therefore not one in which individual brain structures are associated with individual functions (e.g., the amygdala does this, the nucleus accumbens does that) but, rather, one of interconnectivity and the brain working in a highly integrated way.

Eight subcortical brain structures are closely involved in motivation and emotional states. The reticular formation regulates arousal, alertness, and the neural process of

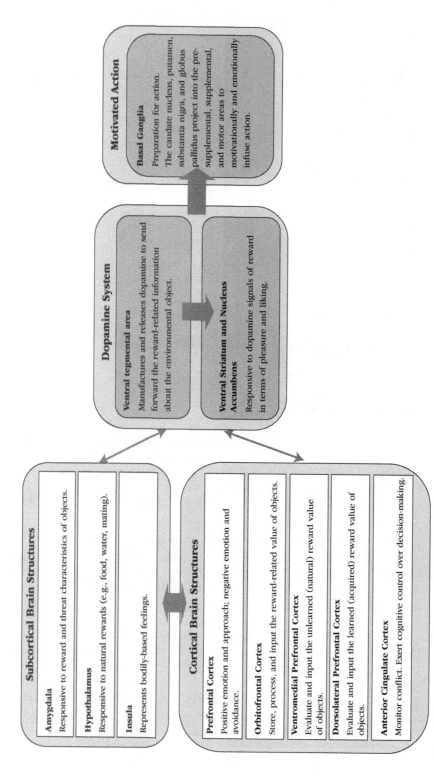

Figure 3.10 Neural Core of Dopamine-Centric Reward-Based Motivated Action

awakening the brain's motivational and emotional concerns. The amygdala detects, learns about, and responds to the stimulus properties of environmental objects, including both threat-eliciting and reward-eliciting associations. The basal ganglia (caudate nucleus, putamen, substantial nigra, and globus pallidus) contribute to the motivational modulation of movement and action. The ventral striatum and nucleus accumbens constitute the brain's reward center. Together, these two structures respond to signals of reward (dopamine release) to produce pleasure and liking. The ventral tegmental area is the starting point in the brain's dopamine-based reward center, because it both manufactures and releases dopamine. The hypothalamus is responsive to natural rewards in the regulation of eating, drinking, and mating and also regulates both the endocrine and autonomic nervous systems. The insula monitors bodily states to produce gut-felt feelings, and it also processes feelings associated with risk, uncertainty, personal agency, and sense of self.

Five cortical brain structures are closely involved in motivation and emotional states. The prefrontal cortex is involved in making plans, setting goals, formulating intentions. Right hemispheric activity is associated with negative affect and "no-go" avoidance motivation, while left hemispheric activity is associated with positive affect and "go" approach motivation. The orbitofrontal cortex stores and processes reward-related values of environmental objects and events to formulate preferences and make choices between options. The ventromedial prefrontal cortex evaluates the unlearned emotional value of basic sensory rewards and internal bodily states and is responsible for emotional control. The dorsolateral prefrontal cortex evaluates the learned emotional value of environmental events and possible courses of action, and it responsible for control over urges and risks during the pursuit of long-term goals. The anterior cingulate cortex monitors motivational conflicts, and it resolves those conflicts by recruiting other cortical brain structures for executive or cognitive control over basic urges and emotions.

While the nervous system relies on neurotransmitters such as dopamine and serotonin to allow communication between brain structures, the endocrine system relies on hormones flowing through the bloodstream to allow communication between bodily organs, such as the heart. While many hormones are important for motivation and emotion, cortisol, testosterone, and oxytocin are particular important. Cortisol produces an energized stress response when the person is exposed to a social-evaluative threat, such as public speaking or relationship conflict. Testosterone produces competitive status-seeking behaviors when men's social status has been questionnaire or threatened. Oxytocin produces an affiliation-based tend-and-befriend stress response when people seek counsel and confide in friends during the stressful events in their lives.

READINGS FOR FURTHER STUDY

Subcortical Brain

CRAIG, A. D. (2009). How do you feel—now? The anterior insula and human awareness. *Nature Review: Neuroscience, 10,* 59–70.

FARRER, C., & FRITH, C. D. (2002). Experiencing oneself vs. another person as being the cause of an action: The neural correlates of the experience of agency. *NeuroImage, 15,* 596–603.

KUHNEN, C. M., & KNUTSON, B. (2005). The neural basis of financial risk taking. *Neuron, 47,* 763–770.

MCCLURE, S. M., LAIBSON, D. I., LOEWENSTEIN, G., & COHEN, J. D. (2004). Separate neural system value immediate and delayed monetary rewards. *Science, 506,* 503–507.

PESSIGLIONE, M., SCHMIDT, L., DRAGANSKI, B., KALISCH, R., LAU, H., DOLAN, R. J., & FRITH, C. D. (2007). How the brain translates money into force: A neuroimaging study of subliminal motivation. *Science, 316,* 904–906.

Cortical Brain

BECHAREA, A., DAMASIO, H., TRANEL, D., & DAMASIO, A. R. (1996). Deciding advantageously before knowing the advantageous strategy. *Science, 275,* 1293–1295.

SUTTON, S. K., & DAVIDSON, R. J. (1997). Prefrontal brain asymmetry: A biological substrate of the behavioral approach and inhibition systems. *Psychological Science, 8,* 204–210.

GALVAN, A., HARE, T. A., PARRA, C. E., PENN, J., VOSS, H., GLOVER, G., & CASEY, B. J. (2006). Earlier development of the accumbens relative to orbitofrontal cortex might underlie risk-taking behavior in adolescents. *Journal of Neuroscience, 26,* 6885–6892.

Hormones

DICKERSON, S. S., & KEMENY, M. E. (2004). Acute stressors and cortisol responses: A theoretical integration and synthesis of laboratory research. *Psychological Bulletin, 130,* 355–391.

HEINRICHS, M., BAUMGARTNER, T., KIRSCHBAUM, C., & EHLERT, U. (2003). Social support and oxytocin interact to suppress cortisol and subjective responses to psychosocial stress. *Biological Psychiatry, 54,* 1389–1398.

Part One

Needs

Chapter 4

Physiological Needs

NEED

    Three Types of Needs

FUNDAMENTALS OF REGULATION

    Physiological Need

    Psychological Drive

    Homeostasis

    Negative Feedback

    Multiple Inputs/Multiple Outputs

    Intraorganismic Mechanisms

    Extraorganismic Mechanisms

    The Homeostatic Mechanism

THIRST

    Physiological Regulation

        Thirst Activation

        Thirst Satiety

        Hypothalamus and Kidneys

    Environmental Influences

HUNGER

    Short-Term Appetite

    Long-Term Energy Balance

        Set-Point Theory

    Environmental Influences

    Self-Regulatory Influences

        Cognitively Regulated Eating Style

        Restraint-Release Situations

    Weight Gain and Obesity

    Comprehensive Model of Hunger

SEX

    Physiological Regulation

    Facial Metrics

Sexual Scripts

Sexual Orientation

Evolutionary Basis of Sexual Motivation

SUMMARY

READINGS FOR FURTHER STUDY

Y ou see an advertisement recruiting volunteers for a new reality show: *Willpower!* The new reality show promotes itself with the tagline: "How mentally tough are you?" You're mentally tough, so, you sign up as a contestant. During episodes 1–4, contestants face the mental challenge to gain 10 percent of their present body weight. Piece of cake—literally. After all, that is what Renee Zellweger basically did for those *Bridget Jones's Diary* movies.

At first, all goes well with challenge 1, as you gain 4 pounds in week 1 and 2 more in week 2. By week 3, however, your appetite wanes. Food is losing its appeal, and your body seems to be putting up defenses to counter the weight gain. As you look at your dinner, you just don't feel the same. The food is not that appealing, and you are surprised by how uncomfortable you feel as you eat the meal. Your active lifestyle has slowed to a sedentary pace, as you exercise less and use elevators more. It becomes increasingly difficult to gain another pound, let alone the 9 still needed to achieve your 10 percent increase. Still, by episode 4, you gain the 10 percent and prove your willpower.

Now comes mental challenge 2. During the next four episodes, contestants are to lose 10 percent of their body weight. You begin a strict diet. You assure the host that, yes, you are strong and have great willpower, saying "Mind over matter" and "It's just a matter of who wants it the most." While too much food took away your appetite, the food deprivation is just plain miserable! Gone are the body's gentle defenses. This time your body is not fooling around. You feel cranky and irritable. You cannot think straight, because your appetite is constantly at the center of your attention. The constant irritation is getting in the way of your daily functioning. Two episodes later, you realize that you might be in over your head on this one. The more you restrain yourself and the more you ignore your bodily cues to eat, the grouchier you feel and the more tempting high-calorie food seems. This really is willower versus bodily appetites. By episode 8, you have not been able to lose the full 10 percent. You get kicked off the show.

Because of your experience, you think about hunger, eating, and weight control a little differently. Your body seems to have an automated guide to how much it should weigh, and when its self-regulatory guides are ignored or outright rejected, then serious motivational states (e.g., hunger, misery) arise and intensify. The thesis of the present chapter is that biological needs, physiological systems, motivational states, and behavior act in concert to achieve stable biological regulation.

A similar research study was carried out with animals, and the results appear in Figure 4.1. For the first 30 days, all animals received a normal diet. Starting at day 30 (point 1), some animals were force fed (line a), some animals were placed on a restricted diet (line c), while other animals continued to receive their normal diet (line b). Three weeks later (day 48; point 2) all animals returned to their normal diets. As you would expect, the force-fed animals gained a lot of weight during days 30–48 (line a) while the restricted-diet animals lost a lot of weight (line c). With the return of the normal diet

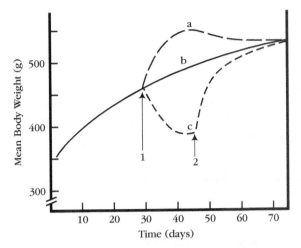

Figure 4.1 Fluctuations in Body Weight over Time for Force-Fed (a), Normally Fed (b), and Food Deprived (c) Animals

Source: From *The Role of the Lateral Hypothalamus in Determining the Body Weight Set Point*, by R. E. Keesey, P. C. Boyle, J. W. Kemnitz, & J. S. Mitchel, 1976, in D. Novin, W. Wyrwicka, & G. A. Bray (Eds.), *Hunger: Basic mechanisms and clinical implications* (pp. 243–255). New York: Raven Press.

(on day 48), the force-fed animals showed little hunger and ate sparingly while the starved animals showed great hunger and ate voraciously. By day 75, the three groups all weighed about the same. That is, irrespective of whether they were force fed or starved, the animals motivationally adapted to their condition, and these reactive motivational states allowed them to return to their normal body weights.

NEED

A need is a condition within the person that is essential and necessary for growth, well-being, and life. When environmental conditions nurture and satisfy our needs, life and health are maintained, growth occurs, and well-being follows. When environmental conditions neglect and frustrate our needs, life, health, growth, and well-being are all put at risk. Need thwarting (no food, no water, no sleep) threatens life and health, halts growth, and disrupts well-being. Because need thwarting is so threatening, the body puts up defenses in the form of motivational and emotional states that provide the impetus to act before serious damage occurs.

Three Types of Needs

Three categories of needs exist. These can be organized within a need structure, as illustrated in Figure 4.2.

Damage can be done to the body, so motives arise from biological needs (e.g., thirst, hunger, sex, pain, sleep, temperature regulation) to energize, direct, and sustain the behavior necessary to avoid tissue damage that would otherwise lead to decay, ill-being, and death. Biological needs are inherent within the effective functioning of biological systems and will

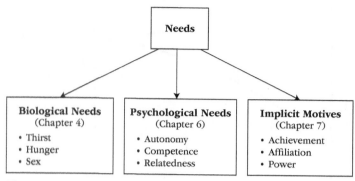

Figure 4.2   Types of Needs

Table 4.1   Three Types of Needs with Their Definitions and Examples

Type of Need	Definition, with Examples
Physiological	A biological condition within the organism that synchronizes brain structures, hormones, and major organs to regulate bodily well-being and to correct bodily imbalances that are potential threats to growth, well-being, and life. Examples include thirst, hunger, and sex.
Psychological	An inherent (inborn) psychological process that underlies the proactive desire to seek out interactions with the environment that can promote personal growth, social development, and psychological well-being. Examples include autonomy, competence, and relatedness.
Implicit	A developmentally acquired (socialized) psychological process to seek out and spend time interacting with those environmental events associated with positive emotion during one's socialization history. Examples include achievement, affiliation, and power.

be discussed in this chapter. Damage can also be to the self, so motives arise from psychological needs to energize, direct, and sustain the behavior necessary to move toward greater growth, well-being, and life. Psychological needs (autonomy, competence, relatedness) are inherent psychological processes within the strivings of human nature and healthy development and will be discussed in Chapter 6. Implicit psychological needs (achievement, affiliation, and power) are developmentally internalized individual differences that people acquire through their unique socioemotional developmental history and will be discussed in Chapter 7. Table 4.1 defines each of these three types of needs.

The distinction between biological and psychological needs is a relatively easy one, because it differentiates bodily needs and physical well-being from psychological needs and mental well-being. The distinction between psychological and implicit needs, however, is more subtle. Psychological needs exist within human nature and are, therefore, inherent in everyone. Everyone needs autonomy, competence, and relatedness, and people are aware of these needs and how their satisfaction versus frustration affects their well-being. Implicit needs arise from our unique personal experiences and therefore vary considerably from one person to the next. Some people experience a very high need for achievement, but little need for either affiliation or power; other people experience a very high need for power but not for either achievement or affiliation. Still others most need affiliation, rather than achievement or power. Because these needs are rooted in early socialization experiences, people are generally not aware of these needs, because they are implicit or unconscious experiences.

All needs generate energetic and persistent behavior. How one need differs from another is therefore through its effects on the direction of behavior (Murray, 1937). For instance, a hunger need is different from a thirst need, not in the amount of energy and persistence it generates but in its ability to direct attention and action toward seeking out food rather than water. Similarly, a competence need is different from a relatedness need not in the amount of motivation energized and sustained but, rather, in the ensuing desire to seek out skill-testing optimal challenges rather than intimate relationships.

Another way that needs differ is that some generate deficiency motivation whereas others generate growth motivation (Maslow, 1987). With deficiency needs, life goes along just fine until some state of deprivation (i.e., it's been 10 hours since your last meal) activates an emergency-like need to interact with the world in a way that will quiet the deficit (i.e., consume food). Growth needs are more subtle. They more gently guide behavior toward a developmental trajectory of growth and well-being. For instance, the need for competence promotes a general desire to seek out opportunities to improve our skills, while the need for relatedness leads us to log onto Facebook in the search of supportive interpersonal relationships (Sheldon, 2011; Sheldon & Schuler, 2011). One telltale sign to differentiate a deficiency-based need from a growth-based need is by the emotions each generates. Deficiency needs typically generate tension-packed, urgency-laden emotions, such as anxiety, frustration, pain, stress, and relief. Growth needs typically generate positive emotions, such as interest, enjoyment, hope, and vitality. These emotions help explain the different purposes behind different types of needs, because deficiency-based biological needs generate negative emotions that grab our full attention until we take the action necessary to prevent decay, ill-being, and death while growth-based psychological needs generate positive emotions that gently encourage us to engage in activities and relationships that foster growth, well-being, and self-actualization.

FUNDAMENTALS OF REGULATION

A half century ago, Clark Hull (1943) created a biologically based theory of motivation referred to as drive theory (see Chapter 2). According to drive theory, physiological deprivations and deficits (e.g., lack of water, food, and sleep) create biological needs. If the need continues unsatisfied, the biological deprivation becomes potent enough to occupy attention and generate psychological drive. *Drive* is a theoretical term used to depict the psychological discomfort (felt tension and restlessness) stemming from the underlying and persistent biological deficit. Drive energizes the animal into action and directs that activity toward those particular behaviors that are capable of servicing (satisfying) bodily needs.

Figure 4.3 illustrates the physiological need—psychological drive—behavioral action process. After drinking a glass of water or having breakfast, an individual experiences a satiated (i.e., full) biological condition, as depicted in (1). As time goes by, the individual evaporates water and expends calories. With this naturally occurring loss of water and nutrients, physiological imbalances or deficits begin to accumulate (2). If the physiological imbalances persist and intensify, then continued deprivation produces a bodily need

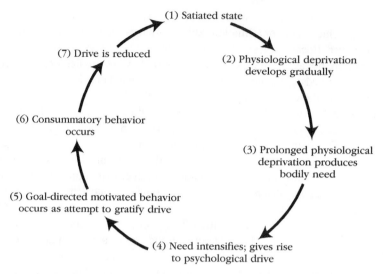

Figure 4.3   Model of Need-Drive-Behavior Sequence

for water or calories (3). In time, the physiological need intensifies enough to produce felt tension and restlessness, which is the psychological drive (4). Once motivated by drive, the person begins to think about and to actually engage in goal-directed action (5). When the thirsty person finds and drinks water, or when the hungry person locates and consumes food, consummatory behavior occurs (6). The water or food intake satisfies and removes the underlying bodily need, which quiets the psychological drive through a process called drive reduction (7). Following drive reduction, the individual returns to a satiated (i.e., unmotivated) state (1), and the whole cyclical process begins to play itself out again.

The cyclical pattern depicting the rise and fall of a psychological drive (Figure 4.3) involves seven core regulatory processes: need, drive, homeostasis, negative feedback, multiple inputs/multiple outputs, intraorganismic mechanisms, and extraorganismic mechanisms.

Physiological Need

Physiological need describes a deficient biological condition. Physiological needs occur with tissue and bloodstream deficits, as from water loss, nutrient deprivation, or physical injury. These deficits range from mild imbalances to life-threatening emergencies. When intense and unaddressed, physiological needs foreshadow and eventually translate into bodily harm and pathology, as someone who is diabetic can tell you (e.g., "I *need* insulin, or I'm in trouble.").

Psychological Drive

Drive is a psychological, not a biological, term. It is the conscious manifestation of an underlying unconscious physiological need. Drive, not the underlying physiological need per se, has motivational properties. For instance, appetite (psychological drive), not low blood sugar or shrunken fat cells (biological need), energizes and directs behavior. When salient enough to grab the individual's attention, drive motivationally readies the individual to engage in goal-directed thoughts and behaviors that are capable of yielding drive reduction.

Homeostasis

Bodily systems show a remarkable capacity for maintaining a steady state of equilibrium. This is true even as these systems perform their functions and are exposed to widely differing and stressful environmental conditions. *Homeostasis* is the term that describes the body's tendency to maintain a stable internal state. The bloodstream, for instance, shows a remarkable constancy in its level of water, salt, sugar, calcium, oxygen, temperature, acidity, proteins, and fats (Cannon, 1932; Dempsey, 1951). People constantly face changing external and internal environments, however, and the mere passage of time can bring conditions of deprivation. Or, people eat, drink, and sleep to excess. Hence, bodily systems are inevitably and continually displaced from homeostasis either by changes in environmental conditions or by one's own consummatory behaviors. Homeostasis is essentially the body's ability to return a system (i.e., bloodstream) to its basal state. To do so, people take compensatory action, and the reason they take compensatory action is that they are motivated by drive to do so. Thus, the body has both a tendency to maintain a steady state as well as the motivational means to do so.

Negative Feedback

Negative feedback refers to homeostasis' physiological stop system (Mook, 1988). People eat and sleep but only until they are no longer hungry or sleepy. While drive activates behavior, negative feedback stops it.

Without feedback and without a way of inhibiting drive-motivated behavior once the underlying need was satiated, human beings would be like the fabled sorcerer's apprentice (from Dukas's poem popularized by Walt Disney's *Fantasia*; Cofer & Appley, 1964). As the story goes, the apprentice, by imitating the sorcerer, learned how to command a broom to bring a bucket of water. The broom obeyed and brought the apprentice a bucket of water. After several buckets, the apprentice had enough water, but the broom continued to bring bucket after bucket after bucket. Most regrettably, the apprentice forgot to learn how to command the broom to quit bringing water. Were the body unable to turn off drive, bodily disaster would result. If people were unable to shut off hunger, they might literally eat themselves to ill-being and death.

Negative feedback systems actually signal satiety well before the physiological need is fully replenished (Adolph, 1980). At first, people eat and drink rapidly, but the rate of eating and drinking decreases quickly over the course of a meal (Spitzer & Rodin, 1981). As people digest food and water, the body displays an amazing aptitude to estimate how much of the food or water, when transformed and transplanted, will be needed to gratify the underlying physiological need. During drinking, for example, the body continuously monitors the volume of fluid ingested on each swallow and it uses that information to predict (unconsciously and automatically) how much water will eventually make its way into the bloodstream and bodily cells. Understanding precisely how the body signals satiety constitutes the study of negative feedback systems.

Multiple Inputs/Multiple Outputs

Drive has multiple inputs, or means of activation. One can feel thirsty, for example, after sweating, eating salty foods, or donating blood, or even at a particular time of day. In much the same way, satiety has multiple outlets, or behavioral responses. When cold, a person can shiver the musculature, put on a jacket, turn up the furnace, or engage in vigorous exercise. Each of these behaviors achieves the same end result—a raised body temperature. The basic idea is that drive arises from a number of different sources (inputs) and motivates a number of different goal-directed behaviors (outputs) until satiety occurs.

The convergence of multiple inputs with multiple outputs, shown in Figure 4.4, is actually what makes drive such an appealing motivational construct. In theoretical terms, drive is an intervening variable, one that integrates the relationships among several otherwise diverse input and output variables (Miller, 1971). Drive is the unobservable motivational concept that stands between ("intervenes" between) observable causes and observable behaviors.

Pain as an intervening variable helps explain what is common among the motivational processes that occur immediately after, for instance, a hammer strikes the hand (Antecedent 1 in the figure), a hand touches the hot stove (Antecedent 2), or a bare foot scrapes across a nail (Antecedent 3) to the time that the person shakes his or her hand frantically (Consequence 1), pours cold water over his or her hand (Consequence 2), or hops around on one foot (Consequence 3). Drive, therefore, intervenes between states of deprivation (input stimuli) and restorative goal-directed actions (output responses).

Consider the theoretical advantage of using drive as an intervening variable for connecting multiple inputs with multiple outputs.[1] Imagine that the three inputs in Figure 4.4 were hours of food deprivation, the tempting smell of fresh popcorn, and hanging out at a party with appealing food on every table. Now imagine that the three outputs were amount of calories consumed, latency to begin eating, and probability of eating. Smelling popcorn

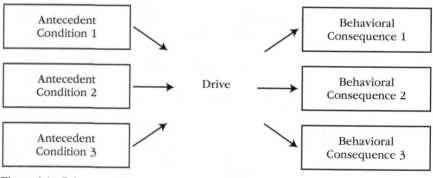

Figure 4.4 Drive as an Intervening Variable

---

[1]The intervening variable approach depicted in Figure 4.4 applies to all motives, not just to drive (recall the theme introduced in Chapter 1). Multiple inputs for the need for achievement, for instance, could be optimal challenge, rapid feedback, and personal responsibility for one's outcomes, while multiple outputs for the need for achievement could be persistence in the face of failure, choice of moderately difficult undertakings, and entrepreneurship.

and attending a party do not cause behaviors like eating a lot of food (amount of calories consumed). We only sometimes eat a lot, and we only sometimes eat quickly. Our motivated behavior depends on the intensity of our hunger (drive), not on the lure of popcorn or on the easy availability of the food. For this reason, motivation psychologists focus on the motivational properties of the intervening variable (drive), rather than on the potential motivational properties of hundreds of individual inputs to drive (hours of deprivation, smell of popcorn, plentiful food, and so on). When you consider what motivates the cluster of behaviors on the right side of Figure 4.4, it is not so much what is happening in the environment (the various antecedent conditions) as it is what is happening in terms of motivation (intensity level of drive).

Intraorganismic Mechanisms

Intraorganismic mechanisms include all the biological regulatory systems within the person that act in concert to activate, maintain, and terminate the biological needs that underlie drive. Brain structures, the endocrine system, and bodily organs constitute the three main categories of intraorganismic mechanisms. For hunger, the principal intraorganismic mechanisms include the hypothalamus (brain structure); glucose and insulin hormones (endocrine system); and the stomach, liver, and pancreas (bodily organs). Together, these bodily mechanisms interact and affect one another in ways that create, maintain, and terminate psychological experience. The study of intraorganismic mechanisms is the study of how internal physiological events cause biological need.

Extraorganismic Mechanisms

Extraorganismic mechanisms include all the environmental influences that play a part in activating, maintaining, and terminating psychological drive. The principal categories of extraorganismic mechanisms are cognitive, environmental, social, and cultural influences. For hunger, extraorganismic influences include beliefs about calories and goals for losing weight (cognitive influences), the smell of food and the time of day (environmental influences), the presence of others and peer pressure to eat or not (social influences), and sex roles and cultural ideals about desirable and undesirable body shapes (cultural influences). The study of extraorganismic mechanisms is the study of how cognitive, environmental, social, and cultural events cause biological need.

The Homeostatic Mechanism

Figure 4.5 graphically represents the homeostatic mechanism, or the "wisdom of the body" (to quote Walter Cannon, 1932). Whether the homeostatic state is the body's water, glucose, or nutrient level, intraorganismic mechanisms engage in an ongoing process of error detection in which rising internal conditions produce negative feedback and satiety or falling internal conditions produce need, drive, and behavioral restoration (multiple outputs). The purpose of Figure 4.5 is both to represent graphically the homeostatic mechanism and to illustrate the interrelations among the seven core regulatory processes of need, drive, homeostasis, negative feedback, multiple inputs/multiple outputs, intraorganismic mechanisms, and extraorganismic mechanisms.

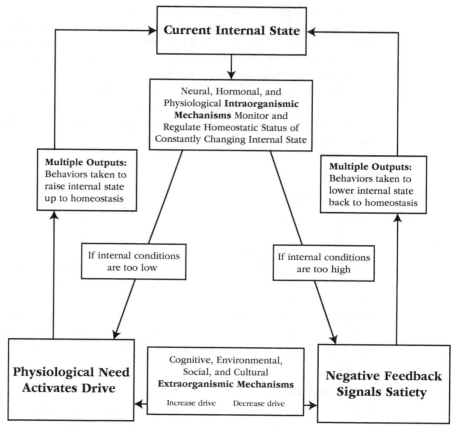

Figure 4.5   The Homeostatic Mechanism

THIRST

Our bodies are about two-thirds water. When our water volume falls by about 2 percent, we feel thirsty. Dehydration occurs with a 3 percent loss of water volume (Weinberg & Minaker, 1995). It is the loss of water below an optimal homeostatic level that creates the biological need that is psychological thirst. We lose water constantly through perspiration, urination, breathing, and even through bleeding, vomiting, and sneezing (i.e., multiple inputs). Without water replenishment, each of us would die in about two days. If you have ever gone more than 24 hours without any water, then you know that the body has reliable and effective intraorganismic mechanisms to grab your attention—your full attention—and motivate goal-directed behaviors to find and consume some water.

Physiological Regulation

The water inside the human body lies in both intracellular and extracellular fluids. The intracellular fluid consists of all the water inside the cells (approximately 40 percent of body weight). The extracellular fluid consists of all the water outside the cells in blood plasma and interstitial fluid (approximately 20 percent of body weight).

Water is water no matter where it is in the body, but the differentiation is important because thirst arises from these two distinct sources. Because thirst arises from both intracellular and extracellular deficits, physiologists endorse the *double-depletion model* of thirst activation (Epstein, 1973). When the intracellular fluid needs replenishment, *osmometric thirst* arises. Cellular dehydration causes osmometric thirst, and cellular hydration stops it. When the extracellular fluid needs replenishment (e.g., after bleeding or vomiting), *volumetric thirst* arises. Hypovolemia (reduction of plasma volume) causes volumetric thirst, and hypervolemia stops it.

Thirst Activation

Consider the standard water deprivation study. Laboratory animals are deprived of water but not food for about 24 hours (Rolls, Wood, & Rolls, 1980). After depriving the animals of water, researchers selectively replace either the intracellular or the extracellular water (using special infusion techniques). The procedure yields three conditions: (1) intracellular replenishment only, (2) extracellular replenishment only, and (3) no replenishment (a control group). The amount of water drunk by animals in the third (control) group serves as a standard of normal thirst. Animals that received full replenishment of their extracellular fluids drank just a bit less than did the animals that received no replenishment at all. That is, they drank as if they were still very thirsty. Animals that received replenishment of their intracellular fluid drank much less. That is, they drank as if they were mostly full. These results suggest that osmometric thirst is the primary cause of thirst activation. Thirst comes mostly from dehydrated cells.

Thirst Satiety

When people drink, they do not drink forever. Something alerts the body to quit drinking. The negative feedback system is important because the body must not only replenish its water deficits, but it must also prevent drinking so much water that cellular dysfunction occurs and threatens death. In this spirit, animals that are not water deprived do not want to drink, and if forced to do so, they just let the water dribble out the side of their mouths without swallowing it (Williams & Teitelbaum, 1956). Humans, of course, often binge when drinking, but such drinking is regulated by factors other than water, such as taste or alcohol.

During drinking, water passes from the mouth and esophagus to the stomach and intestines and is then absorbed into the bloodstream. Through the process of osmosis, water eventually passes from the extracellular fluids into the intracellular fluids to hydrate the cells. The negative feedback mechanism for this satiety must therefore lie in one (or more) of these bodily sites: mouth, stomach, intestines, bloodstream, and cells.

To locate thirst's negative feedback mechanism(s), physiologists devised a number of experiments. In one, animals drank water, but the experimenters arranged for the water to pass through the mouth but not reach the stomach (or intestines, bloodstream, or cells; Blass & Hall, 1976). The animals, on average, drank four times their normal amount of water, but they did eventually stop drinking. Thus, water passing through the mouth provides one specific thirst stop system, albeit a weak one, which is the number of swallows during drinking (Mook & Wagner, 1989): After many swallows (but not necessarily after one drinks a large volume of water), drinking stops.

Subsequent studies arranged for animals to drink so that water passed from the mouth to the stomach but not into the intestines, bloodstream, or cells (Hall, 1973). Animals receiving water into their mouths and stomachs drank twice as much as normal. Thus, the stomach, like the mouth, also has a thirst inhibitory mechanism, albeit another weak one. Other studies allowed animals to drink with water passing into the bloodstream. Pressure receptors exist in walls of the cardiovascular system that allow the brain to know if water levels are above or below normal (homeostatic levels). In another experiment, animals drank a salt solution (Mook & Kozub, 1968). Drinking a salt solution allows much water into the extracellular fluids but little into the intracellular fluids. (Following the principle of osmosis, salty water does not diffuse into intracellular areas.) These animals drank more than normal. Therefore, the cells themselves must also house a negative feedback mechanism. Hence, water consumption does not fully alleviate thirst and stop drinking unless it eventually hydrates bodily cells (Mook, 1996). When taken as a whole, multiple negative feedback systems for thirst satiety exist—in the mouth, stomach, and cells.

Hypothalamus and Kidneys

The mouth, stomach, and cells coordinate thirst activation and satiety, but so do the kidneys, hypothalamus, and specific hormones. The hypothalamus, a subcortical brain structure introduced in Chapter 3, monitors intracellular shrinkage (caused by low-water levels) and releases a hormone into the blood plasma that sends a message to the kidneys to conserve its water reserves (by producing concentrated, rather than diluted, urine). The hypothalamus also contains salt-concentration-sensitive cells that detect above and below normal levels of salt concentration (high salt concentrations correspond to low water levels; low salt concentrations correspond to high water levels). When the hypothalamus detects a low blood volume and a high salt concentration level (both of which are very closely connected to low water), it stimulates the pituitary gland to release the antidiuretic hormone (ADH), which communicates the message to the kidneys to conserve water. While the hypothalamus is managing the involuntary behavior of the kidneys, it also creates the conscious psychological state of thirst that directs attention and behavior toward water-replenishing courses of action. It is in the hypothalamus that the psychological experience of thirst originates, enters into consciousness (by sending a message of awareness to the prefrontal cortex), and generates the motivational urge to drink, which is psychological thirst.

Environmental Influences

For humans, the most important environmental influence for drinking is taste (Pfaffmann, 1960, 1961, 1982). Pure water is tasteless and, therefore, offers no incentive value above and beyond water replenishment. When water is given a taste, however, drinking behavior changes in accordance with the incentive value of the fluid. The incentive values for four tastes appear in Figure 4.6: sweet, sour, salty, and bitter, represented at various stimulus intensities. Using tasteless (pure) water as a baseline (no pleasantness), any taste is slightly pleasant at a very low intensity (even bitter to a small extent). At more meaningful intensities, sucrose-flavored (sweet) water is markedly more pleasant than is tasteless water. Tartaric acid (sour), salt, and quinine-flavored (bitter) water are all markedly more

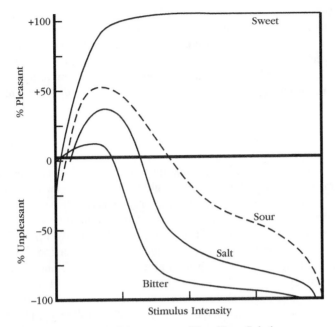

Figure 4.6   Relative Pleasantness of Four Taste Solutions

Source: From *The Pleasures of Sensation*, by C. Pfaffmann, 1960, *Psychological Review, 67*, pp. 253–268. Copyright 1960 by the American Psychological Association. Reprinted with permission.

unpleasant than tasteless water. So because flavored water has incentive value, people over-drink sweet water; homeostatically drink tasteless water; and underdrink sour, salt, and bitter water.[2]

When factors such as a sweet taste offer a high incentive value for drinking, human beings drink excessively and sometimes consume dangerously high amounts, biologically speaking (Rolls et al., 1980). People often drink soft drinks and tea for their taste alone. For water-based drinks that contain alcohol or caffeine, complications via addictions can emerge. Both alcohol and caffeine, therefore, introduce a number of additional physiological processes that motivate people to drink to excess. Furthermore, a number of social and cultural influences surround the drinking of alcoholic and caffeinated beverages that make drinking behavior more complex than thirst-regulated water consumption. Some students on college campuses, for instance, binge-drink alcohol in astonishingly large amounts. Some drugs (e.g., Ecstasy) can also make people feel intensely thirsty and cause them to drink well beyond their physiological need, even to the point of water intoxication and death (Valtin, 2002). Thus, drinking occurs for three reasons: (1) thirst-related water replenishment, which satisfies biological need; (2) non-thirst-related sweet taste, which is a response

---

[2]The relationship between taste and drinking behavior is complicated by the fact that water deprivation affects the perception of the taste of water. Water becomes increasingly more hedonically positive (more rewarding) with increased deprivation, and water becomes increasingly more hedonically aversive with water satiation (Beck, 1979; Williams & Teitelbaum, 1956).

to the attractive incentive value of flavored water; and (3) a non-thirst-related attraction to, or even addiction to, a substance in the water (and not the water itself).

The cultural prescription to drink eight glasses of water a day is another extraorganismic influence on drinking behavior. No scientific evidence, however, supports this advice (Valtin, 2002). This is because food intake provides 20 percent of total water intake while beverages of all kinds provide more than enough to make up for the rest (Rolls, Bell, & Thorwart, 1999).

HUNGER

Hunger is more motivationally complex than thirst. Water loss instigates thirst, and water replenishment satiates it. Hunger, then, might simply involve the cyclical loss and replenishment of food. But, unlike thirst, hunger only loosely follows a "depletion–repletion" model. Food deprivation does activate hunger and eating (i.e., people eat three meals a day to prevent food deprivation). But hunger regulation involves both short-term daily processes operating under homeostatic regulation (e.g., depletion and repletion of blood glucose and calories) but also long-term processes operating under metabolic regulation and stored energy (e.g., fat cells). Hunger and eating are further affected, and substantially so, by cognitive, social, and environmental influences, so much so that an understanding of hunger and eating requires all three of the following: (1) short-term appetite homeostatic-based models, (2) long-term genetic and metabolism energy balance models, and (3) cognitive–social–environmental models (Weingarten, 1985).

Short-Term Appetite

The *glucostatic hypothesis* is a homeostatic-based model of short-term appetite. This model does a good job of accounting for the onset and termination of hunger and eating. The glucostatic (gluco = blood glucose, static = equilibrium or homeostasis) hypothesis argues that blood-sugar levels are critical to hunger—when blood glucose drops, people feel hungry and want to eat (Campfield, Smith, Rosenbaum, & Hirsch, 1996).

Cells require glucose to produce energy. So after a cell uses its glucose to carry out its functions, a physiological need for glucose then arises.[3] The bodily organ that monitors level of blood glucose is the liver, and when blood glucose is low, the liver sends an excitatory signal to the lateral hypothalamus (LH), the brain center responsible for generating the psychological experience of hunger (Anand, Chhina, & Singh, 1962; Wyrwicka, 1988). Stimulation of the LH is important, because its stimulation will lead animals to overeat and, if stimulation is continued, to eat to obesity (Elmquist, Elias, & Saper, 1999).

The brain structure involved in the termination of meals is the ventromedial hypothalamus (VMH). When stimulated, the VMH acts as the brain's satiety center—that is, the VMH is short-term appetite's negative feedback system (Miller, 1960). Without a VMH,

---

[3]Blood glucose is not the full story in the onset of hunger, as people with diabetes will tell you, because they often have both high glucose and high hunger. While people with diabetes have high blood glucose, what they need (and do not have) is high cellular glucose. People with diabetes need insulin because insulin (the hormone they lack) increases cell membrane permeability so that glucose can flow freely from the bloodstream into the cells (Schwartz et al., 2000). In the presence of insulin, blood glucose can then become cellular glucose.

animals become chronic overeaters that double their body weight (Stevenson, 1969). How the VMH gets stimulated in the first place is by the liver's detection of high levels of glucose (Russek, 1971; Schmitt, 1973), stomach distensions (bloated stomach) during eating (Moran, 2000), and the release of the gut peptide cholecystokinin (CCK; Woods, Seeley, Porte, & Schwartz, 1998).

According to the glucostatic hypothesis, appetite rises and falls in response to changes in plasma glucose that, when low, stimulate the LH to increase hunger and that, when high, stimulate the VMH to decrease hunger. Other intraorganismic mechanisms also influence the rise and fall of hunger. The LH, for instance, contains specialized neurons that respond to the rewarding properties of food, such as its taste, and these specialized neurons become activated only when the animal is already somewhat hungry (Rolls, Sanghera, & Roper-Hall, 1979). Short-term appetite also rises and falls in response to nonbrain-based cues, including stomach distensions (Deutsch, Young, & Kalogeris, 1978; McHugh & Moran, 1985) and body temperature (Brobeck, 1960). Concerning body temperature, it is no accident that restaurants routinely run their air conditioners on full blast—because cold temperatures stimulate eating. Likewise, we eat more in the winter than in the summer, not because we are hungry but because we are cold and need the energy to warm up.

The chief nonbrain-based regulator of hunger, however, is the stomach. It empties itself at a calorie-constant rate (about 210 calories per hour), so appetite returns more quickly after a low-calorie meal than after a high-calorie meal (McHugh & Moran, 1985). With a full stomach, people report no hunger; with a stomach that is 60 percent empty, people report a hint of hunger; and with a stomach that is 90 percent empty, people report maximum hunger, even though some food remains in the stomach (Sepple & Read, 1989).[4] One take-home message from this research on stomach distensions is advice that works better than any diet program, which is the 80 percent rule: Stop eating when you feel 80 percent full. This is because it takes a little extra time for the stomach to relay to the brain that it is full (you are actually full when you feel 80 percent full).

Another take-home message is that different foods provide a different feeling of satiety, mostly because they differ in amount of protein, fiber, carbohydrates (sugars, starch), fat, water, and serving size (Holt, Brand-Miller, Petocz, & Farmakalidis, 1995). Food high in protein and fiber (e.g., potatoes, brown pasta) or just protein (e.g., fish) or just fiber (e.g., bran cereal) produce the greatest feeling of satiety (I now feel full), while foods that take little time or effort to eat (e.g., highly palatable foods, such as croissants, cake, donuts, yogurt, and white bread) produce the greatest feeling of lingering hunger (I still feel hungry).

Long-Term Energy Balance

Like glucose, fat (adipose tissue) also produces energy. Just as the body monitors its glucose levels rather precisely, it also monitors its fat cells rather precisely (Faust, Johnson, & Hirsch, 1977a, 1977b). According to the lipostatic (lipo = fatty; static = equilibrium or homeostasis) hypothesis, when the mass of fat stored drops below its homeostatic balance,

---

[4]Deutsch and Gonzalez (1980) further find that the stomach signals not only food volume information but food content information as well. These researchers removed specific nutrients from an animal's food and found that the animal responded by eating foods that had those particular nutrients and refusing foods without those nutrients.

adipose tissue secretes hormones (e.g., ghrelin) into the bloodstream to promote hunger (i.e., weight gain motivation) that increases food intake (Borecki, Rice, Peírusse, Bouchard, & Rao, 1995; Cummings et al., 2002; Wren et al., 2001). Alternatively, when the mass of fat stored increases above its homeostatic balance, adipose tissue secretes hormones (e.g., leptin) into the bloodstream to promote satiety that reduces food intake (Harvey & Ashford, 2003; Schwartz & Seeley, 1997).

Hormones play a critical role in the rise and fall of hunger. Ghrelin is a hormone manufactured in the stomach, circulated in the blood, and detected and monitored by the lateral hypothalamus.[5] Through ghrelin, the lateral hypothalamus receives the message from the stomach and intestines: Nutrients are scarce, send supplies. When that physiological message is translated psychologically, it is a feeling of hunger. Another important hunger-related hormone is leptin. It is manufactured by fat cells throughout the body, circulated in blood, and detected and monitored by the ventromedial hypothalamus (Campfield, Smith, & Burn, 1997a, 1997b; Spiegelman & Flier, 2001). Through leptin, the ventromedial hypothalamus receives the message from the fat cells: Nutrients are abundant, stop supplies. When the physiological message is translated psychologically, it is a feeling of satiety (feeling full; Barzilai et al., 1997).

Consider how this works. It is lunchtime, and some friendly psychologists invite you to join a group of volunteers at an all-you-can-eat buffet (Wren et al., 2001). The lunch is free, and all attendees may eat as much as they would like. But there is a catch. Thirty minutes before the feast, the researchers give some volunteers an intravenous injection of ghrelin while other volunteers receive only a placebo injection. Following the injections, the researchers take a chair, sit back, and watch what happens. What happens is that, while the volunteers with the placebo eat a normal meal, the volunteers with extra ghrelin floating around in their bloodstreams pig out.

Consider a second illustration. Researchers monitored adults' naturally occurring ghrelin over the course of several days (Cummings et al., 2002). After measuring the adults' natural day-to-day levels of ghrelin, the researchers asked some of the adults to start a three-month diet. The diet was carefully designed and included a program of vigorous exercise. It worked. On average, the dieters lost about 20 percent of their body weight, and they maintained their weight loss for another three months. Over this time, the researchers continued to monitor the dieters' levels of ghrelin. Unbeknownst to the dieters, their ghrelin levels continued to rise. Even three months after the diet was over, many dieters still felt "hungry all the time." Why dieters felt this way can be explained by three findings from the study. First, ghrelin rises and falls throughout the normal day—peaking around breakfast, lunch, and dinner. Second, eating food causes a rapid fall in ghrelin. Hence, after we eat breakfast, lunch, or dinner, ghrelin falls rather quickly and rather dramatically. Third, ghrelin was always chronically higher when people were on a diet than it was when people were not on a diet. Hence, the ghrelin level for a non-dieter before a meal is roughly the same as it is for a dieter after a meal. This last finding helps explain why a dieter can feel "hungry all the time."

---

[5]The lateral hypothalamus also manufactures appetite-boosting peptides called orexins (the Greek word for "appetite"; Sakurai et al., 1998). Orexins are powerful appetite boosters, and when injected into the brain of rats, the animals eat three to six times more than control rats.

The message is that diet-induced food deprivation leads the body to generate a potent counterforce against further dieting and food deprivation (i.e., the spike in ghrelin). As one woman who experienced the diet-induced ghrelin spike phrased it, "When I look at a frosted butter cookie, the bells in my head that go off are like standing on the top of a cathedral." From a motivational point of view, the role of ghrelin is to stimulate the brain: "Eat, eat, eat!"

Findings such as these with ghrelin and leptin are very exciting to drug researchers trying to find ways to stimulate appetite, such as people going through chemotherapy (Woods et al., 1998) and to suppress appetite, thus reversing obesity (Campfield, Smith, & Burn, 1998). Unfortunately, leptin administration experiments have not decreased hunger and reversed obesity because animals rather quickly develop resistance to leptin and therefore continue to experience both hunger and obesity even after leptin administration (Myers, Cowley, & Munzberg, 2008). In the same spirit, some food companies seek to postpone the release of insulin by offering low glycemic index foods (this index rank orders carbohydrate-based foods in terms of how much they raise the blood-sugar level), while other food companies offer nutrition bars with a special type of starch to keep blood sugar level constant (to suppress the onset of hunger).

Set-Point Theory

A spin-off theory of the lipostatic hypothesis is the set-point theory (Keesey, 1980; Keesey, Boyle, Kemnitz, & Mitchell, 1976; Keesey & Powley, 1975; Powley & Keesey, 1970). Set-point theory argues that each individual has a biologically determined body weight or "fat thermostat" that is set by genetics either at birth or shortly thereafter. Genetics create individual differences in the number of fat cells per person. In set-point theory, hunger activation and satiety depend on the size (not the number) of one's fat cells, which vary over time. When fat cell size is reduced (e.g., through dieting), hunger arises and persists until feeding behavior allows the fat cells to return to their natural (set-point) size. Hunger therefore is the body's means of defending its genetic set point (Bennett, 1995).

Both the lipostatic hypothesis and set-point theory reflect long-term enduring factors (e.g., genetics, metabolic rates) that regulate the balance between food intake, energy expenditure, and body weight. As to genetics, people inherit relatively consistent metabolic rates (biochemical processes that convert stored energy into expendable energy). People also inherit a number of fat cells and a homeostatic set point for how extended (full) those fat cells should be. While these regulatory processes are relatively constant over time, they can and do change. Set point rises with age, metabolism drops following prolonged caloric restriction (as during a diet), and a chronic excess of food intake can lead to an increase in both fat cell size (lipogenesis) and fat cell number (adipogenesis), and all of these processes can change the set point upwards (Kassirer & Angell, 1998; Keesey, 1989; Mandrup & Lane, 1997).

Environmental Influences

Environmental influences that affect eating behavior include the time of day, stress, and the sight, smell, appearance, and taste of food. Eating behavior increases significantly, for instance, when an individual confronts a variety of foods, a variety of nutrients, and a variety of tastes (Rolls, 1979; Rolls, Rowe, & Rolls, 1982). The mere availability of food variety encourages more eating than does a monotonous diet (Sclafani & Springer, 1976). Even when the individual has only one type of food (e.g., ice cream), variety in the number of flavors available increases food intake (Beatty, 1982). Food availability (e.g., a lot of different foods sitting out on a table at a party) and large portion sizes also lead people to overeat (Hill & Peters, 1998). For food availability, for instance, people nibble here and there when a lot of different foods are sitting out on a table at a party. Each new food brings a new taste, and hence can initiate eating in a way that is independent of hunger. For large portion sizes, people generally eat more when the meal is "super-sized" than when it is not.

Eating is often a social occasion. People eat more when they are in the presence of others (who are also eating) than when they are alone—often 50 percent more (Berry, Beatty, & Klesges, 1985; De Castro, 1991, 1994; De Castro & Brewer, 1992). In the company of others, people eat more, and they eat for longer periods of time (De Castro, 1990), and this is especially true when those others are family and friends (De Castro, 1994). One demonstration of this social facilitation effect involved an experiment with the help of college students participating in an ice-cream tasting experiment. Half the students ate alone, whereas the other half ate in a group of three. Ice-cream eaters also had either one or three flavors from which to choose (a variety manipulation). Table 4.2 lays out the results: Males and females both ate more in the presence of others and in the presence of variety (i.e., 215.6 and 170.8 grams in the presence of three people and three flavors, but only 113.8 and 76.9 grams when alone with a single flavor).

Situational pressure to eat or to diet serves as another environmental influence on eating behavior. Bingeing on food, for instance, is an acquired behavioral pattern under substantial social control (Crandall, 1988). It often occurs in small groups, such as athletic teams (Crago, Yates, Beutler, & Arizmendi, 1985) and cheerleading squads (Squire, 1983), partly because small groups develop and enforce norms about what is appropriate behavior. Deviation from these norms typically results in some form of interpersonal rejection and a reduction in popularity. If eating is an important behavior for the group, then group pressure can become an even more potent eating signal than one's physiology. Another influence on eating is whether our friends are obese. A person's chance of becoming obese increases by

Table 4.2   Ice-cream Intake (in Grams) for Students Alone
versus in Group and with One versus Three Flavors

	Social Setting			
	Alone		Three-Person Group	
	Number of Flavors		Number of Flavors	
	1	3	1	3
Males	113.8	211.1	245.6	215.6
Females	76.9	137.7	128.5	170.8

Source: From "Sensory and social influences on ice cream consumption by males and females in a laboratory setting," by S. L. Berry, W. W. Beatty, and R. C. Klesges, 1985, *Appetite, 6*, pp. 41–45.

over 50 percent if he or she has a friend who recently became obese, and this is especially true with siblings and same-sex friends.

Self-Regulatory Influences

Cognitively Regulated Eating Style

As illustrated by the glucostatic and lipostatic hypotheses, the body defends its weight. Sometimes, however, people come to the conclusion that their physiologically regulated body weight does not measure up well to their personal or cultural aspirations. Rather like a civil war, people decide that it is time for the mind, or will, to begin the revolution to take over and regulate body weight. Successful dieting (in terms of weight-loss goals) requires that the dieter first deaden his or her responsiveness to internal cues (e.g., feeling hungry) and second substitute conscious cognitive controls to supplant, or override, automatic and unconscious physiological controls (Heatherton, Polivy, & Herman, 1989). By dieting, the dieter attempts to bring eating behavior under cognitive, rather than under physiological, control (e.g., "I will eat this much at this time," rather than "I will eat when hungry"). The big problem, however, is that cognitive controls do not feature a negative feedback system. Dieters are therefore highly vulnerable to bingeing. This is so for two reasons. First, we like to think that our cognitive controls and willpower are stronger than our physiological controls and hunger urges. In doing so, we fool ourselves, because we underappreciate how potent and how attention-getting biologically based motives can be (Loewenstein, 1996). Second, environmental events (e.g., alcohol, the presence of others) and our own feelings (e.g., depression, anxiety) can easily distract us away from cognitive control over what we are trying to do. The process in which biological signals overwhelm our well-meant cognitive controls (to the point in which our cognitive controls literally collapse) can be understood by the phenomenon of restraint-release.

Restraint-Release Situations

Under conditions of anxiety, stress, alcohol, depression, or exposure to high-calorie foods, dieters become increasingly susceptible to disinhibition (or "restraint release") of their cognitively regulated eating style (Greeno & Wing, 1994; Polivy & Herman, 1983, 1985). One study, for example, found that people on a diet ate less ice cream than people not dieting, as you would expect, but dieters actually ate more than nondieters when everyone first drank a 15-ounce milk-shake. After the dieters drank the high-calorie food, they became increasingly vulnerable to bingeing (Herman, Polivy, & Esses, 1987), a phenomenon known as restraint release and a pattern of bingeing described as counterregulation (Polivy & Herman, 1985). For dieters, there is truth in the advertising slogan, "You can't eat just one." Similarly, fasting rarely works because it is associated with a major reduction in energy expended (less activity, less motivation to be physically active), decreased metabolism, and fragile cognitive controls that are dangerously vulnerable to restraint release (Lowe, 1993). It is ironic, but dieting and fasting paradoxically create ripe conditions for binge eating.

Counterregulation describes the paradoxical pattern displayed by dieters who generally eat very little yet who eat very much after consuming a high-calorie "preload" (Herman & Mack, 1975; Polivy, 1976; Ruderman & Wilson, 1979; Spencer & Fremouw, 1979; Woody,

Costanzo, Leifer, & Conger, 1981). But consuming high-calorie food is only one of many conditions that unleash the floodgate that is a dieter's bingeing. Depression can also trigger a dieter's restraint release. For instance, depressed dieters typically gain weight, whereas people who are not dieting and are depressed typically lose weight (Polivy & Herman, 1976a). The same pattern holds for anxiety, because anxious dieters eat more than anxious people who are not dieting (Baucom & Aiken, 1981). Stressors produce this same paradoxical effect in which restrained eaters eat more than do unrestrained eaters (e.g., failing at an easy task, speaking before an evaluative audience; Heatherton, Herman, & Polivy, 1991). Alcohol has this same restraint-release effect on dieters as well (Polivy & Herman, 1976b). Taken as a whole, research on social facilitation, social pressure, and restraint-release documents that eating behavior can and often does move away from physiological regulation and toward some type of counterproductive nonphysiological regulation, such as social, cognitive, or emotional regulation (Polivy & Herman, 1985).

Weight Gain and Obesity

Obesity is a medical term that describes a state of increased body weight (adipose tissue) that is of sufficient magnitude to produce adverse health consequences, including an increased risk of heart disease, diabetes, respiratory problems, some cancers, and premature death (Stevens et al., 1998). A whopping 65 percent of American adults are overweight, with 35 percent of all adults qualifying as obese or as morbidly obese (World Health Organization, 2012). Unfortunately, little or no research supports the claim that weight loss produces health benefits (Blackburn, 1995), because the cure for obesity (i.e., weight loss) might very well be worse than the condition itself (Kassirer & Angell, 1998). Therefore, most obesity researchers emphasize prevention (adults in their 20s and 30s often gain a lot of weight) and the cultivation of a healthier lifestyle that centers on exercise (see Box 4) and healthy eating (Otis & Pelletier, 2008).

Other than surgery (see Cummings et al., 2001), the only ways people can prevent or reverse weight gain and obesity are to decrease eating through self-regulatory strategies (e.g., goals, monitoring eating), becoming aware of and monitoring the environmental influences that affect eating, and increasing physical activity to expend calories and fat stores. These three motivations—self-regulation of food intake, mindfulness over one's environmental influences, and exercise motivation—represent voluntary behaviors rather than physiological regulatory processes. Physiological regulatory processes (as described above) affect hunger motivation, and hunger motivation is notoriously difficult to gain conscious control over (see the section entitled "Restraint Release"). The optimistic point to make is that voluntary behaviors such as self-regulation, mindfulness, and exercising are not so difficult to gain conscious control over. So motivating oneself to regulate body weight can be effective to the extent that the person focuses his or her motivation on self-regulation, mindfulness, and exercising.

Comprehensive Model of Hunger

A comprehensive model of hunger that combines short-term and long-term physiological influences with environmental and psychological (self-regulatory) influences appears in Figure 4.7. The two solid horizontal lines connecting hunger to eating represent the

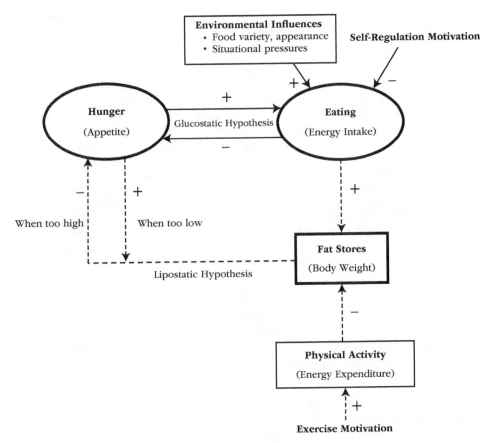

Figure 4.7   Comprehensive Model of Hunger Regulation

glucostatic hypothesis of short-term appetite in which hunger motivates eating (denoted by the + sign) while eating satiates hunger (denoted by the −sign). The dashed lines in the center of the figure represent the lipostatic hypothesis of long-term appetite in which eating increases fat stores while fat stores (when too low) stimulate hunger and fat stores (when too high) stimulate satiety. In addition, physical activity decreases fat stores, environmental influences stimulate eating, and self-regulatory motivation (e.g., goal setting, monitoring one's weight) regulated eating (rather than hunger per se). Overall, the figure identifies the core processes underlying hunger and eating from what can otherwise be a very complex set of relationships.

SEX

In lower animals, sexual motivation and behavior occur only during the female's ovulation period (Parkes & Bruce, 1961). During ovulation, the female secretes a pheromone, and its scent stimulates sexual advances from the male. For the male, injections of testosterone (a hormone) can further increase his sexual behavior. Hence, in the lower animals,

BOX 4   *Obesity Therapy: Reversing Self-Regulation Failure*

Question: Why is this information important?

Answer: Because obesity is a national epidemic.

Body weight and obesity are a lot like the weather: Everybody talks about it, but no one seems to do much about it. One reason people are talking so much about obesity is because it has become a national epidemic in the United States and is threatening to become a global epidemic (World Health Organization, 2012). Among adults in the United States, two-thirds are overweight. Currently, 38 percent of the U.S. population is obese, and that compares to rates of 35 percent in 2006, 33 percent in 1997, 23 percent in 1995, 15 percent in 1980, 14 percent in 1974, and 13 percent in 1962. As you can see, the rates of obesity are rising rapidly (Flegel, Carroll, Kucznarski, & Johnson, 1998; Taubes, 1998). Between 1980 and 2008, obesity rates doubled worldwide and tripled in the United States. Southeast Asia has the lowest obesity problem, by the way, with 14 percent overweight and 3 percent obese (World Health Organization, 2012).

These numbers are based on the measure of body mass index (BMI), which is calculated by dividing the person's weight in kilograms by his or her height in meters squared. A BMI between 18 and 25 constitutes normal; over 25 is overweight; and over 30 is obese (Yanovski & Yanovski, 2002). By this measure, a 5-foot, 10-inch (1.78 m) individual would be considered overweight at 175 pounds (80 kg) and obese at 210 pounds (95 kg).

To prevent weight gain and obesity, one has to know its origins (Jeffrey & Knauss, 1981; Rodin, 1982). Obesity, which is basically just excess body fat, is a multifaceted phenomenon that integrates both genetic (Foch & McClearn, 1980; Price, 1987; Stunkard, 1988) and environmental (Grilo & Pogue-Geile, 1991; Jeffrey & Knauss, 1981) causes and influences. Some environmental influences associated with obesity, for instance, include childrearing (Birch, Zimmerman, & Hind, 1980) and child-feeding (Klesges et al., 1983) practices, low socioeconomic status (Sobal & Stunkard, 1989), high fat content in the diet (Sclafani, 1980), lack of exercise (Stern & Lowney, 1986), and stress (Greeno & Wing, 1994).

Some genetic factors associated with obesity include metabolic efficiency, number of fat cells, liver disorders, and hypothalamic sensitivity (Hill, Pagliassotti, & Peters, 1994), because some bodies are more genetically predisposed to hoard their fat resources than are other bodies.

Our collective genes have not changed substantially in the last quarter century in which the obesity rates have shot through the roof. Therefore, the primary culprits of the obesity epidemic are a culturally engineered environment and lifestyle that promotes overeating on the one hand and physical inactivity on the other (Hill & Peters, 1998). Environments in the United States offer easily available food (when considered in historical context), large portion sizes, and high-fat meals. Environments encourage physical inactivity by reducing people's requirement for physical exertion, such as through advances in transportation and technology (including television, computers, and electronic games). And, unfortunately, increased food intake and decreased physical activity are inextricably linked, such that the heavier we get, the more bothersome physical exercise, even walking, becomes. For instance, carry some extra weight as you go throughout your day (e.g., carry around a gallon of milk), and you will quickly experience a decreased willingness to engage in physical activity.

Pharmaceutical (drug) companies are hard at work trying to create drugs to stimulate weight loss and other drugs to combat weight gain and obesity (Yanovski & Yanovski, 2002). But these drugs have proven difficult to create. One pharmaceutical candidate is leptin (the Greek word for "thin"), but it does not work because people quickly develop a resistance to leptin (El-Haschimi et al., 2000). Physical activity can, however, mitigate the detrimental effects of overeating and protect against weight gain (Birch et al., 1991). Thus, exercise motivation seems centrally important in the effort to reverse the obesity epidemic. To affect the long-term balance between energy intake and energy expenditure, it is the physical activity component of the equation that can be readily altered and subjected to the sort of intervention programs offered by fitness gurus and motivational psychologists.

sex conforms to the cyclical physiological need → psychological drive process shown in Figure 4.3: Time passes, biological need emerges and stimulates psychological drive, and its ensuing consummatory behavior satiates both the psychological drive and the physiological need.

Physiological Regulation

In humans, sexual behavior is influenced, but not determined, by hormones. The sex hormones are the androgens (e.g., testosterone), estrogens, progesterone, and oxytocin. These hormones rise at times, such as a woman's ovulation period, and fall as the person ages past young adulthood into adulthood and old age (Guay, 2001). At age 40, for instance, men's testosterone levels decline by about 1 percent each year. In both men and women, sexual desire and the hormones that underlie it decline steadily beginning in the mid-20s (Laumann, Paik, & Rosen, 1999) such that the hormones and sexual desire of a 40-year-old are about half of that of a 20-year-old (Zumoff, Strain, Miller, & Rosner, 1995).

Although present in both sexes, androgens mostly contribute to the sexual motivation of males (men have $10x$ more testosterone than do women), and estrogens mostly contribute to the sexual motivation of females (Money, Wiedeking, Walker, & Gain, 1976). Even for females, however, androgens play the key role in regulating sexual motivation, with decreases in testosterone (as with aging) foreshadowing decreased sexual desire and increases in testosterone (as with androgen replacement therapy) somewhat reviving it (Apperloo, van der Stege, Hoek, & Schultz, 2003; Davis, 2000; Guay, 2001; Munarriz et al., 2002; Tuiten et al., 2000).

Men and women experience and react to sexual desire very differently (Basson, 2001). In men, the correlation between physiological arousal and psychological desire is high. For instance, the correlation between men's erectile response and their self-reported desire is very high (Meston, 2000). So men's sexual desire can be predicted and explained in the context of their sexual arousal. In the presence of a sexual arousal trigger (e.g., stimulation from a sexual partner), men show a triphasic sexual response cycle: desire, arousal, orgasm (Masters & Johnson, 1966; Segraves, 2001). The triphasic sexual response cycle that describes men's sexual motivation so well—the traditional sex response cycle—appears in the upper half of Figure 4.8. In this model, sexual desire emerges rather spontaneously from an arousal trigger (given appropriate basal support from hormonal levels), and that rising sexual desire then generates accompanying physiological and psychological arousal (in the form of sexual thoughts, fantasies, and a consciously felt urge to be sexual). Such sexual arousal enables orgasm, and with orgasm the traditional response cycle ends with a relatively quick resolution period that returns the man to a baseline state.

In women, the correlation between physiological arousal and psychological desire is low. For instance, the correlation between women's vaginal lubrication and self-reported desire is low and sometimes nonexistent (Meston, 2000). So women's sexual desire cannot be predicted and explained by physiological need (e.g., estrogen, testosterone) or arousal (e.g., genital engorgement). Instead, women's sexual desire is responsive to relationship factors, such as emotional intimacy (Basson, 2001, 2002). The intimacy-based model of sexual desire that describes women's sexual motivation appears in the lower half of Figure 4.8. Emotional intimacy anticipates sexual desire. It is emotional intimacy (not genital engorgement) that takes women from a state of sexual neutrality to being open and responsive to

Traditional Sex Response Cycle

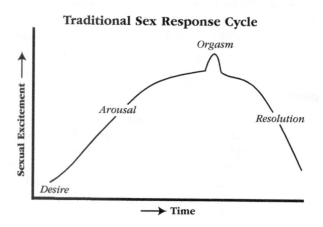

Alternative Sex Response Cycle

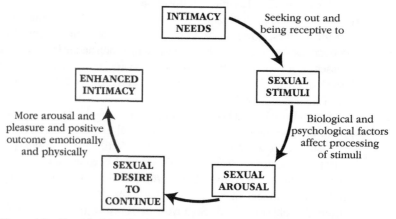

Figure 4.8 Two Models of the Sex Response Cycle: Traditional (Upper) and Alternative (Lower)

Source: From "Using a different model for female sexual response to address women's problematic low sexual desire," by R. Basson, 2001, *Journal of Sex and Marital Therapy, 27,* 395–403.

sexual stimuli. In this context, sexual motivation and behavior reflect closeness and a desire to share with one's partner more than it does an underlying physiological need (Basson, 2003). Sex therefore begins with intimacy needs, not with sexual desire. Furthermore, sexual desire leads to and enhances long-term relationship intimacy, rather than to resolution as in the male sex response cycle.

Desire and arousal are important, but so are pleasure and reward. If sex did not stimulate the brain's reward circuitry, then people might not bother with it so much. Sexual desire is associated with subcortical brain activations in the ventral striatum, nucleus accumbens, ventral tegmental area, hypothalamus, and amygdala (i.e., the subcortical brain's reward center; Chapter 3; Cacioppo, Bianchi-Demicheli, Hatfield, & Rapson, 2012). In comparing desire with love, sexual desire is associated with posterior insula activations (an embodied state), while love is more associated with anterior insula activations (positive subjective feelings).

Sexual behaviors include hand holding, touching, hugging, kissing, cuddling, and the stimulation of reproductive organs, and these behaviors stimulate the hypothalamus to release the hormone oxytocin into the bloodstream. For example, nipple stimulation (e.g., by a romantic partner, by an infant during breastfeeding) is picked up by the hypothalamus, which stimulates the pituitary gland to release oxytocin. When released, oxytocin produces pleasurable feelings that promote social relatedness and bonding. In women, oxytocin is released not only during sex but also during childbirth and breastfeeding, which creates a warm glow underpinning bonding with one's offspring (Lee et al. 2009). Oxytocin release also serves as the biological basis of greater feelings of contentment and calmness and lesser feelings of stress and anxiety, of trust, and of security with one's mate (Marazziti et al., 2006; Meyer, 2007). For both males and females, oxytocin facilitates attraction and bonding to a partner (Feldman, 2012; McCall & Singer, 2012). In males, high levels of oxytocin promote greater commitment to a monogamous relationship (Scheele et al., 2012). For these reasons, oxytocin is often referred to as the "love hormone," although it is more accurate to say that oxytocin release increases trust and decreases fear (Kirsch et al., 2005; Kosfeld et al., 2005). Hence, it is a bit closer to the truth to conclude that oxytocin is the "trust hormone."

In the section on thirst, the advice "to drink eight glasses of water a day" was found to have little empirical support. It is not really good advice. But consider the advice "to have 8 hugs a day." Because hugging leads to oxytocin release, this bit of advice is well taken. Hugging can provide us with a continuous daily supply of hormonal biology that decreases our fear and increases our trust and bonding.

Facial Metrics

Many stimuli arise from a sexual partner—chemical (smell), tactile (touch), auditory (voice), and visual (sight, appearance). The physical attractiveness of a potential partner is perhaps the most potent external stimulus that affects sexual motivation. Western cultures generally rate a slim body build for women as attractive (Singh, 1993a, 1993b). But such standards vary from one culture to the next, largely because these standards are acquired through experience, socialization, and cultural consensus (Mahoney, 1983). That said, some physical characteristics are viewed as universally attractive, including health (e.g., clear skin; Symons, 1992), youthfulness (Cunningham, 1986), and reproductive capacity (Singh, 1993a).

Both men and women rate slim females as attractive. Women's perceptions of male attractiveness, however, have little consensus as to what body shapes or body parts are seen as attractive (Beck, Ward-Hull, & McLear, 1976; Horvath, 1979, 1981; Lavrakas, 1975). The main predictor of women's rating of men's bodies is waist-to-hip ratio (WHR, a measure that ranges typically from 0.7 to 1.0; it is calculated via the narrowest circumference of the waist divided by the widest circumference of the hips/buttocks). Women rate moderately slim WHRs in males as most attractive (Singh, 1995).

The study of people's judgments of the attractiveness of facial characteristics is called *facial metrics* (Cunningham, 1986; Cunningham, Barbee, & Pike, 1990; Cunningham et al., 1995). Consider the face—and its facial metric parameters—shown in Figure 4.9.

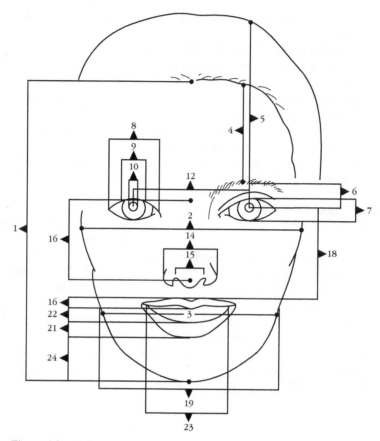

Figure 4.9 Male and Female Facial-Metric Parameters

1, Length of face, distance from hairline to base of chin; 2, Width of face at cheekbones, distance between outer edges of cheekbones at most prominent point; 3, Width of face at mouth, distance between outer edges of cheeks at the level of the middle of the smile; 4, Height of forehead, distance from eyebrow to hairline; 5, Height of upper head, measured from pupil center to top of head estimated without hair; 6, Height of eyebrows, measured from pupil center to lower edge of eyebrow; 7, Height of eyes, distance from upper to lower edge of visible eye within eyelids at pupil center; 8, Width of eyes, inner corner to outer corner of eye; 9, Width of iris, measured diameter of eye; 10, Width of pupil, measured diameter of center of eye; 11, Standardized width of pupil, calculated as a ratio of the width of the pupil to the width of the iris (not shown); 12, Separation of eyes, distance between pupil centers; 13, Cheekbone width, an assessment of relative cheekbone prominence calculated as difference between the width of the face at the cheekbones and the width of the face at the mouth length of the face (not shown); 14, Nostril width, width of nose at outer edges of nostrils at widest point; 15, Nose tip width, width of protrusion at tip of nose, usually associated with crease from nostril; 16, Length of nose, measured from forehead bridge at level of upper edge of visible eye to nose tip; 17, Nose area, calculated as the product of the length of nose and width of nose at the tip length of the face (not shown); 18, Mid-face length, distance from pupil center to upper edge of upper lip, calculated by subtracting from the length of face the height of forehead, height of eyebrows, width of upper lip, height of smile, width of lower lip, and length of chin; 19, Width of cheeks, calculated as an assessment of facial roundness based on the measured width of face at mouth; 20, Thickness of upper lip, measured vertically at center; 21, Thickness of lower lip, measured vertically at center; 22, Height of smile, vertical distance between lips at center of smile; 23, Width of smile, distance between mouth inner corners; 24, Length of chin, distance from lower edge of lower lip to base of chin.

Source: From "Measuring the physical in physical attractiveness: Quasi-experiments on the sociobiology of female facial beauty," by M. R. Cunningham, 1986, *Journal of Personality and Social Psychology, 50*, pp. 925–935. Copyright 1986 by the American Psychological Association. Reprinted with permission.

The questions that link facial metrics with the study of sexual motivation are, On what dimensions do faces vary from each other, and which of those dimensions determine which faces are attractive? Interestingly, different cultures show an impressive convergence in terms of which facial characteristics are considered attractive and which are not.

Faces vary considerably, and Figure 4.9 illustrates 24 different structural characteristics (e.g., eye size, mouth width, cheekbone prominence). Three categories explain which faces are judged attractive: neonatal features, sexual maturity features, and expressive features. Neonatal features correspond to those associated with the newborn infant, such as large eyes and a small nose, and are associated with attractive nonverbal messages of youth and agreeableness (Berry & McArthur, 1985, 1986). Sexual maturity features correspond to those associated with postpubescent status, such as prominent cheekbones and, for males, thick facial and eyebrow hair and are associated with attractive nonverbal messages of strength, status, and competency (Keating, Mazur, & Segall, 1981). Expressive features such as a wide smile/mouth and higher-set eyebrows are means to express positive emotions such as happiness and openness (McGinley, McGinley, & Nicholas, 1978).

Thus, a person's facial features communicate signals of youthfulness/agreeableness, strength/status, and happiness/openness. It is within these perceptions, which are based on implicit facial metric ratings, that a person makes a judgment of how attractive that person's face is. This conclusion raises an interesting slant on the question of whether beauty is in the eye of the beholder. In one sense it is not, because facial metric ratings are objective features of faces that yield pan-cultural consensus as to which faces are beautiful. In another sense, however, it is, because a face is beautiful to the extent that the perceiver sees youthfulness, status, or happiness-openness. It is youthfulness, status, and happiness-openness that are beautiful, and faces just happen to be a conduit to communicate that information about the person.

Facial metrics research proceeds by showing dozens of different faces of men and women (via a PowerPoint presentation) to a group of opposite-sex heterosexual individuals (or same-sex homosexual individuals; Donovan, Hill, & Jankowiak, 1989). The individuals judge each face on a variety of dimensions (e.g., how attractive? how desirous as a sexual partner?), and the experimenters painstakingly measure each face on all the facial-metric dimensions listed in Figure 4.9. With these data in hand, the researchers investigate the correlations that emerge between attractiveness ratings and the various facial characteristics. To get a more personal feel for such an experiment, look at the 25 different faces in Figure 4.10, and you will probably perceive in milliseconds that some of the faces are more attractive than are other faces. Given such different attractiveness perceptions, the question is, Why? Why is one face in Figure 4.10 more attractive than another? Answering this Why? question requires breaking down each face by the 24 facial metrics introduced in Figure 4.9.

Facial metrics predict attractiveness ratings for the faces of women (Cunningham, 1986), men (Cunningham et al., 1990), different cultures (Cunningham et al., 1995), and different ages (Symons, 1992). For women's faces, the facial metrics most associated with physical attractiveness are the neonatal features. Women with large eyes, a small nose, and small chin are seen as youthful and agreeable, hence as physically attractive. After all, there is a reason that every animated character (Bambi), stuffed animal, and Disney princess is drawn with huge eyes, a dot for a nose, and a tiny chin. Sexual maturity (cheekbone prominence) and expressive characteristics (eyebrow height and smile height and width) also add

© Robert Churchill / iStockphoto

Figure 4.10 Casual Smiling Faces - Stock Image; 5X5 Close Ups of Happy, Smiling People

positively to attractiveness ratings of women's faces. For men's faces, the facial metrics most associated with physical attractiveness are the sexual maturity features. Men with a prominent chin length and thick eyebrows are seen as strong and competent, hence physically attractive. Expressive features (smile height and width) also add to attractiveness ratings of men's faces.

Sexual Scripts

A sexual script is one's mental representation of the step-by-step sequence of events that occur during a typical sexual episode (Gagnon, 1974, 1977; Simon & Gagnon, 1986). A sexual script, not unlike a movie script, includes specific actors, the motives and feelings of those actors, and a set of verbal and nonverbal behaviors that should successfully conclude with sexual behavior. In its essence, the sexual script is the individual's storyline of what a typical sexual encounter involves. The young male learns to coordinate his sexual script to coincide with the three linear stages in the sex response cycle of desire (excitement), arousal, and orgasm (see Traditional Sex Response Cycle in Figure 4.8). For females the coordination of sexual script and physical activity is looser, partly because the content of emerging sexual scripts contains little material that is sexual (from the male point of view). The sexual content of the female is more likely to include events such as falling in love (rather than participating in sex).

With dating, both the male and female sexual scripts gain the opportunity of transitioning themselves from independent, fantasy-based scripts into an interpersonal, team-like script. When the couple fails to coordinate their sexual scripts, their sexual episodes will likely be fraught with distress, conflict, and anxiety, and sexual performance is awkward and unsuccessful. But when workable sequences of sexual behavior become coordinated and conventionalized and focused as much on the other as on oneself, the couple's sexual scripts begin to have an adaptive, additive, and reeducative character that brings sexual and relational satisfaction (Simon & Gagnon, 1986).

In addition to harboring sexual scripts to guide their sexual episodes, people also harbor sexual schemas, or cognitive representations of their sexual selves (Andersen & Cyranowski, 1994). Sexual schemas are beliefs about the sexual self that are derived from past experiences that feature both positive approach-oriented thoughts and behaviors (sexual desire and sexual participation) as well as negative avoidance-oriented thoughts and behaviors (sexual anxiety, fear, conservatism, and sexual inhibition). These green-light (positive approach aspects) and red-light (negative avoidance aspects) elements of a person's sexual schema are important because sexual arousal is always a product of competing excitatory (desire) and inhibitory (anxiety) tendencies (Janssen, Vorst, Finn, & Bancroft, 2002).

Sexual Orientation

A key component of postpubescent sexual scripts is the establishment of sexual orientation, or one's preference for sexual partners of the same or other sex. Sexual orientation exists on a continuum, as about one-third of all adolescents have participated in at least one homosexual act (with more boys than girls having done so; Money, 1988). The sexual orientation continuum therefore extends from exclusively heterosexual through a bisexual orientation and continues to an exclusively homosexual orientation. Most adolescents rather routinely commit to a heterosexual orientation, but about 4 percent of males and 2 percent of females do not, and these percentages are higher if one includes a bisexual orientation.

Although not conclusive, research suggests that sexual orientation is not a choice; it is something that happens to the adolescent rather than something that is more deliberate or results from soul-searching (Money, 1988). Part of the explanation for why people develop a homosexual or heterosexual orientation is genetic (see the twin studies by Bailey & Pillard, 1991; Bailey, Pillard, Neale, & Agyei, 1993) and part of the explanation is environmental. Unfortunately, this literature is characterized more by rejected hypotheses than by confirmed ones. For instance, there is little evidence to support the idea that homosexuality emanates from a domineering mother and weak father (Bell, Weinberg, & Hammersmith, 1981) or from exposure to an older same-sex seducer (Money, 1988). The most promising research frontiers in understanding sexual orientation are those in genetics (Bailey & Pillard, 1991; Hamer et al., 1993) and in the prenatal hormonal environment

(Berenbaum & Snyder, 1995; Kelly, 1991; Paul, 1993). For instance, the prenatal (in the womb) hormonal environment (concentrations of androgens, estrogens) predicts adolescent sexual orientation.

Evolutionary Basis of Sexual Motivation

Sexual motivation and behavior have an obvious evolutionary function and basis (reproduction and the survival of the species). In an evolutionary analysis, men and women are hypothesized to have evolved distinct psychological mechanisms that underlie their sexual motivations and mating strategies (Buss & Schmitt, 1993). Compared to women, men have short-term sexual motivations, impose less stringent standards, value sexual accessibility cues such as youth, and value chastity in mates. Compared to men, women value signs of a man's resource, social status, ambition, and promising career potential (Buss & Schmitt, 1993).

Evolutionary psychologists start with the assumptions that sexual behavior is strongly constrained by genes and that genes determine one's mating strategies at least as much as (and often more so than) does rational thought. Furthermore, genes keep the evolutionary message simple: Men want young, attractive mates; women want powerful, high-status mates.[6] Men's and women's different mate-selection preferences appear in Table 4.3

Table 4.3   Gender Differences in Mate Preferences

Variable	Men	Women	Gender Difference?
Physical Appearance			
Is good-looking	3.59	2.58	Yes, greater preference for men
Age			
Is younger than me by 5 years	4.54	2.80	Yes, greater preference for men
Is older than me by 5 years	4.15	5.29	Yes, greater preference for women
Earning Potential			
Holds a steady job	4.27	5.38	Yes, greater preference for women
Earns more than me	5.19	5.93	Yes, greater preference for women
Has more education than me	5.22	5.82	Yes, greater preference for women
Other Variables			
Has been married before	3.35	3.44	No significant gender difference
Has children	2.84	3.11	Yes, greater preference for women
Is of a different religion than me	4.24	4.31	No significant gender difference
Is of a different race than me	3.08	2.84	Yes, greater preference for men

Note: The possible range for each score was 1 (not at all) to 7 (very willing to marry someone who …).
Source: From "Mate selection preferences: Gender differences examined in a national sample," by S. Sprecher, Q. Sullivan, and E. Hatfield, 1994, *Journal of Personality and Social Psychology*, 66, pp. 1074–1080. Copyright 1994 by the American Psychological Association. Adapted with permission.

---

[6]Some differences emerge when examining the preference of homosexuals (Bailey, Gavlin, Agyei, & Gladue, 1994), as homosexual (like heterosexual) males rate the physical attractiveness of their partners as very important but, unlike heterosexual males, they do not show a strong preference for younger partners and are not as prone to sexual jealousy.

(Sprecher, Sullivan, & Hatfield, 1994). The data confirm that, essentially, men find physical attractiveness and youth important in selecting women partners, whereas women find earning potential important in selecting men partners. These data come from asking thousands of unmarried 19- to 35-year-old African American (36 percent) and Caucasian-White (64 percent) men and women the question "How willing would you be to marry someone who … ," which is then answered on a scale ranging from 1 (not at all willing) to 7 (very willing). The table's righthand column summarizes verbally where gender differences do and do not exist.

To appreciate men's and women's different mating strategies, access an online dating service Web site to view the personal ads (Baize & Schroeder, 1995; Harrison & Saeed, 1977; Wiederman, 1993). Men look for something akin to a trophy wife/mate. Likewise, the more attractive the woman is, the more she demands from a potential mate in terms of status and wealth. In turn, the higher the man's social status and wealth, the more he expects in terms of a woman's looks. This same mating strategy preference can be seen during speed-dating (i.e., a series of brief face-to-face interactions with a dozen potential partners). Speed-dating men highly prefer physically attractive women, women highly prefer men with strong earning prospects, and everyone prefers "personable" partners, although these ideal preferences interestingly did not predict follow-up dating behavior (Eastwick & Finkel, 2008).

Although these conclusions are blatantly sexist, they nonetheless represent the expressed preferences of men and women. Such preferences might not be consistent with cultural aspirations, but they are consistent with evolutionary aspirations. However, this sexist mating strategy hypothesis might be limited to only some people. It seems that "likes attract," because women who think a lot about their appearance do strongly prefer men of high status, just as do men who think a lot about their wealth and status are very picky about a woman's youth and looks (Buston & Emlen, 2003). However, when men and women value in themselves factors other than status and attractiveness (e.g., family commitment, sexual fidelity), then they tend to prefer mates with these characteristics as much as mates with high status or attractiveness. Even using an evolutionary perspective, the homely mate can make the best mate if he or she is a great parent to the offspring. Related to this last point, it is interesting to note that while women rate highly muscular men as sexier and more physically dominant, what women rate as most attractive is moderate (not extreme) muscularity, and this is partly because moderately muscular men are expected to be more committed to the relationship than are their highly muscular counterparts (Frederick & Haselton, 2007).

People actually have multiple mating strategies. They consider first the "necessities" and then the "luxuries" (Li, Bailey, Kenrick, & Linsenmeier, 2002). At the "must have" necessities level, men value physical attractiveness and women value status and resources. As they consider possible mates, men really want to know first and foremost that a woman is at least average in physical attractiveness, and women want to know first and foremost that a man is at least average in social status. Both sexes also rate intelligence and kindness as necessities. If the potential mate passes the so-called test at the necessities level, then men and women begin to consider luxuries such as a sense of humor, creativity, and an exciting personality. The conclusion is that men and women possess what amounts to "mating budgets" (men have some level of status to spend and bargain with, while women have some level of attractiveness to spend and bargain with), and these mating budgets are first spent on securing the minimal necessities—must be at least average on intelligence, kindness, and, depending on sex, status or attractiveness—next spent on acquiring a sufficient level of these necessities, and finally spent on luxuries that might make for more interesting interactions but that hold little reproductive value (Kenrick, Groth, Trost, & Sadalla, 1993).

SUMMARY

A need is a condition within the person that is essential and necessary for growth, well-being, and life. Three categories of needs exist, including deficiency-based biological needs (e.g., hunger), growth-oriented psychological needs (e.g., autonomy), and implicit or unconscious psychological needs (e.g., achievement).

Thirst, hunger, and sex are biological needs. The anchor for the chapter was Hull's biologically based drive theory (Figure 4.3). According to drive theory, physiological deprivations and deficits give rise to bodily need states that stimulate neural structures, which in turn give rise to a psychological drive, which motivates the consummatory behavior that results in drive reduction. Then, as time goes by, the physiological deprivations recur, and the cyclical process repeats itself. In outlining the regulatory process for thirst, hunger, and sex, the chapter introduced seven core regulatory processes: physiological need, psychological drive, homeostasis, negative feedback, multiple inputs and outputs, intraorganismic influences, and extraorganismic influences. One concept—that of homeostasis—has dominated motivational neuroscience and its study of physiological needs for the last 50 years.

Thirst is the consciously experienced motivational state that readies the person to perform behaviors necessary to replenish a water deficit. Its activation and satiety are rather straightforward, biologically speaking. Water depletion inside (intracellular thirst) and outside (extracellular thirst) the cells activate thirst. Water restoration satiates thirst, especially when ingested water hydrates the cells. Drinking behavior (that is not necessarily related to thirst) is influenced further by extraorganismic variables, such as a sweet taste, addictions to alcohol and caffeine, and cultural prescriptions such as "drink eight glasses of water per day."

Hunger and eating involve a complex regulatory system of both short-term (glucostatic hypothesis) and long-term (lipostatic hypothesis, including set-point theory) regulation. According to the glucostatic hypothesis, glucose deficiency stimulates eating by activating the lateral hypothalamus, whereas glucose excess inhibits eating by activating the ventromedial hypothalamus. According to the lipostatic hypothesis, a shrunken stomach releases hormones such as ghrelin to stimulate the lateral hypothalamus to generate hunger and motivate eating, while extended fat cells release hormones such as leptin to stimulate the ventromedial hypothalamus to generate satiety and stop eating. Eating behavior (that is not necessarily related to hunger) is influenced further by environmental incentives such as the sight, smell, and taste of food, the presence of others, situational pressures such as a group norm, and the effort to establish a cognitively regulated eating style. Dieting, for instance, represents a person's attempt to supplant involuntary physiological controls for eating with voluntary cognitive controls. Such a cognitively regulated eating style has implications associated with bingeing, restraint release, weight gain, and obesity. One key implication is to learn how potent and attention-getting biologically based needs can be. A comprehensive model of hunger regulation is offered (Figure 4.7).

Sexual motivation rises and falls in response to a host of factors, including hormones, activation of the subcortical brain's reward center, external stimulation, external cues (facial metrics), cognitive scripts, sexual schemas, and evolutionary presses. Sexual motivation in the human male is relatively straightforward because desire reflects physiological forces such as a linear triphasic sexual response cycle (desire–arousal–orgasm), a close correlation between erectile response and psychologically felt desire, relatively homogenous sexual scripts, and stereotypical mating preferences and strategies. Sexual motivation in women is more complex, because women's sexual response cycle is often not linear and revolves around emotional intimacy needs, the correlation between genital response and psychological desire is low, sexual scripts and sexual schemas are heterogeneous and influenced significantly by the hormone oxytocin. Oxytocin, which is released by events such as hugging and stimulation of reproductive areas, decreases fear, increases trust, and promotes intimacy and bonding. For both males and females, sexual orientation is not so much a personal choice as it is a downstream developmental outcome of genetics and hormonal exposure in the prenatal environment.

READINGS FOR FURTHER STUDY

Thirst

TOATES, F. M. (1979). Homeostasis and drinking. *Behavior and Brain Sciences, 2,* 95–102.

Hunger

HOLT, S. H. A., BRAND-MILLER, J. C. B., PETOCZ, P., & FRAMAKALIDIS, E. (1995). A satiety index of common foods. *European Journal of Clinical Nutrition, 49,* 675–690.

KEESEY, R. E., & POWLEY, T. L. (1975). Hypothalamic regulation of body weight. *American Scientist, 63,* 558–565.

POLIVY, J., & HERMAN, C. P. (1985). Dieting and bingeing. *American Psychologist, 40,* 193–201.

SPIEGELMAN, B. M., & FLIER, J. S. (2001). Obesity and the regulation of energy balance. *Cell, 104,* 531–543.

Sex

BASSON, R. (2001). Human sex-response cycles. *Journal of Sex and Marital Therapy, 27,* 33–43.

CACIOPPO, S., BIANCHI-DEMICHELI, F., HATFIELD, E., & RAPSON, R. L. (2012). Social neuroscience of love. *Clinical Neuropsychiatry, 9,* 3–13.

CUNNINGHAM, M. R. (1986). Measuring the physical in physical attractiveness: Quasi-experiments on the sociobiology of female facial beauty. *Journal of Personality and Social Psychology, 50,* 925–935.

HARRISON, A. A., & SAEED, L. (1977). Let's make a deal: An analysis of revelations and stipulations in lonely heart advertisements. *Journal of Personality and Social Psychology, 35,* 257–264.

SCHEELE, D., STRIEPENS, N., GUNTURKEN, O., DEUTSCHLANDER, S., MAIER, K. M., & HURLEMANN, R. (2012). Oxytocin modulates social distance between males and females. *The Journal of Neuroscience, 32,* 16074–16079.

Chapter 5

Extrinsic Motivation

QUASI-NEEDS

EXTRINSIC MOTIVATION

INCENTIVES, CONSEQUENCES, AND REWARDS

    Incentives

    Reinforcers

    Managing Behavior by Offering Reinforcers

    Consequences

        Positive Reinforcers

        Rewards

        Do Rewards Work? Do They Increase Desirable Behavior?

        Negative Reinforcers

        Punishers

        Do Punishers Work? Do They Decrease Undesirable Behavior?

HIDDEN COSTS OF REWARD

    Intrinsic Motivation

    What Is So Great about Intrinsic Motivation?

        Engagement

        Creativity

        Conceptual Understanding/High-Quality Learning

        Optimal Functioning and Well-Being

    Intrinsic Motivation versus Extrinsic Motivation

    Expected and Tangible Rewards

    Implications

    Benefits of Incentives, Consequences, and Rewards

COGNITIVE EVALUATION THEORY

    Two Examples of Controlling and Informational Events

        Praise

        Competition

TYPES OF EXTRINSIC MOTIVATION

    External Regulation

    Introjected Regulation

Identified Regulation

Integrated Regulation

Internalization and Integration

Amotivation

MOTIVATING OTHERS TO DO UNINTERESTING ACTIVITIES

Providing Explanatory Rationales

Suggesting Interest-Enhancing Strategies

SUMMARY

READINGS FOR FURTHER STUDY

Consider three people trying to decide what to do.

The company CEO observes that some employees are engaged and productive while others are not. The CEO decides to create an ABC system in which the top 10 percent of employees are rated as A players, the middle 80 percent are rated as B players, while the bottom 10 percent are rated as C players. To motivate employees, fat raises and generous stock options will be given to the A players, modest annual salary raises to the B players, and nothing to the C players, except a pink slip (a notice slipped into the paycheck to communicate that you are fired). The thinking is that the offering of very attractive incentives and rewards will lead employees to make the motivational adjustments necessary for greater productivity and success. The CEO believes that the most effective way to motivate and engage employees is to implement a company-wide program in which attractive extrinsic incentives and rewards are offered and withheld in a strategic way (based on Byrne & Welsh, 2001).

Miles away, a bus carrying dozens of young men comes to a stop at 1:50 in the morning at the Marine Corps boot camp on Paris Island, South Carolina. Before the men have a chance to step off the bus, a drill instructor charges onto the bus barking orders and giving commands, expecting each word to lead to immediate compliance. The "forming" has begun. For the rest of the evening, the young men will hear as many as 15 commands per minute, such as "Let's go. Now. Move. Move! *Move!*" The emphasis is on heavy discipline, or what they will soon learn is "heavy D." For the next 10 weeks, the drill instructor's commands will be ever present to ensure that the young recruits wake up promptly, dress properly, show proper respect, clean their weapons correctly, and do a hundred other actions the Marine way. Every mistake is met with immediate and severe punishment. If all goes according to plan, what happens over those 11 weeks is that, one by one, a civilian is turned into a Marine (based on Ricks, 1997).

Now consider yourself. You go outside, get in the car, and start up the engine. For some reason, you just cannot find within yourself the motivation to buckle up. But the car manufacturer has anticipated your seatbelt apathy. After a few seconds, a red light first appears on the panel and then several seconds later an irritating "bing, bing, bing" begins that promises to continue until you buckle up. As you sit in the car contemplating whether to buckle up, the red light is on and that irritating noise keeps binging in your ear. If you are like most of us, you too will reach for the seatbelt and buckle up, not in the name of safety but simply to escape from what is irritating (based on Geller, Casali, & Johnson, 1980).

Alluring stock options, loud commands, and obnoxious buzzers illustrate how external events can generate motivational states. These three examples could have been about many other environmental incentives that stir us to action, such as grades in school, frequent flyer mileage points when choosing which airline to fly, or sticker charts and token economies in special education. People do not inherently want to engage in the behaviors required to receive these incentives; rather, the motivation comes from the incentive. Basically, when attractive incentives are at stake, people do what they need to do to obtain the payoff; and when aversive incentives are at stake, people do what they need to do to rid themselves of the irritants. Because incentives and rewards exert such a strong and reliable effect on behavior, people such as CEOs, drill instructors, and automobile manufacturers often embrace extrinsic motivation as a strategy for tilting people's decision making away from apathy and listlessness and toward wanting and action.

Practically every environment we find ourselves in discriminates between desirable and undesirable behaviors. The environment communicates "do this more" and "do that less." Furthermore, practically every environment rewards us in one way or another for performing those desired behaviors and punishes us for performing those undesired behaviors. While driving, for instance, desirable behaviors include staying on your side of the road, driving 30 miles per hour on city streets, and making sure your exhaust pipe is not billowing out a cloud of black smoke. If drivers forego such desirable behaviors, the environment will rather quickly deliver an array of punishers, such as honks of the horn, speeding tickets, and steely-eyed stares from people with pro-environment bumper stickers. As a result, we generally follow our hedonistic tendencies (approach pleasure, avoid pain) and engage in those courses of action that we believe will produce reward and prevent punishment. Over time, we learn which behaviors generally bring us reward and pleasure and which other behaviors bring us punishment and aversion. Following this learning, the environmental objects and events we encounter in daily life come to represent a constant series of either attractive incentives that signal forthcoming reward or aversive incentives that signal forthcoming punishment.

In the other three chapters in this section on needs, motivation is said to arise from inner sources—biological needs (Chapter 4), psychological needs (Chapter 6), and implicit needs (Chapter 7). Biological needs explain why people eat and drink, psychological needs explain why people want choices and intimate relationships, and implicit needs explain why people seek out optimal challenges and try to influence others. To propose that behavior is energized, directed, and authored by inner motivational resources (needs), however, recognizes only part of the story. A person might also engage in these same behaviors out of an environmentally created reason to do so—that is, to obtain extrinsic offerings such as money, a special privilege, or the approval of others. A fruitful and comprehensive analysis of motivated behavior, according to the behavior theorists that will be introduced in this chapter (Baldwin & Baldwin, 1986; Skinner, 1938, 1953, 1986), requires that we add the analysis of how environmental incentives and consequences promote in us a sense of "I want to do that."

One reason why a chapter entitled "Extrinsic Motivation" is included in Part 1 on Needs is because the environmental events that generate extrinsic motivation can also induce within us "quasi-needs."

QUASI-NEEDS

Quasi-needs are situationally induced wants and desires that are not actually full-blown needs in the same sense that physiological, psychological, and implicit needs are. Quasi-needs are so-called needs because they resemble true needs in some ways. For instance, they affect how we think, feel, and act (i.e., affect cognition, emotion, and behavior). Some quasi-needs that affect the thinking, feeling, and acting of college students would be a need for money, a need for a secure job, and a need for a career plan that is capable of gaining the approval of one's parents. Day-to-day circumstances such as shopping, job interviewing, and a visit home create these quasi-needs in us, and these same circumstances constantly remind us of our quasi-needs because we currently do not have the money we need, the job we need, and the approval we need. More often than not, these quasi-needs carry within them a sense of urgency that, at times, can dominate consciousness and perhaps overwhelm and displace other needs.

The definition of a quasi-need is this: An ephemeral, situationally induced desire that creates a tense energy to engage rather immediately and impulsively in that specific behavior that is capable of reducing the situationally induced built-up tension. Examples of common quasi-needs include needing money at the store, a bandage after a cut, and an umbrella in the rain. Rather than existing inside the person as an internal biological or psychological state, quasi-needs originate from situational demands and pressures. Whenever a person satisfies a situational demand or pressure, the quasi-need goes away. When a bill arrives in the mail, we need money; after being rejected, we need self-esteem; upon seeing a store item on sale, we need to possess it; as we age into our late 20s, we need to get married; and so on. Once we get the money, self-esteem, possession, or marriage, however, the situation is such that we no longer need more money, self-esteem, possessions, or marriage proposals. (Some situational pressures, such as a need for money or relief from back pain, however, can recur on a chronic basis.) The fact that quasi-needs disappear once we get what we want, however, is the telltale sign that the need is not a full-blown need. It is not a condition that is essential and necessary for growth, well-being, and life (the definition of a need; Chapter 4). Rather, it is something we introject from the environment for a time that has everything to do with the pressures and demands in the environment and little or nothing to do with the authentic needs of the individual. The proof in this distinction is that any change to the environment leads to a corresponding change in our quasi-need (i.e., if it stops raining, our need for an umbrella fades).

Quasi-needs originate from situational events that promote a psychological sense of tension, pressure, and urgency within us. Hence, quasi-needs are deficiency-oriented and situationally reactive. Quasi-needs are what we lack, yet need, from the environment in a rather urgent way. Thus, the pressured individual says she "needs" a vacation, "needs" to make a good grade on a test, "needs" a haircut, "needs" to find her lost car keys, "needs" a piece of paper to write on, and so on in response to the situational pressure of the moment. The strength of a quasi-need—its potency to gain attention and demand an action—is largely a function of how pressuring and demanding the environment is (e.g., "I just *have* to find my car keys!"). It is this situationally induced psychological context of tension, pressure, and urgency that supplies the motivation for the quasi-need.

EXTRINSIC MOTIVATION

Causal observation of day-to-day behavior suggests that our internal needs are sometimes silent, or at least somewhere on the back burner of consciousness. In schools, students are sometimes apathetic and disinterested in the school's curriculum. At work, employees are sometimes listless and slow to apply themselves. In hospitals, patients sometimes feel little desire to exercise and are reluctant to take their medicines. Such observations suggest that people do not always generate their own motivation from within. Instead, people sometimes turn passive and look to the environment to supply motivation for them. In school, teachers see this lack of inner motivation and, in response, they use grades, stickers, praise, privileges, and threats of doom to motivate their students. At work, employers use paychecks, bonuses, surveillance, competitions, and threats of termination to motivate their employees. In hospitals, doctors use orders, appeals to please loved ones, and implicit threats (e.g., "If you don't exercise more, then. . . .") to motivate their patients. Such are the external events that constitute the incentives and consequences that generate extrinsic motivation.

Extrinsic motivation arises from environmental incentives and consequences, such as food, money, praise, attention, stickers, gold stars, privileges, tokens, approval, scholarships, candy, trophies, extra credit points, certificates, awards, smiles, public recognition, a pat on the back, prizes, and various incentive plans. Extrinsic motivation arises from some consequence that is separate from the activity itself (from a consequence that is extrinsic to—or separate from—the activity). Whenever we act to gain a high academic grade, win a trophy, make a quota, impress our peers, or beat a deadline, our behavior is extrinsically motivated. That is, because we desire to gain attractive consequences and because we desire to avoid unattractive consequences, the presence of incentives and consequences creates within us a sense of wanting to engage in those behaviors that will produce the sought-after consequences.

Extrinsic motivation arises from a "Do this and you will get that" behavioral contract; it exists as an "in order to" motivation (as in, "Do this in order to get that"). The "this" is the requested behavior, and the "that" is the extrinsic incentive or consequence. It is also a "what's in it for me?" type of motivation. Thus, because the answer to these questions is always the offering of an attractive environmental incentive (e.g., get money) or the removal of an aversive environmental incentive (e.g., quiet criticism), extrinsic motivation is an environmentally created reason to initiate or persist in an action.

INCENTIVES, CONSEQUENCES, AND REWARDS

The study of the environmental regulation of motivation revolves around the language of operant conditioning. The term *operant conditioning* refers to the process by which a person learns how to operate effectively in the environment. Operating effectively means learning to engage in behaviors that produce attractive consequences (e.g., approval, money) while also learning not to engage in behaviors that produce aversive consequences (e.g., criticism, rejection). To communicate the language of operant conditioning, Baldwin and Baldwin (1986) offer the following conceptualization of motivated action:

$$S : R \rightarrow C$$

In this three-term model, S, R, and C stand for situational cue (i.e., incentive), behavioral response, and consequence, respectively. The colon between S and R shows that the situational cue sets the occasion for (but does not cause) the behavioral response. The arrow between R and C shows that the behavioral response causes a consequence to happen. Having the attention of a group of friends (S), for instance, does not cause a storyteller to recite jokes (R), but the group does serve as a cue or signal to engage in a class of behaviors like storytelling ($S : R$). Once told, the jokes cause the friends' reactions (C), such that the telling of the jokes causes the audience's subsequent laughter or ridicule ($R \rightarrow C$).

This section is about both sides of the equation above. The first half of the equation ($S : R$) explains the motivational significance of incentives. Incentives are like the "ding, ding, ding" noise in the car trying to get you to buckle up your seatbelt. Incentives solicit, draw out, and even bribe behavior out of people that they would not otherwise freely wish to do—like buckling up the seatbelt. The second half of the equation ($R \rightarrow C$) explains the motivational significance of consequences. Consequences are like the big raises (rewards) and pink slips (punishers) offered in exchange for the work employees do or do not do. Offering an attractive reward in exchange for a behavior makes it more likely that the reward-recipient will repeat that same behavior in the future, such that the reward essentially strengthens the probability of that behavior.

Incentives

An incentive is an environmental event that attracts or repels a person toward or away from initiating a particular course of action. Incentives always precede behavior (i.e., ($S : R$)), and, in doing so, they create in the person an expectation that attractive or unattractive consequences are forthcoming. Some positive incentives might include a smile, an inviting aroma, the presence of friends, and an envelope that looks like it holds a check. Some corresponding negative incentives might include a grimace, a spoiled smell, the presence of enemies, and an envelope that looks like junk mail.

The incentive value of an environmental event is learned through experience. Car noises do not bring heart-stopping fear to people until that noise has proven in the past to be a reliable predictor that disaster is right around the bend. Similarly, the sight of a particular person is not an attractive or aversive incentive until experience teaches us that this person probably brings ridicule and rejection (we learn that one person is an aversive incentive—a bully) or humor and friendship (we learn that another person is an attractive incentive—a friend). It is this learning process (this "conditioning") that shapes our later goal-directed behavior, because positive incentives cue approach behavior while negative incentives cue avoidance behavior.

These examples might appear to confound what constitutes an incentive and what constitutes a consequence. Both are external events that direct behavior, but two important differences exist. Incentives differ from consequences on the basis of (1) when each occurs and (2) how it motivates behavior. Incentives always precede behavior ($S : R$) and attract or repel the initiation of behavior. Consequences always follow behavior ($R \rightarrow C$) and increase or decrease the persistence of behavior.

Reinforcers

From a practical point of view, defining a reinforcer is easy. It is any environmental object or event that increases behavior. If someone smiles while you are talking to her and the steady stream of smiles keeps you talking to her, then the smiling is a reinforcer to your talking. Similarly, if you get a paycheck for going to work and the offering of the paycheck keeps you coming to work, then the paycheck is a reinforcer to your coming to work.

From a theoretical point of view, however, the definition is more difficult. Theoretically, a reinforcer must be defined in a manner that is independent from its effects on behavior.

The problem with defining a reinforcer solely in terms of its effects on behavior is that its definition becomes circular: The cause produces the effect (reinforcers increase behavior), but the effect justifies the cause (increased behavior means that it must be a reinforcer). Hence, in practice, the only way to identify a reinforcer is to actually give it and then wait and see if the reinforcer will increase behavior. Researchers and practitioners, however, have no means of identifying a reinforcer *before* using it. The challenge is therefore to know ahead of time whether the reinforcer will work—that is, will increase behavior (Timberlake & Farmer-Dougan, 1991). To get out of this circular quagmire, the researcher needs to select an extrinsic event never used before on a particular person (e.g., candy bar, field trip to the zoo) and know *a priori* whether it will or will not increase the sought-after desired behavior. In the history of motivation research, each of the following has been used to explain *why* reinforcers increase behavior:

1. It decreases drive (Hull, 1943). Food reinforces behavior because it satiates hunger—it decreases drive.

2. It decreases arousal (Berlyne, 1967). A drug reinforces behavior because it has a calming effect—it decreases anxiety.

3. It increases arousal (Zuckerman, 1979). A rock concert reinforces behavior because it stimulates and excites—it increases arousal.

4. It is attractive to the person (Skinner, 1938). Money reinforces behavior because it is valued—it is attractive to the person.

5. It feels good (Olds, 1969). Electrical stimulation of the nucleus accumbens reinforces behavior because it is pleasurable—it feels good.

6. It makes it possible to do something fun (Premack, 1959). Completing one thing (your homework, a "low-frequency" behavior) makes you eligible to do something you really enjoy doing (your smartphone, a "high-frequency" behavior).

Knowing that a particular environmental event produces one of these effects, the researcher and practitioner alike can explain, in advance, *why* the stimulus will reinforce behavior and, hence, whether it will increase another's behavior.

Managing Behavior by Offering Reinforcers

Consider again a practical perspective. Consider one study that used various reinforcers to encourage an 8-year-old to wear an orthodontic device (Hall et al., 1972). The parents quickly observed that the child had little intrinsic motivation to wear the device, so they sought to create in the child an extrinsic motivation to wear the gear. As shown in Figure 5.1, the parents kept track of the percentage of time their child wore the orthodontic device (five observations per day at random times, such as at breakfast or when leaving for school). Wearing the orthodontic device constituted the desired behavior, at least from the parents' point of view. In the first week (with no positive reinforcer), the child wore the device

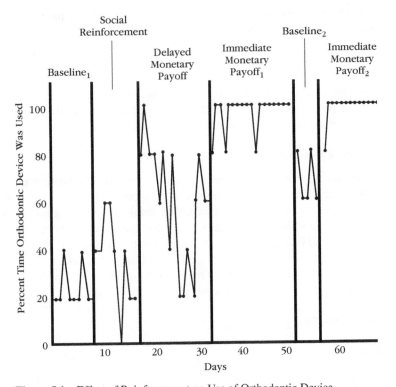

Figure 5.1 Effect of Reinforcement on Use of Orthodontic Device

Source: From "Modification of behavior problems in the home with a parent as observer and experimenter," by R. V. Hall, S. Axelrod, L. Tyler, E. Grief, F. C. Jones, and R. Robertson, 1972, *Journal of Applied Behavior Analysis, 5*, pp. 53–64. Copyright 1972 by the *Journal of Applied Behavior Analysis*. Reprinted with permission.

25 percent of the time. Researchers typically refer to this pre-reinforcer period of time on the left-hand side of Figure 5.1 as the "baseline" measure—how frequently the desired behavior occurs under normal conditions, or how frequently the desired behavior occurs naturally and on its own without the offering of contingent reinforcers.

The parents then began to praise their child each time they saw him wearing the orthodontic gear. Parental praise was the reinforcer for the desired behavior—wearing the orthodontic gear. With praise, the child wore the gear 36 percent of the time. For the next two weeks, the parents administered a delayed monetary reward. Each time the parents saw the child wearing the gear, they promised 25 cents at the end of the month. With money on the line, compliance increased to 60 percent. For a two-week period, the parents next administered an on-the-spot 25-cent reward for any observed compliance. Compliance zoomed to 97 percent. For the next five days, the child received no positive reinforcers for compliance (a second baseline period). Compliance dropped to 64 percent. Finally, for two weeks, the parents reintroduced the immediate 25-cent reward, and the child's compliance returned to a near-100 percent.

This study highlights two considerations about the nature of reinforcers. First, reinforcers vary in their quality. Money worked better than praise. For this child, money was a higher-quality reward than was praise. Second, the immediacy at which a reinforcer is delivered partly determines its effectiveness. Receiving money immediately changed behavior more than did receiving money on a delayed schedule.[1]

Consequences

There are two types of consequences: reinforcers and punishers. Among reinforcers, there are two types—positive and negative. So, overall, there are three types of consequences: positive reinforcers, negative reinforcers, and punishers.

Positive Reinforcers

A positive reinforcer is any environmental stimulus that, when presented, increases the future probability of the desired behavior. Approval, paychecks, and trophies operate as positive reinforcers that occur after saying thank you, working a 40-hour week, and practicing athletic skills. What makes the approval, paycheck, or trophy a positive reinforcer is its capacity to increase the probability that the behaviors of being polite, working hard, or practicing for hours will recur in the future. That is, the person who receives the positive reinforcer becomes more likely to repeat the behavior than the person who receives no such attractive consequence for the same behavior. Additionally offered positive reinforcers in the culture include money, praise, attention, grades, scholarships, approval, prizes, food, awards, trophies, public recognition, and privileges.

Rewards

An extrinsic reward is any offering from one person given to another person in exchange for his or her service or achievement (Craighead, Kazdin, & Mahoney, 1981). Thus, when a teacher promises a special privilege if her students will participate more or when a workplace manager gives a "thumbs up" to acknowledge an employee's successful performance, the teacher and the manager offer a reward (prize, thumbs up) in exchange for another's service (participate more) or achievement (successful performance). Because extrinsic rewards are often confused with positive reinforcers, which are defined by their effects on behavior, rewards and reinforcers need to be distinguished. The distinction is that all positive reinforcers are rewards, while only some rewards function as positive reinforcers (because not all rewards increase behavior). That is, rewards sometimes do and sometimes do not work.

---

[1] In addition to quality and immediacy, four other characteristics of a reward determine what is or is not a reinforcer. First, a reinforcer can be effective for one person but not for another, suggesting that the person/reinforcer fit is as important as is any particular characteristic of the reinforcer per se. Attention and candy might prove effective for young children (and ineffective for adults), whereas a job promotion and stock options might prove effective for adults (and ineffective for young children). Second, the same reinforcer can be effective for a person at one time but ineffective at another time. A cup of coffee might increase behavior early in the morning, but it may prove ineffective at night. Third, reinforcers vary in their intensity. A dollar is typically a more effective reinforcer than is a penny, and a $20 bill is typically a more effective than a dollar. Last, the rewards that administrators (e.g., parents, teachers, employers, therapists, coaches) think will work best often do not correspond to what their recipients actually find to be reinforcing (Green et al., 1988; Pace et al., 1985; Smith, Iwata, & Shore, 1995). For example, a parent might give a child a big hug, thinking the child highly values hugging, although the child might rather have a bowl of chocolate pudding. Thus, six considerations determine a positive reinforcer's effectiveness: (1) its quality, (2) its immediacy, (3) the person/reinforcer fit, (4) the recipient's need for that particular reward, (5) its intensity, and (6) the recipient's perceived value of the reinforcer.

This is a very important practical point to make because people use rewards liberally and often irrespective of whether those rewards actually reinforce behavior. After all, does the teacher's offer of a special privilege really increase students' subsequent classroom engagement, and does the manager's offer of a thumbs up gesture increase worker's job performance? Rewards are therefore best seen as only potential motivators.

Do Rewards Work? Do They Increase Desirable Behavior?

Why do people get so excited about the prospect of receiving an extrinsic reward? Why do rewards enliven positive emotion and facilitate behavior? Six reasons were given earlier in the chapter—because they decrease drive, decrease arousal, increase arousal, are attractive to the person, feel good, and make it possible to do something fun. What all six of these explanations have in common can be understood by returning to Chapter 3 on the neuroscience of motivation. What all behavior-energizing rewards do is trigger dopamine release to signal the possibility of gain (D'Ardenne, McClure, Nystrom, & Cohen, 2008) and, in doing so, activates the behavioral approach system (BAS; Gray, 1990). Environmental stimuli (positive reinforcers, rewards) that increase dopamine generate positive feelings, such as hope and interest, energize approach behavior, direct that behavior toward the attainment of the reward, and sustain that goal-directed action until the reward is attained. Thus, an extrinsic reward enlivens positive emotion and facilitates reward-directed behavior because it signals the opportunity for a personal gain.[2]

In practice, the offering of an extrinsic reward means that personal gain is imminent and that the situation that one is currently involved in has suddenly taken an unexpected turn for the better. Routine and expected life events leave the subcortical brain unexcited, and dopamine release does not occur. However, when events take an unexpected turn for the better (one receives a signal from the environment that personal gain is imminent), then dopamine release and behavioral approach occur as the brain inherently latches onto the environmental signal of the unexpected gain. Therefore, rewards work—rewards increase desired behavior—when they signal in the recipient an unexpected and imminent personal gain. As rewards become routinely predictable (the supervisor gives the same "thumbs up" gesture day-after-day-after-day), they lose their capacity to trigger dopamine release and hence lose their capacity to energize reward-directed behavior (D'Ardenne et al., 2008).

Negative Reinforcers

A negative reinforcer is any environmental stimulus that, when removed, increases the future probability of the desired behavior. Like positive reinforcers, negative reinforcers increase the probability of behavior. Unlike positive reinforcers, negative reinforcers are aversive, irritating stimuli. The shrill ring of the alarm clock is an aversive, irritating stimulus. Stopping the ringing is negatively reinforcing when it increases the probability that the would-be sleeper gets out of bed. In the same way, medicine that removes headache pain is a negative reinforcer that increases the sufferer's willingness to take this same medicine in the

---

[2]This neuroscientific analysis on reward can be considered a modern update on E. L. Thorndike's (1932) well-known law of effect. According to the law of effect, behaviors that have good effects tend to become more frequent, whereas behaviors that have bad effects tend to become less frequent. "Good effects" in a neuroscientific analysis are defined by dopamine release in the subcortical brain's reward center.

future (i.e., removing pain negatively reinforces the act of taking medicine). Additionally offered negative reinforcers in the culture include whining, nagging, crying, surveillance, deadlines, time limits, a pet's incessant meowing or barking, and all sorts of pain.

It is relatively easy to visualize the approach behavior motivated by positive reinforcers. But several examples are needed to illustrate how negative reinforcers motivate escape and avoidance behaviors.

Escape removes a person from an aversive stimulus; avoidance prevents the aversive stimulus from occurring in the first place (Iwata, 1987). Consider how people escape from the sound of the alarm clock by getting out of bed, escape from the car buzzer by buckling a seatbelt, and escape from a whining child by leaving the room. Once we discover which behaviors are effective in removing us from the noise, buzzer, or whining, we tend to repeat these same escape maneuvers when the noise, buzzer, or whining return. We repeat them because we have learned that each is a tried-and-true escape strategy. To prevent the aversive stimuli from occurring in the first place, however, people learn to get out of bed early (to avoid the noise), to buckle up before starting the car (to avoid the buzzer), and to stay away from the child (to avoid the whines). Escape behaviors are reactive against aversive stimuli; avoidance behaviors are anticipatory or proactive in preventing them in the first place.

One illustration that nicely captures how a negative reinforcer motivates both escape and avoidance is the wearing of a postural harness (Azrin et al., 1968), shown in Figure 5.2. An automated shoulder harness to discourage postural slouching sends off a 55-dB tone whenever slouching at the shoulders occurs. Slouching sets off the aversive tone. That is, undesirable behavior sets off a negative reinforcer. To escape it, the wearer must adjust his or her posture accordingly. Noise termination negatively reinforces the escape behavior of thrusting back the shoulder blades. To avoid hearing the tone, the wearer learns that he or she must thrust the shoulders backward. No other postural response will quiet the noise. The motivation to thrust back the shoulders stems not from wanting good posture but, rather, from not wanting to hear that irritating blast of noise. For all 25 adults using such a postural harness in one study, a marked improvement in posture occurred. The postural harness (like a crying baby or a yelling drill sergeant) communicates a nice metaphor for illustrating extrinsic motivation, because the source of motivation (the 55-dB noise) clearly lies outside the individual—literally on the person rather than in him or her.

Punishers

A punisher is any environmental stimulus that, when presented, decreases the future probability of the undesired behavior. Criticism, jail terms, and public ridicule operate as punishers that occur after dressing sloppily, stealing another person's property, and endorsing antisocial attitudes. What makes the criticism, a jail term, or public ridicule a punisher is its capacity to decrease the probability that the behaviors of dressing carelessly, stealing property, and voicing antisocial attitudes will recur in the future. That is, the person who receives the punisher is less likely to repeat the behavior than is the person who receives no such aversive consequence for doing the same thing.

From a behaviorist's point of view, the idea is this: You can engage in the undesirable behavior but suffer the aversive (punishing) consequence, or you can choose not to engage in the undesirable behavior and be spared the aversive (punishing) consequence. It is your strategic choice. That is, you can continue to dress sloppily, steal property, or

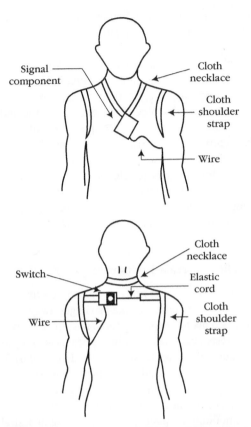

Figure 5.2   Front and Rear View of Person Wearing Postural Harness. The front view in the upper sketch shows the signal component worn around the neck. A wire runs from the component, under the arm, and to the posture switch on the back, which is shown in the lower sketch. The posture switch is attached by the shoulder straps, which are adjusted for the desired posture. Outer garments are worn over the assembly and thereby conceal it from view

Source: From "Behavioral engineering: Postural control by a portable operant apparatus," by N. H. Azrin, H. Rubin, F. O'Brien, T. Ayllon, and D. Roll, 1968, *Journal of Applied Behavior Analysis, 2*, pp. 39–42. Copyright 1968 by the *Journal of Applied Behavior Analysis*. Reprinted with permission.

endorse antisocial attitudes, but you will have to pay the price of doing so (in the form of criticisms, jail terms, and public ridicule).

Much confusion exists in discriminating punishers from negative reinforcers. The reason for the confusion is because both types of consequences utilize aversive stimuli. For instance, when parents yell, complain, and reprimand children for not cleaning their room, do the parents administer an avalanche of negative reinforcers or punishers?

The parent's reprimand is a punisher if its intent is to suppress the child's future room-cluttering behavior. Punishers say, "Stop it!" Punishers say, "Stop what you are doing!"

The reprimand is a negative reinforcer, however, if the child dutifully cleans his or her room to escape from or to avoid the reprimand before it occurs. Negative reinforcers say, "Do it!" Negative reinforcers say, "Do something now so you won't get grief later." Punishers *decrease* (undesirable) behavior; negative reinforcers *increase* (escape and avoidance) behavior.

When most people think of punishers, what comes to mind are aversive punishers. Aversive punishers are *very* commonly used in the culture, but a second type of punisher exists and is widely used—a response cost. Response costs suppress behavior by imposing the cost of losing some attractive resource if one engages in the undesirable behavior. The loss of the attractive resource is a "cost" for the "response" of enacting the undesired behavior. Examples of frequently used response costs include a suspended driver's license to suppress drunk driving, a toy taken away to suppress a child's temper tantrum, taking away a privilege such as watching a favorite television show to suppress ill manners, a $200 ticket to suppress parking in a handicapped space, a $5 fee to suppress using a live teller at the bank, and being grounded to suppress staying out past curfew. While punishers deliver aversive stimuli and response costs remove desirable stimuli, they both send the same message: "Stop it!"

Do Punishers Work? Do They Decrease Undesirable Behavior?

The use of punishers is ubiquitous. To deter and to stop people's undesirable behavior, we criticize, we give cold looks, we complain, we take privileges away, we spank, and we utilize dozens of other extrinsic events to get other people to stop doing whatever undesirable behavior they are doing. But research shows that punishment is actually an ineffective motivational strategy—popular but ineffective (Baldwin & Baldwin, 1986). Worse, punishment reliably generates a number of worrisome and unintentional "side effects," including negative emotionality (it induces crying, screaming, and feeling afraid), an impaired relationship between punisher and punishee, and negative modeling of how to cope with undesirable behavior in others. Overall, not only do punishers not decrease undesirable behavior, they also induce negative emotion, ruin relationships, and teach others to using an ineffective behavior modification strategy.

Perhaps one of the most controversial uses of punishment is corporal punishment, or spanking (Gershoff, 2002). Figure 5.3 addresses the question, Does corporal punishment work? Parents (and others) spank their children for different reasons, but mostly they spank to gain the child's immediate compliance to stop the undesirable behavior. Typically, this is spanking's intended consequence. The first solid upwardly sloped line in Figure 5.3 means that spanking does produce this short-term effect. The figure also identifies a number of unintended consequences of corporal punishment. The second solid downwardly sloped line means that spanking further produces these 10 long-term effects. Children who are spanked are more likely in the future to show aggression, antisocial behavior, poor mental health, poor moral internalization, an impaired parent–child relationship, and, as adults, aggression, poor mental health, abusive behavior, and criminal behavior.

Looking over the consequences of corporal punishment, one sees little merit in spanking as a motivational strategy (Gershoff, 2002). It does yield its intentional consequence (albeit only temporary and perhaps only for minutes), but it also yields a flurry of unintentional, undesirable, and long-term consequences. In fact, a motivational and behavioral analysis of any punisher will yield the same conclusion—it may produce temporary compliance, but it will do so at the cost of a landslide of very developmentally detrimental side effects that makes its use a woefully poor motivational strategy.

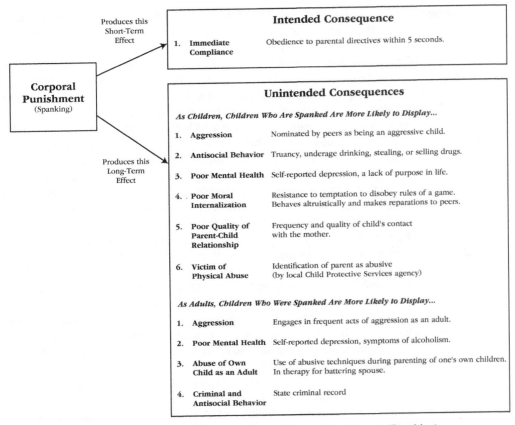

Figure 5.3   Immediate and Long-Term Consequences of Corporal Punishment (Spanking)

Source: From "Corporal punishment by parents and associated child behaviors and experiences: A meta-analytical and theoretical review," By E. T. Gershoff, 2002, *Psychological Bulletin, 128*, 539–579. Copyright 2002 by American Psychological Association. Adapted by permission.

If spanking is not to be recommended, then what does work? In the case of dealing with another person's undesirable behavior, the old adage "Prevention works better than remediation" has never been more true or applicable. Punishment is a remedial strategy. What works is prevention, and prevention works best when the request to stop doing the undesired behavior is offered within the context of a supportive, nurturing, high-quality relationship in which the message is not "stop it, you are irritating me" but, rather, is "I care about you, I'm worried that you are not coping very well, and I want to work collaboratively with you to figure out how to adjust effectively to life so that you will be happy and competent." This latter sentiment concerns a phenomenon known as "internalization" (or "inductive reasoning"), and it will be the subject of the second half of the chapter, but the basic idea is that instead of trying to push aversive motivation onto the person (i.e., punishment) the goal is to transform the quality of the person's motivation away from being unable to energize and direct adaptive behavior to motivation that is able to energize and direct adaptive behavior.

Other preventive strategies are to simply ignore the undesired behavior (because it is simply too difficult to remediate) and, instead, focus on promoting a rival desired behavior to essentially replace the undesired behavior. These strategies include differential rein-forcement (or "catch them being good"), scaffolding (or tutoring in how to cope more effectively), and observational learning (or modeling and then imitating another's desired behavior). These later three strategies are generally effective, and they are effective when the person leaves the role of a "punisher" and, instead, becomes a "reinforcer" (differential reinforcement), a "helpful coach" (scaffolding), or a "role model" (observational learning).

The first tried-and-true alternative to punishment is differential reinforcement, which is a two-step behavior modification strategy in which one first identifies both a desirable and an alternative (substitute) desirable behavior and then, second, ignores the undesirable act (in terms of consequences) while rewarding the desirable act. Differential reinforcement works because the desirable behavior eventually replaces the undesirable behavior, and it does so in a way that does not produce any of punishment's worrisome side effects. Scaf-folding (or tutoring, coaching) is effective in those cases in which the person who engages in undesirable behavior simply does not know how to behave in a more desirable way because of a lack of knowledge or skill (e.g., a novice, a bully, someone who dresses inappropri-ately). Parents, teachers, and others can provide examples, tips, hints, reminders, clues, and prompts—whatever behavioral support the other needs to "get over the hump" and learn a more desirable, adaptive way of behaving. Observational learning is a preventive strategy because undesirable behavior can often be anticipated before it occurs, especially when the parent, manager, or athletic coach has a good deal of experienced-based foresight to know what others undesirable behaviors others tend to do before they do it (e.g., the driving instructor who teachers 10 adolescent drivers a day knows in advance all the unde-sirable things teenage drivers will do even before the teenagers do these things). So, before the undesirable behavior is given the chance to be enacted, a manager can demonstrate and model in advance what desirable and skilled behavior is and looks like. This modeling is fol-lowed by an invitation for the other to imitate and refine the modeled desired way of coping.

HIDDEN COSTS OF REWARD

Okay, punishers do not work. But rewards work, right? To answer this question, we need to introduce another term and another motivational phenomenon—intrinsic motivation.

Intrinsic Motivation

Intrinsic motivation is the inherent propensity to seek out novelty and challenge, to extend and exercise one's capacities, to explore, and to learn (Deci & Ryan, 1985a). It is a nat-ural inclination toward exploration, spontaneous interest, and environmental mastery that emerges from innate strivings for personal growth and from experiences of psychologi-cal need satisfaction. It is the principal source of enjoyment and vitality throughout life (Ryan, 1995).

As illustrated in Figure 5.4, people experience intrinsic motivation because they have psychological needs within themselves. These psychological needs are the subject of Chapter 6. Psychological needs, when they are environmentally supported, nurtured, and satisfied (e.g., "I feel competent doing this task"), spontaneously give rise to the experience of intrinsic motivation. That is, intrinsic motivation is the expression of psychological need satisfaction. As the person fills in a challenging crossword puzzle or travels with a friend, intrinsic motivation arises out of the spontaneous experiences of feeling autonomous,

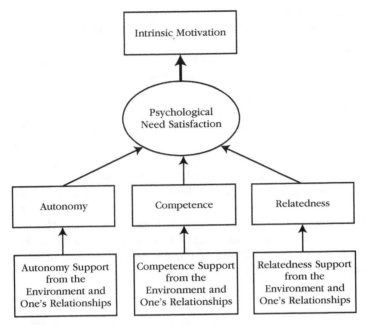

Figure 5.4 Origins of Intrinsic Motivation

feeling competent, and feeling related to others. When intrinsically motivated, the task the person is engaged in provides a steady stream of opportunities for the person to feel free (autonomy), effective (competence), and emotionally close (relatedness). When people feel autonomous, competent, and related to others, they express their intrinsic motivation by saying, "That's interesting," "That's fun," or "I enjoy doing that."

The discussion of intrinsic motivation at this point in the chapter is important because it shows that people have at least two different ways to go about the task of trying to motivate others. One strategy would be to promote extrinsic motivation. The way to promote extrinsic motivation is to offer attractive incentives and consequences to bring desired behavior out of others (or out of oneself). A second strategy, however, would be to promote intrinsic motivation. The way to promote intrinsic motivation is to support in the other person (or in oneself) an experience of psychological need satisfaction—to create environmental opportunities for people to feel free, competent, and emotionally close to others. The benefits of promoting extrinsic motivation are clear—you get compliance and you put yourself in position to manage other people's desired and undesired behaviors (with "manage" meaning that you strategically increase what you view as desired behavior and strategically decrease what you view as undesired behavior). Your child brushes her teeth, your students complete their worksheets, and your employees all show up on time to work. The benefits of promoting intrinsic motivation are not so clear, so a brief discussion of this point is needed.

What Is So Great about Intrinsic Motivation?

When intrinsically motivated, people seek out novelty, they seek out optimal challenges, they exercise and try to extend their talents and capacities, they explore, and they learn.

In other words, when intrinsically motivated, people develop and grow. More specifically, what intrinsically motivated people do is show initiative, pursue their interests, act spontaneously and creatively, strive to learn, strive to extend themselves and their capabilities, process information deeply and conceptually, show greater task persistence, and experience greater positive emotion, vitality, and well-being.

Engagement

The higher a person's intrinsic motivation, the greater will be his or her engagement in the task at hand. People who are intrinsically motivated, for instance, are much more likely than those who are not intrinsically motivated to be active, inquisitive, curious, and playful (Ryan & Deci, 2000a), to explore (Reeve & Nix, 1997), to be proactive and show greater initiative (Reeve, 2013), to exert high effort in the pursuit of their goals (Sheldon & Elliot, 1999), to persist in the face of challenge and failure (Vansteenkiste & Deci, 2003), to persist in the absence of positive feedback (Katz, Assor, Kanat-Maymon, & Bereby-Mayer, 2006), to pay attention in class, to exert effort, and to stay in school (Hardre & Reeve, 2003; Skinner & Belmont, 1993), and to adhere to an exercise program (Ryan, Frederick, Lepes, Rubio, & Sheldon, 1997).

Creativity

Intrinsic motivation enhances spontaneity, originality, personal authenticity, and creativity (Amabile, Hennessey, & Grossman, 1986; Joussemet & Koestner, 1999; Koestner, Ryan, Bernieri, & Holt, 1984). The contribution of intrinsic motivation to creativity is so robust that Teresa Amabile (1983) proposed the following Intrinsic Motivation Principle of Creativity: "People will be most creative when they feel motivated primarily by the interest, enjoyment, satisfaction, and challenge of the work itself—rather than by external pressures."

Conceptual Understanding/High-Quality Learning

Intrinsic motivation enhances a learner's conceptual understanding of what they are trying to learn. When high, intrinsic motivation promotes flexibility in one's way of thinking (McGraw & McCullers, 1979), active information processing (Grolnick & Ryan, 1987), concentration and effective use of learning strategies (Vansteenkiste, Zhou, Lens, & Soenens, 2005), and learning in a way that is conceptual rather than rote (Benware & Deci, 1984; Boggiano et al., 1993; Vansteenkiste et al., 2004, 2005). When intrinsically motivated, learners concentrate, process information deeply, and think about and integrate information in a flexible, conceptual, and less rigid way, rather than engage in rote learning such as memorizing and simply trying to reproduce an other-prescribed right answer.

Optimal Functioning and Well-Being

People who are intrinsically motivated also tend to perform well and enjoy what they do (Black & Deci, 2000; Grolnick & Ryan, 1987), be happy, productive, non-anxious, and well-adjusted (Chirkov & Ryan, 2001; Deci et al., 2001; Vansteenkiste et al., 2005), experience vitality and a sense of being re-energized (Nix, Ryan, Manly, & Deci, 1999), and report high levels of life satisfaction, self-worth, and self-actualization (Kasser & Ryan, 1996, 2001). People who are intrinsically motivated are more likely to say things like

"I feel energized" and "I look forward to each new day" than are people who are extrinsically motivated (Moller, Deci, & Ryan, 2006; Nix et al., 1999).

Intrinsic Motivation versus Extrinsic Motivation

The research on the distinction between intrinsic and extrinsic motivation began with this question: If a person is involved in an intrinsically interesting activity and begins to receive an extrinsic reward for doing it, what happens to his or her intrinsic motivation for that activity? (Deci & Ryan, 1985a, p. 43). For example, what happens to the motivation of the student who reads for the fun of it after she then begins to receive money from her parents for reading? One might suppose that rewarding reading behavior with a monetary prize would add to her motivation. Common sense argues that if a person enjoys reading and is also financially rewarded for it, then the intrinsic (enjoyment) and extrinsic (money) motivations should sum to produce some sort of super-motivation. And if you ask people to make predictions about what happens to a person's motivation under these conditions, increased super-motivation is what most people will predict (Hom, 1994).

Super-motivation does not occur. Rather, the imposition of an extrinsic reward to engage in an intrinsically interesting activity typically undermines (has a negative effect on) future intrinsic motivation (Condry, 1977; Deci, 1971; Deci, Koestner, & Ryan, 1999; Kohn, 1993; Lepper, Greene, & Nisbett, 1973; Wiechman & Gurland, 2009). The reward's adverse effect on intrinsic motivation is termed a "hidden cost of reward" (Lepper & Greene, 1978) because society typically regards rewards as positive contributors to motivation (Boggiano et al., 1987). People use rewards expecting to gain the benefit of increasing another person's motivation and behavior but, in doing so, they often incur the unintentional and hidden cost of undermining that person's intrinsic motivation toward the activity.

Consider what happens in the brain when people are promised attractive rewards if they will engage in an interesting activity (Murayama, Matsumoto, Izuma, & Matsumoto, 2010). In one condition, participants played a challenging game in which they pressed a button when a stopwatch hit an exact time. The task was fun because it was challenging to try to hit the stopwatch button at the precise time—not too soon, not too late, but at just the right time. Participants engaged in this task twice, and their neural activations in the subcortical brain's reward center (ventral striatum, ventral tegmental area; Chapter 3) were measured. During session 1, participants showed significant subcortical brain activations, and they continued to show significant subcortical brain activations during session 2. In other words, the stopwatch task was fun the first time, and it was still fun the second time. In a second condition, participants played the same challenging stopwatch game, but they were promised a monetary reward for doing so during session 1 (e.g., you will gain $2 for each successful trial) but not offered this same reward during session 2. During session 1, when there was reward to be gained, participants showed strong subcortical brain activations. These participants in fact showed stronger subcortical brain activations than did participants who were not promised the reward. During session 2, when the reward was no longer available, the previously strong neural activations of these same participants fully disappeared. Playing the challenging game for no reward after first playing it for reward produced literally nothing in terms of subcortical brain reward activations. Simply put, initially playing the game for an attractive reward undermined the task's later capacity to produce intrinsic motivation.

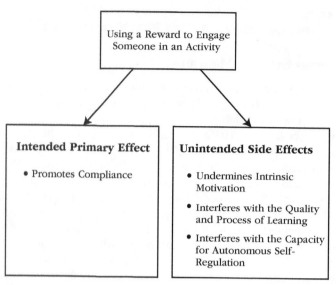

Figure 5.5   Intended and Unintended Effects of Extrinsic Rewards

Extrinsic rewards can have positive effects on motivation and behavior, as illustrated by the earlier postural harness and orthodontic gear examples. But extrinsic forms of motivation almost always come with a price—hidden costs (see Figure 5.5). Undermining intrinsic motivation is a hidden cost of the use of rewards, but there are additional hidden costs as well (Deci & Ryan, 1987; Kohn, 1993). Extrinsic rewards also interfere with the process of learning. In school-based studies, the offering of extrinsic rewards has been shown to distract students' attention from the material they are trying to understand and toward getting the reward. During a learning activity with a reward at stake, the extrinsically motivated student is more likely to attend to factual information and to getting a quick answer (thereby gaining the reward) at the expense of optimally challenging him- or herself, searching for a creative solution, or conceptually understanding the material and its relevance to the person's life (Benware & Deci, 1984; Harter, 1978b; Shapira, 1976; Vansteenkiste et al., 2004, 2005). Extrinsic rewards also interfere with the person's development of autonomous self-regulation (Lepper, 1983; Ryan, 1993). After a history of always being rewarded for doing something (e.g., cleaning your room, mowing the lawn), reward recipients understandably begin to have difficulty regulating their behavior when not offered the reward. The person wonders, "Why should I do it? What is in it for me?" This reward dependency occurs because the presence versus absence of rewards—rather than one's intrinsic motivation and autonomous self-regulation—regulates one's behavior, such as whether to mow the lawn (the initiation of behavior) and when to stop mowing the lawn (when I've done enough to get the reward vs. when the job has been done well; the persistence and quality of behavior).

As a personal example, you might ask yourself when and why you read this textbook— when you are curious and interested to learn about human motivation and emotion (out of intrinsic motivation) or when you have a test tomorrow (out of extrinsic motivation). The more times you read this book out of extrinsic motivation, the rarer and rarer will be those times in the future when you read it out of intrinsic motivation (i.e., your reading has become test-, assignment-, deadline-, and teacher-dependent).

The psychological need for autonomy (Chapter 6) provides one way for understanding the hidden costs of reward (Deci & Ryan, 1987). When experimental participants are paid money (Deci, 1972; Wiechman & Gurland, 2009), promised an award (Lepper et al., 1973), promised a toy (Lepper & Greene, 1975), threatened with a punisher (Deci & Casio, 1972), given a deadline (Amabile, DeJong, & Lepper, 1976), given a directive (Koestner et al., 1984), involved in competitive pressure (Reeve & Deci, 1996), or watched over as they work (i.e., surveillance; Pittman et al., 1980), these participants gradually lose their perception of autonomy and show decreased intrinsic motivation. In other words, when rewards are at stake, the person's reason for engaging in the activity becomes less and less intrinsic (e.g., "I enjoy reading") and more and more extrinsic ("I get money and high grades"; deCharms, 1984). What was once "play" has become "work." What was once "I do it for fun" becomes "I do it for reward." Basically, coercing people to engage in a task, even when using unquestionably attractive rewards like money, instigates a shift in their understanding of why they chose to engage in that task from one of autonomy to one of environment (Deci et al., 1999). You might think that people could engage in a task for both reasons—for intrinsic interest and for extrinsic reward—but being promised and receiving attractive reward instead polarizes people's understanding of why they engaged in the task to the point that they discount the intrinsic reason and replace it with the extrinsic one (Wiechman & Gurland, 2009).

Early experiments by Mark Lepper and his colleagues nicely illustrate the hidden costs of extrinsic rewards (Greene & Lepper, 1974; Lepper & Greene, 1975, 1978; Lepper et al., 1973). Preschool children with a high interest in drawing were grouped into one of three experimental conditions: expected reward, no reward, and unexpected reward. In the expected reward group (extrinsic motivational orientation), children were shown an extrinsic reward—an attractive Good Player certificate featuring the child's name and a big blue ribbon—and asked if they wanted to draw in order to win the reward. Children did find this reward attractive. In the no reward group (intrinsic motivational orientation), children were simply asked if they wanted to draw. In the unexpected reward group, children were asked if they wanted to draw, but they unexpectedly received the Good Player certificate only after the drawing was over. One week later, the experimenters provided the children with another opportunity to draw during their free time. During this second week, children who drew in order to win the certificate (expected reward group) spent significantly less time drawing than did children in the other two groups. In effect, children in the expected reward group lost their intrinsic interest in drawing. The no reward and unexpected reward groups showed no such interest decline. The interest maintenance of the unexpected reward group is important because it shows that the extrinsic motivational orientation (rather than the reward per se) caused children's decreased interest in drawing.

In interpreting these findings, one might feel a bit of skepticism and muse over the fact that the sample of participants included preschoolers, the experimental task was drawing, and the reward was an artificial certificate. Perhaps one might then conclude that the findings have little to do with more complex adult motivations. These findings, however, have been replicated over 100 times using adults, different tasks, and different rewards (see Deci et al., 1999). Such an avalanche of empirical evidence leads to the conclusion that "the undermining effect is a reality after all" (Deci et al., 1999).

In accepting the generality of the negative effects (i.e., "the hidden costs") of an extrinsic motivational orientation (Deci et al., 1999; Deci & Ryan, 1985a; Kohn, 1993; Lepper & Greene, 1978; Rummel & Feinberg, 1988; Sutherland, 1993), one might turn the tables and ask whether rewards always decrease intrinsic motivation. This is precisely what psychologists did ask next. After three decades of research, the conclusion is that extrinsic rewards do generally undermine intrinsic motivation, but not always (Deci et al., 1999; Eisenberger, Pierce, & Cameron, 1999; Rummel & Feinberg, 1988; Wiersma, 1992). In particular, two factors explain which types of rewards decrease intrinsic motivation: expectancy and tangibility.

Expected and Tangible Rewards

People often engage in behaviors in order to receive a reward. In doing so, people expect to receive a reward if they engage in a particular behavior. If, however, the person engages in the behavior with no such knowledge of a reward yet still receives a reward once the task is completed, then the reward is an unexpected one. The earlier study with children drawing for Good Player certificates (Lepper et al., 1973) showed that reinforcers decrease intrinsic motivation only when the person expects that his or her task engagement will yield a reward. The telltale sign that a person expects a reward for task participation is an if–then or in-order-to orientation, such as, "If I read this book, then I can watch TV." Expected rewards undermine intrinsic motivation, while unexpected rewards do not (Greene & Lepper, 1974; Orlick & Mosher, 1978; Pallak, Costomiris, Sroka, & Pittman, 1982).

A second factor in understanding which rewards undermine intrinsic motivation and which do not is the distinction between tangible and verbal rewards. Tangible rewards, such as money, awards, and food, tend to decrease intrinsic motivation, whereas verbal (i.e., intangible) rewards, such as praise and positive feedback on a job well done, do not (Anderson, Manoogian, & Reznick, 1976; Blank, Reis, & Jackson, 1984; Cameron & Pierce, 1994; Deci, 1972; Dollinger & Thelen, 1978; Kast & Connor, 1988; Koestner, Zuckerman, & Koestner, 1987; Sansone, 1989; Swann & Pittman, 1977). In other words, rewards that one can see, touch, feel, and taste generally decrease intrinsic motivation, whereas those that are verbal and symbolic do not.

Implications

The two limiting factors of expectancy and tangibility suggest that rewards decrease intrinsic motivation only when they are expected and tangible. This conclusion is a sort of good news/bad news message. The good news is that extrinsic rewards can be used in a way that does not put intrinsic motivation at risk. The bad news is that our society so often relies on expected and tangible rewards to motivate others. Money, bonuses, paychecks, prizes, trophies, scholarships, privileges, grades, gold stars, awards, honor-roll lists, incentive plans, public recognition, food, frequent flyer miles, and so on are ubiquitous incentives and consequences in Western societies (Kohn, 1993). In practice, therefore, it is not so comforting to say that only expected and tangible extrinsic rewards will decrease intrinsic motivation because so many rewards are offered to people in precisely this way.

Expected, tangible rewards actually put more at risk than just intrinsic motivation (Condry, 1977, 1987; Deci & Ryan, 1987; Kohn, 1993; Wiechman & Gurland, 2009). Extrinsic reinforcers not only decrease intrinsic motivation, they also interfere with both the process and quality of learning (recall Figure 5.5). Rewards shift the learner's goals away from attaining mastery and learning per se in favor of attaining reward and extrinsic gain (Harter, 1978b; Pittman, Boggiano, & Ruble, 1983; Shapira, 1976). Expected and tangible rewards therefore turn extrinsically motivated learners into passive information processors (Benware & Deci, 1984). Expected and tangible rewards further put at risk a learner's flexibility in her way of thinking and problem solving (as she tries to produce a right answer quickly rather than discover an optimal solution; McGraw & McCullers, 1979). Expected, tangible rewards also undermine creativity (Amabile, 1985; Amabile et al., 1986), as people are more creative when they draw and write out of interest than when they draw and write for rewards. And when rewards are involved, learners typically quit as soon as some reward criterion is attained (e.g., reading only the 100 pages required for the test). When rewards are not involved, learners generally persist until curiosity is satisfied, interest is exhausted, or mastery is attained (Condry, 1977; Condry & Chambers, 1978). Thus, not only is intrinsic motivation potentially at risk with the use of expected and tangible rewards, but so is the quality of the learning process (e.g., preference for challenging work, attention, emotional tone, conceptual understanding, cognitive flexibility, and creativity).

A final point is that rewards interfere with the development of autonomous self-regulation (Lepper, 1983; Ryan, 1993). When the social environment tells people what to do and also provides expected and tangible rewards for doing it, people have little difficulty regulating their behavior in rewarding ways. But schools, families, places of work, and other settings often value autonomous self-regulation (i.e., initiative, intrinsic motivation). Learning to depend on rewards can forestall the development of self-regulatory abilities. For instance, students who do not receive rewards for engaging in their academic activities show a close connection between what they are interested in doing and how they spend their time, while children who do receive rewards for engaging in their academic activities show no connection between what they are interested in doing and how they spend their time (Joussemet, Koestner, Lekes, & Houlfort, 2003). This finding occurs because the later students' behavior is regulated by other people's rewards, not by their own interests. If the environment does not offer incentives and consequences, then people with little autonomous self-regulation will have a difficult time finding the needed motivation within themselves. They will be, and they will feel, motivationally empty.

Benefits of Incentives, Consequences, and Rewards

External regulation is not always bad or counterproductive (Covington & Mueller, 2001). Recognizing this, researchers and practitioners alike have tried to use rewards in ways that minimize the sort of detrimental effects illustrated in Figure 5.5. One way to do this, as discussed earlier, is to use rewards that are unexpected and verbal (e.g., praise) and refrain from using those that are expected and tangible (e.g., bribes). A second means is to intentionally limit their use to tasks that have low intrinsic interest but high social importance.

A key practical question is whether extrinsic motivators will have detrimental effects on *un*interesting tasks. In other words, if a person has little or no intrinsic motivation toward the task to undermine, then intrinsic motivation is not likely to be put at risk by the offering of a reward. Indeed, research shows that the negative impact of extrinsic rewards on intrinsic motivation is limited to interesting activities (Deci et al., 1999), because extrinsic rewards have no effect—not an undermining effect, not a facilitating effect—on a person's intrinsic motivation for uninteresting tasks.

Incentives, consequences, and rewards have their benefits. Rewards can make an otherwise uninteresting task suddenly seem worth pursuing. As long as the reward is attractive enough, rewarded individuals will engage in almost any task. Children will eagerly wash dishes if it means that doing so will gain them a new toy. This is typically not so with unrewarded children, because washing dishes is just not an intrinsically interesting thing to do for most children. Without a reward at stake, those dishes stay piled in the sink. In applied settings, behaviorists often promise rewards if their clients perform behaviors like being on time, showing assertiveness, and participating in a group discussion. They do so because their experience tells them that, without a reward at stake, their clients will not engage in these sorts of low-interest behaviors. Consider the value of extrinsic motivators in the following instances in which researchers used rewards to increase socially important but intrinsically uninteresting tasks:

- Developing daily living skills, such as dressing (Pierce & Schreibman, 1994)
- Getting motorists to stop at stop signs (Van Houten & Retting, 2001)
- Increasing participation in recycling (Austira, Hatfield, Grindle, & Bailey, 1993)
- Increasing participation in energy conservation (Staats, Van Leeuwen, & Wit, 2000)
- Motivating children to start their homework (Miller & Kelley, 1994)
- Teaching autistic children to initiate a conversation (Krantz & McClannahan, 1993)
- Increasing the elderly's participation in physical activity (Gallagher & Keenan, 2000)

In each of these examples, an argument can be made that the society's concerns for promoting desirable behavior from its citizens outweighs the concerns for preserving or protecting the individual's autonomy, intrinsic motivation, quality of learning, and autonomous self-regulation. Therefore, some practitioners come to the practical conclusion that it is fine and well to use extrinsic motivators when another person's intrinsic motivation is low (Witzel & Mercer, 2003). This is not, however, necessarily true. Consider the following four reasons not to use extrinsic motivators, even for intrinsically uninteresting endeavors (Kohn, 1993):

1. Extrinsic motivators still undermine the quality of performance and interfere with the process of learning.

2. Using rewards distracts attention away from asking the hard question of why another person is being asked to do an uninteresting task in the first place.

3. There are better ways to encourage participation than extrinsic bribery, as discussed in the last section of the chapter.

4. Extrinsic motivators still undermine the individual's long-term capacity for autonomous self-regulation.

When all is said and done, many people believe that extrinsic motivators simply carry too high a psychological and developmental cost in terms of intrinsic motivation, the process of learning, the quality of learning, and autonomous self-regulation. Plus, there are much better ways to motivate people to engage in uninteresting activities (Jang, 2008; Reeve, Jang, Hardre, & Omura, 2002), as will be discussed in the last section of this chapter.

To this point in the chapter, the practical debate in the effort to motivate others has centered on the wisdom of using extrinsic rewards: Should I promise my child a trip to the toy store if she will first let the doctor give her a shot, or should I not promise such a reward? Two decades of research on this question shows that the critical question is not "Should I give rewards or not?" but instead, "How should I give rewards?" Understanding the motivational and emotional implications of how rewards are offered is the purpose of cognitive evaluation theory.

COGNITIVE EVALUATION THEORY

When people use incentives and consequences, they generally seek to create in others an extrinsic motivation for engaging in that activity. Much of the spirit behind the use of an extrinsic motivator is therefore to shape, influence, or outright control another person's behavior. Sometimes the attempt to control is obvious (e.g., using money to bribe a child to wear orthodontic gear; see Figure 5.1), but other times it is more seductive (e.g., giving free soft drinks at a bar to anyone agreeing to be a designated driver; Brigham, Maier, & Goodner, 1995). Thus, one purpose behind almost any extrinsic motivator is to control another person's behavior—that is, to increase some desirable behavior (or to decrease some undesirable behavior). But there is a second purpose. Incentives and rewards also provide feedback that informs the person about her competence at the task. Rewards such as money, awards, good grades, academic scholarships, and verbal praises not only function to increase behavior (i.e., control behavior) but also to communicate a message of a job well done (i.e., inform competence). This insight on the inherent dual function of rewards raises the practical question of why a person gives rewards to another—Is it to control the other's behavior, or it is to inform the other's competence?

Cognitive evaluation theory asserts that *all* external events have both a controlling aspect and an informational aspect (Deci & Ryan, 1985a). The theory presumes that people have psychological needs for autonomy and competence (Chapter 6). Furthermore, it is the controlling aspect of an external event that affects the person's need for autonomy, whereas it is the informational aspect that affects the person's need for competence. Formally, cognitive evaluation theory exists as the set of three propositions. The theory applies to the offering of incentives and rewards, but it also applies further to the offering of any and all external events.

According to Proposition 1, external events (e.g., offer a choice) that promote an internal perceived locus of causality (PLOC) promote intrinsic motivation because these events involve or satisfy the need for autonomy. External events (e.g., offer a reward) that promote an external PLOC promote extrinsic motivation because these events neglect the need for autonomy and instead establish an if–then contingency between a behavior and a forthcoming consequence. Proposition 1 therefore asks, Is the purpose of the extrinsic event to control another person's behavior? If not, autonomy and intrinsic motivation will be preserved; if so, autonomy and intrinsic motivation will be undermined as extrinsic motivation replaces intrinsic motivation.

According to Proposition 2, external events that increase perceived competence (e.g., offer praise) promote intrinsic motivation, whereas events that decrease perceived competence (e.g., offer criticism) undermine it. Hence, the more an external event communicates positive effectance information, the more likely it is to satisfy the need for competence and increase intrinsic motivation. Proposition 2 therefore asks, Is the purpose of the extrinsic event to inform another person's sense of competence? If so, perceived competence and intrinsic motivation will rise and fall to the extent that the external event communicates positive versus negative effectance information.

The contribution that the first two propositions offer for a comprehensive understanding of the motivational significance of incentives, consequences, and rewards is this: External events affect not only a person's *behavior* but, in addition, a person's *psychological needs*. If the external event is noncontrolling and informational, then it will nurture autonomy and competence and, in doing so, increase an internal perceived locus of causality, a sense of competence, and intrinsic motivation. However, if the external event is controlling and critical, then it will frustrate autonomy and competence and, in doing so, increase an external perceived locus of causality, a sense of incompetence, and extrinsic motivation.

Proposition 3 ties together the first two propositions into a full theoretical statement. According to Proposition 3, the relative salience of whether an event is *mostly controlling* or *mostly informational* determines its effects on intrinsic and extrinsic motivation. Relatively controlling events undermine intrinsic motivation (via their harmful effect on autonomy) and promote extrinsic motivation. Relatively informational events increase intrinsic motivation (via their beneficial effect on competence). It is in Proposition 3 that the usefulness of cognitive evaluation theory becomes apparent. The reader can use cognitive evaluation theory to predict—in advance of its offering—the effect that *any* extrinsic event will have on intrinsic and extrinsic motivations, as discussed more fully in Box 5. The essential question in understanding and in predicting how an external event will affect a person's motivation and behavior becomes, Why am I giving another person this external event—to control behavior or to inform competence?

Two Examples of Controlling and Informational Events

Any external event—praise, money, a scholarship, surveillance, deadlines, interpersonal competition, an attendance policy, a grading system, and so on—can be administered in a relatively controlling way or in a relatively informational way. Consider the two particular cases of praise and competition.

Praise

Consider how praise functions as an extrinsic event sometimes to control another's behavior and sometimes to inform her competence about a job well done (Henderlong & Lepper, 2002). A supervisor using praise, for instance, might communicate praise in an informational way, saying, "Excellent job, your productivity increased by 10%." The supervisor might, however, communicate praise in a controlling way, saying, "Excellent job, you did just as you should." Tagging phrases such as "you should," and "you ought to" onto the praise gives the feedback a tone of pressure (Ryan, 1982). It feels as if the behavior was only pressured compliance (Ryan, Koestner, & Deci, 1991). In contrast, providing clear, specific, and competence-diagnosing feedback typically gives praise a highly informative function (Brophy, 1981). For example, the praise, "Excellent job, I noticed that you greeted the customer warmly and with a sincere tone in your voice," speaks informatively to an employee's sense of competence. The conclusion is that the motivational effect is not in the praise per se but in the way it is administered (Deci & Ryan, 1985a). It is not so much what you say as it is why and how you said it.

| BOX 5 | *Predicting How Any External Event Will Affect Motivation* |

Question: Why is this information important?

Answer: So that you can predict, in advance, what effect *any* external event will have on motivation.

When teachers put stickers on children's homework, they hope the stickers will motivate the children to work hard. When employers give end-of-the-year holiday bonuses, they hope the money and recognition will motivate the workers to work hard. And when street panhandlers wash the windows of a person's car at a traffic stop, they hope the driver will give them some money. The logic is: Since stickers, money, and favors are good and desirable, then the children's, workers,' and drivers' motivation will probably increase in a positive way.

Why a reward is given is at least as important as what is given. A sincere pat on the back can enhance motivation even more than can a big fat check, if the check has strings attached to it. Basically, the purpose behind the reward (Why is this person giving me this reward?) is more important than is the reward itself. Understanding how any external event affects another person's motivation is the domain of cognitive evaluation theory. The theory can be articulated in the accompanying flowchart.

To make sense of the figure, first mentally write in the blank line (on the left) any external event. A teacher, for instance, might be interested in the motivational effects of external events such as stickers, grades, praise, tests, deadlines, video clips, a cooperative learning exercise, a group discussion, a class requirement, or an attendance policy. Next, working from left to right, determine the external event's purpose, or functional significance. Is the external event being offered to control behavior, or is it being offered to inform competence? In particular, which of these two aspects is the relatively more salient one?

If the external event is used largely to control behavior, then its motivational effect will be to decrease autonomy, decrease intrinsic motivation, and increase extrinsic motivation. If the external event is not used to control behavior, then it will not decrease autonomy, not decrease intrinsic motivation, and not increase extrinsic motivation. If the external event is used to communicate a job well done, then its motivational effect will be to increase competence and hence intrinsic motivation. When the external event communicates a job poorly done, however, its motivational effect will be to decrease competence and hence intrinsic motivation.

Notice that in predicting how any external event will affect another person's motivation, the critical question is not what the external event is, but rather, why one person administers it to another.

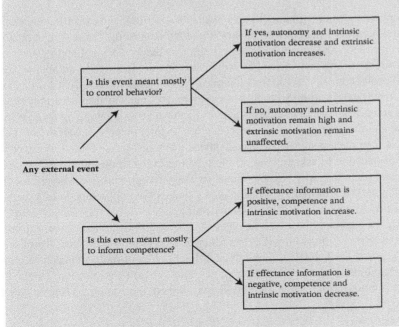

Competition

A second illustration of how the same external event can be administered in a relatively controlling or informational way is interpersonal competition (Reeve & Deci, 1996). When the social context puts a good deal of pressure on winning (with its evaluative audience, screaming coaches, headline-seeking newspaper reporters, championship trophies, scholarship implications, career prospects), competitors usually compete with a sense of contingency, pressure, and doing others' work. When experienced in such a controlling way, competition decreases intrinsic motivation because competitors care relatively little about the task itself and relatively much about the reward of winning (Deci, Betley, et al., 1981; Vallerand, Gauvin, & Halliwell, 1986). The point of the competition ceases to be about the game or sport but, instead, about winning. Even when people win a high-pressure competition, they still show lower intrinsic motivation (Deci, Betley, et al., 1981; Reeve & Deci, 1996). However, when the social context places little emphasis on winning (recreational competition, no audience present, no trophy or scholarship on the line, an autonomy-supportive coach), then competition's informational aspects (e.g., winning, improving, making progress) often become its relatively more salient aspect. Winning, improving, and making progress promote perceived competence and hence increase intrinsic motivation, while losing and the lack of progress undermine perceive competence and hence decrease intrinsic motivation (McAuley & Tammen, 1989; Reeve, Olson, & Cole, 1985). Even after a person loses in competition, intrinsic motivation can still be high if that person feels he or she performed competently (e.g., above a personal standard; Vansteenkiste & Deci, 2003).

The motivational moral of the story is that for intrinsic motivation to flourish, both competence and autonomy must be high (Fisher, 1978), and for both competence and autonomy to be high, the offered external event—such as praise or competition—needs to be presented in a way that is both noncontrolling and informational.

TYPES OF EXTRINSIC MOTIVATION

Cognitive evaluation theory explains changes in people's intrinsic and extrinsic motivation on interesting activities—on activities that are inherently interesting, fun, novel, optimally challenging, enjoyable, and intrinsically appealing. This theory does not apply, however, to inherently uninteresting activities. How individuals acquire (i.e., learn, internalize, and take personal ownership over) the motivation to carry out uninteresting activities is a very important motivational question. Some days we seem to work our way through a daily script that involves going from one uninteresting activity to the next, as we wake up early, take a shower, brush and floss our teeth, make the bed, clean up after ourselves, wait in line, take the bus to work, complete assigned paperwork, attend meetings, and so forth. It is therefore one interesting question to ask why we do these uninteresting things, and it is a second interesting question to ask why we sometimes do these things well and wholeheartedly rather than sloppily and grudgingly. Sometimes we clean up in only a superficial way, but other times we do so with care and attention to detail.

As shown in Figure 5.6, three distinct types of motivation exist: amotivation, extrinsic motivation, and intrinsic motivation (Deci & Ryan, 1985a, 1991; Rigby, Deci, Patrick, & Ryan, 1992; Ryan & Deci, 2000b). These three different types of motivation can be organized along a continuum of perceived locus of causality or self-determination. On the far left-hand side is amotivation, which literally means "without motivation," a state in which

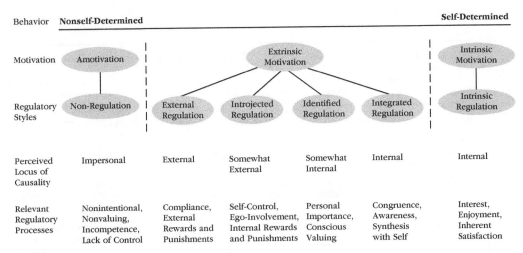

Figure 5.6   Self-Determination Continuum Showing Types of Motivation

Source: Ryan, R. M., & Deci, E. L. (2000b). Self-determination theory and the facilitation of intrinsic motivation, social development, and well-being. *American Psychologist, 55*, 68–78. Copyright 2000 by American Psychological Association. Reprinted by permission.

the person is neither intrinsically nor extrinsically motivated (e.g., a dropout student, disillusioned athlete, or apathetic marriage partner). In the middle of the figure are four types of extrinsic motivation that can be distinguished from one another on the basis of their degree of autonomy: external regulation (not at all autonomous), introjected regulation (somewhat autonomous), identified regulation (mostly autonomous), and integrated regulation (fully autonomous). On the far right-hand side, intrinsic motivation reflects the individual's full endorsement of autonomy and reflects those occasions in which an activity generates spontaneous satisfactions from nurturing the person's psychological needs. Overall, the self-determination continuum varies from amotivation and unwillingness, to compliance, to self-control, to personal valuing, to interest and enjoyment (Ryan & Deci, 2000b).

Identifying types of motivation is important because the amount of autonomy within any motivational state has a substantial effect on what people feel, think, and do. The more autonomous one's motivation is, the more effort the person puts forth, the more freely and willingly that effort is exerted, and the more persistent and productive that effort is in terms of learning, performance, and achievement (Ryan & Connell, 1989), and this is true when people try to lose weight (Williams et al., 1996), regulate their diabetes (Williams, Freedman, & Deci, 1998), recover in an alcohol-treatment program (Ryan, Plant, & O'Malley, 1995), brush and floss their teeth and go to the dentist (Munster Halvari, Halvari, Bjørnebekk, & Deci, 2010), eat healthy foods (Pelletier, Dion, Slovenic-D'Angelo, & Reid, 2004), experience relationship intimacy (Blais, Sabourin, Boucher, & Vallerand, 1990), extend help to others (Weinstein & Ryan, 2010), adhere to an exercise program (Ryan et al., 1997), persist in a competitive sport year after year (Pelletier, Fortier, Vallerand, & Brière, 2001), search for a job when unemployed (Vansteenkiste et al., 2004), and engage themselves in political (Koestner, Losier, Vallerand, & Carducci, 1996) or religious (Ryan, Rigby, & King, 1993) activities. In each case, the type or the quality of motivation matters a great deal. The more autonomous the person's motivation

Table 5.1 Four Types of Extrinsic Motivation, Illustrated by Different Reasons of "Why I Recycle"

Type of Extrinsic Motivation	External Contingency at Stake	The reason I recycle is …	Illustrative Quotation
External Regulation	Incentives, consequences	"to get or to avoid a consequence."	"I recycle to make 5 cents on each can."
Introjected Regulation	Avoid guilt, boost self-esteem	"because I should."	"I recycle because I ought to, if I am going to feel good (rather than guilty) about myself."
Identified Regulation	Valuing, sense of importance	"because it is important."	"I recycle because it is important for a cleaner environment."
Integrated Regulation	Value congruence	"because it reflects my values."	"I recycle because it reflects and expresses who I am and what I believe."

was, the more positive was the person's functioning and the more positive were the person's outcomes.

Table 5.1 focuses specifically on the four types of extrinsic motivation and, to do so, uses the example of recycling (e.g., Why do you recycle?; Pelletier, Tuson, Green-Demers, Noels, & Beaton, 1998). As can be seen by the illustrative quotations, people engage in external regulation largely out of external compulsions, pressured compliance, and to gain an attractive but extrinsic incentive, consequence, or reward (i.e., no autonomy). People engage in introjected regulation largely out of internal compulsions, a pressure-packed sense of self-control, and to avoid internally controlling emotions such as guilt and shame (i.e., little autonomy). However, people who engage in activities out of identified and integrated regulation do so largely because they want and choose to (i.e., they act autonomously). That is, people engage in identified regulation because the activity at hand is seen as important, personally valuable, or personally useful to them (i.e., high autonomy). People engage in integrated regulation because such behaviors reflect their personal values and a sense of who they are—their sense of self (i.e., very high autonomy). In each case, the behavior (e.g., recycling) is extrinsically motivated—it is done in order to receive some outcome that is separate from the activity itself, and what matters is that each type of extrinsic motivation varies in how autonomous or self-determined it is (Ryan & Connell, 1989).

External Regulation

External regulation is the prototype of non-self-determined extrinsic motivation. Externally regulated behaviors are performed to obtain a reward, to avoid a punisher, or to satisfy some external demand. For the person who is externally regulated, the presence versus absence of extrinsic motivators (e.g., rewards, threats) regulates the rise and fall of motivation. A person who is externally regulated typically has a difficult time beginning a task unless there is some external prompt to do so. A student, for instance, begins to study only when a test is coming up or begins to write a term paper only when the deadline nears. Without the test or the deadline, the externally regulated student lacks the motivation necessary to study or to write. Relative to the other three types of extrinsic motivation, people who are motivated through external regulation show poor functioning and poor outcomes (Deci & Ryan, 1987; Kohn, 1993; Ryan & Connell, 1989; Ryan & Deci, 2000a).

Introjected Regulation

Introjected regulation involves taking in, but not truly accepting or self-endorsing, other people's demands to think, feel, or behave in a particular manner. Introjected regulation is essentially being motivated out of guilt and the "tyranny of the shoulds" (Horney, 1937). In essence, the person, acting as a proxy for the external environment, emotionally rewards him- or herself for performing other-defined good behavior (feel proud) and emotionally punishes him- or herself for performing other-defined bad behavior (feel shamed or guilty). Therefore, partial internalization has occurred, but the internalization is kept at an arm's length, so to speak, instead of being really integrated into the self in an authentic and volitional way. The telltale sign that only partial internalization has occurred is that the person feels tension and pressure in carrying out the introjected-motivated behavior (e.g., "I just *have* to study tonight! I *must* clean my room today"). With introjected regulation, the person carries another person's (or society's) prescriptions inside his or her head to such an extent that the introjected voice, not the self per se, generates the motivation to act. Notice, however, that introjected regulation does include the changing of internal structures because the behavior is regulated not by explicit external contingencies but rather by internalized representations of those contingencies (i.e., a parent's voice, cultural expectations).

Identified Regulation

Identified regulation represents mostly internalized and autonomous (or self-determined) extrinsic motivation. With identified regulation, the person voluntarily accepts the merits and utility of a belief or behavior because that way of thinking or behaving is seen as personally important or useful. Thus, if a student comes to believe that extra work in mathematics is important (e.g., it has utility for a career in science) or if an athlete comes to believe that extra practice on his or her technique, posture, or pre-performance routine is important, the motivation to study and to practice are extrinsic but freely chosen. Extra work in mathematics or in sport is extrinsic because these behaviors are instrumental to other aims (a career as a scientist, become a tennis pro), yet they are freely chosen because they are perceived to be useful and valuable for one's life. Exercising, helping others, and cooperating with others provide additional examples of identified regulation, because many people exercise, help, and cooperate freely with others not because they enjoy doing so but because they value what such behaviors can do for them and for their relationships with others (Pavey, Greitemeyer, & Sparks, 2012). Because these ways of thinking and behaving are valued and deemed as personally important, people internalize and identify with them and, by internalizing them, these ways of thinking and behaving become self-determined and freely enacted.

Integrated Regulation

Integrated regulation constitutes the most autonomously endorsed type of extrinsic motivation. While internalization is the process of taking in a value or a way of behaving, integration is the process through which individuals fully transform their identified values and behaviors into the self (Ryan & Deci, 2000a). Integrated regulation is as much a developmental process as it is a type of motivation, because it involves the self-examination necessary to bring new ways of thinking, feeling, and behaving into an unconflicted congruence with the self's preexisting ways of thinking, feeling, and behaving. That is, integration occurs as otherwise isolated identifications (e.g., "Recycling newspapers is not fun, but I want to do it anyway because it is important for the environment.") into coherence and congruence with the existing values of the self (e.g., "I am an environmentalist."). Because it is the most self-determined type of extrinsic motivation, integrated regulation is associated with the most positive outcomes, such as prosocial development and psychological well-being (Ryan & Deci, 2000a; Weinstein, Deci, & Ryan, 2011; Weinstein, Przybylski, & Ryan, 2013).

Internalization and Integration

Internalization refers to the process through which an individual transforms a formerly externally prescribed regulation (rule), behavior, or value into an internally endorsed one (Ryan et al., 1993). Integration refers to the further transformation of that internalized regulation, behavior, or value into the person's sense of self to the point that it actually arises from and emanates out of the self (Ryan & Deci, 2000a). With full integration, the person him- or herself—not the environment—generates the regulation, behavior, or value.

With internalization, a person might "take in" the police person's regulation to stop the car fully at each stop sign, "take in" a parent's prescribed behavior to brush one's teeth for a full 20 seconds, or "take in" a society's value for education or honesty. That is, the person voluntarily adopts the regulation, behavior, or value prescribed by other people (or society). With integration, a person reflects on the merits of these regulations, behaviors, and values and assesses the extent to which they are or are not consistent with his or her own sense of self (Weinstein, Przybylski, & Ryan, 2013). After a period of reflection and a judgment of personal ownership, some internalized regulations are kept at an arm's length: "I know exercising is important; I know it is a healthy thing to do; but it is just not who I am; it is not how I see myself. I value it, but I don't own it." Some other internalizations, however, are fully integrated into the self, and when they are, the self-transformational process that is integration occurs. How autonomous a person is in his or her various regulations, behaviors, and values is important because this degree of internalization and integration is a strong predictor of how prosocial, competent, well-adjusted, and happy that person is (Deci & Ryan, 2000; Downie, Koestner, ElGeledi, & Cree, 2004; Pavey, Greitemeyer, & Sparks, 2012; Pelletier, Dion, Slovinec-D'Angelo, & Reid, 2004).

Amotivation

Recall that three distinct types of motivation were presented in Figure 5.6, and the third type was amotivation (in addition to extrinsic motivation and intrinsic motivation). Amotivation literally means "without motivation" (Legault, Green-Demers, & Pelletier, 2006). It is a

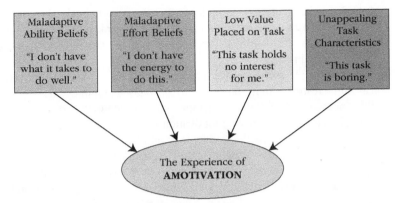

Figure 5.7   Four-Part Experience of Amotivation

state of motivational apathy in which people possess little or no reason (motive) to invest the energy and effort that is necessary to learn or to accomplish something. During class, for instance, the amotivated student tends to sit passively, sleep (or skip class), just act as if he or she is participating, as he or she merely "goes through the motions" of classroom work (Ntoumanis, Pensgaard, Martin, & Pipe, 2004).

Amotivation is actually a rather complicated construct, because it consists of four distinct yet highly intercorrelated aspects (Green-Demers, Legault, Pelletier, & Pelletier, 2008; Legault et al., 2006; Pelletier, Dion, Tuson, & Green-Demers, 1999; Shen et al., 2010). As depicted in Figure 5.7, amotivation includes the four interrelated elements of low ability, low effort, low value, and unappealing task: low ability, which represents a sense of incompetence and the belief that one lacks sufficient ability or aptitude to perform a particular behavior or task; low effort, which represents a lack of desire to expend the energy necessary to enact a particular behavior or task; low value, which represents a lack of perceived importance or usefulness within a particular behavior or task; and unappealing task, which represents the perception that the task at hand is simply a personally unappealing or unattractive thing to do. Amotivation is the worst profile of motivation to possess, because it is a reliable and rather potent predictor of poor functioning. Students who report high amotivation, for instance, tend to show classroom disengagement, poor learning, only superficial coping and learning strategies, poor academic performance, and high dropout rates (Ntoumanis et al., 2004; Pelletier et al., 1999; Shen et al., 2010).

MOTIVATING OTHERS TO DO UNINTERESTING ACTIVITIES

People face a difficult motivational problem when they attempt to motivate others (or themselves) to engage in uninteresting, but worthwhile, activities. Examples of such undertakings might include parents asking their children to wash their hands before dinner, teachers asking students to complete a worksheet of difficult math problems, and workplace managers asking workers to be polite to rude customers. The first solution to such a motivational problem is, typically, to use an incentive to prompt the other person into doing whatever it is you want, as with a parent saying, "If you wash your hands, then you'll get ice cream for dessert; but if you don't wash you hands, then there will be no dessert." In this case, the want of the ice cream motivates compliance, not the personal valuing of washing one's hands. The problem with using expected and tangible rewards is that they yield only compliance, low-quality learning, minimal functioning (poorly washed hands), and a dependence on further external regulation.

When people use incentives, consequences, and rewards to motivate others to engage in an uninteresting activity, they hope to reframe the uninteresting activity away from something "not worth doing" into something that is suddenly "worth doing." That is, the added external contingency creates a motivation to engage in the activity that the activity itself cannot generate (because the activity is so uninteresting). Recognizing that external contingencies are associated with poor functioning and unintended side effects, researchers have explored ways to promote autonomous types of extrinsic motivation. These efforts have produced two motivational strategies to motivate others to engage in and benefit from uninteresting activities—providing an explanatory rationale and suggesting interest-enhancing strategies.

Providing Explanatory Rationales

The first way to promote identified regulation during an uninteresting activity is to offer an explanatory rationale—a verbal explanation of why putting forth effort during the otherwise uninteresting activity might actually be a personally useful and important thing to do (Assor, Kaplan, & Roth, 2002; Deci, Eghrari, Patrick, & Leone, 1994; Husman & Lens, 1999; Jang, 2008; Reeve, Jang, Hardre, & Omura, 2002; Vansteenkiste, Simons, Soenens, & Lens, 2004). Here are two illustrations:

- A parent explains to a child why raking the leaves is an important and necessary thing to do: "*Raking the leaves is important because we need to clean the yard of leaves to invite in and welcome the Halloween trick-or-treaters tonight.*"
- A medical doctor explains why exercising is important for her patient: "*Exercising three times a week is important because it will clean out your arteries by boosting good cholesterol and reducing triglycerides. That will decrease your susceptibility to a heart attack, and it will boost your mood and energy and help you gain control over your weight and diabetes.*"

People who hear a convincing and personally satisfying rationale for why it is important to engage in an uninteresting activity generally put forth greater effort and engagement during that activity than do people who do not hear such an explanatory rationale (Deci et al., 1994; Jang, 2008; Newby, 1991; Reeve et al., 2002; Vansteenkiste et al., 2004). A good rationale takes the other person's perspective and provides information that the person does not already know. The reason why the provision of explanatory rationales works as a motivational strategy is because it can spark some degree of valuing, identified regulation, and internalization.

Suggesting Interest-Enhancing Strategies

The motivational strategy of providing an explanatory rationale applies best to those activities that truly are uninteresting things to do. But a boring task does not always have to be a boring task. While people are engaging (or asked to engage) in relatively uninteresting activities (doing homework, washing clothes, driving cross-country), people can utilize a number of different strategies to foster greater interest (Jang, 2008; Sansone & Smith, 2000; Sansone, Weir, Harpster, & Morgan, 1992). Some widely used "interest-enhancing strategies," for instance, include setting a goal, embedding the activity within a fantasy context, or adding an extra source of stimulation to the task (e.g., playing music, working with a friend; Jang, 2008). In creating a goal to strive for, task engagement becomes more about achieving the goal than it does about the task itself. After all, what is so interesting about athletic activities such as shooting a basketball or hitting a baseball with a bat other than the pursuit of challenging goals?

As one example, when an elementary-grade math teacher wanted to engage her students in a relatively boring fractions lesson, she presented that fractions activity within a "Space Quest" game. While solving fractions in the context of a game, students set a series of goals, worked within a fantasy context, and worked side by side with their friends. Compared to students who learned fractions in a more traditional way, these students found the lesson more interesting and showed better learning as well (Cordova & Lepper, 1996). It was not that the fractions task became any more interesting but, instead, that the acts of pursing a goal, placing the task within a personally meaningful context, and working among friends were able to generate the sense of interest that the task itself was unable to generate.

SUMMARY

Extrinsic motivation arises from an environmentally created reason to initiate an action. External events such as money and frequent-flyer miles generate extrinsic motivation to the extent that they establish a "means to an end" contingency in the person's mind, in which the means is the behavior (going to work, flying a particular airline), and the end is some attractive consequence (money, frequent-flyer points). It is not that people develop a desire to engage in behaviors such as working or flying a particular airline; instead, people want to do whatever it is that the environment will reward them for doing. The reason they engage in the behavior is to get the reward; hence, the motivation is environmentally created (by the presence of the reward).

The study of extrinsic motivation revolves around the three central concepts of incentives, consequences, and rewards. First, an incentive is an environmental event that attracts or repels a person toward or away from a particular course of action. Second, consequences involve reinforcers and punishers. A positive reinforcer (money) is any environmental event that, when presented, increases the probability of that behavior in the future. A negative reinforcer (alarm clock noise) is any environmental event that, when removed, increases the probability of that behavior in the future. A punisher (parking ticket) is any environmental event that, when presented, decreases the probability of that behavior in the future. The chief differences between incentives and consequences are (1) when each occurs and (2) how each motivates behavior. Incentives precede behavior and attract or repel action; consequences follow behavior and increase or decrease the strength of behavior. Third, a reward is any offering from one person given to another person in exchange for his or her service or achievement; rewards sometimes produce the sought-after service or achievement, but other times they do not.

Incentives, consequences, and rewards that are expected and tangible typically undermine motivation by inadvertently producing the three hidden costs of undermining intrinsic motivation, interfering with the quality and process of learning and interfering with the capacity for autonomous self-regulation. Intrinsic motivation is the inherent propensity to seek out novelty and challenge, to extend and exercise one's capacities, to explore, and to learn. It is a natural inclination toward exploration, spontaneous interest, and environmental mastery that emerges from innate strivings for personal growth and from experiences of psychological need satisfaction. When intrinsically motivated, people show strong task engagement, act creatively, learn and process information deeply and conceptually, function well, and experience greater vitality and well-being.

Cognitive evaluation theory provides a way to predict in advance the motivational effects of any extrinsic event. The theory explains how an extrinsic event (e.g., money, grade, deadline) affects intrinsic and extrinsic motivations, as mediated by the extrinsic event's effect on the psychological needs for competence and autonomy. When an extrinsic event is presented in a relatively controlling way (i.e., given to gain compliance), it increases extrinsic motivation but decreases intrinsic motivation because of its detrimental effects on autonomy. When an extrinsic event is presented in a relatively informational way (i.e., given to communicate a message of a job well done), it increases intrinsic motivation because of its favorable effect on competence. Hence, whether an extrinsic event is motivationally constructive or destructive depends on the relative salience of its controlling and informational aspects.

According to self-determination theory, four types of extrinsic motivation exist and can be arranged along a continuum of no autonomy to full autonomy. With external regulation (no autonomy), behaviors are performed to obtain a reward, to avoid a punisher, or to satisfy some external demand. With introjected regulation (low autonomy), the person acts as if he was carrying other peoples' rules and commands inside his head to such an extent that the introjected voice generates self-administered rewards and punishments. With identified regulation (high autonomy), the person has identified with the personal importance of an externally prescribed way of thinking or behaving and has thus accepted it as his or her own way of thinking or behaving. Integrated regulation (full autonomy) involves the self-examination necessary to bring new ways of thinking and behaving into congruence with the preexisting ways of thinking and behaving. A focus on different types of extrinsic motivation puts a spotlight on the phenomenon of internalization, which is the process through which an individual transforms an externally prescribed regulation, behavior, or value into an internally endorsed one, and the effort to arrange the different types of extrinsic motivation along a continuum is important because the more autonomous or self-determined the extrinsic motivation is, the greater is the person's social development, personal adjustment, and psychological well-being.

The chapter ends with the practical problem of motivating others during uninteresting activities. People typically offer rewards so to reframe the uninteresting activity away from something not worth doing into something that is suddenly worth doing. Because this approach is associated with poor functioning and unintended side effects, researchers have explored for ways to promote more autonomous types of extrinsic motivation, such as providing a rationale to explain why the uninteresting activity is important and useful enough to warrant one's volitional engagement and suggesting interest-enhancing strategies such as setting a goal, embedding the activity within a fantasy context, or adding stimulation to the task experience.

READINGS FOR FURTHER STUDY

Extrinsic Motivation

GERSHOFF, E. T. (2002). Corporal punishment by parents and associated child behaviors and experiences: A meta-analytic and theoretical review. *Psychological Bulletin, 128*, 539–579.

HALL, R. V., AXELROD, S., TYLER, L., GRIEF, E., JONES, F. C., & ROBERTSON, R. (1972). Modification of behavior problems in the home with a parent as observer and experimenter. *Journal of Applied Behavior Analysis, 5*, 53–64.

Hidden Costs of Rewards

DECI, E. L., KOESTNER, R., & RYAN, R. M. (1999). A meta-analytic review of experiments examining the effects of extrinsic rewards on intrinsic motivation. *Psychological Bulletin, 125*, 627–668.

HOM, H. L., JR. (1994). Can you predict the overjustification effect? *Teaching of Psychology, 21*, 36–37.

LEPPER, M. R., & GREENE, D. (1975). Turning play into work: Effects of adult surveillance and extrinsic rewards on children's intrinsic motivation. *Journal of Personality and Social Psychology, 31*, 479–486.

MURAYAMA, K., MATSUMOTO, M., IZUMA, K., & MATSUMOTO, K. (2010). Neural basis of the undermining effect of monetary reward on intrinsic motivation. *PNAS, 107*, 20911–20916.

Cognitive Evaluation Theory

KOESTNER, R., RYAN, R. M., BERNIERI, F., & HOLT, K. (1984). Setting limits on children's behavior: The detrimental effects of controlling versus informational styles on intrinsic motivation. *Journal of Personality, 52*, 233–248.

RYAN, R. M., & DECI, E. L. (2000). Self-determination theory and the facilitation of intrinsic motivation, social development, and well-being. *American Psychologist, 55*, 68–78.

Types of Extrinsic Motivation

JANG, H. (2008). Supporting students' motivation, engagement, and learning during an uninteresting activity. *Journal of Educational Psychology, 100*, 798–811.

PAVEY, L., GREITEMEYER, T., & SPARKS, P. (2012). "I help because I want to, not because you tell me to": Empathy increases autonomously motivated helping. *Personality and Social Psychology Bulletin, 38*, 681–689.

Chapter 6

Psychological Needs

PSYCHOLOGICAL NEEDS

Organismic Psychological Needs

Person–Environment Dialectic

Person–Environment Synthesis versus Conflict

Engagement

Developmental Growth

Health

Well-Being

AUTONOMY

The Conundrum of Choice

Supporting Autonomy

Nurturing Inner Motivational Resources

Providing Explanatory Rationales

Listening Empathically, Relying on Informational Language

Displaying Patience

Acknowledging and Accepting Expressions of Negative Affect

Benefits from Autonomy Support

Benefits of Giving and Receiving Autonomy Support

COMPETENCE

The Pleasure of Optimal Challenge

Interdependency between Challenge and Feedback

Optimal Challenge and Flow

Structure

Feedback

Failure Tolerance

RELATEDNESS

Involving Relatedness: Interaction with Others

Satisfying Relatedness: Perception of a Social Bond

Communal and Exchange Relationships

Fruits of Relatedness Need Satisfaction

PUTTING IT ALL TOGETHER: RELATIONSHIPS AND SOCIAL CONTEXTS THAT
SUPPORT PSYCHOLOGICAL NEED SATISFACTION

Engagement

What Makes for a Good Day?

Vitality

SUMMARY

READINGS FOR FURTHER STUDY

Imagine visiting a lake for the afternoon—at a campground or state park, for instance. As you lie on the shore soaking up the sun's rays, you notice a young girl playfully skipping stones across the water's surface. Before each toss, she studiously inspects piles of stones to find the flattest one. With stone in hand and determination on her face, she puts all her effort into the toss. Each time a rock skips according to plan, she smiles and her enthusiasm grows. Each dud brings a somber expression but also increased determination and a revised technique. At first, she tries only to make each stone skip once off the water's surface. After some experimentation, she moves on to develop three or four finely tuned techniques—one very long skip, short skips with many hops, and so forth. And she pretends to throw others, the big and heavy stones, like hand grenades, because these splashes look like explosions in her imagination. Even as the family picnic goes on, her rock skipping continues.

The child is at play. She is intrinsically motivated. For her, an urban child, the lake is a relatively novel setting. It allows her to use her imagination in a way that is different from every day. As she plays, she feels excited, she feels optimally challenged, and she feels a sense of personal causation. Each rock and each toss provides her with a different result. Each new attempt challenges her—"Yeah, but can you do this?"—and affords her an experience that is somehow deeply satisfying, especially when her developing skill results in an improved result. She feels competent, she feels free, she is highly engaged, she learns, she develops skill, and she is happy.

Such intrinsically motivated behavior is more than frivolous play. It is integral to healthy development. The lake setting provides the child with an opportunity to learn to enjoy an activity solely for itself—solely for the experience of interest, enjoyment, and personal causation.

Sports, hobbies, school, work, and travel also offer opportunities for people to engage in activities capable of involving and satisfying their psychological needs. This chapter examines the motivational significance of three psychological needs: autonomy, competence, and relatedness. The theme throughout the chapter is that when people find themselves in environments that support and nurture their psychological needs, then what follows is strong engagement, healthy development, and optimal experience.

PSYCHOLOGICAL NEEDS

People are inherently active (Ryan & Deci, 2007). Doing something and being active is our natural state, because there is never a time when we are not doing something. As children, we push and pull things; we shake, throw, carry, explore, and ask questions about the objects that surround us. As adults, we continue to explore, play, experiment, and engage ourselves. We play games, solve mysteries, read books, visit friends, undertake challenges, pursue hobbies, surf the Web, build new things, and do any number of activities because they are inherently interesting and enjoyable things to do.

When an activity taps into and involves our psychological needs, we feel interest. Interest is the emotion that signals that one's inner psychological needs have been involved by the activity at hand. When an activity satisfies our psychological needs, we feel enjoyment. Enjoyment is the emotion that signals that one's inner psychological needs have been satisfied by the activity at hand. So, as we engage in an activity, we feel task-inspired interest (i.e., "This is so interesting … ") and task-inspired enjoyment (i.e., "This is so much fun … "). But, actually, the underlying motivational cause of engaging our environment is to involve and satisfy our psychological needs. Playing games, solving mysteries, and undertaking challenges are interesting and enjoyable things to do precisely because they are opportunities to involve and satisfy our psychological needs.

Psychological needs are an important addition to the larger analysis of motivated behavior (Deci & Ryan, 2000; Sheldon, 2011). Physiological needs such as thirst and hunger emanate from biological deficits. Drinking and eating are motivationally reactive behaviors in the sense that their purpose is to react against and alleviate a deficit bodily condition. Psychological needs are of a qualitatively different nature. Energy generated by psychological needs is proactive. Psychological needs promote a proactive willingness to seek out and to engage in an environment that we expect will be able to nurture our psychological needs. Because psychological needs motivate exploration and challenge-seeking, they are understood as growth (rather than as deficit) needs.

Organismic Psychological Needs

The three psychological needs of autonomy, competence, and relatedness are organismic psychological needs (Niemiec & Ryan, 2013; Ryan & Deci, 2008). Organismic theories of motivation get their name from the term *organism*, an entity that is alive and in active exchange with its environment (Blais, 1976). The well-being of any organism depends on its environment because the environment offers the resources the organism needs to be well, such as food, water, social support, and intellectual stimulation. Organisms also need environmental resources to grow and to actualize their latent potentials. When environments are supportive and provide what is needed, organisms thrive; when environments are hostile and withhold what is needed, organisms suffer.

Knowing that they need supportive rather than hostile environments, organisms seek out and choose some environments over others, as when a person choses to interact with one person rather than another, to work at one company rather than another, or to drive the car to one location rather than another (Bandura, 2006). And, once in that particular environment, a healthy organism will try to change that environment for the better to make it more supportive (and less frustrating), as when a student expresses his or her preferences, opinions, and interests and lets the teacher know what he or she wants and needs (Reeve & Tseng, 2011a). Environments also constantly change, hence organisms need flexibility to adjust and accommodate to those changes. To adapt and be well, organisms need to learn to substitute a new response for a previously successful but now outdated one (because the environment changed). Hence, organisms need to grow: They need to learn new information, develop new skills, be open to new interests, and discover new and more effective ways of adjusting. Overall, the focus is on how organisms initiate interactions with the environment, how environments change, and how organisms learn, adapt, change, and grow as a function of those environmental transactions.

The opposite of an organismic approach is a mechanistic one. In mechanistic theories, the environment acts on the person and the person reacts. For instance, environments produce heat, and the person responds in a predictable and automatic way—by sweating. Sweating leads to water loss, and when the biological systems detect the loss, thirst arises rather automatically (i.e., mechanistically). Chapter 4 discussed these biologically based rooted needs. The person and the environment relate to one another within a one-way relationship such that the environment acts and the person reacts. The theories of motivation presented in the present chapter reject the mechanistic view of motivation and instead embrace the organismic view.

Person–Environment Dialectic

In a dialectic, the relationship between person and environment is reciprocal (two-way; Deci & Ryan, 1991; Reeve, Deci, & Ryan, 2004). That is, the environment acts on the person and, in doing so, the person changes. And, the person acts on the environment and, in doing so, the environment changes. Both the person and the environment constantly change.

The person–environment dialectic can also be understood as transformational activity (Sameroff, 2009). With transformational activity, what the person does transforms what the environment does (e.g., what the child says to the parent transforms what the parent will in turn say and do toward the child). With ongoing transformational activity (the child transforms teacher activity, and the teacher transforms child activity), the relation between the person and the environment is constantly changing (transforming). The outcome of this person–environment transformation can be characterized as moving toward either greater person–environment synthesis or greater person–environment conflict (as discussed in the next section).

The person–environment dialectic that is embedded within the organismic approach to motivation appears in Figure 6.1. As shown in the left-hand side of Figure 6.1 ("Person"), the person is inherently active. The motivational source of that inherent activity is somewhat complex but essentially involves the person's psychological needs, intrinsic motivation, interests and personal goals, and self-endorsed values (Deci & Ryan, 1985a). This chapter covers psychological needs and personal goals, while the previous chapter (Chapter 5) covered intrinsic motivation and self-endorsed values (i.e., internalized types of extrinsic motivation). Collectively, these motivations represent "inner motivational resources" (Reeve, 1996), and it is these inner motivational resources that motivate the person's agency, challenge-seeking, and engagement, as depicted in the upper arrow in Figure 6.1. As shown in the right-hand side of Figure 6.1 ("Environment"), the environment offers affordances (opportunities), external events (incentives, rewards, consequences, feedback, praise), need-satisfying or need-frustrating relationships, and social and cultural prescriptions such as values, expectations, and advice for how to be happy (Deci & Ryan, 1985a). How supportive versus frustrating the environment is to the person is depicted by the lower arrow in Figure 6.1, because environmental support contributes to the growth and development of future inner motivational resources while environmental frustration undermines and thwarts growth and development of future inner motivational resources.

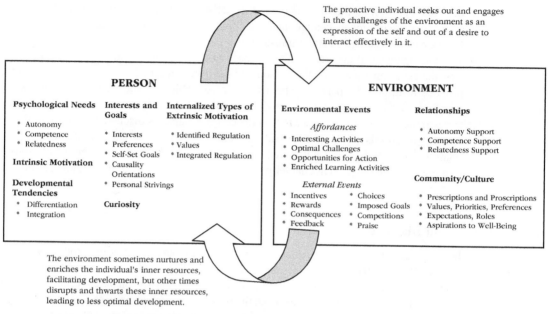

Figure 6.1   Person–Environment Dialectical Framework

Person–Environment Synthesis versus Conflict

The outcome of the person–environment dialectic is an ever-changing synthesis in which the person's needs are fulfilled (or frustrated) by the environment, and the environment produces in the person new forms of motivation. For instance, if you look at the entries in the "Person" box in Figure 6.1, you might notice that some forms of motivation are inherent within the organism, including psychological needs, intrinsic motivation, developmental tendencies, and a sense of curiosity, while some other forms of motivation are learned, acquired, or socialized into the person by the environment, including goals, values, and the two types of extrinsic motivation discussed in Chapter 5—namely, identified regulation and integrated regulation. Overall, the person uses his or her inner motivational resources to interact with and change the environment, while the environment in turn changes and produces new forms of motivation for the person to internalize (i.e., new inner motivational resources). When environments are supportive, the person's inner motivational resources are vitalized, and autonomous forms of extrinsic motivation are internalized (identified regulation, integrated regulation). The outcome of the person–environment interaction is therefore one of synthesis. When environments are frustrating, the person's inner motivational resources are deadened and controlled forms of extrinsic motivation are introjected (introjected regulation, external regulation). The outcome of the person–environment interaction is therefore one of conflict.

Synthesis (person–environment harmony, the forming of a whole) can be seen in people's daily lives in four ways: engagement, developmental growth, health, and well-being. Conflict (person–environment disharmony, a state of clashing or fighting) can be seen in people's daily lives in the four opposite outcomes of defiance, developmental regression and alienation, decay, and ill-being.

Engagement

Engagement refers to how actively involved the person is in the activity at hand (Christenson, Reschly, & Wylie, 2012). When highly engaged, people pay attention, exert effort, persist in the face of challenge and obstacles, think strategically, set goals and make plans, ask questions, and contribute constructively into the flow of whatever they are doing. Organismic theories of motivation argue that the motivation for such initiative is the person's psychological needs (Deci & Ryan, 1985a; White, 1959). The young rock-skipping girl introduced in the chapter's opening vignette ideally illustrates such motivated engagement, because she pursued her own goals (to feel autonomous) and strove for effectance and improvement (to feel competent).

Developmental Growth

Developmental growth refers to how agentic, mature, responsible, authentic, interpersonally connected, self-motivating, efficacious, and self-regulating the person is, while developmental regression refers to how apathetic, immature, irresponsible, pretentious, interpersonally alienated, indolent, helpless, and dependent on others the person is (Ryan & Deci, 2000a). The fruits of personal growth can be seen in developmental outcomes such as effective functioning, deep and enduring interests, learning, talent and skill development, a sense of self-worth, a lack of anxiety and conflict, and personality integration with a sense of wholeness and identity (Niemiec et al., 2006; Sheldon & Kasser, 1995; Vansteenkiste et al., 2005).

Health

Health refers to the functional efficiency of the mind and body and to the absence of illness, disease, and pathology. The variable that best predicts health-related outcomes is the person's behavior (Schroeder, 2007), and people are more likely to initiate and sustain a health-promoting lifestyle when their psychological needs are met (Ryan, Patrick, Deci, & Williams, 2008). The more environments and relationships (e.g., with doctors, dentists, healthcare providers) support the person's psychological needs, the more that person tends toward healthy behaviors, such as eating fruits and vegetables (Shaikh et al., 2011), exercising (Silvia et al., 2011), brushing and flossing (Halvari et al., 2012), and taking prescribed medicine (Williams et al., 2009) and positive health outcomes, such as losing weight (Williams et al., 1996), abstaining from smoking (Williams et al., 2006), improving oral health and dental well-being (Halvari et al., 2013), persisting in alcohol treatment (Ryan, Plant, & O'Malley, 1995), and engaging in effective self-management of one's glucose (Williams, Freedman, & Deci, 1998) and diabetes (Williams et al., 2005, 2009).

Well-Being

Well-being refers generally to positive mental health and more specifically to the presence of positive emotionality, the absence of negative emotionality, having a sense of meaning or purpose, and being satisfied with one's life (Ryan & Deci, 2001; Ryan, Huta, & Deci, 2008). Well-being is the telltale sign of person–environment synthesis, just as ill-being is the telltale sign of person–environment conflict. People who have their psychological needs supported are happier than people who have their psychological needs neglected or frustrated, and the same person is happier on days in which his or her psychological needs are satisfied versus those days when his or her needs are neglected or frustrated (Sheldon, Ryan, & Reis, 1996).

AUTONOMY

When deciding what to do, we desire choice and decision-making flexibility. We want the idea for what we do to be our own—to originate from within us. We want to be the one who determines our actions, rather than have someone coerce us into a particular course of action. We want our behavior to arise out of and express our interests, preferences, wants, and desires in an authentic way. We want to be the one who decides what to do, when to do it, how to do it, when to stop doing it, and whether to do it at all. In other words, we have a need for autonomy.

Autonomy is the psychological need to experience self-direction and personal endorsement in the initiation and regulation of one's behavior (Deci & Ryan, 1985a). Behavior is autonomous (or self-determined) when our interests, preferences, and wants guide our decision-making process to engage or not engage in a particular activity. We are not self-determining (i.e., our behaviors are determined by others) when some outside force takes our sense of choice away and, instead, pressures us to think, feel, or behave in particular ways (Deci, 1980).

The five items listed in Table 6.1 illustrate the experience of autonomy on a daily basis (Weinstein, Przybylski, & Ryan, 2012). Each item assesses the degree of the person's sense of authorship and sense of personal endorsement of what he or she is doing. A synonym for "personal endorsement" would be "congruence," which is a heartfelt affirmative answer to questions such as, Is this *my* decision? Is this *my* behavior? Do I fully agree with this decision and with this course of action? Is this decision and is this behavior congruent with my own personal interests, preferences, and goals? The opposite of congruence would be conflict, because the person thinks, "I'm only doing this because I have to, not because I want to."

The items in Table 6.1 illustrate perceived autonomy as a trait—as an enduring personality characteristic—but perceived autonomy is more typically experienced as a state—as a moment-to-moment experience of personal endorsement versus feeling controlled, pressured, or coerced by outside forces. Thus, perceived autonomy can vary from moment to moment, from situation to situation, and from relationship to relationship, such that the

Table 6.1 Questionnaire Items to Reflect Perceived Autonomy as Authorship and Congruence

1. My decisions represent my most important values and feelings.
2. I strongly identify with the things that I do.
3. My actions are congruent with who I really am.
4. My whole self stands behind the important decisions I make.
5. My decisions are steadily informed by things I want or care about.

Source: Adapted from "The index of autonomous functioning: Development of a scale of human autonomy," by N. Weinstein, A. K. Przybylski, and R. M. Ryan, 2013, *Journal of Research in Personality, 46*, 397–413. Adapted with permission.

person might experience high perceived autonomy while cooking a meal at home with one's family yet low perceived autonomy at work with one's peers and supervisors (or vice versa).

At a moment-to-moment level, three experiential qualities work together to define the subjective experience of autonomy—an internal perceived locus of causality, volition, and perceived choice—as shown in Figure 6.2. *Perceived locus of causality* (PLOC) refers to an individual's understanding of the causal source of his or her motivated actions (Heider, 1958). PLOC exists within a bipolar continuum that ranges from internal to external. This continuum reflects the individual's perception that his or her behavior is initiated by a personal (internal PLOC) or by an environmental (external PLOC) source. For instance, why read a book? If the reason why you read is some motivational agent within the self (interest, value, personal goal), then you read out of an internal PLOC. Your reading emanates from within you—from an inner causality. However, if the reason why you read is some motivational agent in the environment (an assignment, upcoming test, the boss), then you read out of an external PLOC. Your reading comes from an outside force—from an external causality. Some prefer to use the terms "origins" and "pawns" to communicate the distinction between an internal versus an external PLOC (deCharms, 1968, 1976, 1984; Ryan & Grolnick, 1986). Origins "originate" their own intentional behavior. "Pawn," a metaphor taken from the game of chess, captures the experience we feel when powerful people push us around in much the same way that employers boss around their workers, military sergeants command privates, and parents insist that their children behave.

Volition is a heartfelt and unpressured willingness to engage in an activity (Deci, Ryan, & Williams, 1995; Vansteenkiste, Sierens, Soenens, Luyckx, & Lens, 2009). It centers on how free versus coerced people feel while they are doing what they want to do (e.g., playing, studying, talking), and also how free versus coerced they feel while avoiding what they do not want to do (e.g., not smoking, not eating, not apologizing). With volition, the person thinks, "Yes, I freely want to do this" (Deci & Ryan, 1987; Ryan, Koestner, & Deci, 1991). The opposite of volition and feeling free is feeling pressured and coerced into action as in, "Regardless of whether I like it, I simply *have* to do this" (Ryan, 1982; Ryan et al., 1991; Ryan, Mims, & Koestner, 1983).

Perceived choice is a subjective experience that one has decision-making flexibility to act or not to act, or to pursue one course of action rather than another course of action. The opposite of perceived choice is a sense of obligation, rigidity, and inflexibly. This sense of obligation pushes us into a way of thinking, feeling, or behaving that has an emotional tone

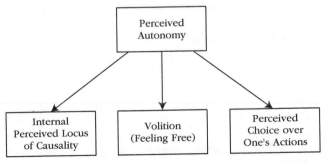

Figure 6.2   Three Subjective Qualities within the Experience of Autonomy

characterized by pressure and "have to," rather than by interest and "want to" as in the case with perceived choice.

The Conundrum of Choice

Providing a person with a choice may be the most obvious and widely used way to support a person's need for autonomy (Flowerday & Schraw, 2000). There is a difference, however, between the environmental event of being offered a choice and the personal experience of true choice. Understanding this difference is an excellent way to understand the nature of the psychological need for autonomy (Patall, 2012).

Providing choices to motivate others is a conundrum (a difficult and complicated problem to solve) because choice sometimes does but other times does not motivate others. Providing choices does generally enhance people's perceived autonomy and intrinsic motivation (Zuckerman et al., 1978). However, not all choices are the same, and not all choices promote autonomy (Patall, Cooper, & Robinson, 2008; Reeve, Nix, & Hamm, 2003; Williams, 1998). Hence, the conundrum is, Does the provision of choice nurture autonomy and intrinsic motivation, or does it not?

A choice among prescribed options offered by others fails to tap into and involve the need for autonomy (e.g., Do you want to listen to country music or to classical music?; Overskeid & Svartdal, 1996; Parker & Lepper, 1992; Schraw, Flowerday, & Reisetter, 1996). For instance, offering people a choice between working on a crossword puzzle or working on an essay activity resulted in no boost in autonomy, engagement, or performance (Flowerday & Schraw, 2003). Likewise, offering students a choice of topics to write about yielded no benefit in terms of later autonomy or performance (Flowerday, Schraw, & Stevens, 2004). In these "either–or" choice offerings, the person is told to make a choice and is even somewhat forced or pressured to make a choice (Moller, Deci, & Ryan, 2006). This is more "picking" than it is "choosing" (Katz & Assor, 2007). Others point out that being given too many options to choose from—such as 80 different shades of blue paint—can be overwhelming and demotivating (Iyengar, 2010). In contrast, it is only when people have a true choice over their actions (e.g., Do you even want to listen to music?), and when they are offered choices that are meaningful to their lives, that they experience a sense of autonomy (Cordova & Lepper, 1996; Katz & Assor, 2007; Reeve et al., 2003; Williams, 1998). When people are allowed to make choices that truly reflect their personal values, goals, and interests, then they do feel a sense of need-satisfying autonomy. Such an experience of autonomy, in turn, leads to positive post-choice functioning in terms of enhanced intrinsic motivation, effort, creativity, preference for challenge, and performance (Moller et al., 2006; Patall et al., 2008).

The act of choosing is both complex and important (Iyengar, 2010; Patall, 2012; Patall, Dent, Oyer, & Wynn, 2013). Choosing is complex because the provision of choice sometimes enhances autonomy and performance but other times it does not (Katz & Assor, 2007; Moller, Deci, & Ryan, 2006). Therefore, there is skill within the art of choosing (Iyengar, 2010). Perhaps the best way to summarize this is through the lens of cognitive evaluation theory, as presented in Chapter 5: Choice—like any other external event—can be offered in either an informational or a controlling way. When offered in an informational way, people give choices to others with the intention of speaking to their preferences and personal goals (e.g., "What would you like to do?"). When offered in a controlling way, people give choices to others in ways that are actually intended to manipulate and control them (e.g., "You can choose to eat your vegetables or to sit here at the dinner table all night long.").

Supporting Autonomy

External events, social contexts, interpersonal relationships, and cultures all vary in how much versus how little they support versus thwart a person's need for autonomy. When these environmental influences tap into, involve, vitalize, and nurture a person's need for autonomy, they are referred to as "autonomy supportive"; when these environmental influences neglect or try to silence and thwart a person's need for autonomy, they are referred to as "controlling" (Deci & Ryan, 1987; Reeve, 2009). Formally, autonomy support is whatever one person says and does to nurture the other's psychological need for autonomy. This is usually done by first taking the other's perspective and then working hard to identify, nurture, and vitalize the other's inner motivational resources (e.g., make a learning activity more interesting or relevant to the student's personal goals), while control is whatever one person says and does to suppress the other's psychological need for autonomy. Behavioral control is usually done by first ignoring or discounting the other's perspective and then pressuring the other toward compliance with a prescribed way of thinking, feeling, or behaving (e.g., "I don't care if you are tired, get the work done by noon, or else."). To distinguish between autonomy support and behavioral control, Table 6.2 provides the definition, enabling conditions, and interpersonal behaviors associated with both autonomy support and behavioral control (Reeve, 2009).

Table 6.2   Enabling Conditions and Interpersonal Behaviors Associated with Autonomy Support and Control

Autonomy Support	Control
Enabling Condition	**Enabling Condition**
Takes the other person's perspective and adopts the other's frame of reference	Takes only one's own perspective and one's frame of reference (while ignoring the other's perspective and frame of reference)
Invites, welcomes, and incorporates the other's thoughts, feelings, and behaviors into the flow of the activity or conversation	Intrudes into and tries to change the other's thoughts, feelings, and behaviors
Supports the other's capacity for autonomous self-regulation	Pressures the other to think, feel, and behave in a prescribed or other-defined "right" way
Interpersonal Behaviors	**Interpersonal Behaviors**
Nurtures inner motivational resources	Relies on environmental sources of motivation
Provides explanatory rationales	Neglects explanatory rationales
Listens empathically, then relies on noncontrolling and informational language	Utters directives, then relies on controlling and pressure-inducing language
Displays patience to allow time for self-paced learning and adjusting to occur	Displays impatience that pushes the other to produce a right answer or a prescribed behavior quickly
Acknowledges and accepts the other's expressions of negative affect	Asserts power to overcome and silence the other's complaints and expressions of negative affect

As shown in the upper left part of Table 6.2, the starting point of any effort to support autonomy in others is to take their perspective and to adopt their frame of reference on the situation. This is usually done through conversation and discussion (e.g., What's interesting? What's most important? What would you like to do? What do you think about this?), although it also involves a good deal of listening, monitoring (e.g., facial expressions, tone of voice), and being flexible and open to others' input, suggestions, and priorities. The lower left part of Table 6.2 shows specifically what autonomy-supportive parents, teachers, coaches, managers, physicians, dentists, personal trainers, clergy, and others say and do while trying to motivate and engage others (i.e., their children, students, athletes, employees, clients, parishioners), while the lower right part of Table 6.2 shows specifically what controlling parents, teachers, coaches, and others say and do while trying to motivate others. Box 6 further provides a self-reflective activity to help you think about the quality of your own autonomy-supportive versus controlling motivating style toward others.

Nurturing Inner Motivational Resources

When teachers place learning activities in front of their students and when employers assign work to their employees, how do they try to spark their students' and employees' initiative, enthusiasm, and motivation to engage themselves productively in the work? People with an autonomy-supportive motivating style seek to vitalize the other person's inner motivational resources. They will present the work to be done so that it is consistent with the other person's interests, preferences, values, personal goals, sense of challenge, and psychological needs. Before presenting the work to the other, they will ask the other, "How can I make this task more interesting? How can I revise this task so that it is personally important to you? How can I restructure the task so that it becomes a more need-satisfying thing to do?" People with a controlling motivating style ignore or discount the other person's inner motivational resources and instead just tell the other what do to. To motivate the other to do what he is told to do, they will offer some environmental source of motivation, such as an incentive, reward, deadline, command, or threat of punishment. By adding the extrinsic motivator, the idea is not to support autonomy but rather to pressure the person into compliance.

Providing Explanatory Rationales

Nurturing inner motivational resources is a helpful motivational strategy when the task at hand is a potentially interesting thing to do, but sometimes we ask others to do relatively uninteresting things. For instance, parents ask their children to clean their rooms, and teachers ask students to follow the rules. To motivate others on uninteresting tasks, people with an autonomy-supportive style communicate the value, worth, meaning, utility, or importance of engaging in these sorts of behaviors, as in "It is important that you follow the rules because we need to respect the rights of everyone in the class and to help everyone feel safe and accepted." Promoting valuing means adding an explanatory "because" to one's request to explain *why* the request or activity is truly worth the other's time and effort. People with controlling styles, however, do not take the time to explain why the activity is worth doing, and say things like, "Just get it done," or a nonexplanatory, "Do it because I told you to." As discussed at the end of Chapter 5, the offering of explanatory rationales allows the other person the opportunity to internalize and voluntarily accept the externally imposed rules, constraints, or limits. Once internalized, people voluntarily (autonomously) put forth effort on even uninteresting (but important) activities (Jang, 2008; Reeve et al., 2002).

BOX 6 *Your Motivating Style*

Question: Why is this topic important?

Answer: To gain insight into your own motivating style toward others.

How do you try to motivate others? What do you say? What would you do? Below are two common motivating styles used by classroom teachers. Imagine yourself in the role of the classroom teacher, read each scenario, and then formulate a sense how much or how little that way of motivating and engaging students describes what you do or would do (based on Reeve et al., 2014).

Teaching Scenario 1: As you plan and prepare for an upcoming lesson, you think about what your students want and need. To support their interest and valuing of the lesson, you prepare some resources in advance. You create a challenging activity for students to do, and you create some engaging questions to pique their interest. As the class period begins, you invite your students' input and suggestions before finalizing the day's lesson plan, letting your students know that you welcome and value their thoughts, ideas, and suggestions. When students encounter difficulties and setbacks, you display patience—giving them the time and space they need to figure out the problem for themselves. When students complain and show little or no initiative, you acknowledge and accept their negative feelings, telling them that you understand why they might feel that way, given the difficulty and complexity of the lesson.

Teaching Scenario 2: As you plan and prepare for an upcoming lesson, you think about what needs to be covered and what students are supposed to learn. As the class period begins, you tell students what to do and then monitor their compliance closely.

To keep students on task, you make sure they follow your directions, obey their assignments, and basically do what they are supposed to do while not doing what they are not supposed to do. When students stray off task, you correct them saying, "You should be working now." To motivate students, you offer little incentives and privileges. When students encounter difficulties and setbacks, you intervene quickly to show and tell them the right way to do it. Overall, you take a "no-nonsense" attitude and make sure students do what you tell them to do, even if it means you need to push and pressure them into doing what they are supposed and required to do.

Motivating style refers to the tone of a person's sentiment and behavior while trying to motivate others to engage in activities; it can be characterized within a bipolar continuum that extends from a highly autonomy supportive through a neutral to a highly controlling style (Deci, Schwartz, Scheinman, & Ryan, 1981; Reeve, 2009, 2011; Su & Reeve, 2011). Teaching scenario 1 represents a highly autonomy-supportive style, while teaching scenario 2 represents a highly controlling style. Did either of these approaches describe your way of motivating others? Whether you tend to motivate and engage others in an autonomy-supportive or controlling way is important because motivating style is a reliable predictor of the sort of outcomes listed in Figure 6.3. In thinking about which teaching scenario above you favored, you can begin to learn about and reflect on your own motivating style. The guidelines in the present chapter may help you in the effort to expand your own style to a more autonomy-supportive style, assuming that you might want to do this.

Listening Empathically, Relying on Informational Language

People are sometimes listless, other times they perform poorly, and other times they behave inappropriately. People who adopt an autonomy-supportive motivating style treat listlessness, poor performance, and inappropriate behavior as motivational problems to be understood and solved rather than as targets for criticism (Deci, Connell, & Ryan, 1989). They listen empathically to understand why the other is struggling motivationally, and they use flexible, noncontrolling, and informational language to work collaboratively with that person to diagnose and solve the motivational problem. For example, a coach

Motivation	Engagement	Development	Learning	Performance	Well-Being
Autonomy	Engagement	Self-Worth	Conceptual Understanding	Grades	Psychological Well-Being
Competence	Persistence	Creativity	Deep Processing	Task Performance	Vitality
Relatedness	Positive Emotion	Preference for Optimal Challenge	Active Information Processing	Standardized Test Scores	School/Life Satisfaction
Intrinsic Motivation	(Less) Negative Emotion		Self-Regulation Strategies		Biological Well-Being
Curiosity	School Retention vs. Dropping Out				
Internalized Values					

Figure 6.3   Benefits from Autonomy Support

might say to her athlete, "I've noticed that your running times have slowed lately. Do you know why this might be?" In contrast, people with a controlling style use a pressuring, rigid, "no-nonsense," and guilt-inducing communication style that says that the other person should, must, ought to, or has to do a certain thing (e.g., "You *should* try harder" or "You *must* finish that project"). People who adopt a controlling motivating style try to motivate others by inducing feelings of guilt, shame, and anxiety for not performing a requested activity (Barber, 1996), by threatening to withdraw their approval (Assor, Roth, & Deci, 2004), by cultivating perfectionist standards (Soenens et al., 2005), and by offering "conditional regard" more generally (Roth, Assor, Niemiec, Ryan, & Deci, 2009).

Displaying Patience

Patience is the calmness one person shows as the other struggles to adjust his behavior from something that is ineffective, indolent, and irresponsible into something that is effective, energized, and responsible. Displaying patience means giving another person the time and space he needs to explore better ways of behaving, to plan and to try out alternative ways of behaving, and to alter personal goals and problem-solving strategies. In practice, what autonomy-supportive patience looks like is a lot of listening, perspective-taking, and postponing of advice until one first deeply understands why the person is acting in an ineffective, indolent, or irresponsible way and second senses that the other is open and ready to hear one's suggestions. Once understood, appropriate and constructive support becomes possible, especially when the other person seems stuck on a problem. This support often involves offering words of encouragement and hints toward progress. In contrast, people who adopt a controlling motivating style impatiently rush in, take over, and show and tell the other person what to do and how to solve the problem (e.g., "Here, let me show you how to do it.").

Acknowledging and Accepting Expressions of Negative Affect

Sometimes people complain, show resistance, and express negative affect about having to engage in uninteresting or difficult tasks. They sometimes show "attitude" when having to do things like clean their rooms, follow rules, run laps, and be nice. People who adopt an autonomy-supportive style listen carefully to these expressions of negative affect and accept them as valid reactions to being asked to do things that seems, to them, uninteresting and not worthwhile. Essentially, autonomy-supportive individuals say "okay," and then work collaboratively with the other person to solve the underlying cause of the negative affect and resistance, usually with the end result of redesigning the uninteresting activity into something that becomes more interesting or appealing to the person. People who adopt a controlling style make it clear that such expressions of negative affect and resistance are unacceptable, saying things such as, "Quit your complaining and just get the work done—or else!" and "It's my way or the highway."

Benefits from Autonomy Support

Receiving autonomy support provides many important benefits. A summary of these benefits appear in Figure 6.3 and include benefits to one's motivation, engagement, development, learning, performance, and well-being. Autonomy support nurtures not only the psychological need of autonomy (Jang, Kim, & Reeve, 2011; Reeve & Jang, 2006), but it also nurtures the full range of inner motivational resources, including competence and relatedness need satisfaction (Baard, Deci, & Ryan, 2004; Cheon, Reeve, & Moon, 2012; Ryan & Grolnick, 1986), intrinsic motivation (Reeve, Nix, & Hamm, 2003), curiosity (Deci, Schwartz et al., 1981), and internalized or self-endorsed values (Grolnick & Ryan, 1987). These experiences of psychological need satisfaction and the vitalization of inner motivational resources then pave the way to gains in and high levels of engagement, development, learning, performance, and well-being (as per Figure 6.3).[1]

Benefits of Giving and Receiving Autonomy Support

The benefits of both giving and receiving autonomy support can be illustrated by thinking about the quality of the relationship you have with several different people in your life. Imagine a close friend and complete the following questions (from Deci, La Guardia et al., 2006):

- My friend believes that I provide him/her with choices and options (giving autonomy support).
- My friend tries to understand how I see things (receiving autonomy support).
- When I am with my friend, I feel free to be who I am (autonomy).

---

[1]Each of the 26 entries listed under the six columns in Figure 6.3 represents a separate empirical study showing that autonomy support was associated with a high level of that dependent measure. For the reference citations associated with each of these studies, please see the 2009 paper by Reeve in the journal *Educational Psychologist*.

- When I am with my friend, I feel like a competent person (competence).
- When I am with my friend, I feel loved and cared about (relatedness).

After completing these questions, ask yourself about the quality of that relationship in terms of relationship satisfaction, closeness, and felt security (versus dismissive, fearful, alienated, and inability to turn to the friend in a time of need). When researchers examined peer relationships, they found that the more one person received autonomy support from the other and the more one person gave autonomy support to the other, the more those in the relationship experience psychological need satisfaction. Further, the more autonomy, competence, and relatedness need satisfaction that relationship was able to produce, the better able was that relationship to produce relationship satisfaction, positive affect, emotional closeness, and felt security, and this was just as true for male friendships as it was for female friendships (Deci et al., 2006).

Consider a second study on the benefits of receiving autonomy support in which schoolchildren painted while their teacher acted in either an autonomy-supportive or a controlling way. In both conditions, teachers imposed a list of rules to follow, including do not mix the paints, clean off the brushes before switching to a new color, and paint only on a particular piece of paper (Koestner et al., 1984). Some children painted under these conditions imposed on them by a controlling teacher. This teacher used controlling, pressuring language that told children to follow the rules. Other children painted under autonomy-supportive conditions. This teacher used informational language that communicated the rationale for each rule so the children could understand why the rules were important and worth following. After the children painted, the researchers measured the quality of their motivation and scored their artwork on various dimensions (see Table 6.3). Children who painted under autonomy-supportive conditions enjoyed the painting more,

Table 6.3   Children's Motivational Benefits from Autonomy-Supportive (Rather Than Controlling) Rules

Dependent Measure		Rules Communicated in a Controlling Way	Rules Communicated in a Autonomy-Supportive Way
Enjoyment	M	4.87	5.57
	(SD)	(0.99)	(0.65)
Free Choice Behavior	M	107.7	257.1
	(SD)	(166.0)	(212.6)
Creativity	M	4.80	5.34
	(SD)	(1.16)	(1.17)
Technical Goodness	M	4.88	5.90
	(SD)	(0.87)	(1.28)
Quality	M	4.84	5.62
	(SD)	(0.68)	(1.06)

Notes: M = Mean, SD = Standard Deviation; Free choice = Intrinsically motivated behavior; All mean differences are significantly different, $p < .05$.
Source: Adapted from "Setting limits on children's behavior: The differential effects of controlling versus informational styles on intrinsic motivation and creativity," by R. Koestner, R. M. Ryan, F. Bernieri, and K. Holt (1984). *Journal of Personality, 52*, 233–248.

were more intrinsically motivated to paint (see "free-choice behavior"), and produced artwork that was creative, technically good, and of high quality. This study follows the spirit of cognitive evaluation theory (Chapter 5) to make it clear that rules per se do not have motivational effects; instead, motivational effect follow from how those rules are communicated and enforced. While controlling rules suffocated the children's artistry, creativity, and enjoyment, autonomy supportive rules actually allowed children's artistry, creativity, and enjoyment to flourish.

COMPETENCE

Everyone wants and strives to be competent. Everyone desires to interact effectively with his or her surroundings, and this desire extends into all aspects of our lives—in school, at work, in relationships, and during recreation and sports. We all want to develop skills and improve our capacities, talents, and potential. When we find ourselves face to face with a challenge, we give the moment our full attention. When given the opportunity to test, expand, and grow and develop our skills, we all want to do well and make progress. When we do so, we feel satisfied, even happy and fulfilled. In other words, we have a need for competence.

Competence is the psychological need to be effective in interactions with the environment, and it reflects the desire to exercise and extend one's capacities and skills and, in doing so, to seek out and master optimal and developmentally appropriate challenges (Deci & Ryan, 1985a). Competence is the psychological need that generates the willingness to seek out optimal challenges, take them on, and exert persistent effort and strategic thinking until we master them. When we engage in a task that offers a level of difficulty and complexity that is precisely right for our current skills and talents, our psychological need for competence is involved; we feel interest. When we make progress on developing and extending our skills, our psychological need for competence is satisfied; we feel enjoyment.

The Pleasure of Optimal Challenge

To confirm that people do indeed derive pleasure and a sense of personal satisfaction from optimal challenge, Susan Harter (1974, 1978b) gave schoolage children anagrams of different difficulty levels and monitored each child's expressed pleasure (through smiling) upon solving each anagram. (An anagram is a word or phrase such as *table*, with its letters rearranged to form another word or phrase, as in *bleat*.) In general, solving anagrams successfully produced greater smiling and higher enjoyment than did failure (Harter, 1974), suggesting that mastery in general gratifies the competence need. In addition, however, some anagrams were very easy (three letters), some were easy (four letters), others were moderately difficult (five letters), and still others were very hard (six letters). As the anagrams increased in difficulty, it took the children longer and longer to solve them, as you might expect, but the critical measure in the study was how much the children smiled after solving the anagrams of different levels of difficulty (Harter, 1978b). A curvilinear inverted-U pattern emerged in which children smiled very little after solving the very easy or easy problems, very much after solving the moderately difficult problems, and only modestly after solving the very hard problems. The central point is that children experience the greatest pleasure following success in the context of optimal (moderate) challenge. In the words of the children, "The fives were just right; they were a challenge, but not too much challenge" and "I liked the hard ones because they gave you a sense of satisfaction, but the really hard ones were just too frustrating" (Harter, 1978b, p. 796).

Interdependency between Challenge and Feedback

Everyone is challenged every day. In school, teachers put examinations in front of students. At work, projects and assignments test a person's writing and creativity skills. On the drive home, the interstate challenges both our patience and our driving skills. If the car breaks down, our automotive repair skills will be put to the test. These situations set the stage for challenge. But setting the stage is not the same thing as actually creating the challenge experience itself. One additional ingredient still needs to be tossed into the equation—feedback. Confronting a test, project, or contest invites challenge, but a person does not *experience* challenge until he or she begins to perform and receive the first glimpse of feedback. It is at that point—facing a challenge and receiving initial performance feedback—that people report the psychological experience of being challenged (Reeve & Deci, 1996). Professional musicians and athletes often echo this insight when they report that their pre-performance feelings of anxiety turn immediately into an experience of challenge with "the first pitch" or "the first keystroke on the piano."

Optimal Challenge and Flow

To determine the conditions that create enjoyment, Mihaly Csikszentmihalyi (1975, 1982, 1990) interviewed and studied hundreds of people he presumed knew what it felt like to have fun: rock climbers, dancers, chess champions, basketball players, surgeons, and others. Later, he studied more representative samples, including working professionals, high school students, assembly-line workers, groups of older adults, and people who generally sat at home and watched television. Irrespective of which sample he studied, Csikszentmihalyi found the essence of enjoyment could be traced to the "flow experience."

Flow is a state of concentration that involves a holistic absorption and deep involvement in an activity (Keller & Bless, 2008). What people say when they are in a state of flow includes, "I am in the zone," "I am totally focused on what I'm doing," and "It feels like everything clicks" (Martin & Jackson, 2008).

Flow is such a pleasurable experience that the person often repeats the activity with the hope of experiencing flow again and again (Csikszentmihalyi & Nakamura, 1989). Flow occurs whenever a person uses his or her skills to rise up to and overcome some challenge. The relationship between task challenge and personal skill appears in Figure 6.4. Although the figures on the left and right side look a bit different at first glance, they are actually two depictions of the same story. Both figures identify the emotional consequences that arise from the different pairings of challenge and skill. When challenge outweighs skill (skill is low, challenge is high; see upper left quadrant of both figures), performers worry that the demands of the task will overwhelm their skills. Being overchallenged threatens competence, and that threat manifests itself emotionally as worry (if moderately overchallenged) or as anxiety (if highly overchallenged). However, when challenge matches skill (challenge and skill are both at least moderately high; see upper right quadrant of both figures), concentration, involvement, and enjoyment rise. If challenges and skills are perfectly matched, the

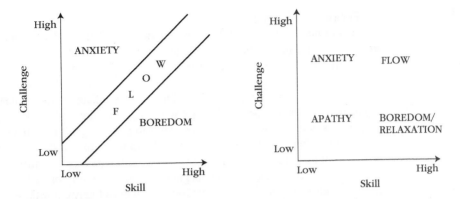

Figure 6.4   Flow Model

Source: Adapted from *Beyond Boredom and Anxiety: The Experience of Flow in Work and Play,* by
M. Csikszentmihalyi, 1975, San Francisco: Jossey-Bass.

experience is one of flow. Csikszentmihalyi calls this "optimal experience." When skill outweighs challenge (skill is high, challenge is low; lower right quadrant of both figures), task
engagement is characterized by reduced concentration, minimal task involvement, and emotional boredom. Being underchallenged neglects competence, and that neglect manifests
itself emotionally as indifference or boredom. The worst profile of experience emanates
from the pairing of low challenge and low skill (the lower left quadrant in both figures). With
both challenge and skill low, literally all measures of emotion, motivation, and cognition are
at their lowest levels—the person simply does not care about the task (Csikszentmihalyi,
Rathunde, & Whalen, 1993). Flow is therefore a bit more complicated than just the balance
of challenge and skill because balancing low skill and low challenge produces apathy. A
more accurate description of how challenge relates to skill is that flow emerges in those situations in which both challenge and skill are high or moderately high (Csikszentmihalyi &
Csikszentmihalyi, 1988; Keller & Bless, 2008).

One way to understand the dynamics of the flow experience, as illustrated in Figure 6.4,
is to imagine three individuals who perform the same moderately difficult task but possess
different levels of skill, with person A being unskilled, person B being moderately skilled,
and person C being highly skilled. Given a somewhat difficult task, unskilled person A will
worry because his skills cannot match the demands and challenges of the task, somewhat
skilled person B will experience flow because his skills equally match with the demands and
challenges of the task, and highly skilled person C will be bored because her skills exceed
the demands and challenges of the task. To alleviate worry, person A has two options:
decrease task difficulty or increase personal skill. If person A is going to experience flow, he
will need to find an easier version of the task, or he will need to learn and practice until he
is able to raise his skill level. If person C is going to experience flow, she will need to find a
more difficult version of task (e.g., a harder math problem to solve, a more proficient tennis
opponent) or she will need to handicap her skill in some way (e.g., solve the math problem
under a time limit, be allowed only one serve rather than the traditional two serves during
a tennis match). People engage in these sorts of strategies of calibrating task difficulty and
personal skill because they want their task participation to involve and satisfy their need for
competence, rather than neglect or frustrate it.

For a concrete example, consider three friends on a snow-skiing outing. Ski slopes offer different difficulty levels such that some slopes are relatively flat (beginner slopes), some are fairly steep (intermediate slopes), and others are downright death-defying (advanced slopes). If the skiers have different levels of skill, Figure 6.4 predicts that the emotional experience will vary for each skier on each slope. The novice skier will enjoy the beginner slopes but will experience mostly worry on the intermediate slopes and heart-stopping anxiety on the advanced slopes. The novice will experience flow only on the beginner slopes. If the novice's time on the beginner slopes starts to produce gains in skill level, however, then he or she will begin to feel the motivational pull to try one of the intermediate slopes (to seek out optimal challenge). The average skier will enjoy the intermediate slopes but will experience mostly boredom on the beginner slopes and worry or perhaps experience anxiety on the advanced slopes. The professional will most likely enjoy the advanced slopes but will experience mind-numbing boredom on the beginner slopes and some boredom on the intermediate slopes. While spending time on the intermediate slopes, the professional will need to adjust his or skill level downward by using only one ski, using shorter skis, skiing backward, or by looking for moguls or whatever other challenges might pop up along the way. The fact that people can adjust both level of skill and level of difficulty means that people can establish the conditions for optimal challenge and hence create the conditions to involve and satisfy their need for competence.

The most important practical implication of flow theory is the following: Given optimal challenge, *any* activity can be enjoyed. Doing electrical work, writing papers, debating issues, sewing, analyzing a play, mowing the lawn, and other such activities do not necessarily make the top of most people's list of must-do activities, but the balance of skill with challenge adds the spice of flow—concentration, absorption, enjoyment, and optimal experience. Consistent with the idea that optimal challenge gives rise to flow, Csikszentmihalyi found in a pair of studies that students actually enjoyed doing their homework and working their part-time jobs more than they enjoyed viewing (challengeless) television programs (Csikszentmihalyi et al., 1993). Furthermore, people more frequently experience enjoyment at (challenging) work than they do during (unchallenging) leisure (Csikszentmihalyi, 1982).

Where an experience of flow comes from and how it feels, once it is actually experienced, appears in Figure 6.5 (Kawabata & Mallett, 2011; Nakamura & Csikszentmihalyi, 2002). The upper portion of the figure (the three boldface ovals) illustrates the origins of flow. The lower portion of the figure (the other six ovals) illustrates the subjective experience of flow. When people enter a task with clear goals and when that task provides them with a steady stream of objective and unambiguous (unbiased) feedback (as occurs with most sports), the person is likely to experience a balance of challenge and skill, hence flow. What the figure adds to the earlier discussion on the origins of flow is to note that (1) enjoyment, concentration, and a feeling of acting in slow motion come largely from the pursuit of a clear goal to strive for and (2) personal control and a Zen-like merging of action and awareness (the task and I are one) come largely from the balance of challenge and skill.

At the ski slopes, for instance, the difficulties on the mountain give the person many clear goals to strive for, such as to get off the ski lift without falling and to maneuver around other skiers and all those trees and patches of ice. This is a key reason *why* skiing is fun. And, it is feedback about one's progress of achieving competent functioning during a challenging task that communicates a sense of personal control and competent need satisfaction. For instance, if you fall on your face as you get off the ski lift, then it is hard not to feel rather unskilled and incompetent, especially if your friends are laughing at you. But if you whiz

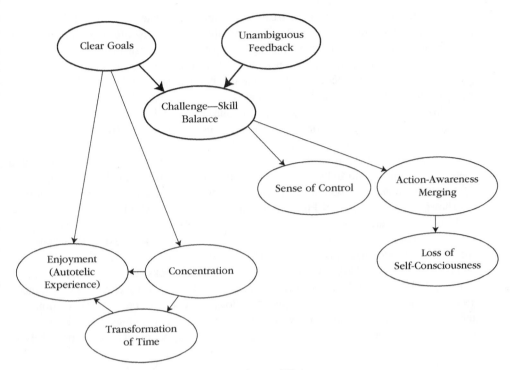

Figure 6.5   Origins (Boldface Ovals) and Experience of Flow

Source: Adapted from "Flow experience in physical activity: Examination of the internal structure of flow from a process-related perspective" by M. Kawabata & C. J. Mallett (2011) in *Motivation and Emotion, 35*, 393–402. Adapted by permission.

more effectively down the slopes on this run than you did on the last run, then it is hard not to feel rather skilled and competent.

In terms of benefits, the experience of flow facilitates and improves performance, and this facilitating effect of flow on performance holds true across a wide range of people and activities, including actors (Martin & Cutler, 2002), athletes (Jackson, Thomas, Marsh, & Smethurst, 2001), students (Engeser & Rheinberg, 2008), and marathon runners (Schuler & Brunner, 2009). The primary reason why flow enhances performance is probably an indirect one, however. That is, the experience of flow is so enjoyable that people want to re-experience it. This desire to re-experience flow leads people to repeat and re-engage in those activities that produce flow, and this persistent involvement with a flow-enabling task then provides a practice and skill-building effect that improves performance over time (Schuler & Brunner, 2009). Rather than increasing performance directly, flow encourages the task involvement necessary to practice and to develop performance-enhancing skill.

Structure

The upper part of Figure 6.5 introduces the interesting idea that environments can be structured to make a flow experience more likely. That is, if the environment provided by teachers, workplace managers, athletic coaches, and so on can be structured to offer both clear goals and clear feedback, then these are the conditions that create both competence psychological need satisfaction and flow. This is generally true, but just offering clear goals and clear feedback has been found to be missing a key piece of the puzzle in helping others experience enjoyment, flow, and competence need satisfaction. People also need skill-building guidance and help. They need optimal challenge, but they also need instruction, coaching, and guidance so that they can figure out how to meet and master that optimal challenge.

This context of clear goals, guidance and help, and clear feedback represents "structure" (Skinner & Belmont, 1993; Jang, Reeve, & Deci, 2010). Figure 6.6 shows one rating sheet to score how much or how little structure teachers provide to students during classroom instruction. Teachers who provide students with a highly structured learning environment do so by offering (1) clear goals, directions, and learning objectives; (2) helpful guidance and mentoring; and (3) clear, constructive, and skill-building feedback (as shown on the right side of Figure 6.6). Similarly, teachers who fail to provide students with such a structured learning environment fail in the effort to provide clear goals, helpful guidance, or constructive feedback (as shown on the left side of Figure 6.6). When environments (e.g., classroom, worksite, athletic field) are structured in a way that offers clear goals and helpful guidance (Hokoda & Fincham, 1995; Nolen-Hoeksema, Wolfson, Mumme, & Guskin, 1995) and well as constructive feedback (Hokoda & Fincham, 1995; Skinner, 1986), people tend to experience enjoyment, flow, and competence need satisfaction (and tend not to experience boredom, worry, and anxiety). In environments characterized by clear goals, helpful guidance, and constructive feedback, people are also more likely to

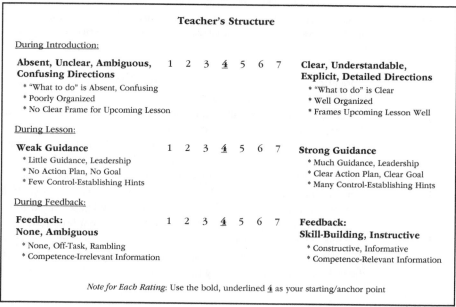

Figure 6.6 Rating Sheet to Score the Three Aspects of Structure: Clear Goals, Helpful Guidance, and Clear Feedback

Source: Adapted from "Engaging students in learning activities: It is not autonomy support or structure, but autonomy support and structure," by H. Jang, J. Reeve, & E. L. Deci (2010), *Journal of Educational Psychology, 102*, 588–600. Copyright by the American Psychological Association. Reprinted by permission.

exert effort, develop skills, solve problems, and make progress (Connell & Wellborn, 1991; Hollembeak & Amorose, 2005; Jang et al., 2010; Ntoumanis, 2005; Skinner, 1991, 1995; Skinner, Zimmer-Gembeck, & Connell, 1998; Taylor & Ntoumanis, 2007).

Feedback

Whether individuals perceive their performance to be competent or incompetent is often an ambiguous undertaking. To make such an evaluation, a performer needs feedback. Feedback comes from one (or more) of the following four sources (from Boggiano & Ruble, 1979; Dollinger & Thelen, 1978; Grolnick, Frodi, & Bridges, 1984; Koestner et al., 1987; Reeve & Deci, 1996; Schunk & Hanson, 1989):

· Task itself

· Comparisons of one's current performance with one's own past performances

· Comparisons of one's current performance with the performance of others

· Evaluations of others

In some tasks, competence feedback is inherent in the performance of the task itself, as in successfully logging onto a computer (or not), repairing a machine (or not), or hitting a tennis ball into the serving area (or not). In most tasks, however, performance evaluation is more ambiguous than a right-versus-wrong performance outcome. In performing social skills, artistic talents, or other such tasks, our own past performances, peer performances, and the evaluations of other people (rather than the task itself) supply the information necessary to make an inference of competence versus incompetence. As for our own past performances, the perception of progress is an important signal of competence (Schunk & Hanson, 1989), just as the perception of a lack of progress signals incompetence. People often feel a sense of competence as they revise their work, as in revising a paper or trying a new version of a song or athletic skill. As to the performance of our peers, doing better than others signals competence, whereas doing worse than others signals incompetence (Harackiewicz, 1979; Reeve & Deci, 1996). Put simply, winning signals competence while losing signals incompetence. As for the evaluation of other people, praise and positive feedback bolsters perceptions of competence, whereas criticism and negative feedback deflates it (Anderson et al., 1976; Blank et al., 1984; Deci, 1971; Dollinger & Thelen, 1978; Vallerand & Reid, 1984).

In summary, performance feedback in its various forms—task-generated, self-generated, social comparisons, and other-generated—supplies the information individuals need to formulate a cognitive evaluation of their perceived level of competence. When these sources of information converge on an interpretation of a job well done, we experience positive feedback that is capable of satisfying the psychological need for competence.

Praise is often used as positive feedback, although it too often fails to produce an authentic experience of competence need satisfaction. In schools, at work, in the home, and on the athletic field, it is routine to hear one person praising the other in hopes of bolstering the other's perceived competence. Praise (verbal positive feedback), however, is only the caboose on this train. A need-satisfying sense of competence comes from optimal challenge, and optimal challenge requires a level of engagement from the person that is rich in concentration, effort, persistence, and strategic thinking, or at least a level of engagement that is proportional to the difficulty of the challenge at hand. As the person engages in an optimal challenge, feedback flows almost naturally from the task, from self-comparisons, from social comparisons, and from the evaluation of others. Hence, in practice, praise is often superfluous information. Rather than praise, what people who are engaged in an optimal challenge really need is helpful and constructive instruction, modeling, coaching, and scaffolding, as expert instruction is one means of increasing one's skill (and therefore increasing one's chances of meeting the optimal challenge). Post-performance praise is fine, but in-performance mentoring that enhances skill is the type of feedback that translates into an authentic experience of competence need satisfaction.

Failure Tolerance

Challenge seeking almost always occurs within a social context. This is important because the main problem with optimal challenge, motivationally speaking, is that people who pursue optimal challenges are as likely to experience failure and frustration as they are to experience success and enjoyment. In fact, one hallmark of optimal challenge is that success and failure are equally likely. Thus, the dread of failure can emotionally squash the competence need-involving qualities of optimal challenge. If intense, the dread of failure can motivate avoidance behaviors so that people go out of their way to escape from being challenged (Covington, 1984a, 1984b). When people are placed into a social context that reacts harshly to failure, they are more likely to avoid challenge than to seek it.

Before people will engage freely in optimally challenging tasks, the social context must tolerate (even value!) failure and error making. Optimal challenge implies that considerable error making will occur, so a prerequisite for challenge seeking is the perception that one is surrounded by a social climate rich in "failure tolerance" or "error tolerance" (Clifford, 1988, 1990). Error tolerance, failure tolerance, and risk taking rest on the belief that we learn more from failure than we do from success. Failure produces unique opportunities for learning because it has its constructive aspects when people identify its causes and when failure feedback prompts people to try new strategies, to seek advice, and to expose themselves to further instruction (Clifford, 1984). People most prefer to seek out optimal challenges (rather than easy successes) when they find themselves in social environments that are autonomy-supportive and failure-tolerant, rather than controlling and failure-intolerant (Clifford, 1990; Deci, Schwartz, et al., 1981).

RELATEDNESS

Everyone needs to belong. Everyone wants friends. Everyone experiences closeness and joy when interacting with a caring, responsive friend. We all go out of our way to form and maintain warm, close, affectionate relationships with others. We all want others to understand us for who we are as individuals, and we want others to accept and to value us. We want others to acknowledge us and to be responsive to our needs. We want relationships with others who really and honestly care for our well-being. We want our relationships to be reciprocal; we want to form not only close, responsive, and caring relationships but we also want the other person to want to form these same sorts of relationships with us. In other words, we have a need for relatedness.

Relatedness is the psychological need to establish close emotional bonds and attachments with other people, and it reflects the desire to be emotionally connected to and interpersonally involved in warm relationships (Baumeister & Leary, 1995;

Carvallo & Gabriel, 2006; Fromm, 1956; Guisinger & Blatt, 1994; Ryan, 1991; Ryan & Powelson, 1991; Sullivan, 1953). It is the psychological need to care and to feel cared for, to love and to feel loved. Because we need relatedness, we gravitate toward people who we trust will care for our well-being, and we drift away from those who we do not trust to look out for our well-being. What people are essentially looking for within need-satisfying relationships is the opportunity to relate the self to another person in an authentic, caring, reciprocal, and emotionally meaningful way (La Guardia & Patrick, 2008; Ryan, 1993).

Because we need relatedness, social bonds form easily (Baumeister & Leary, 1995). Given an opportunity to engage others in face-to-face interaction, people generally go out of their way to create relationships (Brewer, 1979). The emergence of friendships and alliances seems to require little more than proximity and spending time together (Wilder & Thompson, 1980). The more people interact and the more people spend time together, the more likely they are to form friendships. Once social bonds are formed, people are generally reluctant to break them. When we move, when we graduate from school, and when others take their leave of us, we resist the breakup of the relationship. We promise to write and to telephone, we cry, we exchange addresses and phone numbers, and we plan a future occasion to get back together.

Involving Relatedness: Interaction with Others

The primary condition that involves the relatedness need is social interaction. When we are alone, our relatedness need is relatively quiet. It is social interaction that vitalizes the psychological need for relatedness (Carvallo & Gabriel, 2006). But even interactions with strangers can leave the relatedness strangely quiet. So, it is only those social interactions that promise the possibility of warmth, care, and mutual concern that vitalize the relatedness need. Starting a new relationship that promises new opportunities for warmth and care seems to be an especially easy way to involve the need for relatedness. Consider, for instance, the motivational potency of first dates, falling in love, childbirth, fraternity or sorority pledging, and starting anew in school or in employment. Generally speaking, people seek emotionally positive interactions and interaction partners, and in doing so they gain the opportunity to involve or vitalize the psychological need for relatedness.

Satisfying Relatedness: Perception of a Social Bond

Although interaction with others is sufficient for involving the relatedness need, relatedness-need satisfaction requires the creation of a social bond between the self and another. To be satisfying, that social bond needs to be characterized by the perceptions that the other person (1) cares about my welfare and (2) likes me (Baumeister & Leary, 1995). But more than caring and liking, the relationships that deeply satisfy the need for relatedness are those steeped in the knowledge that one's "true self"—one's "authentic self"—has been shown and deemed to be important in the eyes of another person (Deci & Ryan, 1995; Rogers, 1969; Ryan, 1993).

Relationships that do not involve caring, liking, accepting, and valuing do not satisfy the need for relatedness. People who are lonely, for instance, do not lack frequent social contact, and they do not attend less to others. They interact with others, and they notice the changes in facial expression and voice tone as much as do nonlonely people. Rather, those who feel lonely lack close, intimate relationships (Wheeler, Reis, & Nezlek, 1983).

When it comes to relatedness and relationships, quality is more important than quantity (Carstensen, 1993).

Marriages, which are clearly close relationships, are not always emotionally satisfying. Some marriages, although full of social interaction, are also full of conflict, stress, and criticism and basically make the other person's life more difficult than it otherwise would be. Alternatively, supportive marriages, those rich in mutual care and liking, are the emotionally satisfying relationships that lead people to feel happy (Coyne & DeLongis, 1986). Furthermore, youths' relationships with their parents follow the same pattern in that to keep youths' depression at bay, parent–youth relationships not only need to exist, but they also need to be supportive (Carnelley, Pietromonaco, & Jaffe, 1994). Having one's relatedness need satisfied, as opposed to neglected or thwarted, promotes vitality and well-being (Ryan & Lynch, 1989), and it lessens loneliness and depression (Pierce, Sarason, & Sarason, 1991; Windle, 1992). Emotions such as sadness, depression, jealousy, and loneliness exist as telltale signs of a life lived in the absence of intimate, high-quality, relatedness-satisfying relationships and social bonds (Baumeister & Leary, 1995; Williams & Solano, 1983).

Communal and Exchange Relationships

We involve ourselves in many relationships, some of which are more need satisfying than others. The distinction between communal and exchange relationships captures the essence of relationships that do (communal) and do not (exchange) satisfy the relatedness need (Mills & Clark, 1982).

Exchange relationships are those between acquaintances or between people who do business together. Communal relationships are those between persons who care about the welfare of the other, as exemplified by friendships, family, and romantic relationships. What distinguishes exchange from communal relationships are the implicit rules that guide the giving and receiving of benefits, such as money, help, and emotional support (Clark, Mills, & Powell, 1986). In exchange relationships, no obligation exists between interactants to be concerned with the other person's needs or welfare. As they say in the movie *The Godfather*, "It's business." (Incidentally, an "It's business" attitude toward a relationship serves to justify why people act in neglectful and uncaring ways.) In communal relationships, both parties care for the needs of the other, and both feel an obligation to support the other's welfare. Only communal relationships satisfy the relatedness need.

In communal relationships, people monitor and keep track of the other's needs, regardless of any forthcoming opportunities for reciprocity or material gain (Clark, 1984; Clark & Mills, 1979; Clark et al., 1986; Clark, Ouellette, Powell, & Milberg, 1987). For instance, people involved in communal (as compared to exchange) relationships frequently check up on the needs of the other (Clark et al., 1986); resist keeping track (or score) of individual inputs into joint projects (Clark, 1984); are responsive to the other's needs (LeMay, Clark, & Feeney, 2007); provide help when the other feels distressed (Clark et al., 1987); and experience tangible economic gifts as *detrimental* to how friendly, relaxed, and satisfying forthcoming interactions are likely to be (Clark & Mills, 1979). On this latter point, consider the emotional discomfort you might feel after providing a ride home to a close (communal) friend and, upon arrival, were handed $10 for the favor (Mills & Clark, 1982). In communal relationships, what people want and need is relatedness need satisfaction, not a $10 bill.

Fruits of Relatedness Need Satisfaction

The fruits of relatedness need satisfaction are the fruits of any psychological need satisfaction (i.e., autonomy, competence, or relatedness; Moller, Deci, & Elliot, 2010)—namely, engagement, developmental growth, health, and well-being. In terms of engagement, it is a routine finding in the school setting that relatedness to one's teachers, relatedness to one's peers, and relatedness to one's family and community are strong and reliable predictors of students' engagement, including how much effort they put forth during school (Goodenow & Grady, 1993; Furrer & Skinner, 2003) and whether they persist in school versus drop out (Battistich, Solomon, Watson, & Schaps, 1997; Osterman, 2000).

In terms of developmental growth, people function better, are more resilient to stress, and report greater self-esteem and fewer psychological difficulties when their interpersonal relationships support their need for relatedness (Cohen, Sherrod, & Clark, 1986; Lepore, 1992; Osterman, 2000; Ryan, Stiller, & Lynch, 1994; Sarason et al., 1991; Windle, 1992). One key reason that relatedness need satisfaction promotes such positive functioning is because relatedness to others provides the social context in which internalization occurs (Goodenow, 1993; Grolnick, Deci, & Ryan, 1997; Ryan & Powelson, 1991).

When a person feels emotionally connected to and interpersonally involved with another, then he or she believes the other person is truly looking out for his or her welfare, relatedness is high, and internalization occurs willingly. Contrarily, when a person feels emotionally distant from and interpersonally neglected by another, then he or she believes the other person does not care, relatedness is low, and internalization rarely occurs. For instance, children who have a positive relationship with their parents will generally internalize their parents' ways of thinking and behaving. Children with stormy or nonexistent relationships with their parents will generally reject their parents' ways of thinking and behaving and search for a value system elsewhere. High relatedness does not guarantee that internalization will occur. For internalization to occur, the individual must also see the value, meaning, and utility in the other's prescriptions ("do X, believe Y") and proscriptions ("don't do X, don't believe Y"). To internalize a value or to internalize a way of behaving, the person needs to understand why the value or way of acting has merit, as in "Why is it important that I brush my teeth?" Therefore, relatedness is a necessary (but not sufficient) condition for internalization and cultural transmission to occur. Internalization flourishes in relationships that provide a rich supply of (1) relatedness need satisfaction and (2) personally satisfying rationales that explain why the others' prescriptions and proscriptions will benefit the self.

In terms of health, being loved, respected, protected, cared for, and having one's needs meet affects the vasopressin and oxytocin systems (Wisner-Fries et al., 2005). The vasopressin and oxytocin hormones regulate social bonding, stress regulation, and emotional reactivity. For instance, warm touching increases while social neglect decreases the release of these two hormones, and increases in vasopressin and oxytocin lead to positive social behavior and lessened stress while decreases in these hormones leads to negative social behavior and heighten stress.

In terms of well-being, people who experience a steady stream of relatedness need satisfaction in their relationships and in their lives are consistently happier, more enthusiastic, and less stressed, anxious, depressed, and lonely than are those who experience a dearth of relatedness need satisfaction (Baumeister & Leary, 1995). And, the more relatedness need satisfaction that has occurred in one's life, the more the person comes to value and be satisfied by future opportunities for relatedness need satisfaction (Moller, Deci, & Elliot, 2010). When it comes to relatedness need satisfaction, the emotionally rich get richer.

PUTTING IT ALL TOGETHER: RELATIONSHIPS AND SOCIAL CONTEXTS THAT SUPPORT PSYCHOLOGICAL NEED SATISFACTION

Specific aspects of relationships and the social context are noteworthy in their capacity to involve and satisfy the psychological needs. For illustration, Table 6.4 summarizes the prototypical events that involve the needs of autonomy, competence, and relatedness as well as the prototypical events that satisfy these three needs. When involved in activities that offer opportunities for self-direction, optimal challenge, and social interaction, people typically experience need involvement and feel interest. When involved in activities that offer autonomy support, progress feedback, and communal relationships, people typically experience need satisfaction and feel enjoyment.

Engagement

The motivational model of engagement depicted in Figure 6.7 comprehensively illustrates the contribution that relationships and social contexts have for psychological needs (Skinner & Pitzer, 2012; Skinner, Kindermann, Connell, & Wellborn, 2009). Engagement represents how actively involved in an activity the person is, such as when learning in school or practicing skills in music or sports (Christenson et al., 2012). When highly engaged, people show behavioral engagement (on-task attention, effort, persistence), emotional engagement (interest, enjoyment), cognitive engagement (strategic thinking, sophisticated learning strategies), and agentic engagement (constructive contributions into the flow of the activity), as discussed in Chapter 1.

Jim Connell and Ellen Skinner explain the conditions under which people show high and low engagement by tracing the origin of engagement to the three psychological needs. Specifically, they argue that (1) autonomy support enhances engagement because it involves and satisfies the need for autonomy, (2) structure enhances engagement because it involves and satisfies the need for competence, and (3) involvement enhances engagement because it involves and satisfies the need for relatedness. How autonomy support, structure, and involvement are expressed during social interactions (in school, in the home, at work, during athletic practice, on the job site) appear in some detail on the lefthand side of Figure 6.7. The bulleted points listed under Autonomy Support, Structure, and Involvement nicely represent

Table 6.4   Relationship and Social Context Factors that Involve and Satisfy the Three Psychological Needs

Psychological Need	Environmental Condition That Involves the Need	Environmental Condition That Satisfies the Need
Autonomy	Opportunities for self-direction	Autonomy support
Competence	Optimal challenge	Progress feedback
Relatedness	Social interaction	Communal relationships

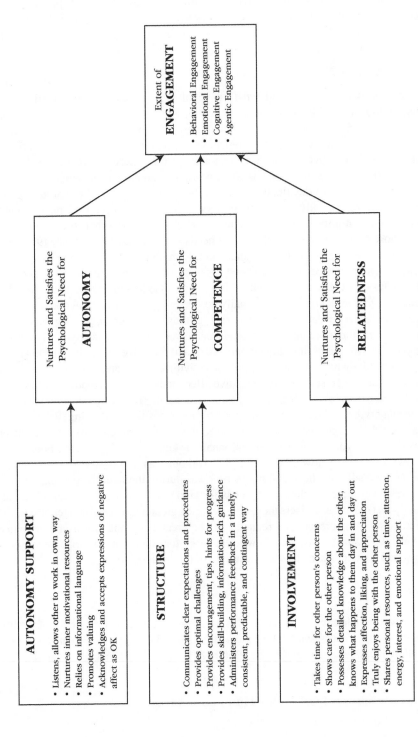

Figure 6.7 Engagement Model to Illustrate the Motivational Significance of Autonomy Support, Structure, and Involvement

the contents of the present chapter. It is within these aspects of a supportive environment (or relationship) that people richly experience engagement-fostering psychological need satisfaction.

What Makes for a Good Day?

Experiences that involve and satisfy psychological needs generate positive emotion and psychological well-being (Reis et al., 2000; Ryan, Bernstein, & Brown, 2010; Ryan & Deci, 2001). Simply put, we feel that we have a good day when the events in our lives work to involve and satisfy our psychological needs, and we feel that we have a bad day when the events in our lives work to neglect and frustrate these needs. So psychological need satisfaction predicts and explains when we do and do not have a "good day."

To study day-to-day fluctuations in well-being, one group of researchers asked college students to keep a daily diary of their moods (joyful, angry) and well-being (vitality, physical symptomatology such as headache frequency). The researchers predicted that good days are those in which one's psychological needs are met (Kasser & Ryan, 1993, 1996; Ryan, Bernstein, & Brown, 2010; Sheldon, Elliot, Kim, & Kasser, 2001; Sheldon, Ryan, & Reis, 1996). Circumstances partly dictated when people had their good days; people had their best days on weekends, for instance. But people also had their best days when they experienced higher levels of autonomy, daily competence, and daily relatedness. For instance, as people spent their days attending classes, talking with friends, playing the cello, or on the job at work, the more internal was their perceived locus of causality (daily autonomy), the more effective they felt (daily competence), and the more they felt close to and connected to others (daily relatedness) during these activities, the greater was their positive affect and vitality and the lesser was their negative affect and physical symptomatology.

These findings confirm that psychological needs provide people with the *psychological nutriments* they need to experience good days and positive well-being (Ryan, 1995; Sheldon et al., 1996). Consider an ordinary trip to the gym to exercise. Imagine at the end of the workout that you completed a questionnaire asking how enjoyable the hour was, why you came to exercise, how challenging the workout was and how much you improved, and what the quality of the social interaction was during the hour. Notice that these questions correspond to the psychological needs for autonomy, competence, and relatedness. In the study that did ask exercisers these questions, the greater the exercisers reported experiencing autonomy, competence, and relatedness, the greater was the exerciser's enjoyment (Ryan et al., 1997). In contrast, people who exercised for other motives (appearance, body image) enjoyed the experience less and worked out for a briefer time.

Vitality

One way people experience a good day is through a subjective experience of vitality. Vitality is the energy that is available to the self (Ryan & Deci, 2008). For instance, consider the following three sentences (Bostic, Rubio, & Hood, 2000; Ryan & Frederick, 1997):

- I feel alive and vital.
- Sometimes I feel so alive I just want to burst.
- I feel energized.

When people have days that allow them to feel autonomous, competent, and interpersonally related, they are significantly more likely to agree with these statements (Kasser & Ryan, 1993, 1996; Sheldon et al., 1996). When people have days that frustrate and thwart their psychological needs, they find these three statements extreme and unrealistic. The conclusion is that psychological need involvement and satisfaction offers us the psychological nutriments we need to feel vital and well, and the presence of vitality is a rather clear signal that are psychological needs are being met and we are well (Ryan & Deci, 2008).

SUMMARY

The study of the three psychological needs of autonomy, competence, and relatedness relies on an organismic approach to motivation, an approach that makes two core assumptions. First, people are inherently active. Second, in the person–environment dialectic, psychological needs provide the person with inherent motivation to engage in the environment, and the environment sometimes supports but other times neglects and frustrates these inner motivational resources. The picture that emerges in an organismic approach to motivation is that human beings possess a natural motivation to learn, grow, and develop in a way that is healthy and mature, and they do so when environments involve and support their psychological needs. When people interact with a motivationally supportive environment, the outcome of the person–environment dialectic is one of synthesis (harmony), because people show strong engagement, developmental growth, health, and well-being. When people interact with a motivationally frustrating environment, the outcome of the person–environment dialectic is one of conflict (disharmony), because people show defiance, developmental regression, decay, and ill-being.

Autonomy is the need to experience self-direction and personal endorsement in the initiation and regulation of one's behavior. When autonomous, people feel a sense of authorship over their thoughts, feelings, and behaviors, and their behavior emanates from an internal perceived locus of causality, a sense of volition, and a sense of perceived choice. External events, social contexts, interpersonal relationships, and cultures all vary in how much versus how little they support versus thwart a person's need for autonomy. People support autonomy in others when they take the other's perspective, nurture inner motivational resources, provide explanatory rationales, rely on informational language, display patience, and acknowledge and accept expressions of negative affect as okay. The benefits to both receiving and giving autonomy support include not only autonomy need satisfaction but also gains in engagement, development, learning, performance, and well-being.

Competence is the need to interact effectively with the environment. It reflects the desire to exercise one's capacities and skills and, in doing so, to seek out and master optimal challenges. The principal environmental event that involves the competence need is optimal challenge. When task challenge and personal skill are both relatively high, people tend to experience flow, which is a psychological state characterized by maximal enjoyment, intense concentration, and full absorption in the task. The principal environmental events that satisfy the competence need are structure, feedback, and failure tolerance. The more environments satisfy people's need for competence, the more willing people are to seek out and try to master optimal challenges that allow them opportunities to develop and grow.

Relatedness is the need to establish close emotional bonds and attachments with other people, and it reflects the desire to be emotionally connected to and interpersonally involved with others in warm, caring relationships. Mere interaction with others is a sufficient condition to involve the need for relatedness. To satisfy relatedness, however, a person needs to confirm that the emerging social bond with another person involves caring, liking, reciprocity, and a sense of exposing one's authentic self and having that authentic self both accepted and valued by the other. A communal relationship represents the type of relationship capable of satisfying the relatedness need. Relatedness need satisfaction is important in the same way that all three of the psychological needs are important—namely, because it predicts engagement, developmental growth, health, and well-being. Relatedness to others is particularly important because it provides the social context that supports internalization, which is the process through which one person takes in and accepts as his or her own another person's belief, value, or way of behaving.

An engagement model of motivation (Figure 6.7) illustrates how relationships and social contexts successfully involve and satisfy (versus neglect and frustrate) the psychological needs for autonomy, competence, and relatedness. Collectively, autonomy support, structure, and involvement are important aspects of the social context because they provide the means through which environments support people's psychological needs. When people experience psychological need satisfaction, they experience the psychological nutriments (psychological need satisfaction) necessary for active engagement, having "a good day," and subjective experiences of vitality and energy.

READINGS FOR FURTHER STUDY

Psychological Needs

RYAN, R. M., & DECI, E. L. (2000). Self-determination theory and the facilitation of intrinsic motivation, social development, and well-being. *American Psychologist, 55*, 68–78.

SHELDON, K. M., RYAN, R. M., & REIS, H. T. (1996). What makes for a good day?: Competence and autonomy in the day and in the person. *Personality and Social Psychology Bulletin, 22*, 1270–1279.

RYAN, R. M., PATRICK, H., DECI, E. L., & WILLIAMS, G. C. (2008). Facilitating health behaviour change and its maintenance: Interventions based on self-determination theory. *The European Health Psychologist, 10*, 2–5.

Autonomy

DECI, E. L., & RYAN, R. M. (1987). The support of autonomy and the control of behavior. *Journal of Personality and Social Psychology, 53*, 1024–1037.

REEVE, J. (2009). Why teachers adopt a controlling motivating style toward students and how they can become more autonomy supportive. *Educational Psychologist, 44*, 159–178.

DECI, E. L., LA GUARDIA, J. G., MOLLER, A. C., SCHEINER, M. J., & RYAN, R. M. (2006). On the benefits of giving as well as receiving autonomy support: Mutuality in close friendships. *Personality and Social Psychology Bulletin, 32*, 313–327.

Competence

HARTER, S. (1978). Pleasure derived from optimal challenge and the effects of extrinsic rewards on children's difficulty level choices. *Child Development, 49*, 788–799.

KELLER, J., & BLESS, H. (2008). Flow and regulatory compatibility: An experimental approach to the flow model of intrinsic motivation. *Personality and Social Psychology Bulletin, 34*, 196–209.

Relatedness

BAUMEISTER, R. F., & LEARY, M. R. (1995). The need to belong: Desire for interpersonal attachments as a fundamental human motivation. *Psychological Bulletin, 117*, 497–529.

CARVALLO, M., & GABRIEL, S. (2006). No man is an island: The need to belong and dismissing avoidant attachment style. *Personality and Social Psychology Bulletin, 32*, 697–709.

Chapter 7

Implicit Motives

IMPLICIT NEEDS

ACQUIRED NEEDS

Social Needs

How Implicit Motives, as Acquired Psychological Needs, Motivate Behavior

ACHIEVEMENT

Origins of the Need for Achievement

Socialization Influences

Developmental Influences

Atkinson's Model

Tendency to Approach Success

Tendency to Avoid Failure

Combined Approach and Avoidance Tendencies

What Achievement Strivings Predict

Achievement for the Future

Dynamics-of-Action Model

Conditions That Involve and Satisfy the Need for Achievement

Moderately Difficult Tasks

Competition

Entrepreneurship

AFFILIATION

The Duality of Affiliation Motivation

Conditions That Involve the Affiliation and Intimacy Duality

Fear and Anxiety

Establishing Interpersonal Networks

Maintaining Interpersonal Networks

Conditions That Satisfy the Affiliation Need

POWER

Conditions That Involve and Satisfy the Need for Power

Leadership and Relationships

Drinking Alcohol

Aggression

Influential Occupations
Prestige Possessions
Power and Goal Pursuit
Is the Implicit Power Motive Bad?
Leadership Motive Pattern
Effectiveness of U.S. Presidents
Four Additional Social Needs

SUMMARY

READINGS FOR FURTHER STUDY

© momentimages Tetra Images/Newscom

© Photodisc / Getty Images

© Digital Vision

Consider the first picture above—the one on the left side. As you look at that picture, let your mind wander wherever it seems to want to go. Then, after a moment's reflection, use the scene in the picture to create an imaginative story that has a beginning, a middle, and an end. Consider who the people in the picture are and what they are thinking and wanting. As you do so, provide an answer to each of the following questions:

· What is happening?
· Who are the people?
· What happened before?
· What are the people thinking about and feeling?
· What do they want?
· What will happen next?

After you write your story to explain what is happening in the first picture, take another 4 or 5 minutes to write an imaginative story about the second picture. Again, let your mind wander to wherever it wants to go as you consider picture 2 and then answer each of the six questions in reference to that second picture (e.g., What is happening? Who are the people?).

Finally, take another 4 or 5 minutes to write an imaginative story for the third picture. Again, let your mind wander and then answer each of the six questions.

Perhaps you feel that it is not necessary to actually write out the stories and, instead, think that you will just continue reading. Okay, but it will be helpful to your understanding of the contents of this chapter in the long run if you will pause to take the time to write the imaginative stories. If you took the time to write imaginative stories, then you have just completed a brief version of the Picture Story Exercise (PSE; Atkinson, 1958; Pang, 2010; Smith, 1992, 2000), the most widely used assessment tool to measure implicit motives. The PSE is a research-based version of the original Thematic Apperception Test (TAT; Morgan & Murray, 1935). The logic underlying the PSE is that a person's needs can be inferred from imaginative material generated in response to an ambiguous cue. In the PSE, research participants are typically shown six pictures. The pictures used in this chapter are intentionally not the same pictures as used in the PSE, because the reader might want to take the PSE under more controlled conditions to produce a valid and interpretable score. But the pictures are similar in spirit to those used in the PSE. Once a person generates a series of six imaginative stories, then trained experts score the contents of the stories using a previously validated coding system. The interested reader can find details on the PSE's scoring system by reading Schultheiss and Pang (2007) or Smith (1992). If the reader is interested in administering the PSE in a personal research project, Pang (2010) provides step-by-step guidelines for how to administer, score, and interpret the PSE.

IMPLICIT NEEDS

Implicit motives are enduring, nonconscious needs that motivate people's behavior toward the attainment of specific social incentives (Schultheiss & Brunstein, 2010). Implicit means unconscious. An implicit motive is a psychological need that is implied or inferred from the person's characteristic thought, emotions, and behavior. The unconscious need exerts a continual and enduring influence on what the person thinks about, feels, and does.

Implicit motives stand in contrast to explicit motives. Explicit motives are people's conscious, readily accessible, and verbally stated motivations. For instance, if someone asked you, "Do you have a strong need for achievement?" "Do you love challenges?" and "Will you persist in the face of failure?" the answers to these questions represent explicit achievement motivation. Explicit motives are assessed with self-report questionnaires. Implicit motives for achievement are different, as they are based on your emotional reactions during a challenging task and whether you really emotionally want to persist in the face of failure. One way to think about the difference between implicit and explicit measures is that with explicit measures people describe themselves (e.g., "I like challenges" and "I do not fear failure") while implicit motives are inferred from what people write in response to the picture cues on the PSE (Schultheiss, Yankova, Dirlikov, & Schad, 2009).

When it comes to predicting people's behavior, implicit motives do a better job than do explicit motives (McClelland, Koestner, & Weinberger, 1989). Hence, the topic of this chapter is not on what people say their motives are but, rather, it is on the unconscious forces (implicit motives) that arise from situational cues that cause emotional reactions that then predict, guide, and explain people's behavior and lifestyle.

What a person "needs" within an implicit motive is to experience a particular pattern of affect or emotion. For instance, a person with a strong need for achievement typically experiences strong interest, enthusiasm, joy, and pride while engaging in a challenging task. A person with little or no need for achievement, on the other hand, does not experience this same pattern of affect. This person typically experiences negative affect, such as anxiety, shame, and embarrassment, while engaging in a challenging task. Hence, people with a strong implicit achievement motivation emotionally "need" to challenge themselves, because challenges are the vehicle to generate a highly desirable pattern of affect and emotion. Similarly, people with a strong affiliation or a strong power implicit motive "need" to involve themselves in close relationships and in opportunities for social impact, respectively, because close relationships are the vehicle to generate positive affect and emotion for the person with a high need for affiliation while opportunities for social influence are the vehicle to generate positive affect and emotion for the person with a high need for power. With that said, look back at the three pictures at the beginning of the chapter. Which one conjures up within you the most positive gut-felt emotion? Why is that? Which picture does nothing for you emotionally? Why?

David McClelland was a pioneer researcher in the field of implicit motives. He traced his doubts about the validity of self-report motivations from his youthful experiences in which he observed consistent contradictions between what people said they would do and what they later actually did. His own example of this contradiction was best represented by listening to what people who attended church on Sunday said they would do during the week and then observing what they actually did and did not do on the other six days of the week (McClelland, 1984). He believed that people's thoughts, feelings, and behaviors were affected by forces that were unknown even to themselves—that is, to unconscious motives. His twofold conclusion was that (1) implicit motives are unconscious and cannot be measured by self-report and (2) implicit motives predicted people's behavior and performance, whereas explicit motives predicted only people's attitudes and values (McClelland, Koestner, & Weinberger, 1989).

ACQUIRED NEEDS

No one is born with a need for achievement, a need for affiliation, or a need for power. Yet each of us develops some or all of these strivings, at least to a degree. Personal experience, socialization opportunities and demands, and our unique developmental history teach us to expect a more positive emotional experience in some situations than in other situations. The anticipation of experiencing such positive emotionality is what leads us to organize our lifestyle around further activity in these domains rather than in other domains. Over time, because of these repeated emotional experiences, we acquire preferences for those particular situations, hobbies, and careers that are associated with our acquired needs. Some of us learn to prefer and enjoy situations that challenge us with explicit standards of excellence (i.e., achievement needs). Others learn to prefer and enjoy situations that afford warm relationship opportunities (i.e., affiliation needs). And others learn to prefer and enjoy situations that allow them to exert influence over others (i.e., power needs).

Chapter 6 presented the motivational literature on inherent psychological needs. All of us need autonomy, competence, and relatedness, because these are universal human needs. In contrast, implicit needs have a social (rather than an innate) origin. Social needs originate from preferences gained through experience and socialization. These needs develop within us as acquired individual differences—as an acquired or a learned part of our personality. This chapter traces the social origins of the need for achievement, affiliation, and power and discusses how each need, once acquired, manifests itself in thought, emotion, action, and lifestyle.

Social Needs

In the acquisition of implicit motives, early childhood experience is of paramount importance. Infants lack language (the word "infancy" literally means "without language"); they also lack cognition and intelligence in the adult sense of these terms. The language of infancy is affect, desire, and emotion. Infants want and feel, rather than think. Desires and feelings represent the language of the unconscious, while thoughts and words represent the language of the conscious. It is during the first two years of life that infants begin to develop preferences to experience strong positive emotion to the attainment of particular classes of incentives.

Throughout infancy and early childhood, children engage in behavior that produces either positive or negative affect. They may walk, climb a stair, or reach for a toy and then experience strong positive emotion such as joy and pride with goal attainment, or frustration and anxiety with goal failure. Experience teaches each of us to expect positive emotional reactions in response to some incentives rather than others (McClelland, 1985). This positive emotionality in the pursuit of a standard of excellence is the emotional and developmental origin of acquiring a preference for situations that offer a standard of excellence. With positive emotion, the child develops a positive goal anticipation upon encountering a new standard of excellence and anticipates joy and pride. Positive emotion to this particular class of incentives (standards of excellence) is the developmental origin of the need for achievement. Of course, children encounter other situations as well. They may involve themselves in close relationships with other people—talking with others, being hugged, and playing cooperatively. Strong positive emotion in these situations can generate an enduring preference for social relationship situations and foster positive goal anticipation in future social settings. Such is the developmental origin of the need for affiliation. Children also involve themselves in situations such as gaining prestige, status, influence, and social power. Strong positive emotions in these situations tend to generate an enduring preference of social influence situations and to foster positive goal anticipation in similar situations. Such is the developmental origin of the need for power.

Once acquired in early childhood, people in later life experience implicit needs as emotional and behavioral potentials that are activated by particular situational incentives (Atkinson, 1982; McClelland, 1985). That is, when an incentive associated with a particular need is present (e.g., a date is an affiliation incentive, an inspirational speech is a power incentive), the person high in that particular need experiences emotional and behavioral activation (i.e., feels hope, seeks interaction). The primary need-activating incentive for each social need appears in Table 7.1.

In an extensive investigation of how people acquire social needs, one group of researchers sought to determine the childrearing antecedents of adult needs for achievement, affiliation, and power (McClelland & Pilon, 1983). The researchers initially scored the parental practices of mothers and fathers of 78 5-year-old boys and girls. When the

Table 7.1 Social Incentive That Activates Each Implicit Motive's Emotional and Behavior Activation Potential

Implicit Motives	Social Incentive That Activates Each Need
Achievement	Doing something well to show personal competence
Affiliation	Opportunity to please others and gain their approval; involvement in a warm and secure relationship
Power	Having impact on others

children grew to the age of 31, the researchers assessed the implicit motives of each adult to see which early socialization experiences, if any, would predict adults' implicit motives. Only a few childrearing antecedents emerged as significant, but the few that did illustrate some early origins. Adults high in the need for achievement generally had parents who imposed high standards. Adults with high needs for affiliation generally had parents who used praise as a socialization technique. Adults with high needs for power generally had parents who were permissive about sex and aggression.

The finding that few childrearing experiences predict adult motives suggests that social needs can and do develop and change over time. For instance, some occupations foster achievement strivings more than do other occupations, because they provide opportunities for moderate challenges, independent work, personal responsibility for outcomes, and rapid performance feedback. People in such achievement-congenial occupations (e.g., entrepreneurs) show marked increases in their achievement strivings over the years compared to people in achievement-noncongenial occupations (e.g., nursing, teaching) (Jenkins, 1987). Similarly, workers in jobs that require assertiveness (e.g., sales) show increases in the need for power over the years (Veroff, Depner, Kulka, & Douvan, 1980). Overall, the development of implicit motives begins in very early childhood and continues throughout life.

How Implicit Motives, as Acquired Psychological Needs, Motivate Behavior

Implicit motives—the needs for achievement, affiliation, and power—are activated and aroused by a specific class of social incentives (i.e., Table 7.1). That is, a teenager plays a game of basketball and, while playing, encounters challenges such as dribbling behind one's back, spinning the ball on an index finger, trying to dunk, or taking shots from the three-point line. If dribbling, spinning, dunking, and shooting produce positive emotions such as interest and pride, then the social incentive of being challenged becomes associated with positive emotion, and an emotion-based preference for challenging situations develops. If dribbling, spinning, dunking, and shooting produce negative emotions such as anxiety and shame, then the social incentive of being challenged becomes associated with negative emotion and no such emotion-based preference for challenging situations develops. Over time, challenging situations and positive emotion go hand in hand, and it is the anticipation of positive emotion in the face of a challenging task that is the implicit motive for achievement.

Notice that implicit motives are mostly reactive in nature. They lie dormant within us until we encounter a potentially need-satisfying incentive that activates a particular pattern of emotionality. For example, picture 1 at the beginning of the chapter often pulls achievement-related emotions and strivings out of those with an implicit motive for achievement. That is, a race is experienced as a standard of excellence, and such an incentive typically conjures up positive emotion and positive goal anticipation in those high in achievement strivings. That same picture and the thought of confronting a standard of excellence will typically generate neutral or negative emotion and negative goal anticipation in those low in achievement strivings. Picture 2 often pulls for affiliation-related emotions and strivings, at least it does so for people with an implicit motive for affiliation. That is, the picture offers a potential social opportunity to make friends, to deepen a friendship, or to reunite with lost friends, and the thought of a warm, close, secure relationship will conjure up positive emotion and positive goal anticipation (a happy ending, such as social acceptance) in those high in affiliation strivings. Similarly, that same picture tends to generate neutral or negative emotion and negative goal anticipation (an unhappy ending, such as rejection) in those low in affiliation strivings. Picture 3 often pulls for power-related emotions and strivings.

Implicit motives are not only reactive, however, as people also learn to anticipate the emergence of social incentives. People learn that particular occupations, organizations, and recreational events, for example, are primarily opportunities for doing well and demonstrating personal competence, for pleasing others and gaining their approval and for participating in warm and secure relationships, or for having an impact on others. Based on this personal experience, people gravitate toward the environments that are capable of activating need-congenial emotions that functionally satisfy their implicit motives. The person high in achievement strivings might enter business to become an entrepreneur or a stockbroker, while the person high in power strivings might enter management, run for political office, or become a stage performer such as a comedian, magician, or entertainer.

Whether social needs are reactive or anticipatory, the core of implicit motives is the desire for particular affective experiences. The fundamental question therefore becomes, In what situations do you feel most strong, fulfilled, and satisfied? What makes you really happy? From this point of view, if you know what sort of activities and environments make you happy, then you have a good insight into the makeup of your own implicit motivation profile. In brief:

- *High achievement strivings*: Feel interest, joy, arousal, excitement, and a sense of opportunity when given a difficult challenge with immediate diagnostic feedback about your performance. Feel happy when you pursue goals such as winning, diagnosing personal competence, and improving the self, as often happens in sports and various domains of risk-taking (e.g., investing in stocks, entrepreneurship).

- *High affiliation strivings*: Feel calmness accompanied by warm, positive affect in situations that offer comfort and interpersonal security (Wirth & Schultheiss, 2006). Feel happy when pursuing activities such as cuddling (family in bed together on a Saturday morning) or just relaxing with a close friend at the beach.

- *High power strivings*: Feel strong, sharp arousal spikes that generate a burst of epinephrine, testosterone, and increased blood pressure and muscle tone (Hall, Stanton, & Schultheiss, 2010). Feel happy when you pursue activities such as riding a rollercoaster and making a persuasive speech in front of a large audience.

The satisfaction of an implicit motive brings immediate affective (emotional) gratification, and it therefore provides a deeply satisfying answer to the following question: What makes you happy?

ACHIEVEMENT

The need for achievement is the desire to do well relative to a standard of excellence. It is the individual's unconscious, but frequently recurring, preference to feel positive affect upon improving his or her performance, making progress on a challenging task, and experiencing "success in competition with a standard of excellence" (McClelland, Atkinson, Clark, & Lowell, 1953). A standard of excellence is any challenge to a person's sense of competence that ends with an objective outcome of success versus failure, win versus lose, or right versus wrong. Competition with a standard of excellence is a broad term that encompasses (following Heckhausen, 1967): competition with a task (e.g., solving a puzzle), competition with the self (e.g., running a race in a personal best time), and competition against others (e.g., becoming the class valedictorian).

What all types of achievement situations have in common is that the person has encountered a standard of excellence and has been energized by it, largely because he or she knows that the forthcoming performance will produce an emotionally meaningful evaluation of personal competence. A "standard of excellence" needs to be defined broadly to include not only meeting an explicit standard of excellence as determined by others (one's teacher, a sales quota, and qualifying time to make the Olympic games), because it also includes attaining a personal best and even a subjective experience that one indeed did rise to a challenge. That said, there are only two outcomes that follow a competition with a standard of excellence: success or failure (Pang, 2010).

When facing standards of excellence, people's emotional reactions vary. Individuals high in the need for achievement generally respond with approach-oriented emotions such as hope, pride, and anticipatory gratification. Individuals low in the need for achievement, however, generally respond with avoidance-oriented emotions such as anxiety, defense, and the fear of failure. People's behavioral responses to standards of excellence also vary. When confronting a standard of excellence, people show differences in choice, latency, effort, persistence, and the willingness to take personal responsibility for the ensuing success/failure outcome (Cooper, 1983). High-need achievers, compared to low-need achievers, choose moderately difficult to difficult versions of tasks instead of easy versions (Kuhl & Blankenship, 1979; Slade & Rush, 1991); they quickly engage in achievement-related tasks rather than procrastinate (Blankenship, 1987); they show more effort and better performance because pride energizes them (Karabenick & Yousseff, 1968; Raynor & Entin, 1982); they persist in the face of difficulty and failure on moderately difficult tasks (Feather, 1961, 1963); and they take a personal responsibility for successes and failures rather than seeking help or advice from others (Weiner, 1980).

As depicted in Figure 7.1, standards of excellence offer people two-edged swords (Covington & Omelich, 1979). A standard of excellence simultaneously arouses in people both the desire to approach it and do well and the desire to avoid it and not embarrass oneself. In part, these standards excite us and we react with approach emotions and strong engagement behavior. These same standards of excellence also bring us anxiety, and we react with

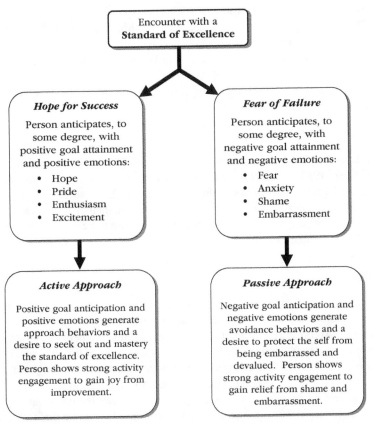

Figure 7.1   Positive versus Negative Emotional Reactions People Experience upon Encountering a Standard of Excellence

avoidance emotions and strong disengagement behavior (although the fear of failure can also motivate effort and persistence as the person strives to avoid or escape from punishing shame and guilt).

Origins of the Need for Achievement

Socialization Influences

Strong and resilient achievement strivings arise, in part, from socialization influences (Heckhausen, 1967; McClelland & Pilon, 1983). Children develop relatively strong achievement strivings when their parents provide the following: independence training (e.g., self-reliance), high performance aspirations, realistic standards of excellence (Rosen & D'Andrade, 1959; Winterbottom, 1958), high ability self-concepts (e.g., "This task will be easy for you"), a positive valuing of achievement-related pursuits (Eccles-Parsons, Adler, & Kaczala, 1982), explicit standards for excellence (Trudewind, 1982), a home environment rich in stimulation potential (e.g., books to read), a wide scope of experiences such as traveling, and exposure to children's readers rich in achievement imagery (e.g., *The Little Engine That Could*; deCharms & Moeller, 1962). After years of investigation, the effort to identify the childhood socialization practices of high-need achievers was only partly successful, however, largely because longitudinal findings began to show that achievement strivings change a great deal from childhood to adulthood and that adult achievement strivings often changed from one decade to the next (Jenkins, 1987; Maehr & Kleiber, 1980).

Developmental Influences

Achievement-related emotions and motivations show a predictable developmental pattern (Stipek, 1984). Children are not born with pride or shame; neither is an innate emotion. Instead, pride emerges from a developmental history of success episodes ending in mastery and task success; shame emerges from a developmental history of failure episodes ending in ridicule (Stipek, 1983). Developmentally, we learn to be pride-prone or shame-prone when facing a standard of excellence.

Atkinson's Model

The initial effort to understand achievement motivation was led by John Atkinson's expectancy *x* value model of achievement behavior, which includes the dynamics-of-action model. Atkinson represented achievement striving and behavior as an inherent struggle of approach versus avoidance. All of us experience standards of excellence as a two-edged sword: Partly we feel excitement and hope and anticipate the pride of a job well done; partly we feel anxiety and fear and anticipate the shame of possible humiliation. Thus, achievement motivation exists as a balance between the emotions and beliefs underlying the tendency to approach success versus the emotions and beliefs underlying the tendency to avoid failure.

John Atkinson (1957, 1964) argued that the need for achievement only partly predicts achievement behavior. Achievement *behavior* depends not only on the individual's dispositional, implicit achievement strivings but also on his or her task-specific probability of success and the incentive for succeeding at that task. For Atkinson, some tasks had high probabilities for success, whereas others had low probabilities for success. Also, some tasks offered greater incentive for success than did others. For instance, consider the classes you are presently taking. Each course has a different probability of success (e.g., a senior-level advanced calculus course is generally harder than is an introductory-level physical education class) and a different incentive value (e.g., doing well in a course in your major is generally valued more than doing well in a course outside your major).

Atkinson's theory features four variables: achievement behavior and its three predictors—need for achievement, probability of success, and incentive for success. Achievement behavior is defined as the tendency to approach success, abbreviated as Ts. The three determining factors of Ts are (1) the strength of a person's need for achievement (Ms, motive to succeed), (2) the perceived probability of success (Ps), and (3) the incentive value of success (Is). Atkinson's model is expressed in the following formula:

$$Ts = Ms \times Ps \times Is$$

Tendency to Approach Success

The first variable in the equation, *Ms*, corresponds to the person's need for achievement. The variable *Ps* is estimated from the perceived difficulty of the task and from the person's perceived ability at that task. The variable *Is* is equal to $1 - Ps$. Therefore, if the probability of success is .25, the incentive for success at that task would be .75 $(1.00 - 0.25)$. That is, incentive value for success during difficult tasks is high whereas it is low during easy tasks. To make sense of the behavioral tendency to approach success (*Ts*), consider a high school wrestler who is scheduled to wrestle two different opponents this week. The first opponent is last year's state champion (*Ps* = .1), so he consequently has a strong incentive to beat the champ (*Is* = $1 - Ps$, which = .9). The second opponent is his equal (*Ps* = .5) so he consequently has a moderate incentive to succeed (*Is* = .5). If we use an arbitrary number like 10 to characterize the wrestler's dispositional need for achievement (*Ms*), Atkinson's theory predicts the wrestler will experience the greater achievement motivation for the second wrestler (*Ts* = 2.50, because $10 \times .5 \times .5 = 2.50$) than for the first wrestler (*Ts* = 0.90, because $10 \times .1 \times .9 = 0.90$), because optimal challenge (*Ps* = .5) provides the richest motivational combination of expectancy of success and incentive for success.

Tendency to Avoid Failure

Just as people have a need for achievement (*Ms*), they also have a motive to avoid failure (*Maf*) (Atkinson, 1957, 1964). The tendency to avoid failure motivates the individual to defend against the loss of self-esteem, the loss of social respect, and the fear of embarrassment (Birney, Burdick, & Teevan, 1969). The tendency to avoid failure, abbreviated *Taf*, is calculated with a formula that parallels that for *Ts*:

$$Taf = Maf \times Pf \times If$$

The variable *Maf* represents the motive to avoid failure, *Pf* represents the probability of failure (which, by definition, is $1 - Ps$), and *If* represents the negative incentive value for failure (*If* = $1 - Pf$). Thus, if an individual has a motive to avoid failure of, say, 10, then the tendency to avoid failure on a difficult task (*Pf* = .9) can be calculated as 0.90 (*Maf* × *Pf* × *If*, which = $10 \times .9 \times .1 = 0.90$).

Combined Approach and Avoidance Tendencies

Atkinson conceptualized *Ms* as a motivational force to seek out achievement situations and *Maf* as a motivational force to escape from (or be anxious about) achievement situations. Thus, to engage in any achievement task is to enter into a risk-taking dilemma in which the person struggles to find a balance between the attraction of pride, hope, and social respect on the one hand versus the repulsion of shame, fear, and social humiliation on the other hand. When *Ts* is greater than *Taf*, the person approaches the opportunity to test personal competence against the standard of excellence, but when *Taf* is greater than *Ts*, the person hesitates or avoids the opportunity altogether. Atkinson's complete formula for predicting the tendency to achieve (*Ta*) and hence for displaying achievement-related behaviors (i.e., choice, latency, effort, and persistence) is as follows:

$$Ta = Ts - Taf = (Ms \times Ps \times Is) - (Maf \times Pf \times If)$$

Although the model can appear to be overwhelming at first, in actuality one needs to know only three variables: the individual's approach motive (Ms), the individual's avoidance motive (Maf), and the probability of success (Ps) on the task at hand. Notice that Is, Pf, and If are all calculated solely from the value of Ps [if $Ps = .3$, then $Is = .7$, $Pf = .7$, and $If = .3$]. If you work through several numerical examples, you will find two general principles that underlie the numerical value for Ta. First, Ta is highest when Ts is greater than Taf and lowest when Taf is greater than Ts (a personality factor). Second, Ta is highest when Ps equals .5 and lowest when Ps is around .9 (task is too easy to generate an incentive to succeed) or .1 (task is too difficult to be motivating).

What Achievement Strivings Predict

People with strong achievement strivings—that is, people in which Ts is greater than Taf—show relatively greater persistence on tasks of moderate difficulty, a preference to engage in moderately difficult tasks, greater attention and effort in these tasks, and better performance on moderately difficult tasks (Cooper, 1983; Pang, 2010). They tend to experience interest and satisfaction for attaining standards of excellence only when they seek achievement for its own sake; they do not derive intrinsic pleasure and satisfaction from attaining excellence that has been externally set or prescribed by others. High achievers also have a strong preference for those achievement tasks that offer concrete, direct, task-related, and immediate performance feedback, largely because they use such feedback as a means to make progress and to improve their future performances.

Achievement for the Future

Not all achievement situations are alike, as some have implications that affect one's future achievement efforts, whereas others have implications only for the present (Husman & Lens, 1999; Raynor, 1969, 1970, 1974, 1981). For example, a track athlete tries to win a race not only to experience the pride of a moment's accomplishment, but a win in today's race might lead to invitations to other important track meets, such as qualifying for the state championships or gaining a college scholarship. Similarly, a student works hard in math class partly out of enjoyment but also partly out of the belief that doing well in math will be instrumental in helping her achieve the long-term goals she has for herself.

"Future achievement orientation" refers to an individual's psychological distance from a long-term achievement goal (e.g., winning the state championship). The importance of future achievement orientation is that, other things being equal, any achievement goal perceived far away in time receives less approach-versus-avoidance weight than does a goal in the very near future. That means future goals generate less approach than do immediate goals. However, future achievement strivings can add to present-day achievement motivation by adding additional future motivation to present motivation (e.g., motivation for today + motivation for next week + motivation for next month + motivation for next year + motivation for one's career; Raynor, 1981). Thus, achievement behavior is a function of not only Ms, Maf, and Ps, but also whether the present achievement will lead toward some future achievement. From this point of view, achievement behavior is a series of steps in a path, and those achievement situations that are psychologically near have more impact on Ta than those that are psychologically far (Gjesme, 1981), although achievement strivings that are psychologically far can nevertheless add to and strengthen *Ta* in the present (Raynor & Entin, 1982).

Future time perspective is the degree to which the individual anticipates and integrates the future into his or her psychological present (Lens, Paixao, Herrera, & Grobler, 2012). Of course, all goals are future oriented, but the temporal distance for some goals is very short (eat three servings of fruit today), while it is very long for other goals (live to be 100 and maintain excellent health in doing so). A focus on only short-term goals tends to lead to maladaptive behaviors such as substance abuse, delinquency, and unsafe sex. In contrast, people with a longer future time perspective will in general be more motivated because they can anticipate not only the present consequences of their current behavior but also its future consequences and because they can further draw on and motivationally benefit from the positive incentive value of their future goal attainments (Husman & Shell, 2008). Such findings have led some researchers to suggest that the effort to extend one's future time perspective during the goal-setting process is a motivationally constructive practice (De Volder & Lens, 1982; Vansteenkiste, Simons, Soenens, & Lens, 2004).

Dynamics-of-Action Model

Atkinson's theory of achievement motivation was an episodic one; its goal was to predict what a person will do at a particular moment (episode) in time. Hence, the theory needed to know only the person's enduring achievement strivings (*Ms*, *Maf*) and the perceived probability of success at the task at hand (*Ps*). The dynamics-of-action model extends Atkinson's episodic view to also explain and predict changes in achievement strivings and behavior over time. In the dynamics-of-action model, achievement behavior occurs within a stream of ongoing behavior (Atkinson & Birch, 1970, 1974, 1978). The stream of behavior is determined largely by three forces: instigation, inhibition, and consummation (Blankenship, 1982, 1987, 1992, 2010).

Instigation is the same as *Ts*. It causes a rise in approach tendencies and occurs by confronting environmental stimuli associated with past reward (i.e., anything that cultivates an increased hope for success). Instigation is the amount of motivation to do something.

Inhibition is the same as *Taf*. It causes a rise in avoidance tendencies and occurs by confronting environmental stimuli associated with past punishment (i.e., anything that cultivates an increased fear of failure). Inhibition is the amount of motivation not to do something.

Instigation and inhibition are synonyms for *Ts* and *Taf*. The one new variable in the dynamics-of-action model is consummation.

Consummation refers to the fact that performing an activity brings about its own cessation (e.g., running, eating, drinking, sleeping, reading this book). The consummatory force decreases the motivation to continue to engage in an ongoing behavior; it is the motivation to stop and take a rest.

Adding consummatory forces allows achievement behavior to be understood as dynamic (changing over time) instead of episodic or static. For instance, your achievement strivings during any one college class change as the class progresses throughout the semester week after week. After 16 weeks, people often feel that they are tired of the class, saying, "Okay, thanks, that's enough. It is now time to do something else."

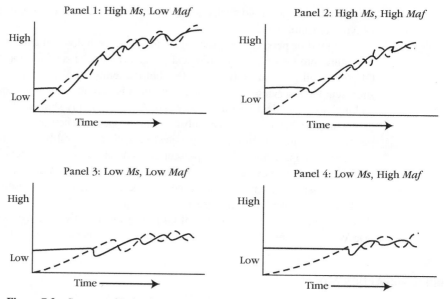

Figure 7.2   Streams of Behavior for People High and Low in *Ms* and *Maf*

Source: From "A computer-based measure of resultant achievement motivation," by V. Blankenship, 1987, *Journal of Personality and Social Psychology, 53*, pp. 361–372. Copyright 1987 by the American Psychological Association. Adapted with permission.

Note: Dashed line represents tendency strength to engage the achievement-related task; solid line represents tendency strength of nonachievement task.

The four panels in Figure 7.2 portray achievement behaviors over time (Blankenship, 1987, 2010). Each panel shows the individual's behavioral preference for an achievement task (a task that arouses both hope for success and fear of failure) and for a nonachievement task (an emotionally neutral task). The four panels correspond to four imaginary people with different levels of instigative and inhibitory forces. Panel 1 shows behavior with high instigation and low inhibition (*Ms* >*Maf*). Panel 2 shows behavior with high levels of both instigation and inhibition (*Ms* = *Maf*, and both are high). Panel 3 shows behavior with low levels of both instigation and inhibition (*Ms* = *Maf*, and both are low). Panel 4 shows behavior with low instigation and high inhibition (*Ms* < *Maf*).

Notice that in Figure 7.2 all four individuals, represented in the four separate panels of the figure, begin interacting first with the nonachievement-related activity (e.g., watching television). The question then becomes, How much time passes until each person starts to engage the achievement task (e.g., studying)? The individual in panel 1 (i.e., high need for achievement) shows the shortest latency for engaging the achievement task (i.e., the quickest achievement behavior), while the individual in panel 4 (i.e., low need for achievement, or high fear of failure) shows the longest latency for engaging the achievement task. The person in panel 4 basically procrastinates. Once achievement behavior has begun, it tends to consume itself, and the individual will eventually return to the nonachievement-related task, which over time will also consume itself (i.e., you can only watch so much television). The motive profiles (*Ms* in relation to *Maf*) explain not only latency to initiate achievement behavior but also its persistence, once begun. Three important messages are communicated in Figure 7.2:

1. Latency to begin an achievement task depends on motive strength (*Ms* versus *Maf*).

2. Persistence on an achievement task depends on motive strength (*Ms* versus *Maf*).

3. Switching to a nonachievement task occurs with rising consumption.

To test the dynamics-of-action empirically, Kuhl and Blankenship (1979) arranged the following early experiment. Participants first completed measures to assess the strengths of their achievement motive and fear of failure. The task involved making choice of how to spend one's time on a reasoning task in which five separate piles of problems lay in front of the participant as he or she sat at a desk. The five piles of problems were clearly labeled as very difficult (*Ps* = .1), difficult (*Ps* = .3), moderately difficult (*Ps* = .5), easy (*Ps* = .7), and very easy (*Ps* = .9). Each pile contained 50 problems, and participants were free to choose among the different levels of difficulties for 50 trials. Participants with strong achievement strivings were very likely to start with the moderately difficult reasoning problems, as predicted by Atkinson's episodic theory of achievement motivation. As predicted by the dynamics-of-action model, however, participants with strong achievement strivings then moved on to spending their time working on the increasingly difficult problems. The preference to move on to more difficult problems occurred because of the consummatory value of success on moderately difficult problems. After a while, success on moderately difficult problems did not generate the same intensity of positive emotion as it did on the earlier trials. So, participants with high achievement strivings preferred to move on to more difficult problems, because these were the ones that were now most capable of generating positive affect.

Follow-up studies changed the focus from task difficulty choices to a focus on latency and persistence (Blankenship, 1982, 1987, 1992). In these studies, high achievers quickly ceased their work on easy tasks while they persisted on difficult tasks in an enduring way. This is because, with difficult tasks, the instigating force remains high while the consummatory force remains low and because, with easy tasks, the instigating force decreases rather quickly while the consummatory force increases quickly. For high achievers, working on difficult tasks over time is the motivational equivalent of sitting down for a nutritious meal, while working on easy tasks is the motivational equivalent of eating a sweet but nonnutritious, nonsatisfying snack.

Conditions That Involve and Satisfy the Need for Achievement

Three situations involve and satisfy the need for achievement: moderately difficult tasks, competition, and entrepreneurship (McClelland, 1985).

Moderately Difficult Tasks

High-need achievers (*Ms* > *Maf*) outperform low-need achievers (*Maf* > *Ms*) on moderately difficult tasks. High-need achievers do not, however, outperform low-need achievers on easy or difficult tasks (Karabenick & Yousseff, 1968; Raynor & Entin, 1982). Performance on a moderately difficult task activates in the high achiever a set of positive emotional and cognitive incentives not socialized into the low achiever. Emotionally, moderately difficult tasks provide an arena for best testing skills and experiencing emotions such as pride and satisfaction. Cognitively, moderately difficult tasks provide an arena for best diagnosing one's sense of competence and level of ability (Trope, 1975, 1983). Hence, moderately challenging tasks provide a mixture of pride from success and information to diagnose abilities that motivates high-need achievers more than it does low-need achievers (Atkinson, 1981; Trope & Brickman, 1975).

Competition

Interpersonal competition captures much of the risk-taking dilemma inherent in achievement settings. It promotes positive emotion, approach behavior, and improved performance in high-need achievers, but negative emotion, avoidance behaviors, and debilitated performance in low-need achievers (Covington & Omelich, 1984; Epstein & Harackiewicz, 1992; Ryan & Lakie, 1965; Tauer & Harackiewicz, 1999). Consider that high-need achievers seek diagnostic ability information (Trope, 1975), seek opportunities to test their skills (Epstein & Harackiewicz, 1992; Harackiewicz, Sansone, & Manderlink, 1985), value competence for its own sake (Harackiewicz & Manderlink, 1984), are attracted to self-evaluation opportunities (Kuhl, 1978), and enjoy demonstrating or proving their ability (Harackiewicz & Elliot, 1993). Competition offers all these attributes and is therefore attractive to high-need achievers (Harackiewicz & Elliot, 1993). For low-need achievers, competition's evaluative pressures arouse mostly anxiety and avoidance (Epstein & Harackiewicz, 1992).

Entrepreneurship

David McClelland (1965, 1987) finds that high-need achievers often display the behavioral pattern of entrepreneurship. He assessed the need for achievement in a group of college students and then waited 14 years to check on the occupational choices they made. Each occupation was classified as either entrepreneurial (e.g., founder of own business, stockbroker) or not (e.g., service personnel). Results confirmed that most entrepreneurs were high-need achievers in college. Entrepreneurship appeals to the high-need achiever because it requires taking moderate risks and assuming responsibility for one's successes and failures. It also provides concrete, rapid performance feedback (e.g., moment-to-moment profits and losses), feedback that generates emotions such as pride and satisfaction, and feedback that allows one to diagnose personal competence and rate of improvement on a continual basis. High-need achievers prefer just about any occupation that offers challenge, independent work, personal responsibility, and rapid performance feedback (Jenkins, 1987; McClelland, 1961).

AFFILIATION

In its early study, the need for affiliation was conceptualized as "establishing, maintaining, or restoring a positive, affective relationship with another person or persons" (Atkinson, Heyns, & Veroff, 1954). According to this definition, the need for affiliation is not the same construct as extraversion, friendliness, or sociability. In fact, early investigators noted that persons high in the need for affiliation were often less popular than persons low in affiliation strivings (Atkinson, Heyns, & Veroff, 1954; Crowne & Marlowe, 1964; Shipley & Veroff, 1952). They were less popular, yet keenly aware of the social networks around them

Table 7.2   Profile of High Intimacy Motivation

Category	Description
Thoughts	Of friends, of relationships
Story Themes	Relationships produce positive affect, reciprocal dialogue, and expressions of commitment, union, and interpersonal harmony
Interaction Style	Self-disclosure; intense listening habits; many conversations.
Autobiography	Themes of love and dialogue are mentioned as personally significant life experiences
Peer Rating	Individual rated as warm, loving, sincere, nondominant
Memory	Enhanced recall with stories involving themes of interpersonal interactions

(i.e., they knew who was friends with whom). Rather than being rooted in extraversion and popularity, the need for affiliation is rooted in a fear of interpersonal rejection (Heckhausen, 1980). People with high-need affiliation tend to interact with others so to avoid negative emotions, such as rejection and anger (Schultheiss & Hale, 2007). They come across not as extraverted, friendly, or sociable but, instead, as "needy," mostly because they spend time seeking reassurance from others. The need for affiliation then can be thought of as the need for approval, acceptance, and security in interpersonal relations.

The more contemporary view of affiliation strivings recognizes its two facets: the need for approval and the need for intimacy. This dual view of affiliation strivings answers the criticism that the former conceptualization was too heavy on rejection anxiety and too light on affiliation interest (Boyatzis, 1973; McAdams, 1980; Weinberger, Cotler, & Fishman, 2010). The call for a more positive conceptualization of affiliation strivings (i.e., intimacy motivation) was answered by giving attention to the motive to engage in warm, close, positive interpersonal relations that hold little fear of rejection (McAdams, 1980, 1982a, 1982b; McAdams & Constantian, 1983; McAdams, Healy, & Kraus, 1984). The intimacy motive reflects a concern for the quality of one's social involvement. It is a willingness to "experience a warm, close, and communicative exchange with another person" (McAdams, 1980). At the core of strong intimacy strivings is the desire and need to share (to self-disclose) one's inner life with a close other—to share one's desires, feelings, goals, and so forth (McAdams, 1989).

A profile of how the need for intimacy expresses itself appears in Table 7.2. An individual with a high need for intimacy thinks frequently about friends and relationships; writes imaginative stories about positive affect-laden relationships; engages in self-disclosure, intense listening, and frequent conversations; identifies love and dialogue as especially meaningful life experiences; is rated by others as warm, loving, sincere, and nondominant; and tends to remember life episodes as those that involve interpersonal interactions. When they are not engaged in social interaction, they typically wish that they were (McAdams & Constantian, 1983).

The Duality of Affiliation Motivation

The need for affiliation has its dark side, because it seems to be mostly about a fear of rejection. It is the anxious need to establish, maintain, and restore interpersonal relations (affiliation need). The need for intimacy has its light side, because it seems to be mostly about an attraction to warm, close relationships. It is the need to engage in warm, close, positive relations (intimacy need). The full picture of affiliation strivings includes a theoretical conceptualization that includes both its positive and negative aspects.

This duality suggests complex developmental antecedents. The best predictor of high affiliative strivings in adults is parental neglect. This infantile neglect explains the adult's fear of rejection and social anxiety. High-intimacy individuals, in contrast, are happy, well-adjusted, and pleasant to be around. From an early age, they smile more, laugh more, and make eye contact during face-to-face conversation. In elementary school, their teachers rate them as cooperative, popular, and friendly (McAdams, Jackson, & Kirshnit, 1984).

Overall, the affiliative motive is complex—it is in fact a two-edged sword (Weinberger et al., 2010). It has its positive dimension in a desire for closeness and a heartfelt pleasure in being with and sharing with others. But it has its negative dimension as well, which includes a fear of rejection and anxiety about relationships. Perhaps this duality is not as surprising as it first may seem, however, when one thinks about how relationships play themselves out in people's developmental and daily lives, as relationships and social interactions offer joy from successfully achieving interpersonal intimacy but also devastating distress from rejection and loss.

Conditions That Involve the Affiliation and Intimacy Duality

The principal condition that involves the need for affiliation is the deprivation from social interaction (McClelland, 1985). Conditions such as loneliness, rejection, and separation raise people's desire, or need, to be with others. Hence, the need for affiliation expresses itself as a deficiency-oriented motive (the deficiency is a lack of social interaction). In contrast, the desire, or need, for intimacy arises from interpersonal caring and concern, warmth and commitment, emotional connectedness, reciprocal dialogue, congeniality, and love (McAdams, 1980). The need for intimacy expresses itself as a growth-oriented motive (the growth opportunity is enriching one's relationships). In the words of Abraham Maslow (1987), the need for affiliation revolves around "deprivation-love," whereas the need for intimacy revolves around "being-love."

Fear and Anxiety

Social isolation and fear-arousing conditions are two situations that increase a person's desire to affiliate with others (Baumeister & Leary, 1995; Schachter, 1959). Under conditions of isolation and fear, people report being jittery and tense, feeling as if they are suffering and are in pain, and seeing themselves as going to pieces. To reduce such anxiety and fear, humans typically adopt the strategy of seeking out others (Rofé, 1984). When afraid, people desire to affiliate for emotional support and to see how others handle the emotions they feel from the fear object. For example, imagine camping out in the wilderness and hearing a sudden, loud noise in the middle of the night. The sudden, unexplained noise might produce fear. While feeling fear and anxiety, people seek out others, partly to see if others seem as afraid and partly to gain emotional and physical support. Having other people around while anxious is comforting, and it helps us clarify the threatening situation, identify possible coping strategies, and help carry out our coping attempts (Kirkpatrick & Shaver, 1988; Kulik, Mahler, & Earnest, 1994). The popularity of mutual support groups (e.g., people with alcoholism, unwed mothers, patients suffering a particular illness, and people facing particular adjustment problems) provides some confirming testimony to the human tendency to seek out others when one is afraid or anxious.

Establishing Interpersonal Networks

To form new friendships, people with a high need for intimacy typically spend time interacting with others, join social groups, and establish stable and long-lasting relationships
(McAdams & Losoff, 1984). As relationships develop, high-need intimacy individuals
come to know more personal information and history about their friends (McAdams,
Healy, & Krause, 1984; McAdams & Losoff, 1984). And they report being more and more
satisfied as their relationships progress, whereas individuals with a low need for intimacy
report being less and less satisfied with their developing relationships (Eidelson, 1980).
Individuals with a high need for intimacy perceive the tightening bonds of friendship as
need involving and as emotionally satisfying, whereas those with a low-need intimacy
perceive the tightening bonds of friendship as stifling and as an entrapment.

Maintaining Interpersonal Networks

Once a relationship has been established, individuals with a high need for affiliation—
involving either affiliation or intimacy motivations—strive to maintain those relationships
by making more telephone calls and paying more visits to their friends (actual and online)
than do those with a low need for affiliation (Boyatzis, 1972; Lansing & Heyns, 1959;
McAdams & Constantian, 1983; Sheldon, Abad, & Hinsch, 2011). One study asked
persons with high and low needs for intimacy to keep a logbook over a two-month period
on which they were to record 10 20-minute friendship episodes (McAdams, Healy, &
Krause, 1984). Those with a high need for intimacy reported more dyadic (vs. larger group)
friendship episodes, more self-disclosure, more listening, and more trust and concern
for the well-being of their friends. Even when thinking and talking about strangers,
high-intimacy-need persons treat others differently than do low-intimacy-need persons,
because they use more positive adjectives when describing others, and they avoid talking
about others in negative terms (McClelland, Constantian, Pilon, & Stone, 1982).

Conditions That Satisfy the Affiliation Need

Because it is largely a deficit-oriented motive, the need for affiliation, when satisfied,
brings out emotions like relief rather than joy. When interacting with others, people high
in the need for affiliation go out of their way to avoid conflict (Exline, 1962), avoid
competitive situations (Terhune, 1968), are unselfish and cooperative (McAdams, 1980),
avoid talking about others in a negative way (McClelland, 1985), and resist making imposing demands on others (McAdams & Powers, 1981). They are sometimes described as
"meek." High-affiliation-need individuals prefer careers that provide positive relationships
and support for others (the helping professions; Sid & Lindgren, 1981), and they perform
especially well under conditions that support their need to be accepted and included
(McKeachie, Lin, Milholland, & Isaacson, 1966). When told that others will be evaluating
them, high-affiliation-need people experience relatively high levels of anxiety via a fear
of rejection (Byrne, 1961). Social acceptance, approval, and reassurance constitute the
need-satisfying conditions for people high in the need for affiliation.

   Because it is largely a growth-oriented motive, people satisfy the need for intimacy
through achieving closeness and warmth in a relationship. Hence, people high in the need for
intimacy more frequently touch others (in a nonthreatening way; McAdams & Powers, 1981),

cultivate deeper and more meaningful relationships (McAdams & Losoff, 1984); find satisfaction in listening and in self-disclosure (McAdams, Healey, & Krause, 1984); and laugh, smile, and make eye contact more during face-to-face interactions (McAdams, Jackson, & Kirshnit, 1984). Such laughing, smiling, and looking lead others to rate high-intimacy-need persons as relatively warm, sincere, and loving human beings (McAdams & Losoff, 1984). Relatedness within a warm, close, reciprocal, and enduring relationship constitutes the need-satisfying condition for people high in the need for intimacy.

POWER

The essence of the need for power is a desire to make the physical and social world conform to one's personal image or plan for it (Winter & Stewart, 1978). People high in the need for power desire to have "impact, control, or influence over another person, group, or the world at large" (Winter, 1973).

Impact allows power-needing individuals to establish power.

Control allows power-needing individuals to maintain power.

Influence allows power-needing individuals to expand their power.

Such power strivings often center on a need for dominance, reputation, status, or position. High-power-strivings individuals not only seek out opportunities for dominance, reputation, status, and social position, but they also find deep emotional satisfaction in being recognized and praised for these power-motive behaviors and outcomes (Fodor, 2010). High-power-need individuals seek to become (and stay) leaders, and they interact with others with a forceful, take-charge style. When they do attain positions of leadership, they feel satisfied and accomplished. This can be seen in high-power-striving individuals' preference for highly competitive sports (e.g., hockey, wrestling) that offer both an opportunity to exercise power and to attain public recognition for effectively enacting power and influencing others (Winter, 1973). When asked to recall the peak experiences in their lives, individuals high in the need for power report life events associated with strong positive emotions that occurred as a result of their impact on others, such as being elected to a leadership position or receiving applause from an audience (McAdams, 1982a).

David Winter (1973) provides two scenarios that illustrate power strivings. In the first, research participants watched a film of an authority figure giving an influential speech (John F. Kennedy's presidential inaugural address), and in the second, another set of participants watched a hypnotist ordering students to behave in particular ways as an audience watched. After these experiences, Winter scored the arousal of their power strivings. As expected, these groups scored higher in power strivings (by writing stories rich in power-related imagery) than did a comparison group who did not view the film or hypnosis session (Winter, 1973).

Others have performed experiments that essentially replicated this procedure, but in addition to measuring power strivings, they added measures of mood and physiological arousal (Steele, 1977). As high-power-need individuals listened to inspirational speeches, their moods became significantly more lively and energetic, and their physiological arousal (measured by epinephrine/adrenaline) showed a striking increase. Based on these findings, the opportunity to involve one's power strivings fills the power-needing individual with a vigor that can be measured via fantasy, mood, and psychophysiological activation (Steele, 1977).

Conditions That Involve and Satisfy the Need for Power

Parents of future power-striving children impose very high developmental standards on their children and are willing to sacrifice their parental affection to get their children to live up to their imposed standards (i.e., the tough-minded, cold, and distant parent). The development of power strivings emerges as a reaction to harsh parental criticism and a thwarting of the psychological need for relatedness (or intimacy). What emerges is then a need for prestige and power to tell the world that he or she is not to be taken lightly and, in fact, is worthy of notice, admiration, and respect (Fodor, 2010).

Four social conditions are noteworthy in their capacity for involving and satisfying the need for power: leadership, aggressiveness, influential occupations, and prestige possessions.

Leadership and Relationships

People with a high need for power seek recognition in groups and find ways for making themselves visible to others, apparently in an effort to establish influence (Winter, 1973). Power-seeking college students, for example, write more letters to the university newspaper, and power-seeking adults willingly take risks in achieving public visibility (McClelland & Teague, 1975; McClelland & Watson, 1973). They argue more frequently with their professors, and they show an eagerness in getting their points across in the classroom (Veroff, 1957). In selecting their friends and coworkers, power-striving individuals generally prefer others who are in a position to be led (Fodor & Farrow, 1979; Winter, 1973). When hanging out with their friends, they tend to adopt an interpersonal orientation that takes on more of a tone of influence than it does a tone of intimacy (McAdams, Healey, & Krause, 1984).

To test the influence of the need for power on tendencies toward leadership, experimenters arranged to have a group of strangers interact with each other for a short time (Foder & Smith, 1982; Winter & Stewart, 1978). Power-seeking individuals talked more and were judged to have exerted more influence. However, the power-seeking individuals were not the best liked, nor were they judged to have contributed the most to getting the job done or for coming to a satisfactory conclusion. In fact, groups that had high-power-need leaders were the ones that produced the poorest decisions. These groups exchanged less information, considered few alternative strategies, and reached poorer final decisions than did groups with a leader low in the need for power. These findings suggest that power-seeking leaders attempt to make others follow their personal plan, even though their assertiveness is often detrimental to group functioning.

In dating relationships, high-power-need men generally fare poorly (Stewart & Rubin, 1976). And they fare no better in marriage, because they generally make poor husbands, at least from the spouse's point of view (McClelland, 1975). In both dating and marriage, high-power-need women do not suffer the same poor outcomes that men do, apparently because they resist using interpersonal relationships as an arena for satisfying their power needs (Winter, 1988). High-power-need men, however, do tend to inflict verbal and physical abuse on their partners (Mason & Blankenship, 1987).

Drinking Alcohol

Drinking alcohol is an opportunity to involve one's need for power as well as to accentuate it (Fodor, 2010). When people drink, they generally report feeling stronger and less inhibited. Thus, people who have strong power motivation typically find drinking alcohol to be a gateway to enhanced personal dominance. It is also a gateway to become disinhibited from social constraints, and particularly to be released from those social constraints that involve aggression and exploitive sex. When drinkers write imaginative stories to the Picture Story Exercise, alcohol consumption leads them to write more power-oriented stories. And people who drink the most are often the power-striving individuals. Thus, power strivings and drinking alcohol seem to go together like peanut butter and jelly.

Aggression

If the need for power revolves around desires for impact, control, and influence, aggression ought to be one means for both involving and satisfying one's power needs. To some extent, the relationship between the need for power and aggression holds true, as men high in power strivings get into more arguments and participate more frequently in competitive sports (McClelland, 1975; Winter, 1973). However, the relationship between the need for power and aggression is diluted because society largely controls and inhibits people's acts of overt aggression. For this reason, aggressive manifestations of the need for power largely express themselves as impulses to (rather than actual acts of) aggression. Males and females with high needs for power report significantly more impulses to act aggressively (McClelland, 1975). When asked, "Have you ever felt like carrying out the following: yelling at someone in traffic, throwing things around the room, destroying furniture or breaking glassware, or insulting clerks in stores?" individuals high in the need for power report significantly more impulses to carry out these acts (Boyatzis, 1973).

Societal inhibitions and restraints largely constrain the power-seeking person's expression of aggression, but when societal inhibitions are removed, high-power-need men are more aggressive than are their low-power-need counterparts (McClelland, 1975; McClelland, Davis, Kalin, & Wanner, 1972; Winter, 1973). Alcohol is one socially acceptable means of gaining a release from societal inhibitions, and power-seeking men do indeed act relatively more aggressively after drinking (McClelland et al., 1972). When life becomes stressful and frustrating, high-power-need individuals sometimes seek alcohol as a means for inflating their sense of control (Cooper, Frone, Russell, & Mudar, 1995). Similarly, power-seeking men, but not power-seeking women, frequently respond to stress and setbacks by inflicting abuse on their intimates (Mason & Blankenship, 1987). This research suggests that people can not only increase power through reputation, prestige, and leadership, but they can also create the perception of heightened power through strategies such as drinking alcohol, risk-taking, gesturing and posturing, using abusive language, using drugs, and driving very fast.

Influential Occupations

People high in the need for power are attracted to occupations such as business executives, teachers/professors, psychologists, journalists, clergy, and international diplomats (Winter, 1973). Each of these occupations shares a common denominator in that the person in the occupational role is in the position to direct the behavior of other people in accordance with some preconceived plan (Winter & Stewart, 1978). People in some of these professions speak to and influence audiences (teachers, journalists, clergy); others have inside information they use to influence people (psychologists, diplomats), while others have a professional status that allows them to tell others what to do (business executives). Furthermore, these careers equip the individual with the rewards and punishments necessary for sanctioning the behavior of others. The teacher, cleric, diplomat, journalist, and business executive, for instance, all have the means for rewarding and punishing other people's compliance or disobedience (through grades, heavenly rewards, deal making, articles, and salaries). Thus, people can involve and satisfy their power strivings through the job they choose.

Prestige Possessions

People high in the need for power tend to amass a collection of power symbols, or "prestige possessions" (Winter, 1973). Power-seeking individuals are more likely to own a rifle or pistol, a convertible car, or a truck that exudes status and power (McClelland, 1975).

Power and Goal Pursuit

Individuals high in the need for power more readily acquire the goals and outcomes they seek than do individuals low in the need for power (Guinote, 2007). Power increases approach tendencies and decreases inhibitory tendencies (Anderson & Berdahl, 2002). High power and taking action go together (Galinsky, Gruenfeld, & Magee, 2003). During negotiations, for instance, high-power individuals are more likely to express anger, and this strategy often gets them what they want, largely because they are seen as tough negotiators who win concessions from others (Sinaceur & Tiedens, 2006).

Is the Implicit Power Motive Bad?

People high in the need for power typically harbor inclinations that are both benevolent and malevolent toward others. Like a superhero, they strive to improve the world. But, like a villain, they strive to make everyone their servant. David Winter devoted his professional life to understanding the implicit power motive, and he offered the following characterization of whether power strivings represented a good or a bad influence on society:

> Power is like fire: It can do useful things; it can be fun to play with and to watch; but it must be constantly guarded and trimmed back, lest it burn and destroy.   (Winter, 1973, p. xviii)

With that metaphor in mind, we can look at the contribution of power strivings to the effectiveness of leaders, such as U.S. presidents.

Leadership Motive Pattern

A special variant of the need for power is the leadership motive pattern (McClelland, 1975, 1985; McClelland & Burnham, 1976; Spangler & House, 1991). Leadership motivation consists of the following threefold pattern: (1) high need for power, (2) low need for affiliation, and (3) high inhibition (McClelland, 1982). Thus, the leadership motive pattern features individuals who desire to exercise influence, are not concerned with being liked, and are well controlled or self-disciplined. For instance, the stereotypical military commander or traditional father figure fits this leadership motive pattern rather well.

Such a constellation of high power, low affiliation, and self-control generally results in effective leaders and managers (Spangler & House, 1991). The characteristic of an internal controlling style (i.e., high inhibition) is important because managers who are high in power, low in affiliation, and high in inhibition are generally productive, successful, and rated highly by workers (McClelland & Burnham, 1976). In contrast, managers who are high in power, low in affiliation, but low in inhibition are often unsuccessful and rated lowly by workers. Apparently, strong self-control leads power-striving managers to internalize characteristics associated with effective management, such as respect for institutional authority and discipline (McClelland, 1975, 1985). So, if one is to be an effective leader, power strivings need to be complemented by self-disciplined inhibition (i.e., power under control). Power under control often gives rise to charismatic leadership and high morale among one's followers (Winter, 2010).

Effectiveness of U.S. Presidents

The leadership motive provides a framework for assessing the effectiveness of U.S. presidents (Spangler & House, 1991; Winter, 1973, 1987, 2005, 2010). Winter (1973, 1987) coded the thematic content of each U.S. president's inaugural address for the social needs of achievement, affiliation, and power and used these scores to predict presidential effectiveness. Presidents generally considered strong by historians—Kennedy, Truman, Wilson, and both Roosevelts—scored relatively high on power needs and relatively low on affiliation needs. Power strivings were a particularly good predictor of "rated greatness" and "made great presidential decisions" (Winter, 1987). Interestingly, achievement strivings were associated with presidential ineffectiveness, because achievement-oriented presidents (e.g., Wilson, Nixon, Carter) were highly active but also frequently frustrated. Power-striving presidents have more success in the office because they use their communication skills, their combative skills, and their sense of humor. They also really enjoy the political scrimmage that is presidential politics (Winter, 2010).

Five variables define presidential effectiveness: direct presidential actions (e.g., entering and avoiding war), perceived greatness, performance on social issues, performance on economic issues, and international relations. To assess each president's needs for power, affiliation, and inhibition, the researchers coded their inaugural speeches, presidential letters, and other speeches. The leadership motive pattern of high power, low affiliation, and high inhibition correlated significantly with all five measures of effectiveness. Apparently, when the United States elects a candidate with personal dispositions consistent with the leadership motive pattern, the nation is electing someone into office who will probably perform quite well, given the rather unique demands and challenges of the office. So how effective each president featured in Figure 7.3 proved to be was rooted, in part, in the quality of their leadership motive pattern.

The leadership motive pattern also predicts when leaders will engage in war and when leaders will pursue peace (Winter, 1993). Of course, war has many nonpsychological causes, but on the psychological side, historical research shows that when leaders express a motive profile of high power and low affiliation, the probability of subsequent war increases. Using British history, British–German World War I communications, and U.S.–Soviet communications during the Cuban Missile Crisis as his database, Winter (1993) found that the motive patterns expressed in speeches foreshadow the coming war-versus-peace decisions. When power imagery rose, war became a historically more likely event. When power imagery fell, war was less likely and ongoing wars tended to end. When affiliation imagery rose, war became a historically less likely event. When affiliation imagery fell, war was more likely to begin (Winter, 1993). According to this research, if you want to forecast whether a nation will enter into, avoid, or exit a war,

© spirit of america / Shutterstock

Figure 7.3   Former U.S. Presidents

read the speeches of the day and look for changes in whether the leaders are promoting influence (power) or relationships (affiliation).

Four Additional Social Needs

Besides those discussed here, other researchers argue for the importance of four additional acquired needs, including the need for cognition (Cacioppo, Petty, Feinstein, & Jarvis, 1996), the need for closure (Webster & Kruglanski, 1994), the need for structure (Neuberg & Newsom, 1993), and the uncertainty orientation (Sorrentino, 2013).

As shown in Box 7, the study of implicit processes extends beyond unconscious motivation to include unconscious attitudes as well.

SUMMARY

Implicit motives are enduring, unconscious needs that motivate people's behavior toward the attainment of specific social incentives. The three implicit motives of achievement, affiliation, and power are learned or acquired through experience and socialization. The social incentive that actives the achievement motive and a corresponding pattern of positive emotion is the opportunity for challenge and doing something well to show personal competence. The social incentive that activates the affiliation motive and a corresponding pattern of positive emotion is the opportunity to be involved in a warm and secure

BOX 7   *Implicit Attitudes*

Question: Why is this information important?

Answer: It expands unconscious processes to include not only motivation but attitudes.

Implicit means implied or inferred. Implicit motivations are inaccessible to conscious awareness and are only inferred from some source of evidence, such as our behavior or psychophysiology. Explicit means fully revealed. What is explicit is known directly and is fully consciously accessible. Just as the implicit-explicit distinction applies to our motivations, it applies to our attitudes (Greenwald, Nosek, & Banaji, 2003; Greenwald, Poehlman, Uhlmann, & Banaji, 2009).

An attitude is an evaluation of an object, person, place, thing, or idea. It is a judgment of good versus bad, like versus dislike, pleasant versus unpleasant. Like motivations, attitudes are both implicit and explicit, and we can have conflicting implicit and explicit attitudes toward the same object. It can be hard to accept the idea that the attitudes we hold are anything but explicit and consciously chosen and filtered. Nevertheless, implicit attitudes do predict our behavior (Greenwald et al., 2009) and well-being (Leavitt et al., 2011). For a demonstration of how pervasive and important implicit attitudes can be, I invite the reader to spend some part of this afternoon interacting with the following website: https://implicit.harvard.edu/implicit/.

This website offers the Implicit Association Test (IAT; Greenwald et al., 2003). The IAT measures attitudes that people are unable (or unwilling) to report, and the IAT is especially insightful when it reveals an implicit attitude that you did not know you had. On this website, you take a 15-minute online test to assess your implicit attitudes toward gender (female-male), weight (fat-thin), sexuality (gay-straight), race (black-white), disability (disabled-abled), skin tone (light skin-dark skin), various world religions, various ethnicities (Asians, Native Americans, Arabs-Muslims), or various people (presidential candidates).

In taking the IAT, attitude objects appear on the screen (young people, old people) and the person presses a key to classify those attitude objects into value categories (good, bad). All pairs are presented (young-good, old-good, young-bad, old-bad), and the computer records the person's reaction time to make each separate categorization. The IAT essentially measures the strength of the association between an attitude object and its evaluation. Fast (easy, quick) reaction times imply a strong association between the two, while slow reaction times (i.e., you have to think about it) imply a weak association. Typically, the reaction time data show that some pairs (old-good, young-bad) are weakly linked while other pairs (old-bad, young-good) are strongly linked. This difference implies a prejudice, or at least a preference for one object over the other. With these reaction times data in hand (the IAT provides individualized feedback), you can compare your implicit attitude with your explicit attitude, as in answering the explicit attitude question, "Which statement best describes you?" (from Greenwald et al., 2003):

___ I strongly prefer young people to old people.
___ I moderately prefer young people to old people.
___ I like young people and old people equally.
___ I moderately prefer old people to young people.
___ I strongly prefer old people to young people.

Sometimes implicit-explicit attitudes agree. But sometimes they conflict. In those latter cases, explicit attitudes tell us only half the story about how we really feel about an attitude object. For the other half of the story, we need to become aware of our implicit attitude. A good place to start is to spend some of your afternoon interacting with the aforementioned website.

relationship and the opportunity to please others and gain their approval. The social incentive that actives the power motive and a corresponding pattern of positive emotion is the opportunity for social influence and having an impact on others.

The need for achievement is the desire to do well relative to a standard of excellence. When facing standards of excellence, people's emotional reactions vary. High need for achievement individuals generally respond with approach-oriented emotions (e.g., hope) and behaviors, whereas low need for achievement individuals (high fear of failure) generally respond with avoidance-oriented emotions (e.g., anxiety) and behaviors. Atkinson's model of achievement and his dynamics-of-action model both explain why high-need achievers choose moderately difficult tasks, engage quickly and enthusiastically in achievement-related tasks, put forth more effort and perform better on moderately difficult tasks, persist in the face of difficulty and failure, and take a personal responsibility for successes and failures. The dynamics-of-action model adds that any stream of ongoing achievement behavior is determined not only by the need for achievement (instigation) and fear of failure (inhibition), but also by the achievement behavior itself (consummation). The conditions that involve and satisfy the implicit achievement motive are moderately difficult tasks, competition, and entrepreneurship.

The need for affiliation has two facets: the need for affiliation (rejection anxiety) and the need for intimacy (affiliation interest). The need for affiliation involves establishing, maintaining, and restoring relationships with others, mostly to escape from and to avoid negative emotions such as disapproval and loneliness. The need for intimacy is the social motive for engaging in warm, close, positive interpersonal relationships that produce positive emotions and hold little threat of rejection. Depriving people of the opportunity for social interaction is the principal condition that involves the need for affiliation, and social acceptance, approval, and reassurance constitute its need-satisfying conditions. Engaging in, developing, and maintaining warm, close relationships involve the need for intimacy, and individuals with high intimacy needs are more likely to join social groups, spend time interacting with others, and form stable, long-lasting relationships that are characterized by self-disclosure and positive affect. People with a high implicit intimacy motive laugh, smile, and make more eye contact during face-to-face interaction, and participating in these warm, reciprocal, and enduring relationships constitutes the condition that satisfies the need for intimacy.

The need for power is the desire to make the physical and social world conform to one's personal image for it. People high in the need for power desire to have impact, control, and influence over others or over the world at large. High-power-need individuals strive for leadership and recognition in small groups, drink alcohol to enhance their sense of dominance, experience frequent impulses of aggression, prefer influential occupations, amass prestige possessions, and generally get what they want during goal pursuit. A special variant of the need for power is the leadership motive pattern, which consists of the threefold pattern of high need for power, low need for intimacy, and high inhibition. Leaders, managers, and U.S. presidents who possess a constellation of needs consistent with the leadership motive pattern (high power, low affiliation, high inhibition) generally perform well as leaders and are rated by others as effective.

READINGS FOR FURTHER STUDY

Picture Story Exercise

PANG, J. S., & SCHULTHEISS, O. C. (2005). Assessing implicit motives in U. S. college students: Effects of picture type and position, gender, and ethnicity, and cross-cultural comparisons. *Journal of Personality Assessment, 85*, 280–294.

SCHULTHEISS, O. C., YANKOVA, D., DIRLIKOV, B., & SCHAD, D. J. (2009). Are implicit and explicit motive measures statistically independent? A fair and balanced test using the picture story exercise and a cue- and response-matched questionnaire method. *Journal of Personality Assessment, 91*, 72–81.

Achievement

ATKINSON, J. W. (1964). A theory of achievement motivation. In *An introduction to motivation* (pp. 240–268). Princeton, NJ: Van Nostrand.

KUHL, J., & BLANKENSHIP, V. (1979). The dynamic theory of achievement motivation: From episodic to dynamic thinking. *Psychological Review, 86*, 141–151.

MCCLELLAND, D. C. (1965). Achievement and entrepreneurship: A longitudinal study. *Journal of Personality and Social Psychology, 1*, 389–392.

Affiliation

MCADAMS, D. P., JACKSON, R. J., & KIRSHNIT, C. (1984). Looking, laughing, and smiling in dyads as a function of intimacy motivation and reciprocity. *Journal of Personality, 52*, 261–273.

MCADAMS, D. P., & LOSOFF, M. (1984). Friendship motivation in fourth and sixth graders: A thematic analysis. *Journal of Social and Personal Relations, 1*, 11–27.

Power

SPANGLER, W. D., & HOUSE, R. J. (1991). Presidential effectiveness and the leadership motive profile. *Journal of Personality and Social Psychology, 60*, 439–455.

STEELE, R. S. (1977). Power motivation, activation, and inspirational speeches. *Journal of Personality, 45*, 53–64.

WINTER, D. G. (2005). Things I've learned about personality from studying political leaders at a distance. *Journal of Personality, 73*, 557–584.

Part Two

Cognitions

Chapter 8

Goal Setting and Goal Striving

COGNITIVE PERSPECTIVE ON MOTIVATION

PLANS OF ACTION

    Corrective Motivation

    Discrepancy

    Affect and Feelings

    Two Types of Discrepancy

GOAL SETTING

    Goal–Performance Discrepancy

        Goal Difficulty

        Goal Specificity

        Goal Congruence

    Difficult, Specific, and Congruent Goals Enhance Performance

    Feedback

    Criticisms

    Long-Term Goal Setting

GOAL STRIVING

    Mental Simulations

    Implementation Intentions

        Getting Started

        Staying on Track

        Resuming

GOAL DISENGAGEMENT

EPILOGUE: FROM WHERE DO GOALS COME?

SUMMARY

READINGS FOR FURTHER STUDY

Mirrors don't lie. Lately, your mirror has been saying you added a few pounds. It is time to lose 10 pounds and get back on the road to physical fitness. You want to take action, but what? when? where? how?

Jogging seems sensible, so you start. At first, jogging is new, even fun, as you enjoy the outdoors and sense of accomplishment. A week goes by, but you do not lose much weight. You begin to wonder how much exercise is enough exercise. Another week goes by and the pressures of everyday living increase and compete for your time and attention. Each day you find it more difficult to find the time and to mobilize the energy to exercise. After a month of lackluster progress, jogging is history.

Your smartphone has some exercise apps, so you check them out. One keeps track of how many steps you take during the day and the smartphone displays your stepping through all sorts of informative graphs and figures. According to the app, fewer than 5,000 steps means you are sedentary. About 9,000 steps means you are fairly active. To lose weight, you need to take at least 12,000 steps per day.

Now you have a goal. No longer are you going to "do your best." Now you are going to take 12,000 steps per day. You wake up the next day bent on taking those 12,000 steps, but your schedule and feet protest that 9,000 steps are enough. Because you cannot quite make it to 12,000 steps, you find yourself devising step-increasing strategies (e.g., take 200 steps around your apartment every few hours, take a lap around the mall prior to shopping, walk up the stairs instead of taking the escalator or elevator). By the end of the third week, you take the 12,000 steps and feel the warm glow of accomplishment. After a month, you boldly decide to try for 15,000 steps per day. You now have a new goal. It will take more effort, more persistence, more focus, and an improved exercise strategy. But because you achieved your earlier goal and because your stamina has increased, you feel up to the lifestyle change. Eagerness has replaced apathy.

Another weight-loss program illustrates these same motivational processes. Dieting is just as ambiguous a task as is exercising—how much can I eat? How many calories is too many? How do I know whether I am making progress? In order to translate general, long-term dieting goals into specific day-to-day action, this popular weight loss program recommends that each person consume foods within a daily point range, depending on the person's current weight. In this system, all foods have a points value, depending on the food's number of calories, grams of fat, and grams of fiber (e.g., two pancakes = 6 points). A daily points goal for a person of 180 pounds might be, for example, between 22 and 27 points. The basic idea is that the person starts each day with a "range of points" goal. The dieter is to plan his or her food choices to eat at least the minimum number of points (to maintain metabolism) but no more than the maximum number of points (to lose weight). Vigorous daily activity (exercise) can increase one's daily points range. The idea is to leave behind the idea of a vague, ambiguous diet and, instead, to focus on a difficult and specific goal, keep track of food points consumed, and achieve this points goal day after day.

COGNITIVE PERSPECTIVE ON MOTIVATION

Cognitions are mental events. Cognitive sources of motivation therefore revolve around a person's constructive ways of thinking. Cognition can be a difficult concept to define (a "messy construct"; Pajares, 1992, p. 307), as it is an umbrella construct that unites together mental constructs such as beliefs, expectations, goals, plans, mindsets, judgments, values, and the self-concept under a single banner that collectively function as causal determinants to action (Gollwitzer & Bargh, 1996). In this section, we investigate the following motivational agents in the cognition → action sequence:

Chapter 8

- Plans of action (Carver & Scheier, 1998)
- Goals (Locke & Latham, 2002)
- Implementation intentions (Gollwitzer, 1999)

Chapter 9

- Growth vs. fixed mindsets (Dweck, 2006)
- Deliberative vs. implementation mindsets (Gollwitzer & Kinney, 1989)
- Promotion vs. prevention orientations (Higgins, 1997)
- Dissonance (Harmon-Jones & Mills, 1999)

Chapter 10

- Perceived control (Skinner, 1996)
- Self-efficacy (Bandura, 1986)
- Mastery beliefs (Diener & Dweck, 1978)
- Expectancy x value (Eccles & Wigfield, 2002)
- Attributions (Weiner, 1986)

Chapter 11

- Self-concept (Markus, 1977)
- Self-regulation (Zimmerman, 2000)
- Self-control (Baumeister & Tierney, 2011)

As we will see, a cognitive mental event such as a goal or an expectancy functions as a "spring to action," a moving force that energizes and directs action in purposive ways (Ames & Ames, 1984). The first motivational spring to action studied was the "plan."

PLANS OF ACTION

The contemporary cognitive study of motivation began in 1960 when a trio of psychologists—George Miller, Eugene Galanter, and Karl Pribram—investigated how plans motivate behavior. According to these pioneers, people have mental representations of the ideal states of their behavior, environmental objects, and events. In other words, people have in mind what an ideal tennis serve looks like (ideal behavior), what an ideal birthday gift would be (ideal environmental object), and what constitutes an ideal night on the town (ideal event). People are also aware of the present state of their behavior, environment, and events. That is, people have the knowledge of their current tennis serve (present behavior), gift (present object), and evening itinerary (present event).

Any mismatch perceived between one's present state and one's ideal state instigates an experience of "incongruity," which has motivational properties. Suffering incongruity, people formulate a plan of action to remove that incongruity (Miller et al., 1960; Newell, Shaw, & Simon, 1958; Powers, 1973). Hence, the essential motivational process underlying a plan is as follows: People have knowledge of both their present and ideal states and any perceived incongruity between the two makes people uncomfortable enough to formulate and act on a plan of action to remove the incongruity so that the present state will change and transform into the ideal state. The incongruity is the motivational "spring to action," and the plan directs behavior toward the pursuit of the ideal state.

The cognitive mechanism by which plans energize and direct behavior is the test–operate–test–exit (TOTE) model, as illustrated in Figure 8.1 (Miller et al., 1960). *Test* means to compare the present state against the ideal. If the present state and the ideal state are the same (are congruous), nothing happens. A mismatch between the two (incongruity), however, springs the individual into action. That is, the mismatch motivates the individual to *operate* on the environment via a planned sequence of action. That is, when you look in the mirror to check if your hair looks okay, you "test" or compare the way your hair presently looks in the mirror against the way you want your hair ideally to look. If your hair looks okay, you say "fine" and walk away from the mirror. But if you see a mismatch between your present hair and your ideal hair, then it is time to "operate" via a plan of action—you comb your hair, take a shower, use hairspray, or just wear a hat. After a period of action, the person again *tests* the present state against the ideal. If the feedback reveals that the incongruity continues to persist, then the person continues to *operate* on the environment (T-O-T-O-T-O, and so on). In daily life, T-O-T-O-T-O looks like, to continue the bad hair day example: Look in mirror—Comb your hair—Look in the mirror for feedback—Comb your hair some more—Look in the mirror again—Comb

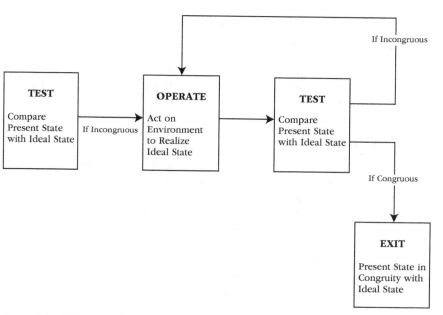

Figure 8.1   Schematic of the TOTE Model

your hair some more, and so on. As long as the incongruity persists, action ("operate") continues. If and when the present matches the ideal, the person *exits* the plan.

Consider a second example of the TOTE model. A painter takes an easel to a waterfall, paints the scenery, compares the canvas to the waterfall, and notices that the two are quite dissimilar. Because the canvas does not yet show a satisfactory representation of the waterfall, the painter operates on the painting to reflect on the canvas the ideal picture in her mind. The painter continually compares (tests) the painting on the canvas to its ideal in her mind. As long as incongruity persists, the painting continues (T-O-T-O-T-O, and so on). Only when the actual and ideal paintings match does the painter exit the plan and cease to paint. The ever-repeated process of comparing the present versus the ideal, followed by incongruity-reducing behavioral adjustments, is a common feature of everyday life.

Overcoming bad hair days and painting waterfalls illustrate the moment-to-moment influence plans have on our motivated behavior—getting started, putting forth effort, persisting over time, and eventually stopping. Dozens of additional illustrations of plans as springs to action are possible, including removing items from a "to do" list, repairing a broken object until it is fixed, driving to a destination, revising a term paper, shopping, saving money for a trip, mowing the lawn, cleaning a sink full of dirty dishes, reading this chapter, and so on.

Plans can also be long term. For instance, how satisfied are you currently with the present state of your career/occupation? Marital status? Capacity to speak a foreign language? Events happen in life that make us aware of the incongruities that exist between our present and our ideal states. Our friend, for instance, might get an "ideal" job, an "ideal" marriage partner, or an "ideal" opportunity to travel or live abroad. When these incongruities cause enough discomfort to stir us into action (as we say to ourselves, "I want the ideal state more than I want my present state"), we formulate plans of action and start down the road of long-term planning of action that is T-O-T-O-T-O.

Corrective Motivation

The plan → action sequence portrays individuals as (1) detecting present-ideal inconsistencies, (2) generating a plan of action to eliminate the incongruity, (3) instigating plan-regulated behavior, and (4) monitoring feedback as to the extent of any remaining present-ideal incongruity. Most researchers (Campion & Lord, 1982; Carver & Scheier, 1998), however, no longer view plans of action as so fixed, static, and mechanical. Rather, plans are adjustable and subject to revision. Given an incongruity between present and ideal, one's plan of action is as likely to change and undergo modification as is one's behavior. The emphasis on modifiable plans is important because it presents human beings as active decision makers who choose one of the following in a given set of circumstances: Act ("Operate") to achieve the ideal state or change and revise an ineffective plan (Carver & Scheier, 1981, 1982). From this point of view, any present-ideal incongruity does not instigate an automatic, mechanical discrepancy-motivated action sequence. Rather, incongruity gives rise to a more general "corrective motivation" (Campion & Lord, 1982).

Corrective motivation activates a decision-making process in which the individual considers many different possible ways for reducing the present-ideal incongruity: change the plan, change behavior (increase effort), or withdraw from the plan altogether. That is, plan-directed behavior is a dynamic, flexible process in which corrective motivation energizes the individual to pursue the most adaptive course. Hence, devising a good plan for removing or reducing incongruity is only the first half of the battle. Actually carrying out the plan is the other half because people all too often encounter problems (e.g., situational constraints, personal inadequacies) while trying to translate their plans into action. Corrective motivation is therefore a dynamic process of going back and forth between the two points listed above—act to achieve the ideal state but also be ready to revise an ineffective plan.

Discrepancy

The more cognitive psychologists worked with "present state versus ideal state" mismatches to study plans and corrective motivation, the more they came to see the larger construct of "discrepancy" as a core motivational construct. The basic idea behind discrepancy (a synonym for "incongruity") is straightforward and can be represented by the magnitude of the arrow below that shows the difference or mismatch between one's present state and one's ideal state.

Present state represents the person's current status of how life is going. The ideal state represents how the person wishes life was going. When the present state falls short of the hoped-for ideal state, a discrepancy is exposed. It is the discrepancy—rather than the ideal state per se—that has motivational properties. Discrepancy creates the sense of wanting to change the present state so that it will move closer and closer toward the ideal state. The motivational question is not so much "What is the ideal state?" as it is "How much of a discrepancy exists between my present vs. ideal states?" Small discrepancies carry little motivational punch, while large discrepancies carry much motivational punch.

Here are a dozen everyday illustrations of discrepancies between what currently is (present state) and what we wish would be (ideal state). For instance, people who are stuck in traffic (present state) wish they were instead driving without interference (ideal state), and the awareness of the mismatch creates a want that motivates people to take action necessary to remove the rather bothersome discrepancy.

Present State	Ideal State
Stuck in traffic	Driving without interference
Poor penmanship	Excellent penmanship
The job you have	The job you want
How skillful you are	How skillful the guy on television is
Empty, blank crossword puzzle	Fully completed crossword puzzle
Current GPA	GPA needed to make the Dean's List
Messy, cluttered desktop	Clean, well-organized desktop
Suffering a headache	Not suffering a headache
Not a member of the team	Member of the team
Having 200 more miles to drive	Being there
10 laps to run around the track	0 laps to run
400 unread pages in this book	0 unread pages

When people ask themselves, "What can I do to increase motivation?" those who study discrepancy-based motivation have a very practical answer: Basically, create an ideal state in your mind. Or, more precisely, create an ideal state in your mind and reflect on the discrepancy that now exists between "what presently is" and "what is desired."

Affect and Feelings

Behavior involves getting from here to there. It involves getting from the present state to the ideal state. But it also matters how quickly or how slowly one gets from here to there. Because the rate of discrepancy reduction matters, affect or feelings are important (Carver & Scheier, 2011).

If a person is making a satisfactory rate of progress to reduce a goal discrepancy (e.g., I need to be at the bus stop before 2:00 pm and, as I walk, I can tell that I am going to arrive early and catch the bus), positive affect arises. If, however, the same person is making an unsatisfactory rate of progress toward discrepancy reduction (I need to be at the bus stop before 2:00 pm but, as I walk, I can tell that I am going to be late and miss the bus), negative affect arises. Positive affect (positive feelings) means that you are doing better at something than you need to be doing; negative affect (negative feelings) means that you are doing worse (Carver & Scheier, 1990, 1998). Thus, feelings such as hope, excitement, eagerness, and enthusiasm signal that you are doing better than you need to, while feelings such as joy, delight, and bliss signal that you are going much better. Similarly, feeling frustrated signals that you are doing worse than you need to, feeling discouraged signals you are doing much worse, feeling sad signals you are doing much, much worse, and feeling depressed signals that you are doing much, much, much worse than you need to being doing (Carver & Scheier, 2011). These later feelings of frustration, irritation, and anxiety make sense because they energize effort and facilitate discrepancy reduction, but feelings such as sadness, despair, and depression mean that effort is perceived as futile and one would be smarter to quit than to persist.

In goal striving, positive affect is more than just a scorecard to tell you that you are doing better than you need to, and negative affect is more than just a scorecard to tell you that you are doing worse than you need to. Affect also energizes behavior. If you are doing worse than you need to be doing, you will not only feel negative affect but you will also push harder—you will start running to catch the bus. If your running gets you back on schedule and you realize that you are now going to be early and catch the bus, then the successful behavior turns off the negative affect. Alternatively, if you are doing better than you need to be doing, then you will probably coast a little—you will not stop walking to catch the bus, but you may ease back a little and perhaps glance in the store windows or pause to check your email on your smartphone (Louro, Pieters, & Zeelenberg, 2007). Thus, affect is not only a discrepancy-reducing scorecard, but it is also a behavioral motivator itself.

Two Types of Discrepancy

Two types of discrepancies exist (Bandura, 1990; Carver & Scheier, 1998). The first is *discrepancy reduction*, which is based on the discrepancy-detecting feedback that underlies plans of action and corrective motivation. Some aspect of the environment (e.g., a boss, scholarship opportunity, athletic opponent, a stopwatch) provides feedback about how well or how poorly current performance matches up with its ideal level. For instance, at work, the supervisor might tell the salesperson that 10 sales are not enough; 15 sales are needed. Likewise, a student might read in a brochure that his current 2.0 GPA is not enough for scholarship eligibility; a GPA of 3.0 is needed. In essence, the environment brings some standard of excellence (an ideal state) to the person's awareness and asks, essentially, "Are you currently performing at this desired level?"

The second type of discrepancy is *discrepancy creation*. Discrepancy creation is based on a "feed-forward" system in which the person looks forward and sets a future, higher goal. The person deliberately and proactively sets a higher goal—an ideal state that does not yet exist except in the performer's mind—and does not require feedback from a boss or a scholarship to impose it. For instance, the salesperson might, for whatever reason, decide to try for 15 sales in one week instead of the usual 10, and the student might decide to try for a 3.0 GPA. Thus, the person creates for him- or herself a new, higher goal to pursue.

The way to think about discrepancy reduction is as a negative feedback loop—a discrepancy arises, action is taken, and negative feedback (discrepancy is getting smaller) terminates that action. A negative feedback loop reduces discrepancies. Alternatively, the way to think about discrepancy creation is as a positive feedback loop—a discrepancy is created, action is taken, and positive feedback energizes further discrepancy creation. A positive feedback loop enlarges discrepancies.

In both cases—discrepancy reduction and discrepancy creation—it is the discrepancy (or incongruity) that provides the motivational basis for action. But two important distinctions between discrepancy reduction and discrepancy creation exist: (1) Discrepancy reduction corresponds to plan-based corrective motivation (discussed in the previous section), whereas discrepancy creation corresponds to goal-setting motivation (discussed in the next section); and (2) discrepancy reduction is reactive, deficiency overcoming, and revolves around a negative feedback system, whereas discrepancy creation is proactive, growth pursuing, and revolves around a positive feedback or "feed-forward" system. As discussed next, goal setting is first and foremost a discrepancy-creating process (Bandura, 1990).

GOAL SETTING

At a general level, a goal is whatever an individual is striving to accomplish (Locke, 1996). When people strive to earn $100, make a 4.0 GPA, graduate from college, sell 100 boxes of Girl Scout cookies, exercise for 30 minutes, or go undefeated in an athletic season, they engage in goal-directed behavior. More specifically, a goal is a future-focused cognitive representation of a desired end state that guides behavior (Hulleman, Schrager, Bodmann, & Harackiewicz, 2010).

Like plans, goals generate motivation by focusing people's attention on the discrepancy (or incongruity) between their present level of accomplishment (no boxes of cookies sold) and their ideal level of accomplishment (100 boxes sold by the end of the month). Researchers refer to this discrepancy between present level of accomplishment and ideal level of accomplishment as a "goal–performance discrepancy" (Locke & Latham, 1990).

Goal–Performance Discrepancy

Generally speaking, people with goals outperform those without goals (Locke, 1996; Locke & Latham, 1990, 2002). And generally speaking, the same person performs better when she has a goal than when she does not have a goal. So people who create goals for themselves and people who accept the goals others set for them perform better than those who do not create or accept such goals. The finding that goals enhance performance is what makes the goal concept an appealing and practical motivational construct.

Consider one study in which elementary-grade students performed sit-ups for 2 minutes (Weinberg, Bruya, Longino, & Jackson, 1988). Some students set a goal for themselves as to how many sit-ups they would accomplish during the 2 minutes (goal-setting group), while others simply completed sit-ups without a predetermined goal (no-goal group). After 2 minutes of exercise, the goal-setting students completed significantly more sit-ups than did the no-goal students. In effect, the presence of a goal motivated exercisers more than did the absence of a goal. The first group of elementary-grade students was not any healthier or athletic than the other group of students. Instead, the presence of a goal energized, directed, and sustained their sit-up performance in a way that the absence of a goal did not.

This same performance-facilitating effect can be found in any number of other studies, because people with goals outperform people without goals, such as in trying to lift weights, learn text information, sell products, shoot archery, conserve natural resources, increase productivity at work, and lose weight (see Locke & Latham's [1990] Table 2.5, which lists 88 different tasks in which goal–performance discrepancies lead to enhanced performance). Goal setting generally enhances performance, but the type of goal one sets is a key determinant in the extent to which a goal translates into performance gains, because goals vary in how difficult they are, how specific they are, and how congruent with the self they are.

Goal Difficulty

Goal difficulty refers to how hard a goal is to accomplish. As goals increase in difficulty, performance increases in a linear fashion (Locke & Latham, 1990; Mento, Steel, & Karren, 1987; Tubbs, 1986). Relative to goals such as scoring 80 on a test, running a mile in 10 minutes, and making one new friend at a social event, more difficult goals would be scoring 90 on a test, running a mile in 8 minutes, and making two new friends. The more difficult the goal, the more it energizes the performer. This is so because people exert effort in proportion to what the goal requires of them. That is, easy goals stimulate little effort, medium goals stimulate moderate effort, and difficult goals stimulate high effort (Earley, Wojnaroski, & Prest, 1987; Locke & Latham, 1984, 1990, 2002). Effort responds to the magnitude of goal difficulty, which is to say that effort responds to the magnitude of the goal–performance discrepancy.

Goal Specificity

Goal specificity refers to how clearly a goal informs the performer precisely what he is to do. Telling a performer to "do your best" sounds like goal setting, but it is actually only an ambiguous statement that does not make clear precisely what the person is to do (Locke & Latham, 1990). On the other hand, telling a writer to have a first draft in one week, a revised draft in two weeks, and a final manuscript in three weeks specifies more precisely what the writer is to do and when she is to do it. Translating a vague goal into a specific goal typically involves restating the goal in numerical terms, although it generally just means being very specific in what you are asking the other person to do (e.g., instead of "be nice," a more specific goal would be to "greet all guests proactively, smile, open your arms, call them by name, offer a refreshment, and tell them that you are glad that they are here").

Goal specificity is important because specific goals draw attention to what one needs to do and reduces ambiguity in thought and variability in performance (Klein, Whitener, & Ilgen, 1990; Locke, Chah, Harrison, & Lustgarten, 1989). As to ambiguous thought, a vague goal such as "study hard" might be interpreted as "read the chapter" by one student but as "read the chapter, take notes, review it, and form a study group to discuss it" by a second student. As to variable performance, a vague goal (e.g., "work quickly" or "read a lot") produces a relatively wide range of performances compared to giving a group of performers a specific goal (e.g., "complete the task in the next 3 minutes" or "read 100 pages"), which produces a relatively narrow range of performances that all hover around the goal level (Locke, Shaw, Saari, & Latham, 1981).

Goal Congruence

All goals are not equal. Some goals are fully endorsed, feel personally authentic, and are whole-heartedly accepted, embraced, and owned by the self; other goals, however, are not at all self-endorsed, feel artificial or socially manufactured, and are taken on without a sense of personal ownership. Self-congruent goals are those that reflect the self's interests, needs, values, and preferences—they are goals that feel authentic and in harmony with the self; self-discrepant goals are those that neglect the self's interests, needs, values, and preferences and instead reflect only social obligations or external pressures—they are goals that feel artificial and conflict with the self (Sheldon & Elliot, 1998, 1999). A goal such as "become a doctor" for one person may by in harmony with the core self (e.g., you tell me to "become a doctor" and, yes, that is something I really want to do), but that same goal for another person might be in conflict with and have little fit with the self (e.g., you tell me to "become a doctor" but, no, that is not something I really want or value).

Goal concordance is important because self-concordant goals allow the person to tap into and draw from personal resources that energize, direct, and sustain goal pursuit (Sheldon & Elliot, 1999). When paired with a goal, personal interests, psychological needs, intrinsic motivation, internalized values, personal preferences, and inner motivational resources in general fuel and sustain greater energy, direction, and persistence. Thus, a person who pursues a self-concordant goal has the motivational support of intrinsic motivation and identified regulation, while a person who pursues a self-discrepant goal lacks these self-generated motivational resources and instead acts only with the motivational support of external or introjected regulation (recall Chapter 6).

Difficult, Specific, and Congruent Goals Enhance Performance

Goals do not always enhance performance. Only those goals that are difficult, specific, and self-congruent do so (Koestner, Lekes, Powers, & Chicoine, 2002; Locke et al., 1981). Anyone who has simply listed a number of goals to accomplish (e.g., a "to do list") knows that there is a difference between having a goal and actually accomplishing it.

The reason difficult, specific, self-concordant goals increase performance while easy, vague, and self-discordant ones do not is motivational. Difficult goals *energize* the performer, specific goals *direct* that energy toward a particular course of action, and concordant goals both *energize* and *direct* the performer (Earley et al., 1987; Sheldon & Elliot, 1999).

Difficult goals energize behavior, which is to say that they increase the performer's effort and persistence. The harder the goal, the greater the output of effort expended to accomplish it (Bandura & Cervone, 1983, 1986; Earley et al., 1987). Difficult goals increase persistence because effort continues and continues until the goal is reached (LaPorte & Nath, 1976; Latham & Locke, 1975). The athlete trying for 45 sit-ups, for example, keeps performing sit-up after sit-up until all 45 are done. Difficult goals also decrease the probability that the performer will be distracted away from the task or will give up prematurely (LaPorte & Nath, 1976). The exerciser with a goal for "45 sit-ups" is more likely to keep going past 30, 35, and 40 sit-ups than is the exerciser with a lesser goal or with a "do my best" goal. With a difficult goal in mind, performers withdraw their effort and persistence only after the goal is accomplished, not when they get bored, frustrated, tired, or distracted.

Specific goals direct attention and strategic planning. Specific goals focus the individual's attention toward the task at hand and therefore away from tasks that are incidental (Kahneman, 1973; Locke & Bryan, 1969; Rothkopf & Billington, 1979). Specific goals tell the performer where to concentrate and precisely what to do (Klein et al., 1990; Latham, Mitchell, & Dossett, 1978; Locke et al., 1989). In studies with students reading texts, for instance, readers with specific goals spent significantly more time looking at their text during a study session than did readers with ambiguous goals, who were more likely to let their eyes wander around the room (Locke & Bryan, 1969; Rothkopf & Billington, 1979). Specific goals also prompt performers to plan a strategic course of action (Latham & Baldes, 1975; Terborg, 1976), and specific goals lead people to use their task knowledge and strategies (Smith, Locke, & Barry, 1990). The weight loss program discussed in the chapter's opening vignette illustrates this point as the dieter needs to invest a good deal of knowledge and deliberate planning into the creation of a strategic plan if he or she is going to successfully limit the day's food intake to 25 points or less. Also, with a specific goal in mind, a performer who is unable to accomplish a goal on a first attempt will tend to drop or revise that strategy by creating a new and improved strategy (Earley et al., 1987; Earley & Perry, 1987).

Self-concordant goals energize behavior, maintain persistence, direct attention, and inspire strategic planning. The reason why a person adopts and pursues a goal matters, as self-concordant goals (e.g., I pursue this goal because it is interesting and important to me) allow performers to draw upon and vitalize inner motivational resources, while goals adopted for external reasons (e.g., social pressure, social obligation, social expectations) or internal pressures (e.g., doing what one "should" or "ought" do) leave these same inner motivational resources untapped. In one study, college students were asked what goals they planned to pursue over the weekend, and they listed goals such as "write a rough draft of my research paper," "show my visiting friend the sights of Montreal," and "clean my room." These goal strivers were also asked why they planned to pursue those particular goals. Participants rated each goal on how self-concordant ("because you really believe that it is an important goal to have—you endorse it freely and value it whole-heartedly") or self-discordant ("because you would feel ashamed, guilty, or anxious if you didn't—you feel that you ought to strive for this") it was (Koestner et al., 2002, p. 235). To complete the study, the researchers then contacted the students after the weekend to ask how much goal progress they had made over the weekend on each goal. Goal concordance predicted goal progress rather well. In a follow-up study, college students were asked what New Year's resolutions (a self-change goal) they made in the first week of January. Again, extent of goal congruence and goal progress were assessed. As before, goal concordance predicted goal progress.

The role that goal difficulty, goal specificity, and goal concordance play in removing goal–performance discrepancies appears in Figure 8.2. People show performance gains for their sought-after goals because difficult goals energize and sustain behavior, because specific goals direct behavior, and because self-concordant goals energize, direct, and sustain behavior.

Goals generate motivation, but motivation is only one of the causes underlying performance. Performance also depends on factors that are not motivational, such as ability, training, coaching, and resources (Locke & Latham, 1984). Because these factors also contribute to the quality of performance, no one-to-one correspondence exists between goals and performance. Thus, if two performers have comparable ability, training, coaching, and resources, then performers with difficult, specific, and self-concordant goals will likely outperform performers without such goals. This is an important practical point because when difficult, specific, and self-concordant goals fail to enhance performance, one might be well advised to focus on factors that are not motivational and that relate to increasing ability (via instruction, practice, role models, videotaped-performance feedback) or resources (via supplying equipment, books, tutors, computers, money).

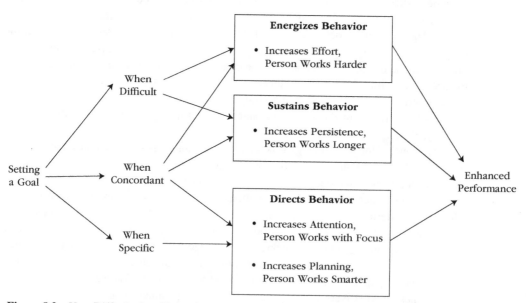

Figure 8.2 How Difficult, Specific, and Self-Concordant Goals Raise Performance to Remove Goal–Performance Discrepancies

Feedback

Difficult, specific, and self-concordant goals enhance performance, but one additional variable is crucial in making goal setting effective: feedback (Erez, 1977). Goal setting translates into increased performance only in the context of timely feedback that documents the performer's progress in relation to the goal (Locke et al., 1981). Feedback, or knowledge of results, allows people to keep track of any progress toward their goal that may occur. In other words, a performer needs both a goal *and* feedback to maximize performance (Bandura & Cervone, 1983; Becker, 1978; Erez, 1977; Strang, Lawrence, & Fowler, 1978; Tubbs, 1986).

Without feedback, performance can be emotionally unimportant and uninvolving. A runner can have a goal to run a mile in 6 minutes, a dieter can have a goal to lose 10 pounds, and a student can have a goal of mastering a subject matter. But if the runner, dieter, and student never gain access to a stopwatch, scale, or examination, respectively, then all the running, dieting, and studying have no way for informing the performer of his or her progress toward goal attainment. But feedback is just information. Just as the goal needs feedback to diagnose progress, the reverse is also true that feedback needs a goal (a standard of performance). It is only within the context of a goal that one can utilize feedback information to judge one's performance as poor (below goal), okay (at goal), or excellent (above goal).

The combination of goals with feedback produces an emotionally meaningful mixture: Goal attainment breeds emotional satisfaction, while goal failure breeds emotional dissatisfaction (Bandura, 1991). Both satisfaction and dissatisfaction have motivational properties. Felt satisfaction contributes favorably to the discrepancy-creating process. When feedback shows the individual that he or she is performing at or above goal level, the individual feels satisfied and competent, competent enough perhaps to create a higher, more difficult goal (the discrepancy-creation process; Wood, Bandura, & Bailey, 1990). Felt dissatisfaction contributes favorably to the discrepancy-reducing process (Carver & Scheier, 1998; Matsui, Okada, & Inoshita, 1983). When performance feedback shows the individual that he or she is performing below goal level, the individual feels dissatisfied and becomes keenly aware of the goal–performance discrepancy, enough perhaps to marshal greater effort toward eliminating the goal–performance incongruity (the discrepancy-reduction process; Bandura & Cervone, 1983, 1986). Feedback therefore provides the emotional punch that continually bathes the goal-setting process within emotional experiences of felt satisfaction and felt dissatisfaction.

The core motivational elements of the goal-setting process appear in summary form in Figure 8.3. The left-hand side of the figure explains why goals enhance performance—namely, because people with goals work harder, longer, smarter, and with more focus (i.e., increased effort, persistence, strategic planning, and attention). The right-hand side explains the motivational process that arises out of feedback in removing goal–performance discrepancies (i.e., discrepancy reduction, new discrepancy creation).

Criticisms

Goal setting has its advantages, but it also has its cautions and pitfalls (Locke & Latham, 1984). A first caution associated with goal setting is that it works best when tasks are relatively uninteresting and require only a straightforward procedure (Wood, Mento, & Locke, 1987), as shown with tasks such as adding numbers (Bandura & Schunk, 1981),

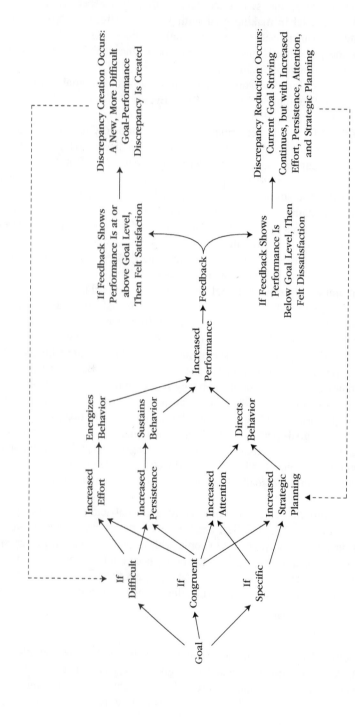

Figure 8.3 Summary of the Goal-Setting Process

typing (Latham & Yukl, 1976), proofreading (Huber, 1985), assembling nuts and bolts (Mossholder, 1980), and sit-ups (Weinberg, Bruya, & Jackson, 1985). Goal setting aids performance on uninteresting, straightforward tasks by generating motivation that the task itself cannot generate (because it is so boring on its own). For tasks that are inherently interesting and require creativity or problem solving, goal setting does not enhance performance (Bandura & Wood, 1989; Earley, Connolly, & Ekegren, 1989; Kanfer & Ackerman, 1989; McGraw, 1978), because inherently interesting tasks generate effort, persistence, attention, and strategic planning on their own.

A second caution associated with goal setting is goal conflict. People rarely pursue only one goal at a time and instead pursue goals that sometimes conflict with one another (Baumeister & Heatherton, 1996). The goal-setting process basically says "pay attention here, not there" and "there" might involve an important goal as well. For instance, one goal to travel in Asia during the summer will likely conflict another goal to save money. In the same spirit, goal pursuit can lead to goal overload and stress (Csikszentmihalyi, 1990; Lazarus, 1991a).

A key pitfall in the applied practice of setting goals for others is that goals are too often administered in ways that are controlling, pressure-inducing, and intrusive and thus can undermine creativity and intrinsic motivation by interfering with one's autonomy, cognitive flexibility, and personal passion for work (Amabile, 1998; Mossholder, 1980).

Long-Term Goal Setting

A student who wants to become a teacher and an athlete who wants to win an Olympic event exemplify individuals involved in long-term goal setting. To accomplish a distant goal, the performer first has to attain several requisite short-term goals. Would-be doctors, for instance, first have to make a high GPA as undergraduates, get accepted into a medical school, raise or borrow a great deal of money, move to a different city, graduate from medical school, complete an internship, join a hospital or partnership, and so forth, all before they can begin their careers as doctors. Thus, goals can be short term or long term or a series of short-term goals linked together into one long-term goal. No significant difference in performance emerges among performers with short-term, long-term, or a mixture of short- and long-term goals (Hall & Byrne, 1988; Weinberg, Bruya, & Jackson, 1985, Weinberg et al., 1988), although all outperform people with no goals.

Instead of affecting performance per se, goal proximity affects persistence and intrinsic motivation. As for persistence, many would-be teachers, Olympians, and doctors eventually forfeit their long-term goals because of a lack of positive reinforcements along the way. During all those years of studying and practicing, the long-term goal of actually being a teacher, Olympian, or doctor never materializes. At 10, the goal striver is not a teacher. At 11, she is still not a teacher. At 12, she is still not a teacher, despite a great deal of goal-striving effort, persistence, attention, and strategic planning. Because the long-term goal striver receives insufficient opportunities for performance feedback and positive reinforcement, his or her persistence would benefit from setting a series of short-term goals that chain together eventually to end in the long-term target goal. Short-term goals provide repeated commitment-boosting opportunities for reinforcement following goal attainment that long-term goals cannot provide (Latham et al., 1978). Short-term goals also provide repeated opportunities for feedback that allow the performer to evaluate performance as being at, above, or below the goal. An athlete trying for a long-term goal such as winning the state championship receives little day-to-day feedback as compared to the athlete trying for a short-term goal such as winning a contest each week.

Several researchers assessed the impact that short- and long-term goals have on intrinsic motivation (Bandura & Schunk, 1981; Harackiewicz & Manderlink, 1984; Mossholder, 1980; Vallerand, Deci, & Ryan, 1985). On uninteresting tasks, short-term goals create opportunities for positive feedback, the experience of making progress, and a means of nurturing a sense of competence, all of which enhance intrinsic motivation (Vallerand et al., 1985). On interesting tasks, however, only long-term goals facilitate intrinsic motivation. For the highly interested performer, short-term goals are typically experienced as superfluous, intrusive, and controlling. People generally prefer to pursue long-term goals in their own way, and this sense of autonomy explains why long-term goals can increase intrinsic motivation (Manderlink & Harackiewicz, 1984; Vallerand et al., 1985).

Additionally, a long-term goal typically exists as a complex cognitive structure (Ortony, Clore, & Collins, 1988). Short-term goals can be thought of as specific behavioral targets, such as to lose 5 pounds, find a job, or make 10 consecutive free throws. To think of long-term goals as cognitive lattice structures, however, consider the long-term goal of an aspiring concert pianist (Ravlin, 1987). At the top of the goal lattice structure are the pianist's most abstract (and long-term) goals. Abstract, long-term goals would be not only "become a concert pianist" but also "have an ideal career," "keep parents happy," and "have a happy family life." At the bottom are the most concrete (and short-term) goals. Concrete, short-term goals would be "pass audition," "get admitted to Indiana University," "become a university student," "graduate from Indiana University," and so forth. Each aspiration is interconnected with the other in the sense that each shares in the musician's overall long-term goal of becoming a concert pianist. Furthermore, each aspiration is connected in a causal flow in which the achievement of a short-term goal increases the probability of attaining the next short-term goal, whereas the failure to achieve one goal decreases the probability of attaining another.

GOAL STRIVING

Goal setting seems so promising, so ripe with potential, as a motivational intervention strategy for helping people accomplish the sorts of things they wish to accomplish (see Box 8). The self-help books in the mega bookstores agree, because they advise readers to set goals and to focus their full attention on these goals. If you want to make better grades, lose 10 pounds, save a ton of money, or be successful in love and work, then you must visualize the goal you want. Think it—be it, they say. Focus on it, visualize it, see the new you with goal in hand. Unfortunately, motivational processes are not that simple, because goal setting needs a great deal of goal striving—effort, persistence, focused attention, and strategic planning—to translate into increased performance and goal attainment. The gap between adopting a goal and actually attaining it can be wide.

| BOX 8 | *Goal Setting and Goal Striving* |

Question: Why is this information important?

Answer: To translate the goals you value into effective action.

What would you like to accomplish? Would you like to increase the number of friends you have? Increase your GPA? Decrease your weight? One means for attaining an objective is goal setting. Effective goal setting entails following and then implementing these sequential procedures:

1. Identify the objective to be accomplished.
2. Define goal difficulty.
3. Clarify goal specificity.
4. Ask why you are pursuing this goal (i.e., evaluate self-goal concordance).
5. Specify how and when performance will be measured.

For instance, consider the goal of getting in shape (to continue the example introduced in the beginning of the chapter). In numerical terms, getting in shape could be represented by taking 12,000 steps per day. Such a goal represents both a difficult and specific course of action. But why adopt a "get in shape" goal? Does such a goal reflect your authentic self, or is this goal simply a socially imposed or "ought to" goal? Checking and recording in a logbook the actual number of steps taken each day before going to sleep specifies how and when performance will be measured.

Identifying the goal gets you halfway home. The other half is to generate goal-attainment strategies that will enable you to translate goal setting into goal attainment:

6. Identify goal-attainment strategies.
7. Create "if-then" implementation intentions.
8. Make performance feedback continuously available.

Identifying goal-attainment strategies means deciding what to do. This means deciding on a strategic plan of action that has a good chance of producing goal attainment. Implementation intentions are also needed to get goal striving started, to stay on course, and to resume goal striving after interruptions. You might decide, for instance, to walk around the neighborhood from 8:00 until 8:30 each morning. While doing so, you would be well advised to keep the pedometer and smartphone with you so to make performance feedback continuously available to know if you are performing at, above, or below goal level.

Given this goal-setting process and the forethought to formulate strategies and implementation intentions, you have now articulated both the goal and the plan of when, where, and how all this goal striving will take place. This is just one example, but you might be surprised by how readily these procedures generalize to other domains that might be important to the objectives you seek.

Mental Simulations

Consider a series of studies designed explicitly to test the advice to "visualize success" (Taylor, Pham, Rivkin, & Armor, 1998). In these studies, participants either (1) focused on the goal they wished to attain, (2) focused on how to attain the goal, or (3) did not focus on anything in particular (a control group). Focusing on the goal actually interfered with goal attainment! Visualizing success backfired. Focusing on how to accomplish the goal, however, did facilitate goal attainment. These data are important because (1) they draw out the distinction between the content of a goal (what one is striving for) and the process of goal striving (the means one uses to attain the goal), and (2) once a goal has been set, it does not inevitably and automatically translate itself into effective performance.

Salespeople know the following trick well: Ask someone to imagine having and using an item and that person will become significantly more likely to go out of his or her way to have and use that item (as in "Just imagine sitting in this beauty, driving it home, and parking this fine machine right in front of your home. Can you see it? Can you feel it?"). In an experimental demonstration of what salespeople already know, researchers found that asking people to work through a mental simulation of attaining a desired end state (a goal) did lead them to purchase that item, which shows a high level of goal commitment (Gregory, Cialdini, & Carpenter, 1982). However, focusing on the rich you, the thin you, or the married you does not get you very far. Visualizing fantasies of success (i.e., wishful thinking) do not produce productive behavior (Oettingen, 1996). Instead of focusing on outcomes (i.e., on goal content), mental simulations need to focus on planning and problem solving (i.e., on goal striving). To illustrate this point, imagine hearing one of the two following instructions (Pham & Taylor, 1999):

Outcome Simulation (Focus on the Goal)

Visualize yourself getting a high grade on your psychology midterm ... imagine how you would feel. It is very important that you see yourself getting a high grade on the psychology midterm and have that picture in your mind.

Process Simulation (Focus on Implementation Intentions)

Visualize yourself studying for the midterm in such a way that would lead you to obtain a high grade on the midterm. As of today and for the remaining days before the midterm, imagine how you would study to get a high grade on your psychology midterm. It is very important that you see yourself actually studying and have that picture in your mind.

The first set of instructions basically asked students to rehearse the joy of success, while the second set of instructions basically asked students to engage in planning and problem solving. Compared to a no-simulation control group, students in the outcome mental simulation condition actually studied less and made poorer scores on the test. Students in the process mental simulation condition studied more and made better test scores. Focusing on success might cultivate hope, but it does not promote productive goal striving. To facilitate action, people need to mentally simulate the goal-striving process—the means by which they will accomplish the end they seek.

Implementation Intentions

When people fail to realize the goals they set for themselves, part of the problem can be explained by how they set the goal (i.e., Is the goal difficult? Is it specific? Is it self-concordant? Is it paired with feedback?). The other part of the problem, however, is simply that people fail to act on the goals they set for themselves (Orbell & Sheeran, 1998). As the old saying goes, "A goal without a plan is just a dream."

An implementation intention is an "if-then" plan that specifies in advance the goal-striving process. Formulating an implementation intention involves deciding *in advance* of one's goal striving the "when, where, and how" goal striving is to occur (Gollwitzer, 1999; Gollwitzer & Oettingen, 2011; Gollwitzer & Sheeran, 2006). Admittedly, the term *implementation intentions* is a bit awkward, but it makes the distinction between two types of intentions—namely, a goal intention (setting a goal) and an implementation intention (striving to accomplish it). A goal intention specifies what one wants to achieve, while an implementation intention specifies when, where, and how one will achieve that goal.

Imagine that you have set a goal, such as making a 4.0 GPA, reading this book, or saving $100 this month. Will these goals come to fruition? Probably not, at least if you fail to develop specific action plans. People in general often fail to specify when they will initiate their goal-directed action, where their goal-directed action will take place, and how they will accomplish their goal, especially in the face of obstacles, distractions, and interruptions. In contrast, when people with a goal take the time to specify implementation intentions, they strongly increase their chance of goal attainment (Aarts, Dijksterhuis, & Midden, 1999; Brandstatter, Lengfelder, & Gollwitzer, 2001; Gollwitzer & Schaal, 1998; Oettingen, Honig, & Gollwitzer, 2000).

To form an implementation intention, a person needs to do two things. First, the person needs to identify a response that will promote goal attainment. For instance, for the student who wants to make an A in a class, what response might cause that A to materialize (e.g., studying, forming a study group)? Second, the person needs to anticipate a suitable occasion to initiate that response. For instance, for the student who believes that studying will cause the A to materialize, then a time for studying needs to be decided upon in advance (e.g., for the two hours after class, I will go to the coffee shop and review my class notes and weekly readings). For the person who wants to exercise more, he might identify taking the stairs to the seventh floor as a response that will promote goal attainment. If so, each time he enters the building and encounters that flight of stairs he encounters a suitable occasion to initiate exercise. In both cases, a strong mental link is formed between the critical situation (after class, entering the building) and the goal-direction action (e.g., studying for two hours, walking up the flight of stairs).

Implementations are simple action plans, but there is some skill to be applied when creating them. To be effective, the person needs to anticipate a situation in which it would be appropriate to initiate goal-striving action. The implementation needs to be tailored to a valued course of action. And, fortunately, the implementation intention can be stated either as an opportunity to act or as a way of overcoming an obstacle. Thus, for the would-be exerciser who enters the same building every day, it is easy to anticipate the daily decision point of "walk up the stairs" versus "take the elevator." If walking was valued as a type of exercise, then "walking up the stairs" would make for an attractive course of action. An opportunity to act would be, "If I see the stairs, then I will walk up them," while a way of overcoming a key obstacle would be, "If I see the elevator doors, then I will say 'no' and turn around." It is a debatable point as to which of these two responses—walking up the stairs versus saying no and turning around—is the more productive of the two or even whether a third response might be more productive, but it is not a debatable point that people who form implementations intentions, especially those that revolve around attractive courses of action, are more likely to attain their goals than people who do not (Adriaanse, De Ridder, & De Wit, 2009; Gollwitzer & Sheeran, 2006).

Implementation intentions take the form of "if-then" statements. The "if" part concerns encountering the critical situational cue, while the "then" part concerns the goal-striving response. It is important to form implementation intentions in advance of encountering the situational cue so that a strong associative link is formed between the situational cue and the goal-striving response. With such a strong link formed in advance, goal-striving behavior can occur instantly and automatically—that is, without deliberation or decision making.

Table 8.1 Examples of Implementation Intentions to Solve Three Self-Regulation Problems Inherent in Goal Striving

---

Getting Started

If it is Sunday afternoon, then I will go to the gym.

If it is April 1st, then I will complete my tax form.

Staying on Track (Avoiding Temptations, Avoiding Distractions)

If I see that the television is on, then I will ignore it.

If new emails pop up in my inbox, then I will ignore them.

Resuming, after an Interruption

After someone drops by to chat, then I will immediately get back to work.

After I end a phone conversation, then the first thing I will do is get back to my term paper.

Many people pause and deliberate on whether they should study, exercise, or practice, and hence consider if they feel like studying, if exercising might be more convenient later in the day, or whether it would be better to practice after the weather improves. The result is that goal striving never gets done. Implementation intentions, in contrast, make goal striving habitual behavior, because one acts immediately and automatically as soon as the key situational cue is encountered, as in "see the stairs, walk the stairs" and "come April 1st, complete tax form." If-then planners act quickly and do not need to consciously intend to act when the critical moment arrives. To get a sense of the if-then character of implementation intentions and to begin to appreciate how people solve fundamental self-regulation problems that interfere with goal striving, Table 8.1 provides some examples of implementation intentions to solve three ever-present self-regulation problems.

The study of implementation intentions is the study of how goals, once set, are effectively acted on (Gollwitzer & Moskowitz, 1996). Implementation intentions play the important role they do in goal achievement because a goal striver needs solutions to the following three inevitable self-regulation problems that work against investing one's effort, persistence, focus, and strategic planning:

- Getting started
- Staying on track
- Resuming

Goal striving has to get started and, once begun, needs to continue over time. Time, however, has a way of opening the door to forgetting to take actions and to any number of temptations, distractions, difficulties, and interruptions. The act of setting implementation intentions is the effort to close the door on these volitional problems. In effect, implementation intentions buffer performers against falling prey to volitional problems.

In the first experiment on implementation intentions, experimenters asked college students going home for the Christmas holidays how they planned to spend their time and what they wanted to get done (e.g., write a paper, read a book, solve a family conflict;

Gollwitzer & Brandstatter, 1997). The experimenters asked half of the students to form explicit implementation intentions for their goal by asking them to pick a specific time and a specific place in which to carry out the goal-directed action (e.g., "On the morning of December 21, I will go to the public library and write the first draft of my 10-page term paper"). The other half of the students were not asked to specify a time and a place for their goal-directed behavior but, instead, were simply encouraged to do their best to accomplish their goal. When students returned, a majority of students in the implementation intentions group had indeed attained their goal, while only a minority of students in the control group had attained their goal. Plus, the more difficult the goal was to accomplish, the more important the forming of implementation intentions was to these completion rates.

Getting Started

Some people exercise every day at a certain time in the afternoon; some people read steadily and persistently when in the library; and some people always stop completely at stop signs. Frequent and consistent pairings of particular situations with particular behaviors lead to strong links between the situation and the behavior. When goal striving is not part of one's routine, however, it is easy to forget to take action. People with good intentions often forget to take their vitamins, forget to send thank-you notes, and forget to work on a project, as in "I had all day to read the chapter, but I just never sat down and read it." In contrast, implementation intentions set up environment–behavior contingencies that lead to automatic, environmentally cued behavior. When the situational cue presents itself (e.g., 7:00 in the morning), the person has a ready-to-go reminder to take her daily vitamin.

Implementation intentions help people get started in their goal striving not only by reminding them to take action but also by making sure that they do not miss a good opportunity to act. The person who wants to eat healthy can form implementations such as, "When I walk in the grocery store, then I will walk first to the fruit section" and "When the waiter comes to take my order, then I will ask for a healthy recommendation." Women who wrote down when and where they would conduct a breast self-examination actually did so 100% of the time during the next month, whereas women who simply had the goal of conducting a breast self-examination during the month did so only 53% of the time (Orbell, Hodgkins, & Sheeran, 1997). The two groups of women had the same goal, yet attained different results, because one group always got started while the other group only sometimes got started. Sometimes there exists only a limited window of opportunity to act (e.g., apply for a scholarship). People who set implementation intentions to take action during that window of opportunity do actually act more often than do people who set a goal but not an implementation intention to act (Dholakia & Bagozzi, 2003).

Implementation intentions further help people get started by helping them overcome a resistance to act. People may have second thoughts or have ambivalent thoughts about eating healthy, climbing the stairs, going to the dentist, or exercising at 6:00 am. The root of the resistance is that short-term benefits (e.g., tasty meal, sleeping in) often win the motivational competition when pitted against long-term benefits (e.g., healthy body). Resistant is a motivational problem (e.g., "Do I really want to do this?"), so implementations solve this problem by getting ahead of the short-term benefit versus long-term benefit dilemma to make acting for long-term benefits automatic (e.g., a habit: "There is no question about it—see the stairs, climb the stairs").

Staying on Track

Once started in the pursuit of a goal, people often face circumstances that were more difficult than they expected. They encounter distractions and demands on their time, and they get interrupted and face the prospect of having to start all over again. But implementation intentions, once set, shield goal striving from potential derailment (Goschke & Dreisbach, 2008; Shah, Friedman, & Kruglanski, 2002; Veling & van Knippenberg, 2006; Wieber et al., 2011).

People often start an exercise program, start writing a paper, and start the effort to learn a foreign language but, in doing so, difficulties, distractions, alternative demands, and interruptions inevitable surface to compete with the goal striving, as in "I started to read the chapter, but then the phone rang and I never did get back to the book." The goal striver needs a shield against these temptations, especially when they are exciting or attractive alternatives (Gollwitzer & Schaal, 1998). Implementation intentions facilitate persistence by helping people anticipate a forthcoming difficulty, temptation, or distraction and therefore form an intention of what they will do once it comes their way (Achtziger, Gollwitzer, & Sheeran, 2008). Dieters and athletes often form implementation intentions to prevent their goal striving from straying off course (Achtziger et al., 2008). For a concrete example, consider the case in which elementary-grade students worked on a homework-like task on the computer while distracting and tempting cartoon videos popped up on the screen. Half of the children were prepared in advance with a goal intention, which was "I will ignore distractions," while the other half were prepared with an implementation intention, which was "If there is a distraction, then I will ignore it" (Wieber et al., 2011, p. 42). Children armed only with a goal intention were frequently derailed from their task and gave into the tempting distractions, while children armed with the implementation intention were more likely to shield their attention and behavior from the distraction to spend more time on task. In a similar study, college students worked on attention-demanding mathematical problems while distracting video clips of television commercials popped up. Just as was the case with the children, college students with an implementation intention (i.e., "If a commercial comes on, then I will ignore it.") prior to solving the mathematics problems solved more problems than did students who did not form the distraction-inhibiting intention (Schaal & Gollwitzer, 1999). Without an implementation intention, students were left vulnerable to distraction. Overall, implementation intentions create a type of close-mindedness that narrows one's field of attention to include goal-directed action but to exclude distractions.

Resuming

Implementation intentions also help people finish up their uncompleted goals. Workers who began to write a letter of correspondence were interrupted, and half were then asked to form an implementation intention while the others were not. When the two groups of workers returned to their desks, those with an intention to finish the letters upon their return (implementation intention) completed their unfinished business to a greater degree than were those who were similarly interrupted but who did not harbor an implementation intention to cope with the interruption.

GOAL DISENGAGEMENT

An essential part of effective goal pursuit is knowing when to stop—knowing when to give up on one goal and switch over to an alternative goal. While the culture proclaims that "winners never quit and quitters never win," such a proclamation applies only to potentially attainable goals. Some goals are unattainable, or become unattainable because of a change in circumstances or personal resources, because the goal conflicts with another goal, or because the person simply has too many goals to pursue. For unattainable goals, we need to add the concept of goal disengagement to our analysis of goal setting and goal striving.

Goal disengagement is the reduction of effort and goal commitment (Wrosch, Scheier, Carver, & Schulz, 2003). Reduction of effort means trying less hard or stopping goal-striving effort altogether; reduction of commitment means reducing the importance that is attached to the goal. Given this definition, it becomes apparent that goal disengagement is essentially the opposite of goal adoption or goal setting.

Life is short, and we all face very real limits in terms of the amount of time and effort we have available to pursue a particular goal. We also have only a limited amount of resources available to us that can be invested in effort, persistence, attention, and strategic planning. For instance, a potential parent can become too old to have a child, an accident or an illness can leave the athlete unable to practice her sport, a person might suffer a financial hardship and simply not have the money available for the goal pursuit, or a student who has a goal to attend Northwestern University may receive a rejection letter in the mail. What makes the concept of goal disengagement important is that ill-advised goal striving has the undesirable consequence of leaving the goal striver highly vulnerable to psychological distress (Wrosch et al., 2003).

As shown in Figure 8.4, people generally have three options once they realize that a sought-after goal is unattainable (e.g., after the student receives the rejection letter from the university). In path 1, the person maintains both effort and commitment to the goal. Because the goal is unattainable, the person is therefore highly vulnerable to failure feedback and psychological distress (e.g., discouragement, despair, depression). In path 2, the person gives up effort but maintains the goal commitment. Again, because the goal is unattainable, the person is highly vulnerable to disillusionment and psychological distress. In path 3, the person violates the cultural axiom that "winners never quit and quitters never win" and gives up both effort and commitment. Somewhat counterintuitively, it is this path that opens up the possibility for psychological well-being. For goal disengagement to transcend into future psychological well-being, the person needs to follow the disengagement of one goal with the adoption of a new, alternative goal (Wrosch, Scheier, Miller, Schulz, & Carver, 2003). To quote Alexander Bell: "When one door closes, another often opens up." Interestingly, the full Alexander Bell quote is actually, "When one door closes, another door opens; but we so often look so long and regretfully upon the closed door, that we do not see the ones which open for us." Disengagement becomes an adaptive course of action when it leads the person to take up a new, alternative, purpose-endowing goal or when it enhances the extent of effort, persistence, attention, and strategic planning invested in one's remaining goals, because disengagement frees up resources for the pursuit of one's remaining goals. If there is not an alternative goal, however, then Wrosch et al. (2003) suggest that this is the worst of all situations, as disengagement brings only a sense of emptiness.

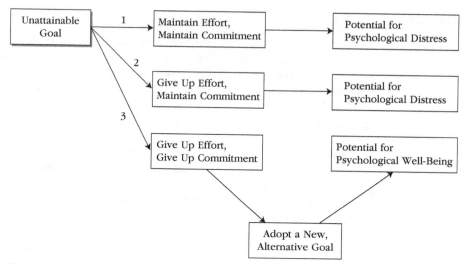

Figure 8.4 Potential for Psychological Distress versus Well-Being from Different Patterns of Goal Disengagement

EPILOGUE: FROM WHERE DO GOALS COME?

Sometimes people assign us goals to pursue. At work, the boss assigns a work goal; at school, the teacher assigns an academic goal; in the gym, the trainer assigns an exercise goal; and at the dentist's office, the dentist assigns an oral hygiene goal. Goal-setting theory was in fact developed in the context of the world of work to help employers (managers) motivate their employees through the assignment of performance-enhancing goals (Locke & Latham, 1984, 1990). These sorts of goals can be understood as other-assigned goals.

Most of the time, however, we generate our own goals to pursue as we seek to give our daily behavior and even our life a sense of purpose. Some self-generated goals originate in our thinking. For instance, a strong sense of self-efficacy prompts people to set goals to strive for (e.g., "I am very confident in my singing skill, so I am going to try to win a talent show"). Valuing also prompts goal setting (e.g., "I value mother earth, so I am going to recycle every day"). Other self-generated goals originate from our personality traits. For instance, extraverts readily adopt goals that revolve around enjoying social attention, while people high in conscientiousness often self-generate self-improvement and personal mastery goals. Still other self-generated goals emerge out of our biological and psychological needs. A hunger need prompts the adoption of a goal to visit a restaurant, just as a related-ness or affiliation need prompts the goal to begin a caring relationship. Goals also arise out of the offering of environmental incentives and attractive role models. A child may watch the financial and social incentives given to a professional athlete and be inspired to adopt the personal goal to become a professional athlete, just as an adolescent might observe a highly skilled role model and then adopt a goal to be able to do what the skilled role model can do.

Whatever its source, a goal represents a future-focused desired end state that guides present behavior. Any goal represents a striving to advance from a present state of affairs to a more ideal state of affairs, and where that sense of an "ideal state" comes from is multifaceted, because it sometimes originates out of an other-assigned goal but other times originates out of a way of thinking, a personality trait, a biological need, a psychological need, an environmental incentive, or an attractive role model.

SUMMARY

The cognitive perspective on motivation focuses on mental processes as causal determinants to action. It concerns itself with the cognition → action sequence. This chapter discusses the motivational significance of three cognitive springs to action: plans, goals, and implementation intentions.

People are routinely aware of both the present state of their behavior and what their behavior might ideally be. The cognitive motivational state of discrepancy arises whenever the person perceives a mismatch between one's present state and one's ideal state. To reduce or remove that discrepancy, people generate a plan of action, which is essentially motivated action to remove the discrepancy. Two types of discrepancies exist: discrepancy reduction and discrepancy creation. Discrepancy reduction corresponds to plan-based corrective motivation, and it is a reactive, deficiency-overcoming motivation that revolves around a negative feedback system. Discrepancy creation corresponds to goal-setting motivation, and it is a proactive, growth-pursuing motivation that revolves around a positive feedback or "feed-forward" system. The rate at which people are able to reduce these discrepancies matter, because positive affect signals that the person is making more progress than what is needed while negative affect signals that the person is making less progress than what is needed to remove the discrepancy.

A goal is generally whatever an individual is striving to accomplish but, more specifically, it is a future-focused cognitive representation of a desired end state that guides behavior. Goals that are difficult, specific, and congruent with the self generally improve performance, and they do so by producing the motivational effects of energizing, directing, and sustaining behavior. With feedback, the person who sets a goal gains the means to evaluate his or her performance as being at, above, or below the level of the goal standard. Performing below goal level generates dissatisfaction that underlies a greater investment of effort, persistence, attention, and strategic planning, while performing above goal level generates satisfaction that underlies a willingness to set more difficult goals in the future. Goals can be short-term, long-term, or a series of short-term goals that chain together into one long-term target goal. Short-term goals generate frequently opportunities for performance feedback, while long-term goals are associated with higher levels of intrinsic motivation.

An implementation intention is an "if-then" plan that specifies the goal-striving process. The "if" part concerns encountering a critical situational cue, while the "then" part concerns specifying the goal-striving response. Formulating an implementation intention involves deciding *in advance* of one's goal striving the "when, where, and how" goal striving is to occur. To form an implementation intention, a person needs to do two things. First, the person needs to identify a response that will lead to goal attainment, such as "To make an A, I will study for two hours a day." Second, the person needs to anticipate a suitable occasion to initiate that response, such as "At 5:00 pm each afternoon, I will study for two hours." People who set implementation intentions in advance of their goal-directed action are significantly more likely to attain or complete their goals than are people who do not set implementation intentions. The three primary reasons why implementation intentions have positive effects on goal striving is because they help performers overcome the volitional problems of getting started, staying on track by shielding one's striving from distractions and temptations, and by prompting the resumption of goal striving following an interruption. Without an implementation intention, people are left vulnerable to distractions, temptations, and interruptions. Overall, implementation intentions create a type of close-mindedness that narrows one's field of attention to include goal-directed action but to exclude distractions.

An essential part of effective goal pursuit is knowing when to stop. Goal disengagement is the reduction of effort and commitment in the face of an unattainable goal. What makes the concept of goal disengagement important is that ill-advised goal striving has the undesirable consequence of leaving the person vulnerable to psychological distress. Goal disengagement becomes an adaptive course of action when it opens up a new opportunity for the person to adopt an alternative, potentially attainable, and purpose-endowing goal. The disengagement from one goal can also have the beneficial effect of freeing up resources for the pursuit of one's remaining goals.

The chapter concluded by asking from where goals come from. Some goals are simply assigned to us, but most goals are self-generated. These goals originate out of a way of thinking, a personality trait, a biological need, a psychological need, an environmental incentive, or an attractive role model.

READINGS FOR FURTHER STUDY

Plans of Action

CARVER, C. S., & SCHEIER, M. F. (1990). Origins and functions of positive and negative affect: A control-process view. *Psychological Review, 97,* 19–35.

Goals

KOESTNER, R., LEKES, N., POWERS, T. A., & CHICOINE, E. (2002). Attaining personal goals: Self-concordance plus implementation intentions equals success. *Journal of Personality and Social Psychology, 83,* 231–244.

LOCKE, E. A. (1996). Motivation through conscious goal setting. *Applied and Preventive Psychology, 5,* 117–124.

LOCKE, E. A., & LATHAM, G. P. (2002). Building a practically useful theory of goal setting and task motivation: A 35-year odyssey. *American Psychologist, 57,* 705–717.

Implementation Intentions

ADRIAANSE, M. A., DE RIDDER, D. T., D., & DE WIT, J. B. F. (2009). Finding the critical cue: Implementation intentions to change one's diet work best when tailored to personally relevant reasons for unhealthy eating. *Personality and Social Psychology Bulletin, 35,* 60–71.

GOLLWITZER, P. M. (1999). Implementation intentions: Strong effects of simple plans. *American Psychologist, 54,* 493–503.

GOLLWITZER, P. M. (2014). Weakness of the will: Is a quick fix possible? *Motivation and Emotion, 38,* 305–322.

GOLLWITZER, P. M., & SHEERAN, P. (2006). Implementation intentions and goal achievement: A meta-analysis of effects and processes. *Advances in Experimental Social Psychology, 38,* 69–119.

WIEBER, F., VON SUCHODOLETZ, A., HEIKAMP, T., TROMMSDORFF, G., & GOLLWITZER, P. M. (2011). If-then planning helps school-age children to ignore attractive distractions. *Social Psychology, 42,* 39–47.

Goal Disengagement

WROSCH, C., SCHEIER, M. F., CARVER, C. S., & SCHULZ, R. (2003). The importance of goal disengagement in adaptive self-regulation: When giving up is beneficial. *Self and Identity, 2,* 1–20.

Chapter 9

Mindsets

FOUR MINDSETS

MINDSET 1: DELIBERATIVE–IMPLEMENTAL

    Deliberative Mindset

    Implemental Mindset

    Downstream Consequences of the Deliberative versus Implemental Mindsets

MINDSET 2: PROMOTION–PREVENTION

    Promotion Mindset

    Prevention Mindset

    Different Definitions of Success and Failure

    Different Goal-Striving Strategies

    Ideal Self-Guides and Ought Self-Guides

    Regulatory Fit Predicts Strength of Motivation and Well-Being

MINDSET 3: GROWTH-FIXED

    Fixed Mindset

    Growth Mindset

    Meaning of Effort

    Origins of Fixed-Growth Mindsets

    Different Fixed-Growth Mindsets Lead to Different Achievement Goals

    Achievement Goals

        Integrating Classical and Contemporary Approaches to Achievement Motivation

        Avoidance Motivation and Ill-Being

MINDSET 4: COGNITIVE DISSONANCE

    Dissonance-Arousing Situations

        Choice

        Insufficient Justification

        Effort Justification

        New Information

    Motivational Processes Underlying Cognitive Dissonance

    Self-Perception Theory

SUMMARY

READINGS FOR FURTHER STUDY

Imagine that you and your friend drive into the 24-hour mega-drugstore on your way to a New Year's Eve party. You need to get a gift for the host of the party. As you drive into the parking lot, cars are everywhere and empty spaces are nowhere. Luckily, a car near the entrance pulls out of a space and you just as quickly drive in. You unbuckle, open the door, and are ready to go inside, but your friend has a different reaction. She is not happy with your choice of parking spaces. Temperatures are freezing, and the walk will be a long one. She wants to drive around and look vigilantly for the perfect spot. For you, the job is done, and it is time to get on with what you came for.

Inside you stand before a wall of wines, champagnes, and a hundred different alcoholic beverages. You grab a good bottle of wine—it is attractive, has a recognizable brand name, and sells for an okay price. With bottle in hand, you turn to your friend. Alas, you again see the cautious let's-think-it-over face. She is looking for the right bottle of wine. Deliberately, she works her way through the options one by one. She does not want to make a mistake and pick the wrong wine, and she points out a couple of shortcomings with your choice. Finally, a wine is selected. You think it is time to check out, but she then asks what the decorative gift bag should be and the whole "pros versus cons" process begins anew. Finally, the two of you make it to the checkout counter, although there is a debate about which line is the right line.

What does this shopping trip with a friend illustrate (based on Kruglanski et al., 2000)? The scenario illustrates that even when two people have the same goal, they can have different strategies for attaining that goal. One approach might be to "just do it" (Kruglanski et al., 2000)—to get on with the task of advancing from a state of not having something to a state of having it (i.e., a parking space, a bottle of wine, a gift bag). If you gain what you need, then things are good. Another approach might be to "do the right thing" (Kruglanski et al., 2000)—to be cautious, to take stock of things, and to make sure that you do not fail to fulfill an important responsibility (i.e., the right parking space, the right bottle of wine, the right gift bag). If you can prevent making a mistake, then things are good. The scenario shows that people with the same goal can nevertheless possess different mindsets that yield different patterns of goal striving.

FOUR MINDSETS

A mindset is a cognitive framework to guide one's attention, information processing, decision making, and thinking about the meaning of effort, success, failure, and one's own personal qualities. Once adopted, a mindset functions as a cognitive motivational system that produces many important downstream consequences in one's thinking, feeling, and acting. That is, the person with one mindset looks at a motivational episode in a fundamentally different way than does the person with a different mindset, and these different ways of thinking yield differences in lifestyle and ways of coping. The present chapter will describe and explain the motivational significance of four mindsets, as introduced in Table 9.1.

Each mindset listed in Table 9.1 provides a pair of contrasting motivational systems that exist simultaneously within each individual. The motivational systems coexist, but people tend toward one motivational system rather than the other. This tendency toward one motivational system or the other occurs sometimes as a result of chronic personality differences and other times occurs as a result of situation-specific circumstances.

Table 9.1   Four Mindsets and Their Associated Motivational Systems

1. DELIBERATIVE–IMPLEMENTAL

Two sequential ways of thinking to differentiate the patterns of thought that occurs during goal-setting versus that which occurs during goal striving.

Deliberative: An open-minded way of thinking to consider the desirability and feasibility of a range of possible goals that one might or might not pursue.

Implemental: A post-decisional closed-minded way of thinking that considers only information related to goal attainment and shields against non-goal-related considerations.

2. PROMOTION–PREVENTION

Two different orientations people adopt during goal striving to distinguish an eager improvement-based regulatory style from a vigilant security-based regulatory style.

Promotion: A focus on advancing the self toward ideals by adopting an eager locomotion behavioral strategy.

Prevention: A focus on preventing the self from not maintaining one's duties and responsibilities by adopting a vigilant behavioral strategy.

3. GROWTH-FIXED

Two contrasting ways of thinking about the nature of one's personal qualities.

Growth: The belief that one's personal qualities are malleable, changeable, and can be developed through effort.

Fixed: The belief that one's personal qualities are fixed, set, and not open to change.

4. CONSISTENCY–DISSONANCE

The near-universal self-view that one is a competent, moral, and reasonable person.

Consistency: Information and behavioral actions that confirm that, yes, one is a competent, moral, and reasonable person.

Dissonance: Information and behavioral actions that suggest that, no, one is actually not a competent, moral, and reasonable person.

MINDSET 1: DELIBERATIVE–IMPLEMENTAL

As emphasized in the previous chapter, one can distinguish between goal setting and goal striving (following Lewin, Dembo, Festinger, & Sears, 1944). This distinction draws attention to a related distinction between motivation and volition (Kuhl, 1984, 1987). Motivation concerns the energization and initial direction of behavior, and it involves all the pre-decisional processes that energize and direct action (e.g., "What should I do tonight? There are so many things to do. Okay, I know what I want. I have decided I will read the textbook."). Volition, on the other hand, concerns the ongoing maintenance and persistence of motivated action, because it involves all the post-decisional processes that sustain ongoing action (e.g., "If I am going to read the textbook, then I must ignore all potential distractions—no television, no web surfing, no telephone chatting."). The two different mindsets—deliberative versus implemental—that underlie goal setting's "phase 1" flow into goal striving's "phase 2" are depicted graphically in Figure 9.1.

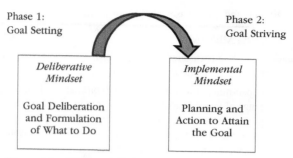

Phase 1:
Goal Setting

Phase 2:
Goal Striving

Deliberative Mindset	*Implemental Mindset*
Goal Deliberation and Formulation of What to Do	Planning and Action to Attain the Goal

Figure 9.1 Different Mindsets to Motivationally Support the Sequential Phases of Goal Setting and Goal Striving

In the study of the deliberative versus implemental mindset, the key distinction is between the initial selection of goals, which involves a great deal of deliberation, and the regulation of the action necessary to bring that chosen goal to fruition, which involves strategic execution and willpower. This distinction can be easily seen in a New Year's resolution as the person first considers the pros and cons of many possible goals (e.g., "start exercising," "stop smoking," or "be nicer to my coworkers") to select and commit to one particular goal; yet, as the calendar turns to February, that chosen goal might not have been realized. Failed New Year resolutions (or any unrealized goal) make it clear that a distinction needs to be made between the deliberative process of setting a goal and the implementation process of actually attaining it. Choosing and setting a goal involves and requires one mindset, while pursuing that goal involves and requires a different mindset.

Deliberative Mindset

People in a deliberative mindset think about what they would like to do—which desire is to be acted on, which goal is to be chosen, which need is to be prioritized, which preference is to be pursued, and which environmental incentive is to be acquired. What the person thinks about (the "mindset") revolves around questions such as how desirable one goal (or desire, need, preference, or incentive) is relative to another. The person asks, "Should I pursue my academic goals tonight, or should I pursue my social-relatedness needs tonight?" The key questions are, "What do I want?" or "What is the most desirable thing for me to do?" In addition to desirability, the person deliberates, considers, and reflects upon how feasible each goal is. The key questions are, "Do I have what it takes to attain goal A, goal B, or goal C?", "How attainable are each of these goals?", and "Is goal A (or B, or C) worth the effort it will take to attain it?" This is a highly open-minded and deliberative process in which many options are considered and each option is worked through a cost and benefits analysis.

In a deliberative mindset, attention is cast wide (Fujita, Gollwitzer, & Oettingen, 2007). The person seeks out and is willing to entertain information related to all possible goals, desires, and incentives. Any information about the desirability and feasibility of a possible goal is welcomed. If planning a vacation, a weekend, or an evening, the person is open-minded and willing to listen to all possible options. A deliberative mindset is most appropriate with motivational questions such as, "Who will I date (or marry)? Which college will I attend? What will be my major, and what will be my profession? Which gift should I purchase? Which menu item should I select? Which course should I take next semester?" During this open-minded deliberation, the person's thinking is rather objective in the evaluation of the pros and cons of possible alternatives.

Implemental Mindset

Once a goal has been set and committed to, the person generally benefits from making a mindset transition from goal setting to goal striving—from a focus on motivation to a focus on volition. Alternative goals are no longer considered, and in fact are now seen as unwanted distractions. Nonchosen goals, desires, needs, preferences, and incentives are now seen as unwelcomed and irrelevant interruptions or temptations that need to be ignored and are now potentially disruptive to and interfering with volition. The thinking and planning transition to questions such as, "Okay, I have decided to date so-and-so, so what do I need to do now?" and "I have selected this particular gift for the birthday party, so what steps do I need to take to get this gift in hand?" The person no longer thinks about the desirability and feasibility of rival goals but, instead, concentrates on getting started and persisting until goal attainment.

In an implemental mindset, the person is closed-minded and attention is focused narrowly to concentrate only on information that is related to goal attainment (Gollwitzer & Bayer, 1999). The mindset is to shield one's thinking against non-goal-related information and considerations. More deliberative thinking will only postpone goal striving, not facilitate it. The thinking is as follows: "This has already been decided. While it was once very constructive to consider my options, it is now counterproductive to do so. What I need to do now is focus and shield myself against distractions." During this closed-minded implementation period, the person's thinking is optimistically biased in the evaluation of the desirability and feasibility of the chosen goal (e.g., my chosen romantic relationship will work out well; Puca, 2001). With an implementation mindset, people raise their forecasted self-efficacy and personal control beliefs about eventual goal attainment (Armor & Taylor, 2003).

The essential point in distinguishing between the two mindsets is that different phases in the motivational process require and benefit from different mindsets. Motivation-rich goal setting benefits from open-minded deliberative thinking, while volition-rich goal-striving benefits from closed mindedness implemental thinking.

Downstream Consequences of the Deliberative versus Implemental Mindsets

The important point to emphasize in making a distinction between the deliberative versus implemental mindset is the following: The implemental mindset is more conducive to goal striving than is the deliberative mindset. When people are in an implemental rather than a deliberative mindset, they persist longer (Brandstatter & Frank, 2002) and perform better (Armor & Taylor, 2003). This is so is because these two mindsets produce different downstream consequences.

To study the downstream consequences of the deliberative versus implemental mindsets, researchers experimentally induced one mindset or the other in participants (see Gollwitzer & Kinney, 1989). To induce a deliberative mindset, participants first identify a goal or personal striving that they are currently considering but have not yet decided on or committed to (e.g., "I'm considering switching my major, but I haven't yet decided whether to change majors or to just stay with this one."). Participants then make a "pros and cons" list of the potential benefits and costs of each possible goal or striving. They also are asked to estimate the probability that these benefits and costs will actually materialize if each goal is or is not pursued. To induce an implemental mindset, participants first identify a goal or striving that they plan to accomplish during a specific period of time (e.g., "By the end of the semester, I will have written my term paper, revised it, and submitted it for a grade."). Participants then make a list of five steps that need to be taken to accomplish that goal. To be specific, participants are asked to write down the specific time and place associated with each of the five goal-attainment strategies.

After one or the other mindset has been induced, participants' thoughts are monitored in a second phase of the study. In a deliberative mindset, people show a "cognitive tuning" toward information expressing the pros and cons (benefits and costs) of one goal vis-à-vis rival goals; in an implementation mindset, people show a "cognitive tuning" toward information related to goal attainment and a step-by-step way of thinking and problem solving (Gollwitzer, Heckhausen, & Steller, 1990). During their implementation mindset, people show a marked drop in thoughts related to the desirability of the chosen goal, and they no longer ponder questions such as "Should I do it, or should I do something else?" (Puca & Schmalt, 2001). While deliberative thinking is valuable and productive for the motivational process of goal setting, it is implemental thinking that is relatively more productive for the volitional process of goal striving.

MINDSET 2: PROMOTION–PREVENTION

Regulatory focus theory proposes that people strive for their goals by using two separate and independent motivational orientations (i.e., mindsets): prevention and promotion (Higgins, 1997, 1998). The first motivational system is an improvement-based regulatory style that involves a promotion focus, while the second motivational system is security-based regulatory style that involves a prevention focus. A promotion focus involves sensitivity to positive outcomes. The striving is to attain what one does not yet have. One strives to approach desired and ideal end states. A prevention focus involves sensitivity to negative outcomes. The striving is to maintain and not lose what one already has. One strives to maintain a sense of duty, obligation, and responsibility. A graphical representation of these two regulatory mindsets appears in Figure 9.2, with the promotion mindset summarized in the upper half of the figure and the prevention mindset summarized in the lower half of the figure. In both cases, the antecedents to adopt or develop the particular mindset appear on the left side of the figure, while its downstream consequences appear on the right side of the figure.

Promotion Mindset

The promotion regulatory focus centers on the possibility of advancement. With a promotion focus, the individual is sensitive to positive outcomes, approaches possibilities of gain, and adopts an eager behavioral strategy of locomotion that might be characterized as "just do it." The concern is with growth, advancement, and accomplishment as the person strives to advance from a neutral state to one of accomplishing a desire, a wish, or an ideal. It means making good things happen. For instance, the person seeks to graduate, develop a

(a) Promotion Mindset

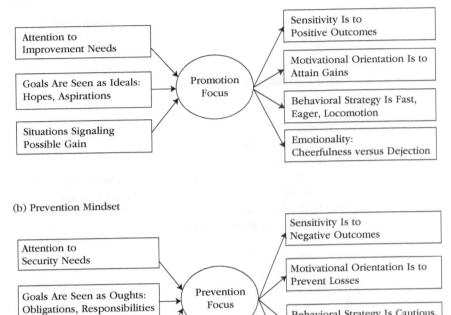

Figure 9.2   Antecedents and Consequences of the Promotion (a) and Prevention (b) Mindsets

new skill, earn extra money, and be supportive of friends. When ideals are realized, the emotional experience is one of being cheerful, including feeling happy and satisfied, but when these sought-after ideals are left unrealized, the emotional experience is one of being dejected, including feeling disappointed, dissatisfied, and sad.

People can adopt a promotion focus either chronically, as in a personality disposition, or it can be induced situationally. An individual who is chronically promotion-focused has been socialized to believe that what matters in life is making good things happen. Parents tend to adopt a bolstering, self-improvement mode in which the child is asked to accomplish ideals and fulfill aspirations (e.g., "My parents told me that they were proud of me when I was trying to be good at something"; Keller, 2008; Manian, Strauman, & Denney, 1998). Those ideals take the form of hopes and aspirations. In addition to parenting, a person's tendency to adopt a promotion focus can be increased by growing up in a promotion-focused culture (e.g., Italy; Fulmer et al., 2010). An individual who is situationally promotion-focused is in an environment that signals possible gains and opportunities for advancement. For instance, to situationally induce a promotion focus, researchers ask participants to think about an ideal: "Describe how your hopes and aspirations are different now from when you were growing up" (Freitas & Higgins, 2002, p. 2).

Prevention Mindset

The prevention regulatory focus centers on responsibility and duty. With a prevention focus, the individual is sensitive to negative outcomes, avoids possibilities of loss, and adopts a vigilant behavioral strategy of caution that might be characterized as "do the right thing." The concern is with safety, security, and responsibility as the person strives to prevent failing to do one's duty, meet one's obligations, and fulfill one's responsibilities. It means being careful to make sure that bad things do not happen. For instance, the person seeks safety and security, to not fail, to not lose money, and to stay in touch and in close contact with friends. When oughts are maintained, the emotional experience is one of being relaxed and feeling calm, but when these ought obligations are lost, the emotional experience is one of being anxious, including feeling agitated, uneasy, afraid, and threatened.

People can adopt a prevention focus either chronically within the personality, or it can be induced situationally. An individual who is chronically prevention-focused has been socialized to see that what matters in life is preventing bad things from happening. Parents tend to adopt a critical, punishing, and restricting mode in which the child is urged to attain safety and meet duties, obligations, and oughts (e.g., "My parents often scolded and criticized me"; Keller, 2008; Manian, Strauman, & Denney, 1998). Doing what one ought to do means taking action to maintain the status quo, not make mistakes, be responsible, and keep danger at bay. In addition to parenting, a person's tendency to adopt a prevention focus can be increased by growing up in a prevention-focused culture (e.g., Japan; Fulmer et al., 2010). An individual who is situationally prevention-focused is in an environment that signals possible losses in terms of one's social obligations and responsibilities. For instance, to situationally induce a prevention focus, researchers ask participants to think about an ought: "Describe how your duties and obligations are different now from when you were growing up."

Different Definitions of Success and Failure

Depending on one's regulatory mindset, success and failure mean different things (Higgins, 1997). For a person with a promotion focus, success means the presence of a gain. The person strives to attain a positive outcome, and that positive outcome takes the form of some type of advancement or improved state of affairs. Success means that change has occurred, and that one has been able to advance a "present state" closer to a desired "ideal state." Success has special meaning—namely, that something good has happened. Failure, on the other hand, means a nongain. It represents an inability to improve upon one's current state. For a person with a promotion focus, failure does not have a special meaning; it is largely a nonevent because the person is still the same as before (e.g., one's present self persists). For the promotion-focused individual, failure is not motivating, while success feeds into and motivationally energizes the system (e.g., re-energizes one's eagerness to accomplish).

For a person with a prevention focus, success means the absence of a loss. The person strives to maintain a satisfactory state. Success means that no change has occurred and that an ought state has been maintained in a satisfactory way. That is, one started with a sense of duty, responsibility, and obligation, and one has taken the actions necessary to prevent their loss. For a person with a prevention focus, success does not have a special meaning; it is largely a non event because the person is still the same as before (e.g., one's ought self persists). Failure, on the other hand, means a loss and that a painful change has occurred. It means that one has not been able to maintain an ought self. Failure has special meaning—namely, that something bad has happened (i.e., has not been prevented). For the prevention-focused individual, success is not motivating, while failure feeds into and motivationally energizes the system (e.g., re-energizes one's vigilance to stay safe).

Different Goal-Striving Strategies

Depending on one's regulatory mindset, goal striving is carried out in one of two different ways. With a promotion focus, the gain-based strategy can be characterized as open-mindedness, exploration, locomotion, acting fast, and eager approach. Locomotion means taking action to move from the present state to an ideal state. It corresponds colloquially with the slogan, "just do it." With a prevention focus, the safety-based strategy can be characterized as being cautious, staying committed, staying the course, protecting one's commitments, playing it safe, assessing where one stands, and being vigilant. Assessment means critically evaluating whether the status quo (an "ought to" standard) has been maintained. It corresponds colloquially with the slogan, "do the right thing."

These two different goal-striving strategies raise the question of which strategy is the better or more productive of the two—is it better to act to accomplish something, or is it better to act responsibly and play it safe? Interestingly, the answer to that question depends on one's regulatory mindset. When the person with a promotion focus pursues a goal such as "earn a high GPA" with eager locomotion, such behaviors "feel right" and produce a greater sense of enjoyment and satisfaction. For instance, for a person with a promotion focus the following strategies feel right (Freitas & Higgins, 2002):

- Complete schoolwork promptly.
- Attend all classes.
- Spend more time in the library.
- Be prepared for tests.
- Increase motivation to earn a high GPA.

However, when the person with a prevention focus pursues a goal such as "earn a high GPA" with vigilant caution, such behaviors "feel right" and produce a greater sense of enjoyment and satisfaction. For instance, for a person with a prevention focus the following strategies feel right (Freitas & Higgins, 2002):

- Stop procrastinating.
- Avoid missing any classes.
- Spend less time at social gatherings/parties.
- Avoid being unprepared for tests.
- Do not lose motivation to earn a high GPA.

Further, when a person with a promotion focuses uses vigilant caution, then those behaviors do not feel right and yield little enjoyment, just as when a person with a prevention focus uses eager locomotion, then those behaviors do not feel right and yield little enjoyment and satisfaction (Freitas & Higgins, 2002). Hence, one behavioral strategy is not necessarily better than the other. Rather, people with a promotion focus enjoy, feel more successful, and are more willing to continue using accomplishment-based eager-infused locomotion actions than they are to use vigilance-based actions, while people with a prevention focus enjoy, feel more successful, and are more willing to continue using safety-infused vigilant actions than they are to use accomplishment-based actions (Higgins, 2000).

Ideal Self-Guides and Ought Self-Guides

An ideal self-guide is a goal (or standard or aspiration) of what one would like to become. Following an ideal self-guide leads the person to adopt a regulatory style oriented toward accomplishment and to a heightened sensitivity to move toward opportunities for positive outcomes. Eager approach behavior is both a natural and an enjoyable means to attain positive outcomes, because the person strives to change, improve, and achieve something new.

An ought self-guide is a goal (or standard or aspiration) specifying what one or others believe you should or must or have to do or be. Following an ought self-guide leads the person to adopt a regulatory style oriented toward responsibility and to a heightened sensitivity to losing what one already has. Cautious vigilance is both a natural and an enjoyable means to prevent negative outcomes, because the person strives to be true to his or her sense of duty, obligation, and responsibility.

Both ideals and oughts are part of the self-system (Higgins, 1987). Some situations and life circumstances incline the person to attend to the possibilities of the idea self, while other situations and life circumstances incline the person to attend to the responsibilities of the ought self. When inclined toward one's ideals some strategies and ways of striving work better, but when inclined toward one's oughts, other strategies and ways of striving work better. For instance, consider an experiment in which some participants were asked to focus on the ideal self: "Please think about something you ideally would like to do. In other words, please think about a hope or an aspiration you currently have" (Freitas & Higgins, 2002, p. 3). Other participants were asked to focus on the ought self: "Please think about something you think you ought to do. In other words, please think about a duty or a responsibility you currently have" (Freitas & Higgins, 2002, p. 3). Next, participants in both conditions were asked to list either five eagerness-related action plans (i.e., "Please list some strategies you could use to make sure everything goes right and helps you realize your hope or aspiration.") or five vigilance-related plans (i.e., "Please list some strategies you could use to avoid anything that could go wrong and stop you from realizing your duty or obligation."). Finally, all participants were asked how enjoyable it would be to perform their listed action plan.

The results appear in Figure 9.3 (from Freitas & Higgins, 2002). Among participants oriented toward ideals, hopes, and aspirations, eagerness action plans were rated as highly enjoyable while vigilant action plans were rated as significantly less enjoyable. Among participants oriented toward oughts, duties, and obligations, the pattern of findings was completely reversed: Vigilant action plans were rated as highly enjoyable while eagerness action plans were rated as significantly less enjoyable. A follow-up study produced similar results in which people with a promotion focus found an activity more interesting when they pursued it for fun rather as a serious activity, while people with a prevention focus found an activity more interesting when they pursue it as a serious activity rather as something done for fun (Higgins et al., 2010).

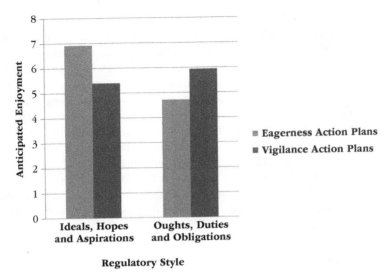

Figure 9.3   Enjoyment of Eagerness and Vigilance Action Plans Depends One One's Regulatory Focus (Hope and Ideals versus Duty and Oughts)

Regulatory Fit Predicts Strength of Motivation and Well-Being

The previous section highlights the importance of regulatory fit, which means that decisions and behaviors feel right when people rely on goal striving means that fit their mindset (i.e., promotion versus prevention mindset; Higgins, 2000, 2005). This sense that something feels right means that one's goal and strategies are matched (promotion matches with eager locomotion; prevention matches with cautious vigilance). Regulatory fit also produces increased motivational strength (Forster, Higgins, & Idson, 1998). That is, people with a promotion focus exert more effort, feel more alert, value the experience more, and actually cope and perform better when they strive with eagerness rather than with vigilance, while people with a prevention focus exert more effort, feel more alert, value the experience more, and cope and perform better when they strive with vigilance rather than with eagerness (Higgins, 2000, 2006; Keller & Bless, 2006). Regulatory fit also contributes positively to psychological well-being because it leads people to feelings of interest, enjoyment, and satisfaction with what they are doing, whereas regulatory misfit interferes with and blocks feelings of interest, enjoyment, and satisfaction with what they are doing.

Such a conclusion acts as a springboard to take the discussion back to the two friends in the chapter-opening vignette who walked into the mega-drugstore with contrasting mindsets. The two friends had the same goals—park, make a purchase, and wrap a gift, but their contrasting mindsets led them to feel that one way of coping was more right than was another way of coping. One friend valued speed, the other valued accuracy. That does not mean that one way of coping (be fast, focus on the big picture, and "just do it") is better or worse than the other way (be accurate, focus on the details, and "do the right thing"); rather, it means that for each person one way of coping feels right and is associated with greater enjoyment and effort than the other way of coping.

Actually, both mindsets are actually necessary for optimal goal striving, and that is true within an individual person and within a couple, team, group, or society. Speed and accuracy almost always trumps speed without accuracy or accuracy without speed (Forster, Higgins, & Bianco, 2003). For instance, the students who make the highest GPAs are those who embrace both a high promotion and a high prevention mindset, and the U. S. Army soldiers who are most likely to complete an advanced training course in the elite Army Rangers unit are those who embrace both a high promotion and a high prevention mindset (Kruglanski et al., 2000). In the pursuit of many different life goals, sometimes what is needed is "taking action" (i.e., "I am a doer.") but other times what is needed is "taking stock" (i.e., "I am a critical person.") (from Kruglanski et al., 2000, p. 798). People have preferred ways of coping and these ways reflect their promotion versus prevention mindset inclinations, but it is almost always true that the same goal can be achieved in different ways. A job well done is one that is done quickly and accurately, and such a job requires the employment of both mindsets.

MINDSET 3: GROWTH-FIXED

The growth-fixed mindset concerns the question of how people think about their personal qualities, such as their intelligence and personality traits. Generally speaking, the way people think about their personal qualities can be characterized in one of two ways (Dweck, 1999, 2006). Some people see personal qualities as fixed and enduring characteristics. The thinking is you are either smart or dumb, an extravert or an introvert, and that is that (i.e., the personal quality is fixed and set). Other people, in contrast, see personal qualities as malleable characteristics that can be increased with effort. You may be dumb or introverted, but you can become smarter or more extraverted with experience, training, effort, practice, and strategic thinking (i.e., the personal quality is malleable and can be changed).

Fixed Mindset

Some people believe that their personal qualities are fixed attributes. They believe that they (and others) are endowed with fixed, set qualities. The thinking is "you either have it, or you don't" in that some people are smart, or creative, or good in mathematics while other people are not. People who hold a fixed mindset are sometimes referred to as "entity theorists," because they believe that there is a physical entity that dwells inside the person (e.g., a good brain, a creative gene) to determine how much of the personality quality a person has.

When people adopt a fixed mindset, they have the sense that if they have a lot of the fixed quality then they are in good shape. For instance, if a person believes that she has a gift for languages, then she will expect to do well in a foreign language class at school. She also believes, however, that if she has little of the fixed personal quality, then she is in bad shape. For instance, she may believe that she lacks athletic genes and therefore expect to do poorly when invited to play a game of basketball.

Growth Mindset

Some people believe that their personal qualities are changeable attributes. They believe that they (and others) can grow, increase, strengthen, and otherwise develop their malleable qualities. The thinking is "the more you try and the more you learn, the better you get" in that all people can become smarter and more creative, at least in proportion to their effort, training, and amount of practice. People who hold a growth mindset are sometimes referred to as "incremental theorists," because the thinking is that personal qualities can be developed incrementally over time.

When people adopt a growth mindset, they have the sense that the more effort they put in, the more they will learn, grow, and develop and the better or higher will be their personal qualities. People with a growth mindset realize that people may start a developmental task with different amounts of the personal quality (intelligence, talent), but they believe that the extent to which they invest effort in the processes of learning, practicing, and training, then they will eventually end up with greater intelligence or greater talent and also that gains in these personal qualities will be explained by the hours and years of learning, practicing, and training invested in the developmental effort.

To gain greater familiarity with the fixed-growth mindset, consider whether you agree or disagree with the following two statements (Dweck, 1999):

- Your intelligence is something about you that you cannot change very much.

- You can always greatly change how intelligent you are.

People with a fixed mindset (i.e., entity theorists) will generally agree with the first statement but disagree with the second. People with a growth mindset (i.e., incremental theorists) will generally agree with the second statement but disagree with the first.

Meaning of Effort

For the person with a fixed mindset, the meaning of effort is "the more you try, the dumber you therefore must be." High effort means low ability. High effort is, in fact, evidence that the performer lacks ability. For the person with a growth mindset, the meaning of effort is that it is a tool, the means by which people turn on and vitalize the development of their skills and abilities. Given this introduction, consider your own reaction to the following:

> You see a puzzle in a science magazine and it's labeled "Test your IQ!" You work on it for a very long time, get confused, start over and over, and finally make progress, but very slowly, until you solve it. How do you feel? Do you feel sort of dumb because it required so much effort? Or, do you feel smart because you worked hard and mastered it?
>
> (Dweck, 1999, p. 39).

In a motivational analysis, the meaning of effort is a crucially important understanding when the individual faces a difficult task, as in the puzzle above (Hong et al., 1999). When facing a difficult task, what one needs is high effort. But marshaling forth high effort poses a motivational dilemma for the person with a fixed mindset. High effort is needed, but high effort is precisely what signals low ability, which is precisely the sort of thing an entity theorist wants most to avoid (Blackwell, Trzesniewski, & Dweck, 2007). People with a fixed mindset do not really believe that high effort will be effective, even on difficult tasks. They say things like, "If you are not good at a subject, working hard won't make you good at it." Actually, what people with a fixed mindset prefer to do is make high grades while coasting along with low effort, because the low effort simply confirms how smart they must be (Covington & Omelich, 1979). Thus, on difficult endeavors, people with a fixed mindset tend to adopt maladaptive motivational patterns by (1) withholding effort,

(2) engaging in self-handicapping to protect the self, and (3) never really understanding or appreciating what effort expenditures can do for them in life (Blackwell et al., 2007; Dweck, 1999; Stipek & Gralinski, 1996; Zuckerman, Kieffer, & Knee, 1998). A person with a growth mindset, however, does truly understand the utility of effort—effort is what becomes learning. Effort is the tool to develop personal qualities. Incremental theorists experience no conflict between the effort challenging tasks require and their willingness to roll up their sleeves and engage in effortful, persistent, and challenging work.

Negative feedback works much the same way as does a difficult task in terms of its effect on people with fixed versus growth mindsets (Hong et al., 1999). When given negative feedback, the person with a fixed mindset tends to attribute poor performance to low ability. With such an interpretation, the typical response is to withdraw effort. On the other hand, when given negative feedback, the person with a growth mindset tends to attribute poor performance to not trying hard enough. With such an interpretation, the typical response is to increase effort. Greater effort is appropriate because one needs to take the remedial action necessary to reverse failure and negative feedback. The bottom line is that difficult tasks, negative feedback, and even effort itself mean different things to entity and incremental thinkers (to people with fixed and growth mindsets). One meaning system embraced by people with the growth mindset is significantly more motivationally adaptive than is the other.

That a growth mindset is more motivationally adaptive than a fixed mindset can be understood not only by difference in the meaning of effort, but also by differences in the meaning of strategies and attributions. When students with a growth mindset reflect on their academic setbacks, they voice compensatory strategies such as, "I would work harder in this class from now on." The attribution being made is that the academic setback was caused by low effort or poor strategy (e.g., "I didn't study hard enough."). Such an optimistic attributional style leads to greater future effort and persistence. When students with a fixed mindset reflect on their academic setbacks, they voice defeatist strategies such as, "I would try not to take this subject ever again." The attribution being made is that the academic setback was caused by low ability (e.g., "I'm just not good at this subject."). Such a pessimistic attributional style leads to lesser future effort and persistence, because the pessimistic attribution simply leaves the person with no good path to success in the class. Rather than look for a good path to success, students with a fixed mindset tend to focus their attention on finding ways to protect their image and self-esteem.

The more adaptive motivational beliefs held by students with a growth mindset have been shown to pay off in terms of performance. One longitudinal study measured students' fixed-growth mindset and then tracked students' academic performance over a two-year period. Students who endorsed a growth mindset showed significantly improved performance two years later, while students who endorsed a fixed mindset showed no such improvement in their performance two years later (Blackwell et al., 2007).

Origins of Fixed-Growth Mindsets

Fixed-growth mindsets are cognitive frameworks that are learned, and this suggests the possibility that entity versus incremental thinking is a product of one's socialization history. One way that children acquire the fixed versus growth mindset is through the praise and criticism they receive from their parents and teachers (Kamins & Dweck, 1999; Mueller & Dweck, 1998) because praise and criticism send children subtle or not-so-subtle signals about the nature of their personal qualities and abilities. With ability praise, parental and teacher feedback essentially judges the child's personal qualities (e.g., you are so smart, you are very bad), and this judgment tends to grow in children a fixed mindset and an entity-oriented meaning system. Alternatively, with effort praise, parental and teacher feedback essentially comments on the child's underlying coping style (e.g., you worked so hard, you did not try as hard as the other kids), and this commentary tends to grow in children a growth mindset and an incremental-oriented meaning system.

In one experimental demonstration of this developmental process, researchers first had young children work on a school-like task. After they completed the task, some children were randomly assigned to receive ability praise ("You must be smart at this"), some received effort praise ("You must have worked really hard"), and some received neither ability praise nor effort praise (a control group). Researchers then measured all children's attributions for their success and tendencies to endorse a fixed or a growth mindset. Children who heard ability praise made more ability attributions and endorsed the fixed mindset, while children who heard effort praise made more effort attributions and endorsed the growth mindset (Mueller & Dweck, 1998). The experiment continued by later giving all children a difficult problem to solve, and the researchers measured children's attributions for failure, intrinsic motivation, and performance. Children who heard ability praise at the beginning of the study made low ability attributions, displayed a large decline in intrinsic motivation, and performed poorly, while children who heard effort praise made low effort attributions, maintained their intrinsic motivation toward the task, and performed better (Mueller & Dweck, 1998).

Ability criticism (e.g., "I'm very disappointed in you") and effort/strategy criticism (e.g., "Perhaps you could think of another way to do it") produce essentially the same effects of ability praise and effort praise, because both are socializing messages about the child's personal qualities or process of coping (Kamins & Dweck, 1999).

Fixed and growth mindsets can also be learned or trained. In an effort to teach students a growth mindset, a team of researchers gave middle-school students an eight-session course in incremental thinking. One session showed neuroscientific evidence that intelligence can be developed as neurons and dendrites form new neural connections. A second session showed how challenging tasks grow brain cells. A third session centered on a group discussion on the topic, "Learning makes you smarter." Compared to students in a control group that did not receive the training, students who were taught incremental thinking were more likely to endorse a growth mindset and to be rated by their teachers as showing more effort and motivation in class; these students also showed a longitudinal increase in their academic performance that students in a control group did not show (Blackwell et al., 2007).

In a study with college students, half of the students were provided with a training experience to show that intelligence is malleable and can grow with learning and experience while another half of the students were placed into a control group that did not receive the same information. In one session, students learned about how the brain can make connections and how it changes and develops in response to challenging activities (which was similar to the study with the middle school students). In a second session, students wrote a letter to a struggling student about how intelligence grows over time with hard work. After learning this information, the students in the experimental group expressed more enjoyment of their academic work and displayed higher GPAs than did students in the control group (Aronson, Fried, & Good, 2002).

Different Fixed-Growth Mindsets Lead to Different Achievement Goals

Fixed-growth mindsets are important to achievement strivings because they guide the type of goals people pursue (Dweck, 1999; Dweck & Elliot, 1983; Elliot & Dweck, 1988). In achievement situations, people with a fixed mindset (entity theorists) generally adopt performance goals. People who adopt performance goals are concerned with looking smart and with not looking dumb. That is, they are concerned with performing well, especially while others are watching. The goal is therefore to use performance as the means to prove that one has much of a desirable characteristic (i.e., intelligence). In contrast, people with a growth mindset (incremental theorists) generally adopt mastery goals in achievement situations. People who adopt mastery goals are concerned with mastering something new or different and with learning or understanding something thoroughly. That is, they are concerned with learning and improving as much as they can. The goal is therefore to use task engagements to improve—to get smarter by learning something new or important.

Both types of goals—performance and mastery—are common in the culture, and both encourage achievement (Elliot & Church, 1997; Harackiewicz et al., 1997). But typically, social settings like the workplace, sports field, and classroom pit these two goals against one another and ask (force?) workers, athletes, and students to pick one goal over the other. People are often asked to choose between courses of action that allow them to:

- Look smart and competent but at the sacrifice of learning something new.
- Learn something new, useful, or important, but at the sacrifice of looking smart or competent.

For instance, when college students select elective courses, they sometimes choose a course in which they can be assured of doing well, looking smart, avoiding errors, and impressing others, or they sometimes choose a course they hope will teach them something new, provide opportunities to learn, and offer an arena to grow their skills. When given such a choice, about half of the population will, on average, select a performance goal while the other half will select a mastery goal.

When people with fixed and growth mindsets face achievement situations, they prefer different goals. This is important because the type of achievement goal one pursues predicts that person's subsequent motivation, emotion, and performance (Ames & Archer, 1988; Stipek & Kowalski, 1989). A series of studies with elementary school, middle school, and college students (Dweck & Leggett, 1988; Mueller & Dweck, 1998) assessed students' fixed versus growth mindsets, and then asked students to choose between tasks that were either: (1) fun and easy, easy enough so mistakes would not occur, or (2) hard, new, and different—confusion and mistakes could occur, but the student would probably learn something useful. The more students endorsed a fixed mindset, the more they chose the performance opportunity (number 1 above). The more students endorsed a growth mindset, the more they chose the learning opportunity (number 2 above).

To test the idea that it is the fixed versus growth mindset that causes people to choose one type of achievement goal over another, researchers situationally manipulated participants' fixed versus growth mindset by asking them to read an informative booklet that provided rather convincing (and true) evidence to support either an entity or an incremental theory of intelligence. The booklet offered passages about the intelligence of notable individuals (including Albert Einstein, Helen Keller, and the child Rubik's Cube champion) as

Table 9.2   Effect of Implicit Theories (Entity, Incremental) on Achievement Goal Choice (Performance-Approach, Performance-Avoidance, Mastery)

	Goal Choice		
Implicit Theory	Performance-Avoidance Goal	Performance-Approach Goal	Mastery Goal
Entity (n = 22)	50.0	31.8	18.2
Incremental (n = 41)	9.8	29.3	60.9

Note: Numbers represent percentages, and the two rows add to 100%.
Source: From "A social-cognitive approach to motivation and personality," by C. S. Dweck and E. L. Leggett, 1988, *Psychological Review*, *95*, pp. 256–273. Copyright 1988 by American Psychological Association. Reprinted by permission.

either a fixed and an inborn trait or as a malleable and an acquired talent. Participants were randomly assigned to read either the entity-touting or the incremental-touting booklet. All participants were then given a choice between a performance-approach goal (task is hard enough to show that you are smart), a performance-avoidance goal (task is easy enough so that you won't get many wrong), or a mastery goal (task is hard, new, and different so that you can learn from it). As shown in Table 9.2, students who read the passage supporting an entity view of intelligence were significantly more likely to pursue a performance goal (81.8%) rather than a mastery goal (18.2%), whereas students who read the passage supporting an incremental view were significantly more likely to pursue the mastery goal (60.9%) rather than a performance goal (39.1%).

These results communicate two conclusions. First, fixed and growth mindsets are malleable and can be changed (as per the booklets). Second, fixed and growth mindsets cause people to pursue either performance or mastery goals (as per the findings reported in Table 9.2). In addition, these findings point to the need to understand what achievement goals are and why they are important.

Achievement Goals

Most theories of achievement motivation (those featured in Chapter 7) treat achievement behavior as a choice: Approach the standard of excellence or avoid it. The core question asks whether the person will approach success or avoid failure, and if so, with what intensity, latency, and persistence that choice will be pursued. Achievement goal researchers, however, are more interested in *why* a person shows achievement behavior rather than *whether* achievement behavior occurs. This is because we so often in daily life do not so much seek out standards of excellence as we have them forced upon us. That is, we are asked, and are often required, to approach a standard of excellence put before us, as happens at school (a test), at work (a sales quota), in sports (an opponent), and so on. In these sorts of settings, approach behavior is taken for granted (because it is required), and the question becomes why people adopt one type of achievement goal rather than another.

This is an important distinction to make because it helps differentiate the concept of "goals" from that of "achievement goals." Goals (e.g., "My goal is to win the tournament.") represent the desired outcome the person strives to attain. Depending on how difficult, how specific, and how self-congruous that goal is, the person will show some level of achievement behavior (i.e., effort). Achievement goals (e.g., "My goal is to develop greater skill.")

Table 9.3 Distinguishing between Mastery and Performance Goals

Adoption of a Mastery Goal	Adoption of a Performance Goal
Develop one's competence	Prove one's competence
Make progress	Display high ability
Improve the self	Outperform others
Overcome difficulties with effort and persistence	Succeed with little apparent effort

are concerned with why the person is trying to achieve something. That is, why is the person trying to win the tournament—is she trying to develop her competence, learn more, and improve her skills (mastery goal), or is she trying to prove her competence and outperform others (performance goal)?

As summarized in Table 9.3, the two main achievement goals are mastery goals and performance goals (Ames & Archer, 1988; Dweck, 1986; Kaplan & Maehr, 2007; Nicholls, 1984; Spence & Helmreich, 1983). The two goals differ from one another in terms of the person's understanding as to what constitutes competence (Elliot & McGregor, 1999). With mastery goals, the person facing the standard of excellence seeks to develop greater competence, make progress, improve the self, and overcome challenges through intense and persistent effort. Achieving a mastery goal means making progress according to a self-set standard. With performance goals, the person facing the standard of excellence seeks to demonstrate or prove competence, display high ability, outperform others, and succeed with little apparent effort. Achieving a performance goal means doing better than others.

The distinction between mastery and performance goals is important because the adoption of mastery goals in an achievement context (e.g., in school, at work, in sports) is associated with positive and productive ways of thinking, feeling, and behaving, whereas the adoption of performance goals in an achievement context is associated with relatively negative and unproductive ways of thinking, feeling, and behaving (Ames & Archer, 1988; Dweck, 1999; Dweck & Leggett, 1988; Harackiewicz & Elliot, 1993; Linnenbrink, 2005; Nolen, 1988; Spence & Helmreich, 1983). The benefits of adopting a mastery, rather than a performance, goal are illustrated in Figure 9.4.

When people adopt mastery goals, compared to when they adopt performance goals, they tend to (1) prefer challenging tasks that they can learn from rather than easy tasks on which they can demonstrate high ability (Ames & Archer, 1988; Elliot & Dweck, 1988), (2) use conceptually based learning strategies such as relating information to existing knowledge rather than superficial learning strategies such as memorizing (Meece, Blumenfeld, & Hoyle, 1988; Nolen, 1988), (3) are more likely to be intrinsically rather than extrinsically motivated (Heyman & Dweck, 1992), and (4) are more likely to ask for help and information from others that will allow them to continue working on their own (Newman, 1991). These adaptive strategies allow those with mastery goals to work harder (increase effort in the face of difficulty rather than turn passive or quit; Elliot & Dweck, 1988), persist longer (Elliot & Dweck, 1988), and perform better (Spence & Helmreich, 1983).

Educational psychologists find the concept of achievement goals to be helpful in understanding students' classroom-based achievement motivation (Ames & Archer, 1988). Part of the reasons achievement goals appeal to educators is that teachers exert a relatively strong influence over their students' achievement goals. What classroom teachers do to promote either mastery goals or performance goals during instruction can be seen in Table 9.4.

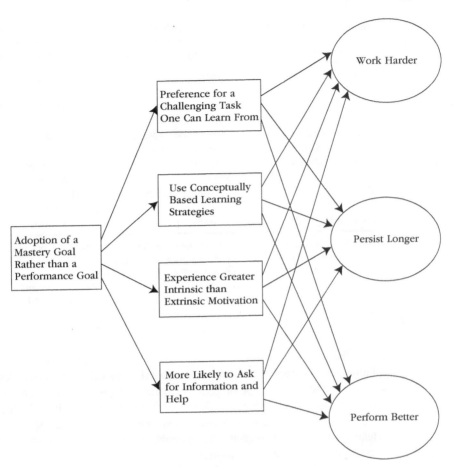

Figure 9.4 Positive and Productive Ways of Thinking, Feeling, and Behaving Associated with Mastery Goals

Hence, to promote mastery rather than performance goals, teachers (and coaches, parents, managers, etc.; see Duda, 2005, for an overview of achievement goals in sport) can define success as improvement, value effort, communicate that satisfaction comes from hard work, focus on how students learn, view errors as a natural and welcomed part of the learning process, explain the utility of effort when trying to learn something new, and assess (grade) students on their extent of improvement and progress. When teachers intentionally create such a learning climate, students are more likely to adopt mastery over performance goals (Maehr & Midgley, 1996; Meece & Miller, 1999).

Integrating Classical and Contemporary Approaches to Achievement Motivation

The classical (Atkinson's theory; Chapter 7) and contemporary (achievement goals) approaches to achievement motivation can be combined and integrated into a single comprehensive model (Elliot, 1997). In the integrated model, mastery goals and two different types of achievement performance goals exist: performance-approach and performance-avoidance.

Table 9.4 Manifestations of Mastery and Performance Goals in the Classroom Context

Climate Dimension	Mastery Goal	Performance Goal
Success defined as	Improvement, progress	High grades, high normative performance
Value placed on	Effort, learning	Normatively high ability
Reasons for satisfaction	Working hard, challenge	Doing better than others
Teacher oriented toward	How students are learning	How students are performing
Views errors or mistakes as	Part of learning	Anxiety eliciting
Focus of attention	Process of learning	Own performance relative to others' performance
Reasons for effort	Learning something new	High grades, performing better than others
Evaluation criteria	Absolute progress	Normative

Note: The table can be interpreted by selecting one classroom climate dimension of interest and then reading across the row for how students with mastery goals rate—what they believe, what they are likely to say—on that dimension and then for how students with performance goals rate on that dimension.
Source: From "Achievement goals in the classroom: Students' learning strategies and motivation processes," by C. Ames and J. Archer, 1988, *Journal of Educational Psychology, 80*, pp. 260–267. Copyright 1988, American Psychological Association. Reprinted by permission.

The classical achievement motivation constructs (achievement motivation, fear of failure, competence beliefs) serve as general, personality-like antecedent conditions that influence the specific type of goals the person adopts in a given achievement setting. For instance, as shown in Figure 9.5, people high in the dispositional need for achievement tend to adopt performance-approach goals, people high in the dispositional fear of failure tend to adopt performance-avoidance goals, and people with task-specific high competency expectancies tend to adopt mastery goals.

Figure 9.5 shows the results from an actual study that tracked participants' achievement strivings, achievement goals, course grades, and intrinsic motivation toward a college course (Elliot & Church, 1997). The need for achievement served as an antecedent for adopting mastery and performance-approach goals, the fear of failure served as an

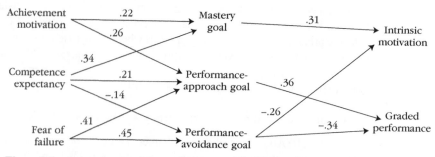

Figure 9.5 Antecedents and Consequences of the Three Achievement Goals

Source: From "A hierarchical model of approach and avoidance achievement motivation," by A. J. Elliot and M. A. Church, 1997, *Journal of Personality and Social Psychology, 72*, pp. 218–232. Copyright 1997, American Psychological Association. Reprinted with permission.

antecedent for adopting performance-approach and performance-avoidance goals (i.e., performance goals in general), and competency expectancies served as an antecedent for adopting mastery and performance-approach goals and for rejecting performance-avoidance goals (notice the negative sign for $-.14$). Furthermore, once these types of achievement goals were adopted, mastery goals increased intrinsic motivation whereas performance-avoidance goals decreased intrinsic motivation while performance-approach goals increased performance whereas performance-avoidance goals decreased performance (Elliot & Church, 1997).

To communicate a better understanding of what performance-approach and performance-avoidance goals are, sample items from the Achievement Goal Questionnaire—Revised (Elliot & Murayama, 2008) are as follows:

- Performance-approach goal: My goal is to perform better than the other students.
- Performance-avoidance goal: My goal is to avoid performing poorly compared to others.
- Mastery goal: My aim is completely master the material presented in this class.

Integrating the classical and contemporary approaches to achievement motivation overcomes, the shortcomings of each individual approach (Elliot, 1997). The problem with the classical approach is that general personality dispositions do a poor job predicting achievement behavior in specific settings. In other words, general personality factors are not necessarily the regulators of achievement behavior in specific life domains such as school, sports, and work. A person might show strong achievement strivings at work yet only the fear of failure in social situations. The problem with the achievement goals approach is that a person is potentially left wondering where these different types of achievement goals come from in the first place. In other words, if you know a basketball player has a performance-approach goal (e.g., to have the highest scoring average on the team), the question remains as to why he or she adopted that particular achievement goal rather than another. Together, the two theories can predict achievement behavior in specific situations (using achievement goals) and can explain from where these achievement goals arise (using personality dispositions and competence perceptions).

Avoidance Motivation and Ill-Being

Most of the discussion on the topic of achievement motivation focuses on its "approach" side, which is the study of whether and why people exert effort and persistence to exceed a standard of excellence. But the fear of failure is important as well, as it functions as a counterforce to achievement strivings by interfering with people's performance, persistence, and emotionality (Birney et al., 1969; Elliot & Sheldon, 1997; Schmalt, 1982). The fear of failure is a functional counterforce because it prompts people to adopt performance-avoidance goals, such as trying to avoid making a mistake, trying to avoid performing poorly, or trying not to embarrass oneself. These avoidance-oriented goals lead people to underperform, quit quickly, and lose interest in what they are doing (Elliot & Church, 1997; Elliot & Harackiewicz, 1996; Roney, Higgins, & Shah, 1995).

Such a relationship (fear of failure → performance-avoidance goals → maladjusted coping style in achievement settings) has important implications for personal adjustment and mental health. The more people fear failure, the more likely they are to adopt performance-avoidance goals. And the more avoidance goals a person harbors, the poorer his subsequent well-being tends to be on measures such as self-esteem, personal control, vitality, life satisfaction, and psychological ill-being (Elliot & Sheldon, 1997). The primary reason well-being suffers when one adopts performance-avoidance goals is that in trying so hard to avoid poor performances, one regulates day-to-day behavior in ways that produce dissatisfaction, negative affect, and little enjoyment or fulfillment. Always trying to avoid embarrassing oneself, even when successfully accomplished, takes its toll on well-being, as highlighted in Box 9.

BOX 9   *Reducing Achievement Anxiety*

Question: Why is this information important?

Answer: So you can reduce anxiety and poor performance in achievement situations.

How much anxiety do you feel while taking tests in school, competing in athletics, making a presentation at work, or working on a project such as repairing something? Whenever we face a standard of excellence—a task that we know will end with a success/failure evaluation from both self and an audience of others—we feel a blend of enthusiasm and a desire to participate mixed in with anxiety and a desire to avoid it all. The athlete running a race, for example, is both eager to test her skills but also hesitant because she might embarrass herself.

The easiest way to reduce anxiety in achievement settings is to change the content of your thoughts. Just before running the race, for instance, an eager runner thinks, "I want to finish the race in under 10 minutes," while the anxious runner thinks, "I'm afraid I'll finish in last place" (Schmalt, 1999). Notice that these thoughts mirror the sample performance-approach and performance-avoidance goals mentioned earlier.

Can control over achievement anxiety really be that simple? Can it really be that straightforward—change your goals and you change your anxiety? Well, no, for two reasons. First, changing the way you think is not as easy as it might first sound. Thoughts are often deeply rooted. Second, achievement situations themselves generate anxiety—time deadlines, presence of an audience, task difficulty, and so on. And our own dispositional neuroticism (emotional instability) further contributes to our anxiety.

But achievement anxiety comes in two forms: cognitive worry and physiological upset ("hyper-emotionality"). The good news is that physiological hyper-emotionality does *not* undermine performance in achievement settings; only cognitive worry does (Elliot & McGregor, 1999). The primary cause of worry in achievement settings are performance avoidance goals. That is, the roots of worry are performance-avoidance goals like, "I just want to avoid making a mistake." So in a sense, these avoidance goals *are* that straightforward. Change your achievement goals and you change your achievement anxiety.

In trying to reduce worry-based anxiety, some productive advice is to change performance-avoidance goals into performance-approach (or mastery) goals. The arousal-based anxiety may remain (e.g., you may still feel nervous or pumped up standing in front of an evaluative audience), but the worry-based anxiety that really debilitates performance will fade in proportion to which performance-avoidance goals are successfully translated into approach-oriented goals.

The preceding advice is precisely the procedure used in experiments on how achievement goals affect motivation, anxiety, and performance. One group of participants is randomly given a performance-approach goal, "Demonstrate you have high ability." A second group of participants is randomly given a performance-avoidance goal, "Don't do worse than others." The first group experiences less anxiety than does the second group (Elliot, 1999; Elliot & Harackiewicz, 1996; Elliot & McGregor, 1999). Experiments such as these make it clear that experimenters can change the contents of our thoughts. It stands to reason that performers can follow this lead and intentionally adopt for themselves anxiety-reducing mastery and performance-approach goals.

A follow-up investigation showed that additional dispositional characteristics predispose people to adopt performance-avoidance goals, including neuroticism and poor life skills (e.g., poor social skills, poor time management; Elliot, Sheldon, & Church, 1997). People high in the fear of failure, high in neuroticism, and low in life-skill competence tend to adopt performance-avoidance goals (e.g., avoid being a boor at parties, avoid being lonely, avoid smoking or drinking). Trying to avoid doing something turns out to be a hard thing to do, relative to trying to do something (e.g., be friendly at parties). When people pursue avoidance goals, they generally perceive that they make little progress in the effort, and it is this perception of a lack of progress that leads to dissatisfaction, negative affectivity, diminished interest, and impaired psychological well-being.

MINDSET 4: COGNITIVE DISSONANCE

Most people see themselves as competent, moral, and reasonable. Most people harbor such a favorable view of themselves that a positive self-view can be understood as a near-universal mindset. This mindset is different from the first three discussed in the present chapter (deliberative–implemental, promotion–prevention, and growth-fixed) in that it is a singular, not a dual, mindset. That is, almost everyone walks around with the mindset "I am a competent, moral, and reasonable person."

While practically everyone walks around with this favorable mindset, it is still the case that people all too often engage in behavior that leaves them feeling stupid, immoral, and unreasonable. For instance, people smoke cigarettes, toss litter, tell white lies, neglect to recycle, drive their cars recklessly, skip classes, act rudely toward strangers, and engage in other such hypocritical conduct. When beliefs about who the self is and what the self does are inconsistent (i.e., believing one thing, yet actually behaving in the opposite way), people experience a psychologically uncomfortable state referred to as "cognitive dissonance" (Aronson, 1969, 1992, 1999; Festinger, 1957; Gerard, 1992; Harmon-Jones & Mills, 1999).

With cognitive consistency, two beliefs are consonant when one follows from the other (a mindset that I am a moral person is consistent with the behavior of telling the truth). With cognitive dissonance, two beliefs are dissonant when one is opposite to the other (a mindset that I am a moral person is dissonant with the behavior of lying). Just how psychologically uncomfortable cognitive dissonance is depends on its magnitude. When intense and uncomfortable enough, dissonance takes on motivational properties, and the person begins to seek ways to eliminate, or at least reduce, the dissonance.

Imagine the following scenario of a woman whose sense of self includes pro-environmental beliefs. She believes in clean water, clean air, clean land, energy conservation, and nature preservation. And she believes that polluted air, polluted land, energy consumption, and overdevelopment are immoral and unreasonable. Her pro-environmental beliefs are all consonant with one another (i.e., believing in clear water is consistent with believing in nature preservation). But suppose she reads an article in the newspaper that says that automobile exhaust fumes are rapidly and irreversibly depleting the ozone layer. Furthermore, according to the article, used automobile tires are littering the rivers and crowding the landfills. Suppose further that this environmentalist drives her car to work every day, and she needs her car for many additional purposes as well. She loves the environment, but she needs her car. She believes one thing about herself, but she behaves in a way that contradicts that self-view. This is an air of hypocrisy, and it is this experience of hypocrisy between self and action that causes dissonance (Aronson, 1999; Fried & Aronson, 1995).

The experience of dissonance is psychologically aversive (Elliot & Devine, 1994). People seek to reduce it (Gerard, 1992; Harmon-Jones & Mills, 1999), and they do so in one of four ways (Festinger, 1957; Harmon-Jones & Mills, 1999; Simon, Greenberg, & Brehm, 1995):

· Remove the dissonant belief.

· Reduce the importance of the dissonant belief.

· Add a new consonant belief.

· Increase the importance of the consonant belief.

Our environmentalist, for instance, might (1) quit driving her car and start riding a bicycle, or she might come to believe that volcano ash, not automobile exhaust, is responsible for the hole in the ozone layer (thereby removing the dissonant belief); (2) trivialize her immoral or unreasonable act of driving by justifying that her driving to work will have no impact on the global condition, especially when considering how much worse pollution is at factories and refineries (thereby reducing the importance of the dissonant belief; Simon et al., 1995); (3) read articles that reassure her that science is hard at work and will soon solve the pollution problem, or she might think of how truly enjoyable and useful it is to drive her car (thereby adding a new consonant belief, or two); or (4) think to herself that car exhaust proves that the city needs more bike trails, and the government needs emission-control device laws for all automobiles (thereby increasing the importance of the consonant belief). How resistant to change these beliefs are depends on (1) how close to reality they are (e.g., Will science really find a solution?), (2) how important or central they are to one's self-view (Simon et al., 1995; Thibodeau & Aronson, 1992), and (3) how much pain and cost must be endured (e.g., How painful will it be to quit driving a car?). Therefore, reality, importance, and personal costs work to support one's current beliefs, while dissonance puts pressure on hypocritical ways of thinking and behaving. It is a psychological competition—reality and self-interest on the one hand versus dissonance on the other—with motivational implications.

Dissonance-Arousing Situations

Human beings frequently encounter information or engage in behavior that is dissonant with their self-view. Four dissonance-arousing circumstances that bring on this hard-to-reconcile "I did one thing, yet believe the opposite" experience include choice, insufficient justification, effort justification, and new information.

Choice

People often choose between alternatives. In some cases, the choice is easy, because the merits of one alternative far outweigh the merits of its rival. In other cases, the choice is not so easy, because both alternatives offer a number of advantages and disadvantages. Once such a difficult choice is made, people experience dissonance (or "post-decision regret"). Dissonance is resolved by appreciating the chosen alternative—viewing it more positively—and by depreciating the rejected alternative—viewing it more negatively

(Brehm, 1956; Gilovich, Medvec, & Chen, 1995; Knox & Inkster, 1968; Younger, Walker, & Arrowood, 1977). To illustrate this process for yourself, simply ask a person both before and after making a difficult choice the following question: "How sure are you that your choice is the correct one?" Whether the choice involves deciding between restaurants, classes, or marriage partners, post-choice decision makers are invariably more confident in the wisdom of their choices than are those still in the decision-making process.[1]

Insufficient Justification

Insufficient justification addresses how people explain actions for which they have little or no external prompting (Festinger & Carlsmith, 1959). For example, people might ask themselves why they donated money to a charity or why they stopped to pick up litter. To justify such unprompted action, people routinely and perhaps necessarily add new consonant beliefs to their favorable self-view mindset, such as "I'm generous" and "I'm an environmentalist."

Effort Justification

During initiation rituals in the military, fraternities, sororities, athletic teams, neighborhood gangs, reality television shows, and other groups, recruits often exert great effort and perform extreme behaviors that must later be justified. Consider the Army private who parachutes out of an airplane as part of boot-camp training. For novice recruits, parachuting is extreme behavior. To justify why they would put their lives on the line like this, privates typically endorse a rather extreme liking for the behavior. Extreme behaviors breed extreme beliefs: "If I did *that*, then I must really *love* this place!" Dissonance theory proposes that the attractiveness of a task increases as a direct function of the magnitude of effort expended to complete it (Aronson & Mills, 1959; Beauvois & Joule, 1996; Rosenfeld, Giacalone, & Tedeschi, 1984). People who engage in extreme behavior need to develop correspondingly extreme values (Aronson, 1988).

New Information

As you read books, listen to the radio, watch television, attend lectures, view Web sites, and interact with others, you expose yourself to opportunities to contradict your beliefs. One group of researchers followed the Seekers, a cult-like group convinced that their city and the entire western coast of the Americas would be destroyed by a great flood on a specific day (Festinger, Riecken, & Schachter, 1956, 1958). On the day before the flood, the group was told that a man would appear at the leader's house at midnight to take them to a flying saucer. Midnight came and passed with no knock on the door, so the Seekers found their cherished belief of doom unequivocally disconfirmed. Given belief disconfirmation, what were the dissonance-suffering Seekers to do? A few did reject their belief and dropped out of the group. Most Seekers, however, were more rationalizing than rational. They saw the disconfirmation as a test of their commitment to the cause (the world was saved because

---

[1] A good illustration of this phenomenon is the often heard (yet absurd) quote from a person looking back on life, "If I had to live my life over again, I wouldn't change a thing—not where I lived, what school I attended, who I married, which career I pursued, nor anything I said or did."

of their faith!) and responded with strong, persistent attempts at proselytizing. By proselytizing, the latter group tried to resolve their dissonance by recruiting new people who
would agree with their beliefs (i.e., add new consonant beliefs). Quite literally, each new
convert allowed the Seekers to reduce their dissonance that the predicted cataclysm never
materialized.

Motivational Processes Underlying Cognitive Dissonance

People engage in all sorts of behaviors that imply that they are incompetent, immoral, or
unreasonable. Inconsistency between what one believes (I am competent) and what one
does (I acted incompetently) creates the cognitive inconsistency that is dissonance. In the
face of dissonance-arousing situational events, like the four discussed above, however, dissonance arises and motivates change in ways of believing or behaving. An overview of the
psychological processes underlying dissonance motivation and people's attempts to reduce
or eliminate it appears in Figure 9.6 (Harmon-Jones & Mills, 1999).

Most dissonance researchers portray dissonance motivation through the analogy of
pain—the person changes beliefs or behaviors in order to eliminate the aversive, persistent, and uncomfortable experience. But dissonance can be used to accomplish productive
social goals too. For instance, using a dissonance framework, researchers have been successful in changing people's attitudes and behaviors toward prosocial causes such as using
condoms during sex (Aronson, Fried, & Stone, 1991), conserving natural resources (e.g.,
water; Dickerson, Thibodeau, Aronson, & Miller, 1992), and reducing prejudice (Leippe &
Eisenstadt, 1994). The conclusion from each of these three experiments may be summarized succinctly as follows: "Saying, or doing, is believing." Beliefs follow from (and act to
justify) what one says and does. For instance, if you join your friend while she walks in the
multiple sclerosis walkathon, your attitude toward people with multiple sclerosis will probably start to change for the better (i.e., add a new consonant belief to justify the effort). The
fact that you walked in a charity's marathon is effort that needs to be justified, especially if
it rained.

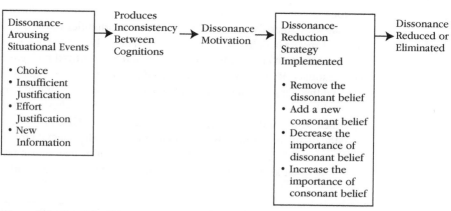

Figure 9.6   Cognitive Dissonance Processes

Self-Perception Theory

Cognitive dissonance theory argues that people develop and change their beliefs in response to a negative motivational–emotional state born in cognitive contradiction (i.e., a core "I am a good person" mindset that is contradicted by behavior that suggests "I am not a good person."). Self-perception theory argues that people develop and change their beliefs for a reason that does not involve a mindset. It offers the alternative interpretation that people develop and change their behavior based simply on self-observation (Bem, 1967, 1972; Bem & McConnell, 1970). For example, we eat squid for whatever reason (maybe we did not know it was squid because the restaurant referred to it as calamari) and after doing so we presume that since we ate squid, we must therefore like it. Both cognitive dissonance theory and self-perception theory revolve around the tenet that "saying, or doing, is believing." The difference between the two theories is that cognitive dissonance theory argues that beliefs change because of negative affect from cognitive inconsistencies, whereas self-perception theory argues that we simply come to believe whatever we do and say.

The dissonance versus self-perception debate generated a great deal of research (Elliot & Devine, 1994; Fazio, Zanna, & Cooper, 1977, 1979; Ronis & Greenwald, 1979; Ross & Shulman, 1973; Snyder & Ebbesen, 1972; Zanna & Cooper, 1976). The conclusion was that both cognitive dissonance and self-perception theories are correct, but each applies to a different set of circumstances. Self-perception theory applies best to situations in which people's beliefs are initially vague, ambiguous, and weak. In such cases, people do indeed draw inferences about themselves from their behavior. On the other hand, dissonance theory applies best to situations in which people's beliefs are initially clear, salient, and strong.

SUMMARY

A mindset is a cognitive framework that guides one's attention, information processing, decision making, and thinking about the meaning of effort, success, failure, and one's own personal qualities. Once adopted, a mindset functions as a cognitive motivational system that produces many important downstream consequences in one's thinking, feeling, and acting. The chapter highlighted four mindsets: deliberative–implemental, promotion–prevention, fixed-growth, and consistency–dissonance.

With the deliberative versus implemental mindset, the key distinction is between the initial selection of goals, which involves a great deal of deliberation, and the volitional regulation of the action necessary to bring that chosen goal to fruition, which involves strategic execution and willpower. In a deliberative mindset, the person is open-minded and attention is cast wide to take in any information about the desirability and feasibility of considered goals. Once a goal has been set and committed to, the person benefits from making a transition from a deliberative to an implemental mindset. In an implemental mindset, the person is closed-minded and attention is focused narrowly to concentrate only on information that is related to goal attainment. When they are in an implemental rather than a deliberative mindset, people generally persist longer and perform better.

Regulatory focus theory proposes that people strive for their goals by using two separate and independent motivational orientations: promotion and prevention. With a promotion mindset, the focus is on advancing the self toward ideals by adopting an eager locomotion behavioral strategy; with a prevention mindset, the focus is on preventing the self from not maintaining one's duties and responsibilities by adopting a vigilant behavioral strategy. The two mindsets lead to different definitions of success, because people with a promotion focus are sensitive to success while people with a promotion focus are sensitive to failure. The two mindsets also lead to different goal-striving strategies, because people with a promotion mindset utilize eager locomotion during goal striving ("just do it"), while people with a prevention mindset utilize cautious vigilance during goal striving ("do the right thing."). Attention to ideal self-guides orient people toward a promotion mindset, while attention to ought self-guides orient people toward a prevention mindset. Both mindsets are necessary for optimal striving, but regulatory fit, in which one's mindset matches one's goal-striving behavioral strategies (promotion with eager locomotion; prevention with cautious vigilance), feels right and leads to more effort, better performance, and enhanced well-being.

The growth-fixed mindset concerns the question of how people think about their personal qualities, such as their intelligence. The growth mindset is the belief that one's personal qualities are malleable, changeable, and can be developed through effort. The fixed mindset is the belief that one's personal qualities are fixed, set, and not open to change. For the person with a fixed mindset, effort is not valued and high levels of effort signal that the person must therefore have low ability; for the person with a growth mindset, effort is highly valued and high levels of effort function as the tool by which people develop and grow their skills and abilities. Fixed-growth mindsets are socialized beliefs, because ability praise from parents and teachers tends to cultivate in children a fixed mindset, whereas effort praise from parents and teachers tends to cultivate in children a growth mindset. A growth mindset can also be taught, and explicit training programs to help students develop a growth mindset have been successful and have helped students develop their qualities and improve their performances. The two mindsets lead to different achievement goals, because people with a fixed mindset tend to adopt performance goals while people with a growth mindset tend to adopt mastery goals. Achievement goals revolve around a person's understanding of what constitutes competence, because performance goals equate competence with outperforming others while mastery goals equate competence with making progress against a self-set standard. Generally speaking, mastery goals yield more productive ways of thinking, feeling, and behaving than do performance goals.

The consistency–dissonance mindset is rooted in the near-universal self-view that "I am a competent, moral, and reasonable person." The basic tenets of cognitive dissonance theory are that people dislike inconsistency, the experience of dissonance is psychologically aversive, and people seek to reduce dissonance by striving to maintain consistency in their beliefs, attitudes, values, and behaviors.

READINGS FOR FURTHER STUDY

Deliberative–Implemental Mindset

Armor, D. A., & Taylor, S. E. (2003). The effects of mindset on behavior: Self-regulation in deliberative and implemental frames of mind. *Personality and Social Psychology Bulletin, 29*, 86–95.

Brandtstadter, J., & Frank, E. (2002). Effects of deliberative and implemental mindsets on persistence in goal-directed behavior. *Personality and Social Psychology Bulletin, 28*, 1366–1378.

Promotion–Prevention Mindset

HIGGINS, E. T. (2005). Value from regulatory fit. *Current Directions in Psychological Science, 14*, 209–213.

FREITAS, A. L., & HIGGINS, E. T. (2002). Enjoying goal-directed action: The role of regulatory fit. *Psychological Science, 13*, 1–6.

Growth-Fixed Mindset

BLACKWELL, L. S., TRZESNIEWSKI, K. H., & DWECK, C. S. (2008). Implicit theories of intelligence predict achievement across an adolescent transition: A longitudinal study and an intervention. *Child Development, 78*, 246–263.

DWECK, C. S. (2008). Can personality be changed? The role of beliefs in personality and change. *Current Directions in Psychological Science, 17*, 391–394.

ELLIOT, A. J., & CHURCH, M. A. (1997). A hierarchical model of approach and avoidance achievement motivation. *Journal of Personality and Social Psychology, 72*, 218–232.

HONG, Y., CHIU, C., DWECK, C. S., LIN, D. M.-S., & WAN, W. (1999). Implicit theories, attributions, and coping: A meaning system approach. *Journal of Personality and Social Psychology, 77*, 588–599.

MUELLER, C. M., & DWECK, C. S. (1998). Praise for intelligence can undermine children's motivation and performance. *Journal of Personality and Social Psychology, 75*, 33–52.

Cognitive Dissonance

HARMON-JONES, E., & MILLS, J. (1999). An introduction to cognitive dissonance theory and an overview of current perspectives on the theory. In E. Harmon-Jones & J. Mills (Eds.), *Cognitive dissonance: Progress on a pivotal theory in social psychology* (pp. 3–21). Washington, DC: American Psychological Association.

Chapter 10

Personal Control Beliefs

MOTIVATION TO EXERCISE PERSONAL CONTROL

    Two Kinds of Expectancy

    Perceived Control: Self, Action, and Control

SELF-EFFICACY

    Sources of Self-Efficacy

        Personal Behavior History

        Vicarious Experience

        Verbal Persuasion

        Physiological State

        Skill and Self-Efficacy: Chicken or the Egg?

    Self-Efficacy Effects on Behavior

        Choice: Selection of Activities and Environments

        Effort and Persistence

        Thinking and Decision Making

        Emotionality

        Learning, Coping, Performing, and Achieving

    Self-Efficacy or the Psychological Need for Competence?

    Empowerment

    Empowering People: Mastery Modeling Program

MASTERY BELIEFS

    Ways of Coping

    Mastery versus Helplessness

LEARNED HELPLESSNESS

    Learning Helplessness

    Application to Humans

    Components

        Contingency

        Cognition

        Behavior

    Helplessness Effects

        Motivational Deficits

        Learning Deficits

        Emotional Deficits

Helplessness and Depression
Attributions and Explanatory Style
Pessimistic Explanatory Style
Optimistic Explanatory Style
Alternative Explanations

REACTANCE THEORY
Reactance and Helplessness

HOPE
EXPECTANCY-VALUE MODEL
SUMMARY
READINGS FOR FURTHER STUDY

What does the future have in store? Will you graduate from college? Will your classes be interesting? Will you pass this course? Will you find this tenth chapter interesting? Will the chapter address important topics, or will it present topics that are only dry and confusing? This winter, will you catch the flu? When you apply for your next job, will you get it? Will you fall in love? Will you fall out of love? If you were to go on a blind date or meet your mate's parents, would these strangers like you? Will you find someone to share your life with, as in marriage? When you drive to school or work tomorrow, will you get stuck in traffic? Will you get a parking ticket? Will you live to see your 50th birthday?

How able are you to cope with what the future brings? Do you have what it takes to graduate? If you underperform on your first exam in this course, can you mount a comeback and still do well in the course? What would happen if you tried to shop online—would it go well? In relationships, can you make another person laugh? Can you cheer up your friends when they feel depressed? Can you defuse arguments? Could you be the life of a party? If a bully insults and pesters you, could you handle the situation? Can you run three miles without stopping to rest? Okay, how about one mile? Can you sing? Could you hit a golf ball on your first try? Could you hit it if an audience was watching?

Our expectancies of what will happen and how well we can cope with life's challenges have important motivational implications. Imagine how motivationally problematic your college experience would be if you expected not to graduate, not to pass a particular course, not to get a job after graduation, and not to understand the professor or this book. Imagine how motivationally problematic your interpersonal relationships would be if you expected others not to like you, not to care about your welfare, or to express only hostility. What if you expected that everyone you met would reject you? Imagine how motivationally problematic your athletic participation would be if you expected only to fail and to embarrass yourself. Imagine how difficult it would be to muster the motivation to run three miles if you knew beforehand that you could not do so.

MOTIVATION TO EXERCISE PERSONAL CONTROL

The focus throughout this chapter is the motivation to exercise personal control over what does and does not happen to you. To some extent, environments are both predictable and responsive to our control attempts. Because this is so, people are often able to figure out what they need to do to exert control over the environment and life's outcomes. The strength with which people try to exercise personal control can be traced to the strengths of their expectancies of being able to do so. Expectancy is a subjective prediction of how likely it is that an event will occur. That event can be an outcome (e.g., losing 10 pounds) or a course of action that brings the outcome to pass (e.g., running 20 minutes on a treadmill without having a heart attack). For instance, when politicians enter an election or athletes enter a competition, they appraise the likelihood that they will win. Before people leap across a creek or tell a risqué joke, they appraise the likelihood of landing on solid ground. In anticipating events and outcomes, people rely on their past experiences and personal resources to make forecasts—expectancies—about what the future holds and how well they will be able to cope with what is to come.

Two Kinds of Expectancy

Two types of expectancies exist: efficacy expectations and outcome expectations (Bandura, 1977, 1986, 1997; Heckhausen, 1977; Peterson et al., 1993). An efficacy expectation (see Figure 10.1) is a judgment of one's capacity to execute a particular act or course of action. The question is, "Can I do it?" An outcome expectation (see Figure 10.1) is a judgment that a given action, once performed, will cause a particular outcome. The question is, "Will it work?" Efficacy expectations estimate the likelihood that an individual can behave in a particular way; outcome expectations estimate how likely it is that certain consequences will follow once that behavior is enacted. For an illustration of these two kinds of expectancy, consider the political candidate who wants to win an election and

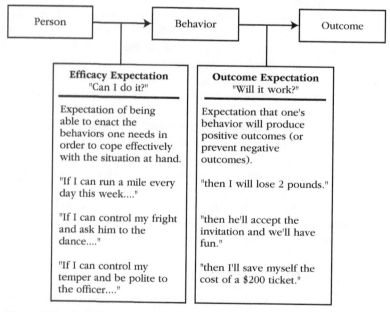

Figure 10.1   Two Kinds of Expectation: Efficacy and Outcome

believes that by giving a convention speech she can win. Efficacy expectations pertain to her confidence that she can "do what it takes" to give a competent speech. Outcome expectancies pertain to her beliefs that once she gives her competent speech, the speech will produce positive outcomes—people will listen, be persuaded by her oratory, and vote for her in the election.

Efficacy and outcome expectations are separate, causal determinants to the initiation and regulation of behavior (Bandura, 1991). Consider the different expectancies that might run through a surgeon's mind in preparing for an operation. The extent to which the surgeon does or does not engage in that operation depends on (1) his efficacy expectation that he can skillfully perform the surgery and (2) his outcome expectation that the surgery, once enacted, will produce certain physical, psychological, emotional, financial, and social benefits for himself and for his patient.

Both efficacy and outcome expectations must be reasonably high before behavior becomes energetic, goal directed, and sustained over time. Thus, an analysis of efficacy and outcome expectancies allows us to understand people's reluctance to engage in activities such as public speaking, dating, athletics, and job interviews. To speak publically, date, compete, or interview, the person must not only be confident in his efficacy to execute these behaviors, he must also be reasonably assured that an effective performance will pay off (i.e., will lead to desired outcomes). Take away either of these positive forecasts and reluctance and avoidance become rather logical ways of acting.

Perceived Control: Self, Action, and Control

Figure 10.1 puts the interrelationships between Person, Behavior, and Outcome at the center of expectancy motivation. Some researchers prefer using the alternative terminology of Self → Action → Control to communicate this same idea (Skinner, 1996), so Figure 10.2 presents this alternative (but interchangeable) terminology. As shown in the figure, the defining relation in the study of perceived control is that of Self (Agent) → Control (Ends). People express this Self → Control relation in everyday questions such as, "Can I improve my health?", "Can I improve my marriage?", and "Can I earn a scholarship?" In other words, perceived control revolves around how the Self (Agent) can exert Control (Ends). Figure 10.2, like Figure 10.1, shows how perceived control can be broken down into the more basic questions of "Can I cope effectively?" (Self → Action) and "Will my coping improve my health, marriage, or scholarship prospects?" (Action → Control).

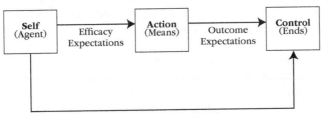

Figure 10.2 *Self → Action → Control* Model of Perceived Control

So, Figures 10.1 and 10.2 communicate the same message, but Figure 10.2 introduces and highlights the larger superordinate construct of perceived control (Self → Control).

SELF-EFFICACY

Efficacy expectations center on questions such as the following: "Can I perform well on this particular task?" and "If things start to go wrong during my performance, do I have the resources within me to cope well and turn things around for the better?" But efficacy expectations and self-efficacy are not quite the same thing. Self-efficacy is a more generative capacity in which the individual (i.e., the "self" in self-efficacy) organizes and orchestrates his or her skills to cope with the demands and circumstances he or she faces. It is the capacity to use one's personal resources well under diverse and trying circumstances. Formally, self-efficacy is defined as one's judgment of how well (or poorly) one will cope with a situation, given the skills one possesses and the circumstances one faces (Bandura, 1986, 1993, 1997).

Self-efficacy is not the same as "ability." Competent functioning requires not only possessing skills (i.e., ability), but also the capacity to translate those skills into effective performance, especially under trying and difficult circumstances. A snow skier might have wondrous slalom, mogul, and downhill racing skills but still perform dismally if the wind blows, the snow ices, or the slopes are crowded with clumsy skiers who keep falling in random ways. Self-efficacy is that generative capacity in which the performer improvises ways to best translate personal abilities into effective performance. Self-efficacy is just as important a determinant of competent functioning as is ability because performance situations often are stressful, ambiguous, and unpredictable, and as one performs, circumstances *always* change (Bandura, 1997). Several studies have tested the comparative predictive power of ability on the one hand and self-efficacy (i.e., perceived capability) on the other hand and found that self-efficacy makes both a significant and a potent contribution to the prediction of performance and outcomes (Collins, 1982; Pajares & Kranzler, 1995).

Consider that most of us can drive a car rather well on the interstate because most of us rate very high on abilities such as steering, braking, negotiating traffic, reciting traffic laws, and finding our destinations. But self-efficacy becomes important when circumstances rise to test our abilities, as when driving in an unreliable car on an unfamiliar road with poorly marked streets, during a snowstorm, as monster trucks whiz by splashing slush that covers the windshield. Even highly skilled drivers sometimes perform dismally because circumstances change in stressful and overwhelming ways. Under trying circumstances, the driver must have what it takes to keep arousal in check, to think clearly in deciding between options, to avoid perils, and perhaps to negotiate or show leadership in enlisting the assistance of the passenger. The same self-efficacy analysis applies to academic test taking (Bandura, Cioffi, Taylor, & Brovillard, 1988), athletic performance (Feltz, 1992), self-defense (Ozer & Bandura, 1990), health-promoting behaviors (Bandura, 1998), and collective agency for solving social problems (Bandura, 1997).

The opposite of efficacy is doubt. For the driver who doubts his or her capacity to cope, then surprises, setbacks, and difficulties will create anxiety (Bandura, 1988), confusion (Wood & Bandura, 1989), negative thinking (Bandura, 1983), and aversive physiological arousal and bodily tension (Bandura et al., 1985). Imagine the unfolding of events that might occur when the self-doubt of an otherwise skilled driver comes face to face with surprises, setbacks, and difficulties. Perhaps an unexpected storm begins (surprise), or the windshield wipers fail (setback), or ice forms on the road (difficulty). Under such trying conditions, doubt can interfere with effective thinking, planning, and decision making to cause anxiety, confusion, arousal, tension, and distress that can spiral performance toward disaster. Of course, surprises, setbacks, and difficulties may not produce poor performance, just as skill, talent, and ability may not produce excellent performance. Rather, extent of self-efficacy (versus self-doubt) is the motivational variable that determines the extent to which a performer copes well (versus poorly) when her skills and abilities are stressed.

Consider the more extended example of trying to present oneself as socially competent as during a job interview, auditioning for a part in a play, or going on a first date. In a self-efficacy analysis, the skills involved in interviewing, auditioning, and dating and the situational demands placed on the performer are complex and multidimensional. The following list describes an adolescent on a first date (Rose & Frieze, 1989) by listing some task demands that need to be coped with (left) as well as the skills needed to successfully cope with those demands (right).

Dating Demand	Dating Skill
Ask for a date	Assertiveness
Make a plan to do something interesting	Creativity
Arrive on time at date's house	Punctuality
Relate warmly to parents or roommates	Sociability
Joke, laugh, and talk	Sense of humor
Impress date	Salesmanship
Be polite	Social etiquette
Understand how other feels	Empathy
Be responsive to the other's needs	Perspective taking
Kiss goodnight	Being romantic

As the adolescent contemplates the date, he asks what specific events will take place. What skills will be needed to perform well? If things go unexpectedly wrong, can he make the necessary corrective adjustments? How does he expect to feel during the date and during each specific event? In this hypothetical situation, the adolescent expects that the overall task at hand will require a dozen or so different skills, such as assertiveness, sociability, and so on. The adolescent also has some expectation of how effectively he can execute each of these skills, and those expectancies might range from woefully incompetent to highly competent. These expectations represent the heart and soul of individual efficacy expectations, as well as one's more general sense of self-efficacy toward the situation at hand: How effective will I be when the situation calls for me to be assertive? Will I feel mostly confidence or mostly doubt? Are my skills hardy enough to get the evening back on track if things go wrong (e.g., parents turn out to be very difficult to relate to)? Just how much social doubt and anxiety the adolescent feels in this particular situation can be predicted by a self-efficacy analysis of his perceived efficacy expectations in each of the 10 task-related demands.

Furthermore, once we know the adolescent's expectancies of efficacy versus doubt in coping with these task demands, we can predict his motivation to go on the date versus avoid it. Boiled down to its essence, self-efficacy predicts the motivational balance between wanting to give it a try on the one hand and anxiety, doubt, and behavioral avoidance on the other.

Sources of Self-Efficacy

Self-efficacy beliefs do not just occur out of the blue; they have causes and historical roots. Self-efficacy beliefs arise from (1) one's personal history in trying to execute that particular behavior or way of coping, (2) observations of similar others who also try to execute that behavior, (3) verbal persuasions (pep talks) from others, and (4) physiological states such as a racing versus a calm heart.

Personal Behavior History

The extent to which a person believes she can competently enact a particular course of action stems from her personal history of trying to enact that course of action in the past (Bandura, 1986, 1997; Bandura, Reese, & Adams, 1982). People learn their current self-efficacy from their interpretations and memories of past attempts to execute the same behavior. Memories and recollections of past attempts to enact the behavior judged as competent raise self-efficacy, whereas memories and recollections of past attempts judged as incompetent lower self-efficacy. For instance, as a child prepares to ride a bicycle, her personal history of being able to actually carry out the cycling behavior on past occasions functions as firsthand information about self-efficacy in the present encounter. Of course, a person's behavior history with regard to any specific course of action changes a bit with each new enactment. How important any one behavioral enactment is to future efficacy depends on the strength of the performer's preexisting expectation. Once one's personal behavior history has produced a strong sense of efficacy, an occasional incompetent enactment will not lower self-efficacy much (or an occasional competent enactment will not raise a strong sense of inefficacy much). If the performer is less experienced (i.e., lacks a behavioral history), however, each new competent or incompetent enactment will inform future efficacy. This is a very important point in teaching situations in which learners are trying out new behaviors and new activities. Of the four sources of self-efficacy, personal behavior history is the most influential (Bandura, 1986).

Vicarious Experience

Vicarious experience involves observing a model enact the same course of action the performer is about to enact (e.g., "You go first, I'll watch"). Seeing others perform masterfully raises an observer's own sense of efficacy (Bandura, Adams, Hardy, & Howells, 1980; Kazdin, 1979). This is so because seeing similar others perform the same behavior initiates a social comparison process (e.g., "If they can do it, so can I"). But vicarious experience works the other way as well, because observing others perform the same behavior clumsily lowers our own sense of efficacy (e.g., "If they can't do it, what makes me think I can?"; Brown & Inouye, 1978). The extent to which a model's enactment affects our own efficacy depends on two factors. First, the greater the similarity between the model and the observer, the greater the impact the model's behavior will have on the observer's efficacy forecast

(Schunk, 1989b). Second, the less experienced the observer is at the behavior (a novice), the greater the impact of the vicarious experience (Schunk, 1989a). Thus, vicarious experience is a potent source of efficacy for relatively inexperienced observers who watch similar others perform.

Verbal Persuasion

Coaches, parents, teachers, employers, therapists, peers, spouses, friends, audiences, clergy, authors of self-help books, infomercials, inspirational posters, happy-face stickers, and songs on the radio often attempt to convince us that we can competently execute a given action—despite our entrenched inefficacy—if we will just try (e.g., "I know you can do it!"). When effective, pep talks persuade the performer to focus more on personal strengths and potentials and less on personal weaknesses and deficiencies. Pep talks shift a performer's attention from sources of inefficacy to sources of efficacy. But verbal persuasion goes only so far if it is contradicted by actual experience (Schunk, 1995). Its effectiveness is limited by the boundaries of the possible (in the mind of the performer) and depends on the credibility, expertise, and trustworthiness of the persuader. Individuals also give themselves pep talks, usually in the form of self-instruction, that can boost efficacy, at least for a little while (Schunk & Cox, 1986). Verbal persuasion works to the extent that it provides the performer with enough of a temporary and provisional efficacy boost to generate the motivation necessary for another try (Schunk, 1991).

Physiological State

Fatigue, pain, muscle tension, mental confusion, and trembling hands are physiological signals that the demands of the task currently exceed the performer's capacity to cope with those demands (Taylor et al., 1985). An abnormal physiological state is a private, yet attention-getting, message that contributes to one's sense of inefficacy. An absence of tension, fear, anxiety, and stress, on the other hand, heightens efficacy by providing first-hand bodily feedback that one can indeed cope adequately with task demands (Bandura & Adams, 1977). The causal direction between efficacy and physiological activity is bidirectional: Inefficacy heightens arousal and heightened arousal feeds back to fuel perceived inefficacy (Bandura et al., 1988). Physiological information communicates efficacy information most when initial efficacy is uncertain (one is performing a task for the first time). When efficacy is relatively assured, people sometimes discount, or even reinterpret, their physiological cues as a positive source of efficacy, as in "I'm pumped up for this" (Carver & Blaney, 1977).

As people face challenging and difficult circumstances and ready themselves to carry out a course of action, these are the four sources of information they rely on to forecast their sense of efficacy during the performance. For a concrete illustration, consider the child at the county swimming pool waiting her turn in line to jump off the high diving board. How eager (motivated) she will be to do so depends on how well she has been able to negotiate the jump in the past, how well or ineptly the divers in the line before her are able to dive, the conversation of encouragement versus ridicule she hears from her friend standing in line with her, and the message of panic versus "cool, calm, and collected" her body sends her as she stands six feet above the water looking down. By itself, none of this information determines her efficacy or her diving forecasts. Instead, through reflective thought, she selects information to attend to, weighs the importance of each, and eventually integrates the multiple (and sometimes contradictory) sources of information into an overall self-efficacy judgment (Bandura, 1997).

While integrating these multiple sources of self-efficacy information into a single judgment is a complex process, the first two sources of efficacy information—personal behavior history and vicarious experience—are generally the stronger sources of efficacy beliefs (Schunk, 1989b). The relative potency of the different sources of efficacy information is important because of its implications for therapeutic strategies for designing motivational interventions for persons with low self-efficacy beliefs (e.g., Ozer & Bandura, 1990). Personal behavior history and vicarious experience are promising therapeutic possibilities, while verbal persuasion and regulating physiological states serve largely as supplemental possibilities.

Skill and Self-Efficacy: Chicken or the Egg?

Self-efficacy beliefs rise and fall with changes in personal behavior history, vicarious experience, verbal persuasion, and physiological state. These changes in self-efficacy, in turn, predict changes in skillful coping. But there is a bit of a chicken-and-egg problem within self-efficacy—namely, does skilled performance (e.g., personal behavior history) increase self-efficacy, does self-efficacy increase skilled performance, or do both of these effects occur? Skilled performance clearly predicts longitudinal changes in self-efficacy beliefs (Bandura, 1997), so the question is whether self-efficacy predicts longitudinal changes in skilled performance. While some research suggests that changes in self-efficacy cause later changes in skilled performance (Caprara, Barbaranelli, Steca, & Malone, 2006), other research shows that self-efficacy does not cause later changes in skilled performance (Stein & Wang, 1988), or does so only mildly (Holzberger, Philipp, & Kunter, 2013). The conclusion seems to be that both effects exist, although the effect that skilled performance has on self-efficacy is stronger than is the effect that self-efficacy has on skilled performance.

Self-Efficacy Effects on Behavior

Once formed, self-efficacy beliefs contribute to the quality of human functioning in multiple ways (Bandura, 1986, 1997). Generally speaking, the more people expect that they can adequately perform an action, the more willing they are to put forth effort and persist in facing difficulties (Bandura, 1989; Bandura & Cervone, 1983; Weinberg, Gould, & Jackson, 1979). In contrast, when people expect that they cannot adequately perform the required task, they are not willing to engage in activities requiring such behavior. Instead, they slacken their effort, prematurely settle for mediocre outcomes, and quit in the face of obstacles (Bandura, 1989). More specifically, self-efficacy beliefs affect (1) the choice of activities and selection of environments, (2) the extent of effort and persistence put forth during performance, (3) the quality of thinking and decision making during performance, and (4) emotional reactions, especially those related to stress and anxiety. The four sources of efficacy and the four effects of strong versus weak self-efficacy beliefs are organized in summary form in Figure 10.3.

Choice: Selection of Activities and Environments

People continually make choices about what activities to pursue and which environments to spend time in. In general, people seek out and approach with excitement those activities and

Sources of Self-Efficacy   *Effects of Self-Efficacy*

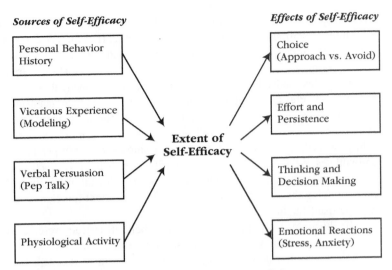

Figure 10.3   Sources and Effects of Self-Efficacy Beliefs

situations that they feel capable of adjusting to or handling, while people shun and actively avoid those activities and situations that they see as likely to overwhelm their coping capacities (Bandura, 1977, 1989). In a self-efficacy analysis, a person will often choose to avoid tasks and environments as a self-protective act for guarding against the possibility of being overwhelmed by demands and challenges. If the student expects a math class or a foreign language class to be overwhelming, confusing, and frustrating, then doubt overwhelms efficacy and produces an avoidance decision, such as withdrawing from class discussions or not enrolling in the class in the first place. The same doubt-plagued avoidance choices apply to social opportunities, such as dating, dancing, participating in sports, selecting (or avoiding) a particular musical instrument, and career paths pursued and shunned.

Doubt-plagued avoidance choices exert a profound and detrimental effect on a person's long-term development (Bandura, 1986). Weak self-efficacy beliefs set the stage for people to shun activities and therefore contribute to their own arrested developmental potentials (Holahan & Holahan, 1987). When people shun an activity out of doubt over personal competence, they participate in the self-destructive process of retarding their own development. If doubt leads people to avoid taking a foreign language class today, then their future likely involves less travel, fewer interactions with international students, narrower culinary preferences, stronger nationalistic beliefs, and so on. Furthermore, the more they avoid such activities, the more entrenched self-doubt becomes because doubters never get the chance to prove themselves wrong and eliminate opportunities to observe expert models or receive instruction. Such a pattern of avoidance progressively narrows people's ranges of activities and settings (Bandura, 1982; Betz & Hackett, 1986; Hackett, 1985).

Effort and Persistence

As people perform, self-efficacy beliefs influence how much effort they exert as well as how long they put forth that effort in the face of adversity (Bandura, 1989). Strong self-efficacy beliefs produce persistent coping efforts aimed at overcoming setbacks and difficulties

(Salomon, 1984). Doubt, on the other hand, leads people to slacken their efforts when they encounter difficulties and perhaps give up altogether (Bandura & Cervone, 1983; Weinberg et al., 1979). Self-doubt also leads performers to settle prematurely on mediocre solutions.

In trying to master complex activities, learning is always fraught with difficulties, obstacles, setbacks, frustrations, rejections, and inequalities, at least to a degree. Self-efficacy plays a pivotal role in facilitating effort and persistence, not because it silences doubt following failure and rejection (because these are expected, normal emotional reactions). Instead, self-efficacy leads to a *quick recovery* of self-assurance following such setbacks (Bandura, 1986). Using examples of persistent writers, scientists, and athletes, Albert Bandura argues that it is the resiliency of self-efficacy in the face of being pounded by uninterrupted failure that provides the motivational support necessary for continuing the persistent effort needed for competent functioning and the development of expertise (Bandura, 1989).

To illustrate this point, Bandura and other self-efficacy researchers quote stories of resiliency from John White's (1978) book *Rejection*. For example, Michael Jordan was cut from his high school basketball team in the tenth grade, Walt Disney was fired by a newspaper editor who said he "lacked imagination," Decca Records turned down a contract with the Beatles saying "We don't like their sound," and J. K. Rowling was rejected by 12 different publishers before *Harry Potter and the Sorcerer's Stone* became an accepted manuscript.

Thinking and Decision Making

People who believe strongly in their efficacy for solving problems remain remarkably efficient in their analytic thinking during stressful episodes, whereas people who doubt their problem-solving capacities think erratically (Bandura & Wood, 1989; Wood & Bandura, 1989), and show both confusion and negative thinking (Bandura, 1983; Wood & Bandura, 1989). To perform their best, people must first use memories of past events to predict the most effective course of action. They must also analyze feedback to assess and to reassess the merit of their plans and strategies. A strong sense of efficacy allows the performer to remain task focused, even in the face of situational stress and problem-solving dead ends. In contrast, self-doubt distracts decision makers away from such task-focused thinking because attention shifts to the deficiencies of the self and the overwhelming demands of the task. In short, doubt deteriorates, whereas efficacy buffers, the quality of a performer's thinking and decision making during a performance.

Emotionality

Before performers begin an activity, they typically spend time thinking about how they will perform. Persons with a strong sense of efficacy attend to the demands and challenges of the task; visualize competent scenarios for forthcoming behaviors; and exude enthusiasm, optimism, and interest. Persons with a weak sense of efficacy, however, dwell on personal deficiencies; visualize formidable obstacles; and exude pessimism, anxiety, and depression (Bandura, 1986, 1988). Once performance begins and things start to go awry, strong self-efficacy beliefs keep anxiety at bay. People who doubt their efficacy, however, are quickly threatened by difficulties, react to setbacks and negative feedback with distress, and see their attention drift toward personal deficiencies and negative emotionality.

Life in general brings any number of potentially threatening events (e.g., examinations, public performances, physical and psychological threats), and perceived self-efficacy plays a central role in determining how much stress and anxiety such events bring to any individual performer. Rather than existing as a fixed property of events, "threat" always depends on the relation a person has to the task (Folkman & Lazarus, 1985; Lazarus & Folkman, 1984). Knowing that one's coping abilities cannot handle an event's perceived demands conjures up thoughts of disaster, emotional arousal, and feelings of distress and anxiety (Bandura et al., 1982, 1985; Lazarus, 1991a). More optimistically, when people plagued with self-doubt undergo therapy-like conditions to enhance their coping capabilities, the intimidating event that once conjured up such an avalanche of doubt, dread, and distress no longer does so (Bandura & Adams, 1977; Bandura et al., 1980, 1982; Ozer & Bandura, 1990). As self-efficacy increases, fear and anxiety slip away. Self-efficacy researchers go so far as to say that the root cause of anxiety is low self-efficacy (Bandura, 1983, 1988). Therefore, any increase in efficacy means a corresponding decrease in anxiety.

Learning, Coping, Performing, and Achieving

Self-efficacy beliefs predict people's learning, coping, performance, and achievement (Bandura, Barbaranelli, Caprara, & Pastorella, 2001; Ozer & Bandura, 1990; Pajares & Graham, 1999; Pietsch, Walker, & Chapman, 2003; Williams & Williams, 2010). The reason why self-efficacy facilitates learning, coping, performing, and achieving is because self-efficacy facilitates the type of active task involvement that is needed to increase and improve one's learning, coping, performing, and achieving—namely, approaching rather than avoiding challenges and opportunities, exerting greater rather than lesser effort, persisting in the face of obstacles rather than giving up, thinking clearly on what needs to be done rather than thinking erratically, negatively, and emotionally, and experiencing constructive emotionality such as hope and interest rather than counterproductive emotionality such as fear and anxiety.

Self-Efficacy or the Psychological Need for Competence?

Self-efficacy and perceived competence (introduced in Chapter 6) are similar, but not theoretically interchangeable, motivational constructs. While they can be experienced and measured in similar ways ("How competent do you feel during badminton?"), an example illustrates the difference between self-efficacy on the one hand and the psychological need for competence on the other. Imagine sitting on a bench at a playground when you see a young girl with a badminton bird, a racket, and a deep desire to bat the bird upwards time and time again (and not miss it). The sheer desire and intrinsic motivation to challenge herself for the spontaneous satisfactions the activity provides shows a proactive, challenge-seeking psychological need for competence. After a few hits, she will begin to reflect on how she is doing and formulate a judgment of her coping capacities and an expectation of how well she will do. If the wind begins to blow or if she improves her technique, then her efficacy judgment will change. The psychological need for competence, however, is more of a developmental constant and may very well motivate her to drop the racket to run over to the monkey bars to seek out and try to master a new challenge.

A second key distinction between self-efficacy and the psychological need for competence is that self-efficacy beliefs are specific to particular tasks and situations, whereas the psychological need for competence is a general pan-situational experience. Even as the person plays a game of tennis, "tennis self-efficacy" is much too broad a way of thinking. Instead of thinking about a general tennis self-efficacy, it is more productive to think about "forehand self-efficacy," "backhand self-efficacy," "serving self-efficacy," "return of serve self-efficacy," "return of serve against a left-handed opponent self-efficacy," and so forth. Similarly, "self-efficacy for writing" needs to be broken down into its component dimensions (Bruning et al., 2013), including "self-efficacy for writing ideation" (e.g., "I can think of many ideas for my writing"), "self-efficacy for writing conventions" (e.g., "I can spell my words correctly"), and "self-efficacy for writing self-regulation" (e.g., "I can focus on my writing for at least one hour"). Coping behaviors are very situation specific, so the self-efficacy expectations that predict them are similarly very situationally specific.

© Ingram Publishing / Newscom

Empowerment

Two practical points about self-efficacy are important to highlight. First, self-efficacy beliefs come from personal behavior history, vicarious experiences, verbal persuasion, and physiological states (e.g., Figure 10.3). What makes this a practical point is that it means high self-efficacy beliefs can be acquired and changed. Second, the level of self-efficacy predicts ways of coping that can be called "competent functioning" or "personal empowerment."

Empowerment involves possessing the knowledge, skills, and beliefs that allow people to exert control over their lives. One example of self-efficacy as empowerment can be found in learning to defend oneself against intimidation and threats from abusive others (Ozer & Bandura, 1990). When threatened, people typically feel anxious, stressed, vulnerable, at risk, and in danger. To empower oneself, people need more than just skills and the knowledge of what to do. People also need self-efficacy beliefs so they can (1) translate their knowledge and skills into effective performance when threatened and (2) exert control over intrusive negative thoughts.

In one study, researchers trained a group of women over a five-week period in self-defense and emotion-management skills. The women felt very afraid for their safety when going out at night because they feared being overpowered by the threats and dangers of night life in San Francisco. The researchers first asked the women to watch expert models defend themselves against assailants (using vicarious experience) and then asked the women to master the modeled behavior while hearing support and encouragement from peers (using verbal persuasion) during simulated attacks (Ozer & Bandura, 1990). The women then enacted the behaviors they had seen modeled and received coaching and corrective feedback as needed (personal behavior history). With each successive week, the women's self-efficacy to control interpersonal threats and to regulate intrusive thinking soared. Once empowered, the women felt less vulnerable and began to engage in activities that were once thought to be too risky (e.g., evening recreation, outdoor exercise). Empowerment occurred as efficacy and engagement replaced doubt and avoidance.

One of the women voiced her empowerment by saying, "I feel freer and more capable than ever. I now make choices about what I will or won't do based on whether or not I want to, not whether or not it is frightening to me" (Ozer & Bandura, 1990). Understandably, the reader might wonder whether the women's increased confidence led them to behave recklessly and put them in harm's way. This did not happen. Instead, the women's generalized avoidance was replaced by flexible, adaptive, confident behavior. Such a program would seemingly be effective in practically any activity that people avoid out of a fear of being overwhelmed by situational challenges, demands, and threats.

Empowering People: Mastery Modeling Program

A formal program to empower people through self-efficacy training is to employ a mastery modeling program. In a mastery modeling program an expert in the skill area works with a group of relative novices to show them how to cope with an otherwise fearsome situation. In the example above, professionals empowered women through self-defense skills. In the school, teachers might use a mastery modeling program to empower children during reading, computers, or public speaking. On the athletic field, coaches might empower athletes with defensive skills and resilient confidence to cope with whatever offense next week's opponent might try. In the hospital and workplace, therapists and managers might empower lonely clients and anxious salespeople with social skills and resilient confidence when interacting with colleagues, clients, and strangers.

In a mastery modeling program, the expert model walks the group of novices through the following seven steps:

1. Expert identifies component skills involved in effective coping and measures novices' efficacy expectation on each component skill.

2. Expert models each component skill, emphasizing the novices' most worrisome skill areas.

3. Novices emulate each modeled skill. Expert provides guidance and corrective feedback, as needed.

4. Novices integrate the individual skills into an overall simulated performance. Expert introduces only mild obstacles and helps novices integrate the different skill components into a coherent overall performance.

5. Novices participate in cooperative learning groups. One person gives a simulated performance while peers watch. As they watch, peers provide encouragement and tips. Each person takes a turn until everyone has performed multiple times.

6. Novices perform individually in a realistic situation that features numerous difficulties, surprises, obstacles, and setbacks while the expert provides modeling and corrective feedback.

7. Expert models confident demeanor and arousal-regulating techniques.

The mastery modeling program is a formal procedure to utilize the four sources of self-efficacy as a means to advance from anxious novices to confident masters. By having novices perform each skill and receive corrective feedback from the expert, the novice builds efficacy through a personal behavior history (step 3). By watching the expert perform (step 2) and by watching similar peers perform (step 5), the novice builds efficacy through vicarious experience. By hearing peers' encouragement and tips (step 5), the novice builds efficacy through verbal persuasion. By observing and imitating the expert's ways of handling performance-debilitating arousal (step 7), the novice builds efficacy through physiological calmness. Then end result is to advance a novice who is easily overwhelmed by a seemingly unpredictable situation to a highly skilled, highly confident coper.

MASTERY BELIEFS

Mastery beliefs reflect the extent of perceived control one has over attaining desirable outcomes and preventing aversive ones (Peterson et al., 1993). When personal control beliefs are strong and resilient, the individual perceives a strong causal link between actions and outcomes. When personal control beliefs are weak and fragile, the individual perceives that personal initiatives and actions produce little effect on what happens.

Ways of Coping

How much mastery over outcomes one possesses depends on how one elects to cope with the situation at hand. Table 10.1 lists many possible ways of coping (Skinner, Edge, Altman, & Sherwood, 2003). People can cope by taking proactive or reactive action, by approaching the problem and taking action or by avoiding it and walking away, singly or in the context of a group or an organization, by focusing on the problem to be solved or by focusing on regulating their emotions, and by additional ways of coping, as illustrated in the table.

Mastery versus Helplessness

Failure means the person was not able to gain control over a desired outcome, and people cope with failure in different ways. A mastery motivational orientation refers to a hardy, resistant portrayal of the self during encounters of failure. With a mastery motivational orientation, the person responds to failure by remaining task-oriented and focused on achieving mastery in spite of difficulties and setbacks (Diener & Dweck, 1978, 1980). On the other

Table 10.1 Ways of Coping

Way of Coping	Illustration
Approach versus Avoidance	Taking action by moving toward and interacting with the problem versus walking away from the problem.
Social versus Solitary	Taking action with a team of others versus acting alone.
Proactive versus Reactive	Taking action to prevent a problem before versus after it occurs.
Direct versus Indirect	Taking action oneself versus enlisting the help of an intermediary who takes the direct action.
Control versus Escape	Take-charge approach versus staying clear of the situation.
Alloplastic versus Autoplastic	Taking action to change the problem versus taking action to change oneself.
Problem Focused versus Emotion Focused	Taking action to manage the problem causing the stress versus regulating one's emotional response to the problem.

hand, a helpless motivational orientation refers to a fragile view of the self during encounters of failure. With a helpless motivational orientation, the person responds to failure by giving up and withdrawing, acting as if the situation were out of his or her control (Dweck, 1975; Dweck & Repucci, 1973).

Most people perform well and stay task focused when working on easy problems and when performing well. However, when tasks turn difficult and challenging—when outcomes are hard to control, the motivational significance of mastery versus helplessness becomes clear. Mastery-oriented persons seize challenges and become energized by setbacks. Helpless-oriented persons shy away from challenges, fall apart in the face of setbacks, and begin to question and then outright doubt their ability. On those occasions in which success feedback slips into failure feedback, mastery-oriented individuals increase their efforts and change their strategies (Diener & Dweck, 1978, 1980). Under these same conditions, helpless-oriented individuals decrease their efforts and begin to condemn their abilities and lose hope for any future successes (Dweck, 1975; Dweck & Repucci, 1973). In sum, during failure feedback, helpless-oriented people focus on why they are failing (low ability), whereas mastery-oriented people focus on how they can remedy the failure (effort, strategy; Diener & Dweck, 1978).

The different reactions to failure feedback for mastery-oriented and failure-oriented performers emanate from a different meaning of failure (Dweck, 1999). Mastery-oriented individuals do not see failure as an indictment of the self. Instead, these individuals, during setbacks and failures, say things like, "The harder it gets, the harder I need to try" and "I love a challenge." Failure feedback is, generally speaking, just information. In fact, failure can be constructive information (Clifford, 1984). Failure feedback suggests that one needs more effort, better strategies, and more resources. Mastery-oriented individuals accept this task-generated information, make the necessary adjustments (more effort, better strategies, more resources), and they therefore actually perform better and more enthusiastically in the face of failure. Helpless-oriented individuals see failure as an indictment of the self. They see failure as a sign of personal inadequacy, one that in turn leads them toward a state of despair.

Perhaps the reader might think the term "helpless" is a bit strong, but research by Carol Dweck (1975) suggests that it is not. When failure rears its ugly head, helpless-oriented people say things like, "I'm no good at things like this" and "I guess I'm not very smart." In other words, they denigrate their abilities and even their self-worth (Diener & Dweck, 1978). Their emotions quickly turn negative, and they start to show unusual ways for dealing with their rising anxiety and doubt, such as acting silly or trying to change the task or its rules (Diener & Dweck, 1978). Their problem-solving strategies collapse into simply making wild guesses or picking answers for random reasons. The self-denigration, negative mood, and immature strategies signal the presence of helplessness, but the telltale sign of helplessness is how *quickly* and how *emphatically* the performer gives up (Dweck, 1999).

LEARNED HELPLESSNESS

Efficacy expectancies are the building blocks of self-efficacy, and outcome expectancies are the building blocks of learned helplessness. When people engage in a task, some outcome is typically at stake. During such task engagement, people make a subjective forecast of how controllable versus uncontrollable the outcome at stake is. For controllable outcomes, a one-to-one relation exists between behavior (what a person does) and outcomes (what happens to that person). For uncontrollable outcomes, a random relationship exists between behavior and outcomes (e.g., "I have no idea what effect, if any, my behavior will have on what happens to me").

When people expect desired outcomes (e.g., making friends, getting a job) or undesired outcomes (e.g., contracting an illness, being fired from a job) are independent of their behavior, they develop a "learned helplessness" over attaining or preventing those outcomes. Learned helplessness is the psychological state that results when an individual expects that life's outcomes are uncontrollable (Mikulincer, 1994; Seligman, 1975).

Boiled down to its essentials, learned helplessness can be understood by the strength of the perceived relation between the person's behavior and the person's fate, or outcome, as represented in Figure 10.4. The relation between one's behavior and one's outcomes can be very high, as represented by a solid and bold arrow between what one does and

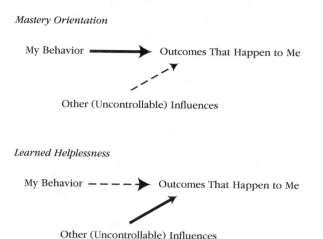

Mastery Orientation

My Behavior ⟶ Outcomes That Happen to Me

Other (Uncontrollable) Influences

Learned Helplessness

My Behavior ⤍ Outcomes That Happen to Me

Other (Uncontrollable) Influences

Figure 10.4   Illustration of the Relationship between Behavior and Outcomes, According to a Mastery Orientation and According to Learned Helplessness

what outcomes occur. The bold solid arrow between behavior and outcomes graphically represents a mastery orientation. In contrast, the relation between one's behavior and one's outcomes can be nonexistent, as represented by the dashed and thin arrow between what one does and what outcomes occur. The thin dashed arrow between behavior and outcomes graphically represents a learned helplessness orientation. With learned helplessness, one's behavior exerts little or no influence over one's outcomes. Instead, other factors outside one's control determine the outcomes, as represented by the bold solid arrow between outside influences and one's outcomes. For example, a job applicant experiencing learned helplessness might perceive that even his efficaciously enacted behaviors during the job interview (acting professionally, demonstrating skills, answering questions well) have nothing to do with whether he is hired by the company. He may perceive that factors outside his control (e.g., poor economy, "who you know," skin color) mostly or even fully determine whether he is hired. Because his behaviors do not control the outcome and because outside, uncontrollable influences do, then the job applicant presumes that he is helpless to influence the hiring decision.

Learning Helplessness

Helplessness is learned. Consider the following experiment with three groups of dogs that were administered either (1) inescapable shock, (2) escapable shock, or (3) no shock (control group) (Seligman & Maier, 1967). Dogs in the two shock groups were placed into a sling and given mild 5-second electric shocks once a day for 64 consecutive days. In the *inescapable shock* group, the shocks occurred randomly, and no response could terminate the shock. Whether the dog barked, howled, or thrashed about frantically, the shock continued for its full 5 seconds. In other words, the shock was inescapable. The outcome (shock) was uncontrollable. In the *escapable shock* group, the dogs could terminate the shock. If the dog pressed a button mounted on the wall (placed just in front of their noses), the shock stopped. The dogs therefore had a response available to escape the shock—push the button. They had to learn the response, but the outcome (shock) was controllable. In the *no-shock control* group, dogs were placed into a sling just like the dogs in the other two conditions were but they received no shocks.

Exposure to inescapable shock, escapable shock, or no shock constituted the first phase—the learning phase—of the two-phase experiment. In the second phase, the dogs in each group were all treated the same. Each dog was placed into a shuttle box in which its two compartments were separated by a wall partition of elbow height. The two compartments were the same size and similar in most respects, except the first compartment had a grid floor through which a mild electrical shock could be delivered while the second compartment was safe from shock. On each trial during phase 2, the dogs were placed into the grid floor compartment and a mild shock was delivered. The onset of this shock was always preceded by a signal (a dimming of the light on the wall). After the lights were dimmed, the electric shock followed 10 seconds thereafter. If the dog jumped over the partition, it escaped the shock. So, for all the dogs, the shock was both predictable and preventable (i.e., controllable) during the second phase of the study. If the dog failed to jump over the partition within 10 seconds, however, the electric shock started and continued for 1 minute.

A summary of the study's procedure and results appears in Table 10.2 (Seligman & Maier, 1967). The dogs in both the escapable shock and no shock groups quickly learned

Table 10.2 Results of a Prototypical Learned Helplessness Study

Experimental condition	Phase 1	Phase 2	Results
Inescapable Shock	Received shock, no coping response could terminate the shock	Received an escapable shock	Failed to escape from the shock
Escapable Shock	Received shock, pressing nose against button could terminate shock	Received an escapable shock	Quickly learned to escape shock by jumping over barrier
Control, No Shock	Received no shocks	Received an escapable shock	Quickly learned to escape shock by jumping over barrier

to escape the shock in the shuttle box. When shocked, these dogs ran about frantically at first and rather accidentally climbed, fell, scrambled, or jumped over the barrier. That is, through trial and error and through the sheer grit of determination, the dogs learned that if they somehow overstepped the barrier, they could escape the shock. After only a few trials, these dogs jumped over the barrier to safety as soon as the warning light dimmed. They learned mastery over very stressful conditions. These dogs learned how to control (prevent) the shock.

The dogs in the inescapable shock group behaved very differently. When shocked, these dogs at first behaved as the other dogs did by running about frantically and howling. However, unlike the dogs in the other two groups, these dogs soon stopped running around and, instead, whimpered until the trial (and shock) terminated. After only a few trials, these dogs gave up trying to escape and passively accepted the shock. On subsequent trials, the dogs failed to make any escape movements at all. What these dogs learned in the sling—that the onset, duration, intensity, and termination of the shock (in phase 1) were all beyond their control—had a carryover effect in the shuttle box: The dogs perceived that escape was beyond their control. These dogs learned helplessness in the face of very stressful conditions.

The startling generalization that emerged from this study is that whenever animals are placed in a situation in which they perceive they have little or no control, they develop the expectation that their future actions will have little or no effect on what happens to them. This learned expectation that one's voluntary behavior will not affect desired outcomes is the heart of learned helplessness.

Application to Humans

The early experiments on learned helplessness used animals as research participants mostly because the uncontrollable events used in these studies included traumatic events, such as electric shock. Later studies found ways to test the extent to which helplessness applied to humans (Diener & Dweck, 1978, 1980; Dweck, 1975; Hiroto, 1974; Hiroto & Seligman, 1975; Mikulincer, 1994; Peterson et al., 1993). In Donald Hiroto's (1974) experiment, irritating noise constituted the aversive, traumatic stimulus event. The results with humans paralleled the results with dogs (see Table 10.2) in that participants in the inescapable noise group sat passively and were unwilling to attempt an escape from the noise, whereas participants in the escapable and no-noise groups learned quickly to escape the noise (by operating a lever). Humans too learned helplessness.

To demonstrate how learned helplessness operates, try to solve problems that vary in how controllable they are: Can you solve academic problems? relationship problems? financial problems? health problems? If your car broke down on the highway, would you try to cope or would you turn passive?

Looking at the sequence of four cards shown in Figure 10.5, consider an experiment in which the participant's task is to figure out which feature the experimenter is looking for—triangle or square, dot or star, shaded or white. A series of 10 cards appear in sequential order and the participant's task is to identify which feature is being tracked. On the first card, he simply guesses "left" or "right," and the experimenter replies "correct" or "incorrect." The same procedure occurs for the following nine cards. For instance, a person who is tracking the hypothesis of "square" would choose right, right, left, and right (in the four cards shown in Figure 10.5).

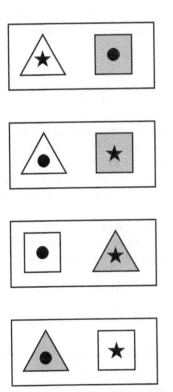

Figure 10.5   Sample of a Problem Used in the Study of Learned Helplessness with Humans

Source: From "An analysis of learned helplessness: Continuous changes in performance, strategy, and achievement cognitions following failure," by C. I. Diener and C. S. Dweck, 1978, *Journal of Personality and Social Psychology, 36*, pp. 451–462. Copyright 1978 by the American Psychological Association. Reprinted with permission.

Now imagine that in one condition, the experimenter (or a computer program) provided authentic feedback such that the participant could, with concentration and effort, use the feedback provided to figure out the answer to the problem. In other words, the problem is controllable, at least with concentration and effort. In a second condition, however, the feedback was random and bogus. With random feedback, the participant could try all the hypotheses in the world and only gain a sense of confusion and frustration for the effort. After several of these problems, the second phase of the study begins as all participants (in both conditions) are asked to solve some moderately difficult problems (e.g., multiplication problems, six-letter anagrams). The consistent finding is that people exposed to solvable problems in the first phase of the study solve significantly more problems in the second phase than do people exposed to unsolvable problems in the first phase (Diener & Dweck, 1978). It is not so much how smart and clever the participant is that matters; instead, it is how responsive and controllable the environment is while one attempts to solve problems.

Components

Learned helplessness theory features three components: contingency, cognition, and behavior (Peterson et al., 1993). Collectively, these three components explain the motivational dynamics that unfold as experience teaches people to expect that the events in their lives will be beyond their personal control.

Contingency

Contingency refers to the objective relation between a person's behavior and the environment's outcomes. The environment can be the home, classroom, workplace, sports field, hospital, interpersonal relationship, psychology laboratory, and so on. Contingency exists on a continuum that ranges from outcomes that occur on a random, noncontingent basis (i.e., uncontrollable outcomes) to outcomes that occur in perfect synchronization with a person's voluntary behavior (i.e., controllable outcomes). That is, how contingent any one environment is can be scored on a continuum that ranges from 0 (uncontrollable outcomes) to 1 (controllable outcomes).

Take a moment to ask yourself what your own experiences have taught you about contingency in the following situations: getting a traffic ticket, getting a job in your hometown, winning a tennis match against a rival, winning the lottery, catching the flu, getting cancer from smoking cigarettes, gaining weight over the holidays, and graduating from college. To characterize the contingency inherent in each of these situations, ask yourself the following: "To what extent does the average person's voluntary, strategic behavior influence the outcomes that occur in these settings?" That is, how much influence does voluntary coping behavior (from people in general, not from you in particular) exert on avoiding a traffic ticket, avoiding the flu, getting a job, winning a contest, winning the lottery, escaping cancer, preventing weight gain, and obtaining a college degree?

Cognition

A good deal of cognitive interpretation takes place between the actual, objective environmental contingencies that exist in the world and a person's subjective understanding of personal control in such environments. Mental events distort the relationship between objective contingencies and subjective control, and these events therefore create some margin of error between objective truth and subjective understanding.

Three cognitive elements are particularly important: biases (e.g., the "illusion of control"); attributions (explanations of *why* we think we do or do not have control); and expectancies, which are the subjective personal control beliefs we carry over from past experiences into our current situation. To illustrate the importance of cognition, ask two people who experience the same environmental contingency why they avoided a traffic ticket, avoided the flu, got a job, and so on. People's outcome beliefs (and hence their replies to your question) stem not only from the objective information about the world (i.e., contingency) but also from each person's unique biases, attributions, and expectancies. Hence, to understand learned helplessness, we need to pay attention not only to objective environmental contingencies (how controllable outcomes really are) but also to subjective personal control beliefs (how controllable the person thinks those outcomes are).

Behavior

Just as contingency exists on a continuum, coping behavior to attain or to prevent outcomes exists on a continuum. In a traumatic event, for instance, people's voluntary coping behavior varies from very passive to very active.

Coping responses can be lethargic and passive, or they can be active and assertive. Lethargy, passivity, and giving up typify a listless, demoralized effort that characterizes the behavior of the helpless individual (recall the passive behavior of the dogs in the inescapable shock group). Alertness, activity, and assertiveness characterize people who are not helpless (who have some expectation of control). To illustrate passive behavior as a component of learned helplessness, consider once again the situations listed earlier (driving on the highway, job hunting, competing against an opponent). Consider your own passive-to-active coping behaviors in the face of such situations and potential outcomes. The job hunter who quits searching for online advertisements, revising her résumé, telephoning prospective employers, and rising early and enthusiastically in the morning to look for a job manifests the listless, demoralized coping behavior that characterizes helplessness.

Helplessness Effects

Learned helplessness occurs when people expect that their voluntary behavior will produce little or no effect on the outcomes they strive to attain or avoid. Once it occurs, it leaves three reliable deficits in its wake: motivational, learning, and emotional (Alloy & Seligman, 1979).

Motivational Deficits

Motivational deficits consist of a decreased willingness to try. Motivational deficits become apparent when a person's willingness to emit voluntary coping responses decreases or disappears altogether. Typically, when people care about an outcome and when the environment is at least somewhat responsive in delivering those outcomes, they act enthusiastically and assertively in bringing about those outcomes. For instance, at the beginning of a season, an athlete might practice diligently and persistently, but after a series of athletic defeats (victory becomes an uncontrollable outcome), willingness to practice wanes. The athlete begins to wonder if the time spent practicing is really worth it. In the aversive-noise learned helplessness experiment described earlier, the experimenters asked participants why they did not use the lever to try to terminate the unpleasant noise (Thorton & Jacobs, 1971). Approximately 60 percent of the participants (from the inescapable noise group) reported that they felt little control over the noise so did not see the point in trying to terminate the noise, saying "Why try?" "Why try?" characterizes the motivational deficit in learned helplessness.

Learning Deficits

Learning deficits consist of an acquired pessimistic set that interferes with one's ability to learn new response–outcome contingencies. Over time, exposure to uncontrollable environments cultivates an expectancy in which people believe that outcomes are generally independent of their actions. Once expectancies take on a pessimistic tone, the person has a very difficult time learning (or, more precisely, relearning) that a new response can affect outcomes. This pessimistic set essentially interferes with, or retards, the learning of future response–outcome contingencies (Alloy & Seligman, 1979).

When students first learn the results from learned helplessness experiments, they frequently wonder why dogs in the inescapable groups do not learn in the second phase of the experiment that jumping over the barrier terminates the shock. Like talking to a laid-off worker who has given up applying for a new job, one wants to yell (to the dog): "Jump! Jump! C'mon boy, just jump!" Consider, however, what the human subjects learned during the noise blast study. The first time they heard the noise, they flinched and jumped, and the second time, they manipulated the lever. Perhaps they perceived that on some trials turning their heads or shifting their weight from side to side coincided with the turning off of the noise. But on later trials, they again turned their heads or shifted their weight, but the noise persisted for its programmed 5 seconds. Gradually, they learned that no response turned off the noise in a reliable way. They tried everything, but nothing worked. Consequently, when they entered the second phase of the experiment with the now-working lever, any positive outcome (turning off the noise) comes across as a "successful accident" and unworthy of being tried again (as were head turning, lever turning, weight shifting, and so forth in the first phase). Compared to the participants in the escapable noise and control groups who quickly learned to discriminate between responses that worked versus responses that did not work, participants in the inescapable noise groups had an unusually difficult time learning an effective coping response.

Emotional Deficits

Emotional deficits consist of affective disruptions in which lethargic, depressive emotional reactions occur in situations that call for active, assertive emotion. In the face of trauma, the natural and typical human response is one of highly mobilized emotion (e.g., fear, anger, assertiveness, frustration). When afraid, people struggle vigorously to overcome, escape, counteract, or do whatever is necessary to cope effectively. Over time, however, an unrelenting onslaught of environmental unresponsiveness leads people to view coping as futile. Once fear-mobilized emotionality is believed to be unproductive, depression-related emotionality takes its place. Once the person becomes convinced that there is nothing that can be done to escape the trauma, the resulting expectation makes energy-mobilizing emotions less likely and makes energy-depleting emotions (e.g., listlessness, apathy, depression) more likely.

Helplessness and Depression

Some clinical psychologists view learned helplessness as a model of naturally occurring unipolar depression (Rosenhan & Seligman, 1984; Seligman, 1975). Learned helplessness and depression are similar in that the same expectations cause both: The individual expects that bad events will occur, and there is nothing she can do to prevent their occurrence (Rosenhan & Seligman, 1984). Learned helplessness and depression also share common symptoms (passivity, low self-esteem, loss of appetite) and therapeutic intervention strategies (time, cognitive behavior modification).

Using the learned helplessness model to understand the etiology of unipolar depression touched off a flurry of research that brought both strong criticism (Costello, 1978; Depue & Monroe, 1978) and strong support (Seligman, 1975). One of the most exciting findings to emerge is that depressed individuals sometimes see the events in their lives as less controllable than do individuals who are not depressed. Such a finding led researchers to wonder whether the depressive tendency of individuals to see their worlds as uncontrollable might be the core cause of unipolar depression. Perhaps the root of depression lies in a depressed individual's inability to recognize that he has more control over his life outcomes than he knows. If so, the therapy recommendation would be clear—namely, increase the person's perceived control beliefs.

Depressed and non-depressed college students (as assessed by a questionnaire) performed a task in which they pushed a button on some trials and did not push it on other trials (Alloy & Abramson, 1979). With a button push, a green light sometimes came on. The point of the study was for the participant to estimate what proportion of time the green light came on. The experimenters controlled the outcome—whether the light came on and when it came on. For one group, the green light came on 75 percent of the time and only when the button was pressed. This was the high-control group. For a second group, the green light came on when the button was pressed 75 percent of the time, but the light also came on 50 percent of the time when no button was pushed. This was the low-control group. In a final group, the green light came on when the button was pressed 75 percent of the time, but it also came on 75 percent of the time when the participants did not push the button. This was the no-control group (because the light came on at the same rate regardless of the participant's button pressing).

Results were most surprising (see Figure 10.6). Depressed individuals accurately judged how much control they had over each situation, as did nondepressed individuals except in one condition, namely in the no-control situation (Alloy & Abramson, 1979). The depressed individuals accurately judged that they had no control in this condition. The light came on in a random way, and they knew it. The nondepressed individuals were the ones who misperceived how much control they had—they overestimated their perceived control.

The most interesting conclusion to draw from Lauren Alloy and Lyn Abramson's (1979, 1982) research is that people with depression are *not* more prone to learned helplessness deficits. Rather, it is the individuals who are not depressed who sometimes believe they have more personal control than they actually have (Taylor & Brown, 1988, 1994). Although the conclusion might sound startling, depressed persons' memories for the positive and negative events in their lives are balanced and equal, whereas the memories of the nondepressed persons harbor biases for recalling more of the positive events (Sanz, 1996). While people misjudge the control they have over the events in their lives

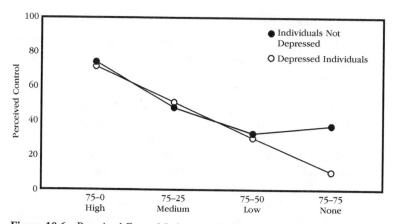

Figure 10.6 Perceived Control Judgments for Depressed and Nondepressed Individuals

Source: From "Judgments of contingency in depressed and nondepressed students: Sadder but wiser?" by L.B. Alloy and L.T. Abramson, 1979, *Journal of Experimental Psychology: General*, *108*, pp. 441–485. Copyright 1979 by the American Psychological Association. Adapted with permission.

(Abramson & Alloy, 1980; Alloy & Abramson, 1979, 1982; Langer, 1975; Nisbett & Ross, 1980), most of the misjudging is done by nondepressed individuals, not by those who are depressed.

Attributions and Explanatory Style

No motivation theory pursues the "why?" question more than does attribution theory. An attribution is a causal explanation for why a particular success-failure outcome occurred (Weiner, 1985, 1986). After a person succeeds or fails, he or she asks why. Why did I make an A on the test? Why did I lose the contest? Why did I get the job, while she did not? Why did I succeed today on the same task that I failed yesterday? There may be an almost limitless number of possible causal attributions, but when explaining their successes and failures, people tend to rely on a small number of attributions, including effort, ability, strategy, luck, and task difficulty (Weiner, 1986), although other common attributions include intelligence, extent of experience, task enjoyment, or help from others (Shell, Colvin, & Bruning, 1995).

Although many different attributions are possible, all attributions can be placed within a three-dimensional causal structure, as illustrated graphically in Figure 10.7. Dimension 1 is locus, which distinguishes between internal versus external causes of outcomes. Dimension 2 is stability, which distinguishes between stable and unstable causes. Dimension 3 is controllability, which distinguishes between controllable and uncontrollable causes.

Explanatory style is a relatively stable, cognitively based personality variable that reflects the way people explain the reasons why bad events happen to them (Peterson & Barrett, 1987; Peterson & Park, 1998; Peterson & Seligman, 1984). Bad events happen to everyone, but people explain these setbacks with attributions that vary in their locus, stability, and controllability. As shown on the right side of Figure 10.7, an *optimistic explanatory style* manifests itself as the tendency to explain bad events with attributions that are unstable and controllable (e.g., "I lost the contest because of a poor strategy"). As shown on the

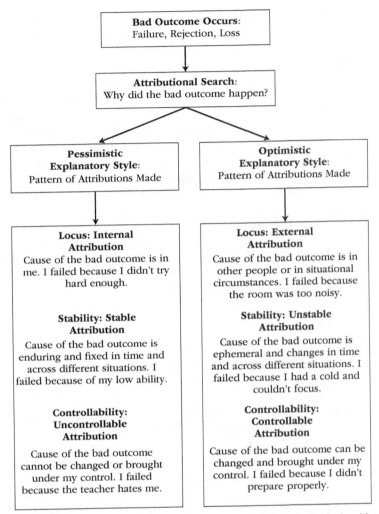

Figure 10.7   Differential Patterns of Attributions Made by Individuals with a Pessimistic versus an Optimistic Explanatory Style

left side of Figure 10.7, a *pessimistic explanatory style* manifests itself as the tendency to explain bad events with attributions that are stable and uncontrollable (e.g., "I lost the contest because I'm too small to compete"). Figure 10.7 shows that attributional optimists and pessimists use all three dimensions of locus, stability, and controllability, but the two attributional dimensions that best distinguish and define attributional pessimists versus attributional optimists are the two shown at the bottom of the figure: stability and controllability.

Pessimistic Explanatory Style

Academic failures, poor physical health, and subpar job performance are common. They happen to us all. Some of us react to such failures by increasing effort and by trying even harder than before. Others react by giving up. A pessimistic explanatory style predisposes people toward the latter response—giving up—in times of failure and setbacks.

When a student with a pessimistic style faces such educational frustrations and failures (e.g., disappointing grades, unintelligible lectures, confusing textbooks), she typically responds with a passive, fatalistic coping style that leads to decreased effort and deteriorating grades (Peterson & Barrett, 1987). As to job performance, one vocation with more than its share of frustrations, failures, and rejections is selling life insurance because only a small percentage of potential clients ever buy a policy. One pair of researchers assessed life insurance agents' explanatory styles and recorded which agents performed well or poorly and which agents stayed on the job or quit (Seligman & Schulman, 1986). The attributionally pessimistic agents were more likely to quit, and those attributional pessimists who continued to work performed significantly worse than did their more optimistic peers.

Overall, a pessimistic explanatory style is associated with academic failure (Peterson & Barrett, 1987), social distress (Sacks & Bugental, 1987), physical illness (Peterson, Seligman, & Vaillant, 1988), impaired job performance (Seligman & Schulman, 1986), depression (Beck, 1976), and even electoral defeat in presidential elections (Zullow, Oettingen, Peterson, & Seligman, 1988).[1]

Optimistic Explanatory Style

The illusion of control is an attributional phenomenon that, over time, fosters an optimistic explanatory style. People with an optimistic explanatory style tend to take substantial credit for their successes but accept little or no blame for their failures (e.g., "It's not my fault that I am unemployed, divorced, broke, and had a car accident last month. I am, however, responsible for my team winning the softball game last night."). As you might expect, depressed individuals rarely have an optimistic style and do not show an illusion of control (Alloy & Abramson, 1979, 1982).

Equipped with the self-serving bias of an illusion of control, people with an optimistic explanatory style readily ignore negative self-related information, impose distorting filters on incoming information, and interpret positive and negative outcomes in self-protecting ways. In one sense, an optimistic explanatory style is delusional. The extent to which a person harbors an optimistic explanatory style is correlated with both a full repertoire of excuses, denials, and self-deceptions (Lazarus, 1983; Sackeim, 1983; Tennen & Affleck, 1987) and narcissism (John & Robins, 1994). Narcissists hold a grandiose sense of self-importance, tend to exaggerate their talents and achievements, and expect to be recognized as superior without commensurate achievements (Kohut, 1971; Millon, 1990; Westen, 1990). But most of us are not narcissists, at least not in the clinical sense of the term. For most of us (depressives and narcissists aside), an optimistic explanatory style is functionally an *asset*, because a "mentally healthy person appears to have the

---

[1] Care must be exercised in interpreting these correlational data, however, because it certainly could be the case that poor grades, nonresponsive partners, and difficulties at work lead individuals toward adopting a pessimistic style. Thus, one can say that a pessimistic style and mental and physical well-being correlate negatively, but one cannot say definitively that a pessimistic style causes mental and physical distress. Researchers continue to investigate the causal status of a pessimistic explanatory style in coping with life's setbacks (Peterson et al., 1993).

enviable capacity to distort reality in a direction that enhances self-esteem, maintains beliefs in personal efficacy, and promotes an optimistic view of the future" (Taylor & Brown, 1988).

Alternative Explanations

The learned helplessness model is not without its critics (Costello, 1978; Weiss, Glazer, & Pohorecky, 1976; Wortman & Brehm, 1975). The central question under debate is just what causes helplessness. In the learned helplessness model, helplessness follows from a cognitive event, namely the expectation of a response → outcome independence (recall Figure 10.4). But, learned helplessness experiments induce participants with trauma, and it could be that traumatic events themselves (e.g., shocks, noise blasts, unsolvable problems) induce helplessness. Through clever and sophisticated research designs (i.e., triadic design with a yoking procedure), researchers found that it was indeed the learned expectation, not the trauma itself, that produces helplessness (Weiss, 1972).

Other researchers argue that the expectation of failure, rather than the expectation of uncontrollability per se, induces helplessness. But investigators' clever research designs showed that failure, more often than not, actually produces a positive motivation (a phenomenon discussed in the next section under "Reactance Theory") and that it is the expectation of uncontrollability, not the expectation of failure, that causes learned helplessness deficits (Winefield, Barnett, & Tiggemann, 1985).

Yet a third possibility is that uncontrollable events induce helplessness deficits not because they are uncontrollable but because they are unpredictable (Winefield, 1982). It is extremely difficult, and probably impossible, to separate uncontrollability from unpredictability, and research shows that predictability does indeed mitigate learned helplessness deficits. The conclusion is that perceived uncontrollability is a necessary, but not a sufficient, condition for inducing learned helplessness deficits. For sufficiency, uncontrollability must coincide with unpredictability (Tiggemann & Winefield, 1987). When life's rejections, losses, failures, and setbacks are perceived to be *both* uncontrollable and unpredictable, people are vulnerable to learned helplessness.

One alternative explanation for why people turn passive and give up in the face of uncontrollable outcomes is that people are actually motivated to remain passive. People are motivated to be passive if they sense that active responding will only make matters worse (Wortman & Brehm, 1975). In the face of a hurricane (an uncontrollable, unpredictable event), for example, it is possible that people are passive and helpless because they believe that negative outcomes will be more likely when they respond compared to when they do not respond. If this is the case, passivity is actually an enlightened and strategic coping response that minimizes trauma. For a second example, imagine the socially anxious person who does not voluntarily engage in social interaction because of a belief that she will only make matters worse by initiating conversations. Perhaps this person is correct. By intentionally not initiating interactions, the anxious person may very well avoid making circumstances worse (by keeping secret her lack of social skill). Thus, looked at in a different light, passivity can be, in some circumstances, a strategic coping response rather than a motivational deficit. This question of whether the exercise of personal control is always desirable is addressed in Box 10.

BOX 10   *Is Personal Control Always Good?*

Question: Why is this information important?

Answer: To answer the questions of, "Is personal control always good?", and "Is more control always better?"

We live in the age of personal control. Indeed, the title of five books featured in this chapter are *Self-Efficacy: The Exercise of Control* (Bandura, 1997), *Learned Helplessness: A Theory for the Age of Personal Control* (Peterson et al., 1993), *Perceived Control, Motivation, and Coping* (Skinner, 1995), *Desire for Control: Personality, Social, and Clinical Perspectives* (Burger, 1992), and *The Psychology of Hope: You Can Get There from Here* (Snyder, 1994).

Generally speaking, people want control, overestimate how much control they have in practically all situations, are optimistic about their ability to achieve control when they do not yet have it, believe they have more skill and greater ability than they actually have, and underestimate how vulnerable they are to overpowering circumstances (Lewinsohn, Mischel, Chaplin, & Barton, 1980; Seligman, 1991; Taylor & Brown, 1988, 1994; Weinstein, 1984, 1993). And people generally benefit from these perceptions and beliefs of control in terms of greater psychological and physical well-being (Bandura, 1997; Rodin & Langer, 1977; Seligman, 1991). The conclusion seems to be the following: Having control is good, and the more control you have, the better (Evans, Shapiro, & Lewis, 1993; Shapiro, Schwartz, & Astin, 1996; Thompson, 1981).

This conclusion presumes, however, that the world is a controllable place. Sometimes people unrealistically desire control, their skills and abilities are not up to par, and they find themselves in uncontrollable situations. In this light, control for *all* situations seems delusional. When you believe you have control when the environment is actually uncontrollable (i.e., the illusion of control) and when you lack the skill necessary to cope with a talent-demanding domain (i.e., low competence), the typical result is futile activity, negative emotion (e.g., depression), and even physical illness (e.g., cardiovascular hyperactivity; Shapiro et al., 1996).

Consider the figure below. People harbor personal control beliefs (i.e., psychological control factors). They bring these beliefs (self-efficacy, mastery beliefs, hope) into situations that vary in how controllable and predictable they are. Some situations match the person's control beliefs, while others do not. Person–environment matches, rather than personal control beliefs per se, predict positive well-being and physical health outcomes. And person–environment mismatches, rather than personal vulnerability beliefs, predict physical illness and mental irregulation. The three-part conclusion is that (1) people sometimes want too much control for their own good, (2) understanding objective control can be as important as boosting perceived control, and (3) control is adaptive and beneficial in controllable environments but potentially maladaptive in uncontrollable environments, such as gambling (Shapiro et al., 1996).

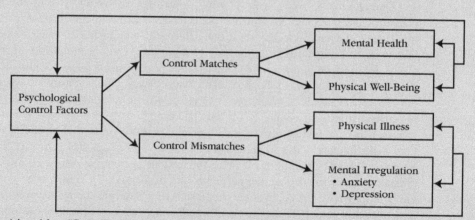

Source: Adapted from "Controlling ourselves, controlling our world: Psychology's role in understanding positive and negative consequences of seeking and gaining control," by D.H. Shapiro Jr., C.E. Schwartz, and J.A. Astin, 1996, *American Psychologist*, *51*, pp. 1213–1230. Copyright 1996 by the American Psychological Association. Adapted with permission.

REACTANCE THEORY

Why do people sometimes do precisely the opposite of what they are told to do? Why do people refuse another person's well-intended favor? Why does propaganda backfire? These are the questions posed by reactance theorists (Brehm, 1966; Brehm & Brehm, 1981). Any instruction, any favor, any advice, no matter how well intended, has the potential to interfere with people's expected freedoms in making up their own minds. When children do precisely what they were told not to do, when gift recipients are more resentful than thankful, and when the targets of propaganda do the opposite of the source's intention, each performs a counter maneuver aimed at reestablishing a threatened freedom. The term *reactance* refers to the psychological and behavioral attempt at reestablishing ("reacting" against) a threatened or eliminated freedom.

Reactance and Helplessness

People experience reactance only if they expect to have control over what happens to them to the point that they react to a loss of control by becoming more active, even aggressive. Both reactance and learned helplessness theories therefore focus on how people react to uncontrollable outcomes. But the two theories suggest that people act in very different ways. Recognizing this discrepancy, Camille Wortman and Jack Brehm (1975) proposed an integrative model of reactance and learned helplessness.

If a person expects to be able to control important outcomes, exposure to uncontrollable outcomes arouses reactance (Wortman & Brehm, 1975). Thus, in the first few trials in a learned helplessness experiment, the person should show vigorous opposition to the uncontrollable environment. Recall that the dogs in the inescapable shock group in the learned helplessness studies first howled, kicked, and generally thrashed about for several trials before eventually becoming helpless. These active, assertive coping efforts usually pay off in life as they enable people and animals to reestablish control. Over time, however, if the environment continues to be uncontrollable, people eventually learn that control attempts are futile. Once a person becomes convinced that reactance behaviors exert little or no influence over the uncontrollable situation, he shows the passivity of helplessness.

The critical difference in predicting whether an individual will show reactance or helplessness is the perceived status of the uncontrollable outcome. As long as the person perceives that coping behavior can affect outcomes, reactance behaviors persist. It is only after the person perceives a response–outcome independence (i.e., the unequivocal loss of a behavioral freedom) that he slips into helplessness. Expectations of control foster reactance; expectations of no control foster helplessness.

For an illustration of reactance and helplessness responses, consider the following experiment (Mikulincer, 1988). One group of participants worked on one unsolvable problem, a second group worked on a series of four unsolvable problems, and a third group did not work on any problems (control group). Mario Mikulincer (1988) reasoned that exposure to one unsolvable problem would produce reactance and actually improve performance, while repeated exposure to unsolvable problems would produce helplessness and impair performance. In the second phase of the experiment, all participants worked on a set of solvable problems. As predicted, participants given one unsolvable problem performed the best, participants given four unsolvable problems performed the worst, and participants not given any problems performed in between these two groups. This finding provides strong support for the ideas that (1) both reactance and helplessness arise from outcome expectancies; (2) reactance is rooted in perceived control, whereas helplessness is rooted in its absence; (3) a reactance response precedes a helplessness response; and (4) reactance enhances performance, whereas helplessness undermines it.

HOPE

Hope emerges out of an integrated two-part cognitive motivational system. When people have both the motivation to pursue their goals and the ways to achieve those goals, they experience hope (Snyder, 1994; Snyder et al., 1991). The first part of hope involves high self-efficacy, or the "I can do it" belief in their capacity to accomplish the goals they set for themselves. The second part of hope involves clear pathways, or the belief that one has multiple and controllable pathways to goal attainment. Together, high self-efficacy supports confidence, while mastery beliefs support optimism. A glance back to Figures 10.1 and 10.2 shows how efficacy expectations and outcome expectations work together; when both are positive, the overall emotional experience is one of hope.

Central (and somewhat uniquely) to the experience of hope is pathway thinking, or the belief that one can generate multiple viable routes to desired goals, as people say to themselves, "I'll find a way to get this done" and "I am not going to let these obstacles stop me" (Snyder, Lapointe, Crowson, & Early, 1998). The athlete preparing for a match or the salesperson trying to close a sale feels hope only when she can generate at least one, and often more than one, controllable routes to the desired goal (scoring points, making a sale). Having multiple pathways to goal attainment is important because environmental obstacles (opponent's strategy, competitor's products) often close off one pathway, suggesting that, "No, you will not be able to do this." Closing a pathway to a goal does not diminish hope if the performer has a number of alternative pathways to the goal. All goals have obstacles to their eventual attainment, so hope follows from knowing that one has more pathways to a goal than the environment has obstacles to block them. Hopeful thinking emerges only out of *both* agentic and pathways thinking (Snyder, 1994).

In college, high-hope freshmen achieve higher GPAs and are more likely to graduate from college five years later than are low-hope freshmen (Snyder, Shorey, et al., 2002). During athletic performance, high-hope track athletes outperform low-hope athletes during stressful competitions (even after controlling for ability; Curry et al., 1997). Facing physical illnesses (e.g., chronic pain, blindness), high-hope patients remain appropriately energized and focused on finding pathways to cope with their illness (Elliot, Witty, Herrick, & Hoffman, 1991; Jackson et al., 1998).

Why do high-hope individuals outperform and outcope their low-hope counterparts? High-hope persons (Snyder, 1994; Snyder et al., 1998; Snyder, Rand, & Sigmond, 2002):

1. Establish specific and short-term, rather than vague and long-term, goals.

2. Set mastery (learning), rather than performance, achievement goals.

3. Rely on self-congruent goals, rather than on self-discordant goals.

4. Engage goals with intrinsic, rather than extrinsic, motivation.

5. Are less easily distracted by external obstacles or by task-irrelevant (distracting) thoughts and negative feelings.

6. Generate multiple pathways and pursue other avenues when stumped rather than stick stubbornly with one approach.

7. Have reservoirs of internally generated determination ("I will get this done"; "Keep going!").

From a cognitive-motivational point of view, high-hope individuals tap into their motivational resources of confidence, self-efficacy, optimism, and mastery beliefs. In doing so, they find the motivational support to overcome life's challenges and obstacles. As one example, Rick Snyder appeared on *Good Morning America* and asked the host, the weatherman, and the show's medical expert to engage in the cold pressor task—submerging their right hand into ice water for as long as they could (as told by Lopez, 2006). After a commercial break, the host asked Snyder what this had to do with hope. He explained that he asked each person to complete the self-report hope scale prior to the show. He then revealed the rank order of hope scores for the three cast members to show how well the hope scores predicted how long each person was able to withstand the numbing pain before quitting.

EXPECTANCY-VALUE MODEL

Not only do expectancies predict effort, persistence, choices, and performance, so do values. Some expectancy-value models of motivation therefore prefer an expectancy-value framework over a pure expectancy model. One example is the Expectancy-Value model of achievement (Eccles & Wigfield, 2002), which appears in graphical form in Figure 10.8. As shown on the right side of Figure 10.8, expectancy and value both predict achievement-related performance and choices, although expectancies more strongly predict performance while values more strongly predict choices (to approach or to avoid the activity) (Eccles et al., 1983; Eccles, Adler, & Meece, 1984; Meece, Wigfield, & Eccles, 1990).

In most (but not all) expectancy-value theories, expectancies correspond to outcomes expectancies. That is, in an achievement task, the individual makes a forecast of how likely is task success versus failure (e.g., a good vs. bad grade, applause vs. ridicule from an audience, acceptance vs. rejection). Expectancies are formed based on the person's past experiences that underlie perceptions of competence, ability beliefs, and task

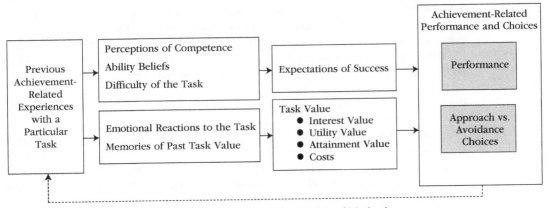

Figure 10.8 Graphical Representation of Expectancy-Value Models of Motivation

difficulty judgments. The new concept in expectancy-value theories, however, is value. Value is defined as the perceived attractiveness of a task, and value is relative in that the value of one task is compared and contrasted to the value of other possible tasks (e.g., how attractive is this particular motivation course, relative to how attractive are the other courses you are taking—or could have potentially taken—this semester)? Value has four components: interest value, utility value, attainment value, and costs.

Interest value is the feeling of interest-enjoyment the person experiences from performing the task. Utility value is how useful the task is in advancing the person's current and future goals, such as career or occupational goals. In the language of Chapter 5, interest value is similar to intrinsic motivation, while utility value is similar to identified regulation or autonomous self-regulation. Attainment value is the personal importance of doing well on the task, which means that doing well affirms or confirms an important part of the person's identity and self-concept (e.g., "I value marathons and choose to run them because doing so confirms my self-view that I am an athlete"). Cost represents the negative aspect of engaging in the task. Engaging in the task, for instance, may produce feelings of anxiety, just as it requires time and effort. Engaging in the task also represents a lost opportunity to engage in alternative tasks (e.g., choosing to read a book means that you will not have time to play basketball, and vice versa). All four aspects of value predict approach versus avoidance choices, such as choosing to engage in a highly valued task and choosing to avoid engaging in a low value task.

Both expectancy and value are mental states. They are cognitive sources of motivation and, like all cognitive sources of motivation, are learned from experience. These learning experiences appear in Figure 10.8 as the left-to-right arrows. But, as shown in the dashed right-to-left line on bottom of the figure, achievement-related performances (success versus failure) and achievement-related choices (approach versus avoidance) feedback to provide the individual with information to revise and update his or her future expectancies and future values.

SUMMARY

The focus throughout the chapter was the motivation to exercise personal control to attain positive outcomes and to prevent negative ones. As people try to control the events in their lives, they acquire two types of expectancies about their control: efficacy and outcome. Efficacy expectations are forecasts about one's capacity to competently enact a particular course of action (e.g., "Can I do it?"). Outcome expectancies are forecasts that a particular outcome will be achieved (or prevented) once a given action is adequately executed (e.g., "Will it work?"). Before people are willing to exert coping efforts to exert personal control, both efficacy and outcome expectancies must be reasonably high.

Self-efficacy is the individual's belief that he "has what it takes" to marshal together the resources needed to cope effectively with the changing and potentially overwhelming demands of a situation. Self-efficacy arises from (1) personal behavior history of trying to execute that particular course of action in the past, (2) observations of similar others as they execute the same behavior, (3) verbal persuasions (or pep talks) from others, and (4) physiological states such as an abnormally fast versus calm heartbeat. Once formed, self-efficacy affects the performer's (1) choice of activities and selection of environments (approach versus avoidance); (2) extent of effort, persistence, and resiliency; (3) the quality of thinking and decision making; and (4) emotional reactions, especially those related to stress and anxiety. Because self-efficacy facilitates approach opportunities, effort, persistence, clear thinking, and positive emotionality, people with high self-efficacy generally learn to cope, perform, and achieve better than do people with low self-efficacy. Because self-efficacy beliefs can be acquired and because self-efficacy beliefs enable such productive ways of thinking, feeling, and behaving, self-efficacy serves as a model for personal empowerment. People who participate in therapy-like conditions (e.g., a mastery modeling program) to build stronger and more resilient self-efficacy beliefs respond by showing flexible, adaptive, and confident engagements with the world. Gains in self-efficacy vanquish anxiety, doubt, and avoidance.

While self-efficacy expectations and beliefs reflect the individual's perceived coping capacities, mastery expectations and beliefs reflect personal control over the environment and the success–failure outcomes it provides. When mastery beliefs are strong and resilient, the individual perceives a strong causal link between personal actions and outcomes. When mastery beliefs are weak and fragile, the individual perceives little or no causal link between personal actions and outcomes and learned helplessness—rather than mastery—occurs.

Learned helplessness is the psychological state that results when an individual expects that events in his or her life are uncontrollable. Helplessness is learned. Three fundamental components explain learned helplessness effects: contingency, cognition, and behavior. Contingency refers to the objective relationship between a person's behavior and the environment's positive or negative outcomes. Cognition includes all those mental processes (e.g., biases, attributions, expectancies) the individual relies on to translate objective environmental contingencies into subjective control beliefs. Behavior refers to the person's voluntary coping behavior, and it varies along a continuum that extends from active and energetic to passive and withdrawing. Once it occurs, helplessness produces profound disruptions in motivation (decreased willingness to try), learning (pessimistic learning set that interferes with learning future response–outcome contingencies), and emotion (emergence of energy-depleting emotions such as depression to replace naturally occurring energy-mobilizing emotions such as frustration).

Reactance theory, like the learned helplessness model, explains how people react to uncontrollable life events. Expectations of controllability foster reactance and activity, whereas expectations of uncontrollability foster helplessness and passivity. When confronting a situation that is difficult to control, individuals show an initial reactance response by becoming increasingly assertive in their psychological and behavioral attempts to reestablish control. If reactance efforts fail to reestablish personal control, individuals then lose their expectation of control and show a subsequent helplessness response.

Hope integrates the personal control beliefs literature by showing how agentic thinking (self-efficacy) and pathway thinking (mastery versus helplessness) function together to provide energy and direction for one's coping efforts. High-hope individuals, who possess resilient self-efficacy and strong mastery motivation, outperform and outcope low-hope individuals in domains such as academics, athletics, and physical illness.

Expectancy-value models supplement the expectancy-based models of motivation with the new motivational concept of value. While expectancy largely predicts performance, value largely predicts approach versus avoidance choice. Value is the perceived attractiveness of a task, and it has four components, including interest value (interest-enjoyment of the task), utility value (perceived importance or usefulness of the task), attainment value (relevance to one's identity or self-concept), and cost (e.g., feelings of anxiety, time and effort, lost opportunity to engage in alternative tasks). Expectancy-value models argue that expectancy and value together predict learning, engagement, and achievement better than does expectancy alone.

READINGS FOR FURTHER STUDY

Perceived Control

Skinner, E. A. (1996). A guide to constructs of control. *Journal of Personality and Social Psychology, 71,* 549–570.

Self-Efficacy

Bandura, A. (1988). Self-efficacy conception of anxiety. *Anxiety Research, 1,* 77–98.
Bandura, A. (1989). Human agency in social cognitive theory. *American Psychologist, 44,* 1175–1184.
Ozer, E. M., & Bandura, A. (1990). Mechanisms governing empowerment effects: A self-efficacy analysis. *Journal of Personality and Social Psychology, 58,* 472–486.

Learned Helplessness

Alloy, L. B., & Abramson, L. V. (1982). Learned helplessness, depression, and the illusion of control. *Journal of Personality and Social Psychology, 42,* 1114–1126.
Diener, C. I., & Dweck, C. S. (1978). An analysis of learned helplessness: Continuous changes in performance, strategy, and achievement cognitions following failure. *Journal of Personality and Social Psychology, 36,* 451–462.

Reactance

Mikulincer, M. (1988). The relationship of probability of success and performance following unsolvable problems: Reactance and helplessness effects. *Motivation and Emotion, 12,* 139–153.
Wortman, C. B., & Brehm, J. W. (1975). Responses to uncontrollable outcomes: An integration of reactance theory and the learned helplessness model. In L. Berkowitz (Ed.), *Advances in experimental social psychology* (Vol. *8,* pp. 277–336). New York: Academic Press.

Hope

Snyder, C. R., Harris, C., Anderson, J. R., Holleran, S. A., Irving, L. M., Sigmon, S. T., et al. (1991). The will and the ways: Development and validation of an individual differences measure of hope. *Journal of Personality and Social Psychology, 60,* 570–585.

Expectancy-Value

Eccles, J. S., & Wigfield, A. (2002). Motivational beliefs, values, and goals. *Annual Review of Psychology, 53,* 109–132.

Chapter 11

The Self and Its Strivings

THE SELF

    The Problem with Self-Esteem

SELF-CONCEPT

    Self-Schemas

    Motivational Properties of Self-Schemas

    Consistent Self

    Self-Verification and Self-Concept Change

    Why People Self-Verify

    Possible Selves

AGENCY

    Self as Action and Development from Within

        Differentiation and Integration

        Internalization and the Integrating Self

    Self-Concordance

    Personal Strivings

SELF-REGULATION

    Self-Regulation: Forethought through Reflection

    Developing More Competent Self-Regulation

    Self-Control

        Energy and Depletion

        Depletion

        Replenishment

        The Limited Strength Model of Self-Control

    Is the Capacity to Exert Self-Control Beneficial to a Successful Life?

IDENTITY

    Roles

    Identity-Establishing Behaviors

    Identity-Confirming Behaviors

    Identity-Restoring Behaviors

WHAT IS THE SELF?

SUMMARY

READINGS FOR FURTHER STUDY

How have you been lately? Reflecting back on the last month, how many days have been happy ones? At school or work, how lively and satisfied have you felt? How are your relationships going? Are they providing you with experiences that leave you energized and fulfilled, or have they left you feeling mostly frustrated? How are your personal finances? How is your health? How are your career prospects?

In the spirit of these questions, consider whether you agree or disagree with each of the following statements:

1. Many of my personal qualities trouble me enough that I wish I could change them.
2. I feel isolated and frustrated in interpersonal relationships.
3. When making important decisions, I rely on the judgments of others.
4. Often I am unable to change or improve my circumstances.
5. My life lacks meaning.
6. I have a sense of personal stagnation that often leaves me bored.

These six statements represent facets of psychological well-being—or ill-being since each item is reverse coded. These six facets of psychological well-being are, in order, *self-acceptance*—positive evaluations of oneself; *positive interpersonal relations*—close, warm relationships with others; *autonomy*—self-determination and personal causation; *environmental mastery*—sense of effectance in mastering circumstances and challenges; *purpose in life*—a sense of meaning that gives life direction and purpose; and *personal growth*—harboring a developmental trajectory characterized by improvement and growth (Ryff, 1989, 1995; Ryff & Keyes, 1995; Ryff & Singer, 2002). Your response to each item above reflects one distinct contour of self-functioning and psychological well-being versus ill-being. To be well psychologically is to possess positive self-regard, positive relationships, autonomy, mastery, purpose, and a trajectory of growth.

Pursuing these qualities is the province of the self. It is what the self does. Table 11.1 describes these six dimensions of self-functioning in greater detail.

THE SELF

In a motivational analysis of the self and its strivings, four problems take center stage (Baumeister, 1987):

1. Defining or creating the self
2. Discovering and developing personal potential
3. Managing and regulating the self
4. Relating the self to society

Table 11.1   Six Dimensions of Psychological Well-Being

Self-Acceptance

High scorer: Possesses a positive attitude toward the self; acknowledges and accepts multiple aspects of self, including good and bad qualities; feels positive about the past.

Low scorer: Feels dissatisfied with self; is disappointed with what has occurred in past life; is troubled about certain qualities; wishes to be different than what he or she is.

Positive Relations with Others

High scorer: Has warm, satisfying, trusting relationships; is concerned about the welfare of others; capable of strong empathy, affection, and intimacy; understands give-and-take of human relationships.

Low scorer: Has few close, trusting relationships; finds it difficult to be warm, open, and concerned about others; is isolated and frustrated in interpersonal relationships; is not willing to make compromises to sustain important ties with others.

Autonomy

High scorer: Is self-determining; is able to resist social pressures to think and act in certain ways; regulates behavior from within; evaluates self by personal standards.

Low scorer: Is concerned about the expectations and evaluations of others; relies on judgments of others to make important decisions; conforms to social pressures to think and act in certain ways.

Environmental Mastery

High scorer: Has a sense of mastery and competence in managing the environment; effectively manages several external activities simultaneously; makes effective use of surrounding opportunities; create contexts suitable to personal needs and values.

Low scorer: Has difficulty managing everyday affairs; feels unable to change or improve surrounding context; is unaware of surrounding opportunities; lacks sense of control over external world.

Purpose in Life

High scorer: Has goals in life and a sense of directedness; feels there is meaning to present and past life; holds beliefs that give life purpose; has aims and objectives for living.

Low scorer: Lacks a sense of meaning in life; has few goals or aims; lacks a sense of direction; does not see purpose in the past; has no outlook or beliefs that give life meaning.

Personal Growth

High scorer: Sees self as growing and expanding; is open to new experiences; has sense of realizing his or her potential; sees improvement in self and behavior over time; is changing in ways that reflect more self-knowledge and effectiveness.

Low scorer: Has a sense of personal stagnation; lacks sense of improvement or expansion over time; feels bored; feels unable to develop new attitudes or behaviors.

Source: "Possible selves in adulthood and old age: A tale of shifting horizons," by C. D. Ryff, 1991, *Psychology and Aging, 6,* 286–295. Copyright 1991 by the American Psychological Association. Reprinted by permission.

In the quest to define or create the self, we wonder about who we are, how others see us, how similar and how different we are from others, and whether we can become the person we want to be. We ask the basic question, "Who am I?" Defining or creating the self shows how *self-concept* energizes and directs behavior. Some aspects of self-definition are simply ascribed to us (e.g., gender). Other aspects, however, must be gained through achievement and through acts of choice (e.g., career, friends, values).

In the quest to discover and develop the self, we explore what does and does not interest us, we internalize the values of those we respect, we strive to create purpose and meaning, we seek to discover and develop our talents, and we devote our time to developing some skills and relationships rather than others. We ask, "What are my goals? Discovering and developing the potential of the self reflects and requires *agency*. Agency means that an agent (the self) has the power and intention to act. It reveals the motivation inherent within the self. Hence, agency communicates a natural motivational force within the person.

In the quest to manage and regulate the self, we reflect on our capacities, set long-term goals to pursue, implement long-term plans and strategies, monitor how well we are accomplishing our goals, and make the adjustments that are needed to achieve both our long-term goals and enhanced future self-functioning. We ask, "Can I exert self-control?" Managing or regulating the self shows how *self-regulation* makes competent functioning more likely. Instead of acting impulsively, the self can delay gratification and suppress short-term rewards and temptations in order to pursue long-term goals that are larger and more rewarding.

In the quest to relate the self to society, we contemplate our place in the social world and which societal roles are (and are not) available to us. We ask, "What is my role?" Relating the self to society shows how *identity* energizes, directs, and sustains behavior. In some respects, society is rigid in the roles it encourages or even allows individuals to pursue. In other respects, however, society is flexible. It gives the individual some choice and personal responsibility in determining who will be one's relationship partners and which social roles will be occupied (e.g., student, mother, politician, teacher).

The Problem with Self-Esteem

Before discussing self-concept, agency, self-regulation, and identity, it will be helpful to pause and challenge a cornerstone belief that many people endorse: Namely, the best way to increase another person's motivation is to increase his or her self-esteem. Teachers, employers, and coaches consistently and enthusiastically say that the way to motivate students, workers, and athletes is to increase their self-esteem. Praise them, reward them, congratulate them, make them feel good about who they are. Then sit back and watch all sorts of wonderful things unfold.

High self-esteem is okay. It is, for instance, correlated positively with being happy (Diener & Diener, 1996). The problem with boosting self-esteem as a motivational intervention, however, is that "there are almost no findings that self-esteem causes anything at all. Rather, self-esteem is caused by a whole panoply of successes and failures .... What needs improving is not self-esteem but improvement of our skills [for dealing] with the world" (Seligman, quoted in Azar, 1994). In other words, in the relation between self-esteem and self-functioning, self-functioning is a cause while self-esteem is only an effect. Self-esteem is essentially a scorecard or a scoreboard to report on how well or how poorly things are going in our lives (Helmke & van Aken, 1995).

Self-esteem and achievement are positively correlated with one another (Bowles, 1999; Davies & Brember, 1999). However, increases in self-esteem do not cause corresponding increases in achievement or productivity; rather, increases in achievement and productivity cause corresponding increases in self-esteem (Helmke & van Aken, 1995; Marsh, 1990; Marsh & Craven, 2006; Marsh et al., 2006). Self-esteem reflects how life is going, but it is not the source of motivation that allows people to make life go well. There is simply no evidence that boosting people's self-esteem will improve their functioning (Baumeister et al., 2003).

Low self-esteem is no bargain, because people low in self-esteem tend to suffer unusually high levels of anxiety. The chief benefit of high self-esteem is that it buffers the self against negative affectivity, such as depression (Alloy & Abramson, 1988) and anxiety (Greenberg et al., 1992; Solomon, Greenberg, & Pyszczynski, 1991). Self-esteem allows people to feel good about themselves, but it does not motivate them to do anything—with one dark exception. People with inflated self-views are significantly more prone to aggression and acts of violence on those occasions when their inflated favorable self-views are threatened (Baumeister, Smart, & Boden, 1996). For instance, when people with very high self-esteem perceive they have just been publicly ridiculed or "dissed," they become unusually prone to acts of retaliatory aggression. They retaliate—sometimes with words but often with actions—to settle the score in a way that perpetuates their inflated favorable self-view. For these two reasons—gains in self-esteem do not cause anything good, and threats to an inflated self-view is a prelude to retaliatory violence—the crusade to boost self-esteem is overrated.

If the above logic is true, then it is worth asking how the "self-esteem movement" got started in the first place. The movement owes its roots to 1986 when the state of California decided to boost the self-esteem of all state residents as a strategy to reduce school failure, welfare dependency, crime, unwanted pregnancy, and drug addiction (California Task Force to Promote Self-Esteem and Personal and Social Responsibility, 1989). The thinking was that virtually all psychological problems were traceable to a person's low self-esteem (Branden, 1984). Following this lead (without any empirical evidence to support it), self-esteem boosting programs exploded on the scene in the form of programs such as Upward Bound, Head Start, the Early Training Project, and in-class pep rallies chanting, "I *am* somebody!" (as well as in popular books of the day, such as *I'm OK, You're OK* and *Awaken the Giant Within*). By the time empirical research caught up with these programs to test their effectiveness, results showed that these programs failed miserably to curb the sort of social problems identified by the California state legislatures (Baumeister et al., 2003; Dawes, 1996; Swann, 1996). The high self-esteem that was being promoted in these self-esteem enhancement programs was fanciful and ephemeral, not something of substance. Programs such as Head Start and Upward Bound are somewhat effective, but their effectiveness works through other components of the program in which children and adolescence work hard and develop new skills that position them well to earn authentic achievements (e.g., complete a difficult obstacle course). When achievements are earned authentically, they signal effective self-functioning, which in turn yields a residual benefit of higher self-esteem.

In the end, the best conclusion to offer is that self-esteem is like happiness. Trying to be happy does not get you very far. Rather, happiness is a byproduct of life's satisfactions, triumphs, and positive relationships (Diener & Biswas-Diener, 2008). In the same spirit, self-esteem is little more than a downstream consequence of the self's adaptive and productive functioning. The same holds true for the six aspects of psychological well-being introduced earlier—self-acceptance, positive interpersonal relationships, autonomy, mastery, purpose, and personal growth. Each is largely a byproduct of other pursuits. This chapter is about those "other pursuits": (1) defining or creating the self (self-concept), (2) discovering and developing the self's potential (agency), (3) managing and regulating the self (self-regulation), and (4) relating the self to society (identity).

SELF-CONCEPT

Self-concepts are individuals' mental representations of themselves. Just as people have mental representations of other people (what teenagers are like), places (what the city of Chicago is like), and events (what Mardi Gras is like), people also have mental representations of themselves (what I am like). The self-concept is constructed from experiences and from reflections on those experiences.

To construct a self-concept, people attend to the feedback they receive in their day-to-day affairs that reveals their personal attributes, characteristics, and preferences. The building blocks people use to construct and define the self come from specific life experiences, such as the following:

- During the group discussion, I felt uncomfortable and self-conscious.
- On the school field trip to the zoo, I did not talk very much.
- At lunch, I avoided sitting with others.

During times of reflection, people do not remember the hundreds of individual life experiences. Rather, over time, people translate their multitude of specific experiences into a general representation of the self (e.g., given my inhibited experiences in groups, at the zoo, and during lunch, I perceive myself as "shy"). It is this general conclusion ("I'm shy"), rather than the specific experiences (in groups, at the zoo, and at lunch), that people remember and use to construct and define the self-concept (Markus, 1977).

Self-Schemas

Self-schemas are cognitive generalizations about the self that are domain specific and learned from past experiences (Markus, 1977, 1983). The earlier generalization of "I'm shy" exemplifies a self-schema. Being shy is both domain specific (relationships with others) and learned from past experiences (during group discussions, field trips, lunchroom conversations). Being shy does not represent the self-concept, but it does represent the self in one particular domain—one's relationships with others.

In athletics, a high school student constructs a domain-specific self-schema by looking back on the week's experiences and recalling his last-place finish in a 100-meter dash, his abandonment of a mile run because of exhaustion, and his repeated crashes into the bar during the high jump competition. In a different domain such as school, however, the same student might recall scoring well on a test, answering all the questions the teacher asked, and having a poem accepted for a school publication. Eventually, if the experiences in athletics and in the classroom are consistent and frequent enough, the student will generalize a self that is, for the most part, incompetent in athletics but skillful in school. These generalizations (athletically inept; intellectually smart) constitute additional domain-specific self-schemas.

The self-concept is a collection of domain-specific self-schemas. Which self-schemas are involved in the definition of the self-concept are those life domains that are most important to the person (Markus, 1977). The major life domains in early childhood, for instance, typically include cognitive competence, physical competence, peer acceptance, and behavioral conduct (Harter & Park, 1984). In adolescence, the major life domains generally include scholastic competence, athletic competence, physical appearance, peer acceptance, close friendships, romantic appeal, and behavioral conduct or morality (Harter, 1990). By college, the major life domains include scholastic competence, intellectual ability, creativity, job competence, athletic competence, physical appearance, peer acceptance, close friendships, romantic relationships, relationships with parents, morality, and sense of humor (Harter, 1990; Neemann & Harter, 1986). This litany of major life domains shows the likely range of self-schemas any one person is likely to possess at different stages in the life cycle. The specific life domains vary from one person to the next, but these domains illustrate the typical age-related structure of the self-concept (Harter, 1988; Kihlstrom & Cantor, 1984; Markus & Sentisk, 1982; Scheier & Carver, 1988).

Motivational Properties of Self-Schemas

Self-schemas generate motivation in two ways. First, self-schemas, once formed, direct an individual's behavior in ways that elicit feedback consistent with the established self-schemas. That is, because a person sees him- or herself as shy, that person directs his or her future behavior in interpersonal domains in ways that produce feedback that will confirm the "I'm shy" self-view. Shy people want and feel comfortable with social feedback that confirms that they are shy, just like humorous people want and feel comfortable with social feedback that confirms that they are humorous. This is so because self-schemas direct behavior in ways that confirm our established self-view. In contrast, feedback that is inconsistent with the established self-schema produces a motivational tension from the inconsistency and self-disconfirmation that leads to resistance and counter-argumentation.

The basic idea behind self-schema consistency is that if a person is told she is introverted when she believes she is extraverted, that contradictory feedback generates a motivational tension. The tension motivates the self to restore consistency. Therefore, people behave in self-schema-consistent ways to prevent feeling an aversive motivational tension. If prevention does not work, then people behave in ways to generate new additional feedback that will restore self-schema consistency.

Second, self-schemas generate motivation to move the present self toward a desired future self. Much like goal setting's discrepancy-creating process (Chapter 8), an ideal possible self initiates goal-directed behavior. Thus, the student who wants to become an actor initiates whatever actions seem necessary for advancing the self from being a "student" to becoming an "actor." "Student" constitutes the present self, while "actor" constitutes the ideal self. Seeking ideal possible selves is a fundamentally different motivational process than is striving to maintain a consistent self-view. Seeking possible selves is a goal-setting process that invites self-concept change and development (see the section "Possible Selves"), whereas seeking a consistent self-view is a verification process that preserves self-concept stability (see the section "Consistent Self").

Consistent Self

Once an individual establishes a well-articulated self-schema in a particular domain, he generally acts to preserve that self-view. Once established, self-schemas become increasingly resistant to contradictory information (Markus, 1977, 1983).

People preserve a consistent self by actively seeking out information consistent with their self-concept and by ignoring information that contradicts their self-view (Swann, 1983, 1985, 1999; Tesser, 1988). It is psychologically disturbing to believe one thing is true about the self yet be told that the reverse is actually the case. Imagine the turmoil of the career politician who loses a local election or the turmoil of the star athlete who does not get drafted into the professional ranks. Inconsistency and contradiction generate an emotional discomfort that signals that consistency needs to be restored. It is this negative affective state that produces the motivation to seek self-confirmatory, and to avoid self-disconfirmatory, information and feedback.

To ensure that other people see us as we see ourselves, we adopt self-presentational signs and symbols that announce who we are (or think we are). Examples of such signs and symbols include the appearances we convey in our physical selves through clothes, dieting, weightlifting, cosmetic surgery, and even our possessions and the kinds of cars we drive. For instance, the person wearing a Green Bay Packers jacket sends a self-presentational message to others along the lines of, "I am a sports enthusiast and an athlete." In doing so, the person strives to develop a social environment that will feed back self-confirmatory information.

Furthermore, in the name of self-schema preservation, we intentionally choose to interact with others who treat us in ways that are consistent with our self-view, and we intentionally avoid others who treat us in ways that are inconsistent with our self-view, a process referred to as "selective interaction" (Robinson & Smith-Lovin, 1992; Swann, Pelham, & Krull, 1989). By choosing friends who confirm our self-view and by keeping our distance from those who contradict that self-view, we make self-confirmatory feedback more likely and we make self-disconfirmatory feedback less likely. Selective interaction explains a key reason why we choose particular friends, roommates, tutors, teachers, teammates, spouses, and so on—namely, because we use social interactions to maintain and verify our self-view (Swann, 1987). Selective interaction also explains why people tend to break up a relationship in which the other person sees the self differently than one sees oneself, as in divorce (De La Ronde & Swann, 1998; Katz, Beach, & Anderson, 1996; Schafer, Wickram, & Keith, 1996). By marrying one person rather than another, the individual selects an interaction partner who will be a source of self-consistent feedback, and by divorcing a marriage partner, the individual might be removing a source of self-discrepant feedback.

Despite preventive efforts, self-discrepant feedback does sometimes occur (as it did for the career politician and star athlete). The first line of defense in the effort to maintain a consistent self is to distort that information until it loses its status as discrepant information. In the face of discrepant self-schema feedback, the individual may ask if the feedback is valid, if the source of the feedback is trustworthy, and how important or relevant this feedback is (Crary, 1966; Markus, 1977; Swann, 1983). For example, a student with a self-view of being intelligent but who fails a college course might functionally discredit that feedback by arguing against (1) its validity (i.e., the student scored as unintelligent only because she was too busy to focus), (2) the professor's judgment (i.e., the student thinks her professor is a nitwit), and (3) its importance or relevance (i.e., the student feels it is not what she knows but who she knows that is important). People also counter disconfirming feedback with compensatory self-inflation (Greenberg & Pyszczynski, 1985), self-affirmation (Steele, 1988), and a barrage of new behaviors to prove one's actual self-view (e.g., "No, no, here let me show you ...."; Swann & Hill, 1982). What all these ways of maintaining self-concept consistency have in common is that they marshal forward counter-examples and counter-explanations to essentially discredit the otherwise self-discrepant feedback. Once invalidated, self-discrepant feedback can be ignored and the self-view preserved.

Self-Verification and Self-Concept Change

An individual's confidence that his or her self-schema is valid and true constitutes "self-concept certainty" (Harris & Snyder, 1986; Swann & Ely, 1984). When high, self-concept certainty anchors stable self-schemas. Discrepant feedback rarely changes a stable self-schema. When low, however, discrepant feedback can eventually instigate self-schema change. Conflict between an uncertain self-schema and discrepant feedback instigates a "crisis self-verification" (Swann, 1983, 1999): How do we verify the accuracy of our self-view, given contradictory feedback and an uncertain self-view? People resolve the self-verification crisis by seeking out additional domain-relevant feedback (Swann, 1983), a sort of "best two out of three to break the tie" approach for figuring out who they are.

The rather complicated self-verification process appears in Figure 11.1. Individuals start with a representation of self (a self-schema) and a preference for self-confirmatory feedback, as illustrated at the top of the figure. As people publically display signs and symbols of who they are (their self-view), their daily social interaction tends to generate a steady stream of routine self-verification.

Things begin to get complicated only after the appearance of self-discrepant social feedback. People handle mild self-discrepant information rather well (Swann & Hill, 1982), as discussed earlier, as people discredit discrepant feedback with counter-evidence and marshal forward compensatory self-affirmations. The effect that potent (strong) disconfirming feedback has on the self-view, however, is not so easily integrated. Its effect depends on self-concept certainty. When self-concept certainty is low (see Figure 11.1), potent feedback *can* overwhelm preexisting self-schemas and instigate self-concept change. When self-concept certainty is high, however, potent feedback is resisted (Swann, Pelham, & Chidester, 1988) and instead counter-argued as but one small piece of information in the context of a lifetime of historical information (e.g., "I was outgoing this time, but I was not outgoing on 100 occasions in the past; therefore, I still think I am shy, all things considered").

The most interesting case, developmentally speaking, occurs when self-concept certainty is moderate. When self-concept certainty is moderate and the person faces potent self-discrepant feedback (as did the politician and athlete), the individual experiences the self-verification crisis. During a self-verification crisis, the individual suspends judgment and seeks out additional feedback. If the additional feedback is very convincing, the self-verification crisis does not change the self-view but instead lowers self-concept certainty. It is the lowered self-concept certainty that makes the person vulnerable to subsequent self-concept change in the future. Notice, for instance, that the only path to "Self-Concept Change" is from low self-concept certainty (as shown on the lower, far right side of the figure). If the additional feedback is self-confirming, the "best two out of three tie"

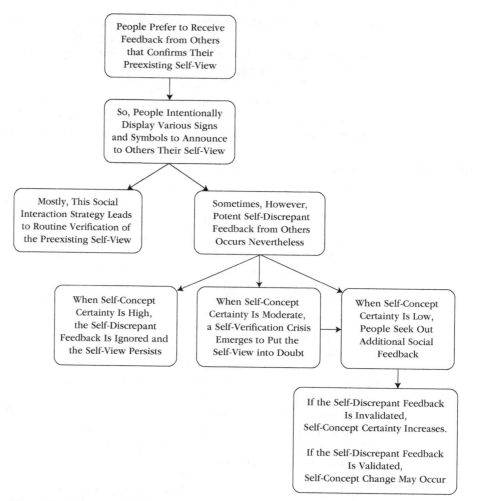

Figure 11.1   Processes Underlying Self-Verification and Self-Concept Change

is broken in favor of the preexisting self-view and the self-verification crisis ends by strengthening self-concept certainty.

Before self-schemas change, (1) self-concept certainty must be low and (2) self-discrepant feedback must be potent and unambiguous—that is, difficult to discredit (Swann, 1983, 1985, 1987). Although self-concept can change, change is the exception rather than the rule. Self-concept change is rare, while self-verification and self-concept consistency are commonplace (see the examples in Box 11).

Why People Self-Verify

People prefer self-verification feedback for cognitive, epistemic, and pragmatic reasons. On the cognitive side, people self-verify because they seek to know themselves (to be true to oneself; Swann, Stein-Seroussi, & Giesler, 1992). Following epistemic concerns, people seek self-verification because verifications of the self bolster perceptions that the world is predictable and coherent (Swann & Pelham, 2002). On the pragmatic side, people self-verify because they wish to avoid interactions that might be fraught with misunderstandings and unrealistic expectations and performance demands; they seek interaction partners who know what to expect from them (Swann, 1992, 1999; Swann & Pelham, 2002).

Possible Selves

Self-schemas sometimes change in response to social feedback (i.e., Figure 11.1). But it is more likely that self-schemas change by a second, more proactive and intentional way. Self-schema change can occur through a deliberate effort to advance the present self toward a desired future possible self. Possible selves represent individuals' ideas of what they would like to become and also what they are afraid they might become (Markus & Nurius, 1986; Markus & Ruvolo, 1989). Some hoped-for selves might include, for instance, the successful self, the creative self, the rich self, the thin self, or the popular self; some feared selves might include the unemployed self, the disabled self, the overweight self, or the rejected self.

Possible selves are mostly social in origin, as the individual observes the selves modeled by others (Markus & Nurius, 1986). The individual sees the current self as his or her "present self" and sees the role model as a desired, future "ideal self." Seeing the discrepancy, the individual makes an inference that he or she could become, just like the successful role model became, that desired self. For instance, a child might watch performers in a musical and aspire to be a singer. One practical illustration of this is a jobs theme park for children in both Tokyo and Seoul ("Kidzania"). This indoor theme park provides an opportunity for children to try out being a pilot, dentist, engineer, and so forth, and it is hugely popular with children (and their parents!).

Possible selves represent the future self. The motivational function of a possible self therefore operates like that of a goal (or personal striving). As a goal—as a desired future end state—a possible self functions as a potent impetus to action in the same way that all goals do—namely, by enhancing effort, increasing persistence, focusing attention, and undertaking strategic planning (see Chapter 8).

Possible selves add an important piece of the puzzle in understanding how the self develops. Possible selves are essentially mental representations of attributes, characteristics, and abilities that the self does not yet possess (e.g., "I would like to become a physician, although I don't know much about human anatomy or surgical techniques"). When the self does not have the evidence or feedback to confirm the emerging possible self, one of two outcomes follows (Markus, Cross, & Wurf, 1990). On the one hand, an absence of supportive evidence (or the presence of disconfirming feedback) will lead the self to reject and abandon the possible self. On the other hand, the possible self can energize and direct action so that the attributes, characteristics, and abilities of the self actually begin to materialize (Cross & Markus, 1994; Nurius, 1991; Oyserman & Markus, 1990). Thus, the possible self's motivational role is to link the present self with ways to become the possible (ideal) self. Hence, an individual pursuing a possible self relies little on the present self-schema and much on the hoped-for self, possibly asking questions such as the following: If I am going to become my possible self, then how should I behave? What activities should I pursue? What education do I need? (Cantor, Markus, Niedenthal, & Nurius, 1986; Markus & Nurius, 1986; Markus & Wurf, 1987). As these questions imply, advancing oneself toward

BOX 11 *Reversing Negative Self-Views*

Question: Why is this information important?

Answer: To help reverse a negative self-view.

A critical question in contexts such as therapy, friendship, and marriage is which type of feedback do people prefer more—self-enhancement (praise) or self-verification (accuracy) (Swann, 1999)? People certainly like praise and adoration, and when they hear it, the praise just feels good. But people also prefer self-verifying feedback; they want to hear the truth about themselves.

For people with a favorable self-view, self-enhancement and self-verification are the same—praise. For people with an unfavorable self-view, however, self-enhancement (praise) and self-verification (criticism) are two very different social messages. This difference is clinically important because research shows that self-verification (not self-enhancement) is a ubiquitous motivation within the strivings of the self-concept. This motivation for self-verification raises the difficult question of how one might go about the task of trying to reverse another person's negative self-view.

What does not help in the effort to reverse another person's unfavorable self-view is to offer compliments and praise. When a person with a negative self-view hears such self-enhancing feedback, she typically becomes motivated to act in a way that proves the validity of the negative self-view (Linehan, 1997; Robinson & Smith-Lovin, 1992). The person with the negative self-view winds up arguing with you and marshaling forth a wealth of often rather convincing evidence to counter your praise. It seems intuitive that praise and adoration would lead to a positive self-view, but it does not when the person possesses a pre-existing negative self-view. A better therapeutic strategy is to attempt to undermine the person's self-concept certainty (e.g., are you sure you are clumsy, stupid, unworthy, and incompetent?), as suggested in Figure 11.1.

Another second strategy is to present extreme self-verification feedback. For instance, Bill Swann (1997) provides the example of challenging an unassertive person's self-view by forwarding the impression that he is a "complete doormat." The hope is that the person will behaviorally resist the extreme version of the identity (e.g., will counter-argue, will show rebuttal "signs and symbols"). Bill Swann has done the same with extreme conservatives, asking, "Why do you think men always make better bosses than women?"

A third strategy for self-concept change is to gain the support of key interaction partners, such as friends, lovers, relatives, and coworkers. Negative self-views are stabilized by interaction partners that provide a steady stream of negative feedback (Swann & Predmore, 1985), and there is some truth to the notion that women with low self-esteem marry men who are highly negative and abusive toward them (Buckner & Swann, 1996) and that aggressive kids have friends who affirm that they are tough, rough, and aggressive. Changing a negative self-view therefore involves changing the social feedback one receives day after day. Hence, gaining the social support of the person's key interaction partners is pivotal if one is to reverse a negative self-view (Swann, 1997, 1999; Swann & Pelham, 2002).

an ideal self requires not only a possible self to strive for but also effective strategies for how one is to get there (Oyserman, Bybee, & Terry, 2006).

The notion of possible selves portrays the self as a dynamic entity with a past, present, and future (Cantor et al., 1986; Day, Borkowski, Punzo, & Howsepian, 1994; Ryff, 1991). The individual without a possible self in a particular domain lacks an important cognitive basis for developing abilities in that domain (Cross & Markus, 1994). Perhaps the reader can look back at his or her own effort devoted to several different college courses and ask the following: What role did the presence versus absence of a relevant possible self play in determining how much effort I put forth, whether I read the textbook, whether I attended class, and whether I enrolled in the course? Part of the reason you put forth high effort, persistence, focused attention, and strategic planning in one particular college course can be traced to the presence of a relevant and important possible self, just as part of the reason why you slacken effort, persistence, attention, and strategic planning in a second college course can be traced to the absence of a relevant and an important possible self. Day-to-day classroom activities and outcomes motivationally matter (e.g., the topic of the day, success/ failure feedback), but the presence versus absence of a relevant, important possible self adds a future time perspective that contributes future-based motivation into today's activity. Exercise (or not) is a second example of this motivational process. The motivation to exercise is rather strong when it adds future-based possible self-motivation (e.g., the strong, healthy, flexible future me) on top of today's activity-specific motivation (e.g., feelings of competence, chance to hang out with your friends) (Vansteenkiste, Simons, Soenens, & Lens, 2004).

AGENCY

The self goes deeper than just cognitive structures (self-concept). The self further possesses an intrinsic motivation that gives it a quality of agency (Ryan, 1993). Agency entails personal causation and action (deCharms, 1987). Agency presents a view of self "as action and development from within, as innate processes and motivations" (Deci & Ryan, 1991).

Self as Action and Development from Within

Chapter 6 discussed the organismic psychological needs of autonomy, competence, and relatedness—needs that provide a natural motivational force to foster agency (i.e., initiative, action). Intrinsic motivation is inseparably coordinated with the active nature of the developing self (Deci & Ryan, 1991). It is the source of motivation that underlies agency because it spontaneously energizes people to pursue their interests, seek out environmental challenges, exercise their skills, and develop their talents—that is, to discover, develop, and fulfill one's potential.

Differentiation and Integration

Differentiation and integration are two developmental processes inherent within the self. Differentiation expands and elaborates the self into an ever-increasing complexity. Integration synthesizes that emerging complexity into a coherent whole, thereby preserving a sense of a single, cohesive self.

Differentiation proceeds as the individual exercises existing interests, preferences, and capacities in such a way that a relatively general and undifferentiated self becomes specialized into several life domains. For an illustration, consider your own history in which you learned that not all computers are alike, not all sports are alike, not all politicians are alike, not all relationships are alike, and not all religions are alike. Minimal differentiation manifests itself in simplicity in which the person has only a unidimensional understanding of a particular domain of knowledge; rich differentiation manifests itself in understanding fine discriminations and unique aspects of a particular life domain. The same holds true for differentiation of the domains of the self-concept. Intrinsic motivation, interests, and preferences motivate the self to interact with the world in such a way that sets the stage for the self to differentiate into an ever-increasing complexity. For instance, the child with an interest in model airplanes skims through catalogues, attends club meetings, talks with peers about model building, subscribes to a topical magazine, experiments with new materials and with various construction techniques, and basically develops specialized skills while learning. It is the self's intrinsic motivation that gives it the agency it needs to skim through catalogues, attend club meetings, talk to peers, and so on, and it is this ongoing and agentic stream of experience that allows the self to differentiate and grow in complexity.

Differentiation does not expand the complexity of the self unabated. Rather, there exists a synthetic tendency to integrate the self's emerging complexity into a single sense of self, into a coherent unity. Integration is an organizational process that brings the self's differentiated parts together into a coherent whole (into a single sense of self, rather than remain as a self characterized by dozens of unrelated or even somewhat contradictory self-schemas).

The notions of agency (via intrinsic motivation), differentiation, and integration argue that the self possesses inherent aspects. Psychological needs and developmental processes provide a starting point for the development of the self. As individuals mature, they gain increasing contact with the social context, and some of these aspects of the social world become assimilated and integrated into the self-system. The motivational portrayal of self-development therefore argues strongly against the idea that the self is merely a passive recipient of the social world's feedback (self-schemas) and identities (places in the social order). The self also actively develops via its inherent agency.

Internalization and the Integrating Self

With its inherent needs and emerging interests, preferences, potentials, and capacities, the self is poised to grow, develop, and differentiate. The need for relatedness, however, keeps the individual close to societal concerns and regulations, and the self therefore develops both toward autonomy and relatedness. The psychological need for relatedness (warm, close relationships with others) is the quality of motivation that supports the individual's proactive motivation to internalize society's rules, values, and concerns. So behaviors, emotions, and ways of thinking originate not only within the self but also within the social context and society. As a person plays, studies, works, performs, and interacts with others, these other people request that the self comply with particular ways of behaving, feeling, and thinking. Thus, intentional acts (i.e., agency) sometimes arise from the self, but intentional acts also sometimes arise from the guidance and recommendations of others. The process through which individuals take in and accept as their own an externally prescribed way of thinking, feeling, or behaving is referred to as internalization (Ryan & Connell, 1989; Ryan et al., 1993). Internalization refers to the process through which an individual transforms a formerly externally prescribed way of behaving or valuing into an internal one (Ryan et al., 1993).

Internalization occurs for two essential reasons. First, internalization occurs from the individual's desire to achieve meaningful relationships with friends, parents, teachers, coaches, employers, clergy, family, and others. Thus, internalization is motivated by the need for relatedness. Second, internalization occurs from the individual's desire to interact effectively with the social world. Thus, internalization is motivated by the need for competence. Much of what the person internalizes promotes his effective functioning (e.g., go to school, brush your teeth, apologize to others). Such internalization has adaptive interpersonal value for the self, because it promotes greater unity between the self and society, such as in the close relationships between parent and child; and it has adaptive intrapersonal value for the self, as it promotes greater effectance in environmental transactions (Ryan, 1993).

The contribution of agency to a portrayal of the self as action and development from within is to recognize that (1) human beings possess a core self, one energized by innate motivation and directed by the inherent developmental processes of differentiation and integration, and (2) not all self-structures are equally authentic, as some self-structures truly reflect the core self while other self-structures only reflect and reproduce the needs and priorities of society (Deci et al., 1994; Deci & Ryan, 1985a, 1991; Ryan, 1991, 1993; Ryan & Connell, 1989). Because some self-structures originate in society, they may produce conflict within the self. Conflict is the opposite of integration. Controlling (pressuring, conflictual) environmental conditions lead the self to ignore innate needs and preferences and, instead, develop a self-structure around the goal of external validation (Hodgins & Knee, 2002). Hence, people who pursue external validation of a socially desirable self might choose a career for the financial wealth, prestige, or social power it offers rather than a career that is more consistent with their intrinsic interests, preferences, and psychological needs.

Self-Concordance

The questions asked by the self-concordance model (Sheldon, 2002) are (1) How do people decide what to strive for in their lives? and (2) How does this personal striving process sometimes nurture the self and promote well-being yet other times go awry and diminish well-being? When people decide to pursue goals that are congruent or "concordant" with their core self, they pursue "self-concordant" goals.

Figure 11.2 graphically illustrates this notion that a person's goals may or may not represent the self's inherent needs, interests, and internalized values (see Sheldon & Elliot, 1998). Following self-determination theory (discussed in Chapter 5), intrinsic goals (goals that arise out of personal interests) and identified goals (goals that arise out of personal conviction or values) represent self-concordant goals. Self-concordant goals reflect and express the integrated, agentic self. Introjected goals (goals that arise out of social obligations—it's what I should do or ought to do) and extrinsic goals (goals that arise out of a desire to be praised or rewarded) represent self-discordant goals. Self-discordant goals reflect and express nonintegrated action that emanates out of controlling internal and external pressures.

The self-concordance model appears in Figure 11.3 (Sheldon & Elliot, 1999). The model begins when the person sets a goal for which to strive. For instance, one person might set the goal of getting married, another might set a goal of graduating high school, while yet another might set a goal of quitting smoking. Some goals reflect and emanate out from the core self's needs, interests, and preferences (self-concordant goals), while other goals do not. Self-concordant goals generate and sustain greater effort (i.e., greater "agency") than do self-discordant goals (Sheldon & Elliot, 1999). Greater effort, especially when sustained over time, increases the likelihood of subsequent goal attainment. Self-concordant motivated goal attainments foster need-satisfying experiences. Just how need-satisfying any one particular goal attainment is, however, depends on the extent to which the goal is a self-concordant one (see the line connecting Goal Self-Concordance × Goal Attainment → Need Satisfying Experience in Figure 11.3). Finally, it is this experience of authentic need-satisfying experiences that increases well-being (i.e., gains in positive mood, vitality, physical health). That is, attaining self-concordant goals provides

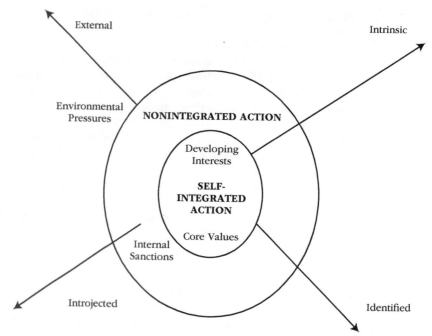

Figure 11.2 Diagrammatic Illustration of Self-Integrated and Nonintegrated Action

Source: From "Goal striving, need satisfaction, and longitudinal well-being: The self-concordance model," by K. M. Sheldon & A. J. Elliot, 1999, *Journal of Personality and Social Psychology*, *76*, 482–497. Copyright 1999 American Psychological Association. Reprinted by permission.

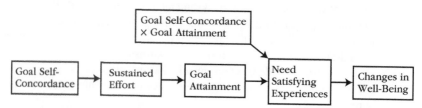

Figure 11.3 Self-Concordance Model

Source: From "Goal striving, need satisfaction, and longitudinal well-being: The self-concordance model," by K. M. Sheldon & A. J. Elliot, 1999, *Journal of Personality and Social Psychology*, *76*, 482–497. Copyright 1999 American Psychological Association. Reprinted by permission.

the self with psychological nutriments that sustain well-being and agency motivation (Ryan, 1995).

A handy self-test exists to determine whether a personal goal is self-concordant or self-discordant—namely, are you striving for something you *want* to do or for something you *have* to do? Self-concordant goals (intrinsic goals, identified goals) emanate out of a sense of authenticity and personal ownership—the person is fully aware that the striving is based on a personal interest, need, or value. Accordingly, the desire to pursue self-concordant goals is embedded in a context of positive affect and "wanting to." Self-discordant goals (extrinsic goals, introjected goals) emanate out of a sense of pressure—that the personal striving is based on an obligation to others or to social demands. Accordingly, the desire to pursue self-discordant goals is embedded in a context of anxiety, pressure, and "having to." In Chapter 6, this distinction was referred to as "perceived locus of causality," as self-concordant goals arise from an internal perceived locus of causality, whereas self-discordant goals arise from an external perceived locus of causality. Thus, self-concordance refers to the sense of heartfelt ownership that people have (or do not have) regarding their goals and strivings.

The act of acquiring a sense of ownership in one's personal goals is a crucial developmental task of the self. A self characterized by agency is proactive and endowed with personal initiative for life improvement and self-expansion, rather than just being reactive to the situational and cultural forces that come along. How self-concordance grows developmentally appears in Figure 11.4. The lefthand side of the figure essentially repeats the self-concordance model depicted earlier in Figure 11.3 (i.e., self-concordant goals → enhanced effort → enhanced goal attainment → need satisfying experiences → increased well-being). But the model in Figure 11.4 extends the self-concordant model because need-satisfying experiences further contribute to the ongoing development of the agentic self by increasing future self-concordance (Sheldon & Houser-Marko, 2001). In doing so, agentic selves participate in an "upward spiral" in which gains in self-concordance contribute to subsequent gains in well-being, personal growth, and happiness (Sheldon & Houser-Marko, 2001).

Personal Strivings

Personal strivings are "what a person is typically or characteristically trying to do" (Emmons, 1989). These strivings represent what an individual is characteristically aiming to accomplish in his day-to-day behavior and over the course of his life (Emmons, 1989, 1996). Personal strivings are not goals per se but, instead, exist as superordinate aspects of the self that organize and integrate the many different goals a person seeks. That is, one personal striving might lead to many different daily goals.

To provide a concrete illustration of personal strivings, one person's self-reported strivings appear in Table 11.2. This woman's strivings are organized around concerns about profession (becoming a teacher, becoming better at my job), personality (being more independent, being more open-minded), relationships (finding a partner, not being so mean), emotion regulation (improving attitude, remaining calm), and well-being (being healthy, losing weight, having more money, traveling more).

All personal strivings are not equal when it comes to their implications for the person's well-being. Instead of striving for what they are interested in and what they value, people often strive for extrinsic and non-self-concordant reasons such as those dictated by social pressure or by an expectation of what others think they should do (Sheldon & Kasser, 1998). Those personal strivings that are not endorsed by the self (e.g., "I *have* to quit smoking") tend to generate conflict and pressure in the person (Sheldon & Elliot, 1999; Sheldon & Houser-Marko, 2001), whereas those personal strivings that cultivate self-concordant goals, personal growth, and subjective well-being (e.g., "I *want* to quit smoking") are those that seek greater autonomy, competence, or relatedness in the person's life (Sheldon, 2001).

Why this is so can be illustrated by an analogy to nutrition (Kasser & Ryan, 2001). Personal strivings that seek to bring greater autonomy, competence, and relatedness into one's life are those that seek to satisfy one's innate psychological needs (see Chapter 6).

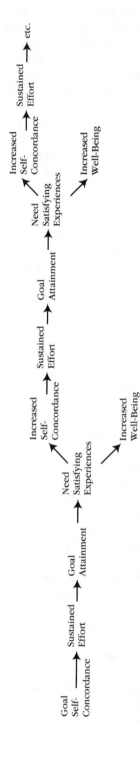

Figure 11.4 Cyclical Path Model for the Self-Concordance Model to Illustrate Developmental Gains in Both Well-Being and Self-Concordance

Note: The "Goal Self-Concordance × Goal Attainment" Box and Its Path/Arrow to "Need Satisfying Experiences" shown in Figure 11.4 has been omitted from this figure for clarity and simplification.

Source: Adapted from Sheldon, K. M., & Houser-Marko, L. (2001). Self-concordance, goal attainment, and the pursuit of happiness: Can there be an upward spiral? *Journal of Personality and Social Psychology, 80,* 152–165. Copyright 2001 American Psychological Association. Adapted with permission.

Table 11.2   One Individual's Personal Strivings

1. Become a teacher
2. Have a better attitude
3. Become more independent
4. Stay healthy
5. Lose weight
6. Have more money
7. Remain calm
8. Find a decent partner
9. Become better at my job
10. Become more open-minded
11. Travel more often
12. Not be so mean

Note: To produce these personal strivings, 12 blank lines were listed down the lefthand side of the page, which began with the following instructions:

> A personal striving is an objective that you are typically trying to accomplish or attain. Personal strivings can be either positive or negative. In other words, a personal striving can be an objective that you typically approach and strive to attain, or it can be an objective that you typically strive to avoid. For instance, a striving you might approach and strive to attain might be "Be a fun person to be around." A striving you might strive to avoid might be "Quit smoking cigarettes."

Striving for these sorts of goals acts like a diet of fruits and vegetables. Extrinsically oriented personal strivings (money, fame) are largely irrelevant to people's innate psychological needs and act like a diet of candy and cookies, a diet that is unable to promote personal growth or subjective well-being.

Furthermore, it is a key point that subjective well-being neither follows from nor depends on actually attaining one's goals or personal strivings. That is, people who attain high levels of fame and fortune are not more psychologically well than are those who do not attain these same sorts of goals (Kasser & Ryan, 2001). Rather, subjective well-being comes from the content of what one is trying to do (Emmons, 1996; Sheldon & Elliot, 1998). When people strive for autonomy, competence, and relatedness aspirations, they are able to create a meaning in their lives that fosters subjective well-being. In the end, subjective well-being is about what one is striving for, not about what one actually attains.

SELF-REGULATION

Self-regulation begins with setting a long-term goal. Long-term goals, such as "graduate college," "learn a foreign language," and "develop a good relationship," do not simply accomplish themselves. Instead, the self needs to exert cognitive, motivational, and emotional effort to advance a hoped-for goal to its desired end state (goal attainment). This process of exerting and managing the self to accomplish a long-term goal is referred to as self-regulation. More formally, self-regulation is the metacognitive planning, implementing, monitoring, and evaluating of one's goal striving efforts (Pintrich, 2000; Zimmerman, 2002).

Self-Regulation: Forethought through Reflection

Self-regulation is a process that occurs over time. It begins with setting a long-term goal and involves each of the following:

- Planning and strategic thinking
- Implementing action and self-control
- Monitoring and checking
- Reflecting and adjusting

Once the self has set a long-term goal to strive for, the attainment of that goal needs to be planned; the individual generates a plan of action, adopts strategies to bring the goal to fruition, and creates implementation intentions. Once the goal-setting process has been established, the individual moves on to goal striving and to self-control. Goal striving requires cognitive, motivational, and emotional work, because plans, strategies, and implementation intentions need to be implemented, while self-control requires suppressing and overriding short-term goal-antagonistic impulses, distractions, and temptations. As goal striving unfolds over time, the individual needs to monitor the goal-performance discrepancy and whether it is being reduced and progress is being made. Finally, the individual needs to reflect on why self-regulation succeeded or failed; once diagnosed, reflected upon, and understood, future self-regulatory efforts need to be revised and updated to better position the individual for future self-regulation success.

As illustrated in Figure 11.5, self-regulation is an ongoing, cyclical process (Zimmerman, 2000). It involves forethought (goal setting, strategic planning), action (goal striving, self-control), and reflection (self-monitoring and self-evaluation that leads to more informed forethought prior to the next performance opportunity). The ongoing, cyclical nature of self-regulation is apparent when reflection on one's self-regulatory successes and failures leads to new and improved forethought—hence, to more effective future self-regulation.

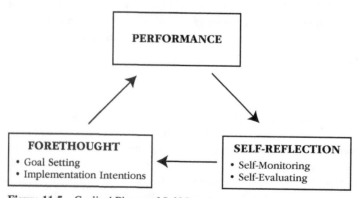

Figure 11.5 Cyclical Phases of Self-Regulation

Developing More Competent Self-Regulation

Everyone engages in self-regulation, but some people do it better than others (Winne, 1997). Most researchers view self-regulation as a skill of the self, a skill that needs to be acquired, improved, and refined (Schunk & Zimmerman, 1997). That self-regulation is an acquired skill is most apparent when people pursue a long-term goal in an unfamiliar domain (e.g., a student enrolls in an honors class for the first time, a couple visits a fancy French restaurant for the first time, an employee begins a new job). In an unfamiliar or unpracticed domain, the individual wonders, "What do I need to do?" and "How can I accomplish my goals?"

As shown in Figure 11.6, self-regulation involves the capacity to carry out the full goal-setting process on one's own (Schunk & Zimmerman, 1997). Gains in self-regulatory competence generally occur within a social learning process and at an observational level in which a relative novice observes the behavior and verbalizations of a relative expert. The novice first imitates the expert model (as illustrated in Figure 11.7), and observation eventually leads to imitation. During a period of imitation, the novice begins to receive social guidance and corrective feedback as to the effectiveness of his imitative behaviors. Adjustments toward ever more effective self-regulation are made. Following a period of social guidance and corrective feedback, the novice begins to internalize the standards of excellence endorsed by the model. At this point, the roots of effective self-regulation begin to take hold. The novice eventually becomes self-regulating in the domain when he no longer needs the expert model and can self-regulate in terms of goal-setting, goal-striving, self-monitoring and self-evaluating. For instance, in learning how to become a competent and self-regulated writer, the novice observes and emulates the expert writer's style and standards, learns to set goals and formulate strategies and implementation intentions, restructures the physical environment to facilitate writing, solicits feedback and tips about writing, and acquires the means to monitor and evaluate his or her own work (Zimmerman & Risemberg, 1997).

Developing competent self-regulation takes a long time (Pressley, 1995). In some sense, self-regulation is only the beginning of expertise. Building expertise requires intensive mentoring and countless hours of deliberate practice on one's own (Ericsson & Charness, 1994; Ericsson, Krampe, & Tesch-Romer, 1993). Independent deliberate practice is very important, but the thesis in the self-regulation literature is that people can acquire, develop, and master complex skills more quickly and more expertly if they

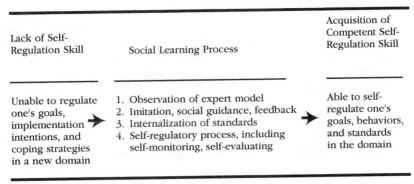

| | | Acquisition of Competent Self- |
Lack of Self-Regulation Skill	Social Learning Process	Regulation Skill
Unable to regulate one's goals, implementation intentions, and coping strategies in a new domain	1. Observation of expert model 2. Imitation, social guidance, feedback 3. Internalization of standards 4. Self-regulatory process, including self-monitoring, self-evaluating	Able to self-regulate one's goals, behaviors, and standards in the domain

Figure 11.6   Summary of the Social Learning Process to Acquire Self-Regulation Skill

Figure 11.7 Acquiring Self-Regulation Skill by First Observing and Imitating an Expert Model

have the benefit of a tutor who models how to set goals, develop strategies, formulate implementation intentions, monitor performance, and evaluate (on one's own) the ongoing goal–performance–feedback process.

Self-Control

Long-term goal pursuit is difficult because people are more attracted to the immediate gratification of short-term rewards than they are to the delay of gratification necessary for longer-term (although larger) rewards. Impulsive behavior is quick and easy—just yield and eat the cookies, drink the alcohol, and play videogames rather than get to work. The problem with these short-term attractions is that they are so often incompatible with, and even antagonistic to, long-term goal pursuit. That is, it is hard to finish your work if you are instead playing a video game. Similarly, to eat healthy, we not only need to consume more fruits and vegetables but simultaneously resist urges to eat chocolate chip cookies, bowls of ice cream, and whatever else is so easy to "grab and go" at the convenience store.

Self-control is the capacity to suppress, restrain, and even override an impulsive desire, urge, behavior, or tendency so to pursue a long-term goal (Bauer & Baumeister, 2011). It is the capacity to interrupt our tendency toward automatic pilot and short-term attractions and, instead, to steer behavior intentionally in the direction of a long-term goal. At a colloquial level, self-control is "willpower" (Baumeister & Tierney, 2011).

To get a feel for self-control in action, consider the radish experiment (Baumeister, Bratslavsky, Muraven, & Tice, 1998). In research on self-control, the basic research paradigm is as follows. Participants in an experimental group first perform some task that requires self-control, while participants in a control group perform a similar task but one that does not require self-control. Next, all participants move to a second, unrelated task that requires self-control. The hypothesis is that, because self-control is depleting, participants who perform the initial self-control task become exhausted and therefore perform more poorly on the follow-up self-control task than do the participants in the control group. In the radish study, the experiments asked all participants to fast for at least three hours prior to the study. When participants walked into the laboratory, the experimenters arranged to have the smell of freshly baked chocolate chip cookies in the air. As participants sat down to begin the study, in front of them on a table was a stack of those fresh chocolate chip cookies and a bowl of raw radishes. Participants in the experimental group were assigned the high self-control task of eating the radishes (and resisting the chocolate chip cookies), while participants in the control group were assigned the no-self-control task of eating the chocolate chip cookies. After five minutes of this, all participants were next taken to another room and given some impossible-to-solve geometry problems (e.g., trace a geometric figure without retracing any lines or lifting the pencil from the paper). The test (the dependent measure) was how long the participants would persist before giving up. On average, participants who ate the chocolate chip cookies persisted for 19 minutes, while participants who at the radishes and suppressed the urge to eat the cookies persisted for only 8 minutes. The radish-consuming participants just did not have the same level of energy available to them to persist on the difficult problems.

Unfortunately, life is a constant task of trying to resist the equivalent of freshly baked chocolate chip cookies. Researchers have now completed about 100 studies using the research paradigm outlined above and, in doing so, have identified the following seven broad spheres of self-control (Baumeister & Vohs, 2007; Hagger, Wood, Stiff, & Chatzisarantis, 2010):

- Suppressing impulses, urges, desires
- Managing and suppressing emotions
- Controlling and suppressing thoughts
- Controlling and fixing attention
- Making decisions and lots and lots of choices
- Managing the impression one is making on others
- Being kind to and dealing with difficult, demanding people

In separate experiments on self-control, researchers have had participants exert self-control by *suppressing impulses, urges, and desires* such as resisting sweets and snacks (Vohs, Baumeister, & Ciarocco, 2005) and the urge to drink or smoke a cigarette (Muraven & Shmueli, 2006); *managing emotions* by suppressing natural emotional reactions such as not crying while watching a very sad movie (Muraven, Tice, & Baumeister, 1998) or suppressing disgust reactions while looking at a contaminated object (Schmeichel, Demaree, Robinson, & Pu, 2006); *controlling thoughts* by suppressing or trying to get rid of an unwanted thought (Muraven, Tice, & Baumeister, 1998); *controlling and fixing attention* by prolonging perseverance, dutifully memorizing words, and engaging in tasks of vigilance (Schmeichel, Vohs, & Baumeister, 2003); *making a lot of decision and choices* concerning trivial and unimportant options (Vohs et al., 2008); *managing the impression one is making* on an audience of others by presenting oneself as a competent and likable person (Vohs, Baumeister, & Ciarocco, 2005); and *being kind to and dealing with difficult, demanding people* by presenting oneself in a way that runs counter to the natural urges that arise when interacting with "high-maintenance" others (Finkel et al., 2006).

Energy and Depletion

The findings from the radish experiment suggest that self-control is more than a skill. It is an energy reserve that seems to exist in only a limited amount. After self-control is exercised, people lose some of their capacity for future self-control. And, as people lose their capacity for self-control, they become increasingly likely to fall prey to impulsive desires, urges, and temptations. This line of thinking led to the proposal of the limited strength model of self-control (Baumeister & Heatherton, 1996; Baumeister, Muraven, & Tice, 2000; Baumeister, Vohs, & Tice, 2007; Muraven, 2012), which can be presented in a series of three propositions:

1. Amount or strength of willpower is critical to the success of self-control.
2. The exertion of self-control depletes some of this resource, and hence,
3. Subsequent attempts at self-control are increasingly likely to fail.

Such a model begs the question as to what is depleted during self-control attempts. The answer seems to be the brain fuel of glucose (Gailliot & Baumeister, 2007; Gailliot et al., 2007).

Glucose is manufactured in the body from food. During digestion, this sugar is produced and released into the bloodstream where it travels to the muscles, heart, liver, immune system, and brain. The brain is a big user of energy; it consumes about 20 percent of the body's glucose-supplied fuel (i.e., calories). Glucose does not actually enter the brain but, instead, it is converted into what the brain does use—namely, neurotransmitters. If the brain runs out of neurotransmitters, then it stops thinking. And if the brain stops thinking, it becomes more impulsive and exerts less executive control. All this complex biology boils down to a simple understanding: "No glucose, no willpower" (Baumeister & Tierney, 2011, p. 49).

Depletion

If the above reasoning is sound, then people who exert self-control should show a significant drop in their glucose level. Research shows that this is precisely what does happen and, further, that the drop in glucose is rather quick and rather large (Gailliot & Baumeister, 2007; Gailliot et al., 2007). That is, if you possess glucose level "X" and then engage in a self-control task such as suppressing a craving, then you will rather quickly have glucose level "less than X." This drop in glucose can be easily confirmed by the use of a glucose meter.

In a depletion experiment, participants engaged in a series of multiple self-control tasks—one after the other. Glucose was depleted rather markedly, which led to poor task performance. In a second study, participants were forewarned that they would be engaging in a series of multiple self-control tasks (i.e., you will be asked to "think hard" and "override impulses"), and the mere anticipation of marshaling forward all the dogged determination that is vigilant self-control was enough to decrease both glucose and task performance (Muraven, Shmueli, & Burkley, 2006).

Replenishment

Self-control depletes glucose but, knowing this, people can consume glucose in advance of a challenging self-control task by drinking a glass of glucose-rich orange juice, lemonade, or a milkshake. Doing so does significantly help people exert effective self-control (Hagger et al., 2010). Glucose does not have to be consumed via a sugary drink, but this is the fastest way to get glucose to the brain (as a diabetic will tell you). Low-sugar, high-protein foods (nuts, fruits, fish, meat, cheese) work just as well, but they take longer to produce brain fuel. Such a nutritional effect leads self-control researchers to the practical advice that you eat a good breakfast before embarking on any day that will require a fair amount of self-control.

Self-control depletes glucose, but it does so only when self-control means suppressing an attractive short-term urge (eat sweets, smoke a cigarette, play videogames) in order to pursue a less inherently attractive long-term goal (study for hours, complete a long list of chores, control one's temper during a negotiation). Interestingly, glucose depletion and poor performance do not occur if the person is first placed in a positive mood state, as by watching and laughing with a humorous film (Tice, Baumeister, Shmueli, & Muraven, 2007). Glucose depletion and poor performance also do not occur when people pursue long-term goals that satisfy the psychological needs of autonomy, competence, and relatedness (Muraven, 2008). In fact, long-term goal pursuit that produces episodes of psychological need satisfaction actually vitalizes (increases) energy and performance, rather than depletes them (Moller, Deci, & Ryan, 2006; Muraven, Gagne, & Rosman, 2008).

Self-control strength can also be enhanced through practice (Baumeister, Gailliot, De Wall, & Oaten, 2006). For instance, participants practiced self-control exercises for two weeks by working daily either to monitor and improve their posture or to monitor their food eaten each day (Muraven, Baumeister, & Tice, 1999). Monitoring one's posture requires self-control because one needs to constantly override the habit of slouching (as while sitting, standing); monitoring one's daily food consumption requires self-control because one needs to restrain a "grab and go" eating style. After two weeks of self-control practice, trained participants showed less self-control depletion than did a control group of untrained participants. Results were particularly strong for those who monitored their posture. In an education setting, students were trained to exert daily self-control over their studying by keeping to a regular study schedule. While untrained students in a control group showed depletion during the course examination period, the trained students in the experimental group actually showed self-control replenishment, rather than depletion (Oaten & Cheng, 2006). Relaxation also buffers people from self-control depletion and self-regulation failure (Tyler & Burns, 2008).

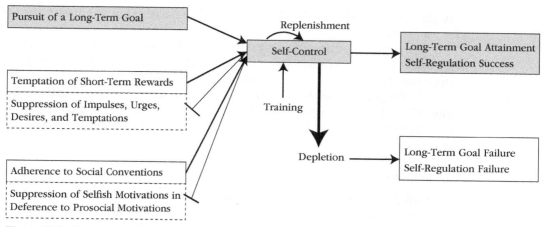

Figure 11.8   Full Limited Strength Model of Self-Control

The Limited Strength Model of Self-Control

A graphical representation of the limited strength model of self-control appears in Figure 11.8. Effective self-control is the use of willpower to help translate the pursuit of a long-term goal into gain attainment. This core purpose of self-regulation appears in the upper three shaded boxes of Figure 11.8. But self-control is a limited resource that is depleted by suppressing goal-antagonistic impulses, urges, desires, emotions, and thoughts. Self-control is further depleted by forcing oneself to adhere to social conventions (i.e., suppressing selfish motivations to realize prosocial motivations). Suppressing, restraining, and overriding impulses and short-term attractions deplete self-control strength, as depicted in the thick downward vertical line. Depletion, in turn, predicts and explains long-term goal and self-regulation failure, just as self-control predicts and explains long-term goal attainment and self-regulation success. The limited strength model also explains how self-control might be increased, as through nutritional replenishment, a positive mood, and psychological need satisfaction, and also how it might be buffered or toughened up, as through training and practice.

One entry that was not drawn into in Figure 11.8 still needs to be considered and discussed. The upper left of the figure features the box "Pursuit of a Long-Term Goal," but people rather frequently try to pursue more than one long-term goal at a time. College students, for instance, try persistently to achieve academically, but they also at the same time try earnestly and diligently to get their finances in order, repair upset and fragile relationships, and diet to lose weight. So, additional boxes for "Pursuit of Long-Term Goal 2" and "Pursuit of Long-Term Goal 3" could be added to Figure 11.8. The problem with multiple long-term goal pursuit is that it is an all-too reliable path to self-depletion and self-regulation failure. The problem is that studying for four hours every day necessarily entails effortfully suppressing a lot of short-term urges, desires, and attractions, just as dieting and trying to lose weight entails effortfully suppressing a lot of short-term urges, desires, and attractions, and just as trying to stay agreeable with a conflictual and irresponsible close other entails effortfully suppressing a lot of short-term urges, desires, and attractions. It is simply too depleting to pursue multiple long-term goals simultaneously. Research shows that it is best to pursue one long-term goal at a time and to invest one's limited capacity for self-control toward that single long-term goal (Shmueli & Prochaska, 2009).

Is the Capacity to Exert Self-Control Beneficial to a Successful Life?

The enduring capacity to resist the immediate gratification of a short-term attraction in the service of a delayed gratification of a larger long-term goal is a personality variable with one of the best track records of predicting who does (and who does not) live a successful life (Mischel, 1974; Mischel & Ayduk, 2004; Mischel, Shoda, & Peake, 1988). Realizing just how important self-control is in the effort to navigate a successful life began with the humble marshmallow study.

In the marshmallow study, a young child is brought into a room, shown a marshmallow (or cookie, or attractive sweet of his or her choice), and offered the following deal: You may eat the marshmallow whenever you want to, but if you hold off and do not eat the marshmallow and instead wait until I return to the room in 15 minutes, then you will get a second marshmallow to eat along with this one. When tested on their capacity to delay such immediate gratification, some children ate the marshmallow right away while others were able to wait the full 15 minutes. Then, the researchers waited until all the children were young adults to see how they were doing in terms of academic achievement, peer popularity, physical health, proneness to aggression, susceptibility to various addictions, and other indicators of a successful life. Results were clear. The children who showed high self-control had higher grade point averages, higher standardized test scores, were socially more popular, were objectively healthier, were prosocial rather than antisocial, and were generally free of the abuses of drugs and alcohol, compared to the children who showed low self-control (i.e., immediate gratification). Follow-up research linked trait-like self-control capacity to less relationship conflict (Finkel & Campbell, 2001), less overspending (Vohs & Faber, 2007), less violence (Stucke & Baumeister, 2006), and less obesity (Tangney, Baumeister, & Boone, 2004). These results show the benefits of self-control, but they just as clearly testify to the perils of impulsivity and the lack of self-control capacity.

IDENTITY

A final major aspect of the self is identity. Identity is the means by which the self relates to society, as it captures the essence of who one is within a cultural context (Deaux, Reid, Mizrahi, & Ethier, 1995; Gecas & Burke, 1995). Of course, people have unique personality traits and strivings, but people are also members of social and cultural groups. Cultures and social groups offer a variety of different identities that their individual members might occupy. Once a person inhabits a role (e.g., student, mother, salesperson, musician, liberal, Southerner), that identity then prescribes the person to display some behaviors (identity-confirming behaviors) while avoiding other behaviors (identity-disconfirming behaviors).

Roles

A role consists of cultural expectations for behavior from persons who hold a particular social position (Gross, Mason, & McEachern, 1958). Each of us holds a number of differ- ent social positions (roles), and which role we inhabit at any given time depends on the situation we are in and the people with whom we are interacting. For instance, in a college classroom, you probably assume the role of "student" as you interact with other "students" and a "professor." From a sociological point of view, it is not so much that Joe is interacting with Mary, Sue, and Jamar (individuals with unique motives and personalities) as it is that an inhabitant of the "professor" role interacts with several inhabitants of the "student" role. When you leave the classroom and go to your job at the psychology clinic, the role you occupy is very likely to change as you might assume the role of a "counselor" as you interact with "clients." At home, your role and the roles of those you interact with might again change as you assume the role of "mother" (or father) who interacts with a "daughter."

While assuming one role rather than another, people change how they act. They change the topic of their conversation, the vocabulary they use, the tone of their voice, and so forth. Even though "Mary" is still the same person, she converses in different ways when she finds herself in the role of "professor" rather than "mother." Behavior varies to such an extent from one role to the next that it makes more sense to speak of a person's set of identities rather than his or her single identity.

Identity-Establishing Behaviors

Individuals have many identities, and they present to others the particular identity that is most appropriate for the situation. For instance, if you telephone an office, the person who answers your call is likely assuming a role of a receptionist. Figuring out who you are (what role the situation places you in) and who it is you are talking to is a burden placed on the person answering the phone. The receptionist wonders, "Who am I talking to? A potential customer? An established client? A researcher? Someone from the media? The boss?" Once that key question has been answered, the receptionist then knows how to behave, what to say, what to expect from the other person, which behaviors are appropriate and which other behaviors are inappropriate, and also how the conversation will go. Once social interaction partners know that an "established client" is telephoning a "receptionist," the client expresses thoughts, feelings, and behaviors that are consistent with a client role, just as the receptionist expresses thoughts, feelings, and behaviors that are consistent with a receptionist role. At that point, social interaction proceeds smoothly.

Sociologists refer to this process of figuring out roles as the "definition of the situation" (Goffman, 1959; Gonas, 1977). Whenever people participate socially, their first task is to define the roles for the self and others. Once identities have been established, the situation has been defined and smooth social interaction can proceed.

Identity-Confirming Behaviors

Human beings possess a wide range of potential behaviors, but only a subset of those behaviors are appropriate and expected in any one particular setting. Precisely which behaviors and emotions are most appropriate is determined by the identity the person inhabits. Once that situationally and culturally appropriate identity has been established, people's behavior can be predicted and understood. Nice identities lead people to behave in nice ways, powerful identities lead people to behave in powerful ways, passive identities lead people to behave in passive ways, and so on. Identities direct behavior, and behaviors feedback to maintain and confirm that identity (Heise, 1979; Robinson & Smith-Lovin, 1992). The corresponding prescription for how to motivate others is therefore the following: If you want people to be nice, place them into an identity that the culture sees as nice ("helper"). If you want people to be assertive, place them into an identity that the culture sees as assertive ("leader"). If a teacher wants her students to show strong initiative and creativity, she might put them into the role of "detectives." An athletic coach can generate extra initiative from an athlete by putting him or her in the role of "team captain."

Identity-Restoring Behaviors

If a person behaves in an identity-inconsistent way (e.g., a mother scolds her child), she can restore the original identity either through restorative behaviors (e.g., nurture and soothe the child) or restorative emotions (e.g., display remorse or guilt). That is, both behavioral displays and emotional displays provide identity-relevant information of who that person is.

Consider how people use strategic emotion displays to restore their temporarily discon-firmed identities (Robinson, Smith-Lovin, & Tsoudis, 1994). Emotion displays act as public identity cues such that good people who act bad should show sorrow if they are truly good people (just as bad people who act bad should show no such sorrow if they are truly bad people). If a good person commits a bad act and does not show remorse, an observer is left to wonder if that person really is a good person. Good people should display deep remorse following a deviant act, whereas bad people should display little post-deviance remorse. Notice here that the behavior is known, the emotion is observed, and the underlying iden-tity is the only unknown. The mental calculus is to use the behavior and the emotion to figure out what the underlying character (identity) of the person must be. Hence, behaviors and emotions can be used to restore one's temporarily disconfirmed identity.

As an example, ask yourself "how good?", "how active?", and "how powerful?" are the following identities (social roles): teacher, principal, babysitter, elementary grade student, cheerleader, actor, nurse, CEO, accountant, lawyer, policeperson, and librarian. A cheer-leader who is not highly active, a CEO who is not highly powerful, and a nurse who is not highly good are just strange—are identity disconfirming. A cheerleader who acts in a lifeless way, a CEO who acts in a wimpy way, and a nurse who acts in a cruel way all need to counter-behave and to counter-emote to quickly restore that they really are lively, pow-erful, and nice, respectively. If not, then society (social interaction partners) will question whether each person really is a cheerleader, CEO, or nurse.

Overall, the motivational and emotional implications are that, once the individual finds his or her place in society, society expects him or her to behave and to emote in a way that is consistent with that identity. Hence, the cultural identity itself has motivational and emotional ramifications.

WHAT IS THE SELF?

Answering the question, "What is the self?" is a tall order, but a motivational analysis can help by explaining what the self does and how well it does it. At one level, the self is a social being that needs to be described and understood. Knowing one's personal qualities and pri-vate self reflects the *self-concept*, and knowing one's social roles and public self reflects *identity*. The self is also an agent, an actor with initiative and personal causation. The self has a reservoir of resources such as intrinsic motivation that acts as wellsprings for personal strivings. These wellsprings reflects *agency*, or the agentic self. The *phenomenological self* is that which is aware of its own subjective experience (e.g., "I feel conflicted about my job") and functioning (e.g., "I am doing well at school; I'm making fast progress"). The process of managing one's experience and long-term goals is *self-regulation*, and the process of suppressing dysregulation and impulsivity is *self-control*. Finally, the self is also a bit of a historian and prognosticator (Prebble, Addis, & Tippett, 2013). The self is a biographer-historian who creates a life story that endows the self with a sense of coherence and meaning, and the self is also a prognosticator who strives to create and then realize a desired future self.

Overall, the self is both complex (multifaceted) and busy. From a motivational point of view, the emphasis is partly on what the self is but it is mostly on what the self does—and how well it does it. Hence, a motivational analysis of the self asks if the self is happy, engaged, productive, flourishing, and fully functioning, or if it is depressed, indolent, ineffective, floundering, and overwhelmed. That answer depends on the health of the self in terms of its self-concept, identities, agency, phenomenology, and capacity for self-regulation and self-control.

SUMMARY

Four core problems occupy the self: defining and creating the self, discovering and developing personal potential, managing or regulating the self, and relating the self to society. This chapter presented these problems as self-concept (defining the self), agency (developing personal potential), self-regulation (managing the self), and identity (relating the self to society).

Self-schemas are cognitive generalizations about the self that are domain specific and learned from past experience. The self-concept is a collection of domain-specific self-schemas (e.g., how people mentally represent their personal characteristics in domains such as athletic competence and interpersonal relationships). Self-schemas generate motivation in two ways: the consistent self and the possible self. For the consistent self, self-schemas direct behavior to confirm the self-view and to prevent episodes that generate feedback that might disconfirm that self-view. In other words, behavior is used to solicit feedback that verifies the existing self-concept. For the possible self, the individual observes others and proactively forecasts a future possible self that he or she would like to become. Possible selves are higher-order long-term goals in that they energize, direct, and sustain the motivation necessary to develop the present self toward the hoped-for future self.

The self goes deeper than cognitive structures (self-concept) in that it has an intrinsic motivation, or agency, of its own. Agency entails personal causation and action from within. Agency energizes the developmental processes of differentiation and integration. Differentiation occurs as the self exercises its intrinsic interests, preferences, and capacities to grow and expand the self into an ever-increasing complexity. Integration occurs as these differentiated parts of the self are brought together into a sense of coherence or unity. The process is a dynamic one in which intrinsic motivation, differentiation, integration, and the internalization of social prescriptions all contribute to the ongoing development and growth of the self. The self-concordance model illustrates the motivational and developmental benefits of pursuing life goals that emanate out of personal agency and the integrated self, as self-goal congruence generates enhanced effort, greater psychological well-being, and developmental gains in future self-concordance.

Personal strivings constitute the superordinate goals people try to accomplish. Research on personal strivings reveals that well-being is more about what one strives for than it is about what one actually obtains in life.

Self-regulation involves the metacognitive monitoring of how one's goal-setting progress is going. Self-regulation begins with setting a long-term goal and proceeds through planning and strategic thinking, implementing action and self-control, monitoring and checking, and reflecting and revising. Self-regulatory processes are typically acquired and improved upon through a social learning process in which a novice observes, imitates, and then internalizes the competent self-regulatory skills of an expert model. Acquiring a greater capacity for effective self-regulation increases the person's capacity to carry out the goal-setting process on his or her own.

Self-control is the capacity to suppress, restrain, and override an impulsive, short-term urge, desire, or temptation so to pursue a long-term but larger goal. Colloquially, self-control is the same as willpower. Self-control is easily and quickly depleted while people struggle to override their immediate urges, desires, emotions, and unwanted thoughts. According to the limited strength model of self-control, the biological basis of self-control is the brain fuel of glucose and the assertion that "no glucose, no willpower." Glucose and the capacity for future self-control are depleted by the exercise of self-control but replenished by food, positive mood states, and goal pursuits that produce episodes of psychological need satisfaction. Longitudinal research shows rather impressively that the childhood capacity for high self-control predicts a successful life, compared to the life outcomes displayed by children with only a minimal capacity for self-control.

Identity is the means by which the self relates to society, and it captures the essence of who the self is within a cultural context. Once people assume social roles (e.g., mother, teacher), they act to establish, confirm, and restore the cultural meaning of that role-identity. People with nice identities engage in nice behaviors, just as people with powerful identities engage in powerful behaviors. Thus, a physician is helpful and kind, rather than hostile or cruel, because these behaviors exemplify the good and powerful identity of a doctor. Cultural identities (social roles) motivate identity-establishing, identity-confirming, and identity-restoring thoughts, behaviors, and emotions.

READINGS FOR FURTHER STUDY

Self-Functioning

BAUMEISTER, R. F. (1987). How the self became a problem: A psychological review of historical research. *Journal of Personality and Social Psychology, 52,* 163–176.

RYFF, C. D. (1989). Happiness is everything, or is it?: Explorations on the meaning of psychological well-being. *Journal of Personality and Social Psychology, 57,* 1069–1081.

Self-Concept

MARKUS, H. (1977). Self-schemata and processing information about the self. *Journal of Personality and Social Psychology, 35,* 63–78.

SWANN, W. B., JR. (1987). Identity negotiation: Where two roads meet. *Journal of Personality and Social Psychology, 53,* 1038–1051.

Agency

DECI, E. L., & RYAN, R. M. (1991). A motivational approach to self: Integration in personality. In R. Dienstbier (Ed.), *Nebraska Symposium on Motivation: Perspectives on motivation* (Vol. *38,* pp. 237–288). Lincoln: University of Nebraska.

SHELDON, K. M., & ELLIOT, A. J. (1999). Goal striving, need satisfaction, and longitudinal well-being: The self-concordance model. *Journal of Personality and Social Psychology, 76,* 482–497.

Self-Regulation

ZIMMERMAN, B. (2002). Attaining self-regulation: A social cognitive perspective. In M. Boekaerts, P. R. Pintrich, & M. Zeidner (Eds.), *Handbook of self-regulation* (pp. 13–39). San Diego, CA: Academic Press.

Self-Control

BAUMEISTER, R. F., VOHS, K. D., & TICE, D. M. (2007). The strength model of self-control. *Current Directions in Psychological Science, 16,* 351–355.

BAUMEISTER, R. F., BRATSLAVSKY, E., MURAVEN, M., & TICE, D. M. (1998). Ego depletion: Is the active self a limited resource? *Journal of Personality and Social Psychology, 74,* 1252–1265.

Identity

ROBINSON, D. T., & SMITH-LOVIN, L. (1992). Selective interaction as a strategy for identity maintenance: An affect control model. *Social Psychology Quarterly, 55,* 12–28.

Part Three

Emotions

Chapter 12

Nature of Emotion:
Six Perennial Questions

SIX PERENNIAL QUESTIONS

WHAT IS AN EMOTION?

    Definition
    Relation between Emotion and Motivation
        Emotion as Motivation
        Emotion as Readout

WHAT CAUSES AN EMOTION?

    Two-Systems View
    Chicken-and-Egg Problem
    What Ends an Emotion?

HOW MANY EMOTIONS ARE THERE?

    Biological Perspective
    Cognitive Perspective
    Reconciliation of the Numbers Issue
        Emotion Families (Reconciliation Strategy 1)
        Basic Emotions and Emotion Schemas (Reconciliation Strategy 2)

WHAT GOOD ARE THE EMOTIONS?

    Coping Functions
    Social Functions
    Why We Have Emotions

CAN WE CONTROL OUR EMOTIONS?

    Emotion Regulation Strategies
        Situation Selection
        Situation Modification
        Attentional Focus
        Reappraisal
        Suppression

WHAT IS THE DIFFERENCE BETWEEN EMOTION AND MOOD?

Everyday Mood

Positive Affect

Conditions that Make Us Feel Good

Benefits of Feeling Good

SUMMARY

READINGS FOR FURTHER STUDY

According to Chinese fortune cookies, the great philosophers, the Bible, Roosevelt (FDR) speeches, Vulcans, and the Dalai Lama, emotions such as anger and fear rarely pay off. Most of the time, these sources say, emotions lead to destructive results. Fear leads to paralysis. Anger leads to shoving and to blurting out words that we later regret. The suggestion is that we should ignore these meddling emotions. Emotion researchers, in contrast, see these emotions as constructive responses to fundamental life tasks. Fear and anger might feel bad, and they might sometimes steer us astray, but even the hottest of emotions exists as a necessary tradeoff in humans' emotion-laden quest for survival, adaptation, and mental health.

Emotion researchers are an open-minded bunch, so they decided to pack their bags, board an airplane to Dharamsala, and visit the Dalai Lama to hear a second opinion about "destructive emotions" (see Goleman, 2003). After all, it does make a good deal of sense to think of some emotions as potentially dangerous. You do not want to be in the same car with an anger-prone driver who fumes, speeds, weaves in and out, and grips the steering wheel like he is strangling the life out of other drivers' throats. This driver could benefit from a chat with the Dalai Lama.

So what wisdom did the Dalai Lama have to offer? A lot, it turns out. Buddhist thought organizes itself around the goal of recognizing, lessening, and then fundamentally transforming destructive emotions, particularly the big three of craving, agitation, and hatred. These emotions apparently are those that are most harmful to self and others. They have their place in survival and adapting to threatening situations, but since saber tooth tigers are no longer in the neighborhood, anger, fear, and the like may cost us more than they provide in benefits.

Through years of meditation, Buddhist monks learn how to translate their craving into contentment, their agitation into calm, and even their hatred into compassion. In the West, people lessen their negative emotions mostly with medicines (e.g., a pill for anxiety, a drug for depression). In the East, those who practice meditation turn their negative emotions into positive ones, because anger can, potentially, be focused into compassion just as resentment can be willed into love and respect for the other. Our biology has indeed prepared us to act emotionally to important life events, because everyone feels sad with loss and fear with threat. But a lot happens in the split second that occurs between the onset of a threat and the initiation of a constructive or a destructive emotional response. Discovering what happens in this split second of time opens up the possibility of being able to translate a biologically destructive reaction into a constructive way of coping. That is what Western emotion researchers learned from the Dalai Lama, and they have been studying what happens during that split second of time ever since.

SIX PERENNIAL QUESTIONS

Emotions arise as reactions to important life events. Once activated, emotions generate feelings, arouse the body to action, generate motivational states, and produce recognizable facial expressions. To understand this process, Chapter 12 discusses the nature of emotion, Chapter 13 focuses on the biological and cognitive events that occur within that split second between life event and emotional response, and Chapter 14 then looks at individual emotions one-by-one. Here, to understand the nature of emotion, Chapter 12 asks and answers the following six perennial questions in the study of emotion:

1. What is an emotion?
2. What causes an emotion?
3. How many emotions are there?
4. What good are the emotions?
5. Can we control our emotions?
6. What is the difference between emotion and mood?

WHAT IS AN EMOTION?

Emotions are more complex than first meets the eye. At first glance, we all know emotions as feelings. We know joy and fear because the feeling aspect of these emotions is so salient, so obvious. It may in fact be impossible not to notice emotion's feeling aspect during threat (fear) or during progress toward a goal (joy). But, in the same way that the nose is only part of the face, feelings are only part of the emotion.

Emotions are multidimensional. They exist as subjective, biological, purposive, and expressive phenomena (Izard, 1993; Mauss et al., 2005). In part, emotions are feeling states, because they lead to feeling a particular way, such as angry or joyful. But emotions are also biological reactions—energy-mobilizing response systems that prepare the body for adapting to whatever situation one faces. Emotions are also agents of purpose, much like hunger has purpose, that generate urges and impulses to action. Anger, for instance, creates a motivational impulse to do what we might not otherwise do, such as fight an enemy or protest an injustice. And, emotions are social-expressive phenomena. When emotional, we send recognizable facial, postural, and vocal signals that communicate the quality and intensity of our emotionality to others.

Given the four-part character of emotion, it is apparent that the concept is going to elude a straightforward definition (Izard, 2010; Mulligan & Scherer, 2012). The difficulty in defining emotion might puzzle you at first because emotions seem so straightforward in everyday experiences. Everyone knows what it is like to experience joy and anger, so the reader might ask, "What's the problem?" (Widen & Russell, 2010). The problem is the following: "Everyone knows what emotion is, until asked to give a definition" (Fehr & Russell, 1984). None of these separate dimensions—subjective, biological, purposive, or expressive—adequately defines emotion. Each of these four dimensions simply emphasizes a different aspect of emotion. To understand and to define emotion, it is necessary to study each of emotion's four dimensions and how they interact with one another.

Emotion's four dimensions (or components) appear in Figure 12.1. The figure shows four boxes, and each box corresponds to a separate aspect. The feeling component gives emotion its subjective experience that has both meaning and personal significance.

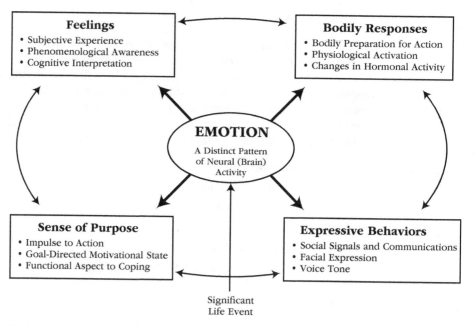

Figure 12.1   Four Components of Emotion

In both intensity and quality, emotion is felt and experienced at the subjective (or "phenomenological") level.

The bodily response component includes activation of our neural and biological response systems, including the activity of the brain and endocrine (hormonal) systems as they prepare and regulate the body's adaptive coping behavior during emotion. Brain activation, physiological activation, changes in hormonal activity, and bodily preparation for action are so intertwined with emotion that any attempt to imagine an angry or a disgusted person who is not bodily prepared for action is not possible. When emotional, our body is prepared for action, and that is true in terms of our brain, physiology (heart rate, epinephrine in the bloodstream), and musculature (alert posture, clenched fist).

The purposive component gives emotion its goal-directed character to deeply want to take the action necessary to cope with the circumstances at hand. The purposive aspect generates an impulse to action that explains why people want to do what they do during an emotion.

The expressive behavior component is emotion's communicative aspect. Through postures, gestures, vocalizations, and facial expressions, our private experiences become public expressions. Through such expressive behavior, we nonverbally signal to others how we feel and how we interpret the present situation. For instance, as a person opens a private letter, we watch her face and listen to the tone of her voice to read her emotions. Emotions therefore engage our whole person—our feelings, bodily arousal, sense of purpose, and nonverbal communications.

Definition

Emotions are short-lived, feeling–purposive–expressive–bodily responses that help us adapt to the opportunities and challenges we face during important life events. Figure 12.1

adds two more emotion features. Emotions arise as responses to the significant events in our lives, so Figure 12.1 includes an activating path from "significant life event" to "emotion." Figure 12.1 also includes the box "Distinct pattern of neural (brain) activity" within the concept of emotion to communicate that significant life events produce in us a distinct pattern of brain activity and also that it is this brain activity that gets everything going—that interrupts and changes our attention and information processing (what we are thinking about) to generate, guide, and coordinate the four aspects of emotion depicted in Figure 12.1. Thus, a significant life event occurs and produces a distinct pattern of neural activity that, in turn, generates and coordinates the emotional reaction that is a feeling–purposive–expressive–bodily reaction to that life event.

Defining emotion requires more than a "sum of its parts" definition. A "sum of the parts" approach allows us to describe (rather than define) emotion. As to description, Carroll Izard (2010) asked 34 leading emotion researchers to define the term *emotion;* he pulled together their replies into the following description (Izard, 2010, p. 367):

> Emotion consists of neural circuits (that are at least partially dedicated), response systems, and a feeling state/process that motivates and organizes cognition and action.
>
> Emotion also provides information to the person experiencing it, and may include antecedent cognitive appraisals and ongoing cognition including an interpretation of its feeling state, expressions, or social-communicative signals, and may motivate approach or avoidant behavior, exercise control/regulation of responses, and be social or relational in nature.

To define (and not just describe) emotion, we need to draw attention to the four double-sided arrows that link together the four component boxes in Figure 12.1. Emotion is the psychological construct that unites and coordinates these four aspects of experience into a synchronized pattern. That is why the term *emotion* appears in Figure 12.1 as a separate construct from its individual components. Emotion is not any of its individual components but is, instead, what choreographs the feeling, bodily response, purposive, and expressive components into a coherent reaction to an eliciting event. For instance, in the case of fear, the eliciting event might be steep ski slopes, while the reaction includes feelings, bodily responses, goal-directed desires, and all-too-public nonverbal communications. Thus, the threatened skier feels scared (feeling aspect), is "pumped up" (bodily response aspect), strongly desires self-protection (purposive aspect), and shows tensed eyes and pulled-back corners of the mouth (expressive aspect). Fear is what synchronizes and coordinates this complex pattern of reactivity to an environmental danger.

This description of what an emotion is highlights how different aspects of experience complement and coordinate with one another (Averill, 1990; LeDoux, 1989; Mauss et al., 2005). For instance, what people feel correlates with how they move the muscles of their face. What they want to do (sense of purpose) coordinates with how bodily prepared they are to do it. Similarly, the way you move your face is coordinated with your physiological reactivity, such that lowering your brow and pressing your lips firmly together coincides with increased heart rate and a raised skin temperature (Davidson et al., 1990). These interrelationships and the intercoordination among the four components of emotion are shown graphically in Figure 12.1 by the thin, curved lines that connect each aspect of emotion to each of the other three aspects. The two-way arrows communicate that changes in one aspect (component) correlates with changes in the other three aspects of emotion.

Figure 12.2 provides a concrete illustration of the otherwise abstract principle shown in Figure 12.1. Using sadness as an example, separation or failure is a common eliciting life

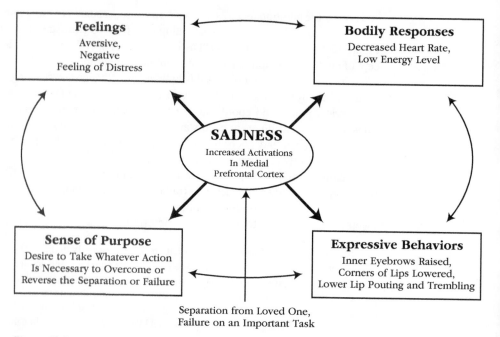

Figure 12.2   Four Components of Sadness

event. As an emotional reaction to separation or failure, sadness gets started with brain activity in the medial prefrontal cortex (Pelletier et al., 2003; Phan, Wager, Taylor, & Liberzon, 2002) and, with the onset of sadness, the aversive feeling arises and influences and co-occurs with lethargic bodily responses, with a sense of purpose (to reverse the separation or failure), and the readily recognized sad facial expression. Hence, emotions are the synchronized brain-based systems that coordinate feeling, bodily response, purpose, and expression so to ready the individual to adapt successfully to life circumstances. "Emotion" is the word psychologists use to name this coordinated, synchronized process.

One team of researchers explicitly tested how much versus how little each of emotion's four components were intercorrelated (Mauss et al., 2005). They had participants view video clips designed to include either joy (watch a puppy playing) or sadness (watch a boy crying over his father's death). As participants watched one of the video clips—and hence experienced one of the two emotions—researchers recorded second-to-second changes of their feelings, bodily responses (e.g., heart rate), motivational urges, and facial expressions. They then calculated intercorrelations among all possible pairs of these four aspects of emotions (i.e., the curved arrows between the boxes in Figures 12.1 and 12.2). Results showed that all pairs of emotion components were positively intercorrelated and that the correlation between feelings and facial expression was particularly high for both emotions.

With that rather extended preface, here is Robert Levenson's (1994a, p. 123) answer the age-old question, "What is an emotion?":

Emotions are short-lived psychological-physiological phenomena that represent efficient modes of adaptation to changing environmental demands.

Relation between Emotion and Motivation

Emotions relate to motivation in two ways. First, emotions are one type of motive. Like all other motives (e.g., needs, cognitions), emotions energize, direct, and sustain behavior. Anger, for instance, energizes subjective, physiological, hormonal, and muscular resources (i.e., energizes behavior) to achieve a particular goal or purpose (i.e., directs behavior), such as overcoming an obstacle to a valued goal. This energy and direction are maintained (persist) until either the eliciting event itself is removed or the anger-motivated coping behaviors successfully change the obstacle into a nonobstacle. From this perspective, emotional reactions fit the Chapter 1 definition of a motive very well (i.e., "those internal processes that give behavior its energy, direction, and persistence"). Second, emotions serve as an ongoing "readout" system to indicate how well or how poorly personal adaptation is going. Joy, for instance, signals social inclusion and goal progress, whereas distress signals social exclusion and goal failure.

Emotion as Motivation

Most emotion researchers agree that emotions function as one type of motive. Some researchers, however, go further. They argue that emotions constitute the *primary* motivational system (Izard, 1991, 2007; Tomkins, 1962, 1963, 1984). Throughout the 100-year history of psychology, the biological drives (hunger, thirst, sleep, sex, and pain) were considered to be the primary motivators (Hull, 1943, 1952). Air deprivation provides one example. Being deprived of air generates a physiological drive that can capture the person's full attention, energize the most vigorous of action, and direct behavior decidedly toward a single purpose. Accordingly, it seems logical to conclude that air deprivation produces a potent and primary homeostatic motive for taking whatever action is necessary in gaining the air needed to reestablish homeostasis (see Chapter 4). Emotion researcher Silvan Tomkins, however, called this reasoning, this apparent truism, a "radical error." According to Tomkins (1970), the loss of air produces a strong emotional reaction—one of fear or terror. It is this terror that provides the motivation to act. Thus, the terror, not the air deprivation or threat to homeostasis per se, is the causal and immediate source of the motivated action that follows. Take away the emotion, and you take away the motivation.

Emotion as Readout

Emotions read out the person's ever-changing motivational states and personal adaptation status (Buck, 1988). Positive emotions signal that "all is well" and reflect the involvement and successful satisfaction of our needs and goals; negative emotions act as a warning signal that "all is not well" and reflect the neglect and frustrated thwarting of our needs and goals (Carver & Scheier, 1998; Frijda, 1986; Oatley & Jenkins, 1992). As an illustration, consider sexual motivation and how emotion provides an ongoing progress report ("readout") that facilitates some behaviors and inhibits others. During attempts at sexual gratification, positive emotions such as interest and joy signal that all is well and facilitate further sexual conduct. Negative emotions such as disgust, anger, and guilt signal that all is not well and inhibit further sexual conduct. Positive emotions (interest, joy) during motivated action provide a metaphorical green light for continuing to pursue that goal or need satisfaction; negative emotions (disgust, guilt) provide a metaphorical red light for stopping the pursuit of that goal or need satisfaction.

WHAT CAUSES AN EMOTION?

When we encounter a significant life event, an emotion arises, as shown in Figure 12.3. Upon encountering a significant life event (a potential threat, a potential opportunity), the brain processes this event with a distinct pattern of neural activity (LeDoux, 2012; Panksepp, 1998). For example, walking into the dark leads to amygdala activation that becomes fear. This brain activity leads sets in motion the cognitive and biological processes that collectively generate, guide, and coordinate the critical components of emotion, including feelings, bodily responses, goal-directed purpose, and expressive behavior.

In the effort to explain what causes an emotion, many different viewpoints come into play, including those that are biological, psycho-evolutionary, neuroscientific, psychophysical, cognitive, clinical, developmental, psychoanalytical, social, sociological, and cultural. Despite this diversity, most of the answer to this question revolves around one central debate: biology versus cognition. Together, the cognitive and biological perspectives provide a relatively comprehensive picture of the emotion process. Nonetheless, acknowledging that both cognitive and biological aspects underlie emotion begs the question as to which is primary: biological or cognitive factors (Lazarus, 1982, 1984, 1991a, b; Scherer & Ekman, 1984; Zajonc, 1980, 1981, 1984). If emotions are largely biological, they should emanate from a causal biological core, such as subcortical brain circuits. For the biological theorist, emotions can and do occur without a prior cognitive event, but they cannot occur without a prior biological event. Biology, not cognition, is therefore primary. If emotions are largely cognitive, however, they should emanate from causal mental events, such as appraisals and interpretations of what the situation means. For the cognitive theorist, individuals cannot respond emotionally unless they first cognitively appraise the meaning and personal significance of an event: Is the event important to me? Is it relevant to my well-being? Interpretative cognitive appraisal, not biology, is therefore primary.

So, which side is correct? Or, which side is more correct? Emotion researchers have struggled for answers to this question, and two helpful answers have emerged.

Two-Systems View

One answer is that both cognition and biology cause emotion. According to Buck (1984), human beings have two synchronous systems that activate and regulate emotion.

One system is an innate, spontaneous, biologically driven system that reacts automatically and involuntarily to emotional stimuli. A second system is an experience-based cognitive system that reacts interpretatively by evaluating the meaning or personal significance of the emotional stimuli. The physiological emotion system came first in humankind's

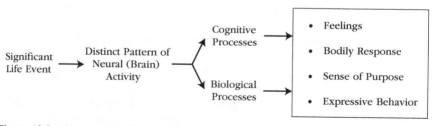

Figure 12.3 Causes of the Emotion Experience

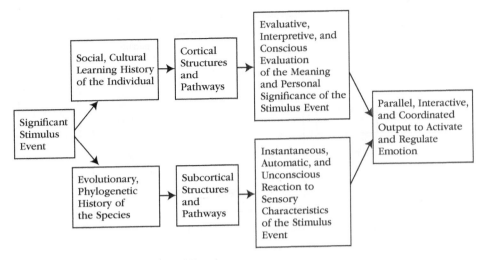

Figure 12.4 Two-Systems View of Emotion

evolution (i.e., the subcortical brain), whereas the cognitive emotion system came later as human beings became increasingly cerebral and social (i.e., the cortical brain). Together, the primitive biological system and the contemporary cognitive system combine to provide a highly adaptive, two-system emotion mechanism.

The two-systems view appears in Figure 12.4 (Buck, 1984). The lower system is biological and traces its origins to the ancient evolutionary history of the species. Sensory information is processed rapidly, automatically, and unconsciously by subcortical brain structures and pathways. The second system is cognitive and depends on the unique learning history of the individual. Sensory information is processed evaluatively, interpretatively, and consciously by cortical pathways. The two emotion systems are complementary (rather than competitive) and work together to activate and regulate emotional experience.

Robert Levenson (1994a) takes the two-systems view of emotion a bit farther by hypothesizing how the biological and cognitive emotion systems interact. The biological system serves basic problems by generating time-tested and highly automatic ways of generating emotion (i.e., general emotional reactions), while the cognitive system is highly flexible and open to learning and personal experience so that it can generate emotion to solve novel and situationally specific problems (Levenson, 1999). Instead of existing as parallel systems, the two systems influence, complement, and back-up one another. Panksepp (1994) adds that basic emotions such as fear, anger, and disgust arise primarily from the biological system (from subcortical structures and pathways in Buck's [1984] terminology). Other emotions such as gratitude, hope, and resentment arise primarily from personal experience, social modeling, and cultural contexts. These emotions arise primarily from the cognitive system's appraisals, expectancies, and attributions (from cortical structures and pathways in Buck's terminology).

Chicken-and-Egg Problem

Robert Plutchik (1985) sees the cognition versus biology debate as a chicken-and-egg quandary. Emotion should not be conceptualized as cognitively caused or as biologically caused.

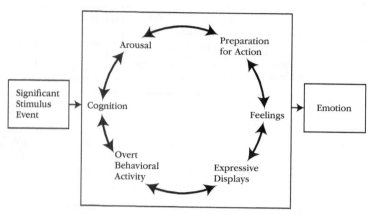

Figure 12.5 Feedback Loop in Emotion

Rather, emotion is a process, a chain of events that aggregate into a complex feedback system. The elements in Plutchik's feedback loop are cognition, arousal, feelings, preparations for action, expressive displays, and overt behavioral activity (i.e., recall the multi-dimensional aspects of emotion from Figures 12.1 and 12.2). One possible representation of Plutchik's emotion feedback loop appears in Figure 12.5. The recursive feedback system begins with a significant life event and concludes with emotion. Mediating between event and emotion is a complex interactive chain of events. To influence emotion, one can intervene at any point in the feedback loop. Change the cognitive appraisal from "this is beneficial" to "this is harmful," and the emotion will change. Change the quality of the arousal (as through exercise, a drug, or mediation), and the emotion will change. Change bodily expression (e.g., facial musculature, bodily posture), and the emotion will change, and so on.

Plutchik's (1985) solution to the cognition–biology debate enters into the complex world of dialectics, in which each aspect of emotion is both cause and effect and the final outcome is due to the dynamic interplay among the six forces in the figure. The most important theme to extract from a chicken-and-egg analysis is that cognitions do not directly cause emotions any more than biological events do. Together, cognition, arousal, preparation for action, feelings, expressive displays, and overt behavioral activity constitute the cauldron of experience that causes, influences, and regulates emotion. Others echo this emotion-as-a-process view by emphasizing that all emotional experiences exist as episodes that occur over time, as the different components continually rise and fall and exert influences on one another (Scherer, 1994b, 2013).

What Ends an Emotion?

Emotions arise as reactions to significant life events and to the biological and cognitive processes that these events set in motion. Emotions end, on the other hand, for two reasons. First, emotions end upon the removal of the significant life event. If looking at a needle in the doctor's office makes us feel fear, then walking out the doctor's office and leaving the needle behind is a good way to end the fear (although emotion-eliciting events very often recur in daily life and hence reactivate the emotion; Verduyn et al., 2009). Similarly, when circumstances perceived as unjust and unfair are revised to be just and fair, then our initially aroused anger fades appropriately away (Lerner, Goldberg, & Tetlock, 1998). Second, emotions generate coping behaviors, and these coping behaviors are often successful in managing and altering the significant life event. That is, upon seeing a spider, people often feel fear. But opening the window and tossing the spider out will fundamentally change (remove) the fear. Here, the coping action of tossing the spider out the window is what brings the fear to its end.

HOW MANY EMOTIONS ARE THERE?

The cognition–biology debate indirectly raises another important question: How many emotions are there? A biological orientation emphasizes basic emotions (e.g., anger, fear) and downplays the importance of secondary or acquired emotions. A cognitive orientation acknowledges the importance of the basic emotions, but it stresses that much of what is interesting about emotional experiences arises from individual, social, and cultural experiences. A cognitive orientation emphasizes the complex (secondary, acquired) emotions. Ultimately, any answer to the "How many emotions are there?" question depends on whether one favors a biological or a cognitive orientation.

Biological Perspective

The biological perspective typically emphasizes basic emotions, with a lower limit of two (Solomon, 1980) or three (Gray, 1994) to an upper limit of eight (Plutchik, 1980). Each biological theorist has a very good reason for proposing a specific number of emotions, although each proposal is based on a different emphasis. Ten major research traditions in the biological study of the emotions can be identified and offered to represent the biological perspective on emotions. Table 12.1 organizes these 10 biological perspectives side-by-side by listing the specific number of basic emotions proposed by each theorist, the rationale for that proposal, the theorist's name(s), and a supportive reference citation for further reading.

Richard Solomon (1980) identifies two hedonic, unconscious brain systems that exist such that any pleasurable experience is automatically and reflexively opposed by a

Table 12.1 Number of Basic Emotions Specified by 10 Biologically-Oriented Emotion Theorists

Number of Emotions	Rationale for That Proposed Number of Basic Emotions	Supportive Reference
2	Hedonic, unconscious "opponent" brain systems	Solomon (1980)
3	Animal brain circuits	Gray (1994)
4	Essential life pursuits	Stein and Trabasso (1992)
5	Brain circuits	Vytal and Hamann (2010)
6	Patterns of neural firing	Tomkins (1970)
6	Hard-wired, functional solutions to survival-relevant challenges	Levenson (2011)
7	Criteria specified by differential emotion theory	Izard (2011)
7	Brain circuits	Panksepp (1998)
7	Emotion families	Ekman and Cordaro (2011)
8	Emotion–behavior syndromes	Plutchik (1980)

counter-aversion experience, just as any aversive experience is automatically and reflexively opposed by a counter-pleasurable process (e.g., fear is countered by, and quickly replaced by, the "opponent process" of euphoria, as during sky diving).

Jeffrey Gray (1994) proposes three basic emotions based on the number of separate brain circuits he identified on an anatomical basis: the behavioral approach system (joy), the fight-or-flight system (anger/fear), and the behavioral inhibition system (anxiety).

Nancy Stein and Tom Trabasso (1992) stress the four emotions of happiness, sadness, anger, and fear because these emotions reflect reactions to life's essential pursuits: attainment (happiness), loss (sadness), obstruction (anger), and uncertainty (fear). Here the number of emotions in based on the number of key life events that activate the emotion.

Katherine Vytal and Stephan Hamann (2010) identify five emotions—happiness, sadness, fear, anger, and disgust, because of their analysis of about 100 different neuroimaging brain studies. They find that these five emotions produce distinct patterns of brain activity.

Silvan Tomkins (1970) distinguishes six emotions—interest, fear, surprise, anger, distress, and joy—because he finds six distinct patterns of neural firing produce these different emotions. For instance, interest is a slowly gradual increase in the rate of neural firing, fear is a rapid increase in the rate of neural firing, and surprise is a sudden surge in the rate of neural firing.

Robert Levenson (2011) also suggests six basic emotions—enjoyment, anger, disgust, fear, surprise, and sadness—because that is how many emotions are distinct, hard-wired, and functional in that each basic emotion is a general solution to a particular survival-relevant challenge.

Carroll Izard (1991) lists seven emotions on the basis of the criteria specified for a basic emotion within his differential emotions theory: interest, joy, sadness, anger, disgust, surprise, and fear. To identify basic emotions, he pays particularly close attention to the emotions of infants, as infants clearly show a limited number of discrete emotions despite their rather serious cognitive shortcomings (i.e., limited to no language, vocabulary, memory).

Jaak Panksepp (1998) proposes seven emotions—seeking, fear, anger/rage, lust, care, sadness/grief, and play. He proposed that these emotions are basic based on the finding of seven separate neuroanatomical, emotion-generating pathways within the subcortical brain.

Paul Ekman (Ekman & Cordaro, 2011) proposes seven basic emotions—fear, anger, sadness, surprise, disgust, happiness, and contempt. His list of emotions features this particular number of seven emotions because each is associated with a corresponding universal (cross-cultural) facial expression. These emotions also have very rapid onsets, brief durations, and can occur automatically/involuntarily.

Finally, Robert Plutchik (1980) lists eight emotions—anger, disgust, sadness, surprise, fear, acceptance, joy, and anticipation. Each of these emotions corresponds to an emotion–behavior syndrome common to all living organisms (e.g., fear corresponds to protection, as will be discussed in Table 12.2).

Each of these 10 research traditions agree that (1) a small number of basic emotions exists, (2) basic emotions are universal to all human beings (and animals), and (3) basic emotions are products of biology and evolution. All these theorists also argue that when we are experiencing an emotion, a cascade of automatic changes occur—with or without our awareness or consent, because preset signals emerge in our feelings, on our face, in the tone of our voice, within our autonomic nervous and endocrine systems, in our motivational urges, and in our thoughts and memories. Where the 10 traditions diverge is in their specifications of what constitutes the precise biological core that orchestrates emotional experience.

Cognitive Perspective

The cognitive perspective asserts firmly that human beings experience a greater number of emotions than the half-dozen or so highlighted by the biological tradition. Cognitive theorists grant that, yes of course, there are only a limited number of neural brain circuits, essential life pursuits, and hard-wired reactions to survival-relevant challenges. They point out, however, that several different emotions can arise from the same biological reaction. For instance, a single physiological response, such as a rapid rise in heart rate and blood pressure, can serve as the biological basis for anger, jealousy, or envy. High blood pressure and an appraisal of injustice produce anger; high blood pressure and an appraisal that one's relationship is in peril produce jealousy; and high blood pressure and an appraisal that another person is in a superior position produce envy. In each case, the biology is the same, but the emotions are different because the cognitive activity is different.

Instead of specifying a specific number of basic emotions (e.g., from 2 to 8) like the biologically oriented emotion theorists, cognitive emotion theorists argue that cognitive activity is a necessary prerequisite to emotion and, because this is so, an almost limitless number of emotions exist. This is so because all cognitive theorists share the assumption that "emotions arise in response to the meaning structures of given situations; different emotions arise in response to different meaning structures" (Frijda, 1988). How the cognitive theories of emotion differ is in how they portray the way people generate and interpret the meaning of a situation. That is, a life event occurs, a split second of time follows, and then some cognitively informed and situationally appropriate emotional reaction follows. In that split second of time, different cognitive emotion theories have identified a variety of different cognitive appraisals that take place to generate the emotion (Arnold, 1960; Ellsworth, 2013; Frijda, 2007; Lazarus, 1991a; Oatley & Johnson-Laird, 1987; Ortony, Clore, & Collins, 1988; Roseman, 1984; Scherer, 2009; Smith & Ellsworth, 1985; Weiner, 1986). Notice in the list of references in the previous sentence that 10 different cognitively oriented emotion theories and their distinct programs of research can be identified to represent a cognitive perspective on emotion. Each of these research traditions will be featured in Chapter 13.

Richard Lazarus was a pioneer in the cognitive perspective to understanding emotion, and his basic argument was that without an understanding of the personal relevance of an event's potential impact on personal well-being, there is no reason to respond emotionally. Stimuli appraised as irrelevant do not elicit emotional reactions. For Lazarus (1991a, b), the individual's cognitive appraisal of the meaning of an event (rather than the event itself) sets the stage for emotional experience. That is, a car passing you in traffic is not likely to call up your fear or shame unless its way of passing leads you to think that your well-being or self-image has in some way been put at risk. The emotion-generating process begins not with the event and not with one's biological reaction to it, but instead with the cognitive appraisal of its meaning.

Reconciliation of the Numbers Issue

Everyone—biologically and cognitively minded researchers—agrees that there are dozens of emotions. Everyone agrees that guilt and pride and gratitude are emotions; the biologically minded emotion theorist simply argues that these are not basic emotions. The debate therefore centers on whether some emotions are more basic or more fundamental than are others (Ekman & Davidson, 1994). One way to reconcile this debate is to argue that each basic emotion is not a single emotion but rather a *family* of related emotions (Ekman, 1994; Ekman & Cordaro, 2011). A second way to reconcile this debate is to distinguish first-order emotions (basic emotions) from second-order emotions (cognitively enriched emotion schemas) (Izard, 2011).

Emotion Families (Reconciliation Strategy 1)

Each basic emotion is not a single emotion but, rather, is a family of emotions that revolve around a particular theme. For instance, anger is a basic emotion, but anger is also a family of emotions that includes all emotions related to a "destroy obstacles" theme—namely, hostility, rage, fury, outrage, annoyance, resentment, envy, and frustration. Similarly, joy is a basic emotion, but joy is also a family of emotions that includes all emotions related to a "making progress on a goal" theme—namely, satisfaction, relief, enthusiasm, contentment, amusement, and pride. Each member of a family shares many of the characteristics of the basic emotion—its physiological bodily preparation, its subjective feeling state, its expressive signals, and its motivational urge to action (recall Figure 12.2). There are a limited number of these basic emotion families rooted in biology and evolution (as argued by the biologically minded theorists), but also there are a number of variations of these basic emotions via learning, socialization, and culture (as argued by the cognitively minded theorists).

Emotion families can also be understood from a cognitive perspective. An analysis of the English language led one group of researchers to conclude that emotion knowledge involves five basic emotion families: anger, fear, sadness, joy, and love (Shaver et al., 1987). While a child's emotional repertoire might include only anger, fear, sadness, joy, and love, greater experience and socialization allows the child to learn increasingly finer distinctions within the causes and consequences of these five basic emotions. The child learns that different situations give rise to different variations of the basic emotion. For instance, it takes learning, experience, and socialization to understand all the following varieties of fear: alarm, shock, fright, horror, terror, panic, hysteria, mortification, anxiety, nervousness, tension, uneasiness, apprehension, worry, dread, and perhaps others. Thus, fear is the basic emotion, while greater sophistication with different types of situations, with different interpretations of situations, and with language, social interaction, and enculturation lead to fear variations as secondary emotions.

Any answer to the question of how many emotions there are forces one to commit to a level of specificity (Averill, 1994), which means that emotions can be conceptualized at a general level such as a family (e.g., anger) or at a situation-specific level (e.g., hostility, envy, frustration). The specific characteristics of a basic emotion that can be utilized to make this distinction between what is basic and general versus what is not (i.e., what is specific, personal, and situational) includes the following (based on

Ekman, 1992; Ekman & Davidson, 1994; Ekman & Cordaro, 2011). All basic emotions feature a(n):

1. Distinct facial expression
2. Distinct pattern of physiology
3. Automatic (unlearned) appraisal
4. Distinct antecedent cause
5. Inescapable (inevitable) activation
6. Presence in other primates
7. Rapid onset
8. Brief duration
9. Distinct subjective experience (feeling state)
10. Distinct cognition (thoughts, images, memories)

Using these criteria, Ekman and Cordaro (2011) argue that the following seven basic emotions meet all the criteria to warrant the status of a basic emotion that serves as the foundational starting point for the development of an emotion family: anger, fear, surprise, sadness, disgust, happiness, and contempt. Several other emotions come close to meeting the above 10 qualifying criteria, but they only meet most—not all—of the above criteria. Included in this "almost basic emotion" category are guilt, shame, embarrassment, interest, love, and hate.

Upon seeing a list of emotions that includes only anger, fear, surprise, sadness, disgust, happiness, and contempt, one is likely to ask the question, "Where are emotions like jealousy, hope, love, anxiety, depression, aggression, and worry?" Biologically minded theories generally do not consider these basic emotions for the following reasons (Ekman, 1992):

1. Many emotions are experienced-based derivatives of a basic emotion (e.g., anxiety is a derivative of fear).
2. Many emotion terms actually better describe moods (e.g., irritation).
3. Many emotion terms actually better describe attitudes (e.g., hatred).
4. Many emotion terms actually better describe personality traits (e.g., hostile).
5. Many emotion terms actually better describe disorders (e.g., depression).
6. Some emotions are blends of basic emotions (e.g., romantic love blends interest, joy, and the sex drive).
7. Many emotion terms refer to only one specific aspect of a basic emotion (e.g., what elicits the emotion [homesickness] or to how a person who experiences a basic emotion behaves [aggression]).

Basic Emotions and Emotion Schemas (Reconciliation Strategy 2)

Basic emotions can be conceptualized as subcortical brain circuits that are rooted in evolutionary adaptation to major life tasks that have automatic connections with feelings, expressions, bodily preparations, and motivational action tendencies (Barrett, 2006;

Izard, 2007). In his differential emotions theory, Carroll Izard (1991, 2007, 2009, 2011) postulates that basic emotions can be identified by meeting seven criteria. Each basic emotion:

1. Is present at birth or emerges during infancy.
2. Requires only simple or minimal cognitive processing for its activation.
3. Is derived through evolutionary processes.
4. Features a unique feeling state: its own unique subjective, phenomenological quality.
5. Features a unique expression: its own unique facial-expressive signal.
6. Features a unique function: It serves its own unique purpose.
7. Features a unique motivational force important to survival and well-being.

The six basic emotions that fulfill each of these seven postulates from differential emotions theory are interest, joy (enjoyment, happiness, contentment), sadness, anger, disgust, and fear. Izard remains ambivalent about the inclusion/exclusion of a seventh emotion—namely contempt. Unlike all other biologically oriented emotion theorists, Izard (2007, 2011) proposes that people infrequently experience these six or seven basic emotions after early childhood. Instead, these basic emotions serve as developmental building blocks for more complex emotions termed *emotion schemas*. After childhood, emotion schemas serve as the principal motivational and regulatory system for the person's behavior and action.

Emotion schemas develop out of a dynamic interplay among basic emotions, cognitive appraisals, and higher-order cognition (e.g., self-concept, emotion knowledge). After early development, emotion schemas—but not basic emotions per se—function as the central source of human motivation (Izard, 2007), because basic emotions combine with cognition to produce complex emotion schemas. The sadness emotion schema, for instance, retains the core sad feeling but it also adds sad-related and experience-based thoughts and memories. Such an emotion schema might be activated by an experience of loss or failure, but it might also be activated by appraisals, memories, past learning experiences, thoughts, images, and information processing more generally. While the feeling, expression, action tendency, and bodily preparations are developmentally constant elements of any emotion schema, the content of an emotion schema changes over time. Because cognition is differentiated and complex, the person develops many dozens of emotion schemas, as cognitive content becomes more and more central to the emotion while the basic feeling–purpose–bodily preparation-expressive behavior core becomes less and less central.

Thus, Carroll Izard's reconciliation of the numbers question is to recognize two categories of emotion—first-order basic emotions and second-order emotion schemas. Infants start with a full repertoire of pure first-order basic emotions and no second-order emotion schemas, while adults possess no first-order basic emotions and a full repertoire of second-order emotion schemas. The number of emotion schemas the adult's uses to interact with the world is a large number, and that number is determined by the richness of the person's experience, cognition, and emotion differentiation.

WHAT GOOD ARE THE EMOTIONS?

While feeling the angst of sadness, anger, shame, pity, embarrassment, or jealousy, people understandably ask themselves, "What purpose do emotions serve—what good are they?"

It is not uncommon for people who feel aversive emotions to wish that their emotion would just go away and leave them alone. Who wants to feel sad? Who wants to feel ashamed?

Work on the utility or function of emotion began with Charles Darwin's *The Expression of Emotions in Man and Animals* (1872), a less famous effort than his 1859 work on the evolution of species. In his work on emotions, Darwin argued that emotions help animals adapt to their surroundings. Displays of emotion help adaptation much in the same way that displays of physical characteristics (e.g., height) do. For example, the dog baring its teeth in defense of its territory helps it cope with hostile situations (by warding off opponents). Such expressiveness is functional, and emotions are therefore candidates for natural selection.

Coping Functions

Emotions do not just occur out of the blue. They occur and affect the person for a reason. From a functional point of view, emotions evolved because they helped animals deal with fundamental life tasks (Ekman, 1994a; Levenson, 2011; Plutchik, 1970, 1980; Tooby & Cosmides, 1990). To survive, animals must explore their surroundings, vomit harmful substances, develop and maintain relationships, attend immediately to emergencies, avoid injury, reproduce, fight, and both receive and provide caregiving. Each of these behaviors is emotion produced, and each facilitates the individual's adaptation to changing physical and social environments.

Fundamental life tasks are universal human predicaments, such as loss, threat, and achievement (Johnson-Laird & Oatley, 1992). The emotion during a life task energizes and directs behavior in adaptive ways (e.g., after goal interference, assertively confronting and overcoming the barrier or restriction proved more effective than did other courses of action). Of course, there are many possible ways of coping, so what emotions functionally do is to prioritize some ways of acting over other ways of acting (e.g., "Do this!") to optimize the individual's capacity to adjust to the changes in the physical and social environment (Keltner & Gross, 1999). That is, emotion and emotional behavior provide animals with ingrained and automated ways for coping with major challenges and threats to their welfare (Tooby & Cosmides, 1990).

As shown in Table 12.2, emotions serve at least 10 distinct purposes. When something happens to interfere with the pursuit of an important goal, we feel anger—the functional

Table 12.2 Functional View of Emotional Behavior

Fundamental Life Task	Emotion	Coping Function (Purpose of the Emotion)
Goal progress, attainment	Joy	Soothe, play
Separation or failure	Sadness	Reverse the separation or failure
Interference with goal pursuit	Anger	Overcome barriers and restrictions
Threat or danger present	Fear	Protect, avoid
Spoiled object	Disgust	Repulsion
Novelty, need-involvement	Interest	Explore, take in information
Achievement	Pride	Acquire skills, persist
Judging another as inferior	Contempt	Maintain the social hierarchy
Feelings of inferiority	Shame	Protect, restore the self
Behaving inadequately	Guilt	Reconsider and change that behavior

purpose of which is to overcome that barrier or restriction. When we encounter a threatening or dangerous situation, we feel fear—the functional purpose of which is to protect the self, as by defending, feeling, or avoiding. When we behave in a socially inadequate way, we feel guilt—the functional purpose of which is to prompt us to reconsider that behavior and to change it into something more adequate. For every major life task, human beings evolved a corresponding, adaptive emotional reaction. The function of emotion is therefore to prepare us with an automatic, very quick, and historically successful response to life's fundamental tasks.

The logic and line of reasoning that underlies a functional perspective on emotion is this: There is no such thing as a "bad" emotion. Joy is not necessarily a good emotion, and anger and fear are not necessarily bad emotions. *All* emotions are beneficial because they direct attention and channel behavior to where it is needed, given the circumstances one faces. Any one person might not wish to feel anger, disgust, or fear, but it sure is handy to have the motivational readiness to fight when you need to, reject when you need to, and explore when you need to. From this point of view, fear, anger, disgust, sadness, and all other emotions are good. Situations and circumstances might be bad–but not the emotional reaction per se. Anger turns us into activists who are ready to change injustice into justice (Solomon, 1990), just as fear motivates protection, disgust motivates rejection, and so forth. Even embarrassment is functionally good, because it helps the person maintain a positive self-image in the eyes of the audience in the moments that immediately follow a social blunder (Semin & Manstead, 1982). Emotions are therefore positive, functional, purposive, and adaptive organizers of behavior.

Other biologically oriented emotion researchers stress greater flexibility in emotional ways of coping than is otherwise apparent from Table 12.2 (Frijda, 1994). That is, while fear essentially motivates protective behavior, it also readies us for additional and more flexible actions, including preventing the dangerous event from occurring in the first place or suppressing activity until the threat passes. Likewise, anger essentially motivates destructive action, but it also prepares us to enforce social norms or to discourage anger-causing events before they occur. Individual experience and cultural learning over time greatly expand the behavioral actions and strategies that can successfully serve the "Coping Function" column in Table 12.2. This increased flexibility is important because it makes it clear that emotional responses are more flexible than are reflexes (Scherer, 1984b).

Social Functions

In addition to serving coping functions, emotions serve social functions (Izard, 1989; Keltner & Haidt, 1999; Manstead, 1991; Rime, 2009). The assumption is that people are social by nature. Being social, emotions play a functional role in helping people navigate their social interactions and interpersonal relationships to solve important social problems. Emotions

1. Communicate our feelings to others.
2. Influence how others interact with us.
3. Invite, smooth, and facilitate social interaction.
4. Create, maintain, and dissolve relationships.

Emotional expressions are potent, nonverbal messages that communicate our feelings to others. Through emotional expressions, infants nonverbally communicate what they cannot communicate verbally, as through the face (Fridlund, 1992), voice (Scherer, 1986), and emotional behavior in general (Huebner & Izard, 1988). At birth, infants are capable of expressing joy, interest, and disgust; by 2 months, infants can also express sadness and anger; and by 6 months, infants can express fear (Izard, 1989). Throughout infancy, interest, joy, sadness, disgust, and anger represent almost 100 percent of emotion-based facial expressions (Izard et al., 1995). Caregivers reliably recognize and can accurately interpret these facial expressions (Izard et al., 1980). Infant facial expressions therefore guide caretakers' emotion-specific care (Huebner & Izard, 1988).

The emotional expressions of one person can prompt selective behavioral reactions from a second person (Camras, 1977; Coyne, 1976a, b; Frijda, 1986; Klinnert et al., 1983). In a conflict situation over a toy, for instance, a child who expresses anger or sadness is much more likely to keep the toy than is a child who expresses no such emotion (Camras, 1977; Reynolds, 1982). The emotional expression nonverbally communicates to others what one's probable forthcoming behavior is likely to be (Keltner & Haidt, 1999). If the toy is taken away, the anger-expressing child communicates a probable forthcoming attack, whereas the sadness-expressing child communicates a probable barrage of tears. The signal that one is likely to attack or cry often succeeds in regaining the lost toy (or preventing the toy from being taken in the first place). Hence, in the context of social interaction, emotions serve multiple functions, including informative ("This is how I feel"), forewarning ("This is what I am about to do"), and directive ("This is what I want you to do") functions (Ekman, 1993; Schwartz & Clore, 1983). In this way, emotional expressions communicate social incentives (joy smile), social deterrents (angry face), and unspoken messages (embarrassment face) that smooth and coordinate social interactions (Fernald, 1992; Keltner & Buswell, 1997; Tronick, 1989).

Emotional expressions are also used to invite, smooth, and facilitate social interaction. Ethnologists studying smiling in primates found that chimpanzees use the voluntary smile sometimes to deflect potentially hostile behavior from dominant animals and other times to maintain or increase friendly interactions (van Hooff, 1962, 1972). Just as primates smile (bare their teeth) to appease dominants, young children smile when approaching a stranger, and children are more likely to approach a stranger who smiles than a stranger who does not smile (Connolly & Smith, 1972). Adults who are embarrassed socially are also likely to smile, or at least to show a goofy grin on their face (Harris, 2006). In addition, the smile is a universal greeting display (Eibl-Eibesfeldt, 1972; van Hooff, 1972) that seems to say, nonverbally, "I am friendly; I would like us to be friends." In each of these instances, smiling is socially, rather than emotionally, motivated.

The idea that a smile can be socially motivated leads to the question of whether smiling is typically an emotional expression of joy or a social expression of friendliness (Fernandez-Dols & Ruiz-Belba, 1995; Kraut & Johnston, 1979). To test this hypothesis, Robert Kraut and Robert Johnston (1979) observed people smiling while bowling, while watching a hockey match, and while walking down the street. The researchers wondered whether people smiled more often when engaged in social interaction or when experiencing a joy reaction to a positive event (a good bowling score, a goal for their hockey team, sunny weather). Generally speaking, bowlers, spectators, and pedestrians were more likely to smile socially (to smooth social interactions) than emotionally (in response to positive outcomes).

Just as the emotional expressions of interest and joy bring people together and encourage interaction (Abe & Izard, 1999), emotional expressions of anger, disgust, and fear push people apart. Contempt is an especially toxic emotion that dissolves relationships (Gottman, 1994). Anger, disgust, fear, and contempt can also prevent relationships from forming in the first place.

Why We Have Emotions

Life is full of challenges, stresses, and problems to be solved, and emotions exist as solutions to these challenges, stresses, and problems. By coordinating and orchestrating feelings, arousal, purpose, and expression, emotions "establish our position vis-à-vis our environment" (Levenson, 1999) and "equip us with specific, efficient responses that are tailored to problems of physical and social survival" (Keltner & Gross, 1999).

Some argue that emotions serve no useful purpose. They argue that emotions disrupt ongoing activity, disorganize behavior, and rob us of our rationality and logic (Hebb, 1949; Mandler, 1984). These emotion researchers grant that while emotions served important evolutionary functions thousands of years ago, they no longer do so in the modern world (e.g., Buss et al., 1998). This position stands in stark contrast to the assertion that emotions prioritize behavior in ways that optimize adjustment to the demands we face. Everyone agrees that emotions affect the way we think, feel, and behave. So, the question hinges on whether emotions are adaptive and functional or maladaptive and dysfunctional (see Box 12).

The reason that both sides of the "functional versus dysfunctional" question makes sense is because both are correct. Emotions exist as both a masterpiece of evolutionary design (as pointed out by emotion theorists) and also as excess baggage in the age of reason (as pointed out by Stoics, Buddhists, and others).

Human emotion operates within a two-system design (Levenson, 1999). The biological core of the emotion system is one that humans share with other animals, and this is the part of the emotion system that evolved to solve fundamental life tasks. Because only a few life tasks are truly fundamental, the emotion system responds in a stereotypical way that recruits and orchestrates a limited but highly appropriate set of responses. This way of responding can be characterized as "time-tested recipe" (to borrow an example from Levenson, 1999, and to capture the spirit of the content featured in Table 12.2). When situationally appropriate, these automated ways of responding to problems can be highly adaptive. But they can also be situationally inappropriate when activated under other circumstances. After all, attacking one's opponents is not always the best way to handle a situation. For emotions to be adaptive across many different situations, they need to be regulated and controlled.

As Robert Levenson (1999) points out, in the modern world, tigers rarely jump out at us, people rarely steal our food, and wild beasts rarely threaten to kill our young. Today's threats are on a smaller scale and therefore do not require the same sort of massive mobilization of our emotion systems. Becoming competent in regulating one's emotions generally improves with experience, and it constitutes a lifelong undertaking (Carstensen, 1995; Gross, 2002). In the end, whether emotions serve us well depends on how able we are to self-regulate our emotion systems such that we experience regulation *of* emotion rather than regulation *by* emotion (Gross, 1999).

| BOX 12 | *Emotion's Role in Development* |

Question: Why is this information important?

Answer: To appreciate why Vulcans could never be smarter than humans.

In science fiction (i.e., *Star Trek*), Vulcans are a race of people who deny and reject their emotions. They constantly seek to overcome their emotions. Vulcans are also a very smart race, full of logic, intelligence, abstract thinking, and amazing cognitive development. Vulcans accomplish these lofty cognitive attainments, they believe, because they reject their emotions.

Rejecting emotions to enrich cognitive development is more fiction than it is science. The emotion system is a critical ally in the development of the cognitive system. What if the Vulcan infant refused to smile or show spontaneous interest? The poor little guy's quantity and quality of social interaction with caretakers would nose-dive. The social smile recruits caregivers' approach and interaction. Without frequent smiling, the Vulcan infant would not have the means of gaining a steady stream of stimulation and challenge from others that is necessary for optimal cognitive development, perspective taking, role playing, and rule internalization.

Interest is an emotion that arises from environmental novelty and complexity. Without interest, the Vulcan would lack an inner motivational resource to explore her physical surroundings—to pick things up, shake them, toss them, and conduct all sorts of little experiments on the world. Infants who express positive emotions such as interest and joy bring caretakers close to them, and the relationship with an attachment figure is the infant's springboard for increasing exploration, increasing play, reducing wariness of strangers, and gaining an increased sociability with others outside the infant–caregiver relationship (Colin, 1996).

Anger during the "terrible twos" helps foster the preschool child's sense of self-reliance (Dunn & Munn, 1987). Imagine the Vulcan child without the capacity for anger when goals were obstructed. He or she would show little or no protest against restraints and discomforts. He or she would feel little motivation to engage in the thinking and problem solving necessary for figuring out how to cope so to reverse and overcome obstacles.

Sadness, shame, guilt, sympathy, and empathy are emotional ingredients in the development of prosocial behavior. Without the information provided by these emotions, the Vulcan child would be slow to learn what would be wrong with taking a prized toy from another child. Empathy and sadness allow the child ways to understand the deleterious consequences to the other child (Davidson, Turiel, & Black, 1983). Shame and guilt make it painful to violate social rules and moral standards. Shame tells the self that one is acting in a way that is inadequate or unacceptable to others (Orth, Berking, & Burkhardt, 2006). Guilt motivates reparative behaviors that help maintain our relationships with others (Zeelenberg & Breugelmans, 2008).

Emotions facilitate and fuel cognitive development (Abe & Izard, 1999; Larson & Asmussen, 1991). One interesting analysis of this process appears in *The Diary of Anne Frank*. Her writings consistently showed that experiences of intense emotion were quickly followed by gains in higher levels of thinking (Haviland & Kramer, 1991). Emotional experiences (e.g., fear, anger, disgust, sadness) contribute motivationally to the adolescent's active mental construction of the self-concept, the discovery of meaning, consideration of ideal and possible selves, and abstract thinking in general. In this way, emotions fuel cognitive development.

CAN WE CONTROL OUR EMOTIONS?

The tone of the chapter thus far has been that emotions are functional assets that generate automatic and effective coping responses that help us solve life's fundamental problems. That is, emotions are fundamentally good. But those who study emotion regulation point out that emotions are not always helpful and can in fact sometimes hurt as well as help (Gross, 1998, 2008). Emotions hurt us when they are situationally inappropriate, when they come at the wrong time, or when they occur at the wrong level of intensity. It is at these times

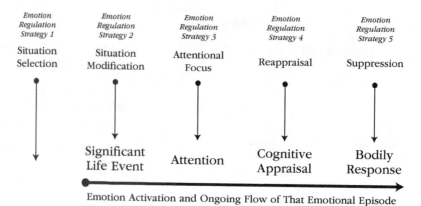

Figure 12.6 Flow of a Typical Emotion Episode and Five Opportunities to Regulate That Emotion

when we wish to intervene to take control to regulate or change our emotions. Emotions are often automatic reactions, but that does not mean that there are not numerous opportunities within the flow of an emotional episode to intervene to change the course it takes.

Emotion regulation refers to how we try to influence which emotions we have, when we have them, and how we experience and express the emotions we have (Gross, 2008). Emotion regulation also refers to what part of the emotion we try to gain control over—our feelings, our bodily response, our motivational urge, or our expressive display, and emotion regulation further involves efforts to change an emotion's latency, magnitude, and duration (i.e., when it begins, what intensity level it reaches, and how long it lasts). To illustrate how and when people attempt to intervene to regulate an emotion, James Gross breaks down the flow of an emotional episode, as depicted graphically in Figure 12.6. An emotion begins with a situation, or what the chapter has referred to as a significant life event. Once in an emotional situation, there is typically some degree of management or modification of that situation. The person also directs attention toward or away from the significant life event. Those situations that are attended to are appraised, interpreted, and reappraised. A coping response follows, and such action can change any part of the emotional episode. As a brief illustration, your telephone may ring and your friend invites you to lunch. First, you decide to answer the phone or not, and second you may (or may not) suggest an alternative activity. During the conversation, you may attend fully to your friend and the plan for the afternoon, or you may just daydream or doodle on a piece of paper. During the conversation, you make a flurry of appraisals: "Is the invitation good or bad? Is the invitation familiar or unexpected? Is anything important at stake?" All these appraisals will be reassessed during the lunch. And, during the lunch, you will display many coping responses, such as expressing your thanks, offering self-disclosure, enlisting your friend's support for something you are trying to do, or other responses. The point is that you will have many opportunities for emotion regulation during almost every emotional episode, and these opportunities for emotion regulation are depicted by the downward vertical lines at the top of Figure 12.6.

Emotion Regulation Strategies

Five opportunities to intervene to regulate an emotional episode are possible and are identified in the upper half of Figure 12.6: situation selection, situation modification, attentional focus, reappraisal, and suppression. The first four emotion regulation strategies are proactive, while the last strategy is reactive to the emotional experience (Gross, 2002; Gross & Thompson, 2007). There are probably a hundred different emotion regulation strategies, so the five strategies featured in Figure 12.6 represent categories or families of strategies.

Figure 12.6 presents five discrete emotion regulation strategies, although people tend to use multiple emotion regulation strategies during any one emotional episode (Aldao & Nolen-Hoeksema, 2013). Further, some strategies are more effective than are others. For instance, reappraisal and attentional focus regulate negative emotion rather effectively while suppression generally does not (Augustine & Hemenover, 2009). And, some people have more emotion regulation strategies than do others; for instance, women generally have a wider range of emotion regulation strategies than do men (Nolen-Hoeksema, 2012).

Situation Selection

The earliest opportunity to intervention to influence the trajectory of an emotional experience is situation selection. Situation selection is taking action to make one emotional experience more or less likely. Sometimes, situation selection is a strategic effort to prevent an emotion from launching (e.g., "If I go there, I'll feel sad. So, I just won't go."). More generally, however, situation selection involves deciding what to do, where to go, who to spend time with, which activities to engage in, which appointments to keep, what to do after work, what to do during free time, and how to schedule a Saturday afternoon. By selecting one situation rather than another, we tip the odds significantly whether we will encounter this or that significant life. By selecting which life events to expose ourselves to, we significantly bias which emotions we will and will not experience. If we visit a friend, we will likely feel joy; if we clean the bathroom, we will likely feel disgust; and if we go to the job interview, we will likely experience multiple emotions such as interest and fear while also preventing other emotions such as regret.

Situation Modification

Life's significant events unfold over time. The confrontation with a bully starts with fear, but the situation can take several twists and turns as each actor works to modify the situation. Upon seeing the bully's angry face and posture, we can modify that situation by expressing challenge or appeasement, by telling a joke or hurling an insult, by bringing along a big friend or coping alone, or other strategies. In the same way, classrooms that start off boring do not have to stay that way, because students can make suggestions to change the schedule of events. And, conversations that begin as heated arguments do not have to be a breeding ground for anger, resentment, and contempt, if one or both partners will intervene to modify the flow of the argument by apologizing, showing concern, offering support, soliciting advice, or behaving in a prosocial rather than in an antisocial way. Situation modification essentially involves problem-focused coping (Lazarus & Folkman, 1984), efforts to establish primary control over a situation (Rothbaum, Weisz, & Snyder, 1982), and the search for social support (Mikulincer, Shaver, & Pereg, 2003). Sometimes, situations are modified by simply leaving them (Aldao, Nolen-Hoeksema, & Schweizer, 2010).

Attentional Focus

Situation selection and situation modification are rather active emotion regulation strategies. Changing one's attentional focus does not change the situation but, rather, redirects one's attention within that situation. Within any emotional experience, there are always multiple aspects of that experience that we might potentially attend to. Sitting in class, you might attend to the content of the lesson, to the professor's funny tie, to the person sitting next to you, to the temperature in the room, to the scene happening outside the window, or you can distract yourself by drawing or checking emails on your smartphone. If you are stuck in a long line, you might attend to the frustratingly long line or to the interesting conversation your friend can provide. When a child faces a threatening situation such as the dentist's office, the child can think of something else, such as the promise of an ice cream cone afterwards or the cartoon playing on the television set. Many attentional focus strategies are possible, but distraction seems to be many people's favorite. Drawing, for instance, seems to be an effective attentional regulating strategy to lessen negative emotionality (Dalebroux, Goldstein, & Winner, 2008; Drake & Winner, 2013). The opposite of distraction would be rumination. Rumination (i.e., persistent focus) over positive events is referred to as "savoring," and it can produce positive benefits (Bryant, 1989), but rumination over negative events is usually a poor emotion regulation strategy that simply increases the duration and intensity of a negative emotion such as distress or fear or anger (Bushman, 2002; Spasojevic & Alloy, 2001).

Reappraisal

Reappraisal is defined as "changing the way an individual thinks about a potentially emotion-eliciting situation in order to modify its emotional impact" (John & Gross, 2004, p. 1302). The thoughts that can be changed (reappraised) include both how one thinks about the situation (e.g., primary appraisal) and how to cope with it (e.g., secondary appraisal). Reappraisal involves changing a situation's meaning. If someone bumps you in the hallway, you may feel angry, unless you take the time to think about why the event occurred. If the bump is reappraised as an accident, your anger may dissipate. If the bump is reappraised as empathy—because the person is so overworked and has to rush to keep the boss from yelling at her, your anger may turn to sympathy, pity, and even to prosocial behavior such as helping the other (Gross & John, 2003). In other situations, we may take a tragic turn of events (e.g., a cancer diagnosis) and, after some reflection and reappraisal, see the once-distressing event as a blessing that can be a springboard to bring us closer to a loved one or to the true meaning in our life. One particularly effective reappraisal strategy is the "negative functional reappraisal" in which the person recognizes that the event is bad, but not tragic, as in "It is frustrating to be hassled but I can stand the frustration of being hassled" (Crista, Tatar, Nagy, & David, 2012). Reappraisal can be used either to down-regulate or change a negative emotion, or it can be used to up-regulate a positive emotion. In general, reappraisal is a highly effective emotion regulation strategy, because people who tend to use reappraisal also tend toward better psychological, social, and physical well-being (Gross & John, 2003; Karademas, Tsalikou, & Tellarou, 2010).

Suppression

Suppression is unlike the previous four emotion regulation strategies in that it is used to modify an already occurring emotional experience, including any or all of its components of feeling, bodily activation, sense of purpose, or expression. Suppression is a strategy to down-regulate one or more of these four aspects of emotion, such as to lessen a feeling or a bodily activation, as by taking a deep breath or trying to inhibit a facial expression.

Suppression mostly involves "do nots," as in do not laugh at the politically incorrect joke, do not show anger toward the boss, do not show your fear during a job interview, and do not cry during the sad movie. Unlike the previous emotion regulation strategies, suppression is generally a poor strategy, because it often backfires and also produces troubling social side effects. Suppression backfires when we try to suppression an emotion or a component of emotion, because it usually produces more, not less, of that emotion or emotion component (e.g., it increases, rather than decreases, heart rate; Gross & Levenson, 1993). Suppression also tends to lead to social costs, because we typically feel more uncomfortable with interaction partners who try to suppress their emotions, rather than express them naturally (Butler et al., 2003). Generally, suppression is a rather blunt strategy, and what works best in emotion regulation is a flexible, situation-specific, and situationally sensitive intervention effort.

Overall, emotion regulation is a skill, and the more people have of this skill the better they seem to function. That is, the quality of people's emotion regulation skill predicts the quality of their functioning in various domains, such as having high-quality peer relationships (Lopes, Salovey, Cote, & Beers, 2005), high-quality relationships with teachers (Grazziano, Reavis, Keane & Calkins, 2007), and strong academic achievement (Gumora & Arsenio, 2002).

WHAT IS THE DIFFERENCE BETWEEN EMOTION AND MOOD?

A sixth fundamental question on the nature of emotion asks, "What is the difference between emotion and mood?" (Ekman & Davidson, 1994; Russell & Barrett, 1999). Several distinguishing criteria can be listed (Goldsmith, 1994), but three seem especially telling: different antecedents, different action-specificity, and different time course.

First, emotions and moods arise from different antecedent causes. Emotions emerge from significant life situations and from appraisals of their significance to our well-being. Moods, on the other hand, emerge from processes that are ill-defined and are oftentimes unknown (Goldsmith, 1994). Moods often occupy the background of consciousness, whereas emotions are clearly in its foreground (Rosenberg, 1998). Second, as to different action-specificity, emotions mostly influence behavior and direct specific courses of action. Moods, however, mostly influence cognition and direct what the person thinks about (Davidson, 1994). Third, as to different time course, emotions emanate from short-lived events that last for seconds or perhaps minutes, whereas moods emanate from mental events that last for hours or perhaps days. Hence, moods are more enduring than are emotions (Ekman, 1994a).

Everyday Mood

Most people have about 1,000 waking minutes in their day, but only a few of these actually include a prototypical emotion such as anger, fear, or joy (Clark, Watson, & Leeka, 1989; Watson & Clark, 1994). In contrast, the average person generally experiences an ever-present stream of moods, or "affect." Although emotions are relatively rare in daily experience, people are always feeling something. What they typically feel is a mood, a way of feeling that often exists as an aftereffect of a previously experienced emotional episode (Davidson, 1994).

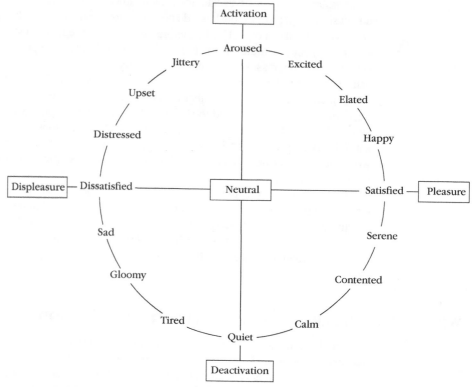

Figure 12.7   Circumplex Model of Affect

Mood—or affect—is a simple, nonreflective feeling state. It is a mental state, but it is not a cognitive state, because there is no specific object that is focused on or interpreted. Instead, mood acts as a barometer of our underlying psychological and physiological functioning (Thayer, 1996). It is also ever-present in consciousness. Mood exists as a blend of two dimensions: valence and arousal (Russell, 2003; Yik, Russell, & Steiger, 2011). Valance refers to a dimension of pleasure versus displeasure; arousal refers to a dimension of activation versus deactivation. Together, mood is simply feeling good or bad, drowsy or energized. A depiction of James Russell's circumplex of affect appears in Figure 12.7.

On the *x*-axis is the dimension of valence, or displeasure-to-pleasure, on the *y*-axis is the dimension of valance, or deactivation-to-activation, and in the middle of the circumplex is a neutral affective state that is neither displeasurable nor pleasurable and neither deactivated nor activated. As one moves away from the center point out to the edge of the circumplex, mood takes on a sense of valence and arousal, as one can feel both positive and activated (elated), both positive and deactivated (contented), both negative and activated (upset), or both negative and deactivated (gloomy). Some mood researchers prefer to rotate the circumplex 45 degrees so that "energetic arousal" (elation) is at the top of the circumplex, accompanied by "tense tiredness," "calm tiredness," and "calm energy" (Thayer, 1996, 2012). Other emotion researchers prefer to combine positive and activation into "positive affect" and negative and deactivation into "negative affect (Watson & Tellegen, 1985).

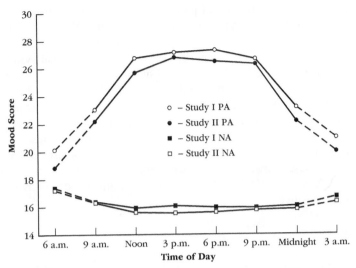

Figure 12.8   Levels of Positive Affect (PA) and Negative Affect (NA) as a Function of Time of Day in Two Studies

The circumplex does a good job of describing the experience (the phenomenology) of affect, because one need only know two variables to determine a person's mood—how positive do you feel? And how aroused (activated) do you feel? From the answers to these two questions, the person's specific mood state can be identified, using the circumplex model in Figure 12.7. Where mood gets complicated is in the finding that positive and negative mood are independent—not opposite—ways of feeling (Diener & Emmons, 1984; Diener & Iran-Nejad, 1986). For example, during a job interview, people often report feeling both positive and negative affects simultaneously. The job interviewee typically feels both happy and distressed, both excited and tense, at the same time. Positive affect also varies systematically in accordance with the sleep–wake cycle, while negative affect does not (Watson, Wiese, Vaidya, & Tellegen, 1999). As shown in Figure 12.8, level of positive affect is quite low upon waking. It increases rapidly throughout the morning, and positive affect continues to rise gradually throughout the afternoon until it hits its peak from 6:00 P.M. to 9:00 P.M. Positive affect then declines rapidly throughout the late evening as it returns to its early-morning low level (Clark et al., 1989).

Positive affect reflects pleasurable engagement. It is a "go" system (Thayer, 2012). It exists as a person's current level of pleasure, enthusiasm, and progress toward goals. People who feel high positive affect typically feel enthusiastic and experience energy, alertness, and optimism, whereas those who feel low positive affect typically feel lethargic, apathetic, and bored.

Negative affect reflects unpleasant engagement. It is a "stop" system (Thayer, 2012). People who feel high negative affect typically experience dissatisfaction, nervousness, and irritability, whereas those who feel low negative affect are calm and relaxed. These feelings of alertness versus boredom (positive affect) and irritability versus relaxation (negative affect), rather than prototypical emotional states such as joy and fear, constitute the essential nature of everyday, ongoing affective experience—our everyday mood.

Positive and negative affect pertain not only to moods but also to broad cognitive, motivational, biological, and behavioral systems (Clark, Watson, & Mineka, 1994). Positive affect reflects a reward-driven, appetitive motivational system (Fowles, 1988), whereas negative affect reflects a punishment-driven, aversive motivational system (Gray, 1987a, b). Basically, positive affect and a good mood support approach behavior, while negative affect and a bad mood support stopping and withdrawal (Thayer, 2012; Watson et al., 1999). The positive affect system has its own neural substrate—dopaminergic pathways. These pathways are activated by the expectancy of desirable events (Ashby et al., 1999; Wise, 1996) and generate positive affect and approach behavior (without impacting negative feelings). The negative affect system has its own neural substrate—serotonergic and noradrenergic pathways. These pathways are activated by the expectancy of negative outcomes (MacLeod, Byrne, & Valentine, 1996) and generate negative affect and withdrawal behavior (without impacting positive feelings).

Positive Affect

Positive affect refers to the everyday, low-level, general state of feeling good (Isen, 1987). It is the warm glow that so often accompanies everyday pleasant experiences such as walking in the park on a sunny day, receiving an unexpected gift or good news, listening to music, or making progress on a task. Although we focus on the park scenery, good news, pleasant music, or positive feedback, the mild good feeling arises subconsciously. We may smile more, whistle while we walk, daydream about happy memories, or talk more excitedly, but the positive feelings typically remain outside our conscious attention. In fact, if someone brings the pleasant mood to our attention ("My, aren't we in a good mood today!"), such attention paradoxically is the beginning of the end of the positive affect.

This lack of awareness of the positive affect stands in contrast to the more intense, attention-grabbing positive emotions, such as joy. The purpose of an emotion is to capture attention and direct coping behavior (so the person can adapt to situational demands effectively). Positive affect is more subtle. It affects neither attention nor behavior. Instead, positive affect subtly influences the information-processing flow—what we think about, the decisions we make, creativity, judgments, risk-taking, and so on (Isen, 1987, 2002).

Conditions that Make Us Feel Good

People have difficult times explaining why they feel good. If pressed, they typically say that life is generally going well. Mood researchers, on the other hand, have learned which conditions lead people to feel good, and most of these conditions create positive affect in ways that leave people unaware of the causal source of their good moods (Isen, 1987). Consider these positive affect-inducing experimental manipulations of a small gain, amusement, or pleasure: find money (Isen & Levin, 1972), receive a gift of a bag of candy (Isen & Geva, 1987; Isen, Niedenthal, & Cantor, 1992), receive a free product sample (Isen, Clark, & Schwartz, 1976), receive a candy bar (Isen, Daubman, & Nowicki, 1987; Isen, Johnson, Mertz, & Robinson, 1985), learn that a performance was successful (Isen, 1970), receive a cookie (Isen & Levin, 1972), receive refreshments such as orange juice (Isen et al., 1985), a random act of kindness (Wilson, Centerbar, Kermer, & Gilbert, 2005), receive positive feedback (Isen, Rosenzweig, & Young, 1991), think about positive events

(Isen et al., 1985), experience sunny weather (Kraut & Johnston, 1979), watch an amusing film (Isen & Nowicki, 1981), or rate funny cartoons (Carnevale & Isen, 1986).

Once instigated by an eliciting event (e.g., receiving a small gift), the warm glow of a positive mood continues for up to 20 minutes (Isen et al., 1976). Because we enjoy feeling good, happy people make decisions and act in ways that maintain their good moods for longer than 20 minutes (Forest, Clark, Mills, & Isen, 1979; Isen, Shalker, Clark, & Karp, 1978). More often than not, however, some rival event or interrupting task distracts our attention away from the positive affect-inducing event. That is, we lose our positive mood by engaging in neutral and aversive events (e.g., boring work, congested traffic, bad news, a risk turned sour).

Benefits of Feeling Good

Compared to people in a neutral mood, people exposed to conditions that allow them to feel good are more likely to help others (Isen & Levin, 1972), act sociably (i.e., initiate conversations; Batson et al., 1979), express greater liking for others (Veitch & Griffitt, 1976), be more generous to others (Isen, 1970) and to themselves (Mischel, Coates, & Raskoff, 1968), take risks (Isen & Patrick, 1983), act more cooperatively and less aggressively (Carnevale & Isen, 1986), solve problems in creative ways (Isen et al., 1987), persist in the face of failure feedback (Chen & Isen, 1992), make decisions more efficiently (Isen & Means, 1983), and show greater intrinsic motivation on interesting activities (Isen & Reeve, 2005). Consider two illustrations of the benefits of feeling good.

Positive affect facilitates our willingness to help others (Isen & Levin, 1972). A group of researchers conducted a field study at a local mall in which they randomly filled a telephone booth's coin return slot with change. Their thinking was that everyone would check the coin slot after making their telephone call and those who found the spare change would feel good while those that found only an empty coin slot would continue to feel their regular day-to-day mood. After each participant left the telephone booth, the researchers arranged to have a young woman walk by and "accidently" drop an armful of books. If positive affect facilitates helping others, then the participants who received the spare change should be significantly more likely to help the woman than would the participants who did not receive the small gift of spare change. Results appear in Table 12.3. People in their normal and regular daily mood (did not receive the small gift) almost never helped (only 1 out of 25 helped). People in a good mood, however, almost always helped (fully 14 out of 16 helped). These results show that a very mild, pleasant feeling dramatically increased people's willingness to help a stranger in need.

Table 12.3 Effect of Positive Affect on Helping Others

Condition	Females		Males	
	Helped	Did Not Help	Helped	Did Not Help
Positive Affect (Did Receive Dime)	8	0	6	2
Neutral Affect (Did Not Receive Dime)	0	16	1	8

Source: From "The effect of feeling good on helping: Cookies and kindness," by A. M. Isen & P. F. Levin, (1972), *Journal of Personality and Social Psychology, 21*, pp. 384–388. Copyright 1972 American Psychological Association. Reprinted by permission.

Positive affect also facilitates cognitive flexibility (Isen et al., 1992) and creative problem solving (Estrada, Isen, & Young, 1994, 1997; Isen et al., 1987). Alice M. Isen and her colleagues (1987) induced positive or neutral affect in groups of college students and then asked them to solve one of two problem-solving tasks requiring creativity—the candle task (Dunker, 1945) or the Remote Associates Test (RAT; Mednick, Mednick, & Mednick, 1964). In the candle task, the participant receives a pile of tacks, a candle, and a box of matches and the instructions to attach the candle to the wall (a cork board) so that the candle can burn without dripping wax on the floor. In the RAT, the participant sees three words (*soul*, *busy*, *guard*) and is asked to generate a fourth word that relates to the other three (in this case, *body*). Positive affect participants solved the creativity-demanding candle task and gave creative (unusual or "remote") associates to the RAT (Isen et al., 1987). In contrast, the candle task stumped the neutral affect participants, and they gave routine, stereotypical responses to the RAT. Thus, there are inherent information processing advantages conferred by feeling good (Aspenwall, 1998).

The explanation as to *how* and *why* positive affect facilitates creativity, decision-making efficiency, sociability, prosocial behavior, persistence, and so on is not as straightforward as it might first appear to be. Being a mood rather than an emotion, positive affect influences cognitive processes, such as memories, judgments, and problem-solving strategies. It therefore influences the contents of working (short-term) memory by biasing what the individual thinks about and what memories and expectations come to mind (Isen, 2008; Yang, Yang, & Isen, 2013). When feeling good, positive affect essentially serves as a retrieval cue to put the spotlight on positive material stored in memory (Isen et al., 1978; Laird, Wagener, Halal, & Szegda, 1982; Nasby & Yando, 1982; Teasdale & Fogarty, 1979). As a result, people who feel good have ready access to happy thoughts and positive memories (compared to people who feel neutral). With happy thoughts and pleasant memories salient in one's mind, people show increased creativity, help others more, show persistence in the face of failure, make decisions efficiently, show high intrinsic motivation, and so on. This helps explain why short-term positive affect helps people be successful in a wide range of areas in their lives, including marriage, friendship, income, work, and health (Lyubomirsky, King, & Diener, 2005).

SUMMARY

This chapter addresses six questions central to understanding the nature of emotion. The first question asks, "What is an emotion?" Emotions have a four-part character in that they feature dimensions of feeling, bodily preparation for action, motivational purpose, and expressive behavior. Feelings give emotions a subjective, phenomenological component. Bodily preparation includes biological activity that prepares the body for adaptive coping behavior. The purposive component generates an impulse to action that gives emotion a goal-directed sense of motivation to take a specific course of action. The expressive behavior component of emotion is its communicative aspect, as through a facial expression. Emotion is the psychological construct that coordinates and unifies these four aspects of experience into a synchronized, adaptive pattern.

The second question asks, "What causes an emotion?" This question asks what activates an emotion and investigates whether emotion is primarily a biological or a cognitive phenomenon. According to the biological perspective, emotions arise from the activation of neural circuits in the subcortical brain. According to the cognitive perspective, emotions arise from appraisals and interpretations of the personal meaning of the emotion-causing event. Both sides of the biology–cognition debate marshal together an impressive array of evidence to support their positions. Both biology and cognition play a pivotal role in the activation and regulation of emotion, and researchers specify two ways that biology and cognition together cause emotion: as two parallel emotion systems and as a dynamic, dialectical process.

The third question asks, "How many emotions are there?" The answer depends on one's perspective. According to the biological perspective, human beings possess somewhere between two and eight basic emotions (e.g., fear, anger, sadness, disgust, joy). These researchers illustrate how basic emotions emerge from subcortical neural circuits, essential life pursuits, and hardwired functions to solve survival-relevant challenges. According to the cognitive perspective, human beings possess a richer, more personalized, and more diverse emotional repertoire. These researchers illustrate how an almost limitless number of complex emotions are acquired through personal experience, and they can explain complex emotions such as gratitude, hope, and resentment. One strategy to reconcile this numbers issue is to think of basic emotions as families of emotion that contain one core basic emotion and its many derivative complex emotions. A second strategy is to differentiate biologically basic emotions from cognitively enriched emotion schemas.

The fourth question asks, "What good are the emotions?" It highlights that emotions serve a purpose. From a functional point of view, emotions evolved as biological reactions that helped us adapt successfully to fundamental life tasks, such as facing a threat. The coping functions of emotion include the motivational tendencies that stem from each emotion, such that enjoyment motivates playing, anger motivates fighting, and so forth. The social functions of emotion include communicating our feelings to others, influencing how others interact with us, inviting and smoothing social interaction, and creating and dissolving interpersonal relationships. Emotions can facilitate or interfere with coping effectiveness, depending largely on how able we are to experience regulation of emotion rather than regulation by emotion.

The fifth question asks, "Can we control our emotions?" Emotions are often automatic reactions, but there are nevertheless numerous opportunities within the flow of an emotional episode to intervene to change the course it takes. Emotion regulation refers to how we try to influence which emotions we have, when we have them, and how we experience and express the emotions we have. Five emotion regulation strategies are common. Situation selection is taking action to approach or avoid a known emotion-eliciting situation. Situation modification is modifying the emotion-eliciting situation so that it becomes more likely to produce positive emotions and less likely to produce negative emotions. Attentional focus includes effective strategies such as distraction, drawing, and savoring, but also ineffective ones such as rumination. Reappraisal refers to changing how one appraises the meaning emotion-eliciting event, as a threatening situation can be reinterpreted as a beneficial one. Suppression is a strategy to down-regulate a negative emotion or one of its components. Overall, emotion regulation is a skill that predicts people's functioning in terms of interpersonal relationships and personal productivity.

The sixth and final question asks, "What is the difference between emotion and mood?" Emotions arise in response to a specific event, motivate specific adaptive behaviors, and are short-lived. Moods arise from ill-defined sources, affect cognitive processes, and are long-lived. Mood exists as a blend of the two dimensions of valence (pleasure versus displeasure) and arousal (activation versus deactivation). Together, mood is simply feeling good or bad, drowsy or energized. The benefits of a positive affect state are many and include being more sociable, cooperative, creative, persistent during failure, efficient in decision making, and intrinsically motivated during interesting tasks. Positive affect exerts these beneficial effects by affecting cognitive processes such as memories and judgments—that is, what comes to mind. As a result, people who feel good have greater access to happy thoughts and positive memories and therefore behave in ways that reflect easy access to happy thoughts (e.g., more creative, more helpful).

READINGS FOR FURTHER STUDY

What Is an Emotion?

IZARD, C. E. (2010). The many meanings/aspects of emotion: Definitions, functions, activation, and regulation. *Emotion Review, 2*, 363–370.

MAUSS, I. B., LEVENSON, R. W., McCARTER, L., WILHELM, F. H., & GROSS, J. J. (2005). The tie that binds? Coherence among emotion experience, behavior, and physiology. *Emotion, 5*, 175–190.

What Causes an Emotion?

JOHNSON-LAIRD, P. N., & OATLEY, K. (1992). Basic emotions, rationality and folk theory. *Cognition and Emotion, 6*, 201–223.

How Many Emotions Are There?

EKMAN, P., & CORDARO, D. (2011). What is meant by calling emotions basic? *Emotion Review, 3*, 364–370.

MOORS, A., ELLSWORTH, P. C., SCHERER, K. R., & FRIJDA, N. H. (2013). Appraisal theories of emotion: State of the art and future development. *Emotion Review, 5*, 119–124.

Functions of Emotion

CARSTENSEN, L. L., GOTTMAN, J. M., & LEVENSON, R. W. (1995). Emotional behavior in long-term marriage. *Psychology and Aging, 10*, 140–149.

Mood and Positive Affect

ISEN, A. M., DAUBMAN, K. A., & NOWICKI, G. P. (1987). Positive affect facilitates creative problem-solving. *Journal of Personality and Social Psychology, 51*, 1122–1131.

RUSSELL, J. A. (2009). Emotion, core affect, and psychological construction. *Cognition and Emotion, 23*, 1259–1283.

Emotion Regulation

GROSS, J. J. (2002). Emotion regulation: Affective, cognitive, and social consequences. *Psychophysiology, 39*, 281–291.

DRAKE, J. E., & WINNER, E. (2013). How children use drawing to regulate their emotions. *Cognition and Emotion, 27*, 512–520.

Chapter 13

Aspects of Emotion

BIOLOGICAL ASPECTS OF EMOTION

    James–Lange Theory

    Contemporary Perspective

    Brain Activity Activates Individual Emotions

    Facial Feedback Hypothesis

        Facial Musculature
        Test of the Facial Feedback Hypothesis
        Are Facial Expressions of Emotion Universal across Cultures?
        Skill in Recognizing Emotional Facial Expressions

COGNITIVE ASPECTS OF EMOTION

    Appraisal

        Definition
        From Perception to Appraisal
        From Appraisal to Emotion
        From Felt Emotion to Action

    Complex Appraisal

        Primary Appraisal
        Secondary Appraisal
        Motivation

    Appraisal as a Process

    Emotion Differentiation

    Emotion Knowledge

    Attributions

    Emotions Affect Cognition

SOCIAL ASPECTS OF EMOTION

    Social Interaction

    Social Sharing of Emotion

    Cultural Construction of Emotion

SUMMARY

READINGS FOR FURTHER STUDY

Try to look sad—try to produce a sad facial expression. As you try this, attend to the changing sensations you feel from the movements of your facial musculature. If you just pouted out the lower lip and pulled down the corners of your mouth, then you probably did not feel too sad. So, try this again.

Produce a second sad facial expression. But this time move not only your lower lip and corners of your mouth but also move your eyebrows inward and upward at the same time. Moving your eyebrows inward and upward will take some skill, so pretend that you have a couple of golf tees attached to the inner corners of the eyebrows. Pretend these golf tees are about two inches apart and pointing out from your face in a parallel way (imagine that the base of each tee rests on the inner eyebrow with its tip extending outward). Now move your eyebrows inward and upward until the tips of the golf tees touch. Now try to move all three of these muscles together—touch the golf tees together, pout your lower lip, and turn the corners of your mouth down (Larsen, Kasimatis, & Frey, 1992).

Did you feel anything change? Did you sense a hint of a sad feeling coming on? Did your heart rate accelerate a little? Any vague urge to cry? If so, the feeling will be mild because a posed facial expression is not as authentic and emotion-producing as is a spontaneous facial expression.

As important life events come our way, these events activate biological and cognitive reactions in us. The resulting biological and cognitive processes generate emotion. And the emotion readies us to cope adaptively with the important life event before us. An outline of the most important biological and cognitive processes involved in emotion appears in Table 13.1. The first half of this chapter overviews these biological processes (left-hand side), while the second half of the chapter overviews these cognitive processes (right-hand side).

BIOLOGICAL ASPECTS OF EMOTION

Emotions are, in part, biological reactions to important life events. The list of biological events in Table 13.1 is important because these entries identify what the body is doing to react to and to prepare for emotion-eliciting events. Facing a situation of personal significance (e.g., a threat), the body prepares itself to cope effectively (e.g., gets ready to run) by (1) activating the heart, lungs, and muscles (autonomic nervous system) and releasing hormones into the bloodstream (endocrine system); (2) stimulating subcortical brain structures such as the amygdala; and (3) expressing a unique pattern of the facial musculature (facial feedback). With these biological systems engaged, the person experiences emotion and is ready to cope with the impending threat. Table 13.1 also identifies the central cognitive aspects of emotion—appraisal, knowledge, and attribution, and these will be detailed and discussed in the second half of the chapter.

Table 13.1   Biological and Cognitive Aspects of Emotion

Biological Aspects	Cognitive Aspects
1. Autonomic nervous system	**1.** Appraisals
2. Subcortical brain circuits	**2.** Knowledge
3. Facial feedback	**3.** Attributions

Emotion study began about 100 years ago by asking what role the autonomic nervous system played in the subjective experience of emotion. The first theory of emotion, the James–Lange theory, asked whether the different emotions each had unique bodily reactions associated with them. We all know that fear and joy feel different, but do fear and joy also have their own unique bodily reactions? Do our heart, lungs, and hormones behave one way when we are afraid yet another way when we experience joy? And if so, do these biological differences explain why the emotions we experience are different? Does the pattern of activity in our heart, lungs, and hormones cause the felt fear and felt joy?

James–Lange Theory

Personal experience suggests that we experience an emotion and that the felt emotion is quickly followed by bodily changes. As soon as we see the flashing red lights and hear the siren of a police car, fear arises and the feeling of fear subsequently makes our heart race and our palms sweat. The sequence of events seems to be stimulus → emotion → bodily reaction. William James (1884, 1890, 1894) argued against this common view. He suggested that our bodily changes do not follow the emotional experience; rather, emotional experience follows from and depends on our bodily responses to the flashing lights and siren sounds. Hence, bodily changes cause emotional experience: stimulus → bodily reaction → emotion.

James's theory rested on two assumptions: (1) The body reacts uniquely (discriminatorily) to different emotion-eliciting events, and (2) the body does not react to nonemotion-eliciting events. To appreciate James's hypotheses, think of your body's physiological responses to a shower that suddenly and unexpectedly turns cold. The physiological reaction—the increased heart rate, quickened breath, and widened eyes—begins before you have time to think about why your heart is racing and why your eyes are widening. The body reacts and the ensuing emotional reactions are on us before we are aware of what is happening. James argued that such instantaneous bodily reactions occur in patterns. Each different pattern caused a different emotion. Further, if the bodily changes did not occur, then the ensuing emotion would not occur.

The James–Lange theory of emotions quickly became popular, but it also met with criticism (Cannon, 1927).[1] Critics argued that the sort of bodily reactions James referred to were actually part of the body's general mobilizing fight-or-flight response that did not vary from one emotion to the next (Cannon, 1929; Mandler, 1975; Schachter, 1964).[2] These critics also argued that emotional experience was quicker than physiological reactions. That is, while a person feels anger in a tenth of a second, it takes this person's nervous system a full second or so to activate important glands and send excitatory hormones through the bloodstream. These critics contended that the role of physiological arousal was to augment, rather than to cause, emotion (Newman, Perkins, & Wheeler, 1930). Critics concluded that

---

[1] At the same time James presented his ideas, a Danish psychologist, Carl Lange (1885), proposed essentially the same (but more limited) theory. For this reason, the idea that emotions emanate from our interpretation of patterns of physiological arousal is traditionally called the James-Lange theory (Lange & James, 1922).

[2] For instance, does a person experience specific emotions after taking a stimulant drug known to induce bodily changes—increase heart rate, minimize gastrointestinal activity, and dilate the bronchioles? Drug-induced visceral stimulation leads people to feel "as if afraid" or "as if going to weep without knowing why" rather than afraid or sad per se (i.e., people feel generally aroused but not specifically afraid).

the contribution of physiological changes to emotional experience was small, supplemental, and relatively unimportant.

Contemporary Perspective

In the face of criticism, James's ideas faded out of favor, and rival theories of emotion emerged and became popular (e.g., see Schachter & Singer, 1962). Nonetheless, James' insights continue to guide contemporary study (Ellsworth, 1994; Lang, 1994), and contemporary research now supports the physiological specificity of a few emotions (Buck, 1986; Levenson, 1992; Schwartz, 1986). Paul Ekman, Robert Levenson, and Wallace Friesen (1983), for example, studied whether each of several emotions does or does not have a unique pattern of bodily changes. These researchers recruited people who could experience emotions on command (professional actors) and asked each to relive five different emotions—anger, fear, sadness, joy, and disgust—while the researchers measured for emotion-specific patterns of physiological activity. Distinct differences in heart rate (HR), skin temperature (ST), and skin conductance (SC) emerged. With anger, HR and ST both increased. With fear, HR increased while ST decreased. With sadness, HR increased while SC decreased. With joy, HR, ST, and SC were all low and stable. And with disgust, both HR and ST decreased. Just as James suspected, different emotions did indeed produce distinguishable patterns of bodily activity.

Persuasive evidence exists for distinctive autonomic nervous system (ANS) activity associated with anger, fear, sadness, and disgust (Ekman & Davidson, 1993; Ekman et al., 1983; Levenson, 1992; Levenson, Carstensen, Friensen, & Ekman, 1991; Levenson, Ekman, & Friesen, 1990; Sinha & Parsons, 1996; Stemmler, 1989). Of course, autonomic nervous system activity extends beyond just HR, ST, and SC. Autonomic nervous system activity also involves vasodilation (blushing), stimulation of the lacrimal glands (crying), pupil dilation and constriction, stimulation of the salivary glands, stimulation of hair follicles, and so on. When these aspects of autonomic nervous system activation are included, ANS activity can distinguish between at least six emotions—namely, anger, fear, sadness, disgust, happiness, and embarrassment (Matsumoto et al., 2008). These patterns of ANS activity supposedly emerged because they were able to recruit ways of behaving that proved to be adaptive. For instance, blushing facilitated embarrassment-motivated appeasement behaviors to help maintain a positive self-image in the eyes of others, despite the social blunder that caused the embarrassment in the first place. In the same way, in a fight that arouses anger, increased heart rate and skin temperature facilitate strong, assertive behavior. Some implications of emotion-distinctive ANS activity are discussed in Box 13.

Only a few emotions have distinct ANS patterns, however. If no specific pattern of behavior has survival value for an emotion, there is little reason for the development of a specific pattern of ANS activity (Ekman, 1992, 1994a). For instance, what is the most adaptive behavioral pattern to jealousy? to hope? For these emotions, no single adaptive activity seems universally most appropriate, because adaptive coping depends more on the specifics of the situation than on the emotion itself. That said, new research is beginning to show that positive emotions (e.g., enthusiasm, awe, love, amusement) also show qualitatively distinct ANS patterns of activity (Shiota et al., 2011).

In discussing the James–Lange theory of emotion, the fundamental question is whether the physiological arousal causes, or just follows, emotion activation. This question is important because if arousal causes emotion, then the study of physiological arousal becomes the

BOX 13   *Affective Computing*

Question: Why is this information important?

Answer: To prepare yourself for the coming technology that will read your emotions.

The finding that emotions show autonomic nervous system (ANS) specificity has intriguing implications for coming technology. If changes in blood pressure and skin temperature can reliably distinguish between the emotions of anger, fear, sadness, joy, and disgust, then machines that read our emotions are not far away.

Imagine electronic sensors built into steering wheels, smartphones, tablets, wristwatches, and the handles of bicycles, pilot simulators, computer joysticks, and golf clubs that constantly monitor the user's ANS activity while driving, talking, and so on. Imagine too electronic sensors in a device held by audience members during plays, lectures, musical performances, and political debates.

Soon, you will not need to imagine such technology, because scientists in the new field of "affective computing" are hard at work building such devices. One particularly interesting invention is the "emotion mouse" (Azar, 2000). It functions like an ordinary computer mouse, except it has special sensors for monitoring heart rate, skin temperature, hand movements, and skin conductance. The computer monitors the data collected by the emotion mouse and analyzes these data as a means to infer the user's emotional state.

If a computer can read a user's emotions, then it gains the capacity to adjust its programming to the user's emotionality. A computer game can be made more or less challenging. A tutorial can be adjusted to decrease fear, say by re-presenting familiar information rather than new information. An online counseling session can provide emotional feedback regarding the feelings of a client at different points in the conversation.

But even the best emotion mouse will still be limited to monitoring only five or six emotions (i.e., only the emotions that show ANS specificity). To expand the computer's ability to monitor and analyze additional emotions, a digital camera or a camera built into a smartphone or tablet could monitor and analyze facial expressions. Such a camera could monitor movements of the user's face—the user's frontalis, corrugators, orbicularis oculi, zygomaticus, nasalis, depressors, orbicularis oris, and quadratus labii (see Figure 13.2). With these facial movements, the computer gains the data necessary to infer both the presence and the intensity of anger, fear, distress, disgust, joy, interest, and contempt.

Researchers have already developed the software needed to analyze and interpret a user's facial muscles called "FACS" for facial action coding system (Ekman & Friesen, 1978). Computers using this software are about as accurate as (and much faster than) people who score the same facial movements (Cohn, Zlochower, Lien, & Kanade, 1999). The ability of computers to instantly recognize people's emotional expressions appears to be only a matter of time (Ekman & Friesen, 1975; Ekman & Rosenberg, 1997). It will not be long before your automobile, television set, or wristwatch will ask how it can help you, because it will know that you are significantly more distressed now than you were 10 minutes ago.

---

cornerstone for any understanding of emotion. But if arousal merely follows and augments emotion, physiological activity is therefore much less important—noteworthy, but not vital. Contemporary researchers generally agree that physiological arousal accompanies, regulates, and sets the stage for emotion, but it does not directly cause it. The modern perspective is that emotions recruit biological and physiological support to enable adaptive behaviors such as fighting, fleeing, and nurturing (Levenson, 1994b).

Endocrine activity also plays a role in emotion (Panksepp, 1998). Opiates promote social bonding by producing a strong positive emotionality (love). Brain exogenous opiates (morphine) and brain endogenous opiates (endorphins) both alleviate sadness and separation distress. In addition, oxytocin and prolactin play a key role in alleviating sadness and separation distress, and they further contribute positively to joy, love, contentment, attraction, and social bonding (Marazziti, Dall'osso, & Baroni, 2007). The two hormones of adrenaline (epinephrine) and cortisol support the fight-or-flight stress reaction (Kemeny & Shestyuk, 2008). Just as emotion involves a good deal of autonomic nervous system activity, it also involves a good deal of endocrine (hormonal) activity.

Brain Activity Activates Individual Emotions

Just as early researchers looked for emotion-specific patterns of physiological activity, contemporary researchers search for emotion-specific patterns in brain activity (Gray, 1994; LeDoux, 1996; Panksepp, 1998; Panksepp & Biven, 2011; Vytal & Hamann, 2010). For instance, Jeffrey Gray's (1994) neuroanatomical findings (with nonhuman mammals) document the existence of three distinct neural circuits in the brain, each of which regulates a distinctive pattern of emotional behavior: (1) a *behavioral approach system* that readies the animal to seek out and interact with attractive environmental opportunities, (2) a *fight-or-flight system* that readies the animal to flee from some aversive events but to defend aggressively against other events, and (3) a *behavioral inhibition system* that readies the animal to freeze in the face of aversive events. These three neural circuits underlie the four emotions of joy, fear, rage, and anxiety.

When emotion researchers use the methods of neuroscience to scan brain activity during the emotional experience, they use various techniques to activate emotions and then scan the brain to monitor its reaction (PET and *f*MRI; recall Chapter 3). For instance, researchers ask participants to view an emotion-eliciting film, and they then observe closely what each participant's brain does to generate an emotional reaction (Vytal & Hamann, 2010). Their finding for five basic emotions can be summarized as follows (Vytal & Hamann, 2010):

- Happiness Nine identifiable brain areas are activated, primarily the right superior temporal gyrus and rostral anterior cingulate cortex.
- Sadness Thirty-five identifiable brain areas are activated, primarily the left medial frontal gyrus and the caudate anterior cingulate cortex.
- Anger Thirteen identifiable brain areas are activated, primarily the left inferior frontal gyrus and parahippocampal gyrus.
- Fear Eleven identifiable brain areas are activated, primarily the left amygdala and insula.
- Disgust Sixteen identifiable brain areas are activated, primarily the right anterior insula and right inferior frontal gyrus.

These neuroscience-based data support the conclusion that basic emotions are associated with specific, characteristic, and discriminable patterns of brain activity.

The activation of any particular subcortical brain area is important because biologically minded emotion researchers assume that within each brain structure must be a certain set of specific instructions (metaphorically speaking) to guide the coordinated activity that is an emotional reaction (Ekman & Cordaro, 2011; Ohman & Mineka, 2011). The onset of the person's subjective feelings, motivational impulses, autonomic nervous system activity, and expressive signals occurs so quickly and in such a coherent and coordinated way that researchers confidently assume that stimulated brain areas must be implementing an emotion program that is specific to each individual basic emotion. The assumption is that there are somewhere between three and eight brain areas with specific instructions to guide each family of emotions.

These emotion programs can be traced to our evolutionary past, but they are also open systems to include learning from experience and culture. It is important to note that such "instructions" embedded with a subcortical brain structure are not lengthy scripts but, rather, consist of something more like the following. The brain area features a very fast pattern detector that monitors what is happening in the immediate second of time (e.g., seeing unexpected movement activates threat) and also a very fast output generator (e.g., accelerate heart rate, dilate the pupils; Levenson, 2011). Thus, what the amygdala brain structure does is detect that class of stimuli that signal threat and quickly generate the bodily systems necessary to produce a freezing reaction. What detects the threat and what mobilizes the bodily reaction is the ancient and evolutionary-developed emotion program (set of instructions) stored in the amygdala (LeDoux, 1996, 2000).

A second perspective on the nature of these subcortically stored emotion programs is that they are situation-detecting algorithms that lie dormant until activated by specific constellations of situational cues that were identified in one's ancestral past (Tooby & Cosmides, 2008). An analogy that speaks to the nature of these emotion programs is hunger. The hypothalamus has the capacity to detect low blood sugar and then generate output motivation to find and consume food. When a situation is detected by an emotion program that is consistent with cues related to a fundamental life task (e.g., a threat, a new area to explore), these anciently stored algorithms detect those signals to activate the corresponding basic emotion. Some of what is detected is rather straightforward (e.g., "snake detected!"), while some of what is detected is more complicated because it involves neural connections that add information from personal experience and learning.

Facial Feedback Hypothesis

According to the facial feedback hypothesis, the subjective aspect of emotion stems from feelings engendered by (1) movements of the facial musculature, (2) changes in facial temperature, and (3) changes in glandular activity in the facial skin. Therefore, emotions are "sets of muscle and glandular responses located in the face" (Tomkins, 1962). In other words, emotion is the awareness of proprioceptive feedback from facial behavior.

Upon being introduced to the facial feedback hypothesis, the reader might be a bit skeptical—"C'mon, smiling makes you happy?" But consider the following sequence of events depicted in Figure 13.1 to understand how sensations from the face feed back to the cortical brain to produce subjective emotional experience (Izard, 1991). Exposure to an external (loud noise) or internal (memory of being harmed) event increases the rate of neural firing quickly enough to activate a subcortical emotion program such as fear (1 in Figure 13.1). The subcortical brain structure possesses an emotion-specific program (2). When activated, these programs send impulses to the basal ganglia and facial nerve to generate discrete facial expressions (3). Within microseconds of the displayed fear facial expression (4), the brain interprets the proprioceptive stimulation (which muscles are contracted, which muscles are relaxed, changes in blood flow, changes in skin temperature, change in glandular secretions; 5). This particular pattern of facial feedback is cortically integrated—made sense of—as the subjective feeling of fear (6). Only then does the frontal lobe of the cortex become aware of the emotional state at a conscious level.

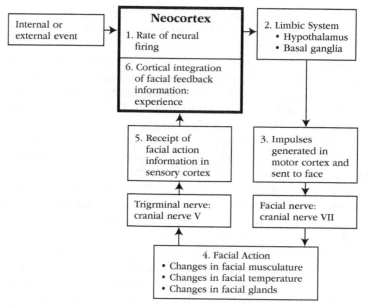

Figure 13.1   Sequence of the Emotion-Activating Events According to the Facial Feedback Hypothesis

Quickly thereafter, the whole body joins the facial feedback to become involved in amplifying and sustaining the activated fear experience.

Facial feedback does one job: emotion activation (Izard, 1989, 1994). Once an emotion is activated, it is the emotion program, not the facial feedback, that recruits further cognitive and bodily participation to maintain the emotional experience past the first split-second of time. The person then becomes aware of and monitors not her facial feedback but her changes in heart rate, respiration, muscle tonus, posture, and so on.

Facial action also changes brain temperature, such that facial movements associated with negative emotion (sadness) constrict breathing, raise brain temperature, and produce negative feelings, whereas facial movements associated with positive emotion (happiness) enhance breathing, cool brain temperature, and produce positive feelings (McIntosh, Zajonc, Vig, & Emerick, 1997; Zajonc, Murphy, & Inglehart, 1989). To make sense of this, make a sad facial expression and see if the facial action around the nose does not constrict your air flow a bit. Also, make a joy facial expression and see if that facial action (e.g., raising the cheeks) does not encourage and open up nasal air flow. The changing brain temperatures do have (mild) emotional consequences.

Facial Musculature

There are 80 facial muscles, 36 of which are involved in facial expression. For purposes of exposition, however, the eight facial muscles shown in Figure 13.2 are sufficient for differentiating among the basic emotions (for more information, see Ekman &

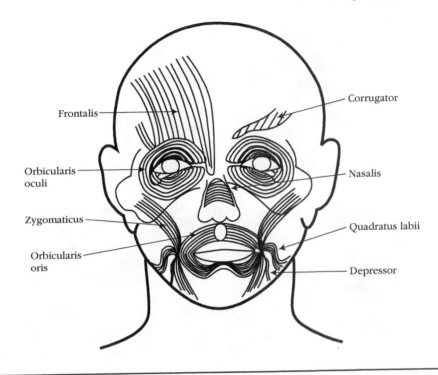

Facial Muscle	Anger	Fear	Disgust	Sadness	Joy
Frontalis (Forehead)	n/a	contracts, producing forehead wrinkles	n/a	n/a	n/a
Corrugator (Eyebrows)	draws eyebrows in and down	raises inner corners of eyebrows	n/a	raises and draws together inner corners of eyelids	n/a
Orbicularis Oculi (Eyes)	tenses lower eyelids upward	raises upper eyelids, tenses lower eyelids	n/a	raises upper inner corner of eyelids	relaxes, showing wrinkles below eyes
Nasalis (Nose)	n/a	n/a	wrinkles nose	n/a	n/a
Zygomaticus (Cheeks)	n/a	n/a	raises cheeks	n/a	1. pulls corners of lip back and up; 2. raises cheeks, showing Crow's feet below eyes
Orbicularis Oris (Lips)	presses lips firmly together	n/a	raises upper lip	n/a	n/a
Quadratus Labii (Jaw)	n/a	pulls lips backward	n/a	n/a	n/a
Depressor (Mouth)	n/a	n/a	n/a	pull corners of lips down	n/a

Figure 13.2 Eight Major Facial Muscles Involved in the Expression of Emotion

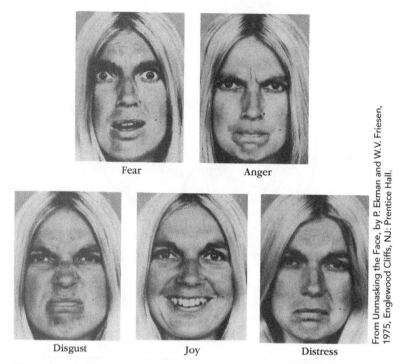

Fear   Anger

Disgust   Joy   Distress

From Unmasking the Face, by P. Ekman and W.V. Friesen, 1975, Englewood Cliffs, NJ: Prentice Hall.

Figure 13.3 Facial Expressions for Five Emotions

Friesen, 1975; Izard, 1971). The upper face (the eyes and forehead) has three major muscles: the frontalis (covers the forehead), corrugator (lies beneath each eyebrow), and orbicularis oculi (surrounds each eye). The middle face has two major muscles: the zygomaticus (extends from the corners of the mouth to the cheekbone) and the nasalis (wrinkles the nose). The lower face has three major muscles: the depressor (draws the corners of the mouth downward), the orbicularis oris (circular muscle surrounding the lips), and the quadratus labii (draws the corners of the mouth backward).

Patterns of facial behavior produce discrete emotional expressions. Anger, fear, disgust, distress, and joy, for instance, all have a recognizable facial expression. These facial expressions are described muscle-by-muscle in words in Figure 13.2 and in pictures in Figure 13.3 (Ekman & Friesen, 1975). Two additional emotions are associated with a particular pattern of facial behavior: interest (Reeve, 1993) and contempt (Ekman & Friesen, 1986). The interest expression is illustrated in the faces of the gallery who are tracking the flight of the golf ball in Figure 13.4 (e.g., the man seventh from the left wearing a dark striped shirt). For interest, the orbicularis oculi open the eyelids and the orbicularis oris slightly parts the lips open. For contempt, the zygomaticus unilaterally raises the corner of one lip upward. In contempt, the person "snarls" upward one side of the upper lip (a la Elvis Presley). Pride too can be universally recognized, although pride expresses itself beyond the face (i.e., small smile, head tilted slightly back, expanded posture, arms lifted and extended high; Tracy & Robins, 2004, 2007).

© Debby Wong / Shutterstock

Figure 13.4   Some Facial Expressions of Interest

Test of the Facial Feedback Hypothesis

Feedback from facial behavior, when transformed into conscious awareness, constitutes the experience of emotion (Laird, 1974; Tomkins, 1962, 1963). This is the facial feedback hypothesis (FFH). Investigations to test the validity of the FFH have used two different methodologies, because there are two testable versions of the FFH—the strong version and the weak version (McIntosh, 1996; Rutledge & Hupka, 1985).

In its strong version, the FFH proposes that manipulating one's facial musculature into a pattern that corresponds to an emotion display (e.g., see Figure 13.3) will activate that emotional experience. In other words, frowning the lips and raising the inner eyebrows inward and upward activates sadness (recall the example at the beginning of this chapter). In empirical tests, an experimenter instructs a participant to contract and relax specific muscles of the face and, with a particular facial expression displayed, complete a questionnaire to assess emotional experience. For example, in one study, participants were instructed to (1) "raise your brows and pull them together," (2) "now raise your upper eyelids," and (3) "now also stretch your lips horizontally, back toward your ears" (Ekman et al., 1983). So posed, the participants were asked about their emotional state (fear, in this case) on a questionnaire. Research has both supported (Laird, 1974, 1984; Larsen et al., 1992; Rutledge & Hupka, 1985; Strack, Martin, & Stepper, 1988) and refuted (McCaul, Holmes, & Solomon, 1982; Tourangeau & Ellsworth, 1979) the strong version of the FFH.

One area of consensus is that a posed facial musculature produces reliable changes in physiological reactions, such as changes in cardiovascular and respiratory rates (Ekman et al., 1983; Tourangeau & Ellsworth, 1979). It is still debated whether the posed facial musculature produces emotional experience, but most studies suggest that it does produce at least a small effect (Adelmann & Zajonc, 1989; Izard, 1990; Laird, 1984; Matsumoto, 1987; Rutledge & Hupka, 1985).

In its weaker (more conservative) version, the FFH proposes that facial feedback modifies the intensity of (rather than causes) the emotion. Thus, managing one's facial musculature into a particular emotional display will augment (exaggerate) but will not necessarily activate (cause) the emotional experience. In other words, if you intentionally smile when you are already joyful, then you will feel a more intense joy. In one experiment, participants either exaggerated or suppressed their spontaneous facial expressions while watching a video, which depicted either a pleasant, a neutral, or an unpleasant scenario (Zuckerman, Klorman, Larrance, & Spiegel, 1981). Exaggerating naturally occurring facial expressions did augment both emotional and physiological experience, just as suppressing naturally occurring facial expressions softened both emotional and physiological experience (Lanzetta, Cartwright-Smith, & Kleck, 1976).

Unlike its stronger version, the weaker version of the FFH has received a consensus of support (McIntosh, 1996; Soussignan, 2002). These results highlight the two-way street between the emotions we feel and the emotions we express: Emotions activate facial expressions, and facial expressions, in turn, feed back to exaggerate and suppress the emotions we feel. Critics contend, however, that the contribution of such facial feedback is small and that other factors are more important (Matsumoto, 1987).

Are Facial Expressions of Emotion Universal across Cultures?

The facial feedback hypothesis assumes that facial expressions are innate. But much facial behavior is surely learned. It is a rare individual who has not learned to express the polite smile and to inhibit the angry face while talking with the boss. But the fact that some facial behavior is learned (and therefore under voluntary control) does not rule out the possibility that facial behavior also has a genetic, innate component, as proposed by the proponents of the FFH.

A series of cross-cultural investigations tested the proposition that human beings display similar facial expressions regardless of cultural differences (Ekman, 1972, 1994b; Izard, 1994). In each of these studies, representatives from diverse nationalities looked at three photographs, each showing a different facial expression (Ekman, 1972, 1993; Ekman & Friesen, 1971; Ekman, Sorenson, & Friesen, 1969; Izard, 1971, 1980, 1994). From these photographs, participants chose, via a multiple-choice format, the photograph they thought best expressed a particular emotion. For example, participants were shown photographs of three faces, one expressing anger, one expressing joy, and one expressing fear. The participants selected the picture they thought showed what a face would look like when the person encountered an injustice or obstacle to a goal (i.e., anger). The research question is whether persons from different cultures would agree on which facial expressions correspond with which emotional experiences. The finding that people from different cultures (different cultures, different languages, different nationalities) match the same facial expressions with the same emotions is evidence that facial behavior is cross-culturally universal (Ekman, 1994b;

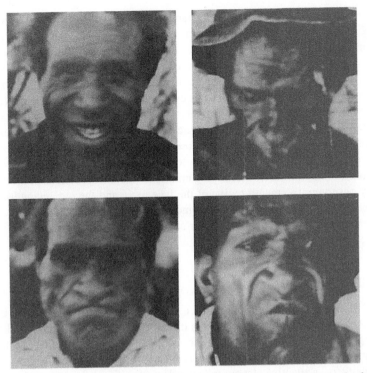

Figure 13.5   Which Facial Expression Shows Disgust? The photograph of the New Guinea native expressing disgust appears in the lower-right corner. Clockwise from the bottom-left are expressions of anger, joy, and distress. From "Universal and Cultural Differences in Facial Expression of Emotion" by P. Ekman, 1972, in J. R. Cole (Ed.), Nebraska Symposium on Motivation (Vol. 19, pp. 207–283), Lincoln: University of Nebraska Press.

Ekman & Friesen, 1971; Izard, 1971).[3] This is evidence that emotion-related facial behavior has an innate, unlearned component.

To test yourself as the participants in the cross-cultural experiments were tested, take a look at the photographs shown in Figure 13.5. The photographs show four different expressions of a New Guinea native (someone from a different culture than you). Your task is to identify the face that just encountered a contaminated object (i.e., disgust).

Skill in Recognizing Emotional Facial Expressions

With explicit training, people can learn how to recognize emotional facial expressions in others (Hurley, 2012; Matsumoto & Hwang, 2011). Some facial expressions are easier to recognize than are others. Joy (happiness) is generally the easiest facial expression of

---

[3]Research with infants supports the idea that facial behavior has a strong innate component (Izard et al., 1980) because presocialized infants show distinct, identifiable facial expressions. Blind children, who lack opportunity to learn facial expressions from others through modeling and imitation, show the same recognizable facial expressions as do children of the same age who can see (Goodenough, 1932). Severely mentally handicapped children, who have difficulty learning new motor behaviors, also show full expressions of the emotions (Eibl-Eibesfeldt, 1971).

emotion to recognize, while fear tends to be the most difficult to recognize accurately (Calvo & Lundqvist, 2008; Montagne et al., 2007; Russell, 1994). People in Western cultures (e.g., United States, Europe) tend to recognize facial expressions of emotion more accurately than do people in Eastern cultures (e.g., Asia; Russell, 1994). These East–West differences seem to arise because of culture-specific patterns of observation. Eastern observers mostly look at a person's eye region when trying to judge a facial expression of emotion, whereas Western observers mostly look at a person's mouth region (Jack et al., 2009). This is an important difference because the eye region provides more ambiguous information about emotion than does the mouth region (Calvo & Nummenmaa, 2008). From these data, it seems possible to conclude that if you were interested in improving your skill in accurately identifying emotional facial expressions in others, you could do so by observing the mouth region of the face more and the eye region less. This conclusion seems to be especially true for emotions such as fear and sadness. Looking into the eyes seems necessary, however, for anger accuracy and looking in the nose region seems necessary for disgust accuracy.

COGNITIVE ASPECTS OF EMOTION

For those who study emotion from a cognitive perspective, biological events are not necessarily the most important aspects of emotion. Cognitive theorists acknowledge the biological contribution to emotion (Parkinson, 2012), but they further argue that emotion and emotion activation are both deeply immersed within cognitive activity. These theorists see emotions as adaptive responses that reflect cognitive appraisals and cognitive mental representations (e.g., the self-concept) that interpret environmental events as being significant to one's well-being, and they tend to focus on complex emotions. They point out that an emotion such as "disappointment" cannot be explained by ANS activity or changes in facial expressions but, instead, by a cognitive understanding of what it means to not have what you expected you would have (van Dijk, Zeelenberg, & van der Pligt, 1999). Similarly, "shame" is not activated by subcortical brain structures but, rather, by a cognitive evaluation that the self is inferior or damaged in some important way (Tangney & Dearing, 2002).

Appraisal

The central construct in a cognitive understanding of emotion is appraisal (Moors, Ellsworth, Scherer, & Frijda, 2013).

Definition

Appraisal is a cognitive process that evaluates the significance of environmental events in terms of one's well-being (e.g., "Is this situation significant to me?"). Well-being is driven by the individual's goals, needs, values, beliefs, and attachments or personal relationships. That is, appraisal involves basically everything the person cares about.

Appraisal also affects each aspect of an emotional episode, including the feeling state, sense of purpose, bodily preparation, and expressive signals (Frijda, 2007; Reisenzein, 1994). Because appraisal causes a change in each aspect of an emotion, appraisal theorists conclude that appraisal causes emotion (Moors, 2013).

Appraisals change over time. Appraisals change as the person's perception of the environment changes, and appraisals change as the person's perception of the person–environment interaction changes. As appraisals change, so do the person's feelings, bodily readiness, action tendencies (sense of purpose), expressive signals, and coping behaviors. These changed emotional reactions typically produce changes in the environment and changes in the person–environment interaction, which again change the person's appraisals. The overall picture is that the emotion process is continuous and recursive, not a quick burst of activity that lasts for only a second or two.

Consider a child who sees a man approaching. Immediately and automatically, the child appraises the meaning of the man's approach as probably "good" or probably "bad." The appraisal is an evaluation of the environment that is based on the salient characteristics of the man approaching (gender, facial expression, pace of approach), expectations of who might be approaching, beliefs of what approaching people typically do, and memories of approaching people in the past. It is not the approaching man per se that explains the quality of the child's emotional reaction, but rather, it is how the child expects that the approaching man will affect her well-being that gives life to her emotion. If she sees the approaching man smiling and waving and if she remembers the man is her friend, then she will likely appraise the event as a good one. If she sees the approaching man ranting and raving and if she remembers the man is the neighborhood bully, then she will likely appraise the event as a bad one. These appraisals lead to specific action tendencies (motivations), expressive signals, bodily changes that mobilize coping responses, and the instrumental behavior that is coping. If the child did not appraise the personal relevance of the approaching man, she would not have had an emotional reaction to the man in the first place because events that are irrelevant to well-being do not generate emotions (Lazarus, 1991a; Ortony & Clore, 1989; Ortony et al., 1988). This example illustrates the four central beliefs that are shared by all appraisal emotion theorists (Ellsworth, 2013; Frijda, 2007; Lazarus, 1991a; Oatley & Johnson-Laird, 1987; Ortony et al., 1988; Roseman, 1984; Scherer, 2009; Smith & Ellsworth, 1985; Weiner, 1986):

1. Without an antecedent cognitive appraisal of the event, emotions do not occur.
2. The appraisal, not the event itself, causes the emotion.
3. Emotion is a process.
4. If the appraisal changes, even if the situation does not, then the emotion will change.

One of the earliest cognitive theorists was Magda Arnold (1960, 1970). She specified how appraisals, brain activity, and arousal work together to produce emotion by focusing on three questions: (1) How does the perception of an object or event produce a good or bad appraisal? (2) How does the appraisal generate emotion? and (3) How does felt emotion express itself in action? Arnold's pioneering appraisal theory of emotion is summarized in Figure 13.6 (see also Cornelius, 2006).

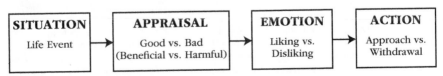

Figure 13.6   Arnold's Appraisal Theory of Emotion

From Perception to Appraisal

According to Arnold, people categorically appraise stimulus events and objects as positive or negative. This good/bad appraisal was simply a gut-felt evaluation of the stimulus event.

She recognized that the duration of time between the presentation of a stimulus and the onset of an emotional reaction to that stimulus was so remarkably brief that the appraisal process that took place between stimulus and emotional reaction must therefore be fairly simple (and hence fast). To substantiate her ideas, Arnold paid particularly close attention to the neurological pathways in the brain. In all encounters with the environment, subcortical brain structures (e.g., the amygdala) automatically appraise the hedonic tone of sensory information. For instance, a harsh sound instantaneously is appraised as intrinsically unpleasant (bad), while the smell of a rose is appraised as intrinsically pleasant (good). Recent neuroanatomical research confirms Arnold's claim that the subcortical brain (and amygdala in particular) is the focal brain center that appraises the emotional significance of sensory stimuli (Berridge & Kringelbach, 2008; LeDoux, 2012). In addition, most stimuli are further appraised cortically by adding information processing and hence expectations, memories, beliefs, goals, judgments, and attributions (Davidson & Irwin, 1999; Ochsner & Gross, 2005). Full appraisal therefore draws on both subcortical and cortical evaluations of the stimulus event in terms of sensory information and in terms of the person's goals and preferences.

From Appraisal to Emotion

Once an object has been appraised as good or bad (as beneficial or harmful), an experience of liking or disliking follows immediately and automatically. For Arnold, the liking or disliking is the felt emotion. Contemporary research has backed up Arnold's belief that the like–dislike appraisal is both fast and automatic (Moors, De Houwer, & Eelen, 2004).

From Felt Emotion to Action

Liking generates a motivational tendency to approach the emotion-generating object; disliking generates a motivational tendency to avoid it. This motivational tendency represents an action readiness to approach versus avoid.

During appraisal, the individual relies on memory and imagination to generate a number of possible courses of action in dealing with the liked or disliked object. When a particular course of action is decided upon, the subcortical brain generates autonomic and endocrine system reactions (Kapp, Pascoe, & Bixler, 1984; LeDoux, Iwata, Cicchetti, & Reis, 1988), general arousal (Krettek & Price, 1978), and the muscles that control facial expressions (Holstedge, Kuypers, & Dekker, 1977). Through its effects on these biological systems, emotions produce action.[4]

---

[4]One important feature of Arnold's theory is that emotion is defined in terms of motivation. The tendency to approach or avoid gives the emotion a directional force, while the physiological changes in the muscles and viscera give emotion its energy. A second important feature of Arnold's theory treats emotion as a unitary construct, because she preferred to talk about emotion forces of approach and avoidance, of attraction and repulsion, and of liking and disliking more than she did of specific emotions such as anger, sadness, or pride.

Complex Appraisal

Like Arnold, Richard Lazarus emphasized the cognitive processes that intervene between important life events (environmental conditions) and physiological and behavioral reactivity. While following Arnold's ideas as a road map, Lazarus expanded her general good/bad appraisal into a more complex conceptualization of appraisal (Lazarus, 1968, 1991a; Lazarus & Folkman, 1984). "Good" appraisals were conceptualized into several types of benefit, while "bad" appraisals were differentiated into several types of harm and into several types of threat. Lazarus's (1991a) complex appraisals framework appears in Figure 13.7.

In articulating a more complex portrayal of appraisal, Lazarus pointed out that people evaluate whether the situation they face has personal relevance for their well-being. When well-being is at stake, people then evaluate the potential harm, threat, or benefit they face. For Lazarus (1991a), these appraisals take the form of questions such as: Is this event relevant to my well-being? Is this event consistent with my goals? How deeply does this event touch my self-esteem? Given these appraisals of personal relevance, goal congruence, and ego involvement, people appraise situations as particular kinds of harm, as particular kinds of threat, or as particular kinds of benefit (Lazarus, 1991a, 1994).

The appraisal process does not end with an assessment of personal relevance, goal congruence, and ego involvement. Perceived coping abilities continue to alter how people

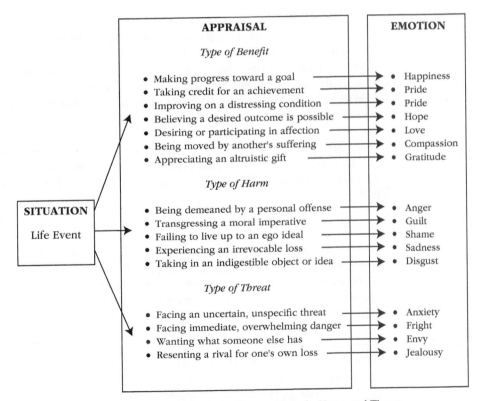

Figure 13.7   Lazarus's Complex Appraisals: Types of Benefit, Harm, and Threat

interpret (appraise) the situations they face (Folkman & Lazarus, 1990; Lazarus, 1991a, b). The person asks him- or herself, can I cope with the potential benefit, threat, or harm I face? Can I bring the benefit to fruition, and can I prevent the harm or threat? Anticipated coping changes the way a situation is appraised (if I can cope with the threat, then it is not really much of a threat). A changed appraisal leads to a changed emotion. Overall, then, people first appraise their relationship to the life event ("primary appraisal") and then appraise their coping potential within that event ("secondary appraisal").

Primary Appraisal

Primary appraisal involves an estimate of whether one has anything at stake in the encounter (Folkman et al., 1986). The following are potentially at stake in primary appraisal: (1) health, (2) self-esteem, (3) a goal, (4) financial state, (5) respect, and (6) the well-being of a loved one. In other words, primary appraisals ask whether one's physical or psychological well-being, goals and financial status, or interpersonal relationships are at stake during a particular encounter. As soon as one of these is at stake, an "ordinary life event" becomes an emotion-generating "significant life event." For instance, when driving a car and it swerves on ice, the cognitive system immediately generates the primary appraisal that much is now at stake—personal health, reputation as a skillful driver, a valuable possession (the car), and the physical and psychological well-being of one's passenger.

Secondary Appraisal

Secondary appraisal, which occurs after some reflection, involves the person's assessment for coping with the possible benefit, harm, or threat (Folkman & Lazarus, 1990). Coping involves the person's cognitive, emotional, and behavioral efforts to manage the benefit, harm, or threat. For instance, imagine the coping options for a musician scheduled to perform for an audience. The musician might solicit advice from a mentor, practice throughout the night, find a means of escape, make a plan of action and follow through, copy another musician's style, joke and make light of the event's significance, and so forth. The musician's emotional experience will depend not only on his initial appraisal of the potential benefit, harm, or threat within the evening's performance, but also on his reflection on the potential efficacy of his coping strategies to realize the benefit or prevent the harm or threat.

Motivation

Lazarus's portrayal of emotion is a motivational one. A person brings personal motives (goals, well-being) into a situation. When personal motives are at stake, emotions follow. Furthermore, emotions constantly change as primary and secondary appraisals change. The whole emotion process is characterized not so much by the linear sequence of life event → appraisal → emotion as it is by the ongoing change in the status of one's personal motives. Life events offer potential benefits, harms, and threats to well-being, and ongoing coping efforts have important implications for the extent to which those benefits, harms, and threats are realized. So, the individual's personal motives (goals, well-being) lie at the core of the emotion process and the individual continually makes primary and secondary appraisals about the status of those personal motives as events unfold and coping efforts are implemented.

Lazarus labels his emotion theory as a cognitive–motivational–relational one (Lazarus, 1991b). *Cognitive* communicates the importance of appraisal, *motivational* communicates the importance of personal goals and well-being, and *relational* communicates that emotions arise from one's relation to environmental threats, harms, and benefits.

Appraisal as a Process

The appraisal framework to understand emotion was proposed by Arnold, developed by Lazarus, and brought to its maturity by present-day emotion theorists. Inspired by Lazarus' concept of a complex appraisal, cognitively based emotion theorists worked to develop an increasingly sophisticated understanding of the appraisal process (Ellsworth, 2013; Frijda, 2007; Lazarus, 1991a; Johnson-Laird & Oatley, 1989; Oatley & Johnson-Laird, 1987; Ortony et al., 1988; Roseman, 1984, 1991; Roseman & Evdokas, 2004; Scherer, 2009; Smith & Ellsworth, 1985; Weiner, 1986). Like Lazarus, these researchers showed rather clearly that different appraisals caused different emotions. Each appraisal theorist embraced the life event → appraisal → emotion sequence, but they differed on how many dimensions of appraisal are necessary to explain emotional experience. Arnold used appraisal to explain two emotions (like and dislike), Lazarus used primary and secondary appraisals to explain approximately 15 emotions (see Figure 13.7), yet cognitive emotion theorists ultimately seek to use appraisals to explain *all* emotions.

These cognitive theorists believe that each emotion can be described by a unique pattern of appraisals. The thinking is that if one were able to know the full pattern of a person's appraisals, then it would be a rather straightforward task to predict which ensuing emotion the person would experience. The following list of additional appraisals represents the thinking of most cognition-minded emotion theorists (Moors et al., 2013):

Arnold's Appraisal:
Valence   Is the event good or bad?

Lazarus's Appraisals:
Goal Relevance   Is the event relevant to my goals and well-being?
Coping Potential   Can I cope successfully with the event?

Additional Appraisals:
Goal Congruence   Is the event facilitating my goal attainment?
Novelty   Did I expect the event to happen?
Agency   Who caused the event: self? others? circumstances?
Self/Norm Compatibility   Is the event okay on a moral level?

The four new additional appraisals are goal congruence, novelty, agency, and self/norm compatibility. *Goal congruence* is an evaluation of whether the external event is working to facilitate (versus block, thwart) one's progress toward goal attainment or motive satisfaction. *Novelty* is detection of a change in the environment, and the detection of such a change recruits greater attention and information processing. The environment can change in different ways, including stimulus novelty (i.e., a new object appears in a familiar context) and contextual novelty (i.e., a familiar object appears in a new context). *Agency* is an attribution of the cause of the event, because events can be caused by the self, by someone else, or by impersonal circumstances. *Self/Norm compatibility* is an evaluation of how compatible versus incompatible (how acceptable versus unacceptable) the event is with one's self-concept or personal standards. Together, these appraisals provide a rather comprehensive picture of the sort of appraisals people across many different cultures use (Scherer, 1997a).

Consider how a combination of several different appraisals can produce one specific emotion. Sadness, for instance, is a combination of the following four appraisals: (1) A valued goal is at stake (goal relevance); (2) no progress was made toward the goal (low goal congruence); (3) the goal was lost (unpleasant intrinsic value); and (4) it is not possible to regain what was lost (low coping potential). That is, high personal relevance + low goal congruence + unpleasant intrinsic value + low coping potential = sadness. If the appraisal pattern were to change so that low coping potential was re-evaluated to be high coping potential, then anger would replace sadness, as anger = high personal relevance + low goal congruence + unpleasant intrinsic value + high coping potential.

The ultimate goal of the appraisal emotion theorists is perhaps now apparent. They are hard at work to construct a decision tree in which all possible patterns of appraisal lead to a single emotion (Scherer, 1993, 1997b). That is, if the person makes appraisals X, Y, and Z, then emotion A will surely and inevitably follow.

Emotion Differentiation

The strong suit of an appraisal theory of emotion is its ability to explain emotion differentiation. Emotional differentiation is the phenomenon in which people experience different emotions for the same event. It also concerns how the same person can experience different emotions for the same event at different times. Emotional differentiation is actually the number one contribution that appraisal theory makes to the study of emotion. Unlike the biological perspective that explains how everyone experiences the same emotion to the same fundamental life event (i.e., everyone feels sad after the loss of a valued object), the appraisal theory of emotion can explain how different emotions emerge from the same event. Emotional differentiation occurs because different people appraise the same event differently and also because the same person appraises the same event differently at two different times.

Emotional differentiation occurs even within a single emotional episode. Those who use a neuroscientific perspective to study the appraisal process (Brosch & Sander, 2013) examine the appraisal process during an emotional episode on a millisecond-to-millisecond basis. They find that when the person encounters an external event, that stimulus event is very quickly appraised for its novelty and goal relevance, based largely on its sensory information. These two appraisals begin about one-tenth of a second after stimulus exposure and they feed-forward this novelty and goal relevance evaluative information to other brain areas for further processing. Brain structures such as the amygdala then orchestrate further appraisals and information processing as the stimulus event is appraised for goal congruence and agency. These appraisals occur about one-half of a second after stimulus exposure. As the appraisal process continues, information processing expands from just sensory stimulus information to learned associations and eventually to the accessing of stored information such as self/norm compatibility and predictive forecasts of the future, as with coping potential. Because these later appraisals feed back to combine with the earlier appraisals, the emotion may change—may undergo emotion differentiation. After several evaluative iterations and several seconds of time, the appraisal pattern begins to stabilize to

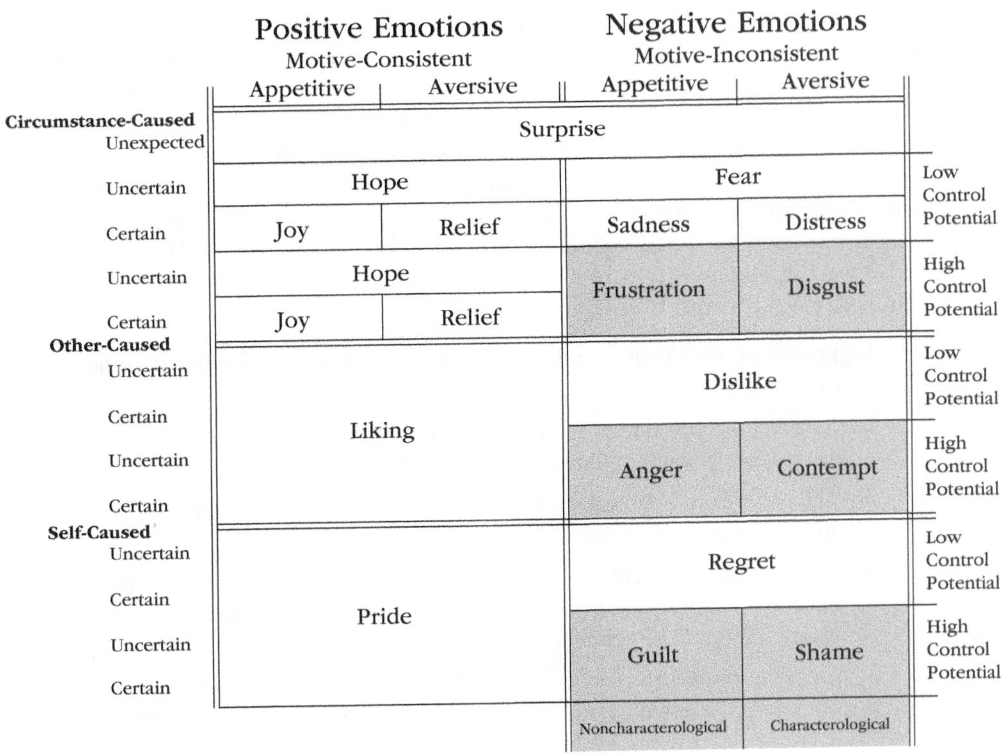

	Positive Emotions Motive-Consistent		Negative Emotions Motive-Inconsistent		
	Appetitive	Aversive	Appetitive	Aversive	
Circumstance-Caused Unexpected	Surprise				
Uncertain	Hope		Fear		Low Control Potential
Certain	Joy	Relief	Sadness	Distress	
Uncertain	Hope		Frustration	Disgust	High Control Potential
Certain	Joy	Relief			
Other-Caused Uncertain	Liking		Dislike		Low Control Potential
Certain					
Uncertain			Anger	Contempt	High Control Potential
Certain					
Self-Caused Uncertain	Pride		Regret		Low Control Potential
Certain					
Uncertain			Guilt	Shame	High Control Potential
Certain					
			Noncharacterological	Characterological	

Figure 13.8   Appraisal Decision Tree to Differentiate among 17 Emotions

Source: From "Appraisal determinants of emotions: Constructing a more accurate and comprehensive theory," by I. J. Roseman, A. A. Antoniou, and P. E. Jose, 1996, *Cognition and Emotion, 10*, pp. 241–277. Reprinted by permission of Psychology Press, Ltd.

the point that the person settles on what the stimulus event means for his or her goals and well-being.

Figure 13.8 depicts one possible decision tree to show how the six earlier-mentioned appraisal dimensions can differentiate among 17 different emotions (Roseman, 2011, 2013; Roseman, Antoniou, & Jose, 1996). The appraisal dimensions are shown on the border of the figure, while the differentiated emotions appear in the boxes inside the figure. The appraisal dimensions on the left side of the figure represent *agency* (circumstance-caused, other-caused, self-caused) and *novelty* (unexpected, uncertain, certain). The appraisal dimensions on the top of the figure represent *goal congruence* (motive-consistent, motive-inconsistent) and *intrinsic value* (appetitive, aversive). The appraisal dimension on the right side of the figure represents *coping potential* (low versus high). And Roseman adds one additional appraisal dimension on the bottom of the figure to evaluate the source of the event (noncharacterological, characterological). Admittedly, the figure can be difficult to follow, but it does get one point across rather well—namely, that in an emotional episode, people engage in a good deal of cognitive appraisal to interpret what is happening to them and as any of these interpretations (appraisals) change so does the person's emotional experience.

An appraisal decision tree such as the one depicted in Figure 13.8 will never predict ensuing emotions correctly 100 percent of the time (Oatley & Duncan, 1994). Appraisal theorists generally agree that knowing a person's particular configuration of appraisal allows them about a 65–70 percent accuracy rate in predicting people's emotions (Reisenzein & Hofman, 1993). Critics are a bit tougher in stating these odds—one researcher put the odds at only about 25 percent, a little higher for anger, a little lower for sadness, fear, and guilt (Tong, 2010). Five reasons explain why appraisals are not sufficient for emotion and, hence, why appraisal theory cannot explain emotional reactions with 100 percent accuracy (Berkowitz & Harmon-Jones, 2004; Fischer, Shaver, & Carnochan, 1990; Reisenzein & Hofman, 1993; Scherer, 1997b):

1. Processes other than appraisal contribute to emotion (as discussed in the first half of this chapter).

2. Appraisals often function only to intensify (rather than cause) the emotion (e.g., low coping potential intensifies, but does not cause, anger).

3. The patterns of appraisals for many emotions overlap (e.g., guilt and shame have similar patterns of appraisal).

4. Developmental differences exist among people such that children experience only general emotions (e.g., joy), whereas socialized adults generally experience a richer variety of appraisal-specific emotions (e.g., pride, relief, gratitude).

5. Emotion knowledge and causal attributions (the next two topics in this chapter) represent additional cognitive factors beyond appraisal that affect emotion.

Emotion Knowledge

Infants and young children understand and distinguish between only a few basic emotions. They learn to name the few basic emotions of anger, fear, sadness, joy, and love (Kemper, 1987; Shaver et al., 1987). As people gain experience with different situations, they learn to discriminate shades within a single emotion. The shades of joy, for instance, include happiness, relief, optimism, pride, contentment, and gratitude (Ellsworth & Smith, 1988). The shades of anger include fury, hostility, vengefulness, rage, aggravation, and wrath (Russell & Fehr, 1994). These distinctions are stored cognitively in hierarchies of basic emotions and their derivatives. Thus, the number of different emotions any one person can distinguish constitutes her *emotion knowledge* (Shaver et al., 1987).

Emotion knowledge is the ability to differentiate emotional experience into discrete categories (anger versus fear) and to differentiate one particular basic emotion into its various shades (anger versus irritation, frustration, hostility, and rage) (Barrett, Gross, Christensen & Benvenuto, 2001). It refers to the level of complexity individuals rely on to identity, label, and mentally represent their emotional experience (Lischetzke et al., 2005). People with low emotion knowledge tend to think about emotions in global terms (e.g., "I feel good"), whereas people with high emotion knowledge tend to use specific and situationally specific terminology (Barrett, 2004; Feldman, 1995). Hence, emotion knowledge is rather literally people's knowledge and understanding of their own emotional experiences.

The depth, complexity, and sophistication of a person's emotion knowledge is important because greater emotion knowledge leads to greater psychological well-being

(Palmer, Donaldson, & Stough, 2002; Tugade, Fredrickson & Barrett, 2004) and to better emotion regulation strategies. With sophisticated emotion knowledge, the person targets some particular emotions for regulation (Barrett & Gross, 2001) and facilitates the choosing and implementation of a strategy that has the best chance of regulating that emotion successfully. Sophisticated emotion knowledge also decreases emotional variability (Thompson, Dizen, & Berenbaum, 2009), and it decreases negative emotional variability in particular (Pond et al., 2012), because people with sophisticated emotion knowledge know clearly what they are feeling, what did and what did not cause them to feel that way, and which behavior and which coping strategies will most effectively deal with the emotion-eliciting event at hand.

One person's hypothetical (computer-generated) emotion knowledge appears in Figure 13.9. At the most general level, the figure shows that the person differentiates positive (left side) from negative (right side) emotions. At the next level, the middle of the figure shows that the person represents emotion with the basic emotion categories of love, joy, surprise, anger, sadness, and fear. For this person, these are his or her six basic emotions (or emotion families). With experience, the individual learns shades of these basic emotions (listed on the lower part of the figure). For instance, the individual depicted in the figure understands three shades of love—affection, lust, and longing—and six shades of sadness—suffering, depression, disappointment, shame, neglect, and sympathy. The asterisk in each column of emotion words denotes the prototype within the shades of that emotion.

Much of the diversity of emotion experience comes from learning fine distinctions among emotions and the specific situations that cause them. For example, an individual who has just lost out to a rival might potentially experience distress, anger, fear, disgust, or jealousy (Hupka, 1984). One learns that these emotions can coincide. One also learns that other emotions (e.g., love, joy) are far removed from this cluster of emotional experience. Finally, one learns the differences between shades of anger—the differences that allow for distinctions among jealousy, hate, irritation, and so on. Eventually, a lifetime of such learning produces finer and more sophisticated emotion knowledge. It is this reservoir of emotion knowledge that enables the individual to appraise situations with high discrimination and therefore to respond to each life event with a specialized and highly appropriate emotional reaction (rather than with general ones).

Attributions

Attribution theory rests on the assumption that people very much want to explain why they experienced a particular life outcome (Heider, 1958; Jones & Davis, 1965; Kelley, 1967, 1973; Weiner, 1980, 1985, 1986). Following an outcome, we ask: "Why did I fail that chemistry examination? Why did the Yankees win the World Series? Why did Suzy drop out of school? Why is this person rich while that person is poor? Why didn't I get that job? Why didn't Frank return my telephone call?"

An attribution is the reason the person uses to explain an important life outcome (Weiner, 1985, 1986). It is the causal explanation to answer why an outcome occurred. For instance, if we answer the question, "Why did I fail that chemistry test?" by saying, "because I didn't study for it," then "low effort" is the attribution to explain the failure. Attributions are important because the explanation we use generates emotional reactions. Following positive outcomes, people generally feel happy, and following negative outcomes,

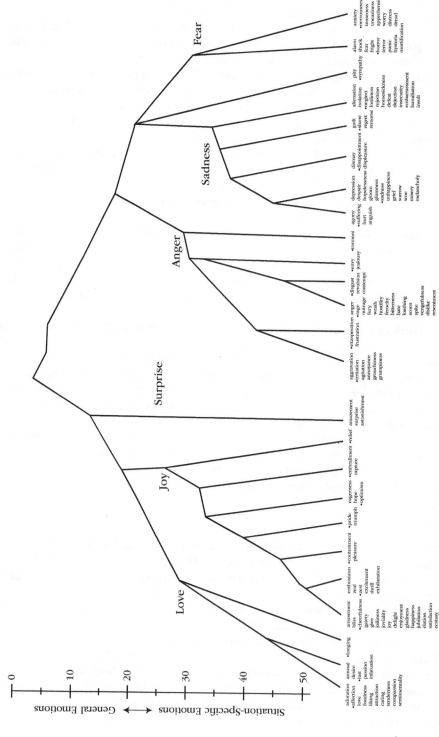

Figure 13.9 Hypothetical Representation of One Person's Emotion Knowledge

Source: From "Emotion knowledge: Further exploration of a prototype approach," by P. Shaver, J. Schwartz, D. Kirson, and C. O'Conner, 1987, *Journal of Personality and Social Psychology, 52,* pp. 1061–1086. Copyright © 1987 by American Psychological Association. Adapted with permission.

people generally feel sad or frustrated. In his attributional theory of emotion, Bernard Weiner (1985, 1986) refers to the outcome-dependent emotional reaction as a "primary appraisal of the outcome." Basic emotions of happy and sad simply follow good and bad outcomes (Weiner, Russell, & Learman, 1978, 1979). Attribution theory proposes that in addition to these primary outcome-generated emotional reactions, people further explain why they succeeded or failed. Once the outcome has been explained, new emotions surface to differentiate the general happy–sad initial emotional reaction into specific secondary emotions. The attribution of why the outcome occurred constitutes the "secondary appraisal of the outcome." The sequence of events in Weiner's attribution theory of emotion appears in Figure 13.10.

As depicted in Figure 13.10, seven emotions occur in reliable ways as a function of the attributional information-processing flow (Weiner, 1985, 1986; Weiner & Graham, 1989). The attributional roots to the seven emotions are as follows:

Pride	Attributing a positive outcome to an internal cause. "I succeeded because of my outstanding effort."
Gratitude	Attributing a positive outcome to an external cause. "I succeeded because of help from my teammates."
Hope	Attributing a positive outcome to a stable cause. "I do well in sports because I am athletic by nature."
Anger	Attributing a negative outcome to an external-controllable cause. "I lost because my opponent cheated."
Pity (Sympathy)	Attributing a negative outcome to an external-uncontrollable cause. "I lost my job because of the poor economy."
Guilt	Attributing a negative outcome to an internal-controllable cause. "I lost because I didn't put forth much effort."
Shame	Attributing a negative outcome to an internal-uncontrollable cause. "I was rejected because I am ugly."

Notice that in each of these seven emotions (three positive, four negative), the attributional analysis of why the outcome came to pass is causally prior to the specific emotion. For instance, the fundamental assertion of an attributional analysis of emotion is that if the attribution was to change, then the emotion would change as well (i.e., change the attribution, change the emotion). If a student feels pride because she feels her effort won her a scholarship, and if the student then learns that the real reason she won the scholarship was because of someone's strong support of her application during a meeting, then the experienced emotion flows from pride into gratitude. The outcome is the same (she won the scholarship), but when the attribution changed so did the emotional reaction.

Appraisal theorists begin their analysis with relatively simple appraisals, such as whether an event signifies harm, threat, or danger (Lazarus, 1991a). They continue with progressively more complex appraisals, such as self/norm compatibility. Cognitive theorists then add emotion knowledge to explain further how people make fine-tuned appraisals. In his attributional analysis, Bernard Weiner (1982, 1986) adds yet one more type of appraisal to help explain emotion—the post-outcome appraisal of why the outcome occurred. Thus, the role of cognition is not only to appraise the meaning of the life event

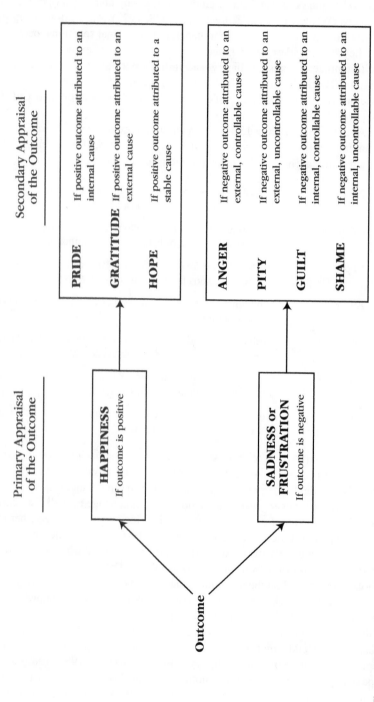

Figure 13.10 Attribution Theory of Emotion

(appraisal) but also to appraise why the life outcome turned out the way it did (attribution). When taken as a whole, preoutcome appraisals such as potential benefit, harm, versus threat explain some emotional processes, yet postoutcome appraisals (attributions) explain additional emotional processes (Leon & Hernandez, 1998).

Emotions Affect Cognition

The theme of the second part of this chapter has been that cognition affects emotion. But it works the other way too, because emotion affects cognition. That is, emotional states and emotional episodes affect and cause cognitive events such as attentional engagement, judgment, decision making, interpretation, risk taking, reasoning, short-term working memory, and long-term memory storage and retrieval (Angie, Connelly, Waples, & Kligyte, 2011; Blanchette & Richards, 2010; Derakshan & Eysenck, 2010; Lench, Flores & Bench, 2011; Lerner & Keltner, 2001; Yegiyan & Yonelinas, 2011). While this is a very important point, it is not all that surprising, because emotions have such robust effects. Emotions affect and coordinate people's feeling states, bodily preparation for action, motivational sense of purpose, expressive signals, *and* cognition. Further, the effect that individual emotions have on cognitive events is about the same in magnitude as the effect of emotion on feeling states, bodily preparation for action, motivational sense of purpose, and expressive signals (Lench et al., 2011).

This finding—that emotion changes cognition—might lead some to think that the four components of emotion should be expanded from four to five. That is, the emotional components of feeling, purpose, bodily preparation, and expressive signals should add the fifth component of cognition. But that would be a conceptual mistake. Cognition, like coping behavior, is a result of emotion, rather than one of its component aspects. So, the overall emotion process is as follows: A significant life event occurs and is appraised, then a feeling state, motivational sense of purpose, autonomic nervous and endocrine system activity, and expressive signals quickly follow. This complex reaction then causes the behavioral and cognitive activity that becomes the person's adaptive functioning toward the significant life event.

SOCIAL ASPECTS OF EMOTION

Other people are typically our most frequent source of day-to-day emotion (Oatley & Duncan, 1994). We experience a greater number of emotions when interacting with others than when we are alone.

Social Interaction

If you kept track of which events and experiences caused your emotional reactions—another person's action, an action of your own, something you read or saw—you would likely discover that interactions with others triggered most of your emotions (Oatley & Duncan, 1994). Emotions are intrinsic to interpersonal relationships. They also play a central role in creating (joy), maintaining (sadness), and dissolving (anger) interpersonal relationships, as emotions draw us together and emotions push us apart (Fischer & Manstead, 2008; Levenson, Carstensen, & Gottman, 1994; Levenson & Gottman, 1983).

Other people not only directly cause emotions to stir in us, but they also affect us indirectly, as through *emotional contagion*. Emotional contagion is "the tendency to automatically mimic and synchronize expressions, vocalizations, postures, and movements with those of another person and, consequently, to converge emotionally" (Hatfield, Cacioppo, & Rapson, 1993a). The three propositions of mimicry, feedback, and contagion explain how, during social interaction, the emotions of others indirectly create emotions in us (Hatfield, Cacioppo, & Rapson, 1993b):

Mimicry: "In conversation, people automatically mimic and synchronize their movements with the facial expressions, voices, postures, movements, and instrumental behaviors of other people."

Feedback: "Emotional experience is affected, moment to moment, by the activation of and feedback from facial, vocal, postural, and movement mimicry."

Contagion: "Consequently, people tend to 'catch' other people's emotions."

As we are exposed to the emotional expressions of others, we tend to mimic their facial expressions (Dimberg, 1982; Strayer, 1993), speech style (Hatfield et al., 1995), and posture (Bernieri & Rosenthal, 1991). Once mimicry occurs, the facial feedback hypothesis illustrates how mimicry (of not only the face, but also voice and posture) can affect the observer's emotional experience, and hence lead to a contagion effect.

Social Sharing of Emotion

During social interaction, we not only expose ourselves to a rich source of emotionally eliciting events and to emotional contagion effects, but we also put ourselves into a conversational context that provides an opportunity to re-experience and relive past emotional experiences, a process referred to as the social sharing of emotion (Rimé, 2009; Rimé, Mesquita, Philippot, & Boca, 1991). Social sharing of emotion is a conversational event in which one person that has experienced an emotional episode talks openly with person about the circumstances of the event and his or her feelings and emotional reactions. In social sharing, the person gains attention and elicits empathy, but he or she also undertakes a reflective effort to unpack the emotional material (e.g., contextual circumstances, antecedent causes, emotional processes, interpretation of events, consequences), put labels on that emotional material, organizes it into an emotional story that communicates what happened and what obstacles were encountered, and shares what was felt and thought. Social sharing occurs following the vast majority of emotional episodes (about 90 percent of the time; Rimé, 2009), more often involves positive emotional episodes rather than negative ones, and is most likely to occur on the same day as the emotional episode (about 60 percent of the time; Rimé, 2009), although social sharing also takes place days, weeks, months, or even years after the eliciting emotional event.

When people share their emotions, they typically do so by recounting the full account of what happened during the emotional episode, what it meant, and how the person felt throughout. Just sharing a negative emotional episode (i.e., talking about it, or just venting) is not sufficient to dissipate that emotion (Rimé, 2009). Rather, people share emotions in different ways and with different effects. One major way people share their emotional experiences is social-affectively, when the speaker solicits and the listener provides support, comfort, validation, and empathy. Another major way people share their emotional experience is in terms of cognitive sharing when the speaker asks for and the listener stimulates the cognitive work necessary to recover from the felt sadness, fear, or anger episode.

Social-Affective Sharing:	Listening; understanding; unconditional positive regard; comforting; offering consolation; caring; reassuring; perspective taking and empathy; revalidating self-esteem; providing social and concrete help and assistance.
Cognitive Sharing:	Reframing the event; reappraising the emotional episode; creating meaning; encouraging the abandonment of failed goals; reprioritizing one's goals and motives.

People share their emotions with others primarily to better regulate those emotions. Social-affective sharing helps regulate emotion, especially negative emotion, by temporarily alleviating emotional distress. It is particularly beneficial in the early stages of the emotional event, because it does generally provide a state of temporary relief from one's distress, fear, anger, anxiety, insecurity, or sense of helplessness. But social-affective sharing is not sufficient to attain emotional recovery. Emotional recovery—getting over and getting beyond the distress, fear, or anger—requires cognitive sharing in which the other person helps the person reframe or reappraise the emotional event. Cognitive sharing is something more akin to therapy, because it provides an opportunity for reappraisal, deeper understanding, and more effective coping. Cognitive sharing helps bring distressing emotional episodes to an end (Brans et al., 2013). Importantly, if the social sharing of emotion involves only social-affective sharing (and not cognitive sharing), then it tends to produce a temporary distress relief but not much more. Part of the reason for this is because most listeners are not all that skilled in helping the person work cognitively and competently through the emotional episode (Nils & Rimé, 2012).

Social sharing of emotion contributes to some level of relief from the emotional distress, and it contributes to eventual emotional recovery, but it does more. The social sharing of an emotional experience by one person with another instigates an interpersonal dynamic that brings the two people closer together. This interpersonal dynamic is illustrated graphically in Figure 13.11. According to Rimé (2009), person 1 experiences an emotion and conversationally shares it with person 2. Person 2 then reacts with interest, because emotional stories are viewed as inherently interesting events. Person 1 takes person 2's expressed interest as a social signal to socially share more. Listening to social sharing that is elaborative enough to produce a full emotional story functions as an emotion-eliciting situation for person 2 (Strack & Coyne, 1983). The social sharing then begins to generate a social connection between the two interactants, because it is in experiences such as perceived similarity and greater empathy that a social connection is facilitated and begins to open the pair up to nonverbal communications such as eye contact, vocal mimicry, and touching intimacy. This enhanced relationship leads person 2 to a greater desire to help person 1 work through social-affective support and cognitive restructuring. Helping leads person 2 to like person 1 more, and the received interpersonal support leads person 1 to like person 2 more. Hence, what began as the social sharing of an emotional experience evolves into a closer and more positive interpersonal relationship between speaker and listener. It is in these times of sharing our emotions that we build and maintain the relationships that are central to our lives (Edwards, Manstead, & MacDonald, 1984), such as in friendship and marriage (Noller, 1984).

Overall, the conclusions from the social sharing of emotion are as follows: (1) Social sharing of emotion is the norm in emotional experience, not the occasional exception that

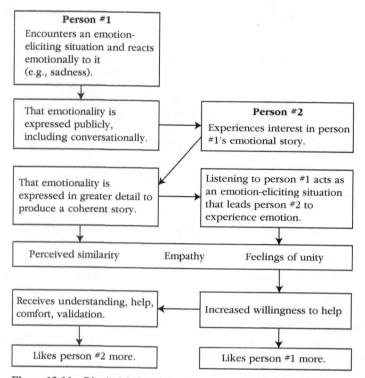

Figure 13.11 Rimé's Model of the Interpersonal Dynamics in the Social Sharing of an Emotional Experience

people only sometimes do; (2) social sharing sets the stage for interpersonal dynamics that bring the sharer and the listener closer together; (3) social-affective sharing is commonplace but generally yields little benefit beyond temporary relief; and (4) cognitive sharing stimulates the cognitive work necessary for emotional healing and recovery (Rimé, 2009). More generally, research on the social sharing of emotion makes the larger point that emotional episodes are social experiences. This research also challenges the common view that emotion is a short-lived, intrapersonal experience, because it argues alternatively that emotional experiences routinely endure for days, weeks, and even years, partly because they are retold and relived through this process of social sharing.

Cultural Construction of Emotion

Because appraisal contributes to a cognitive understanding of emotion and because social interaction contributes to a social understanding of emotion, the cultural context in which we live contributes to a cultural understanding of emotion. Social psychologists, sociologists, and others argue that emotion is not necessarily a private, biological, intrapsychic phenomenon. Instead, they contend that many emotions originate within both social interaction and a cultural context (Manstead, 1991; Rimé, 2009; Stets & Turner, 2008).

Those who study the cultural construction of emotion point out that if you changed the culture you lived in, then your emotional repertoire would also change (Mascolo, Fischer, & Li, 2003). Consider, for instance, the emotional repertoire of people in the

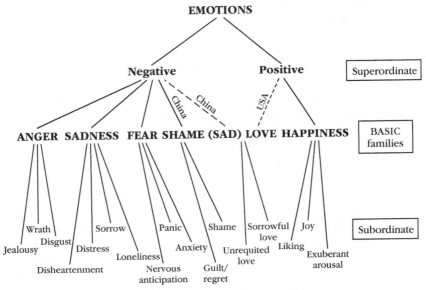

Figure 13.12   Cluster Analysis of Basic Emotion Families in Chinese and English

Source: From "Cross-cultural similarities and differences in emotion and its representation: A prototype approach," by P. R. Shaver, S. Wu, & J. C. Schwartz, 1992, in M. S. Clark (Ed.), *Review of Personality and Social Psychology*, *13*, pp. 231–251. Thousand Oaks, CA: Sage.

United States and China. Chinese infants are less emotionally reactive and expressive than are American infants, probably because Chinese parents emphasize and expect emotional restraint whereas American parents emphasize and expect emotional expression. Similarly, the expression of some negative relational emotions—primarily anger—is strictly prohibited in cultures that are highly collectivistic, including China (Fok et al., 2008).

In the same spirit, Figure 13.12 graphically illustrates the similar and dissimilar basic emotions for people from both cultures. The solid lines to anger, sadness, fear, and happiness illustrate that members of both cultures see essentially the same meaning within these emotional experiences. The dashed lines to shame and love illustrate that members from the two cultures see different meanings within these emotions. For Chinese, love is not necessarily a positive emotion. The meaning of love is much closer to "sad love," and it is often considered to be a negative emotion. For people in China, shame is considered to be a basic emotion. Thus, people in the United States find meaning in two positive emotions and three negative emotions, whereas people in China find meaning in one positive emotion and five negative emotions. (The 17 subordinate emotions—jealousy, wrath, disgust, etc.—are from the Chinese participants, not from the American participants.)

If you are an English-speaking reader and are surprised that Chinese-speaking participants understand love ("sad love") as a negative emotion, then the point helps illustrate the cultural basis of emotion. In traditional Chinese culture, parents sometimes arrange their children's marriages. In these cases, marriages function as the joining of two extended families, in addition to the joining of two people. When one anticipates an arranged marriage, romantic love takes on meaning as a potentially disruptive force that can separate a son or daughter from his or her parents (Potter, 1988). If embraced, romantic love therefore has the potential to break down the proper respect and deference that sons and daughters are expected to show their parents (Russell & Yik, 1996). The experience of romantic love therefore takes on a negative valence and is better represented by the experience of "sad love."

The case of East versus West in romantic love has an additional complexity in that Westerners generally lack the emotional complexity shown by Easterners (Kitayama, Markus, & Kurokawa, 2000). Emotional complexity is the experience of positive and negative emotion to the same event. While men and women from the East report comparable levels of positively valenced romantic love, Easterners tend to report that the negative emotions of shame, contempt, and anger accompany their experience of romantic love while Westerners do not report this same emotional complexity (Shiota et al., 2010). For Westerners, the experience of positive and negative emotions are strongly negatively correlated (i.e., if you feel one, you rarely feel the other), while positive and negative emotions are often bundled together in the emotional experience of Easterners.

Cultures also offer children storybooks to read and immerse their lives into. Preschoolers in the United States generally prefer exciting stories, whereas preschoolers in China prefer calm stories. Furthermore this exposure to exciting storybooks is part of what leads U.S. children to prefer exciting affect as ideal while exposure to calm storybooks is part of what leads Chinese children to prefer calm affect as ideal (Tsai, Louie, Chen, & Uchida, 2007). Societies also clearly socialize their members' emotional experiences and expressions (Chen, 1993, Stipek, 1999). Still, limits exist as to how much a culture can socialize particular emotions into its constituents. Consider the claim that in some cultures people exchange romantic partners without jealousy. Biology-minded theorists argue that sharing a sexual partner would surely produce jealousy, and appraisal theorists might make a similar argument (see Figure 13.7). But can people be socialized to not experience jealousy during the exchange of romantic partners? Is culture that dominant? The short answer is, basically, no (Reiss, 1986). Cultures *do* vary as to which behaviors signal jealousy, which signs of affection justify jealousy, and how people express jealousy, but the emotional angst of sexual jealousy occurs in all cultures (Reiss, 1986). Like many other basic emotions, jealousy is universal, although many of its nuances (causes, expressions) vary from one culture to the next.

Culture does not necessarily mean "nationality," because culture can consist of any group of people with shared beliefs, practices, and values. How people learn to manage their emotions in microcultures can be seen in professionals who interact frequently, closely, and intimately with the public, such as physicians (Smith & Kleinman, 1989), hairstylists (Parkinson, 1991), and airline flight attendants (Hochschild, 1983). In these microcultures, socialization pressures to manage one's emotions mostly revolve around a theme of coping with aversive feelings in ways that are both socially desirable and personally adaptive (Saarni, 1997). Physicians, for instance, are not supposed to feel either attraction or disgust for their patients, irrespective of how beautiful or revolting their appearance might be. Therefore, during their medical school training (i.e., during their enculturation into the professional society), physicians must learn affective neutrality, a detached concern for their patients. As a case in point, medical students learn emotion-regulating strategies such as the following during procedures such as a pelvic, rectal, and breast examinations and while blood is spewing out of an artery during surgery, dissections, and autopsies (Smith & Kleinman, 1989):

Transform the emotional contact into something else.

Mentally transform intimate bodily contact into a cold step-by-step procedure.

Accentuate the positive.

Identify the satisfaction in learning or the opportunity to practice medicine.

Laugh about it.

Joke about it, because joking exempts the doctor from admitting weakness.

Consider also hairstylists (Parkinson, 1991). To be professionally successful, hairstylists need to develop an open communication style characterized by expressiveness, affect intensity, empathy, poise, frequent positive facial expressions, and a concealment of negative emotions. Furthermore, the more natural and spontaneous the hairstylist appears to clients, the better the job goes. How do hairstylists learn to manage their emotions in this way? The problem hairstylists face is, essentially, how they can acquire an open interaction style with clients who are often uptight and socially remote. Part of the job of being a hairstylist is to figure this out, and the ones who do develop these emotion management skills report higher job satisfaction.

Flight attendants need to adopt an open interaction style similar to that of the hairstylist. To do so, the flight attendant frequently uses "deep-acting" methods that are not too unlike the methods stage actors use during a 2-hour performance. Using deep-acting methods, the flight attendant replaces her natural and spontaneous emotional reactions with an emotional repertoire characterized by constant courtesy to clients (Hochschild, 1983). In all these cases—medical students, hairstylists, and flight attendants—people learn to manage their private, spontaneous feelings and express them in publicly scripted and socially desirable ways of acting. Doing so facilitates smooth professional interactions with their clients (Manstead, 1991).

SUMMARY

Three central aspects of emotion exist: biological, cognitive, and social–cultural. The chapter begins with a biological analysis of emotion because emotions are, in part, biological reactions to important life events. They serve coping functions that allow the individual to prepare to adapt effectively to important life circumstances. Emotions energize and direct bodily actions (e.g., running, fighting) by affecting (1) the autonomic nervous system and its regulation of the heart, lungs, and muscles; (2) neural brain circuits such as those in the subcortical brain; and (3) facial feedback and discrete patterns of the facial musculature.

Research on the biological underpinnings of emotion identify that the activation of between two and eight basic emotions can be understood from a biological perspective. For instance, the basic emotions of anger, fear, sadness, and disgust show autonomic nervous system specificity in that the pattern of heart rate, skin temperature, and skin conductance is different for each emotion. Similarly, the basic emotions of anger, fear, sadness, disgust, and sadness are associated with a specific subcortical brain area. The facial feedback hypothesis asserts that the subjective aspect of emotion is actually the awareness of proprioceptive feedback from facial action. According to the strong version of this hypothesis, posed facial expressions activate specific emotions, such that smiling activates joy. According to the weak version of this hypothesis, exaggerated and suppressed facial expressions augment and attenuate naturally occurring emotion. Although research is mixed on the strong version, evidence confirms the validity of the weaker version.

The central construct in a cognitive understanding of emotion is appraisal. Appraisal is a cognitive process that evaluates the significance of environmental events in terms of the person's goals and well-being. Cognitively minded appraisal emotion researchers embrace all of the following beliefs: (1) Without an antecedent cognitive appraisal of the event, emotions do not occur; (2) the appraisal, not the event itself, causes the emotion; (3) emotion is a process; and (4) if the appraisal changes, even if the situation does not, then the emotion will change. To explain virtually all complex emotions—not just the two to eight basic emotions emphasized by the biologically minded theorists—cognitive emotion researchers emphasize seven appraisals. Environmental events are evaluated in terms of their valence (is the event good or bad?), goal relevance (is the event relevant to my goals and well-being?), coping potential (can I cope successfully with the event?), goal congruence (is the event facilitating my goal attainment?), novelty (did I expect the event to happen?), agency (who caused the event?), and self-norm compatibility (is the event okay on a moral level?). Different patterns of these appraisals produce different emotions and explain why two different people can experience different emotions even to the same event.

In a social and cultural analysis of emotion, other people are our richest sources of emotional experiences. During social interaction, we often "catch" other people's emotions through a process of emotion contagion that involves mimicry, feedback, and, eventually, contagion. We also share and relive our emotional experiences during conversations with others, a process referred to as the social sharing of emotion. Social sharing of emotion is commonplace, brings the sharer and the listener closer together, usually provides only temporary distress relief, but can potentially stimulate the cognitive work necessary for emotional healing and recovery. In the cultural construction of emotion, cultural forces socialize how members of that culture experience, express, and manage (i.e., suppress) their emotional expressions toward ways that are socially acceptable and away from ways that are genuinely felt.

READINGS FOR FURTHER STUDY

Biological Aspects of Emotion

Ekman, P., & Cordaro, D. (2011). What is meant by calling emotions basic? *Emotion Review, 3,* 364–370.

Izard, C. E. (2007). Basic emotions, natural kinds, emotion schemas, and a new paradigm. *Perspectives on Psychological Science, 2,* 260–280.

Levenson, R. W. (1992). Autonomic nervous system differences among emotions. *Psychological Science, 3,* 23–27.

McIntosh, D. N. (1996). Facial feedback hypotheses: Evidence, implications, and directions. *Motivation and Emotion, 20,* 121–147.

Cognitive Aspects of Emotion

Lazarus, R. S. (1991). Progress on a cognitive-motivational-relational theory of emotion. *American Psychologist, 46,* 819–834.

Lazarus, R. S., & Smith, C. A. (1988). Knowledge and appraisal in the cognition-emotion relationship. *Cognition and Emotion, 2,* 281–300.

Moors, A., Ellsworth, P. C., Scherer, K. R., & Frijda, N. H. (2013). Appraisal theories of emotion: State of the art and future development. *Emotion Review, 5*, 119–124.

Scherer, K. R. (1993). Studying the emotion-antecedent appraisal process: An expert system approach. *Cognition and Emotion, 7*, 325–355.

Shaver, P., Schwartz, J., Kirson, D., & O'Connor, C. (1987). Emotion knowledge: Further exploration of a prototype approach. *Journal of Personality and Social Psychology, 52*, 1061–1086.

Social Aspects of Emotion

Rimé, B. (2009). Emotion elicits the social sharing of emotion: Theory and empirical review. *Emotion Review, 1*, 60–85.

Chapter 14

Individual Emotions

BASIC EMOTIONS

Fear

Anxiety

Posttraumatic Stress Disorder

Phobias

Anger

Disgust

Contempt

Sadness

Depression

Emotional Preparation for Threat and Harm

Joy

Interest

Emotional Preparation for Motive Involvement and Satisfaction

SELF-CONSCIOUS EMOTIONS

Shame

Guilt

Embarrassment

Pride

Triumph

Interrelations among Shame, Guilt, Pride, and Hubris

COGNITIVELY COMPLEX EMOTIONS

Envy

Gratitude

Disappointment and Regret

Hope

Schadenfreude

Empathy

Compassion

SUMMARY

READINGS FOR FURTHER STUDY

Crash! Sitting in your car waiting for the red light to turn green, another car hits you from behind. Luckily, the car was traveling at only 10 mph and you are not hurt. Your car is probably not so lucky, so you get out, walk to the back of the car, and take a look. As you look, the other driver exits and starts to approach the scene. This is a critical moment. What is this guy thinking? What is he feeling? What will he do? How will the interaction go? From your point of view, the accident was clearly his fault, but you wonder how the interaction will go nevertheless. Will it be a friendly chat or an aggressive provocation?

Crashing is certainly a significant life event—an emotion-eliciting event. So, emotional expressive signals will be sent. Fortunately, you know what the other driver is feeling and what actions he is most likely to take. You know this because you read his facial, vocal, and postural signals. If you read his expressive signals, then you can infer both his emotional state and what he most wants to do (i.e., his action tendencies, as summarized in Table 14.1). Processing this emotion knowledge, your job in the next two seconds will be to prepare yourself for as constructive a face-to-face interaction as is possible. Incidentally, while most people think that "be pleasant" is the most constructive expression during such a confrontation, expressing anger is probably the smarter and more constructive thing to do (Ford & Tamir, 2012).

This third chapter on emotion examines 20 individual emotions. The first section presents the seven basic emotions of fear, anger, disgust, contempt, sadness, joy, and interest. The second section presents the five self-conscious emotions of shame, guilt, embarrassment, pride, and triumph. The third section presents the eight cognitively complex emotions of envy, gratitude, disappointment, regret, hope, schadenfreude, empathy, and compassion.

Table 14.1 The Motivational Urge (Action Tendency) Associated with 17 Emotions

Individual Emotion	Motivational Urge or Action Tendency
Fear	Flee; protect oneself.
Anger	Overcome obstacles; right an illegitimate wrong.
Disgust	Reject; get rid of; get away from.
Contempt	Maintain the social hierarchy.
Sadness	Repair a loss or failure.
Joy	Continue one's goal striving; play; engage in social interaction.
Interest	Explore; seek; acquire new information; learn.
Pride (Authentic)	Acquire further skill; persist at challenging tasks.
Shame	Restore the self; protect the self.
Guilt	Make amends.
Embarrassment	Appease others; communicate blunder was unintended.
Envy (Benign)	Move up; improve one's position.
Gratitude	Act prosocially; grow the relationship.
Regret	Undo a poor decision or behavior.
Hope	Keep engaged in the pursuit of a desired goal.
Empathy	Act prosocially; help the other.
Compassion	Reduce suffering.

BASIC EMOTIONS

Fear, anger, disgust, contempt, sadness, joy, and interest are relatively easy emotions to understand, because they are ubiquitous experiences. Basic emotions are an inherent part of everyone's emotional repertoire, regardless of age, gender, culture, or historical time period. These emotions have clear and identifiable antecedents, and they produce reliable downstream behavioral, cognitive, and social effects.

Fear

Fear arises from a person's interpretation that the situation is dangerous and a threat to one's well-being. The most common fear-activating situations are those rooted in the anticipation of physical or psychological harm, a vulnerability to danger, or an expectation that one's coping abilities will not be able to match up to forthcoming circumstances. Physical and psychological threats can come from biological (snakes, spiders) or sociocultural (angry facial expressions, strangers, racial out-group members) dangers, although we are more prepared to fear the former and a bit more flexible in our fear of the latter (Mallan, Lipp, & Cochrane, 2013). That said, slithering snakes seem to have a special capacity to elicit fear in us (Ohman & Mineka, 2003), because no object is more quickly detected by the human brain than is a snake in the grass. A close runner-up, however, is a threatening facial expression (Ohman & Mineka, 2001). What these stimulus situations have in common is that both are rather clear signals of imminent pain, threat, and danger.

The perception that one can do little to cope with an environmental threat or danger is at least as important a source of fear as is any actual characteristic of the threatening situation itself (Bandura, 1983). Fear is therefore mostly about a perceived vulnerability to being overwhelmed by a threat or danger. That fear can be calmed by coping potential says something important about the nature and experience of fear—namely, that it is not necessarily an automatic process. The fact that an appraisal of high coping potential can calm fear means that the cortical brain can take some of the fire (fear) out of the subcortical brain.

Fear motivates protection. It functions as a warning signal for forthcoming physical or psychological harm that manifests itself in an impulse to freeze or flee (as in the "flight" part of the fight-or-flight response). The individual trembles, perspires, looks around, and feels nervous tension to protect the self. Fear is the emotion system that signals our vulnerability (often in no uncertain terms). Protection motivation manifests itself either through escape or withdrawal. Fleeing puts physical (or psychological) distance between the self and whatever is feared. If fleeing is not possible, fear motivates freezing—being quiet and still.

On a more positive note, fear can provide the motivational support for learning new coping responses that remove the person from encountering danger in the first place. Few highway drivers in a torrential rainfall, for instance, need to be reminded to pay attention to the slippery road (fear activates coping efforts), and experienced drivers are better at coping with such a danger than are novice drivers (fear facilitates the learning of adaptive responses). Fear therefore warns us of our vulnerability, but it also facilitates learning how to cope.

Anxiety

Anxiety is a close ally of fear (Ohman, 2008). Fear and anxiety are both aversive emotional states that arise from a threat to one's well-being. One key difference is that fear has an identifiable threat whereas anxiety does not. We are afraid of snakes and heights, but we are anxious about the future. A second key difference is that fear motivates a specific course of coping, because we run from the snake and avoid the steep roof. Anxiety, on the other hand, is a state of undirected arousal and tension. This distinction makes it clear that fear is largely a functional emotion and a motivational asset, while anxiety is more of an "on alert" negative emotionality that does not typically advance our coping effectiveness.

Posttraumatic Stress Disorder

A second fear ally is posttraumatic stress disorder (Ohman, 2008). Posttraumatic stress disorder arises from an experience (or experiences) of extreme danger that elicits intense fear (fright, terror) that has fear-related short-term consequences but also trauma-related long-term consequences. The typical antecedents are living through terrorism, torture, major accidents, or a natural disaster (e.g., a hurricane). In each of these cases, one sees others killed in a context of widespread violence (e.g., bombs exploding, homes destroyed). The object that causes the fright is clear (the trauma), but the person feels anxiety and stress because he or she cannot predict when the fear experience will be re-experienced in the form of vivid flashbacks. Thus, being anxious, the person with a posttraumatic stress disorder finds it difficult to sleep or to concentrate on daily activities. Like anxiety, it is very difficult to turn off the fear aroused by a past trauma because there exists no clear effective coping response (i.e., one cannot go back in time and undo the trauma).

Phobias

A final close ally of fear is the clinical phobia (Ohman, 2008). Although it sometimes seems that the number of potential phobias is limitless, a careful analysis reveals four categories of phobias (Arrindell et al., 1991). The first category of common adult phobias is fear about "interpersonal events and situations." This first category includes fears of criticism, rejection, and interpersonal conflict, especially violent conflict. The second category is fear about "death, injuries, illnesses, blood, and surgical procedures." This second category includes fears of bodily injury, illness, and death. The third category includes fears of "animals." This category includes domestic animals, but it more often involves creepy and crawly animals. The fourth category is "agoraphobic fears." This category includes getting lost in crowds, entering closed spaces, and being alone. Collectively, all four phobias make evolutionary sense, because social situations can escalate out of control to produce psychological and physical injury, death and illness are self-evident, animals can be predators, and agoraphobic fears stem from being separated from a secure base or one's family.

Anger

Anger is a ubiquitous emotion (Averill, 1982). When people describe their most recent emotional experience, anger is the emotion that often comes to mind (Scherer & Tannenbaum, 1986). The core antecedent of anger is the presence of an obstacle to one's goal pursuit, so anger's key function is to prepare the person to overcome such obstacles. Said a little differently, anger arises from any interference with our pursuit of a goal we care about, although anger can also arise from interference with minor goals as occurs when stuck in traffic behind a slow-moving vehicle (Stephens & Groeger, 2011). It is also triggered by someone attempting to do us harm, physically or psychologically. In these cases, anger prepares the person to remove the obstacle or to stop the harm. It also includes a wish to hurt the person who is attempting to do us harm. Anger also arises from a betrayal of trust, being rebuffed, receiving unwarranted criticism, suffering a lack of consideration from others, and cumulative annoyances (Fehr et al., 1999). Anger further is caused rather directly by aversive conditions, such as pain (Berkowitz & Harmon-Jones, 2004). Overall, anger arises from restraint, as in the interpretation that one's plans, goals, or well-being have been interfered with by some outside force (e.g., barriers, obstacles, interruptions). The essence of anger is the belief that the situation is not what it should be; that is, the restraint, interference, or criticism is illegitimate (de Rivera, 1981).

Anger is the most passionate emotion. The angry person becomes stronger and more energized (as in the "fight" part of the fight-or-flight response). Anger arises when people want to keep control of something that is theirs (Levenson, 2011). It motivates self-defense, and it regulates social interactions to defend the self and whatever belongs to the self. One way anger produces its functional effects is by increasing the person's sense of control (Lerner & Keltner, 2001). Thus, when people do act out their anger, research shows a surprising success rate (Tafrate, Kassinove, & Dundin, 2002). People (e.g., politicians) who express anger generally get more respect and status following a wrong than do people who express sadness or guilt (Tiedens & Linton, 2001). This is because anger makes people more attuned to the injustices of what other people do (Keltner, Ellsworth, & Edwards, 1993), and because it often clarifies relationship problems, energizes political agendas, and spurs a culture to change for the better, as occurred with the civil rights movement, the woman's suffrage movement, and Americans' national response to the September 11, 2001, terrorists attacks (Tavris, 1989).

Anger is not only the most passionate emotion, it is also the most dangerous, because its purpose is to destroy barriers in the environment. About one-half of anger episodes include yelling or screaming, and about 10 percent of anger episodes lead to aggression (Tafrate et al., 2002). When anger prompts aggression, it produces needless destruction and injury, as when we shove a rival, curse at a teammate, or thoughtlessly damage property. For these reasons, they key downside of anger is that is repels others (Marsh, Ambady, & Kleck, 2005). This seemingly contradictory state—anger repels others, yet it is also an effective way of coping—means that how we regulate anger is very important (Eisenberg et al., 1994). People who can effectively regulate their anger to regulate their bodily activation (Denson, Grisham, & Moulds, 2011) to produce constructive rather than destructive responses inside a provocative encounter function better socially than do those who do not show this same self-regulatory skill (Eisenberg et al., 1997).

Disgust

Disgust is the oldest emotion. Its original, primitive function was to prevent the oral incorporation of offensive substances (Rozin & Fallon, 1987). It is healthy if one can produce a strong repulsion urge against foods that smell or look spoiled or infested with bugs, and that emotion needs to be strong enough to fully counter-urge hunger. Disgust involves feeling repulsed by and motivated to get rid of or get away from a contaminated, deteriorated, or spoiled object. Just what that object is depends on development and culture (Rozin, Haidt, & McCauley, 1993; Rozin, Lowery, & Ebert, 1994). Its purpose is rejection (Rozin, Haidt, & McCauley, 2008).

Nine domains of disgust antecedents have been validated: food, bodily waste products, animals, sexual behaviors, contact with death or corpses, violations of the exterior of the body (gore, deformity), poor hygiene, contact with unsavory people, and moral offenses (Haidt, McCauley, & Rozin, 1994). What this list of disgust elicitors suggests is that the oldest emotion began as a repulsion to contaminated foods but developed gradually into a general rejection system that protects the self from a wide range of potential contaminants (Rozin et al., 2008). This developmental trajectory applies both to the history of the species and to the individual. In infancy, for instance, the cause of disgust is limited to bitter or sour tastes. In childhood, disgust reactions expand to include psychologically acquired revulsions and generally any object deemed to be offensive (Rozin & Fallon, 1987). By adulthood, disgust arises from any object deemed to be contaminated in some way, including bodily contaminations (germs, poor hygiene, illness), interpersonal contaminations (physical contact with undesirable people, sleeping in a hotel bed on which the linens have not been changed), and moral contaminations (child abuse, incest, infidelity) (Rozin et al., 1994). Disgust elicitors can also easily contaminate other objects. Seeing a dead cockroach touching your food will trigger disgust and pretty much contaminate the whole plate of food, emotionally speaking (Rozin, Millman, & Nemeroff, 1986).

At the core of disgust is the identification of substances that are deteriorated or contaminated in some way, but that core can be expanded by socialization experiences. Physical contamination represents the prototype of disgust elicitors, but contamination extends to the social and moral domains. Acts of social deviance can elicit disgust (Rozin, Haidt, & Fincher, 2009). Unfair treatment is also a reliable disgust elicitor (Chapman, Kim, Susskind, & Anderson, 2009). Ideas and values can become contaminated and produce moral disgust (Haidt, 2007). A good example over the last decade has been to think of smoking not as a personal preference but as a disgusting moral value (Rozin & Singh, 1999). With moral contaminations, people recruit the disgust emotion and pair it with an object or event so to remove any temptation to interact further with that object or event (as process called "moralization"; Rozin, 1999). This moralization process can also explain vegetarian's lack of desire to eat meat (Rozin, Markwith, & Stoess, 1997). In this sense, disgust becomes a moral emotion (Rozin et al., 2008). Individuals high in disgust sensitivity hold relatively harsh moral judgments, including conservative attitudes about sexuality and gays—to the point of homophobia (Olatunji, 2008; Inbar, Pizarro, Knobe, & Bloom, 2009). It is not so much that people high in disgust sensitivity are inherently homophobic as it is that they tend to be morally hypervigilant and hence focused rather strongly on avoiding contact with what they believe to be potential moral offenders (Jones & Fitness, 2008).

Because disgust is phenomenologically aversive, it paradoxically plays a positive motivational role in our lives. Feeling disgusted, we wish to avoid contaminated objects, and we learn the coping behaviors needed to prevent encountering (or creating) conditions that produce disgust. Therefore, because people wish to avoid putting themselves into disgusting situations, they change personal habits and attributes, discard waste and sanitize their surroundings, and reappraise their thoughts and values. They wash the dishes, brush their teeth, take showers, and exercise to avoid an out-of-shape or "disgusting" body.

Sometimes of course it is too late, as we bite into the apple to only later see the worm within. In this case, rejection gets you only so far. So, the second function of disgust is to generate a proactive desire to cleanse (Zhong & Liljenquist, 2006). If the cleansing is successful—if we wash our hands, brush our teeth, and go to the doctor, then the cleansing often eliminates the earlier-felt disgust.

Contempt

Contempt arises from a sense of being morally superior to another person. It involves a negative evaluation of the other person's behavior, although it typically goes deeper to mean that the other person is judged to be unworthy in some way. Interestingly, contempt is an inherently social emotion, because it occurs only during social interaction. It has a strong experiential overlap with disgust, but contempt is a unique emotion in that is has its own distinct antecedents (a sense of moral superiority to another) and its own unique cross-cultural facial expression (Ekman & Friesen, 1986; Ekman & Heider, 1988; Matsumoto, 1992; Matsumoto & Ekman, 2004). A contempt facial expression shows a unilateral lip raise and tightening. Such an expression occurs in a situation such as hearing a person brag about an accomplishment for which he was were not responsible (i.e., taking credit for something that he did not actually do; Matsumoto & Ekman, 2004).

The function of contempt is to maintain the social hierarchy. A contempt expression signals one's dominance and superiority over the other. Such a signal can, however, lead to very destructive social consequences. When it occurs in the context of marriage, it is considered toxic to the relationship, especially when expressed by the husband, and it predicts the future dissolution of the marriage with rather high accuracy (Gottman & Silver, 1999).

Sadness

Sadness (or distress) is the most negative, aversive emotion. Sadness arises principally from experiences of separation or failure, although it is particularly closely related to an experience of permanent loss. To feel sad, the loss needs to involve a close attachment. Separation—the loss of a loved one through death, divorce, circumstances (e.g., travel), or argument—is distressing. We also experience separation from a place (hometown) and from a valued job, position, or status. In loss-induced sadness, there is an acute feeling of resignation. Failure also leads to sadness, as in failing an examination, losing a contest, or being rejected from a group's membership. Even failure outside of one's volitional control can cause distress, as in war, illness, accidents, and economic depression (Izard, 1991).

Sadness turns our attention inward and promotes personal reflection. Bodily arousal decreases substantially, and this deactivation state facilitates reflection and taking the time to take stock of our life plans and goals to accommodate that which has been lost (Bonanno & Keltner, 1997; Welling, 2003). But sadness also occurs with temporary and with partial loss (not just with permanent loss), and in these cases sadness motivates the person to take the action necessary to restore the environment to its state before the distressing situation. Following separation, the rejected lover apologizes, sends flowers, or telephones in an effort to repair the broken relationship. Following failure, a performer practices to restore confidence and to prevent the recurrence of a similar failure. That is, because we feel sad, we are more likely to apologize and to offer reparations. Unfortunately, many separations and failures cannot be restored. Under hopeless conditions, the person behaves not in an active, vigorous way but in an inactive, lethargic way that essentially leads to withdrawal.

One beneficial aspect of sadness is that it indirectly facilitates the cohesiveness of social groups (Averill, 1968). Because separation from significant people causes sadness and because sadness is such an uncomfortable emotion, its anticipation motivates people to stay cohesive with their loved ones (Averill, 1979). If people did not miss others so much, then they would be less motivated to go out of their way to maintain social cohesion. Similarly, if the student or athlete did not anticipate the possibility of suffering failure-induced distress, she would be less motivated to prepare and practice. So, while sadness feels miserable, it can motivate and maintain productive behaviors.

Depression

Sadness can slip into depression (Bonanno, Goorin, & Coifman, 2008). Sadness has its benefits, because it can motivate reparative behavior, and it can give off expressive signals that bring sympathy, caring, and helping from others. Depression, however, has few benefits and gives off expressive signals that push people away (Coyne, 1976a).

The key trigger that slips sadness toward depression appears to be rumination. When rumination is piled on top of a sadness from a permanent loss, the result is often depression (Nolen-Hoeksema, Wisco, & Lyubomirsky, 2008; Spasojevic & Alloy, 2001). Rumination accompanies sadness when the person experiences emotion overproduction—that is, when the person simultaneously feels sad but also angry, afraid, ashamed, and discouraged (Hervas & Vazquez, 2011). Anger adds irritation with the self, discouragement adds disappointment with the self, and when these self-derogating thoughts and feelings are added onto of sadness, then the resulting emotional overproduction leads to rumination and to depression vulnerability. Unlike acute sadness that can promote reflection and reparative coping, rumination-based depression impairs problem solving, distracts attention, stimulates negative thinking, erodes social support, and replaces reparative coping behaviors with self-harm and destructive binging behaviors (Nolen-Hoeksema et al., 2008).

Emotional Preparation for Threat and Harm

The themes that organize the otherwise diverse emotions of fear, anger, disgust, and sadness are threat and harm. When threatening and potentially harmful events are anticipated, we feel fear. During the struggle to fight off or to reject the threatening event, we feel anger and disgust. Once the harm has materialized, we feel sadness. Fear motivates fleeing, escaping, and avoiding. Anger motivates fighting and vigorous counterdefense. Disgust motivates rejection of the object or event. Sadness brings resignation. Hence, fear, anger, disgust, and sadness work collectively to endow the individual with an emotion system that provides effective emotional preparation to cope with all aspects of threat and harm.

Joy

The events that bring joy include desirable outcomes—success at a task, personal achievement, progress toward a goal, getting what we want, gaining respect, receiving love or affection, receiving a pleasant surprise, or experiencing pleasurable sensations (Ekman & Friesen, 1975; Izard, 1991; Shaver et al., 1987). Joy is the emotional evidence that things are going well (e.g., success, achievement, progress, respect, love). The causes of joy—desirable outcomes related to personal success and interpersonal relatedness—are essentially the opposite of the causes of sadness (failure, separation/loss). How joy affects us also seems to be the opposite of how sadness affects us. When sad, we feel lethargic, withdrawn, and turn inward; when joyous, we feel enthusiastic, outgoing, and expand outward. When sad, we are often pessimistic; when joyous, we turn optimistic.

The function of joy is threefold. First, joy facilitates our willingness to engage in social activities. Smiles of joy facilitate social interaction (Haviland & Lelwica, 1987), and if the smiles keep coming, they help relationships form and strengthen over time (Langsdorff, Izard, Rayias, & Hembree, 1983). Few experiences are as potent and as rewarding as are the smile and interpersonal inclusion it facilitates. Joy is therefore a social glue that bonds relationships, such as infant and mother, lovers, coworkers, and teammates.

Second, joy has a "soothing function" (Fredrickson et al., 2000; Levenson, 1999). It is the positive feeling that makes life pleasant and balances experiences of frustration, disappointment, and general negative affect. Joy can undo life's stress and negative emotionality. Job stress predicts burnout, for instance, but joy at work counters stress to effectively prevent burnout from occurring (Gloria, Faulk, & Steinhardt, 2013). Joy also has a way of undoing the distressing effects of aversive emotions, as when parents sing and make funny faces to soothe distressed infants and when lovers show affection to soothe away an otherwise conflictual exchange (Carstensen, Gottman, & Levenson, 1995). Hence, the second function of joy is to preserve psychological well-being, even as distressing events keep coming our way, and this is true even for people who are dealing with suicidal thoughts (Joiner et al., 2001).

Third, joy creates the urge to play and to be creative. Unlike negative emotions that narrow attention onto the immediate stimulus at hand, joy has the opposite effect of broadening our attention, thoughts, and behaviors (Fredrickson, 1998; Fredrickson & Branigan, 2005). During joyful play, we jump around aimlessly, do unpredictable things, and open up in creative ways. Such activity tends to build our social resources (we make friends) and our intellectual resources (we gain new knowledge and greater intellectual complexity). Because joy broadens attention, cognition, and behavior and because joy builds our social and intellectual resources, it helps transform people into more creative, knowledgeable, resilient, healthy, and socially integrated individuals (Lyubomirsky, King, & Diener, 2005).

Joy is also a family of positive emotions. Some specific shades of a joy theme include amusement (a positive emotional response to something found to be funny), wonder (a response to something that is both incredible and incomprehensible), pride (a response to success at a difficult task), contentment (sitting back and savoring a positive state of affairs), and even schadenfreude (felt joy when an enemy suffers a setback).

Interest

Interest is the most prevalent emotion in day-to-day functioning (Izard, 1991). Some level of interest is ever-present. Because this is so, increases and decreases in interest usually involve a shifting of interest from one event, thought, or action to another. So, interest is not so much activated as it is redirected, although its magnitude certainly rises and falls from moment to moment in response to changes in the environment (Mouratidis, Vansteenkiste, Sideris, & Lens, 2011). What grabs interest is the presence of environmental novelty—stimulus change, novelty, uncertainty, complexity, puzzles and curiosities, challenges, and discoveries (Berlyne, 1966; Izard, 1991; Silvia, 2006) and any opportunity to gain new information, develop greater understanding, and learn (Izard, 2007; Silvia, 2008) and also those that involve our needs or well-being (Deci, 1992b). What most people find interesting are those things they appraise as novel-complex, although people additionally need to feel competent that they can eventually make sense of the newness, novelty, and complexity that stands before them, as with modern art or a class lecture (Silvia, 2005).

Interest creates the urge to explore, investigate, seek, manipulate, and extract information from the objects that surround us. It motivates exploration, and it is in these acts of turning things around, upside down, over, and about that we gain the information we seek. Interest creates a vitalizing type of motivation that supports eager interaction with environmental opportunities to explore and learn (Mouratidis et al., 2011). The benefits of exploring, taking in new information, and developing greater understanding is that one expands the self in the process. A person's interest in an activity also determines how much attention is directed to that activity and how well that person processes, comprehends, and remembers relevant information (Hidi, 1990; Renninger, Hidi, & Krapp, 1992; Renninger & Wozniak, 1985; Schiefele, 1991; Shirey & Reynolds, 1988). Interest therefore enhances learning (Alexander, Kulikowich, & Jetton, 1994). It is difficult to learn a foreign language, allocate time to read a book, or engage in most any learning activity without emotional support from interest. As a case in point, when interested, students persist longer at learning activities, spend more time studying, read more deeply, remember more of what they read, and make better grades (Silvia, 2006).

Interest is important for two key reasons. First, it motivates environmental engagement, as reviewed in the previous paragraph. In doing so, interest promotes learning, skill development, knowledge acquisition, and achievement (Schiefele, 1991; Schraw & Lehman, 2001; Silvia, 2006). Second, interest replenishes personal resources (Thoman, Smith, & Silvia, 2011). Exploring and learning require a great deal of engagement and re-engagement, and the expenditure of all this effort and concentration can be tiring. Prolonged environmental engagement can exhaust people. But interest-motivated engagement is a strangely different kind of engagement. When people engage in a learning task without the motivational support of interest, over time they typically experience a type of motivational and cognitive exhaustion that makes it harder and harder to persist and to continue to concentrate. However, when people engage in the same learning task with the motivational support of interest, they often experience a type of motivational and cognitive vitality that energizes further engagement (Thoman et al., 2011). That is, interest-fueled engagement counteracts exhaustion by replenishing—rather than by draining—motivational (e.g., capacity to persist) and cognitive (e.g., capacity to concentrate) resources.

Emotional Preparation for Motive Involvement and Satisfaction

The themes that organize the positive emotions of interest and joy are motive involvement and satisfaction. When a beneficial event related to our needs and well-being is anticipated, we feel interest. When the beneficial event materializes into motive satisfaction, we feel joy (or enjoyment). Interest motivates the exploratory behavior and task engagement necessary for promoting contact with the potentially motive-satisfying event. Interest also prolongs task engagement so we can put ourselves in a position to experience motive satisfaction. Joy adds to and somewhat replaces interest once motive satisfaction occurs (Izard, 1991). Joy then promotes ongoing task persistence and subsequent reengagement behaviors with the motive-satisfying event. Together, interest and joy provide the emotional support to be fully involved in an activity to the point that we are emotionally prepared to experience motive involvement and satisfaction (Reeve, 1989).

SELF-CONSCIOUS EMOTIONS

Shame, guilt, embarrassment, and pride do not arise in response to clear and specific antecedents in the same way that fear, anger, and joy do. Rather, events occur that have implications for the evaluation of the self, and it is this process of evaluating the self that gives rise to the cluster of self-conscious emotions. That is, rather than tracing the origins of these four emotions to a particular "significant life event," these emotions arise out of cognitive processes that revolve around the evaluation of the self (Lewis, 2008). It is in this process of self-evaluation that the self-conscious emotions arise.

Shame

Shame is an overwhelmingly powerful emotion that is associated with feelings of inferiority, a sense of worthlessness, and a damaged self-image (Tangney & Dearing, 2002). It arises after the violation of standards associated with morality and competent functioning. For instance, behaving inappropriately while drunk, laughing at a joke during a somber funeral, or hurting others emotionally are moral violations, while failing an examination or performing very poorly in a sport or musical performance are violations of competent functioning (de Hooge, Zeelenberg, & Breugelmans, 2010). Failing at an easy task is particularly likely to induce shame (Chao, Cheng, & Chio, 2011). Such moral and performance failures signal that something is wrong with the self. This message makes shame an "ugly" emotion, one that is accompanied by intense pain, confusion in thought, an inability to speak, strong withdrawal tendencies, rumination, and essentially a global (emotional) attack on the self (Keltner & Buswell, 1996; Orth, Berking, & Burkhardt, 2006; Tangney, 1991, 1999). In this sense, the function of shame is that of a moral barometer to provide immediate and salient feedback about how well or how poorly one's self stands up to moral and performance-based standards of acceptability.

Shame generates two motives—one to protect the self and another to restore the threatened self (de Hooge, Zeelenberg, & Breugelmans, 2010, 2011). A model of how these dual motives generate the behavior necessary to deal with a threatened positive self-view appears in Figure 14.1. Performance-based displays of incompetence and moral transgressions create the impression of an inferior, worthless, or damaged self, and it is this threatened positive self-view that gives rise to shame. Shame then generates the two motives to protect the self and to restore the self. To protect the self, the self withdraws, hides, and avoids taking action that may cause further damage to the self. The person who feels ashamed prefers to work alone, and he or she may use this time alone to initiate private attempts to restore the self (Chao et al., 2011). To restore the self publically, the self seeks out an opportunity for a second chance to demonstrate that the self is morally good and competent. As shown in Figure 14.1, it is sometimes impossible, too difficult, or too risky (too punishing) to take the action necessary to restore the threatened self. If it is impossible to make amends (e.g., the behavior cannot be undone or there are no more opportunities for a second chance), then the person will withdraw, hide, and avoid taking action that may cause further damage to

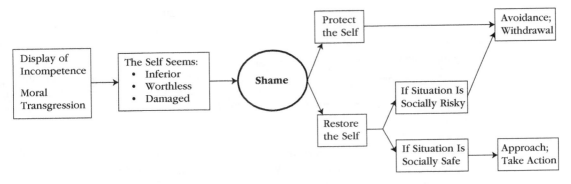

Figure 14.1   Dual Motivational Model of Shame

the self. But if restoration of the self is possible, then the shame-generated motive to restore the self leads to behavior designed to make amends and restore the positive self-view.

In empirical tests of the dual motive model of shame, researchers find that the motive to restore the self is stronger than is the motive to protect the self (de Hooge et al., 2010). For instance, after a performance failure or after enacting socially inappropriate behavior, people are more likely to feel a strong urge to repair their self-image and to make amends (i.e., try the task a second time) but only a moderate urge to protect the self and not make the self-presentation worse than it already is. This is because shame primarily generates a motive to regain the positive image that one has (hopefully temporarily) lost. Despite the stronger motive to restore the self, people who experience shame are more likely to withdraw from the situation, avoid taking a second chance, and hide. This is because it is so often impossible, too difficult, or too socially risky to take the action one needs to try to restore the self. Under these conditions, the strength of the motive to restore the self declines, while the strength of the motive to protect the self rises. As a result, behavioral avoidance and withdrawal often follow the experience of shame, because the person decides it is best to just prevent further damage to one's self-image.

The model in Figure 14.1 helps deepen our understanding of the specific emotion of shame, but it goes further in that it helps deepen our understanding of emotion more generally. If any emotion is qualified to be labeled as a "bad" emotion, it is "ugly" shame. Yet its functional purpose is to motivate behaviors to restore a positive view of the self that has just been threatened or challenge by one's own moral violation or display of incompetence (de Hooge et al., 2010).

Guilt

While similar to shame in many respects, guilt lacks the negative intensity of shame. It does not involve an ugly attack on the self. Guilt arises after the person evaluates his behavior (not himself) as a failure. The focus during guilt is on the self's behaviors and action, rather than on the self's worth per se. Guilt signals that one's behavior has caused harm, loss, or distress to a relationship partner (Tangney, Miller, Flicker, & Barlow, 1996; Zeelenberg & Breugelmans, 2008). Guilt does not produce confusion in thought, an inability to speak, strong withdrawal tendencies, rumination, and a global attack on the self (as with shame). Instead, it produces the thought necessary to focus on the hurt or distress caused to a relationship partner (Tangney et al., 1996; Zeelenberg & Breugelmans, 2008). The person who feels guilty focuses on the worth of the behavior and on what needs to be done to undo the hurtful consequences of the behavior. Thus, guilt-generated behaviors often involve making amends, apologizing, confessing, and basically doing whatever needs to be done to undo the distressing consequences of the behavior. In this sense, the function of guilt is that of a moral barometer to provide immediate and salient feedback about the worth and acceptability of one's behavior. Guilt means that the behavior needs to be reconsidered and changed.

Guilt often goes hand in hand with taking the perspective of others and with empathy. To evaluate the consequences of the "bad behavior," people engage in both perspective taking and empathic understanding. When combined with perspective taking and empathy, guilt often leads to an effective course of action, such as apologizing or making amends.

Embarrassment

Embarrassment signals that "something is amiss" and that some aspect of the self needs to be hidden, or at least carefully self-monitored. It occurs after a social blunder that is committed in front of an audience of others, a blunder that suggests that the actor may possess some personal deficiency, as occurs when forgetting someone's name (a mental lapse), tripping or stumbling (a physical pratfall), or suffering some bodily dysfunction such as uncontrollably spitting out one's beverage through the nose while laughing uncontrollably (a lack of reasonable control over one's physical functions). But embarrassment is not caused by the social blunder per se but, rather, by the anticipation of a negative evaluation by others (i.e., a cognitive appraisal). Hence, we become embarrassed when we perceive that the social image we wish to project to others has been put at risk by our social blunder and others are beginning to form a negative impression of us (Harris, 2006).

Somewhat curiously, embarrassment also occurs even in positive social situations (e.g., others are congratulating us). Thus, it is probably more accurate to say that embarrassment arises when we anticipate a disruption of smooth social interaction at a time when there is no clear guideline as to what socially appropriate behavior would be in that situation. So, the embarrassed person being congratulated, handed an award, being sung to, or just being called on during class just stands there with a goofy grin on her face, not knowing what to do next. Actually, what the person is doing for several seconds is suppressing her emotionality (as evidenced by increase heart rate, increased blood pressure; Harris, 2001), rather than acting in a socially smooth fashion.

The essential functions of embarrassment are to appease the audience, take action to repair the negative self-impression, and communicate implicitly that the social blunder will not occur again. To appease the audience, the embarrassed person averts her eyes, blushes, acts submissively, apologizes, promises not to do it again, and engages in self-grooming. Appeasing the audience is essential behavior because such gestures signal to the audience that the social blunder was an unintentional act, an accident that will not be repeated. So, when embarrassed, people engage in a flurry of appeasement behavior (Keltner, 1995; Keltner & Buswell, 1997), and they look down, gaze their eyes to the left, attempt to control a smile (show the goofy grin), and touch the face or hair (Keltner, 1995). This inexplicable urge to touch the face, hair, or scalp is a curious act, but you might notice it after committing some social blunder (e.g., accidently cutting off another driver on the highway). Interestingly, a display of embarrassment is very often successful, as those who show embarrassment (i.e., those who blush; Dijk, de Jong, & Peters, 2009) and those who go out of their way to appease the audience (Semin & Manstead, 1982) are rated more positively than those who enact the same social blunder but who do not show embarrassment. Thus, embarrassment works. It has remedial value. The functional conclusion is that it is unwise to hide one's embarrassment after committing a social blunder (Dijk et al., 2011), which might be a good thing to remember the next time you trip over a cord, spill coffee on someone, knock over a stack of boxes at the supermarket, drive your bicycle into the bushes, or greet a stranger enthusiastically.

Pride

Pride is a self-related emotion. Feelings of pride in one's achievement, success, and positive functioning maintain and boost self-esteem and alert the self and others that one is worthy of acceptance and status, much in the same way that shame attacks self-esteem and alerts self and others that one is unworthy of acceptance or status. People express pride with a slight (not a large) smile, tilting the head slightly back, expanding the chest, and raising their arms upward in the air (Tracy & Matsumoto, 2008; Tracy & Robins, 2004). Such an "expansive" posture makes one appear larger and therefore attracts attention to the self. It is also worth noting that this pride expression is readily recognized by children (Tracy, Robins, & Lagattuta, 2005) and is naturally expressed by those who are blind (and hence could not have easily learned the expression through socialization; Tracy & Matsumoto, 2008).

Pride is a complex emotion that has a dual nature—it has two facets. On the one hand, pride in one's success promotes achievement behavior, an authentic and heartfelt self-esteem, and prosocial behaviors such as volunteering and altruism (Tracy & Robins, 2007; Wubben, De Cremer, & van Dijk, 2012). On the other hand, pride has a dark side (i.e., Dante referred to it as one of the seven deadly sins). Pride can be associated with narcissism and contribute to aggression, relationship conflict, and antisocial behaviors such as manipulating others (Campbell, 1999; Tracy & Robins, 2007; Wubben et al., 2012). This dual view of pride as confidence, success, and achievement versus arrogance, conceit, and self-aggrandizement had lead researches to refer to the former as "authentic pride" and to the later as "hubris pride" (Tracy & Robins, 2007).

Authentic pride revolves around subjective experiences of accomplishing, achieving, succeeding, feeling confident, and being productive and fulfilled, and it is rooted in internal, unstable, and controllable attributions (e.g., "I won because I practiced hard to develop my skills."); hubristic pride revolves around subjective experiences of being snobbish, stuck-up, conceited, arrogant, egotistical, and smug, and it is rooted in internal, stable, and uncontrollable attributions (e.g., "I won because I am the greatest of all time"; Tracy & Robins, 2007). Interestingly, authentic and hubristic pride do not have different antecedents—both are caused by success and accomplishment. Where they differ is in how success is appraised and attributed. They also differ in their paths to prosocial versus antisocial behavior. Authentic pride is prosocial, because it plays a clear motivational role in the acquisition of skills and persevering on difficult tasks (Williams & DeSteno, 2008). Because of this motivational effect, authentic pride allows people to develop the proficiency, self-efficacy, conscientiousness, and leadership that allows them to help others, such as cooperating rather than acting selfishly (Williams & DeSento, 2009; Wubben et al., 2012). Hubristic pride is antisocial, because it contributes to a narcissistic quest for status and domination and to uncaring and exploitive behaviors. Because of this, hubristic pride tends people toward abusing others, such as acting selfishly, aggressively, and with hostility and exploitation rather than with care (Campbell, Bush, Brunell, & Shelton, 2005; Tracy, Cheng, Robins, & Trzesniewski, 2009; Wubben et al., 2012).

Triumph

Triumph is the emotional reaction that follows victory in a competitive situation (Matsumoto & Hwang, 2012, 2014). The triumphant victor displays both (1) self-expressive behavior—arms raised above the shoulders and away from the body, chest and torso pushed out while leaning back, mouth open, head tilt back or up, a smile, and a thumbs-up gesture and (2) social dominance—making a fist, thrusting a fist pump, and shouting, as found with competitive athletes who win an intense competition (Matsumoto & Hwang, 2014). These behaviors signal victory, dominance, and social power over the defeated and, in doing so, inform an audience of others about one's achieved victory. A triumph display communicates that one is socially dominant and that others should avoid future challenges and instead take their relatively submissive place within the social hierarchy. Dominance is different from pride in that pride reflects a successful evaluation of a specific action or body of work, whereas triumph signals social dominance that has an air of aggression, tension release, and a taunting of opponents that seeks to put them in their place. Triumph is much closer to hubristic pride that it is to authentic pride.

Interrelations among Shame, Guilt, Pride, and Hubris

Just as shame and guilt exist as two negative self-conscious emotions that have different antecedents and consequences (Tangney & Dearing, 2002), pride and hubris also exist as two positive self-conscious emotions that have different antecedents and consequences (Tracy & Robins, 2007). Guilt arises from failing to enact a specific achievement or prosocial action, and in a similar way pride arises from successfully enacting a specific achievement or prosocial action. Shame arises from the failure of the global self, and in a similar way hubris arises from the success of the global self. Thus, with both guilt and pride the self is separated from the behavioral action and that behavior is what is compared to the standard. With both shame and hubris the self is equated with the behavioral action and it is the self that is compared to the standard.

COGNITIVELY COMPLEX EMOTIONS

Envy

Envy is a painful emotion caused by the good fortune of others (van de Ven, Zeelenberg, & Pieters, 2009). It is an unpleasant emotional experience that arises when one person perceives that another has an advantage over him or her while also desiring what the other has (Parrott & Smith, 1993). That perceived advantage may be that the envied other possesses a special quality (a better job), an achievement (won a prestigious award), or a possession (the latest sports car). It is a highly social emotion, as it is embedded in social comparison of the self with what others have (Smith & Kim, 2007). Envy brings with it the goal to level the difference between the self and the envied other, a goal that may be accomplished either by moving oneself up to the level of the other or by pulling the other back down to one's own level.

Just as pride has two facets—one constructive and one destructive, so does envy. Benign envy generates a moving-up motivation, and it is aimed at improving one's position. The positive facet of (benign) envy leads to constructive behavior aimed at moving up to the same superior position currently held by the envied person. It carries with it the seeds of motivation to improve oneself (Cohen-Charash, 2009; van de Ven et al., 2009). Malicious envy generates a pulling-down motivation, although it too is aimed at improving one's position. The negative facet of (malicious) envy leads to destructive behavior aimed at pulling down the envied person. It does not carry with it any seed of improvement motivation. The key difference between the two types of envy is the appraisal of deservedness (van de Ven, Zeelenberg, & Pieters, 2012). With benign envy, the person believes that the other person deserves his or her superior position. This view of envy is rooted in a belief that self-improvement is possible, the world is a fair and just place, and the other person is to be admired because he or she worked hard to attain that superior position. Benign envy typically inspires people to work harder to attain for themselves what the currently superior person has (e.g., it motivates upward social mobility, working hard, and "keeping up with the Joneses"). With malicious envy, however, the person believes that the other does not deserve his or her superior position—that the other person has benefitted from some undeserved advantage (van de Ven et al., 2012). This inequality is perceived as unjust and unfair, and it is accompanied by feelings of ill-will, resentment, frustration, and anger. It often leads to behaviors designed to damage the position of the envied person (van de Ven et al., 2009).

To better appreciate the distinction between the two types of envy, consider the following scenario (from van de Ven, Zeelenberg, & Pieters, 2009, p. 420):

> Niels and Rik play in the first team of a good soccer club. Marcel, a teammate of Niels and Rik, is selected to play for a professional team. Niels feels benign envy toward Marcel, Rik feels malicious envy.

Participants are then asked, who (Niels or Rik) is more likely to hope Marcel succeeds as a professional, and also who is more likely to commit a foul against Marcel during the next game? In addition, participants are asked who is motivated to start practicing more and who is more likely to aspire to become a professional himself. Overwhelmingly, participants infer that Niels wishes Marcel well, will practice more, and aspires to become a professional like Marcel, and participants infer that Rik will more likely aggress (commit a foul) against Marcel in the next game (van de Ven et al., 2009).

A similar study asked college students to describe a person they knew well who was better than they were at something. After describing this person, they were then asked, "Compared to last semester, how many hours more or less do you plan to spend on your studying in the upcoming semester?" (van de Ven, Zeelenberg, & Pieters, 2011, p. 786). Those who described a benignly envied other said that they would study more this semester than did those who described a malicious envied other.

Somewhat counterintuitively, envy can motivate prosocial behavior from the one who is envied. The fear of being envied can lead people to act prosocially in a proactive attempt to ward off the potentially destructive effects of malicious envy. So, the envied person helps others, but this behavior functions more as an appeasement strategy than it does as altruism.

The general rule is that people who are well off do not help more or less than do people who are less well off, but people who are well off ("advantaged") become more likely to help others when they have reasons to suspect malicious envy from others (van de Ven, Zeelenberg, & Pieters, 2010).

Gratitude

Gratitude is a positive emotion that arises upon receiving something of value (gift, help, assistance, guidance) from another person (McCullough, Kilpatrick, Emmons, & Larson, 2001). For gratitude to arise, that assistance (the receipt of something of value) needs to be voluntarily given, given at some cost to the giver, and done intentionally (McCullough, Kimeldorf, & Cohen, 2008; Tsang, 2006). For instance, if your car breaks down because of a flat tire and another motorist stops to help even though it is raining and he has to use his own spare tire to get you on your way, then you are likely to feel gratitude at such an act of kindness. Gratitude is a benefit detector; it is an emotional readout that one has benefitted from the generosity and prosocial behavior of another (McCullough et al., 2008).

Acts of kindness are as likely to activate the negative emotion of indebtedness in us as they are to activate the positive emotion of gratitude (Algoe, Gable, & Maisel, 2010; Tsang, 2006). Because this is so, the processes that explain when we feel indebted versus when we feel gratitude are summarized in Figure 14.2. The distinction between the two emotional experiences begins when the recipient focuses either on the giver's kindness or on the benefit received (i.e., the money, the car repair). A focus on the kindness leads the recipient to focus on the thoughtfulness of the giver, on the positive qualities of the giver, and, most importantly, on the fact that the giver was responsive to the needs of the self. It is this focus on the other person's responsiveness to the self that gives rise to the positive emotion of gratitude, which promotes a caring orientation. This focus on being cared for builds what was termed in Chapter 6 as a "communal relationship" (benefits are given in a noncontingent "no strings attached" way), because the person feels a greater connection and closeness to the benefactor and the relationship between the two grows toward greater intimacy and satisfaction. A focus on the benefit, on the other hand, leads the recipient to focus on what was received and the need and necessity to repay the gift. A focus on the benefit per se and the incurred debt that now needs to be repaid gives rise to the negative emotion of indebtedness, which promotes a reciprocity motivation. This focus on reciprocity leads toward a relationship orientation that was termed in Chapter 6 as an "exchange relationship" (benefits are given in a contingent "with strings attached" way), because the person adopts a business-like "tit for tat" (this for that) orientation toward the relationship partner.

To think about the emotional dynamics portrayed in Figure 14.2, consider a simple act of kindness. Imagine that you and a colleague are working together on a project. After a short break, your colleague returns with two sodas, one of which is for you (from Regan, 1971). What do you feel? What are the downstream implications of this small act of kindness?

Gratitude is an important social emotion because it reinforces generosity and prosocial behavior (e.g., hugging, saying "thank you"), it motivates beneficiaries to behave prosocially, and it promotes and builds positive interpersonal relationships. Gratitude therefore both signals and motivates generosity and cooperation between two people. In an exchange of generosity, both the benefactor and the beneficiary experience positive affect and greater relationship satisfaction (Algoe, 2012; Algoe, Fredrickson, & Gable, 2013).

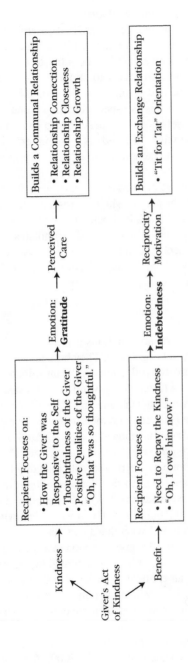

Figure 14.2 Sequence of Relationship-Based Events in Gratitude versus Indebtedness

People who experience gratitude, compared to those who do not, have a positive perception of their benefactor, experience a boost in relationship satisfaction, are more likely to act prosocially (e.g., cooperate), spend more time with the benefactor, and experience a sense of healing within a relationship that is otherwise hurting (Algoe et al., 2010; Bartlett et al., 2012; Gottman & Silver, 1999; Lambert & Fincham, 2011; McCullough, Emmons, & Tsang, 2002). This relationship satisfaction boost from gratitude applies not only to the one who receives the kindness but to the one who gives it as well (Lambert et al., 2010). Gratitude also seems to stimulate personal reflection in which the person reconsiders how helpful and giving he or she should be toward others in the future (Bartlett & DeSteno, 2006), and this is especially true as one reflects on the perspective, needs, and desires of the benefactor—the person who caused the sense of gratitude to occur in the first place. In this sense, gratitude is a crucial emotional catalyst if the relationship is to grow from a business-like exchange relationship into one that is communal, intimate, and caring.

Gratitude also sometimes acts as a motivation for "upstream reciprocity" (Nowak & Roch, 2007) in which the person who receives a benefit then decides to pay back the benefit by giving back not to the original beneficiary but, rather, to the neighborhood, community, or world. This occurs when gratitude stimulates an experience of social integration (e.g., "I love helping people") and, together, the emotional gratitude and the social integration motivate the person's prosocial behavior to pass on the benefit to self to an upstream third party (Froh, Bono, & Emmons, 2010).

Disappointment and Regret

Disappointment and regret are emotions that are intrinsic to decision making (Chua et al., 2009; van Dijk & Zeelenberg, 2002). They both arise from the nonoccurrence of a desired outcome, and both involve reflection on "what might have been" had things turned out differently than they did (Zeelenberg, van Dijk, Manstead, & van de Pligt, 1998).

Disappointment arises when comparing the outcome one received versus a better outcome that might have resulted from the same action or the same choice. With disappointment, a positive outcome was planned and anticipated, an action was taken or a choice was made, but the positive outcome did not materialize. That is, the person anticipated passing the test, but did not. Or, the person anticipated getting the job, but did not. Regret is different from disappointment in that the person believes that he or she could have acted differently or could have made a different choice, but did not. Regret arises with the nonoccurrence of a desired outcome caused by a wrong behavior or a bad choice: "I took action, it turned out bad, and now I wish that I had acted differently or that I had made a different choice." Regret arises after poor decision making and self-regulation such as "I did not study enough, and now I regret it" and "I wasted my money shopping, and I now regret it." Thus, regret involves an element of personal responsibility in which the "I" in "*I* made a bad choice" is emphasized. When the nonoccurrence of the positive outcome is attributed only to unfavorable circumstances, then the person experiences disappointment, not regret (Gilovich & Medvec, 1994).

Regret and disappointment produce a different pattern of feelings, thoughts, motivations, and action tendencies (Chua et al., 2009; Zeelenberg, van Dijk, Manstead, & van de Pligt, 1998, 2000). These different downstream consequences appear in Table 14.2. Disappointment involves an acceptance of the negative outcome that is accompanied by

Table 14.2   Different Consequences of Regret versus Disappointment

	Regret	Disappointment
Feelings	I should have known better.	I feel powerless.
	Strong dislike of the outcome.	Moderate dislike of the outcome.
Thoughts	I made a mistake.	My expectancy was disconfirmed.
Motivation	I want a second chance.	This is nothing I want to do.
	I want to undo what happened.	
Action Tendency	I want to correct my mistake.	This is nothing I want to do.

feelings of powerlessness and by motivation and action tendencies that revolve around doing nothing. Regret, on the other hand, involves blaming the self and generating the motivation and action tendencies to reverse the self-caused negative outcome (I want to correct my mistake). Regret is experienced as a painful lesson that things would have been better had a different choice been made, so it therefore functions as an emotional cue to take future decision-making opportunities more seriously. Regret can therefore be functional in guiding future decision making, although it can also be dysfunctional and lead to severe psychological distress (Epstude & Roese, 2008). Thus, while regret and disappointment are similar emotions—both follow the nonoccurrence of a desired outcome—they differ in their implications for what the person will do in the near future with regret motivating restorative behavior and disappointment leading to resignation and inertia.

Hope

Hope arises with a wish that a desired goal will be attained (Bruininks & Malle, 2005). Hope is rooted in the desire for some future outcome that is of particular importance to the person, and it typically involves a wish for an attractive goal (e.g., I hope I get accepted into my favorite college), an attractive event (e.g., I hope I get tickets to the big game), or a desired relationship (e.g., I hope I get back together with my boyfriend). The motivational function of hope is to keep the person focused on the goal, to keep the person going, to keep the person engaged in the pursuit of the desired goal, and to act as a counter-force to negative feelings that are otherwise associated with doubt that the desired future goal will ever materialize (Bruininks & Malle, 2005).

Schadenfreude

Schadenfreude is a German word that entails taking pleasure at the misfortune of others. When others suffer a setback, the person who feels schadenfreude smiles a bit and takes some measure of pleasure in the other's suffering. Schadenfreude typically arises when the other person is disliked (Hareli & Weiner, 2002), envied (Smith et al., 1996), falls from grace (van Dijk et al., 2006), or has achieved in a way that is perceived to be undeserved and resented (Feather & Sherman, 2002).

Empathy

Empathy is triggered by another person's emotional state or situational circumstances, and it involves the observer feeling what the actor feels. Empathy occurs as an emotional transformation process in which the observed emotional state of another becomes one's own emotional experience. Its phenomenology includes feeling moved by and compassionate or sympathetic toward the other (Eisenberg & Fabes, 1990; Niezink et al., 2012). The essence of empathy is, first, feeling what the other feels and, second, experiencing an other-oriented desire for the other to feel better.

Empathy, or empathic concern, arises from two principle antecedents (Hoffman, 2008). First, empathy arises from mimicry, in which one's own facial expression, voice tone, and posture change in synchrony with the other person's facial, vocal, and postural expressions. The mimicked resulting muscle movements then trigger feedback within oneself to activate the neural structures that create the emotion in oneself (Regenbogen et al., 2012). This is a rather involved social-communicative process, but recent evidence suggests that the same effect occurs through mirror neurons. With mirror neurons, the same neural pattern that is involved in self-generating one's own emotion is also involved in observing someone else feel that same emotion. That is, observing another's facial expression is all it takes to feel her emotion, at least to the extent that observing that emotional expression activates mirror neurons to activate the same emotion in oneself. A similar process occurs when simply hearing about another's distress or when reading about another's distress (e.g., in a letter or email). If the listener uses the conversation or letter to generate visual and auditory images of the other's emotional facial, vocal, and postural expressions, then the mirror neurons may be activated in the same way they are activated with direct observation.

Second, empathy arises from perspective taking. Perspective taking is imaging one-self in another's place. Perspective taking does not involve experiencing the other person's emotional state, but instead involves understanding the other person's feelings. Perspective taking combines two skills—namely, suppressing one's own perspective and then understanding the perspective of the other (Davis, 2004). Because perspective taking is an antecedent to empathy and not empathy itself, some researchers make the distinction between cognitive empathy that involves perspective taking and understanding what the other is thinking versus emotional empathy that involves other-focused feelings such as concern, sympathy, and compassion that lead to altruistic prosocial behaviors (Hoffman, 2000; Shamay-Tsoory, Aharon-Peretz, & Perry, 2009).

An experience of empathy typically heightens the perceptions of closeness toward the other, and it creates an approach-based prosocial motivational orientation toward the other. People engage in more prosocial behavior when they feel empathy toward the other, compared to when they do not. And people engage in a high level of prosocial behavior when they feel strong empathy toward the other, while they engage in only a moderate level of prosocial behavior when they feel only mild empathy toward the other. And people feel greater empathy and help more when they combine both perspective taking and other-concern (e.g., "imagine yourself as the other person") than when they rely only on perspective taking without the affective kick that comes from empathic concern (e.g., "imagine the other") (Myers, Laurent, & Hodges, 2013).

Empathy is distinct from personal distress. Personal distress is a self-focused aversive motivational response to anther's distress. Because personal distress feels aversive, people are more likely to ignore the other's distress, walk away from it, and distance themselves from the person in need more than they are to remain in the situation, continue to experience that personal stress, and take the time to help the other. While empathy generates an approach-based prosocial motivation to help, personal distress generates only a rather egotistical desire to relieve one's own distress in an indirect way by first removing the distress of the other.

As highlighted in Box 14, empathy is an important prosocial emotion that both facilitates cooperation and helping on the one hand and acts as a counterforce or outright antidote to antisocial behavior such as aggression. But, as the emotions of schadenfreude and personal distress both make clear, empathy does not always follow from observing others' emotional states, because dislike and resentment toward the other (as occurs with

---

| BOX 14 | *Will You Help Me? Will I Help You?* |

Question: Why is this information important?

Answer: It shows that prosocial behavior is often emotion motivated.

Helping is necessarily an emotion-motivated prosocial behavior. It would be nice if people routinely helped others, but helping is typically a personally costly thing to do. The one who helps makes a sacrifice (e.g., time, effort, money, etc.) or puts oneself at risk in some important way. To overcome these costs of helping, we need the motivational support of prosocial emotion.

Will I Help You?

When we find ourselves in the role of "the helper," whether we help depends in a large part on how we feel. Positive affect and emotions such as gratitude are both robust predictors of helping motivation and behavior (Bartlett & DeSteno, 2006). When we feel gratitude, our thoughts are prosocial (e.g., "Oh, that was so thoughtful of her.") and prosocial thinking gives the proverbial green light to helping in a way that neutral thinking does not (Emmons & McCullough, 2004). Helping also depends on where our attention is directed. When self-focused (what I am feeling, the costs I might incur), the would-be helper tends to feel sympathy or pity toward the other. Neither emotion is a reliable predictor of helping, as both emotions are more likely to motivate escape and avoidance than staying and helping. When other-focused (what the other is feeling, what the other needs), the would-be helper tends to feel empathy. Empathy is a very good predictor of helping (Dovidio, Piliavin, Schroeder, & Penner, 2006). People who feel empathy are moved to help. Emotions such as compassion and guilt sometimes do and sometimes do not move us to help. When our attention is other-focused, compassion and guilt do

tend to move us to helping; when our attention is self-focused, these same emotions tend to backfire and undermine helping, as they are experienced as something aversive that we need to get rid of (often by escaping or leaving).

Will You Help Me?

When we find ourselves in the role of the one requesting help, whether we receive aid depends in large part on the emotion we express. When a person who requests help simultaneously displays a neutral (unemotional) facial and vocal expression, onlookers typically feel little inclination to help. Similarly, when a person who requests help displays an inappropriate emotion such as anger (e.g., "I'm mad and upset that you are not helping me!"), onlookers again typically feel little inclination to help. Expressions of anger simply do not fit the script for a request to help, and the onlooker rightly suspects that the person in need will turn on the helper and blame him or her for their current predicament (e.g., "I'm in need, and it is your fault (not mine)"; Kuppens & Van Mechelen, 2007). However, when a person who requests help simultaneously displays an appropriate emotion such as sadness or disappointment, onlookers typically do feel an inclination to help. The reason why emotions such as sadness and disappointment seem so appropriate to a person requesting help is because these emotions tell us that the other person is truly in need—that they are powerless, have little control over the situation, cannot cope with the situation by oneself (are dependent on others), and are resigned to their sad fate—unless some nice person comes along to help. In other words, facial and vocal expressions of sadness, distress, and discouragement act as effective assistance signals (Eisenberg, 2000; Van Dorn, Van Kleef, & van der Pligt, 2014; Van Kleef, De Dreu, & Manstead, 2006).

schadenfreude) tend to block one's capacity for empathy as does a self-related concern (as occurs with personal distress). But, if the person makes an intentional effort at other-focused perspective taking and if mimicry occurs (or mirror neurons are activated), then empathy is likely to occur. Through empathy, we can feel what others feel. If we can feel what others feel and if we have a good deal of emotion knowledge about what motivational urges are associated with each individual emotional state, then we will be well positioned to deeply understand others and to respond to them in a highly emotionally appropriate way.

Compassion

Compassion is a complex emotion, partly because it is peculiarly both a positive and a negative emotion. People generally think of compassion as a positive emotion, but when they are actually experiencing it then feels like a negative emotion (Condon & Barrett, 2013). Compassion is a positive emotion when it connotes caring and when the focus is on the one who is cared for, while compassion is a negative emotion when it is tightly paired with distress and suffering and when one focuses on that personal distress. The mixed status of compassion is probably due to the fact that compassion can be elicited by another's experience of suffering but also by another's heart-warming experience. To depict a heart-warming experience within a context of suffering, researchers asked participants to listen to a two-minute audiotape of (1) a woman telling about her sister's death in a subway accident and her most prized possession of a voicemail left by her sister that said "I love you," and (2) a husband and wife discussing the man's Alzheimer's, his love for his grandson, and the woman's gratefulness for being able to take care of her husband during the difficult disease (Condon & Barrett, 2013). Both stories elicited significant increases in felt compassion, but both stories also elicited significant gains in feelings of personal distress (i.e., feeling distressed, troubled, upset).

The conclusion is that while compassion itself is thought of as a positive emotion, the sympathy it entails toward another's suffering (e.g., poverty, vulnerable infants) brings along an element of psychological distress (Condon & Barrett, 2013; Simon-Thomas et al., 2012). Further, this pairing of positively valenced compassion with negatively valenced distress is probably inherent in the complex emotional experience that is compassion since its function is to reduce another's suffering in a heartfelt way.

SUMMARY

This chapter examined 20 individual emotions that were grouped into the three categories of basic emotions, self-conscious emotions, and cognitively complex emotions.

The emotional dynamics of seven basic emotions were detailed. Fear arises from a perceived danger, a threat to one's well-being, and from a perceived vulnerability of being overwhelmed, and its functional purpose is to protect the self as by fleeing. Three close emotional allies of fear include anxiety, posttraumatic stress disorder, and phobias. Anger arises from the presence of an obstacle to one's goal pursuit and from the sense that the situation is not what is should be. Anger's functional purpose is to overcome the obstacle and to right the illegitimate wrong. Disgust arises as repulsion against a contaminated object such as food, but it can also arise from cognitive, social, and moral contaminants. The function of disgust is to reject the contaminated object. Contempt arises from feeling morally superior to another person, and its function is to maintain the social order. Sadness arises from an experience of separation or loss, and its function is to repair and reverse that loss or failure, if possible. Sadness can slip into depression when it is accompanied by emotional overproduction and rumination. Joy arises from desirable outcomes such as making progress toward a goal or getting what we want, and its function is to engage in social interaction and to continue one's goal striving. Interest arises from environmental novelties, opportunities to gain new information, and need-involvement opportunities. Its function is to vitalize and replenish exploration, engagement, and learning.

The emotional dynamics of five self-conscious emotions were detailed. Shame arises from violations of standards associated with morality and competent functioning that lead to a perception that the self is inferior or damaged in some way. Shame's functional purpose is to restore the self, although shame also generates a motive to protect the self. Guilt arises from the perception that one's behavior caused harm, loss, or distress to a relationship partner, and its function is to make amends. Embarrassment follows a social blunder and signals that something is amiss with the self. Its function is to appease the audience and communicate that the blunder was an accident rather than evidence of an enduring personal inadequacy. Pride arises from success and achievement, and it has the two facets of authentic pride and hubristic pride. Its function is to motivate the persistence necessary to acquire new skills and persist in challenging activities. Triumph is an emotional reaction to competitive victory and leads to an expressive display of both self-expression and social dominance.

The emotional dynamics of eight cognitively complex emotions were detailed. Envy is the painful emotion that arises from the good fortunes of others, and its function is to level the status of self and others. With benign envy, the person is motivated to move the self up to the level of the other; with malicious envy, the person is motivated to pull the other back down to the self's level. Gratitude arises from a gift to the self that comes at a cost to the giver, and it functions as a benefit detector. People who feel gratitude report a positive perception of their benefactor, experience a rise in relationship satisfaction, and are motivated to act prosocially. Disappointment and regret are two decision-making emotions that arise from the nonoccurrence of a positive outcome. While disappointment leads to resignation and inertia, regret is experienced as a painful lesson that things could have been better and it therefore motivates taking future decision-making opportunities more seriously. Hope arises with a wish that a desired goal will be attained, and it motivates persistence in the pursuit of that desired goal. Schadenfreude arises from taking pleasure at the misfortune of others. Empathy is feeling the emotional state of another, and it arises from both mimicry and perspective taking. Empathy heightens the perception of closeness with the other and motivates a prosocial (helping) orientation toward the other. Compassion is both a positive and negative emotion. When paired with an experience of another's suffering, it feels like a negative emotion, but when paired with both suffering and a heartwarming experience it feels like a positive emotion. In both cases the function of compassion is to reduce the other's suffering.

READINGS FOR FURTHER STUDY

Basic Emotions

MATSUMOTO, D., & EKMAN, P. (2004). The relationship among expressions, labels, and descriptions of contempt. *Journal of Personality and Social Psychology, 87*, 529–540.

ROZIN, P., MARKWITH, M., & STOESS, C. (1997). Moralization and becoming a vegetarian: The transformation of preferences into values and the recruitment of disgust. *Psychological Science, 8*, 67–73.

STEPHENS, A. N., & GROEGER, J. A. (2011). Anger-congruent behavior transfers across driving situations. *Social Psychological and Personality Science, 2*, 592–599.

THOMAN, D. B., SMITH, J. L., & SILVIA, P. J. (2011). The resource replenishment function of interest. *Social Psychological and Personality Science, 2,* 592–599.

Self-Conscious Emotions

HARRIS, C. R. (2006). Embarrassment: A form of social pain. *American Scientist, 94,* 524–533.

TRACY, J. L., & ROBINS, R. W. (2007). The psychological structure of pride: A tale of two facets. *Journal of Personality and Social Psychology, 92,* 506–525.

WILLIAMS, L. A., & DESTENO, D. (2008). Pride and perseverance: The motivational role of pride. *Journal of Personality and Social Psychology, 94,* 1007–1017.

Cognitively Complex Emotions

ALGOE, S. B., GABLE, S. L., & MAISEL, N. (2010). It's the little things: Everyday gratitude as a booster shot for romantic relationships. *Personal Relationships, 17,* 217–233.

CONDON, P., & BARRETT, L. F. (2013). Conceptualizing and experiencing compassion. *Emotion, 13,* 817–821.

VAN DE VEN, N., ZEELENBERG, M., & PIETERS, R. (2000). Leveling up and down: The experiences of benign and malicious envy. *Emotion, 9,* 419–429.

Part Four

Applied Concerns

Chapter 15

Growth Motivation and Positive Psychology

HOLISM AND POSITIVE PSYCHOLOGY

    Holism

    Positive Psychology

SELF-ACTUALIZATION

    Hierarchy of Human Needs

        Deficiency Needs versus Growth Needs

        Research on the Need Hierarchy

    Encouraging Growth

ACTUALIZING TENDENCY

    Organismic Valuing Process

    Emergence of the Self

    Conditions of Worth

    Conditional Regard as a Socialization Strategy

        Congruence

    Fully Functioning Individual

HUMANISTIC MOTIVATIONAL PHENOMENA

    Causality Orientations

    Growth-Seeking versus Validation Seeking

    Relationships

        Helping Others

        Relatedness to Others

    Freedom to Learn

    Self-Definition and Social Definition

    Problem of Evil

POSITIVE PSYCHOLOGY

    Happiness and Well-Being

    Eudaimonic Well-Being

    Optimism

Meaning

Positivity

INTERVENTIONS

CRITICISMS

SUMMARY

READINGS FOR FURTHER STUDY

Each of us is born with a temperament. Our inherited dispositional temperament predisposes us to act in ways that are naturally inhibited and reserved or in ways that are naturally adventurous. Some of us are born to be introverts while some of us are born to be extraverts.

But cultures have preferences for about how people should behave. For instance, the typical college campus culture in the United States values extraversion, emotional intensity, and being exciting and entertaining while it relatively devalues introversion, emotional calm, and being a wallflower. Thus, students hear two messages of how to behave socially—one from their biological temperament and another from cultural priorities. This dual message is not much of a problem for extraverts: Just act naturally and the culture will value you. It is a problem, however, for introverts. Interestingly, the reverse is typically true in the East, because nations such as China and South Korea culturally value introversion over extraversion.

What happens when biological disposition contradicts socialization preference? What happens when an experience feels right and natural, but the culture devalues anyone who gravitates toward that experience? Should the introvert follow the cultural press and reject his inner nature and try to substitute a more socially acceptable extraverted style in its place?

Introverts who act like extraverts do experience some of the positive emotional benefits of extraversion (e.g., having fun at a party; Lucas et al., 2000). And, what is wrong with the individual's effort to be sensitive to, adjust to, and accommodate to her culture? Humanistic psychology is willing to answer that question. It argues that rejecting one's nature in favor of social priorities puts personal growth and psychological well-being at risk.

Imagine yourself in the following experiment (Ford, 1991a). The experiment begins by asking you to self-report your temperament on questionnaires assessing phenomena such as activity level and extraversion. The experimenter also asks for permission to send identical questionnaires to one of your parents (i.e., your primary caretaker), asking him or her to complete each questionnaire in terms of how you behaved during the preschool ages of 3–5 years. The ages 3–5 are important because toddlerhood is old enough for temperament to express itself and be observed by parents yet also young enough to precede the heavy socialization that occurs after toddlers venture out of the house. The study's prediction is that adults who express something other than their natural childhood temperament will show present-day maladjustment. That is, the prediction is that when the culture tries to replace a person's devalued inner nature with a socially valued style—that is, tries to socialize the introvert into an extravert, then maladjustment follows.

To index maladjustment, the experimenter also asks you to complete questionnaire measures of anxiety, depression, hostility, feelings of inadequacy, and physical/somatic troubles. To test the humanistic hypothesis, the experimenter computes a discrepancy score of the difference between your expressed temperament as an adult and your parent's rating of your temperament as a child. Results showed the greater the discrepancy, the greater the adult's maladjustment. People who were pressured—willingly or unwillingly—into acting in ways that contradicted their biologically based temperaments suffered.

These findings set the stage for the theme of the present chapter: "If this essential core (inner nature) of the person is frustrated, denied, or suppressed, sickness results" (Maslow, 1968). To Abraham Maslow's theme, we can add its logical complement: If this essential core is appreciated, supported, and nurtured, health results.

The everyday choice to follow "one's inner nature" versus "cultural priorities" is not a neutral choice. Social preferences and social priorities are communicated and enforced as desirable ways of acting by all sorts of social advocates, including incentives, rewards, approval, love, advertising messages, social demands, norms, expectations, and all the people we hear each day that tell us what we should, ought to, have to, and must be. The social message is strong. Inner guides, in contrast, are subtle. Unlike the culture around us, inner guides have no organized lobby to persuade us what to do. So, in everyday living, our inner guides are relatively quiet while social expectations and cultural priorities are relatively loud.

It is easy to hear the culture's priorities, but it might not be so psychologically healthy to unquestioningly follow them. For instance, people who choose to devote their lives to the pursuit of the "American dream" (the pursuit of money, fame, and popularity) suffer more psychological distress (anxiety, depression, narcissism) than do people who pursue inner guides like personal growth for its own sake. This is true even when those who pursue the American dream do actually attain the money, fame, and popularity they seek (Kasser, 2002; Kasser & Ryan, 1993, 1996). Humanistic psychology plays a key role in motivation by asking people to pause, listen to their inner guides, and consider the wisdom of coordinating their inner guides (interests, preferences, values) with their day-to-day lifestyle. Research on positive psychology adds that inner guides like meaning, authenticity, and the passion to learn add reservoirs of strength and wellness and, further, that it is the effort to develop these personal strengths, rather than the effort to realize cultural priorities, that makes us happy (Fredrickson, 2009; Seligman, 2002, 2011).

HOLISM AND POSITIVE PSYCHOLOGY

Human motives can be understood from many different perspectives, ranging from the most objective viewpoints of objectivism (Diserens, 1925), behaviorism (Watson, 1919), and logical positivism (Bergmann & Spence, 1941) to the most subjective viewpoints of existentialism (May, 1961), gestalt psychology (Goldstein, 1939; Perls, 1969), and holism (Aristotle, *On the Soul*). Along with existentialism and gestalt psychology, holism asserts that a human being is best understood as an integrated, organized whole rather than as a series of differentiated parts. It is the whole organism that is motivated rather than just some part of the organism, such as the stomach or brain. In holism, any event that affects one system affects the entire person. To borrow a phrase from Maslow, it is John Smith who desires food, not John Smith's stomach.

In modern parlance, holism sees little value in a "bottom-up" approach (i.e., focus on specific, individual motives, one at a time, and in relative isolation from one another) and, instead, prefers a "top-down" approach (i.e., focus on general, all-encompassing motives, seeing how the master motives govern the more specific ones). Both the bottom-up and the top-down approaches to motivation study have merit. This chapter, however, highlights the top-down approach (while Chapters 3 and 4 highlighted the bottom-up approach).

Holism

Holism derives its name from "whole" or "wholeness" and therefore concerns itself with the study of what is healthy or unbroken. In contrast, a broken view of personality emphasizes human beings as fragmented sets of structures or forces that oppose one another. For instance, a broken view speaks of the conflict between an ideal self and an actual self (Chapter 9) or the conflict between the biological desire for food and the social demand for a slim figure (Chapter 4). In psychoanalytic theory (see Chapter 16), a broken self manifests itself in a sort of psychological competition among the three personality structures of id, ego, and superego (i.e., psychodynamics). In contrast, humanism identifies strongly with the holistic perspective, because it stresses top-down master motives, such as the self and its strivings toward fulfillment.

In a nutshell, humanistic psychology is about discovering human potential and encouraging its development. To accomplish this, the humanistic perspective concerns strivings (1) toward growth and self-realization and (2) away from facade, self-concealment, and the pleasing of others (Rogers, 1966). In every page authored by humanistic thinkers, the reader can hear a commitment to personal growth as the ultimate motivational force.

Positive Psychology

Positive psychology is an emerging and rapidly growing field in psychology (Seligman & Csikszentmihalyi, 2000; Lopez & Snyder, 2009; Snyder & Lopez, 2002). It seeks to articulate the vision of the good life (psychologically speaking), and it uses the empirical methods of psychology to understand what makes life worth living. The goal is to show what actions lead to experiences of well-being, to the development of individuals who are optimistic and resilient, and to the creation of nurturing and thriving institutions and communities. The subject matter of positive psychology is therefore the investigation of positive subjective experiences such as happiness, well-being, optimism, meaning, resilience, authenticity, open-mindedness, compassion, gratitude, creativity, wisdom, good citizenship, a strong work ethic, and the nurturance of others.

Positive psychology is not a subfield of humanistic psychology. It chooses the same subject matter as does humanistic psychology, so the two fields do substantially overlap one another. What sets positive psychology apart from humanistic psychology is not its subject matter but is, instead, its strong reliance on hypothesis-testing, data-based empirical research. Positive psychology is the more scientifically rigorous of the two fields of study. As one positive psychologist put it, "Positive psychology is psychology, and psychology is science" (Peterson, 2006).

Positive psychology looks at a person and asks, "What could be?" As a field, positive psychology realizes both that people routinely fall short of "what could be" and also the epidemic-like prevalence of pathologies such as depression, substance abuse, school and workplace apathy, and violence. It further realizes the important role played by the effort to cure or reverse these human pathologies. Mostly, however, positive psychology devotes attention to the proactive building of personal strengths and competencies. To prevent sickness, people need to inoculate themselves with strengths such as hope, optimism, and meaning. The question is less "How can we correct people's weaknesses?" and more "How can we develop and amplify people's strengths?" How can families, schools, corporations, governments, and interpersonal relationships be restructured to better develop human strengths?

SELF-ACTUALIZATION

Self-actualization is an inherent developmental striving. It is a process of leaving behind timidity, defensiveness, and a dependence on others that is paired with the parallel process of moving toward the courage to create, to view life realistically, and to achieve autonomous self-regulation. It is "an underlying flow of movement toward constructive fulfillment of its inherent possibilities" (Rogers, 1980). It is an ever-fuller realization of one's talents, capacities, and potentialities (Maslow, 1987).

The two fundamental directions that characterize self-actualization as a process are autonomy and openness to experience. *Autonomy* means moving away from heteronomy and toward an ever-increasing capacity to depend on one's self and to regulate one's own thoughts, feelings, and behaviors so to move toward greater self-realization (Deci & Ryan, 1991). *Openness* means receiving information (including feelings) such that it is neither repressed, ignored, or filtered, nor distorted by wishes, fears, or past experiences (Mittelman, 1991). Through openness, one leaves behind timidity and defensive appraisals and moves toward greater mindfulness, courage, and realistic appraisals.

Hierarchy of Human Needs

The cornerstone of Maslow's understanding of motivation is the proposition that human needs can be organized into clusters. The arrangement of these need clusters, Maslow felt, was best communicated visually by a hierarchy, as illustrated in Figure 15.1. The first set of

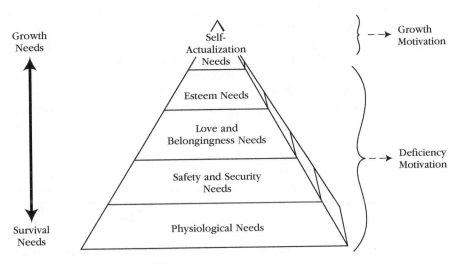

Figure 15.1   Maslow's Need Hierarchy

needs contains basic physiological needs, as discussed in Chapter 4. All the other needs in the hierarchy are psychological needs (safety and security, love and belongingness, esteem, and self-actualization). The hierarchical presentation conveys three themes about the nature of human needs (Maslow, 1943, 1987).

1. Needs arrange themselves in the hierarchy according to potency or strength. The lower the need is in the hierarchy, the stronger and more urgently it is felt.

2. The lower the need is in the hierarchy, the sooner it appears in development. Young people experience only the lower needs in the hierarchy, while older people are more likely to experience the full range of the hierarchy.

3. Needs in the hierarchy are fulfilled sequentially, from lowest to highest, from the base of the pyramid to its apex.

Theme 1 proposes that the survival-based needs (at the bottom of the hierarchy) dominate as the strongest motives, whereas the self-actualization needs (at the top) are the weakest. Here, Maslow makes the point that self-actualization needs are relatively quiet urges that are easily overlooked in the rush of one's day-to-day affairs. Theme 2 communicates that the lower needs (e.g., safety and security) characterize needs typical of nonhuman animals and of children, whereas the higher needs (e.g., esteem) are uniquely human and pertain to adults. Theme 3 stipulates that satisfying lower needs is a prerequisite to satisfying higher needs. Hence, before people experience the needs for esteem and self-actualization, they must first sufficiently gratify their physiological, safety, and belongingness needs.

Deficiency Needs versus Growth Needs

Biological disturbances (e.g., thirst, hunger) and needs for safety, belongingness, and esteem are collectively referred to as deficiency needs. Deficiency needs are like vitamins; people need them because their absence inhibits growth and development. The presence of any of the deficiency needs indicated that the individual was in a state of deprivation, whether that state of deprivation involved food, job security, group membership, or social status. Maslow (1971) characterized such deprivation as human sickness, a term he used to connote a failure to move toward growth and actualization.

Given satisfaction of all deficiency needs, growth needs surface and render the person restless, discontent, and wanting something more from life. The person no longer feels hungry, insecure, isolated, or inferior, but instead needs a need to fulfill personal potential. Growth needs—or self-actualization needs—provide energy and direction to become what one is capable of becoming: "A musician must make music, an artist must paint, a poet must write, if he is to be ultimately happy. What a man can be, he must be. This need we may call self-actualization" (Maslow, 1943). Putting the sexist language aside, it can be difficult to pinpoint precisely what self-actualization needs are and are not. One can understand physiological needs by thinking of hunger and thirst, but self-actualization is a more abstruse term. It is actually a master motive that coalesces the following 14 "metaneeds" or "B-values": truth, beauty, wholeness, spontaneity, justice, simplicity, humor, transcendence, uniqueness, perfection, completion, richness or totality, effortlessness, and autonomy (Maslow, 1971).

One way to discover what self-actualization needs are is to pay attention to the pathological state that arises from their absence (Maslow, 1971). For instance, when deprived of the need for wholeness, the person feels a sense that one's world is falling apart in chaos and disintegration. When deprived of a sense of aliveness, the person suffers apathy and just goes through the motions day after day. A man deprived of the need for uniqueness might speculate that his wife could easily find another mate that would be just as good a husband as he. In other words, sometimes it is easier to hear people's pathological states of disintegration, deadness, sameness, dishonesty, humorlessness, and despair than it is to hear people's needs to grow, to develop, and to become the person they are capable of becoming.

Research on the Need Hierarchy

Maslow's need hierarchy was, and still is, wildly popular. It has been embraced as a modus operandi in education, business, management, the workplace, psychotherapy, and the health professions of medicine, nursing, and geriatrics (Cox, 1987). The need hierarchy can still be found in practically all introductory psychology textbooks. It also fits nicely with both personal experience and common sense. Despite its tremendous popularity, research has actually found very little empirical support for the need hierarchy (Wahba & Bridwell, 1976). That is, children are not more occupied with physiological and safety needs, while adults are not more occupied with esteem and actualization needs (Goebel & Brown, 1981). Also, college students prioritize their needs as follows (from least to most important): esteem, security, self-actualization, belongingness, and physical/physiological (Mathes, 1981). Overall, the pattern of findings casts considerable doubt on the hierarchy's validity.

The only finding with some empirical support is the conceptualization of a dual-level (not a five-level) hierarchy. In a dual-level hierarchy, the only distinction is between deficiency and growth needs (Wahba & Bridwell, 1976), and when researchers make this distinction, they do find some empirical support for the two-level hierarchy (Sheldon et al., 2001). Thus, three conclusions from research on the need hierarchy are to:

1. Reject the five-level hierarchy.
2. Collapse the physiological, safety, belongingness, and esteem needs into the single category of deficiency needs.
3. Hypothesize a simplified, two-level hierarchy distinguishing only between deficiency and growth needs.

Given these conclusions, take a second look at Figure 15.1. In your mind's eye, erase the three horizontal lines that separate the physiological, safety, belongingness, and esteem needs. With these lines erased, you will see one large triangle that includes the full range of the deficiency needs and one small triangle at the top for the self-actualization needs. Such a conceptualization does tend to fit the data well.

Encouraging Growth

When talking and theorizing about deficiency needs, Maslow made some mistakes. But when talking about growth needs, he was much more in his element, and many of his ideas about growth needs have indeed stood the test of time.

Maslow estimated that less than 1 percent of the population ever reached self-actualization. Because the self-actualization needs were supposedly innate, one is left wondering why everyone does not ultimately self-actualize. In some cases, Maslow reasoned, people fail to reach their potential because of a nonsupportive internal (e.g., chronic back pain) or external (e.g., neglect, abuse) environment. In other cases, the person was responsible for her own lack of growth (i.e., each of us fears our own potential, which Maslow termed the "Jonah complex," after the timid Biblical merchant who tried to flee his great calling). Like Maslow, all humanistic thinkers continue to emphasize that the process of self-emergence is an inherently stressful and anxiety-provoking process, because it always makes the person face the insecurities of personal responsibility. When a person works toward self-emergence, she typically feels isolated and, to some degree, alone, or what Erich Fromm (1941) called the "unbearable state of powerlessness and aloneness." Facing such insecurity and having the personal responsibility for one's own personal growth, many people—like Jonah—seek escape (Fromm, 1941). The popular musical *The Sound of Music* illustrates this process for two young identity-seeking adults, as Liesl sings "I'll need someone older and wiser showing me what to do," while Rolf becomes an automaton within the powerful authoritarian military force of the day. Liesl's search for someone to show her the way and Rolf's submission to a powerful authority represent two common but self-actualizing-thwarting "take the safe route" life choices.

Ever the counselor and clinician, Maslow (1971) offered several everyday behaviors for encouraging growth, as listed in Table 15.1. Maslow further stressed the importance of

Table 15.1   Six Behaviors That Encourage Self-Actualization

1. Make Growth Choices

See life as a series of choices, forever a choice toward progression and growth versus regression and fear. The progression-growth choice is a movement toward self-actualization, whereas the regression-fear choice is a movement away from self-actualization. For instance, enroll in a difficult but skill-building college course rather than in a safe and "easy A" course.

2. Be Honest

Be honest rather than not, especially when in doubt. Take responsibility for your choices and the consequences of those choices. For instance, at a bookstore, pick a book that reflects your personal (but not necessarily popular) interest rather than a book featured on the best seller's list.

3. Situationally Position Yourself for Peak Experiences

Set up conditions to make peak experiences more likely. Get rid of false notions and illusions. Use your intelligence. If you are talented and interested in playing the piano, then spend more and more time in that domain and less and less time in more socially rewarding domains in which you lack talent and interest.

4. Give Up Defensiveness

Identify defenses and find the courage to give them up. For instance, instead of using fantasies to prop up the self and to keep anxiety at bay, drop the indulgent fantasy and get to work on developing the skills needed to actually become that sort of person.

5. Let the Self Emerge

Perceive within yourself and listen to that inner voice. Shut out the noises of the world. Instead of only looking to others to tell you what to do and who to become, listen to your own personal interests and aspirations of what you want to do and who you want to become.

6. Be Open to Experience

Experience fully, vividly, selflessly with full concentration and total absorption. Experience without self-consciousness, defenses, or shyness. Be spontaneous, original, and open to experience.

relationships—intimate and fulfilling relationships rather than the all-too-common super-ficial ones—as the soil for cultivating peak experiences (Hardeman, 1979). Setting up conditions to foster growth in our lives involved not only enacting the sort of behaviors listed in Table 15.1 but also immersing our lives in relationships that support both autonomy and openness.

ACTUALIZING TENDENCY

Humanistic psychology's emphasis on holism and self-actualization can be represented by Carl Rogers's (1951) oft-cited quotation: "The organism has one basic tendency and striving—to actualize, maintain, and enhance the experiencing self." Fulfillment of phys-iological needs maintains and enhances the organism, as does the fulfillment of needs for belongingness and social status. Furthermore, a motive such as curiosity enhances and actu-alizes the person via greater learning and the development of new interests. Overall, Rogers (1959, 1963) recognized the existence of individual motives, but he emphatically stressed the holistic proposition that all human needs serve the collective purpose of maintaining, enhancing, and actualizing the person.

Rogers, like Maslow, believed that the actualizing tendency was innate, a continual presence that quietly guides the individual toward genetically determined potentials. This forward-moving pattern of development was characterized by "struggle and pain," and Rogers offered the following illustration for communicating the self-actualizing tendency's ever-present path toward development and growth. The 9-month-old infant has the genetic potential to walk but must struggle to advance from crawling to walking. The struggle to make those first steps inevitably includes wobbling, falling, and feeling frustrated, hurt, and disappointed. Despite the struggle and pain, the child nevertheless persists toward walking and away from crawling. The pain and disappointment undermine and discour-age the child's motivation to walk, but the actualization tendency, "the forward thrust of life," supports the child ever forward.

Organismic Valuing Process

The actualization tendency's "forward thrust of life" has a partner. That partner was the "organismic valuing process," an inherent capacity to judge for oneself whether a specific experience promotes or reverses growth (Rogers, 1964). It is also an inherent capacity to judge what is important and essential for a more fulfilling life. All experiences within the struggle and pain of actualizing one's potential are evaluated by the organismic valuing process. Experiences perceived as maintaining or enhancing the person are positively val-ued and feel right. Such growth-promoting experiences are given the metaphorical green light by the organismic valuation process and are subsequently approached. Experiences perceived as regressive are valued negatively and feel wrong. Such growth-blocking expe-riences are given the metaphorical yellow or red light by the organismic valuing process and are therefore subsequently avoided. In effect, the organismic valuing process provides an experiential feed-forward system that allows the individual to coordinate life experiences in accordance with the actualization tendency.

The actualizing tendency motivates the individual to want to undertake new and challenging experiences, and the organismic valuing process provides the interpretive information needed for deciding whether the new undertaking is growth-promoting. The feed-forward system of the organismic valuing process is an interesting addition to a motivational analysis of behavior because it complements the many feedback systems already discussed (i.e., physiological stop system in Chapter 4, goal-feedback system in Chapter 8). With a feedback system, information follows behavior to affect continuing motivation and persistence; with a feed-forward system, information precedes behavior to communicate a proverbial green, yellow, or red light as to one's *intention* to act and, hence, applies to the initiation (rather than the persistence) of behavior.

The organismic valuing process sounds like an appealing asset, but it is important to ask, Is there really such a thing? Kennon Sheldon and his colleagues designed a series of experiments to empirically test the validity of this process (Sheldon, Arndt, & Houser-Marko, 2003). In one study, they asked participants to rate growth-promoting aspirations ("intrinsic goals," such as personal growth and helping others) and growth-debilitating aspirations ("extrinsic goals," such as material possessions and social popularity). Then, 20 minutes later these same participants were asked to reflect on how important these two categories of goals were to them. After some reflection, people increased their rating of how important their intrinsic aspirations were. In another study, they again asked participants to rate the importance of growth-promoting aspirations and growth-debilitating aspirations, but this time they waited six weeks to ask participants to reconsider how important these goals were to their lives. After six weeks, people increased their rating of how important their intrinsic aspirations were and they decreased their rating of how important their extrinsic aspirations were. What this means is that, over time, people do tend to move toward goals and aspirations that are growth-promoting, and they do tend to move away from goals and aspirations that are growth-debilitating. As the authors conclude, "In short, it appears that people really do have some idea about what kinds of goals are most likely to be beneficial for their subjective well-being, presumably because they possess an organismic valuing process" (Sheldon et al., 2003, p. 860).

Emergence of the Self

The actualizing tendency characterizes the individual as a whole. Part of the actualizing tendency differentiates itself to become aware of its own experience. That differentiated experience becomes "the self," and it represents an awareness of being, an awareness of experience, and an awareness of one's own functioning (Rogers, 1959). With the emergence of the self, a person grows in complexity, and the organismic valuing process begins to apply not only to the organism as a whole but also to the self in particular. The most important motivational implication of the emergence of the self is that the actualizing tendency begins to express itself in part toward that portion of the organism conceptualized as the self. This means that the individual gains a second major motivational force in addition to the actualizing tendency, namely the self-actualizing tendency. Notice that actualization and self-actualization are not the same thing (Ford, 1991b), as the actualizing tendency and the self-actualizing tendency can sometimes work at odds with one another, as discussed in the next section.

The emergence of the self prompts the emergence of the need for positive regard— approval, acceptance, and love from others. The need for positive regard is of special significance because it makes the individual sensitive to the feedback of others (criticisms and praises). Over time, evaluating the self from other people's points of view becomes a rather automated and internalized process.

Conditions of Worth

Soon after birth, children begin to learn the "conditions of worth" on which their behavior and personal characteristics (the self) are judged as either positive and worthy of acceptance or negative and worthy of rejection. Eventually, because the need for positive regard sensitizes the individual to attend to the acceptances and rejections of others, the child internalizes parental conditions of worth into the self structure. Throughout development, the self structure expands beyond parental conditions of worth to include societal conditions of worth as well. By adulthood, the individual learns from parents, friends, teachers, clergy, spouses, coaches, employers, and others what behaviors and which characteristics are good and bad, right and wrong, beautiful and ugly, desirable and undesirable.

According to Rogers (1959), all of us live in two worlds—the inner world of organismic valuing and the outer world of conditions of worth. To the extent to which one internalizes conditions of worth, these acquired conditions of worth gain the capacity to substitute for, and even replace, the innate organismic valuing process. When governed by conditions of worth, individuals necessarily divorce themselves from their inherent means of coordinating experience with the actualizing tendency. No longer is experience judged in accordance with the innate organismic valuing process. Rather, experience is judged in accordance with societal conditions of worth.

Rogers viewed the child's movement toward conditions of worth and away from organismic valuing as antithetical to the development of the actualizing and the self-actualizing tendencies. When the developing individual adheres to conditions of worth, he moves farther away from an inherent ability to make the behavioral choices necessary to actualize the self. The overall process and consequences of adherence to either the organismic valuing process or socialized conditions of worth are summarized in Figure 15.2.

The way not to interfere with organismic valuing is to provide "unconditional positive regard," rather than the "conditional positive regard" that emanates from conditions of worth. If given unconditional positive regard, a child has no need to internalize societal conditions of worth. Experiences are judged as valuable to the extent that they enhance oneself (see upper half of Figure 15.2). If parents approve of, love, and accept their child for who she naturally is (i.e., unconditional positive regard) rather than for who the parents wish her to be (i.e., conditional positive regard), then the child and the child's self-structure will be a relatively transparent representation of her inherent preferences, talents, capacities, and potentialities. With conditions of worth, in contrast, experiences are judged as valuable to the extent that they are approved of by others (see lower half of Figure 15.2).

In the absence of salient conditions of worth, no conflict exists between the actualizing tendency and the self-actualizing tendency, and the two motivational tendencies remain unified (Rogers, 1959). Internalized conditions of self-worth, however, create motivational conflict. With conditional self-regard, tension and internal confusion emerge because some aspects of behavior are regulated by the actualizing tendency, while others are regulated by the self-actualizing tendency (Ford, 1991b; Rogers, 1959). Self-actualization, when evaluated and directed via conditions of worth rather than organismic valuation, can paradoxically lead a person to develop in a way that is incongruent, conflicting, and maladaptive (Ford, 1991b). Thus, self-actualization does not necessarily lead to and result in health

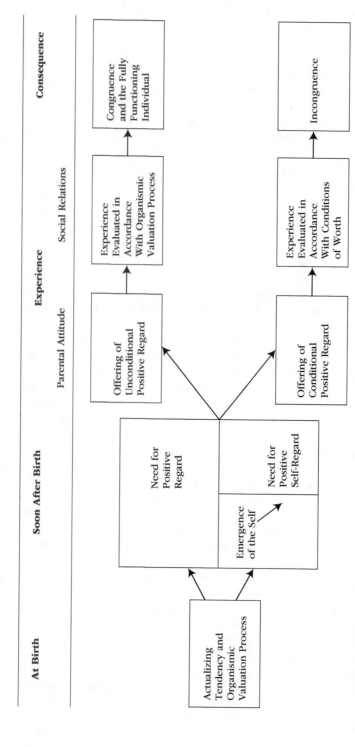

Figure 15.2 Rogerian Model of the Process of Self-Actualization

and growth. Mental health and personal growth occur only when the actualizing tendency and the self-actualizing tendency are in synchronization and when all experiences are evaluated within an internal frame of reference.

Parents, for instance, are placed in difficult positions when their child expresses a somewhat socially undesirable characteristic, such as shyness, irritability, or an explosive temper (e.g., recall the chapter's opening vignette). Conditional positive regard implies rejection and retraining so to promote social inclusion and popularity. The difficult position the parents face manifests itself in the dilemma of avoiding psychological costs (e.g., depression) versus avoiding social costs (e.g., peer rejection) to the developing child (Dykman, 1998).

To test Rogers' ideas (i.e., the model summarized in Figure 15.2), researchers assessed parents' childrearing practices and how these parental way of relating to children affected the child's creative potential—both in present time and longitudinally 10 years later (Harrington, Block, & Block, 1987). Researchers first assessed the extent to which parents supported their child's actualizing tendency ("I encourage my child to be curious, to explore, and to question things") and parents' thwarting of the actualizing tendency ("I do not allow my child to question my decisions"). They also assessed the child's creativity and self-expressiveness ("Is resourceful in initiating activities" versus "Gives up and withdraws where possible in terms of adversity"). For both mothers and fathers, parenting style predicted their child's current creative potential and, 10 years later, their adolescent's creative potential.

Conditional Regard as a Socialization Strategy

To socialize children and adolescents, adults (parents, teachers) sometimes go about the effort by creating "internal compulsions" within socializees to do what the adult wants them to do and to believe what the adult wants them to believe (Assor et al., 2004; Assor, Kaplan, Kanat-Mayman, & Roth, 2005; Roth et al., 2009). The prototype of such a pressuring socialization strategy is conditional regard, which is the offering of parental love for child obedience and the withdrawal of parental love for child disobedience. Conditional regard, a synonym of conditions of worth, comes in two forms—positive and negative.

- *Positive conditional regard* is giving love and affection for obedience and achievement. Here, parents provide more attention and affection when the child acts as told to act. When the child cleans her room and makes good grades, parents pour on the attention and affection.

- *Negative conditional regard* is taking away love and affection for disobedience and failure. Here, parents provide less attention and affection when then child fails to act as told. When the child messes his room and makes poor grades, parents turn cold and distant.

When parents use positive conditional regard as a socialization strategy, their children tend to take in feelings of internal compulsion (e.g., perfectionism; see Box 15) and adopt a grade-focused engagement in school (e.g., I have to prove myself). When parents use negative conditional regard as a socialization strategy, their children tend to resent their parents (e.g., anger, anxiety) and become amotivated toward school, showing academic apathy and even school dropout (Roth et al., 2009). These two parental socialization strategies may increase the child's temporary compliance, but they also produce worrisome costs in terms of their children's emotional and academic functioning and well-being. The researchers also

| BOX 15 | *Perfectionism as Conditions of Worth* |

Question: Why is this information important?

Answer: It invites you to examine the origins and implications of your own sense of perfectionism.

Nowhere in the industrialized world is the suicide rate higher for young men than it is in New Zealand. The everyday cultural expectations these men face stress inflated standards of masculinity, self-reliance, total emotional control, and unbound excellence in school and sports. From a humanistic perspective, these young men are asked to internalize societal conditions of worth characterized by perfectionism.

High personal standards are not bad. High standards generally cultivate both achievement strivings and good work habits (Frost, Marten, Lahart, & Rosenblate, 1990). In "normal perfectionism," people remain capable of experiencing pleasure and satisfaction in their work (Hamachek, 1978; Timpe, 1989). But perfectionism, like ice cream, comes in flavors, including "self-oriented perfectionism," "socially prescribed perfectionism," and "neurotic perfectionism" (Hewitt & Flett, 1991a, b).

Self-oriented perfectionism features exceedingly high, self-imposed, unrealistic standards that are paired with extreme self-criticism and an unwillingness to accept failure and personal flaws. When the self-oriented perfectionist does experience failure, self-criticism and depression are likely aftershocks.

Socially prescribed perfectionism is rooted in one's belief that other people hold exaggerated and unrealistic expectations for the self that are difficult, if not impossible, to meet—yet must be met if one is to gain acceptance and approval (Hewitt & Flett, 1991a, b). These imposed standards are not only external to the self, but they are also uncontrollable.

Failure to live up to these external-uncontrollable standards therefore ushers forth anxiety, helplessness, and suicidal thoughts (Blatt, 1995).

When relationships (as with parents and teachers) are supportive and nurturing, both self-oriented and socially prescribed dimensions of perfectionism can facilitate constructive strivings (Nystul, 1984). When relationships are not supportive, however, these two types of perfectionism often collapse into "neurotic perfectionism" (Hamachek, 1978), which is essentially the *intense* need to avoid failure. With neurotic perfectionism, no performance is good enough, and even well-done jobs yield little or no satisfaction. Deep feelings of inferiority throw the individual into an endless cycle of self-defeating, excessive striving accompanied by self-criticism, self-attack, and intense negative feelings. In general, neurotic perfectionism is associated with a wide range of psychopathology—depression (Hewitt & Dyck, 1986; LaPointe & Crandell, 1980), suicide (Adkins & Parker, 1996; Delisle, 1986; Shaffer, 1977), and eating disorders (Brouwers & Wiggum, 1993; Druss & Silverman, 1979; Katzman & Wolchik, 1984).

Neurotic perfectionism grows out of childhood experiences with disapproving parents whose love is conditional on how well the child behaves and performs (Hamachek, 1978). These parents incessantly urge their child to do better. The child never feels satisfied because his behaviors and performances never hit his parents' moving target of being good enough to earn approval and love. The result is a constant quest to avoid mistakes. And, typically, the harsh parental standards become internalized into a self-critical voice that uses the withdrawal of self-love as a means of personal punishment. Such a voice of neurotic perfectionism is the antithesis of organismic valuing.

---

tested the outcomes associated with a third parenting strategy, autonomy support (Chapter 6), and found that this socialization strategy produced feelings of valuing their schoolwork and an interest-focused engagement in school, social outcomes consistent with a Rogerian perspective on parenting.

Congruence

Congruence and incongruence describe the extent to which the individual denies and rejects (incongruence) or accepts (congruence) the full range of his or her personal characteristics, abilities, desires, and beliefs (Sheldon & Kasser, 1995). Psychological incongruence is essentially the extent of discrepancy or difference between "the self as perceived and the actual experience of the organism" (Rogers, 1959). The individual might perceive him- or herself as having one set of characteristics and one set of feelings but then publicly express a different set of characteristics and a different set of feelings. Conflict between experience–expression reveals incongruence; harmony between experience–expression reveals congruence.

When people move toward identifying with external conditions of worth, they adopt facades. A facade is essentially the social mask a person wears, and it relates to ways of behaving that have little to do with inner guides and much to do with a social front to hide behind (Rogers, 1961). Consider the unauthentic smile (the social facade of acting happy and friendly). Introverts often find themselves wearing the facade of the unauthentic smile on a regular basis, as when they force themselves to smile for hours at a social gathering. Doing so on a regular basis—acting one way yet feeling another way—predicts prone- ness to maladjustment, including anxiety, depression, self-doubt, and hypoassertiveness (Ford, 1995). Adopting a socially desirable facade carries psychological costs.

Fully Functioning Individual

According to Rogers, when fully functioning, the individual lives in close and confident relationship to the organismic valuing process, trusting that inner direction. Congruence is a constant companion. Furthermore, the fully functioning individual spontaneously com- municates inner impulses both verbally and nonverbally. He or she is open to experience, accepts the experiences as they are, and expresses those experiences in an unedited man- ner. The fully functioning individual is authentic. To characterize the moment-to-moment experience of the fully functioning individual, Figure 15.3 illustrates the sequential process of a motive's emergence, acceptance, and unedited expression.

HUMANISTIC MOTIVATIONAL PHENOMENA

Causality Orientations

People vary in their understandings of what causes and what regulates their behavior. Some people adopt a general orientation that their inner guides initiate and regulate their behavior; others adopt a general orientation that social guides and environmental incentives initiate and regulate their behavior. To the extent that individuals habitually rely on internal guides (e.g., needs, interests), individuals have an *autonomy causality orientation*. To the extent

Emergence	Acceptance	Expression
Onset of innate desire, impulse, or motive →	Desire, impulse, or motive is accepted "as is" into consciousness →	Unedited communication of desire, impulse, or motive

Figure 15.3   Fully Functioning as the Emergence, Acceptance, and Expression of a Motive

that individuals habitually rely on external guides (e.g., social cues), they have a *control causality orientation*.

The autonomy orientation involves a high degree of experienced choice with respect to the initiation and regulation of behavior (Deci & Ryan, 1985b; Hagger & Chatzisarantis, 2011). When autonomy oriented, people's behavior proceeds with a full sense of volition and an internal locus of causality. Needs, interests, and personally valued goals initiate the person's behavior, and needs, interests, and self-endorsed goals regulate his or her decision in persisting or quitting. In making a choice of college majors or careers to pursue, external factors such as salary and status are not irrelevant influences, but autonomy-oriented individuals pay closer attention to their needs and feelings than they do public opinion and environmental contingencies.

The control orientation involves a relative insensitivity to inner guides, as control-oriented individuals prefer to pay closer attention to environmental incentives and social expectations (Deci & Ryan, 1985b; Hagger & Chatzisarantis, 2011). When control oriented, people make decisions in response to the presence and quality of incentives, rewards, social expectations, and social concerns (e.g., pleasing others). Social demands, such as what *should* be done, and environmental factors, such as pay, status, and extrinsic rewards are very important. When researchers ask control-oriented individuals what they aspire to, the goals that energize and direct their behavior involve the pursuit of financial and material success (Kasser & Ryan, 1993).

The General Causality Orientations Scale (Deci & Ryan, 1985b) measures causality orientations by presenting a series of 12 vignettes (short stories). Each vignette presents a situation and lists responses to that situation, one of which is autonomy oriented and the other of which is control oriented. (A third scale to assess the impersonal orientation is not discussed here.) For instance, one of the vignettes presents the following situation:

> *You have been offered a new position in a company where you have worked for some time. The first question that is likely to come to mind is:*
> *I wonder if the new work will be interesting? (Autonomy)*
> *Will I make more money at this position? (Control)*

Causality orientations reflect extent of autonomy and self-determination in the personality. An autonomy causality orientation is a developmental outcome from a personal history of having one's psychological needs satisfied on a consistent basis. Hence, self-determination theory explains the origins and dynamics of causality orientations (Chapter 5; Deci & Ryan, 1985a). The autonomy-oriented personality is characterized by intrinsic motivation and identified regulation, because the forces that cause behavior are personal needs and interests (intrinsic motivation) as well as beliefs and values that have been integrated into the self (identified regulation). A person with an autonomy causality orientation uses information to make choices, and this tendency to do so applies generally across many different situations. The control-oriented personality is characterized by extrinsic regulation and introjected regulation, because the forces that cause behavior are environmental rewards and punishers (extrinsic regulation) and beliefs and values that have been forced onto the self (introjected regulation). A control causality orientation is a developmental outcome from a personal history of having one's psychological needs thwarted on a consistent basis. A person with a control causality orientation uses environmental signals as controls and demands on his or her behavior, and this tendency to be controlled

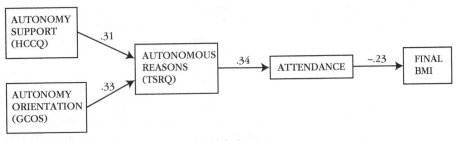

Figure 15.4 Model of Self-Determined Weight Loss

Source: Adapted from "Motivational predictors of weight loss and weight-loss maintenance," by G. C. Williams, V. M. Grow, E. R. Freedman, R. M. Ryan, and E. L. Deci, 1996, *Journal of Personality and Social Psychology, 70,* pp. 115–126. Copyright 1996 by American Psychological Association. Adapted with permission.

by external contingencies applies generally across many different situations (Hagger & Chatzisarantis, 2011).

Because of its close relationship to self-determination in personality, the autonomy orientation, like self-determination in general, correlates positively with measures of positive functioning, such as self-actualization, ego development, self-esteem, openness to experience, attitude–behavior congruence, and acceptance of one's true feelings (Deci & Ryan, 1985b; Koestner, Bernieri, & Zuckerman, 1992; Scherhorn & Grunert, 1988). This is true in domains as diverse as religion, education, prosocial behavior, and health care (Ryan & Connell, 1989; Ryan et al., 1993; Williams et al., 1996).

When people seek to change their behavior, they typically rely on either internal guides (personal goals) or external guides (relationship pressures) to do so. While participating in a weight-loss program, for instance, people can generally rely on both internal and external support for assistance and motivation for changing their behavior (Williams et al., 1996). After the program ends, however, people lose much of their external support (the staff, the structure of the program) for changing their behavior. Researchers therefore reasoned that the more autonomy oriented the participants were, the more likely it was that they would stay in the program from one week to the next, lose weight during the program, and, most importantly, maintain their weight loss after the program ended (i.e., maintain the behavior change). How autonomy-oriented individuals succeeded in maintaining their behavior change appears in Figure 15.4. The more autonomy oriented the participants were (and the more autonomy supportive the staff–patient interactions were), the more these participants relied on relatively autonomous reasons for losing weight, such as identified regulation ("It is important to my health that I lose more weight") rather than external regulation ("My spouse will divorce me if I don't lose more weight"). Rooting weight loss motivation in autonomous reasons promoted week-to-week attendance, and the more frequently they attended meetings the more successful they were in losing weight and maintaining that weight loss, as indicated in the figure by a decline (−.23) in their final body mass index (BMI).

Growth-Seeking versus Validation Seeking

When people identify with and internalize societal conditions of worth, they do more than just adopt socially desirable facades. Quasi-needs emerge. A quasi-need (see Chapter 4) emerges to the extent that the individual *needs* social approval—directly or symbolically—during social interaction. Valuing oneself via societal conditions of worth leads people into processes of validation-seeking. For the person who *needs* the approval of others to feel good about him- or herself, fulfilling others' conditions of worth leads to external validation, whereas failing to live up to others' conditions of worth leads to a perceived lack of personal worth, competence, and likeability.

During social interaction, people who seek external validation often use interpersonal situations to test or measure their personal worth, competence, or likability. That is, other people—one's peers, employers, teachers, and romantic partners—are seen as potential sources of external validation that can be used as social yardsticks to measure one's personal worth (Dykman, 1998). Positive outcomes generally leave the validation-seeking individual feeling rather accepted and validated. The adjustment problems surface following negative outcomes because these problems imply a lack of personal worth, competence, or likability.

In contrast, growth-seeking individuals center their personal strivings around learning, improving, and reaching personal potential. Seeking personal growth leads one to adopt a pattern of thinking in which situations and relationships are seen as opportunities for personal growth, learning, or self-improvement. Unlike validation-seeking individuals, however, negative interpersonal outcomes (e.g., exclusion, rejection, failure) fail to usher in adjustment problems because such outcomes identify and communicate information about life areas that are in need of improvement.

The Goal Orientation Inventory (GOI; Dykman, 1998) measures validation-seeking and growth-seeking strivings as relatively enduring personality characteristics. In taking the GOI, the respondent is asked to agree or disagree on whether the item describes how he or she thinks and acts in general:

> *Instead of just enjoying activities and social interactions, most situations to me feel like a major test of my basic worth, competence, or likability. (Validation-Seeking).*
> *Personal growth is more important to me than protecting myself from my fears. (Growth-Seeking)*

The distinction between striving for validation versus growth is important because it predicts vulnerability to mental health difficulties. For instance, the more people strive for validation, the more likely they are to suffer anxiety during social interaction, fear of failure, low self-esteem, poor task persistence, and high depression (see the first column of numbers in Table 15.2). In contrast, the more people strive for personal growth, the more likely they are to experience low interaction anxiety, low fear of failure, high self-esteem, high task persistence, and low depression (see the second column of numbers in Table 15.2).

This distinction between validation-seeking and growth-seeking is another way of expressing Maslow's distinction between deficiency and growth needs. Seeking validation is the pursuit to restore one's deficiency needs, whereas seeking growth is the pursuit of looking for opportunities to realize one's potential. The distinction also expresses a climate of conditional positive regard versus a climate of unconditional positive regard.

Relationships

The extent to which individuals develop toward congruence and adjustment depends greatly on the quality of their interpersonal relationships. At one extreme, relationships take on a

Table 15.2   Correlations with Indices of Psychological Well-Being for the Two Goal Orientations of Validation-Seeking and Growth-Seeking

Dependent Measure	Validation-Seeking Scale of the GOI	Growth-Seeking Scale of the GOI
Interaction anxiety	.46**	−.48**
Social anxiety	.42**	−.41**
Fear of failure	.50**	−.48**
Self-esteem	.59**	−.56**
Task persistence	−.40**	.55**
Depression	.38**	−.36**
Self-actualization:		
Time competence scale	−.51**	.20*
Inner directedness scale	−.56**	.31**

$*p < .05$; $**p < .01$. N ranged from 101 to 251 for each correlation reported above.

Note: The personality scale for each measure listed above was as follows: Interaction anxiety, Interaction Anxiousness Scale (Leary, 1983); social anxiety, Social Anxiety Subscale of the Self-Consciousness Scale (Fenigstein, Scheier, & Buss, 1975); fear of failure, Fear of Failure Scale (Dykman, 1998); self-esteem (reverse scored), Rosenberg's Self-Esteem Scale (Rosenberg, 1965); task persistence, Hope Scale (Snyder et al., 1991); depression, Beck Depression Inventory (Beck et al., 1979); and self-actualization, Personality Orientation Inventory (Shostrom, 1964, 1974).

Source: From "Integrating cognitive and motivational factors in depression: Initial tests of a goal-orientation approach," by B. M. Dykman, 1998, *Journal of Personality and Social Psychology, 74*, pp. 139–158. Copyright 1998 by American Psychological Association. Adapted with permission.

controlling, coercive tone as others force their agendas on the individual, pushing him or her toward heteronomy and socially prescribed conditions of worth. At the other extreme, relationships take on a supportive, nurturing tone as others take the individual's perspective and provide the support needed to allow for greater autonomy. Only the latter relationships nurture the actualizing tendency.

In humanistic therapy, for example, a client moves toward health and psychological congruence when his or her therapist brings the following characteristics into the relationship: warmth, genuineness, empathy, acceptance, and confirmation of the other person's capacity for self-determination (Kramer, 1995; Reeve, 2006; Rogers, 1973, 1995). *Warmth* involves care, love, and the process of enjoying spending time with the other person. *Genuineness* involves being fully present in and open to the relationship's here and now, offering personal authenticity rather than a professional facade of being a therapist, or "the expert." *Empathy* relates to listening to and hearing all the messages the other is sending and also truly understanding and willingly adopting the other's perspective on experience. Empathy occurs as one person enters into the private perceptual world of the other and becomes thoroughly at home in that world. *Acceptance* means that each person in the relationship experiences a basic acceptance and trust from the other (unconditional positive regard). Finally, *confirmation of the other person's capacity for self-determination* acknowledges that the other person is capable and competent and possesses an inherently positive developmental direction. Within a humanistic framework, these five characteristics reflect the quality of an interpersonal relationship.

Helping Others

Relationships become constructive when they help advance each person toward becoming more mature, better integrated, and open to experience (Rogers, 1995). Helping, in the humanistic tradition, does not involve an expert rushing in to solve the problem, to fix things, to advise people, or to mold and manipulate them in some way. Instead, helping involves letting the other person discover, and then be, him- or herself. This last insight is the antithesis of conditions of worth.

Relatedness to Others

One index of healthy psychosocial development is the extent to which the individual accepts social conventions, accommodates the self to the society, internalizes cultural values, cooperates with others, and shows respect for others. Rather than being independent, selfish, and socially detached, self-actualizers are actually good citizens. What motivates the willingness to accommodate the self to others is the need for relatedness (Goodenow, 1993; Grolnick, Deci, & Ryan, 1997; Ryan & Powelson, 1991). Interpersonally, relatedness (Chapter 6) refers to a need-satisfying experience in which one feels emotionally connected to, interpersonally involved with, liked by, respected by, and valued by another person. When this is so, relatedness is high and internalization of external regulations occurs willingly (Ryan & Powelson, 1991) and children show volitional social engagement (Furrer & Skinner, 2003).

But relatedness can come with a price—a hidden agenda in which one person asks for compliance from the other before granting love or approval (Gruen, 1976). Conditions of worth, for instance, essentially mean that the other person's (or society's) love, approval, care, and emotional connectedness are contingent on compliance with socialization standards and norms. But there is another type of relatedness between people besides a conformity-demanding conditional positive regard—namely, the unconditional acceptance and support (Hodgins, Koestner, & Duncan, 1996; Ryan, 1993). The quality of relatedness in early attachments (infant and caretaker) depends on how sensitive and responsive caregivers are to the infant's needs and initiatives (Colin, 1996). The paradoxical conclusion that emerged from Mary Ainsworth's classic program of research on infant attachment was that infants who received warm, need-satisfying, responsive, sensitive care from mothers did not become dependent or needy; instead, parental nurturance enabled and even liberated the child's autonomy (Ainsworth, 1989). Relationships rich in relatedness similarly facilitate autonomy in adults (Hodgins, Koestner, & Duncan, 1996). In contrast, when others provide contingent conditions of worth, people often forgo autonomy in order to preserve relatedness. In optimal development, neither autonomy nor relatedness is sacrificed or forgone (Ryan, 1993).

Freedom to Learn

Rogers continually lamented contemporary educational practices. He did not like the idea of a "teacher" because he felt that the only learning that really mattered was self-initiated learning (Rogers, 1969). Little of consequence occurs when a teacher gives out heaps of information for students to digest. Instead of "teacher," Rogers preferred "facilitator," a term that describes the classroom leader as one who creates and then supports an atmosphere conducive to students' learning. Learning does not follow teaching. Rather, learning follows having one's interests, goals, and aspirations identified and supported. Personal initiative and self-evaluation are of prime importance. Thus, education is not something a teacher can give to (or force on) a student. Rather, education must be acquired by the student through an investment of his energies and interests.[1]

Self-Definition and Social Definition

Self-definition and social definition are personality processes related to how individuals conceptualize who they are (Jenkins, 1996; Stewart, 1992; Stewart & Winter, 1974). Socially defined individuals accept external definitions of who they are. Self-defined individuals resist these external definitions and instead favor internal definitions of the self.

Self-definition and social definition processes are particularly instructive in the developing identities of women (Jenkins, 1996). Compared to their socially defined counterparts, self-defined women are more autonomous in their interpersonal relationships (they depend less on others) and social roles (they prefer nontraditional occupations). They organize their goals around self-determined aspirations, including their own personal decisions to get married or not and to have children or not. They are less invested in so-called traditional roles, such as wife and mother. In contrast, socially defined women prefer to work with and depend on others. They prefer traditional female roles both at home and at work. They are typically willing to compromise in terms of their own personal plans, college-degree aspirations, career persistence, and relationships. Decisions and experience flow not from the self but, instead, from social sources. And by depending on others, socially defined married women hope for husbands who can provide them with a life that is stimulating and challenging.

Problem of Evil

Much of the spirit of humanistic psychology follows the questionnable assumption that "human nature is inherently good." But do we as a society dare trust people who follow their inner guides? Freedom and self-determination are fine if human nature is benevolent, cooperative, and warmhearted, but what if human nature is malevolent, selfish, and aggressive? What if human nature is evil, or at least partly evil?

Humanistic thinkers wrestle with the nature of evil (Goldberg, 1995; Klose, 1995). The discussion typically takes one of two forms. On the one hand, the discussion asks *how much* of human nature is evil? This question asks, If family, political, economic, and social systems were benevolent and growth-promoting, then would human evil be reduced to zero or would some residual ferociousness remain? (Maslow, 1987). On the other hand, the discussion tries to understand evildoers (e.g., murderers, rapists) who confess to enjoying what they do and express a willingness to continue doing such acts (Goldberg, 1995).

Evil is the deliberate, intentional infliction of painful suffering on another person without respect for his or her humanity or personhood. Rogers's conviction was that evil was not inherent in human nature. He argued that if caretakers provided enough nurturance and acceptance and if they established a genuine connectedness with those they cared for, then people would inevitably choose good over evil (Rogers, 1982). Hence, human

---

[1]Golfer Ben Hogan, in a Rogerian spirit, gave the following reply to answer why he had not written another instructional book: "Golf is a game that cannot be taught; it must be learned."

beings behave malevolently only to the extent that they have been injured or damaged by experience. Violence reflects a history of relationships steeped in power and control (Muehlenhard & Kimes, 1999), while altruism reflects a history of relationships steeped in empathy and care (Batson, 1991).

Other humanists see more ambiguity in human nature. They assume that both benevolence *and* malevolence are part of everyone. In this view, under one set of social conditions, the actualizing tendency pairs itself with life-affirming values and adopts constructive ways for relating and behaving; but under another set of conditions, the actualizing tendency pairs itself with malicious values and leads to cruelty and destructive behavior (May, 1982). Thus, a person needs a value system (standards of right and wrong) to support and complement the organismic valuing process. If adults (parents) do not provide a child with a benevolent value system, then that child will grab a value system wherever it is available, be it among equally confused peers on the street, the college fraternity world, or Wall Street (Maslow, 1971). The recent study of suicide terrorists shows that these individuals were pretty much normal people who were intensely committed to a cause and to a set of values that they saw as greater than themselves (Atran, 2003). If a society cannot provide a benevolent value system for all its members, then it must build safeguards and structures into its social systems to renounce cruelty and to counter impulses to do evil (Bandura, 1999).

A motivational analysis of a terrorist is possible (Kruglanski & Orehek, 2011; Kruglanski et al., 2009). Terrorists, especially suicide bombers, feel that they will achieve something of tremendous significance through their acts of terrorism and suicide. Terrorism and suicide are perceived to be the path to heroism. Experiences of discrimination, personal problems, and humiliation that have nothing to do with the terrorist conflict are usually in the past of the individual terrorist, but the terrorist believes that these problems can be compensated for—even trumped in one swift act—by an act of perceived heroism. The act of perceived heroism is something—anything—that is held in extremely high regard by their community. In terrorism, this "something" takes the form of self-sacrifice for the sake of the community's cause. Underlying the act of terrorism is typically a social component (desire to be part of the group), an emotional component (many terrorists are recruited by first being shown films of atrocities being committed against the community), and an ideological component (a set of beliefs that condone violence for the sake of the in-group). It is the ideological component that serves as the person's acquired malevolent value system.

When people *desire* to act in ways that promote evil, they possess a malevolent personality (Goldberg, 1995). The descent into a malevolent personality is a slippery course of choices (Baumeister & Campbell, 1999; Fromm, 1964; Goldberg, 1995). Evil develops as follows (Staub, 1999): (1) Adults shame and scorn the child such that the child comes to the conclusion that he or she is flawed and incompetent as a human being; (2) the child incubates a negative self-view and comes to prefer lies and self-deceit over critical self-examination; (3) a transition occurs from being a victim to becoming an insensitive perpetrator; (4) the person initiates experimental malevolence; and (5) the malevolent personality is forged through a rigid refusal to engage in critical self-examination (Staub, 1999). The self becomes unwilling to examine itself (e.g., scapegoating is often used to preserve one's positive self-image; Baumeister et al., 1996), and intimidation tactics are used to foster the self-aggrandizement that counteracts the need for self-examination (Goldberg, 1995).

This view argues that evil springs out of a damaged concept of self. Evil's cause seems to have its origin in enculturation, not in human nature. It is difficult to determine whether evil is inherent in human nature. Within a supportive interpersonal climate, people's choices move them in the direction of greater socialization, improved relationships, and toward what is healthy and benevolent (Rogers, 1982). Therefore, as murder, war, and prejudice continue unabated throughout human history, the culprit might not be the evil in human nature but, alternatively, the sickness in culture. As long as society offers people choices, the possibility remains that its members will internalize a pathological value system that makes possible the descent into evil and the forging of a malevolent personality (May, 1982).[2]

POSITIVE PSYCHOLOGY

Positive psychology looks at people's mental health and the quality of their lives to ask, "What could be?" (Seligman & Csikszentmihalyi, 2000). It seeks to build people's strengths and competencies. It does not ask that people put on rose-colored glasses or adopt Pollyanna as a role model. Instead, positive psychology makes the case that strengths are as important as are weaknesses, resilience is as important as is vulnerability, and the lifelong task to cultivate wellness is as important as is an intervention attempt to remedy pathology. The fundamental assertion within positive psychology is that good mental health requires more than the absence of mental illness. Many people simply feel empty—not ill but floundering more than flourishing. Positive psychology tries to encourage flourishing—high levels of emotional, psychological, and social well-being that grows out of continuous self-growth, high-quality relationships, and a purposive and meaningful life (Keyes, 2007; Seligman, 2011).

A sampling of the human strengths that comprise the subject matter of positive psychology appears in Table 15.3 (Lopez & Snyder, 2009; Snyder & Lopez, 2002; Peterson & Park, 2009). The building of the strengths in Table 15.3 yield two interrelated outcomes: (1) greater personal growth and well-being and (2) lesser human sickness

Table 15.3   Personal Strengths Investigated as the Subject Matter of Positive Psychology

* Happiness	* Love of learning
* Meaning	* Wisdom
* Resilience	* Authenticity
* Flow	* Open-mindedness
* Curiosity	* Autonomy
* Optimism	* Forgiveness
* Zest	* Compassion
* Hope	* Gratitude
* Self-efficacy	* Humor
* Goal-setting	* Spirituality

---

[2]A final question asks whether human evil can be healed. One constant in humanistic thinking is that it never condemns without an affirmation of hope. But the malevolent personality is a tough one. Four reasons exist to explain the difficulty in healing evil: (1) the malevolent personality's closed nature (unwillingness to engage in critical self-examination), (2) the rarity of the malevolent personality's genuine motivation to change, (3) the odds against the malevolent personality finding those supportive conditions in which motivation for personal change can take root and fulfill itself, and (4) the strong influence of the individual's choice to change or not (Klose, 1995).

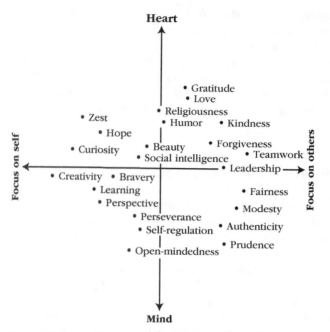

Figure 15.5 Two Dimensional Representation of Two Dozen Human Strengths

Source: From "Classifying and measuring strengths of character," by C. Peterson & N. Park, 2009, *Oxford handbook of positive psychology*, pp. 25–33, edited by C. R. Snyder & S. J. Lopez, Oxford University Press. Copyright 2009 by Oxford University Press.

(e.g., depression, suicide) from ever taking root within the personality. Rather than just listing human strengths, another way of thinking about human strengths is to map out them out visually in a two-dimensional space of "heart versus mind" and "self versus other" (Peterson & Park, 2009). This two-dimensional representation appears in Figure 15.5, and it is useful for two primary reasons. First, it implies that people need to make tradeoffs in their pursuit of personal strengths, because moving toward heart or self may necessitate less attention to mind and other, and vice versa. That is, it may be difficult to strive to develop greater gratitude and kindness (other and heart) while one is simultaneously striving to develop creativity and self-regulation (self and mind). Second, the strengths listed in the top half of the figure tend life toward happiness, while the strengths in the bottom half of the figure tend life toward meaning and achievement. Either way, if the human strengths listed in Table 15.3 are the developmental causes of greater happiness and greater meaning, then it is important to be clear about what happiness and meaning are.

Happiness and Well-Being

Happiness is a subjective state of being mentally well. People who are happy believe that their lives are going well. They believe that the current events in their lives are going well, and they particularly believe that things are going well in those life domains that are most important to them, such as work, health, or relationships. So, happiness is mostly the presence of positive emotion and the absence of negative emotion. But happiness also has a cognitive component because people not only emotionally feel happy or unhappy, but they also step back and evaluate their lives to judge how well or how poorly things are going. This process of stepping back to reflect on how things are going represents life satisfaction. Overall, to define happiness, motivation and emotion researchers use the synonymous "subjective well-being" (Diener & Biswas-Diener, 2008; Diener, Emmons, Larsen, & Griffin, 1985; Diener & Seligman, 2004; Diener, Suh, Lucas, & Smith, 1999). The nature and structure of subjective well-being are illustrated graphically in Figure 15.6 (based on Bettencourt & Sheldon, 2001; Sheldon & Elliot, 1999; Sheldon & Niemiec, 2006).

Most people are mildly happy most of the time (Diener & Diener, 1996). This is not because they have a lot of money and material wealth but, rather, because they find their work engaging, are making some progress in the life goals that are important to them, are healthy, and are enmeshed in loving social relationships. Material wealth is mildly correlated with happiness, but the important conclusion about the money-happiness relation is this: "It is generally good for your happiness to *have* money, but toxic to your happiness to *want* money too much" (Diener & Biswas-Diener, 2008, p. 111). Wanting money too much leads to materialism, and materialism is negatively correlated, even toxic to happiness and subjective well-being (Kasser, 2002). Such a conclusion comes from comparing the subjective well-being of wealthy and impoverished people (Diener, Horwitz, & Emmons, 1985) and from comparing wealthy and impoverished nations (Diener, Diener, & Diener, 1995).

Consider the subjective well-being of the following people who face difficult circumstances in their lives: urban poor, people who live in a slum, sex workers, and rural peasants in a third world country (Cox, 2012), homeless migrants in China (Nielsen, Smyth, & Zhai, 2010; people with a mental disorder (e.g., a phobia; Bergsma, Vennhoven, ten Have, & de Graaf, 2011), people with a physical disorder (e.g., multiple sclerosis; Barak & Achiron, 2011), and people who work long hours for low wages (e.g., Beijing taxi drivers; Nielsen, Paritski, & Smyth, 2010). Most of the people studied in these samples were just as happy as the average person, but the important insight to be gained from studying the subjective well-being of those who face difficult circumstances is that the causes of happiness are the same in everyone. As these studies show, almost regardless of life circumstances, happiness

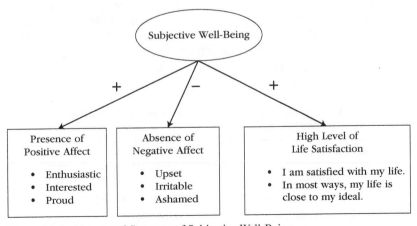

Figure 15.6 Nature and Structure of Subjective Well-Being

flows out of subjective appraisals of one's health, life achievements, feeling safe and secure, the quality of one's personal relationships, and feeling part of one's community.

Other research adds these two important points about happiness: (1) subjective well-being is a process—happiness comes from doing, rather than from having and (2) subjective well-being is beneficial to effective life functioning—the happier people are the better is their future health, work engagement, and relationship satisfaction (Diener & Biswas-Diener, 2008). This latter point is a fundamental one to those who study positive psychology as it supports the conclusion that happiness does not just feel good but it also has a positive causal effect on life success in terms of health, work, and relationships. The road from life success to happiness turns out to be a two-way street.

Eudaimonic Well-Being

Well-being comes in two forms: subjective well-being and eudaimonic well-being (Ryan & Deci, 2001). While subjective well-being (happiness) is the experience of positive affect, the absence of problems and negative affect, and a judgment of life satisfaction (Figure 15.6), eudaimonic well-being is the experience of seeking out challenges, exerting effort, being fully engaged and experiencing flow in what one is doing, acting on one's true values, and feeling fully alive and authentic (Ryan & Deci, 2001). In its essence, eudaimonic well-being is self-realization. Aristotle defined eudaimonic well-being as activity spent in the pursuit of excellence, and positive psychologists might suggest that eudaimonia is the active engagement in a meaningful life, even if that active engagement takes one through hardships and long periods of the absence of positive affect episodes. That is because eudaimonia is more about engagement, meaning, and self-realization than it is about happiness per se. Previously discussed motivational processes that represent eudaimonic well-being include the fully functional individual (Rogers), self-actualization (Maslow), psychological need satisfaction (Chapter 6), and positive self-functioning (Chapter 11). Those who study eudaimonic well-being do not argue that it is more important than hedonic well-being but, rather, that any analysis of psychological well-being needs to include both happiness and meaning—that is, both subjective (hedonic) well-being and personal growth (Compton, Smith, Cornish, & Qualls, 1996).

In thinking about eudaimonic well-being, the question is not so much Are you happy? as it is Do you live a meaningful, purposive life characterized by enthusiasm and clear goals? One way to assess level of eudaimonic well-being is the Purpose in Life Test (Schulenberg & Melton, 2010). As shown in Table 15.4, the PLT assesses one part a purposive life and one part an exciting life.

In the study of the antecedents of eudaimonic well-being, research emphasizes two: life pursuits (the pursuit of personal goals) and the quality of one's close relationships. In

Table 15.4   Items Representing the Two Factors of the Purpose in Life Test

A Purposive Life	An Exciting Life
· Life purpose	· Excitement in living
· Clear goals in life	· Newness of each day
· Life goal completion	· Capacity to discover meaning

terms of what one strives for in life, the pursuit of self-endorsed (as opposed to societally imposed) goals foreshadows eudaimonic well-being (Sheldon & Elliot, 1999; Sheldon & Kasser, 1998). Self-endorsed, or self-concordant, goals are those that fulfill basic psychological needs (autonomy, competence, relatedness) and are aligned with one's true self. This is so because the subjective experience of autonomy, competence, and relatedness functions as the "psychological nutriments" that underlie personal growth and eudaimonic well-being (Sheldon & Kasser, 1998). Of course, many people do not pursue intrinsic, psychological-need satisfying goals, and instead pursue "wealth, fame, and fortune" (i.e., "the American dream"). While the pursuit of extrinsic, materialistic goals is common, it is nevertheless a functional obstacle to eudaimonic well-being (Kasser & Ryan, 1996). The problem with pursuing wealth, fame, and fortune is that such pursuits have the side effect of moving people away from the pursuit of intrinsic, psychological-need satisfying goals (Kasser, 2002). The pursuit of materialistic goals also tends to take people away from the relationships in their lives, because people do what they need to do to earn money and fame (e.g., workaholics, materialists), rather than spend time involved in close relationships.

In terms of the quality of one's relationships, the psychological need that most reliably forecasts eudaimonic well-being is relatedness. Relatedness satisfaction explains why the presence of warm, trusting, intimate, and supportive interpersonal relationships in one's life are such solid predictors of eudaimonic well-being (DeNeve, 1999). For most positive psychologists, the pursuit of high-quality relationships is a rock-bottom fundamental to well-being.

Optimism

Most people are neither realistic nor accurate in how they think. Most of us think we are better than average, and most of us think we are better than average in all sorts of domains (e.g., driving, teaching, honesty, you name it). Many of us harbor within us a positivity bias. This pervasive tendency to see ourselves in a positive light is associated with well-being and enhanced performance (Taylor, 1989; Taylor & Brown, 1988). Optimism is basically expecting positive future events in one's life, while pessimism is basically expecting negative future life events (Peterson, 2000; Scheier & Carver, 1985, 1993). Optimists tend to believe that their actions will lead to positive outcomes. Believing this, they tend to exert greater effort to attain those sought-after outcomes and then tend to use relatively effective, proactive, and preventive problem-solving strategies while trying to do so (Carver, Scheier, Miller, & Fulford, 2009).

As an illustration, imagine asking a group of 13-year-olds about their optimism, asking "What is your attitude toward your future?", waiting three decades, and then finding them at age 43 to ask how their life is going (Daukantaite & Bergman, 2005). What these researchers found was that adolescent optimism was a rather strong predictor of adult well-being and life satisfaction. These researchers continued to following these participants until age 49 (Daukantaite & Zukauskiene, 2012). So, when their participants were 43, they assessed adult optimism by asking questions such as:

· Thoughts about my future give me good feelings.
· Even when I find myself in a difficult situation, I am convinced everything will turn out in the end.

These researchers found, once again, that the more optimistic the person was at 43, the more satisfied and happy that same person was at 49.

Of course, wishful thinking can do more harm than good (Oettingen, 1996), and it is often illusory (Freud, 1927). Still, empirical evidence supports the conclusion that people who are optimistic live more worthwhile lives than do people who are not optimistic. Optimists experience better psychological and physical health (Scheier & Carver, 1992), undertake more health-promoting behaviors (Peterson et al., 1998), show greater persistence and more effective problem solving, and are more socially popular (Peterson, 2000). The reason this is so is because optimism gives people a sense of hope and motivation that their future can indeed be improved, as in increasing school achievement, improving personal health, and growing in an interpersonal relationship (Seligman, 1991). Positive psychologists counter their critics by pointing out the difference between optimism and delusion—arguing that optimism is responsive to reality while delusions are not (Taylor, Collins, Skokan, & Aspinwall, 1989).

Optimism can be taught and learned (Seligman, Reivich, Jaycox, & Gillham, 1995). Optimism is generally taught through the enactment of the cognitive strategy that is the optimistic explanatory style (discussed in Chapter 10). Peterson (2006) argues that learned optimism is hard work and provides the example of the "hot seat technique." In this therapeutic strategy, the person creates dozens of index cards, with each card listing a different event capable of pushing the person's proverbial buttons and leaving him or her feeling burned out and helpless (e.g., the boss ignores you when passing by in the hallway). With each new card (event) the person is to try to identify the immediate, automatic, and pessimistic thoughts that are triggered. Then, just as rapidly, the person is to evaluate the evidence for the pessimistic thought and then generate an alternative and optimistic interpretation of the event (e.g., a negative outcome that is an attributionally unstable and controllable; recall Figure 10.10). When equipped with greater optimism, the more positive expectations and emotions open the door to ways of coping and performing that are more productive than are the competing ways of coping and performing.

Meaning

Existentialism is the study of the isolation and meaninglessness of the individual in an indifferent universe. Existentialism has been studied in one of two ways—the gloom and doom pessimism of Sartre or the optimism and sense of purpose of Victor Frankl. Although Frankl predated positive psychology, his logotherapy (logo = meaning) made popular the contention that, while there was no meaning to life in general, there was great meaning within each individual life. For Frankl, meaning was a need—a need of discovery and accomplishment that was as fundamental to humanity as hunger. When confronted with the awareness of the existential vacuum ("my life is meaningless"), Frankl argued that this awareness simply signaled that our will toward meaning was alive and well (just as hunger signals a need for food).

From a positive psychology point of view, it is important to understand meaning and how to cultivate it, because positive psychologists seek to elevate people's lives so beyond "merely tolerable" to deeply vital, fulfilling, and meaningful. A life without meaning is a life that becomes, at best, merely tolerable. A meaningful life is a life with purpose and significance (Steger, 2009). To give today's activity and struggle a sense of purpose, it helps if the person generates future-oriented goals, such as trying to graduate high school, fall in love during a summer vacation, or go to heaven in the afterlife. Connecting the activity of the day with a future goal effectively endows day-to-day activity with a sense of purpose it otherwise would not have. Significance often comes out of finding meaning in one's work/achievement, relationships, spirituality, or self-transcendence (e.g., one's children) (Emmons, 2003). But purpose and significance not only need to be found within a life, but they need to be created as well. The process of writing, for instance, if often beneficial to discovering and creating meaning in one's life by telling a story about how individual life events can be integrated into a larger, overarching understanding of personal values, strengths, and meaning (Baumeister & Vohs, 2002; King & Pennebaker, 1996).

Creating meaning is an active process in which people interpret the events in their lives (Taylor, 1983), find the benefit in these events (Davis, Nolen-Hoeksema, & Larsen, 1998), and discover the significance of what happens to them (Park & Folkman, 1997). That is, people create meaning in response to a health crisis (e.g., cancer), the loss of a loved one, academic failure, unemployment, and career burnout (Baumeister & Vohs, 2002). As Frankl often said (paraphrasing), success is not our greatest achievement but, rather, it is facing a difficult life challenge with dignity and integrity. People who successfully create meaning within a crisis typically do so by first framing the event as a burden or bad event. They then explain how that bad event set in progress a developmental trajectory in which the bad event is ultimately translated into a positive outcome. In doing so, they essentially use the burden as a springboard to create a self-endowed with strengths such as purpose, moral goodness, and strong efficacy (McAdams, Diamond, de St. Aubin, & Mansfield, 1997). In contrast, people who do not counter life's burdens with purpose, moral goodness, and efficacy (i.e., meaning) are significantly more likely to suffer mental pathology in the wake of the bad event (McAdams, 1993, 1996). From this point of view, the act of creating meaning helps prevent future sickness (e.g., depression).

Positivity

Positivity represents the positive emotions in life: joy, gratitude, serenity, interest, hope, pride, amusement, inspiration, awe, and love (Fredrickson, 2009). These emotions function differently than do their negative counterparts. Negative emotions such as anger, disgust, and fear grab and intensely narrow our attention toward the aversive environmental object. If we are casually eating a meal and a bug walks onto our plate, we quickly and strongly experience disgust that arrests our full attention to what that bug is doing and how we can get rid of both the bug and the now-spoiled meal. The cluster of positive emotions that represents positivity works differently. Positive emotions are subtle, and they broaden—rather than narrow—attention.

The "broaden-and-build" theory of positivity proposes that positive emotional experiences first broaden the person's momentary thought-action repertoires, and this greater open-mindedness second leads to actions that build or growing the sort of personal resources listed in Table 15.3 and Figure 15.5 (Cohn & Fredrickson, 2009; Fredrickson, 2009). "Broaden" means that people become more open-minded and more cognitively flexible, as the positive emotionality widens or expands what thoughts come to mind (Isen & Daubman, 1984), thereby enhancing creativity (Isen et al., 1985), problem solving

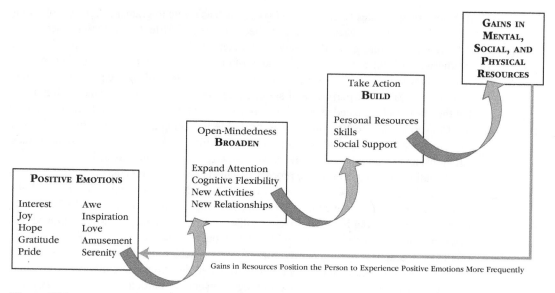

Figure 15.7 The Broaden-and-Build Theory of Positive Emotions

(Isen, Daubman, & Nowicki, 1987) and the urges to explore and play (Isen & Reeve, 2005). This broadening of cognition and experience allows people to engage in the sort of actions that build mental resources (facilitate learning), social resources (facilitate relationships), and physical resources (facilitate health) (Fredrickson, 2009). Gains in mental, social, and physical resources then, in turn, increase the likelihood and frequency at which the person experiences positive emotions in the future. Figure 15.7 graphically illustrates the processes that take place with the broaden-and-build theory of positive emotions. As you can see, the events in Figure 15.7 depict an upward spiral to positive functioning because positive emotions engender ways of thinking and acting that grow the sort of strengths that make it more likely to experience positive emotions in the first place.

The broaden-and-build theory of positive emotion was created to explain the conditions under which people flourish and grow, rather than flounder and stagnate. To flourish it seems that we need our experiences of positive emotions to outweigh our experiences of negative emotions. In her early work, Fredrickson observed people and groups and noted when flourishing and personal/social growth occurred and when it did not. She found that a stream of experience in which positive emotions occurred at least three times as often as did negative experiences was the tipping point to positivity. For Fredrickson (2009), the three-to-one ratio of positive emotions to negative emotions (the exact ratio was 2.9 to 1) was a necessary condition for positive emotions to accumulate and compound on each other in such a way as to create the crucial tipping point at which floundering became flourishing. This raises the interesting practical question of what one might do during the day to reach this tipping point to positivity. Hence, we turn to the topic of interventions and therapy within the positive psychology framework.

INTERVENTIONS

Compared to other programs of therapy (e.g., cognitive-behavioral therapy), positive psychology does not yet have a host of validated intervention techniques. To lay the foundation on which to build such techniques, one group of authors created and recommended the following four "happiness exercises" (Seligman, Steen, Park, & Peterson, 2005):

1. *Gratitude visit.* Write and deliver a letter of gratitude to someone who has been especially kind to you but was never really thanked.

2. *Three good things in life.* At the end of each day, write down three things that went well and identify the cause of each.

3. *You at your best.* Write about a time when you functioned at your best. Reflect on the personal resources that made that functioning possible.

4. *Identify signature strengths.* Identify up to five personal signature strengths (from a list such as the one in Table 15.3) and find a way to use each in a new way.

In testing the benefits of these therapeutic interventions, the general empirical strategy has been to assess the baseline psychological well-being (happiness) and ill-being (depression) of members of the community, have these individuals carry out one of the above exercises for several weeks, and then reassess participants' psychological well-being and ill-being over time (one week later, one month later, six months later) to see how completing each exercise produced a longitudinal increase in well-being and a longitudinal decrease in ill-being.

Consider the gratitude exercise, which has generally been the most effective of the four exercises listed above (Seligman et al., 2005). One research team asked college students to write letters of gratitude once a week for four weeks (Toepfer, Cichy, & Peters, 2012). They were asked to write nontrivial letters of gratitude (*not* "thank you notes") that expressed heartfelt appreciation for someone's valuable and altruistically intended aid. Compared to a control group of participants, those who wrote and delivered letters of gratitude experienced increases in happiness and life satisfaction and decreases in depression. The conclusion seems to be that happy people tend to be grateful people (Watkins, 2008).

Another research team worked collaboratively with Portuguese elementary school students and their teachers and parents to build these children's psychological strength of hope (Marques, Lopez, & Pais-Ribeiro, 2011). For these researchers, hope is the threefold capacity to conceptualize a goal to seek, generate a specific strategy to attain that goal, and grow the confidence needed to sustain the effort necessary to attain the goal (e.g., set a goal, endorse a mastery belief, grow self-efficacy, respectively; Snyder, 2002). Students were invited to participate in a five-week "Building Hope for the Future" intervention in which students conceptualized a clear future goal to strive for, generated a range of possible goal-attainment strategies, and learned how to reappraise obstacles into challenges. Children's hope, life satisfaction, and self-worth were assessed prior to the intervention (a baseline measure), immediately after the intervention ended, six months later, and again 18 months later. As shown in Figure 15.8, the children who participated in the intervention showed significant gains in hope (CHS scores), life satisfaction (not pictured), and self-worth (SWS scores). Further, these gains were maintained more than a year after the intervention ended.

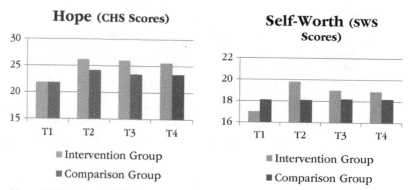

Figure 15.8 Hope (CHS Scores in Left Panel) and Self-Worth (SWS Scores in Right Panel) Scores over Time for Children Who Did and Did Not Participate in the "Building Hope for the Future" Intervention

The benefits gained from these positive psychology "strengths interventions" are somewhere between small and moderate, but never large (Quinlan, Swain, & Vella-Brodrick, 2012). Interventions that ask people to identify their strengths, such as the four listed above, generally produced only small benefits. The strength interventions that tend to produce moderate benefits are those that go beyond identifying strengths to also further grow and develop those strengths, as was done in the "Building Hope for the Future" intervention summarized above.

CRITICISMS

After spending a few hours reading Maslow, Rogers, or an article on positive psychology, it is easy to feel good and optimistic about yourself and about human beings in general. For instance, if you read any one of the 15 chapters in Rogers's (1980) *A Way of Being*, you will likely experience a sense of personal enrichment. Still, one must square the optimism of humanism and positive psychology with daily reality to wonder if it is overly naive to conceptualize human nature as intrinsically good. If human nature is something to be nurtured rather than constrained, then one wonders why hatred, prejudice, crime, exploitation, and war persist throughout human history without interruption (Geller, 1982). Perhaps people are not so intrinsically honorable and trustworthy. Perhaps people have within themselves not only positive human potentialities but also the potential to destroy themselves and others (Baumeister & Campbell, 1999; May, 1982; Staub, 1999). One can imagine the potentially adverse consequences of a parent or a government that presupposes benevolent inner guides and therefore gives wide latitude to misbehaving children or citizens (Bandura, 1999). There is some practical truth to the notion that "bad is stronger than good" (Baumeister, Bratslavsky, Finkenauer, & Vohs, 2001). It seems that the humanistic view emphasizes only one part of human nature.

A second criticism is that humanistic theorists use a number of vague and ill-defined constructs. It is difficult to pinpoint precisely what an "organismic valuing process" and a "fully functioning individual" are, for example. Any theoretical construct that evades a precise operational definition must remain scientifically dubious. For this reason, humanistic views on motivation have been harshly criticized (Daniels, 1988; Neher, 1991), and these criticisms were instrumental to the rise and eventual popularity of positive psychology.

A third criticism questions how one is to know what is *really* wanted or what is *really* needed by the actualizing tendency (Geller, 1982). Early learning and socialization can also yield the personal conviction that a way of thinking or behaving is right and natural. For example, if a person is 100 percent confident that abortion is bad, wrong, and something to be refused, then how is that person to know for sure that such a preference is a product of the organismic valuing process rather than an internalization of societal conditions of worth? Knowledge of right and wrong can be difficult to trace back to the origins of its true source (although enhanced "mindfulness" can help a great deal in this regard). If standards of right and wrong are introjected from infancy, a person can be self-deceived into thinking that his preferences are his own rather than his parents'.

SUMMARY

Humanistic psychology stresses the notions of inherent potentialities, holism, and strivings toward personal fulfillment. In practice, humanistic psychology is about identifying and developing human potential. Positive psychology looks at people's lives to ask, What could be? In practice, positive psychology seeks to build people's strengths so to cultivate psychological wellness.

Self-actualization refers to the full realization and use of one's talents, capacities, and potentialities. In his need hierarchy, Maslow made the distinction between deficiency needs and growth needs. For Rogers, one fundamental need—the actualizing tendency—subsumed and coordinated all other motives so as to serve the fundamental purpose of enhancing and actualizing the self. With socialization, children learn societal conditions of worth on which their behavior and personal characteristics are judged. As a consequence, all of us live in two worlds—the inner world of the actualizing tendencies and organismic valuation and the outer world of social priorities, conditions of worth, and conditional regard. When people move away from organismic valuing and toward external conditions of worth, they adopt facades and reject or deny personal characteristics, preferences, and beliefs. The terms *congruence* and *incongruence* describe the extent to which an individual denies and rejects personal qualities (incongruence) or accepts the full range of his or her personal characteristics and desires (congruence). The congruent, fully functioning individual lives in close proximity to the actualizing tendency and therefore experiences a marked sense of autonomy, openness to experience, and personal growth.

Causality orientations reflect the extent of self-determination in the personality and concern differences in people's understanding of what causes and regulates their behavior. For the person with an autonomy–causality orientation, behavior arises in response to needs and interests with a full sense of personal choice. For the person with a control-causality orientation, inner guides are relatively ignored as behavior arises in response to external expectations and controls and signals of pay, status, and extrinsic reward. Autonomy-oriented individuals experience relatively greater positive functioning than do control-oriented individuals, including greater attitude-behavior congruence and longer-term maintenance of behavioral changes such as losing weight.

A strong commitment to societal conditions of worth leads people into a process of seeking validation from others. In social interaction, validation-seeking individuals strive to prove their self-worth, competence, and likability. Validation-seeking individuals are more vulnerable to experiencing anxiety and depression. In contrast, growth-seeking individuals center their strivings on learning, improving, and reaching personal potential.

Interpersonal relationships support the actualizing tendency in at least four ways: helping others (as in therapy), relating to others in authentic ways, promoting the freedom to learn (as in education), and defining the self. Interpersonal relationships characterized by warmth, genuineness, empathy, acceptance, and confirmation of the other person's capacity for self-determination provide the social climate that optimally supports the actualization tendency. Another problem with which humanistic thinkers wrestle is that of evil—namely, how much of human nature is inherently evil and why do some people enjoy inflicting suffering on others? Some humanistic thinkers argue that human nature is inherently good and evil arises only when experience injures and damages the person. Other humanists assume that both benevolence and malevolence are inherent in everyone—that human nature needs to internalize a benevolent value system before it can avoid evil.

Positive psychology looks at people's mental health and the quality of their lives to ask, What could be? It seeks to build people's strengths, and it makes the study of these strengths its subject matter. Positive psychology places a particular importance on happiness, which involves both subjective well-being—positive affect, absence of negative affect, life satisfaction—and eudaimonia—self-realization through the effortful pursuit of authenticity and personal growth. Flourishing is more than the absence of mental illness and depends on well-being that grows out of continuous personal growth, high-quality relationships, and a life characterized by purpose, optimism, meaning, and eudaimonic well-being. To cultivate these strengths, positive psychology therapy offers "happiness exercises" such as gratuity visits.

The chapter concludes by offering a number of criticisms of a humanistic understanding of motivation, including Pollyanna optimism, imprecise scientific concepts, and unknown origins of inner guides.

READINGS FOR FURTHER STUDY

Humanistic Theorists

HARDEMAN, M. (1979). A dialogue with Abraham Maslow. *Journal of Humanistic Psychology, 19*, 23–28.

ROGERS, C. R. (1959). A theory of therapy, personality, and interpersonal relationships, as developed in the client-centered framework. In S. Koch (Ed.), *Psychology: A study of science* (Vol. 3, pp. 184–256). New York: McGraw-Hill.

ROGERS, C. R. (1995). What understanding and acceptance mean to me. *Journal of Humanistic Psychology, 35*, 7–22.

Empirical Tests of Humanistic Hypotheses

DECI, E. L., & RYAN, R. M. (1985). The General Causality Orientations Scale: Self-determination in personality. *Journal of Research in Personality, 19*, 109–134.

DYKMAN, B. M. (1998). Integrating cognitive and motivational factors in depression: Initial tests of a goal-orientation approach. *Journal of Personality and Social Psychology, 74*, 139–158.

SHELDON, K. M., ARNDT, J., & HOUSER-MARKO, L. I. (2003). In search of the organismic valuing process: The human tendency to move towards beneficial goal choices. *Journal of Personality, 71*, 835–869.

Positive Psychology

MARQUES, S. C., LOPEZ, S. J., & PAIS-RIBEIRO, J. L. (2011). "Building hope for the future": A program to foster strengths in middle-school students. *Journal of Happiness Studies, 12*, 139–152.

SELIGMAN, M. E. P., & CSIKSZENTMIHALYI, M. (2000). Positive psychology: An introduction. *American Psychologist, 55*, 5–14.

SELIGMAN, M. E. P., STEEN, T. A., PARK, N., & PETERSON, C. (2005). Positive psychology progress: Empirical validation of interventions. *American Psychologist, 60*, 410–421.

TOEPFER, S. M., CICHY, K., & PETERS, P. (2012). Letters of gratitude: Further evidence for author benefits. *Journal of Happiness Studies, 13*, 187–201.

Chapter 16

Unconscious Motivation

PSYCHODYNAMIC PERSPECTIVE

    Psychoanalytic Becomes Psychodynamic

    Dual-Instinct Theory

    Contemporary Psychodynamic Theory

THE UNCONSCIOUS

    Freudian Unconscious

    Adaptive Unconscious

    Implicit Motivation

    Priming

PSYCHODYNAMICS

    Repression

    Suppression

    Do the Id and Ego Actually Exist?

EGO PSYCHOLOGY

    Ego Development

    Ego Defense

    Ego Effectance

OBJECT RELATIONS THEORY

CRITICISMS

SUMMARY

READINGS FOR FURTHER STUDY

Imagine accompanying your friend on his visit to a psychiatrist. To begin the session, your friend undergoes hypnosis. Once hypnotized, the psychiatrist suggests that your friend brought a newspaper with him to the session and that once he awakes, he will want to read it. In actuality, your friend brought no newspaper. Furthermore, the therapist suggests that upon his awakening, he will look for the newspaper but will be unable to find it. The therapist tells your friend that, after several minutes of searching, an idea will occur to him that another person has taken his newspaper—that the other person has, in fact, stolen it.

The therapist also suggests that your friend's discovery will provoke him to anger. Furthermore, the therapist tells your friend to direct that anger toward the thief. Unfortunately for you, the psychiatrist next tells your friend that you are that thief. The therapist tells your friend that, in his fit of anger, he will first insist and will then demand that you return his newspaper. To conclude the hypnosis session, the psychiatrist tells your friend that he will forget that the source of all this (mis)information was actually a series of suggestions given to him by the therapist.

Your friend awakens. He begins to chat leisurely and cheerily about the day's events, and then remarks, "Incidentally, that reminds me of something I read in today's newspaper. I'll show you." Your friend looks around, does not see his newspaper, and begins to search for it. You begin to feel a hint of anxiety because you have been with your friend all day and know that he has neither read nor purchased a paper. Then, suddenly, he turns toward you with piercing eyes. Accusingly, your friend announces that you took his newspaper, and he now wants it back. You are starting to think coming along was not such a good idea and rather sheepishly say that you know nothing of the newspaper. But your friend persists. He is truly upset. With his anger piqued, your friend forcefully accuses you of stealing his newspaper. He goes further, saying that you took it because you are too cheap to buy one of your own. To substantiate his accusation, he says someone saw you steal his newspaper and told him about it.

This is no longer funny. Your friend *really* believes you stole his newspaper, and he really wants it back.

What does this hypnosis session illustrate (based on Fromm, 1941)? The scenario illustrates that human beings can have thoughts, feelings, and emotions that they subjectively feel are their own but, in fact, have been introjected from another source. Your friend wanted something—to show you an item in the newspaper. He thought something—you stole his newspaper. And he felt something—anger against an alleged thief. But your friend's wants, thoughts, and feelings were not his own in the sense that they did not originate within him. Yet, your friend surely acted as if those wants, thoughts, and feelings were his own. Such a demonstration of the posthypnotic suggestion testifies to the paradox that while we can be sure of what we want, think, and feel, we can also have little idea as to the source of what we want, think, and feel. The whole scenario bears witness to the idea that motivation can arise from a source that lies outside of conscious awareness and volitional intent.

PSYCHODYNAMIC PERSPECTIVE

In contrast to humanism (Chapter 15), the psychodynamic approach presents a largely deterministic and pessimistic image of human nature. Psychoanalysis is deterministic in that it holds that the ultimate cause of motivation and behavior derives from biologically endowed and socially acquired impulses that determine our desires, thoughts, feelings, and behaviors, regardless of whether we like it. Psychoanalysis is further deterministic in that personality changes little after puberty. Thus, many of the motivational impulses of an adult can be traced to events that took place in childhood. Motivation comes across as something that happens to us, rather than as something we choose or create. Psychoanalysis is also relatively pessimistic in tone, because it places the spotlight on sexual and aggressive urges, conflict, anxiety, repression, defense mechanisms, and a host of emotional burdens, vulnerabilities, and shortcomings of human nature. It sees anxiety as inevitable and the collapse of personality as a matter of degree rather than as an exceptional event that happens to only a few of us. We are all dogged by guilt, anxiety is our constant companion, narcissism and homophobia are common, and distortions of reality are modus operandi. It is not a pretty picture, Freud said, but it is reality. In his mind, Freud was not a pessimist; he was a realist.

Psychoanalysis is strangely appealing and wonderfully popular. Part of its appeal is that, in reading psychoanalytic theory, the reader comes face to face with some difficult aspects of human nature. According to psychoanalysis, people "are more interested in getting sexual pleasure than they will admit" and people have "blind rages, wild lusts, and parasitic infantile longings" (Holt, 1989). These mysterious aspects of human nature present us with a psychological riddle that pulls in our curiosity. Who can resist wanting to learn more about a theory that reveals the secrets of the mind—secret crushes and jealousies, fantasies and desires, memories of things done and not done, and all sorts of hidden intrigue and despair?

Part of the appeal of psychoanalysis is that it makes the unconscious its subject matter. Thus, psychoanalysis willingly goes "where no theory has gone before" (to paraphrase *Star Trek*)—into dreams, hypnosis, inaccessible memories, fantasy, and all the hidden forces that shape our motives and behaviors without our awareness and without our consent. In doing so, psychoanalysis offers a chance to talk about a deeply interesting subject matter—the content of our own private subjective experience and why unwanted desires and fears make their home there.

Psychoanalytic Becomes Psychodynamic

Decades ago, the terms *psychoanalytic* and *psychodynamic* could be used as synonyms. A growing number of scholars, however, found themselves in the uncomfortable position of being very interested in the study of unconscious mental processes but not wanting to study those motivational processes within a Freudian framework. They rejected the explanatory power of Sigmund Freud's dual-instinct theory of motivation (discussed next), for instance, yet they focused on the empirical study of unconscious mental processes, broadly defined as motivation, affect, feelings, needs, motives, and even intuition and hunches. Today, *psychoanalytic* refers to practitioners who remain committed to most traditional Freudian principles. *Psychodynamic* refers to the study of dynamic unconscious mental processes. In other words, one can study unconscious mental processes (e.g., prejudice, depression, thought suppression, defense mechanisms) inside or outside the Freudian tradition. That is, many researchers study psychodynamic processes without embracing the psychoanalytic approach.

Figure 16.1 graphically communicates the idea that unconscious motivation can be studied inside or outside of a Freudian understanding of the unconscious. Under psychodynamic unconscious motivational processes, researchers study either the adaptive unconscious or implicit motives. Chapter 7 presented the findings and conclusions concerning the implicit motives of achievement, affiliation, and power. This chapter adds the empirical study of the adaptive unconscious. This is a nice addition to the goal of understanding motivation and emotion because the adaptive unconscious has proven to be a rich storehouse of mental activity. One example of the productivity of this research tradition has been the Implicit Association Test (recall Box 7).

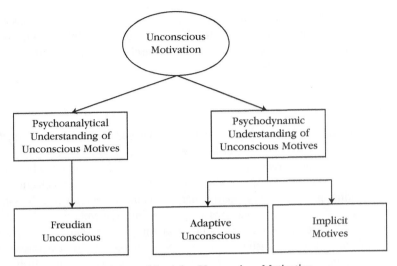

Figure 16.1   Three Ways of Studying Unconscious Motivation

Imagine sitting in front of a computer to take the Implicit Association Test (IAT; Greenwald & Farnham, 2000; Lane, Banaji, Nosek, & Greenwald, 2007; https://implicit .harvard.edu/implicit/demo). Images appear on the screen, and you are to press a key as rapidly as you can to categorize the stimulus into one group category or another. What the IAT is measuring is how long it takes you to make that categorization (latency of response). Specifically, the IAT involves four steps:

1. Press one of two keys (*e* or *i*) for faces of Black or White. For instance, each time a face for the race of White appears, press *e*; each time a face for the race Black appears, press *i*.

2. Press one of two keys (*e* or *i*) for words representing a positive (happy) or a negative (rotten) valence. For instance, each time a positive word appears, press *e*; each time a negative word appears, press *i*.

3. Press *e* each time an image of White or negative word appears; press *i* each time an image of Black or positive appears.

4. Press *i* each time an image of Black or negative word appears; press *i* each time an image of White or positive appears.

Faster key presses for [Black + positive and White + negative] than for [White + positive and Black + negative] in steps 3 and 4 indicate a stronger association of Black than White with a positive valence. Another name for "stronger association" is prejudice. These *automatically activated associations* as measured by the IAT do not correlate with people's self-report attitudes, and this lack of correspondence suggests a difference between conscious or explicit prejudice versus unconscious or implicit prejudice. IAT scores using different sets of images predict a wide range of outcomes, including not only racial prejudice but also gender prejudice, obesity prejudice, age prejudice, nationality prejudice, and several other prejudices. IAT scores also do a good job of predicting brand preferences (e.g., Coke vs. Pepsi, Apple vs. Samsung), political preferences, and even the anxieties and phobias people hold (Greenwald, Poehlman, Uhlmann, & Banaji, 2009).

The present chapter largely discusses psychodynamic unconscious motivation in ways that are not necessarily based in traditional Freudian principles. But to understand the foundation of the psychoanalytical perspective, the chapter begins where Freud began—namely, his controversial dual-instinct theory.

Dual-Instinct Theory

A physician by training, Sigmund Freud viewed motivation as regulated by impulsive biological forces. The human body was seen as a complex energy system organized for the purpose of increasing and decreasing its energies through behavior. Some behaviors increased bodily energy (eating, breathing), while other behaviors depleted energy (working, playing). Some bodily energy was mental energy, and the mind needed mental energy to perform its functions (e.g., thinking, remembering). The mind received this psychic energy from the body's physical energy. The source of all physical energy was biological drive (or instinct), which was a biologically rooted force "emanating within the organism and penetrating to the mind" (Freud, 1915). Hence, instinctual bodily drives explained the source of all motivation.

For Freud, there were as many biological drives as there were different bodily demands (e.g., food, water, sleep). But Freud recognized that there were too many different bodily needs to list. Instead of compiling a comprehensive taxonomy of bodily drives, Freud (1920, 1927) emphasized two general categories: instincts for life and instincts for death.

The first class of instincts—Eros, the life instincts—are the more easily defined of the two. Eros instincts maintain life and ensure individual and collective (species) survival. Thus, instincts for food, water, air, sleep, and the like all contribute to the life and survival of the individual. These are instincts for self-preservation. Instincts for sex, nurturance, and affiliation contribute to the life and survival of the species, a reproductive emphasis Freud borrowed from Darwin (Ritvo, 1990). These are instincts for species preservation. Freud understood the biological drives in the same spirit as the present book presented thirst, hunger, and sex as core biological needs in Chapter 4. In his discussions of the life instincts, Freud (1917) gave primary emphasis to sex, although he conceptualized sex quite broadly as "pleasure seeking" (including thumb-sucking, being tickled, being rocked, being caressed, being tossed in the air, rhythmic stimulation, masturbation, and sexual contact).

The second class of instincts—Thanatos, the death instincts—push the individual toward rest, inactivity, and energy conservation. An absence of any bodily disturbance could be achieved only through total rest, which was death. In discussing the death instincts, Freud gave primary emphasis to aggression. When focused on the self, aggression manifests itself in self-criticism, sadism, depression, suicide, masochism, alcoholism, drug addiction, and unnecessary risk taking such as gambling. When focused on others, aggression manifests itself in anger, hate, prejudice, verbal insult, cruelty, rivalry, revenge, murder, and war. For example, a hostile joke about an ethnic group represented an expression of the Thanatos (Freud, 1905).

These bodily based instinctual drives toward life and death—sex and aggression—provide the energy to motivate behavior. But people did not just impulsively act on their inborn sexual and aggressive energies. Instead, the individual learned from experience to direct his or her behavior toward need-satisfying aims. Through experience, which is a synonym for "psychosexual development" or "personality," the individual learns defensive reactions for managing her ever-present sexual and aggressive energies. One's habitual, learned manner of defense is what Freud meant by the ego. Thus, instinctual drives provide the energy for behavior, while the ego provides its direction—attain biological (instinctual) satisfaction in the most socially appropriate and in the least anxiety-provoking way. Recall that motivation study concerns all those forces that energize and direct behavior, and for Freud energy came from the biological drives while direction came from ego defense that managed the bodily and mental energy that arose from these biological drives.

The dual-instinct theory of motivation represents psychoanalysis, circa 1930. Times have changed. Few contemporary psychoanalysts understand motivation as a function of the dual-instinct theory (Kolb, Cooper, & Fishman, 1995; Westen, 1991), and this has been true for several decades (Berkowitz, 1962). No contemporary theorist endorses the validity of the thanatos. Notice, for instance, that none of Freud's death instincts (biological drives) were included in Chapter 4.

The goal of psychoanalytic therapy has always been to understand the confusing activities of the unconscious and therefore free the ego to deal with reality. To do so, contemporary psychodynamic therapists focus more and more on cognitive and interpersonal forces, and less and less on biological and intrapersonal forces (Wegner, 1989; Westen, 1998). Contemporary psychodynamic therapists and researchers do not write much about ids and egos, and they do not spend much of their time undertaking archaeological-like expeditions in search of lost memories that will lead to a discovery of the patient's present-day psychopathology (Kolb et al., 1995; Mitchell, 1988; Wachtel, 1993; Westen, 1998). Instead, the contemporary focus is decidedly interpersonal because it centers on helping people recognize, improve upon, or outright run away from problematic interpersonal relationships (Hazan & Shaver, 1987; Loevinger, 1976; Scharff & Scharff, 1995; Westen et al., 1991). For example, a common problem in psychodynamic therapy is recognizing and developing the skill necessary to overcome the chronic tendency to involve oneself in intimate relationships with the wrong kind of person (Greenberg & Mitchell, 1983; Westen et al., 1991).

Contemporary Psychodynamic Theory

A lot has changed since Freud. Today, four postulates define psychodynamic theory, research, and practice (Westen, 1998). That these principles are contemporary, as opposed to classically Freudian, is important for two reasons. First, psychodynamic thought has had time to put Freud's insightful propositions to empirical tests to see which postulates do, and which postulates do not, stand the objective tests of time and empirical evaluation. Second, most readers will be more familiar with Freud's classical psychoanalysis than they will be with the contemporary approach, a fact that makes it necessary to review the following core postulates (Westen, 1998):

1. *The Unconscious.* Much of mental life is unconscious.

2. *Psychodynamics.* Mental processes operate in parallel with one another.

3. *Ego Development.* Healthy development involves moving from an immature, socially dependent personality to one that is more mature and interdependent with others.

4. *Object Relations Theory.* Mental representations of self and others form in childhood that guide the person's later social motivations and relationships.

The first postulate emphasizes the unconscious. It argues emphatically that thoughts, feelings, and desires exist at the unconscious level. Thus, because unconscious mental life affects behavior, people can behave in ways that are inexplicable, even to themselves.

The second postulate emphasizes psychodynamics. It argues that motivational and emotional processes frequently operate in parallel with one another—people commonly want and fear the same thing at the same time. It is the rule, not the exception, that people have conflicting feelings that motivate them in opposing ways. Hence, people commonly harbor divergent conscious and unconscious racial (Fazio, Jackson, Dunton, & Williams, 1995) and gender (Banaji & Hardin, 1996) attitudes that produce simultaneous approach and avoidant behavior. That is, a person can be both highly prejudiced (unconsciously) and not at all prejudiced (consciously) at the same time.

The third postulate emphasizes ego development. Contemporary ego psychologists focus on how we developmentally leave behind our immature, fragile, egocentric, and narcissistic beginnings in life to become relatively mature, resilient, empathic, and socially responsible beings.

The fourth postulate highlights object relations theory. It argues that stable personality patterns begin to form in childhood as people construct mental representations of the self and others. Once formed, these beliefs about self and others shape enduring patterns of motivation (relatedness, anxiety) that guide the adult's interpersonal activity and quality of relationships.

THE UNCONSCIOUS

The first core postulate of the contemporary psychodynamic study is the existence and importance of the unconscious. In the early years, scientific psychology had a difficult time with the empirical exploration of the unconscious. After all, if the unconscious is hidden from both private consciousness and public observation, then how can a researcher ever gain access to it? This problem is not an insurmountable one, however, any more than concepts such as electrons are insurmountable to those who study physics. Like unconscious mental processes, electrons and the expanding universe are also difficult, but not impossible, to measure and to study scientifically.

Freud believed that the individual must express strong unconscious urges and impulses, although in a disguised and socially acceptable form. The unconscious is therefore a "shadow phenomenon" that cannot be known directly but can be inferred only from its indirect manifestations (Erdelyi, 1985). Believing the unconscious constituted the "primary process" while consciousness was but a "secondary process," Freud and his colleagues explored the contents and processes of the unconscious in a number of creative ways, including hypnosis, free association, dream analysis, humor, projective tests, errors and slips of the tongue, and so-called accidents (Exner, 1986; Freud, 1905, 1914, 1920, 1927, 1932; Murray, 1943).

It has been a rocky and emotionally charged 100-year debate, but the conclusion that much of mental life is unconscious is now largely and widely accepted as true (Kahneman, 2011; Westen, 1998; Wilson, 2002). The idea that people have motives and intentions that lie outside of their everyday awareness is readily accepted by motivation researchers (Bargh & Chartrand, 1999; Wegner, 1994). Instead of debating whether some of mental life is unconscious, the debate now centers on three different portrayals of the unconscious. The three views can be called the Freudian unconscious, the adaptive unconscious, and implicit motivation. Just as Freud used methods such as hypnosis and slips of the tongue, modern-day psychologists use methods such as subliminal activation, priming, selective attention, unconscious learning, procedural learning, and implicit memory to study various aspects of the non-Freudian unconscious (Bargh, Chen, & Burrows, 1996; Greenwald & Farnham, 2000; Kihlstrom, 1987; Lane et al., 2007; Steele & Aronson, 1995).

Freudian Unconscious

The division of mental life into what is conscious and what is unconscious is the fundamental premise of psychoanalysis (Freud, 1923). Freud rejected the idea that consciousness was the essence of mental life and therefore divided the mind into three components: conscious, preconscious, and unconscious. The conscious (i.e., short-term memory, consciousness) includes all the thoughts, feelings, sensations, memories, and experiences that a person is aware of at any given time. The preconscious stores all the thoughts, feelings, and memories that are absent from immediate consciousness but can be retrieved into consciousness with a little prompting (e.g., you are aware of but are not currently thinking about your name or what color ink these words are printed in). The most important, and by far the largest, component of mental life is the unconscious. The unconscious is the mental storehouse of inaccessible instinctual impulses, repressed experiences, childhood (before language) memories, and strong but unfulfilled wishes and desires (Freud, 1915, 1923).

To illustrate the Freudian view of the unconscious, consider unconscious activity during dreaming. For Freud, daily tensions continually mounted in the unconscious and were vented during dreaming. Because dreams vent unconscious tensions, dreams provided an opportunity for accessing the unconscious' wishful core. Assuming that the person could recall his or her dreams, dream analysis began by asking the individual to report a dream's storyline and ended with the therapist's interpretation of the underlying meaning of the dream. A dream's storyline represents its manifest content (its face value and defensive facade), while the symbolic meanings of the events in the storyline represent its latent content (its underlying meaning and wishful core). Because the explicit expression of unconscious wishes would be anxiety-provoking and ego-threatening (and would awaken the dreamer), the unconscious expresses its impulses through the latent and symbolic, rather than the obvious and manifest.

As one illustration, consider the following dream reported by one of Freud's patients (Freud, 1900):

A whole crowd of children—all of her brothers, sisters, and cousins of both sexes—were romping in a field. Suddenly, they all grew wings, flew away, and disappeared.

The patient first had this dream as a young child and continued to have this same dream repeatedly into adulthood. In the dream, all of the patient's brothers, sisters, and cousins flew away, and she alone remained in the field. According to Freud, the dream does not make much sense at the manifest level, and to gain an understanding of its meaning and significance, the analysis must take place within the latent content, using the technique of free association. At the latent level, the dream is (for this particular person) a death wish from the Thanatos. According to Freud, the dreamer is wishing that her brothers, sisters, and cousins would all sprout wings and fly away like butterflies (a child's view of the soul leaving the body upon death), leaving her to the full attention and affection of her parents.

Before we can conclude that dreams function to vent unconscious wishes, however, we must acknowledge what contemporary research has discovered since Freud. In addition to somewhat serving a venting function, dreams further serve (1) *neurophysiological activity* in that the brain stem (not unconscious wishes) produces random neural input for the neocortex to process and make sense of (Crick & Mitchison, 1986); (2) a *memory consolidating function* as memories of the day are moved from short-term into long-term memory (Greenberg & Perlman, 1993); (3) a *stress-buffering or coping function* by providing an opportunity to pair defense mechanisms against threatening events such as job stress (Koulack, 1993); and (4) a *problem-solving function* in that, during dreaming, people process information, organize ideas, and arrive at creative constructions for solving their problems (Winson, 1992). While some evidence supports the idea that dreams provide an outlet for venting wishes and tensions (Fisher & Greenberg, 1996) and that nightmares are associated with anxiety symptoms (Levin & Nielsen, 2007), it is also true that Freud's concept of the dream was too limited. Dreams express unconscious wishes, but dreams are also neurophysiological, cognitive, coping, and problem-solving events that have little to do with unconscious wishes (Fisher & Greenberg, 1996; Levin, 1990; Moffitt, Kramer, & Hoffman, 1993).

Adaptive Unconscious

The empirical study of the non-Freudian unconscious began with a patient with epilepsy. Because of the debilitating severity of his daily seizures, he had his hippocampus removed and, as a result, had amnesia. He was brought into a laboratory for several consecutive days to practice a motor skill. As he walked into the laboratory each new day, he had absolutely no memory of being there before, no memory of the people who worked there, and no memory of the motor skill he practiced each day. Still, he showed rather marked improvement in the motor skill day after day. This experiment suggested the existence of an adaptive unconscious.

In his popular book, *Stranger to Ourselves*, Timothy Wilson (2002) described the nature of the adaptive unconscious through the analogy of an airplane. Most of the time, the pilot just puts the plane on automatic pilot. On automatic pilot, the plane does a fine job of attending to its environment, initiating efficient action, setting goals, and keeping a mechanical eye out for signals of danger. Every once in a while, the pilot breaks in to make an intentional change or adjustment. The adaptive unconscious runs on automatic pilot as it carries out countless computations and innumerable adjustments during acts such as tying your shoes, driving a car, or playing the piano.

An illustrative YouTube video shows New York City commuters climbing a flight of stairs to exit the subway. A surprisingly large number of commuters rather unexpectedly stumble and trip over the same stair. Looking at the flight of stairs, everything seems normal and routine. Still, person after person catches their foot on one particular stair, stumbles awkwardly, and then looks around in a startled way (e.g., "What the ... ?"). To investigate, engineers measured each step and, sure enough, the stumble-inducing step was ever so slightly higher than the other stairs. The elevated height was not enough for the conscious mind to notice, but it was elevated just enough to cause a disruption in the adaptive unconscious' automatic task of climbing a flight of stairs. Like the automatic pilot on the airplane, the adaptive unconscious is so skilled at monitoring and carrying out its tasks that we do not even notice that it is doing its job—until we stumble and trip. Then, we need the conscious mind to jump in a figure out what went wrong and what to do about it. A second, common, and related illustration of when the adaptive unconscious recruits the conscious mind occurs as you near the end of a moving walkway (e.g., at the airport). Automatically (unconsciously), you intuit if your natural stride will land you safely over the end of the electric walkway or whether you will need a stutter half-step to land comfortably. If you intuit that your natural step will be okay, then the adaptive unconscious lets you continue to listen to music, daydream, or talk with your friend, but if your intuition signals that you might trip and stumble without corrective action, it interrupts what your conscious mind is doing and recruit it to pay attention and solve the problem before the moving walkway end.

This automatic pilot analogy suggests that the conscious mind is "in charge" while the adaptive unconscious does the low-level janitorial work. But a closer study of the adaptive unconscious shows that it does all the same high-level executive work that the conscious mind does, such as setting goals, interpreting events, and making judgments. The current thinking about the relation between the conscious and unconscious mind is that they do basically the same things, but in two different ways. The conscious mind is an effortful, deliberate, and slow system; the unconscious mind—the adaptive unconscious—is an automatic, instantaneous, and fast system. For instance, when you try to solve a math problem ($12 \times 16 = ?$), thinking is effortful, deliberate, and slow, but when you glance at someone's facial expression of emotion, thinking is automatic, instantaneous, and fast. Perhaps the best way to characterize these two ways of thinking is to say that the mind uses two very different strategies to make sense of most any situation (Gladwell, 2005).

Table 16.1 lists a dozen defining features of the adaptive unconscious, also called System 1, and the corresponding features of the conscious mind, also called System 2 (based on Kahneman, 2011):

Table 16.1   Defining Features of the Adaptive Unconscious versus the Conscious Mind

Adaptive Unconscious (Unconscious Mind) System 1	Conscious Mind System 2
Automatic	Controlled
Intuitive	Analytical, logical
Fast, quick	Slow
Rash, uncontrollable	Thoughtful, controllable
Involuntary, unintentional	Voluntary, intentional
Effortless	Effortful
Emotional	Rational
Efficient, but impulsive	Self-control, Self-regulation
Thoughts come to mind automatically	Thoughts have to be effortfully produced
First impressions	Reflective judgment
Not open to education and training	Open to education and training

Sometimes these two systems process information about the world in ways that complement another (e.g., I had an initial hunch, and the hunch provided to be true), but other times these two systems process information that contradicts with the other (e.g., I had an initial hunch, but subsequent information makes me now doubt the validity of that hunch). Most of the time, however, the adaptive unconscious (System 1) is doing the thinking—making judgments, generating feelings, monitoring how things are going, forming impressions, and doing so automatically and effortlessly. For instance, consider all the automatic skilled action you carry out unconsciously (and skillfully!) moment by moment, as in walking, writing, typing, driving, reading people's faces, reading people's body language, and so on. Sometimes, however, System 1 needs some help. It finds that help by recruiting System 2 thinking. For instance, you walk into a room or run into a friend at the bookstore and immediately sense that something is not right. You cannot put your finger on what is wrong or what is different. Your intuition and gut feeling tells you that something is wrong, something is different, something has changed. At that point, System 1 calls in System 2 into to help out—to conduct an effortful, deliberate, Sherlock Holmes-like investigation and analysis to identify just what the adaptive unconscious noticed in the blink of an eye.

The adaptive unconscious is very good at what it does. Because it is so skilled at what it does, this part of the unconscious deserves its "adaptive" moniker. The adaptive unconscious is highly skilled at appraising the environment, setting goals, making judgments, and initiating action, and it can do all these things even while we are consciously thinking about something else. You can carry out a conversation with a friend for instance, while driving a car, monitoring traffic, listening to music, drinking a beverage, and so forth.

The adaptive unconscious has rather special talents. As one case in point, consider the experiment in which college students were shown only a 2-second muted video clip of an instructor and asked to rate his or her teaching effectiveness based on what they saw in that very brief slice of action (Ambady, Bernieri, & Richeson, 2000). Ratings were also taken from the students of these same instructors who had taken a semester-long course. Students who saw only the quickest slice of the instructor's teaching made just as valid judgments of the instructor's effectiveness as did students who spent four months in the classroom with the same instructor. These students could not tell you why they made the ratings they did, but their intuition told them something important about how effective or ineffective each instructor was likely to be. People are also able to make accurate judgments of other people's emotions with only a microsecond of exposure to the person's facial expressions, despite the fact that they cannot tell you what piece of information they are using to make such judgments (Ekman, 1993). The judgments made by the adaptive unconscious often turn out to be right (Gladwell, 2005).

Implicit Motivation

The best way to introduce the concept of implicit motivation is to contrast it with conscious motivation. Implicit motivation refers to all those motives, emotions, attitudes, and judgments that operate outside a person's conscious awareness and that are fundamentally distinct from self-report motives, emotions, attitudes, and judgments (McClelland, Koestner, & Weinberger, 1989). Motivational constructs such as goals, intentions, and self-concept represent a conscious, self-report, "explicit" type of motivation. "Implicit," in contrast, describes motivational processes that are indirect, implied, or not well understood.

Unconscious implicit motives are difficult to articulate (difficult to measure with self-report questionnaires) and therefore need to be measured indirectly (Schultheiss & Pang, 2007).

Whereas explicit motives are those linked with learned values and cognitively elaborated aspects of the self-concept (e.g., "I like difficult tasks"; "It is important to persist in the face of difficulty"), implicit motives are linked to emotional experiences. The social needs reviewed in Chapter 7 illustrated implicit motivations well (e.g., needs for achievement, affiliation, and power). When we actually encounter difficult tasks and when we have an opportunity to persist versus quit in the face of difficulty, we experience emotion and affect that predicts our resulting behavior rather well. That is, during difficulty and challenge we feel good and energized or we feel bad and anxious, and these emotional reactions (rather than our conscious values) predict behavior well.

Implicit motives orient, direct, and select attention such that people automatically attend to environmental events that have emotional associations (McClelland, 1985; Schultheiss & Hale, 2007). That is, those who harbor positive affect associated with achievement orient, direct, and select their attention when the environment offers them an opportunity to do something well and to show personal competence. Similarly, those who harbor positive affect associated with power orient, direct, and select their attention when the environment offers them an opportunity to have an impact on others (recall Table 7.1).

Whether implicit motivational processes predict behavior depends on the degree to which individuals exercise awareness of the events going on around them that affect their motivation and how they respond to these events in terms of thoughts, emotions, and behavior (Bargh, 1997). Hence, mindfulness explains when implicit motives affect behavior, while mindlessness explains when implicit motives fail to affect behavior (Levesque & Brown, 2007). Mindfulness is a receptive attention to and awareness of present events and experiences; it is a noninterference with one's experience in which the person allows inputs to enter awareness in a simple noticing of what is taking place (Brown & Ryan, 2003). With the emotional activation of implicit motivation and with the openness of high mindfulness, people are able to regulate their behavior in implicit and productive ways (Brown, Ryan, & Creswell, 2007). This is an important point to make because it shows how conscious and unconscious motivation can potentially work together in a harmonious and productive way (rather than as opposing id versus ego forces).

Priming

Priming is the procedure that evokes an implicit response from an individual upon exposure to a stimulus that is outside his or her conscious awareness. While priming occurs outside of the person's conscious awareness, the prime itself can be delivered unconsciously or consciously. An example of an unconsciously delivered prime might be a word that is flashed so briefly on a computer screen (e.g., 30 msec) that it is not recognized, although it still produces an implicit effect. An example of a consciously delivered prime might occur as the person is asked to judge if a dot appears above or below a word, a word whose content induces an implicit effect (e.g., the words "good" or "pleasant" might produce implicit positive feelings). Primes that activate a mental representation of a behavior (outside the person's awareness) prepare people to enact behaviors consistent with that mental representation. For instance, the smell of a cleaning solution, the sight of a briefcase, and viewing a library painting lead people to engage in cleaning behavior, competitive behavior, and hushed conversation, compared to the absence of these primes, although participants in these studies reported being unaware of the aroma, briefcase, or painting (Aarts & Dijksterhuis, 2003; Holland, Hendriks, & Aarts, 2005; Kay, Wheeler, Bargh, & Ross, 2004). These findings show that nonconscious primes prepare (i.e., motivate) action.

To appreciate the capacity of a prime to prepare action, consider the cleaning study (Holland, Hendriks, & Aarts, 2005). For the primary manipulation, participants completed a routine task in a cubicle with or without the presence of a citrus scent of an all-purpose cleaner. The scent was rather mild; participants did not even notice it or report having any conscious thoughts about cleaning while exposed to the scent. Participants were then moved to a room without any scent. They sat at a table and were instructed to eat a crumbly biscuit. As they did, crumbs fell onto the tabletop. The dependent measure was simply the extent to which the participant kept his or her table clean. Participants in the scent condition cleaned the table more often than did participants in the no-scent control condition. This study shows that unconsciously activated thoughts can guide a person's behavior in ways that are consistent with those thoughts even as the thoughts remain unconscious and the person is not aware that he is actually cleaning the table or why he is doing so.

Primes influence a range of unconscious motivations. Primes have been shown to activate implicit motives such as power and affiliation (Schultheiss, 2008), outcome expectancies (Custers, Aarts, Oikawa, & Elliot, 2009), autonomous motivations (Hodgins, Yacko, & Gottlieb, 2006), and so forth. For instance, students who were asked to solve language puzzles populated by achievement-related words ("win") outperformed and outpersisted students who were asked to solve the same language puzzles populated by neutral words when both groups worked on a second task unrelated to the language-puzzle task (Bargh et al., 2001). This means that the nonconscious activation of the motivational state promotes behavioral activation if the motivational state itself is associated with positive valence (Aarts, Custers, & Marien, 2008; Custers & Aarts, 2005). That is, primes facilitate motivated action by activating mental representations of action (i.e., the subliminal presentation of the words "exert" and "vigorous"), implicit motivational states, and positive affect; furthermore, these effects occur even though participants are unaware of the presentation of the primes.

Priming produces its impressive effects by offering environmental cues that activate automatic associations the person already holds. This is very different from trying to put a new thought into a person's mind, as advertisers try when they flash subliminal information in a movie (e.g., "Eat popcorn," "Drink Coke"; Morse & Stoller, 1982), or when department stores try to broadcast anti-shoplifting subliminal messages over the public address system ("If you steal, you will get caught"; Loftus & Klinger, 1992). These subliminal directives do not work. The unconscious might recognize and understand the message in some way, but actually acting on the directive is a whole different matter.

One group of researchers tested the validity of widely available subliminal audiotapes designed to enhance memory or boost self-esteem (Greenwald, Spangenberg, Pratkanis, & Eskenazi, 1991). The audiotapes play subliminal messages (e.g., "You're the best"; "I love you") over relaxing material (e.g., popular music, nature sounds of the forest) to improve the daily listener's self-esteem. The researchers recruited college-age volunteers who wanted to increase their self-esteem or improve their memory. Each volunteer completed initial measures of their self-esteem and memory, listened daily to the audiotape for five weeks, and completed follow-up measures of their self-esteem and memory. In a nutshell, results showed that the audiotapes did not work. Like the "Eat popcorn" and "If you steal, you will get caught" messages, the "I love you" subliminal messages were not processed in a way that affected thoughts or behaviors (Greenwald et al., 1991).

PSYCHODYNAMICS

The second core postulate of the contemporary psychodynamic study is psychodynamics, or the clashing and conflict of thoughts and desires. Freud observed that people often engaged in behavior that they clearly did not wish to do (e.g., ritualized hand washing). Because people sometimes did what they did not want to do, he reasoned that motivation must be more complex than that which follows intentional volition. Conscious volition must have to wrestle with an unconscious counterwill. Following this line of reasoning, Freud (1917) conceptualized people as being of two minds: "The mind is an arena, a sort of tumbling-ground, for the struggle of antagonistic impulses." People have ideas and wills, but people also have counterideas and counterwills. When the conscious (ego's) will and the unconscious (id's) counterwill are of roughly equal strength, a sort of internal civil war ensues in which neither is completely satisfied. The mental combatants can be diagrammed as follows:

$$\text{Will} \rightarrow \leftarrow \text{Counterwill}$$

Freud's depiction of the human mind was one of conflict—idea versus counteridea, will versus counterwill, desire versus repression, excitation versus inhibition, and cathexis (sexual attraction) versus anticathexis (guilt). This clashing of forces is what is meant by the term *psychodynamics*.

For Freud, psychodynamics concerned the conflict between the personality structures of the id and ego (and superego, which is not discussed here). The motivations of the id were unconscious, involuntary, impulse-driven, and hedonistic, because the id obeyed the pleasure principle: Obtain pleasure and avoid pain and do so at all costs and without delay. The motivations of the ego were partly conscious and partly unconscious, steeped in defenses, and organized around the delay of gratification, because the ego obeyed the reality principle: Hold pleasure seeking at bay until a socially acceptable need-satisfying object can be found. Today, psychoanalysts point out that wishes, fears, values, goals, emotions, thoughts, and motives are never in harmony, and mental conflict is an inevitable constant (e.g., one wants and fears the same thing, as during a job interview, a marriage proposal, or in contemplating attending tomorrow's motivation class). As a case in point, Drew Westen (1998) points out that children's feelings toward their parents almost *have* to be riddled in conflict since parents provide not only security, comfort, and love but also frustration, distress, and disappointment.

Repression

When most readers think of psychodynamics, what comes to mind are concepts like the id, ego, libido, and the Oedipal complex (Boneau, 1990). But, when Freud himself defined psychodynamics, the central concept was repression (Freud, 1917).

Freud envisioned the unconscious as an overcrowded apartment and the conscious as a reception room to prepare oneself for going out into the public world. Repression is the security guard checking each thought's identification card to judge whether it was fit to enter the public world.

Because many motivations reside in the unconscious, people necessarily remain unaware of their own motivations. In addition, people go out of their way to remain unaware of these motivations. This is what Timothy Wilson (2002) meant by the title of his book, *Stranger to Ourselves*. People cannot bear to know things about themselves that contradict either their self-view or public opinion. Awareness of one's true motives would generate conflict with either the ideal self or what society regards to be a respectable person. Thus, repression—the tough-minded security guard who turns down most unconscious thoughts' request to exit the overcrowded apartment—constituted the foundation of psychodynamics (Fromm, 1986).

Repression is the process of forgetting information or an experience by ways that are unconscious, unintentional, and automatic. It is the ego's psychodynamic counterforce to the id's demanding and distressing wishes, desires, ideas, or memories. When unconscious impulses try to surface, anxiety emerges as a danger signal. It is this anxiety that moves the unconscious mind to repression (Freud, 1959; Holmes, 1974, 1990).

Repression is tremendously difficult to study empirically because you have to ask people about things they do not remember. Studying repression is similar to figuring out whether the light stays on after you close the refrigerator door. Research on repression has not yet produced impressive understandings (Erdelyi, 1985, 1990; Erdelyi & Goldberg, 1979), but research on the related mental control process of suppression has been enlightening.

Suppression

The ability to stop a thought is beyond the human mind. No one can stop a thought. Instead, people try to suppress the thought once it has already occurred. Suppression is the process of removing a thought from the mind by ways that are conscious, intentional, and deliberate (Wegner, 1992).

Suppression routinely fails.[1] When we try to suppress a thought, all we get for our trouble is a lesson that we have less control over our thoughts than we care to admit (Wegner, 1989). Like a balloon held under water, thoughts and emotions can be suppressed for only a while.

Consider the psychodynamics of the following:

- Do not *think* about something (today's dental appointment).
- Do not *do* something (go all day without smoking a cigarette).
- Do not *want* something (food while on a diet).
- Do not *remember* something (forget a deeply humiliating experience).

When such thoughts enter our consciousness, our thinking halts itself because the thought precedes something that we wish not to happen. That is, the self-instruction of "don't think about that candy bar" precedes the undesired act of eating the candy bar.

---

[1] Suppressing a thought given by an external source (i.e., another person) is something that lies beyond the capacity of the human mind to suppress. People's own, self-generated intrusive thoughts are a different story (Kelly & Kahn, 1994). The number-one strategy that works with self-generated intrusive thoughts is distraction (Wegner, 1989). With familiar intrusive thoughts, people generally have a rich network of thoughts they have used previously to distract themselves from their unwanted thoughts (Kelly & Kahn, 1994). But a psychodynamic rebound effect always occurs when thoughts are generated by an outside agent, like an experimenter saying not to think of a white bear (Wegner et al., 1987) or a friend asking you to keep a secret (Lane & Wegner, 1995). With externally induced intrusive thoughts, people lack the experience they need to suppress them.

With the stream of thought interrupted—halted, in fact—the unwanted thought lingers out there in consciousness all by itself with a spotlight on it. We can suppress that thought for a few seconds, but there is a curious tendency for that thought to pop up again (Wegner, 1989; Wegner, Schneider, Carter, & White, 1987).

Consider a laboratory experiment in which college students were asked not to think of a white bear (Wegner et al., 1987). Dan Wegner's decision to ask participants to suppress the thought of a white bear came from a Tolstoy quote in which, for nineteenth-century Russians, being attacked by a white bear while walking through the countryside was a real danger, something similar to what contemporary drivers do when they try not to think of the possibility of a drunk driver suddenly swerving toward them. Each participant sat alone at a table with a bell on it (like the old-fashioned umbrella-shaped bells seen on hotel counters). For the first 5 minutes, the participant said whatever popped into mind. "Free association" was easy. For the next 5 minutes, however, the participant was asked explicitly not to think of a white bear, but if she did think of the bear, she was to ring the bell as a signal that the unwanted thought had accidentally popped into her mind. During a final 5-minute period, the participant once again was to say whatever popped into mind (i.e., free association). In this last period, participants experienced a "rebound effect" in which a lot of bell ringing occurred—certainly more white bears popped to mind after the suppression effort than before it.

These results contradict common sense. Thought suppression not only failed, but it produced an obsessive preoccupation about those white bears (the rebound effect). Paradoxically, suppression did not lead to serenity and peace of mind; rather, it led to obsession.

People rely on thought suppression to control their thoughts and actions in practically all areas of life. People rely on thought suppression for behavioral self-control, as in the effort to abstain from eating certain foods (Polivy & Herman, 1985) or consuming addictive substances (Marlatt & Parks, 1982). People rely on thought suppression to keep a secret (Pennebaker, 1990) or to deceive another person (DePaulo, 1992). People rely on thought suppression for self-control over pain (Cioffi, 1991) and fear (Rachman, 1978). And people use thought suppression to avoid making public the inner workings of their mind and its socially offensive wants, desires, and intentions (Wegner & Erber, 1993).

People rely on thought suppression for good reasons. Many of our private thoughts would produce public confusion (to put it nicely) if they were allowed to be freely expressed. Thought suppression turns potential social conflict into a private mental struggle of wanted versus unwanted thoughts (Wegner, 1992). We learn quickly that thought suppression can be a social ally in preventing us from just blurting out our thoughts, as sometimes happens when we are stressed (Jacobs & Nadel, 1985) or impaired by drugs or alcohol (Steele & Josephs, 1990).

All this makes for interesting psychodynamics. An unwanted thought pops to mind, so we suppress it. But conscious thought suppression activates an unconscious counterprocess. While the conscious mind is busy suppressing the unwelcomed thought, the unconscious mind is just as busy searching and detecting for the presence of the thought to be suppressed. The unconscious mind keeps vigilant search over whether those white bears have returned. The unconscious monitoring process ironically keeps the to-be-suppressed thought activated, which is the very thing that the conscious intention was trying to avoid. Continued suppression actually, in time, builds a rather potent counterforce that drives the unwanted thought toward an obsession (e.g., the dieter who tries not to think of food is vulnerable to thinking only about food; Polivy & Herman, 1985). According to Dan Wegner (1989, 1992), the way out of the thought suppression quagmire is to stop suppressing and, instead, focus on and think about the unwanted thought. Paradoxically, only those unconscious thoughts that we welcome into consciousness are we able to forget (Frankl, 1960). If that does not work, distraction (go to a movie, spend time gardening) is the second best strategy to avoid a thought.

Do the Id and Ego Actually Exist?

Given the preceding discussion on psychodynamics, an interesting question arises: What does contemporary empirical research have to say about the scientific status of the id and ego? Is the human brain organized such that part exists as a cauldron of innate and impulsive desires and emotions, while another part exists as an executive control center that perceives the world and learns and adapts to it?

The conscious awareness responsible for executive control over mental life is a relatively new evolutionary development that has been structurally superimposed over a primitive and motivationally rich information-processing system (Reber, 1992). Subcortical brain structures (e.g., amygdala, ventral striatum, and nucleus accumbens) generate automatic and impulsive wants, needs, desires, and subjective experiences of pleasure–unpleasure. The subcortical brain makes for a pretty fair id. The frontal lobes of the neocortex qualify as the brain structure that corresponds to the ego, because it performs all those functions that reflect choice, decision making, self-control, delay of gratification, and intellectual problem solving. Further, the prefrontal cortical brain projects neural pathways into the subcortical brain structures (see Figure 3.3 for a graphical representation of the cortical and subcortical brain). Unilateral and bidirectional neural interconnections are everywhere (e.g., the amygdala both excites and is inhibited by the prefrontal cortex). The picture that emerges corresponds to a pattern of psychodynamics, of forces and counterforces, of excitations and inhibitions, and of subcortical activation and cortical inhibition.

Contemporary neuroscientists further confirm that the emotion-generating amygdala is present at birth while the memory-generating hippocampus matures later. Hence, early childhood experiences can leave an emotional memory imprint (implicit learning) without a corresponding episodic (conscious) memory.

EGO PSYCHOLOGY

The third core postulate of the contemporary psychodynamic study is ego psychology. Freud postulated that all psychical energy originated in the id. At birth, the infant was all id, while the ego was only in the beginning processes of formation (Freud, 1923). Throughout infancy, the ego developed from perceiving instincts to curbing them. The id was force; the ego—the personality—developed to become its counterforce.

The neo-Freudians saw ego functioning as much more. Heinz Hartmann (1958, 1964), the "father of ego psychology," saw the ego involved in a developmental process that made it increasingly independent from its id origins. For Hartmann, the ego, unlike the id, developed through learning and experience. Learning occurred because the child engaged in a tremendous amount of manipulative, exploratory, and experimental activity (such as grasping, walking, and thinking), all of which provided the ego with information about itself and its surroundings. With feedback from its manipulative, exploratory, and experimental activity, the ego began to acquire ego properties—language, memory, intentions, complex ideas, and so on—that facilitated its ability to adapt successfully to the realities, demands, and constraints of the world. Hartmann conceptualized that because of its ability to learn, adapt, and grow, the mature ego was mostly autonomous from the id. Neo-Freudians studied the motivational dynamics of the "autonomous ego."

Ego Development

Defining ego is difficult because it is not so much a thing as it is a developmental process. The essence of ego development is a developmental progression toward what is possible in terms of psychological growth, maturity, adjustment, prosocial interdependence, competence, and autonomous functioning (Hartmann, 1958; Loevinger, 1976). From its infantile origins, the ego develops along the following trajectory (Loevinger, 1976):

- Symbiotic
- Impulsive
- Self-protective
- Conformist
- Conscientious
- Autonomous

During the (infantile) symbiotic stage, the ego is extremely immature and constantly overwhelmed by impulses. The ego is symbiotic in the sense that its welfare depends on and is wholly provided for by its caretaker, not by itself. With language, the symbiotic ego begins to differentiate itself from the caretaker but remains extremely immature. In the impulsive stage, external forces (parental constraints, rules), and not the ego per se, curb the child's impulses and desires. Self-control emerges when the child first anticipates consequences and understands that rules exist. The ego then internalizes these consequences and rules in guiding its self-protective defensive capabilities. During the conformist stage, the ego internalizes group-accepted rules, and the anxiety of group disapproval becomes a potent counterforce against one's impulses. The conscientious ego has a conscience, an internalized set of rules, and a prosocial sense of responsibility to others. The conscience functions as a set of internal standards to curb and counter impulses. The autonomous ego is one in which thoughts, plans, goals, and behaviors originate from within the ego and its resources, rather than from id impulses or from other people's (including society's) demands and pressures (Ryan, 1993). The autonomous ego is self-motivating and self-regulating.

Ego development is important to motivation study in two ways. First, the ego develops to defend against anxiety. If the ego is unable to manage the demands of the id, superego, and environment, then it experiences anxiety. Anxiety is the emotional reaction in which the ego is "obliged to admit its weakness" (Freud, 1964, p. 78). Ego development therefore means mature defenses against anxiety (as discussed below in the section "Ego Defense"). Second, the ego develops to empower the person to interact more effectively and more proactively with its surroundings. By growing its sense of competence, the ego gains an increasing capacity not only to deal effectively with environmental challenges but also to generate its own inner motivation and become self-motivating (as discussed below in the section "Ego Effectance").

Ego Defense

The day-to-day existence of the ego is one of vulnerability. The person who makes a group presentation is in a state of vulnerability. The person who goes out on a date is in a state of vulnerability. The person who tries to learn something new is in a state of vulnerability. The person who tries to hold biological desire in check is in a state of vulnerability. The person who tries to do everything his parents and society approve of (satisfy the ego ideal) and tries to resist doing anything his parents and society disapprove of (satisfy the conscience) is in a state of vulnerability. The ego is always in a state of vulnerability.

Through its defense mechanisms, the ego buffers consciousness against potentially overwhelming levels of anxiety originating from conflict with id impulses (neurotic anxiety), superego demands (moral anxiety), and environmental dangers (realistic anxiety). The role that defense mechanisms play in keeping psychopathology at bay appears in Figure 16.2, which shows that conflict emanating from the environment, id, and superego will rather inevitably create anxiety and, eventually, distress and depression if the conflicts are not defended against. Id demands in the form of biological impulses ("Obtain pleasure, avoid pain!") generate neurotic anxiety; environmental demands ("Adapt to threats and dangers!") generate reality anxiety; and superego demands ("Always be perfect!") generate moral anxiety. How much anxiety (or how much "serenity of consciousness") and how much energy the ego has left over for its own development depends on the maturity level of its defense mechanisms, or coping strategies. Without mature defense mechanisms, anxiety from the id, superego (ego ideal, conscience), and environment would overwhelm the ego's capacity to cope, which would result in psychopathology. Fourteen such defense mechanisms appear in Table 16.2, along with a definition and example for each (American Psychiatric Association, 2013; A. Freud, 1946; Vaillant, 2000).

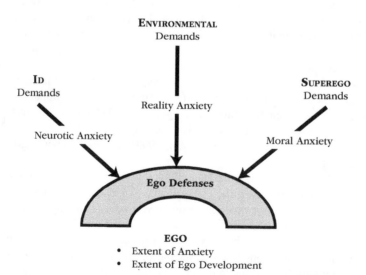

Figure 16.2   Role of Defense Mechanisms in Buffering the Ego from Anxiety-Generating Events

Table 16.2   Ego Defense Mechanisms

Defense Mechanism	Definition (with *example in italics*)
Denial	Ignoring or refusing to acknowledge an unpleasant external reality. *Preoccupation with work so there is no attention paid to the messages of rejection coming from a problematic personal relationship.*
Fantasy	Gratifying a frustrated desire by imaging omnipotent achievement. *Imagining oneself to be a courageous national hero who performs incredible feats to win the admiration of all.*
Projection	Assigning one's own unacceptable desire or impulse onto someone else. *The anxiety of "I am failing this course because I am unintelligent" is expressed as "This textbook is stupid" or "The teacher is an idiot."*
Displacement	Anxiety release onto a substitute object when doing so against the source of the anxiety could be harmful. *Discharging aggression toward a father figure (the boss) onto an anxiety-manageable object, such as the household dog. The worker kicks the dog as a substitute for the father figure.*
Identification	Taking on the characteristics of someone viewed as successful. *Seeing the nation adore a celebrity and then adjusting one's appearance (hair style, mode of dress) to be loved and treated like the celebrity.*
Regression	Returning to an earlier stage of development when anxious. *Using baby talk to gain another's nurturance and sympathy to win an anxiety-provoking argument.*
Reaction formation	Expressing the strong opposite of one's true feelings or motives. *Expressing strong optimism ("Everything will work out just fine") in the face of the grim realities of world hunger or interpersonal rejection.*
Rationalization	Justifying a disturbing or an unacceptable thought or feeling by selecting a logical reason to think or feel that way. *Producing an acceptable reason to justify one's hatred for a particular group of people, such as "because they lie and cheat all the time."*
Anticipation	Forecasting future danger in small steps so to cope with the danger gradually rather than all in one avalanche. *A person anticipates a probable future loss by dealing with the loss one step at a time—making a list of things to do, practicing what one will say at different stages of the danger, etc.*
Humor	Capacity to not take oneself too seriously, as in accepting one's shortcoming and talking about it in a socially acceptable way. *A cartoon exaggerates an anatomical feature of a high-ranking politician that allows readers to laugh at, yet also feel affection for, the authority figure.*
Sublimation	Transforming a socially unacceptable anxiety into a source of energy that is made socially acceptable and productive—even exciting. *Lust or sexual impulses are channeled into love, sexual foreplay, or work that is manual, creative, or scientific.*

Defense mechanisms exist in a hierarchical ordering from least to most mature, from least to most adaptive (Vaillant, 1977, 1992, 1993). At the most immature level, defense mechanisms deny reality or invent an imaginary one. Defense mechanisms such as denial and fantasy are the most immature because the individual fails even to recognize external reality. At the second level are defenses such as projection in which the person recognizes reality but copes by casting its disturbing aspects away from the self. At the third level of maturity are the most common defenses, including rationalization and reaction formation. These defenses deal effectively with short-term anxiety but fail to accomplish any long-term gain in adjustment (because reality is repressed rather than accommodated). Rationalization, for example, temporarily excuses unacceptable desires, but it fails to provide the means for coping with the problem that produced the anxiety in the first place. Level four defenses are the most adaptive and mature and include mechanisms such as sublimation and humor. Sublimation accepts unconscious impulses but effectively channels these impulses into socially beneficial outlets, such as the creative energy that produces a painting or a poem (making unconscious impulses both socially acceptable and personally productive). Humor allows the person to look directly at what is painful or anxiety-provoking and deal with it in a socially acceptable way (Freud, 1905; Vaillant, 2000). Still, like all defenses, humor does not transform reality but instead transforms only the perception of reality (to alleviate subjective distress; Lefcourt & Martin, 1986; Nezu, Nezu, & Blissett, 1988).

To test his ideas that the maturity level of one's defenses reflects ego strength and predicts life adjustment, Vaillant (1977) followed the lives of 56 men over a 30-year period. He interviewed each man in his college-age years, and independent testers classified each man as using predominantly mature (levels 3 and 4) or predominantly immature (levels 1 and 2) defense mechanisms as a personal style against distress and anxiety. The study sought to determine how these two groups of men would fare in life, and the research assessed each man's life adjustment 30 years later in four categories: career, social, psychological, and medical. Ego strength, as indexed by maturity level of defense mechanisms, successfully discriminated men who suffered under the burden of career, social, psychological, and medical problems from those who did not (see Table 16.3). Mature defense mechanisms allowed the men to live a well-adjusted life, show psychosocial maturity, find and keep a fulfilling job, develop a rich and stable friendship pattern, avoid divorce, avoid the need for psychiatric visits, avoid psychopathology and mental illnesses, and so on. A second, similar longitudinal study with men and women from diverse backgrounds showed that the maturity level of one's defenses predicted—30 years later—income level, job promotions, psychosocial adjustments, social supports, joy in living, physical functioning, and marital satisfaction (Vaillant, 2000).

One illustration of how mature defense mechanisms promote well-being appears in Figure 16.3 (Cui & Vaillant, 1996). On the horizontal x-axis, the graph shows the extent to which adults in the study used mature defense mechanisms (with five representing the most mature defense mechanisms). The y-axis plots the study's dependent measure, depression. The diagonal line with the o's shows the depression scores for those adults who lived very stressful lives (poverty, physical disability, loss of a loved one). The four adults with highly stressful lives and immature defense mechanisms were very likely to experience depression (75%), whereas the nine adults with equally stressful lives but mature defense mechanisms were essentially inoculated against depression (0%). Adults who did not live stressful lives did not experience depression (as shown by the straight horizontal

Table 16.3   Relationship between Maturity of Defense Mechanisms and Life Adjustment

	Predominant Adaptive Style (%)	
	Mature (N = 25)	Immature (N = 31)
Overall Adjustment		
1) Top third in adult adjustment	60%	0%
2) Bottom third in adult adjustment	4%	61%
3) "Happiness" (top third)	68%	16%
Career Adjustment		
1) Income over $20,000/year	88%	48%
2) Job meets ambition for self	92%	58%
3) Active public service outside job	56%	29%
Social Adjustment		
1) Rich friendship pattern	64%	6%
2) Marriage in least harmonious quartile or divorced	28%	61%
3) Barren friendship pattern	4%	52%
4) No competitive sports (age 40–50)	24%	77%
Psychological Adjustment		
1) 10+ psychiatric visits	0%	45%
2) Ever diagnosed mentally ill	0%	55%
3) Emotional problems in childhood	20%	45%
4) Worst childhood environment (bottom fourth)	12%	39%
5) Fails to take full vacation	28%	61%
6) Able to be aggressive with others (top fourth)	36%	6%
Medical Adjustment		
1) 4+ adult hospitalizations	8%	26%
2) 5+ days sick leave/year	0%	23%
3) Recent health poor by objective exam	0%	36%
4) Subjective health consistently judged excellent since college	68%	48%

N = sample size.
Source: From *Adaptation to Life* (p. 87), by G. E. Vaillant, 1977, Boston: Little, Brown & Company. Copyright 1977 by George E. Vaillant.

line with the *x*'s). Thus, depression occurred when people used immature defenses to cope with life stress. When life was not stressful or when adults used mature defenses, depression was avoided. This same conclusion (mature defenses prevent sickness) was also found in preventing posttraumatic stress disorder after combat (Lee, Vaillant, Torrey, & Elder, 1995).

Ego Effectance

Ego effectance concerns the individual's competence in dealing with environmental challenges, demands, and opportunities (Harter, 1981; White, 1959). Effectance motivation begins during infancy as an undifferentiated source of ego energy. With its diffuse energy, emerging properties (e.g., grasping, crawling, walking, language) and acquired skills (e.g., penmanship, social skills), the ego attempts to deal satisfactorily with the circumstances and stressors that come its way. In the process of adapting and developing,

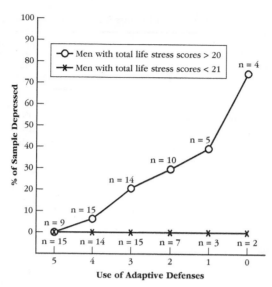

Figure 16.3 Likelihood of Depression as a Function of Life Stress and the Maturity Level of One's Defense Mechanisms

Source: From "The antecedents and consequences of negative life events in adulthood: A longitudinal study," by X. Cui & G.E. Vaillant, 1996, *American Journal of Psychiatry, 152,* 21–26. Copyright 1996 American Psychiatric Association. http://psychiatryonline.org. Reprinted by permission.

the ego gains the motivational resource of effectance motivation, or the proactive desire to interact effectively with the environment (see Chapter 6).

Ego effectance develops into more than just a defensive coping response to life's demands. As the child exercises skills, he or she begins to learn how to produce successful changes in the environment. The child learns how to use crayons, climb trees, cross streets, hold the attention of adults, feed him- or herself, use a computer, make new friends, ride a bicycle, and a hundred other tasks. When successful, such interactions produce a sense of being effective, a perception of competence, and feelings of satisfaction and enjoyment. The ego aggregates these perceptions and feelings into a general sense of competence. With each successful transaction with the environment (a friend is made, a tree house is constructed), effectance motivation grows. The greater the effectance motivation, the stronger the desire to seek out new and challenging interactions with the environment. Effectance motivation grows into the proactive, initiative-rich desire to intentionally change one's environment and one's life for the better. In this sense, ego effectance functions as "ego offense" (to complement the earlier discussed "ego defense").

OBJECT RELATIONS THEORY

The fourth and final core postulate of the contemporary psychodynamic study is object relations theory. The study of unconscious motivation began with a rather single-minded focus on sexual and aggressive drives. Over time, thinking about unconscious motivation became less biological and more interpersonal. Emphasis on the biological need for sexual gratification, for instance, gradually gave way to an emphasis on the psychological need for relatedness (Horney, 1939). Central to the object relations theory are the infant's need for attachment to the caregiver and the adult's subsequent interpersonal connectedness to the important people in his or her life.

"Object relations" is an awkward term. But the term is less awkward than it might at first appear to be once its etiology is told. Freud used the word "object" to refer to the gratification target of one's drives. Therefore, object relations theory studies how people satisfy their need for relatedness through their mental representations of and actual attachments to social and sexual objects (i.e., other people). Object relations theory studies how people relate to objects (others) to satisfy that emotional and psychological need for relatedness.

Object relations theory focuses on the nature and the development of mental representations of the self and others and on the affective processes (wishes, fears) associated with these representations (Bowlby, 1969; Eagle, 1984; Greenberg & Mitchell, 1983; Scharff & Scharff, 1995; Westen, 1990). In particular, object relations theory focuses on how childhood mental representations of one's caretakers are captured within the personality and persist into adulthood (Main, Kaplan, & Cassidy, 1985; van IJzendoorn, 1995). What persists into adulthood are mental representations of self and others, such as the following: Am I lovable or unlovable? Am I worthy of other people's attention and care or unworthy of such affection and investment? Are other people warm and caring or selfish and unreliable? Can other people be trusted? Can you depend on others when you need them to be there for you?

Object relations often stress the impact that parental abuse or neglect has on the infant's emerging mental representations of self and others (Blatt, 1994; Luborsky & Crits-Christoph, 1990; Strauman, 1992; Urist, 1980). In essence, the bond between mother (caregiver) and child becomes the child's template for self and for other mental representations. When one's primary caretaker is warm, nurturing, responsive, available, and trustworthy, the parental object satisfies the infant's need for relatedness, communicates a message of approval, and nonverbally sends a message about relationships that encourages secure and affectionate relations; when one's primary caretaker is cold, abusive, unresponsive, neglectful, and unpredictable, the parental object frustrates the infant's need for relatedness, communicates a message of disapproval, and nonverbally sends a message about relationships that encourages insecurity, mistrust, and anxiety (Ainsworth, Blehar, Waters, & Wall, 1978; Sullivan, 1953).

A positive mental model of self predicts adult levels of self-reliance, social confidence, and self-esteem (Feeney & Noller, 1990; Klohnen & Bera, 1998). Similarly, as shown in Box 16, secure mental models of others predict the quality of one's adult romantic relationships (Feeney & Noller, 1990; Hazan & Shaver, 1987), including whether that person ever marries and, if so, how long that person stays committed to that marriage (Klohnen & Bera, 1998). Alternatively, a childhood of interpersonal traumas (e.g., physical abuse, serious neglect, sexual molestation) and parental psychopathology (e.g., depression, anxiety, substance abuse, violent marital interaction) predict the child's later adulthood dysfunctional relationships (Mickelson, Kessler, & Shaver, 1997).

For a concrete example, consider a schematic of one female's mental representation of men, which is depicted in Figure 16.4 (Westen, 1991). The young woman suffered from rather severe depression and social isolation, and she reported a childhood history in which she characterized her parents as openly contemptuous of one another. Her mother constantly spoke of the ways in which she was victimized by her husband and three sons. In the course of psychotherapy, the woman's mental representation of her expected and

BOX 16   *Love as an Attachment Process*

Question: Why is this information important?

Answer: To understand how your own early attachments manifest themselves in your current (adult) romantic love relationships.

Consider the following three-item, multiple-choice question. Read each statement carefully, and then check the one that best describes you:

— I find it easy to get close to others. I am comfortable depending on others. I am comfortable having other people depend on me. I don't worry about being abandoned, and I don't worry about someone getting too close to me.

— I am somewhat uncomfortable being close to others. I find it difficult to trust others completely. I find it difficult to allow myself to depend on others. I become nervous when anyone gets too close, and I get nervous when others want me to be more intimate with them than I feel comfortable being.

— I find that others are reluctant to get as close as I would like. I worry that others don't really love me or that others don't really want to stay with me. I want to merge completely with others, especially love partners, and this desire sometimes scares people away.

Like object relations theory, attachment theory argues that affectionate bonds develop between infants and their caretakers and that these affectionate bonds, whether positive or negative, carry forward into adulthood, affecting the adult's relationships with lovers (Bowlby, 1969, 1973, 1980). In both object relations theory and attachment theory, infants have a psychological need for relatedness that strongly motivates them to desire close, affectionate bonds with their caregivers. Based on the quality of the care infants receive, they form mental models of how interaction partners relate to them that can be characterized by secure, anxious, or avoidant attachment (Ainsworth et al., 1978).

Which of the three statements above best resonated with your own experience? The three statements characterize, in order, a secure, an avoidant, and an anxious attachment style. About 55 percent of adults classify themselves as secure, about 20 percent classify themselves as anxious, and about 25 percent classify themselves as avoidant, respectively (Hazan & Shaver, 1987; Shaver & Hazan, 1987).

Cindy Hazan and Phillip Shaver (1987) gave the above multiple-choice question to about 600 adults in the Denver, Colorado, area and asked them also to complete questionnaires about their attachment history, beliefs about love, and experiences with a current partner. The three attachment groups experienced adult romantic love very differently.

Securely attached adults experienced love as a trilogy of friendship, trust, and happiness. They accepted and supported their partner, and their relationships endured over the years. Avoidantly attached adults experienced love as a fear of intimacy and commitment and reported a marked absence of a positive emotion from the relationship. This is the approach to romantic love heard every 15 minutes on television soap operas, "He is afraid of commitment." Anxiously attached lovers experienced love as an obsession, a desire for constant reunion and reciprocation, and as an extreme attraction and an extreme jealousy that produced emotional highs and lows. Obsessive preoccupations might play out well in soap operas, but in real life, they generally lead to "needy, clingy" partners who are troubled by frequent episodes of loneliness and whose relationships are less likely to last than are those of securely attached lovers.

To articulate how infantile experiences color the adult mind, Freud compared Ancient Rome (the child) with modern-day Rome (the adult) (see *Civilization and Its Discontents*, 1958, pp. 15–20). Under the great twenty-first-century metropolis lie centuries of ruins that have been buried after a repeated series of traumas such as fires, earthquakes, and invasions. Like the metaphor of Ancient Rome, the psychological traumas of infancy, childhood, and adolescence harbor still-smoldering anger, frustration, sadness, craving, longing, and a fear of mistrust and commitment that carry forward into and color subsequent adult mental models of romantic love.

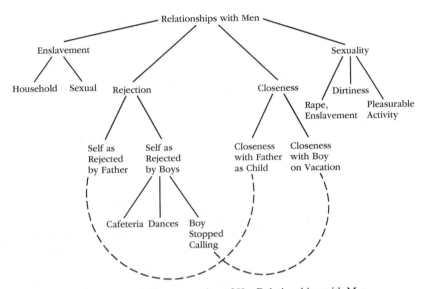

Figure 16.4   One Woman's Representation of Her Relationships with Men

Source: From "Social cognition and object relations," by D. Westen, 1991, *Psychological Bulletin, 109,* pp. 429–455. Copyright 1991 by American Psychological Corporation. Reprinted with permission.

actual relationships with men became apparent. Her mental representation, as inferred by the psychotherapist and as illustrated in Figure 16.4, contains aspects of a psychological need for relatedness (closeness, sexuality), but it also contains an ample supply of abuse (enslavement), anger and resentment (rejection), and conflict (close to, yet also rejected by, father).

The feelings associated with men are difficult to represent in a figure, but they also are part of the woman's object ("men") relations. As you might suspect, the woman's conflicting needs and feelings led her to adopt an interpersonal style toward men that was extremely anxious and avoidant.

According to object relations theory, the quality of any one's mental representations of relationships (e.g., Figure 16.4) can be characterized by three chief dimensions: (1) unconscious tone (benevolent vs. malevolent), (2) capacity for emotional involvement (selfishness/narcissism vs. mutual concern), and (3) mutuality of autonomy with others.

First, mental representations possess an unconscious affective tone (Westen, 1991). This affective coloring of the object world ranges from understanding relationships as good-benevolent versus bad-malevolent. Second, mental representations possess an unconscious capacity for emotional involvement (Westen, 1991). This capacity ranges from a narcissistic, exploitive, and unilateral orientation toward relationships to a more mature relatedness based on mutual concern, respect, and eagerness to invest in the relationship. Third, mental representations possess a capacity for the mutuality of autonomy (Urist, 1980). At its higher level (mutuality of autonomy), objects are viewed as having an autonomous existence vis-à-vis one another, and relationships present no risk to the integrity and autonomy of the participants (Ryan, Avery, & Grolnick, 1985; Urist, 1977).

Research on object relations theory underscores the fundamental motivational significance of people's psychological need for relatedness. When this need is nurtured through warm and responsive care, a person develops positive mental models of him- or herself, of significant others, and of relationships in general. Positive object relations, in turn, enable the person to develop, and to relate to others, in ways that are healthy, growth-oriented, and resistant to psychopathology. When this need for relatedness is frustrated or ignored through cold, rejecting, and unresponsive care, however, a person develops maladaptive mental models that leave him or her vulnerable to psychopathology and to developing primarily defense-oriented motivational orientations and interpersonal relationships.

CRITICISMS

Despite its intrigue, the most devastating criticism against a Freudian contribution to the study of human motivation and emotion is that many of his concepts are not scientifically testable (Crews, 1996; Eysenck, 1986). Without scientific tests, such concepts are best taken with skepticism and understood metaphorically rather than as credible scientific constructs. In science, theoretical constructs that have not yet stood the test of objective experimentation must remain guilty until proven innocent, invalid until proven valid. For this reason, psychoanalytic thinkers have spent the last 50 years finding ways to test Freud's ideas and, once accomplished, glean his many ideas into a core set of postulates like the four mentioned earlier in the chapter. Some (but certainly not all) of Freud's ideas have indeed stood the test of empirical validation (Fisher & Greenberg, 1977; Masling, 1983; Silverman, 1976). Other ideas and phenomena have been reinterpreted in ways that do not rely on psychoanalytic concepts (e.g., consider Brown's (1991) analysis of the tip-of-the-tongue phenomenon and Wegner's (1994) analysis of mental control). But on many points about human motivation and emotion, Freud was simply wrong (e.g., his theory of superego formation; Fisher & Greenberg, 1977).

A second criticism is that although psychoanalytic theory is a wonderful interpretive device for events that occurred in the past, it is woeful as a predictive device. For instance, suppose a person has a dream about siblings dying (as discussed earlier in the chapter). For one person, the dream might be best interpreted as a wish for her siblings to die. For a second person, however, the dream might be best interpreted (via reaction formation) as a wish for her siblings to survive. For yet another person, the siblings' deaths or survivals might represent sentiments associated with a third party, for instance, one's own children. All these post hoc (after the fact) interpretations make sense in psychoanalysis. The theory, however, is very poor at predicting a priori (before the fact) that a person will have a dream specifically about siblings sprouting wings and flying off into the sky. For the theory to be predictive, it must allow us to anticipate when a person will or will not have a particular type of dream, or use a particular defense mechanism, or achieve a particular level of ego development, or commit suicide, or any other course of action. A scientific theory must be able to predict what will happen in the future. It is hard to trust a theory that explains only the past. It is even harder to apply such a theory in productive ways to real-life settings, such as schools or the workplace.

In the neo-Freudian years, the ego psychologists have taken these criticisms to heart. They respect both the insight of Freud and the criticisms levied against his subjective (nonscientific) methods of data collection. The contemporary study of thought suppression, ego development, defense mechanisms, and effectance motivation use more rigorous scientific research methods and strive to build a theoretical framework that values a priori prediction over post hoc explanations. These trends can be seen even more clearly in contemporary investigations of the adaptive unconscious. The study of priming, for instance, uses experimental research methods (e.g., random assignment of participants into either experimental and control groups), objective dependent measures (e.g., reaction times), and multiple replications using different stimuli and different samples. The subject matter since Freud is pretty much the same (the unconscious), but the research methods are decidedly more objective and scientific.

To illustrate how motivation researchers have used objective scientific methods to advance their understanding of unconscious motivation, consider Timothy Wilson's (2002) reflections on "Freud's genius" and "Freud's myopia":

What Is the Nature of the Unconscious?

Freudian insight: The unconscious is a storehouse of infantile desires that must be repressed and kept out of consciousness because of its anxiety-provoking properties.

Contemporary view: Yes, but the adaptive unconscious is much more. It continually sizes up the world, generates gut feelings, makes judgments, sets goals, learns, and carries out innumerable tasks and procedures automatically and skillfully.

Why Does the Unconscious Exist?

Freudian insight: People have a long list of unacceptable desires, so they develop defenses to avoid knowing what their unconscious motives and feelings are.

Contemporary view: The mind is a well-designed system in which the adaptive unconscious does a great deal of automatic thinking and coping, while the conscious mind steps into help when reflective, analytical thinking is needed.

SUMMARY

Psychoanalysis makes for a strangely appealing study. By studying the unconscious and by embracing a rather pessimistic view of human nature, psychoanalysis opens the door to study topics such as traumatic memories, inexplicable addictions, anxieties about the future, dreams, hypnosis, inaccessible and repressed memories, fantasies, masochism, repression, self-defeating behaviors, suicidal thoughts, overwhelming impulses for revenge, and all the hidden forces that shape our needs, feelings, and ways of thinking and behaving that we would probably not want our neighbors to know about us. The subject matter of psychoanalysis strangely reflects what seems to be so popular in contemporary movies (hence, in contemporary society): sex, aggression, psychopathology, revenge, and the like.

The father of the psychoanalytic perspective was Sigmund Freud. His view of motivation presented a biologically based model in which the two instinctual drives of sex and aggression supplied the body with its physical and mental energies. But a lot has changed since Freud. Today, the following four postulates define psychodynamic theory, research, and practice:

1. *The Unconscious.* Much of mental life is unconscious.

2. *Psychodynamics.* Mental processes operate in parallel with one another.

3. *Ego Development.* Healthy development involves moving from an immature, socially dependent personality to one that is more mature and interdependent with others.

4. *Object Relations Theory.* Mental representations of self and others form in childhood that guide the person's later social motivations and relationships.

The first core postulate is the existence and importance of the unconscious. The idea that people have motives, desires, intentions, impulses, affect, and feelings that lie outside their everyday awareness is widely accepted today. So the debate mostly concerns how to understand what the unconscious is. The Freudian unconscious is the mental storehouse of inaccessible instinctual impulses, repressed experiences, childhood (before language) memories, and strong but unfulfilled wishes and desires. The adaptive unconscious runs on "automatic pilot" and rather automatically appraises the environment, sets goals, makes judgments, and initiates action, all while we are consciously thinking about something else. It is also very good (very adaptive) at what it does. Implicit motivation is rooted in past emotional associations that lie outside of our conscious awareness. As people encounter various environmental events (e.g., a challenge, an authority figure), they experience implicitly cued emotional reactions (affect, desire, anxiety) that orients, directs, and selects their attention and produces affectively consistent thoughts, feelings, and behaviors.

The second postulate of a contemporary psychodynamic understanding of motivation and emotion is that mental processes operate in parallel with one another, such that people commonly want and fear the same thing at the same time. This is the postulate of psychodynamics. It is the rule, not the exception, that people have conflicting feelings that motivate them in opposing ways. Hence, people commonly harbor divergent conscious and unconscious racial attitudes, gender biases, and love/hate (approach/avoidance) relationships with their parents, their jobs, and practically everything else in their lives.

The third postulate is that of ego development. Healthy development involves moving from an immature, socially dependent personality to one that is more mature and socially responsible. To develop and to overcome immaturity and vulnerability, the ego must gain resources and strengths, including resilient defense mechanisms for coping successfully with the inevitable anxieties of life (e.g., ego defense) and a sense of competence that provides a generative capacity for changing the environment for the better (e.g., ego effectance). The ego develops motives of its own by moving through the following developmental progression: symbiotic, impulsive, self-protective, conformist, conscientious, and autonomous. The maturity level of a person's ego defenses and competence motivation predicts life adjustment well.

The fourth postulate of a contemporary psychodynamic understanding is that mental representations of self and others form in childhood to guide adult social motivations and interpersonal relationships. This is the postulate of object relations. It argues that lifelong personality patterns begin to form in childhood as people construct mental representations of the self, others, and relationships. Once formed, these beliefs form the basis of motivational states (e.g., relatedness, anxiety) that guide the course of the adult's interpersonal relationships. Positive mental models of oneself, for instance, predict adult levels of self-reliance, social confidence, self-esteem, and loving and committed partnerships. Negative mental models, on the other hand, forecast dysfunctional interpersonal relationships.

The chapter concludes by offering a number of criticisms of a psychodynamic understanding of motivation and emotion, including relying on scientifically untestable constructs and a theoretical perspective that works better to explain and interpret the past rather than to explain and predict the future. Contemporary researchers take these criticisms seriously, and rely on experimental methods, objective dependent measures, and replication of results. Priming research illustrates a contemporary psychodynamic approach.

READINGS FOR FURTHER STUDY

Overview

WESTEN, D. (1998). The scientific legacy of Sigmund Freud: Toward a psychodynamically informed psychological science. *Psychological Bulletin, 124*, 333–371.

The Unconscious

AARTS, H., CUSTERS, R., & MARIEN, H. (2008). Preparing and motivating behavior outside of awareness. *Science, 319*, 1639.

AMBADY, N., BERNIERI, F., & RICHESON, J. (2000). Towards a histology of social behavior: Judgmental accuracy from thin slices of behavior. In M. P. Zanna (Ed.), *Advances in Experimental Social Psychology*, 201–272.

BARGH, J. A., GOLLWITZER, P. M., LEE-CHAI, K., BARNDOLLAR, K., & TROTSCHEL, R. (2001). The automated will: Nonconscious activation and pursuit of behavioral goals. *Journal of Personality and Social Psychology, 82*, 1014–1027.

HOLLAND, R. W., HENDRICKS, M., & AARTS, H. (2005). Smells like clean spirit: Nonconscious effects of scent on cognition and behavior. *Psychological Science, 16*, 689–693.

Psychodynamics

WEGNER, D. M., SCHNEIDER, D. J., CARTER, S., III, & WHITE, L. (1987). Paradoxical effects of thought suppression. *Journal of Personality and Social Psychology, 53*, 5–13.

WEGNER, D. M. (1992). You can't always think what you want: Problems in the suppression of unwanted thoughts. In M. P. Zanna (Ed.), *Advances in Experimental Social Psychology* (Vol. 25, pp. 193–225). San Diego, CA: Academic Press.

Ego Development

VAILLANT, G. E. (2000). Adaptive mental mechanisms: Their role in a positive psychology. *American Psychologist, 55*, 89–98.

WHITE, R. W. (1959). Motivation reconsidered: The concept of competence. *Psychological Review, 66*, 297–333.

Object Relations Theory

HAZAN, C., & SHAVER, P. (1987). Romantic love conceptualized as an attachment process. *Journal of Personality and Social Psychology, 52*, 511–524.

Chapter 17

Interventions

APPLYING PRINCIPLES OF MOTIVATION AND EMOTION

    Explaining Motivation and Emotion

    Predicting Motivation and Emotion

    Solving Motivational and Emotional Problems

    Practice Problems

FOUR STATE-OF-THE-ART INTERVENTIONS

    Intervention 1: Supporting Psychological Need Satisfaction

    Intervention 2: Increasing a Growth Mindset

    Intervention 3: Promoting Emotion Knowledge

    Intervention 4: Cultivating Compassion

WISDOM GAINED FROM A SCIENTIFIC STUDY OF MOTIVATION AND EMOTION

The title of the book is *Understanding Motivation and Emotion*. For 16 chapters, the goal has been to increase your capacity to understand and explain human motivation and emotion. That is a fine goal. But now it is time to get practical. Now it is time to use that understanding to improve people's lives. If you are a motivation and an emotion specialist, the way to improve people's lives is to design and then implement a high-quality intervention to strengthen people's motivational and emotional resources.

An intervention is a step-by-step plan of action to alter some existing condition. In the context of motivation and emotion study, an intervention is a step-by-step plan of action to enrich people's motivational and emotional resources and, in doing so, promote life outcomes that people care deeply about, such as enhanced engagement, skill acquisition, performance, and well-being.

Each chapter presented a number of experimental manipulations used to alter people's motivation or emotion in a temporary or momentary way. The use of short-term experimental manipulations is very important in motivation and emotion study because they provide an ideal context for researchers to test their theoretical predictions about motivation and emotion's antecedents, processes, and consequences. For instance, Table 17.1 lists one exemplary experimental manipulation taken from each of the previous content-based chapters to show how one particular motivation or emotion can be changed on a short-term basis. Collectively, these examples are important because they make the point that motivation and emotion are malleable and can be changed and strengthened.

Table 17.1   Chapter-by-Chapter Listing of One Featured Experimental Manipulation for Each Chapter

Chapter	Motivation/Emotion	Experimental Manipulation
3	Trust	Squirt of a nasal spray of the oxytocin hormone.
4	Sexual Attraction	Facial metrics of large eyes, small nose, and small chin.
5	Extrinsic Motivation	Offering a scholarship for making very high grades.
6	Autonomy	Opportunity to pursue an interest or a personal goal.
7	Power	Elected into a position of leadership.
8	Discrepancy	Goal to strive for.
9	Growth Mindset	Story about how hard Einstein worked to become so smart.
10	Self-Efficacy	Exposure to a highly competent role model.
11	Self-Control Depletion	Resisting an attractive temptation for five minutes.
12	Positive Affect	Receiving a small unexpected gift.
13	Sadness	Viewing a film about a son at his dad's funeral.
14	Embarrassment	Committing a social blunder in front of an audience.
15	Incongruence	Parental negative conditional regard.
16	Obsession	Keep a secret about the person to whom you are talking.

Successfully demonstrating that motivational and emotional resources are malleable and can be strengthened is important theoretically. From a more practical point of view, however, short-term boosts to people's motivation and emotion are not enough. What is needed in applied settings such as the schools, the workplace, in therapy, in healthcare, in the home, and on the athletic field, is a long-term effort to build people's enduring motivational and emotional resources. To produce these changes, one needs to go beyond brief experimental manipulations to employ step-by-step, state-of-the-art intervention programs. In this chapter, we present four such exemplary interventions, one each to show how needs, cognitions, emotions, and applied life pursuits can be strengthened in an enduring way.

APPLYING PRINCIPLES OF MOTIVATION AND EMOTION

It is actually difficult to design a highly effective intervention without first having a solid theoretical framework to guide and inform its design. So, step 1 in designing a successful intervention is to double-check the depth and sophistication of one's theoretical understanding of motivation and emotion. Thus, before presenting specific illustrations of how motivation and emotion theory has been translated successfully into practice, we need to determine our intellectual readiness to design a state-of-the-art intervention. To assess that readiness, consider your current confidence in answering the three following questions:

1. Can you explain why people do what they do?
2. Can you predict in advance how conditions will affect motivation and emotion?
3. Can you apply motivational principles to solve practical problems?

Explaining Motivation and Emotion

Explaining the reasons for behavior—explaining why we do what we do—requires the ability to generate psychologically satisfying answers to questions such as, Why did he do that? Why does she want that? Why is he so afraid of or so resistant to a particular course of action? Answers to these questions lie in understanding the source of motivation and how motives, once aroused, intensify, change, and fade.

To explain why we do what we do, Chapter 1 listed 31 motivation theories (see Table 1.5). Each theory provides a piece of the puzzle that is the grand effort to explain human wants, desires, emotions, and strivings. Collectively, these theories address most of the circumstances in which the reader might be interested. Having an empirically validated theory at your side will help you explain why a particular motivational phenomenon rises, persists, and declines, and which particular conditions in the person, in the environment, in the social context, and in the culture affect that phenomenon. With such a theory in mind, it becomes easier to answer questions such as the following: Why do people set high goals for themselves? Why do people procrastinate when it is so obvious that there is work to be done? Why do people engage in risky behaviors such as parachute jumping or driving really fast? Motivation and emotion theories provide a means to understand and explain why we do what we do and why we want what we want.

Predicting Motivation and Emotion

Can you predict changes in people's motivation and emotion *before they occur*? Can you predict the rise and fall of motivational and emotional states? Which antecedents energize, direct, and sustain which motivations and emotions? Biological, psychological, environmental, interpersonal, social, and cultural conditions all change, so the question is, Can you predict how changes in these antecedents will produce corresponding changes in motivation and emotion?

Quiz yourself on how 10 different antecedents covered in the earlier chapters can be expected to change motivation and emotion. For each antecedent, check whether a helpful theory comes to mind that allows you to predict what effect that condition might have on motivation and emotion:

- 24 hours of deprivation (from food, people)
- threatening "anger face" emotional display
- smell a cleaning solution
- expected, tangible reward (e.g., money)
- highly competent role model
- standard of excellence
- unresponsive, uncontrollable environment
- autonomy-supportive teacher
- obstacle to one's goal
- failure in front of others at and easy task

Solving Motivational and Emotional Problems

The more you understand the principles of motivation and emotion, the greater will be your capacity to find workable solutions to real-world motivational and emotional problems.

Solving such problems means empowering people toward more intentional action, optimal experience, positive functioning, goal attainment, positive emotion, a resilient sense of self, and healthy development and away from impulsive action, habitual experience, counterproductive functioning, goal failure, negative emotion, a fragile sense of self, and maladaptive or dysfunctional development.

Empowering self and others involves identifying, nurturing, and utilizing strengths while also identifying, challenging, and repairing weaknesses and vulnerabilities. Quiz yourself again, this time by asking what you might do to promote the following 10 constructive motivational states in self and others:

- Resilient self-efficacy beliefs
- Autonomy need satisfaction
- Flow experience
- A fully functioning individual
- Mastery motivational orientation
- Difficult, specific, and self-congruent goals
- Mastery goals
- Ego development
- Joy
- Gratitude

And, quiz yourself by asking what you might do to overcome the following 10 motivational pathologies in self and others:

- Restraint release that leads to binge eating
- Hidden costs of reward
- Learned helplessness
- Fixed mindset
- Depleted self-control
- Pessimistic explanatory style
- Thought suppression
- Immature defense mechanisms
- Hubristic pride
- Malicious envy

Practice Problems

Consider the five case studies featured in Box 17. These case studies are offered as a practice opportunity to think about how to solve common motivational and emotional problems. In each case, a person faces a different problem. The child finds it difficult to generate the motivation she needs to engage in an uninteresting, devalued course of action. The salesperson faces the challenge of maintaining her confidence, interest, optimism, and hope

---

BOX 17   *Five Practice Case Studies*

Question: Why is this information important?

Answer: To practice understanding and solving motivational and emotional problems.

Consider five case studies in which a different person faces a motivational or an emotional issue. Use each case study to practice the threefold task of (1) explaining, (2) predicting, and (3) applying motivation and emotion. The goal is to explain why the person's motivation is what it is, predict how his or her motivation would change in response to different events, and propose an intervention to affect the person's motivation and emotion for the better.

Child at Home

A child resists brushing her teeth at night before going to bed. She does not like it. She does not do it. And, when she does brush her teeth, she does it poorly and only half-heartedly (e.g., she just plays with the water). But her parents see high value in her brushing and they encourage her to do so, although they dread having to deal with their daughter's resistance night after night.

Employee at Work

A sales representative for a large company receives a monthly sales quota and is told that everything is fine so long as she meets or exceeds her quota. She feels that she has the skills for the job, but 90 percent of the calls she makes fail to produce a sell. The day-to-day job experience is one of rejection and frustration. She is thinking about quitting and looking for another job.

Athlete or Musician

An athlete (or musician) performs well, and she very much enjoys her sport (instrument). She loves to play and practice, but she would like to develop her talents further, much further in fact. For some reason, her rate of improvement is laboriously slow and often nonexistent. She wants to become an elite performer, but it does not seem to be happening.

Medical Patient

A physician tells a patient to lose 40 pounds or risk a heart attack. The patient understands the need to make a lifestyle change. Although he knows the physician is right, he is nevertheless pessimistic that he will ever take his physician's advice and make the lifestyle change. Exercise and a healthy diet are just not his thing. He doubts that the lifestyle change is really worth the fuss.

Suffering Student

A student is taking a class he thought would be easy. He only sometimes pays attention in class, and he only sometimes reads the textbook. On the mid-term exam, he does so poorly that he feels ashamed of himself. He cannot possibly tell anyone how poorly he performed. He has lost all motivation for the second half of the course and wishes he could just stop going.

---

in the face of frequent failure and potential burnout. The athlete wants to develop talent and enhance performance, but she is having a difficult time doing so. The patient faces the difficult, energy-demanding task of initiating and maintaining a lifestyle change. And, the student faces the very painful emotional state that comes from feedback that suggests that something is wrong with the self.

In reading each case study, pursue the three earlier listed objectives—namely, explain motivation, predict motivation, and solve motivational problems. First, attempt to diagnose why the person is currently experiencing that particular motivational experience. You will not, of course, have access to the important details of his or her situation, but you can still generate a number of possible hypotheses. Second, once you have several hypotheses to work with, identify the key sources of the person's motivation. What conditions could affect a change in the person's motivation? Third, apply your knowledge of motivation and emotion to generate a productive course of action to help each person generate the energy and direction needed to solve the motivational or emotional issue.

FOUR STATE-OF-THE-ART INTERVENTIONS

One reason why motivation and emotion study is important is because researchers have been able to design and implement successful interventions to improve people's lives. Below are four success stories in the effort to translate motivation and emotion theory into very practical state-of-the-art intervention programs. The first intervention illustrates a need-based intervention, the second illustrates a cognition-based intervention, the third an emotion-based intervention, and the fourth an applied life concern intervention.

Intervention 1: Supporting Psychological Need Satisfaction

In many classrooms, students receive instruction in a way that ignores their psychological needs. That is, teachers ask students to write papers, complete projects, and learn new skills in ways that leave students' psychological needs dormant. As featured in Chapter 6, students—like everybody else—possess the three psychological needs for autonomy, competence, and relatedness, and these three needs energize and vitalize their classroom engagement and learning. Recognizing this, one group of researchers developed an intervention program to help teachers develop a motivating style capable of supporting students' psychological needs. Specifically, the researchers developed, implemented, and tested the merits of an autonomy supportive intervention program (ASIP; Cheon, Reeve, & Moon, 2012).

What autonomy-supportive teachers do during instruction is take their students' perspective, listen empathically to what students say, and utilize instructional strategies such as nurturing inner motivational resources, providing explanatory rationales, using informational language, displaying patience, and acknowledging and accepting students' expressions of negative affect. These are not commonly occurring classroom events, but these instructional strategies can be learned. The intervention program provided to teachers to help them learn how to be more autonomy supportive appears on the lower half of Figure 17.1. The experimentally designed, longitudinally based empirical study implemented to test the validity and efficacy of the intervention appears on the upper half of Figure 17.1.

The study recruited 21 experienced middle- and high-school Korean teachers and randomly assigned them into either the experimental or control condition. For the 10 teachers in the experimental group, the autonomy-supportive intervention program (ASIP) was delivered in three parts. Part 1 was a three-hour workshop offered prior to the beginning of the semester. During the workshop, teachers learned what autonomy support is, why it is important, and how to implement it in the classroom. To learn the "how to" of autonomy support, teachers watched and discussed videotapes of other teachers modeling the five autonomy-supportive instructional behaviors. Part 2 was a two-hour group discussion that took place one month into the semester. In the discussion, teachers shared their actual experiences with trying to implement autonomy-supportive teaching in their own classrooms. Part 3 was another two-hour group discussion, and it took place in the second half of the semester. Teachers shared and exchanged their ideas, experiences, and instructional strategies. To assess the validity and effectiveness of the intervention program, the students of teachers in both conditions completed questionnaires to report their perceptions of their teacher's motivating style as well as their own motivation and classroom functioning at the beginning (Time 1, or T1), middle (T2), and end (T3) of the semester. In addition, a group

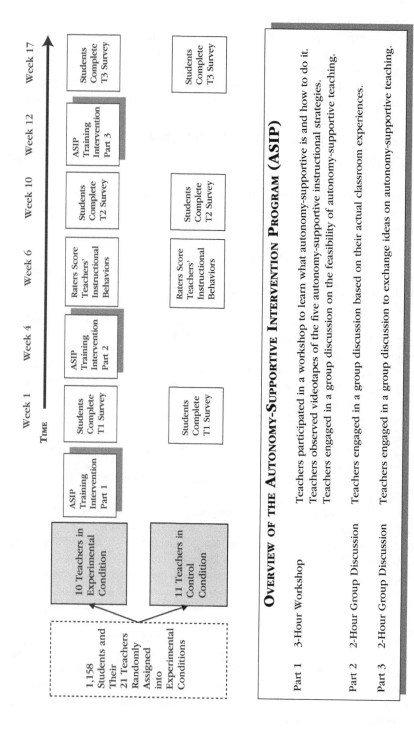

Figure 17.1 Design of an Intervention to Support Students' Psychological Needs during Instruction

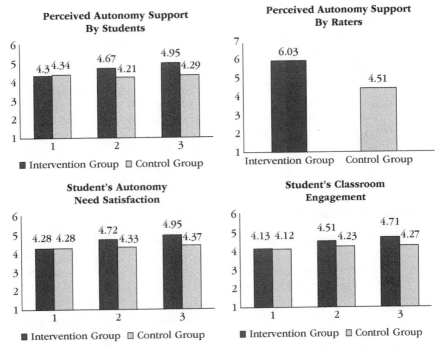

Figure 17.2 Results Showing that the Intervention Was Successful (Two Upper Panels) and Beneficial for Students (Two Lower Panels)

of trained raters visited each teacher's classroom midway through the semester (Week 6) to rate objectively how frequently teachers actually used each of the five autonomy-supportive instructional behaviors during instruction.

Results from the semester-long ASIP appear in Figure 17.2. The upper two figures report the evidence that the intervention produced its intended effect, while the lower two figures report the evidence that the intervention produced positive benefits. As shown in the upper left panel, students of teachers in the control group reported that their teachers' autonomy support did not change throughout the semester (4.34 = 4.21 = 4.29), while students of teachers in the experimental group reported that their teachers became increasingly more autonomy supportive (4.30 -> 4.67 -> 4.95). As shown in the upper right panel, the trained raters scored the teachers in the experimental group as enacting significantly more autonomy-supportive instructional behaviors than did teachers in the control group (6.03 > 4.51). Together, these two figures confirm that the intervention produced its intended effect in helping teachers in the experimental group teach in a more autonomy-supportive way.

The lower two figures report the evidence that the intervention produced positive benefits. As shown in the lower left panel, students in the control group reported a level of autonomy need satisfaction that did not change throughout the semester (4.28 = 4.33 = 4.37), while students in the experimental group reported a steadily increasing level of autonomy need satisfaction (4.28 -> 4.72 -> 4.95). As shown in the lower right panel, students in the control group reported a level of classroom engagement that did not change throughout the semester (4.12 = 4.23 = 4.27), while students in the experimental group reported a steadily increasing level of classroom engagement (4.13 -> 4.51 -> 4.71). Although not shown in Figure 17.2, students of teachers in the experimental group also showed steadily increasing levels of competence need satisfaction, relatedness need satisfaction, autonomous motivation, perceived skill development, and academic achievement, whereas the students of teachers in the control group did not.

In a supplemental analysis, the researchers showed that the reason why students showed end-of-semester gains in all these positive course outcomes could be explained by their increased mid-semester psychological need satisfaction. That is, the intervention allowed teachers to be more autonomy supportive, which allowed students to experience greater psychological need satisfaction during class, which in turn explained why students showed such positive end-of-course outcomes. Overall, this intervention is a success story because it shows that teachers can learn how to support students' psychological need satisfaction.

Intervention 2: Increasing a Growth Mindset

Adolescent aggression is a problem, especially when it takes on a violent tone. Some adolescent aggression is unprovoked, but most occurs as retaliation to peer conflict, social exclusion, and victimization. In a conflict, adolescents generally make a personality-like analysis of the other person's character. When a victim sees the other as a trait-like "bully," then the thinking is that the other cannot change. This belief leads to aggressive retaliation, because harming the aggressor seems deserved. When a victim sees the other as someone who can change, then this belief tends to reduce aggressive retaliation and open up the possibility for a prosocial response. To the extent that this is true, then adolescents who embrace a fixed mindset—a belief that people cannot change their personalities—would be more likely to be aggressive than would adolescents who embrace a growth mindset, as discussed in Chapter 11. Recognizing this, one group of researchers developed an intervention program to help adolescents endorse a growth mindset in thinking about people's personality. Specifically, the researchers developed, implemented, and tested the merits of a growth mindset workshop (Yeager, Trzesniewski, & Dweck, 2013). The intervention program provided to help adolescence adopt a growth-oriented mindset appears on the lower half of Figure 17.3. The experimentally designed, longitudinally based empirical study implemented to test the validity and efficacy of the intervention appears on the upper half of Figure 17.3.

The study recruited 111 ninth- and tenth-grade students in several different high schools in the San Francisco area, and classrooms of students were randomly assigned into either the experimental or control condition. For the three classrooms of students in the experimental group, the growth mindset intervention was delivered over three consecutive weeks. In Week 1, students attended lectures and engaged in activities to teach them the science of a growth mindset, including the key idea that the brain changes with learning. In Week 2, students attended lectures and engaged in activities to teach them that personalities live in brains and brains can change. In Week 3, students attended lectures to teach them that thoughts and feelings can also change, and they engaged in activities to help them think about peer conflict and aggression. To assess the validity and effectiveness of the intervention program, students completed a questionnaire assessing the growth mindset two weeks before the start of the intervention and again two weeks after the intervention ended (week 5). In Week 7, students played a "cyberball" activity in which they suffered an experience of peer exclusion. After the peer exclusion experience, participants were given

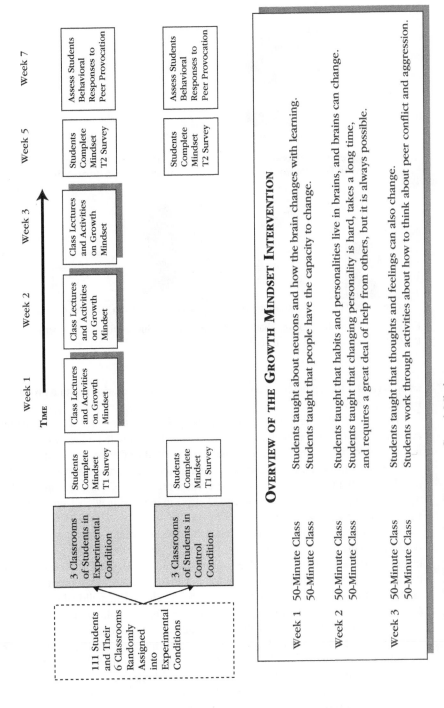

Figure 17.3 Design of an Intervention to Increase a Growth Mindset

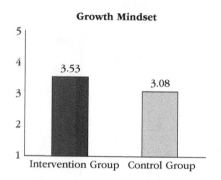

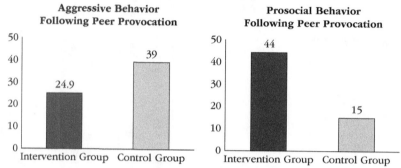

Figure 17.4 Results Showing that the Intervention Was Successful (Two Upper Panels) and Beneficial for Students (Two Lower Panels)

an opportunity to behave in an aggressive (aggressive retaliation) or in a prosocial (write a friendly note) way.

Results from the three-week intervention appear in Figure 17.4. The single upper figure reports the evidence that the intervention produced its intended effect, while the lower two figures report the evidence that the intervention produced positive benefits. As shown in the upper panel, adolescents in the experimental group endorsed the growth mindset significantly more than did adolescents in the control group (3.53 > 3.08). This result confirms that the intervention produced its intended effect in increasing adolescents' endorsement of a personality-based growth mindset.

The lower two figures report evidence that the intervention produced positive benefits. As shown in the lower left panel, when adolescents were provoked by peer exclusion, those in the experimental group showed less aggressive behavior than did adolescents in the control group (24.9 < 39.0). As shown in the lower right panel, when provoked, adolescents in the experimental group showed more prosocial behavior than did adolescents in the control group (44.0 > 15.0). Although not shown in Figure 17.4, the adolescents' classroom teachers rated how aggressive each student had been over the last few weeks, with aggression being defined as making fun of other students, hitting, slapping, pushing, threatening, excluding, insulting, and spreading rumors. Teachers rated adolescents in the experimental group as significantly less aggressive than they rated adolescents in the control group.

Overall, the study showed that a school-based intervention that taught adolescents the science of the growth mindset was able to take the anger- and aggression-based edge out of peer conflict so that aggressive retaliation became less likely while a prosocial behavior response became more likely. This intervention is a success story because it shows that adolescents can learn the growth mindset.

Intervention 3: Promoting Emotion Knowledge

Children with unsophisticated emotion knowledge are at risk of developing maladaptive behavior problems. Emotion knowledge involves a child's capacity to recognize emotional expressions in others, produce a correct label for those emotional expressions, and articulate the causes of basic emotions. Maladaptive behavior problems include interpersonal conflict, classroom disruptive behavior, aggressive behavior, and the absence of social competence. If children could develop their emotion knowledge and learn how to better utilize their positive emotions (interest, joy), then they would be better positioned to regulate their negative emotions (fear, anger) and maladaptive behavior problems. Recognizing this, one group of researchers developed an intervention program within the context of a Head Start preschool program to deliver an "Emotions Course" and an "Emotion-Based Prevention Program" to promote children's emotion knowledge (Izard et al., 2008).

In the Emotions Course, children engage in activities (e.g., a puppet show) that provide opportunities to label basic emotions. Children also draw faces of emotional expressions to depict both the different emotions and different intensity levels of those emotions. The point of the Emotions Course is to increase children's skill in decoding or recognizing emotional expressions in others. In the Emotion-Based Prevention Program, children engage in activities that create mild emotions (reading books about characters that have emotional episodes) as teachers help them articulate their feeling states, understand the causes of these emotions, and take action to regulate them. To regulate anger, for instance, children are taught to hug a pillow (to reduce anger-generated arousal), take three deep breaths, and then use words to negotiate. The intervention program provided to promote children's emotion knowledge appears on the lower half of Figure 17.5. The experimentally designed, longitudinally based empirical study implemented to test the validity and efficacy of the intervention appears on the upper half of Figure 17.5.

The study recruited 177 preschool students and their 26 teachers who were involved in a low-income preschool Head Start program in the rural mid-Atlantic states, and teachers were randomly assigned into either the experimental or control condition. For the 15 teachers in the experimental group, the Emotions Course (EC) and Emotion-Based Prevention (EBP) Program were delivered in three parts. Part 1 was a two-hour workshop before the semester began to help teachers learn how to teach the Emotions Course in their classrooms. For Part 2, a member from the research team observed the teacher's classroom on a biweekly basis and then provided a post-class consultation to refine and improve the teacher's delivery of the EC and EBP. In Part 3, researchers met with the parents of the 177 children on a monthly basis to discuss the EC content and its instructional strategies. In these meetings, parents discussed teachers' instructional techniques to help children understand, regulate, and utilize basic emotions. The validity and effectiveness of the intervention program were assessed in three ways: (1) Children took an emotion knowledge test (e.g., view a photograph of an emotional facial expression and identify which emotion it is); (2) teachers rated the children on both emotion knowledge and frequency of expressing positive emotions (interest, joy) during class; and (3) trained raters objectively scored the frequency with which each child displayed negative emotional

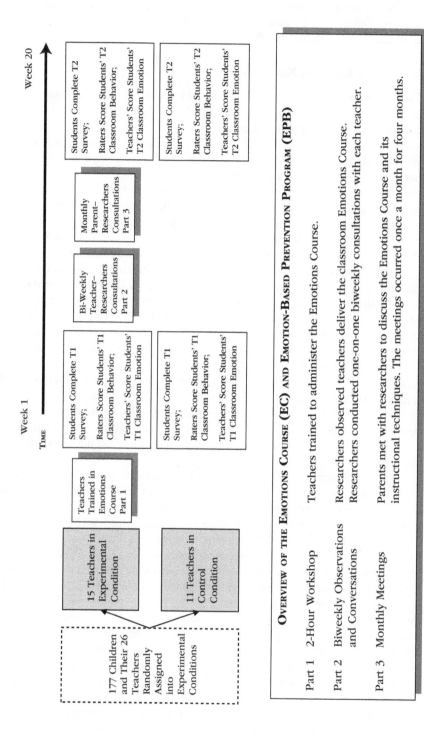

Figure 17.5 Design of an Intervention to Promote Emotion Knowledge

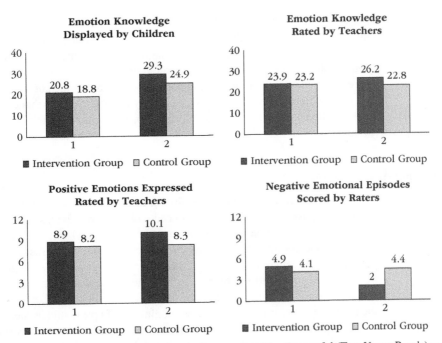

Figure 17.6   Results Showing that the Intervention Was Successful (Two Upper Panels) and Beneficial for Students (Two Lower Panels)

episodes during class. All these measures were scored the week before the intervention began (T1) and again at the end of the intervention (T2).

Results from the 20-week EC and EBP intervention program appear in Figure 17.6. The two upper figures report evidence that the intervention produced its intended effect, while the lower two figures report the evidence that the intervention produced positive benefits. As shown in the upper left panel, children in the control group showed greater emotion knowledge (because they were now older; 18.8 -> 24.9) while children in the experimental group showed a significantly greater gain in their emotion knowledge (20.8 -> 29.3). As shown in the upper right panel, teachers rated children in the control group as showing the same emotion knowledge after 20 weeks (23.2 = 22.8), while teachers rated children in the experimental group as showing a significant increase in their emotion knowledge after 20 weeks (23.9 -> 26.2). Together, these two figures confirm that the intervention produced its intended effect in helping children in the experimental group increase their emotion knowledge.

The lower two figures report the evidence that the intervention produced positive benefits. As shown in the lower left panel, teachers rated that the children in the control group expressed the same frequency of positive emotions after 20 weeks (8.2 = 8.3), while teachers rated that the children in the experimental group expressed positive emotions significantly more frequently after 20 weeks (8.9 -> 10.1). As shown in the lower right panel, raters scored the children in the control group as displaying the same number of negative emotional episodes after 20 weeks (4.1 = 4.4), while raters scored the children in the experimental group as displaying a significantly lower number of negative emotional episodes after 20 weeks (4.9 -> 2.0). Although not shown in Figure 17.6, teachers rated children in their class as displaying fewer post-intervention negative emotions and more post-intervention social competence, while parents rated the children in the experimental group as displaying less post-intervention aggressive behavior and less post-intervention depressive behavior at home that did parents of children in the control group.

Overall, this intervention is a success story because it shows that children can increase their emotion knowledge and, when they do, they increase their capacity for effective emotion regulation.

Intervention 4: Cultivating Compassion

Compassion is the recognition of suffering in others and the desire to alleviate that suffering. Compassion is positively associated with positive affect, social connectedness, and kindness to self and others, while it is negatively associated with negative affect and stress. While many emotion researchers recognized compassion as a prosocial emotion, it is not yet clear how compassion might be cultivated. Recognizing this, one group of researchers developed an intervention program to help members of a community cultivate a greater capacity for compassion. Specifically, the researchers developed, implemented, and tested the merits of a compassion cultivation training (CCT) program (Jazaieri et al., 2013a, b).

Compassion can be trained, and it is trained by mental exercises such as meditation. The week-by-week mental exercises included in the CCT program appear in the lower part of Figure 17.7. While the first week was an introductory week, the next six weeks included meditation-based mental exercises that included settling and focusing the mind, embracing loving-kindness for a loved one, embracing loving-kindness for oneself, embracing a shared common humanity and developing a greater appreciation of others, and cultivating compassion for others. The last two weeks added new compassion cultivating exercises. The intervention program provided to help community members cultivate greater compassion toward others and self appears on the lower half of Figure 17.7. The experimentally designed, longitudinally based empirical study implemented to test the validity and efficacy of the intervention appears on the upper half of Figure 17.7.

The study recruited 100 middle-aged members from the San Francisco area community and randomly assigned them into either the experimental or control condition. For the 60 participants in the experimental group, the cultivating compassion training (CCT) program was delivered over the course of nine consecutive weeks. To assess the validity and effectiveness of the intervention program, participants in both conditions completed questionnaires assessing compassion for others, compassion for self, several measures of affect (e.g., worry, stress, happiness), and several measures of emotion regulation strategies (e.g., cognitive reappraisal, cognitive suppression) once before the intervention began and again for a second time after the intervention ended 10 weeks later.

Results from the nine-week CCT program appear in Figure 17.8. The upper two figures report the evidence that the intervention produced its intended effect, while the lower two figures report the evidence that the intervention produced positive benefits. As shown in the upper left panel, participants in the control group reported an unchanged level of compassion for others 10 weeks later (2.94 = 3.05), while participants in the experimental group reported a level of compassion for others that was significantly higher 10 weeks later (2.76 -> 3.29). As shown in the upper right panel, participants in the control group

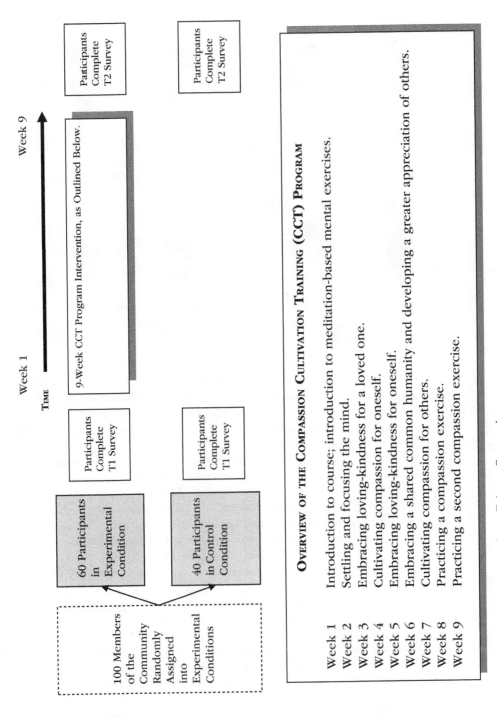

Week 1 → Week 9

TIME

100 Members of the Community Randomly Assigned into Experimental Conditions

60 Participants in Experimental Condition → Participants Complete T1 Survey → 9-Week CCT Program Intervention, as Outlined Below. → Participants Complete T2 Survey

40 Participants in Control Condition → Participants Complete T1 Survey → Participants Complete T2 Survey

OVERVIEW OF THE COMPASSION CULTIVATION TRAINING (CCT) PROGRAM

Week 1 Introduction to course; introduction to meditation-based mental exercises.
Week 2 Settling and focusing the mind.
Week 3 Embracing loving-kindness for a loved one.
Week 4 Cultivating compassion for oneself.
Week 5 Embracing loving-kindness for oneself.
Week 6 Embracing a shared common humanity and developing a greater appreciation of others.
Week 7 Cultivating compassion for others.
Week 8 Practicing a compassion exercise.
Week 9 Practicing a second compassion exercise.

Figure 17.7 Design of an Intervention to Enhance Compassion

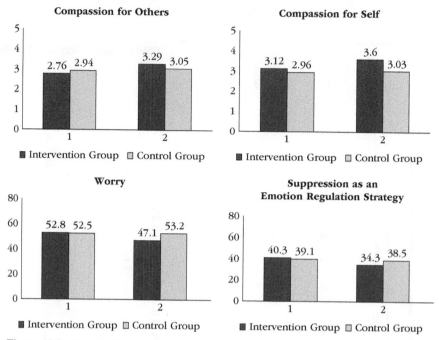

Figure 17.8   Results Showing that the Intervention Was Successful (Two Upper Panels) and Beneficial for Students (Two Lower Panels)

reported that their compassion for self did not change 10 weeks later (2.96 = 3.03), while participants in the experimental group reported that their compassion for self increased 10 weeks later (3.12 -> 3.60). Together, these two figures confirm that the intervention produced its intended effect in helping middle-age members of the community cultivate a greater capacity for compassion.

The lower two figures report the evidence that the intervention produced positive benefits. As shown in the lower left panel, participants in the control group reported that their worry emotionality did not change 10 weeks later (52.5 = 53.2), while participants in the experimental group reported that their worry emotionality decreased significantly (52.8 -> 47.1). As shown in the lower right panel, participants in the control group reported that their reliance on suppression as an emotion regulation strategy did not change 10 weeks later (39.1 = 38.5), while participants in the experimental group reported that their reliance on suppression as an emotion regulation strategy decreased significantly (40.3 -> 34.3). Although not shown in Figure 17.8, participants in the experimental group did not report any greater increase in happiness or any greater reliance on reappraisal as an emotion regulation strategy than did participants in the control group.

Overall, this intervention is a success story because it shows that people from the community can learn how to cultivate a greater capacity for compassion. The intervention did produce positive benefits, but it is worth noting that these benefits were not as widespread and not of the same magnitude as observed in the first three interventions. This fourth intervention study did, however, show an effect not observed in the other three interventions—namely, a dosage effect. That is, participants who completed the

CCT intervention program engaged in varying hours of meditation with some engaging in only the minimum required hours while others engaging in many more extra hours of mediation practice. Hours of meditation practice correlated significantly (negatively) with post-intervention worry and suppression. That is, the more one meditated, the less was her subsequent worry and suppression.

WISDOM GAINED FROM A SCIENTIFIC STUDY OF MOTIVATION AND EMOTION

The book's almost 500 pages have reported a barrage of theories and empirical findings. In this final section, it is time to go beyond the collection of knowledge and reflect so to draw out the wisdom that might be gained from the effort to understand motivation and emotion. Here, are 17 pearls of wisdom—one extracted from each of the 17 chapters. Your own reflection on the key take-away from each chapter might lead you to generate a different list from the one below, but perhaps the effort to generate such a list will help you open the door to seeing, understanding, and appreciating the wider implications of motivation and emotion study.

Chapter 1	Human wants and desires can be discovered using scientific methods.
Chapter 2	What we don't yet know about motivation and emotion exceeds what we do know.
Chapter 3	The brain is as much about motivation and emotion as it is about cognition and thinking.
Chapter 4	We underestimate how powerful biological urges can be when we are not currently experiencing them.
Chapter 5	Quality of motivation is as important as is quantity of motivation.
Chapter 6	To flourish, motivation needs supportive conditions, especially supportive relationships.
Chapter 7	Implicit (unconscious) motives predict behavior better than do explicit (conscious) motives.
Chapter 8	We do not do our best when we "try to do our best"; rather, we do our best when we have a specific action plan to pursue a difficult, specific, and self-congruent goal.
Chapter 9	Two people with the same goal but a different mindset will pursue that goal in different ways.
Chapter 10	Competent, enthusiastic functioning requires the two core beliefs of "I can do it" and "It will work."
Chapter 11	Boosting self-esteem is a poor motivational strategy. What works is exerting self-control over short-term urges so to pursue a long-term goal.
Chapter 12	All emotions are good; all emotions serve a functional purpose.
Chapter 13	Other people are the source of most of our emotions.
Chapter 14	The more sophisticated and complex our emotional repertoire is, the more likely we are to have the right emotion for every situation.
Chapter 15	Encouraging growth is more productive than is curing weakness.
Chapter 16	Motivation often arises from a source outside of conscious awareness.
Chapter 17	There is nothing so practical as a good theory.

REFERENCES

Aarts, H., & Dijksterhuis, A. (2003). The silence of the library: Environment, situational norm, and social behavior. *Journal of Personality and Social Psychology, 84*, 18–28.

Aarts, H., Custers, R., & Marien, H. (2008, March 21). Preparing and motivating behavior outside of awareness. *Science, 319*, 1639.

Aarts, H., Dijksterhuis, A., & Midden, C. (1999). To plan or not to plan: Goal achievement of interrupting the performance of mundane behavior. *European Journal of Social Psychology, 29*, 971–979.

Abe, J. A. A., & Izard, C. E. (1999). The developmental functions of emotions: An analysis in terms of differential emotions theory. *Cognition and Emotion, 13*, 523–549.

Abramson, L. Y., & Alloy, L. B. (1980). Judgment of contingency: Errors and their implications. In A. Baum & J. Singer (Eds.), *Advances in environmental psychology: Applications of personal control* (Vol. 2, pp. 111–130). Hillsdale, NJ: Erlbaum.

Achtziger, A., Gollwitzer, P. M., & Sheeran, P. (2008). Implementation intentions and shielding goal strivings from unwanted thoughts and feelings, *Personality and Social Psychology Bulletin, 34*, 381–393.

Adelmann, P. K., & Zajonc, R. B. (1989). Facial efference and the experience of emotion. *Annual Review of Psychology, 40*, 249–280.

Adkins, K. K., & Parker, W. (1996). Perfectionism and suicidal preoccupation. *Journal of Personality, 64*, 529–543.

Adolph, E. F. (1980). Intakes are limited: Satieties. *Appetite, 1*, 337–342.

Adolphs, R., Tranel, D., Damasio, H., & Damasio, A. (1994). Impaired recognition of emotion in facial expressions following bilateral damage to the human amygdala. *Nature, 372*, 669–672.

Adriaanse, M. A., De Ridder, D. T. D., & De Wit, J. B. F. (2009). Finding the critical cue: Implementation intentions to change one's diet work best when tailored to personally relevant reasons for unhealthy eating. *Personality and Social Psychology Bulletin, 35*, 60–71.

Aggleton, J. P. (1992). The functional effects of amygdala lesions in humans: A comparison with findings from monkeys. In J. P. Aggleton (Ed.), *The amygdala: Neurobiological aspects of emotion, memory, and mental dysfunction* (pp. 485–503). New York: Wiley.

Agnati, L. F., Bjelke, B., & Fuxe, K. (1992). Volume transmission in the brain. *American Scientist, 80*, 362–373.

Ainsworth, M. D. S. (1989). Attachments beyond infancy. *American Psychologist, 44*, 709–716.

Ainsworth, M. D. S., Blehar, M. C., Waters, E., & Wall, S. (1978). *Patterns of attachment: A psychological study of the strange situation.* Hillsdale, NJ: Erlbaum.

Aldao, A., & Nolen-Hoeksema, S. (2013). One versus many: Capturing the use of multiple emotion regulation strategies in response to an emotion-eliciting stimulus. *Cognition and Emotion, 27*, 753–760.

Aldao, A., Nolen-Hoeksema, S., & Schweizer, S. (2010). Emotion-regulation strategies across psychopathology: A meta-analytic review. *Clinical Psychology Review, 30*, 217–237.

Alexander, P. A., Kulikowich, J. M., & Jetton, T. L. (1994). The role of subject-matter knowledge and interest in the processing of linear and nonlinear text. *Review of Educational Research, 64*, 201–252.

Algoe, S. B. (2012). Find, remind, and bind: The functions of gratitude in everyday relationships. *Social and Personality Psychology Compass, 6*, 455–469.

Algoe, S. B., Fredrickson, B. L., & Gable, S. L. (2013). The social functions of the emotion of gratitude via expression. *Emotion, 13,* 605–609.

Algoe, S. B., Gable, S. L., & Maisel, N. (2010). It's the little things: Everyday gratitude as a booster shot for romantic relationships. *Personal Relationships, 17,* 217–233.

Alloy, L. B., & Abramson, L. T. (1979). Judgment of contingency in depressed and nondepressed students: Sadder but wiser? *Journal of Experimental Psychology: General, 108,* 441–485.

Alloy, L. B., & Abramson, L. T. (1982). Learned helplessness, depression, and the illusion of control. *Journal of Personality and Social Psychology, 42,* 1114–1126.

Alloy, L. B., & Abramson, L. Y. (1988). Depressive realism: Four theoretical approaches. In L. B. Alloy (Ed.), *Cognitive processes in depression* (pp. 223–265). New York: Guilford Press.

Alloy, L. B., & Seligman, M. E. P. (1979). On the cognitive component of learned helplessness and depression. *Psychology of Learning and Motivation, 13,* 219–276.

Amabile, T. M. (1983). *The social psychology of creativity.* New York: Springer-Verlag.

Amabile, T. M. (1985). Motivation and creativity: Effect of motivational orientation on creative writers. *Journal of Personality and Social Psychology, 48,* 393–399.

Amabile, T. M. (1998). How to kill creativity. *Harvard Business Review, 76,* 76–87.

Amabile, T. M., DeJong, W., & Lepper, M. R. (1976). Effects of externally-imposed deadlines on subsequent intrinsic motivation. *Journal of Personality and Social Psychology, 34,* 92–98.

Amabile, T. M., Hennessey, B. A., & Grossman, B. S. (1986). Social influences on creativity: The effects of contracted-for reward. *Journal of Personality and Social Psychology, 50,* 14–23.

Ambady, N., Bernieri, F. J., & Richeson, J. A. (2000). Toward a histology of social behavior: Judgmental accuracy from thin slices of the behavioral stream. In M. P. Zanna (Ed.), *Advances in Experimental Social Psychology, 32,* 201–271.

American Psychiatric Association (2013). *Diagnostic and statistical manual of mental disorders* (5th ed.). Arlington, VA: American Psychiatric Publishing.

Ames, C. A., & Archer, J. (1988). Achievement goals in the classroom: Student learning strategies and motivational processes. *Journal of Educational Psychology, 80,* 260–267.

Ames, R., & Ames, C. A. (1984). Introduction. In R. Ames & C. A. Ames (Eds.), *Research on motivation in education: Student motivation* (Vol. *1,* pp. 1–11). Orlando, FL: Academic Press.

Anand, B. K., Chhina, G. S., & Singh, B. (1962). Effect of glucose on the activity of hypothalamic feeding centers. *Science, 138,* 597–598.

Andersen, B. L., & Cyranowski, J. M. (1994). Women's sexual self-schema. *Journal of Personality and Social Psychology, 67,* 1079–1100.

Anderson, C. A. (1989). Temperature and aggression: Ubiquitous effects of heat on occurrence of human violence. *Psychological Bulletin, 106,* 74–106.

Anderson, C., & Berdahl, J. L. (2002). Experience of power: Examining the effects of power on approach and inhibition tendencies. *Journal of Personality and Social Psychology, 83,* 1362–1377.

Anderson, R., Manoogian, S. T., & Reznick, J. S. (1976). The undermining and enhancing of intrinsic motivation in preschool children. *Journal of Personality and Social Psychology, 34,* 915–922.

Andreassi, J. L. (2007). *Psychophysiology: Human behavior and physiological response* (5th ed.). Mahwah, NJ: Lawrence Erlbaum.

Angie, A. D., Connelly, S., Waples, E. P., & Kligyte, V. (2011). The influence of discrete emotions on judgement and decision-making: A meta-analytic review. *Cognition and Emotion, 25,* 1393–1422.

Apperloo, M. J. A., van der Stege, J. G., Hoek, A., & Schultz, W. C. M. W. (2003). In the mood for sex: The value of androgens. *Journal of Sex and Marital Therapy, 29,* 87–102.

Appley, M. H. (1991). Motivation, equilibration, and stress. In R. A. Dienstbier (Ed.), *Nebraska Symposium on Motivation* (Vol. *38,* pp. 1–67). Lincoln: University of Nebraska Press.

Arana, F. S., Parkinson, J. A., Hinton, E., Holland, A. J., Owen, A. M., & Roberts, A. C. (2003). Dissociable contributions of the human amygdala and orbitofrontal cortex to incentive motivation and goal selection. *Journal of Neuroscience, 23*, 9632–9638.

Armor, D. A., & Taylor, S. E. (2003). The effects of mindset on behavior: Self-regulation in deliberative and implemental frames of mind. *Personality and Social Psychology Bulletin, 29*, 86–95.

Arnett, J. (1991). Still crazy after all these years: Reckless behavior among young adults aged 23–27. *Personality and Individual Differences, 12*, 1305–1313.

Arnold, M. B. (1960). *Emotion and personality* (Vols. 1 & 2). New York: Columbia University Press.

Arnold, M. B. (1970). Perennial problems in the field of emotion. In M. B. Arnold (Ed.), *Feelings and emotions* (pp. 169–185). New York: Academic Press.

Aronson, E. (1969). The theory of cognitive dissonance: A current perspective. In L. Berkowitz (Ed.), *Advances in experimental social psychology* (Vol. *4*, pp. 1–34). New York: Academic Press.

Aronson, E. (1988). *The social animal* (5th ed.). San Francisco: W. H. Freeman.

Aronson, E. (1992). The return of the repressed: Dissonance theory makes a comeback. *Psychological Inquiry, 3*, 303–311.

Aronson, E. (1999). Dissonance, hypocrisy, and the self-concept. In E. Harmon-Jones & J. Mills (Eds.), *Cognitive dissonance: Progress on a pivotal theory in social psychology* (pp. 103–126). Washington, DC: American Psychological Association.

Aronson, E., & Mills, J. (1959). The effect of severity of initiation on liking for a group. *Journal of Abnormal and Social Psychology, 59*, 177–181.

Aronson, E., Fried, C. B., & Stone, J. (1991). Overcoming denial and increasing the intention to use condoms through the induction of hypocrisy. *American Journal of Public Health, 81*, 1636–1637.

Aronson, J., Fried, C., & Good, C. (2002). Reducing the effects of stereotype threat on African American college students by shaping theories of intelligence. *Journal of Experimental Social Psychology, 38*, 113–125.

Arrindell, W. A. Pickersgill, M. J., Merckelbach, H., Ardon, M. A., & Cornet, F. C. (1991). Phobic dimensions: III. Factor analytic approaches to the study of common phobic fears: An updated review of findings obtained with adult subjects. *Advances in Behaviour Research and Therapy, 13*, 73–130.

Ashby, F. G., Isen, A. M., & Turken, A. U. (1999). A neuropsychological theory of positive affect and its influence on cognition. *Psychological Review, 106*, 529–550.

Aspinwall, L. G. (1998). Rethinking the role of positive affect in self-regulation. *Motivation and Emotion, 22*, 1–22.

Assor, A., Kaplan, H., & Roth, G. (2002). Choice is good, but relevance is excellent: Autonomy-enhancing and suppressing teaching behaviors predicting students' engagement in schoolwork. *British Journal of Educational Psychology, 27*, 261–278.

Assor, A., Kaplan, H., Kanat-Maymon, Y., & Roth, G. (2005). Directly controlling teacher behaviors as predictors of poor motivation and engagement in girls and boys: The role of anger and anxiety. *Learning and Instruction, 15*, 397–413.

Assor, A., Roth, G., & Deci, E. L. (2004). The emotional costs of parents' conditional regard: A self-determination theory analysis. *Journal of Personality, 72*, 47–88.

Atkinson, J. W. (1957). Motivational determinants of risk-taking behavior. *Psychological Review, 64*, 359–372.

Atkinson, J. W. (1958). *Motives in fantasy, action, and society: A method of assessment and study.* Oxford, UK: Van Nostrand.

Atkinson, J. W. (1964). A theory of achievement motivation. In J. W. Atkinson, *An introduction to motivation* (pp. 240–268). New York: Van Nostrand.

Atkinson, J. W. (1981). Studying personality in the context of an advanced motivational psychology. *American Psychologist, 36*, 117–128.

Atkinson, J. W. (1982). Motivational determinants of thematic apperception. In A. J. Stewart (Ed.), *Motivation and society* (pp. 3–40). San Francisco: Jossey-Bass.

Atkinson, J. W., & Birch, D. (1974). The dynamics of achievement-oriented activity. In J. W. Atkinson & J. O. Raynor (Eds.), *Motivation and achievement* (pp. 271–325). Washington, DC: Van Nostrand Reinhold.

Atkinson, J. W., & Birch, D. (1978). *Introduction to motivation* (2nd ed.). New York: Van Nostrand.

Atkinson, J. W., & Birch, D. (Eds.). (1970). *The dynamics of action*. New York: Wiley.

Atkinson, J. W., Bongort, K., & Price, L. H. (1977). Explorations using computer simulation to comprehend TAT measurement of motivation. *Motivation and Emotion, 1*, 1–27.

Atkinson, J. W., Heyns, R. W., & Veroff, J. (1954). The effect of experimental arousal of the affiliation motive on thematic apperception. *Journal of Abnormal and Social Psychology, 49*, 405–410.

Atran, S. (2003). Genesis of suicide terrorism. *Science, 299*, 1534–1539.

Augustine, A. A., & Hemenover, S. H. (2009). On the relative effectiveness of affect regulation strategies: A meta-analysis. *Cognition and Emotion, 23*, 1181–1220.

Austira, J., Hatfield, D. B., Grindle, A. C., & Bailey, J. S. (1993). Increasing recycling in office environments: The effects of specific, informative cues. *Journal of Applied Behavior Analysis, 26*, 247–253.

Averill, J. R. (1968). Grief: Its nature and significance. *Psychological Bulletin, 70*, 721–748.

Averill, J. R. (1979). The functions of grief. In C. Izard (Ed.), *Emotions in personality and psychopathology* (pp. 339–368). New York: Plenum Press.

Averill, J. R. (1982). *Anger and aggression: An essay on emotion*. New York: Springer-Verlag.

Averill, J. R. (1990). Emotions as related to systems of behavior. In N. L. Stein, B. Leventhal, & T. Trabasso (Eds.), *Psychological and biological approaches to emotion* (pp. 385–404). Hillsdale, NJ: Erlbaum.

Averill, J. R. (1994). In the eyes of the beholder. In P. Ekman & R. J. Davidson (Eds.), *The nature of emotion: Fundamental questions* (pp. 7–14). New York: Oxford University Press.

Azar, B. (1994, October). Seligman recommends a depression vaccine. *APA Monitor, 27*, 4.

Azar, B. (2000, January). Two computer programs "face" off. *Monitor on Psychology*, pp. 48–49.

Azrin, N. H., Rubin, H., O'Brien, F., Ayllon, T., & Roll, D. (1968). Behavioral engineering: Postural control by a portable operant apparatus. *Journal of Applied Behavior Analysis, 2*, 39–42.

Baard, P. P., Deci, E. L., & Ryan, R. M. (2004). A motivational basis of performance and well-being in two work settings. *Journal of Applied Social Psychology, 34*, 2045–2068.

Bailey, J. M., & Pillard, R. C. (1991). A genetic study of the male sexual orientation. *Archives of General Psychiatry, 48*, 1089–1096.

Bailey, J. M., Gavlin, S., Agyei, Y., & Gladue, B. A. (1994). Effects of gender and sexual orientation on evolutionary relevant aspects of human mating psychology. *Journal of Personality and Social Psychology, 66*, 1081–1093.

Bailey, J. M., Pillard, R. C., Neale, M. C., & Agyei, Y. (1993). Heritable factors influence sexual orientation in women. *Archives of General Psychiatry, 50*, 217–223.

Baize, H. R., & Schroeder, J. E. (1995). Personality and mate selection in personal ads: Evolutionary preferences in a public mate selection process. *Journal of Social Behavior and Personality, 10*, 517–536.

Baldwin, J. D., & Baldwin, J. I. (1986). *Behavior principles in everyday life* (2nd ed.). Englewood Cliffs, NJ: Prentice Hall.

Banaji, M., & Hardin, C. (1996). Automatic stereotyping. *Psychological Science, 7*, 136–141.

Bancroft, J. (2002). Biological factors in human sexuality. *Journal of Sex Research, 39*, 15–21.

Bandura, A. (1977). Self-efficacy: Toward a unifying theory of behavioral change. *Psychological Review, 84*, 191–215.

Bandura, A. (1982). Self-efficacy mechanism in human agency. *American Psychologist, 37*, 122–147.

Bandura, A. (1983). Self-efficacy mechanisms of anticipated fears and calamities. *Journal of Personality and Social Psychology, 45*, 464–469.

Bandura, A. (1986). Self-efficacy. In A. Bandura, (Ed.) *Social foundations of thought and action: A social cognitive theory* (pp. 390–453). Englewood Cliffs, NJ: Prentice Hall.

Bandura, A. (1988). Self-efficacy conception of anxiety. *Anxiety Research, 1*, 77–98.

Bandura, A. (1989). Human agency in social cognitive theory. *American Psychologist, 44*, 1175–1184.

Bandura, A. (1990). Conclusion: Reflections on nonability determinants of competence. In R. J. Sternberg & J. Kolligian Jr. (Eds.), *Competence considered* (pp. 315–362). New Haven, CT: Yale University Press.

Bandura, A. (1991). Self-regulation of motivation through anticipatory and self-regulatory mechanisms. In R. A. Dienstbier (Ed.), *Nebraska Symposium on Motivation: Perspectives on motivation* (Vol. *38*, pp. 69–164). Lincoln: University of Nebraska Press.

Bandura, A. (1993). Perceived self-efficacy in cognitive development and functioning. *Educational Psychologist, 28*, 117–148.

Bandura, A. (1997). *Self-efficacy: The exercise of control.* New York: W. H. Freeman.

Bandura, A. (1998). Health promotion from the perspective of social cognitive theory. *Psychological Health, 13*, 623–649.

Bandura, A. (1999). Moral disengagement in the perpetration of inhumanities. *Personality and Social Psychology Review, 3*, 193–209.

Bandura, A. (2006). Toward a psychology of human agency. *Perspectives on Psychological Science, 1*, 164–180.

Bandura, A., & Adams, N. E. (1977). Analysis of self-efficacy theory of behavioral change. *Cognitive Therapy and Research, 1*, 287–308.

Bandura, A., & Cervone, D. (1983). Self-evaluative and self-efficacy mechanisms governing the motivational effects of goal systems. *Journal of Personality and Social Psychology, 45*, 1017–1028.

Bandura, A., & Cervone, D. (1986). Differential engagement of self-reactive influences in cognitive motivation. *Organizational Behavior and Human Decision Processes, 38*, 92–113.

Bandura, A., & Schunk, D. H. (1981). Cultivating competence, self-efficacy, and intrinsic interest through proximal self-motivation. *Journal of Personality and Social Psychology, 41*, 586–598.

Bandura, A., & Wood, R. E. (1989). Effect of perceived controllability and performance standards on self-regulation of complex decision making. *Journal of Personality and Social Psychology, 56*, 805–814.

Bandura, A., Adams, N. E., Hardy, A. B., & Howells, G. N. (1980). Tests of the generality of self-efficacy theory. *Cognitive Therapy and Research, 4*, 39–66.

Bandura, A., Barbaranelli, C., Caprara, G. V., & Pastorelli, C. (2001). Self-efficacy beliefs as shapers of children's aspirations and career trajectories. *Child Development, 72*, 187–206.

Bandura, A., Cioffi, D., Taylor, C. B., & Brouillard, M. E. (1988). Perceived self-efficacy in coping with cognitive stressors and opioid activation. *Journal of Personality and Social Psychology, 55*, 479–488.

Bandura, A., Reese, L., & Adams, N. E. (1982). Microanalysis of action and fear arousal as a function of differential levels of perceived self-efficacy. *Journal of Personality and Social Psychology, 43*, 5–21.

Bandura, A., Taylor, C. B., Williams, S. L., Mefford, I. N., & Barchas, J. D. (1985). Catecholamine secretion as a function of perceived coping self-efficacy. *Journal of Consulting and Clinical Psychology, 53*, 406–414.

Barak, Y., & Achiron, A. (2011). Happiness and personal growth are attainable in interferon-beta-1a treated multiple sclerosis patients. *Journal of Happiness Studies, 12*, 887–895.

Barber, B. K. (1996). Parental psychological control: Revisiting a neglected construct. *Child Development, 67*, 3296–3319.

Bargh, J. A., & Chartrand, T. L. (1999). The unbearable automaticity of being. *American Psychologist*, *54*, 462–479.

Bargh, J. A. (1997). The automaticity of every day life. In R. S. Wyer & T. K. Srull (Eds.), *Advances in Social Cognition* (Vol. *10*, pp. 1–61). Hillsdale, NJ: Lawrence Erlbaum.

Bargh, J. A., Chen, M., & Burrows, L. (1996). Automaticity of social behavior: Direct effects of trait construct and stereotype activation on action. *Journal of Personality and Social Psychology*, *71*, 230–244.

Bargh, J. A., Gollwitzer, P. M., Lee-Chai, K., Barndollar, K., & Trotschel, R. (2001). The automated will: Nonconscious activation and pursuit of behavioral goals. *Journal of Personality and Social Psychology*, *82*, 1014–1027.

Barrett, L. F. (2004). Feelings or words? Understanding the content in self-report ratings of emotional experience. *Journal of Personality and Social Psychology*, *87*, 266–281.

Barrett, L. F. (2006). Are emotions natural kinds? *Perspectives on Psychological Science*, *1*, 28–58.

Barrett, L. F., & Gross, J. J. (2001). Emotional intelligence: A process model of emotion representation and regulation. In T. J. Mayne, & G. A. Bonanno (Eds.), *Emotions: Current issues and future directions* (pp. 286–310). New York: Guilford Press.

Barrett, L. F., Gross, J. J., Christensen, T. C., & Benvenuto, M. (2001). Knowing what you're feeling and knowing what to do about it: Mapping the relation between emotion differentiation and emotion regulation. *Cognition and Emotion*, *15*, 713–724.

Bartlett, M. Y., & DeSteno, D. (2006). Gratitude and prosocial behavior: Helping when it costs you. *Psychological Science*, *17*, 319–325.

Bartlett, M. Y., Condon, P., Cruz, J., Baumann, J., & Desteno, D. (2012). Gratitude: Prompting behaviours that build relationships. *Cognition and Emotion*, *26*, 2–13.

Bartz, J. A., Zaki, J., Bolger, N., & Ochsner, K. N. (2011). Social effects of oxytocin in humans: Context and person matter. *Trends in Cognitive Science*, *15*, 301–309.

Barzilai, N., Wang, J., Massilon, D., Vuguin, P., Hawkins, M., & Rossetti, L. (1997). Leptin selectively decreases visceral adiposity and enhances insulin action. *Journal of Clinical Investigation*, *100*, 3105–3110.

Bassett, D. S., & Gazzaniga, M. S. (2011). Understanding complexity in the human brain. *Trends in Cognitive Science*, *15*, 200–209.

Basson, R. (2001). Human sex-response cycles. *Journal of Sex and Marital Therapy*, *27*, 33–43.

Basson, R. (2002). Women's sexual desire—disordered or misunderstood? *Journal of Sex and Marital Therapy*, *28*, 17–28.

Basson, R. (2003). Commentary on "In the mood for sex—The value of androgens." *Journal of Sex and Marital Therapy*, *29*, 177–179.

Batson, C. D. (1991). *The altruism question: Toward a social-psychological answer*. Hillsdale, NJ: Erlbaum.

Batson, C. D., Coke, J. S., Chard, F., Smith, D., & Taliaferro, A. (1979). Generality of the "glow of goodwill": Effects of mood on helping and information acquisition. *Social Psychology Quarterly*, *42*, 176–179.

Battistich, V., Solomon, D., Watson, M. E., & Schaps, E. (1997). Caring school communities. *Educational Psychologist*, *32*, 137–151.

Baucom, D. H., & Aiken, P. A. (1981). Effect of depressed mood on eating among obese and nonobese dieting and nondieting persons. *Journal of Personality and Social Psychology*, *41*, 577–585.

Bauer, I. M., & Baumeister, R. F. (2011). Self-regulatory strength. In K. D. Vohs & R. F. Baumesiter (Eds.), *Handbook of self-regulation: Research, theory, and applications* (2nd ed., pp. 64–82). New York: Guilford Press.

Baumeister, R. B., & Heatherton, T. F. (1996). Self-regulation failure: An overview. *Psychological Inquiry*, *7*, 1–15.

Baumeister, R. F. (1987). How the self became a problem: A psychological review of historical research. *Journal of Personality and Social Psychology, 52*, 163–176.

Baumeister, R. F., & Campbell, W. K. (1999). The intrinsic appeal of evil: Sadism, sensational thrills, and threatened egotism. *Personality and Social Psychology Review, 3*, 210–221.

Baumeister, R. F., & Heatherton, T. F. (1996). Self-regulation failure: An overview. *Psychological Inquiry, 7*, 1–15.

Baumeister, R. F., & Leary, M. R. (1995). The need to belong: Desire for interpersonal attachments as a fundamental human motivation. *Psychological Bulletin, 117*, 497–529.

Baumeister, R. F., & Tierney, J. (2011). *Willpower: Rediscovering the greatest human strength*. New York: Penguin Books.

Baumeister, R. F., & Vohs, K. D. (2002). The pursuit of meaningfulness in life. In C. R. Snyder & S. J. Lopez(Eds.), *Handbook of positive psychology* (pp. 608–618). New York: Oxford University Press.

Baumeister, R. F., & Vohs, K. D. (2007). Self-regulation, ego depletion, and motivation. *Social and Personality Psychology Compass, 1*, 115–128.

Baumeister, R. F., Bratslavsky, E., Finkenauer, C., & Vohs, K. D. (2001). Bad is stronger than good. *Review of General Psychology, 5*, 323–370.

Baumeister, R. F., Bratslavsky, E., Muraven, M., & Tice, D. M. (1998). Ego depletion: Is the active self a limited resource? *Journal of Personality and Social Psychology, 74*, 1252–1265.

Baumeister, R. F., Campbell, J. D., Krueger, J. I., & Vohs, K. D. (2003). Does high self-esteem cause better performance, interpersonal success, happiness, or healthier lifestyles? *Psychological Science in the Public Interest, 4*, 1–44.

Baumeister, R. F., Gailliot, M. T., De Wall, C. N., & Oaten, M. (2006). Self-regulation and personality: How interventions increase regulatory success, and how depletion moderates the effects of traits on behavior. *Journal of Personality, 74*, 1773–1801.

Baumeister, R. F., Muraven, M., & Tice, D. M. (2000). Ego depletion: A resource model of volition, self-regulation, and controlled processing. *Social Cognition, 18*, 130–150.

Baumeister, R. F., Smart, L., & Boden, J. M. (1996). Relation of threatened egotism to violence and aggression: The dark side of self-esteem. *Psychological Review, 103*, 5–33.

Baumeister, R. F., Vohs, K. D., & Tice, D. M. (2007). The strength model of self-control. *Current Directions in Psychological Science, 16*, 351–355.

Baxter, M. G., & Murray, E. A. (2002). The amygdala and reward. *Nature Reviews: Neuroscience, 3*, 863–873.

Beach, F. A. (1955). The descent of instinct. *Psychological Review, 62*, 401–410.

Beatty, W. W. (1982). Dietary variety stimulates appetite in females but not in males. *Bulletin of the Psychonomic Society, 19*, 212–214.

Beauvois, J. L., & Joule, R. V. (1996). *A radical dissonance theory*. London: Taylor & Francis.

Bechara, A., Damasio, H., Tranel, D., & Damasio, A. R. (1996). Deciding advantageously before knowing the advantageous strategy. *Science, 275*, 1293–1295.

Beck, A. T. (1976). *Cognitive therapy and the emotional disorders*. New York: International Universities Press.

Beck, A. T., Rush, A. J., Shaw, B. R, & Emery, G. (1979). *Cognitive therapy of depression*. New York: Guilford Press.

Beck, R. C. (1979). Roles of taste and learning in water regulation. *Behavioral and Brain Sciences, 1*, 102–103.

Beck, S. P., Ward-Hull, C. I., & McLear, P. M. (1976). Variable related to women's somatic preferences of the male and female body. *Journal of Personality and Social Psychology, 34*, 1200–1210.

Becker, L. J. (1978). Joint effect of feedback and goal setting on performance: A field study of residential energy conservation. *Journal of Applied Psychology, 63*, 428–433.

Behrens, T. E. J., Fox, P., Laird, A., & Smith, S. M. (2013). What is the most interesting part of the brain? *Trends in Cognitive Science, 17*, 2–4.

Bell, A. P., Weinberg, M. S., & Hammersmith, S. K. (1981). *Sexual preference: Its development in men and women*. Bloomington: Indiana University Press.

Bem, D. J. (1967). Self-perception: An alternative interpretation of cognitive dissonance phenomena. *Psychological Review, 74*, 183–200.

Bem, D. J. (1972). Self-perception theory. In L. Berkowitz (Ed.), *Advances in experimental social psychology* (Vol. 6, pp. 1–62). New York: Academic Press.

Bem, D. J., & McConnell, H. K. (1970). Testing the self-perception explanation of dissonance phenomena: On the salience of premanipulation attitudes. *Journal of Personality and Social Psychology, 14*, 23–31.

Benjamin, L. T., Jr., & Jones, M. R. (1978). From motivational theory to social cognitive development: Twenty-five years of the Nebraska Symposium. In L. T. Benjamin & M. R. Jones (Eds.), *Nebraska Symposium on Motivation* (Vol. 26, pp. ix–xix). Lincoln: University of Nebraska Press.

Bennett, W. I. (1995). Beyond overeating. *New England Journal of Medicine, 332*, 673–674.

Benware, C., & Deci, E. L. (1984). The quality of learning with an active versus passive motivational set. *American Educational Research Journal, 21*, 755–765.

Berenbaum, S. A., & Snyder, E. (1995). Early hormonal influences on childhood sex-typed activity and playmate preferences: Implications for the development of sexual orientation. *Developmental Psychology, 31*, 31–42.

Bergmann, G., & Spence, K. W. (1941). Operationalism and theory construction. *Psychological Review, 48*, 1–14.

Bergsma, A., Veenhoven, R., ten Have, M., & de Graaf, R. (2011). Do they know how happy they are? On the value of self-rated happiness of people with a mental disorder. *Journal of Happiness Studies, 12*, 793–806.

Berkowitz, L. (1962). *Aggression: A social psychological analysis*. New York: McGraw-Hill.

Berkowitz, L., & Harmon-Jones, E. (2004). Toward an understanding of the determinants of anger. *Emotion, 4*, 107–130.

Berlyne, D. E. (1966). Curiosity and exploration. *Science, 153*, 25–33.

Berlyne, D. E. (1967). Arousal and reinforcement. In D. Levine (Ed.), *Nebraska Symposium on Motivation* (Vol. 15, pp. 1–110). Lincoln: University of Nebraska Press.

Berlyne, D. E. (1975). Behaviourism? Cognitive theory? Humanistic psychology? To Hull with them all. *Canadian Psychological Review, 16*, 69–80.

Bernard, L. C., & Lac, A. (2013). Testing a multidimensional model of putative evolved human motives. *Motivation and Emotion, 37*, 564–582.

Bernard, L. L. (1924). *Instinct: A study of social psychology*. New York: Holt.

Bernieri, F. J., & Rosenthal, R. (1991). Interpersonal coordination: Behavior matching and interactional synchrony. In R. S. Feldman & B. Rimeí (Eds.), *Fundamentals of nonverbal behavior* (pp. 401–432). New York: Cambridge University Press.

Berridge, K. C. (2004). Motivation concepts in behavioral neuroscience. *Physiology & Behavior, 81*, 179–209.

Berridge, K. C., & Kringelbach, M. (2008). Affective neuroscience and pleasure: Reward in humans and animals. *Psychopharmacology, 191*, 391–431.

Berridge, K. C., & Robinson, T. E. (1995). The mind of an addict brain: Neural sensitization of wanting and liking. *Current Directions in Psychological Science, 4*, 71–76.

Berridge, K. C., & Robinson, T. E. (1998). What is the role of dopamine in reward: hedonic impact, reward learning, or incentive salience? *Brain Research Review, 28*, 309–369.

Berry, D. S., & McArthur, L. Z. (1985). Some components and consequences of a babyface. *Journal of Personality and Social Psychology, 48*, 312–323.

Berry, S. L., Beatty, W. W., & Klesges, R. C. (1985). Sensory and social influences on ice cream consumption by males and females in a laboratory setting. *Appetite, 6,* 41–45.

Best, J. R., Miller, P. H., & Jones, L. L. (2009). Executive functions after age 5: Changes and correlates. *Developmental Review, 29,* 180–200.

Bettencourt, B., & Sheldon, K. M. (2001). Social roles as vehicles for psychological need satisfaction within groups. *Journal of Personality and Social Psychology, 81,* 1131–1143.

Betz, N. E., & Hackett, G. (1986). Applications of self-efficacy theory to understanding career choice behavior. *Journal of Social and Clinical Psychology, 4,* 279–289.

Bindra, D. (1959). *Motivation: A systematic reinterpretation.* New York: Ronald Press.

Bindra, D. (1979). *Motivation, the brain, and psychological theory.* Unpublished manuscript, Psychology Department, McGill University, Montreal.

Birch, H. G. (1956). Sources of odor in maternal behavior in animals. *American Journal of Orthopsychiatry, 26,* 279–284.

Birch, L. L., Johnson, S. L., Anderson, G., Peters, J. C., & Schulte, M. C. (1991). The variability of young children's energy-intake. *New England Journal of Medicine, 324,* 232–235.

Birch, L. L., Zimmerman, S. I., & Hind, H. (1980). The influence of social affective context on the formation of children's food preferences. *Child Development, 51,* 856–861.

Birney, R. C., Burdick, H., & Teevan, R. C. (1969). *Fear of failure.* New York: Van Nostrand.

Black, A. E., & Deci, E. L. (2000). The effects of instructors' autonomy support and students' autonomous motivation on learning organic chemistry: A self-determination theory perspective. *Science Education, 84,* 740–756.

Blackburn, G. (1995). Effect of degree of weight loss on health benefits. *Obesity Research, 3,* 211S.

Blackwell, L. S., Trzesniewski, K. H., & Dweck, C. S. (2007). Implicit theories of intelligence predict achievement across an adolescent transition: A longitudinal study and an intervention. *Child Development, 78,* 246–263.

Blais, A. (1976). Concept of development in personality theory. In J. Loevinger (Ed.), *Ego development* (pp. 29–53). San Francisco: Jossey-Bass.

Blais, M. R., Sabourin, S., Boucher, C., & Vallerand, R. J. (1990). Toward a motivational model of couple happiness. *Journal of Personality and Social Psychology, 59,* 1021–1031.

Blanchard, D. C., & Blanchard, R. J. (1972). Innate and conditioned reactions to threat in rats with amygdaloid lesions. *Journal of Comparative and Psychological Psychology, 81,* 281–290.

Blanchette, I., & Richards, A. (2010). The influence of affect on higher level cognition: A review of research on interpretation, judgement, decision making and reasoning. *Cognition and Emotion, 24,* 561–595.

Blandler, R. (1988). Brain mechanisms of aggression as revealed by electrical and chemical stimulation: Suggestions of a central role for the midbrain periaqueductal grey region. In A. N. Epstein & J. M. Sprague (Eds.), *Progresses in psychobiology and physiological psychology* (Vol. *13,* pp. 67–154). San Diego, CA: Academic Press.

Blank, P. D., Reis, H. T., & Jackson, L. (1984). The effects of verbal reinforcements on intrinsic motivation for sex-linked tasks. *Sex Roles, 10,* 369–387.

Blankenship, V. (1982). The relationship between consummatory value of success and achievement task difficulty. *Journal of Personality and Social Psychology, 42,* 911–924.

Blankenship, V. (1987). A computer-based measure of resultant achievement motivation. *Journal of Personality and Social Psychology, 53,* 361–372.

Blankenship, V. (1992). Individual differences in resultant achievement motivation and latency to and persistence at an achievement task. *Motivation and Emotion, 16,* 35–63.

Blankenship, V. (2010). Computer-based modelling, assessment, and coding of implicit motives. In O. C. Schultheiss & J. C. Brunstein (Eds.), *Implicit motives* (Chapter 7, pp. 186–208). New York: Oxford University Press.

Blass, E. M., & Hall, W. G. (1976). Drinking termination: Interactions among hydrational, orogastric, and behavioral controls in rats. *Psychological Review, 83,* 356–374.

Blatt, S. J. (1994). *Therapeutic change: An objects relations approach.* New York: Plenum Press.

Blatt, S. J. (1995). The destructiveness of perfectionism: Implications for the treatment of depression. *American Psychologist, 50,* 1003–1020.

Boggiano, A. K., & Ruble, D. N. (1979). Competence and the overjustification effect: A developmental study. *Journal of Personality and Social Psychology, 37,* 1462–1468.

Boggiano, A. K., Barrett, M., Weiher, A. W., McClelland, G. H., & Lusk, C. M. (1987). Use of the maximal-operant principle to motivate children's intrinsic interest. *Journal of Personality and Social Psychology, 53,* 866–879.

Boggiano, A. K., Flink, C., Shields, A., Seelbach, A., & Barrett, M. (1993). Use of techniques promoting students' self-determination: Effects on students' analytic problem-solving skills. *Motivation and Emotion, 17,* 319–336.

Bolles, R. C. (1972). A motivational view of learning, performance, and behavior modification. *Psychological Review, 81,* 199–213.

Bolles, R. C. (1975). *A theory of motivation* (2nd ed.). New York: Harper & Row.

Bonanno, G. A., & Keltner, D. (1997). Facial expressions of emotion and the course of conjugal bereavement. *Journal of Abnormal Psychology, 106,* 126–137.

Bonanno, G. A., Goorin, L., & Coifman, K. G. (2008). Sadness and grief. In M. Lewis, J. M. Haviland-Jones, & L. F. Barrett (Eds.), *Handbook of emotions* (3rd ed., pp. 797–810). New York: Guilford Press.

Boneau, C. A. (1990). Psychological literacy: A first approximation. *American Psychologist, 45,* 891–900.

Borecki, I. B., Rice, T., Pérusse, L., Bouchard, C., & Rao, D. C. (1995). Major gene influence on the proximity to store fat in trunk versus extremity depots: Evidence from the Quebec family study. *Obesity Research, 3,* 1–8.

Bostic, T., Rubio, D., & Hood, M. (2000). A validation of the subjective vitality scale using structural equation modeling. *Social Indicators Research, 53,* 313–324.

Botvinick, M. M. et al., (2001). Cognitive monitoring and cognitive control. *Psychological Review, 108,* 624–652.

Botvinick, M. M., Cohen, J. D., & Carter, C. S. (2004). Conflict monitoring and anterior cingulate cortex: An update. *Trends in Cognitive Science, 8,* 539–546.

Bowlby, J. (1969). *Attachment and loss: Vol. 1. Attachment.* New York: Basic Books.

Bowlby, J. (1973). *Attachment and loss: Vol. 2. Separation: Anxiety and anger.* New York: Basic Books.

Bowlby, J. (1980). *Attachment and loss: Vol. 3. Loss, sadness, and depression.* New York: Basic Books.

Bowles, T. (1999). Focusing on time orientation to explain adolescent self concept and academic achievement: Part II. Testing a model. *Journal of Applied Health Behavior, 1,* 1–8.

Boyatzis, R. E. (1972). *A two factor theory of affiliation motivation.* Unpublished doctoral dissertation, Harvard University.

Boyatzis, R. E. (1973). Affiliation motivation. In D. C. McClelland & R. S. Steele (Eds.), *Human motivation: A book of readings.* Morristown, NJ: General Learning Press.

Branden, N. (1984). *The six pillars of self-esteem.* New York: Bantam Books.

Brandstatter, V., Lengfelder, A., & Gollwitzer, P. M. (2001). Implementation intentions and efficient action initiation. *Journal of Personality and Social Psychology, 81,* 946–960.

Brandtstadter, J., & Frank, E. (2002). Effects of deliberative and implemental mindsets on persistence in goal-directed behavior. *Personality and Social Psychology Bulletin, 28,* 1366–1378.

Brans, K., van Mechelen, I., Rime, B., & Verduyn, P. (2013). The relation between social sharing and the duration of emotional experience. *Cognition and Emotion, 27,* 1023–1041.

Brehm, J. W. (1956). Postdecision changes in the desirability of alternatives. *Journal of Abnormal and Social Psychology, 52*, 384–389.

Brehm, J. W. (1966). *A theory of psychological reactance*. New York: Academic Press.

Brehm, J. W., & Self, E. A. (1989). The intensity of motivation. *Annual Review of Psychology, 40*, 109–131.

Brehm, S. S., & Brehm, J. W. (1981). *Psychological reactance: A theory of freedom and control*. New York: Academic Press.

Brewer, M. B. (1979). Ingroup bias in the minimal intergroup situation: A cognitive-motivational analysis. *Psychological Bulletin, 86*, 307–324.

Brigham, T. A., Maier, S. M., & Goodner, V. (1995). Increased designated driving with a program of prompts and incentives. *Journal of Applied Behavior Analysis, 28*, 83–84.

Brobeck, J. R. (1960). Food and temperature. *Recent Progress in Hormone Research, 16*, 439.

Brophy, J. (1981). Teacher praise: A functional analysis. *Review of Educational Research, 51*, 5–32.

Brosch, T., & Sander, D. (2013). Comment: The appraising brain: Towards a neuro-cognitive model of appraisal processes in emotion. *Emotion Review, 5*, 163–168.

Brouwers, M., & Wiggum, C. D. (1993). Bulimia and perfectionism: Developing the courage to be imperfect. *Journal of Mental Health Counseling, 15*, 141–149.

Brown, A. S. (1991). A review of the tip-of-the-tongue experience. *Psychological Bulletin, 109*, 204–223.

Brown, E. S., & Suppes, T. (1998). Mood symptoms during corticosteroid therapy: A review. *Harvard Review of Psychiatry, 5*, 239–246.

Brown, I., Jr., & Inouye, D. K. (1978). Learned helplessness through modeling: The role of perceived similarity in competence. *Journal of Personality and Social Psychology, 36*, 900–908.

Brown, J. S. (1961). *The motivation of behavior*. New York: McGraw-Hill.

Brown, K. W., & Ryan, R. M. (2003). The benefits of being present: Mindfulness and its role in psychological well-being. *Journal of Personality and Social Psychology, 84*, 822–848.

Brown, K. W., Ryan, R. M., & Creswell, J. D. (2007). Mindfulness: Theoretical foundations and evidence for its salutary effects. *Psychological Inquiry, 18*, 211–237.

Bruininks, P., & Malle, B. F. (2005). Distinguishing hope from optimism and related affective states. *Motivation and Emotion, 29*, 327–355.

Bruning, R., Dempsey, M., Kauffman, D. F., McKim, C., & Zumbrunn, S. (2013). Examining dimensions of self-efficacy for writing. *Journal of Educational Psychology, 105*, 25–38.

Bryant, F. B. (1989). A four-factor model of perceived control: Avoiding, coping, obtaining, and savoring. *Journal of Personality, 57*, 773–797.

Buck, R. (1984). *The communication of emotion*. New York: Guilford Press.

Buck, R. (1986). The psychology of emotion. In J. LeDoux & W. Hirst (Eds.), *Mind and brain: Dialogues in cognitive neuroscience* (pp. 275–300). New York: Cambridge University Press.

Buck, R. (1988). *Human motivation and emotion*. New York: Wiley.

Buckner, C. E., & Swann, W. B. Jr. (1996, August). *Physical abuse in close relationships: The dynamic interplay of couple characteristics*. Paper presented at the annual meeting of the American Psychological Association, Washington, DC.

Bugental, J. F. T. (1967). *Challenges and humanistic psychology*. New York: McGraw-Hill.

Burger, J. M. (1992). *Desire for control: Personality, social, and clinical perspectives*. New York: Plenum Press.

Burnham, T. C., Chapman, J. F., Gray, P. B., McIntyre, M. H., Lipson, S. F., & Ellison, P. T. (2003). Men in committed, romantic relationships have lower testosterone. *Hormones and Behavior, 44*, 119–122.

Bush, G. et al. (2002). Dorsal anterior cingulate cortex: A role in reward-based decision making. *Proceedings of the National Academy of Science: USA, 99*, 523–528.

Bushman, B. J. (2002). Does venting anger feed or extinguish the flame?: Catharsis, rumination, distraction, anger, and aggressive responding. *Personality and Social Psychology Bulletin, 28,* 724–731.

Buss, D. M., & Schmitt, D. P. (1993). Sexual strategies theory: An evolutionary perspective on human mating. *Psychological Review, 100,* 204–232.

Buss, D. M., Haselton, M. G., Shackelford, T. K., Bleske, A. L., & Wakefeld, J. C. (1998). Adaptations, exaptations, and spandrels. *American Psychologist, 53,* 533–548.

Buston, P. M., & Emlen, S. T. (2003). Cognitive processes underlying human mate choice: The relationship between self-perception and mate preference in Western society. *Proceedings of the National Academy of Sciences, 100,* 8805–8810.

Butler, E. A., Egloff, B., Wilhelm, F. W., Smith, N. C., Erickson, E. A., & Gross, J. J. (2003). The social consequences of expressive suppression. *Emotion, 3,* 48–67.

Byrne, D. (1961). Anxiety and the experimental arousal of affiliation need. *Journal of Abnormal and Social Psychology, 63,* 660–662.

Byrne, J., & Welsh, J. (2001). *Jack: Straight from the gut.* New York: Warner Books.

Cacioppo, J. T., Petty, R. E., Feinstein, J. A., & Jarvis, W. B. G. (1996). Dispositional differences in cognitive motivation: The life and times of individuals varying in the need for cognition. *Psychological Bulletin, 119,* 197–253.

Cacioppo, S., Bianchi-Demicheli, F., Hatfield, E., & Rapson, R. L. (2012). Social neuroscience of love. *Clinical Neuropsychiatry, 9,* 3–13.

California Task Force to Promote Self-Esteem and Personal and Social Responsibility. (1989). *Toward a state of self-esteem.* Sacramento: California State Department of Education.

Calvo, M. G., & Lundqvist, D. (2008). Facial expressions of emotion (KDEF): Identification under different display-duration conditions. *Behavior Research Methods, 40,* 109–115.

Calvo, M. G., & Nummenmaa, L. (2008). Detection of emotional faces: Salient physical features guide effective visual search. *Journal of Experimental Psychology: General, 137,* 471–494.

Cameron, J., & Pierce, W. D. (1994). Reinforcement, reward, and intrinsic motivation: A meta-analysis. *Review of Educational Research, 64,* 363–423.

Campbell, W. K., Bush, C. P., Brunell, A. B., & Shelton, J. (2005). Understanding the social costs of narcissism: The case of the tragedy of the commons. *Personality and Social Psychology Bulletin, 31,* 1358–1368.

Campfield, L. A., Smith, F. J., & Burn, P. (1997a). OB protein: A hormonal controller of central neural networks mediating behavioral, metabolic and neuroendocrine responses. *Endocrinology and Metabolism, 4,* 81–102.

Campfield, L. A., Smith, F. J., & Burn, P. (1997b). The OB protein (leptin) pathway: A link between adipose tissue mass and central neural networks. *Hormone and Metabolic Research, 28,* 619–632.

Campfield, L. A., Smith, F. J., Rosenbaum, M., & Hirsch, J. (1996). Human eating: Evidence for a physiological basis using a modified paradigm. *Neuroscience and Biobehavioral Reviews, 20,* 133–137.

Campion, M. A., & Lord, R. G. (1982). A control systems conceptualization of the goal-setting and changing process. *Organizational Behavior and Human Performance, 30,* 265–287.

Camras, L. (1977). Facial expressions used by children in a conflict situation. *Child Development, 48,* 1431–1435.

Cannon, W. B. (1927). The James-Lange theory of emotion: A critical examination and an alternative theory. *American Journal of Psychology, 39,* 106–124.

Cannon, W. B. (1929). *Bodily changes in pain, hunger, fear, and rage.* New York: Appleton.

Cannon, W. B. (1932). *The wisdom of the body.* New York: W. W. Norton.

Cantor, N., Markus, H., Niedenthal, P., & Nurius, P. (1986). On motivation and the self-concept. In R. M. Sorrentino & E. T. Higgins (Eds.), *Handbook of motivation and cognition* (Vol. *1,* pp. 96–121). New York: Guilford Press.

Caprara, G. V., Barbaranelli, C., Steca, P., & Malone, P. S. (2006). Teachers' self-efficacy beliefs as determinants of teachers' job satisfaction. *Journal of Educational Psychology*, *95*, 473–490.

Cardinal, R. N., Parkinson, J. A., Hall, J., & Everitt, B. J. (2002). Emotion and motivation: The role of the amygdala, ventral striatum, and prefrontal cortex. *Neuroscience and Biobehavioral Reviews*, *26*, 321–352.

Carlsmith, J. M., Ellsworth, P. C., & Aronson, E. (1976). *Methods of research in social psychology.* New York: Random House.

Carnelley, K. B., Pietromonaco, P. R., & Jaffe, K. (1994). Depression, working models of others, and relationship functioning. *Journal of Personality and Social Psychology*, *66*, 127–140.

Carnevale, P. J. D., & Isen, A. M. (1986). The influence of positive affect and visual access on the discovery of integrative solutions in bilateral negotiation. *Organizational Behavior and Human Decision Processes*, *37*, 1–13.

Carstensen, L. L. (1993). Motivation for social contact across the life span. In J. Jacobs (Ed.), *Nebraska Symposium on Motivation: Developmental perspectives on motivation* (Vol. *40*, pp. 209–254). Lincoln: University of Nebraska Press.

Carstensen, L. L. (1995). Evidence for a life-span theory of socioemotional selectivity. *Current Directions in Psychological Science*, *4*, 151–156.

Carstensen, L. L., Gottman, J. M., & Levenson, R. W. (1995). Emotional behavior in long-term marriage. *Psychology and Aging*, *10*, 140–149.

Carvallo, M., & Gabriel, S. (2006). No man is an island: The need to belong and dismissing avoidant attachment style. *Personality and Social Psychology Bulletin*, *32*, 697–709.

Carver, C. S. (2006). Approach, avoidance, and the self-regulation of affect and action. *Motivation and Emotion*, *30*, 105–110.

Carver, C. S., & Blaney, P. H. (1977). Avoidance behavior and perceived control. *Motivation and Emotion*, *1*, 61–63.

Carver, C. S., & Scheier, M. F. (1981). *Attention and self-regulation: A control theory approach to human behavior.* New York: Springer-Verlag.

Carver, C. S., & Scheier, M. F. (1982). Control theory: A useful conceptual framework for personality: Social, clinical, and health psychology. *Psychological Bulletin*, *92*, 111–135.

Carver, C. S., & Scheier, M. F. (1990). Origins and functions of positive and negative affect: A control-process view. *Psychological Review*, *97*, 19–35.

Carver, C. S., & Scheier, M. F. (1998). *On the self-regulation of behavior.* Cambridge, UK: Cambridge University Press.

Carver, C. S., & Scheier, M. F. (2011). Self-regulation of action and affect. In K. D. Vohs & R. F. Baumeister (Eds.), *Handbook of self-regulation: Research, theory, and applications* (2nd ed., Chpt. 1, pp. 3–21). New York: Guilford Press.

Carver, C. S., & White, T. L. (1994). Behavioral inhibition, behavioral activation, and affective responses to impending reward and punishment: The BIS/BAS scales. *Journal of Personality and Social Psychology*, *67*, 319–333.

Carver, C. S., Scheier, M. F., Miller, C. J., & Fulford, D. (2009). Optimism. In S. J. Lopez & C. R. Snyder (Eds.), *Oxford handbook of positive psychology* (2nd ed., pp. 303–311). New York: Oxford University Press.

Chao, Y.-S., Cheng, Y.-Y., & Chiou, W.-B. (2011). The psychological consequences of experiencing shame: Self-sufficiency and mood-repair. *Motivation and Emotion*, *35*, 202–210.

Chapman, H. A., Kim, D. A., Susskind, J. M., & Anderson, A. K., (2009). In bad taste: Evidence from the oral origins of moral disgust. *Science*, *323*, 1222–1226.

Chen, M., & Isen, A. M. (1992). *The influence of positive affect and success on persistence on a failed task.* Unpublished manuscript, Cornell University.

Chen, R. (1993). Responding to compliments: A contrastive study of politeness strategies between American English and Chinese speakers. *Journal of Pragmatics*, *20*, 49–75.

Cheon, S. H., Reeve, J., & Moon, I. S. (2012). Experimentally based, longitudinally designed, teacher-focused intervention to help physical education teachers be more autonomy supportive toward their students. *Journal of Sport and Exercise Psychology, 34*, 365–396.

Chirkov, V. I., & Ryan, R. M. (2001). Parent and teacher autonomy-support in Russian and U.S. adolescents: Common effects on well-being and academic motivation. *Journal of Cross Cultural Psychology, 32*, 618–635.

Christenson, S. L., Reschly, A. L., & Wylie, C. (Eds.). (2012). *Handbook of research on student engagement.* New York: Springer Science.

Chua, H. F., Gonzales, R., Taylor, S. F., Welsh, R. C., & Liberzon, I. (2009). Decision-related loss: Regret and disappointment. *NeuroImage, 47*, 2031–2040.

Cioffi, D. (1991). Beyond attentional strategies: A cognitive-perceptual model of somatic interpretation. *Psychological Bulletin, 109*, 25–41.

Clark, L. A., Watson, D., & Leeka, J. (1989). Diurnal variation in the positive affects. *Motivation and Emotion, 13*, 205–234.

Clark, L. A., Watson, D., & Mineka, S. (1994). Temperament, personality, and the mood and anxiety disorders. *Journal of Abnormal Psychology, 103*, 103–116.

Clark, M. S. (1984). Record keeping in two types of relationships. *Journal of Personality and Social Psychology, 47*, 549–557.

Clark, M. S., & Mills, J. (1979). Interpersonal attraction in exchange and communal relationships. *Journal of Personality and Social Psychology, 37*, 12–24.

Clark, M. S., Mills, J., & Powell, M. C. (1986). Keeping track of needs in communal and exchange relationships. *Journal of Personality and Social Psychology, 51*, 333–338.

Clark, M. S., Ouellette, R., Powell, M. C., & Milberg, S. (1987). Recipient's mood, relationship type, and helping. *Journal of Personality and Social Psychology, 53*, 94–103.

Clifford, M. M. (1984). Thoughts on a theory of constructive failure. *Educational Psychologist, 19*, 108–120.

Clifford, M. M. (1988). Failure tolerance and academic risk-taking in ten-to twelve-year-old students. *British Journal of Educational Psychology, 58*, 15–27.

Clifford, M. M. (1990). Students need challenge, not easy success. *Educational Leadership, 48*, 22–26.

Cofer, C. N., & Appley, M. H. (1964). *Motivation: Theory and research.* New York: Wiley.

Cohen, S., Sherrod, D. R., & Clark, M. S. (1986). Social skills and the stress-protective role of social support. *Journal of Personality and Social Psychology, 50*, 963–973.

Cohen-Charash, Y. (2009). Episodic envy. *Journal of Applied Social Psychology, 39*, 2128–2173.

Cohn, J. F., Zlochower, A. J., Lien, J., & Kanade, T. (1999). Automated face analysis by feature point tracking has high concurrent validity with manual FACS coding. *Psychophysiology, 36*, 35–43.

Cohn, M. A., & Fredrickson, B. L. (2009). Positive emotions. In S. J. Lopez, & C. R. Snyder (Eds.) (2009). *Oxford handbook of positive psychology* (2nd ed.; pp. 13–24). New York: Oxford University Press.

Colin, V. L. (1996). *Human attachment.* New York: McGraw-Hill.

Collins, J. L. (1982, March). *Self-efficacy and ability in achievement behavior.* Paper presented at the annual meeting of the American Educational Research Association, New York.

Compton, W. C., Smith, M. L., Cornish, K. A., & Qualls, D. L. (1996). Factor structure of mental health measures. *Journal of Personality and Social Psychology, 71*, 406–413.

Condon, P., & Barrett, L. F. (2013). Conceptualizing and experiencing compassion. *Emotion, 13*, 817–821.

Condry, J. (1977). Enemies of exploration: Self-initiated versus other-initiated learning. *Journal of Personality and Social Psychology, 35*, 459–477.

Condry, J. (1987). Enhancing motivation: A social development perspective. *Advances in Motivation and Achievement: Enhancing Motivation, 5*, 23–49.

Condry, J., & Chambers, J. (1978). Intrinsic motivation and the process of learning. In M. R. Lepper & D. Greene (Eds.), *The hidden costs of reward: New perspectives on the psychology of human motivation* (pp. 61–84). Hillsdale, NJ: Erlbaum.

Connell, J. P., & Wellborn, J. G. (1991). Competence, autonomy, and relatedness: A motivational analysis of self-system processes. In M. R. Gunnar & L. A. Sroufe (Eds.), *Self processes in development: Minnesota Symposium on Child Psychology* (Vol. 23, pp. 167–216). Chicago: University of Chicago Press.

Connolly, K., & Smith, P. K. (1972). Reactions of pre-school children to a strange observer. In N. G. Blurton-Jones (Ed.), *Ethological studies of child behavior*. Cambridge, UK: Cambridge University Press.

Cooper, M. L., Frone, M. R., Russell, M., & Mudar, P. (1995). Drinking to regulate positive and negative emotions: A motivational model of alcohol use. *Journal of Personality and Social Psychology, 69*, 990–1005.

Cooper, W. H. (1983). An achievement motivation nomological network. *Journal of Personality and Social Psychology, 44*, 841–861.

Cordova, D. I., & Lepper, M. R. (1996). Intrinsic motivation and the process of learning: Beneficial effects of contextualization, personalization, and choice. *Journal of Educational Psychology, 88*, 715–730.

Cornelius, R. R. (2006). Magda Arnold's Thomistic theory of emotion, the self-ideal, and the moral dimension of appraisal. *Cognition and Emotion, 20*, 976–1000.

Costello, C. G. (1978). A critical review of Seligman's laboratory experiments on learned helplessness and depression in humans. *Journal of Abnormal Psychology, 87*, 21–31.

Covington, M. (1984a). Motivation for self-worth. In R. Ames & C. A. Ames (Eds.), *Research on motivation in education* (Vol. 1, pp. 77–113). New York: Academic Press.

Covington, M. (1984b). The self-worth theory of achievement motivation: Findings and implications. *Elementary School Journal, 85*, 5–20.

Covington, M. V., & Mueller, K. J. (2001). Intrinsic versus extrinsic motivation: An approach/ avoidance reformulation. *Educational Psychology Review, 13*, 157–176.

Covington, M. V., & Omelich, C. L. (1979). Effort: The double-edged sword in school achievement. *Journal of Educational Psychology, 71*, 169–182.

Covington, M. W., & Omelich, C. L. (1984). Task-oriented versus competitive learning structures: Motivational and performance consequences. *Journal of Educational Psychology, 76*, 1038–1050.

Cox, K. (2012). Happiness and unhappiness in the developing world: Life satisfaction among sex workers, dump-dwellers, urban poor, and rural peasants in Nicaragua. *Journal of Happiness Studies, 13*, 103–128.

Cox, R. (1987). The rich harvest of Abraham Maslow. In A. Maslow, *Motivation and personality* (3rd ed., pp. 245–271). New York: Harper & Row.

Coyne, J. C. (1976a). Depression and the response of others. *Journal of Abnormal Psychology, 85*, 186–193.

Coyne, J. C. (1976b). Towards an interactional description of depression. *Psychiatry, 39*, 28–40.

Coyne, J. C., & DeLongis, A. (1986). Going beyond social support: The role of social relationships in adaptation. *Journal of Consulting and Clinical Psychology, 54*, 454–460.

Cragg, L., & Nation, K. (2008). Go or no-go? Developmental improvements in the efficiency of response inhibition in mid-childhood. *Developmental Science, 11*, 819–827.

Crago, M., Yates, A., Beutler, L. E., & Arizmendi, T. G. (1985). Height–weight ratios among female athletes: Are collegiate athletics the precursors to an anorexic syndrome? *International Journal of Eating Disorders, 4*, 79–87.

Craig, A. D. (2003). Interoception: The sense of the physiological condition of the body. *Current Opinion in Neurobiology, 13*, 500–505.

Craig, A. D. (2009a). How do you feel? Interoception: The sense of the physiological condition of the body. *Nature Review: Neuroscience, 3*, 655–666.

Craig, A. D. (2009b). How do you feel—now? The anterior insula and human awareness. *Nature Review: Neuroscience, 10*, 59–70.

Craighead, W. E., Kazdin, A. E., & Mahoney, M. J. (1981). *Behavior modification: Principles, issues, and applications.* Boston: Houghton Mifflin.

Crandall, C. S. (1988). Social cognition of binge eating. *Journal of Personality and Social Psychology, 55*, 588–598.

Crary, W. G. (1966). Reactions to incongruent self-experiences. *Journal of Consulting Psychology, 30*, 246–252.

Crews, F. (1996). The verdict on Freud. *Psychological Science, 7*, 63–67.

Crick, F., & Mitchison, G. (1986). REM sleep and neural networks. *Journal of Mind and Behavior, 7*, 229–250.

Crista, I. A., Tatar, A. S., Nagy, D., & David, D. (2012). The bottle is half empty and that's bad, but not tragic: Differential effects of negative functional reappraisal. *Motivation and Emotion, 36*, 550–563.

Cross, S. E., & Markus, H. R. (1994). Self-schemas, possible selves, and competent performance. *Journal of Educational Psychology, 86*, 423–438.

Cross, S. E., & Markus, H.R. (1991). Possible selves across the life span. *Human Development, 34*, 230–255.

Crowne, D. P., & Marlowe, D. (1964). *The approval motive.* New York: Wiley.

Csikszentmihalyi, M. (1975). *Beyond boredom and anxiety: The experience of flow in work and play.* San Francisco: Jossey-Bass.

Csikszentmihalyi, M. (1982). Toward a psychology of optimal experience. *Review of Personality and Social Psychology, 3*, 13–36.

Csikszentmihalyi, M. (1990). *Flow: The psychology of optimal experience.* New York: Harper & Row.

Csikszentmihalyi, M., & Csikszentmihalyi, I. (Eds.). (1988). *Optimal experiences: Psychological studies of flow in consciousness.* New York: Cambridge University Press.

Csikszentmihalyi, M., & Nakamura, J. (1989). The dynamics of intrinsic motivation: A study of adolescents. In C. A. Ames & R. Ames (Eds.), *Research on motivation in education* (Vol. 3, pp. 45–61). San Diego, CA: Academic Press.

Csikszentmihalyi, M., Rathunde, K., & Whalen, S. (1993). *Talented teenagers: The roots of success and failure.* New York: Cambridge University Press.

Cui, X., & Vaillant, G. E. (1996). The antecedents and consequences of negative live events in adulthood: A longitudinal study. *American Journal of Psychiatry, 152*, 21–26.

Cummings, D. E., Weigle, D.S., Frayo, R. S., Breen, P. A., Ma, M. K., Dellinger, E. P., et al. (2002). Plasma ghrelin levels after diet-induced weight loss or gastric bypass surgery. *New England Journal of Medicine, 346*, 1623–1630.

Cunningham, M. R. (1986). Measuring the physical in physical attractiveness: Quasi-experiments on the sociobiology of female facial beauty. *Journal of Personality and Social Psychology, 50*, 925–935.

Cunningham, M. R., Barbee, A. P., & Pike, C. L. (1990). What do women want?: Facialmetric assessment of multiple motives in the perception of male facial physical attractiveness. *Journal of Personality and Social Psychology, 59*, 61–62.

Cunningham, M. R., Roberts, A. R., Barbee, A. P., Druen, P. B., & Wu, C. (1995). Their ideas of beauty are, on the whole, the same as ours: Consistency and variability in the cross-cultural perception of female physical attractiveness. *Journal of Personality and Social Psychology, 68*, 261–279.

Cunningham, W., & Zelazo, P. D. (2007). Attitudes and evaluation: A social cognitive neuroscience perspective. *Trends in Cognitive Sciences, 11*, 97–104.

Curry, L. A., Snyder, C. R., Cook, D. L., Ruby, B. C., & Rehm, M. (1977). The role of hope in student-athlete academic and sport achievement. *Journal of Personality and Social Psychology, 73*, 1257–1267.

Custers, R., & Aarts, H. (2005). Positive affect as implicit motivator: On the nonconscious operation of behavioral goals. *Journal of Personality and Social Psychology, 89*, 129–142.

Custers, R., Aarts, H., Oikawa, M., & Elliot, A. (2009). The nonconscious road to perceptions of performance: Achievement priming augments outcome expectancies and experienced self-agency. *Journal of Experimental Social Psychology, 45*, 1200–1208.

D'Amato, M. R. (1974). Derived motives. *Annual Review of Psychology, 25*, 83–106.

D'Ardenne, K., McClure, S. M., Nystrom, L. E., & Cohen, J. D. (2008). BOLD responses reflecting dopaminergic signals in the human ventral tegmental area. *Science, 319*, 1264–1267.

Dalebroux, A., Goldstein, T. R., & Winner, E. (2008). Short-term mood repair through art-making: Attention redeployment is more effective than venting. *Motivation and Emotion, 32*, 288–295.

Damasio, A. R. (1994). *Descartes' error*. New York: Grosset/Putnam.

Damasio, A. R. (1996). The somatic marker hypothesis and the possible functions of the prefrontal cortex. *Philosophical Transactions of the Royal Society B: Biological Sciences, 35*, 1413–1420.

Daniels, M. (1988). The myth of self-actualization. *Journal of Humanistic Psychology, 28*, 7–38.

Darwin, C. A. (1859). *On the origin of species by means of natural selection*. London: John Murray.

Darwin, C. A. (1872). *The expression of the emotions in man and animals*. London: John Murray.

Daukantaite, D., & Bergman, L. R. (2005). Childhood roots of women's subjective well-being: The role of optimism. *European Psychologist, 10*, 287–297.

Daukantaite, D., & Zukauskiene, R. (2012). Optimism and subjective well-being: Affectivity plays a secondary role in the relationship between optimism and global life satisfaction in the middle-aged women. Longitudinal and cross-cultural findings. *Journal of Happiness Studies, 13*, 1–16.

Davidson, K. J. (1994). Un emotion, mood, and related affective constructs. In P. Ekman & R.N. Davidson (Eds.). *The nature of emotion: Fundamental questions* (pp. 51–55). New York: Oxford University Press.

Davidson, P., Turiel, E., & Black, A. (1983). The effects of stimulus familiarity in the use of criteria and justification in children's social reasoning. *British Journal of Developmental Psychology, 1*, 49–65.

Davidson, R. J. (2004). What does the prefrontal cortex "do" in affect? Perspectives on frontal EEG asymmetry research. *Biological Psychology, 67*, 219–233.

Davidson, R. J. (2012). *The emotional life of your brain*. New York: Hudson Street Press.

Davidson, R. J., & Irwin, W. (1999). The functional neuroanatomy of emotion and affective style. *Trends in Cognitive Science, 3*, 11–21.

Davidson, R. J., & Sutton, S. K. (1995). Affective neuroscience: The emergence of a discipline. *Current Opinion in Neurobiology, 5*, 217–224.

Davidson, R. J., Ekman, P., Saron, C., Senulis, J., & Friesen, W. V. (1990). Approach/ withdrawal and cerebral asymmetry. *Journal of Personality and Social Psychology, 58*, 330–341.

Davies, J., & Brember, I. (1999). Reading and mathematics attainments and self-esteem in years 2 and 6—an eight-year cross-sectional study. *Educational Studies, 25*, 145–157.

Davis, C. G., Nolen-Hoeksema, S., & Larsen, J. (1998). Making sense of loss and benefiting from the experience: Two construals of meaning. *Journal of Personality and Social Psychology, 75*, 561–574.

Davis, M. (1992). The role of the amygdala in conditioned fear. In J. P. Aggleton (Ed.), *The amygdala: Neurobiological aspects of emotion, memory, and mental dysfunction* (pp. 255–305). New York: Wiley.

Davis, M. H. (2004). Empathy: Negotiating the border between self and other. In L. Z. Tiedens & C. W. Leach (Eds.), *The social life of emotions* (pp. 19–42). New York: Cambridge University Press.

Davis, M., Hitchcock, J. M., & Rosen, J. B. (1987). Anxiety and the amygdala: Pharmacological and anatomical analysis of the fear-potentiated startle paradigm. *Psychology of Learning and Motivation, 21,* 263–305.

Davis, S. (2000). Testosterone and sexual desire in women. *Journal of Sex Education and Therapy, 25,* 25–32.

Dawes, R. M. (1996). *House of cards: Psychology and psychotherapy built on myth.* New York: Free Press.

Day, J. D., Borkowski, J. G., Punzo, D., & Howsepian, B. (1994). Enhancing possible selves in Mexican American students. *Motivation and Emotion, 18,* 79–103.

De Castro, J. M. (1990). Social facilitation of duration and size but not rate of the spontaneous meal intake of humans. *Physiology and Behavior, 47,* 1129–1135.

De Castro, J. M. (1991). Social facilitation of the spontaneous meal size of humans occurs on both weekdays and weekends. *Physiology and Behavior, 49,* 1289–1291.

De Castro, J. M. (1994). Family and friends produce greater social facilitation of food intake than other companions. *Physiology and Behavior, 56,* 445–455.

De Castro, J. M., & Brewer, E. M. (1992). The amount eaten in meals by humans is a power function of the number of people present. *Physiology and Behavior, 51,* 121–125.

De Hooge, I. E., Zeelenberg, M., & Breugelmans, S. M. (2010). Restore and protect motivations following shame. *Cognition and Emotion, 24,* 111–127.

De Hooge, I. E., Zeelenberg, M., & Breugelmans, S. M. (2011). A functionalist account of shame-induced behavior. *Cognition and Emotion, 25,* 939–946.

De La Ronde, C., & Swann, W. B., Jr. (1998). Partner verification: Restoring shattered images of our intimates. *Journal of Personality and Social Psychology, 75,* 374–382.

de Rivera, J. (1981). The structure of anger. In J. de Rivera (Ed.), *Conceptual encounter: A method for the exploration of human experience.* Washington, DC: University Press of America.

De Volder, M., & Lens, W. (1982). Academic achievement and future time perspective as a cognitive-motivational concept. *Journal of Personality and Social Psychology, 42,* 566–571.

Deaux, K., Reid, A., Mizrahi, K., & Ethier, K. A. (1995). Parameters of social identity. *Journal of Personality and Social Psychology, 53,* 281–295.

deCharms, R. (1968). *Personal causation.* New York: Academic Press.

deCharms, R. (1976). *Enhancing motivation: Change in the classroom.* New York: Irvington.

deCharms, R. (1984). Motivation enhancement in educational settings. In R. E. Ames & C. A. Ames (Eds.), *Research on motivation in education: Student motivation* (Vol. 1, pp. 275–310). New York: Academic Press.

deCharms, R. (1987). The burden of motivation. In M. L. Maehr & D. A. Kleiber (Eds.), *Advances in motivation and achievement: Enhancing motivation* (Vol. 5, pp. 1–21). Greenwich, CT: JAI Press.

deCharms, R., & Moeller, G. H. (1962). Values expressed in American children's readers: 1800–1950. *Journal of Abnormal and Social Psychology, 64,* 136–142.

Deci, E. L. (1971). Effects of externally mediated rewards on intrinsic motivation. *Journal of Personality and Social Psychology, 18,* 105–115.

Deci, E. L. (1972). Intrinsic motivation, extrinsic reinforcement, and inequity. *Journal of Personality and Social Psychology, 22,* 113–120.

Deci, E. L. (1975). *Intrinsic motivation.* New York: Plenum Press.

Deci, E. L. (1980). *The psychology of self-determination.* Lexington, MA: Lexington Books.

Deci, E. L. (1992a). On the nature and function of motivation theories. *Psychological Science, 3,* 167–171.

Deci, E. L. (1992b). The relation of interest to the motivation of behavior: A self-determination theory perspective. In K. A. Renninger, S. Hidi, & A. Krapp (Eds.), *The role of interest in learning and development* (pp. 43–60). Hillsdale, NJ: Erlbaum.

Deci, E. L. (1995). *Why we do what we do: Understanding self-motivation*. New York: Penguin Books.

Deci, E. L., & Casio, W. F. (1972, April). *Changes in intrinsic motivation as a function of negative feedback and threats*. Paper presented at the meeting of the Eastern Psychological Association, Boston.

Deci, E. L., & Ryan, R. M. (1985a). The General Causality Orientations Scale: Self-determination in personality. *Journal of Research in Personality, 19,* 109–134.

Deci, E. L., & Ryan, R. M. (1985b). *Intrinsic motivation and self-determination in human behavior*. New York: Plenum Press.

Deci, E. L., & Ryan, R. M. (1987). The support of autonomy and the control of behavior. *Journal of Personality and Social Psychology, 53,* 1024–1037.

Deci, E. L., & Ryan, R. M. (1991). A motivational approach to self: Integration in personality. In R. Dienstbier (Ed.), *Nebraska Symposium on Motivation: Perspectives on motivation* (Vol. 38, pp. 237–288). Lincoln: University of Nebraska Press.

Deci, E. L., & Ryan, R. M. (1995). Human autonomy: The basis for true self-esteem. In M. Kernis (Ed.), *Efficacy, agency, and self-esteem* (pp. 31–49). New York: Plenum Press.

Deci, E. L., & Ryan, R. M. (2000). The "what" and "why" of goal pursuits: Human needs and the self-determination of behavior. *Psychological Inquiry, 11,* 227–268.

Deci, E. L., Betley, G., Kahle, J., Abrams, L., & Porac, J. (1981). When trying to win: Competition and intrinsic motivation. *Personality and Social Psychology Bulletin, 7,* 79–83.

Deci, E. L., Eghrari, H., Patrick, B. C., & Leone, D. R. (1994). Facilitating internalization: The self-determination theory perspective. *Journal of Personality, 62,* 119–142.

Deci, E. L., Koestner, R., & Ryan, R. M. (1999). A meta-analytic review of experiments examining the effects of extrinsic rewards on intrinsic motivation. *Psychological Bulletin, 125,* 627–668.

Deci, E. L., La Guardia, J. G., Moller, A. C., Scheiner, M. J., & Ryan, R. M. (2006). On the benefits of giving as well as receiving autonomy support: Mutuality in close friendships. *Personality and Social Psychology Bulletin, 32,* 313–327.

Deci, E. L., Ryan, R. M., & Williams, G. C. (1995). Need satisfaction and the self-regulation of learning. *Learning and Individual Differences, 8,* 165–183.

Deci, E. L., Ryan, R. M., Gagne', M., Leone, D. R., Usunov, J., & Kornazheva, B. P. (2001). Need satisfaction, motivation, and well-being in the work organizations of a former Eastern Bloc country: A cross-cultural study of self-determination. *Personality and Social Psychology Bulletin, 27,* 930–942.

Deci, E. L., Schwartz, A., Scheinman, L., & Ryan, R. M. (1981). An instrument to assess adult's orientations toward control versus autonomy in children: Reflections on intrinsic motivation and perceived competence. *Journal of Educational Psychology, 73,* 642–650.

Deci, E. L., Spiegel, N. H., Ryan, R. M., Koestner, R., & Kauffman, M. (1982). Effects of performance standards on teaching styles: Behavior of controlling teachers. *Journal of Educational Psychology, 74,* 852–859.

Delisle, J. (1986). Death with honors: Suicide among gifted adolescents. *Journal of Counseling and Development, 64,* 558–560.

Dember, W. N. (1965). The new look in motivation. *American Scientist, 53,* 409–427.

Dember, W. N. (1974). Motivation and the cognitive revolution. *American Psychologist, 29,* 161–168.

Dempsey, E. W. (1951). Homeostasis. In S. S. Stevens (Ed.), *Handbook of experimental psychology* (pp. 209–235). New York: Wiley.

DeNeve, K. M. (1999). Happy as an extraverted clam?: The role of personality for subjective well-being. *Current Directions in Psychological Science, 8,* 141–144.

Denson, T. F., Grisham, J. R., Moulds, M. L. (2011). Cognitive reappraisal increases heart rate variability in response to anger provocation. *Motivation and Emotion, 35,* 14–22.

DePaulo, B. (1992). Nonverbal behavior and self-presentation. *Psychological Bulletin, 111,* 203–243.

Depue, R. A., & Monroe, S. M. (1978). Learned helplessness in the perspective of the depressive disorders: Conceptual and definitional issues. *Journal of Abnormal Psychology, 87*, 3–20.

Derakshan, N., & Eysenck, M. W. (2010). Introduction to the special issue: Emotional states, attention, and working memory. *Cognition and Emotion, 24*, 189–199.

Descartes, R. (1970). *The passions of the soul.* Paris: Vrin. (Original work published in 1649).

Deutsch, J. A., & Gonzalez, M. F. (1980). Gastric nutrient content signals satiety. *Behavior Neural Biology, 30*, 113–116.

Deutsch, J. A., Young, W. G., & Kalogeris, T. J. (1978). The stomach signals satiety. *Science, 201*, 165–167.

Dholakia, U. M., & Bagozzi, R. P. (2003). As time goes by: How goal and implementation intentions influence enactment of short-fuse behaviors. *Journal of Applied Social Psychology, 33*, 889–922.

Di Chiara, G. (1998). A motivational learning hypothesis of the role of mesolimbic dopamine in compulsive drug use. *Journal of Psychopharmacology, 12*, 54–67.

Dickerson, C., Thibodeau, R., Aronson, E., & Miller, D. (1992). Using cognitive dissonance theory to encourage water conservation. *Journal of Applied Social Psychology, 22*, 841–854.

Dickerson, S. S., & Kemeny, M. E. (2004). Acute stressors and cortisol responses: A theoretical integration and synthesis of laboratory research. *Psychological Bulletin, 130*, 355–391.

Dickinson, A., & Balleine, B. (2002). The role of learning in the operation of motivational systems. In C. R. Gallistel (Ed.), *Stevens' handbook of experimental psychology: Learning, motivation, and emotion* (Vol. *3*, pp. 497–534). New York: Wiley.

Diener, C. I., & Dweck, C. S. (1978). An analysis of learned helplessness: Continuous changes in performance, strategy, and achievement cognitions following failure. *Journal of Personality and Social Psychology, 36*, 451–462.

Diener, C. I., & Dweck, C. S. (1980). An analysis of learned helplessness: II. The processing of success. *Journal of Personality and Social Psychology, 39*, 940–952.

Diener, E., & Biswas-Diener, R. (2008). *Happiness: Unlocking the mysteries of psychological wealth.* Malden, MA: Blackwell Publishing.

Diener, E., & Diener, C. (1996). Most people are happy. *Psychological Science, 7*, 181–185.

Diener, E., & Emmons, R. A. (1984). The independence of positive and negative affect. *Journal of Personality and Social Psychology, 47*, 105–1117.

Diener, E., & Iran-Nejad, A. (1986). The relationship in experience between various types of affect. *Journal of Personality and Social Psychology, 50*, 1031–1038.

Diener, E., & Seligman, M. E. P. (2002). Very happy people. *Psychological Science, 13*, 81–84.

Diener, E., & Seligman, M. E. P. (2004). Beyond money: Toward an economy of well-being. *Psychological Science in the Public Interest, 5*, 1–31.

Diener, E., Diener, M., & Diener, C. (1995). Factors predicting the subjective well-being of nations. *Journal of Personality and Social Psychology, 69*, 851–864.

Diener, E., Emmons, R. A., Larsen, R. J., & Griffin, S. (1985). The satisfaction with life scale. *Journal of Personality Assessment, 49*, 71–75.

Diener, E., Horwitz, J., & Emmons, R. A. (1985). Happiness of the very wealthy. *Social Indicators Research, 16*, 263–274.

Diener, E., Suh, E. M., Lucas, R. E., & Smith, H. L. (1999). Subjective well-being: Three decades of progress. *Psychological Bulletin, 125*, 276–302.

Dienstbier, R. A. (1991). Introduction. In R. A. Dienstbier (Ed.), *Nebraska Symposium on Motivation* (Vol. *38*, pp. ix–xiv). Lincoln: University of Nebraska Press.

Dijk, C., de Jong, P. J., & Peters, M. L. (2009). The remedial value of blushing in the context of transgressions and mishaps. *Emotion, 9*, 287–291.

Dijk, C., Koenig, B., Ketelaar, T., & De Jong, P. J. (2011). Saved by the blush: Being trusted despite defecting. *Emotion, 11*, 313–319.

Dimberg, U. (1982). Facial reactions to facial expressions. *Psychophysiology, 19*, 643–647.

Diserens, C. M. (1925). Psychological objectivism. *Psychological Review, 32*, 121–125.

Dollinger, S. J., & Thelen, M. H. (1978). Over-justification and children's intrinsic motivation: Comparative effects of four rewards. *Journal of Personality and Social Psychology, 36*, 1259–1269.

Donovan, J. M., Hill, E., & Jankowiak, W. R. (1989). Gender, sexual orientation, and truth or consequences in studies of physical attractiveness. *Journal of Sex Research, 26*, 264–271.

Dovidio, J. F., Piliavin, J. A., Schroeder, D. A., & Penner, L. A. (2006). *The social psychology of prosocial behavior*. Mahwah, NJ: Lawrence Erlbaum.

Downie, M., Koestner, R., ElGeledi, S., & Cree, K. (2004). The impact of cultural internalization and integration on well-being among tricultural individuals. *Personality and Social Psychology Bulletin, 30*, 305–314.

Drake, J. E., & Winner, E. (2013). How children use drawing to regulate their emotions. *Cognition and Emotion, 27*, 512–520.

Druss, R. G., & Silverman, J. A. (1979). Body image and perfectionism of ballerinas. *General Hospital Psychiatry, 2*, 115–121.

Duda, J. (2005). Motivation in sport: The relevance of competence and achievement goals. In A. J. Elliot & C. S. Dweck (Eds.), *Handbook of competence and motivation* (Chapter 18, pp. 318–335). New York: Guilford Press.

Duffy, E. (1957). Psychological significance of the concept of arousal or activation. *Psychological Review, 64*, 265–275.

Dunker, K. (1945). On problem-solving. *Psychological Monographs, 58*, Whole No. 5.

Dunlap, K. (1919). Are there any instincts? *Journal of Abnormal Psychology, 14*, 35–50.

Dunn, J., & Munn, P. (1987). Development of justification in disputes with mother and sibling. *Developmental Psychology, 23*, 791–798.

Dweck, C. S. (1975). The role of expectancies and attributions in the alleviation of learned helplessness. *Journal of Personality and Social Psychology, 31*, 674–685.

Dweck, C. S. (1986). Motivational processes affecting learning. *American Psychologist, 41*, 1040–1048.

Dweck, C. S. (1999). *Self-theories: Their role in motivation, personality, and development*. Philadelphia: Psychology Press.

Dweck, C. S. (2006). *Mindset: The new psychology of success*. New York: Random House.

Dweck, C. S. (2008). Can personality be changed? The role of beliefs in personality and change. *Current Directions in Psychological Science, 17*, 391–394.

Dweck, C. S., & Elliot, E. S. (1983). Achievement motivation. In P. Mussen & E. M. Hetherington (Eds.), *Handbook of child psychology* (pp. 643–692). New York: Wiley.

Dweck, C. S., & Leggett, E. L. (1988). A social-cognitive approach to motivation and personality. *Psychological Review, 95*, 256–273.

Dweck, C. S., & Repucci, N. D. (1973). Learned helplessness and reinforcement responsibility in children. *Journal of Personality and Social Psychology, 25*, 109–116.

Dykman, B. M. (1998). Integrating cognitive and motivational factors in depression: Initial tests of a goal-orientation approach. *Journal of Personality and Social Psychology, 74*, 139–158.

Eagle, M. (1984). *Recent developments on psychoanalysis*. New York: McGraw-Hill.

Earley, P. C., & Perry, B. C. (1987). Work plan availability and performance: An assessment of task strategy priming on subsequent task completion. *Organizational Behavior and Human Decision Processes, 39*, 279–302.

Earley, P. C., Connolly, T., & Ekegren, G. (1989). Goals, strategy development and task performance: Some limits on the efficacy of goal setting. *Journal of Applied Psychology, 74*, 24–33.

Earley, P. C., Wojnaroski, P., & Prest, W. (1987). Task planning and energy expended: Exploration of how goals influence performance. *Journal of Applied Psychology, 72*, 107–113.

Eastwick, P. W., & Finkel, E. J. (2008). Sex differences in mate preferences revisited: Do people know what they initially desire in a romantic partner? *Journal of Personality and Social Psychology, 94*, 245–264.

Eccles, J. S., & Wigfield, A. (2002). Motivational beliefs, values, and goals. *Annual Review of Psychology, 53*, 109–132.

Eccles, J. S., Adler, T. F., & Meece, J. L. (1984). Sex differences in achievement: A test of alternate theories. *Journal of Personality and Social Psychology, 46*, 26–43.

Eccles-Parsons, J. E., Adler, T. F., & Kaczala, C. M. (1982). Socialization of achievement attitudes and beliefs: Parental influences. *Child Development, 53*, 310–321.

Eccleston, C., & Crombez, G. (1999). Pain demands attention: A cognitive-affective model of the interruptive function of pain. *Psychological Bulletin, 125*, 356–366.

Edwards, R., Manstead, A. S. R., & MacDonald, C. J. (1984). The relationship between children's sociometric status and ability to recognize facial expressions of emotion. *European Journal of Social Psychology, 14*, 235–238.

Eibl-Eibesfeldt, I. (1971). *Love and hate*. London: Methuen.

Eibl-Eibesfeldt, I. (1972). Similarities and differences between cultures in expressive movements. In R. A. Hinde (Ed.), *Nonverbal communication*. Cambridge, UK: Cambridge University Press.

Eibl-Eibesfeldt, I. (1989). *Human ethology*. New York: Aldine De Gruyter.

Eidelson, R. J. (1980). Interpersonal satisfaction and level of achievement: A curvilinear relationship. *Journal of Personality and Social Psychology, 39*, 460–470.

Eisenberg, N. (2000). Emotion, regulation, and moral development. *Annual Review of Psychology, 51*, 665–697.

Eisenberg, N., & Fabes, R. A. (1990). Empathy: Conceptualization, measurement, and relation to prosocial behavior. *Motivation and Emotion, 14*, 131–149.

Eisenberg, N., Fabes, R. A., Nyman, M., Bernzweig, J., & Pinuelas, A. (1994). The relations of emotionality and regulation to children's anger-related reactions. *Child Development, 65*, 109–128.

Eisenberg, N., Fabes, R. A., Shepard, S. A., Murphy, B. C., Guthrie, I. K., Jones, S., et al. (1997). Contemporaneous and longitudinal prediction of children's social functioning from regulation and emotionality. *Child Development, 68*, 642–664.

Eisenberger, R., Pierce, W. D., & Cameron, J. (1999). Effects of reward on intrinsic motivation: Negative, neutral, and positive: Comment on Deci, Koestner, and Ryan (1999). *Psychological Bulletin, 125*, 677–691.

Ekman, P. (1972). Universal and cultural differences in facial expression of emotion. In J. R. Cole (Ed.), *Nebraska Symposium on Motivation* (Vol. 19, pp. 207–284). Lincoln: University of Nebraska Press.

Ekman, P. (1992). An argument for basic emotions. *Cognition and Emotion, 6*, 169–200.

Ekman, P. (1993). Facial expression and emotion. *American Psychologist, 48*, 384–392.

Ekman, P. (1994a). All emotions are basic. In P. Ekman & R. J. Davidson (Eds.), *The nature of emotion: Fundamental questions* (pp. 15–19). New York: Oxford University Press.

Ekman, P. (1994b). Strong evidence for universals in facial expressions: A reply to Russell's mistaken critique. *Psychological Bulletin, 115*, 268–287.

Ekman, P., & Cordaro, D. (2011). What is meant by calling emotions basic? *Emotion Review, 3*, 364–370.

Ekman, P., & Davidson, R. J. (1993). Voluntary smiling changes regional brain activity. *Psychological Science, 4*, 342–345.

Ekman, P., & Davidson, R. J. (Eds.). (1994). *The nature of emotion: Fundamental questions* (pp. 20–24). New York: Oxford University Press.

Ekman, P., & Friesen, W. V. (1971). Constants across cultures in facial expressions of emotion. In J. K. Cole (Ed.), *Nebraska Symposium on Motivation* (pp. 207–283). Lincoln: University of Nebraska Press.

Ekman, P., & Friesen, W. V. (1975). *Unmasking the face.* Englewood Cliffs, NJ: Prentice Hall.

Ekman, P., & Friesen, W. V. (1978). *Facial action coding system.* Palo Alto, CA: Consulting Psychologists Press.

Ekman, P., & Friesen, W. V. (1986). A new pan-cultural facial expression of emotion. *Motivation and Emotion, 10,* 159–168.

Ekman, P., & Heider, K. G. (1988). The universality of a contempt expression: A replication. *Motivation and Emotion, 12,* 303–308.

Ekman, P., & Rosenberg, E. (1997). *What the face reveals.* New York: Oxford University Press.

Ekman, P., Levenson, R. W., & Friesen, W. V. (1983). Autonomic nervous system activity distinguishes between emotions. *Science, 221,* 1208–1210.

Ekman, P., Sorenson, E. R., & Friesen, W. V. (1969). Pan-cultural elements in facial displays of emotion. *Science, 164,* 86–88.

El-Haschimi, K., Pierroz, D. D., Hileman, S. M., Bjorbake, C., & Flier, J. S. (2000). Two defects contribute to hypothalamic leptin resistance in mice with diet-induced obesity. *Journal of Clinical Investigation, 105,* 1827–1832.

Elliot, A. J. (1997). Integrating the "classic" and "contemporary" approaches to achievement motivation: A hierarchical model of approach and avoidance achievement motivation. In M. L. Maehr & P. R. Pintrich (Eds.), *Advances in motivation and achievement* (Vol. *10,* pp. 143–179). Greenwich, CT: JAI Press.

Elliot, A. J. (1999). Approach and avoidance motivation and achievement goals. *Educational Psychologist, 34,* 169–189.

Elliot, A. J. (2006). The hierarchical model of approach-avoidance motivation. *Motivation and Emotion, 30,* 111–116.

Elliot, A. J., & Church, M. (1997). A hierarchical model of approach and avoidance achievement motivation. *Journal of Personality and Social Psychology, 72,* 218–232.

Elliot, A. J., & Devine, P. G. (1994). On the motivational nature of cognitive dissonance: Dissonance as psychological discomfort. *Journal of Personality and Social Psychology, 66,* 382–394.

Elliot, A. J., & Harackiewicz, J. (1996). Approach and avoidance goals and intrinsic motivation: A mediational analysis. *Journal of Personality and Social Psychology, 70,* 461–475.

Elliot, A. J., & McGregor, H. (1999). Test anxiety and the hierarchical model of approach and avoidance achievement motivation. *Journal of Personality and Social Psychology, 76,* 628–644.

Elliot, A. J., & Murayama, K. (2008). On the measurement of achievement goals: Critique, illustration, and application. *Journal of Educational Psychology, 100,* 613–628.

Elliot, A. J., & Sheldon, K. (1997). Avoidance achievement motivation: A personal goals analysis. *Journal of Personality and Social Psychology, 73,* 171–185.

Elliot, E., & Dweck, C. (1988). Goals: An approach to motivation and achievement. *Journal of Personality and Social Psychology, 54,* 5–12.

Elliot, T. R., Witty, T. E., Herrick, S., & Hoffman, J. T. (1991). Negotiating reality after physical loss: Hope, depression, and disability. *Journal of Personality and Social Psychology, 61,* 608–613.

Ellison, P. T. (2001). *On fertile ground: A natural history of reproduction.* Cambridge, MA: Harvard University Press.

Ellsworth, P. C. (1994). William James and emotion: Is a century of fame worth a century of misunderstanding? *Psychological Review, 101,* 222–229.

Ellsworth, P. C. (2013). Appraisal theory: Old and new questions. *Emotion Review, 5,* 125–131.

Ellsworth, P. C., & Smith, C. A. (1988b). Shades of joy: Patterns of appraisal differentiating pleasant emotions. *Cognition and Emotion, 2,* 301–331.

Elmquist, J. K., Elias, C. F., & Saper, C. B. (1999). From lesions to leptin: hypothalamic control of food intake and body weight. *Neuron, 22,* 221–232.

Emmons, R. A. (1989). The personal striving approach to personality. In L. A. Pervin (Ed.), *Goal concepts in personality and social psychology* (pp. 87–126). Hillsdale, NJ: Erlbaum.

Emmons, R. A. (1996). Striving and feeling: Personal goals and subjective well-being. In P. M. Gollwitzer & J. A. Bargh (Eds.), *The psychology of action: Linking cognition and motivation to behavior* (pp. 313–337). New York: Guilford Press.

Emmons, R. A. (2003). Personal goals, life meaning, and virtue: Wellsprings of a positive life. In C. Keyes & J. Haidt (Eds.), *Flourishing: Positive psychology and the well-lived life* (pp. 105–128). Washington, DC: American Psychological Association.

Emmons, R. A. (2003). Personal goals, life meaning, and virtue: Wellsprings of a positive life. In C.L.M. Keyes (Ed.), *Flourishing: The positive person and the good life* (pp. 105–128). Washington, DC: American Psychological Association.

Emmons, R. A., & McCullough, M. E. (2004). *The psychology of gratitude.* New York: Oxford University Press.

Engeser, S., & Rheinberg, F. (2008). Flow, moderators of challenge-skill balance, and performance. *Motivation and Emotion, 32,* 158–172.

Epstein, A. N. (1973). Epilogue: Retrospect and prognosis. In A. N. Epstein, H. R. Kissileff, & E. Stellar (Eds.), *The neuropsychology of thirst: New findings and advances in concepts* (pp. 315–332). New York: Wiley.

Epstein, J. A., & Harackiewicz, J. H. (1992). Winning is not enough: The effects of competition and achievement orientation on intrinsic interest. *Personality and Social Psychology Bulletin, 18,* 128–138.

Epstude, K., & Roese, N. J. (2008). The functional theory of counterfactual thinking. *Personality and Social Psychology Review, 2,* 168–192.

Erdelyi, M. H. (1985). *Psychoanalysis: Freud's cognitive psychology.* New York: W. H. Freeman.

Erdelyi, M. H. (1990). Repression, reconstruction, and defense: History and integration of the psychoanalytic and experimental frameworks. In J. L. Singer (Ed.), *Repression and dissociation* (pp. 1–31). Chicago: University of Chicago Press.

Erdelyi, M. H., & Goldberg, B. (1979). Let's not sweep repression under the rug: Toward a cognitive psychology of repression. In J. F. Kilstrom & F. J. Evans (Eds.), *Fundamental disorders of memory.* Hillsdale, NJ: Erlbaum.

Erez, M. (1977). Feedback: A necessary condition for the goal setting performance relationship. *Journal of Applied Psychology, 62,* 624–627.

Ericsson, K. A., & Charness, N. (1994). Expert performance: Its structure and acquisition. *American Psychologist, 49,* 725–747.

Ericsson, K. A., Krampe, R. T. C., & Tesch-Romer, C. (1993). The role of deliberate practice in the acquisition of expert performance. *Psychological Review, 100,* 363–406.

Estrada, C. A., Isen, A. M., & Young, M. J. (1994). Positive affect improves creative problem-solving and influences reported source of practice satisfaction in physicians. *Motivation and Emotion, 18,* 285–299.

Estrada, C. A., Isen, A. M., & Young, M. J. (1997). Positive affect influences integration of information and decreases anchoring in reasoning among physicians. *Organizational Behavior and Human Decision Making Processes, 72,* 117–135.

Evans, G. E., Shapiro, D. H., & Lewis, M. (1993). Specifying dysfunctional mismatches between different control dimensions. *British Journal of Psychology, 84,* 255–273.

Exline, R. V. (1962). Need affiliation and initial communication behavior in problem solving groups characterized by low interpersonal visibility. *Psychological Reports, 10,* 79–89.

Exner, J. E., Jr. (1986). *The Rorschach: A comprehensive system* (2nd ed., Vol. 1). New York: Wiley Interscience.

Eysenck, H. J. (1986). Can personality study ever be scientific? *Journal of Social Behavior and Personality, 1,* 3–19.

Farrer, C., & Frith, C. D. (2002). Experiencing oneself vs. another person as being the cause of an action: The neural correlates of the experience of agency. *NeuroImage, 15,* 596–603.

Farrer, C., Franck, N., Georgieff, N., Frith, C. D., Decety, J., & Geannerod, M. (2003). Modulating the experience of agency: a positron emission tomography study. *NeuroImage, 18,* 324–333.

Faust, I. M., Johnson, P. R., & Hirsch, J. (1977a). Adipose tissue regeneration following lipectomy. *Science, 197,* 391–393.

Faust, I. M., Johnson, P. R., & Hirsch, J. (1977b). Surgical removal of adipose tissue alters feeding behavior and the development of obesity in rats. *Science, 197,* 393–396.

Fazio, R. H., Jackson, J. R., Dunton, B., & Williams, C. J. (1995). Variability in automatic activation as an unobtrusive measure of racial attitudes: A bona fide pipeline? *Journal of Personality and Social Psychology, 69,* 1013–1027.

Fazio, R. H., Zanna, M., & Cooper, J. (1977). Dissonance and self-perception: An integrative view of each theory's proper domain of application. *Journal of Experimental Social Psychology, 13,* 464–479.

Fazio, R. H., Zanna, M., & Cooper, J. (1979). On the relationship of data to theory: A reply to Ronis and Greenwald. *Journal of Experimental Social Psychology, 15,* 70–66.

Feather, N. T. (1961). The relationship of persistence at a task to expectation of success and achievement related motives. *Journal of Abnormal and Social Psychology, 63,* 552–561.

Feather, N. T. (1963). Persistence at a difficult task with alternative tasks of intermediate difficulty. *Journal of Abnormal and Social Psychology, 66,* 604–609.

Feather, N. T., & Sherman, R. (2002). Envy, resentment, schadenfreude, and sympathy: Reactions to deserved and undeserved achievement and subsequent failure. *Personality and Social Psychology Bulletin, 28,* 953–961.

Feeney, J. A., & Noller, P. (1990). Attachment style as a predictor of adult romantic relationships. *Journal of Personality and Social Psychology, 58,* 281–291.

Fehr, B., & Russell, J. A. (1984). Concept of emotion viewed from a prototype perspective. *Journal of Experimental Psychology: General, 113,* 464–486.

Fehr, B., Baldwin, M., Collins, L., Patterson, S., & Benditt, R. (1999). Anger in close relationships: An interpersonal script analysis. *Personality and Social Psychology Bulletin, 25,* 299–312.

Feldman, L. A. (1995). Valence focus and arousal focus: Individual differences in the structure of affective experience. *Journal of Personality and Social Psychology, 69,* 153–166.

Feldman, R. (2012). Oxytocin and social affiliation in humans. *Hormones and Behavior, 61,* 380–391.

Feltz, D. L. (1992). Understanding motivation in sport: A self-efficacy perspective. In G. C. Roberts (Ed.), *Motivation in sport and exercise* (pp. 93–105). Champaign, IL: Human Kinetics.

Fenigstein, A., Scheier, M. F., & Buss, A. H. (1975). Public and private self-consciousness: Assessment and theory. *Journal of Consulting and Clinical Psychology, 43,* 522–527.

Fernald, A. (1992). Human maternal vocalizations to infants as biologically relevant signals: An evolutionary perspective. In J. H. Barkow, L. Cosmides, & J. Tooby (Eds.), *The adapted mind* (pp. 391–428). New York: Oxford University Press.

Fernandez-Dols, J. M., & Ruiz-Belba, M. A. (1995). Are smiles a sign of happiness? Gold medal winners at the Olympic games. *Journal of Personality and Social Psychology, 69,* 1113–1119.

Feshbach, S. (1984). The personality of personality theory and research. *Personality and Social Psychology Bulletin, 10,* 446–456.

Festinger, L. (1957). *A theory of cognitive dissonance.* Stanford, CA: Stanford University Press.

Festinger, L., & Carlsmith, J. M. (1959). Cognitive consequences of forced compliance. *Journal of Abnormal and Social Psychology, 58,* 203–210.

Festinger, L., Riecken, H. W., & Schachter, S. (1956). *When prophecy fails*. Minneapolis: Minnesota University Press.

Festinger, L., Riecken, H. W., & Schachter, S. (1958). When prophecy fails. In E. E. Maccoby, T. M. Newcomb, & E. L. Hartley (Eds.), *Readings in social psychology* (pp. 156–163). New York: Holt, Rinehart & Winston.

Finkel, E. J., & Campbell, W. K. (2001). Self-control and accommodation in close relationships: An interdependence analysis. *Journal of Personality and Social Psychology, 81*, 263–277.

Finkel, E. J., Dalton, A. N., Campbell, W. K., Brunell, A. B., Scarbeck, S. J., & Chartrand, T. L. (2006). High-maintenance interaction: Inefficient social coordination impairs self-regulation. *Journal of Personality and Social Psychology, 91*, 456–475.

Fischer, H., Andersson, J. L. R., Furmark, T., Wik, G., & Fredrikson, M. (2002). Right-sided human prefrontal brain activation during acquisition of conditioned fear. *Emotion, 2*, 233–241.

Fischer, K. W., Shaver, P. R., & Carnochan, P. (1990). How emotions develop and how they organise development. *Cognition and Emotion, 4*, 81–127.

Fischer, A. H., & Manstead, A. S. R. (2008). Social functions of emotion. In M. Lewis, J. M. Haviland-Jones, & L. F. Barrett (Eds.), *Handbook of emotions* (3rd ed., pp. 456–468). New York: Guilford Press.

Fisher, C. D. (1978). The effects of personal control, competence, and extrinsic reward systems on intrinsic motivation. *Organizational Behavior and Human Performance, 21*, 273–288.

Fisher, S., & Greenberg, R. P. (1977). *The scientific credibility of Freud's theories and therapy*. New York: Basic Books.

Fisher, S., & Greenberg, R. P. (1996). *Freud scientifically reappraised: Testing the theories and therapy*. New York: Wiley.

Fiske, S. T. (2004). Mind the gap: In praise of informal sources of formal thinking. *Personality and Social Psychology Review, 8*, 132–137.

Flegel, K. M., Carroll, M. D., Kucznarski, R. J., & Johnson, C. L. (1998). Overweight and obesity in the United States: Prevalence and trends, 1960–1994. *International Journal of Obesity Relat. Metabolism Disorder, 22*, 39–47.

Flowerday, T., & Schraw, G. (2000). Teacher beliefs about instructional choice: A phenomenological study. *Journal of Educational Psychology, 92*, 634–645.

Flowerday, T., & Schraw, G. (2003). Effect of choice on cognitive and affective engagement. *Journal of Educational Research, 96*, 207–215.

Flowerday, T., Schraw, G., & Stevens, J. (2004). The role of choice and interest in reader engagement. *Journal of Experimental Education, 72*, 93–114.

Foch, T. T., & McClearn, G. E. (1980). Genetics, body weight, and obesity. In A. E. Stunkard (Ed.), *Obesity* (pp. 48–61). Philadelphia: W. B. Saunders.

Fodor, E. M. (2010). Power motivation. In O. C. Schultheiss & J. C. Brunstein (Eds.), *Implicit motives* (Chapter 1, pp. 3–29). New York: Oxford University Press.

Fodor, E. M., & Farrow, D. L. (1979). The power motive as an influence on the use of power. *Journal of Personality and Social Psychology, 37*, 2091–2097.

Fodor, E. M., & Smith, T. (1982). The power motive as an influence on group decision making. *Journal of Personality and Social Psychology, 42*, 178–185.

Fok, H. K., Hui, C. M., Bond, M. H., Matsumoto, D., & Yoo, S. H. (2008). Integrating personality, context, relationship, and emotion type into a model of display rules. *Journal of Research in Personality, 42*, 133–150.

Folkman, S., & Lazarus, R. S. (1985). If it changes it must be a process: Study of emotion and coping during three stages of a college examination. *Journal of Personality and Social Psychology, 48*, 150–170.

Folkman, S., & Lazarus, R. S. (1990). Coping and emotion. In N. Stein, B. Leventhal, & T. Trabasso (Eds.), *Psychological and biological approaches to emotion* (pp. 313–332). Hillsdale, NJ: Erlbaum.

Folkman, S., Lazarus, R. S., Dunkel-Schetter, C., DeLongin, A., & Gruen, R. J. (1986). Dynamics of a stressful encounter: Cognitive appraisal, coping, and encounter outcomes. *Journal of Personality and Social Psychology, 50,* 992–1003.

Ford, B. Q., & Tamir, M. (2012). When getting angry is smart: Emotional preferences and emotional intelligence. *Emotion, 12,* 685–689.

Ford, J. G. (1991a). Inherent potentialities of actualization: An initial exploration. *Journal of Humanistic Psychology, 31,* 65–88.

Ford, J. G. (1995). The temperament/actualization concept: A perspective on constitutional integrity and psychological health. *Journal of Humanistic Psychology, 35,* 57–67.

Forest, D., Clark, M. S., Mills, J., & Isen, A. M. (1979). Helping as a function of feeling state and nature of the helping behavior. *Motivation and Emotion, 3,* 161–169.

Forster, J., Higgins, E. T., & Bianco, A. T. (2003). Speed/accuracy decisions in task performance: Built-in trade-off or separate strategic concerns. *Organizational Behavior and Human Decision Processes, 90,* 148–164.

Forster, J., Higgins, E. T., & Idson, C. I. (1998). Approach and avoidance strength as a function of regulatory focus: Revisiting the "goal looms larger" effect. *Journal of Personality and Social Psychology, 75,* 1115–1131.

Fowles, D. C. (1988). Psychophysiology and psychopathology: A motivational approach. *Psychophysiology, 25,* 373–391.

Frankl, V. E. (1960). Paradoxical intention: A logotherapeutic technique. *American Journal of Psychotherapy, 14,* 520–525.

Frederick, D. A., & Haselton, M. G. (2007). Why is muscularity sexy?: Tests of the fitness indicator hypothesis. *Personality and Social Psychology Bulletin, 33,* 1167–1183.

Fredricks, J. A., Blumenfeld, P. C. & Paris, A. H. (2004). School engagement: Potential of the concept, state of the evidence. *Review of Educational Research, 74,* 59–109.

Fredrickson, B. L. (1998). What good are positive emotions? *Review of General Psychology, 2,* 300–319.

Fredrickson, B. L. (2009). *Positivity: Top-notch research reveals the 3-to-1 ratio that will change your life.* New York: Three Rivers Press.

Fredrickson, B. L., & Branigan, C. (2005). Positive emotions broaden thought-action repertoires: Evidence for the broaden-and-build model. *Cognition and Emotion, 19,* 313–332.

Fredrickson, B. L., Mancuso, R. A., Branigan, C., & Tugade, M. (2000). The undoing effect of positive emotions. *Motivation and Emotion, 24,* 237–258.

Freitas, A. L., & Higgins, E. T. (2002). Enjoying goal-directed action: The role of regulatory fit. *Psychological Science, 13,* 1–6.

Freud, A. (1946). *The ego and mechanisms of defense.* New York: International Universities Press.

Freud, S. (1914 [Original work published 1901]). *Psychopathology of everyday life* (A. A. Brill, Trans.). New York: Macmillan.

Freud, S. (1915). Instincts and their vicissitudes. In *Collected papers of Sigmund Freud* (Vol. *4,* pp. 60–83). London: Hogarth Press.

Freud, S. (1917 [Original work published 1905]). *Wit and its relation to the unconscious* (A. A. Brill, Trans.). New York: Moffat, Yard.

Freud, S. (1920 [Original work published 1917]). *A general introduction to psychoanalysis* (J. Riviére, Trans.). New York: Liveright.

Freud, S. (1922 [Original work published 1920]). *Beyond the pleasure principle* (J. Strachey, Trans.). London: Hogarth Press.

Freud, S. (1927 [Original work published 1923]). *The ego and the id* (J. Rivieére, Trans.). London: Hogarth Press.

Freud, S. (1932 [Original work published 1900]). *The interpretation of dreams* (A. A. Brill, Trans.). London: Allen & Irwin.

Freud, S. (1949 [Original work published 1915]). Instincts and their vicissitudes. In J. Riviére (Trans.), *Collected papers of Sigmund Freud* (Vol. *4*, pp. 60–83). London: Hogarth Press.

Freud, S. (1959 [Original work published 1926]). Inhibitions, symptoms, and anxiety (A. Strachey & J. Strachey, Trans.). In J. Strachey (Ed.), *The standard edition of the complete psychological works of Sigmund Freud* (Vol. *20*). London: Hogarth Press.

Freud, S. (1961 [Original work published 1927]). Humour. In J. Strachey (Ed.), *The standard edition of the complete psychological works of Sigmund Freud* (Vol. *21*). London: Hogarth Press.

Freud, S. (1964). New introductory lectures on psychoanalysis. In J. Strachey (Ed. & Trans.), *The standard edition of the complete psychological works of Sigmund Freud*. London: Hogarth Press.

Fridlund, A. J. (1992). The behavioral ecology and sociality of human faces. In M. S. Clark (Ed.), *Emotion*. Newbury Park, CA: Sage.

Fried, C. B., & Aronson, E. (1995). Hypocrisy, misattribution, and dissonance reduction. *Personality and Social Psychology Bulletin, 21*, 925–933.

Frijda, N. H. (1986). *The emotions*. New York: Cambridge University Press.

Frijda, N. H. (1988). The laws of emotion. *American Psychologist, 43*, 349–358.

Frijda, N. H. (1994). Universal antecedents exist, and are interesting. In P. Ekman & R. J. Davidson (Eds.), *The nature of emotion: Fundamental questions* (pp. 155–162). New York: Oxford University Press.

Frijda, N. H. (2007). *The laws of emotion*. Mahwah, NJ: Erlbaum.

Froh, J. J., Bono, G., & Emmons, R. (2010). Being grateful is beyond good manners: Gratitude and motivation to contribute to society among early adolescents. *Motivation and Emotion, 34*, 144–157.

Fromm, E. (1941). *Escape from freedom*. New York: Rinehart.

Fromm, E. (1956). *The art of loving*. New York: Harper & Brothers.

Fromm, E. (1964). *The heart of man*. New York: Harper & Row.

Fromm, E. (1986). *For the love of life*. New York: Free Press.

Frost, R. O., Marten, P., Lahart, C., & Rosenblate, R. (1990). The dimensions of perfectionism. *Cognitive Therapy and Research, 14*, 449–468.

Fujita, K., Gollwitzer, P. M., & Oettingen, G. (2007). Mindsets and pre-conscious open-mindedness to incidental information. *Journal of Experimental Social Psychology, 43*, 48–61.

Fulmer, C., Gelfand, M., Kruglanski, A., Kim-Prieto, C., Diener, E., Pierro, A., & Higgins, E. T. (2010). On "feeling right" in cultural contexts: How person-culture match affects self-esteem and subjective well-being. *Psychological Science, 21*, 1563–1569.

Furrer, C., & Skinner, E. A. (2003). Sense of relatedness as a factor in children's academic engagement and performance. *Journal of Educational Psychology, 95*, 148–162.

Gable, S. L., Reis, H. T., & Elliot, A. J. (2000). Behavioral activation and inhibition in everyday life. *Journal of Personality and Social Psychology, 78*, 1135–1149.

Gagnon, J. H. (1974). Scripts and the coordination of sexual conduct. In J. K. Cole & R. Diensteiber (Eds.), *Nebraska Symposium on Motivation* (Vol. *21*, pp. 27–59). Lincoln: University of Nebraska Press.

Gailliot, M. T., & Baumeister, R. F. (2007). The physiology of willpower: Linking blood glucose to self-control. *Personality and Social Psychology Review, 11*, 303–327.

Gailliot, M. T., Baumeister, R. F., DeWall, C. N., Maner, J. K., Plant, E. A., Tice, D. M., Brewer, L. E., & Schmeichel, B. J. (2007). Self-control relies on glucose as a limited energy source: Willpower is more than a metaphor. *Journal of Personality and Social Psychology, 92*, 325–336.

Gallagher, M., & Chiba, A. A. (1996). The amygdala and emotion. *Current Opinion in Neurobiology,* *6,* 221–227.

Gallagher, S. M., & Keenan, M. (2000). Independent use of activity materials by the elderly in a residential setting. *Journal of Applied Behavior Analysis, 33,* 325–328.

Galvan, A. (2010). Adolescent development of the reward system. *Frontiers of Human Neuroscience,* *4,* 6.

Galvan, A., Hare, T. A., Parra, C. E., Penn, J, Voss, H., Glover, G., et al. (2006). Earlier development of the accumbens relative to orbitofrontal cortex might underlie risk-taking behavior in adolescents. *Journal of Neuroscience, 26,* 6885–6892.

Gardner, H. (1985). *The mind's new science: A history of the cognitive revolution.* New York: Basic Books.

Gatinsky. A. D. Grvenfeld, D. H. & Magee, J. C. (2003). Power and action. *Journal of Personality and Social Psychology, 85,* 453–466.

Gazzaniga, M. S., Ivry, R., & Mangun, G. R. (2008). *Cognitive neuroscience: The biology of the mind* (3rd ed.). New York: W. W. Norton.

Gecas, V., & Burke, P. J. (1995). Self and identity. In K. S. Cook, G. A. Fine, & J. S. House (Eds.), *Sociological perspectives on social psychology* (pp. 41–67). Boston: Allyn & Bacon.

Geller, E. S., Casali, J. G., & Johnson, R. P. (1980). Seat belt usage: A potential target for applied behavior analysis. *Journal of Applied Behavior Analysis, 13,* 669–675.

Geller, L. (1982). The failure of self-actualization theory: A critique of Carl Rogers and Abraham Maslow. *Journal of Humanistic Psychology, 22,* 56–63.

Gerard, H. (1992). Dissonance theory: A cognitive psychology with an engine. *Psychological Inquiry,* *3,* 323–327.

Gershoff, E. T. (2002). Corporal punishment by parents and associated child behaviors and experiences: A meta-analytic and theoretical review. *Psychological Bulletin, 128,* 539–579.

Gilovich, T., & Medvec, V. H. (1994). The temporal pattern to the experience of regret. *Journal of Personality and Social Psychology, 67,* 357–365.

Gilovich, T., Medvec, V. H., & Chen, S. (1995). Commission, omission, and dissonance reduction: Coping with regret in the Monty Hall problem. *Personality and Social Psychology Bulletin, 21,* 182–190.

Gjesme, T. (1981). Is there any future in achievement motivation? *Motivation and Emotion, 5,* 115–138.

Gladwell, M. (2005). *Blink: The power of thinking without thinking.* New York: Back Bay Books.

Gladwin, T. E., Figner, B., Crone, E. A., & Wiers, R. W. (2011). Addiction, adolescence, and the integration of control and motivation. *Developmental Cognitive Neuroscience, 1,* 364–376.

Gloria, C. T., Faulk, K. E., & Steinhardt, M. A. (2013). Positive affectivity predicts successful and unsuccessful adaptation to stress. *Motivation and Emotion, 37,* 185–193.

Goebel, B. L., & Brown, D. R. (1981). Age differences in motivation related to Maslow's need hierarchy. *Developmental Psychology, 17,* 809–815.

Goffman, E. (1959). *The presentation of self in everyday life.* Garden City, NY: Doubleday.

Goldberg, C. (1995). The daimenic development of the malevolent personality. *Journal of Humanistic Psychology, 35,* 7–36.

Goldsmith, H. H. (1994). Parsing the emotional domain from a developmental perspective. In P. Ekman & R. J. Davidson (Eds.), *The nature of emotion: Fundamental questions* (pp. 68–73). New York: Oxford University Press.

Goldstein, K. (1939). *The organism.* New York: American Book Company.

Goleman, D. (2003). *Destructive emotions: How can we overcome them?* New York: Bantam Books.

Gollwitzer, P. M. (1999). Implementation intentions: Strong effects of simple plans. *American Psychologist, 54,* 493–503.

Gollwitzer, P. M., & Bargh, J. A. (Eds.). (1996). *The psychology of action: Linking cognition and motivation to behavior.* New York: Guilford Press.

Gollwitzer, P. M., & Bayer, U. (1999). Deliberative versus implemental mindsets in the control of action. In S. Chaiken & Y. Trope (Eds.), *Dual-process theories in social psychology* (pp. 403–422). New York: Guilford Press.

Gollwitzer, P. M., & Brandstatter, V. (1997). Implementation intentions and effective goal pursuit. *Journal of Personality and Social Psychology, 73,* 186–199.

Gollwitzer, P. M., & Kinney, R. F. (1989). Effects of deliberative and implemental mind-sets on illusion of control. *Journal of Personality and Social Psychology, 56,* 531–542.

Gollwitzer, P. M., & Moskowitz, G. B. (1996). Goal effects on action and cognition. In E. T. Higgins & A. W. Kruglanski (Eds.), *Social psychology: Handbook of basic principles* (pp. 361–399). New York: Guilford Press.

Gollwitzer, P. M., & Oettingen, G. (2011). Planning promotes goal striving. In K. D. Vohs & R. F. Baumeister (Eds.), *Handbook of self-regulation: Research, theory, and applications* (2nd ed., pp. 162–185). New York: Guilford Press.

Gollwitzer, P. M., & Schaal, B. (1998). Metacognition in action: The importance of implementation intentions. *Personality and Social Psychology Review, 2,* 124–136.

Gollwitzer, P. M., & Sheeran, P. (2006). Implementation intentions and goal achievement: A meta-analysis of effects and processes. *Advances in Experimental Social Psychology, 38,* 69–119.

Gollwitzer, P. M., Heckhausen, H., & Steller, B. (1990). Deliberative versus implemental mind-sets: Cognitive tuning toward congruous thoughts and information. *Journal of Personality and Social Psychology, 59,* 1119–1127.

Gonas, G. (1977). Situation versus frame: The interactionist and the structuralist analysis of everyday life. *American Sociological Review, 42,* 854–867.

Goodenough, F. L. (1932). Expressions of emotions in a blind-deaf child. *Journal of Abnormal and Social Psychology, 27,* 328–333.

Goodenow, C. (1993). The psychological sense of school membership among adolescents: Scale development and educational correlates. *Psychology in the Schools, 30,* 79–90.

Goodenow, C., & Grady, K. E. (1993). The relationship of school belonging and friends' values to academic motivation among urban adolescent students. *Journal of Experimental Education, 62*(1), 60–71.

Goschke, T., & Dreisbach, G. (2008). Conflict-triggered goal shielding: Response conflicts attenuate background monitoring for prospective memory cues. *Psychological Science, 19,* 25–32.

Gottman, J. (1994). *Why marriages succeed or fail … and how you can make yours last.* New York: Fireside.

Gottman, J. M., & Silver, N. (1999). *The seven principles for making marriage work.* New York: Crown Publishers.

Gray, J. A. (1987a). Perspectives on anxiety and impulsivity: A commentary. *Journal of Research in Personality, 21,* 493–509.

Gray, J. A. (1987b). *The psychology of fear and stress* (2nd ed.). Cambridge, UK: Cambridge University Press.

Gray, J. A. (1990). Brain systems that mediate both emotion and cognition. *Cognition and Emotion, 4,* 269–288.

Gray, J. A. (1994). Three fundamental emotion systems. In P. Ekman & R. J. Davidson (Eds.), *The nature of emotion: Fundamental questions* (pp. 243–247). New York: Oxford University Press.

Gray, P. B., Chapman, J. F., Burnham, T. C., McIntyre, M. H., Lipson, S. F., & Ellison, P. T. (2004). Human male pair bonding and testosterone. *Human Nature—An Interdisciplinary Biosocial Perspective, 15,* 119–131.

Gray, P. B., Kahlenberg, S. M., Barrett, E. S., Lipson, S. F., & Ellison, P. T. (2002). Marriage and fatherhood are associated with lower testosterone in males. *Evolution and Human Behavior*, *23*, 193–201.

Grazziano, P. A., Reavis, R. D., Keane, S. P., & Calkins, S. D. (2007). The role of emotion regulation in children's early academic success. *Journal of School Psychology*, *45*, 3–19.

Green, C. W., Reid, D. H., White, L. K., Halford, R. C., Brittain, D. P., & Gardner, S. M. (1988). Identifying reinforcers for persons with profound handicaps: Staff opinion versus systematic assessment of preferences. *Journal of Applied Behavior Analysis*, *21*, 31–43.

Greenberg, J. R., & Mitchell, S. (1983). *Object relations in psychoanalytic theory*. Cambridge, MA: Harvard University Press.

Greenberg, J. R., & Pyszczynski, T. (1985). Compensatory self-inflation: A response to the threat to self-regard of public failure. *Journal of Personality and Social Psychology*, *49*, 273–280.

Greenberg, J. R., Solomon, S., Pyszczynski, T., Rosenblatt, A., Burling, J., Lyon, D., et al. (1992). Why do people need self-esteem? Converging evidence that self-esteem serves an anxiety-buffering function. *Journal of Personality and Social Psychology*, *63*, 913–922.

Greenberg, R., & Pearlman, C. (1993). An integrated approach to dream theory: Contributions from sleep research and clinical practice. In A. Moffitt, M. Kramer, & R. Hoffman (Eds.), *The functions of dreaming* (pp. 363–380). Albany: State University of New York.

Green-Demers, I., Legault, L., Pelletier, D., & Pelletier, L. G. (2008). Factorial invariance of the academic amotivation inventory across gender and grade in a sample of Canadian high school students. *Educational and Psychological Measurement*, *68*, 862–880.

Greene, D., & Lepper, M. R. (1974). Effects of extrinsic rewards on children's subsequent intrinsic interest. *Child Development*, *45*, 1141–1145.

Greeno, C. G., & Wing, R. R. (1994). Stress-induced eating. *Psychological Bulletin*, *115*, 444–464.

Greenwald, A. G., & Farnham, S. D. (2000). Using the Implicit Association Test to measure self-esteem and self-concept. *Journal of Personality and Social Psychology*, *79*, 1022–1038.

Greenwald, A. G., Nosek, B. A., & Banaji, M. R. (2003). Understanding and using the Implicit Association Test: I. An improved scoring algorithm. *Journal of Personality and Social Psychology*, *85*, 197–216.

Greenwald, A. G., Poehlman, T. A., Uhlmann, E. L., & Banaji, M. R. (2009). Understanding and using the Implicit Association Test: III. Meta-analysis of predictive validity. *Journal of Personality and Social Psychology*, *97*, 17–41.

Greenwald, A. G., Spangenberg, E. R., Pratkanis, A. R., & Eskenazi, J. (1991). Double-blind tests of subliminal self-help audiotapes. *Psychological Science*, *2*, 119–122.

Gregory, L. W., Cialdini, R. B., & Carpenter, K. M. (1982). Self-relevant scenarios as mediators of likelihood estimates and compliance: Does imagining make it so? *Journal of Personality and Social Psychology*, *43*, 89–99.

Grilo, C. M., & Pogue-Geile, M. F. (1991). The nature of environmental influences on weight and obesity: A behavior genetics analysis. *Psychological Bulletin*, *110*, 520–537.

Grolnick, W. S., & Ryan, R. M. (1987). Autonomy in children's learning: An experimental and individual difference investigation. *Journal of Personality and Social Psychology*, *52*, 890–898.

Grolnick, W. S., Deci, E. L., & Ryan, R. M. (1997). Internalization within the family: The self-determination perspective. In J. E. Grusec & L. Kuczynski (Eds.), *Parenting and children's internalization of values: A handbook of contemporary theory* (pp. 135–161). New York: Wiley.

Grolnick, W. S., Frodi, A., & Bridges, L. (1984). Maternal control styles and the mastery motivation of one-year-olds. *Infant Mental Health Journal*, *5*, 72–82.

Gross, J. J. (1998). The emerging field of emotion regulation: An integrative review. *Review of General Psychology*, *2*, 271–299.

Gross, J. J. (1999). Emotion regulation: Past, present, future. *Cognitive and Emotion*, *13*, 551–573.

Gross, J. J. (2002). Emotion regulation: Affective, cognitive, and social consequences. *Psychophysiology*, *39*, 281–291.

Gross, J. J. (2008). Emotion regulation. In M. Lewis, J. M. Haviland-Jones, & L. F. Barrett (Eds.), *Handbook of emotions* (pp. 497–512). New York: Guilford Press.

Gross, J. J., & John, O. P. (2003). Individual differences in two emotion regulation processes: Implications for affect, relationships, and well-being. *Journal of Personality and Social Psychology*, *85*, 348–362.

Gross, J. J., & Levenson, R. W. (1993). Emotional suppression: Physiology, self-report, and expressive behavior. *Journal of Personality and Social Psychology*, *64*, 970–986.

Gross, J. J., & Thompson, R. A. (2007). Emotion regulation: Conceptual foundations. In J. J. Gross (Ed.), *Handbook of emotion regulation* (pp. 3–24). New York: Guilford Press.

Gross, N., Mason, W. S., & McEachern, A. W. (1958). *Explorations in role analysis: Studies of the school superintendency role*. New York: Wiley.

Gruen, A. (1976). Autonomy and compliance: The fundamental antithesis. *Journal of Humanistic Psychology*, *16*, 61–69.

Guay, A. T. (2001). Decreasing testosterone in regularly menstrating women with decreased libido: A clinical observation. *Journal of Sex and Marital Therapy*, *27*, 513–519.

Guinote, A. (2007). Power and goal pursuit. *Personality and Social Psychology Bulletin*, *33*, 1076–1087.

Guisinger, S., & Blatt, S. J. (1994). Individuality and relatedness: Evolution of a fundamental dialectic. *American Psychologist*, *49*, 104–111.

Gumora, G., & Arsenio, W. F. (2002). Emotionality, emotion regulation, and school performance in middle school children. *Journal of School Psychology*, *40*, 395–413.

Hackett, G. (1985). The role of mathematics self-efficacy in the choice of math-related majors of college women and men: A path analysis. *Journal of Counseling Psychology*, *32*, 47–56.

Haggbloom, S. J., Warnick, R., Warnick, J. E., Jones, V. K., Yarbrough, G. L., Russell, T. M., et al. (2002). The 100 most eminent psychologists of the 20th century. *Review of General Psychology*, *6*, 139–152.

Hagger, M. S., & Chatzisarantis, N. L. (2011). Causality orientations moderate the undermining effect of rewards on intrinsic motivation. *Journal of Experimental Social Psychology*, *47*, 485–489.

Hagger, M. S., Wood, C., Stiff, C., & Chatzisarantis, N. L. D. (2010). Ego depletion and the strength model of self-control: A meta-analysis. *Psychological Bulletin*, *136*, 495–525.

Haidt, J. (2007). The new synthesis in moral psychology. *Science*, *316*, 998–1002.

Haidt, J., McCauley, C. R., & Rozin, P. (1994). A scale to measure disgust sensitivity. *Personality and Individual Differences*, *16*, 701–713.

Haidt, J., McCauley, C., & Rozin, P. (1994). Individual differences in sensitivity to disgust: A scale sampling seven domains of disgust elicitors. *Personality and Individual Differences*, *16* (5), 701–713.

Hall, H. K., & Byrne, A. T. J. (1988). Goal setting in sport: Clarifying recent anomalies. *Journal of Sport and Exercise Psychology*, *10*, 184–198.

Hall, J. F. (1961). *Psychology of motivation*. Philadelphia: J. B. Lippincott.

Hall, J. L., Stanton, S. J., & Schultheiss, O. C. (2010). Biopsychological correlates of implicit motives. In O. C. Schultheiss & J. C. Brunstein (Eds.), *Implicit motives* (pp. 279–307). New York: Oxford University Press.

Hall, R. V., Axelrod, S., Tyler, L., Grief, E., Jones, F. C., & Robertson, R. (1972). Modification of behavior problems in the home with a parent as observer and experimenter. *Journal of Applied Behavior Analysis*, *5*, 53–64.

Hall, W. G. (1973). A remote stomach clamp to evaluate oral and gastric controls of drinking in the rat. *Physiology and Behavior*, *173*, 897–901.

Halvari, A. E. M., Bjørnebekk, G., Halvari, H., & Deci, E. L. (2012). Self-determined motivational predictors of increases in dental behaviors, decreases in dental plaque, and improvement in oral health: A randomized clinical trial. *Health Psychology, 31*(6), 777–788.

Halvari, A. E. M., Halvari, H., Bjørnebekk, G., & Deci, E. L. (2013). Oral health and dental well-being: Testing a self-determination theory model. *Journal of Applied Social Psychology, 43*, 275–292.

Hamachek, D. E. (1978). Psychodynamics of normal and neurotic perfectionism. *Psychology, 15*, 27–33.

Hamann, S. B., Ely, T. D., Hoffman, J. M., & Kilts, C. D. (2002). Ecstasy and agony: Activation of the human amygdala in positive and negative emotion. *Psychological Science, 13*, 135–141.

Hamer, D. H., Hu, S., Magnuson, V. L., Hu, N., & Pattatucci, A. M. L. (1993). A linkage between DNA markers on the X chromosome and male sexual orientation. *Science, 261*, 321–327.

Hampton, A. N., & O'Doherty, J. P. (2007). Decoding the neural substrates of reward-related decision making with fMRI. *PNAS, 104*, 1377–1382.

Harackiewicz, J. (1979). The effects of reward contingency and performance feedback on intrinsic motivation. *Journal of Personality and Social Psychology, 37*, 1352–1363.

Harackiewicz, J. M., & Elliot, A. J. (1993). Achievement goals and intrinsic motivation. *Journal of Personality and Social Psychology, 65*, 904–915.

Harackiewicz, J. M., & Manderlink, G. (1984). A process analysis of the effects of performance-contingent rewards on intrinsic motivation. *Journal of Experimental Social Psychology, 20*, 531–551.

Harackiewicz, J. M., Barron, K. E., Carter, S. M., Lehto, A. T., & Elliot, A. J. (1997). Predictors and consequences of achievement goals in the college classroom: Maintaining interest and making the grade. *Journal of Personality and Social Psychology, 73*, 1284–1295.

Harackiewicz, J. M., Sansone, C., & Manderlink, G. (1985). Competence, achievement orientation, and intrinsic motivation: A process analysis. *Journal of Personality and Social Psychology, 48*, 493–508.

Hardeman, M. (1979). A dialogue with Abraham Maslow. *Journal of Humanistic Psychology, 19*, 23–28.

Hardre, P. L., & Reeve, J. (2003). A motivational model of rural students' intentions to persist in, versus drop out of, high school. *Journal of Educational Psychology, 95*, 347–356.

Hareli, S., & Weiner, B. (2002). Dislike and envy as antecedents of pleasure at another's misfortune. *Motivation and Emotion, 26*, 257–277.

Harlow, H. F. (1953). Motivation as a factor in the acquisition of new responses. In M. R. Jones (Ed.), *Nebraska Symposium on Motivation* (Vol. *1*, pp. 24–49). Lincoln: University of Nebraska Press.

Harmon-Jones, E., & Mills, J. (1999). An introduction to cognitive dissonance theory and an overview of current perspectives on the theory. In E. Harmon-Jones & J. Mills (Eds.), *Cognitive dissonance: Progress on a pivotal theory in social psychology* (pp. 3–21). Washington, DC: American Psychological Association.

Harper, R. M., Frysinger, R. C., Trelease, R. B., & Marks, J. D. (1984). State-dependent alteration of respiratory cycle timing by stimulation of the central nucleus of the amygdala. *Brain Research, 306*, 1–8.

Harrington, D. M., Block, J. H., & Block, J. (1987). Testing aspects of Carl Roger's theory of creative environments: Child-rearing antecedents of creative potential in young adolescents. *Journal of Personality and Social Psychology, 52*, 851–856.

Harris, C. R. (2001). Cardiovascular responses to embarrassment and effects of emotional suppression in a social setting. *Journal of Personality and Social Psychology, 81*, 886–897.

Harris, C. R. (2006). Embarrassment a form of social pain. *American Scientist, 94*, 524–533.

Harris, R. N., & Snyder, C. R. (1986). The role of uncertain self-esteem in self-handicapping. *Journal of Personality and Social Psychology, 51*, 451–458.

Harrison, A. A., & Saeed, L. (1997). Let's make a deal: An analysis of revelations and stipulations in lonely hearts advertisements. *Journal of Personality and Social Psychology, 35*, 257–264.

Harter, S. (1974). Pleasure derived by children from cognitive challenge and mastery. *Child Development, 45*, 661–669.

Harter, S. (1978a). Effectance motivation reconsidered: Toward a developmental model. *Human Development, 21*, 34–64.

Harter, S. (1978b). Pleasure derived from optimal challenge and the effects of extrinsic rewards on children's difficulty level choices. *Child Development, 49*, 788–799.

Harter, S. (1981). A model of mastery motivation in children: Individual differences and developmental changes. In W. A. Collin (Ed.), *Aspects of the development of competence* (Vol. *14*, pp. 215–255). Hillsdale, NJ: Erlbaum.

Harter, S. (1988). The construction and conservation of the self: James and Cooley revisited. In D. K. Lapsle & F. C. Power (Eds.), *Self, ego, and identity: Integrative approaches* (pp. 43–60). New York: Springer-Verlag.

Harter, S. (1990). Causes, correlates and the functional role of global self-worth: A life-span perspective. In R. J. Sternberg & J. Kolligian, Jr. (Eds.), *Competence considered* (pp. 67–97). New Haven, CT: Yale University Press.

Harter, S., & Park, R. (1984). The pictorial perceived competence scale for young children. *Child Development, 55*, 1969–1982.

Hartmann, H. (1958). *Ego psychology and the problem of adaptation* (D. Rapaport, Trans.). New York: International Universities Press.

Hartmann, H. (1964). *Essays on ego psychology: Selected problems in psychoanalytic theory.* New York: International Universities Press.

Harvey, J., & Ashford, M. L. J. (2003). Leptin in the CNS: Much more than a satiety signal. *Neuropharmacology, 44*, 845–854.

Hatfield, E., Cacioppo, J. T., & Rapson, R. L. (1993a). *Emotional contagion.* Cambridge, UK: Cambridge University Press.

Hatfield, E., Cacioppo, J. T., & Rapson, R. L. (1993b). Emotional contagion. *Current Directions in Psychological Science, 2*, 96–99.

Hatfield, E., Hsee, C. K., Costello, J., Weisman, M. S., & Denney, C. (1995). The impact of vocal feedback on emotional experience and expression. *Journal of Social Behavior and Personality, 10*, 293–312.

Haviland, J. J., & Lelwica, M. (1987). The induced affect response: Ten-week old infants' responses to three emotion expressions. *Developmental Psychology, 23*, 997–1004.

Haviland, J. M., & Kramer, D. A. (1991). Affect-cognition relationships in adolescent diaries: The case of Anne Frank. *Human Development, 34*, 143–159.

Hayden, B. Y., Nair, A. C., McCoy, A. N., & Platt, M. L. (2008). Posterior cingulate cortex mediates outcome-contingent allocation behavior. *Neuron, 60*, 19–25.

Hazan, C., & Shaver, P. (1987). Romantic love conceptualized as an attachment process. *Journal of Personality and Social Psychology, 52*, 511–524.

Heatherton, T. F., Herman, C. P., & Polivy, J. (1991). Effects of physical threat and ego threat on eating behavior. *Journal of Personality and Social Psychology, 60*, 138–143.

Heatherton, T. F., Polivy, J., & Herman, C. P. (1989). Restraint and internal responsiveness: Effects of placebo manipulations of hunger state on eating. *Journal of Abnormal Psychology, 98*, 89–92.

Hebb, D. O. (1949). *The organization of behavior.* New York: Wiley.

Hebb, D. O. (1955). Drives and the C.N.S.: Conceptual nervous system. *Psychological Review, 62*, 245–254.

Heckhausen, H. (1967). *The anatomy of achievement motivation.* New York: Academic Press.

Heckhausen, H. (1977). Achievement motivation and its constructs: A cognitive model. *Motivation and Emotion, 1*, 283–329.

Heckhausen, H. (1980). *Motivation and Handeln*. New York: Springer-Verlag.

Heider, F. (1958). *The psychology of interpersonal relations*. New York: Wiley.

Heinrichs, M., Baumgartner, T., Kirschbaum, C., & Ehlert, U. (2003). Social support and oxytocin interact to suppress cortisol and subjective responses to psychosocial stress. *Biological Psychiatry, 54*, 1389–1398.

Heise, D. R. (1979). *Understanding events: Affect and the construction of social action*. New York: Cambridge University Press.

Helmke, A., & van Aken, M. A. G. (1995). The causal ordering of academic achievement and self-concept of ability during elementary school: A longitudinal study. *Journal of Educational Psychology, 87*, 624–637.

Henderlong, J., & Lepper, M. R. (2002). The effects of praise on children's intrinsic motivation: A review and synthesis. *Psychological Bulletin, 128*, 774–795.

Herman, C. P., & Mack, D. (1975). Restrained and unrestrained eating. *Journal of Personality, 43*, 647–660.

Herman, C. P., Polivy, J., & Esses, J. M. (1987). The illusion of counter-regulation. *Appetite, 9*, 161–169.

Hervas, G., & Vazquez, C. (2011). What else do you feel when you feel sad? Emotional overproduction, neuroticism and rumination. *Emotion, 11*, 881–895.

Hewitt, P. L., & Dyck, D. G. (1986). Perfectionism, stress, and vulnerability to depression. *Cognitive Therapy and Research, 10*, 137–142.

Hewitt, P. L., & Flett, G. L. (1991a). Dimensions of perfectionism in unipolar depression. *Journal of Abnormal Psychology, 100*, 98–101.

Hewitt, P. L., & Flett, G. L. (1991b). Perfectionism in the self and social contexts: Conceptualization, assessment, and association with psychopathology. *Journal of Personality and Social Psychology, 60*, 456–470.

Heyman, G. D., & Dweck, C. S. (1992). Achievement goals and intrinsic motivation: Their relation and their role in adaptive motivation. *Motivation and Emotion, 16*, 231–247.

Hidi, S. (1990). Interest and its contribution as a mental resource for learning. *Review of Educational Research, 60*, 549–571.

Hidi, S., & Renninger, A. K. (2006). The four-phase model of interest development. *Educational Psychologist, 41*, 111–127.

Higgins, E. T. (1987). Self-discrepancy: A theory relating self and affect. *Psychological Review, 94*, 319–340.

Higgins, E. T. (1997). Beyond pleasure and pain. *American Psychologist, 52*, 1280–1300.

Higgins, E. T. (1998). Promotion and prevention: Regulatory focus as a motivational principle. *Advances in Experimental Social Psychology, 46*, 1–46.

Higgins, E. T. (2000). Making a good decision: Value from fit. *American Psychologist, 55*, 1217–1230.

Higgins, E. T. (2005). Value from regulatory fit. *Current Directions in Psychological Science, 14*, 209–213.

Higgins, E. T. (2006). Value from hedonic experience and engagement. *Psychological Review, 113*, 439–460.

Higgins, E. T., Cesario, J., Hagiwara, N., Spiegel, S., & Pittman, T. S. (2010). Increasing or decreasing interest in activities: The role of regulatory fit. *Journal of Personality and Social Psychology, 98*, 559–572.

Hilgard, E. R. (1987). *Psychology in America: A historical survey*. San Diego, CA: Harcourt Brace Jovanovich.

Hill, J. O., & Peters, J. C. (1998). Environmental contributions to the obesity epidemic. *Science, 280*, 1371–1374.

Hill, J. O., Pagliassotti, M. J., & Peters, J. C. (1994). Genetic determinants of obesity. In C. Bouchard (Ed.), *Genetic determinants of obesity* (pp. 35–48). Boca Raton, FL: CRC Press.

Hiroto, D. S. (1974). Locus of control and learned helplessness. *Journal of Experimental Psychology, 102*, 187–193.

Hiroto, D. S., & Seligman, M. E. P. (1975). Generality of learned helplessness in man. *Journal of Personality and Social Psychology, 31*, 311–327.

Hochschild, A. R. (1983). *The managed heart.* Berkeley: University of California Press.

Hodgins, H. S., & Knee, C. R. (2002). The integrating self and conscious experience. In E. L. Deci & R.M. Ryan (Eds.), *Handbook of self-determination* (pp. 65–86). Rochester, NY: University of Rochester Press.

Hodgins, H. S., Koestner, R., & Duncan, N. (1996). On the compatibility of autonomy and relatedness. *Personality and Social Psychology Bulletin, 22*, 227–237.

Hodgins, H. S., Yacko, H. A., & Gottlieb, E. (2006). Autonomy and nondefensiveness. *Motivation and Emotion, 30*, 283–293.

Hoebel, B. G. (1976). Brain stimulation reward and aversion in relation to behavior. In A. Wauquier & E. T. Rolls (Eds.), *Brain stimulation reward* (pp. 355–372). New York: Elsevier.

Hoffman, M. L. (2000). *Empathy and moral development: Implications for caring and justice.* New York: Cambridge University Press.

Hoffman, M. L. (2008). Empathy and prosocial behavior. In M. Lewis, J. M. Haviland-Jones, & L. F. Barrett (Eds.), *Handbook of emotions* (3rd ed., pp. 440–455). New York: Guilford Press.

Hogg, M. A. (2010). Influence and leadership. In S. T. Fiske, D. T. Gilbert, & G. Lindzey (Eds.), *Handbook of social psychology* (5th ed., pp. 1166–1207). Hoboken, NJ: Wiley.

Hokoda, A., & Fincham, F. D. (1995). Origins of children's helpless and mastery achievement patterns in the family. *Journal of Educational Psychology, 87*, 375–385.

Holahan, C. K., & Holahan, C. J. (1987). Self-efficacy, social support, and depression in aging: A longitudinal analysis. *Journal of Gerontology, 42*, 65–68.

Holland, R. W., Hendriks, M., & Aarts, H. (2005). Nonconscious effects of scent on cognition and behavior. *Psychological Science, 16*, 689–693.

Hollembeak, J., & Amorose, A. J. (2005). Perceived coaching behaviors and college athletes' intrinsic motivation: A test of self-determination theory. *Journal of Applied Sport Psychology, 17*, 20–36.

Holmes, D. S. (1974). Investigation of repression: Differential recall of material experimentally or naturally associated with ego threat. *Psychological Bulletin, 81*, 632–653.

Holmes, D. S. (1990). The evidence for repression: An examination of sixty years of research. In J. L. Singer (Ed.), *Repression and dissociation* (pp. 85–102). Chicago: University of Chicago Press.

Holstedge, G., Kuypers, H. G. J. M., & Dekker, J. J. (1977). The organization of the bulbar fibre connections to the trigeminal, facial, and hypoglossal motor nuclei: II. An autoradiographic tracing study in cat. *Brain, 100*, 265–286.

Holt, E. B. (1931). *Animal drive and the learning process.* New York: Holt.

Holt, R. R. (1989). *Freud reappraised: A fresh look at psychoanalytic theory.* New York: Guilford Press.

Holt, S. H. A., Brand-Miller, J. C. B., Petocz, P., & Farmakalidis, E. (1995). A satiety index of common foods. *European Journal of Clinical Nutrition, 49*, 675–690.

Holzberger, D., Philipp, A., & Kunter, M. (2013). How teachers' self-efficacy is related to instructional quality: A longitudinal analysis. *Journal of Educational Psychology, 105*, 774–786.

Hom, H. L., Jr. (1994). Can you predict the overjustification effect? *Teaching of Psychology, 21*, 36–37.

Hong, Y., Chiu, C., Dweck, C. S., Lin, D. M.-S., & Wan, W. (1999). Implicit theories, attributions, and coping: A meaning system approach. *Journal of Personality and Social Psychology, 77*, 588–599.

Horney, K. (1937). *The neurotic personality of our time.* New York: W. W. Norton.

Horney, K. (1939). *New ways in psychoanalysis*. New York: W. W. Norton.

Horowitz, M. J., Wilner, N., Kaltreidr, N., & Alvarez, W. (1980). Signs and symptoms of post-traumatic stress disorder. *Archives of General Psychology*, *37*, 85–92.

Horvath, T. (1979). Correlates of physical beauty in men and women. *Social Behavior and Personality*, *7*, 145–151.

Horvath, T. (1981). Physical attractiveness: The influence of selected torso parameters. *Archives of Sexual Behavior*, *10*, 21–24.

Huber, V. L. (1985). Effects of task difficulty, goal setting, and strategy on performance of a heuristic task. *Journal of Applied Psychology*, *70*, 492–504.

Huebner, R. R., & Izard, C. E. (1988). Mothers responses to infants facial expressions of sadness, anger, and physical distress. *Motivation and Emotion*, *12*, 185–196.

Huettel, S. A., et al. (2006). Neural signatures of economic preferences for risk and ambiguity. *Neuron*, *49*, 765–775.

Hull, C. L. (1943). *Principles of behavior*. New York: Appleton-Century-Crofts.

Hull, C. L. (1952). *A behavior system: An introduction to behavior theory concerning the individual organism*. New Haven, CT: Yale University Press.

Hulleman, C. S., Schrager, S. M., Bodmann, S. M., & Harackiewicz, J. M. (2010). A meta-analytic review of achievement goal measures: Different labels for the same constructs or different constructs with similar labels? *Psychological Bulletin*, *136*, 422–449.

Hupka, R. B. (1984). Jealousy: Compound emotion or label for a particular situation. *Motivation and Emotion*, *8*, 141–155.

Hurley, C. M. (2012). Do you see what I see? Learning to detect micro expressions of emotion. *Motivation and Emotion*, *36*, 371–381.

Husman, J., & Lens, W. (1999). The role of the future in student motivation. *Educational Psychologist*, *34*, 113–125.

Husman, J., & Shell, D. F. (2008). Beliefs and perceptions about the future: A measurement of future time perspective. *Learning and Individual Differences*, *18*, 166–175.

Hwang, H. C., & Matsumoto, D. (2014, Dominance threat display for victory and achievement in competitive context. *Motivation and Emotion*, *38*, 206–214.

Hyman, S. E., & Malenka, R. C. (2001). Addiction and the brain: The neurobiology of compulsion and its persistence. *Nature Reviews: Neuroscience*, *2*, 695–703.

Inbar, Y., Pizarro, D. A., Knobe, J., & Bloom, P. (2009). Disgust sensitivity predicts intuitive disapproval of gays. *Emotion*, *9* (3), 435–439.

Isen, A. M. (1970). Success, failure, attention, and reactions to others: The warm glow of success. *Journal of Personality and Social Psychology*, *15*, 294–301.

Isen, A. M. (1987). Positive affect, cognitive processes, and social behavior. In L. Berkowitz (Ed.), *Advances in experimental social psychology* (Vol. *20*, pp. 203–253). New York: Academic Press.

Isen, A. M. (2002). A role for neuropsychology in understanding the facilitating influence of positive affect on social behavior and cognitive processes. In C. R. Snyder & S. J. Lopez (Eds.), *Handbook of positive psychology* (pp. 528–540). New York: Oxford University Press.

Isen, A. M. (2008). Some ways in which positive affect influences decision making and problem solving. In M. Lewis, J. M. Haviland-Jones, & L. F. Barrett (Eds.), *Handbook of emotions* (pp. 548–573). New York: Guilford Press.

Isen, A. M., & Daubman, K. A. (1984). The influence of affect on categorization. *Journal of Personality and Social Psychology*, *47*, 1206–1217.

Isen, A. M., & Geva, N. (1987). The influence of positive affect on acceptable level of risk: The person with a large canoe has a large worry. *Organizational Behavior and Human Decision Processes*, *39*, 145–154.

Isen, A. M., & Levin, P. F. (1972). The effect of feeling good on helping: Cookies and kindness. *Journal of Personality and Social Psychology*, *21*, 384–388.

Isen, A. M., & Means, B. (1983). The influence of positive affect on decision-making strategy. *Social Cognition, 2*, 18–31.

Isen, A. M., & Nowicki, G. P. (1981). *Positive affect and creative problem solving.* Paper presented at the annual meeting of the Cognitive Science Society, Berkeley, CA.

Isen, A. M., & Patrick, R. (1983). The effects of positive feelings on risk-taking: When the chips are down. *Organizational Behavior and Human Performance, 31*, 194–202.

Isen, A. M., & Reeve, J. (2005). The influence of positive affect on intrinsic and extrinsic motivation: Facilitating enjoyment of play, responsible work behavior, and self-control. *Motivation and Emotion, 29*, 295–323.

Isen, A. M., Clark, M. S., & Schwartz, M. F. (1976). Duration of the effects of good mood on helping: Footprints in the sands of time. *Journal of Personality and Social Psychology, 34*, 385–393.

Isen, A. M., Daubman, K. A., & Nowicki, G. P. (1987). Positive affect facilitates creative problem-solving. *Journal of Personality and Social Psychology, 51*, 1122–1131.

Isen, A. M., Johnson, M. M. S., Mertz, E., & Robinson, G. F. (1985). The influence of positive affect on the unusualness of word associations. *Journal of Personality and Social Psychology, 48*, 1413–1426.

Isen, A. M., Niedenthal, P., & Cantor, N. (1992). An influence of positive affect on social categorization. *Motivation and Emotion, 16*, 65–68.

Isen, A. M., Rosenzweig, A. S., & Young, M. J. (1991). The influence of positive affect on clinical problem solving. *Medical Decision Making, 11*, 221–227.

Isen, A. M., Shalker, T., Clark, M., & Karp, L. (1978). Affect, accessibility of material in memory, and behavior: A cognitive loop? *Journal of Personality and Social Psychology, 36*, 1–12.

Iwata, B. A. (1987). Negative reinforcement in applied behavior analysis: An emerging technology. *Journal of Applied Behavior Analysis, 20*, 361–378.

Iyengar, S. (2010). *The art of choosing.* New York: Twelve.

Izard, C. E. (1971). *The face of emotion.* New York: Appleton-Century-Crofts.

Izard, C. E. (1980). Cross-cultural perspectives on emotion and emotion communication. In H. Triandis & W. J. Lonner (Eds.), *Handbook of cross-cultural psychology* (Vol. *3*). Boston: Allyn & Bacon.

Izard, C. E. (1989). The structure and functions of emotions: Implications for cognition, motivation, and personality. In I. S. Cohen (Ed.), *The G. Stanley Hall lecture series* (Vol. *9*, pp. 39–63). Washington, DC: American Psychological Association.

Izard, C. E. (1990). Facial expressions and the regulation of emotions. *Journal of Personality and Social Psychology, 58*, 487–498.

Izard, C. E. (1991). *The psychology of emotions.* New York: Plenum Press.

Izard, C. E. (1993). Four systems for emotion activation: Cognitive and noncognitive development. *Psychological Review, 100*, 68–90.

Izard, C. E. (1994). Innate and universal facial expressions: Evidence from developmental and cross-cultural research. *Psychological Bulletin, 115*, 288–299.

Izard, C. E. (2007). Basic emotions, natural kinds, emotion schemas, and a new paradigm. *Perspectives on Psychological Science, 2*, 260–280.

Izard, C. E. (2009). Emotion theory and research: Highlights, unanswered questions, and emerging issues. *Annual Review of Psychology, 60*, 1–25.

Izard, C. E. (2010). The many meanings/aspects of emotion: Definitions, functions, activation, and regulation. *Emotion Review, 2*, 363–370.

Izard, C. E. (2011). Forms and functions of emotions: Matters of emotion-cognition interactions. *Emotion Review, 3*, 371–378.

Izard, C. E., Fantauzzo, C. A., Castle, J. M., Haynes, O. M., Rayias, M. F., & Putnam, P. H. (1995). The ontogeny and significance of infants' facial expressions in the first nine months of life. *Developmental Psychology, 31*, 997–1013.

Izard, C. E., Huebner, R. R., Risser, D., McGinnes, G., & Dougherty, L. (1980). The young infant's ability to reproduce discrete emotion expressions. *Developmental Psychology, 16*, 132–140.

Izard, C. E., King, K. A., Trentacosta, C. J., Morgan, J. K., Laurenceau, J.-P., Krauthamer-Ewing, S. E., & Finlon, K. J. (2008). Accelerating the development of emotion competence in Head Start children: Effects on adaptive and maladaptive behavior. *Development and Psychopathology, 20*, 369–397.

Jack, R. E., Blais, C., Scheepers, C., Schyns, P. G., & Caldara, R. (2009). Cultural confusions show that facial expressions are not universal. *Current Biology, 19*, 1543–1548.

Jackson, S. A., Thomas, P. R., Marsh, H. W., & Smethurst, C. J. (2001). Relationships between flow, self-concept, psychological skills, and performance. *Journal of Applied Sport Psychology, 13*, 129–153.

Jackson, W. T., Taylor, R. E., Palmatier, A. D., Elliott, T. R., & Elliot, J. L. (1998). Negotiating the reality of visual impairment: Hope, coping, and functional ability. *Journal of Clinical Psychology in Medical Settings, 5*, 173–185.

Jacobs, W. J., & Nadel, L. (1985). Stress induced recovery of fears and phobias. *Psychological Review, 92*, 512–531.

James, W. (1884). What is an emotion? *Mind, 9*, 188–205.

James, W. (1890). *The principles of psychology* (2 vols.). New York: Henry Holt.

James, W. (1894). The physical basis of emotion. *Psychological Review, 1*, 516–529.

Jang, H. (2008). Supporting students' motivation, engagement, and learning during an uninteresting activity. *Journal of Educational Psychology, 100*, 798–811.

Jang, H., Kim, E. J., & Reeve, J. (2012). Longitudinal test of self-determination theory's motivation mediation model in a naturally-occurring classroom context. *Journal of Educational Psychology, 104*, 1175–1188.

Jang, H., Reeve, J., & Deci, E. L. (2010). Engaging students in learning activities: It is not autonomy support or structure, but autonomy support and structure. *Journal of Educational Psychology, 102*, 588–600.

Janssen, E., Vorst, H., Finn, P., & Bancroft, J. (2002). The sexual inhibition (SIS) and Sexual excitation (SES) scales: I. Measuring sexual inhibition and excitation proneness in men. *Journal of Sex Research, 39*, 114–126.

Jazaieri, H., Jinpa, G. T., McGonigal, K., Rosenberg, E. L., Finkelstein, J., Simon-Thomas, E., Cullen, M., Doty, J. R., Gross, J. J., & Goldin, P. R. (2013a). Enhancing compassion: A randomized controlled trial of a compassion cultivation training program. *Journal of Happiness Studies*.

Jazaieri, H., McGonigal, K., Jinpa, T., Doty, J. R., Gross, J. J., & Goldin, P. R. (2013b). A randomized controlled trial of compassion cultivation training: Effects on mindfulness, affect, and emotion regulation. *Motivation and Emotion*.

Jeffrey, D. B., & Knauss, M. R. (1981). The etiologies, treatments, and assessments of obesity. In S. N. Haynes & L. Gannon (Eds.), *Psychosomatic disorders: A psychophysiological approach to etiology and treatment* (pp. 269–319). New York: Praeger.

Jenkins, S. R. (1987). Need for achievement and women's careers over 14 years: Evidence for occupational structural effects. *Journal of Personality and Social Psychology, 53*, 922–932.

Jenkins, S. R. (1996). Self-definition in thought, action, and life path choices. *Personality and Social Psychology Bulletin, 22*, 99–111.

John, O. P., & Gross, J. J. (2004). Healthy and unhealthy emotion regulation: Personality processes, individual differences, and life span development. *Journal of Personality, 72*, 1301–1333.

John, O. P., & Robins, R. W. (1994). Accuracy and bias in self-perception: Individual differences in self-enhancement and the role of narcissism. *Journal of Personality and Social Psychology, 66*, 206–219.

Johnson-Laird, P. N., & Oatley, K. (1989). The language of emotions: An analysis of a semantic field. *Cognition and Emotion, 3*, 81–123.

Johnson-Laird, P. N., & Oatley, K. (1992). Basic emotions, rationality and folk theory. *Cognition and Emotion, 6*, 201–223.

Joiner, T. E., Pettit, J. W., Perez, M., & Burns, A. B. (2001). Can positive emotion influence problem-solving among suicidal adults? *Professional Psychology: Research and Practice, 32*, 507–512.

Jones, A., & Fitness, J. (2008). Moral hypervigilance: The influence of disgust sensitivity in the moral domain. *Emotion, 8* (5), 613–627.

Jones, E. E., & Davis, K. E. (1965). From acts to dispositions: The attribution process in person perception. In L. Berkowitz (Ed.), *Advances in experimental social psychology* (Vol. 2, pp. 214–266). New York: Academic Press.

Josephs, R. A., et al. (2003) Status, testosterone, and human intellectual performance: Stereotype threat as status concern. *Psychological Science, 14*, 158–163.

Josephs, R. A., et al. (2006). The mismatch effect: When testosterone and status are at odds. *Journal of Personality and Social Psychology, 90*, 999–1013.

Joussemet, M., & Koestner, R. (1999). Effect of expected rewards on children's creativity. *Creativity Research Journal, 12*, 231–239.

Joussemet, M., Koestner, R., Lekes, N., & Houlfort, N. (2003). Introducing uninteresting tasks to children: A comparison of the effects of rewards and autonomy support. *Journal of Personality, 72*, 139–166.

Kagan, J. (1972). Motives and development. *Journal of Personality and Social Psychology, 22*, 51–66.

Kahneman, D. (1973). *Attention and effort.* Englewood Cliffs, NJ: Prentice Hall.

Kahneman, D. (2011). *Thinking, fast and slow.* New York: Farrar, Straus & Giroux.

Kamins, M., & Dweck, C. S. (1999). Person vs. process praise and criticism: Implications for contingent self-worth and coping. *Developmental Psychology, 35*, 835–847.

Kanfer, R., & Ackerman, P. L. (1989). Motivation and cognitive abilities: An integrative aptitude treatment interaction approach to skill acquisition. *Journal of Applied Psychology, 74*, 657–690.

Kaplan, A., & Maehr, M. L. (2007). The contributions and prospects of goal orientations theory. *Educational Psychology Review, 19*, 141–184.

Kapp, B. S., Gallagher, M., Underwood, M. D., McNall, C. L., & Whitehorn, D. (1982). Cardiovascular responses elicited by electrical stimulation of the amygdala central nucleus in the rabbit. *Brain Research, 234*, 251–262.

Kapp, B. S., Pascoe, J. P., & Bixler, M. A. (1984). The amygdala: A neuroanatomical systems approach to its contributions to aversive conditioning. In N. Buttlers & L. R. Squire (Eds.), *Neuropsychology of memory* (pp. 473–488). New York: Guilford Press.

Karabenick, S. A., & Yousseff, Z. I. (1968). Performance as a function of achievement level and perceived difficulty. *Journal of Personality and Social Psychology, 10*, 414–419.

Karademas, E. C., Tsalikou, C., & Tellarou, M.-C. (2010). The impact of emotion regulation and illness-focused coping strategies on the relation of illness-related negative emotions to subjective health. *Journal of Health Psychology, 16*, 510–519.

Kasser, T. (2002). *The high price of materialism.* Cambridge, MA: MIT Press.

Kasser, T., & Ryan, R. M. (1993). A dark side of the American dream: Correlates of financial success as a central life aspiration. *Journal of Personality and Social Psychology, 65*, 410–422.

Kasser, T., & Ryan, R. M. (1996). Further examining the American dream: Differential correlates of intrinsic and extrinsic goals. *Personality and Social Psychology Bulletin, 22*, 280–287.

Kasser, T., & Ryan, R. M. (2001). Be careful what you wish for: Optimal functioning and the relative attainment of intrinsic and extrinsic goals. In P. Schmuck & K. M. Sheldon (Eds.), *Life goals and well-being: Toward a positive psychology of human striving.* Seattle, WA: Hogrefe & Huber.

Kassirer, J. P., & Angell, A. (1998). Losing weight: An ill-fated New Year's resolution. *New England Journal of Medicine, 338*, 52–54.

Kast, A., & Connor, K. (1988). Sex and age differences in response to informational and controlling feedback. *Personality and Social Psychology Bulletin, 14*, 514–523.

Katz, I., & Assor, A. (2007). When choice motivates and when it does not. *Educational Psychology Review, 19*, 429–442.

Katz, I., Assor, A., Kanat-Maymon, Y., & Bereby-Meyer, Y. (2006). Interest as a motivational resource: Feedback and gender matter, but interest makes the difference. *Social Psychology of Education, 9*, 27–42.

Katz, J., Beach, S. R. H., & Anderson, P. (1996). Self-enhancement versus self-verification: Does spousal support always help? *Cognitive Therapy and Research, 20*, 345–360.

Katzman, M., & Wolchik, S. (1984). Bulimia and binge eating in college women: A comparison of personality and behavioral characteristics. *Journal of Consulting and Clinical Psychology, 52*, 423–428.

Kawabata, M., & Mallett, C. J. (2011). Flow experience in physical activity: Examination of the internal structure of flow from a process-related perspective. *Motivation and Emotion, 35*, 393–402.

Kay, A. C., Wheeler, S. C., Bargh, J. A., & Ross, L. (2004). Material priming: The influence of mundane objects on situational construal and competitive behavioral choice. *Organizational Behavior and Human Decision Processes, 95*, 83–96.

Kazdin, A. E. (1979). Imagery elaboration and self-efficacy in the covert modeling treatment of unassertive behavior. *Journal of Consulting and Clinical Psychology, 47*, 725–733.

Keating, C. F., Mazur, A., & Segall, M. H. (1981). A cross-cultural exploration of physiognomic traits of dominance and happiness. *Ethology and Sociobiology, 2*, 41–48.

Keesey, R. E. (1980). A set-point analysis of the regulation of body weight. In A. J. Stunkard (Ed.), *Obesity* (pp. 144–165). Philadelphia: W. B. Saunders.

Keesey, R. E. (1989). Physiological regulation of body-weight and the issue of obesity. *Medical Clinics of North America, 73*, 15–27.

Keesey, R. E., & Powley, T. L. (1975). Hypothalamic regulation of body weight. *American Scientist, 63*, 558–565.

Keesey, R. E., Boyle, P. C., Kemnitz, J. W., & Mitchell, J. S. (1976). The role of the lateral hypothalamus in determining the body weight set point. In D. Novin, W. Wyrwicka, & G. A. Bray (Eds.), *Hunger: Basic mechanisms and clinical implications* (pp. 243–255). New York: Raven Press.

Keller, J. (2008). On the development of self-regulatory focus: The role of parenting styles. *European Journal of Social Psychology, 38*, 354–364.

Keller, J., & Bless, H. (2006). Regulatory fit and cognitive performance: The interactive effect of chronic and situational self-regulatory mechanisms on cognitive test performance. *European Journal of Social Psychology, 36*, 393–405.

Keller, J., & Bless, H. (2008). Flow and regulatory compatibility: An experimental approach to the flow model of intrinsic motivation. *Personality and Social Psychology Bulletin, 34*, 196–209.

Kelley, H. H. (1967). Attribution theory in social psychology. In D. Levine (Ed.), *Nebraska Symposium on Motivation* (Vol. *15*, pp. 192–238). Lincoln: University of Nebraska Press.

Kelley, H. H. (1973). The process of causal attribution. *American Psychologist, 28*, 107–128.

Kelly, A. E., & Kahn, J. H. (1994). Effects of suppression of personal intrusive thought. *Journal of Personality and Social Psychology, 66*, 998–1006.

Kelly, D. D. (1991). Sexual differentiation of the nervous system. In E. R. Kandel, J. H. Schwartz, & T. M. Jessell (Eds.), *Principles of neural science* (3rd ed., pp. 959–973). Norwalk, CT: Appleton & Lange.

Keltner, D. (1995). Signs of appeasement: Evidence for the distinct displays of embarrassment, amusement, and shame. *Journal of Personality and Social Psychology, 68*, 441–454.

Keltner, D., & Buswell, B. N. (1996). Evidence for the distinctiveness of embarrassment, shame, and guilt: A study of recalled antecedents and facial expressions of emotion. *Cognition and Emotion, 10*, 155–171.

Keltner, D., & Buswell, B. N. (1997). Embarrassment: Its distinct form and appeasement functions. *Psychological Bulletin, 122*, 250–270.

Keltner, D., & Gross, J. J. (1999). Functional accounts of emotions. *Cognitive and Emotion, 13*, 467–480.

Keltner, D., & Haidt, J. (1999). Social functions of emotions at four levels of analysis. *Cognitive and Emotion, 13*, 505–521.

Keltner, D., Ellsworth, P. C., & Edwards, K. (1993). Beyond simple pessimism: Effects of sadness and anger on social perception. *Journal of Personality and Social Psychology, 64*, 740–752.

Kemeny, M. E., & Shestyuk, A. (2008). Emotions, the neuroendocrine and immune systems, and health. In M. Lewis, J. M. Haviland-Jones, & L. F. Barrett (Eds.), *Handbook of emotions* (3rd ed., pp. 661–675). New York: Guilford Press.

Kemper, T. D. (1987). How many emotions are there?: Wedding the social and the autonomic components. *American Sociological Review, 93*, 263–289.

Kenrick, D. T., Groth, G. E., Trost, M. R., & Sadalla, E. K. (1993). Integrating evolutionary and social exchange perspectives on relationship: Effects of gender, self-appraisal, and involvement level on mate selection criteria. *Journal of Personality and Social Psychology, 64*, 951–969.

Keyes, C. L. M. (2007). Promoting and protecting mental health as flourishing: A complementary strategy for improving national mental health. *American Psychologist, 62*, 95–108.

Kihlstrom, J. F. (1987). The cognitive unconscious. *Science, 237*, 1445–1452.

Kihlstrom, J. F., & Cantor, N. (1984). Mental representations of the self. In L. Berkowitz (Ed.), *Advances in experimental and social psychology* (Vol. *17*, pp. 2–47). New York: Academic Press.

Kimble, G. A. (1990). Mother nature's bag of tricks is small. *Psychological Science, 1*, 36–41.

King, L. A., & Pennebaker, J. W. (1996). Thinking about goals, glue, and the meaning of life. In R. S. Wyer (Ed.), *Advances in social cognition* (Vol. *9*, pp. 97--106). Mahwah, NJ: Erlbaum.

Kirkpatrick, L. A., & Shaver, P. (1988). Fear and affiliation reconsidered from a stress and coping perspective: The importance of cognitive clarity and fear reduction. *Journal of Social and Clinical Psychology, 7*, 214–233.

Kirsch, P., Esslinger, C., Chen, Q., et al. (2005). Oxytocin modulates neural circuitry for social cognition and fear in humans. *Nature, 435*, 673–676.

Kirschbaum, C., Klauer, T., Filipp, S., & Hellhammer, D. H. (1995). Sex-specific effects of social support on cortisol and subjective responses to acute psychological stress. *Psychosomatic Medicine, 57*, 23–31.

Kirschbaum, C., Wolf, O. T., May, M., Wippich, W., & Hellhammer, D. H. (1996). Stress- and treatment-induced elevations of cortisol levels associated with impaired declarative memory in healthy adults. *Life Science, 58*, 1475–1483.

Kitayama, S., Markus, H. R., & Kurokawa, M. (2000). Culture, emotion, and well-being: Good feelings in Japan and the United States. *Cognition and Emotion, 14*, 93–124.

Klein, H. J., Whitener, E. M., & Ilgen, D. R. (1990). The role of goal specificity in the goal-setting process. *Motivation and Emotion, 14*, 179–193.

Klesges, R. C., Coates, T. J., Brown, G., Sturgeon-Tillisch, J., Moldenhauer-Klesges, L. M., Holzer, B., et al. (1983). Parental influences on children's eating behavior and relative weight. *Journal of Applied Behavioral Analysis, 16*, 371–378.

Klien, G. (1954). Need and regulation. In M. R. Jones (Ed.), *Nebraska Symposium on Motivation* (Vol. *2*, pp. 224–274). Lincoln: University of Nebraska Press.

Kling, A. S., & Brothers, L. A. (1992). The amygdala and social behavior. In J. P. Aggleton (Ed.), *The amygdala: Neurobiological aspects of emotion, memory, and mental dysfunction* (pp. 353–377). New York: Wiley.

Klinnert, M. D., Campos, J. J., Sorce, J. F., Emde, R. N., & Suejda, M. (1983). Emotions as behavior regulators: Social referencing in infancy. In R. Plutchik & H. Kellerman (Eds.), *Emotion: Theory, research, and experience, emotions in early development* (Vol. *2*, pp. 57–86). New York: Academic Press.

Klohnen, E. C., & Bera, S. (1998). Behavioral and experiential patterns of avoidantly and securely attached women across adulthood: A 31-year longitudinal perspective. *Journal of Personality and Social Psychology, 74*, 211–223.

Klose, D. A. (1995). M. Scott Peck's analysis of human evil: A critical review. *Journal of Personality and Social Psychology, 35*, 37–66.

Knock, D., & Erst, F. (2007). Resisting the power of temptations: The right pre-frontal cortex and self-control. *Annals of the New York Academy of Science, 1104*, 123–134.

Knox, R. E., & Inkster, J. A. (1968). Postdecision dissonance at post time. *Journal of Personality and Social Psychology, 8*, 319–323.

Koestner, R., Bernieri, F., & Zuckerman, M. (1992). Self-regulation and consistency between attitudes, traits, and behaviors. *Personality and Social Psychology Bulletin, 18*, 52–59.

Koestner, R., Lekes, N., Powers, T. A., & Chicoine, E. (2002). Attaining personal goals: Self-concordance plus implementation intentions equals success. *Journal of Personality and Social Psychology, 83*, 231–244.

Koestner, R., Losier, G. F., Vallerand, R. J., & Carducci, D. (1996). Identified and introjected forms of political internalization: Extending self-determination theory. *Journal of Personality and Social Psychology, 70*, 1025–1036.

Koestner, R., Ryan, R. M., Bernieri, F., & Holt, K. (1984). Setting limits on children's behavior: The differential effects of controlling versus informational styles on intrinsic motivation and creativity. *Journal of Personality, 52*, 233–248.

Koestner, R., Zuckerman, M., & Koestner, J. (1987). Praise, involvement, and intrinsic motivation. *Journal of Personality and Social Psychology, 53*, 383–390.

Kohn, A. (1993). *Punished by rewards: The trouble with gold stars, incentive plans, A's, praise, and other bribes*. Boston: Houghton Mifflin.

Kohut, H. (1971). *The analysis of self*. New York: International Universities Press.

Kolb, J., Cooper, S, & Fishman, G. (1995). Recent developments in psychoanalytic technique: A review. *Harvard Review of Psychiatry, 3*, 65–74.

Kosfeld, M., Heinrichs, M., Zak, P. J., Fischbacher, U., & Fehr, E. (2005). Oxytocin increases trust in humans. *Nature, 435*, 673–676.

Koulack, D. (1993). Dreams and adaptation to contemporary stress. In A. Moffitt, M. Kramer, & R. Hoffman (Eds.), *The functions of dreaming* (pp. 321–340). Albany: State University of New York Press.

Kramer, P. D. (1993). *Listening to Prozac*. New York: Penguin Books.

Kramer, R. (1995). The birth of client-centered therapy: Carl Rogers, Otto Rank, and "The Beyond." *Journal of Humanistic Psychology, 35*, 54–110.

Krantz, P. J., & McClannahan, L. E. (1993). Teaching children with autism to initiate to peers: Effects of a script-fading procedure. *Journal of Applied Behavior Analysis, 26*, 121–132.

Kraut, R. E., & Johnston, R. E. (1979). Social and emotional messages of smiling: ethological approach. *Journal of Personality and Social Psychology, 37*, 1539–1553.

Krettek, J. E., & Price, J. L. (1978). Amygdaloid projections to subcortical structures within the basal forebrain and brainstem in the rat and cat. *Journal of Comparative Neurology, 178*, 225–254.

Kruglanski, A. W. & Orehek, E. (2011). The role of quest for significance in motivating terrorism. In J. Forgas, A. Kruglanski, & K. Williams (Eds.), *Social conflict and aggression*. New York: Psychology Press.

Kruglanski, A. W., Chen, X., Dechesne, M., Fishman, S., & Orehek, E. (2009). Fully committed: Suicide bombers' motivation and the quest for personal significance. *Political Psychology, 30*, 331–557.

Kruglanski, A. W., Thompson, E. P., Higgins, E. T., Atash, M. N., Pierro, A., Shah, J. Y., & Spiegel, S. (2000). To "do the right thing" or to "just do it": Locomotion and assessment as distinct self-regulatory imperatives. *Journal of Personality and Social Psychology, 79*, 793–815.

Kuhl, J. (1978). Standard setting and risk preference: An elaboration of the theory of achievement motivation and an empirical test. *Psychological Review, 85,* 239–248.

Kuhl, J. (1984). Motivational aspects of achievement motivation and learned helplessness: Toward a comprehensive theory of action control. In B. A. Maher & W. B. Maher (Eds.), *Progress in experimental personality research* (Vol. *13,* pp. 99–171). New York: Academic Press.

Kuhl, J. (1987). Action control: The maintenance of motivational states. In F. Halisch & J. Kuhl (Eds.), *Motivation, intention, and volition* (pp. 279–291). Berlin, Germany: Springer.

Kuhl, J., & Blankenship, V. (1979). The dynamic theory of achievement motivation. *Psychological Review, 86,* 141–151.

Kuhn, T. S. (1962). *The structure of scientific revolutions.* Chicago: University of Chicago Press.

Kuhn, T. S. (1970). *The structure of scientific revolutions* (2nd ed.). Chicago: University Press.

Kuhnen, C. M., & Knutson, B. (2005). The neural basis of financial risk taking. *Neuron, 47,* 763–770.

Kulik, J. A., Mahler, H. I. M., & Earnest, A. (1994). Social comparison and affiliation under threat: Going beyond the affiliative-choice paradigm. *Journal of Personality and Social Psychology, 66,* 301–309.

Kuo, Z. Y. (1921). Giving up instincts in psychology. *Journal of Philosophy, 17,* 645–664.

Kuppens, P., & Van Mechelen, I. (2007). Interactional appraisal models for the anger appraisals of threatened self-esteem, other-blame, and frustration. *Cognition and Emotion, 21,* 56–77.

La Guardia, J. G., & Patrick, H. (2008). Self-determination theory as a fundamental theory of close relationships. *Canadian Psychology, 49,* 201–209.

Laird, J. D. (1974). Self-attribution of emotion: The effects of expressive behavior on the quality of emotional experience. *Journal of Personality and Social Psychology, 29,* 475–486.

Laird, J. D. (1984). Facial response and emotion. *Journal of Personality and Social Psychology, 47,* 909–917.

Laird, J. D., Wagener, J. J., Halal, M., & Szegda, M. (1982). Remembering what you feel: The effects of emotion on memory. *Journal of Personality and Social Psychology, 42,* 646–657.

Lambert, N. M., & Fincham, F. D. (2011). Expressing gratitude to a partner leads to more relationship maintenance behavior. *Emotion, 11,* 52–60.

Lambert, N., Clark, M., Durtschi, J., Fincham, F. D., & Graham, S. M. (2010). Benefits of expressing gratitude: Expressing gratitude to a partner changes one's view of the relationship. *Psychological Science, 21,* 574–580.

Lane, J. D., & Wegner, D. M. (1995). The cognitive consequences of secrecy. *Journal of Personality and Social Psychology, 69,* 237–253.

Lane, K. A., Banaji, M. R., Nosek, B. A., & Greenwald, A. G. (2007). Understanding and using the Implicit Association Test: IV. What we know (so far). In B. Wittenbrink & N. S. Schwarz (Eds.), *Implicit measures of attitudes: Procedures and controversies* (pp. 59–102). New York: Guilford Press.

Lang, P. J. (1994). The varieties of emotional experience: A mediation of James–Lange theory. *Psychological Review, 101,* 211–221.

Lange, C. (1922 [Original work published 1885]). The emotions. In K. Dunlap (Ed.), *The emotions* (Istar A. Haupt, Trans.; pp. 33–90). Baltimore: Williams & Wilkins.

Lange, R. D., & James, W. (1922). *The emotions.* Baltimore: Williams & Wilkins.

Langer, E. (1975). The illusion of control. *Journal of Personality and Social Psychology, 32,* 311–328.

Langsdorff, P., Izard, C. E., Rayias, M., & Hembree, E. (1983). Interest expression, visual fixation, and heart rate changes in 2-to 8-month old infants. *Developmental Psychology, 19,* 375–386.

Lansing, J. B., & Heyns, R. W. (1959). Need affiliation and frequency of four types of communication. *Journal of Abnormal and Social Psychology, 58,* 365–372.

Lanzetta, J. T., Cartwright-Smith, J. E., & Kleck, R. E. (1976). Effects of nonverbal dissimulation of emotional experience and autonomic arousal. *Journal of Personality and Social Psychology, 33,* 354–370.

LaPointe, K. A., & Crandell, C. J. (1980). Relationship of irrational beliefs to self-reported depression. *Cognitive Therapy and Research, 4*, 247–250.

LaPorte, R. E., & Nath, R. (1976). Role of performance goals in prose learning. *Journal of Educational Psychology, 68*, 260–264.

Larsen, R. J., Kasimatis, M., & Frey, K. (1992). Facilitating the furrowed brow: An unobtrusive test of the facial feedback hypothesis applied to unpleasant affect. *Cognition and Emotion, 6*, 321–338.

Larson, R., & Asmussen, L. (1991). Anger, worry, and hurt in early adolescence: An enlarging world of negative emotion. In M. Colton & S. Gore (Eds.), *Adolescent stress: Causes and consequences* (pp. 21–42). New York: Aldine de Gruyter.

Latham, G. P., & Baldes, J. J. (1975). The practical significance of Locke's theory of goal setting. *Journal of Applied Psychology, 60*, 122–124.

Latham, G. P., & Locke, E. A. (1975). Increasing productivity with decreasing time limits: A field replication of Parkinson's law. *Journal of Applied Psychology, 60*, 524–526.

Latham, G. P., & Yukl, G. A. (1976). Effects of assigned and participative goal setting on performance and job satisfaction. *Journal of Applied Psychology, 61*, 166–171.

Latham, G. P., Mitchell, T. R., & Dossett, D. L. (1978). Importance of participative goal setting and anticipated rewards on goal difficulty and job performance. *Journal of Applied Psychology, 63*, 163–171.

Laumann, E. O., Paik, A., & Rosen, R. C. (1999). Sexual dysfunction in the United States: Prevalence and predictors. *Journal of the American Medical Association, 281*, 537–544.

Lavrakas, P. J. (1975). Female preferences for male physiques. *Journal of Research in Personality, 9*, 324–334.

Lazarus, R. S. (1966). *Psychological stress and the coping process.* New York: McGraw-Hill.

Lazarus, R. S. (1968). Emotions and adaptation: Conceptual and empirical relations. In W. J. Arnold (Ed.), *Nebraska Symposium on Motivation* (Vol. *16*, pp. 175–266). Lincoln: University of Nebraska Press.

Lazarus, R. S. (1982). Thoughts on the relations between emotion and cognition. *American Psychologist, 37*, 1019–1024.

Lazarus, R. S. (1983). The costs and benefits of denial. In S. Bresnitz (Ed.), *The denial of stress* (pp. 1–32). New York: International Universities Press.

Lazarus, R. S. (1984). On the primacy of cognition. *American Psychologist, 39*, 124–129.

Lazarus, R. S. (1991a). *Emotion and adaptation.* New York: Oxford University Press.

Lazarus, R. S. (1991b). Progress on a cognitive–motivational–relational theory of emotion. *American Psychologist, 46*, 819–834.

Lazarus, R. S. (1994). Universal antecedents of the emotions. In P. Ekman & R. J. Davidson (Eds.), *The nature of emotion: Fundamental questions* (pp. 163–171). New York: Oxford University Press.

Lazarus, R. S., & Folkman, S. (1984). *Stress, appraisal, and coping.* New York: Springer-Verlag.

Leary, M. R. (1983). Social anxiousness: The construct and its measurement. *Journal of Personality Assessment, 47*, 66–75.

Leavitt, K., Fong, C. T., & Greenwald, A. G. (2011). Asking about well-being gets you half an answer: Intra-individual processes of implicit and explicit job attitudes. *Journal of Organizational Behavior, 32*, 672–687.

LeDoux, J. E. (1989). Cognitive-emotional interactions in the brain. *Cognition and Emotion, 3*, 267–289.

LeDoux, J. E. (1996). *The emotional brain.* New York: Simon & Schuster.

LeDoux, J. E. (2000). Emotion circuits in the brain. *Annual Review of Neuroscience, 23*, 155–184.

LeDoux, J. (2012). A neuroscientist's perspective on the debates about the nature of emotion. *Emotion Review, 4*, 375–379.

LeDoux, J. E. (2013). The slippery slope of fear. *Trends in Cognitive Science, 17*, 155–156.

LeDoux, J. E., Iwata, J., Cicchetti, P., & Reis, D. J. (1988). Different projections of the central amygdaloid nucleus mediate autonomic and behavioral correlates of conditioned fear. *Journal of Neuroscience, 8*, 2517–2529.

LeDoux, J. E., Romanski, L. M., & Xagoraris, A. E. (1989). Indelibility of subcortical emotional memories. *Journal of Cognitive Neuroscience, 1*, 238–243.

Lee, H. J., Macbeth, A. H., Pagani, J. H., & Young, W. S. (2009). Oxytocin: The great facilitator of life. *Progress in Neurobiology, 88*, 127–151.

Lee, K. A., Vaillant, G. E., Torrey, W. C., & Elder, G. H. (1995). A 50-year prospective study of the psychological sequelae of World War II combat. *American Journal of Psychiatry, 152*, 516–522.

Lee, W., & Reeve, J. (2013). Self-determined, but not non-self-determined, motivation predicts activations in the anterior insular cortex: an fMRI study of personal agency. *Social, Cognitive, and Affective Neuroscience, 8*, 538–545.

Lefcourt, H. M., & Martin, R. A. (1986). *Humor and life stress: An antidote to adversity.* New York: Springer-Verlag.

Legault, L., Green-Demers, I., & Pelletier, L. G. (2006). Why do high school students lack motivation in the classroom? Toward an understanding of academic amotivation and the role of social support. *Journal of Educational Psychology, 98*, 567–582.

Leippe, M. R., & Eisenstadt, D. (1994). Generalization of dissonance reduction: Decreasing prejudice through induced compliance. *Journal of Personality and Social Psychology, 67*, 395–413.

LeMay, E. P., Jr., Clark, M. S., & Feeney (2007). Projection of responsiveness to needs and the construction of satisfying communal relationships. *Journal of Personality and Social Psychology, 92*, 834–853.

Lench, H. C., Flores, S. A., & Bench, S. W. (2011). Discrete emotions predict changes in cognition, judgment, experience, behavior, and physiology: A meta-analysis of experimental emotion elicitations. *Psychological Bulletin, 137*, 834–855.

Lens, W., Paixao, M. P., Herrera, D., & Grobler, A. (2012). Future time perspective as a motivational variable: Content and extension of future goals affect the quantity and quality of motivation. *Japanese Psychological Research, 54*, 321–333.

Leon, I., & Hernandez, J. A. (1998). Testing the role of attribution and appraisal in predicting own and other's emotions. *Cognition and Emotion, 12*, 27–43.

Lepore, S. J. (1992). Social-conflict, social support, and psychological distress: Evidence of cross-domain buffering effects. *Journal of Personality and Social Psychology, 63*, 857–867.

Lepper, M. R. (1983). Social-control processes and the internalization of social values: An attributional perspective. In E. T. Higgins, D. N. Ruble, & W. W. Hartup (Eds.), *Social cognition and social development* (pp. 294–330). New York: Cambridge University Press.

Lepper, M. R., & Greene, D. (1975). Turning play into work: Effects of adult surveillance and extrinsic rewards on children's intrinsic motivation. *Journal of Personality and Social Psychology, 31*, 479–486.

Lepper, M. R., & Greene, D. (Eds.). (1978). *The hidden costs of reward.* Hillsdale, NJ: Erlbaum.

Lepper, M. R., Greene, D., & Nisbett, R. E. (1973). Undermining children's intrinsic interest with extrinsic rewards: A test of the overjustification hypothesis. *Journal of Personality and Social Psychology, 28*, 129–137.

Lerner, J. S., & Keltner, D. (2001). Fear, anger, and risk. *Journal of Personality and Social Psychology, 81*, 146–159.

Lerner, J. S., Goldberg, J. H., & Tetlock, P. E. (1998). Sober second thoughts: The effects of accountability, anger, and authoritarianism on attributions of responsibility. *Personality and Social Psychology Bulletin, 24*, 563–574.

Levenson, R. W. (1992). Autonomic nervous system differences among emotions. *Psychological Science, 3*, 23–27.

Levenson, R. W. (1994a). Human emotion: A functional view. In P. Ekman & R. J. Davidson (Eds.), *The nature of emotion: Fundamental questions* (pp. 123–126). New York: Oxford University Press.

Levenson, R. W. (1994b). The search for autonomic specificity. In P. Ekman & R. J. Davidson (Eds.), *The nature of emotion: Fundamental questions* (pp. 252–257). New York: Oxford University Press.

Levenson, R. W. (1999). The intrapersonal functions of emotion. *Cognitive and Emotion, 13,* 481–504.

Levenson, R. W. (2011). Basic emotion questions. *Emotion Review, 3,* 379–386.

Levenson, R. W., & Gottman, J. M. (1983). Marital interaction: Physiological linkage and affective exchange. *Journal of Personality and Social Psychology, 45,* 587–597.

Levenson, R. W., Carstensen, L. L., & Gottman, J. M. (1994). Influence of age and gender on affect, physiology, and their interrelations: A study of long-term marriages. *Journal of Personality and Social Psychology, 67,* 56–68.

Levenson, R. W., Carstensen, L. L., Friesen, W. V., & Ekman, P. (1991). Emotion, physiology, and expression in old age. *Psychology and Aging, 6,* 28–35.

Levenson, R. W., Ekman, P., & Friesen, W. V. (1990). Voluntary facial action generates emotion-specific autonomic nervous system activity. *Psychophysiology, 27,* 363–384.

Levesque, C., & Brown, K. W. (2007). Mindfulness as a moderator of the effect of implicit motivational self-concept on day-to-day behavioral motivation. *Motivation and Emotion, 31,* 284–299.

Levin R., & Nielsen, T. A. (2007). Disturbed dreaming, posttraumatic stress disorder, and affect distress: A review and neurocognitive model. *Psychological Bulletin, 133,* 482–528.

Levin, R. (1990). Psychoanalytic theories of the function of dreaming: A review of the empirical literature. In J. Masling (Ed.), *Empirical studies of psychoanalytic theories* (Vol. *3,* pp. 1–53). Hillsdale, NJ: Analytic Press.

Lewin, K., Dembo, T., Festinger, L., & Sears, P. S. (1944). Level of aspiration. In J. McHunt (Ed.), *Personality and the behavior disorders* (Vol. *1,* pp. 333–378). New York: Ronald.

Lewinsohn, P. M., Mischel, W., Chaplin, W., & Barton, R. (1980). Social competence and depression: The role of illusory self-perceptions. *Journal of Abnormal Psychology, 89,* 203–212.

Lewis, M. (2008). Self-conscious emotions: Embarrassment, pride, shame, and guilt. In M. Lewis, J. M. Haviland-Jones, & L. F. Barrett (Eds.), *Handbook of emotions* (3rd ed., pp. 742–756). New York: Guilford Press.

Li, N. P., Bailey, J. M., Kenrick, D. T., & Linsenmeier, J. A. W. (2002). The necessities and luxuries of mate preferences: Testing the tradeoffs. *Journal of Personality and Social Psychology, 82,* 947–955.

Liljeholm, M., & O'Doherty, J. P. (2012). Contributions of the striatum to learning, motivation, and performance: An associative account. *Trends in Cognitive Science, 16,* 467–475.

Lim, M. M., & Young, L. J. (2006). Neuropeptidergic regulation of affiliative behavior and social bonding in animals. *Hormones and Behavior, 50,* 506–517.

Lindsley, D. B. (1957). Psychophysiology and motivation. In M. R. Jones (Ed.), *Nebraska Symposium on Motivation* (Vol. 5, pp. 44–105). Lincoln: University of Nebraska Press.

Lindzey, G. (Ed.). (1958). *Assessment of human motives.* New York: Rinehart.

Linehan, M. M. (1997). Self-verification and drug abusers: Implications for treatment. *Psychological Science, 8,* 181–183.

Linnenbrink, E. A. (2005). The dilemma of performance-approach goals: The use of multiple goal contexts to promote students' motivation and learning. *Journal of Educational Psychology, 97,* 197–213.

Lischetzke, T., Cuccodoro, G., Gauger, A., Todeschini, L., & Eid, M (2005). Measuring affective clarity indirectly: Individual differences in response latencies of state. *Emotion, 5,* 431–445.

Locke, E. A. (1968). Toward a theory of task motivation and incentives. *Organizational Behavior and Human Performance, 3,* 157–189.

Locke, E. A. (1996). Motivation through conscious goal setting. *Applied and Preventive Psychology, 5,* 117–124.

Locke, E. A., & Bryan, J. F. (1969). The directing function of goals in task performance. *Organizational Behavior and Human Performance, 4*, 35–42.

Locke, E. A., & Latham, G. P. (1984). *Goal-setting: A motivational technique that works!* Englewood Cliffs, NJ: Prentice Hall.

Locke, E. A., & Latham, G. P. (1990). *A theory of goal setting and task performance.* Englewood Cliffs, NJ: Prentice Hall.

Locke, E. A., & Latham, G. P. (2002). Building a practically useful theory of goal setting and task motivation. *American Psychologist, 57*, 705–717.

Locke, E. A., Chah, D. O., Harrison, S., & Lustgarten, N. (1989). Separating the effects of goal specificity from goal level. *Organizational Behavior and Human Decision Processes, 43*, 270–287.

Locke, E. A., Shaw, K. N., Saari, L. M., & Latham, G. P. (1981). Goal setting and task performance: 1969–1980. *Psychological Bulletin, 90*, 125–152.

Loevinger, J. (1976). Stages of ego development. In J. Loevinger (Ed.), *Ego development* (pp. 13–28). San Francisco: Jossey-Bass.

Loewenstein, G. (1996). Out of control: Visceral influences on behavior. *Organizational Behavior and Human Decision Processes, 65*, 272–292.

Loftus, E. F., & Klinger, M. R. (1992). Is the unconscious smart or dumb? *American Psychologist, 47*, 761–765.

Lopes, P. N., Salovey, P., Cote, S. & Beers, M. (2005). Emotion regulation and the quality of social interaction. *Emotion, 5*, 113–118.

Lopez, S. J. (2006). C. R. Snyder (1944–2006). *American Psychologist, 61*, 719.

Lopez, S. J., & Snyder, C. R. (Eds.) (2009). *Oxford handbook of positive psychology* (2nd ed.). New York: Oxford University Press.

Lorenz, K. (1965). *Evolution and modification of behavior: A critical examination of the concepts of the "learned" and the "innate" elements of behavior.* Chicago: University of Chicago Press.

Louro, M. J., Pieters, R., & Zeelenberg, M. (2007). Dynamics of multiple-goal pursuit. *Journal of Personality and Social Psychology, 93*, 174–193.

Lowe, M. R. (1993). The effects of dieting on eating behavior: A three-factor model. *Psychological Bulletin, 114*, 100–121.

Luborsky, L., & Crits-Christoph, P. (1990). *Understanding transference: The core conflictual relationship theme method.* New York: Basic Books.

Lucas, R. E., Diener, E., Grob, A., Suh, E. M., & Shao, L. (2000). Cross-cultural evidence for the fundamental features of extraversion. *Journal of Personality and Social Psychology, 79*, 452–468.

Lyubomirsky, S. L., King, L., & Diener, E. (2005). The benefits of frequent positive affect: Does happiness lead to success? *Psychological Bulletin, 131*, 803–855.

Lyubomirsky, S., King, L., & Diener, E. (2005). The benefits of frequent positive affect: Does happiness lead to success? *Psychological Bulletin, 131*, 803–855.

MacLeod, A. K, Byrne, A., & Valentine, J. D. (1996). Affect, emotional disorder, and future directed thinking. *Cognition and Emotion, 10*, 69–86.

Madsen, K. B. (1959). *Theories of motivation.* Copenhagen: Munksgaard.

Maehr, M. L., & Kleiber, D. A. (1980). The graying of achievement motivation. *American Psychologist, 36*, 787–793.

Maehr, M. L., & Midgley, C. (1996). *Transforming school cultures.* Boulder, CO: Westview Press.

Mahoney, E. R. (1983). *Human sexuality.* New York: McGraw-Hill.

Main, M., Kaplan, N., & Cassidy, J. (1985). Security in infancy, childhood, and adulthood: A move to the level of representation. In I. Bretherton & E. Waters (Eds.), Growing points of attachment theory and research. *Monographs of the Society for Research in Child Development, 50*, 67–104.

Mallan, K. M., Lipp, O. V., & Cochrane, B. (2013). Slithering snakes, angry men and out-group members: What and whom are we evolved to fear? *Cognition and Emotion, 27*, 1168–1180.

Malmo, R. B. (1959). Activation: A neurological dimension. *Psychological Review, 66*, 367–386.

Manderlink, G., & Harackiewicz, J. M. (1984). Proximal versus distal goal setting and intrinsic motivation. *Journal of Personality and Social Psychology, 47*, 918–928.

Mandler, G. (1975). *Mind and emotion*. New York: Wiley.

Mandler, G. (1984). *Mind and body: Psychology of emotion and stress*. New York: W. W. Norton.

Mandrup, S., & Lane, M. D. (1997). Regulating adipogenesis. *Journal of Biology and Chemistry, 272*, 5367–5370.

Manian, N. Strauman, T. J., & Denney, N. (1998). Temperament, recalled parenting styles and self-regulation: Testing the developmental postulates of self-discrepancy theory. *Journal of Personality and Social Psychology, 75*, 1321–1332.

Manstead, A. S. R. (1991). Emotion in social life. *Cognition and Emotion, 5*, 353–362.

Marazziti, D., Dall'Osso, B., Baroni, S., et al. (2006). A relationship between oxytocin and anxiety of romantic attachment. *Clinical Practice and Epidemiology in Mental Health, 2*, 28.

Markus, H. (1977). Self-schemata and processing information about the self. *Journal of Personality and Social Psychology, 35*, 63–68.

Markus, H. (1983). Self-knowledge: An expected view. *Journal of Personality, 51*, 543–565.

Markus, H., & Sentisk, K. (1982). The self in social information processing. In J. Suls (Ed.), *Psychological perspectives on the self* (Vol. *1*, pp. 41–60). Hillsdale, NJ: Erlbaum.

Markus, H., & Wurf, E. (1987). The dynamic self-concept: A social psychological perspective. *Annual Review of Psychology, 38*, 299–337.

Markus, H., Cross, S., & Wurf, E. (1990). The role of self-esteem in competence. In R. J. Sternberg & J. Kolligian (Eds.), *Competence considered* (pp. 205–225). New Haven, CT: Yale University Press.

Markus, H., & Nurius, P. (1986). Possible selves. *American Psychologist, 41*, 954–969.

Markus, H., & Ruvolo, A. P. (1989). Possible selves: Personalized representations of goals. In L. A. Pervin (Ed.), *Goal concepts in personality and social psychology* (pp. 211–241). Hills-dale, NJ: Erlbaum.

Marlatt, G. P., & Parks, G. A. (1982). Self-management of addictive behaviors. In P. Karoly & F. H. Kanfer (Eds.), *Self-management and behavior change* (pp. 443–488). New York: Pergamon.

Marques, S. C., Lopez, S. J., & Pais-Ribeiro, J. L. (2011). "Building hope for the future": A program to foster strengths in middle-school students. *Journal of Happiness Studies, 12*, 139–152.

Marsh, A. A., Ambady, N., & Kleck, R. E. (2005). The effects of fear and anger facial expressions on approach- and avoidance-related behaviors. *Emotion, 5*, 119–124.

Marsh, H. W. (1990). Causal ordering of academic self-concept and academic achievement: A multivariate, longitudinal panel analysis. *Journal of Educational Psychology, 82*, 646–656.

Marsh, H. W., & Craven, R. G. (2006). Reciprocal effects of self-concept and performance from a multidimensional perspective: Beyond seductive pleasure and unidimensional perspectives. *Perspectives on Psychological Science, 1*, 133–163.

Marsh, H. W., Trautwein, U., Ludtke, O., Koller, O., & Baumert, J. (2006). Integration of multidimensional self-concept and core personality constructs: Construct validation and relations to well-being and achievement. *Journal of Personality, 74*, 403–456.

Martin, A. J., & Jackson, S. A. (2008). Brief approaches to assessing task absorption and enhanced subjective experience: Examining "short" and "core" flow in diverse performance domains. *Motivation and Emotion, 32*, 141–157.

Martin, J. J., & Cutler, K. (2002). An exploratory study of flow and motivation in theatre actors. *Journal of Applied Sport Psychology, 14*, 344–352.

Mascolo, M. F., Fischer, K. W., & Li, J. (2003). Dynamic development of component systems of emotions: Pride, shame, and guilt in China and the United States. In R. J. Davidson, K. R. Scherer, & H. H. Goldsmith (Eds.), *Handbook of affective sciences* (pp. 375–408). New York: Oxford University Press.

Masling, J. (Ed.). (1983). *Empirical studies of psychoanalytic theories*. Hillsdale, NJ: Analytic Press.

Maslow, A. H. (1943). A theory of human motivation. *Psychological Review, 50*, 370–396.

Maslow, A. H. (1954). *Motivation and personality*. New York: Harper.

Maslow, A. H. (1968). *Toward a psychology of being*. New York: Van Nostrand.

Maslow, A. H. (1971). *The farther reaches of human nature*. New York: Viking Press.

Maslow, A. H. (1987). *Motivation and personality* (3rd ed.). New York: Harper & Row.

Mason, A., & Blankenship, V. (1987). Power and affiliation motivation, stress, and abuse in intimate relationships. *Journal of Personality and Social Psychology, 52*, 203–210.

Masters, W. H., & Johnson, V. E. (1966). *Human sexual response*. Boston: Little, Brown.

Mathes, E. W. (1981). Maslow's hierarchy of needs as a guide for living. *Journal of Humanistic Psychology, 21*, 69–72.

Matsui, T., Okada, A., & Inoshita, O. (1983). Mechanism of feedback affecting task performance. *Organizational Behavior and Human Performance, 31*, 114–122.

Matsumoto, D. (1987). The role of facial response in the experience of emotion: More methodological problems and a meta-analysis. *Journal of Personality and Social Psychology, 52*, 769–774.

Matsumoto, D. (1992). More evidence for the universality of a contempt expression. *Motivation and Emotion, 16*, 363–368.

Matsumoto, D., & Ekman, P. (2004). The relationship among expressions, labels, and descriptions of contempt. *Journal of Personality and Social Psychology, 87*, 529–540.

Matsumoto, D., & Hwang, H. S. (2011). Evidence for training the ability to read microexpressions of emotion. *Motivation and Emotion, 35*, 181–191.

Matsumoto, D., & Hwang, H. S. (2012). Evidence for a nonverbal expression of triumph. *Evolution and Behavior, 33*, 520–529.

Matsumoto, D., Keltner, D., Shiota, M. N., O'Sullivan, M., & Frank, M. (2008). Facial expressions of emotion. In M. Lewis, J. M. Haviland-Jones, & L. F. Barrett (Eds.), *Handbook of emotions* (3rd ed., pp. 211–234). New York: Guilford Press.

Matsumoto, K. et al. (2003). Neural correlates of goal-based motor selection in the prefrontal cortex. *Science, 301*, 229–232.

Mauss, I. B., Levenson, R. W., McCarter, L., Wilhelm, F. H., & Gross, J. J. (2005). The tie that binds? Coherence among emotion experience, behavior, and physiology. *Emotion, 5*, 175–190.

May, R. (1982). The problem of evil: An open letter to Carl Rogers. *Journal of Humanistic Psychology, 22*, 10–21.

May, R. (Ed.). (1961). *Existential psychology*. New York: Random House.

McAdams, D. P. (1980). A thematic coding system for the intimacy motive. *Journal of Research in Personality, 14*, 413–432.

McAdams, D. P. (1982a). Experiences of intimacy and power: Relationships between social motives and autobiographical memory. *Journal of Personality and Social Psychology, 42*, 292–302.

McAdams, D. P. (1982b). Intimacy motivation. In A. J. Stewart (Ed.), *Motivation and society*. San Francisco: Jossey-Bass.

McAdams, D. P. (1989). *Intimacy: The need to be close*. New York: Doubleday.

McAdams, D. P. (1993). *The stories we live by: Personal myths and the making of the self*. New York: Morrow.

McAdams, D. P. (1996). Personality, modernity, and the storied self: A contemporary framework for studying persons. *Psychological Inquiry, 7*, 295–321.

McAdams, D. P., & Constantian, C. A. (1983). Intimacy and affiliation motives in daily living: An experience sampling analysis. *Journal of Personality and Social Psychology, 45*, 851–861.

McAdams, D. P., & Losoff, M. (1984). Friendship motivation in fourth and sixth graders: A thematic analysis. *Journal of Social and Personal Relationships, 1*, 11–27.

McAdams, D. P., & Powers, J. (1981). Themes of intimacy in behavior and thought. *Journal of Personality and Social Psychology, 40*, 573–587.

McAdams, D. P., Diamond, A., de St. Aubin, E., & Mansfield, E. (1997). Stories of commitment: The psychosocial construction of generative lives. *Journal of Personality and Social Psychology, 72,* 678–694.

McAdams, D. P., Healy, S., & Krause, S. (1984). Social motives and patterns of friendship. *Journal of Personality and Social Psychology, 47,* 828–838.

McAdams, D. P., Jackson, R. J., & Kirshnit, C. (1984). Looking, laughing, and smiling in dyads as a function of intimacy motivation and reciprocity. *Journal of Personality, 52,* 261–273.

McAuley, E., & Tammen, V. V. (1989). The effect of subjective and objective competitive outcomes on intrinsic motivation. *Journal of Sport and Exercise Psychology, 11,* 84–93.

McCall, C., & Singer, T. (2012). The animal and human neuroendocrinology of social cognition, motivation and behavior. *Nature Neuroscience, 15,* 681–688.

McCaul, K. D., Holmes, D. S., & Solomon, S. (1982). Facial expression and emotion. *Journal of Personality and Social Psychology, 42,* 145–152.

McClelland, D. C. (1961). *The achieving society.* Princeton, NJ: Van Nostrand.

McClelland, D. C. (1965). Achievement and entrepreneurship: A longitudinal study. *Journal of Personality and Social Psychology, 1,* 389–392.

McClelland, D. C. (1975). *Power: The inner experience.* New York: Irvington.

McClelland, D. C. (1978). Managing motivation to expand human freedom. *American Psychologist, 33,* 201–210.

McClelland, D. C. (1982). The need for power, sympathetic activation, and illness. *Motivation and Emotion, 6,* 31–41.

McClelland, D. C. (1984). *Motives, personality, and society. Selected papers.* New York: Praeger.

McClelland, D. C. (1985). *Human motivation.* San Francisco: Scott, Foresman.

McClelland, D. C. (1987). Characteristics of successful entrepreneurs. *Journal of Creative Behavior, 21,* 219–233.

McClelland, D. C. (Ed.). (1955). *Studies in motivation.* New York: Appleton-Century-Crofts.

McClelland, D. C., & Burnham, D. H. (1976, March–April). Power is the great motivator. *Harvard Business Review,* 100–110.

McClelland, D. C., & Pilon, D. A. (1983). Sources of adult motives in patterns of parent behavior in early childhood. *Journal of Personality and Social Psychology, 44,* 564–574.

McClelland, D. C., & Teague, G. (1975). Predicting risk preferences among power-related tasks. *Journal of Personality, 43,* 266–285.

McClelland, D. C., & Watson, R. I., Jr. (1973). Power motivation and risk-taking behavior. *Journal of Personality, 41,* 121–139.

McClelland, D. C., Atkinson, J. W., Clark, R. A., & Lowell, E. L. (1953). *The achievement motive.* New York: Appleton-Century-Crofts.

McClelland, D. C., Constantian, C., Pilon, D., & Stone, C. (1982). Effects of child-rearing practices on adult maturity. In D. C. McClelland (Ed.), *The development of social maturity.* New York: Irvington.

McClelland, D. C., Davis, W. B., Kalin, R., & Wanner, E. (1972). *The drinking man: Alcohol and human motivation.* New York: Free Press.

McClelland, D. C., Koestner, R., & Weinberger, J. (1989). How do self-attributed and implicit motives differ? *Psychological Review, 96,* 690–702.

McClure, S. M., Laibson, D. I., Loewenstein, G., & Cohen, J. D. (2004). Separate neural system value immediate and delayed monetary rewards. *Science, 506,* 503–507.

McClure, S. M., York, M. K., & Montague, P. R. (2004). The neural substrate of reward processing in humans: The modern role of *f*MRI. *Neuroscientist, 10,* 260–268.

McCullough, M. E., Kilpatrick, S. D., Emmons, R. E., & Larsen, D. B. (2001). Is gratitude a moral affect? *Psychological Bulletin, 127,* 249–266.

McCullough, M. E., Kimeldorf, M. B., & Cohen, A. D. (2008). An adaptation for altruism? The social causes, social effects, and social evolution of gratitude. *Current Directions in Psychological Science, 17*, 281–285.

McCullough, M.E., Emmons, R.A., & Tsang, J. (2002). The grateful disposition: A conceptual and empirical topography. *Journal of Personality and Social Psychology, 82*, 112–127.

McDonald, A. J. (1998). Cortical pathways to the mammalian amygdala. *Progress in Neurobiology, 55*, 257–332.

McDougall, W. (1908). *Introduction to social psychology.* London: Methuen.

McDougall, W. (1926). *Introduction to social psychology.* Boston: Luce and Co.

McEwen, B. S. (1998). Protective and damaging effects of stress mediators. *New England Journal of Medicine, 338*, 171–179.

McGinley, H., McGinley, P., & Nicholas, K. (1978). Smiling, body position and interpersonal attraction. *Bulletin of the Psychonomics Society, 12*, 21–24.

McGraw, K. O. (1978). The detrimental effects of reward on performance: A literature review and a prediction model. In M. R. Lepper & D. Greene (Eds.), *The hidden costs of reward* (pp. 33–60). New York: Wiley.

McGraw, K. O., & McCullers, J. C. (1979). Evidence of detrimental effects of extrinsic incentives on breaking a mental set. *Journal of Experimental Social Psychology, 15*, 285–294.

McHugh, P. R., & Moran, T. H. (1985). The stomach: A conception of its dynamic role in satiety. In J. M. Sprague & A. N. Epstein (Eds.), *Progress in psychobiology and physiological psychology* (Vol. *11*, pp. 197–232). Orlando, FL: Academic Press.

McIntosh, D. N. (1996). Facial feedback hypotheses: Evidence, implications, and directions. *Motivation and Emotion, 20*, 121–147.

McIntosh, D. N., Zajonc, R. B., Vig, P. S., & Emerick, S. W. (1997). Facial movement, breathing, temperature, and affect: Implications of the vascular theory of emotional efference. *Cognition and Emotion, 11*, 171–195.

McKeachie, W. J. (1976). Psychology in America's bicentennial year. *American Psychologist, 31*, 819–833.

McKeachie, W. J., Lin, Y., Milholland, J., & Issacson, R. (1966). Student affiliation motives, teacher warmth, and academic achievement. *Journal of Personality and Social Psychology, 4*, 457–461.

McNally, R. J. (1992). Disunity in psychology: Chaos or speciation? *American Psychologist, 47*, 1054.

Mednick, M. T., Mednick, S. A., & Mednick, E. V. (1964). Incubation of creative performance and specific associative priming. *Journal of Abnormal and Social Psychology, 69*, 84–88.

Meece, J. L., & Miller, S. D. (1999). Changes in elementary school children's achievement goals for reading and writing: Results from a longitudinal and an intervention study. *Scientific Studies of Reading, 3*, 207–229.

Meece, J. L., Wigfield, A., & Eccles, J. S. (1990). Predictors of math anxiety and its consequences for young adolescents' course enrollment intentions and performance in mathematics. *Journal of Educational Psychology, 82*, 60–70.

Meece, J., Blumenfeld, P., & Hoyle, R. (1988). Students' goal orientations and cognitive engagement in classroom activities. *Journal of Educational Psychology, 80*, 514–523.

Mento, A. J., Steel, R. P., & Karren, R. J. (1987). A meta-analytic study of the effects of goal setting on task performance: 1966–1984. *Organizational Behavior and Human Decision Processes, 39*, 52–83.

Meston, C. M. (2000). The psychophysiological assessment of female sexual function. *Journal of Sex Education and Therapy, 25*, 6–16.

Meyer, D. (2007). Selective serotonin reuptake inhibitors and their effects on relationship satisfaction. *The Family Journal, 15*, 392–397.

Mickelson, K. D., Kessler, R. C., & Shaver, P. R. (1997). Adult attachment in a nationally representative sample. *Journal of Personality and Social Psychology, 73*, 1092–1106.

Mikulincer, M. (1988). The relationship of probability of success and performance following failure: Reactance and helplessness effects. *Motivation and Emotion, 12,* 139–152.

Mikulincer, M. (1994). *Human learned helplessness: A coping perspective.* New York: Plenum Press.

Mikulincer, M., Shaver, P. R., & Pereg, D. (2003). Attachment theory and affect regulation: The dynamics, development, and cognitive consequences of attachment-related strategies. *Motivation and Emotion, 27,* 77–102.

Miller, D. L., & Kelley, M. L. (1994). The use of goal setting and contingency contracting for improving children's homework performance. *Journal of Applied Behavior Analysis, 27,* 73–84.

Miller, E. K., & Cohen, J. D. (2001). An integrative theory of prefrontal cortex function. *Annual Review of Neuroscience, 24,* 167–202.

Miller, G. A., Galanter, E. H., & Pribram, K. H. (1960). *Plans and the structure of behavior.* New York: Holt, Rinehart & Winston.

Miller, N. E. (1948). Studies of fear as an acquirable drive: 1. Fear as motivation and fear-reduction as reinforcement in the learning on new responses. *Journal of Experimental Psychology, 38,* 89–101.

Miller, N. E. (1959). Liberalization of basic S-R concepts: Extensions to conflict behavior, motivation, and social learning. In S. Koch (Ed.), *Psychology: A study of a science* (Vol. 2, pp. 196–292). New York: McGraw-Hill.

Miller, N. E. (1960). Motivational effects of brain stimulation and drugs. *Federation Proceedings, Federation of American Societies for Experimental Biology, 19,* 846–853.

Miller, N. E. (1971). *Neal E. Miller: Selected papers.* Chicago: Aldine Atherton.

Millon, T. (1990). The disorders of personality. In L. A. Pervin (Ed.), *Handbook of personality: Theory and research* (pp. 339–370). New York: Guilford Press.

Mills, J., & Clark, M. S. (1982). Communal and exchange relationships. In L. Wheeler (Ed.), *Review of personality and social psychology* (Vol. 3, pp. 121–144). Beverly Hills, CA: Sage.

Mirenowicz, J., & Schultz, W. (1994). Importance of unpredictability for reward responses in primate dopamine neurons. *Journal of Neurophysiology, 72,* 1024–1027.

Mischel, W. (1974). Processes in delay of gratification. In L. Berkowitz (Ed.), *Advances in experimental social psychology* (Vol. 7, pp. 249–292). San Diego, CA: Academic Press.

Mischel, W., & Ayduk, O. (2004). Willpower in a cognitive-affective processing system: The dynamics of delay of gratification. In R. F. Baumeister & K. Vohs (Eds.), *Handbook of self-regulation: Research, theory, and applications* (pp. 99–129). New York: Guilford Press.

Mischel, W., Coates, B., & Raskoff, A. (1968). Effects of success and failure on self-gratification. *Journal of Personality and Social Psychology, 10,* 381–390.

Mischel, W., Shoda, Y., & Peake, P. (1988). The nature of adolescent competencies predicted by preschool delay of gratification. *Journal of Personality and Social Psychology, 54,* 687–696.

Mitchell, S. (1988). *Relational concepts in psychoanalysis.* Cambridge, MA: Harvard University Press.

Mittelman, W. (1991). Maslow's study of self-actualization: A reinterpretation. *Journal of Humanistic Psychology, 31,* 114–135.

Moffitt, A., Kramer, M., & Hoffman, R. (1993). *The functions of dreaming.* Albany: State University of New York.

Mogenson, G. J., & Calaresu, F. R. (1973). Cardiovascular responses to electrical stimulation of the amygdala in the rat. *Experimental Neurology, 39,* 166–180.

Moller, A. C., Deci, E. L., & Elliot, A. J. (2010). Person-level relatedness and the incremental value of relating. *Personality and Social Psychology Bulletin, 36,* 754–767.

Moller, A. C., Deci, E. L., & Ryan, R. M. (2006). Choice and ego-depletion: The moderating role of autonomy. *Personality and Social Psychology Bulletin, 32,* 1024–1036.

Moltz, H. (1965). Contemporary instinct theory and the fixed action pattern. *Psychological Review, 72,* 27–47.

Money, J. (1988). *Gay, straight, and in-between: The sexology of erotic orientation*. New York: Oxford University Press.

Money, J., Wiedeking, C., Walker, P. A., & Gain, D. (1976). Combined antiandrogenic and counseling program for treatment of 46 XY and 47 XYY sex offenders. In E. J. Sachar (Ed.), *Hormones, Behavior, and Psychopathology, 66*, 105–109.

Montagne, B., Kessels, R. P., De Haan, E. H., & Perrett, D. I. (2007). The Emotion Recognition Task: A paradigm to measure the perception of facial emotional expressions of different intensities. *Perceptual and Motor Skills, 104*, 589–598.

Montague, P. R., Dayan, P., & Sejnowski, T. J. (1996). A framework for mesencephalic dopamine systems based on predictive Hebbian learning. *Journal of Neuroscience, 16*, 1936–1947.

Mook, D. G. (1988). On the organization of satiety. *Appetite, 11*, 27–39.

Mook, D. G. (1996). *Motivation: The organization of action* (2nd ed.). New York: W. W. Norton.

Mook, D. G., & Kozub, F. J. (1968). Control of sodium chloride intake in the nondeprived rat. *Journal of Comparative and Physiological Psychology, 66*, 105–109.

Mook, D. G., & Wagner, S. (1989). Orosensory suppression of saccharin drinking in rat: The response, not the taste. *Appetite, 13*, 1–13.

Moors, A. (2013). On the causal role of appraisal in emotion. *Emotion Review, 5*, 132–140.

Moors, A., De Houwer, J., & Eelen, P. (2004). Automatic stimulus-goal comparisons: Support from motivational affective priming studies. *Cognition and Emotion, 18*, 29–54.

Moors, A., Ellsworth, P. C., Scherer, K. R., & Frijda, N. H. (2013). Appraisal theories of emotion: State of the art and future development. *Emotion Review, 5*, 119–124.

Moran, T. H. (2000). Cholecystokinin and satiety: Current perspectives. *Nutrition, 16*, 858–865.

Morgan, C. D., & Murray, H. A. (1935). A method of examining fantasies: The Thematic Apperception Test. *Archives in Neurology and Psychiatry, 34*, 219–274.

Morse, R. C., & Stoller, D. (1982, September). The hidden message that breaks habits. *Science Digest*, p.28.

Moruzzi, G., & Magoun, H. W. (1949). Brain stem reticular formation and activation of the EEG. *EEG and Clinical Neurophysiology, 1*, 455–473.

Mossholder, K. W. (1980). Effects of externally mediated goal setting on intrinsic motivation: A laboratory experiment. *Journal of Applied Psychology, 65*, 202–210.

Mouratidis, A. A., Vansteenkiste, M., Sideridis, G., & Lens, W. (2011). Vitality and interest- enjoyment as a function of class-to-class variation in need-supportive teaching and pupils' autonomous motivation. *Journal of Educational Psychology, 103*, 353–366.

Muehlenhard, C. L., & Kimes, L. A. (1999). The social construction of violence: The case of sexual and domestic violence. *Personality and Social Psychology Review, 3*, 234–245.

Mueller, C. M., & Dweck, C. S. (1997). *Implicit theories of intelligence: Malleability beliefs, definitions, and judgments of intelligence*. Unpublished data.

Mueller, C. M., & Dweck, C. S. (1998). Intelligence praise can undermine motivation and performance. *Journal of Personality and Social Psychology, 75*, 33–52.

Mulligan, K., & Scherer, K. R. (2012). Toward a working definition of emotion. *Emotion Review, 4*, 345–357.

Munarriz, R., Talakoub, L., Flaherty, E., Gioia, M., Hoag, L., Kim, N. N., et al. (2002). Androgen replacement therapy with dehydroepiandrosterone for androgen insufficiency and female sexual dysfunction: Androgen and questionnaire results. *Journal of Sex and Marital Therapy, 28*, 165–173.

Munster Halvari, A. E., Halvari, H., Bjørnebekk, G., & Deci, E. L. (2010). Motivation and anxiety for dental treatment: Testing a self-determination theory model of oral self-care behaviour and dental clinic attendance. *Motivation and Emotion, 34*, 15–33.

Muraven, M. (2008). Autonomous self-control is less depleting. *Journal of Research in Personality, 42*, 763–770.

Muraven, M. (2012). Ego depletion: Theory and evidence. In R. M. Ryan (Ed.), *The Oxford handbook of human motivation* (pp. 111–126). New York: Oxford University Press.

Muraven, M., & Shmueli, D. (2006). The self-control costs of fighting the temptation to drink. *Psychology of Addictive Behaviors, 20*, 154–160.

Muraven, M., Baumeister, R. F., & Tice, D. M. (1999). Longitudinal improvement of self-regulation through practice: Building self-control strength through repeated exercise. *Journal of Social Psychology, 139*, 446–457.

Muraven, M., Gagne, M., & Rosman, H. (2008). Helpful self-control: Autonomy support, vitality, and depletion. *Journal of Experimental Social Psychology, 44*, 573–585.

Muraven, M., Shmueli, D., & Burkley, E. (2006). Conserving self-control strength. *Journal of Personality and Social Psychology, 91*, 524–537.

Muraven, M., Tice, D. M., & Baumeister, R. F. (1998). Self-control as a limited resource: Regulatory depletion patterns. *Journal of Personality and Social Psychology, 74*, 774–789.

Murayama, K., Matsumoto, M., Izuma, K., & Matsumoto, K. (2010). Neural basis of the undermining effect of monetary reward on intrinsic motivation. *PNAS Early Edition*, 1–6. doi: 10.1073/pnas.1013305107.

Murray, H. A. (1937). Facts which support the concept of need or drive. *Journal of Personality, 3*, 115–143.

Murray, H. A. (1938). *Explorations in personality*. New York: Oxford University Press.

Murray, H. A. (1943). *Thematic apperception test*. Cambridge, MA: Harvard University Press.

Myers, M. G., Cowley, M.A., & Munzberg, H. (2008). Mechanisms of leptin action and leptin resistance. *Annual Review of Physiology, 70*, 537–556.

Myers, M. W., Laurent, S. M., & Hodges, S. D. (2014). Perspective taking instructions and self-other overlap: Different motives for helping. *Motivation and Emotion, 38*, 224–234.

Nakamura, J., & Csikszentmihalyi, M. (2002). The concept of flow. In C. R. Snyder & S. J. Lopez (Eds.), *Handbook of positive psychology* (pp. 89–105). Oxford, UK: Oxford University Press.

Nasby, W., & Yando, R. (1982). Selective encoding and retrieval of affectively information. *Journal of Personality and Social Psychology, 43*, 1244–1255.

Neemann, J., & Harter, S. (1986). *The self-perception profile for college students* [Manual]. Denver, CO: University of Denver.

Neher, A. (1991). Maslow's theory of motivation: A critique. *Journal of Humanistic Psychology, 31*, 89–112.

Neuberg, S. L., & Newsom, J. T. (1993). Personal need for structure: Individual differences In the desire for simpler structure. *Journal of Personality and Social Psychology, 65*, 113–131.

Newby, T. J. (1991). Classroom motivation: Strategies of first-year teachers. *Journal of Educational Psychology, 83*, 195–200.

Newell, A., Shaw, J. C., & Simon, H. A. (1958). Elements of a theory of human problem solving. *Psychological Review, 65*, 151–166.

Newman, E. B., Perkins, F. T., & Wheeler, R. H. (1930). Cannon's theory of emotion: A critique. *Psychological Review, 37*, 305–326.

Newman, R. S. (1991). Goals and self-regulated learning: What motivates children to seek academic help? In M. L. Maehr & P. R. Pintrich (Eds.), *Advances in motivation and achievement* (Vol. 7, pp. 151–183). Greenwich, CT: JAI Press.

Nezu, A. M., Nezu, C. M., & Blissett, S. E. (1988). Sense of humor as a moderator of the relation between stressful events and psychological distress: A prospective analysis. *Journal of Personality and Social Psychology, 54*, 520–525.

Nicholls, J. G. (1984). Achievement motivation: Conceptions of ability, subjective experience, task choice, and performance. *Psychological Review, 91*, 328–346.

Nielsen, I., Paritski, O., & Smyth, R. (2010). Subjective well-being of Beijing taxi drivers. *Journal of Happiness Studies, 11*, 721–733.

Nielsen, I., Smyth, R., & Zhai, Q. (2010). Subjective well-being of China's off-farm migrants. *Journal of Happiness Studies, 11*, 315–333.

Niemiec, C. P., & Ryan, R. M. (2013). What makes for a life well lived? Autonomy and its relation to full functioning and organismic wellness. In S. David, I. Boniwell, & A. Conley Ayers (Eds.), *Oxford handbook of happiness* (pp. 214–226). Oxford, UK: Oxford University Press.

Niemiec, C. P., Lynch, M. F., Vansteenkiste, M., Bernstein, J., Deci, E. L., & Ryan, R. M. (2006). The antecedents and consequences of autonomous self-regulation for college: A self-determination theory perspective on socialization. *Journal of Adolescence, 29*, 761–775.

Niezink, L. F., Siero, F. W., Dijkstra, P., Buunk, A. P., & Barelds, D. P. (2012). Empathic concern: Distinguishing between tenderness and sympathy. *Motivation and Emotion, 36*, 544–549.

Nils, F., & Rimé, B. (2012). Beyond the myth of venting: Social sharing modes determine emotional disclosure. *European Journal of Social Psychology, 42*, 672–681.

Nisbett, R. E., & Ross, L. (1980). *Human inference: Strategies and shortcomings of social judgment.* Englewood Cliffs, NJ: Prentice Hall.

Nix, G. A., Ryan, R. M., Manly, J. B., & Deci, E. L. (1999). Revitalization through self-regulation: The effects of autonomous and controlled motivation on happiness and vitality. *Journal of Experimental Social Psychology, 35*, 266–284.

Nolen, S. B. (1988). Reasons for studying: Motivational orientations and study strategies. *Cognition and Instruction, 5*, 269–287.

Nolen-Hoeksema, S. (2012). Emotion regulation and psychopathology: The role of gender. *Annual Review of Clinical Psychology, 8*, 61–87.

Nolen-Hoeksema, S., Wisco, B. E., & Lyubomirsky, S. (2008). Rethinking rumination. *Perspectives in Psychological Science, 3*, 400–424.

Nolen-Hoeksema, S., Wolfson, A., Mumme, D., & Guskin, K. (1995). Helplessness in children of depressed and nondepressed mothers. *Developmental Psychology, 31*, 377–387.

Noller, P. (1984). *Nonverbal communication and marital interaction.* Oxford, UK: Pergamon.

Nowak, M. A., & Roch, S. (2007). Upstream reciprocity and the evolution of gratitude. *Proceedings of the Royal Society B: Biological Sciences, 274*, 604–609.

Ntoumanis, N. (2005). A prospective study of participation in optional school physical education using a self-determination theory framework. *Journal of Educational Psychology, 97*, 444–453.

Ntoumanis, N., Pensgaard, A., Martin, C., & Pipe, K. (2004). An idiographic analysis of amotivation in compulsory school physical education. *Journal of Sport & Exercise Psychology, 26*, 197–214.

Nurius, P. (1991). Possible selves and social support: Social cognitive resources for coping and striving. In J. A. Howard & P. L. Callero (Eds.), *The self-society interface: Cognition, emotion, and action* (pp. 239–258). New York: Cambridge University Press.

Nystul, M. S. (1984). Positive parenting leads to self-actualizing children. *Individual Psychology: The Journal of Adlerian Theory, Research, and Prentice, 40*, 177–183.

Oaten, M., & Cheng, K. (2006). Improved self-control: The benefits of a regular program of academic study. *Basic and Applied Social Psychology, 28*, 1–16.

Oatley, K., & Duncan, E. (1994). The experience of emotions in everyday life. *Cognition and Emotion, 8*, 369–381.

Oatley, K., & Jenkins, J. M. (1992). Human emotions: Function and dysfunction. *Annual Review of Psychology, 43*, 55–85.

Oatley, K., & Johnson-Laird, P. N. (1987). Toward a cognitive theory of emotions. *Cognition and Emotion, 1*, 29–50.

Ochsner, K. N., & Gross, J. J. (2005). The cognitive control of emotion. *Trends in Cognitive Science, 9*, 242–249.

O'Doherty, J. (2004). Reward representations and reward-related learning in the human brain: Insights from human neuroimaging. *Current Opinion in Neurobiology, 14*, 769–776.

Oettingen, G. (1996). Positive fantasy and motivation. In P. M. Gollwitzer & J. A. Bargh (Eds.), *The psychology of action: Linking cognition and motivation to behavior* (pp. 236–259). New York: Guilford Press.

Oettingen, G., Honig, G., & Gollwitzer, P. M. (2000). Effective self regulation of goal attainment. *International Journal of Education Research, 33*, 705–732.

Ohman, A. (2008). Fear and anxiety. In M. Lewis, J. M. Haviland-Jones, & L. F. Barrett (Eds.), *Handbook of emotions* (3rd ed., pp. 709–729). New York: Guilford Press.

Ohman, A., & Mineka, S. (2001). Fears, phobias, and preparedness: Toward an evolved module of fear and fear learning. *Psychological Review, 108*, 483–522.

Ohman, A., & Mineka, S. (2003). The malicious serpent: Snakes as a prototypical stimulus for an evolved module of fear. *Current Directions in Psychological Science, 12*, 2–9.

Olatunji, B. O. (2008). Disgust, scrupulosity and conservative attitudes about sex: Evidence for a mediational model of homophobia. *Journal of Research in Personality, 42*(5), 1364–1369.

Olds, J. (1969). The central nervous system and the reinforcement of behavior. *American Psychologist, 24*, 114–132.

Olds, J., & Milner, P. (1954). Positive reinforcement produced by electrical stimulation of septal area and other regions in the rat brain. *Journal of Comparative and Physiological Psychology, 47*, 419–427.

Olds, M. E., & Fobes, J. L. (1981). The central basis of motivation: Intracranial self-stimulation studies. *Annual Review of Psychology, 32*, 523–574.

Orbell, S., & Sheeran, P. (1998). "Inclined abstainers": A problem for predicting health-related behavior. *British Journal of Social Psychology, 37*, 151–165.

Orbell, S., Hodgkins, S., & Sheeran, P. (1997). Implementation intentions and the theory of planned behavior. *Personality and Social Psychology Bulletin, 23*, 945–954.

Orlick, T. D., & Mosher, R. (1978). Extrinsic rewards and participant motivation in a sport related task. *International Journal of Sport Psychology, 9*, 27–39.

Orth, U., Berking, M., & Burkhardt, S. (2006). Self-conscious emotions and depression: Rumination explains why shame, but not guilt, is maladaptive. *Personality and Social Psychology Bulletin, 32*, 1608–1619.

Ortony, A., & Clore, G. L. (1989). Emotion, mood, and conscious awareness. *Cognition and Emotion, 3*, 125–137.

Ortony, A., Clore, G. L., & Collins, A. (1988). *The cognitive structure of emotions*. Cambridge, UK: Cambridge University Press.

Osterman, K. F. (2000). Students' need for belonging in the school community. *Review of Educational Research, 70*, 323–367.

Otis, N., & Pelletier, L. G. (2008). Women's regulation styles for eating behaviors and outcomes: The mediating role of approach and avoidance food planning. *Motivation and Emotion, 32*, 55–67.

Overskeid, G., & Svartdal, F. (1996). Effects of reward on subjective autonomy and interest when initial interest is low. *Psychological Record, 46*, 319–331.

Oyserman, D., & Markus, H. (1990). Possible selves and delinquency. *Journal of Personality and Social Psychology, 59*, 112–125.

Oyserman, D., Bybee, D., & Terry, K. (2006). Possible selves and academic outcomes: How and when possible selves impel action. *Journal of Personality and Social Psychology, 91*, 188–204.

Ozer, E. M., & Bandura, A. (1990). Mechanisms governing empowerment effects: A self-efficacy analysis. *Journal of Personality and Social Psychology, 58*, 472–486.

Pace, G. M., Ivancis, M. T., Edwards, G. L., Iwata, B. A., & Page, T. J. (1985). Assessment of stimulus preference and reinforcer value with profoundly retarded individuals. *Journal of Applied Behavior Analysis, 18*, 249–255.

Pajares, F., & Graham, L. (1999). Self-efficacy, motivation constructs, and mathematics performance of entering middle school students. *Contemporary Educational Psychology, 24*, 124–139.

Pajares, F., & Kranzler, J. (1995). Self-efficacy beliefs and general mental ability in mathematical problem-solving. *Contemporary Educational Psychology, 20,* 426–443.

Pajares, M. F. (1992). Teachers' beliefs and educational research: Cleaning up a messy construct. *Review of Educational Research, 62,* 307–332.

Pallak, S. R., Costomiris, S., Sroka, S., & Pittman, T. S. (1982). School experience, reward characteristics, and intrinsic motivation. *Child Development, 53,* 1382–1391.

Palmer, B., Donaldson, C., & Stough, C. (2002). Emotional intelligence and life satisfaction. *Personality and Individual Differences, 33,* 1091–1100.

Pang, J. S. (2010). The achievement motive: A review of theory and assessment of achievement, hope of success, and fear of failure. In O. C. Schultheiss & J. C. Brunstein (Eds.), *Implicit motives* (Chapter 2, pp. 30–70). New York: Oxford University Press.

Panksepp, J. (1994). The basics of basic emotion. In P. Ekman & R. J. Davidson (Eds.), *The nature of emotion: Fundamental questions* (pp. 20–24). New York: Oxford University Press.

Panksepp, J. (1998). *Affective neuroscience.* New York: Oxford University Press.

Panksepp, J. (1998). *Affective neuroscience: The foundations of human and animal emotions.* New York: Oxford University Press.

Panksepp, J., & Biven, L. (2011). *The archaeology of mind: Neuroevolutionary origins of human emotions.* New York: Norton.

Park, C. L., & Folkman, S. (1997). Meaning in the context of stress and coping. *Review of General Psychology, 1,* 115–144.

Parker, L. E., & Lepper, M. R. (1992). Effects of fantasy contexts on children's learning and motivation: Making learning more fun. *Journal of Personality and Social Psychology, 62,* 625–633.

Parkes, A. S., & Bruce, H. M. (1961). Olfactory stimuli in mammalian reproduction. *Science, 134,* 1049–1054.

Parkinson, B. (1991). Emotional stylists: Strategies of expressive management among trainee hairdressers. *Social Psychology Quarterly, 5,* 419–434.

Parkinson, B. (2012). Piecing together emotion: Sites and time-scales for social construction. *Emotion Review, 4,* 291–298.

Parrott, W. G., & Smith, R. H. (1993). Distinguishing the experiences of envy and jealousy. *Journal of Personality and Social Psychology, 64,* 906–920.

Patall, E. A. (2012). The motivational complexity of choosing: A review of theory and research. In R. Ryan (Ed.), *Oxford handbook of human motivation* (pp. 249–279). New York: Oxford University Press.

Patall, E. A., Cooper, H., & Robinson, J. C. (2008). The effects of choice on intrinsic motivation and related outcomes: A meta-analysis of research findings. *Psychological Bulletin, 134,* 270–300.

Patall, E. A., Dent, A. L., Oyer, M., & Wynn, S. R. (2013). Student autonomy and course value: The unique and cumulative roles of various teacher practices. *Motivation and Emotion, 37,* 14–32.

Paul, J. P. (1993). Childhood cross-gender behavior and adult homosexuality: The resurgence of biological models of sexuality. *Journal of Homosexuality, 24,* 41–54.

Paulus, M. P., & Stein, M. B. (2006). An insular view of anxiety. *Biological Psychiatry, 60,* 383–387.

Pavey, L., Greitemeyer, T., & Sparks, P. (2012). "I help because I want to, not because you tell me to": Empathy increases autonomously motivated helping. *Personality and Social Psychology Bulletin, 38,* 681–689.

Pecina, S., & Berridge, K. C. (2005). Hedonic hot spot in nucleus accumbens shell: Where do u-opiods cause increased hedonic sweeters? *Journal of Neuroscience, 25,* 11777–11786.

Pelletier, L. G., Dion, S. C., Slovenic-D'Angelo, M., & Reid, R. (2004). Why do you regulate what you eat? Relationship between forms of regulation, eating behaviors, sustained dietary behavior change, and psychological adjustment. *Motivation and Emotion, 28,* 245–277.

Pelletier, L. G., Dion, S., Tuson, K., & Green-Demers, I. (1999). Why do people fail to adopt environmentally protective behaviors? Toward a taxonomy of environmental amotivation. *Journal of Applied Social Psychology, 29,* 2481–2504.

Pelletier, L. G., Fortier, M. S., Vallerand, R. J., & Brière, N. M. (2001). Associations among perceived autonomy support, forms of self-regulation, and persistence: A prospective study. *Motivation and Emotion, 25,* 279–306.

Pelletier, L. G., Tuson, K., Green-Demers, I., Noels, K., & Beaton, A. (1998). Why are you doing things for the environment? The Motivation Toward the Environment Scale (MTES). *Journal of Applied Social Psychology, 28,* 437–468.

Pelletier, M., Bouthillier, A., Levesque, J., Carrier, S., Breault, C., Paquette, V., Mensour, B., Leroux, J.-M., Beaudoin, G., Bourgouin, P., & Beauregard, M. (2003). Separate neural circuits for primary emotions? Brain activity during self-induced sadness and happiness in professional actors. *Brain Imaging, 14,* 111–116.

Pennebaker, J. W. (1990). *Opening up.* New York: Morrow.

Perls, F. S. (1969). *Gestalt therapy verbatim.* Lafayette, CA: Real People Press.

Pessiglione, M., et al. (2007). How the brain translates money into force: A neuroimaging study of subliminal motivation. *Science, 316,* 904–906.

Peters, R. S. (1958). *The concept of motivation.* London: Routledge & Kegan Paul.

Peterson, C. (2000). The future of optimism. *American Psychologist, 55,* 44–55.

Peterson, C. (2006). *A primer in positive psychology.* New York: Oxford University Press.

Peterson, C., & Barrett, L. C. (1987). Explanatory style and academic performance among university freshmen. *Journal of Personality and Social Psychology, 53,* 603–607.

Peterson, C., & Park, C. (1998). Learned helplessness and explanatory style. In D. F. Barone, V. B. Van Hasselt, & M. Hersen (Eds.), *Advanced personality* (pp. 287–310). New York: Plenum Press.

Peterson, C., & Park, N. (2009). Classifying and measuring strengths of character. In S. J. Lopez, & C. R. Snyder (Eds.) (2009). *Oxford handbook of positive psychology* (2nd ed.; pp. 25–33). New York: Oxford University Press.

Peterson, C., & Seligman, M. E. P. (1984). Causal explanations as a risk factor for depression: Theory and evidence. *Psychological Review, 91,* 347–374.

Peterson, C., Maier, S. F., & Seligman, M. E. P. (1993). *Learned helplessness: A theory for the age of personal control.* New York: Oxford University Press.

Peterson, C., Seligman, M. E. P., & Vaillant, G. E. (1988). Pessimistic explanatory style is a risk factor for physical illness: A thirty-five year longitudinal study. *Journal of Personality and Social Psychology, 55,* 23–27.

Peterson, C., Seligman, M. E. P., Yurko, K. H., Martin, L. R., & Friedman, H. S. (1998). Catastophizing and untimely death. *Psychological Science, 9,* 49–52.

Pfaffmann, C. (1960). The pleasures of sensation. *Psychological Review, 67,* 253–268.

Pfaffmann, C. (1961). The sensory and motivating properties of the sense of taste. In M. R. Jones (Ed.), *Nebraska Symposium on Motivation* (Vol. 9, pp. 71–108). Lincoln: University of Nebraska Press.

Pfaffmann, C. (1982). Taste: A model of incentive motivation. In D. W. Pfaff (Ed.), *The physiological mechanisms of motivation* (pp. 61–97). New York: Springer-Verlag.

Pham, L. B., & Taylor, S. E. (1999). From thought to action: Effects of process-versus outcome-based mental simulations on performance. *Personality and Social Psychology Bulletin, 25,* 250–260.

Phan, K. L., Wager, T., Taylor, S. F., & Liberzon, I. (2002). Functional neuroanatomy of emotion: A meta-analysis of emotion activation studies in PET and fMRI. *NeuroImage, 16,* 331–348.

Philadelphia: W. B. Saunders. Sclafini, A., & Springer, D. (1976). Dietary obesity in adult rats: Similarities to hypothalamic and human obesity syndromes. *Physiology and Behavior, 17,* 461–471.

Pierce, G. R., Sarason, B. R., & Sarason, I. G. (1991). General and specific support expectations and stress as predictors of perceived supportiveness: An experimental study. *Journal of Personality and Social Psychology, 63,* 297–307.

Pierce, K. L., & Schreibman, L. (1994). Teaching daily living skills to children with autism in unsupervised settings through pictorial self-management. *Journal of Applied Behavior Analysis, 27,* 471–481.

Pietsch, J., Walker, R., Chapman, E. (2003). The relationship among self-concept, self-efficacy and performance in mathematics during secondary school. *Journal of Educational Psychology*, *95*(3), 589–603.

Pintrich, P. R. (2000). The role of goal orientation in self-regulated learning. In M. Boekaerts, P. Pintrinch, & M. Zeidner (Eds.), *Handbook of self-regulation, research, and applications* (pp. 451–502). Orlando, FL: Academic Press.

Pintrich, P. R. (2003). A motivational science perspective on the role of student motivation in learning and teaching contexts. *Journal of Educational Psychology*, *95*, 667–686.

Pittman, T. S., & Heller, J. F. (1988). Social motivation. *Annual Review of Psychology*, *38*, 461–489.

Pittman, T. S., Boggiano, A. K., & Ruble, D. N. (1983). Intrinsic and extrinsic motivational orientations: Limiting conditions on the undermining and enhancing effects of reward on intrinsic motivation. In J. Levine & M. Wang (Eds.), *Teacher and student perceptions: Implications for learning* (pp. 319–340). Hillsdale, NJ: Erlbaum.

Pittman, T. S., Davey, M. E., Alafat, K. A., Wetherill, K. V., & Kramer, N. A. (1980). Informational versus controlling verbal rewards. *Personality and Social Psychology Bulletin*, *6*, 228–233.

Plutchik, R. (1970). Emotions, evolution, and adaptive processes. In M. B. Arnold (Ed.), *Feelings and emotions* (pp. 3–24). New York: Academic Press.

Plutchik, R. (1980). *Emotion: A psychoevolutionary analysis*. New York: Harper & Row.

Plutchik, R. (1985). On emotion: The chicken-and-egg problem revisited. *Motivation and Emotion*, *9*, 197–200.

Polivy, J. (1976). Perception of calories and regulation of intake in restrained and unrestrained subjects. *Addictive Behaviors*, *1*, 237–243.

Polivy, J., & Herman, C. P. (1976a). Clinical depression and weight change: A complex relation. *Journal of Abnormal Psychology*, *85*, 338–340.

Polivy, J., & Herman, C. P. (1976b). Effect of alcohol on eating behavior: Influences of mood and perceived intoxication. *Journal of Abnormal Psychology*, *85*, 601–606.

Polivy, J., & Herman, C. P. (1983). *Breaking the diet habit*. New York: Basic Books.

Polivy, J., & Herman, C. P. (1985). Dieting and binging. *American Psychologist*, *40*, 193–201.

Pollak, L. H., & Thoits, P. A. (1989). Processes in emotional socialization. *Social Psychology Quarterly*, *52*, 22–34.

Pond, R. S Jr., Kashdan, T. B., DeWall, N., Savostyanova, A., Lambert, N. M., & Ficham, F. D. (2012). Emotion differentiation moderates aggressive tendencies in angry people: A daily diary analysis. *Emotion*, *12*, 326–337.

Potter, S. H. (1988). The cultural construction of emotion in rural Chinese social life. *Ethos*, *16*, 181–208.

Powers, S. I., Pietromonaco, P. R., Gunlicks, M., & Sayer, A. (2006). Dating couples' attachment styles and patterns of cortisol reactivity and recovery in response to a relationship conflict. *Journal of Personality and Social Psychology*, *90*, 613–628.

Powers, W. T. (1973). *Behavior: The control of perception*. Chicago, IL: Aldine.

Powley, T. L., & Keesey, R. E. (1970). Relationship of body weight to the lateral hypothalamus feeding syndrome. *Journal of Comparative and Clinical Psychology*, *70*, 25–36.

Prebble, S. C.., Addis, D. R., & Tipett, L. J. (2013). Autobiographical memory and sense of self. *Psychological Bulletin*, *139*, 815–840.

Premack, D. (1959). Toward empirical behavior laws: I. Positive reinforcement. *Psychological Review*, *66*, 219–233.

Pressley, M. (1995). More about the development of self-regulation: Complex, long-term, and thoroughly social. *Educational Psychologist*, *30*, 207–212.

Price, R. A. (1987). Genetics of human obesity. *Annals of Behavioral Medicine*, *9*, 9–14.

Puca, R. M. (2001). Preferred difficulty and subjective probability in different action phases. *Motivation and Emotion*, *25*, 307–326.

Puca, R. M., & Schmalt, H. (2001). The influence of the achievement motive on spontaneous thoughts in pre- and postdecisional action phases. *Personality and Social Psychology Bulletin, 27*, 302–308.

Quattrone, C. A. (1985). On the congruity between internal states and action. *Psychological Bulletin, 98*, 3–40.

Quinlan, D., Swain, N., & Vella-Brodrick, D. A. (2012). Character strengths interventions: Building on what we know for improved outcomes. *Journal of Happiness Studies, 13*, 1145–1163.

Rachman, S. (1978). *Fear and courage.* San Francisco: Freeman.

Ramamurthi, B. (1988). Stereotactic operation in behaviour disorders. *Amygdalotomy and hypothalamotomy. Acta Neurochir, 44* (Suppl.), 152–157.

Rand, A. (1964). The objectivist ethics. In A. Rand, *The virtue of selfishness.* New York: Signet.

Rapaport, D. (1960). On the psychoanalytic theory of motivation. *Nebraska symposium on motivation* (Vol. *8*, pp. 173–247). Lincoln: University of Nebraska Press.

Ravlin, S. B. (1987). *A computer model of affective reactions to goal-relevant events.* Unpublished master's thesis, University of Illinois, Urbana–Champaign.

Raynor, J. O. (1969). Future orientation and motivation of immediate activity: An elaboration of the theory of achievement motivation. *Psychological Review, 76*, 606–610.

Raynor, J. O. (1970). Relationship between achievement-related motives, future orientation, and academic performance. *Journal of Personality and Social Psychology, 15*, 28–33.

Raynor, J. O. (1974). Future orientation in the study of achievement motivation. In J. W. Atkinson & J. O. Raynor (Eds.), *Motivation and achievement.* Washington, DC: V. H. Winston.

Raynor, J. O. (1981). Future orientation and achievement motivation: Toward a personality functioning and change. In G. d'Ydexezlle & W. Lens (Eds). *Cognition in human motivation and learning* (pp 199–231). Hillsdale, NJ: Lawrence Erlbaum.

Raynor, J. O., & Entin, E. E. (1982). *Motivation, career striving, and aging.* New York: Hemisphere.

Reber, A. (1992). The cognitive unconscious: An evolutionary perspective. *Consciousness and Cognition, 1*, 93–133.

Reeve, J. (1989). The interest-enjoyment distinction in intrinsic motivation. *Motivation and Emotion, 13*, 83–103.

Reeve, J. (1993). The face of interest. *Motivation and Emotion, 17*, 353–375.

Reeve, J. (1996). *Motivating others: Nurturing inner motivational resources.* Needham Heights, MA: Allyn & Bacon.

Reeve, J. (2006). Teachers as facilitators: What autonomy-supportive teachers do and why their students benefit. *Elementary School Journal, 106*, 225–236.

Reeve, J. (2009). Why teachers adopt a controlling motivating style toward students and how they can become more autonomy supportive. *Educational Psychologist, 44*, 159–178.

Reeve, J. (2011). Teaching in ways that support students' autonomy. In D. Mashek & E. Hammer (Eds.), *Enhancing teaching and learning* (Chapter 5, pp. 90–103). Hoboken, NJ: Wiley-Blackwell.

Reeve, J. (2013). How students create motivationally supportive learning environments for themselves: The concept of agentic engagement. *Journal of Educational Psychology, 105*, 579–595.

Reeve, J., & Deci, E. L. (1996). Elements of the competitive situation that affect intrinsic motivation. *Personality and Social Psychology Bulletin, 22*, 24–33.

Reeve, J., & Jang, H. (2006). What teachers say and do to support students' autonomy during learning activities. *Journal of Educational Psychology, 98*, 209–218.

Reeve, J., & Lee, W. (2012). Neuroscience and human motivation. In R. M. Ryan (Ed.), *The Oxford handbook of motivation* (Chapter 21, pp. 365–380). New York: Oxford University Press.

Reeve, J., & Nix, G. (1997). Expressing intrinsic motivation through acts of exploration and facial displays of interest. *Motivation and Emotion, 21*, 237–250.

Reeve, J., & Tseng, M. (2011a). Agency as a fourth aspect of student engagement during learning activities. *Contemporary Educational Psychology, 36*, 257–267.

Reeve, J., & Tseng, C.-M. (2011b). Cortisol reactivity to a teacher's motivating style: The biology of being controlled versus supporting autonomy. *Motivation and Emotion, 35*, 63–74.

Reeve, J., Vansteenkiste, M., Assor, A., Ahmad, I., Cheon, S. H., Jang, H., Kaplan, H., Moss, J. D., Olaussen, B. S., & Wang, C. K. J. (2013). The beliefs that underlie autonomy-supportive and controlling teaching: A multinational investigation. *Motivation and Emotion, 38*, 93–110.

Reeve, J., Deci, E. L., & Ryan, R. M. (2004). Self-determination theory: A dialectical framework for understanding the sociocultural influences on student motivation. In D. M. McInerney & S. Van Etten (Eds.), *Research on sociocultural influences on motivation and learning: Big theories revisited* (Vol. *4*, pp. 31–59). Greenwhich, CT: Information Age.

Reeve, J., Jang, H., Hardre, P., & Omura, M. (2002). Providing a rationale in an autonomy-supportive way as a strategy to motivate others during an uninteresting activity. *Motivation and Emotion, 26*, 183–207.

Reeve, J., Nix, G., & Hamm, D. (2003). Testing models of the experience of self-determination in intrinsic motivation and the conundrum of choice. *Journal of Educational Psychology, 95*, 375–392.

Reeve, J., Olson, B. C., & Cole, S. G. (1985). Motivation and performance: Two consequences of winning and losing in competition. *Motivation and Emotion, 9*, 291–298.

Regan, D. T. (1971). Effects of a favor and liking on compliance. *Journal of Experimental Social Psychology, 7*, 627–639.

Regenbogen, C., Schneider, D. A., Finkelmeyer, A., Kohn, N., Derntl, B., Kellermann, T., Gur, R. E., Schneider, F., & Habel, U. (2012). The differential contribution of facial expressions, prosody, and speech content to empathy. *Cognition and Emotion, 26*, 995–1014.

Reifman, A. S., Larrick, R. P., & Fein, S. (1991). Temper and temperature on the diamond: The heat-aggression relationship in major league baseball. *Personality and Social Psychology Bulletin, 17*, 580–585.

Reis, H. T., Sheldon, K. M., Gable, S. L., Roscoe, R., & Ryan, R. M. (2000). Daily well-being: The role of autonomy, competence, and relatedness. *Personality and Social Psychology Bulletin, 26*, 419–435.

Reisenzein, R. (1994). Pleasure-arousal theory and the intensity of emotions. *Journal of Personality and Social Psychology, 67*, 525–539.

Reisenzein, R., & Hofman, T. (1993). Discriminating emotions from appraisal-relevant situational information: Baseline data for structural models of cognitive appraisals. *Cognition and Emotion, 7*, 271–293.

Reiss, I. L. (1986). A sociological journey into sexuality. *Journal of Marriage and the Family, 48*, 233–242.

Renninger, K. A., & Wozniak, R. H. (1985). Effect of interest on attentional shift, recognition, and recall in young children. *Developmental Psychology, 21*, 624–632.

Renninger, K. A., Hidi, S., & Krapp, A. (Eds.). (1992). *The role of interest in learning and development*. Hillsdale, NJ: Erlbaum.

Reynolds, P. C. (1982). Affect and instrumentality: An alternative view on Eibl-Eibesfeldt's human ethology. *Behavioral and Brain Science, 5*, 267–268.

Ricks, T. E. (1997). *Making the corps*. New York: Scribner.

Rigby, C. S., Deci, E. L., Patrick, B. P., & Ryan, R. M. (1992). Beyond the intrinsic-extrinsic dichotomy: Self-determination in motivation and learning. *Motivation and Emotion, 16*, 165–185.

Rimé, B. (2009). Emotion elicits the social sharing of emotion: Theory and empirical review. *Emotion Review, 1*, 60–85.

Rimé, B., Mesquita, B., Philippot, P., & Boca, S. (1991). Beyond the emotional event: Six studies on the social sharing of emotion. *Cognition and Emotion, 5*, 435–465.

Ritvo, L. B. (1990). *Darwin's influence on Freud: A tale of two sciences*. New Haven, CT: Yale University Press.

Roberts, G. C. (Ed.). (1992). *Motivation in sport and exercise*. Champaign, IL: Human Kinetics Books.

Robinson, D. T., & Smith-Lovin, L. (1992). Selective interaction as a strategy for identity maintenance: An affect control model. *Social Psychology Quarterly, 55*, 12–28.

Robinson, D. T., Smith-Lovin, L., & Tsoudis, O. (1994). Heinous crime or unfortunate accident?: The effects of remorse on responses to mock criminal confessions. *Social Forces, 73*, 175–190.

Robinson, T. E., & Kolb, B. (1997). Persistent structural modifications in nucleus accumbens and prefrontal cortex neurons produced by previous experience with amphetamine. *Journal of Neuroscience, 17*, 8491–8497.

Rodin, J. (1981). Current status of the external-internal hypothesis for obesity. *American Psychologist, 36*, 361–372.

Rodin, J. (1982). Obesity: Why the losing battle? In B. B. Wolman (Ed.), *Psychological aspects of obesity: A handbook* (pp. 30–87). New York: Van Nostrand Reinhold.

Rodin, J., & Langer, E. J. (1977). Long-term effects of a control-relevant intervention with the institutionalized aged. *Journal of Personality and Social Psychology, 35*, 897–902.

Rofé, Y. (1984). Stress and affiliation: A utility theory. *Psychological Review, 91*, 251–268.

Rogers, C. R. (1951). *Client-centered therapy: Its current practice, implications, and theory*. Boston: Houghton Mifflin.

Rogers, C. R. (1959). A theory of therapy, personality, and interpersonal relationships, as developed in the client-centered framework. In S. Koch (Ed.), *Psychology: A study of a science* (Vol. *3*, pp. 184–256). New York: McGraw-Hill.

Rogers, C. R. (1961). *On becoming a person*. Boston: Houghton Mifflin.

Rogers, C. R. (1963). Actualizing tendency in relation to motives and to consciousness. In M. R. Jones (Ed.), *Nebraska Symposium on Motivation* (Vol. *11*, pp. 1–24). Lincoln: University of Nebraska Press.

Rogers, C. R. (1964). Toward a modern approach to values: The valuing process in the mature person. *Journal of Abnormal and Social Psychology, 68*, 160–167.

Rogers, C. R. (1966). *A therapist's view of personal goals* [Brochure]. Wallingford, PA: Pendle Hill.

Rogers, C. R. (1969). *Freedom to learn: A view of what education might become*. Columbus, OH: Merrill.

Rogers, C. R. (1973). My philosophy of interpersonal relationships and how it grew. *Journal of Humanistic Psychology, 13*, 3–15.

Rogers, C. R. (1980). *A way of being*. Boston: Houghton Mifflin.

Rogers, C. R. (1982). Notes on Rollo May. *Journal of Humanistic Psychology, 22*, 8–9.

Rogers, C. R. (1995). What understanding and acceptance mean to me. *Journal of Humanistic Psychology, 35*, 7–22.

Rolls, B. J. (1979). How variety and palatability can stimulate appetite. *Nutrition Bulletin, 5*, 78–86.

Rolls, B. J., Bell, E. A., & Thorwart, M. L. (1999). Water incorporated into a food but not served with a food decreases energy intake in lean women. *American Journal of Clinical Nutrition, 70*, 448–455.

Rolls, B. J., Rowe, E. T., & Rolls, E. T. (1982). How sensory properties of food affect human feeding behavior. *Physiology and Behavior, 29*, 409–417.

Rolls, B. J., Wood, R. J., & Rolls, E. T. (1980). Thirst: The initiation, maintenance, and termination of drinking. In J. M. Sprague & A. N. Epstein (Eds.), *Progresses in psychobiology and physiological psychology* (Vol. *9*, pp. 263–321). New York: Academic Press.

Rolls, E. T. (1999). *The brain and emotion*. Oxford, UK: Oxford University Press.

Rolls, E. T., Sanghera, M. K., & Roper-Hall, A. (1979). Latency of activation of neurons in the lateral hypothalamus and substantia innominata during feeding in the monkey. *Brain Research, 164,* 121–135.

Roney, C., Higgins, E. T., & Shah, J. (1995). Goals and framing: How outcome focus influences motivation and emotion. *Personality and Social Psychology Bulletin, 21,* 1151–1160.

Ronis, D., & Greenwald, A. (1979). Dissonance theory revised again: Comment on the paper by Fazio, Zanna, and Cooper. *Journal of Experimental Social Psychology, 15,* 62–69.

Rose, S., & Frieze, I. H. (1989). Young singles scripts for a first date. *Gender and Society, 3,* 258–268.

Roseman, I. J. (1984). Cognitive determinants of emotion: A structural theory. In P. Shaver (Ed.), *Review of personality and social psychology: Emotions, relationships, and health* (Vol. 5, pp. 11–36). Beverly Hills, CA: Sage.

Roseman, I. J. (1991). Appraisal determinants of discrete emotions. *Cognition and Emotion, 5,* 161–200.

Roseman, I. J. (2011). Emotional behaviors, emotivational goals, emotion strategies: Multiple levels of organization integrate variable and consistent responses. *Emotion Review, 3,* 434–443.

Roseman, I. J. (2013). Appraisal in the emotion system: Coherence in strategies for coping. *Emotion Review, 5,* 141–149.

Roseman, I. J., & Evdokas, A. (2004). Appraisals cause experienced emotions: Experimental evidence. *Cognition and Emotion, 18,* 1–28.

Roseman, I. J., Antoniou, A. A., & Jose, P. E. (1996). Appraisal determinants of emotions: Constructing a more accurate and comprehensive theory. *Cognition and Emotion, 10,* 241–277.

Rosen, B., & D'Andrade, R. C. (1959). The psychological origins of achievement motivation. *Sociometry, 22,* 185–218.

Rosenberg, E. L. (1998). Levels of analysis and the organization of affect. *Review of General Psychology, 2,* 247–270.

Rosenberg, M. (1965). *Society and the adolescent self-image.* Princeton, NJ: Princeton University Press.

Rosenfeld, P., Giacalone, R. A., & Tedeschi, J. T. (1984). Cognitive dissonance and impression management explanations for effort justification. *Personality and Social Psychology Bulletin, 10,* 394–401.

Rosenhan, D. L., & Seligman, M. E. P. (1984). *Abnormal psychology.* New York: W. W. Norton.

Ross, M., & Shulman, R. (1973). Increasing the salience of initial attitudes: Dissonance versus self-perception theory. *Journal of Personality and Social Psychology, 28,* 138–144.

Roth, G., Assor, A., Niemiec, C. P., Ryan, R. M., & Deci, E. L. (2009). The emotional and academic consequences of parental conditional regard: Comparing conditional positive regard, conditional negative regard, and autonomy support as parenting practices. *Developmental Psychology, 45,* 1119–1142.

Rothkopf, E. Z., & Billington, M. J. (1979). Goal-guided learning from text: Inferring a descriptive processing model from inspection times and eye movements. *Journal of Educational Psychology, 71,* 310–327.

Roy, M., Shohamy, D., & Wager, T. D. (2012). Ventromedial prefrontal-subcortical systems and the generation of affective meaning. *Trends in Cognitive Science, 16,* 147–156.

Rozin, P. (1999). The process of moralization. *Psychological Science, 10,* 218–221.

Rozin, P., & Fallon, A. E. (1987). A perspective on disgust. *Psychological Review, 94,* 23–41.

Rozin, P., & Singh, L. (1999). The moralization of cigarette smoking in America. *Journal of Consumer Behavior, 8,* 321–337.

Rozin, P., Haidt, J., & Fincher, K. (2009). From oral to moral. *Science, 323,* 1179–1180.

Rozin, P., Haidt, J., & McCauley, C. R. (1993). Disgust. In M. Lewis & J. Haviland (Eds.), *Handbook of emotions* (pp. 575–594). New York: Guilford Press.

Rozin, P., Haidt, J., & McCauley, C. R. (2008). Disgust. In M. Lewis, J. M. Haviland-Jones, & L. F. Barrett (Eds.), *Handbook of emotions* (3rd ed., pp. 757–776). New York: Guilford Press.

Rozin, P., Lowery, L., & Ebert, R. (1994). Varieties of disgust faces and the structure of disgust. *Journal of Personality and Social Psychology, 66*, 870–881.

Rozin, P., Markwith, M., & Stoess, C. (1997). Moralization and becoming vegetarian: The transformation of preferences into values and the recruitment of disgust. *Psychological Science, 8*, 67–73.

Rozin, P., Millman, L., & Nemeroff, C. (1986). Operation of the laws of sympathetic magic in disgust and other domains. *Journal of Personality and Social Psychology, 50*, 703–712.

Ruckmick, C. A. (1936). The psychology of feeling and emotion. New York: McGraw-Hill.

Ruderman, A. J., & Wilson, G. T. (1979). Weight, restraint, cognitions, and counter-regulation. *Behaviour Therapy and Research, 17*, 581–590.

Rummel, A., & Feinberg, R. (1988). Cognitive evaluation theory: A meta-analytic review of the literature. *Social Behavior and Personality, 16*, 147–164.

Russek, M. (1971). Hepatic receptors and the neurophysiological mechanisms controlling feeding behavior. In S. Ehrenpreis (Ed.), *Neuroscience research*. New York: Academic Press.

Russell, J. A. (1994). Is there universal recognition of emotion from facial expression? A review of cross-cultural studies. *Psychological Bulletin, 115*, 102–141.

Russell, J. A. (2003). Core affect and the psychological construction of emotion. *Psychological Review, 110*, 145–172.

Russell, J. A., & Barrett, L. F. (1999). Core affect, prototypical emotional episodes, and other things call emotion: Dissecting the elephant. *Journal of Personality and Social Psychology, 76*, 805–819.

Russell, J. A., & Fehr, B. (1994). Fuzzy concepts in a fuzzy hierarchy: Varieties of anger. *Journal of Personality and Social Psychology, 67*, 186–205.

Russell, J. A., & Yik, M. S. M. (1996). Emotion among the Chinese. In M. H. Bond (Ed.), *The handbook of Chinese psychology* (pp. 166–188). Hong Kong: Oxford University Press.

Rutledge, L. L., & Hupka, R. B. (1985). The facial feedback hypothesis: Methodological concerns and new supporting evidence. *Motivation and Emotion, 9*, 219–240.

Ryan, E. D., & Lakie, W. L. (1965). Competitive and noncompetitive performance in relation to achievement motive and manifest anxiety. *Journal of Personality and Social Psychology, 1*, 342–345.

Ryan, R. M. (1982). Control and information in the intrapersonal sphere: An extension of cognitive evaluation theory. *Journal of Personality and Social Psychology, 43*, 450–461.

Ryan, R. M. (1991). The nature of the self in autonomy and relatedness. In J. Strauss & G. R. Goethals (Eds.), *The self: Interdisciplinary approaches* (pp. 208–238). New York: Springer-Verlag.

Ryan, R. M. (1993). Agency and organization: Intrinsic motivation, autonomy, and the self in psychological development. In J. E. Jacobs (Ed.), *Nebraska Symposium on Motivation: Developmental perspectives on motivation* (Vol. 40, pp. 1–56). Lincoln: University of Nebraska Press.

Ryan, R. M. (1995). Psychological needs and the facilitation of integrative processes. *Journal of Personality, 63*, 397–427.

Ryan, R. M. (2007). *Motivation and Emotion*: A new look and approach for two reemerging fields. *Motivation and Emotion, 31*, 1–3.

Ryan, R. M. (2013, June). *Closing remarks, questions and answers*. Keynote presentation at the 5th International Conference on Self-Determination Theory, Rochester, NY.

Ryan, R. M., & Connell, J. P. (1989). Perceived locus of causality and internalization: Examining reasons for acting in two domains. *Journal of Personality and Social Psychology, 57*, 749–761.

Ryan, R. M., & Deci, E. L. (2000a). Intrinsic and extrinsic motivations: Classic definitions and new directions. *Contemporary Educational Psychology, 25*, 54–67.

Ryan, R. M., & Deci, E. L. (2000b). Self-determination theory and the facilitation of intrinsic motivation, social development, and well-being. *American Psychologist, 55*, 68–78.

Ryan, R. M., & Deci, E. L. (2001). On happiness and human potentials: A review of research on hedonic and eudaimonic well-being. *Annual Review of Psychology, 52*, 141–166.

Ryan, R. M., & Deci, E. L. (2007). Active human nature: Self-determination theory and the promotion and maintenance of sport, exercise, and health. In M. S. Hagger & N. L. D. Chatzisarantis (Eds.), *Intrinsic motivation and self-determination in exercise and sport* (pp. 1–19). Champaign, IL: Human Kinetics.

Ryan, R. M., & Deci, E. L. (2008). Self-determination theory and the role of basic psychological needs in personality and the organization of behavior. In O. P. John, R. W. Robbins, & L. A. Pervin (Eds.), *Handbook of personality: Theory and research* (pp. 654–678). New York: The Guilford Press.

Ryan, R. M., & Frederick, C. M. (1997). On energy, personality, and health: Subjective vitality as a dynamic reflection of well-being. *Journal of Personality, 65*, 529–565.

Ryan, R. M., & Grolnick, W. S. (1986). Origins and pawns in the classroom: Self-report and projective assessments of individual differences in children's perceptions. *Journal of Personality and Social Psychology, 50*, 550–558.

Ryan, R. M., & Lynch, J. (1989). Emotional autonomy versus detachment: Revisiting the vicissitudes of adolescent and young adulthood. *Child Development, 60*, 340–356.

Ryan, R. M., & Powelson, C. L. (1991). Autonomy and relatedness as fundamental to motivation and education. *Journal of Experimental Education, 60*, 49–66.

Ryan, R. M., Avery, R. R., & Grolnick, W. S. (1985). A Rorschach assessment of children's mutuality of autonomy. *Journal of Personality Assessment, 49*, 6–12.

Ryan, R. M., Bernstein, J. H., & Brown, K. W. (2010). Weekends, work, and well-being: Psychological need satisfactions and day of the week effects on mood, vitality, and physical symptoms. *Journal of Social and Clinical Psychology, 29*, 95–122.

Ryan, R. M., Frederick, C. M., Lepes, D., Rubio, N., & Sheldon, K. M. (1997). Intrinsic motivation and exercise adherence. *International Journal of Sport Psychology, 28*, 335–354.

Ryan, R. M., Huta, V., & Deci, E. L. (2008). Living well: A self-determination theory perspective on eudaimonia. *Journal of Happiness Studies, 9*, 139–170.

Ryan, R. M., Koestner, R., & Deci, E. L. (1991). Ego-involved persistence: When free-choice behavior is not intrinsically motivated. *Motivation and Emotion, 15*, 185–205.

Ryan, R. M., Mims, V., & Koestner, R. (1983). Relation of reward contingency and interpersonal context to intrinsic motivation: A review and test using cognitive evaluation theory. *Journal of Personality and Social Psychology, 45*, 736–750.

Ryan, R. M., Patrick, H., Deci, E. L., & Williams, G. C. (2008). Facilitating health behaviour change and its maintenance: Interventions based on self-determination theory. *The European Health Psychologist, 10*, 2–5.

Ryan, R. M., Plant, R. W., & O'Malley, S. (1995). Initial motivations for alcohol treatment: Relations with patient characteristics, treatment involvement and dropout. *Addictive Behaviors, 20*, 586–596.

Ryan, R. M., Rigby, S., & King, K. (1993). Two types of religious internalization and their relations to religious orientations and mental health. *Journal of Personality and Social Psychology, 65*, 586–596.

Ryan, R. M., Stiller, J., & Lynch, J. H. (1994). Representations of relationships to teachers, parents, and friends as predictors of academic motivation and self-esteem. *Journal of Early Adolescence, 14*, 226–249.

Ryff, C. D. (1989). Happiness is everything, or is it?: Explorations on the meaning of psychological well-being. *Journal of Personality and Social Psychology, 57*, 1069–1081.

Ryff, C. D. (1991). Possible selves in adulthood and old age: A tale of shifting horizons. *Psychology and Aging, 6*, 286–295.

Ryff, C. D. (1995). Psychological well-being in adult life. *Current Directions in Psychological Science, 4*, 99–104.

Ryff, C. D., & Keyes, C. L. M. (1995). The structure of psychological well-being revisited. *Journal of Personality and Social Psychology, 69,* 719–727.

Ryff, C. D., & Singer, B. (2002). From social structure to biology: Integrative science in pursuit of human health and well-being. In C. R. Snyder & S. J. Lopez (Eds.), *Handbook of positive psychology* (pp. 541–555). New York: Oxford University Press.

Saarni, C. (1997). Coping with aversive feelings. *Motivation and Emotion, 21,* 45–63.

Sabatinelli, D., Bradley, M. M., Lang, P. J., Costa, V. D., & Versace, F. (2007). Pleasure rather than salience activates human nucleus accumbens and medial prefrontal cortex. *Journal of Neurophysiology, 98,* 1374–1379.

Sackeim, H. A. (1983). Self-deception, self-esteem, and depression: The adaptive value of lying to oneself. In J. Masling (Ed.), *Empirical studies of psychoanalytic theories* (Vol. *1,* pp. 101–157). Hillsdale, NJ: Analytic Press.

Sacks, C. H., & Bugental, D. B. (1987). Attributions as moderators of affective and behavioral responses to social failure. *Journal of Personality and Social Psychology, 53,* 939–947.

Sakurai, T., Amemiya, A., Ishii, M., Matsuzaki, I., Chemelli, R. M., Tanaka, H., et al. (1998). Orexins and orexin receptors: A family of hypothalamic neuropeptides and G protein-coupled receptors that regulate feeding behavior. *Cell, 92,* 573–585.

Salomon, G. (1984). Television is "easy" and print is "tough": The differential investment of mental effort in learning as a function of perceptions and attributions. *Journal of Educational Psychology, 76,* 647–658.

Sameroff, A. (Ed.) (2009). *The transactional model of development: How children and contexts shape each other.* Washington, DC: American Psychological Association.

Sansone, C. (1989). Competence feedback, task feedback, and intrinsic interest: The importance of context. *Journal of Experimental Social Psychology, 25,* 343–361.

Sansone, C., & Smith, J. L. (2000). Self-regulating interest: When, why, and how. In C. Sansone & J. M. Harackiewicz (Eds.), *Intrinsic motivation: Controversies and new directions* (pp. 343–373). New York: Academic Press.

Sansone, C., Weir, C., Harpster, L., & Morgan, C. (1992). Once a boring task always a boring task?: Interest as a self-regulatory mechanism. *Journal of Personality and Social Psychology, 63,* 379–390.

Sanz, J. (1996). Memory biases in social anxiety and depression. *Cognition and Emotion, 10,* 87–105.

Sarason, B. R., Pierce, G. R., Shearin, E. N., Sarason, I. G., Waltz, J. A., & Poppe, L. (1991). Perceived social support and working models of self and actual others. *Journal of Personality and Social Psychology, 60,* 273–287.

Schaal, B., & Gollwitzer, P. M. (1999). *Implementation intentions and resistance to temptation.* Unpublished manuscript, New York University.

Schachter, S. (1959). *The psychology of affiliation.* Stanford, CA: Stanford University Press.

Schachter, S. (1964). The interaction of cognitive and physiological determinants of emotion. In L. Berkowitz (Ed.), *Advances in experimental social psychology* (Vol. *1,* pp. 49–80). New York: Academic Press.

Schachter, S., & Singer, J. E. (1962). Cognitive, social, and physiological determinants of emotional states. *Psychological Review, 69,* 379–399.

Schafer, R. B., Wickram, K. A. S., & Keith, P. M. (1996). Self-concept disconfirmation, psychological distress, and marital happiness. *Journal of Marriage and the Family, 58,* 167–177.

Scharff, J. S., & Scharff, D. E. (1995). *The primer of object relations therapy.* Northvale, NJ: Jason Aronson.

Scheele, D., Striepens, N., Gunturkun, O., Deutschlander, S., Maier, W., Kendrick, K. M., & Hurlemann, R. (2012). Oxytocin modulates social distance between males and females. *Journal of Neuroscience, 32,* 16074–16079.

Scheier, M. F., & Carver, C. S. (1985). Optimism, coping, and health: Assessment and implications of generalized outcome expectations. *Health Psychology, 4*, 219–247.

Scheier, M. F., & Carver, C. S. (1988). A model of behavioral self-regulation: Translating intention into action. In L. Berkowitz (Ed.), *Advances in experimental social psychology* (Vol. *21*, pp. 303–346). New York: Academic Press.

Scheier, M. F., & Carver, C. S. (1992). Effects of optimism on psychological and physical well-being: Theoretical overview and empirical update. *Cognitive Therapy and Research, 16*, 201–228.

Scheier, M. F., & Carver, C. S. (1993). On the power of positive thinking: The benefits of being optimistic. *Current Directions in Psychological Science, 2*, 26–30.

Scherer, K. R. (1984b). On the nature and function of emotion: A component process approach. In K. Scherer & P. Ekman (Eds.), *Approaches to emotion* (pp. 293–318). Hillsdale, NJ: Erlbaum.

Scherer, K. R. (1986). Vocal affect expression: A review and a model for future research. *Psychological Bulletin, 99*, 143–165.

Scherer, K. R. (1993). Studying the emotion-antecedent appraisal process: An expert systems approach. *Cognition and Emotion, 7*, 325–355.

Scherer, K. R. (1994). Toward a concept of modal emotions. In P. Ekman & R. J. Davidson (Eds.), *The nature of emotion: Fundamental questions* (pp. 25–31). New York: Oxford University Press.

Scherer, K. R. (1997a). The role of culture in emotion-antecedent appraisal. *Journal of Personality and Social Psychology, 73*, 902–922.

Scherer, K. R. (1997b). Profiles of emotion-antecedent appraisal: Testing theoretical predictions across cultures. *Cognition and Emotion, 11*, 113–150.

Scherer, K. R. (2009). The dynamic architecture of emotion: Evidence for the component process model. *Cognition and Emotion, 23*, 1307–1351.

Scherer, K. R. (2011). The nature and dynamics of relevance and valence appraisals: Theoretical advances and recent evidence. *Emotion Review, 5*, 150–162.

Scherer, K. R., & Ekman, P. (1984). *Approaches to emotion*. Hillsdale, NJ: Erlbaum.

Scherer, K. R., & Tannenbaum, P. H. (1986). Emotional experience in everyday life. *Motivation and Emotion, 10*, 295–314.

Scherhorn, G., & Grunert, S. C. (1988). Using the causality orientations concept in consumer behavior research. *Journal of Consumer Psychology, 13*, 33–39.

Schiefele, U. (1991). Interest, learning, and motivation. *Educational Psychologist, 26*, 299–323.

Schmalt, H. D. (1982). Two concepts of fear of failure motivation. *Advances in Test Anxiety Research, 1*, 45–52.

Schmeichel, B. J., Demaree, H. A., Robinson, J. L., & Pu, J. (2006). Ego depletion by response exaggeration. *Journal of Experimental Social Psychology, 42*, 95–102.

Schmeichel, B. J., Vohs, K. D., & Baumeister, R. F. (2003). Intellectual performance and ego depletion: Role of the self in logical reasoning and other information processing. *Journal of Personality and Social Psychology, 85*, 33–46.

Schmitt, M. (1973). Influences of hepatic portal receptors on hypothalamic feeding and satiety centers. *American Journal of Physiology, 225*, 1089–1095.

Schraw, G., & Lehman, S. (2001). Situational interest: A review of the literature and directions for future research. *Educational Psychology Review, 13*, 23–52.

Schraw, G., Flowerday, T., & Reisetter, M. F. (1996). The role of choice in reader engagement. *Journal of Educational Psychology, 90*, 705–714.

Schroeder, S. (2007). We can do better—improving the health of the American people. *New England Journal of Medicine, 357*, 1221–1228.

Schulenberg, S. E., & Melton, A. M. A. (2010). A confirmatory factor-analytic evaluation of the Purpose in Life Test: Preliminary psychometric support for a replicable two-factor model. *Journal of Happiness Studies, 11*, 95–111.

Schuler, J., & Brunner, S. (2009). The rewarding effect of flow on performance in a marathon race. *Psychology of Sport and Exercise, 10*, 168–174.

Schultheiss, O. C. (2008). Implicit motives. In O. P. John, R. W. Robins, & L. A. Pervin (Eds.), *Handbook of personality: Theory and research* (3rd ed., pp. 603–633). New York: Guilford.

Schultheiss, O. C., & Brunstein, J. C. (Eds.) (2010). *Implicit motives.* New York: Oxford University Press.

Schultheiss, O. C., & Hale, J. A. (2007). Implicit motives modulate attentional orienting to perceived facial expressions of emotion. *Motivation and Emotion, 31*, 13–24.

Schultheiss, O. C., & Pang, J. S. (2007). Measuring implicit motives. In R. W. Robins, R. C. Fraley, & R. F. Krueger (Eds.), *Handbook of research methods in personality psychology* (pp. 322–344). New York: Guilford Press.

Schultheiss, O. C., Yankova, D., Dirlikov, B., & Schad, D. J. (2009). Are implicit and explicit motive measures statistically independent? A fair and balanced test using the Picture Story Exercise and a cue- and response-matched questionnaire measure. *Journal of Personality Assessment, 91*, 72–81.

Schultz, D. P., & Schultz, S. E. (2011). *A history of modern psychology* (9th ed.). Belmont, CA: Wadsworth.

Schultz, W. (2000). Multiple reward signals in the brain. *Nature Reviews: Neuroscience, 1*, 199–207.

Schultz, W., Tremblay, L., & Hollerman, J. R. (2000). Reward processing in primary orbitofrontal cortex and basal ganglia. *Cerebral Cortex, 10*, 272–283.

Schunk, D. H. (1989a). Self-efficacy and achievement behaviors. *Educational Psychology Review, 1*, 173–208.

Schunk, D. H. (1989b). Self-efficacy and cognitive skill learning. In C. A. Ames & R. Ames (Eds.), *Research on motivation in education: Goals and cognition* (Vol. *3*, pp. 13–44). San Diego, CA: Academic Press.

Schunk, D. H. (1991). Self-efficacy and academic motivation. *Educational Psychologist, 26*, 207–231.

Schunk, D. H. (1995). Self-efficacy and education and instruction. In J. E. Maddux (Ed.), *Self-efficacy, adaptation, and adjustment: Theory, research, and application* (pp. 281–303). New York: Plenum.

Schunk, D. H., & Cox, P. D. (1986). Strategy training and attributional feedback with learning disabled students. *Journal of Educational Psychology, 78*, 201–209.

Schunk, D. H., & Hanson, A. R. (1989). Self-modeling and children's cognitive skill learning. *Journal of Educational Psychology, 83*, 155–163.

Schunk, D. H., & Zimmerman, B. J. (1997). Social origins of self-regulatory competence. *Educational Psychologist, 32*, 195–208.

Schwartz, G. E. (1986). Emotion and psychophysiological organization: A systems approach. In M. G. H. Coles, E. Ponchin, & S. W. Proges (Eds.), *Psychophysiology: Systems, processes, and applications* (pp. 354–377). New York: Guilford Press.

Schwartz, M. W., & Seeley, R. J. (1997). Neuroendocrine responses to starvation and weight loss. *New England Journal of Medicine, 336*, 1802–1811.

Schwartz, M. W., Woods, S. C., Porte, D., Jr., Seeley, R. J., & Baskin, D. G. (2000). Central nervous system control of food intake. *Nature, 404*, 661–671.

Schwartz, N., & Clore, G. L. (1983). Mood, misattribution, and judgments of well-being: Informative and directive functions of affective states. *Journal of Personality and Social Psychology, 45*, 513–523.

Sclafani, A. (1980). Dietary obesity. In A. J. Stunkard (Ed.), *Obesity* (pp. 166–181).

Segal, E. M., & Lachman, R. (1972). Complex behavior or higher mental process: Is there a paradigm shift? *American Psychologist, 27*, 46–55.

Segraves, R. T. (Ed.) (2001). Historical and international context of nosology of female sexual disorders [Special issue]. *Journal of Sex and Martial Therapy, 27* (2).

Seligman, M. E. P. (1975). *Helplessness: On depression, development, and death.* San Francisco: W. H. Freeman.

Seligman, M. E. P. (1991). *Learned optimism.* New York: Alfred A. Knopf.

Seligman, M. E. P. (2002). *Authentic happiness.* New York: Free Press.

Seligman, M. E. P. (2011). *Flourish.* New York: Free Press.

Seligman, M. E. P., & Csikszentmihalyi, M. (2000). Positive psychology: An introduction. *American Psychologist, 55,* 5–14.

Seligman, M. E. P., & Maier, S. F. (1967). Failure to escape traumatic shock. *Journal of Experimental Psychology, 94,* 1–9.

Seligman, M. E. P., & Schulman, P. (1986). Explanatory style as a predictor of productivity and quitting among life insurance agents. *Journal of Personality and Social Psychology, 50,* 832–838.

Seligman, M. E. P., Reivich, K., Jaycox, L., & Gillham, J. (1995). *The optimistic child.* New York: Houghton Mifflin.

Seligman, M. E. P., Steen, T. A., Park, N., & Peterson, C. (2005). Positive psychology progress: Empirical validation of interventions. *American Psychologist, 60,* 410–421.

Semin, J. R., & Manstead, A. S. R. (1982). The social implications of embarrassment displays and restitution. *European Journal of Social Psychology, 12,* 367–377.

Sepple, C. P., & Read, N. W. (1989). Gastrointestinal correlates of the development of hunger in man. *Appetite, 13,* 183–191.

Shaffer, D. (1977). Suicide in childhood and early adolescence. *Journal of Child Psychology and Psychiatry, 45,* 406–451.

Shah, J. Y., Friedman, R., & Kruglanski, A. W. (2002). Forgetting all else: On the antecedents and consequences of goal shielding. *Journal of Personality and Social Psychology, 83,* 1261–1280.

Shaikh, A. R., Vinokur, A. D., Yaroch, A. L., Williams, G. C., & Resnicow, K. (2011). Direct and mediated effects of two theoretically based interventions to increase consumption of fruits and vegetables in the healthy body healthy spirit trial. *Health Education & Behavior, 38,* 492–501.

Shamay-Tsoory, S., Aharon-Peretz, J., & Perry, D. (2009). Two systems for empathy: A double dissociation between emotional and cognitive empathy in inferior frontal gyrus versus ventromedial prefrontal lesions. *Brain, 132,* 617–627.

Shapira, Z. (1976). Expectancy determinants of intrinsically motivated behavior. *Journal of Personality and Social Psychology, 34,* 1235–1244.

Shapiro, D. H., Schwartz, C. E., & Astin, J. A. (1996). Controlling ourselves, controlling our world: Psychology's role in understanding positive and negative consequences of seeking and gaining control. *American Psychologist, 51,* 1213–1230.

Shaver, P., & Hazan, C. (1987). Being lonely, falling in love: Perspectives from attachment theory. *Journal of Social Behavior and Personality, 2,* 105–124.

Shaver, P., Schwartz, J., Kirson, D., & O'Connor, C. (1987). Emotion knowledge: Further exploration of a prototype approach. *Journal of Personality and Social Psychology, 52,* 1061–1086.

Sheffield, F. D., & Roby, T. B. (1950). Reward value of a non-nutritive sweet taste. *Journal of Comparative and Physiological Psychology, 43,* 471–481.

Sheldon, K. M. (2001). The self-concordance model of healthy goal striving: When personal goals correctly represent the person. In P. Schmuck & K. M. Sheldon (Eds.), *Life goals and well-being: Towards a positive psychology of human striving* (pp. 18–36). Seattle, WA: Hogrefe & Huber.

Sheldon, K. M. (2002). The self-concordance model of healthy goal striving: When personal goals correctly represent the person. In E. L. Deci & R. M. Ryan (Eds.), *Handbook of self-determination* (pp. 65–86). Rochester, NY: University of Rochester Press.

Sheldon, K. M. (2011). Integrating behavioral-motive and experiential requirement perspectives on psychological needs: A two process model. *Psychological Review, 118,* 552–569.

Sheldon, K. M., & Houser-Marko, L. (2001). Self-concordance, goal attainment, and the pursuit of happiness: Can there be an upward spiral? *Journal of Personality and Social Psychology, 80,* 152–165.

Sheldon, K. M., & Kasser, T. (1995). Coherence and congruence: Two aspects of personality integration. *Journal of Personality and Social Psychology, 68,* 531–543.

Sheldon, K. M., & Kasser, T. (1998). Pursuing personal goals: Skills enable progress but not all progress is beneficial. *Personality and Social Psychology Bulletin, 24,* 1319–1331.

Sheldon, K. M., & Niemiec, C. P. (2006). It's not just the amount that counts: Balanced need satisfaction also affects well-being. *Journal of Personality and Social Psychology, 91,* 331–341.

Sheldon, K. M., & Schuler, J. (2011). Wanting, having, and needing: Integrating motive disposition theory and self-determination theory. *Journal of Personality and Social Psychology, 101,* 1106–1123.

Sheldon, K. M., Abad, N., & Hinsch, C. (2011). A two-process view of Facebook use and relatedness need-satisfaction: Disconnection drives use, and connection rewards it. *Psychology of Popular Media Culture, 1,* 2–15.

Sheldon, K. M., Arndt, J., & Houser-Marko, L. I (2003). In search of the organismic valuing process: The human tendency to move towards beneficial goal choices. *Journal of Personality, 71,* 835–869.

Sheldon, K. M., Ryan, R. M., & Reis, H. T. (1996). What makes for a good day?: Competence and autonomy in the day and in the person. *Personality and Social Psychology Bulletin, 22,* 1270–1279.

Sheldon, K., M., & Elliot, A. J. (1998). Not all personal goals are personal: Comparing autonomous and controlled reasons as predictors of effort and attainment. *Personality and Social Psychological Bulletin, 24,* 546–557.

Sheldon, K., M. , & Elliot, A. J. (1999). Goal striving, need-satisfaction, and longitudinal wellbeing: The self-concordance model. *Journal of Personality and Social Psychology, 76,* 482–497.

Sheldon, K., M. , Elliot, A. J., Kim, Y., & Kasser, T. (2001). What is satisfying about satisfying events?: Testing 10 candidate psychological needs. *Journal of Personality and Social Psychology, 80,* 325–339.

Shell, D. F., Colvin, C., & Bruning, R. H. (1995). Self-efficacy, attribution, and outcome expectancy mechanisms in reading and writing achievement: Grade-level and achievement-level differences. *Journal of Educational Psychology, 87,* 386–398.

Shen, B., Wingert, R. K., Li, W., Sun, H., & Rukavina, P. B. (2010). An amotivation model in physical education. *Journal of Teaching in Physical Education, 29,* 72–84.

Shiota, M. N., Campos, B., Gonzaga, G. C., Keltner, D., & Peng, K. (2010). I love you but … : Cultural differences in emotional complexity during interaction with a romantic partner. *Cognition and Emotion, 24,* 786–799.

Shiota, M. N., Neufeld, S. L., Yeung, W. H., Moser, S. E., & Perea, E. F. (2011). Feeling good: Autonomic nervous system responding in five positive emotions. *Emotion, 11,* 1368–1378.

Shipley, T. E., Jr., & Veroff, J. (1952). A projective measure of need for affiliation. *Journal of Experimental Psychology, 43,* 349–356.

Shirey, L. L., & Reynolds, R. E. (1988). Effect of interest on attention and learning. *Journal of Educational Psychology, 80,* 159–166.

Shmueli, D., & Prochaska, J. J. (2009). Resisting tempting foods and smoking behavior: Implications from a self-control theory perspective. *Health Psychology, 28,* 300–306.

Shostrom, E. L. (1964). An inventory for the measurement of self-actualization. *Educational and Psychological Measurement, 24,* 207–218.

Shostrom, E. L. (1974). *Manual for the Personal Orientation Inventory.* San Diego, CA: EDITS.

Sid, A. K. W., & Lindgren, H. C. (1981). Sex differences in achievement and affiliation motivation among undergraduates majoring in different academic fields. *Psychological Reports, 48,* 539–542.

Silva, M. N., Markland, D. A., Carraca, E. V., Vieira, P. N., Coutinho, S. R., Minderico, C. S., Matos, M. G., Sardinha, L. B., & Teixeira, P. J. (2011). Exercise autonomous motivation predicts 3-yr weight loss in women. *Medicine and Science in Sports and Exercise, 43,* 728–737.

Silverman, L. H. (1976). Psychoanalytic theory: The reports of my death are greatly exaggerated. *American Psychologist, 31,* 621–637.

Silvia, P. J. (2005). What is interesting? Exploring the appraisal structure of interest. *Emotion, 5,* 89–102.

Silvia, P. J. (2006). *Exploring the psychology of interest.* New York: Oxford University Press.

Silvia, P. J. (2008). Interest-The curious emotion. *Current Directions in Psychological Science, 17,* 57.

Simon, L., Greenberg, J., & Brehm, J. (1995). Trivialization: The forgotten mode of dissonance reduction. *Journal of Personality and Social Psychology, 68,* 247–260.

Simon, W., & Gagnon, J. H. (1986). Sexual scripts: Permanence and change. *Archives of Sexual Behavior, 15,* 97–120.

Simon-Thomas, E. R., Godzik, J., Castle, E., Antonenko, O., Ponz, A., Kogan, A., & Keltner, D. (2012). An *f*MRI study of caring vs. self-focus during induced compassion and pride. *Social Cognitive and Affective Neuroscience, 7,* 635–648.

Sinaceur, M., & Tiedens, L. Z. (2006). Get mad and get more than even: When and why anger expression is effective in negotiations. *Journal of Experimental Social Psychology, 42,* 314–322.

Singer, T., Critchley, H. D., & Preuschoff, K. (2009). A common role of insula in feelings, empathy, and uncertainty. *Trends in Cognitive Science, 13,* 334–340.

Singh, D. (1993a). Adaptive significance of female physical attractiveness: Role of waist-to-hip ratio. *Journal of Personality and Social Psychology, 65,* 293–307.

Singh, D. (1993b). Body shape and women's attractiveness: The critical role of waist-to-hip ratio. *Human Nature, 4,* 297–321.

Singh, D. (1995). Female judgment of male attractiveness and desirability for relationships: Role of waist-to-hip ratio and financial status. *Journal of Personality and Social Psychology, 69,* 1089–1101.

Sinha, R., & Parsons, O. A. (1996). Multivariate response patterning of fear and anger. *Cognition and Emotion, 10,* 173–198.

Skinner, B. F. (1938). *The behavior of organisms.* New York: Appleton-Century-Crofts.

Skinner, B. F. (1953). *Science and human behavior.* New York: Macmillan.

Skinner, B. F. (1986). What is wrong with daily life in the Western world? *American Psychologist, 41,* 568–574.

Skinner, E. A. (1991). Development and perceived control: A dynamic model of action in context. In M. Gunnar & L. A. Sroufe (Eds.), *Minnesota Symposium on Child Psychology* (Vol. 23). Hillsdale, NJ: Erlbaum.

Skinner, E. A. (1995). *Perceived control, motivation, and coping.* Newbury Park, CA: Sage.

Skinner, E. A. (1996). A guide to constructs of control. *Journal of Personality and Social Psychology, 71,* 549–570.

Skinner, E. A., & Belmont, M. J. (1993). Motivation in the classroom: Reciprocal effects of teacher behavior and student engagement across the school year. *Journal of Educational Psychology, 85,* 571–581.

Skinner, E. A., Edge, K., Altman, J., & Sherwood, H. (2003). Searching for the structure of coping: A review and critique of category systems for classifying ways of coping. *Psychological Bulletin, 129,* 216–269.

Skinner, E. A., Kindermann, T. A., Connell, J. P., & Wellborn, J. G. (2009). Engagement and disaffection as organizational constructs in the dynamics of motivational development. In K. Wentzel & A. Wigfield (Eds.), *Handbook of motivation at school* (pp. 223–245). Mahwah, NJ: Erlbaum.

Skinner, E. A., Zimmer-Gembeck, M. J., & Connell, J. P. (1998). Individual differences and the development of perceived control. *Monographs of the Society for Research in Child Development, 63* (Serial no. 254).

Skinner, E., A., & Pitzer, J. R. (2012). Developmental dynamics of student engagement, coping, and everyday resilience. In S. L. Christenson, A. Reschly, & C. Wylie (Eds.), *Handbook of research on student engagement* (Chapter 2, pp. 21–44). New York: Springer.

Skinner, E., Kindermann, T. A., Connell, J. P., & Wellborn, J. G. (2009). Engagement as an organizational construct in the dynamics of motivational development. In K. Wentzel & A. Wigfield (Eds.), *Handbook of motivation at school* (pp. 223–245). Mahwah, NJ: Lawrence Erlbaum.

Slade, L. A., & Rush, M. C. (1991). Achievement motivation and the dynamics of task difficulty choices. *Journal of Personality and Social Psychology, 60*, 165–172.

Smith, A. C., III, & Kleinman, S. (1989). Managing emotions in medical school: Students' contacts with the living and the dead. *Social Psychology Quarterly, 52*, 56–69.

Smith, C. A., & Ellsworth, P. C. (1985). Patterns of cognitive appraisal in emotion. *Journal of Personality and Social Psychology, 48*, 813–838.

Smith, C. P. (2000). Content analysis and narrative analysis. In H. T. Reis & C. M. Judd (Eds.), *Handbook of research methods in social and personality psychology* (pp. 313–335). New York: Cambridge University Press.

Smith, C. P. (Ed.) (1992). *Motivation and personality: Handbook of thematic content analysis*. New York: Cambridge University Press.

Smith, K. S., Tindell, A. J., Aldridge, J. W., & Berridge, K. C. (2009). Ventral pallidum roles in reward and motivation. *Brain Research, 196* (2), 155–167.

Smith, K., Locke, E., & Barry, D. (1990). Goal setting, planning and organizational performance: An experimental simulation. *Organizational Behavior and Human Decision Processes, 46*, 118–134.

Smith, R. G., Iwata, B. A., & Shore, B. A. (1995). Effects of subject-versus experimenter-selected reinforcers on the behavior of individuals with profound developmental disabilities. *Journal of Applied Behavior Analysis, 28*, 61–71.

Smith, R. H., & Kim, S. H. (2007). Comprehending envy. *Psychological Bulletin, 133*, 46–64.

Smith, R. H., Turner, T. J., Garonzik, R., Leach, C. W., Urch-Druskat, V., & Weston, C. M. (1996). Envy and schadenfreude. *Personality and Social Psychology Bulletin, 22*, 158–168.

Snyder, C. R. (1994). *The psychology of hope: You can get there from here*. New York: Free Press.

Snyder, C. R. (2002). Hope theory: Rainbows in the mind. *Psychological Inquiry, 13*, 249–275.

Snyder, C. R., & Lopez, S. J. (Eds.) (2002). *Handbook of positive psychology*. New York: Oxford University Press.

Snyder, C. R., Harris, C., Anderson, J. R., Holleran, S. A., Irving, L. M., Sigmond, S. T. et al. (1991). The will and the ways: Development and validation of an individual-differences measure of hope. *Journal of Personality and Social Psychology, 60*, 570–585.

Snyder, C. R., Lapointe, A. B., Crowson, J. J., Jr., & Early, S. (1998). Preferences of high-and low-hope people for self-referential input. *Cognition and Emotion, 12*, 807–823.

Snyder, C. R., Rand, K. L., & Sigmon, D. R. (2002). Hope theory: A member of the positive psychology family. In C. R. Snyder & S. J. Lopez (Eds.), *Handbook of positive psychology* (pp. 257–276). New York: Oxford University Press.

Snyder, C. R., Shorey, H. S., Cheavens, J., Pulvers, K. M., Adams, V. H. III, & Wiklund, C. (2002). Hope and academic success in college. *Journal of Educational Psychology, 94*, 820–826.

Snyder, M., & Ebbesen, E. B. (1972). Dissonance awareness: A test of dissonance theory versus self-perception theory. *Journal of Experimental Social Psychology, 8*, 502–517.

Sobal, J., & Stunkard, A. J. (1989). Socioeconomic status and obesity: A review of the literature. *Psychological Bulletin, 105,* 260–275.

Soenens, B., Vansteenkiste, M., Duriez, B., Luyten, P., & Goossens, L. (2005). Maladaptive perfectionistic self-representations: The mediational link between psychological control and adjustment. *Personality and Individual Differences, 38,* 487–498.

Solomon, R .C. (1990). *A passion for justice.* New York: Addison-Wesley.

Solomon, R. L. (1980). The opponent-process theory of motivation: The costs of pleasure and the benefits of pain. *American Psychologist, 35,* 691–712.

Solomon, S., Greenberg, J., & Pyszczynski, T. (1991). A terror management theory of social behavior: The psychological functions of self-esteem and cultural worldviews. In M. P. Zanna (Ed.), *Advances in experimental social psychology* (Vol. *24,* pp. 93–159). San Diego, CA: Academic Press.

Somerville, L. H., Hare, T., & Casey, B. J. (2010). Frontostriatal maturation predicts cognitive-control failure to appetitive cues in adolescents. *Journal of Cognitive Neuroscience, 23,* 2123–2134.

Sorrentino, R. M. (2013). Looking for B = f(P, E): The exception still forms the rule. *Motivation and Emotion, 37,* 4–13.

Sorrentino, R. M., & Higgins, E. T. (1986). Motivation and cognition. In R. M. Sorrentino & E. T. Higgins (Eds.), *Handbook of motivation and cognition: Foundations of social behavior* (pp. 3–19). New York: Guilford Press.

Soussignan, R. (2002). Duchenne smile, emotional experience, and autonomic reactivity: A test of the facial feedback hypothesis. *Emotion, 2,* 52–74.

Spangler, W. D., & House, R. J. (1991). Presidential effectiveness and the leadership motive profile. *Journal of Personality and Social Psychology, 60,* 439–455.

Spasojevic, J., & Alloy, L. B. (2001). Rumination as a common mechanism relating depressive risk factors to depression. *Emotion, 1,* 25–37.

Spence, J. T., & Helmreich, R. L. (1983). Achievement-related motives and behavior. In J. T. Spence (Ed.), *Achievement and achievement motives: Psychological and sociological approaches* (pp. 10–74). San Francisco: W. H. Freeman.

Spencer, J. A., & Fremouw, W. J. (1979). Binge eating as a function of restrained and weight classification. *Journal of Abnormal Psychology, 88,* 262–267.

Spiegelman, B. M., & Flier, J. F. (2001). Obesity and the regulation of energy balance. *Cell, 104,* 531–543.

Spitzer, L., & Rodin, J. (1981). Human eating behavior: A critical review of studies in normal weight and overweight individuals. *Appetite, 2,* 293–329.

Sprecher, S., Sullivan, Q., & Hatfield, E. (1994). Mate selection preferences: Gender differences examined in a national sample. *Journal of Personality and Social Psychology, 66,* 1074–1080.

Squire, S. (1983). *The slender balance.* New York: Pinnacle.

Staats, H., van Leeuwen, E., & Wit, A. (2000). A longitudinal study of informational interventions to save energy in an office building. *Journal of Applied Behavior Analysis, 33,* 101–104.

Stacey, C. L., & DeMartino, M. F. (Eds.). (1958). *Understanding human motivation.* Cleveland, OH: Howard Allen.

Stansbury, K., & Gunnar, M. R. (1994). Adrenocortical activity and emotion regulation. *Monographs of the Society for Research in Child Development, 52,* 318–327.

Staub, E. (1999). The roots of evil: Social conditions, culture, personality, and basic human needs. *Personality and Social Psychology Review, 3,* 179–192.

Steele, C. M. (1988). The psychology of self-affirmation: Sustaining the integrity of the self. In L. Berkowitz (Ed.), *Advances in experimental social psychology* (Vol. *20,* pp. 261–302). New York: Academic Press.

Steele, C. M., & Aronson, J. (1995). Stereotype threat and the intellectual test performance of African Americans. *Journal of Personality and Social Psychology, 69,* 797–811.

Steele, C. M., & Josephs, R. A. (1990). Alcohol myopia: Its prized and dangerous effects. *American Psychologist, 45*, 921–933.

Steele, R. S. (1977). Power motivation, activation, and inspirational speeches. *Journal of Personality, 45*, 53–64.

Steger, M. F. (2009). Meaning in life. In S. J. Lopez & C. R. Snyder (Eds.), *Oxford handbook of positive psychology* (2nd ed., pp. 679–687). Oxford, UK: Oxford University Press.

Stein, M., K., & Wang, M. C. (1988). Teacher development and school improvement: The process of teacher change. *Teaching and Teacher Education, 4*, 171–187.

Stein, N. L., & Trabasso, T. (1992). The organisation of emotional experience: Creating links among emotion, thinking, language and intentional action. *Cognition and Emotion, 6*, 225–244.

Stemmler, G. (1989). The autonomic differentiation of emotions revisited: Convergent and discriminant validity. *Psychophysiology, 26*, 617–632.

Stephens, A. N., & Groeger, J. A. (2011). Anger-congruent behaviour transfers across driving situations. *Cognition and Emotion, 25*, 1423–1438.

Stern, J. S., & Lowney, P. (1986). Obesity: The role of physical activity. In K. D. Brownell & J. P. Foreyt (Eds.), *Handbook of eating disorders: Physiology, psychology, and treatment of obesity, anorexia, and bulimia* (pp. 145–158). New York: Basic Books.

Stets, J. E., & Turner, J. H. (2008). The sociology of emotions. In M. Lewis, J. M. Haviland-Jones, & L. F. Barrett (Eds.), *Handbook of emotions* (3rd ed., pp. 32–46). New York: Guilford Press.

Stevens, J., Cai, J., Pamuk, E. R., Williamson, D. F., Thun, M. J., & Wood, J. L. (1998). The effect of age on the association between body-mass index and mortality. *New England Journal of Medicine, 338*, 1–7.

Stevenson, J. A. F. (1969). Neural control of food and water intake. In W. Haymaker, E. Anderson, & W. J. H. Nauta (Eds.), *The hypothalamus.* Springfield, IL: Thomas.

Stewart, A. J. (1992). Self-definition and social definition: Personal styles reflected in narrative style. In C. P. Smith (Ed.), *Motivation and personality: Handbook of thematic content analysis.* New York: Cambridge University Press.

Stewart, A. J., & Rubin, Z. (1976). Power motivation in the dating couple. *Journal of Personality and Social Psychology, 34*, 305–309.

Stewart, A. J., & Winter, D. G. (1974). Self-definition and social definition in women. *Journal of Personality, 42*, 238–259.

Stipek, D. J. (1983). A developmental analysis of pride and shame. *Human Development, 26*, 42–56.

Stipek, D. J. (1984). Young children's performance expectations: Logical analysis or wishful thinking? In J. G. Nicholls (Ed.), *The development of achievement motivation* (pp. 33–56). Greenwich, CT: JAI Press.

Stipek, D. J. (1999). Differences between Americans and Chinese in the circumstances evoking pride, shame, and guilt. *Journal of Cross-Cultural Psychology, 29*, 616–629.

Stipek, D. J., & Gralinski, H. (1996). Children's beliefs about intelligence and school performance. *Journal of Educational Psychology, 88*, 397–407.

Stipek, D. J., & Kowalski, P. S. (1989). Learned helplessness in task-orienting versus performance-orienting testing conditions. *Journal of Educational Psychology, 81*, 384–391.

Strack, F., & Coyne, J. C. (1983). Shared and private reaction to depression. *Journal of Personality and Social Psychology, 44*, 798–806.

Strack, F., Martin, L. L., & Stepper, S. (1988). Inhibiting and facilitating conditions of the human smile: Unobtrusive test of the facial feedback hypothesis. *Journal of Personality and Social Psychology, 54*, 768–777.

Strang, H. R., Lawrence, E. C., & Fowler, P. C. (1978). Effects of assigned goal level and knowledge of results on arithmetic computation: A laboratory study. *Journal of Applied Psychology, 63*, 446–450.

Straub, W. F., & Williams, J. M. (Eds.). (1984). *Cognitive sport psychology*. Lansing, NY: Sport Science Associates.

Strauman, T. (1992). Self-guides, autobiographical memory, and anxiety and dysphoria: Toward a cognitive model of vulnerability to emotional distress. *Journal of Abnormal Psychology, 101,* 87–95.

Strayer, J. (1993). Children's concordant emotions and cognitions in response to observed emotions. *Child Development, 64,* 188–201.

Stroud, L. R., Salovey, P., & Epel, E. S. (2002). Sex differences in stress responses: Social rejection versus achievement stress. *Biological Psychiatry, 52,* 318–327.

Stucke, T. S., & Baumeister, R. F. (2006). Ego depletion and aggressive behavior: Is the inhibition of aggression a limited resource? *European Journal of Social Psychology, 36,* 1–13.

Stunkard, A. J. (1988). Some perspectives on human obesity: Its causes. *Bulletin of New York Academy of Medicine, 64,* 902–923.

Su, Y., & Reeve, J. (2011). A meta-analysis of the effectiveness of intervention programs designed to support autonomy. *Educational Psychology Review, 23,* 159–188.

Sullivan, H. S. (1953). *The interpersonal theory of psychiatry.* New York: W.W. Norton.

Susman, E. J. (2006). Psychobiology of persistent antisocial behavior: Stress, early vulnerabilities, and the attenuation hypothesis. *Neuroscience and Biobehavioral Reviews, 30,* 376–389.

Sutherland, S. (1993). Impoverished minds. *Nature, 364,* 767.

Sutton, S. K., & Davidson, R. J. (1997). Prefrontal brain asymmetry: A biological substrate of the behavioral approach and inhibition systems. *Psychological Science, 8,* 204–210.

Swann, W. B., Jr. (1983). Self-verification: Bringing social reality into harmony with self. In J. Suls & A. Greenwald (Eds.), *Psychological perspectives on the self* (Vol. 2, pp. 33–66). Hillsdale, NJ: Erlbaum.

Swann, W. B., Jr. (1985). The self as architect of social reality. In B. Schlenker (Ed.), *The self and social life* (pp. 100–125). New York: McGraw-Hill.

Swann, W. B., Jr. (1987). Identity negotiation: Where two roads meet. *Journal of Personality and Social Psychology, 53,* 1038–1051.

Swann, W. B., Jr. (1992b). Why people self-verify. *Journal of Personality and Social Psychology, 62,* 392–401.

Swann, W. B., Jr. (1996). *Self-traps: The elusive quest for higher self-esteem.* New York: Freeman.

Swann, W. B., Jr. (1997). The trouble with change: Self-verification and allegiance to the self. *Psychological Science, 8,* 177–180.

Swann, W. B., Jr. (1999). *Resilient identities: Self, relationships, and the construction of social reality.* New York: Basic Books.

Swann, W. B., Jr., & Ely, R. J. (1984). A battle of wills: Self-verification versus behavioral confirmation. *Journal of Personality and Social Psychology, 46,* 1287–1302.

Swann, W. B., Jr., & Hill, C. A. (1982). When our identities are mistaken: Reaffirming self-conceptions through social interactions. *Journal of Personality and Social Psychology, 43,* 59–66.

Swann, W. B., Jr., & Pelham, B. W. (2002). The truth about illusions: Authenticity and positivity in social relationships. In C. R. Snyder & S. J. Lopez (Eds.), *Handbook of positive psychology* (pp. 366–381). New York: Oxford University Press.

Swann, W. B., Jr., & Pittman, T. S. (1977). Initiating play activity in children: The moderating influence of verbal cues on intrinsic motivation. *Child Development, 48,* 1125–1132.

Swann, W. B., Jr., & Predmore, S. C. (1985). Intimates as agents of social support: Sources of consolation or despair? *Journal of Personality and Social Psychology, 49,* 1609–1617.

Swann, W. B., Jr., Pelham, B. W., & Chidester, T. (1988). Change through paradox: Using self-verification to alter beliefs. *Journal of Personality and Social Psychology, 54,* 268–273.

Swann, W. B., Jr., Pelham, B. W., & Krull, D. S. (1989). Agreeable fancy or disagreeable truth: Reconciling self-enhancement and self-verification. *Journal of Personality and Social Psychology*, *57*, 782–791.

Swann, W. B., Jr., Stein-Seroussi, A., & Giesler, B. (1992). Why people self-verify. *Journal of Personality and Social Psychology*, *62*, 392–401.

Symons, D. (1992). What do men want? *Behavioral and Brain Sciences*, *15*, 113.

Szpunar, K. K., Watson, J. M., & McDermott, K. B. (2007). Neural substrates of envisioning the future. *Proceedings of the National Academy of Science U.S.A., 104*, 642–647.

Tafrate, R. C., Kassinove, H., & Dundin, L. (2002). Anger episodes in high-and low-trait anger community adults. *Journal of Clinical Psychology*, *58*, 1573–1590.

Tangney, J. P. (1991). Moral affect: The good, the bad, and the ugly. *Journal of Personality and Social Psychology*, *61*, 598–607.

Tangney, J. P. (1999). The self-conscious emotions: Shame, guilt, embarrassment and pride. In T. Dalgleish & M. J. Power (Eds.), *Handbook of cognition and emotion* (pp. 541–568). Chichester, England: John Wiley & Sons.

Tangney, J. P., & Dearing, R. L. (2002). *Shame and guilt*. New York: Guilford Press.

Tangney, J. P., Baumeister, R. F., & Boone, A. L. (2004). High self-control predicts good adjustment, less pathology, better grades, and interpersonal success. *Journal of Personality*, *72*, 271–322.

Tangney, J. P., Miller, R. S., Flicker, L., & Barlow, D. H. (1996). Are shame, guilt, and embarrassment distinct emotions? *Journal of Personality and Social Psychology*, *70*, 1256–1269.

Taubes, G. (1998). Obesity rates rise, experts struggle to explain why. *Science*, *280*, 1367–1368.

Tauer, J. M., & Harackiewicz, J. M. (1999). Winning isn't everything: Competition, achievement orientation, and intrinsic motivation. *Journal of Experimental Social Psychology*, *35*, 209–238.

Tavris, C. (1989). *Anger: The misunderstood emotion*. New York: Simon & Schuster.

Taylor, C. B., Bandura, A., Ewart, C. K., Miller, N. H., & DeBusk, B. F. (1985). Exercise testing to enhance wives' confidence in their husbands' cardiac capabilities soon after clinically uncomplicated acute myocardial infarction. *American Journal of Cardiology*, *55*, 635–638.

Taylor, I. M. & Ntoumanis, N. (2007). Teacher motivational strategies and student self-determination in physical education. *Journal of Educational Psychology*, *99*, 747–760.

Taylor, S. E. (1983). Adjustment to threatening events: A theory of cognitive adaptation. *American Psychologist*, *38*, 1161–1173.

Taylor, S. E. (1989). *Positive illusions: Creative self-deception and the healthy mind*. New York: Basic Books.

Taylor, S. E., & Brown, J. D. (1988). Illusion and well-being: A social psychological perspective on mental health. *Psychological Bulletin*, *103*, 193–210.

Taylor, S. E., & Brown, J. D. (1994). Positive illusions and well-being revisited: Separating fact from fiction. *Psychological Bulletin*, *116*, 21–27.

Taylor, S. E., Collins, R. L., Skokan, L. A., & Aspinwall, L. G. (1989). Maintaining positive illusions in the face of negative information: Getting the facts without letting them get to you. *Journal of Social and Clinical Psychology*, *8*, 114–129.

Taylor, S. E., Pham, L. B., Rivkin, I. D., & Armor, D. A. (1998). Harnessing the imagination: Mental simulation, self-regulation, and coping. *American Psychologist*, *53*, 429–439.

Taylor, S. E., Seeman, T. E., Eisenberger, N. I., Kozanian, T. A., Moore, A. N., & Moons, W. G. (2010). Effects of a supportive or an unsupportive audience on biological and psychological response to stress. *Journal of Personality and Social Psychology*, *98*, 47–56.

Teasdale, J. D., & Fogarty, S. J. (1979). Differential effects of induced mood on retrieval of pleasant and unpleasant events from episodic memory. *Journal of Abnormal Psychology*, *88*, 248–257.

Tennen, H., & Affleck, G. (1987). The costs and benefits of optimistic explanations and dispositional optimism. *Journal of Personality*, *55*, 377–393.

Terborg, J. R. (1976). The motivational components of goal setting. *Journal of Applied Psychology*, *61*, 613–621.

Terhune, K. W. (1968). Studies of motives, cooperation, and conflict within laboratory microcosms. In G. H. Snyder (Ed.), *Studies in international conflict* (Vol. *4*, pp. 29–58). Buffalo, NY: University of Buffalo.

Tesser, A. (1988). Toward a self-evaluation maintenance model of social behavior. In L. Berkowitz (Ed.), *Advances in experimental social psychology* (Vol. *21*, pp. 181–227). New York: Academic Press.

Thayer, R. E. (1996). *The origin of everyday moods*. New York: Oxford University Press.

Thayer, R. E. (2012). Moods of energy and tension that motivate. In. R. M. Ryan (Ed.), *The Oxford handbook of human motivation* (pp. 408–419). New York: Oxford University Press.

Thibodeau, R., & Aronson, E. (1992). Taking a closer look: Reasserting the role of the self-concept in dissonance theory. *Personality and Social Psychology Bulletin*, *18*, 591–602.

Thoman, D. B., Smith, J. L., & Silvia, P. J. (2011). The resource replenishment function of interest. *Social Psychological and Personality Science*, *2*, 592–599.

Thompson, R. J., Dizen, M., & Berenbaum, H. (2009). The unique relations between emotional awareness and facets of affective instability. *Journal of Research in Personality*, *43*, 875–879.

Thompson, S. (1981). Will it hurt less if I can control it?: A complex answer to a simple question. *Psychological Bulletin*, *90*, 89–101.

Thorndike, E. L. (1932). *The fundamental of learning*. New York: Teachers College Press.

Thorton, J. W., & Jacobs, P. D. (1971). Learned helplessness in human subjects. *Journal of Experimental Psychology*, *87*, 369–372.

Tice, D. M., Baumeister, R. F., Shmueli, D., & Muraven, M. (2007). Restoring the self: Positive affect helps improve self-regulation following ego depletion. *Journal of Experimental Social Psychology*, *43*, 379–384.

Tiedens, L. Z., & Linton, S. (2001). Judgment under emotional certainty and uncertainty: The effects of specific emotions on information processing. *Journal of Personality and Social Psychology*, *81*, 973–988.

Tiggemann, M., & Winefield, A. H. (1987). Predictability and timing of self-report in learned helplessness experiments. *Personality and Social Psychology Bulletin*, *13*, 253–264.

Timberlake, W., & Farmer-Dougan, V. A. (1991). Reinforcement in applied settings: Figuring out ahead of time what will work. *Psychological Bulletin*, *110*, 379–391.

Timpe, R. L. (1989). Perfectionism: Positive possibility or personal pathology. *Journal of Psychology and Christianity*, *8*, 23–24.

Toepfer, S. M., Cichy, K., & Peters, P. (2012). Letters of gratitude: Further evidence for author benefits. *Journal of Happiness Studies*, *13*, 187–201.

Tolman, E. C. (1923). The nature of instinct. *Psychological Bulletin*, *20*, 200–218.

Toman, W. (1960). *An introduction to the psychoanalytic theory of motivation*. New York: Pergamon Press.

Tomkins, S. S. (1962). *Affect, imagery, and consciousness: The positive affects* (Vol. *1*). New York: Springer.

Tomkins, S. S. (1963). *Affect, imagery, and consciousness: The negative affects* (Vol. *2*). New York: Springer.

Tomkins, S. S. (1970). Affect as the primary motivational system. In M. B. Arnold (Ed.), *Feelings and emotions* (pp. 101–110). New York: Academic Press.

Tomkins, S. S. (1984). Affect theory. In K. R. Scherer & P. Ekman (Eds.), *Approaches to emotion* (pp. 163–196). Hillsdale, NJ: Erlbaum.

Tong, E. M. W. (2010). The sufficiency and necessity of appraisals for negative emotions. *Cognition and Emotion*, *24*, 692–701.

Tooby, J., & Cosmides, L. (1990). The past explains the present: Emotional adaptations and the structure of ancestral environment. *Ethology and Sociobiology, 11*, 375–424.

Tooby, J., & Cosmides, L. (2008). The evolutionary psychology of the emotions and their relationship to internal regulatory variables. In M. Lewis, J. M. Haviland-Jones, & L. F. Barrett (Eds.), *Handbook of emotions* (3rd ed., pp. 114–137). New York: Guilford Press.

Tourangeau, R., & Ellsworth, P. C. (1979). The role of facial response in the experience of emotion. *Journal of Personality and Social Psychology, 37*, 1519–1531.

Tracy, J. L., & Matsumoto, D. (2008). The spontaneous expression of pride and shame: Evidence for biologically innate nonverbal displays. *PNAS, 105*, 11655–11660.

Tracy, J. L., & Robins, R. W. (2004). Show your pride: Evidence for a discrete emotion expression. *Psychological Science, 15*, 194–197.

Tracy, J. L., & Robins, R. W. (2007). The psychological structure of pride: A tale of two facets. *Journal of Personality and Social Psychology, 92*, 506–525.

Tracy, J. L., & Robins, R. W. (2008). The nonverbal expression of pride: Evidence for cross-cultural recognition. *Journal of Personality and Social Psychology, 94*, 516–530.

Tracy, J. L., Cheng, J. T., Robins, R. W., & Trzesniewski, K. H. (2009). Authentic and hubristic pride: The affective core of self-esteem and narcissism. *Self and Identity, 8*, 196–213.

Tracy, J. L., Robins, R. W., & Lagattuta, K. H. (2005). Can children recognize the pride expression? *Emotion, 5*, 251–257.

Tronick, E. Z. (1989). Emotions and emotional communication in infants. *American Psychologist, 44*, 112–119.

Trope, Y. (1975). Seeking information about one's own ability as a determinant of choice among tasks. *Journal of Personality and Social Psychology, 32*, 1004–1013.

Trope, Y. (1983). Self-assessment in achievement behavior. In J. Suls & A. G. Greenwald (Eds.), *Psychological perspectives on the self* (Vol. 2, pp. 93–121). Hillsdale, NJ: Erlbaum.

Trope, Y. (2004). Theory in social psychology: Seeing the forest and the trees. *Personality and Social Psychology Review, 8*, 193–200.

Trope, Y., & Brickman, P. (1975). Difficulty and diagnosticity as determinants of choice among tasks. *Journal of Personality and Social Psychology, 31*, 918–925.

Trudewind, C. (1982). The development of achievement motivation and individual differences: Ecological determinants. In W. Hartrup (Ed.), *Review of child development research* (Vol. 6, pp. 669–703). Chicago: University of Chicago Press.

Tsai, J. L., Louie, J. Y., Chen, E. E., & Uchida, Y. (2007). Learning what feelings to desire: Socialization of ideal affect through children's storybooks. *Personality and Social Psychology Bulletin, 33*, 17–30.

Tsang, J. (2006). Gratitude and prosocial behavior: An experimental test of gratitude. *Cognition and Emotion, 20*, 138–148.

Tubbs, M. E. (1986). Goal-setting: A meta-analytic examination of the empirical evidence. *Journal of Applied Psychology, 71*, 474–483.

Tugade, M. M., Fredrickson, B. L., & Barrett, L. F. (2004). Psychological resilience and positive emotion granularity: Examining the benefits of positive emotions on coping and health. *Journal of Personality, 72*, 1161–1190.

Tuiten, A., van Honk, J., Koppeschaar, H., Bernaards, C., Thijssen, J., & Verbaten, R. (2000). Time course of effects of testosterone administration on sexual arousal in women. *Archives of General Psychiatry, 57*, 149–153.

Turner, J. H. (1987). Toward a sociological theory of motivation. *American Sociological Review, 52*, 15–27.

Tyler, J. M., & Burns, K. C. (2008). After depletion: The replenishment of the self's regulatory resources. *Self and Identity, 7*, 305–321.

Urist, J. (1977). The Rorschach test and the assessment of object relations. *Journal of Personality Assessment, 41*, 3–9.

Urist, J. (1980). Object relations. In R. W. Woody (Ed.), *Encyclopedia of clinical assessment* (Vol. 2, pp. 821–833). San Francisco: Jossey-Bass.

Vaillant, G. E. (1977). *Adaptation to life*. Boston: Little, Brown.

Vaillant, G. E. (1992). *Ego mechanisms of defense: A guide for clinicians and researchers*. Washington, DC: American Psychiatric Association.

Vaillant, G. E. (1993). *The wisdom of the ego*. Cambridge, MA: Harvard University Press.

Vaillant, G. E. (2000). Adaptive mental mechanisms: Their role in a positive psychology. *American Psychologist, 55*, 89–98.

Vallerand, R. J. (1997). Toward a hierarchical model of intrinsic and extrinsic motivation. In M. P. Zanna (Ed.), *Advances in experimental social psychology* (Vol. 29, pp. 271–360). San Diego, CA: Academic Press.

Vallerand, R. J., & Reid, G. (1984). On the causal effects of perceived competence on intrinsic motivation: A test of cognitive evaluation theory. *Journal of Sport Psychology, 6*, 94–102.

Vallerand, R. J., Deci, E. L., & Ryan, R. M. (1985). Intrinsic motivation in sport. In K. B. Pandolf (Ed.), *Exercise and sport sciences reviews* (Vol. 15, pp. 389–425). New York: Macmillan.

Vallerand, R. J., Gauvin, L. I., & Halliwell, W. R. (1986). Negative effects of competition on children's intrinsic motivation. *Journal of Social Psychology, 126*, 649–656.

Valtin, H. (2002). "Drink at least eight glasses of water a day." Really? Is there scientific evidence for "8 × 8"? *American Journal of Physiology: Regulatory, Integrative, and Comparative Physiology, 283*, R993–R1004.

Van de Ven, N., Zeelenberg, M., & Pieters, R. (2009). Leveling up and down: The experiences of benign and malicious envy. *Emotion, 9*, 419–429.

Van de Ven, N., Zeelenberg, M., & Pieters, R. (2010). Warding off the evil eye: When the fear of envy increases prosocial behavior. *Psychological Science, 21*, 1671–1677.

Van de Ven, N., Zeelenberg, M., & Pieters, R. (2011). Why envy outperforms admiration. *Personality and Social Psychology Bulletin, 37*, 784–795.

Van de Ven, N., Zeelenberg, M., & Pieters, R. (2012). Appraisal patterns of benign envy and related emotions. *Motivation and Emotion, 36*, 195–204.

Van Dijk, W. W., & Zeelenberg, M. (2002). Investigating appraisal patterns of regret and disappointment. *Motivation and Emotion, 26*, 321–331.

Van Dijk, W. W., Ouwerkerk, J. W., Goslinga, S., Nieweg, M., & Gallucci, M. (2006). When people fall from grace: Reconsidering the role of envy in schadenfreude. *Emotion, 6*, 156–160.

Van Dijk, W. W., Zeelenberg, M., & van Der Plight, J. (1999). Not having what you want versus having what you do not want: The impact of type of negative outcome on the experience of disappointment and related emotions. *Cognition and Emotion, 13*, 129–148.

Van Doorn, E. A., Van Kleef, G. A., & Van der Pligt, J. (2014). How emotional expressions shape prosocial behavior: Interpersonal effects of anger and disappointment on compliance with requests. *Motivation and Emotion*.

van Hooff, J. A. R. A. M. (1962). Facial expressions in higher primates. *Symposium of the Zoological Society of London, 8*, 97–125.

van Hooff, J. A. R. A. M. (1972). A comparative approach to the phylogeny of laughter and smiling. In R. A. Hinde (Ed.), *Non-verbal communication*. Cambridge, UK: Cambridge University Press.

Van Houten, R., & Retting, R. A. (2001). Increasing motorist compliance and caution at stop signs. *Journal of Applied Behavior Analysis, 34*, 185–193.

van IJzendoorn, M. H. (1995). Adult attachment representations, parental responsiveness, and infant attachment: A meta-analysis on the predictive validity of the adult attachment interview. *Psychological Bulletin, 117*, 387–403.

Van Kleef, G. A., De Dreu, C. K. W., & Manstead, A. S. R. (2006). Supplication and appeasement in conflict and negotiation: The interpersonal effects of disappointment, worry, guilt, and regret. *Journal of Personality and Social Psychology, 91*, 124–142.

Van Veen, V., Cohen, J. D., Botvinick, M. M., Stenger, V. A., & Carter, C. S. (2001). Anterior cingulate cortex, conflict monitoring, and levels of processing. *NeuroImage, 14*, 1302–1308.

Vansteenkiste, M., & Deci, E. L. (2003). Competitively contingent rewards and intrinsic motivation: Can losers remain motivated? *Motivation and Emotion, 27*, 273–299.

Vansteenkiste, M., Lens, W., De Witte, S., De Witte, H., & Deci, E. L. (2004). The "why" and "why not" of job search behavior: Their relation to searching, unemployment experience, and well-being. *European Journal of Social Psychology, 34*, 345–363.

Vansteenkiste, M., Sierens, E., Soenens, B., Luyckx, K., & Lens, W. (2009). Motivational profiles from a self-determination perspective: The quality of motivation matters. *Journal of Educational Psychology, 101*, 671–688.

Vansteenkiste, M., Simons, J., Lens, W., Sheldon, K. M., & Deci, E. L. (2004). Motivating learning, performance, and persistence: The synergistic role of intrinsic goals and autonomy-support. *Journal of Personality and Social Psychology, 87*, 246–260.

Vansteenkiste, M., Simons, J., Lens, W., Soenens, B., & Matos, L. (2005). Examining the motivational impact of intrinsic versus extrinsic goal framing and autonomy-supportive versus internally-controlling communication style on early adolescents' academic achievement. *Child Development, 76*, 483–501.

Vansteenkiste, M., Simons, J., Soenens, B., & Lens, W. (2004). How to become a persevering exerciser? Providing a clear, future intrinsic goal in an autonomy supportive way. *Journal of Sport and Exercise Psychology, 26*, 232–249.

Vansteenkiste, M., Zhou, M., Lens, W., & Soenens, B. (2005). Experiences of autonomy and control among Chinese learners: Vitalizing or immobilizing? *Journal of Educational Psychology, 97*, 468–483.

Veitch, R., & Griffitt, W. (1976). Good news–bad news: Affective and interpersonal effects. *Journal of Applied Social Psychology, 6*, 69–75.

Veling, H., & van Knippenberg, A. (2006). Shielding intentions from distraction: Forming an intention induces inhibition of distracting stimuli. *Social Cognition, 24*, 409–425.

Verduyn, P., Delvaux, E., Van Coillie, H., Tuerlinckx, F., & Van Mechelen, I. (2009). Predicting the duration of emotional experience: Two experience sampling studies. *Emotion, 9*, 83–91.

Veroff, J. (1957). Development and validation of a projective measure of power motivation. *Journal of Abnormal and Social Psychology, 54*, 1–8.

Veroff, J., Depner, C., Kulka, R., & Douvan, E. (1980). Comparison of American motives: 1957 versus 1976. *Journal of Personality and Social Psychology, 39*, 1249–1262.

Vohs, K. D., & Faber, R. J. (2007). Spent resources: Self-regulatory resource availability affects impulse buying. *Journal of Consumer Research, 33*, 537–547.

Vohs, K. D., Baumeister, R. F., & Ciarocco, N. J. (2005). Self-regulation and self-presentation: Regulatory resource depletion impairs impression management and effortful self-presentation depletes regulatory resources. *Journal of Personality and Social Psychology, 88*, 632–657.

Vohs, K. D., Baumeister, R. F., Schmeichel, B. J., Twenge, J. M., Nelson, N. M., & Tice, D. M. (2008). Making choices impairs subsequent self-control: A limited-resource account of decision making, self-regulation, and active initiative. *Journal of Personality and Social Psychology, 94*, 883–898.

Vroom, V. H. (1964). *Work and motivation.* New York: Wiley.

Vytal, K., & Hamann, S. (2010). Neuroimaging support for discrete neural correlates to basic emotions: A voxel-based meta-analysis. *Journal of Cognitive Neuroscience, 22*, 2864–2885.

Wachtel, P. (1993). *Therapeutic communication.* New York: Guilford Press.

Wahba, M. A., & Bridwell, L. G. (1976). Maslow reconsidered: A review of research on the need hierarchy theory. *Organizational Behavior and Human Performance, 15,* 212–240.

Walton, M. E. et al. (2003). Functional specialization within medial frontal cortex of the anterior cingulate for evaluating effort-related decisions. *Journal of Neuroscience, 23,* 6475–6479.

Watkins, P. C. (2008). *The psychology of gratitude.* New York: Oxford University Press.

Watson, D., & Clark, L. A. (1994). The vicissitudes of mood: A schematic model. In P. Ekman & R. J. Davidson (Eds.), *The nature of emotion: Fundamental questions* (pp. 400–405). New York: Oxford University Press.

Watson, D., & Tellegen, A. (1985). Toward a consensual structure of mood. *Psychological Bulletin, 98,* 219–235.

Watson, D., Wiese, D., Vaidya, J., & Tellegen, A. (1999). The two general activation systems of affect: Structural findings, evolutionary considerations, and psychobiological evidence. *Journal of Personality and Social Psychology, 76,* 820–838.

Watson, J. B. (1919). *Psychology from the standpoint of a behaviorist.* Philadelphia: Lippincott.

Watson, J. B. (1924). *Behaviorism.* New York: W. W. Norton.

Webster, D. M., & Kruglanski, A. W. (1994). Indivdual differences in the need for cognitive closure. *Journal of Personality and Social Psychology, 67,* 1049–1062.

Wegner, D. M. (1989). *White bears and other unwanted thoughts.* New York: Guilford Press.

Wegner, D. M. (1992). You can't always think what you want: Problems in the suppression of unwanted thoughts. In M. P. Zanna (Ed.), *Advances in experimental social psychology* (Vol. 25, pp. 193–225). San Diego, CA: Academic Press.

Wegner, D. M. (1994). Ironic processes of mental control. *Psychological Review, 101,* 34–52.

Wegner, D. M., & Erber, R. (1993). Hyperaccessibility of suppressed thoughts. *Journal of Personality and Social Psychology, 63,* 903–912.

Wegner, D. M., Schneider, D. J., Carter, S., III, & White, T. (1987). Paradoxical effects thought suppression. *Journal of Personality and Social Psychology, 53,* 5–13.

Weinberg, A., & Minaker, K. (1995). Council of Scientific Affairs, American Medical Association: Dehydration evaluation and management in older adults. *Journal of the American Medical Association, 274,* 1552–1556, 1995.

Weinberg, R. S., Bruya, L., & Jackson, A. (1985). The effects of goal proximity and goal specificity on endurance performance. *Journal of Sport Psychology, 7,* 296–305.

Weinberg, R. S., Bruya, L., Longino, J., & Jackson, A. (1988). Effect of goal proximity and specificity on endurance performance of primary-grade children. *Journal of Sport and Exercise Psychology, 10,* 81–91.

Weinberg, R. S., Gould, D., & Jackson, A. (1979). Expectations and performance: An empirical test of Bandura's self-efficacy theory. *Journal of Sport Psychology, 1,* 320–331.

Weinberger, J., Cotler, T., & Fishman, D. (2010). The duality of affiliative motivation. In O. C. Schultheiss & J. C. Brunstein (Eds.), *Implicit motives* (Chapter 3, pp. 71–88). New York: Oxford University Press.

Weiner, B. (1972). *Theories of motivation: From mechanism to cognition.* Chicago: Rand McNally.

Weiner, B. (1979). A theory of motivation for some classroom experiences. *Journal of Educational Psychology, 71,* 3–25.

Weiner, B. (1980). *Human motivation.* New York: Holt, Rinehart & Winston.

Weiner, B. (1982). The emotional consequences of causal attributions. In M. S. Clark & S. T. Fiske (Eds.), *Affect and cognition* (pp. 185–209). Hillsdale, NJ: Erlbaum.

Weiner, B. (1985). An attributional theory of achievement motivation and emotion. *Psychological Review, 92,* 548–573.

Weiner, B. (1986). *An attributional theory of motivation and emotion.* New York: Springer-Verlag.

Weiner, B. (1990). History of motivational research in education. *Journal of Educational Psychology, 82,* 616–622.

Weiner, B., & Graham, S. (1989). Understanding the motivational role of affect: Life-span research from an attributional perspective. *Cognition and Emotion, 3*, 401–409.

Weiner, B., Russell, D., & Learman, D. (1978). Affective consequences of causal ascriptions. In J. Harvey, W.J. Ickes, & R. F. Kidd (Eds.), *New directions in attribution research* (Vol. 2, pp. 59–88). Hillsdale, NJ: Erlbaum.

Weiner, B., Russell, D., & Learman, D. (1979). The cognition-emotion process in achievement-related context. *Journal of Personality and Social Psychology, 37*, 1211–1220.

Weingarten, H. P. (1985). Stimulus control of eating: Implications for a two-factor theory of hunger. *Appetite, 6*, 387–401.

Weinstein, N. D. (1984). Why it won't happen to me: Perceptions of risk factors and susceptibility. *Health Psychology, 3*, 431–457.

Weinstein, N. D. (1993). Optimistic biases about personal risks. *Science, 155*, 1232–1233.

Weinstein, N., & Ryan, R. M. (2010). When helping helps: Autonomous motivation for prosocial behavior and its influence on well-being for the helper and recipient. *Journal of Personality and Social Psychology, 98*, 222–244.

Weinstein, N., Deci, E. L., & Ryan, R. M. (2011). Motivational determinants of integrating positive and negative past identities. *Journal of Personality and Social Psychology, 100*, 527–544.

Weinstein, N., Przybylski, A. K., & Ryan, R. M. (2012). The index of autonomous functioning: Development of a scale of human autonomy. *Journal of Research in Personality, 46*, 397–413.

Weinstein, N., Przybylski, A. K., & Ryan, R. M. (2013). The integrative process: New research and future directions. *Current Directions in Psychological Science, 22*, 69–74.

Weiss, J. M. (1972). Psychological factors in stress and disease. *Scientific American, 226*, 104–113.

Weiss, J. M., & Simson, P. G. (1985). Neurochemical basis of stress-induced depression. *Psychopharmacology Bulletin, 21*, 447–457.

Weiss, J. M., Glazer, H. I., & Pohorecky, L. A. (1976). Coping behavior and neurochemical changes in rats: An alternative explanation for the original learned helplessness experiments. In G. Serban & A. King (Eds.), *Animal models in human psychobiology*. New York: Plenum Press.

Welling, H. (2003). An evolutionary function of the depressive reaction: The cognitive map hypothesis. *New Ideas in Psychology, 21*, 147–156.

Westen, D. (1990). Psychoanalytic approaches to personality. In L. Pervin (Ed.), *Handbook of personality: Theory and research* (pp. 21–65). New York: Guilford Press.

Westen, D. (1991). Social cognition and object relations. *Psychological Bulletin, 109*, 429–455.

Westen, D. (1998). The scientific legacy of Sigmund Freud: Toward a psychodynamically informed psychological science. *Psychological Bulletin, 124*, 333–371.

Westen, D., Klepser, J., Ruffins, S. A., Silverman, M., Lifton, N., & Boekamp, J. (1991). Object relations in childhood and adolescence: The development of working representations. *Journal of Consulting and Clinical Psychology, 59*, 400–409.

Whalen, P. J. (1999). Fear, vigilance, and ambiguity: Initial neuroimagining studies of the human amygdala. *Current Directions in Psychological Science, 7*, 177–187.

Whalen, P. J. (2007). The uncertainty of it all. *Trends in Cognitive Science, 11*, 499–500.

Wheeler, L., Reis, H. T., & Nezlek, J. (1983). Loneliness, social interaction, and sex roles. *Journal of Personality and Social Psychology, 45*, 943–953.

White, J. (1978). *Rejection*. Boston: Addison-Wesley.

White, R. W. (1959). Motivation reconsidered: The concept of competence. *Psychological Review, 66*, 297–333.

White, R. W. (1960). Competence and the psychosexual stages of development. In M. R. Jones (Ed.), *Nebraska Symposium on Motivation* (Vol. 8, pp. 97–141). Lincoln: University of Nebraska Press.

Wicker, B., Keysers, C., Plailly, J., Royet, J., Gallese, V., & Rizzolatti, G. (2003). Both of us disgusted in my insula: The common neural basis of seeing and feeling disgust. *Neuron, 40*, 655–664.

Widen, S. C., & Russell, J. A. (2010). Descriptive and prescriptive definitions of emotion. *Emotion Review, 2,* 377–378.

Wieber, F., von Suchodoletz, A., Heikamp, T., Trommsdorff, G., & Gollwitzer, P. M. (2011). If-then planning helps school-age children to ignore attractive distractions. *Social Psychology, 42,* 39–47.

Wiechman, B. M., & Gurland, S. T. (2009). What happens during the free-choice period? Evidence of a polarizing effect of extrinsic rewards on intrinsic motivation. *Journal of Research in Personality, 43,* 716–719.

Wiederman, M. W. (1993). Evolved gender differences in mate preferences: Evidence from personal advertisements. *Ethology and Sociobiology, 13,* 331–352.

Wiersma, U. J. (1992). The effects of extrinsic rewards in intrinsic motivation: A meta-analysis. *Journal of Occupational and Organizational Psychology, 65,* 101–114.

Wilder, D. A., & Thompson, J. E. (1980). Intergroup contact with independent manipulations of in-group and out-group interaction. *Journal of Personality and Social Psychology, 38,* 589–603.

Williams, D. R., & Teitelbaum, P. (1956). Control of drinking by means of an operant conditioning technique. *Science, 124,* 1294–1296.

Williams, G. C., Freedman, Z. R., & Deci, E. L. (1998). Supporting autonomy to motivate glucose control in patients with diabetes. *Diabetes Care, 21,* 1644–1651.

Williams, G. C., Grow, V. M., Freedman, Z. R., Ryan, R. M., & Deci, E. L. (1996). Motivational predictors of weight loss and weight-loss maintenance. *Journal of Personality and Social Psychology, 70,* 115–126.

Williams, G. C., King, D., Nelson, C. C., & Glasgow, R. E. (2005). Variation in perceived competence, glycemic control, and patient satisfaction: Relationship to autonomy support from physicians. *Patient Education and Counseling, 57,* 39–45.

Williams, G. C., Patrick, H., Niemiec, C. P., Williams, L. K., Divine, G., Lafata, J. E., Heisler, M., Tunceli, K., & Pladevall, M. (2009). Reducing the health risks of diabetes: How self-determination theory may help improve medication adherence and quality of life. *The Diabetes Educator, 35,* 484–492.

Williams, G. C., Sharp, D., Levesque, C. S., Kouides, R. W., Ryan, R. M., & Deci, E. L. (2006). Testing a self-determination theory intervention for motivating tobacco cessation: Supporting autonomy and competence in a clinical trial. *Health Psychology, 25,* 91–101.

Williams, J. G., & Solano, C. H. (1983). The social reality of feeling lonely: Friendship and reciprocation. *Personality and Social Psychology Bulletin, 9,* 237–242.

Williams, L. A., & DeSteno, D. (2008). Pride and perseverance: The motivational role of pride. *Journal of Personality and Social Psychology, 94,* 1007–1017.

Williams, L. A., & DeSteno, D. (2009). Pride: Adaptive social emotion or seventh sin? *Psychological Science, 20,* 284–288.

Williams, S. (1998). An organizational model of choice: A theoretical analysis differentiating choice, personal control, and self-determination. *Genetic, Social and General Psychology Monographs, 124,* 465–492.

Williams, T., & Williams, K. (2010). Self-efficacy and performance in mathematics: Reciprocal determinism in 33 nations. *Journal of Educational Psychology, 102*(2), 453–466.

Wilson, T. D. (2002). *Strangers to ourselves: Discovering the adaptive unconscious.* Cambridge, MA: Harvard University Press.

Wilson, T. D., Centerbar, D. B., Kermer, D. A., & Gilbert, D. T. (2005). The pleasures of uncertainty: Prolonging positive moods in ways people do not anticipate. *Journal of Personality and Social Psychology, 88,* 5–21.

Windle, M. (1992). Temperament and social support in adolescence: Interrelations with depression and delinquent behavior. *Journal of Youth and Adolescence, 21,* 1–21.

Winefield, A. H. (1982). Methodological differences in demonstrating learned helplessness in humans. *Journal of General Psychology, 107*, 255–266.

Winefield, A. H., Barnett, A., & Tiggemann, M. (1985). Learned helplessness deficits: Uncontrollable outcomes or perceived failure? *Motivation and Emotion, 9*, 185–195.

Winne, P. H. (1997). Experimenting to bootstrap self-regulated learning. *Journal of Educational Psychology, 88*, 397–410.

Winson, J. (1992). The function of REM sleep and the meaning of dreams. In J. W. Barron, M. N. Eagle, & D. L. Wolitzky (Eds.), *Interface of psychoanalysis and psychology* (pp. 347–356). Washington, DC: American Psychological Association.

Winter, D. G. (1973). *The power motive.* New York: Free Press.

Winter, D. G. (1987). Leader appeal, leader performance, and the motive profiles of leaders and followers: A study of American presidents and elections. *Journal of Personality and Social Psychology, 52*, 196–202.

Winter, D. G. (1988). The power motive in women and men. *Journal of Personality and Social Psychology, 54*, 510–519.

Winter, D. G. (1993). Power, affiliation, and war: Three tests of a motivational model. *Journal of Personality and Social Psychology, 65*, 532–545.

Winter, D. G. (2005). Things I've learned about personality from studying political leaders at a distance. *Journal of Personality, 73*, 557–584.

Winter, D. G. (2010). Political and historical consequences of implicit motives. In O. C. Schultheiss & J. C. Brunstein (Eds.), *Implicit motives* (Chapter 14, pp. 407–432). New York: Oxford University Press.

Winter, D. G., & Stewart, A. J. (1978). Power motivation. In H. London & J. Exner (Eds.), *Dimensions of personality.* New York: Wiley.

Winterbottom, M. (1958). The relation of need for achievement to learning experience in independence and mastery. In J. Atkinson (Ed.), *Motives in fantasy, action, and society* (pp. 453–478). Princeton, NJ: Van Nostrand.

Wirth, M. M., & Schultheiss, O. C. (2006). Effects of affiliation arousal (hope of closeness) and affiliation stress (fear of rejection) on progesterone and cortisol. *Hormones and Behavior, 50*, 786–795.

Wise, R. A. (1996). Addictive drugs and brain stimulation reward. *Annual Review of Neuroscience, 19*, 319–340.

Wise, R. A. (2002). Brain reward circuitry: Insights from unsensed incentives. *Neuron, 36*, 229–240.

Wise, R. A., & Bozarth, M. A. (1984). Brain reward circuitry: Four circuit elements wired in apparent series. *Brain Research Bulletin, 12*, 203–208.

Wismer-Fries, A. B., Ziegler, T. E., Kurian, J. R., Jacoris, S., & Pollak, S. D. (2005). Early experience in humans is associated with changes in neuropeptides critical for regulating social behavior. *Proceedings of the National Academy of Science, 102*, 17237–17240.

Witzel, B. S., & Mercer, C. D. (2003). Using rewards to teach children with disabilities. Implications for motivation. *Remedial and Special Education, 24*, 88–96.

Wood, R. E., & Bandura, A. (1989). Impact of conceptions of ability on self-regulatory mechanisms and complex decision making. *Journal of Personality and Social Psychology, 56*, 407–415.

Wood, R. E., Bandura, A., & Bailey, T. (1990). Mechanisms governing organizational performance in complex decision-making environments. *Organizational Behavior and Human Decision Processes, 46*, 181–201.

Wood, R. E., Mento, A. J., & Locke, E. A. (1987). Task complexity as a moderator of goal effects: A meta-analysis. *Journal of Applied Psychology, 72*, 416–425.

Woods, S. C., Seeley, R. J., Porte, D., Jr., & Schwartz, M. W. (1998). Signals that regulate food intake and energy homeostasis. *Science, 280*, 1378–1383.

Woodworth, R. S. (1918). *Dynamic psychology.* New York: Columbia University Press.

Woody, E. Z., Costanzo, P. R., Leifer, H., & Conger, J. (1981). The effects of taste and caloric perceptions on the eating behavior of restrained and unrestrained subjects. *Cognitive Research and Therapy, 5*, 381–390.

World Health Organization (2012). *World health statistics, 2012.* Geneva, Switzerland: Word Health Organization Press. Full report is available at: http://www.who.int/gho/publications/world_health_statistics/2012/en/

Wortman, C. B., & Brehm, J. W. (1975). Responses to uncontrollable outcomes: An integration of reactance theory and the learned helplessness model. In L. Berkowitz (Ed.), *Advances in experimental social psychology* (Vol. 8, pp. 277–336). New York: Academic Press.

Wren, A. M., Seal, L. J., Cohen, M. A., Brynes, A. E., Frost, G. S., Murphy, K. G., et al. (2001). Ghrelin enhances appetite and increases food intake in humans. *The Journal of Clinical Endocrinology and Metabolism, 86*, 59–92.

Wrosch, C., Scheier, M. F., Carver, C. S., & Schulz, R. (2003). The importance of goal disengagement in adaptive self-regulation: When giving up is beneficial. *Self and Identity, 2*, 1–20.

Wrosch, C., Scheier, M. F., Miller, G. E., Schulz, R., & Carver, C. S. (2003). Adaptive self-regulation of unattainable goals: Goal disengagement, goal reengagement, and subjective well-being. *Personality and Social Psychology Bulletin, 29*, 1494–1508.

Wubben, M. J. J., De Cremer, D., & van Dijk, E. (2012). Is pride a prosocial emotion? Interpersonal effects of authentic and hubristic pride. *Cognition and Emotion, 26*, 1084–1097.

Wyrwicka, W. (1988). *Brain and feeding behavior.* Springfield, IL: Charles C. Thomas.

Yang, H., Yang, S., & Isen, A. M. (2013). Positive affect improves working memory: Implications for controlled cognitive processing. *Cognition and Emotion, 27*, 474–482.

Yanovsky, S. Z., & Yanovsky, J. A. (2002). Drug therapy: Obesity. *New England Journal of Medicine, 346*, 591–602.

Yeager, D. S., Trzesniewski, K. H., & Dweck, C. S. (2013). An implicit theory of personality intervention reduces adolescent aggression in response to victimization and exclusion. *Child Development, 84*, 970–988.

Yegiyan, N. S., & Yonelinas, A. P. (2011). Encoding details: Positive emotion leads to memory broadening. *Cognition and Emotion, 25*, 1255–1262.

Yerkes, R. M., & Dodson, J. D. (1908). The relation of strength of stimulus to repidity of habit formation. *Journal of Comparative Neurology and Psychology, 18*, 459–482.

Yik, M., Russell, J. A., & Steiger, J. H. (2011). A 12-point circumplex structure of core affect. *Emotion, 11*, 705–731.

Young, P. T. (1961). *Motivation and emotion: A survey of the determinants of human and animal activity.* New York: Wiley.

Young, P. T. (1966). Hedonic organization and regulation of behavior. *Psychological Review, 73*, 59–86.

Younger, J. C., Walker, L., & Arrowood, A. J. (1977). Postdecision dissonance at the fair. *Personality and Social Psychology Bulletin, 3*, 284–287.

Zajonc, R. B. (1980). Feeling and thinking: Preferences need no inferences. *American Psychologist, 35*, 151–175.

Zajonc, R. B. (1981). A one-factor mind about mind and emotion. *American Psychologist, 36*, 102–103.

Zajonc, R. B. (1984). On the primacy of affect. *American Psychologist, 39*, 117–123.

Zajonc, R. B., Murphy, S. T., & Inglehart, M. (1989). Feeling and facial efference: Implications of the vascular theory of emotions. *Psychological Review, 96*, 395–416.

Zak, P. J. et al. (2007). Oxytocin increases generosity in humans. *PLoS ONE 2*, e1128.

Zanna, M. P., & Cooper, J. (1976). Dissonance and the attribution process. In J. H. Harvey, W. J. Ickes, & R. F. Kidd (Eds.), *New directions in attribution research* (Vol. 1, pp. 199–217). Hillsdale, NJ: Erlbaum.

Zeelenberg, M., & Breugelmans, S. M. (2008). The role of interpersonal harm in distinguishing regret from guilt. *Emotion, 8,* 589–596.

Zeelenberg, M., van Dijk, W. W., Manstead, A. S. R., & van de Pligt, J. (1998). The experience of regret and disappointment. *Cognition and Emotion, 12,* 221–230.

Zeelenberg, M., van Dijk, W. W., Manstead, A. S. R., & van de Pligt, J. (2000). On bad decisions and disconfirmed expectancies: The psychology of regret and disappointment. *Cognition and Emotion, 14,* 521–541.

Zhong, C. B., & Liljenquist, K. (2006). Washing away your sins: Threatened morality and physical cleansing. *Science, 313,* 1451–1452.

Zhou, F.-M., Liang, Y., Salas, R., Zhang, L., DeBiasi, M., & Dani, J. A. (2005). Corelease of dopamine and serotonin from striatal dopamine terminals. *Neuron, 46,* 65–74.

Zimmerman, B. J. (2000). Attaining self-regulation: A social cognitive perspective. In M. Boekaerts, P. R. Pintrich, & M. Zeidner's (Eds.), *Handbook of self-regulation* (pp. 13–39). San Diego, CA: Academic Press.

Zimmerman, B. J. (2002). Becoming a self-regulated learner: An overview. *Theory into Practice, 41,* 64–70.

Zimmerman, B. J., & Risemberg, R. (1997). Become a proficient writer: A social cognitive perspective. *Contemporary Educational Psychology, 22,* 73–101.

Zuckerman, M. (1979). *Sensation-seeking: Beyond the optimal level of arousal.* Hillsdale, NJ: Erlbaum.

Zuckerman, M. (1994). *Behavioral expressions and biosocial bases of sensation seeking.* New York: Cambridge University Press.

Zuckerman, M., Kieffer, S. C., & Knee, C. R. (1998). Consequences of self-handicapping effects on coping, academic performance, and adjustment. *Journal of Personality and Social Psychology, 74,* 1619–1628.

Zuckerman, M., Klorman, R., Larrance, D. T., & Spiegel, N. H. (1981). Facial, autonomic, and subjective components of emotion: The facial feedback hypothesis versus the externalizer-internalizer distinction. *Journal of Personality and Social Psychology, 41,* 929–944.

Zuckerman, M., Porac, J., Lathin, D., Smith, R., & Deci, E. L. (1978). On the importance of self-determination for intrinsically-motivated behavior. *Personality and Social Psychology Bulletin, 4,* 443–446.

Zullow, H. M., Oettingen, G., Peterson, C., & Seligman, M. E. P. (1988). Pessimistic explanatory style in the historical record: CAVing LBJ, presidential candidates, and East versus West Berlin. *American Psychologist, 43,* 673–682.

Zumoff, B., Strain, G. W., Miller, L. K., & Rosner, W. (1995). Twenty-four-hour mean plasma testosterone concentration declines with age in normal premenopausal women. *Journal of Clinical Endocrinology and Metabolism, 80,* 1429–1430.

AUTHOR INDEX

A

Aarts, H., 231, 478, 495
Abad, N., 201
Abe, J. A. A., 356, 357
Abramson, L. Y., 291, 292, 294, 302, 307
Achiron, A., 455
Achtziger, A., 234
Ackerman, P. L., 227
Adams, N. E., 274, 275, 279
Addis, D. R., 332
Adelmann, P. K., 380
Adkins, K. K., 444
Adler, T. F., 191, 299
Adriaanse, M. A., 231, 238
Adolph, E. F., 89
Adolphs, R., 62
Affleck, G., 294
Aggleton, J. P., 61, 62
Agnati, L. F., 67
Agyei, Y., 111, 112
Aharon-Peretz, J., 424
Aiken, P. A., 102
Ainsworth, M. D. S., 450, 489, 490
Aldao, A., 359
Aldridge, J. W., 64
Alexander, P. A., 413
Algoe, S. B., 420, 422, 428
Alloy, L. B., 289–292, 294, 302, 307, 360, 411
Altman, J., 282
Amabile, T. M., 132, 135, 137, 227
Ambady, N., 408, 476, 495
Ames, C. A., 20, 254, 256, 258
Amorose, A. J., 173
Anand, B. K., 96
Andersen, B. L., 110
Anderson, A. K., 409
Anderson, C., 205
Anderson, C. A., 22
Anderson, J. R., 302
Anderson, P., 310
Anderson, R., 136, 173
Andreassi, J. L., 14

Angell, A., 99, 102
Angie, A. D., 395
Antoniou, A. A., 389
Applerloo, M. J. A., 105
Appleseed, J., 42
Appley, M. H., 28, 39, 40, 45, 50, 89
Aquinas, T., 29
Arana, F. S., 72
Archer, J., 20, 254, 256, 258
Arizmendi, T. G., 100
Aristotle, 29, 433, 456
Armor, D. A., 229, 243, 266
Arndt, J., 440, 464
Arnett, J., 57
Arnold, M. B., 349, 384–386
Aronson, E., 15, 253, 261–264, 473
Arrindell, W. A., 406
Arrowood, A. J., 263
Arsenio, W. F., 361
Ashby, F. G., 68, 364
Ashford, M. L. J., 98
Asmussen, L., 357
Aspinwall, L. G., 366, 458
Assor, A., 132, 148, 160, 164, 443
Astin, J. A., 296
Atkinson, J. W., 12, 19, 20, 26, 36, 39, 45, 185, 187, 190, 192, 193, 195, 198, 209, 257
Atran, S., 452
Augustine, A. A., 359
Austira, J., 138
Averill, J. R., 341, 350, 407, 411
Avery, R. R., 491
Axelrod, S., 123, 151
Ayduk, O., 329
Ayllon, T., 127
Azar, B., 8, 306, 373
Azrin, N. H., 126, 127

B

Baard, P. P., 165
Bagozzi, R. P., 233
Bailey, J. M., 111–113
Bailey, J., 138

Bailey, T., 225
Baize, H. R., 112
Baldes, J. J., 223
Baldwin, J. D., 118, 120, 128
Baldwin, J. I., 118, 120, 128
Balleine, B., 66, 72
Banaji, M. R., 208, 469, 472
Bancroft, J., 75, 111
Bandura, A., 26, 36, 39, 41, 45, 154, 215, 219, 220, 223, 225, 227, 228, 270, 271, 272, 274–281, 296, 302, 406, 452, 462
Barak, Y., 455
Barbaranelli, C., 276, 279
Barbee, A. P., 107
Barber, B. K., 164
Bargh, J. A., 215, 472, 473, 477, 478, 495
Barlow, D. H., 415
Barndollar, K. 495
Baroni, S., 374
Barrett, L. C., 292, 294, 295
Barrett, L. F., 351, 361, 390, 391, 426, 428
Barry, D., 223
Bartlett, M. Y., 422, 425
Barton, R., 296
Bartz, J. A., 75
Barzilai, 98
Bassett, D. S., 55
Basson, R., 105, 106, 115
Batson, C. D., 365, 452
Battistich, V., 177
Baucom, D. H., 102
Bauer, I. M., 324
Baumeister, R. F., 8, 26, 174–177, 182, 200, 215, 227, 304, 307, 324–327, 329, 333, 334, 452, 459, 462
Baxter, M. G., 61, 62
Bayer, U., 243
Beach, F. A., 31
Beach, S. R. H., 310
Beatles, 278

Beaton, A., 144
Beatty, W. W., 100
Beauvois, J. L., 263
Bechara, A., 63, 80
Beck, A. T., 294, 449
Beck, R. C., 95
Beck, S. P., 107
Becker, L. J., 225
Beers, M., 361
Behrens, T. E. J., 53
Bell, A. G., 235
Bell, A. P., 111
Bell, E. A., 96
Belmont, M. J., 132, 172
Bem, D. J., 265
Bench, S. W., 395
Benjamin, L. T., Jr., 40, 45, 50
Bennett, W. I., 99
Benvenuto, M., 390
Benware, C., 132, 134, 137
Bera, S., 489
Berdahl, J. L., 205
Berenbaum, H., 391
Berenbaum, S. A., 111
Bereby-Mayer, Y., 132
Bergma, A., 455
Bergman, L. R., 457
Bergmann, G., 433
Berking, M., 357, 414
Berkowitz, L., 390, 408, 471
Berlyne, D. E., 26, 37, 38, 41, 122,
    413
Bernard, L. C., 5
Bernard, L. L., 32
Bernieri, F. J., 396, 476
Bernieri, F., 132, 151, 166, 447, 495
Bernstein, J. H., 180
Berridge, K. C., 42, 44, 62, 64, 66,
    384
Berry, D. S., 109
Berry, S. L., 100
Best, J. R., 57
Betley, G., 142
Bettencourt, B., 455
Betz, N. E., 277
Beutler, L. E., 100
Billington, M. J., 223
Bianchi-Demicheli, F., 106, 115
Bianco, A. T., 250
Bindra, D., 36, 42
Birch, D., 12, 26, 195

Birch, H. G., 32
Birch, L. L., 104
Birney, R. C., 193, 259
Biswas-Diener, R., 307, 455, 456
Biven, L., 374
Bixler, M. A., 384
Bjelke, B., 67
Bjornebekk, G., 143
Black, A., 357
Black, A. E., 132
Blackburn, G., 102
Blackwell, L. S., 251–253, 267
Blais, M. R., 143, 154
Blanchard, D. C., 62
Blanchard, R. J., 62
Blanchette, J., 395
Blandler, R., 61
Blaney, P. H., 275
Blank, P. D., 136, 173
Blankenship, V., 190, 195–197, 203,
    204, 209
Blass, E. M., 93
Blatt, S. J., 175, 444, 489
Blehar, M. C., 489
Bless, H., 168, 169, 182, 249
Blissett, S. E., 486
Block, J., 443
Block, J. H., 443
Blumenfeld, P. C., 13, 256
Bodmann, S. M., 220
Bloom, P., 409
Boca, S., 396
Boden, J. M., 307
Boggiano, A. K., 132, 133, 137, 173
Bolger, N., 75
Bolles, R. C., 12, 26, 35, 37, 49, 50
Boneau, C. A., 479
Bongort, K., 19, 20
Bonanno, G. A., 410, 411
Bono, G., 422
Boone, A. L., 329
Borecki, I. B., 98
Borkowski, J. G., 314
Bostic, T., 180
Botvinick, M. M., 74
Bouchard, C., 98, 143
Bowlby, J., 489, 490
Bowles, T., 307
Boyatzis, R. E., 199, 201, 204
Boyle, P. C., 85, 99
Bozarth, M. A., 76

Brand-Miller, J. C. B., 97, 114
Branden, N., 307
Brandstatter, J., 266
Brandstatter, V., 231, 233, 243
Branigan, C., 412
Brans, K., 397
Bratslavsky, E., 325, 334, 462
Brehm, J. W., 26, 39, 262, 263, 295,
    297, 302
Brehm, S. S., 297
Brember, I., 307
Breugelmans, S. M., 357, 414–416
Brewer, E. M., 100
Brewer, M. B., 175
Brickman, P., 198
Bridges, L., 173
Bridwell, L. G., 437
Briere, N. M., 143
Brigham, T. A., 139
Brobeck, J. R., 97
Brophy, J., 140
Brosch, T., 388
Brothers, L. A., 61
Brouillard, M. E., 272
Brouwers, M., 444
Brown, A. S., 492
Brown, D. R., 437
Brown, E. S., 75
Brown, I., Jr., 274
Brown, J. D., 291, 295, 296, 457
Brown, J. S., 36, 45
Brown, K. W., 180, 477
Bruce, H. M., 103
Bruininks, P., 423
Brunell, A. B., 418
Bruing, R., 280
Bruning, R. H., 292
Brunner, S., 171
Brunstein, J. C., 26, 185
Bruya, L., 221, 227
Bryan, J. F., 223
Bryant, F. B., 360
Bryne, A. T. J., 227
Buck, R., 343, 344, 345, 372
Buckner, C. E., 314
Bugental, D. B., 41, 294
Bumgartner, T., 75, 80
Burdick, H., 193
Burger, J. M., 296
Burke, P. J., 329
Burkhardt, S., 357, 414

Burkley, E. 327
Burn, P., 98, 99
Burnham, D. H., 205, 206
Burnham, T. C., 75
Burns, K. C., 327
Burrows, L., 473
Bush, C. P., 418
Bush, G., 74
Buss, A. H., 449
Buss, D. M., 111, 356
Buston, P. M., 113
Buswell, B. N., 355
Bybee, D., 314
Byrne, A., 364
Byrne, D., 117, 201

C
Cacioppo, J. T., 106, 115, 207, 396
Calaresu, F. R., 61
Calkins, S. D., 361
Calvo, M. G., 382
Cameron, J., 124, 136
Campbell, J. D., 8
Campbell, W. K., 329, 418, 452, 462
Campfield, L. A., 96, 98, 99
Campion, M. A., 217
Camras, L. A., 355
Cannon, W. B., 89, 91, 371
Cantor, N., 309, 313, 314, 364
Caprara, G. V., 276, 279
Cardinal, R. N., 61, 63
Carducci, D., 143
Carlsmith, J. M., 15, 263
Carnelley, K. B., 176
Carnevale, P. J. D., 365
Carnochan, P., 390
Carpenter, K. M., 230
Carroll, M. D., 104
Carstensen, L. L., 176, 356, 368, 372, 395, 412
Carter, C. S., 74
Carter, J., 206
Carter, R., 57
Carter, S., III, 481, 495
Cartwright-Smith, J. E., 380
Carvallo, M., 175, 182
Carver, C. L., 71
Carver, C. S., 21, 215, 217, 219, 225, 235, 238, 275, 309, 343, 457, 458
Casali, J. G., 117

Casey, B. J., 57, 80
Casio, W. F., 135
Cassidy, J., 489
Centerbar, D. B., 364
Cervone, D., 223, 225, 276, 278
Chah, D. O., 222
Chambers, J., 137
Chao, Y.-S., 414
Chaplin, W., 296
Chapman, E., 279
Chapman, H. A., 409
Charness, N., 323
Chartrand, T. L., 472
Chatzisarantis, N. L., 325, 446, 447
Chen, E. E., 400
Chen, M., 365, 473
Chen, R., 400
Chen, S., 263
Cheng, J. T., 418
Cheon, S. H., 165, 501
Chhina, G. S., 96
Chiba, A. A., 61
Chicoine, E., 222, 238
Chiou, W. B., 414
Chirkov, V. I., 132
Chiu, C., 267
Christenson, S. L., 12, 13
Christenson, T. C., 390
Chua, H. F., 422
Church, M. A., 254, 258, 259, 261, 267
Cialdini, R. B., 230
Cichy, K., 461, 465
Cioffi, D., 272, 481
Clark, M. S., 176, 177, 361, 363–365
Clark, R. A., 190
Clifford, M. M., 174, 283
Clore, G. L., 228, 349, 355, 383
Coates, B., 365
Cochrane, B., 406
Cofer, C. N., 28, 40, 50, 89
Cohen, A. D., 420
Cohen, J. D., 70, 74, 79, 125
Cohen, S., 177
Cohen-Charash, Y., 419
Cohn, J. F., 373
Cohn, M. A., 459
Coifman, K. G., 411

Cole, S. G., 142
Colin, V. L., 357, 450
Collins, A., 228, 349
Collins, J. L., 272
Collins, R. L., 458
Colvin, C., 292
Compton, W. C., 456
Condon, P., 426, 428
Condry, J., 133, 136, 137
Conger, J., 102
Connell, J. P., 13, 143–145, 163, 173, 178, 316, 317, 447
Connelly, S., 395
Connolly, K., 355
Connolly, T., 227
Connor, K., 136
Constantian, C. A., 199, 201
Cook, D. L., 298
Cooper, H., 160, 194
Cooper, J., 265
Cooper, M. L., 204
Cooper, S, 471
Cooper, W. H., 190
Copernicus, 44
Cornish, K. A., 456
Cordaro, D., 350, 351, 368, 374, 402
Cordova, D. I., 149, 160, 347, 348
Cornelius, R. R., 383
Cosmides, L., 353, 375
Costanzo, P. R., 102
Costello, C. G., 291
Costello, J., 295
Costomiris, S., 136
Cote, S., 361
Cotler, T., 199
Covington, M., 137, 174, 190, 198, 251
Cowley, M. A., 99
Cox, K., 455
Cox, P. D., 275
Cox, R., 437
Coyne, J. C., 176, 355, 397, 411
Craig, A. D., 68, 69, 79
Craighead, W. E., 124
Cragg, L., 57
Crago, M., 100
Crandall, C. S., 100
Crandell, C. J., 444
Crary, W. G., 310
Craven, R. G., 8, 307
Cree, K., 146

Creswell, J. D., 477
Crews, F., 492
Crick, F., 474
Crista, I. A., 360
Critchley, H. D., 69
Crits-Christoph, P., 489
Crombez, G., 18
Crone, E. A., 57
Cross, S. E., 313, 314
Crowne, D. P., 198
Crowson, J. J., Jr., 298
Csikszentmihalyi, I., 169
Csikszentmihalyi, M., 22, 26, 39,
    168–170, 227, 434, 453
Cui, X., 486, 488
Cummings, D. E., 98, 102
Cunningham, M. R., 107–109, 115
Cunningham, W., 73
Curry, L. A., 298
Custers, R., 478, 495
Cutler, K., 171
Cyranowski, J. M., 110

D
D'Amato, M. R., 41
D'Andrade, R. C., 191
D'Ardenne, K., 125
Dalebroux, A., 360
Dall'Osso, B., 374
Damasio, A., 62, 63, 73, 80
Damasio, H., 62, 63, 80
Daniels, M., 462
Darwin, C. A., 31, 47, 50, 353, 470
Daubman, K. A., 364, 368, 460
Daukantaite, D., 457
David, D., 360
Davidson, R. J., 52, 70, 72, 73, 80,
    341, 350, 351, 357, 361, 372, 384
Davies, J., 307
Davis, C. G., 459
Davis, K. E., 391
Davis, M., 61
Davis, M. H., 424
Davis, S., 105
Davis, W. B., 204
Dawes, R. M., 307
Day, J. D., 314
Dayan, P., 65
Dearing, R. L., 382, 414, 418
De Castro, J. M., 100
De Cremer, D., 417

De Dreu, C. K. W., 425
De Hooge, I. E., 414, 415
De Houwer, J., 384
De Jong, P. J., 417
De La Ronde, C., 310
De Ridder, D. T. D., 231, 238
de Rivera, J., 408
de St. Aubin, E., 459
De Steno, D., 417, 422, 425, 428
De Volder, M., 195
De Wall, C. N., 327
De Wit, J. B. F., 231, 238
Deaux, K., 329
deCharms, R., 135, 159, 192, 315
Deci, E. L., 8, 17, 20, 21, 23, 26, 39,
    40, 45, 130, 132–137, 139, 140,
    142, 143, 145, 146, 148, 151,
    153–155, 157–161, 163–168,
    172–175, 177, 178, 180–182,
    228, 315, 317, 327, 333, 413,
    435, 446, 447, 450, 456, 464
DeJong, W., 135
Dekker, J. J., 384
Delisle, J., 444
DeLongis, A., 176
Demaree, H. A., 326
DeMartino, M. F., 36
Dember, W. N., 37, 41, 50
Dembo, T., 241
Dempsey, E. W., 89
DeNeve, K. M., 457
Denson, T. F., 408
Dent, A. L., 160
DePaulo, B., 481
Depner, C., 188
Depue, R. A., 291
Derakshan, N., 395
Derryberry, D., 45
Descartes, R., 30, 47, 48, 50
Deutsch, J. A., 97
Deutschlander, S., 115
Devine, P. G., 262, 265
Dholakia, U. M., 233
Di Chiara, G., 66
Diamond, A., 459
Dickerson, C., 264
Dickerson, S. S., 75, 80
Dickinson, A., 66, 72
Diener, C. I., 282–284, 286–288,
    302, 366, 455
Diener, C., 215, 306, 455

Diener, E., 306, 307, 363, 412, 455,
    456
Dienstbier, R. A., 45
Dijk, C., 417
Dijksterhuis, A., 231, 478
Dimberg, U., 396
Dion, S. C., 143, 146, 147
Dirlikov, B., 185, 209
Diserens, C. M., 433
Disney, W., 89, 278
Dizen, M., 391
Dodson, J. D., 38
Dolan, R. J., 80
Dollinger, S. J., 136, 173
Donaldson, C., 391
Donovan, J. M., 109
Dossett, D. L., 223
Douvan, E., 188
Dovidio, J. F., 425
Downie, M., 146
Draganski, B., 80
Drake, J. E., 360, 368
Dreisbach, G., 234
Druss, R. G., 444
Duda, J., 257
Duffy, E., 38
Duncan, E., 390, 395
Duncan, N., 450
Dundin, L., 408
Dukas, 89
Dunker, K., 366
Dunlap, K., 32
Dunn, J., 357
Dunton, B., 472
Dweck, C. S., 26, 45, 215, 250–256,
    267, 282–284, 286–288, 302,
    504
Dyck, D. G., 444
Dykman, B. M., 443, 448, 449, 464

E
Eagle, M., 489
Earley, P. C., 221, 223, 227
Early, S., 298
Earnest, A., 200
Eastwick, P. W., 112
Ebbesen, E. B., 265
Ebert, R., 409
Eccles, J. S., 215, 299, 302
Eccles-Parsons, J. E., 191
Eccleston, C., 18

Edge, K., 282
Edwards, K., 408
Edwards, R., 397
Eelen, P., 384
Eghrari, H., 148
Ehlert, U., 75, 80
Eibl-Eibesfeldt, I., 33, 355, 381
Eidelson, R. J., 201
Einstein, A., 40, 44, 254
Eisenberg, N., 408, 424, 425
Eisenberger, R., 136
Eisenstadt, D., 264
Ekegren, G., 227
Ekman, P., 12, 47, 50, 344, 347,
    348, 350, 351, 353, 355, 361,
    368, 372–374, 376, 378–381,
    402, 410, 411, 427, 476
Elder, G. H., 487
ElGeledi, S., 146
El-Haschimi, K., 104
Elias, C. F., 96
Elliot, A., 478
Elliot, A. J., 20, 21, 26, 70, 132,
    177, 178, 180, 198, 222, 223,
    254, 256–262, 265, 267, 317,
    318, 321, 334, 455, 457
Elliot, E. S., 254, 256
Elliot, T. R., 298
Ellison, P. T., 75
Ellsworth, P. C., 15, 349, 368, 372,
    379, 380, 382, 383, 387, 390,
    403, 408
Elmquist, J. K., 96
Ely, R. J., 311
Ely, T. D., 61
Emerick, S. W., 376
Emlen. S. T., 113
Emmons, R. A., 319, 321, 363,
    455, 459
Emmons, R. E., 420, 422, 425
Engeser, S., 171
Entin, E. E., 190, 195, 197
Epel, E. S., 75
Epstein, A. N., 93
Epstein, J. A., 198
Epstude, K., 423
Erber, R., 481
Erdelyi, M. H., 472, 480
Erez, M., 225
Ericsson, K. A., 323
Erst, F., 73, 74

Eskenazi, J., 478
Esses, J. M., 101
Estrada, C. A., 366
Ethier, K. A., 329
Evans, G. E., 296
Evdokar, A., 387
Everitt, B. J., 61
Exline, R. V., 201
Exner, J. E., Jr., 472
Eysenck, H. J., 492
Eysenck, M. W., 395

F
Fabes, R. A., 424
Faber, R. J., 329
Fallon, A. E., 408, 409
Farmakalidis, E., 97
Farmer-Dougan, V. A., 122
Farnham, S. D., 469, 473
Farrer, C., 69, 79
Farrow, D. L., 203
Faulk, K. E., 412
Faust, I. M., 97
Fazio, R. H., 265, 472
Feather, N. T., 190, 423
Feeney, J. A., 176, 489
Fehr, B., 339, 390, 408
Fein, S., 22
Feinberg, R., 136
Feinstein, J. A., 207
Feldman, L. A. 107, 390
Feltz, D. L., 272
Fenigstein, A., 449
Fernald, A., 355
Fernandez-Dols, J. M., 355
Feshbach, S., 43
Festinger, L., 36, 39, 45, 241,
    261, 263
Figner, B., 57
Filipp, S., 75
Fincham, F. D., 172, 422
Fincher, K., 409
Finkel, E. J., 112, 326, 329
Finkenauer, C., 462
Finn, P., 111
Fischer, A. H., 395
Fischer, H., 70
Fischer, K. W., 390, 398
Fisher, C. D., 142
Fisher, S., 474, 492
Fishman, D., 199

Fishman, G., 471
Fiske, S. T., 5
Fitness, J., 409
Flegel, K. M., 104
Flett, G. L., 444
Flicker, L., 415
Flier, J. F., 98
Flier, J. S., 115
Flores, S. A., 395
Flowerday, T., 160
Fobes, J. L., 76
Foch, T. T., 104
Foder, E. M., 202, 203
Fogarty, S. J., 366
Fok, H. K., 399
Folkman, S., 279, 359, 385,
    386, 459
Ford, B. Q., 405
Ford, J. G., 432, 440, 441, 445
Forest, D., 365
Forster, J., 249, 250
Fortier, M. S., 143
Fowler, P. C., 225
Fowles, D. C., 364
Fox, M. J., 28
Fox, P., 53
Framakalidis, E., 114
Frank, E., 243, 266
Frankl, V. E., 458, 482
Frederick, C. M., 132, 180
Frederick, D. A., 113
Fredricks, 13
Fredrickson, B. L., 26, 391, 412,
    420, 433, 459, 460
Freedman, E. R., 447
Freedman, Z. R., 142, 157
Freitas, A. L., 245, 247, 248, 267
Fremouw, W. J., 101
French, J. D., 60
Freud, A., 484
Freud, S., 29, 32, 34, 36, 49, 458,
    468, 470, 472, 473, 478, 480,
    482, 483, 486, 490, 493
Frey, K., 370
Fridlund, A. J., 355
Fried, C. B., 253, 262, 264
Friedman, R., 234
Friesen, W. V., 12, 372, 373, 378,
    380, 381, 410, 411
Frieze, I. H., 273

Frijda, N. H., 343, 349, 354, 355, 368, 382, 383, 387, 403
Frith, C. D., 69, 79, 80
Frodi, A., 170–173
Froh, J. J., 422
Fromm, E., 175, 438, 452, 467, 480
Frone, M. R., 204
Frost, R. O., 444
Frysinger, R. C., 61
Fulmer, C., 245, 246
Fujita, F., 242
Fulford, D., 457
Furrer, C., 177, 450
Fuxe, K., 67

G
Gable, S. L., 70, 71, 420, 428
Gabriel, S., 175, 182
Gagne, M., 327
Gagnon, J. H., 110
Gailliot, M. T., 326, 327
Gain, D., 105
Galanter, E. H., 41, 215
Galinsky, A. D., 205
Gallagher, M., 61
Gallagher, S. M., 138
Galvan, A., 57, 80
Gardner, H., 40
Gauvin, L. I., 142
Gavlin, S., 112
Gazzaniga, M. S., 52, 55
Gecas, V., 329
Geller, E. S., 117
Geller, L., 462, 463
Gerard, H. B., 261, 262
Gershoff, E. T., 128, 129, 151
Geva, N., 364
Giacalone, R. A., 263
Giesler, B., 312
Gilbert, D. T., 364
Gillham, J., 458
Gilovich, T., 263
Gjesme, T., 194
Gladue, B. A., 112
Gladwell, M., 475, 476
Gladwin, T. E., 57
Glazer, H. I., 295
Gloria, C. T., 412
Glover, G., 80
Goebel, B. L., 437
Goffman, E., 330

Goldberg, B., 480
Goldberg, C., 451, 452
Goldberg, J. H., 347
Goldsmith, H. H., 361
Goldstein, K., 433
Goldstein, T. R., 360
Goleman, D., 338
Gollwitzer, P. M., 215, 230–234, 238, 242–244, 495
Gonas, G., 330
Gonzalez, M. F., 97
Good, C., 253
Goodenough, F. L., 381
Goodenow, C., 177, 450
Goodner, V., 139
Goschke, T., 234
Gottlieb, E., 478
Gottman, J. M., 356, 368, 395, 410, 412, 422
Gould, D., 276
Graaf, R., 455
Grady, K. E., 177
Graham, L, 279
Graham, S., 393
Gralinski, H., 252
Gray, J. A., 125, 347, 348, 364, 374
Gray, P. B., 75
Grazziano, P. A., 361
Green, C. W., 124
Greenberg, J. R., 262, 307, 311
Greenberg, R. P., 471, 474, 489, 492
Green-Demers, I., 144, 146, 147
Greene, D., 133, 135, 136, 151
Greeno, C. G., 101, 104
Greenwald, A. G., 208, 265, 469, 473, 478
Greitemeyer, T., 145, 146, 151
Gregory, L. W., 230
Grief, E., 123, 151
Griffin, S. 455
Griffitt, W., 365
Grilo, C. M., 104
Grindle, A. C., 138
Grisham, J. R., 408
Grobler, A., 195
Groeger, J. A., 408, 428
Grolnick, W. S., 132, 159, 165, 173, 177, 450, 491
Gross, J. J., 73, 353, 356–361, 366, 368, 384, 390, 391
Gross, N., 329

Grossman, B. S., 132
Groth, G. E., 113
Grow, V. M., 447
Gruen, A., 450
Gruenfeld, D. H., 205
Grunert, S. C., 447
Guay, A. T., 105
Guinote, A., 205
Guisinger, S., 175
Gumora, G., 361
Gunlicks, M., 75
Gunnar, M. R., 75
Gunturkun, O., 115
Gurland, S. T., 133, 135, 136
Guskin, K., 172

H
Hackett, G., 277
Haggbloom, S. J., 36
Hagger, M. S., 325, 327, 446, 447
Haidt, J., 354, 355, 409
Halal, M., 366
Hale, J. A., 199, 477
Hall, H. K., 227
Hall, J., 61
Hall, J. F., 36
Hall, J. L., 189
Hall, R. V., 122, 123, 151
Hall, W. G., 93, 94
Halliwell, W. R., 142
Halvari, H., 143, 157
Hamachek, D. E., 444
Hamann, S., 347, 348, 374
Hamann, S. B., 61
Hamer, D. H., 111
Hamm, D., 160, 165
Hammersmith, S. K., 111
Hampton, A. N., 64
Hanson, A. R., 173
Harackiewicz, J., 173, 198, 220, 228, 254, 256, 259, 260
Hardeman, M., 439, 464
Hardin, C., 472
Hardre, P. L., 132, 138, 148
Hardy, A. B., 274
Hare, T., 57
Hare, T. A., 80
Hareli, S., 423
Harlow, H. F., 36, 45
Harmon-Jones, E., 26, 215, 261, 262, 264, 267, 390, 408

Harper, R. M., 61
Harpster, L., 149
Harrington, D. M., 443
Harris, C., 302
Harris, C. R., 355, 416, 428
Harris, R. N., 311
Harrison, A. A., 112, 115
Harrison, S., 222
Harter, S., 26, 39, 134, 137, 167, 168, 182, 309, 487
Hartmann, H., 482, 483
Harvey, J., 98
Haselton, M. G., 113
Hatfield, D. B., 138
Hatfield, E., 106, 112, 115, 396
Haviland, J. J., 412
Haviland, J. M., 357
Hayden, B. Y., 64, 74
Hazan, C., 471, 489, 490, 495
Healy, S., 199, 201–203
Heatherton, T. F., 101, 102, 227, 326
Hebb, D. O., 35, 37, 38, 356
Heckhausen, H., 190, 191, 199, 244, 270
Heider, F., 159, 391
Heider, K. G., 410
Heikamp, T., 238
Heinrich, M., 75, 80
Heise, D. R., 330
Heller, J. F., 44
Hellhammer, D. H., 75
Helmke, A., 306, 307
Helmreich, R. L., 256
Hembree, E. A., 412
Hemenover, S. H., 359
Henderlong, J., 140
Hendricks, M., 478, 495
Hennessey, B. A., 132
Herman, C. P., 44, 101, 102, 115, 481, 482
Hernandez, J. A., 395
Herrera, D., 195
Herrick, S., 298
Hervas, G., 411
Hewitt, P. L., 444
Heyman, G. D., 256
Heyns, R. W., 198, 201
Hidi, S., 26, 213
Higgins, E. T., 42, 44, 45, 215, 244–250, 259, 267
Hilgard, 41

Hill, C. A., 311
Hill, E., 109
Hill, J. O., 100, 104
Hind, H., 104
Hinsch, C., 201
Hiroto, D. S., 286
Hirsch, J., 96, 97
Hitchcock, J. M., 61
Hochschild, A. R., 400, 401
Hodges, S. D., 424
Hodgins, H. S., 317, 450, 478
Hodgkins, S., 233
Hoebel, B. G., 76
Hoek, A., 105
Hoffman, J. M., 61
Hoffman, J. T., 298
Hoffman, M. L., 424
Hoffman, R., 474
Hofman, T., 390
Hogan, B., 451
Hogg, M. A., 11
Hokoda, A., 172
Holahan, C. J., 277
Holahan, C. K., 277
Holland, R. W., 478, 495
Hollembeak, J., 173
Holleran, S. A., 302
Hollerman, J. R., 11
Holmes, D. S., 379, 480
Holstedge, G., 384
Holt, E. B., 32
Holt, K., 132, 151, 166
Holt, R. R., 468
Holt, S. H. A., 97, 114
Holzberger, D., 276
Hom, H. L., Jr., 133, 151
Hong, Y., 251, 252, 267
Honig, G., 231
Hood, M., 180
Horney, K., 145, 489
Horowitz, M. J., 455
Horvath, T., 107
Houlfort, N., 137
House, R. J., 205, 206, 209
Houser-Marko, L., 319, 320, 440, 464
Howells, G. N., 274
Howsepian, B., 314
Hoyle, R., 256
Huber, V. L., 227
Huebner, R. R., 355

Huettel, S. A., 69
Hull, C. L., 33–37, 49, 50, 87, 112, 343
Hulleman, C. S., 220
Hupka, R. B., 379, 380, 391
Hurlemann, R., 115
Hurley, C. M., 381
Husman, J., 148, 194, 195
Huta, V., 157
Hwang, H. C., 381, 418
Hyman, S. E., 66

I
Idson, C. I., 249
Ilgen, D. R., 222
Inbar, Y., 409
Inglehart, M., 376
Inkster, J. A., 263
Inoshita, O., 225
Inouye, D. K., 274
Iran-Nejad, A., 363
Irving, L. M., 302
Irwin, W., 73, 384
Isaacson, R. L., 201
Isen, A. M., 21, 26, 68, 364–366, 368, 460
Ivry, R., 52
Iwata, B. A., 124, 126
Iwata, J., 384
Iyengar, S., 160
Izard, C. E., 10, 20, 26, 47, 50, 339, 341, 343, 347, 348, 350, 352, 354–357, 368, 375, 376, 378, 380, 381, 402, 410–413, 507
Izuma, K., 133, 151

J
Jack, R. E., 382
Jackson, A., 221, 276
Jackson, J. R., 472
Jackson, L., 136
Jackson, R. J., 200, 202, 209, 227
Jackson, S. A., 168, 171
Jackson, W. T., 298
Jacobs, P. D., 290
Jacobs, W. J., 481
Jaffe, K., 176
James, W., 31–33, 36, 47, 50, 371, 372
Jang, H., 138, 148, 149, 151, 162, 165, 172, 173

Jankowiak, W. R., 109
Janssen, E., 111
Jarvis, W. B., G., 207
Jaycox, L., 458
Jazaieri, H., 510
Jeffrey, D. B., 104
Jenkins, J. M., 343
Jenkins, S. R., 5, 188, 192, 198, 451
Jetton, T. L., 413
John, O. P., 294, 360
Johnson, C. L., 104
Johnson, M. M. S., 364
Johnson, P. R., 97
Johnson, R. P., 117
Johnson, V. E., 105
Johnson-Laird, P. N., 349, 353, 368, 383, 387
Johnston, R. E., 22, 355, 365
Joiner, T. E., 412
Jonah, 438
Jones, A., 409
Jones, E. E., 391
Jones, F. C., 123, 151
Jones, L. L., 57
Jones, M. R., 40, 45, 50
Jordan, M., 278
Jose, P. E., 389
Josephs, R. A., 75, 481
Joule, R. V., 263
Joussemet, M., 132, 137

K
Kaczala, C. M., 191
Kagan, J., 44
Kahn, J. H., 480
Kahneman, D., 223, 472
Kalin, R., 204
Kalisch, R., 80
Kalogeris, T. J., 97
Kamins, M., 252, 253
Kanade, T., 373
Kanat-Mayman, Y., 132, 443
Kanfer, R., 227
Kaplan, H., 148, 256, 443
Kaplan, N., 489
Kapp, B. S., 61, 384
Karabenick, S. A., 190, 197
Karademas, E. C., 360
Karp, L., 365
Karren, R. J., 221

Kasser, T., 132, 157, 180, 181, 319, 321, 433, 445, 455, 457
Kassinove, H., 370, 408
Kassirer, J. P., 99, 102
Kast, A., 136
Katz, I., 132, 160
Katz, J., 310
Katzman, M., 444
Kawabata, M., 170, 171
Kay, A. C., 478
Kazdin, A. E., 123, 274
Keane, S. P., 361
Keating, C. F., 109
Keenan, M., 138
Keesey, R. E., 85, 99, 115
Keith, P. M., 310
Keller, J., 168, 169, 182, 245, 246, 249
Keller, H., 254
Kelley, H. H., 391
Kelley, M. L., 138
Kelly, A. E., 480
Kelly, D. D., 111
Keltner, D., 353–356, 395, 408, 410, 414, 416
Kemeny, M. E., 75, 80, 374
Kemnitz, J. W., 85, 99
Kemper, T. D., 390
Kendrick, K. M., 115
Kennedy, J. F., 202, 206
Kenrick, D. T., 113
Kermer, D. A., 364
Kessler, R. C., 489
Keyes, C. L. M., 23, 304, 453
Kieffer, S. C., 252
Kihlstrom, J. F., 309, 473
Kilpatrick, S. D., 420
Kilts, C. D., 61
Kim, E. J., 165
Kim, D. A., 409
Kim, S. H., 418
Kim, Y., 180
Kimble, G. A., 21
Kimeldorf, M. B., 420
Kimes, L. A., 452
Kindermann, T. A., 13, 178
King, K., 143
King, L., 366, 412
King, L. A., 459
Kinney, R. F., 215, 243
Kirkpatrick, L. A., 200

Kirschbaum, C., 75, 80
Kirsch, P., 107
Kirshnit, C., 199, 202, 209
Kirson, D., 392, 403
Kitayama, S., 400
Klauer, T., 75
Kleck, R. E., 380, 408
Kleiber, D. A., 192
Klein, H. J., 222, 223
Kleinman, S., 400
Klesges, R. C., 100, 104
Klien, G., 36
Kligyte, V., 395
Kling, A. S., 61
Klinger, M. R., 478
Klinnert, M. D., 355
Klohnen, E. C., 489
Klorman, R., 380
Klose, D. A., 451
Knauss, M. R., 104
Knee, C. R., 252, 317
Knobe, J., 409
Knock, D., 73, 74
Knox, R. E., 263
Knutson, B., 69, 79
Koch, S., 50
Koestner, R., 8, 132, 133, 135–137, 140, 143, 146, 151, 159, 166, 173, 185, 186, 222, 224, 238, 447, 450, 476
Kohn, A., 133, 134, 136, 138, 145
Kohut, H., 294
Kolb, B., 66
Kolb, J., 471
Kosfeld, M., 76, 107
Koulack, D., 474
Kowalski, P. S., 254
Kozub, F. J., 94
Kramer, D. A., 357
Kramer, M., 474
Kramer, P. D., 68
Kramer, R., 449
Krampe, R. T. C., 323
Krantz, P. J., 138
Kranzler, J., 272
Krapp, A., 413
Krause, S., 199, 201–203
Kraut, R. E., 22, 355, 365
Krettek, J. E., 384
Kringelbach, M., 62, 64, 384
Krueger, J. I., 8

Kruglanski, A. W., 207, 234, 240, 250, 452
Krull, D. S., 310
Kucznarski, R. J., 104
Kuhl, J., 190, 197, 198, 209, 241
Kuhn, T. S., 43
Kuhnen, C. M., 69, 79
Kulik, J. A., 200
Kulikowich, J. M., 413
Kulka, R., 188
Kunter, M., 276
Kuo, Z. Y., 32, 50
Kuppens, P., 424
Kurokawa, M., 400
Kuypers, H. G. J. M., 384

L
La Guardia, J. G., 165, 175, 182
Lac, A., 5
Lau, H., 80
Lachman, R., 40
Lahart, C., 444
Laibson, D. L., 74, 79
Laird, A., 53
Laird, J. D., 366, 379, 380
Lagattuta, K. H., 417
Lakie, W. L., 198
Lama, D., 338
Lambert, N. M., 422
Lane, J. D., 473, 480
Lane, K. A., 469
Lane, M. D., 99
Lang, P. J., 372
Lange, C., 371, 372
Langer, E. J., 292, 296
Langsdorff, P., 412
Lansing, J. B., 201
Lanzetta, J. T., 380
Lapointe, A. B., 298
LaPointe, K. A., 444
LaPorte, R. E., 223
Larrance, D. T., 380
Larrick, R. P., 22
Larsen, D. B., 420
Larsen, J., 459
Larsen, R. J., 357, 370, 379, 453
Latham, G. P., 26, 41, 44, 215, 220–225, 227, 228, 236, 238
Laumann, E. O., 105
Laurent, S. M., 424
Lavrakas, P. J., 107

Lawrence, E. C., 225
Lazarus, R. S., 26, 41, 47, 50, 227, 279, 294, 344, 349, 359, 383, 385–387, 393, 402
Learman, D., 393
Leary, M. R., 174–177, 182, 200, 449
Leavitt, K., 208
LeDoux, J. E., 61, 62, 341, 344, 374, 375, 384
Lee, H. J., 107
Lee, K. A., 487
Lee, W., 52, 68, 69
Lee-Chal, K., 107
Leeka, J., 361
Lefcourt, H. M., 486
Legaut, L., 146, 147
Leggett, E. L., 254–256
Lehman, S., 413
Leifer, H., 102
Leippe, M. R., 264
Lekes, N., 137, 222, 238
Lelwica, M., 412
LeMay, E. P. Jr., 176
Lench, H. C., 395
Lengfelder, A., 231
Lens, W., 132, 148, 159, 194, 195, 315, 412
Leon, I., 395
Leone, D. R., 148
Lepes, D., 132
Lepore, S. J., 177
Lepper, M. R., 133–137, 140, 149, 151, 160
Lerner, J. S., 347, 395, 408
Levenson, R. W., 342, 345, 347, 348, 353, 356, 361, 366, 372, 373, 375, 395, 402, 408, 412
Levesque, C., 477
Levin, P. F., 365
Levin, R., 364, 474
Lewinsohn, P. M., 296
Lewin, K., 25, 36, 241
Lewis, M., 296, 414
Li, J., 398
Li, N. P., 113
Liberzon, I., 342
Lien, J., 373
Liesl, 438
Liljeholm, M., 63
Liljenquist, K., 410

Lim, M. M., 75
Lin, D. M.-S., 267
Lin, Y., 201
Lindgren, H. C., 201
Lindsley, D. B., 36–38
Linehan, M. M., 314
Linnenbrink, E. A., 256
Linsenmeier, J. A. W., 113
Linton, S., 408
Lipp, O. V., 406
Lischetzke, T., 390
Locke, E. A., 26, 39, 41, 44, 215, 220, 224, 225, 236, 238
Loevinger, J., 471, 483
Loewenstein, G., 74, 79, 101
Loftus, E. F., 478
Longino, J., 221
Lopes, P. N., 361
Lopez, S. J., 299, 434, 453, 461, 465
Lord, R. G., 217
Lorenz, K., 33
Losier, G. F., 143
Losoff, M., 201, 202, 209
Louie, J. Y., 400
Louro, M. J., 219
Lowe, M. R., 101
Lowell, E. L., 190
Lowery, L., 409
Lowney, P., 104
Luborsky, L., 489
Lucas, R. E., 432, 455
Lundquist, D., 382
Lustgarten, N., 222
Luyckx, K., 159
Lynch, J. H., 176, 177
Lyubomirsky, S., 366, 411, 412

M
MacDonald, C. J., 397
Mack, D., 101
MacLeod, A. K, 364
Madsen, K. B., 36
Maehr, M. L., 192, 256, 257
Magee, J. C., 205
Magoun, H. W., 37
Mahler, H. I. M., 200
Mahoney, E. R., 107
Mahoney, M. J., 123
Maier, S. F., 17, 26, 285
Maier, S. M., 139

Maier, W., 115
Main, M., 489
Maisel, N., 420, 428
Malenka, R. C., 66
Mallan, K. M., 406
Malle, B. F., 423
Mallett, C. J., 170, 171
Malmo, R. B., 38
Malone, P. S., 276
Manderlink, G., 198, 228
Mandler, G., 356, 371
Mandrup, S., 99
Manian, N., 245, 246
Mangun, G. R., 52
Manly, J. B., 132
Manoogian, S. T., 136
Mansfield, E., 459
Manstead, A. S. R., 354, 395, 397, 398, 401, 417, 422, 425
Marazziti, D., 107, 374
Marien, H., 478, 495
Marks, J. D., 61
Markus, H., 39, 41, 215, 308–310, 313, 314, 333, 400
Markwith, M., 409, 427
Marlatt, G. P., 481
Marlowe, D., 198
Marques, S. C., 461, 465
Marsh, A. A., 408
Marsh, H., 8, 171, 307
Martin, A. J., 168
Martin, C., 147
Martin, J. J., 171
Martin, L. L., 379
Martin, P., 444
Martin, R. A., 486
Mascolo, M. F., 398
Masling, J., 492
Maslow, A. H., 29, 36, 40, 41 45, 87, 200, 433, 435–439, 448, 451, 452, 456, 462, 463
Mason, A., 203, 204
Mason, W. S., 329
Masters, W. H., 105
Mathes, E. W., 437
Matsui, T., 225
Matsumoto, D., 372, 380, 381, 410, 417, 418, 427
Matsumoto, K., 74, 133, 151
Matsumoto, M., 133, 151
Mauss, I. B., 339, 341, 342, 368

May, R., 433, 452, 453, 462
Mazur, A., 109
McAdams, D. P., 199–203, 209, 459
McArthur, L. Z., 109
McAuley, E., 142
McCall, C., 107
McCarter, L., 368
McCaul, K. D., 379
McCauley, C. R., 409
McClannahan, L. E., 138
McClearn, G. E., 104
McClelland, D. C., 36, 41, 45, 185–187, 190, 191, 197, 198, 200, 201, 203–206, 209, 476, 477
McClure, S. M., 64, 74, 79, 125
McConnell, H. K., 265
McCoy, A. N., 64
McCullough, M. E., 420, 422, 425
McCullers, J. C., 132, 137
McDermott, K. B., 56
McDonald, A. J., 61
McDougall, W., 32
McEachern, A. W., 329
McEwen, B. S., 75
McGinley, H., 109
McGinley, P., 109
McGraw, K. O., 132, 137, 227
McGregor, H., 256, 260
McHugh, P. R., 97
McIntosh, D. N., 376, 379, 380, 402
McKeachie, W. J., 41, 201
McLear, P. M., 107
McNally, R. J., 43
Mead, M., 47
Means, B., 365
Mednick, E. V., 366
Mednick, M. T., 366
Mednick, S. A., 366
Medvec, V. H., 263
Meece, J., 256, 257, 299
Melton, A. M. A., 456
Mento, A. J., 221, 225
Mercer, C. D., 138
Mertz, E., 364
Mesquita, B., 396
Meston, C. M., 105
Meyer, D., 107
Mickelson, K. D., 489
Midden, C., 231
Midgley, C., 257

Mikulincer, M., 284, 286, 297, 302, 359
Milberg, S., 176
Milholland, J., 201
Miller, C. J., 457
Miller, D., 264
Miller, D. L., 138
Miller, E. K., 70
Miller, G. A., 215, 216
Miller, G. E., 235
Miller, L. K., 90
Miller, N. E., 35–37, 41, 96
Miller, P. H., 57
Miller, S. D., 257
Miller, R. S., 415
Millman, L., 409
Millon, T., 294
Mills, J., 26, 176, 215, 261–264, 267, 365
Milner, P., 76
Mims, V., 159
Minaker, K., 92
Mineka, S., 364, 374, 406
Mirenowicz, J., 66
Mischel, W., 30, 296, 329, 365
Mitchell, J. S., 85, 99
Mitchell, S., 471, 489
Mitchell, T. R., 223
Mitchison, G., 474
Mittelman, W., 435
Mizrahi, K., 329
Moeller, G. H., 192
Moffitt, A., 474
Moller, A. C., 133, 160, 177, 178, 182, 327
Moltz, H., 33
Money, J., 105, 111
Monroe, S. M., 291
Montague, B., 382
Montague, P. R., 64, 65
Mook, D. G., 89, 94
Moon, I. S., 165, 501
Moors, A., 368, 382, 384, 387, 403
Moran, T. H., 97
Morgan, C., 149
Morgan, C. D., 185
Morgenson, G. J., 61
Morse, R. C., 478
Moruzzi, G., 37
Mosher, R., 136
Moskowitz, G. B., 232

Mossholder, K. W., 227, 228
Moulds, M. L., 408
Mouratidis, A. A., 412, 413
Mowrer, H., 45
Mudar, P., 204
Muehlenhard, C. L., 452
Mueller, C. M., 252–254, 267
Mueller, K. J., 137
Mulligan, K., 339
Mumme, D., 172
Munarriz, R., 105
Munn, P., 357
Munster-Halvari, A. E., 143
Munzberg, H., 99
Muraven, M., 325–327, 334
Murayama, K., 133, 151, 259
Murphy, S. T., 376
Murray, E. A., 61, 62
Murray, H. A., 37, 87, 185, 472
Myers, M., 424
Myers, M. G., 99

N
Nadel, L., 481
Nagy, D., 360
Nair, A. C., 64
Nakamura, J., 168, 170
Nasby, W., 366
Nath, R., 223
Nation, K., 57
Neale, M. C., 111
Neemann, J., 309
Neher, A., 463
Nemeroff, C., 409
Neuberg, S. L., 207
Newby, T. J., 148
Newell, A., 216
Newman, E. B., 371
Newman, R. S., 256
Newsom, J. T., 207
Nezlak, J., 175
Nezu, A. M., 486
Nezu, C. M., 486
Nicholas, K., 109
Nicholls, J. G., 254
Niedenthal, P. M., 364
Niedenthal, P., 313
Nielsen, I., 455
Nielsen, T. A., 474
Niemiec, C. P., 154, 157, 164, 455
Niezink, L. F., 424

Nils, F., 397
Nisbett, R. E., 133, 292
Nix, G. A., 132, 133, 160, 165
Nixon, M., 206
Noels, K., 144
Nolen, S. B., 256
Nolen-Hoeksema, S., 172, 359, 411, 459
Noller, P., 397, 489
Nosek, B. A., 208, 469
Nowicki, G. P., 364, 365, 368, 460
Ntoumanis, N., 147, 173
Nummenmaa, L., 382
Nurius, P., 313
Nystrom, L. E., 125
Nystul, M. S. 444

O
O'Brien, F., 127
O'Connor, C., 392, 403
O'Doherty, J., 56, 63, 64, 72
Oaten, M., 327
Oatley, K., 343, 349, 353, 368, 383, 387, 390, 395
Ochsner, K. N., 73, 75, 384
Oettingen, G., 230, 231, 242, 294, 458
Ohman, A., 374, 407, 408
Oikawa, M., 478
Okada, A., 225
Olatunji, B. O., 409
Olds, J., 37, 45, 76, 77, 122
Olson, B. C., 142
Omelich, C. L., 190, 198, 251
O'Malley, S., 143, 157
Omura, M., 138, 148
Orbell, S., 230, 233
Orehek, E., 452
Orlick, T. D., 136
Orth, U., 357, 414
Ortony, A., 228, 349, 383, 387
Osterman, K. F., 177
Otis, N., 102
Ouellette, R., 176
Overskeid, G., 160
Oyer, M., 160
Oyserman, D., 313, 314
Ozer, E. M., 272, 276, 279–281, 302

P
Pace, G. M., 124
Pagliassotti, M. J., 104

Paik, A., 105
Pais-Ribeiro, J. L., 461, 465
Paixao, M. P., 195
Pajares, M. F., 214, 272, 279
Pallak, S. R., 136
Palmer, B., 391
Pang, J. S., 185, 190, 194, 209, 476
Panksepp, J., 344, 345, 347, 348, 373, 374
Paris, A. H., 13
Park, C. L., 459
Park, C., 292, 453
Park, N., 454, 461, 465
Park, R., 309
Parker, L. E., 160
Parker, W., 444
Parkes, A. S., 103
Parkinson, B., 382, 400, 401
Parkinson, J. A., 61
Parks, G. A., 481
Parra, C. E., 80
Parrott, W. G., 418
Parsons, O. A., 372
Pascoe, J. P., 384
Pastorella, C., 279
Patall, E. A., 160
Patrick, B. C., 142, 148, 157, 175, 182
Patrick, R., 365
Paul, J. P., 111
Paulus, M. P., 69
Pavey, L., 145, 146, 151
Pavlov, I., 36
Peake, P., 329
Pearlman, C., 474
Pecina, S., 64
Peirusse, L., 98
Pelham, B. W., 310, 311, 313, 314
Pelletier, D., 147
Pelletier, L. G., 21, 102, 143, 144, 146, 147, 342
Penn, J., 80
Pennebaker, J. W., 459, 481
Penner, L. A., 425
Pensgaard, A., 147
Pereg, D., 359
Perkins, F. T., 371
Perls, F. S., 433
Perry, D., 424
Perry, B. C., 223
Pert, C. B., 67
Pessiglione, M., 63, 64, 80

Peters, D., 461, 465
Peters, J. C., 100, 104
Peters, M. L., 417
Peters, R. S., 36
Peterson, C., 17, 26, 270, 282, 286, 288, 292, 294, 296, 434, 453, 454, 457, 458, 461, 465
Petocz, P., 97
Petty, R. E., 207
Pfaffmann, C., 37, 94, 95
Pham, L. B., 229, 230
Phan, K. L., 342
Philipp, A., 276
Philippot, P., 396
Piaget, J., 36
Pierce, G. R., 176
Pierce, K. L., 138
Pierce, W. D., 136
Pieters, R., 219, 418–420, 428
Pietsch, J., 279
Pietromonaco, P. R., 75, 176
Pike, C. L., 107
Pillard, R. C., 111
Pilon, D. A., 187, 191, 201
Pintrich, P. R., 43, 44, 50, 321
Pipe, K., 147
Pittman, T. S., 44, 135–137
Pitzer, J. R., 178
Piviavin, J. A., 425
Pizarro, D. A., 409
Plant, R. W., 143, 157
Plato, 29, 48
Platt, M. L., 64
Plutchik, R., 345–348, 353
Poehlman, T. A., 208, 469
Pogue-Geile, M. F., 104
Pohorecky, L. A., 295
Polivy, J., 41, 44, 101, 102, 115, 481, 482
Pollyanna, 464
Pond, R. S. Jr., 391
Porte, D., Jr., 97
Potter, S. H., 399
Powell, M. C., 176
Powelson, C. L., 175, 177, 450
Powers, J., 201
Powers, S. I., 75
Powers, T. A., 222, 238
Powers, W. T., 216
Powley, T. L., 99, 115
Pratkanis, A. R., 478
Prebble, S. C., 332

Predmore, S. C., 314
Premack, D., 122
Pressley, E., 378
Pressley, M., 323
Prest, W., 221
Preuschoff, K., 69
Pribram, K. H., 41, 215
Price, J. L., 384
Price, L. H., 19, 20
Price, R. A., 104
Prochaska, I. J., 329
Przybylski, A. K., 146, 158
Pu, J., 326
Puca, R. M., 243, 244
Punzo, D., 314
Pyszczynski, T., 307, 311

Q
Qualls, D. L., 456
Quattrone, C. A., 15
Quinlan, D., 462

R
Rachman, S., 13, 481
Ramamurthi, B., 62
Rand, A., 30
Rand, K. L., 298
Rao, D. C., 98
Rapaport, D., 40
Rapson, R. L., 106, 115, 396
Raskoff, A., 365
Rathunde, K., 169
Ravlin, S. B., 228
Rayias, M., 412
Raynor, J. O., 190, 194, 195, 197
Read, N. W., 97
Reavis, R. D., 361
Reber, A., 482
Reese, L., 274
Reeve, J., 13, 52, 68, 69, 75, 132, 135, 138, 142, 148, 154, 155, 160–163, 165, 168, 172, 173, 182, 365, 378, 414, 449, 460, 501
Regan, D. T., 420
Regenbogen, C., 424
Rehm, M., 298
Reid, A., 329
Reid, G., 173
Reid, R., 143, 146
Reifman, A. S., 22
Reis, D. J., 384

Reis, H. T., 70, 136, 158, 175, 180, 182
Reis, I. L., 400
Reisenzein, R., 382, 390
Reisetter, M. F., 160
Reivich, K., 458
Renninger, K. A., 26, 413
Repucci, N. D., 283
Reschly, A. L., 12, 157
Retting, R. A., 138
Reynolds, P. C., 355
Reynolds, R. E., 413
Reznick, J. S., 136
Rheinberg, F., 171
Rice, T., 98
Richards, A., 395
Richeson, J. A., 475, 495
Riecken, H. W., 263
Ricks, T. E., 117
Rigby, S., 142, 143
Rimé, B., 354, 396–398, 403
Risemberg, R., 323
Ritvo, L. B., 470
Rivkin, I. D., 229
Roberts, G. C., 44
Robertson, R., 123, 151
Robins, R. W., 294, 378, 417, 418, 428
Robinson, D. T., 310, 314, 330, 331, 334
Robinson, G., F., 364
Robinson, J. C., 160
Robinson, J. L., 326
Robinson, T. E., 64, 66
Roby, T. B., 36
Roch, S., 422
Rodin, J., 42, 89, 104, 296
Roese, N. J., 423
Rofe', Y., 200
Rogers, C. R., 26, 36, 37, 41, 175, 435, 439–445, 449–451, 453, 456, 462–464
Rolf, 438
Roll, D., 127
Rolls, B. J., 93, 95, 96, 100
Rolls, E. T., 61, 62, 93, 97, 100
Romanski, L. M., 62
Roney, C., 259
Ronis, D., 265
Roosevelt, F. D., 206, 338
Roosevelt, T., 206
Roper-Hall, A., 97

Rose, S., 273
Roseman, H., 327
Roseman, I. J., 349, 383, 387, 389
Rosen, B., 191
Rosen, J. B., 61
Rosen, R. C., 105
Rosenbaum, M., 96
Rosenberg, E., 373
Rosenberg, E. L., 361
Rosenberg, M., 449
Rosenblate, R., 444
Rosenfeld, P., 263
Rosenhan, D. L., 291
Rosenthal, R., 396
Rosenzweig, A. S., 364
Ross, L., 292, 478
Ross, M., 265
Roth, G., 148, 164, 443
Rothkopf, E. Z., 223
Rotter, J. B., 45
Rowe, E. T., 100
Rowling, J. K., 278
Roy, M., 73
Rozin, P., 408, 409, 427
Rubin, H., 127
Rubin, Z., 203
Rubio, D., 180
Rubio, N., 132
Ruble, D. N., 137, 173
Ruby, B. C., 298
Ruckmick, C. A., 30
Ruderman, A. J., 101
Ruiz-Belba, M. A., 355
Rummel, A., 136
Rush, M. C., 190
Russek, M., 97
Russell, D., 393
Russell, J. A., 339, 361, 362, 368,
   382, 390, 400
Russell, M., 204
Rutledge, L. L., 379, 380
Ruvolo, A. P., 313
Ryan, E. D., 198
Ryan, R. M., 8, 20–23, 26, 40, 45,
   50, 130, 132–137, 139, 140, 142,
   143, 145, 146, 151, 153–155,
   157–161, 163–167, 175–177,
   180–182, 228, 315–319, 321,
   327, 333, 433, 435, 446, 447,
   450, 456, 464, 477, 483, 491
Ryff, C. D., 304, 305, 314, 333

S
Saari, L. M., 222, 400
Sabatinelli, 64
Sabourin, S., 143
Sackeim, H. A., 294
Sacks, C. H., 294
Sadalla, E. K., 113
Saeed, L., 112, 115
Sakurai, T., 98
Salomon, G., 278
Salovey, P., 75, 361
Sameroff, A., 155
Sander, D., 388
Sanghera, M. K., 97
Sansone, C., 136, 149, 198
Sanz, J., 291
Saper, C. B., 96
Sarason, B. R., 176, 177
Sarason, I. G., 176
Sayer, A., 75
Schaal, B., 231, 234
Schachter, S., 36, 47, 200, 263,
   371, 372
Schad, D. J., 185, 209
Schafer, R. B., 310
Schaps, E., 177
Scharff, D. E., 471, 489
Scharff, J. S., 471, 489
Scheele, D., 107, 115
Scheier, M. F., 215, 217, 219, 225,
   235, 238, 309, 339, 343, 449,
   457, 458
Scheiner, M. J., 182
Scheinman, L., 163
Scherer, K. R., 344, 346, 349, 354,
   355, 368, 383, 387, 388, 390,
   403, 407
Scherhorn, G., 447
Schiefele, U., 413
Schmalt, H. D., 244, 259, 260
Schmeichel, B. J., 326
Schmit, L., 80
Schmitt, D. P., 111
Schmitt, M., 97
Schneider, D. J., 481, 495
Schrager, S. M., 220
Schraw, G., 160, 413
Schreibman, L., 138
Schroeder, D. A., 425
Schroeder, J. E., 112
Schroeder, S., 157

Schulenberg, S. E., 456
Schuler, J., 87, 171
Schulman, P., 294
Schultheiss, O. C., 26, 185, 189,
   199, 209, 476, 477, 478
Schultz, D. P., 31
Schultz, R., 235, 238
Schultz, W., 11, 64, 66
Schultz, W. C. M. W., 105
Schunk, D. H., 173, 225, 228, 275,
   276, 323
Schwartz, A., 163, 165, 174
Schwartz, C. E., 296
Schwartz, G. E., 372
Schwartz, J., 392, 403
Schwartz, J. C., 399
Schwartz, M. F., 364
Schwartz, M. W., 96–98
Schwartz, N., 355
Schweizer, S., 359
Sclafani, A., 100, 104
Sears, P. S., 241
Seeley, R. J., 97, 98
Segal, E. M., 40
Segall, M. H., 109
Segraves, R. T., 105
Sejnowski, T. J., 65
Self, E. A., 26
Seligman, M. E. P., 8, 17, 22, 26, 39,
   41, 284–286, 289–292, 294, 296,
   306, 433, 434, 453, 455, 458,
   461, 465
Semin, J. R., 354, 417
Sentisk, K., 309
Sepple, C. P., 97
Shaffer, D., 444, 490
Shah, J., 259
Shah, J. Y., 234
Shaikh, A. R., 157
Shalker, T., 365
Shamay-Tsoory, S., 424
Shapira, Z., 134, 137
Shapiro, D. H., 296
Shaver, P. R., 200, 350, 359, 390,
   392, 399, 403, 411, 471,
   489, 495
Shaw, J. C., 216
Shaw, K. N., 222
Sheeran, P., 230, 231, 233,
   234, 238
Sheffield, F. D., 36

Sheldon, K. M., 26, 87, 132, 154, 157, 158, 180–182, 201, 222, 223, 259–261, 317–321, 334, 437, 440, 445, 455, 457, 464
Shell, D. F, 195, 292
Shelton, J., 418
Shen, B., 147
Sherman, R., 423
Sherrod, D. R., 177
Sherwood, H., 282
Shestyuk, A., 374
Shiota, M. N., 372, 400
Shipley, T. E., Jr., 198
Shirey, L. L., 413
Shmueli, D., 325, 327, 329
Shoda, Y., 329
Shohamy, D., 73
Shore, B. A., 124
Shorey, H. S., 298
Shostrom, E. L., 449
Shulman, R., 265
Sid, A. K. W., 201
Sideridis, G., 412
Sierens, E., 159
Sigmon, S. T., 298, 302
Silver, N., 410, 422
Silverman, J. A., 444
Silverman, L. H., 492
Silvia, P. J., 157, 413, 428
Simon, H. A., 216
Simon, L., 262
Simon, W., 110
Simon-Thomas, E. R., 426
Simons, J., 148, 195, 315
Simson, P. G., 68
Sinaceur, M., 205
Singer, B., 304
Singer, J. E., 372
Singer, T., 69, 107
Singh, B., 96
Singh, D., 107
Singh, L, 409
Sinha, R., 372
Skinner, B. F., 36, 122
Skinner, E. A., 13, 118, 132, 172, 173, 177, 178, 215, 271, 282, 296, 302, 450
Skokan, L. A., 458
Slade, L. A., 190
Slovinec-D'Angelo, M., 143, 146
Smart, L., 307
Smethurst, C. J., 171

Smith, A. C., III, 400
Smith, C. A., 349, 383, 387, 390, 402
Smith, C. P., 185
Smith, F. J., 96, 98, 99
Smith, H. L., 455
Smith, J. L., 149, 413, 428
Smith, K., 223
Smith, K. S., 64
Smith, M. L., 456
Smith, P. K., 355
Smith, R. G., 124
Smith, R. H., 418, 423
Smith, S. M., 53
Smith, T., 203
Smith-Lovin, L., 310, 314, 330, 331, 334
Smyth, R., 455
Snyder, C. R., 296, 298, 299, 302, 311, 434, 449, 453, 461
Snyder, E., 111
Snyder, M., 265
Sobal, J., 104
Socrates, 29
Soenens, B., 132, 148, 159, 164, 195, 315
Solano, C. H., 176
Solomon, D., 177
Solomon, R. C., 354
Solomon, R. L., 26, 347
Solomon, S., 307, 379
Somerville, L. H., 57
Sorenson, E. R., 380
Sorrentino, R. M., 42, 44, 45, 207
Soussignan, R., 380
Spangenberg, E. R., 411, 478
Spangler, W. D., 205, 206, 209
Sparks, P., 145, 146, 151
Spasojevic, J., 360
Spence, J. T., 256
Spence, K. W., 35, 433
Spencer, J. A., 101
Spiegel, N. H., 380
Spiegelman, B. M., 98, 115
Spitzer, L., 89
Sprecher, S., 112
Springer, D., 100
Squire, S., 100
Sroka, S., 136
Staats, H., 138
Stacey, C. L., 36
Stansbury, K., 75

Stanton, S. J., 189
Staub, E., 452, 462
Steca, P., 276
Steel, R. P., 221
Steele, C. M., 311, 473, 481
Steele, R. S., 202, 209
Steen, T. A., 461, 465
Steger, M. F., 458
Stein, N. L., 347, 348
Steinhardt, M. A., 412
Stein-Seroussi, A., 312
Steller, B., 244
Stemmler, G., 372
Stephens, A. N., 408, 428
Stepper, S., 379
Stern, J. S., 104
Stets, J. E., 398
Stevens, J., 102, 160
Stevenson, J. A. F., 97
Stewart, A. J., 202–204, 451
Stiff, C., 325
Stiller, J., 177
Stipek, D. J., 192, 252, 254, 400
Stoess, C., 409, 427
Stoller, D., 478
Stone, C., 201
Stone, J., 264
Stough, C., 391
Strack, F., 379, 397
Strain, G. W., 105
Strang, H. R., 225
Straub, W. F., 44
Strauman, T., 489
Strauman, T., J., 245, 246
Strayer, J., 396
Striepens, N., 115
Stroud, L. R., 75
Stucke, T. S., 329
Stunkard, A. J., 104
Su, Y.-L., 163
Suh, E. M., 455
Sullivan, H. S., 175, 489
Sullivan, Q., 112
Suppes, T., 75
Susman, E. J., 75
Susskind, J. M., 409
Sutherland, S., 136
Sutton, S. K., 52, 72, 80
Svartdal, F., 160
Swain, N., 462
Swann, W. B., Jr., 136, 307, 310–314, 333

Symons, D., 107, 109
Szegda, M., 366
Szpunar, K. K., 56

T
Tafrate, R. C., 408
Tamir, M., 405
Tammen, V. V., 142
Tangney, J. P., 329, 382, 414–416, 418
Tannenbaum, P. H., 407
Tatar, A. S., 360
Taubes, G., 42, 104
Tauer, J. M., 198
Tavris, C., 408
Taylor, C. B., 272, 275, 291
Taylor, I. M., 173
Taylor, S. E., 75, 229, 230, 243, 266, 295, 296, 457–459
Taylor, S. F., 342
Teague, G., 203
Teasdale, J. D., 366
Tedeschi, J. T., 263
Teevan, R. C., 193
Teitelbaum, P., 93, 95
Tellarou, M.-C., 360
Tellegen, A., 362, 363
Tennen, H., 294
tenHave, M., 455
Terborg, J. R., 223
Terhune, K. W., 201
Terry, K., 314
Tesch-Romer, C., 323
Tesser, A., 310
Tetlock, P. E., 347
Thayer, R. E., 362–364
Thelen, M. H., 136, 173
Thibodeau, R., 262, 264
Thoman, D. B., 413, 428
Thomas, P. R., 171
Thompson, J. E., 175
Thompson, R. A., 359
Thompson, R. J., 391
Thompson, S., 296
Thorndike, E. L., 36, 125
Thorton, J. W., 290
Thorwart, M. L., 96
Tice, D. M., 26, 325–327, 334
Tiedens, L. Z., 205, 408
Tierney, J., 215, 325, 326
Tiggemann, M., 295
Timberlake, W., 122

Timpe, R. L., 444
Tindell, A. J., 64
Tipett, L. J., 332
Toates, F. M., 113
Toepfer, S. M., 461, 465
Tolman, E. C., 32, 36
Tolstoy, 481
Toman, W., 36
Tomkins, S. S., 47, 50, 343, 347, 348, 375, 379
Tong, E. M., W., 390
Tooby, J., 353, 375
Torrey, W. C., 487
Tourangeau, R., 379, 380
Trabasso, T., 347, 348
Tracy, J. L., 378, 417, 418, 428
Tranel, D., 62, 63, 80
Trelease, R. B., 61
Tremblay, L., 11
Trommsdorff, G., 238
Tronick, E. Z., 355
Trope, Y., 5, 198
Trost, M. R., 113
Trotschel, R., 495
Trudewind, C., 191
Truman, H. S., 206
Trzesniewski, K. H., 251, 267, 418, 504
Tsai, J. L., 400
Tseng, C., 13, 75, 154
Tsoudis, O., 331
Tubbs, M. E., 221, 225
Tucker, D., 45
Tugade, M. M., 391
Tuiten, A., 105
Turiel, E., 357
Turken, A. U., 68
Turner, J. H., 43, 398
Tuson, K., 144, 147
Tyler, L., 123, 151
Tyler, J. M., 327

U
Uchida, Y., 400
Uhlmann, E. L., 208, 469
Urist, J., 489, 491

V
Vaidya, J., 363
Vaillant, G. E., 294, 484, 486–488, 495
Valentine, J. D., 364

Vallerand, R. J., 20, 142, 143, 173, 228
Valtin, H., 95, 96
van Aken, M. A. G., 306, 307
Van de Ven, N., 418–420, 428
van der Plight, J., 382, 422, 425
van der Stege, J. G., 105
van Dijk, W. W., 382, 417, 422, 423
Van Doorn, E. A., 425
van Hooff, J. A. R. A. M., 355
Van Houten, R., 138
van IJzendoorn, M. H., 489
Van Kleef, G. A., 425
Van Knippenberg, A., 234
Van Leeuwen, E., 138
Van Mechelen, I., 425
Van Veen, V., 74
Vansteenkiste, M., 132, 134, 142, 143, 148, 157, 159, 195, 315, 412
Vazquez, C., 411
Veenhoven, R., 455
Veitch, R., 365
Veling, H., 234
Vella-Brodrick, D. A., 462
Verduyn, P., 346
Veroff, J., 188, 198, 203
Vig, P. S., 376
Vohs, K. D., 8, 26, 325, 326, 329, 334, 459, 462
Von Suchadoletz, A., 238
Vorst, H., 111
Voss, I. I., 80
Vroom, V. H., 39, 44
Vytal, K., 347, 348, 374

W
Wachtel, P., 471
Wagener, J. J., 366
Wager, T., 342
Wager, T. D., 73
Wagner, S., 94
Wahba, M. A., 437
Walker, L., 263
Walker, P. A., 105
Walker, R., 279
Wall, S., 489
Walton, M. E., 74
Wan, W., 267
Wang, M. C., 276
Wanner, E., 204
Waples, E. P., 395
Ward-Hull, C. I., 107

Waters, E., 489
Watkins, P. C., 461
Watson, D., 361–364
Watson, J. B., 32, 36, 433
Watson, J. M., 56
Watson, M. E., 177
Watson, R. I., Jr., 203
Webster, D. M., 207
Wegner, D. M., 471, 472, 480–482, 492, 495
Weinberg, A., 92
Weinberg, M. S., 111
Weinberg, R. S., 221, 227, 276, 278
Weinberger, J., 185, 186, 199, 200, 476
Weiner, B., 20, 26, 35, 39–41, 44, 45, 50, 190, 215, 292, 349, 383, 387, 391, 393
Weiner, B., 423
Weingarten, H. P., 96
Weinstein, N., 143, 146, 158
Weinstein, N. D., 296
Weir, C., 149
Weiss, J. M., 68, 295
Wellborn, J. G., 13, 173, 178
Weller, H., 410
Welsh, J., 117
Wertheimer, M., 36
Westen, D., 26, 294, 471, 472, 479, 489, 491, 495
Whalen, P. J., 62
Whalen, S., 169
Wheeler, L., 175
Wheeler, R. H., 371
Wheeler, S. C., 478
White, J., 278
White, L., 495
White, R. W., 36, 39, 40, 157, 487, 495
White, T. L., 71
White, T., 481
Whitener, E. M., 222
Wicker, B., 68
Wickram, K. A. S., 310
Widen, S. C., 339
Wieber, F., 234, 238
Wiechman, B. M., 133, 135, 136
Wiedeking, C., 105
Wiederman, M. W., 112
Wiers, R. W., 57
Wiersma, U. J., 136
Wiese, D., 363

Wigfield, A., 215, 299, 302
Wiggum, C. D., 444
Wilder, D. A., 175
Wilhelm, F. H., 368
Williams, C. J., 472
Williams, D. G., 93, 95
Williams, G. C., 143, 157, 159, 160, 182, 447
Williams, J. G., 176
Williams, J. M., 44
Williams, K., 279
Williams, L. A., 417, 428
Williams, T., 279
Wilson, G. T., 101
Wilson, T. D., 364, 472, 474, 479, 493
Wilson, W., 206
Windle, M., 176, 177
Winefield, A. H., 295
Wing, R. R., 101, 104
Winne, P. H., 323
Winner, L. A., 360, 368
Winson, J., 474
Winter, D. G., 202–206, 209, 451
Winterbottom, M., 191
Wirth, M. M., 189
Wisco, B. E., 411
Wise, R. A., 64, 76, 364
Wisner-Fries, A. B., 177
Wit, A., 138
Witty, T. E., 298
Witzel, B. S., 138
Wojnaroski, P., 221
Wolchik, S., 444
Wolfson, A., 172
Wood, C., 325
Wood, R. E., 225, 227, 272, 278
Wood, R. J., 93
Woods, S. C., 97, 99
Woodworth, R. S., 33
Woody, E. Z., 101
Wortman, C. B., 26, 295, 297, 302
Wozniak, R. H., 413
Wren, A. M., 98
Wrosch, 235, 238
Wu, S., 399
Wubben, M. J. J., 417, 418
Wundt, W., 36
Wurf, E., 313
Wylie, C., 12, 157
Wynn, S. R., 160
Wyrwicka, W., 96

X
Xagoraris, A. E., 62

Y
Yacko, H. A., 478
Yando, R., 366
Yankova, D., 185, 209
Yang, H., 366
Yang, S., 366
Yanovsky, J. A., 104
Yanovsky, S. Z., 104
Yates, A., 100
Yeager, D. S., 504
Yegiyan, N. S., 395
Yerkes, R. M., 37
Yik, M. S. M., 362, 400
Yonelinas, A. P., 395
York, M. K., 64
Young, L, J., 75
Young, M. J., 364, 366
Young, P. T., 36, 37, 40
Young, W. G., 97
Younger, J. C., 263
Yousseff, Z. I., 190, 197
Yukl, G. A., 227

Z
Zajonc, R. B., 344, 376, 380
Zak, J., 75
Zak, P. J., 76
Zanna, M. P., 265
Zeelenberg, M., 219, 357, 382, 414, 415, 416, 418–420, 422, 428
Zelazo, P. D., 73
Zellweger, R., 84
Zhai, Q., 455
Zhong, C. B., 410
Zhou, F.-M., 68
Zhou, M., 132
Zimmer-Gembeck, M. J., 173
Zimmerman, B. J., 215, 322, 323, 334
Zimmerman, S. I., 104
Zlochower, A. J., 373
Zuckerman, M(arvin), 26, 122
Zuckerman, M(iron), 136, 160, 252, 380, 447
Zukauskiene, R., 457
Zullow, H. M., 294
Zumoff, B., 105

Subject Index

A

A Way of Being, 462
ABC system, 117
Absorption, 170, 171
Ability, 253, 272, 299
Ability praise and criticism, 253
Academic achievement, 361
Achievement, need for, 4, 39, 90,
  187–198, 477
  Atkinson's model, 39, 192–197
  competition, 198
  conditions that involve and
    satisfy, 197–198
  entrepreneurship, 198
  moderately difficulty tasks, 197,
    198
  origins, 191. 192
  tendency to avoid failure, 193,
    194
  tendency to approach success,
    193, 194
Achievement anxiety, 193–197, 260
Achievement behavior, 192, 196
Achievement for the future (see
  Future achievement)
Achievement goals, 26, 254–261
  mastery goals, 254–259
  performance-approach goals, 255,
    257–259
  performance-avoidance goals,
    255, 257–261
Achievement Goal Questionnaire,
  259
Acquired needs, 186–190
Active nature of the person, 39, 40,
  315
Actualizing tendency, 439–445, 463
Adaptation, 16, 17
Adaptive unconscious, 468, 469,
  474–476, 493
Adherence, 132, 143
Adipogenesis, 99
Adjustment, 484–487
Adrenal gland, 67

Adrenaline (see Epinephrine)
Advice, 155
Affect (*see* Mood), 219, 361–366
  circumplex model, 362, 363
Affective computing, 373
Affective neuroscience, 52
Affiliation, need for (*see* Intimacy),
  187–189, 198–202, 205, 206,
  477, 478
  conditions that involve and
    satisfy, 200–202
  duality of, 199, 200
  establishing and maintaining
    interpersonal networks, 201
  fear/anxiety, 200
Affordances, 155
Agency, 13, 69, 155, 157, 306,
  315–321, 331, 387, 389
Aggression, 204, 309, 408, 418,
  425, 470, 471, 504–507
Agitation, 338
Air deprivation, 343
Alarm clock, 125
Alcohol (Alcoholism), 95, 101, 102,
  143
Alcohol treatment, 143
Alienation, 156
American dream, 433, 457
Amotivation, 142, 143, 146, 147,
  443
Amusement, 459, 460
Amygdala, 52, 53, 58, 59, 61–63,
  70, 78, 106, 374, 388, 482
Anagrams, 167
Androgens, 105
Anger, 338, 350–353, 372–374,
  378, 390, 393, 394, 405, 407,
  408, 425
Anterior cingulate cortex, 58, 59,
  74, 78, 374
Antidiuretic hormone (ADH), 94
Anti-depressant drugs, 68
Anxiety, 101, 102, 190–193, 200,
  276–279, 407, 480, 483, 484

Appeasement, 416, 417
Appetite, 96, 97, 99
Applications, 5–6, 497–500
Appraisal (in emotion), 349, 360,
  370, 382–390, 393–395
  Arnold's theory, 383, 384, 387
  attributional, 393–395
  cognitive-motivational-relational,
    387
  decision tree, 389
  definition, 382
  Lazarus' theory, 385–387
  negative functional reappraisal,
    360
  primary, 360, 386
  secondary, 360, 386
  reappraisal, 358, 360
  time course, 389
Approach motivation, 20, 21,
  70–72, 190–197, 364
Arousal, 26, 37, 38, 105, 106, 122,
  189, 362
  inverted-U hypothesis, 38
  optimal level of, 38
Aspirations, 440
Attachment (styles), 75, 450, 488,
  490
Attainment value, 299, 300
Attention, 17, 18, 74, 132, 157, 223,
  224, 325, 326, 413
Attitude, 208
Attribution, 252, 289, 292–295,
  370, 391, 393–395
  emotion and, 391, 393–395
  explanatory style, 295, 296
  learned helplessness,
    291–295
Authentic pride, 405, 417, 418
Authenticity, 453
Autism, 138
Automatically activated
  associations, 469, 478
Autonomic nervous system, 66–68,
  370–373

Autonomous self-regulation, 134, 137, 138, 161, 478

Autonomy (Perceived autonomy), 131, 135, 139, 143, 154, 158–167, 178–181, 305, 435, 450, 453, 497, 501–504

Autonomy causality orientation, 445–447

Autonomy support (Supporting autonomy), 131, 161–167, 174, 444, 501–504
  benefits of, 164–167
  enabling conditions, 161
  giving, 165, 166

Autonomy-supportive intervention program (ASIP), 501–504

Autonomy-supportive strategies:
  acknowledges and accepts negative affect, 161, 165, 501
  displays patience, 161, 164, 501
  listens empathically, 161, 163, 501
  nurtures inner motivational resources, 161, 162, 501
  perspective taking, 161, 162, 501
  provides explanatory rationales, 161, 162, 501
  relies on informational language, 161, 163, 501

Avoidance, 126–128

Avoidance motivation, 20, 21, 70–72, 126–128, 259–261, 364

Awards, 135

Awe, 459, 460

B

Back to the Future, 28

Basal ganglia, 58, 59, 63–66, 78, 376

Baseball, 22

Basic emotion criteria, 351, 352

Behavior, 12, 13, 19, 20, 120, 289

Behavioral approach system (BAS), 71, 72, 348, 374

Behavioral inhibition system (BIS), 71, 72, 348, 374

Behaviorism, 433

Belongingness needs (*see* Relatedness), 435–437

Benefit, 385, 386, 420

Benign envy, 419

Biological needs (see Physiological needs)

Bodily gestures, 13

Body Mass Index (BMI), 104, 447

Bonding, 107, 175

Bottom-up approach, 433, 434

Brain, 14, 15, 42, 51–74, 76, 78, 91, 326, 374, 375, 384, 388, 474, 482, 513

Brain activations, 14, 15, 53–55, 347, 348, 374, 375

Brain's reward center, 63–66, 133, 482

Bridget Jones's Diary, 84

Broaden-and-build, 26, 412, 459, 460

Buddhist thought, 338

Bully, 359

C

Caffeine, 95

Calm (calmness), 189, 282, 338

Cardiovascular activity, 14, 380

Caring, 175, 176

Causality orientations, 445–447

Causality Orientations Scale, General, 445, 446

CEOs, 117

Challenge, 130, 167–171, 174, 188, 189, 413

Challenge seeking, 154–156

Challenge-skill balance, 168–171

Child-rearing practices, 187, 188

Choice(s), 13, 72, 74, 159–161, 197, 262, 263, 276, 277, 299, 438

China, 399, 400, 455

Cingulate cortex (see Anterior cingulated cortex)

Circumplex model of affect, 362, 363

Civilization and Its Discontents, 490

Civil rights movement, 408

Cognition and Emotion, 45

Cognitions, 9, 10, 13, 40, 41, 228, 288, 289

Cognitive approach to motivation, 40, 41, 214, 215, 228, 299, 300

Cognitive control, 74

Cognitive dissonance, 26, 39, 215, 241, 261–265

dissonance-arousing situations, 262–265

self-perception theory, 265

Cognitive evaluation theory, 26, 39, 139–142

Cognitive neuroscience, 52

Cognitive revolution, 39–41

Cognitive sharing of emotion, 397, 398

Cognitively-regulated eating style, 101

Commands, 117

Commitment, 235, 236

Communal relationships, 176, 420–422

Compassion, 338, 405, 426, 453, 510–513

Competence, 4, 130, 139, 154, 164, 167–174, 178–181, 279, 280, 316, 488

Competence support, 130

Competition, 75, 135, 142, 190, 198, 418

Compliance, 123, 128, 129, 131, 443, 450

Concentration, 132, 170, 171

Conceptual learning/understanding, 132

Conditional regard, 443, 444

Conditional positive regard, 441, 442, 450

Conditions of worth, 441–444

Conflict, 74, 76, 156–158, 317, 445, 479, 504

Congruence, 146, 158, 442, 444

Consequences, 120, 121, 124–130, 137, 138

Consistent self, 261–263, 309–313

Consummation, 195–197

Contagion, 396

Contempt, 351–353, 356, 378, 405, 410

Contingency, 288

Control (*see* Personal control)

Control causality orientation, 445–447

Controlling motivating style, 161, 163

Conundrum of choice, 160, 161

Coping (with stress, failure, or threat), 41, 279, 280, 289, 297, 386, 387, 389, 406
Corporal punishment (*see* Spanking)
Corrective motivation, 217, 218
Cortical brain, 55–59, 78, 482
Cortisol, 68, 374
Counterregulation, 101, 102
Craving, 338
Creativity, 132, 166, 167, 366, 412, 460
Costs, 299, 300, 361
Criticism, 252, 253
Culture, 155, 156, 329–332, 380, 381, 432, 433, 452, 453
Cultural aspects of emotion, 47, 380, 381, 398–401
Curiosity, 156, 164, 453
Cyberball activity, 504

D
Dating, 110, 112, 203, 273
Deadlines, 135
Decay, 156
Decision making, 74, 276–278, 366, 422, 423
Decision-making flexibility, 366
Deep-acting methods, 401
Defense mechanisms, 484–487
Defiance, 156
Deficiency needs, 87, 435–437
Definition of the situation, 330
Delay of gratification, 72, 329
Deliberative-Implemental mindset, 215, 241–244
Depletion (see Ego depletion)
Depression, 41, 68, 101, 102, 290–292, 449, 486–488
Desire (sexual), 105, 106
Desire for Control: Personality, Social, and Clinical Perspectives, 296
Destructive emotions, 338
Developmental growth, 156, 157, 164, 177
Developmental regression, 156
Diabetes, 143, 157
Dialectic, 154–156
Diary of Anne Frank The, 357
Diet (dieting), 84, 85, 98–101, 214

Differential emotions theory, 26, 347, 352
Differentiation, 156, 315, 316
Differential reinforcement, 130
Directives, 135
Disappointment, 382, 412, 413, 425
Discrepancy, 215–220, 497
   affect and feelings, 219
   discrepancy creation, 220, 225, 226, 309
   discrepancy reduction, 219, 220, 225, 226
Disgust, 315–353, 372–374, 378, 405, 408–410, 459
Distraction, 360
Dissonance (*see* Cognitive dissonance)
Distress (*see* Sadness), 235, 236, 378, 424, 426
Dominance, 202–206, 410, 418
Dopamine, 57, 64–68, 70, 78, 125
Double-depletion model, 93
Doubt, 272–274
Dreams and dream analysis, 473, 474, 492
Drinking, 93–96
Drive, 26, 33–38, 88–92, 122
   as intervening variable, 90, 91
   drive, cue, response, reward, 35
   Freud's theory, 33, 34
   Hull's theory, 34–38, 87, 88
   induction, 36
   reduction, 35–37
   theory, 33–82
Drugs, 66, 68, 95, 104
Dorsolateral prefrontal cortex, 52, 53, 58, 59, 73, 74, 78
Dual-instinct theory, 468, 470, 471
Dual-level hierarchy, 437
Dual process model, 56, 57
Dynamics of action model, 19, 20, 26, 195–197

E
Eating, 100, 101, 103
Education, 23, 24
Electroencephalogram (EEG), 54, 72
Effectance motivation, 26, 39, 487, 488
Efficacy expectations, 270–272

Effort, 13, 132, 157, 235, 236, 251, 252, 276–278, 317–320
Effort justification, 263, 264
Ego, 471, 479, 480, 482–488
Ego defense, 484–487
Ego depletion, 26, 326–329
Ego development, 26, 471, 472, 483, 484
Ego effectance, 487, 488
Ego offense, 488
Ego psychology, 482–488
Electrodermal activity, 14
Embarrassment, 190–193, 372, 405, 416, 417, 497
Emotion, 45
Emotion(s), 9, 10, 13, 20, 47, 48, 225, 276–279, 331, 337–426, 513
   appraisal, 349
   as motivation system, 343
   as readout system, 343
   aspects of, 369–401
   attributions and, 391, 393–395
   basic emotions, 393, 406–414, 507
   biological perspective, 344, 345, 347–349, 370–382
   chicken-and-egg problem, 345, 346
   cognitive perspective, 344, 345, 349, 382–395
   cognitively complex emotions, 418–426
   criteria for basic emotions, 351, 352
   cultural construction of, 398–401
   definition, 2, 10, 339–342
   developmental function of, 357
   effect on cognition, 395
   history of, 47–48
   intercoordination of the four components of emotion, 341, 342
   function, 352–357, 412
   functional vs. dysfunctional, 356
   James-Lange theory, 371–374
   mood and, 361–364
   motivation, 343, 386
   multidimensional nature, 10, 339–342
   perennial questions, 339–366

Emotion(s) (*con't.*)
  primary motivation system, 343
  readout, 343
  social perspective, 395–401
  social sharing, 396–398
  time-tested recipes, 356
  two-systems view of, 344, 345,
   356
Emotion-behavior syndrome, 347,
  348
Emotion differentiation, 388–390
Emotion families, 347, 350
Emotion knowledge, 390–392,
  507–510
Emotion mouse, 373
Emotion program, 375, 376
Emotion regulation, 357–361, 510
Emotion regulation strategies,
  357–361, 400, 401
  attentional focus, 358–360
  reappraisal, 358, 360
  situation modification, 358, 359
  situation selection, 358, 359
  suppression, 358, 360, 361
Emotion schemas, 350, 352
Empathy, 397, 398, 405, 416,
  423–426, 449
Empowerment, 280–282
Endocrine (hormonal) system,
  66–68, 74, 91, 373, 374
Endorphins, 57
Energy conservation, 138
Engagement, 12–14, 132, 155–157,
  164, 177–180, 362, 363, 413,
  503, 504
Enjoyment, 130, 154, 166, 167, 170,
  171, 488
Enthusiasm, 191
Entity theorists, 250, 254, 255
Entrepreneurship, 188, 189, 198
Envy, 405, 418–420
Epinephrine (Adrenaline), 189, 374
Eros, 470
Error tolerance (*see* Failure
  tolerance)
Escape, 126–128
Essential life pursuits, 347, 348
Estrogens, 105
Eudaimonic well-being, 456, 457
Evil, 30, 451–453

Evolutionary approach to emotion,
  344, 345, 375
Evolutionary basis of sexual
  motivation, 111–113
Exchange relationships, 176,
  420–422
Excitement, 189, 190, 192, 456
Exercise, 3, 4, 23, 24, 157, 180, 214,
  221
Existentialism, 433, 458
Expectancy, 41, 136, 137, 155,
  269–272, 289, 299, 300
  efficacy, 270, 271
  outcome, 270, 271
Expectancy *x* Value model, 26, 39,
  192, 215, 299, 300
Expected rewards, 125, 135
Expert(ise), 323
Explanatory style, 292–296
  optimistic, 293–295
  pessimistic, 293–295
Exploration, 131, 132, 154, 413, 460
External events, 9, 11, 139–142,
  155, 156, 160
External regulation, 4, 137,
  143–145, 318, 446
Extraorganismic mechanisms, 91,
  92, 96
Extraversion, 198, 432, 433
*Expression of Emotions in Man and
  Animals, The*, 353
Expressions of motivation, 12–15
Extrinsic goals, 440, 457
Extrinsic motivation, 20, 116–149,
  497
  external regulation, 143–145
  identified regulation, 143–145
  integrated regulation, 143–146
  introjected regulation, 143–145
  intrinsic motivation and, 20,
   133–137
  problems with, 133–139
  types of, 142–146

F

Facial action coding system (FACS),
  373
Facial expression of emotion, 13,
  47, 61, 340–342, 348, 351,
  355, 370, 375–385
  skill in recognizing, 381, 382

Facial feedback, 370, 371, 375–382
Facial feedback hypothesis, 26,
  375–382
Facial musculature, 376–378
  currugator, 377, 378
  depressor, 377, 378
  frontalis, 377, 378
  nasalis, 377, 378
  orbicularis oculi, 377, 378
  orbicularis oris, 377, 378
  quadrates labii, 377, 378
  zygomaticus, 377, 378
Facial metrics, 107–110
Facilitator, 450
Failure, 246, 247, 282, 283,
  293–295, 342, 410, 414, 459
Failure tolerance, 174
Fantasia, 89
Fantasy, 149
Fear, 191, 199, 200, 279, 290, 341,
  351–353, 372–374, 378, 379,
  382, 405, 481
  anxiety and, 407
  phobias, 407
  posttraumatic stress disorder, 407
Fear of failure, 190–197, 259, 261,
  449
Feedback, 168–174, 189, 225, 396
Feelings, 68, 69, 219
Fiber, 97
Fight-or-flight, 76, 374, 406, 408
Fixed mind set, 241, 250–255
Flexibility, 132, 154, 159, 366
Flight attendants, 400, 401
Flourishing, 453, 460
Flow, 4, 26, 39, 168–171, 453
Forgiveness, 453
Forward thrust of life, 439
Framework to understand
  motivation and emotion, 15, 16
Freedom to learn, 450, 451
Freezing, 61
Freud's instinct theory, 33, 34
Freudian unconscious, 468–474,
  493
Fully functioning individual, 445,
  462
Functional magnetic resonance
  imaging (fMRI), 52–54, 374
Functions of emotion, 352–357
  coping functions, 353, 354

social functions, 354–356
Fundamental life tasks, 353, 375
Future achievement, 194, 195

G
Gestalt psychology, 433
Ghrelin, 98, 99
Glucose, 54, 91, 96, 157, 326–328
Glucostatic hypothesis, 96, 97, 103
Glycemic index, 99
Goal(s), 4, 41, 70, 71, 155, 156,
    170–173, 215, 236, 237,
    319–321, 456, 513
Goal congruence, 222–226, 387,
    389
Goal difficulty, 221–226
Goal disengagement, 235, 235
Goal mechanisms, 221–226
Goal origins, 236, 237
Goal proximity, 227, 228
Goal relevance, 387
Goal-setting, 26, 39, 149, 220–229,
    241–243, 321, 322, 453, 513
Goal specificity, 221–226
Goal Orientation Inventory (GOI),
    448
Goal-Performance discrepancy,
    220–222. 225
Goal pursuit, 205
Goal striving, 228–234, 241–244,
    322, 347, 348
Good Morning America, 299
Grand theories of motivation, 30–38
    drive, 33–38
    instinct, 31–33
    will, 30, 31
Gratitude, 393, 394, 405, 420–425,
    453, 459, 460, 461
Gratuity visit, 461
Green Bay Packers, 310
Growth mindset, 241, 250–255
Growth-Fixed mindset, 215, 241,
    250–261, 497, 504–507
    achievement goals, 254–261
    increasing a growth mindset, 253,
        504–507
    meaning of effort, 251, 252
    origins, 252, 253
Growth seeking, 447–449
Growth motivation, 87, 154,
    436–439

Growth needs, 435–439
Growth-seeking, 447–449
Guilt, 350, 353, 393, 394, 405, 415,
    416, 418
Gut feelings, 68, 69, 186, 384,
    476

H
Habit (H), 35
Hair stylists, 400, 401
Happiness, 351, 372, 374, 453–457
Harm, 385, 386, 411
*Harry Potter and the Sorcerer's
    Stone*, 278
Hate (hatred), 338
Health, 156, 157, 177, 458
Heart rate, 372
Hedonism, 118
Helping others, 21, 22, 143, 365,
    425, 450
Help seeking, 425
Helplessness (*see* Learned
    helplessness)
Hidden costs of reward, 130–138
Hierarchy of human needs, 435–437
History of emotion study, 45, 46
History of motivation study, 28–48
History of science, 43
Holism, 433, 434
Homeostasis, 89, 91, 92
Homework, 138
Homophobia, 409
Homosexual orientation, 111
Hope, 190–192, 298, 299, 393, 394,
    405, 423, 453, 459–462
    efficacy and outcome
        expectations, 298, 299
Hope for success, 190–194
Hormones, 14, 74–76, 98, 103, 105,
    111
    cortisol, 75
    oxytocin, 75
    testosterone, 75
Hot seat technique, 458
Hubristic pride, 417, 418
Hugging, 107
Hull's drive theory (*see* Drive)
Human nature, 22, 23, 451–453,
    462, 478, 468
Humanism, 41, 432–434

Humanistic psychology, 41, 433,
    434, 445–453
Humanistic therapy, 449
Humor, 453
Hunger, 90, 91, 96–104
    comprehensive model of, 102,
        103
    environmental influences on, 100,
        101
    long-term energy balance, 97–99
    restraint release situations, 101,
        102
    self-regulation failure, 104
    self-regulatory influences,
        101–104
    set-point theory, 99
    short-term appetite, 96, 97
Hypnosis, 466, 467
Hypothalamus, 58, 59, 61, 66–68,
    78, 91, 94, 96–98, 106, 107,
    376
Hypothalamic-pituitary-adrenocortical
    system, 75

I
Id, 479, 482, 484
Ideal self guides, 248, 249
Ideal state (vs. present state),
    215–220, 246, 248, 249, 313
Identified regulation, 143–145, 148,
    318, 446
Identity, 306, 329–331
If-then plans (*see* Implementation
    intentions)
Ill-being, 156, 157, 259–261
Illusion of control, 294
Implementation intentions, 215,
    229–234, 243, 244, 322
    getting started, 232, 234
    resuming, 232, 234
    staying on track, 232, 234
Implicit Associations Test, 208, 469
Implicit attitudes, 208
Implicit motives, 26, 183–208, 476,
    477, 513
    achievement, 190–198, 477
    affiliation, 198–202, 477
    measuring, 184, 185
    power, 202–207, 477
Implicit needs, 86, 185, 186

Incentive, 8, 24, 35–37, 72, 94, 95, 118, 120, 121, 137, 138, 188, 189, 192
Incentive motivation (K), 35, 36
Incongruence, 442, 445, 497
Incongruity (*see* Discrepancy)
Incremental theorists, 251, 254, 255
Indebtedness, 420, 421
Influence, 11, 202–207, 354
Inhibition, 195–197, 205, 206
Initiation rituals, 263
Initiative, 132
Inner motivational resources, 155, 156
Inspiration, 459, 460
Instigation, 195–197
Instinct, 31–33, 470, 471
Insufficient justification, 263, 264
Insula (Insular cortex), 52, 53, 58, 59, 68, 69, 78, 107, 374
Insulin, 91, 96, 99
Integrated regulation, 143–146
Integrated self, 316, 317
Integration, 146, 156, 315–317
Intelligence, 250, 251, 254
Interest, 26, 130, 154–156, 189, 318, 352, 353, 378, 379, 405, 412–414, 459, 460
Interest value, 299, 300
Interest-enhancing strategies, 148, 149
Internal compulsions, 443
Internalization, 145, 146, 177, 316, 317, 323, 450
Intervening variable, 18, 19
Interventions, 461, 462, 496–513
    building hope for the future, 461, 462
    cultivating compassion, 510–513
    developing self-regulation, 323
    emotion course, 507–510
    increasing a growth mindset, 253, 504–507
    gratuity visit, 461
    promoting emotion knowledge, 507–510
    supporting psychological need satisfaction, 501–504
    three good things in life, 461
Intimacy (need for), 105, 106, 143, 175, 176, 199–202

Intimacy-based model of sexual desire, 105, 106
Intraorganismic mechanisms, 91, 92
Intrinsic goals, 440, 457
Intrinsic motivation, 4, 20, 39, 130–144, 155, 156, 164, 228, 318, 446
    benefits of, 131–133
    extrinsic motivation and, 20, 133–137
Intrinsic motivation principle of creativity, 132
Introjected regulation, 4, 143–145, 318, 446
Introversion (*see* Extraversion)
Involvement (*see* Relatedness support)

J
James-Lange theory of emotion, 371–374
Jonah complex, 438
Journal of Educational Psychology, 46
Journal of Sport and Exercise Psychology, 46
Journal of Experimental Psychology, 36
Journal of Personality and Social Psychology, 46
Joy(ful), 189, 352, 353, 372–374, 378, 381, 390, 405, 411–414, 459, 460

K
Kidneys, 94
Kidzania, 313
Kindness, 420, 421, 510
Knowledge, 370

L
Latency, 13, 196, 197
Law of effect, 125
Leadership motive pattern, 205–207
Learned helplessness, 26, 39, 282–298
    alternative explanations, 295
    applications to humans, 286–288
    attributions and, 292–295
    components, 288, 289

deficits from, 289–292
depression and, 291, 292
effects of, 289–292
emotional deficits, 290
learning deficits, 29
motivational deficits, 289, 290
origins of, 284–288
telltale sign, 284
vs. mastery, 282–284
vs. reactance, 297, 298
two-phase experimental paradigm, 285, 286
Learned Helplessness: A Theory for the Age of Personal Control, 296
Learned optimism, 458
Learning, 132, 164, 279, 413, 450, 451, 453
Learning goals (*see* Mastery goals)
Leptin, 98, 99, 104
Life satisfaction, 157
Liking, 66, 175
Limited strength model of self-control, 328, 329
Lipogenesis, 99
Lipostatic hypothesis, 97–99, 103
Little Engine that Could, The, 192
Liver, 91
Logical positivism, 433
Logotherapy, 458
Long-term goal setting, 227, 228, 321–323, 328
Loss, 411, 459
Love, 200, 399, 400, 435–437, 459, 460, 490
Love hormone, 107

M
Maladjustment, 432, 433
Malevolent personality, 452
Malicious envy, 419, 420
Marriage, 176, 310, 410
Marines, 117
Marshmallow study, 329
Mastery beliefs, 215, 282–296
    vs. helplessness, 282–284
Mastery (Learning) goals, 254–259
Mastery modeling program, 281, 282

Mastery motivation, 20, 284–288
Materialism, 455
Mating (Mating strategies), 111–113
Meaning, 157, 453, 456, 458, 459
Meaning of effort, 251, 252
Mechanistic approach to motivation, 155
Medial prefrontal cortex, 342
Meditation, 510–513
Mental health (*see* Health)
Mental simulations, 229, 230
Mind-body dualism, 29, 30
Mindfulness, 477
Mimicry, 396, 424–426
Minitheories of motivation, 39–43
Mirror neurons, 424, 426
Moderately difficult tasks, 190–198
Money, 123, 124, 135, 455
Mood, 361–366
Moralization, 409
Motivated and emotional brain, 51–80
Motivating others, 24
Motivating others on uninteresting activities, 147–149
    providing explanatory rationales, 148
    suggesting interest-enhancing strategies, 148, 149
Motivating style, 163, 253
Motivation, 1–334, 431–513
    definition, 2, 9
    expressions of, 12–15
    relation to emotion, 343
    subject matter, 9–11
    themes, 16–25
    vs. influence, 11
    why study?, 2, 3
Motivation and Emotion, 40
Motivational intensity, 26
Motivational neuroscience, 52
Motivational science, 4–6
Motives, 9–11
Multiple inputs/multiple outputs, 90–92

N
Nebraska Symposium on Motivation, 45
Need, 9, 10, 85–88
    definition, 10, 85, 86
    types of, 85–87
Need for closure, 207
Need for cognition, 207
Need for structure, 207
Need-satisfying experiences, 317–320
Negative affect (Negative emotion), 157, 362–364, 455, 509, 510
Negative conditional regard, 443
Negative emotionality (*see* Negative affect)
Negative feedback, 89, 92–94, 96, 219, 220, 252
    stop system, 363
Negative reinforcers, 125–128
Neural firing in emotion, 347, 348
Neuroscience, 51–78, 133
Neurotransmitters, 57, 326
Neurotransmitter pathways, 57
New Guinea, 381
New Year's resolution, 242
Noise, 286, 287
Norepinephrine (Noreadrenaline), 57
Novelty, 130, 131, 387, 389, 412
Nucleus accumbens, 52, 53, 58, 59, 63–66, 78, 106, 122

O
Obesity, 99, 101, 102, 104
Observational learning, 130, 323
Objectivism, 433
Objects relations theory, 471, 472, 488–492
Obsession, 481, 482, 497
Occular activity, 14
Occupations, 198, 204, 205
On the Soul, 433
Openness, 435, 438, 453, 459
Operant conditioning, 120
Opponent process theory, 4, 26, 347, 348
Optimal challenge, 131, 167–171, 174
    flow, 168–171
    pleasure of, 167, 168

Optimal functioning, 132, 133, 272–274
Optimal level of arousal, 38
Optimism, 71, 453, 457, 458
Optimistic explanatory style, 292–295
Orbitofrontal cortex, 58, 59, 65, 73, 78
Organismic psychological needs, 154, 155
Organismic valuation process, 439–442, 445, 462
Origins and pawns, 159
Orthodontic device, 122, 123
Osmometric thirst, 93
Osmosis, 93
Ought self-guides, 248, 249
Outcome expectations, 270–272, 478
Ovulation, 103, 105
Oxytocin, 75, 76, 107, 373
Oxygen, 54

P
Pain, 61, 68, 90, 481
Pancreas, 91
Paradigm (Paradigm shift), 43
Parasympathetic nervous system, 68
Parenting style, 246
Parents, 122–124, 147, 148, 246, 399, 432, 433, 441–445, 479, 489
Passion, 47
Passions of the Soul, The, 47
Pathway thinking, 298, 299
Peak experiences, 438
Pep talks (*see* Verbal persuasion)
Perceived control, 215, 271, 272, 282
Perceived Control, Motivation, and Coping, 296
Perceived locus of causality, 158, 159
Perennial questions in emotion study, 337–366
    can we control our emotions?, 357–361
    how many emotions are there?, 347–352
    what causes an emotion?, 344–347

Perennial questions in emotion
  study (*con't.*)
  what is an emotion?, 339–342
  what is the difference between
    emotion and mood?, 361–366
  what good are the emotions?,
    352–357
Perennial questions in motivation
  study, 6–9
  what could be?, 434, 453
  what causes behavior?, 6, 7
  why does behavior vary in its
    intensity, 7–9, 40
  why try?, 290
  why we do what we do, 8, 497
Perfectionism, 444
Performance, 164, 171, 221–224,
  299
Performance goals, 254–261
  performance-approach goals, 255,
    257–259
  performance-avoidance goals,
    255, 257–261
Persistence (Perseverance), 13, 132,
  157, 196, 197, 227, 276–278,
  449
Person-environment dialectic,
  155–157
Personal behavior history, 274, 276,
  277, 282
Personal control beliefs, 4, 268–300
Personal goals, 155, 156, 447
Personal growth, 305, 453
Personal strivings, 319, 321
Perspective taking, 161, 162, 424,
  426
Pessimism, 71
Pessimistic explanatory style, 293,
  294
PET scan, 54, 374
Phenomenological self, 331
Pheromone, 103
Philosophical origins of
  motivational concepts, 29, 30
Phobias, 407
Physical attractiveness, 107–110
Physical activity, 138
Physicians, 400, 401
Physiological needs, 83–113,
  435–437

definition, 86, 88
fundamentals of regulation,
  87–92
multiple inputs/multiple outputs,
  90, 91
Physiological state, 260, 275, 276
Picture Story Exercise (PSE), 184,
  185
Pituitary gland, 67
Pity (*see* Sympathy), 393, 394, 425
Plan, 41, 215–220, 322
Play(ing), 135, 412, 460
Pleasure, 68, 76, 77, 167, 168, 362,
  470, 482
Pleasure principle, 479
Positive affect (Positive emotion), 4,
  26, 157, 189, 219, 362–366,
  455, 460, 497, 509
Positive conditional regard, 443
Positive emotionality (*see* Positive
  affect)
Positive psychology, 433–435,
  453–462
Positive regard, 440–444
Positive reinforcer, 124
Positivity, 459, 460
Possible selves, 4, 313–315
Post-decision regret, 262
Post-hypnotic suggestion, 467
Posttraumatic stress disorder, 407
Posture (Postural harness), 126, 127,
  327
Power, 187–189, 202–207, 418,
  477, 478, 497
  alcohol, 203, 204
  aggression, 204
  conditions that involve and
    satisfy, 203–205
  goal pursuit, 205
  influential occupations, 204,
    205
  impact, control, and influence,
    202
  is it bad?, 205
  leadership, 203
  leadership motive pattern,
    205–207
  prestige possessions, 205
Practice, 326, 327
Praise, 8, 140, 173, 174, 252,
  253

Preconscious mind, 473
Prefrontal cortex, 58, 59, 65, 69–72,
  78
Prejudice, 208, 469
Presidents, 206, 207
Pressure, 119, 142, 144, 227,
  443
Prestige possessions, 205
Prevention focus, 240, 241,
  244–250
Pride (Proud), 190–192, 350, 353,
  393, 394, 405, 417, 418, 459,
  460
Priming, 473, 477, 478
Probability of response, 13
Problem-solving, 460, 474
Procrastination, 196
Prolactin, 373
Promotion focus, 240, 241, 244–250
Promotion-Prevention mindset, 215,
  241, 244–250
Protein, 97
Psychoanalytic perspective, 468,
  434
Psychodynamic perspective,
  467–472
  criticisms of, 492, 493
  dual-instinct theory, 470–472
Psychodynamics, 26, 471, 472,
  479–482
Psychological needs, 86, 130, 131,
  152–181, 446, 457, 501–504
Psychological nutriments, 180,
  457
Psychological Review,
  36, 45
Psychological Science, 45
Psychological well-being (*see*
  Well-being)
*Psychology of Hope: You Can Get
  There From Here*, 296
Psychophysiology, 14
Punishers, 126–130, 135
Punishment, 126–130, 364
  corporal, 128–130
  does it work?, 128–130
  side effects, 128–130
Purpose (in life), 157, 305, 340, 342,
  456
Purpose in Life Test, 456

Q

Quasi-needs, 119, 447
Questions in motivation and emotion study (see Perennial questions in motivation/emotion study)
Questionnaires, 15

R

Radish experiment, 325
Rationale, 148
Reactance, 26, 39, 297, 298
  vs. helplessness, 297, 298
Reality principle, 479
Reappraisal, 358, 360
Reciprocity, 420, 421
Regret, 405, 422, 423
Regulatory focus theory, 244–250
Recycling, 138, 144
Reinforcers, 121–124
Rejection, 278
Rejection anxiety, 199, 200
Relatedness, 4, 130, 154, 164, 174–181, 316, 450, 457, 491, 492
  benefits, 177, 178
  communal vs. exchange relationships, 176
  conditions that involve and satisfy, 175, 176
Relatedness support, 130, 457
Relationships, 155, 156, 174–179, 198–203, 354, 356, 361, 395–398, 412, 420–422, 448–450, 457, 471, 488–492
Remote Associates Test (RAT), 366
Replenishment, 327, 328
Repression, 479, 480
Resiliency, 453
Respiration, 61, 380
Response cost, 128
Restraint release, 101, 102
Reticular formation, 57–60
Rewards (Extrinsic rewards), 8, 62–66, 73, 76, 77, 124–126, 130–139, 141, 364
  benefits, 137, 138
  brain's reward center, 63–66, 76, 77
  do rewards work?, 125
  expected, 136
  hidden costs, 130–138

  tangible, 136
Risk-taking (Risk-accepting), 69, 189, 198
Role(s), 329, 330
Rumination, 360, 411

S

Sad(ness), 342, 351–353, 370, 374, 379, 388, 405, 410, 411, 425, 497
Sad love, 399, 400
Safety and security, 435–437
Salesperson, 230
Satiety, 89, 92, 96, 97
Scaffolding, 130
Schadenfreude, 423
Saying, or doing, is believing, 264, 265
School, 41, 120
Seat belts, 117
Security, 189
Seekers, 263, 264
Selective interaction, 310
Self, 69, 304–306, 331, 332, 440–443
  problems of the self, 304, 306
  what is it?, 331, 332, 440–442
Self and its strivings, 303–332
Self as action and development from within, 315–317
Self-acceptance, 305
Self-actualization, 26, 435–439, 449
Self-concept, 41, 215, 306, 308–315, 331
Self-concept certainty, 311, 312
Self-concept change, 311–315
Self-concordance, 26, 222–226, 317–321, 457
Self-control, 206, 215, 322, 324–329, 332, 481, 497, 513
  benefits, 329
  depletion, 326–328, 497
  limited strength model, 328, 329
  replenishment, 327, 328
Self-control strength, 327–329
Self-definition, 451
Self-determination (*see* Autonomy)
Self-determination theory, 26, 142–147
Self-discrepancy feedback, 310–314
Self-endorsed values, 155, 156

Self-efficacy, 26, 39, 215, 272–282, 453, 497
  competent functioning, 276–282
  effects on behavior, 276–279
  empowerment, 280–282
  mastery modeling program, 281–282
  sources, 274–277
  vs. need for competence, 279, 280
Self-Efficacy: The Exercise of Control, 296
Self-enhancement, 314
Self-esteem, 8, 306–308, 414, 415, 417, 435–437, 449, 513
Self-esteem movement, 307
Self-handicapping, 252
Self-instruction, 275
Self-functioning (Dimensions of well-being), 304–306
Self/Norm compatibility, 387
Self-perception theory, 265
Self-presentational signs and symbols, 310
Self-realization, 456
Self-regulation, 215, 306, 321–323, 332
Self-regulation failure, 323, 328
Self-report, 15
Self-schemas, 39, 308–315
Self-verification, 311–315
Serenity, 459, 460
Sensation seeking, 26
Separation (Loss), 342, 410
Serotonin, 57, 68
Set-point theory, 99
Sex, 75, 103–114, 470, 471, 497
  evolutionary basis, 111–113
  facial metrics, 107–110
  intimacy-based model, 105–107
  physiological regulation of, 105–107
Sexual motivation, 343
Sexual orientation, 111
Sexual response cycle, 105, 106, 111
Sexual scripts, 110, 111
Shame, 191, 192, 353, 382, 393, 394, 405, 414, 415, 418
Shocks, 285, 286
Significant life event, 341, 344, 386
Sit-ups, 221, 223
Skeletal muscle activity, 14

Skiing (Skiers), 170

Skill, 168–171, 413, 487, 488

Skill in recognizing emotional facial expressions, 381, 382

Skin conductance, 372

Skin temperature, 372

Smiles (Smiling), 167, 168, 355, 412, 445

Smoking, 409

Social-Affective sharing of emotion, 397, 398

Social blunder, 416, 417

Social context, 9, 11

Social definition, 451

Social facilitation, 100

Social interaction, 174–179, 354, 355

Social needs, 187, 188, 207, 477

Social sharing of emotion, 396–398

Social support, 75

Sociability, 198

Socially relevant questions, 39, 41–43

Society for the Study of Motivation, 45

Socioemotional competence, 74

Sound of Music, The, 438

Space Quest game, 149

Spanking, 128, 129

Spirituality, 453

Sports, 23, 24

Spring to action, 215

Standard of excellence, 190, 191

Star Trek, 357, 468

Status (status-seeking), 75, 202–206

Stomach, 91, 93, 94, 97

Stranger to Ourselves, 474, 480

Strategic planning, 223, 224, 226

Striatum, 58, 59, 63–66, 78, 106

Stress (and coping), 26, 41, 75, 100, 276–279, 474, 487, 488

Structure, 171–173

Struggle and pain, 439

Subcortical brain, 55–59, 78, 133, 348, 351, 370, 375, 384, 482

Subjective well-being (*see* Well-being)

Subliminal activation, 473, 478

Success, 246, 247

Suicide bombers, 452

Super-motivation, 133

Supporting autonomy (*see* Autonomy support)

Suppression, 325–328, 358, 360, 361, 480–482, 512, 513

Surgeon, 54

Surprise, 351

Sympathetic nervous system, 61, 67

Sympathy (Pity), 393, 394, 425, 426

Synthesis, 156

System 1, 475, 476

System 2, 475, 476

T

Taste, 94, 95, 100

Teachers, 450, 451, 476, 501–504

Temperament, 432, 433

Tend and befriend stress response, 75, 76

Temperature regulation, 90, 97

Temptation (resisting), 73, 325, 328

Tendency to approach success (Ts), 192–197

Tendency to avoid failure (Taf), 193–197

Tennis, 280

Tension, 119

Terrorists (attacks), 408, 452

Testosterone, 105, 189

Thanatos, 470

Themes in motivation study, 16–25

  motivation and emotion benefit adaptation and functioning, 16, 17

  motivation and emotion direct attention, 17, 18

  motivation and emotion are "intervening variables", 18, 19

  motivation study reveals what people want, 22, 23

  motives vary over time and influence the ongoing stream of behavior, 19, 20

  there is nothing so practical as a good theory, 25, 26, 513

  to flourish, motivation needs supportive conditions, 23, 24, 513

  types of motivation exist, 20, 21, 513

  we are not always consciously aware of the motivational basis of our behavior, 21, 22

  when trying to motivate others, what is easy to do is rarely what is effective, 24

Theories of Motivation: From Mechanism to Cognition, 41

Theory, 5, 6, 25, 26, 492

Therapy, 23, 24

Thirst, 90, 92–96

  activation, 93

  environmental influences, 94–96

  hypothalamus, 94

  kidneys, 94

  physiological regulation of, 92–94

  satiety, 93, 94

  taste, 93, 94

Thought suppression (*see* Suppression)

Threat (Danger, Harm), 61–63, 75, 385, 386, 406, 407, 411

Three good things in life, 461

Three-to-one ratio, 460

Time-tested recipe, 356

Top-down approach, 433, 434

TOTE unit, 216, 217

Transformational activity, 155

Triumph, 418

Trust, 75, 497

Tyranny of the shoulds, 144

U

Uncertainty, 69

Uncertainty orientation, 207

Unconditional positive regard, 441, 442, 493

Unconscious, 471–476

Unconscious motivation, 21, 22, 466–493

Uncontrollable events and outcomes, 284–292, 295–298

Undermining effect, 133–137

Unexpected rewards, 125, 136

Unifying themes (see Themes in motivation study)

U.S. presidents (see Presidents)

Utility value, 299, 300

V

Valence, 362, 387
Validation-seeking, 447–449
Value (Values), 4, 155, 156, 164,
    299, 300, 318, 452
Vegetarian, 409
Ventral striatum (see Striatum)
Ventral tegmental area (VTA), 58,
    59, 63–66, 78, 106
Ventromedial prefrontal cortex, 58,
    59, 73, 78
Verbal persuasion (pep talks),
    275–277, 282
Vicarious experience,
    274–277, 282
Violence, 22, 309
Vitality, 130, 132, 133,
    180, 181

Volition, 159
Volumetric thirst, 93
Vulcans, 298, 357

W

Waist-to-hip ratio, 107
Wall Street, 75
Wanting, 66
War, 206, 207
Ways of coping, 282, 283
Weight gain (see Obesity)
Weight loss (weight control), 143,
    447
Well-being, 132, 133, 156–158,
    164, 177, 180, 181, 235, 236,
    249, 250, 259–261, 304, 305,
    317–320, 382, 385, 386, 412,
    413

What makes for a good day?,
    180
What might have been, 422
Will (Willpower), 30–32, 241, 325,
    326, 479
Wisdom, 453, 513
Wishful thinking, 458
Women's suffrage movement,
    408
Work, 23, 24, 41, 120
Worry, 260, 512, 513
Writing, 280, 323

Y

YouTube video, 474

Z

Zeitgeist, 40

Printed in the USA
J095946SCI021015   01S29053000000000260